Treat this book with care and respect.

*It should become part of your personal
and professional library. It will
serve you well at any number
of points during your
professional care*

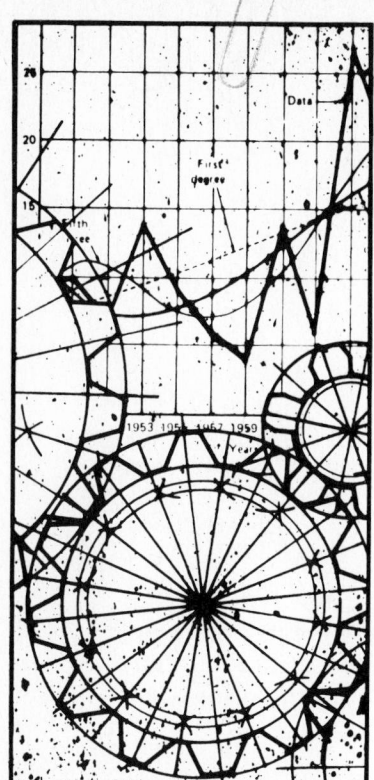

Statistical Analysis for Administrative Decisions

Third Edition

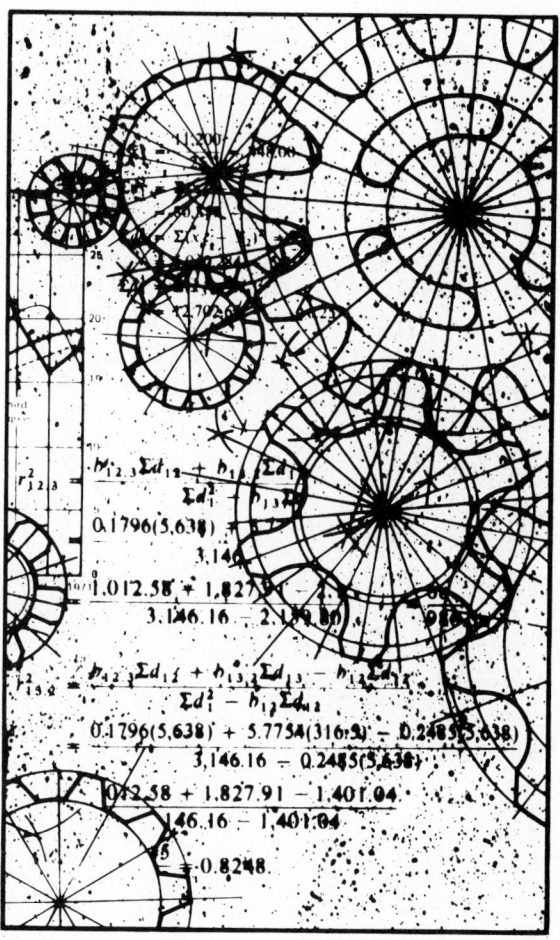

Charles T. Clark

Professor
  of Business Statistics
The University of Texas
  at Austin

Lawrence L. Schkade

Professor
  of Business Administration
  and Urban Studies
The University of Texas
  at Arlington

M27

Published by

SOUTH-WESTERN PUBLISHING CO.

CINCINNATI   WEST CHICAGO, ILL.   DALLAS   PELHAM MANOR, N.Y.   PALO ALTO, CALIF.

ISBN: 0–538–13270–1

Library of Congress Catalog Card Number: 77–87407

123456D432109

Printed in the United States of America

Preface

The objective of this edition of STATISTICAL ANALYSIS FOR AD-MINISTRATIVE DECISIONS is basically the same as that of the second edition in that it has been written for use as a text for courses on modern statistical concepts and their application to problems of administration in business, industry, government, and other types of organizations and for use as a reference for administrators who wish to use statistical methods in making decisions. The concepts and methods presented in this edition range from elementary to advanced in degree of sophistication and comprise a significant portion of the methodology that is called quantitative methods. The level of presentation presumes no mathematical preparation beyond college algebra and no previous background in digital computers. Topics that are more advanced than these basic levels are developed fully in the book.

The writing of this edition has provided the opportunity to improve upon the second edition by presenting more recent data in illustrations and problems, altering the emphasis for selected topics, adding the presentation of new concepts, simplifying some of the notation, and increasing the readability of the manuscript. Thanks to the interest and kindness of a large number of students, instructors, and administrators who used the second edition, many valuable comments and suggestions were contributed, and these were utilized in the preparation of this edition.

The increase in the use of statistical and other quantitative methods and the application of computers in the decision-making process in recent years has been dramatic. This edition reflects the trend by presenting statistical concepts that are used in making administrative decisions and by illustrating how digital computers are utilized in the application of statistical methods. The availability of computers for problem solving has led to the development of new statistical methods and to the modification of some of the traditional manual computational methods. A selection of these new statistical methods is included in this edition. It is not necessary, however, that a computer be used in conjunction with this book, for the topical presentation is designed to be utilized either with or without a computer.

The style of presentation reflects an approach to the exposition of statistical concepts that highlights clarity and understandability, and it has been developed on the basis of extensive combined teaching and consulting experience. For example, to clarify further the differences in and applications of descriptive statistics and parametric and nonparametric methods, greater emphasis is placed on the quality of data and levels of measurement in this edition. The discussion of selected topics has been condensed and the organization of topics has been changed slightly to enhance readability.

The organization of this book is similar to that of the preceding edition. The symbols and notation in this book are consistent with those recommended by the American Statistical Association. Study questions and problems are included at the end of each chapter. An extensive group of statistical tables are included in the appendix. The examples and problems in this book have been selected to present understandable and realistic situations. The study questions are designed to focus attention on important concepts and relationships developed in the discussions. Solutions to most of the odd-numbered problems are provided in the back of the book as reinforcements to the reader when solving the problems at the end of each chapter. The selected readings contain brief comments concerning other books that offer similar or more extensive presentations of the topics included in each of the chapters.

The authors are indebted to many persons for their interest and encouragement in the preparation of this manuscript. In particular, appreciation is expressed to Dr. John R. Stockton, who suggested the writing of this book; to Pearl Clark for her valuable assistance in editing the manuscript; and to Catherine Goode and David Schkade for assisting with problem solutions.

The authors are also indebted to the Literary Executor of the late Sir Ronald A. Fisher, F.R.S., Cambridge, to Dr. Frank Yates, F.R.S., Rothamsted, and to Messrs. Oliver and Boyd, Ltd., Edinburgh, for their permission to reprint Tables III and IV from their book *Statistical Tables for Biological, Agricultural and Medical Research,* and Tables III and V-A from *Statistical Methods for Research Workers;* to Dr. Stephen P. Shao, Old Dominion University, and the publisher for permission to reprint Table B from his book *Mathematics of Finance;* to the Editors of the *Annals of Mathematical Statistics* for their permission to publish data included in Table 12.2; and to Dr. Robert Schlaifer and the President and Fellows of Harvard College for permission to publish the tables of the Unit Normal Loss Function that appear in *Probability and Statistics for Business Decisions* by Robert Schlaifer, published by the McGraw-Hill Book Company in 1959.

Contents

Part 1
Statistical Data and Descriptive Measures

Chapter 1
The Nature of Statistics

Statistics is a discipline which is made up of a body of methods and techniques for quantitatively expressing and interpreting knowledge. It is especially designed to treat the complexities and uncertainties of the business and administrative world. Today, more and more administrative and scientific decisions are made on the basis of information presented in quantitative form.

As organizations grow in size and complexity, the administrator is forced to make many decisions, some of which involve millions of dollars. Actions must be taken on the basis of the facts available about the organization and the economic, political, and physical aspects of the external environment that affect the organization.

Modern statistical methods provide one of the most useful and necessary sets of tools for decision making. It is the purpose of this book to introduce briefly the basic statistical techniques, to present some of the more advanced methods for statistical decision making, and to give students an understanding of the power of statistical analysis in helping to summarize and obtain useful information from data.

Important applications of probability and statistics are found in almost all fields of endeavor. Success stories involving the use of statistical analysis can be found in such diverse areas as health and medicine, government, space programs, business, and weather research, to name only a few. The following examples are mentioned briefly to whet the student's appetite for what is to come.

In 1954 the largest and most expensive statistical experiment in the history of medicine was carried out to test the effectiveness of the Salk vaccine as protection against paralysis or death from poliomyelitis. It involved over a million young children, cost more than $5 million, and led to a notable triumph in the battle against disease. Statistical techniques are now frequently used to test the safety and effectiveness of new drugs before they are marketed.

The 1936 national election provided for the first time an excellent example of how election polling can be used as a kind of "acid test" on the effectiveness of statistical techniques used in opinion measurement now applied in marketing. An election represents one of the few situations in which the forecast produced by the statistician can be compared to the actual (voting) results. For the 11 national elections since 1948, the average error in the Gallup Poll has been only 1.6%.

Probability and statistics have played an important role in the development of *reliability theory*. The Apollo space vehicle would not have been possible without the ability to test the final complex system statistically rather than to test it by performing a mission. This same reliability theory developed for the space program is now being applied to the manufacture of household appliances, automobiles, telephones, power supplies, and so on. For example, the five-year guarantee given now by some automobile manufacturers resulted from their determination of the reliability of components included in the guarantee.

The great variability in rainfall in the United States from one year to the next has always been a major problem for the nation's farmers. The need for accurate quantitative predictions of rainfall amounts has led to the use of a technique called *multiple discriminant analysis* to predict the probability of precipitation. Statisticians were also called on to design and conduct experimental programs to establish whether or not various cloud-seeding techniques can reliably increase precipitation to meet the needs of a growing and thirsty population.

THE DECISION-MAKING PROCESS IN ADMINISTRATION

The decision-making process in business follows essentially the same basic steps used for problem solving in physics, engineering, or chemistry. In business and in the social sciences the variables are often more numerous and more difficult to measure and control than in the physical sciences, but the steps are the same. They are:

1. Simplification
2. Building a decision model
3. Testing the model
4. Using the model to find a solution

Simplification

The ancient Greeks in the fourth, fifth, and sixth centuries before Christ made a great discovery. They learned how mathematical reasoning could be used to simplify and explain the things they observed in nature. When they saw that the heavenly bodies are spheres, the surfaces of lakes are flat, light travels in a straight line, and the sides of a house form a rectangle, they began to study lines, planes, circles, triangles, and rectangles as abstractions.

In their study of geometry the Greeks observed that certain basic facts are obvious. A straight line is the shortest distance between two points in a plane. Or, all the points on the circumference of a circle are equidistant from the center. They reasoned that if some new facts could be derived, these facts would apply to all those physical objects with the same basic properties. If the area of a triangle could be shown by reasoning to be one half the base times the altitude, then a carpenter could use this abstract idea to determine how much lumber is needed to enclose the end of a gable roof.

By dealing first with abstractions that strip away all the nonessential details of a situation, it is possible to reason with the remaining basic relationships and to use this reasoning to cover a multitude of complex cases. Better still, the basic reasoning may produce other meaningful information that is entirely unforeseen.

Building a Decision Model

Simplification is but the first step in the decision-making process. The decision maker next turns to the task of taking the essential factors in the problem and arranging them in a *model*, which is a representation of reality designed to explain it and used to predict or to control it.

While the mathematician leads in the use of abstract concepts and models, mathematical ways of thinking about essential relationships have long been used by the physical scientist. This kind of thinking is rapidly being adopted by the social scientist and the business executive.

■ *Example.* Mathematicians who see an object dropped from a tower can estimate with great accuracy the time it will take the object to reach the ground. They use a simple model,

$$d = 16t^2$$

where *d* is the distance in feet from the top of the tower to the ground and *t* is the time in seconds it takes the object to fall. The mathematicians disregard the resistance of air since the distance the object falls is not great. Further, they ignore the weight of the object since they know that when air resistance is not considered, all objects fall at the same rate under the pull of gravity. The entire physical problem is now a simple problem of algebra; they need only to insert a value for *d* in the equation and solve for *t*.

From the above-mentioned example, several characteristics of a model can be pointed out:

1. It is a simplified representation of an actual situation.
2. It need not be complete or exact in all respects.

3. It concentrates on the most essential relationships and ignores the less essential ones.
4. It is more easily understood than the empirical situation and, hence, permits the problem to be more readily solved with a minimum of time and effort.
5. It can be used again and again for like problems or can be modified if necessary to solve new ones with added complications.

The statistical formulas used in this book can be thought of as mathematical models capable of providing the decision maker with useful tools for the important and arduous task of making decisions. Some of these models are quite simple, while others are complex.

A great deal of exciting work is being done on the frontiers of modern business decision making. Those individuals charged with the responsibility of guiding the destiny of large corporations have been faced with a growing problem in recent years. Too often they find that facts gathered in the traditional manner are so long in preparation that the decisions they are designed to guide must be made before all the facts are available. To solve this problem, research and planning personnel in many large organizations are working to develop complex models of their firm or industry, programmed for a large computer and capable of giving approximate answers to far-reaching questions long before these same answers could come through conventional organizational channels. This is model building in its most sophisticated form — simulation.

Testing the Model

The real test of any model is whether it predicts outcomes with usable accuracy. If the formula $d = 16t^2$ does not predict accurately the time it will take an object dropped from a tower to hit the ground, the formula must be replaced by one that can predict with the needed accuracy. An oversimplification of the empirical situation may have led to the development of a model that ignores elements essential to its functioning as a predictor. Even if all the essential elements have been identified, the model must be tested to see if the correct relationships between these essentials have been established. Certainly, as models become more complex, a great deal of testing may be necessary to establish that they will work.

In the field of statistics many of the models used are ones that have withstood the test of time and are known to be reliable within given limits. The task of the student is to understand what the limitations of a given model are and how it can be used to produce the required results. A simple model such as the arithmetic mean has been used for many years and its characteristics are well known. Some of the more sophisticated models are still being tested in order to learn what they will do.

Using the Model to Find a Solution

One of the difficulties encountered in a brief discussion of models is that there are many kinds of models and they have many uses. Further, they involve many different levels of abstraction. In statistics a model may be a simple descriptive measure of a frequency distribution or it may be used to accept or reject a sample as being drawn from a given larger group. Such tests are necessary because, regardless of how precise a system of measurement may be, there are always elements of chance at work that introduce random variation.

The statistician may use a model to determine which variables are pertinent to changes occurring in some dependent variable and to what extent each shares in the process. At a higher level of abstraction, there are simulation models that operate on a problem-solving sequence in which the input for one stage is the output from a previous stage. Such problems are solved through the application of the so-called *Monte Carlo* methods.

The very nature of human thought is such that model building, model testing, and model application to solve problems are an integral part of any organized thought process.

WHAT IS STATISTICS?

Much of the confusion that arises in the public mind about statistics comes from the fact that the word *statistics* has two meanings.

1. When the administrator asks for the most recent statistics on population and housing for a state, the request is for facts. These facts are in quantitative form and are, strictly speaking, *statistical data.*
2. When a business manager asks a quality control engineer to explain how statistics can be used to determine whether a shipment of parts should be accepted for use or returned to the supplier as unsatisfactory after inspecting only a few parts, the manager is asking about a *statistical method.*

To the scientist, the engineer, the business executive, or any other person engaged in problem-solving activities, the second sense of the word statistics is also important. It refers to the vast and ever-growing body of methods for collecting, summarizing, analyzing, and interpreting quantitative facts. These techniques are a part of the scientific method and can be applied in many fields of endeavor. In this book the prime emphasis will be on the application of statistical methods to the solution of administrative and business problems.

The word *statistic* should also be mentioned here for completeness. Throughout this text, when the word statistic is used in the singular, it will have a meaning completely different from the two just given. Statistic will be used to refer to an arithmetic mean, a median, a standard deviation, or some other descriptive measure computed from a sample. Of course, it is possible to use the word in the plural in this sense also.

Descriptive and Inductive Statistics

The word statistics has been defined as meaning both "statistical data" and "statistical methods." A further distinction is often made between descriptive statistics and inductive statistics. The term *descriptive statistics* is confined to the treatment of data for the purpose of describing their characteristics. This term is distinct from the term *inductive statistics,* which involves making forecasts, estimations, or judgments about some larger group of data than that actually observed or about some future happening based on a study of historical data. The arithmetic mean of a sample of observations is a descriptive measure, but if it is used to estimate the arithmetic mean of the larger group from which the sample was drawn, inductive techniques are involved.

The foundation of inductive statistics is probability. Examples of inductive techniques are the use of probability theory to estimate the likelihood that a sample has been drawn from a given universe, to forecast sales, or to predict the action of one variable based on its previous relationship with other variables. The whole idea of using probability theory to solve scientific or business problems on a formal, wide-scale basis is relatively recent but is of rapidly growing importance.

■ *Example.* To point up the distinction between descriptive statistics and inductive statistics, imagine a manufacturer who is studying a report made by the quality control department of a shipment of parts received by the firm for an assembly operation. The shipment is from one of the manufacturer's regular suppliers and contains 10,000 parts. The inspectors have checked 200 of these parts drawn at random from the shipment.

The inspection shows 12 out of the 200 parts examined are defective. This is 6% of the sample total. As long as the executive is interested only in this sample percent of defective parts, he or she is dealing with descriptive statistics.

Imagine further that there is a contract between the supplier and the manufacturer which states that the manufacturer will not accept any shipment of parts with more than 5% defective. Since the sample percent of defectives is 6%, the manufacturer may decide that the percent of defectives in the entire shipment is too high and may reject the entire lot. Just as soon as the manufacturer generalizes about the proportion of defective parts of the entire shipment of 10,000 from the results obtained from an inspection of only 200 of the parts, the focus has moved into the domain of inductive statistics. The manufacturer has generalized about the quality of the group when having information about only a part of it.

The generalization that the manufacturer must make in the example above is not an easy one. He or she must recognize that the inspectors may have gotten a "bad" sample which has 6% defectives. If another sample of 200 parts were selected, "chance" might dictate that it would contain only 4% defectives. If the difference between the sample percent and the critical 5% for the whole shipment had been large, the decision might be easier to make. Also, if the sample had been much larger, it would be reasonable to assume that it might be more representative of the whole group. Finally, the way in which the sample was drawn is important. If only parts from the top of each box had been selected, these might be the ones most subject to damage. Only an experiment that is properly designed and carefully conducted can be used as the basis for generalization.

Statistical Laws

In discussing models, the formula

$$d = 16t^2$$

was used to describe an important law of falling bodies. Using Newton's laws of motion, one can compute exactly where the falling object will hit the ground beneath the tower. On the other hand, if a six-sided die is rolled on the table, there are no laws to predict whether the top face will stop as a one, two, three, four, five, or six. However, it is possible to predict that if the die is rolled a great many times, the one will appear on top about one sixth of the time. The distinction that is made between these two situations is the distinction between a *causal law* and a *statistical law*.

Even though the causal law permits an estimate of the exact spot where the object will fall, the problem is not that simple. If an experiment is carried out repeatedly, it will be observed that the actual hits will form a certain pattern about the predicted spot. Only if all physical conditions could be perfectly controlled in the empirical experiment would the dispersion of the actual hits be reduced to zero. The law is called "causal" because it is theoretically possible to control simultaneously all the physical conditions and to compute mathematically an exact answer.

In the case of the rolling die, the Newtonian laws of motion are still in effect, but the ability to predict the outcome of a single roll is not present. For one roll, or even a few rolls, the pattern of the outcomes is not predictable. It is necessary to fall back on the frequency with which different values occur in a great many trials to compute the probability that a one will occur in any one trial. The prediction in this case is based on a "statistical law."

In a sense there are statistical laws that allow for controlled conditions in such a manner that they permit the expression of a causal law. On the other hand, there are statistical laws, such as the laws for rolling a die, in which the conditions cannot be controlled. These laws must continue to be expressed as statistical laws. It is with the latter group that this book is concerned.

Populations and Samples

Another distinction that must be made early in a preliminary discussion of the field of statistics is the difference between a population and a sample. A *population* or a *universe* (the terms are used synonymously) can be defined as each and every member of some group. The group that constitutes a population can be determined in many ways. For example, the population of City A may be defined as all those persons living within the city limits. In this case a political boundary is used to designate the group. The population of sophomore students at College B may be defined as all the students having 30 or more but fewer than 60 hours of college course credit and registered in College B during the current semester. The definition of the population should be clear and complete.

Any descriptive measure of the characteristics of a population is called a *parameter*. For example, the total number of persons living in City A or the average age of the sophomores registered in College B is a parameter.

Once the population has been defined, a *sample* can be described as some of the members of the population. Some of the residents of City A or some of the sophomores at College B would constitute a sample. There are, of course, many possible samples of a given size that might be drawn from any population of any size.

As has already been mentioned, a *statistic* is a descriptive measure of some characteristic of a sample. For example, the average age of a sample of sophomores from College B is a statistic.

Much of the work in inductive statistics is concerned with the problems involved in using a statistic to estimate a parameter.

VARIABLES

A basic building block with which the statistician deals is the variable. Statistical data are the result of successive observations of some characteristic of a group. The characteristic being observed is the *variable*. The observations, which are recorded as the corresponding magnitudes or numbers, are the *values of the variable*.

A variable in which the several possible magnitudes differ by clearly defined steps is called a *discrete variable*. A discrete variable can assume only certain values, often integers, and no intermediate values. For example, the number of rooms in a house or the number of automobiles sold during the month of August is a discrete variable.

When the values of a variable are obtained by measuring from a continuous scale, the variable is said to be a *continuous variable*. Such measures as weight, time, distance, or volume involve measurement on a continuous scale. For any two measurements, no matter how close together, a third measurement can always be found that lies between the first two if a more precise measurement is taken. A continuous variable always has an infinite number of values that need not be whole numbers but which may be carried to as many decimal places as the accuracy of the measurement will justify.

A variable that is derived as a ratio of two other variables, such as income per capita, miles per hour, or units per day of production, is called a *derived variable*.

The individual values of a variable in a population are designated by a capital X, and the number of observations is designated by a capital N. The N observations may be designated as

$$X_1, X_2, \ldots, X_N.$$

The values of a variable in a sample are designated by a lowercase x, and the number of observations is designated by a lowercase n. The n observations may be designated as

$$x_1, x_2, x_3, \ldots, x_n.$$

■ *Example.* Six workers performing an assembly operation turn out 14, 16, 12, 10, 15, and 13 parts each in an hour. The variable X has six values, which can be denoted as follows:

X: $X_1 = 14$, $X_2 = 16$, $X_3 = 12$, $X_4 = 10$, $X_5 = 15$, and $X_6 = 13$.

The group of six workers constitutes a universe, so capital X's have been used to denote each observation of the variable. Since only completed parts are counted, the variable is discrete.

Assume that a sample of three workers from the group is selected and the average time each worker takes to assemble one part is computed. If the times are 4.3, 3.7, and 4.6 minutes, the variable x has three values as follows:

x: $x_1 = 4.3$, $x_2 = 3.7$, $x_3 = 4.6$.

Since the group of three workers constitutes a sample, lowercase x's have been used to denote each observation of the variable. The values of the variable are measured on a continuous scale, time, and the variable is continuous.

ACCURACY OF STATISTICAL DATA

The statistician is confronted with two problems in dealing with statistical data. Care should be taken not to present quantitative facts in a manner that leaves the impression that they are more accurate than they actually are. On the other hand, the statistician must be careful not to discard any accuracy that can be justified.

■ *Example.* If a news report states that unemployment during the past month increased by 257,115 persons as a result of a strike in the automobile industry, the reader is given the impression that the count is an exact one. Actually, it is probably an estimate compiled from new claims for unemployment compensation from several states, reports of layoffs made by the companies involved, and statements made by union officials. A statement to the effect that unemployment has risen approximately a quarter of a million persons would be more justified by the nature of the data. However, a statement by an official of the Texas Employment Commission in Austin that 23,121 new claims for unemployment compensation were filed during the past week would most likely be the result of an actual count made from reports from local offices of the commission. Even in this case it might be helpful to know that all the local offices reported so that no "estimates" had to be made by someone in Austin to fill in gaps in the report.

It must be recognized that additional accuracy in data is often secured only at additional cost, which may or may not be justified by the use to be made of the data. Many administrative decisions require only information that is approximate. The business executive may need to know only in a general way the changes that have occurred in inventories, sales, and employment, or the shifts that have been noted in consumer demand. Data that purport to be more accurate than they are, are not only deceptive but unnecessary as well.

Exact and Approximate Numbers

The values of a discrete variable are *exact numbers*. In many cases an exact number is one that results from the counting of distinct physical objects or occurrences. While the concept of an exact number is simple, the mechanics of arriving at such a number may be complex. For example, census counts may be made of the population of a large city. Individuals are distinct units and can be counted; but because they are constantly moving about and in and out of the city limits, the census count may be only a good approximation of the true population that is never known.

A datum which is arrived at by the measurement of some characteristic is always an *approximate number*. The fact that it is approximate does not mean it is inaccurate. If a student weighs on a drug store scale and reads a weight of 174 pounds, the number 174 is an approximate number, rounded to the nearest full pound. It is an approximate number because the variable, weight, is a continuous variable. If the scale is reasonably accurate, so is the value of the observation. If the same student weighs on a very sensitive scale in the Physics Department and reads a weight of 174.25 pounds, the observed weight may be more accurate than before but the number is still approximate.

Rounding

To avoid the impression of greater accuracy than actually exists, numbers are often rounded to drop unnecessary digits. If an estimate of a city's population is made from the number of water meter connections, it might be better to round an estimate of 121,144 to 120,000. The use of zeros implies that the number is approximate.

Rounding cannot always be accomplished by changing other digits to zeros, however. To do so might induce a downward bias in the data, as demonstrated in the following example.

■ *Example.* If a governmental agency interested in the average age of its employees used the age at last birthday to compute the average, the average would undoubtedly be too small. It would be more accurate to round the age of each employee to the nearest birthday before computing the average. In some cases the age recorded for an employee would be less than the true age, and in other cases, more; but most of the inaccuracies would be canceled out in the final average.

The following rules are usually used in rounding:

1. When the first of the digits to be rounded to zero is less than five, make no change in the last digit retained.
2. When the first of the digits to be rounded to zero is more than five, or five followed by some digits not all zero, increase the last digit retained by one.
3. When the first of the digits to be rounded to zero is five, or five followed by zeros only, make no change in the last digit retained if it is even, but increase it by one if it is odd.

■ *Example.* Given the following measurements, the rules for rounding would be applied as shown below to round to two digits in each case:

Rule	Original number	Number rounded to two digits
1	2.713	2.7
2	2.768	2.8
3	2.75	2.8
3	2.85	2.8
2	2.85001	2.9
3	2.850000	2.8
1	2.74995	2.7

Significant Digits

After rounding, any digit other than a zero is always *significant*. If sales for the month have been recorded as 3,427 units, each of the four digits is significant. This means that the only problem of significance is with zeros. The following rules may be used to determine if a zero is significant:

1. A zero that falls between two significant digits is always significant.
2. A zero that falls after a significant digit is always significant if the number contains a decimal point.
3. A zero that falls before the first significant digit is not significant.
4. A zero that falls after the last significant digit of a whole number may or may not be significant. A dot placed above the last significant zero makes it and all the zeros that precede it significant.

■ Example. The rules of significant digits are used to interpret the zeros in the following numbers:

Rule	Number	Number of significant digits
2	12.740	5
3	0.00743	3
1	60,501	5
4	3,000	1 to 4
4	3,00ò	4
4	3,0ò0	3
2	3,000.	4
1	609	3
4	60,900	3 to 5
2	1.2000	5
1	200.003	6

Computation with Rounded Numbers

Once the number of significant digits is determined for rounded numbers used in computation, two simple rules govern the number of significant digits that may be carried in the answer.

1. In addition or subtraction, digits to the right of the place in which the last significant digit occurs in any of the numbers are not significant and should not be carried in the sum or remainder.
2. In multiplication or division, the product or quotient should contain no more significant digits than that number with the least number of significant digits used in the calculations.

■ Example. The rules for computation with rounded numbers are used to determine the proper number of significant digits in the following computations:

Rule	Computations	Answer to be shown as
1. (addition)	2.743	
	*172.6	
	14.76	
	190.103	190.1
1. (subtraction)	145.268	
	* 19.3	
	125.968	126.0

2. (multiplication)

$$
\begin{array}{r}
172.43 \\
*\ \underline{\hspace{4mm}1.2} \\
34486 \\
\underline{17243\hspace{4mm}} \\
206.916
\end{array}
$$

210**

2. (division)

$$*3.1\overline{)47.12}\ 15.2$$

$$
\begin{array}{r}
\underline{31}\ \\
161 \\
\underline{155} \\
62 \\
\underline{62}
\end{array}
$$

15

* This number determines the number of significant digits that may be carried in each answer.
** Although only two significant digits can be justified in the answer, it is necessary to add the zero, which is not significant, to keep from changing the value of the number.

It should be stressed that in problems involving several computational steps, more than the maximum number of significant digits may be used in intermediate answers.

TYPES OF STATISTICAL DATA

In order to produce statistical data one must assign numbers to observations in such a way that the numbers can be analyzed by manipulating them according to a certain set of rules. This analysis will reveal new information about the observations that are being measured.

For example, if statisticians collect data on years of experience of machine operators and then manipulate these data by performing algebraic operations (adding, dividing, etc.) to compute the average (arithmetic mean) and the measure of dispersion (standard deviation), they are assuming that they have a high enough level of measurement to justify the use of these statistical measures.

If, on the other hand, these statisticians have gathered data on the different kinds of machine operators in the firm, they have a lower level of measurement which is qualitative and which will not justify the computation of a mean or a standard deviation.

The distinction between types of data or levels of measurement is fundamental in determining the kinds of statistical methods that are appropriate for summarizing and analyzing the data.

All data measurements can be classified into one of four major categories:

1. Nominal data
2. Ordinal data
3. Interval data
4. Ratio data

Nominal Data

The weakest level of measurement exists when observations are assigned to groups simply on the basis of a difference in kind. When the observations in one group have certain characteristics in common that differentiate them from items in other groups, the data are said to be *nominal data.*

■ *Example.* Employees in an office might be classified as male or female. In recording these data in the personnel file, a one might be used to represent a male and a zero to represent a female. The data are nominal and are represented by the numbers one and zero.

■ *Example.* A numbering system in an office building could produce nominal data. The first digit of a three-digit number might designate the floor number, while the last digit might indicate whether the office is on the north or the south side of the building, depending on whether the digit is odd or even.

The only types of descriptive statistical methods that can be used with nominal data are the mode, frequency counts, bar charts, or any kind of one-to-one transformation where one set of symbols is substituted for some other.

There are also appropriate tests of hypotheses for nominal data, such as the chi-square test, which will be discussed in a later chapter in this book.

Ordinal Data

The second level of measurement exists when all the observations can be placed into separate categories and each category has a known relationship to every other category. If the order of relationship is such that category A is greater than category B for all pairs of categories, a complete rank ordering of classes is possible and the data are considered to be *ordinal data.*

■ *Example.* The classification of faculty rank in a university is made so that professor > associate professor > assistant professor > instructor.[1]

■ *Example.* Ten workers may be ranked from 1 to 10 by their supervisor in the order in which the supervisor thinks they deserve merit increases in pay.

■ *Example.* A homemaker may rank six brands of household detergent in the order in which she prefers to use them to do the family wash.

---

[1] The symbol ">" is read "greater than."

The most appropriate statistic for describing central tendency (the average) for ordinal data is the median. Since it is an average based on position, it is not influenced by the relative size of the difference between any two categories. This and other statistical measures appropriate to ordinal data will be discussed in later chapters.

Interval Data

Interval data have all the characteristics of ordinal data, but the scale is one for which equal units are used. If, for example, the measure goes from 1 to 50, the difference between 10 and 20 is the same as the difference between 20 and 30 because the interval of 10 is the same for both. The naming of this type of measurement arises from the fact that the measurements of a variable are sufficiently precise to permit one to know just how large the interval is between any two observations.

■ *Example.* A classic example is temperature which can be measured on either of two interval scales, Fahrenheit or centigrade. The zero point on the scale is arbitrary and is different for each scale.

The interval measure is much stronger than that for ordinal data and, as a result, more useful descriptive statistics can be computed when this measure is used. The interval scale is often called a *quantitative scale* and can be used to compute means, standard deviations, and many other measures which will be explained in later chapters.

Ratio Data

Ratio data have all the characteristics of interval data and the ratio scale has an absolute true zero point as the origin. Not only are the intervals between values known, but also the ratio between any two points on the scale can be determined regardless of what type of ratio scale is used.

■ *Example.* The length of an object can be measured on several scales. Regardless of whether the scale is in inches or centimeters, both scales have the same origin of zero. Since 1 inch = 2.54 centimeters, the ratio of 10 inches to 25.4 centimeters is the same as 100 inches to 254 centimeters. The ratio between any two lengths is the same regardless of which ratio scale is used.

The ratio scale is another type of quantitative scale and will justify the use of statistical measures such as the geometric mean.

The concept of the differences between the kinds of data or levels of measurement will be discussed further in Chapter 2 and will be important to an understanding of tests of significance in later chapters.

STUDY QUESTIONS

1-1. Explain briefly the meaning of each of the following terms:
a. model
b. Monte Carlo methods
c. statistics
d. statistical data
e. statistical method
f. statistic
g. descriptive statistics
h. inductive statistics
i. causal law
j. statistical law
k. population
l. universe
m. parameter
n. sample
o. variable
p. values of the variable
q. discrete variable
r. continuous variable
s. derived variable
t. exact number
u. approximate number
v. significant digit
w. nominal data
x. ordinal data
y. interval data
z. quantitative scale
aa. ratio data

1-2. Discuss the steps in the decision-making process. How does the application of these steps to administrative problems differ from their application to engineering or physical science problems?

1-3. Distinguish between the terms descriptive statistics and inductive statistics. Give two examples of each.

1-4. For the following variables distinguish between those that are continuous and those that are discrete:
a. Number of absences students have in a history class
b. Weight of castings in a foundry
c. Time required to assemble 100 TV sets
d. Grades on an accounting quiz
e. Height of six-month-old fig bushes in a nursery
f. Machines requiring repair in a factory in one day

1-5. Give three examples of a derived variable. What is the advantage of using a derived variable?

1-6. Discuss the difference between a population and a sample. Give examples of three populations, being careful that each is precisely and accurately defined.

1-7. If you wish to take a sample of dwelling units from the population of all dwelling units in a city, how would you define the term, "dwelling unit"? Why would it be necessary to have an exact definition?

1-8. Why is it necessary to distinguish between exact and approximate numbers in dealing with statistical data? Why is rounding necessary in dealing with approximate numbers? What is the danger of too much rounding?

1-9. Indicate the type or level of measurement used with each of the following sets of observations:
   a. Measurement of the amount of air in four automobile tires, measured in pounds per square inch.
   b. Order in which sports cars finish a 500-mile race.
   c. Make and model of computers used by 100 colleges and universities.
   d. Amounts spent by 75 shoppers in a supermarket.
   e. Temperature readings at 37 locations in a state all taken at noon of the same day.

PROBLEMS

1-1. How many significant digits are there in each of the following numbers?
   a. 16,730
   b. 512 thousand
   c. 0.0016
   d. 100,001.10
   e. 17.0
   f. 0.76
   g. 250,000
   h. 13 million
   i. .760

1-2. Round each of the following numbers so that it contains four significant digits:
   a. 0.05580
   b. 3,780,467
   c. 9,876,500
   d. 2,679.50
   e. 765,900
   f. .0004298
   g. 10.00001
   h. 437.000
   i. 999,999

1-3. If all the numbers used in the following computations are approximate, round the results to the appropriate number of significant digits:
   a. $\sqrt{2.73} = 1.6522712$
   b. $(49)^2 = 2,401$
   c.
      742.37
      22.4
      1,377.2379
      2,142.0079
   d. $1,748 \div 3 = 582.6666$
   e. $(4,782)(3.8) = 18,171.6$
   f.
      948.231
      −56.8
      891.431

SELECTED READINGS

Costis, Harry G. *Statistics for Business.* Columbus, Ohio: Charles E. Merrill Publishing Company, 1972.
   Many of the ideas in this chapter are presented in a slightly different light in Chapters 1 and 2 of the Costis book.
Fisher, Sir Ronald A. *Statistical Methods for Research Workers,* 14th ed. New York: Hafner Press, 1973.
   The introduction in this book makes most interesting reading for any student studying the science of statistics.

Stockton, John R., and Charles T. Clark. *Introduction to Business and Economic Statistics,* 5th ed. Cincinnati: South-Western Publishing Co., 1975.

    The first few chapters of this book provide a more complete introduction to the field of statistics as it relates to the business executive.

Tanur, Judith M., Frederick Mosteller, et al. *Statistics: A Guide to the Unknown.* San Francisco: Holden-Day, Inc., 1972.

    A series of 44 essays collected and edited by a committee of the American Statistical Association to illustrate past accomplishments in the field of statistics. A delightful, nontechnical book showing how widely statistical tools are applied.

Walker, Helen M. *Mathematics Essential in Elementary Statistics, A Self-Teaching Manual,* rev. ed. New York: Henry Holt and Company, 1951.

    This is a self-teaching manual of great value to the student who wishes to review the elementary mathematical concepts necessary to an understanding of statistics.

Chapter 2
Statistical Description

It is pointed out in Chapter 1 that the kinds of analysis that can be made of data are dependent on the level of measurement of those data. The level of measurement will play an important part in this chapter in selecting the appropriate descriptive statistical measure to use under a given set of circumstances. The areas of descriptive analysis discussed in this chapter fall into four categories:

1. Measures of central tendency
2. Measures of absolute dispersion
3. Measures of relative dispersion
4. Measures of shape

ANALYSIS OF UNGROUPED DATA

The first part of this chapter deals with the analysis of individual observations at all levels of measurement. The emphasis is on the appropriate measure to use based on the type of data and the information needed to solve a particular problem.

Measures of Central Tendency

Most measures of central tendency are referred to as "averages." One speaks of the "average student" or the "average starting salary," often without being very specific as to exactly what this means. The use of "average" is an attempt to find one single figure to describe a whole group of figures.

Since there are several different kinds of averages in statistics, the use of precise terminology is necessary. Each average must be clearly defined and labeled to avoid ambiguity and confusion. This chapter deals with measures of central tendency such as the arithmetic mean, geometric mean, median, and mode. Also, the measures of location known as quartiles, deciles, and percentiles are discussed briefly.

Mode. The *mode* can be defined as the most frequently occurring value. It may be viewed as a single value that is most representative of all the values in a distribution of the values of some variable.

The mode can be used with data at any level of measurement, but it is the only average which can be used appropriately to describe nominal data.

■ *Example.* An insurance agency classifies insurance policies by type of payment used and comes up with the following categories:

Type of Plan	Number of Policies
Monthly	59
Prepaid Monthly	85
Quarterly	12
Prepaid Quarterly	32
Annually	5
Semiannually	7
Total	200

The mode is found in the second group because it is the type of payment that occurs most often. Note that the data are measured on a nominal scale and that the type of payment falls into groups or classes. Thus, the mode is more appropriately called the *modal class*, which is the class containing the greatest number of items.

■ *Example.* If the starting salaries made by 10 graduating seniors on their first jobs were in the following amounts, the fact that the greatest number started at $700 per month would make that figure the mode:

Name	Starting salary	Starting salary (array)	
Anderson	$825	$660	
Lopez	700	680	
Cleveland	680	700	
Dawson	700	700	← Mode = $700
Emerson	660	700	
Franklin	700	700	
Goldman	775	725	
Harris	730	730	
Chung	725	775	
Jackson	700	825	

When there are only a few values in a group of values, it is quite possible that there will be no two of them alike; hence, there will be no mode. It is also possible that there may be two or more modes. In these cases, it is clear that the mode cannot be used as a measure of central tendency.

Median. When the measurement of a group of observations is at least ordinal in nature, the observations can be ranked or sorted into an array. In an *array* the various values of the variable are arranged in order of magnitude with each individual value retaining its original identity. If a value appears more than once, it is listed separately each time it occurs. While the array is one of the simplest ways of organizing data, it has many useful applications in statistical analysis if the number of items is not too large.

The *median* is defined as the value of the middle item of a group of items that form an array. The median can be defined as the item occupying the $\frac{(N + 1)}{2}$ position. This is the point in the array at which the items divide into two groups of equal size. The value of the middle item is the median, which is an average determined by position or rank in an array of items. While its value is affected by the position of each item in the array, the median is not unduly influenced by a few very large or a few very small items. Note the effect of the extreme value in the following examples.

Finding the median for ungrouped data is a matter of arranging the items in an array and then finding the middle item and noting its value. This can be a tedious job if the number of items is large. For example, if 1,000 items are to be arranged by size, the task might take several hours if done by hand but only seconds if accomplished by a computer.

■ *Example.* The following shows the location of the median time required by five workers to perform an assembly operation:

Worker	Time (in minutes)	Time (in array)
1	25	23
2	26	25
3	130	26 → Median
4	23	28
5	28	130

A strict application of the definition of the median leads to two problems that need special consideration because, technically, the median is indeterminate. The first of these problems arises when there are an even number of items. The second problem appears when two or more items in the center of the array have the same value. These special cases are discussed in the following two examples.

■ Example.

An even number of items:	Time (in minutes)

$$
\begin{array}{c}
23 \\
25 \\
\left.\begin{array}{c} 26 \\ 28 \end{array}\right\} \rightarrow \text{Median} = \dfrac{26 + 28}{2} = 27 \text{ minutes} \\
30 \\
132
\end{array}
$$

When there are an even number of items in the distribution, the median is taken as a value halfway between the two middle items.

■ Example.

An odd number of items with identical items at the center:	Time (in minutes)

$$
\begin{array}{c}
23 \\
25 \\
\boxed{26} \rightarrow \text{Median} = 26 \text{ minutes} \\
26 \\
28
\end{array}
$$

In the example above the value 26 is taken as the median even though two of the values are smaller and only one is larger.

Arithmetic Mean. Averages other than the mode and the median, such as the arithmetic mean, are possible when data measurement is at the interval or ratio level. As discussed in Chapter 1, the interval scale has an arbitrary zero, and the ratio scale has a true zero.

Because it is easily understood, the best known, and most useful, the arithmetic mean is the most often used average in statistics. The *arithmetic mean* can be defined as the sum of the values of a variable divided by the number of values. To compute the mean of the values of a variable X, such as $X_1, X_2, X_3, \ldots , X_N$, the following equation can be used:

$$
\mu = \frac{\Sigma X}{N} \quad \text{..(2.1)}
$$

where
μ is the arithmetic mean
X is the value of an individual observation of the variable
ΣX is "the sum of" the values of the variable[1]
N is the number of values being averaged.

---

[1] See Technical Note No. 1 at the end of this chapter.

■ *Example.* If a car owner purchases gasoline six times during the month in the following amounts, 5.4, 9.8, 7.6, 8.2, 8.7, and 10.1 gallons, the arithmetic mean of the purchases is:

$$\mu = \frac{5.4 + 9.8 + 7.6 + 8.2 + 8.7 + 10.1}{6} = \frac{49.8}{6} = 8.3 \text{ gallons.}$$

The arithmetic mean has an additional property. If the total and the number of values being averaged are known, it is not necessary to know the values of the individual items to compute the mean.

■ *Example.* If the total payroll for a retail store with 43 employees is $18,608.25, then:

$$\mu = \frac{\$18,608.25}{43} = \$432.75.$$

The fact that an arithmetic mean can be computed does not always imply that it is a meaningful or useful average.

■ *Example.* If the numbers on the jerseys of five football players are 16, 23, 30, 28, and 10, the arithmetic mean of 21.4 is completely meaningless. The data in this example are measured on the nominal scale, and the use of the arithmetic mean is not appropriate.

■ *Example.* If five sales representatives travel 25, 35, 28, 850, and 32 miles in visiting customers one week:

$$\mu = \frac{25 + 35 + 28 + 850 + 32}{5} = 194 \text{ miles.}$$

This figure is neither typical of the distance traveled by the sales representatives who make all of their calls in a single district of town, nor is it typical of one sales representative who travels throughout the state to visit customers. The arithmetic mean has the one weakness of being unduly influenced by unusually large or unusually small values in a distribution. For example, the median of 27 minutes is much more typical of the times shown in a previous example than would be the mean time of 44 minutes. It would be meaningless to say that the arithmetic mean of all army ranks is corporal, since the ranks of private, corporal, sergeant, etc., are ordinal data and cannot be used to compute a mean.

The arithmetic mean has another familiar property that will be useful to remember. The sum of the deviations of the values from their mean is zero, and the sum of the squared deviations of the values about the mean is a minimum. That is to say, the sum of the squared deviations is less than the sum of the squared deviations about any other value. The advantages of this characteristic will be apparent in later chapters in this text.

■ **Example.** For the following values the arithmetic mean is 8, and the sum of the values about 8 is 0.

Values of X	$X - \mu$	$(X - \mu)^2$
2	−6	36
4	−4	16
4	−4	16
6	−2	4
10	2	4
10	2	4
12	4	16
12	4	16
12	4	16
72	0	128

$$\mu = \frac{72}{9} = 8$$

$$\Sigma(X - \mu) = 0$$

$\Sigma(X - \mu)^2 = 128$ is a minimum sum of squares

Weighted Arithmetic Mean. Formula 2.1 assumes that the values being averaged are all of equal importance. This is not always the case, however. For example, the grade on a three-hour final examination is more important than the grade on a one-hour quiz in determining the final grade in a course. To compute the mean of the values of the variable X when each value has an assigned weight, such as $w_1 X_1, w_2 X_2, w_3 X_3, \ldots , w_N X_N$, the following equation can be used:

$$\mu = \frac{\Sigma w X}{\Sigma w} \dots\dots\dots\dots\dots\dots\dots\dots\dots\dots(2.2)$$

where
   w is the weight assigned each value of X.

■ **Example.** In the case of a student's final grade, the weighted arithmetic mean might be computed as shown in the following table:

TABLE 2.1

Computation of Weighted Arithmetic Mean, Semester Grade of One Student

Work	Grade X	Weight w	wX
Homework problems	79	5	395
Laboratory reports	85	10	850
First hour quiz	72	15	1,080
Second hour quiz	68	15	1,020
Third hour quiz	81	15	1,215
Term report	89	10	890
Final examination	75	30	2,250
Total	...	100	7,700

$$\mu = \frac{\Sigma w X}{\Sigma w} = \frac{7,700}{100} = 77.$$

An analogy of this characteristic is illustrated graphically in Figure 2.1, where blocks of equal weight representing the values of X are distributed along a bar (assumed to have no weight) marked with a scale of all possible values of the variable. When the bar is placed on a fulcrum, it will be in balance only if the fulcrum is located at that point on the scale corresponding to the arithmetic mean of the values. The arithmetic mean corresponds to the point on the scale for which the sum of the products of the weights times their respective distances to the left of the mean (negative values) is exactly offset by the sum of the products of the weights and their respective distances to the right of the mean (positive values). Thus, the sum of deviations of X about the mean is zero, or $\Sigma(X - \mu) = 0$.

FIGURE 2.1

The Arithmetic Mean of a Set of Points Is Its Balance Point

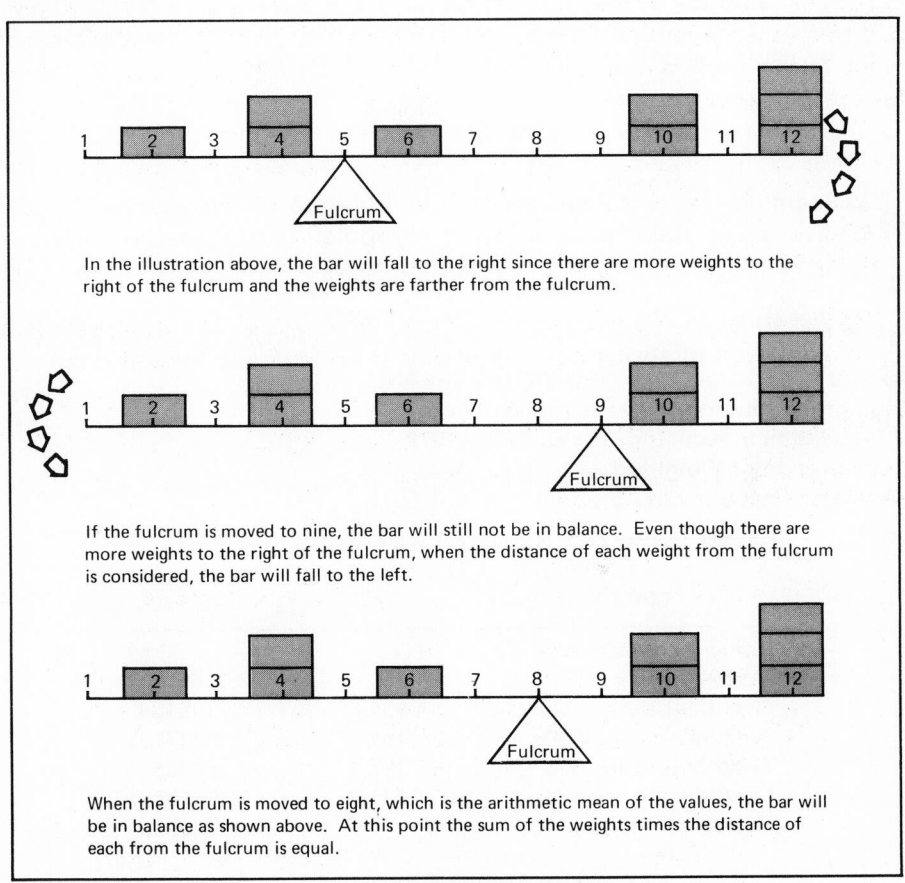

In the illustration above, the bar will fall to the right since there are more weights to the right of the fulcrum and the weights are farther from the fulcrum.

If the fulcrum is moved to nine, the bar will still not be in balance. Even though there are more weights to the right of the fulcrum, when the distance of each weight from the fulcrum is considered, the bar will fall to the left.

When the fulcrum is moved to eight, which is the arithmetic mean of the values, the bar will be in balance as shown above. At this point the sum of the weights times the distance of each from the fulcrum is equal.

In order to simplify the arithmetic involved, it is customary to assign weights so that they total either 1 or 100. This is not a requirement however.

Geometric Mean. In addition to the median, the mode, and the arithmetic mean, it is possible to average observations using the geometric mean when the measurement of data is on a ratio scale. This mean is often used to average ratios and percents, and it is particularly valuable in computing index numbers. The *geometric mean* can be defined as the Nth root of the product of N values of a variable. If the variable X has values $X_1, X_2, X_3, \ldots, X_N$, the geometric mean of these values can be computed as follows:

$$G = \sqrt[N]{X_1 \cdot X_2 \cdot X_3 \cdot \ldots \cdot X_N} \ldots\ldots\ldots\ldots\ldots\ldots\ldots\ldots(2.3)$$

where
  G is the geometric mean
  X is the value of the individual observation of the variable
  N is the number of values being averaged.

When N is more than two, the geometric mean can be most easily computed by using logarithms and the following formula:

$$\log G = \frac{\Sigma \log X}{N} \ldots\ldots\ldots\ldots\ldots\ldots\ldots\ldots\ldots\ldots\ldots(2.4)$$

■ *Example.* Table 2.2 shows the computation of the geometric mean of five ratios. Each ratio shows the population of Houston, Texas, as a percentage of the figure 10 years before.

TABLE 2.2

COMPUTATION OF THE GEOMETRIC MEAN,
Percentage Change from Previous 10 years
of Population in Houston, Texas, 1920–1970

Year	Population (in thousands)	Percent of previous 10 years X	Log X
1920	138	...	...
1930	292	211.6	2.325516
1940	385	131.8	2.119915
1950	596	154.8	2.189771
1960	938	157.4	2.197005
1970	1,233	131.4	2.118595
Total			10,950802

Source: United States Bureau of Census.

$$\log G = \frac{\Sigma \log X}{N} = \frac{10.950802}{5} = 2.190160$$
$$\text{antilog } 2.190160 = 154.94$$
$$G = 154.94$$
$$\text{Average rate of increase} = 154.94\% - 100.00\%$$
$$= 54.94\%$$

The nature of the formula for the geometric mean (see Formula 2.3) is such that if any of the values being averaged is zero, the product of the values will be zero, and the geometric mean cannot be computed. It is also meaningless to compute the geometric mean if negative values are involved. These difficulties can usually be overcome, however, by using care in selecting the way in which the values are expressed when they are to be averaged using the geometric mean. It would be inappropriate to use an arithmetic mean to average the percentages in this example since each percentage has a different base, and the arithmetic mean would have an upward bias. That is to say, it would be too large.

While the geometric mean can be computed from grouped data, this is seldom necessary and will not be discussed in this book.

Other Measures of Location. Quartiles, deciles, and percentiles are other summary measures of a distribution that are important as locators for data measured at or above the ordinal level. Just as the median is a value that divides a distribution so that half of the items are smaller and the other half are larger than the median, quartiles divide the distribution into quarters; deciles divide it into tenths; and percentiles divide it into hundredths.

To calculate quartiles of ungrouped data, the items must be ranked in an array. The *second quartile* is the same as the median and is found in exactly the same manner. The *first quartile* (Q_1) is that value which divides the items less than the median in half. The third quartile (Q_3) is that value which divides the items greater than the median in half.

■ *Example.* The location of quartiles for ungrouped data is shown below:

Salaries (Array)		Salaries (Array)	
$420		$420	
430		428	$\leftarrow \boxed{Q_1} = \frac{428 + 432}{2} = \$430$
435	$\leftarrow Q_1$ First Quartile = $435	432	
438		438	$\leftarrow \boxed{Md} = \frac{438 + 440}{2} = \$439$
441		440	
445	$\leftarrow Q_2$ Second Quartile or Median = $445	445	$\leftarrow \boxed{Q_3} = \frac{445 + 449}{2} = \$447$
447		449	
490		450	

$$500 \leftarrow Q_3 \boxed{\text{Third Quartile}} = \$500$$
510
515

Deciles and percentiles can be located by following the same general procedures used to determine the location of quartiles. The computation and, hence, the use of these measures is greatly facilitated when the data are grouped into a frequency distribution.

Measures of Absolute Dispersion

Measures of dispersion are measures of scatter about an average. Measures of *absolute* dispersion, as distinguished from measures of *relative* dispersion, are in the same units as the data whose scatter they measure. For example, the scatter of salaries about an average is measured in dollars and cents, and the variation of time required for workers to do an assembly operation is measured in minutes and seconds. Measures of absolute dispersion cannot be used to compare the scatter in one distribution with that in another distribution when the averages of the distributions differ in size or the units of measure differ in kind.

The following measures of absolute dispersion are discussed here:

1. Range
2. Interquartile range
3. Quartile deviation
4. Variance and standard deviation

Measures of dispersion are not defined for nominal data since at this level of measurement, data are obtained from several distinct categories rather than being observations of a single random variable.

Measures such as the range, interquartile range, and quartile deviation may be used to describe scatter in observations at an ordinal or higher level of measurement.

Range. The *range* is the simplest of all measures of dispersion and is used with interval or ratio data. It can be defined as:

1. The difference between the largest and the smallest values of some variable, or
2. The largest and the smallest values themselves.

For example, a firm has 25 accountants on its payroll, and the monthly salaries of these accountants vary from a low of $650 to a high of $1,050. The range can be defined either as $400 or as $650 to $1,050 per month. The latter expression gives more information, however.

An advantage of the range is its easy computation, but it tells nothing about what lies in between the largest and the smallest values. In the case of the accountants' salaries, 24 of them might be earning $650 per month and the remaining one, $1,050. Or there might be only one earning $650 and the other 24 earning $1,050. The average salary in each case would be quite different.

Interquartile Range. The *interquartile range* describes the extent of the scatter or dispersion of the middle 50% of the values in a distribution. As shown below, this type of range is defined as the distance between the first and the third quartiles:

$$QR = Q_3 - Q_1 \dots\dots\dots\dots\dots\dots\dots\dots(2.5)$$

where
QR is the interquartile range.

■ *Example.* If a personnel director is making a study of salaries paid secretaries in a community, the range may be an unusable measure since it will be influenced by the extremes at both the high and the low ends of distribution. Some secretaries may have the title but lack adequate skills, so they will be paid very low salaries. At the upper end of the scale, however, are jobs requiring much more ability and training than normally required of a secretary; hence, these secretaries will be better paid. The interquartile range is not influenced by the extremes of very high or very low salaries. Since it is based on location and not directly on quantitative magnitude, it measures the spread in salaries of the most significant group, that which lies in the middle of the distribution.

Quartile Deviation. The *quartile deviation* is defined as one-half the distance between the first and the third quartiles. Its formula is:

$$Q = \frac{Q_3 - Q_1}{2} \dots\dots\dots\dots\dots\dots\dots(2.6)$$

where
Q is the quartile deviation.

The quartile deviation can be computed from a frequency distribution with an open-end class when it might not be possible to compute other types of measures. For example, we will find later in this chapter that a standard deviation cannot be computed from a frequency distribution with an open-end class.

Variance and Standard Deviation. The most useful measures of dispersion and those with the most desirable mathematical properties are variance and standard deviation. These measures may be used with data measured on either an interval or a ratio scale. *Variance* may be defined as the arithmetic mean of the squared deviations of the individual items about their mean. The square root of variance is called *standard deviation*. This measure is particularly useful when dealing with the normal distribution (see Chapter 5).

For ungrouped data, the formulas for variance and standard deviation are written as follows:

$$\sigma^2 = \frac{\Sigma(X - \mu)^2}{N} \quad\text{............................(2.7)}$$

$$\sigma = \sqrt{\frac{\Sigma(X - \mu)^2}{N}} \quad\text{............................(2.8)}$$

where
σ^2 is the variance of a universe
σ is the standard deviation of a universe.[2]

Algebraically equivalent expressions of Formulas 2.7 and 2.8 that are often easier to use in manual calculations are as follows:[3]

$$\sigma^2 = \frac{\Sigma X^2}{N} - \left(\frac{\Sigma X}{N}\right)^2 \quad\text{............................(2.9)}$$

$$\sigma = \sqrt{\frac{\Sigma X^2}{N} - \left(\frac{\Sigma X}{N}\right)^2} \quad\text{............................(2.10)}$$

■ *Example.* Both Formulas 2.8 and 2.10 are used in Table 2.3 to illustrate the computation of the standard deviation for ungrouped data.

Formula 2.8

$$\mu = \frac{33.6}{8} = 4.2$$

$$\sigma = \sqrt{\frac{\Sigma(X - \mu)^2}{N}} = \sqrt{\frac{5.72}{8}} = \sqrt{0.715}$$

$$\sigma = \sqrt{0.715} = 0.846 \text{ or } 846 \text{ hours.}$$

Formula 2.10

$$\sigma = \sqrt{\frac{\Sigma X^2}{N} - \left(\frac{\Sigma X}{N}\right)^2} = \sqrt{\frac{146.84}{8} - \left(\frac{33.6}{8}\right)^2} = \sqrt{0.715}$$

$$\sigma = \sqrt{0.715} = 0.846 \text{ or } 846 \text{ hours.}$$

---

[2] The Greek lowercase sigma (σ) is used to denote the standard deviation of a universe of items. The letter s is used to denote the standard deviation of a sample. The relationship between σ and s is discussed in detail in Chapter 6 which deals with sampling distributions.

[3] These expressions are derived by computing the square of $\Sigma(X - \mu)^2$ and summing to give $\Sigma X^2 - 2\mu\Sigma X + N\mu^2$. Substituting this expression into Formula 2.7 gives $\sigma^2 = \dfrac{\Sigma X^2}{N} - \dfrac{2\mu\Sigma X^2}{N} + \dfrac{\mu^2}{N}$. Since $\mu = \dfrac{\Sigma X}{N}$, $\sigma^2 = \dfrac{\Sigma X^2}{N} - \dfrac{2\Sigma X}{N}\left(\dfrac{\Sigma X}{N}\right) + \left(\dfrac{\Sigma X}{N}\right)^2 = \dfrac{\Sigma X^2}{N} - 2\left(\dfrac{\Sigma X}{N}\right)^2 + \left(\dfrac{\Sigma X}{N}\right)^2 = \dfrac{\Sigma X^2}{N} - \left(\dfrac{\Sigma X}{N}\right)^2$.

TABLE 2.3

**Computation of Standard Deviation, Ungrouped Data,
Length of Life of Eight Experimental Light Bulbs**

Bulb	Length of life (thousands of hours) X	$X - \mu$	$(X - \mu)^2$	X^2
1	2.9	−1.3	1.69	8.41
2	5.6	1.4	1.96	31.36
3	4.2	0	0	17.64
4	3.3	− .9	.81	10.89
5	4.8	.6	.36	23.04
6	5.0	.8	.64	25.00
7	3.7	− .5	.25	13.69
8	4.1	− .1	.01	16.81
Total	33.6	0	5.72	146.84

Formulas 2.9 and 2.10 save time over Formulas 2.7 and 2.8 in that they make it unnecessary first to compute the mean and then to compute the squared deviations about that mean.

Measures of Relative Dispersion

Measures of relative dispersion express the degree of dispersion or variation as a percentage of the average about which they are computed. These measures are normally used to compare the variation in one distribution with that of another.

■ *Example.* An investor, trying to decide between one of two stocks, wishes to select the one with less fluctuation in price. The standard deviation of closing prices for each stock for one month is as follows:

Stock	A	B
Standard deviation in prices for one month	$1.50	$12.00

With no further information, the investor might purchase stock *A*, for its price shows the smaller variation.

While there are many measures of relative dispersion, the *coefficient of variation* is the most commonly used. It shows the standard deviation as a percent of the arithmetic mean. The formula is written as:

$$V = \frac{\sigma}{\mu} \cdot 100 \dots\dots\dots\dots\dots\dots\dots\dots(2.11)$$

where

    σ is the standard deviation

    μ is the arithmetic mean.

> ■ *Example.* Assume that in the preceding stock example, stock A had an average (mean) price of $5 a share and stock B had an average price of $75 a share. As shown below, the computation of the coefficient of variation for each stock might cause the investor to purchase B rather than A.

$$V \text{ (for stock } A) = \frac{1.50}{5.00} \cdot 100 = 30\%$$

$$V \text{ (for stock } B) = \frac{12.00}{75.00} \cdot 100 = 16\%.$$

Measures of Shape

In addition to knowing a measure of central tendency and the dispersion in a distribution, it is often helpful to know more about its shape. For example, in selecting a proper sample design, one of the factors to be considered is the shape of the universe from which the sample will be drawn. The two most important measures of shape are measures of *skewness* and measures of *kurtosis*. Skewness describes the lack of symmetry in a distribution, and kurtosis describes the peakedness of the distribution.

Pearsonian Coefficients of Skewness. Two expressions for measuring skewness are named after the statistician, Karl Pearson. These formulas are based on the knowledge that with a symmetrical distribution the values of the mean, the median, and the mode are equal. However, the greater the degree of skewness of a distribution, the greater the difference between these measures, with the arithmetic mean being farthest in the direction of the extreme values in the longer tail. The mode remains with the greatest concentration of items, and the median falls roughly two thirds of the distance from the mode to the mean. These relationships are illustrated in Figure 2.2.

The formulas for computing the coefficients of skewness are:

$$Sk = \frac{\mu - Mo}{\sigma} \quad \dots\dots\dots\dots\dots\dots\dots\dots\dots\dots\dots (2.12)$$

$$Sk = \frac{3(\mu - Md)}{\sigma} \quad \dots\dots\dots\dots\dots\dots\dots\dots (2.13)$$

where

    Sk is the coefficient of skewness

    μ is the arithmetic mean

    Mo is the mode

    Md is the median

    σ is the standard deviation.

FIGURE 2.2

**Relationship of the Mean, Median, and Mode
as Determined by the Direction of the Skewness**

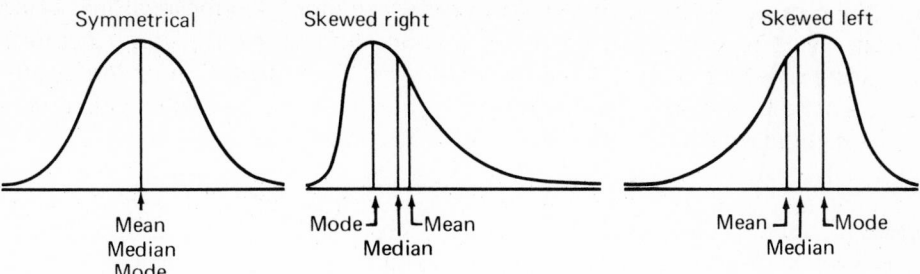

The reason for giving the two formulas is that in some cases either the mode or the median of a distribution may be available but not the other measure.

■ *Example.* A distribution has the following values:

$$\mu = 17.2 \qquad Md = 19.4$$
$$Mo = 23.7 \qquad \sigma = 10.6$$

The coefficient of skewness is computed as:

$$Sk = \frac{17.2 - 23.7}{10.6} = -0.61$$

or as:

$$Sk = \frac{3(17.2 - 19.4)}{10.6} = -0.62.$$

The negative sign indicates that the tail of this distribution is to the left and the distribution is skewed to the smaller values. If the sign had been positive, the distribution would be skewed to the right. The fact that the two measures are not exactly the same indicates that the pattern of relationships among the three averages is not always the same for all distributions, and the coefficients are estimates of the degree of skewness.

Kurtosis. Kurtosis is that property of a distribution which expresses its relative peakedness. A distribution with normal peakedness is said to be *mesokurtic*. A distribution which is flatter than normal is called *platykurtic*, and one which is more peaked than normal is *leptokurtic*. An example of each type is shown in Figure 2.3.

ANALYSIS OF FREQUENCY DISTRIBUTIONS

The analysis of data discussed in the first part of this chapter was limited to ungrouped data, which require that the value of each individual observation be known. The remainder of this chapter will deal with the

FIGURE 2.3

**Classification of Distributions Based on
Degree of Peakedness**

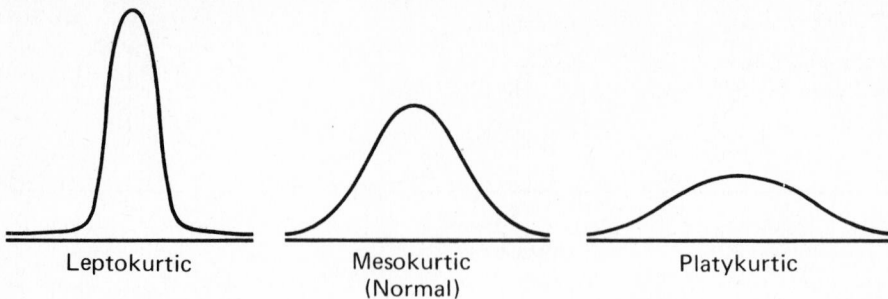

| Leptokurtic | Mesokurtic (Normal) | Platykurtic |

organization of data through the creation, presentation, and analysis of frequency distributions.

Organization of Data

As a practical matter, a large amount of empirical data in raw form is very difficult to comprehend. Frequently the first step in analyzing a set of empirical data is to organize the observations into a logical arrangement. One of the most useful forms of organization is the frequency distribution, which makes it possible to summarize and describe data to make them more useful and understandable. A frequency distribution may be used as follows:

1. Data may be presented as a *statistical table* in which the grouping of observations by size helps to show the characteristics of the data more clearly than would a study of the individual observations.
2. The frequency distribution may be shown as a figure. A *figure* presents statistical data in picture form to emphasize their principal characteristics.
3. Estimates of central tendency, dispersion, and other descriptive measures can be computed more easily from a frequency distribution than may be possible from the individual observations, especially when a computer is not available to do the tedious computations.

The Frequency Distribution

When the values of a variable result from the counting or measuring of some characteristic and when these observations are grouped into classes showing the number of observations in each class, the resulting table is called a *frequency distribution*.

■ *Example.* A milk company clerk records the number of quarts of milk purchased by 64 families on a particular route during one month. The results are shown in Table 2.4.

To permit the clerk to understand better the meaning of the observations, these data might be arranged into a frequency distribution such as that shown in Table 2.5.

TABLE 2.4

**Number of Quarts of Milk Purchased
by 64 Families in One Month**

19	16	22	9	22	12	39	19
14	23	6	24	16	18	7	17
20	25	28	18	10	24	20	21
10	7	18	28	24	20	14	23
25	34	22	5	33	23	26	29
13	36	11	26	11	37	30	13
8	15	22	21	32	21	31	17
16	23	12	9	15	27	17	21

TABLE 2.5

**NUMBER OF QUARTS OF MILK PURCHASED BY
64 FAMILIES IN ONE MONTH,
A Frequency Distribution**

Number of quarts purchased	Number of families
5–9	7
10–14	10
15–19	13
20–24	18
25–29	8
30–34	5
35–39	3
Total	64

In the example above, the groupings 5–9, 10–14, . . . , 35–39 are called *class intervals*. The class interval is the width of each class and is five for each class in the foregoing example; *e.g.*, for the first class, the number of quarts can be 5, 6, 7, 8, or 9. The number of families recorded for each class, *i.e.*, 7, 10, . . . , are the *frequencies*. The *lower class limits* are the values 5, 10, . . . , and 35; the *upper class limits* are the values 9, 14, . . . , 39. The *class midpoints* are those values, such as 7, 12, . . . , 37, that fall halfway between the upper and the lower class limits. Because of the gaps between the upper limit of one class and the lower limit of the next, the values 9.5, 14.5, . . . , and 39.5 are called the *real class limits*. These values often appear in formulas, in preference to the stated class limits, because they permit more accurate computation of the descriptive measures desired.

It is also important to note that the values of the variable used in this example are integers. Setting up a frequency distribution for these data is relatively simple because there is a definite break in the values of the variables since they are whole numbers.

The values of the observations of a continuous variable present some additional complications, as demonstrated by the following examples.

■ *Example.* A milk company clerk makes a careful study of the length of time a driver spends making 64 deliveries on a new route. The observations are recorded in the following frequency distribution.

TABLE 2.6

Time Required to Make Deliveries to 64 Customers

Time required to make a delivery (in minutes)	Number of deliveries
1 and under 2	12
2 and under 3	22
3 and under 4	13
4 and under 5	6
5 and under 6	5
6 and under 7	4
7 and under 8	2
Total	64

For the third class in this distribution:
    The class interval is 3 and under 4 minutes, or 1 minute.
    The frequency is 13 deliveries.
    The lower class limit is 3 minutes.
    The upper class limit is up to but not including 4 minutes.
    The class midpoint is 3.5 minutes.

The previous distribution has the advantage of having the stated class limits the same as the real class limits.

■ *Example.* If the clerk making the study had rounded each observation to the nearest tenth of a minute and had then grouped the observations into a frequency distribution, the table might look like Table 2.7.

For the third class in this distribution:
    The class interval is 3 to 3.9 minutes.
    The frequency is 12 deliveries.

TABLE 2.7

**Time Required to Make Deliveries to
64 Customers**

Time required to make a delivery (in minutes)	Number of deliveries
1–1.9	11
2–2.9	23
3–3.9	12
4–4.9	7
5–6.9	5
7–9.9	3
10 and over	3
Total	64

The real lower class limit is 2.95 minutes, which is the shortest time that would be rounded to 3 minutes for inclusion in the third class. The real upper class limit is a time just under 3.95 minutes, which would be rounded downward for inclusion in the third class. The class midpoint is 3.45 minutes, halfway between the class limits of 3.95 and 2.95.

In the last example using continuous data, the class interval was not the same for all classes, and the last class, "10 and over," was written as an *open-end class*. While there are advantages to having all class intervals the same length and in not having open-end classes, it is not always possible to do this in dealing with economic and business data. Equal class intervals often make computation of various statistical measures easier, but when the data are positively skewed with a few very large values, using equal class intervals could result in many classes in the frequency distribution with very few or with no observations.

In setting up a frequency distribution, the most important consideration is the number of classes to be used. If there are too few classes, pertinent characteristics of the data are lost through too much summarization. If there are too many classes, the distribution is difficult to work with and there is not enough summarization.

It is logical to assume that the number of observations to be classified is an important factor in determining the number of classes. Judgment must also be used to secure logical class limits and a frequency distribution best designed to meet the needs for which it is intended.

As the number of observations grows very large, there is a slight increase in the number of classes called for; but it is seldom that more than about 20 classes will be used.

A frequency distribution arranged to show the number of observations above or below a given figure is known as a *cumulative frequency distribution*. Such a distribution may take the shape of either a "more than" or a "less than" cumulative frequency distribution.

■ *Example.* The observations in Table 2.8 demonstrate both forms of a cumulative frequency distribution.

TABLE 2.8

Quarts of Milk Purchased by 64 Families in One Month

Number of quarts purchased	Number of families	Number of quarts purchased	Number of families
Less than 10	7	More than 35	3
Less than 15	17	More than 30	8
Less than 20	30	More than 25	16
Less than 25	48	More than 20	34
Less than 30	56	More than 15	47
Less than 35	61	More than 10	57
Less than 40	64	More than 5	64

Graphic Presentation

All types of statistical data may be presented in graphic form. There are literally hundreds of different charts and graphs that can be used effectively to emphasize important facts and relationships in statistical data. The discussion in this book is limited to the histogram and the frequency polygon. These have the greatest application in later chapters. The selected readings at the end of this chapter give other sources of a more complete discussion of graphic presentation.

The Histogram. A *histogram* is a bar chart of continuous data that have been grouped into a frequency distribution. Since there are no gaps between the class limits, there are no gaps between the bars of the histogram. It is an accepted practice to use vertical bars in any chart of a frequency distribution.

■ *Example.* The data in Table 2.6 are presented in Figure 2.4 as a histogram.
The bars have been plotted so that the height of each represents the frequency within that class. The tallest bar is the second one from the left, which shows that there were 22 deliveries that required between two and three minutes each. Since all the class intervals in this distribution are the same, all the bars have the same width.

FIGURE 2.4

**Time Required to Make Deliveries to
64 Customers**

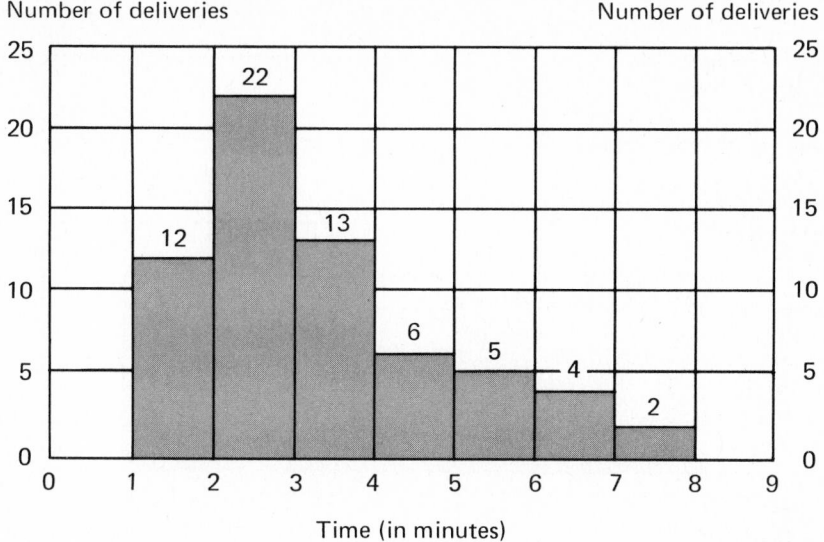

The height of the bar may also be thought of in a slightly different way. Since the standard unit in this distribution is a class interval, the frequency per interval unit is referred to as the *frequency density.*

Suppose the distribution of delivery times has been arranged into classes of varying widths as shown below.

TABLE 2.9

**Time Required to Make Deliveries to
64 Customers**

Time required to make a delivery (in minutes)	Number of deliveries	Frequency ÷ interval	Frequency density
1 and under 2	12	12 ÷ 1	12
2 and under 3	22	22 ÷ 1	22
3 and under 4	13	13 ÷ 1	13
4 and under 6	11	11 ÷ 2	5.5
6 and under 8	6	6 ÷ 2	3

When the distribution in Table 2.9 is plotted as a histogram in Figure 2.5, the frequency, which is the number of units in the class, represents the *area* of each bar. The frequency density, which is the number of units per minute, represents the *height* of the bar.

FIGURE 2.5

Time Required to Make Deliveries to 64 Customers

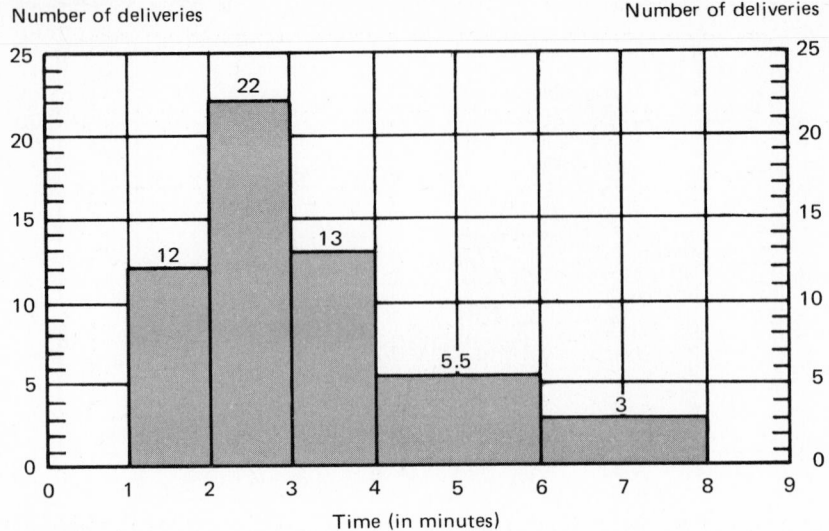

The Frequency Polygon. If the midpoints of the class intervals are connected by straight lines, and if the lines are brought to the baseline in the vacant class at either end of the distribution, the resulting chart is a *frequency polygon*.

■ *Example.* The histogram shown in Figure 2.4 has been converted into a frequency polygon in Figure 2.6.

Central Tendency

When observations are grouped into frequency distributions, only estimates of measures of central tendency and dispersion can be calculated. These estimates are based on the assumption that the items in an interval are evenly distributed in each interval and that the midpoint of each class interval is a good representation of all the values in that interval. To the extent that this is not true, there will be some grouping error in the estimates, although this error usually is not large enough to be of consequence.

Mode, Grouped Data. In a frequency distribution, the class with the greatest number of items is the modal class. If the data are plotted as a histogram, the easiest value to find to represent the mode is the midpoint of the modal class. This is called the *crude mode*. When the frequencies of the two classes lying immediately on either side of the modal class are approximately equal, the crude mode is a good estimate and can be arrived at by inspection. When one of the classes adjacent to the modal class has

FIGURE 2.6

**Time Required to Make Deliveries to
64 Customers**

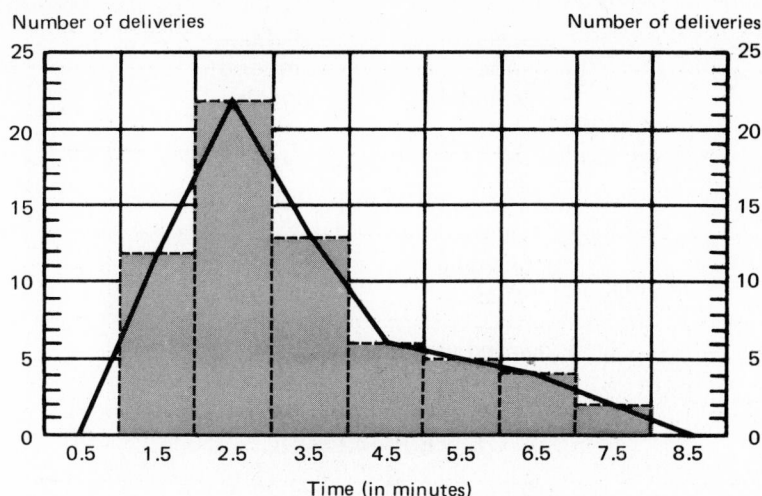

substantially more items than the class immediately on the other side of the modal class, it is reasonable to expect that the mode will not be centered in the modal class but will be drawn in the direction of the adjacent class with the most items. In the example shown in Table 2.10, the modal class is clearly that of "age 30–39"; but it should be greater than the midpoint of that class since there are more life insurance agents represented in the "40–49" age bracket than in the "20–29" age group.

The following formula can be used to locate the mode in a frequency distribution:

$$Mo = L_{Mo} + \frac{d_1}{d_1 + d_2} i_{Mo} \dots\dots\dots\dots\dots\dots\dots\dots(2.14)$$

where
   Mo is the mode
   L_{Mo} is the real lower limit of the modal class
   d_1 is the difference between the number of items in the modal class and the class that immediately precedes it
   d_2 is the difference between the number of items in the modal class and the class that immediately follows it
   i_{Mo} is the class interval of the modal class.

The mode can be located in an open-end frequency distribution since it is necessary to know only the number of items in the extremes of the distribution and not their values.

■ *Example.* Table 2.10 illustrates the location of the mode.

TABLE 2.10

**Location of the Mode, Grouped Data,
Ages of Life Insurance Agents in a
Midwestern Company**

Age (years)	Number of agents
20–29	24
30–39	60
40–49	42
50–59	31
60 or older	19
Total	176

Source: Hypothetical data.

$$d_1 = 60 - 24 = 36$$
$$d_2 = 60 - 42 = 18$$
$$Mo = 29.5 + \frac{36}{36 + 18}\, 10 = 29.5 + 6.7$$
$$Mo = 36.2 \text{ years.}$$

FIGURE 2.7

Location of the Mode, Graphic Method

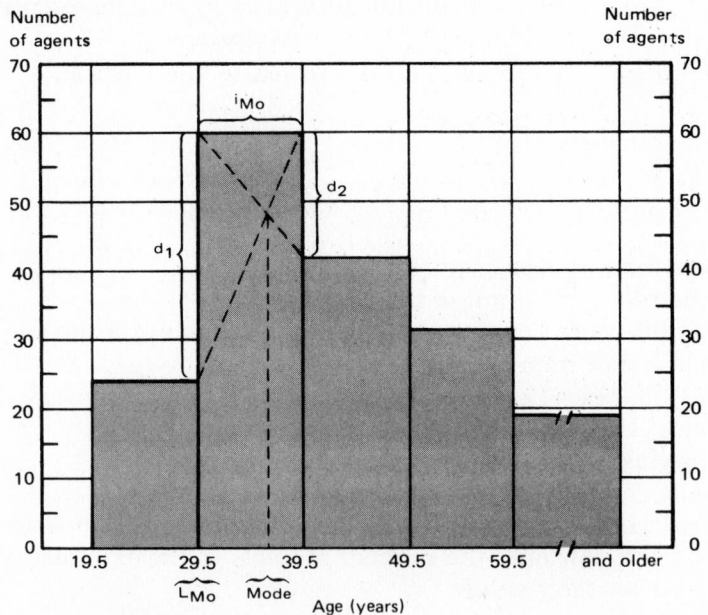

Source: Table 2.10.

Median, Grouped Data. When a large number of items are involved, the mechanical job of sorting the items into an array can be extremely tedious and time consuming. Under these conditions, it may be much more expedient first to classify the items in a frequency distribution and then to estimate the median. If the data to be analyzed are already grouped and the individual observations are not available, the median must be estimated.

The median can be estimated for data in a frequency distribution by use of the following formula:

$$Md = L_{Md} + \frac{\frac{N}{2} - F_{L_{Md}}}{f_{Md}} \, i_{Md} \quad \dots\dots\dots\dots\dots\dots(2.15)$$

where

Md is the median

L_{Md} is the real lower limit of the median class

$F_{L_{Md}}$ is the cumulative frequency less than the real lower limit of the median class

f_{Md} is the frequency of the median class

i_{Md} is the class interval of the median class

N is the number of items in the distribution.

■ *Example.* The data in Table 2.11 demonstrate how to estimate the median from a frequency distribution. This is largely a matter of interpolation to find a value which lies within the median class.

TABLE 2.11

Location of the Median, Grouped Data, Ages of Life Insurance Agents in a Midwestern Company

Age (years)	Number of agents f	Cumulative number F
20–29	24	24
30–39	60	84
40–49	42	126
50–59	31	157
60 or older	19	176
Total	176	.....

Source: Table 2.10.

$$Md = 39.5 + \frac{\frac{176}{2} - 84}{42} \, 10$$

$$Md = 39.5 + 0.95 = 40.45.$$

The first step is to determine the class within which the median falls. This determination is easy if a cumulative frequency column is added to the work sheet showing for each class the number of items in that class and in all preceding classes. Since there are 176 items in the distribution, the middle item is found to be

$$\frac{N}{2} = \frac{176}{2} = 88.$$

Since there are an even number of items in the distribution, the value of the item that represents the median lies halfway between items number 88 and 89. Because there are 84 items in the first two classes and 126 items in the first three, the third class will contain the median and is called the "median class."

Under certain conditions the median has two advantages over the arithmetic mean. The median is a more representative average than the mean for a distribution that is badly skewed, and it can be located in a frequency distribution that has an open-end class, i.e., "60 or older." Many distributions of economic data have both these characteristics.

Arithmetic Mean, Grouped Data. The arithmetic mean of grouped data can be computed using Formula 2.16.

$$\mu = \frac{\Sigma fm}{N} \dots\dots\dots\dots\dots\dots\dots\dots\dots\dots\dots\dots\dots\dots\dots\dots(2.16)$$

where
  f is the number of items in each class
  m is the midpoint of each class interval
  N is the total number of items in the distribution.

■ *Example.* Table 2.12 is a frequency distribution of the size of gasoline purchases made by 256 customers at a service station. In computing the mean of this frequency distribution, it is assumed that the midpoint of each class is representative of the items in that class. While some items will be larger and some smaller, a uniform distribution of items within each interval is usually assumed.

The formula for grouped data is actually a weighted arithmetic mean with the class midpoint, m, representing X for all the items in that class, and the frequency, f, for each class being used as the weight, w, for that class.

The preceding method can be used to estimate the mean regardless of whether the class intervals are the same for all classes. If, however, the frequency distribution has an open-end class such as "14.0 and over," it is impossible to estimate the mean unless the values of the individual items in that class are known. In an open-end class there is no way to determine the midpoint. Since many economic data are classified in open-end frequency distributions, the statistician is forced to refer to the original data before they were grouped, or to use some other average.

TABLE 2.12

Computation of the Arithmetic Mean, Grouped Data;
Purchases of Gasoline by 256 Customers

Purchases of gasoline (in gallons)	Number of purchases f	Gallons purchased (midpoint) m	fm
0.0–1.9	9	0.95	8.55
2.0–3.9	22	2.95	64.90
4.0–5.9	57	4.95	282.15
6.0–7.9	64	6.95	444.80
8.0–9.9	46	8.95	411.70
10.0–11.9	33	10.95	361.35
12.0–13.9	18	12.95	233.10
14.0–15.9	7	14.95	104.65
Total	256	...	1,911.20

$$\mu = \frac{1,911.20}{256} = 7.47 \text{ gallons.}$$

Measures of Dispersion

The measures of absolute and relative dispersion can also be estimated from frequency distributions.

Standard Deviation, Grouped Data. There are two methods of computing the standard deviation from grouped data. The longer of the two methods can be used in all cases regardless of whether the class intervals are the same for all classes. The shortcut method of computing the standard deviation is now seldom used and is not shown here. The standard deviation has the same limitation as the mean and the average deviation: it cannot be computed from a frequency distribution with an open-end class.

The long formula is written as follows:

$$\sigma = \sqrt{\frac{\Sigma f(m - \mu)^2}{N}} \quad \dots\dots\dots\dots\dots\dots\dots(2.17)$$

where
  f is the frequency of each class
  m is the midpoint of each class interval
  μ is the arithmetic mean
  N is the sum of f.

■ Example. Table 2.13 shows the computation of the standard deviation of grouped data using the so-called long method.

TABLE 2.13

Computation of Standard Deviation (Long Method for Grouped Data), Length of Life of Eighty Experimental Light Bulbs

Length of life (thousands of hours)	Number of bulbs f	Class midpoint m	$m - \mu$	$(m - \mu)^2$	$f(m - \mu)^2$
2 and under 3	4	2.5	−2.125	4.516	18.064
3 and under 4	16	3.5	−1.125	1.266	20.256
4 and under 5	33	4.5	−0.125	0.016	0.528
5 and under 6	20	5.5	0.875	0.766	15.320
6 and under 7	7	6.5	1.875	3.516	24.612
Total	80	...	...	...	78.780

Note: The μ of the above distribution is 4.625.

$$\sigma = \sqrt{\frac{\Sigma f(m - \mu)^2}{N}} = \sqrt{\frac{78.780}{80}} = \sqrt{0.98475}$$

$\sigma = 0.992$ or 992 hours.

Technical Note: Subscripts and Summations. Statistical formulas are written with two objectives in mind:

1. To provide a symbolic notation for expressing relationships clearly and concisely with a minimum of writing.
2. To present a general form that can be used with many different kinds of data.

As in mathematics, the first letters of the alphabet such as a, b, and c are used to represent constants. The last letters of the alphabet such as x, y, and z are used to represent variables.

If the statistician is interested in the hourly rates of machine-tool operators, X may be used to represent the rate, which is a variable and which can take on as many values as there are operators. If there are four operators, their rates may be referred to as X_1, X_2, X_3, and X_4. If the statistician wishes to refer to a rate in general from this group, X_i might be used, where i is a variable subscript that can take on any one of the four values of X (i.e., X_1, X_2, X_3, or X_4).

There are several advantages to this arrangement. For example, if the statistician wishes to indicate the sum of the values of the variable, it may be written as

$$\sum_{i=1}^{4} X_i$$

which is the total of the four rates, where X_i goes from X_1 through X_4. The Greek capital letter Σ (sigma) is used to denote sum.

This can be written in more general terms as

$$\sum_{i=1}^{n} X_i$$

which refers to the total of all the values of the variable, where X_i goes from X_1 through the last value of X_n, whatever it may be.

The notation

$$\sum_{i=3}^{n-2} X_i$$

can be used to indicate the sum of the values of the variable, beginning with the third one and including all but the last two.

The following problem deals with a rectangular array of values.

Ratings of Service Stations by Professional Shoppers

	Rater A	Rater B	Rater C	Rater D
Station 1	47	78	82	61
Station 2	62	50	75	94
Station 3	59	63	92	76
Station 4	57	88	77	80

The variable rating can be represented by a double subscript notation in which the first subscript denotes the row, and the second subscript, the column. Such a rectangular array of entries appearing in rows and columns is called a *matrix*.

Ratings of Service Stations by Professional Shoppers

	Rater A	Rater B	Rater C	Rater D
Station 1	X_{11}	X_{12}	X_{13}	X_{14}
Station 2	X_{21}	X_{22}	X_{23}	X_{24}
Station 3	X_{31}	X_{32}	X_{33}	X_{34}
Station 4	X_{41}	X_{42}	X_{43}	X_{44}

When referring to the value of the variable represented by X_{23}, the statistician is referring to the rating of Station 2 made by Rater C, which is 75 points. If the statistician wishes to refer to a rating in general, the notation X_{ij}, where i stands for the ith row, and j stands for the jth column, can be used. The sum of all the ratings for Station 3 can be written as

$$\sum_{j=1}^{4} X_{3j} = 59 + 63 + 92 + 76 = 290.$$

The sum of all the ratings made by Rater D can be written as

$$\sum_{i=1}^{4} X_{i4} = 61 + 94 + 76 + 80 = 311.$$

The sum of all the ratings made on all four stations can be written as

$$\sum_{i=1,\,j=1}^{4}\sum X_{ij} = 47 + 78 + 82 + 61 + \\ 62 + 50 + 75 + 94 + \\ 59 + 63 + 92 + 76 + \\ 57 + 88 + 77 + 80 = 1{,}141.$$

A matrix with m rows and n columns can be written as

$$X_{11}\,X_{12}\,\ldots\,X_{1n} \\ X_{21}\,X_{22}\,\ldots\,X_{2n} \\ \cdot\quad\cdot\quad\cdots\quad\cdot \\ X_{m1}\,X_{m2}\,\ldots\,X_{mn},$$

and its sum can be written as

$$\sum_{i=1}^{m}\sum_{j=1}^{n}X_{ij}.$$

STUDY QUESTIONS

2-1. Explain briefly the meaning of each of the following statistical terms:

a. mode
b. modal class
c. array
d. median
e. arithmetic mean
f. weighted arithmetic mean
g. geometric mean
h. measures of dispersion
i. absolute dispersion
j. range
k. quartile deviation
l. variance
m. standard deviation
n. relative dispersion
o. coefficient of variation
p. skewness
q. kurtosis
r. mesokurtic
s. leptokurtic

t. platykurtic
u. statistical table
v. figure
w. frequency distribution
x. class interval
y. frequencies
z. lower class limits
aa. upper class limits
ab. class midpoint
ac. real class limits
ad. open-end class
ae. cumulative frequency distribution
af. histogram
ag. frequency density
ah. area of a bar in a histogram
ai. height of a bar in a histogram
aj. frequency polygon
ak. crude mode

2-2. Under what conditions would you use each of the following averages?

a. arithmetic mean
b. geometric mean

2–3. Under what conditions would each of the following be the most appropriate average to use to describe a distribution?
 a. arithmetic mean
 b. median
 c. mode

2–4. What averages may be used with nominal and ordinal data? Explain.

2–5. What is the greatest weakness of each of the following averages?
 a. arithmetic mean
 b. mode
 c. geometric mean

2–6. If a frequency distribution is skewed positively (to the right), what is the normal relationship between the arithmetic mean, the median, and the mode?

2–7. Of what practical use are measures of absolute dispersion? Give two examples.

2–8. When is it preferable to use measures of relative dispersion when considering scatter? Give two examples.

2–9. What is a frequency distribution? When is it a useful way of organizing data? What problems are involved in determining the number of classes to be used?

2–10. What is a histogram? What advantages does its use provide in the analysis of statistical data?

2–11. Two frequency polygons can be compared with one another if they both have the same class intervals and the same total frequencies. If the class intervals are the same but the total frequencies are different for two distributions, can you suggest a way to compare them?

2–12. Why is an arithmetic mean computed from a frequency distribution only an estimate of the true value? Under what conditions can it not be computed at all? What other averages can you use when you cannot estimate the mean?

2–13. If a frequency distribution has an open-end class, what measure of absolute dispersion can be computed? Is it possible to measure skewness and kurtosis for such a distribution?

2–14. Give an example of a distribution that would normally be negatively skewed and give an example of a distribution that would normally be positively skewed. Into which category would most economic data fall?

PROBLEMS

2–1. The following prices for a gallon of unleaded regular gasoline were secured from one service station in each of 10 U.S. cities in August, 1976.

City	Cents per gallon
Anchorage	82
Baltimore	66
Boston	64
Dallas	60
Honolulu	73
Los Angeles	66
New York	66
San Francisco	67
Seattle	64
Washington	68

a. Compute the arithmetic mean of the values.
b. Compute the median of the values.
c. Compute the mode of the values.
d. Which of the averages do you consider to be the most appropriate average for these data? Why?

2-2. Mary can type a standard form letter in 14 minutes, Jim can type the same letter in 12 minutes, but it takes Sue 18 minutes to do the same job.
a. What is the average number of minutes required to type the form letter?
b. What is the average number of letters typed per hour per person?
Hint: Use a weighted mean.

2-3. Four suppliers of parts needed in an assembly operation quote the following prices:

Supplier	Price per dozen
A	$0.85
B	0.80
C	0.70
D	0.90

a. If 1,000 dozen parts are purchased from each supplier, what is the average cost per dozen?
b. If $500 is spent buying parts from each supplier, what is the average cost per dozen?
c. Compare the two answers computed above and explain any difference.

2-4. The table below gives the number of master policies for group life insurance in force in the United States for selected years for the period 1920 through 1970:

Year	Number of master policies (in thousands)	Percentage of number of master policies of previous 10 years
1920	6	. . .
1930	20	333.33

1940	22	110.00
1950	56	254.55
1960	182	325.00
1970	303	166.48

Source: *Life Insurance Fact Book* (New York: Institute of Life Insurance, 1971), p. 29.

a. Compute the geometric mean of the percentages to determine the average percent change for each year over the value 10 years before.
b. Is the geometric mean the proper average to use in this problem? Support your answer.
c. Use the answer found in (a) to estimate the number of master policies (in thousands) that will be in force in 1980.
d. If there was a constant rate of growth in the number of master policies between 1960 and 1970, estimate the number (in thousands) in 1965.

2–5. Nonagricultural employment for the years 1972 through 1976 is shown below for a rural county close to a large industrial city.

Year	Number employed	Number as percent of previous year X
1972	932	. . .
1973	1,163	124.79
1974	1,097	94.33
1975	1,212	110.48
1976	1,433	118.23

a. Compute the arithmetic mean of the percentages.
b. Compute the geometric mean of the percentages. Is this value larger or smaller than the arithmetic mean? Would you expect it to always be so? Explain.

2–6. The data in the table below have been gathered to describe some of the characteristics of a production process to better understand what is happening.

Measurements of a critical
dimension of sixty parts

15.4	5.2	12.3	18.1	19.0	12.0
10.4	15.1	19.8	21.5	24.6	13.3
5.5	11.2	6.8	25.3	9.8	22.0
21.7	24.8	13.7	21.9	24.9	19.7
7.1	22.5	26.7	30.7	22.4	18.6
15.3	18.2	19.5	7.0	14.8	11.3
8.4	27.2	32.6	27.8	16.5	29.3
23.3	10.6	14.0	17.8	20.1	16.7
16.2	34.5	11.8	18.0	14.7	23.4
19.5	20.8	24.9	17.4	19.5	17.2

Unit: .001 inches in excess of 6.500 inches

Compute the following descriptive measures:
- a. Arithmetic mean
- b. Median
- c. Mode
- d. Range
- e. Standard deviation
- f. Quartile deviation
- g. Coefficient of variation
- h. Skewness using the mean, median, and the standard deviation.

2-7. The following observations represent service lives (in hours) of seven flashlight batteries: 53, 60, 49, 52, 57, 61, and 55.
- a. Find the range.
- b. Compute the quartile deviation.
- c. Compute the standard deviation. How does it compare with the quartile deviation?
- d. Compute the coefficient of variation using the mean and the standard deviation.

2-8. During four successive months a homemaker pays the following prices for eggs: 82¢, 75¢, 79¢, and 91¢ per dozen.
- a. What is the average cost per dozen eggs if eight dozen are bought each month?
- b. What is the average cost per dozen if $10.00 per month is spent on eggs?

2-9. Six measurements of the diameter of a cylinder are recorded as 11.61, 11.29, 12.14, 11.97, 12.03, and 11.88 inches.
- a. Find the arithmetic mean of the measurements.
- b. Find the standard deviation of the measurements.
- c. Find the coefficient of variation.

2-10. The number of days of sick leave taken by 20 employees in an office over a three-year period are: 30, 12, 23, 42, 37, 32, 22, 15, 26, 35, 48, 31, 26, 25, 38, 28, 24, 13, 21, and 23.
- a. Arrange the observations into a frequency distribution ranging from 10 to 50 with 4 equal class intervals.
- b. Draw a histogram of the distribution.
- c. Draw a frequency polygon of the distribution.
- d. Estimate the mean of the distribution.
- e. Estimate the median of the distribution.
- f. Estimate the mode of the distribution.
- g. Estimate the standard deviation of the distribution.

2-11. Use the data from Problem 2-6 for this problem.
- a. Put the 60 observations into a frequency distribution ranging from 5 to 35 with 6 equal class intervals. These should be 5 and under 10, 10 and under 15, etc.
- b. Draw a histogram of the distribution.
- c. Draw a frequency polygon of the distribution.

d. Estimate the mean of the distribution.
e. Estimate the median of the distribution.
f. Estimate the mode of the distribution.
g. Estimate the standard deviation of the distribution.
h. Compare the estimated values for the mean, median, mode, and standard deviation with those computed in Problem 2–6. What are the differences? Why are there differences?

2–12. The following distribution shows the sales of a clerk in the sporting goods department of a large department store during a single day:

$54.00	10.00	49.00	2.23	52.19	22.50	13.00	20.00
42.00	16.67	17.78	25.00	5.00	10.10	73.67	.05
.19	66.03	23.17	29.99	48.80	27.17	3.98	26.89
45.00	.11	15.11	3.00	6.33	14.14	56.11	13.67
12.13	33.72	18.43	75.00	58.00	28.47	4.78	30.00
10.04	.06	24.20	4.17	12.00	5.42	11.22	1.19
.27	59.61	9.23	26.03	7.18	57.25	5.10	38.85
36.17	2.00	6.77	5.26	8.82	4.77	.17	.49

a. Place the observations into a frequency distribution with 8 classes. The last class should be an open-end class such as "$60.00 and over."
b. Compute two measures of central tendency for the distribution, keeping in mind that the last class has an open end.

2–13. The frequency distribution below shows the purchase orders for a small manufacturing plant during the month of October:

Size of order (in dollars)	Number of orders
under 10	15
10 and under 20	22
20 and under 30	24
30 and under 40	19
40 and under 50	16
50 and under 60	9
60 and under 70	3
70 and under 80	2
80 and under 90	1
Total	111

a. For the class with the largest frequency find:
(1) the class midpoint   (4) the upper class limit
(2) the class frequency   (5) the class interval
(3) the lower class limit
b. Make a "more than" cumulative frequency distribution. How many orders were $50 and greater?

c. Make a "less than" cumulative frequency distribution. How many orders were less than $60?
d. Draw a histogram of the frequency distribution.
e. Draw a frequency polygon. Since the first class begins with zero and there can be no vacant class at the beginning of the chart, bring the chart line to the base line at zero.

SELECTED READINGS

Boot, John C. G., and Edwin B. Cox. *Statistical Analysis for Managerial Decisions,* 2d ed. New York: McGraw-Hill Book Company, Inc., 1974.
 Chapter 5 of this text gives a very simple introductory discussion of the most important measures of central tendency and dispersion.
Chou, Ya-lun. *Statistical Analysis with Business and Economic Applications,* 2d ed. New York: Holt, Rinehart and Winston, Inc., 1975.
 Chapters 2 and 3 of this text give a very complete discussion of measures of central tendency, variation, and skewness for both grouped and ungrouped data.
Richmond, Samuel B. *Statistical Analysis,* 2d ed. New York: The Ronald Press Company, 1964.
 Chapter 3 discusses the arithmetic mean and the standard deviation, which are considered to be the most important average and measure of dispersion. Chapter 4 discusses other averages and other measures of dispersion.
Stockton, John R., and Charles T. Clark. *Introduction to Business and Economic Statistics,* 5th ed. Cincinnati: South-Western Publishing Co., 1975.
 Chapters 3 and 4 cover the definition, computation, uses, and chief characteristics of the principal averages and measures of dispersion, of skewness, and of kurtosis.

Part 2

Probability and Probability Distributions

Chapter 3

Probability

Descriptive statistics, discussed in Chapter 2, provide methods for summarizing a body of data. Descriptive statistics can be computed for a universe when complete data for that universe are available. When it is not feasible or desirable to collect complete universe data, summary statistics can be computed from an appropriate sample drawn from the universe. Sample statistics are computed as the basis for making judgments about the nature of the universe. This process of making judgments or inferences on the basis of sample statistics is called *statistical inference*. Making a decision based on a statistical test of a universe characteristic involves a given degree of risk, or error, which may be expressed in terms of a numerical probability.

Sampling and statistical inference, which are discussed in Part III and Part IV, draw heavily on the theory of probability. This theory enables one to draw conclusions about the probable composition of a sample based on a mathematical model of the universe. Statistical inference, on the other hand, is concerned with making an inference about the composition of a universe on the basis of a sample statistic.

The study of probability poses three kinds of problems: (1) defining and interpreting what is meant by probability; (2) using known probabilities to calculate others; and (3) obtaining numerical probabilities. The discussion in this chapter is limited to a consideration of the first two problems; the third is discussed later in the chapters on estimation and inference. The present discussion is further limited to the topics of probability theory that are most helpful in understanding sampling and statistical inference. Probability theory — including topics from set theory, rules for calculating probabilities, revision of probabilities, and mathematical expectation — is presented in the following sections.

THE MEANING OF PROBABILITY

The concept of probability is particularly useful in administration as well as in personal life when a decision or judgment is made concerning a situation for which the outcome is uncertain. A business executive may decide that the chances are excellent that a new product will succeed; a manager reflects on past experience to estimate the completion date of a research project; a construction foreman schedules work crews based on the judgment that rain is not likely on a given day. Each of these situations involves uncertainty and each of the decisions is essentially a prediction of an outcome, made with some degree of confidence that the prediction will be substantiated. Probability theory offers a means for mathematically formulating predictions of uncertain outcomes, and it is important to distinguish between some interpretations of probability and the mathematical deductions obtained from the postulates of probability.

A probability may be interpreted as a fraction or proportion of outcomes or values of a variable that has a particular characteristic.

■ *Example.* The probability of obtaining a three on one toss of a fair die is the fraction $\frac{1}{6}$, for one face of the die has the characteristic of having three dots and there are six faces or possible outcomes that can occur with equal likelihood.

■ *Example.* A study of weather records for a city in the Southwest indicates that the high daily temperature was 100° F or more on a total of 200 days during the months of June for the past 10 years. The estimate of the probability that the temperature will be 100° F or more on a day in June is the proportion 200/300 = 0.67.

The odds associated with an outcome or value of a variable are related to probability. The odds that an event will happen is the ratio of the number of ways or times the event can or did occur to the number of ways or times the outcome cannot or did not occur. In the preceding examples, the odds that a three will be obtained from one toss of a die are 1 to 5 or the number of ways a three can occur (1) as opposed to the number of ways a three cannot be obtained (5). Similarly, the estimate of the odds that the temperature will be 100° F or more on a day in June are 200 to 100 (or 2 to 1), where the number of days of 100° F or greater temperatures (200) is compared to the number of days with temperatures of less than 100° F (300 − 200 = 100).

Preliminary Ideas

There are a few basic concepts that will facilitate the presentation of a formal definition of probability. The first of these concepts is that of an experiment. In order to apply the concepts of probability and statistics to administrative problems, it is necessary to obtain data for analysis. Any process of observation is called an *experiment*. Thus, tossing dice, observing the percent of defective items in a lot of manufactured articles, or recording the arrivals of patients at a hospital may be looked on as experiments.

In these instances the numbers that turn up on the dice, the condition of a manufactured product as being acceptable or defective, or the number of arrivals at a hospital per time unit are called the possible outcomes of experiments. Each of the outcomes that can occur in a single trial of an experiment is called an *elementary event*.

■ *Example.* A trial of an experiment consists of tossing a die. The elementary events or outcomes of a toss of a die are the numbers 1 through 6 on the faces of the die. Any one of the events can occur in a single trial.

The die-tossing example points to an important concept in that the numbers 1 through 6 comprise the complete list of possible events. A group of events that constitutes a complete list of possible events which can occur, one of which is bound to occur in a trial of an experiment, is said to be *collectively exhaustive*. If the occurrence of any one of the events on the list of possible events precludes the occurrence of any other, the possible events are *mutually exclusive*.

■ *Example.* A supermarket has five counters for checking out customers. The check-out process at any one of the counters constitutes an event that must be performed at any one (collectively exhaustive) but only one (mutually exclusive) of the counters.

Associated with each of the elementary events is an entity called an *elementary unit* or an *observation*. The totality of elementary units is termed the *universe* or the *population*. Consider a bin of mass-produced parts that contains a mixture of acceptable and defective items. A trial of an experiment is performed by selecting a part at random from the bin, observing whether the part is acceptable or defective, and replacing the part in the bin. The simple events are the two possible outcomes — acceptable or defective. The universe of elementary units includes all the parts in the bin. Associated with each elementary unit are two possible outcomes — acceptable or defective.

Experiments involve making a limited number of trials when more extensive experimentation is impossible, impractical, or uneconomical. The process of making a finite number of trials by randomly selecting elementary units from a universe is called *simple random sampling*. Data obtained from simple random samples are frequently used to calculate averages or measures of dispersion. A statistic thus computed serves as the basis for estimating a universe parameter or making an inference about the composition or characteristics of the universe.

■ *Example.* A sample is taken from a large inventory of one-pound boxes of granulated sugar. A trial is performed by randomly selecting a box of sugar (elementary unit), weighing the contents, and recording the weight (elementary event). A total of $n = 50$ trials is made and the average weight of the sampled boxes is found to be 16.1 ounces, or slightly more than the intended weight of 16.0 ounces for the universe of inventory items. Management is now faced with deciding whether the average weight of all boxes is more than 16.0 ounces.

■ *Example.* A marketing research team, seeking to determine what percent of customers in an area prefers the firm's brand of detergent, randomly selects 400 homemakers and asks each of them which brand is preferred. The tabulation shows that 15% of the sampled customers favor the firm's brand. The sample percent serves as an estimate of the percent of all customers in the area who prefer this brand of detergent.

Objective Probability

The *objective* interpretation of probability is based on two different approaches to the meaning of probability, which employ abstract reasoning or experience to determine probabilities.

Equiprobable Events. The concept of *equiprobable events,* also called the *principle of insufficient reason,* suggests that if there is no reason to favor any one of the possible outcomes of a situation to any other, then the outcomes should be considered equally likely to occur.

■ *Example.* A fair coin is tossed and an individual is asked to state the probability that a head will appear. The answer will most likely be $\frac{1}{2}$ if there is no evidence to suggest that the sides of the coin are not equally likely to occur.

But what is the basis for stating that a side of a fair coin will turn up with a probability of $\frac{1}{2}$? There are two possible outcomes of a toss of a fair coin, but only one of the outcomes is desired. The ratio of the number of ways in which the desired outcome can occur to the total number of possible outcomes is $\frac{1}{2}$, the probability of the desired outcome.

The determination of this probability does not require that one toss the coin many times to gain experience, for the symmetry of the probabilities of the outcomes is seen intuitively from the assumption of a fair coin. Probabilities determined by using intuitive judgment or abstract reasoning are determined by what is called the *a priori method* of calculating probabilities.

The application of the concept of equiprobable outcomes is limited to situations where equal probabilities can be assumed, such as drawing from a fair deck of cards or tossing a fair die. For these situations probabilities can be determined by the a priori method, and extensive experimental data are not required.

Relative Frequency. It is not possible to calculate a priori probabilities for every experiment. In fact, many experiments are performed to estimate the probability of an event by determining the relative frequency. The relative frequency obtained from a finite number of trials provides a numerical value with which to estimate the probability of an event. The longer the series of trials, the closer relative frequencies are expected to approximate the probabilities of the respective outcomes of the experiment.

■ *Example.* In a game played with a standard deck of playing cards, a player observes that a high card denoted *H* (ace, king, queen, or jack) is dealt on a single draw from a full deck of cards less often than a low card (10 or less) denoted *L*. For 100 trials of the experiment, each consisting of randomly drawing a card from a full deck of well-shuffled cards, the player obtains the results shown in groups of 10 draws in Table 3.1. The columns in the table show the number of high cards *H* for each group of 10 draws, the cumulative totals of high cards $\Sigma H = m$, the cumulative number of trials *n*, and the relative frequency of drawing high cards $\dfrac{m}{n}$.

TABLE 3.1

Results of 100 Random Draws from a Standard Deck of Playing Cards

Trial numbers	Events	Number of high cards H	Cumulative number of high cards $\Sigma H = m$	Cumulative number of trials n	Relative frequency $\dfrac{m}{n}$
1–10	H L L L L H L L L L	2	2	10	0.200
11–20	H H H L L L H L L H	5	7	20	0.350
21–30	L L H L H L L H L H	4	11	30	0.367
31–40	L L L L L L H L L L	1	12	40	0.300
41–50	L H H L L L L L L L	2	14	50	0.280
51–60	L L H L H L L H L H	4	18	60	0.300
61–70	H H L H L H L H H L	6	24	70	0.343
71–80	L L L L H L L L L H L	2	26	80	0.325
81–90	L H H L L L H L L L	3	29	90	0.322
91–100	L L L H L L L L L L	1	30	100	0.300

An important property of the example above is illustrated in Figure 3.1 by the horizontal line drawn at a relative frequency of $\frac{16}{52} = 0.308$, the proportion of a deck of cards consisting of high cards. As *n*, the number of trials, becomes large, the deviations of the relative frequencies about the horizontal line at 0.308 tend to decrease. This tendency for the relative frequencies to converge on the proportion 0.308, that is, for the fluctuations to decrease as

FIGURE 3.1

**Relative Frequency of Drawing High Cards
in Cumulative Trials**

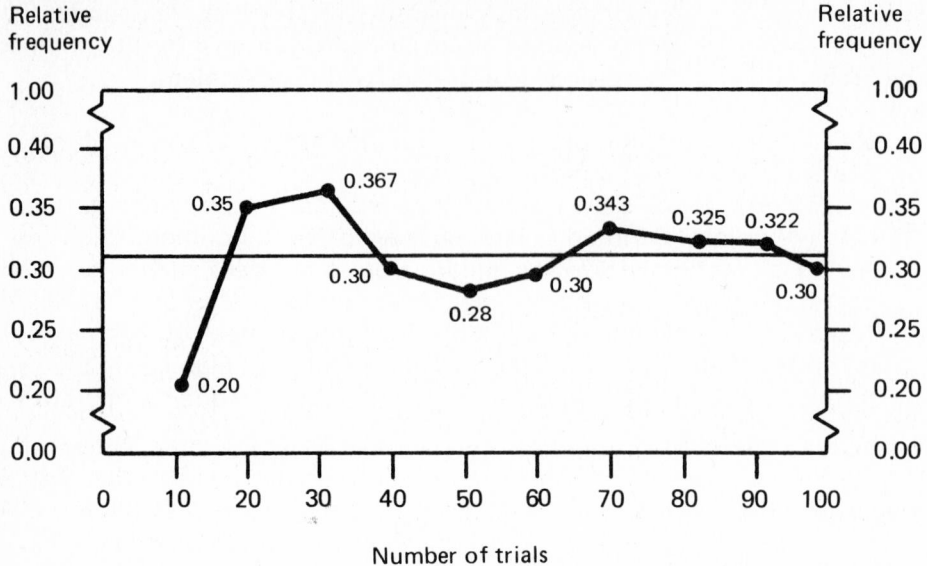

Number of trials

n becomes large, illustrates what is called *statistical regularity*. Thus, for a very large n, the relative frequency would very closely approximate a number P, the probability of the occurrence of an event. For the previous example the event, drawing a high card, is denoted by H; and $P(H)$ is the probability of drawing a high card; and $P(H) = 0.308$.

The relative frequency $\frac{m}{n}$ determined from 100 trials of the experiment of drawing cards is 0.300 and closely approximates $P(H) = 0.308$. In this particular example $P(H)$ is calculated a priori since the number of high cards and the total number of cards are known. Although relative frequencies are sometimes used as probabilities, the values of the two quantities $P(H)$ and $\frac{m}{n}$ are not necessarily the same.

■ *Example.* A marketing analyst uses simple random sampling to estimate what proportion of customers who enter a department store buys appliances. Of 100 customers sampled, 8 purchased appliances. The estimate of the probability that a customer entering the store will purchase an appliance is $\frac{m}{n} = \frac{8}{100} = 0.08$, assuming the universe proportion remains constant while the sample is drawn (statistical regularity).

Viewing a relative frequency or probability as a proportion suggests three basic properties of these measures of uncertainty. First, the ratio of the number of occurrences to the number of trials cannot be less than zero or more than one. It follows that the probability of an event A, which is one of the set of mutually exclusive and collectively exhaustive events of an experiment, is in the range

$$0 \le P(A) \le 1 \quad\text{...................................(3.1)}$$

Second, since the events are collectively exhaustive, one of the elementary events must occur on a trial. The probability that the event which occurs is not A is

$$P(A') = 1 - P(A) \quad\text{................................(3.2)}$$

where A' is the nonoccurrence of A.

A third property is illustrated by examining the nature of the event A'. Suppose the event A denotes an elementary event from a list of several mutually exclusive and collectively exhaustive events. Then A' denotes an event composed of the group of mutually exclusive events other than A and is called a *compound event*. The occurrence of any of the events other than A constitutes the nonoccurrence of A, that is, the occurrence of A'. Thus, $P(A')$ is the sum of the probabilities of all the elementary events except A.

■ *Example.* A dealer who sells appliances in a variety of colors finds that 60% of all customers buy white; 20% buy brown; 10% buy green; and 10% buy yellow. The probability that a customer selected at random will buy a white appliance is $P(W) = 0.60$. The probability that a customer will select a color other than white, $P(W')$, is the sum of the probabilities for the remaining elementary events, or $P(B) + P(G) + P(Y) = 0.20 + 0.10 + 0.10$. The probability of the compound event non-white is $P(W') = 0.40$.

The three important properties are expressed by the following axioms of probability theory:

1. A probability is a number between 0 and 1 that is assigned to an event.
2. The sum of the probabilities of the mutually exclusive and collectively exhaustive events of an experiment must total 1.
3. The probability of an event composed of a group of mutually exclusive events is equal to the sum of the probabilities of the events.

A probability or a relative frequency of zero is interpreted to mean that the occurrence of an event is highly unlikely rather than strictly impossible. At the other extreme of $P(A) = 1$, a similar interpretation is made in that an event is not assumed to be strictly certain to occur; but for all practical purposes, certainty is a reasonable assumption.

The Limit of a Relative Frequency. The relative frequency approach to probability uses the ratio $\dfrac{m}{n}$ as an estimate of the probability $P(A)$ of an event A for a large value of n. This approach is modified by the limit of the relative frequency concept, which states that the probability $P(A)$ of an event A exists and that

$$\lim_{n \to \infty} \frac{m}{n} = P(A),$$

which is read: the probability $P(A)$ is the limit of the relative frequency $\dfrac{m}{n}$ as the number of trials n becomes very large.

The relative frequency approach, on which much of probability theory is based, will be used extensively in the following discussion.

The relative frequency approach to probability is summarized by four principal characteristics: (1) the assumption of a large number of trials of an experiment; (2) the presumption of statistical regularity; (3) the use of empirical information gained from experience; and (4) the use of a relative frequency to estimate probability. For certain kinds of problems, the first two characteristics become limitations. In some situations probabilities are estimated before trials can be made. In this manner, subjective estimates are assigned as probabilities to events for which there is no actual or reliable experience. For example, a manufacturer wishes to experiment with a new process and makes a decision to undertake the untried process on the basis of an 80–20 chance estimate that the process will be profitable.

Subjective Probability

The view that the concept of probability has meaning only in instances when trials of an experiment can be repeated under uniform conditions presently enjoys considerable favor. How does one deal with problems for which repeated trials are impossible, impractical, or uneconomical? Are probabilities pertinent in such situations? The *subjective* or *personalistic* interpretation of probability is a view of probability as a numerical expression of personal judgment or belief with respect to a particular proposition. With practice, "rational" individuals can think abstractly about their beliefs concerning the elements of a situation that are not certain, regardless of how they may feel about any other aspects of the situation. Further, if different rational individuals are confronted with the same information, their degree of belief and personal probability estimates for the same event may be different.

This is not to say, however, that a rational individual will assign probabilities arbitrarily. Rather, probabilities are assigned to real world events on the basis of experience with such events and, in general, rational individuals with similar experiences for given events will assign roughly the same probability. Thus, if an individual appraising the probability of an event feels that the event would occur with a relative frequency p for many trials made under uniform conditions, that individual will assign a probability p to the event.

■ *Example.* A veteran contractor submits a proposal for constructing an office building and believes there is a 50–50 chance of being awarded the contract. Thus, the contractor assigns a subjective probability of $p = 0.50$ to the event that the contract will be received.

The subjective approach to probability uses probabilities as "weights" that are assigned to events. In this manner an individual expresses degree of belief in the likelihood of the outcomes of a situation, one and only one of which is certain to occur.

■ *Example.* An industrial relations manager expresses a belief in the likelihood of each of the possible outcomes of current labor negotiations by weighting each of the outcomes. Reflecting on past experiences in similar negotiations, the manager assigns the following subjective probabilities as weights:

Event	Probability
Settlement	0.60
Arbitration	0.30
Strike	0.10
	1.00

The nature of some administrative problems is such that historical frequencies of outcomes are not available or are impossible to obtain. If a product is to be marketed for the first time, there is no past experience of selling the product with which to determine the likelihood of success. However, it is possible to visualize the probabilities involved as relative frequencies in an imaginary series of trials, even if it is not possible to perform repeated trials. Where, historically, there is no precedent for assigning probabilities, but subsequent trials are possible, an initial probability estimate can be made subjectively and later modified in terms of experience. This technique of revising probabilities will be considered in a later discussion of Bayes' Theorem. With successive revisions, the long-run probabilities obtained subjectively will approximate those determined solely from objective data.

SETS, RANDOM VARIABLES, AND PROBABILITY

The role of probability in statistical inference and other statistical decision problems is subtle. The concept of sets, however, offers a very useful mathematical model with which to present probability. In this section, topics from set theory are introduced to amplify the concepts of probability previously discussed and to provide insight into the relationships among events, sample spaces, random variables, axioms of probability, and Bayes' Theorem.

Sets and Events

Sets. The concept of a set has great significance in the study of probability, for all mathematics can be developed from this fundamental notion. A *set* is a well-defined collection of entities, whether real or imaginary. By this definition, the employees of a firm form a set. Similarly, we may speak of the set of the theories of the origin of the universe, the set of insured automobiles in an area, or the set of outcomes of an experiment. These illustrations are examples of *discrete* sets, since each collection of entities is comprised of a finite number of elements. This discussion will be essentially limited to the consideration of discrete sets.

A set can be identified in two different ways. The elements of a set can be designated by means of a *description,* where, by means of a rule, it can be determined whether a given object is in a set. Alternatively, a set can be identified by a *listing,* which enumerates all the elements of the set.

■ *Example.* A set of elementary units is described by a rule stating that the set consists of pieces of pasteboard or plastic which are a deck of playing cards. Another set is defined by listing the four suits of a deck of cards, the set of elementary events.

A listing of a set is customarily enclosed with braces. For the latter example, the listing is {clubs, diamonds, hearts, spades}. The set of elementary events of an experiment is called a *universal set.*

Set Operations. In many instances only a particular portion of the elements of a universal set is of interest. Any part of a universal set is called a *subset.* Any subset of a universal set of outcomes of an experiment is called an *event.*

■ *Example.* The set of all possible outcomes of a trial of an experiment consisting of a toss of a fair die is the universal set {1, 2, 3, 4, 5, 6}.

■ *Example.* There are 36 possible elementary events that can occur in a trial of an experiment in which a pair of fair dice are tossed. The subset of elementary events in which the sum of the numbers on the faces of the dice is seven is {(1, 6), (2, 5), (3, 4), (4, 3), (5, 2), (6, 1)}.

Subsets of a universal set are sometimes easier to visualize if presented graphically. One form of graphic presentation is the *Venn diagram,* in which the universal set is represented by a rectangle and the subsets are shown as circular portions of the rectangle. See Figure 3.2.

FIGURE 3.2

Venn Diagram of the Subsets of Hearts and Kings

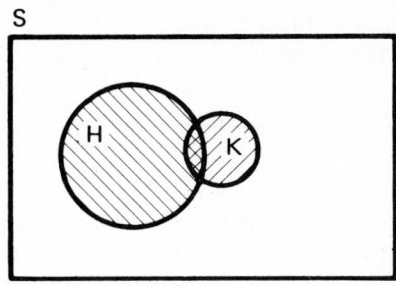

■ *Example.* Consider the universal set S as a deck of 52 playing cards with a subset of hearts H and a subset of kings K. The set of all cards is represented by the rectangle and the subset of cards that are either hearts or kings is represented by the areas enclosed by the circles H and K in Figure 3.2.

The subset of elements that are in either H or K is the shaded area in Figure 3.2. This area is called the *union* of H and K and is denoted by $H \cup K$, which is read "H cup K," "H or K," or "H union K." The doubly cross-hatched portion, where the circles H and K overlap, represents elements that are in both subsets. This portion is called the *intersection* of H and K and is denoted by $H \cap K$, which is read "H cap K," "H and K," or "H intersection K." For the previous example, $H \cap K$ consists of a single element, the king of hearts.

Subsets from a universal set can be designated so that the subsets contain no common elements. When shown graphically, these sets do not intersect, since the occurrence of an element in one subset precludes its presence in the other. Sets that contain only elements which are not common (mutually exclusive) to another set are called *disjoint*. To complete the designation of the areas in a diagram, the elements in a universal set S that are not included in one or more subsets of interest are denoted by S', which is called the *complement*.

■ *Example.* The subsets of hearts and diamonds from a set of playing cards S are shown by the circles H and D in Figure 3.3. These circles do not overlap since a card must be either a heart or a diamond and cannot be both. The cards in the deck that are not hearts or diamonds, $S - H \cup D$, are represented by the shaded portion S' in the rectangle.

The presentation of sets by means of diagrams is useful for suggesting the relationships that exist in the combination of two or more sets in terms of unions, intersections, and complements. Proofs of the results, however, are based on the algebra of sets involving a series of theorems that are beyond the scope of this discussion.

FIGURE 3.3

Diagram of Disjoint Subsets *H* and *D*, and S′, The Complement of the Subsets

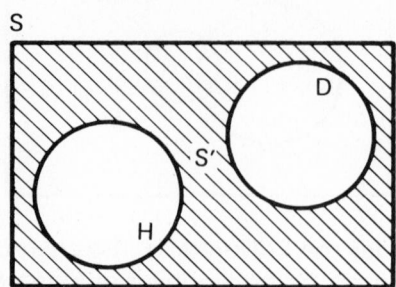

Random Variables and Functions

Random Variables. The concept of a *variable* was introduced in Chapter 1 and in a general way in the discussion of descriptive statistics in Chapter 2. In those discussions a variable was associated with a series of values that expresses observed characteristics of elementary units and provides the basis for computing a summary statistic, such as an average or a measure of dispersion. Similarly, in this chapter the idea of a variable is suggested by observing values such as those obtained by tossing dice, sampling the weights of boxes of sugar, or randomly selecting customers in a survey. In each of these instances the specific outcome of a trial is not known in advance, but some information is available concerning the relative frequency of each outcome. Trials made from processes of this type where the events are not identical or individually predictable with certainty are termed *stochastic processes* or *chance processes*. Making repeated trials of an experiment involving stochastic processes yields results or events. A quantity that takes on a definite value or property for every possible elementary event is called a *random variable,* also referred to as a *chance variable* or a *stochastic variable*. Random variables are of two types: *continuous* and *discrete*. A continuous variable can assume an infinite number of values, while a discrete variable can take on only a specified finite number of values.

■*Example.* An experiment is performed where the trials consist of: (a) taking a random sample (a stochastic process) of metal castings (elementary units), (b) determining the weight of each casting (continuous variable), and (c) deciding that the casting is of an acceptable or unacceptable weight (discrete variable). The weight of a casting (observed value of a continuous random variable, an event) can be determined to the fraction of a pound such as 5.61825 . . . pounds, while there are only two specified outcomes, acceptable or unacceptable, for the discrete variable.

This discussion is principally concerned with discrete random variables, although in later chapters continuous variables will be applied or used as approximations for discrete variables.

Sets and Functions. The concept of a discrete variable can be related to the concept of sets by stating that a variable is a range of values, each of which can be associated with a set of objects.

■ *Example.* Consider the outcome of an experiment in which two fair dice are tossed. The value three of a discrete variable is associated with the elementary events {1, 2} or {2, 1}. The value three of the discrete variable is also associated with the compound event {(1, 2), (2, 1)}. The set of all values for the random variable is the number associated with the universal set of events {2, 3, 4, 5, 6, 7, 8, 9, 10, 11, 12}. Remembering that the elementary outcomes of a toss of two fair dice have equal probabilities of $\frac{1}{36}$ and that the probability corresponding to a compound event is equal to the sum of the probabilities of the component elementary events, the probability associated with the event {(1, 2), (2, 1)} is $\frac{1}{36} + \frac{1}{36} = \frac{1}{18}$. For the possible events corresponding to a trial of an experiment, there is a set of probabilities such that for each event (subset) there is a corresponding numerical probability.

The relationship between the elements of one set and those of another can be described by a rule called a *function*. The rule can be expressed verbally or in mathematical terms.

■ *Example.* If a worker is paid under a piecework incentive plan, one might consider the wage as a function of output. Accordingly, a "high wage" corresponds to "high output" and a "low wage" is associated with "low output" in terms of a function, which in this case is a verbal rule.

The set of all possible levels of output that a worker can achieve is called the *domain*. For each output level there is a corresponding wage, and the set of wage amounts forms a set called the *range*. If the worker's wage is different for each level of output, then the relationship between the sets is called a *point function,* which assigns a value or an element in the range of each "point" or element in the domain.

■ *Example.* An incentive plan states that a worker is paid $0.05 for each unit of output produced. The function or transformation relating a worker's wage W with output P is the set function $W = \$0.05P.$

There are many situations where the domain consists of one or more sets rather than single points or elements, and the corresponding range is one or more real numbers. A function with a domain and a range of this type is called a *set function*.

Sample Space. A fundamental concept in the theory of sampling is the identification of the elementary events or *sample points* from which sample observations can be selected. A *sample space* of an experiment is defined as the set of sample points so that each point corresponds to one and only one possible elementary event.

■ *Example.* In an experiment a fair coin is tossed twice, and for each toss, one of two possible outcomes, a head *H* or a tail *T* occurs. The sample space or domain of elementary events is the universal set of sample points {(*H*, *H*), (*H*, *T*), (*T*, *H*), (*T*, *T*)}. The number of tails *T* that can be obtained is the range {0, 1, 2} of a discrete random variable. The elements of the range correspond to the subsets {(*H*, *H*)}, {(*H*, *T*), (*T*, *H*)}, and {(*T*, *T*)}.

Note in the example that each number of tails which can be obtained in two tosses of the coin corresponds to a subset of events. The sample space of the example experiment is shown graphically in the left-hand diagram in Figure 3.4, and the range corresponding to the sample space is in the right-hand diagram. The subset of the two sample points {(*T, H*), (*H, T*)} enclosed by the dotted line corresponds to the unit subset {1} from the range of the number of tails obtained. The lines associating these subsets in Figure 3.4 represent a counting rule — a function.

FIGURE 3.4

Sample Space and Range of Tosses of a Fair Coin

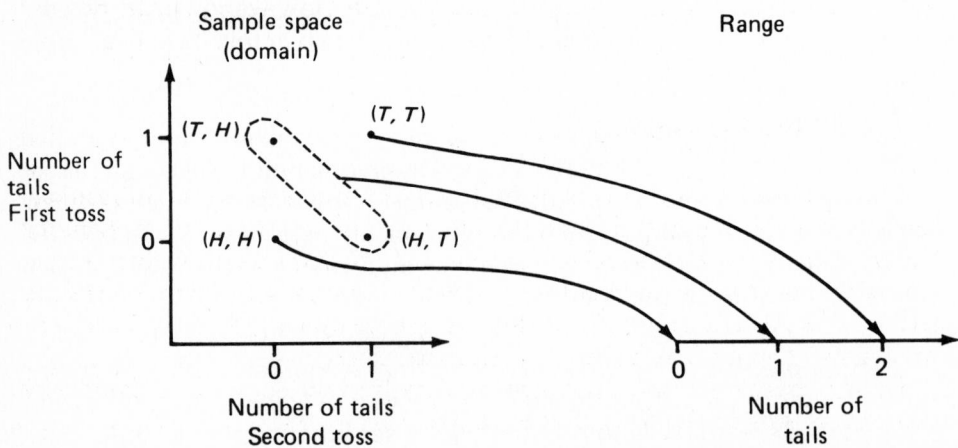

Another function of greater interest here is that which associates the subsets of outcomes with probabilities. The function can be evaluated a priori by comparing the number of sample points in a subset with the number of points in the sample space. The fraction of outcomes in which one tail occurs is $\frac{2}{4} = \frac{1}{2}$. Similarly, the fraction of outcomes giving no tails is $\frac{1}{4}$; for two tails, the ratio is $\frac{1}{4}$. The function that transforms subsets of a sample space into probabilities is represented by the rectangle in Figure 3.5. This function can be expressed mathematically in general form by $P(r) = \binom{n}{r} p^r (1 - p)^{n-r}$. This expression denotes binomial probabilities, which are discussed in detail in Chapter 4.

The correspondence between subsets of the sample space of an experiment and values of a random variable can be expressed by selecting an appropriate function. The principal objective in many statistics problems is that of discovering what function should be assigned to a sample space.

FIGURE 3.5

Transformation of Subsets of a Sample Space to Probabilities

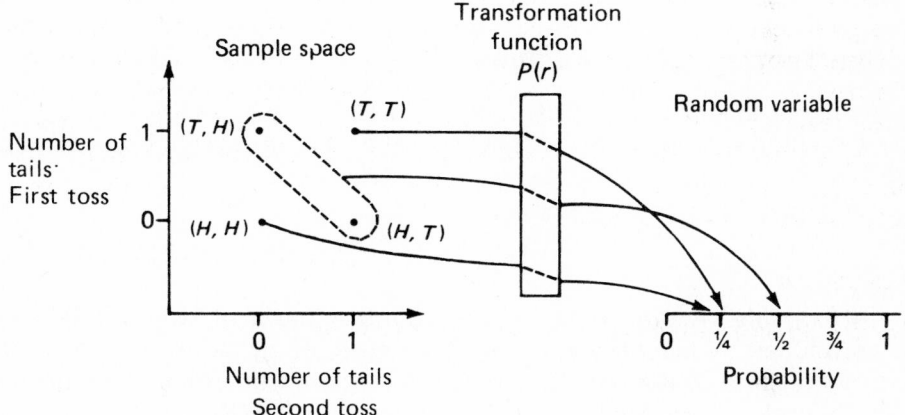

RULES OF PROBABILITY

The axioms of probability introduced in the section on preliminary ideas serve as a basis for considering the interpretation of probability. These axioms do not, however, provide a sufficient basis for formulating the wide spectrum of probability problems encountered in administration, but in this section additional rules are presented to provide a more comprehensive approach to calculating probabilities.

By way of review, the axioms previously introduced are associated with concepts of sets in the following example.

■ **Example.** Consider an experiment consisting of two tosses of a fair coin. The points of the sample space and the related probabilities are listed as follows:

Sample points	Event	A priori probability
(H, H)	A_1	$P(A_1) = \frac{1}{4}$
(H, T)	A_2	$P(A_2) = \frac{1}{4}$
(T, H)	A_3	$P(A_3) = \frac{1}{4}$
(T, T)	A_4	$P(A_4) = \frac{1}{4}$
		1.0

The a priori probabilities are expressed by the probability set function, $P(A_i) = \frac{1}{4}$. Thus, $P(A_1) = \frac{1}{4}$ and $P(A_1') = 1 - P(A_1) = 1 - \frac{1}{4} = \frac{3}{4}$. Let B_1 denote the event "head on first toss," and $P(B_1) = P(A_1 \cup A_2) = P(A_1) + P(A_2) = \frac{1}{4} + \frac{1}{4} = \frac{1}{2}$.

The example illustrates the axioms of probability previously introduced. These are summarized as follows:

I. $0 \leq P(A_i) \leq 1$
II. $P(A_1) + P(A_2) + \ldots + P(A_k) = 1$
III. $P(A_1') = 1 - P(A_1)$

The Special Rule of Addition

A fourth axiom is illustrated by the result $P(B_1) = P(A_1) + P(A_2)$ of the foregoing example. This axiom, known as the *Special Rule of Addition*, states:

For k mutually exclusive events

$$P(A_1 \cup A_2 \cup \ldots \cup A_k) = P(A_1) + P(A_2) + \ldots + P(A_k) \quad \ldots\ldots(3.3)$$

■ **Example.** A bin contains 400 identical parts of which 120 were produced by Machine A, 80 by Machine B, 96 by Machine C, and 104 by Machine D. If a part is selected at random from the bin, the probability that it was produced by Machine A or B or D is $P(A \cup B \cup D)$ = $P(A) + P(B) + P(D) = \frac{120}{400} + \frac{80}{400} + \frac{104}{400} = \frac{76}{100} = 0.76$. The selection of a part at random implies that each of the 400 parts in the bin has an equal chance of $\frac{1}{400}$ of being selected. Suppose we are interested in the selection of a part produced by Machine A. The selection of any one of the parts produced by Machine A constitutes the occurrence of the event of interest. The probability of the event is the sum of the probabilities for the 120 parts or $P(A) = 120(\frac{1}{400}) = \frac{120}{400} = 0.30$.

The General Rule of Addition

In many instances experimental events are not mutually exclusive, for the subsets corresponding to the events may have common elements.

■ *Example.* In two tosses of a fair coin, the probability of either the event "head on first toss," denoted B_1, or the event "head on second toss," denoted B_2, is $P(B_1 \cup B_2) = \frac{1}{2} + \frac{1}{2} - \frac{1}{4} = \frac{3}{4}$. The intersection $B_1 \cap B_2$ of the subsets as shown in Figure 3.6 is the common element $\{(H, H)\}$, where a head occurs on each toss. It is apparent from Figure 3.6 that $P(B_1 \cup B_2)$ does not equal $P(B_1) + P(B_2)$, for B_1 and B_2 have a common element $\{(H, H)\}$ whose probability should not be added twice.

These results can be summarized by the *General Rule of Addition,* which states:

If B_1 and B_2 are events, then

$$P(B_1 \cup B_2) = P(B_1) + P(B_2) - P(B_1 \cap B_2) \quad \dots\dots\dots\dots(3.4)$$

FIGURE 3.6

Diagram of Intersecting Subsets

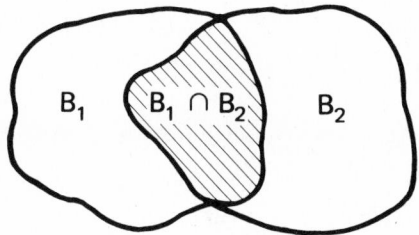

This rule applies to the addition of probabilities whether the events are mutually exclusive or not. If events are mutually exclusive, then the corresponding subsets are disjoint and the last term $P(B_1 \cap B_2)$ is zero. For events not mutually exclusive, $P(B_1 \cap B_2)$ is greater than zero and less than or equal to one.

The Special Rule of Multiplication

The rules of addition provide the basis for finding the probability of a compound event. A compound event can occur in more than one way because there are two or more elementary events in the subset of events that correspond to the compound event. The occurrence of *any one* of the elementary events constitutes the occurrence of the compound event. For example, the compound event of drawing a heart from a deck of cards occurs if any of the 13 heart cards is drawn. Not all probability problems are of this nature, since one may wish to determine the probability of a *succession* of elementary events. This type of probability is called a *joint probability.*

■ *Example.* A production supervisor randomly assigns five operators to five machines. From experience it is known that, on the average, each of the operators spends about one-tenth of the time waiting for raw material. The operators include two men and three women. The probability that at any moment during the working day the operator of a randomly selected machine will be *both* male and waiting for material is $P(\text{male}) \cdot P(\text{waiting}) = (\frac{2}{5}) \cdot (\frac{1}{10}) = \frac{2}{50}$, as shown by the probability tree in Figure 3.7.

Before generalizing the results in Figure 3.7, it is important to recognize an assumption that is implicit in the example; namely, that the selection of a male or a female operator in no way influences the likelihood that the worker is operating a machine or waiting for material. Events of this type are said to be *statistically independent.* Similarly, the outcomes of tosses of a coin are usually considered to be independent.

A general statement of the joint probability of independent events is given by the *Special Rule of Multiplication,* which states:

For k independent events $A_1, A_2, \ldots, A_k$, the probability that all these events will occur is

$$P(A_1 \cap A_2 \cap \ldots \cap A_k) = P(A_1) \cdot P(A_2) \cdot \ldots \cdot P(A_k) \ldots\ldots\ldots(3.5)$$

FIGURE 3.7

Tree Diagram Showing Calculation of Joint Probabilities

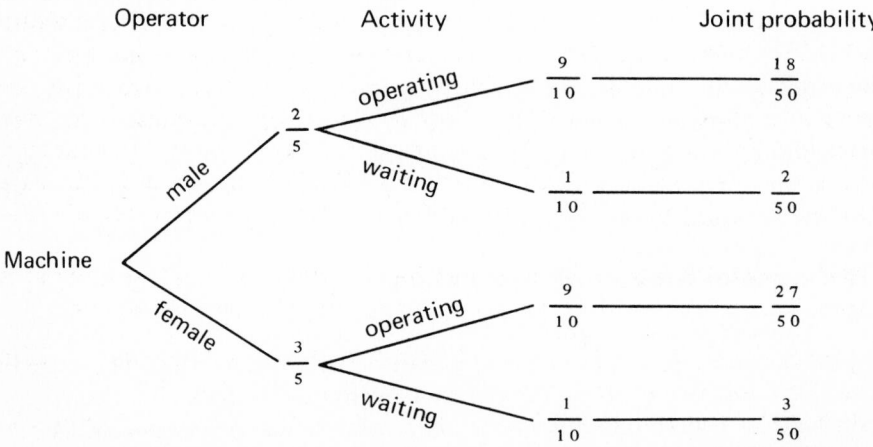

■ *Example.* Records of an airline indicate that $\frac{1}{3}$ of its flight attendants are blondes, $\frac{1}{2}$ are college graduates, and $\frac{3}{4}$ have more than one year of service. The probability that a randomly selected attendant is blonde *and* a college graduate *and* has more than a year of service is, assuming independence, $(\frac{1}{3}) \cdot (\frac{1}{2}) \cdot (\frac{3}{4}) = \frac{1}{8}$.

The Special Rule of Multiplication also applies to problems that involve sampling with replacement. Such a sample is drawn from a group of items by randomly selecting an item from the group and replacing it prior to drawing the next item. When sampling is done in this manner, the probability of selecting any given item in the group remains constant for all draws made in selecting the sample.

■ *Example.* A bowl contains four red balls and six white balls. A sample of three balls is drawn with replacement. The probability of drawing three white balls on successive draws is $P(W \cap W \cap W) = (\frac{6}{10})(\frac{6}{10})(\frac{6}{10}) = 0.216$. The probability of drawing one red ball and two white balls in a sample of three, where order is not specified, is computed by use of the multiplication and addition rules. The permutations corresponding to the combination one red and two white balls are: *RWW, WRW,* and *WWR.* The probability of any one of the sequences occurring in the sample is $(\frac{4}{10})(\frac{6}{10})(\frac{6}{10}) = (\frac{6}{10})(\frac{4}{10})(\frac{6}{10}) = (\frac{6}{10})(\frac{6}{10})(\frac{4}{10}) = 0.144$. Since there are three equally probable outcomes that correspond to the combination of one red and two white balls, the probability of obtaining this combination is $3(0.144) = 0.432$.

In reality, administrative problems often involve statistical dependence, in which the probability of one event is conditional on the occurrence of another. The following section takes up problems of this type.

Conditional Probability

Problems frequently arise that deal with the probabilities for only a portion of instead of the complete sample space. The probability of an event depends on what portion of the sample space is considered. The probability of randomly selecting from the population of all employees one having a college degree is different from the probability of selecting from the employees in managerial capacities one who is a college graduate. The managerial employees constitute a subpopulation defined by special conditions along with those attached to the total population. The probabilities associated with events in a subpopulation are defined as *conditional probabilities.*

■ *Example.* An automobile dealer has 10 cars for use as demonstrators. The characteristics of the cars are summarized as follows:

	Station wagons (B)	Sedans (B')	Total
Automatic transmission (A)	3	4	7
Standard transmission (A')	1	2	3
	4	6	10

If all the cars are available for use, the sample space S is 10 for the random selection of a vehicle. The probability of an event A, the selection of a car with an automatic transmission, is $P(A) = \frac{7}{10}$; the probability of event B, the random choice of a station wagon, is $P(B) = \frac{4}{10}$.

Now assume that a customer asks to drive a station wagon. The sample space is reduced from $S = 10$ to the subpopulation $B = 4$. The conditional probability of A (a car with an automatic transmission) given that the car is a station wagon is $P(A \mid B) = \frac{3}{4}$, the probability of A associated with the reduced sample space B. The term $P(A \mid B)$ is read: the probability that an event A will occur, given the condition that event B has already occurred. The original sample space S is depicted in Figure 3.8 by the rectangle shown in two parts. The reduced sample space B is represented by the right-hand portion of the rectangle. The shaded portion of both parts of the rectangle is the subset A, the vehicles with automatic transmissions.

FIGURE 3.8

Diagram of an Original and Reduced Sample Space

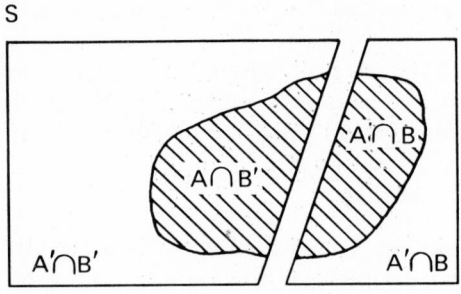

The result $P(A \mid B) = \frac{3}{4}$ is verified by considering that $P(A \mid B)$ is equal to $P(A \cap B)$, the proportion of all cars that are station wagons with automatic transmissions divided by $P(B)$, the proportion of cars that are station wagons, which is written

$$P(A \mid B) = \frac{P(A \cap B)}{P(B)} = \frac{\frac{3}{10}}{\frac{4}{10}} = \frac{3}{4}$$

More formally, if A and B are not independent events, the *conditional probability* of an event A relative to an event B, given that A and B are events from the same sample space and $P(A) \neq 0$, is expressed by

$$P(A \mid B) = \frac{P(A \cap B)}{P(B)} \quad\dots\dots\dots\dots\dots\dots\dots\dots\dots\text{(3.6)}$$

An assumption of the foregoing example was that the sample points had equal probabilities, but this assumption is not a requirement. Conditional probabilities can be very usefully applied to more general problems of assigning probabilities in a sample space.

The General Rule of Multiplication

Probabilities can be assigned to a sample space by means of a rearrangement of the terms in Formula 3.6 as illustrated by the following examples.

■ **Example.** In a toolroom of a plant there are six identical power drills, four in working order (*W*) and two that are defective (*D*). The toolroom clerk receives a requisition for two drills. The drills are selected randomly for issue. The sample space for the experiment is

$$S = (W_1,W_2), (W_1,D_2), (D_1,W_2), (D_1,D_2)$$

representing the possible outcomes of selecting two drills. The probability that the first drill selected is in working order is $W_1 = \frac{4}{6}$. Given that the first drill selected is in working order, the probability that the second drill selected is also in working order is $W_2 = \frac{3}{5}$. Substituting these values into Formula 3.6 gives

$$\frac{3}{5} = \frac{P(W_2 \cap W_1)}{\frac{4}{6}}, \text{ and}$$

$$P(W_2 \cap W_1) = (\tfrac{3}{5})(\tfrac{4}{6}) = \tfrac{2}{5}.$$

Similarly, the probabilities of the other possible outcomes are shown as follows:

		Second drill		
		W_2	D_2	Total
First	W_1	$\frac{2}{5}$	$\frac{4}{15}$	$\frac{2}{3}$
drill	D_1	$\frac{4}{15}$	$\frac{1}{15}$	$\frac{1}{3}$
		$\frac{2}{3}$	$\frac{1}{3}$	1

■ **Example.** A contractor submits separate contract bids for the plumbing and heating of a building. The contractor estimates subjectively that there is a $\frac{1}{2}$ chance of being awarded the plumbing contract, event *A*. Further, the contractor estimates that there is a $\frac{2}{3}$ chance of also receiving the heating contract, event *B*, if the plumbing contract is received. Should the contractor not receive the plumbing contract, the contractor nevertheless feels that there is a $\frac{1}{4}$ chance of receiving the heating contract. The probabilities for the intermediate and the final events are shown in Figure 3.9.

The foregoing example provides an intuitive illustration of the *General Rule of Multiplication*, which states:

If A and B are events, the probability that both will occur is expressed by

$$P(A \cap B) = P(B) \cdot P(A \mid B) \dots\dots\dots\dots\dots(3.7)$$

It is also true that $P(A \cap B) = P(A) \cdot P(B \mid A)$. If A and B are independent, then $P(A \cap B) = P(A) \cdot P(B) = P(B) \cdot P(A)$.

Formula 3.7 is illustrated in Figure 3.9, where the probability that neither the plumbing nor the heating contract will be received is $P(A' \cap B') = P(A') \cdot P(B' | A') = (\frac{1}{2}) \cdot (\frac{3}{4}) = \frac{3}{8}$.

FIGURE 3.9

Tree Diagram of Sequential Events Involving Conditional Probabilities

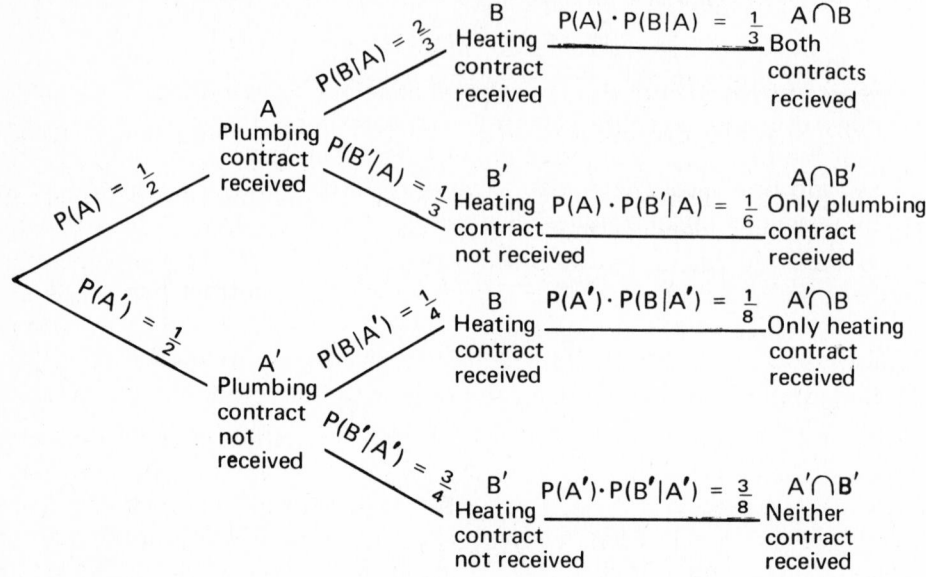

The Rule of Elimination

Suppose the contractor in the preceding example wishes to determine the probability of receiving the heating contract whether or not the plumbing contract is received. There are two conditions in which the heating contract can be received, and the probability of either of these outcomes occurring is the sum of the joint probabilities $P(A) \cdot P(B | A) + P(A') \cdot P(B | A') = (\frac{1}{2})(\frac{2}{3}) + (\frac{1}{2})(\frac{1}{4}) = \frac{11}{24}$.

The general form of this type of calculation is given by the *Rule of Elimination*, which states:

If $A_1, A_2, \ldots, A_k$ are mutually exclusive events, then

$$P(B) = P(A_1) \cdot P(B | A_1) + P(A_2) \cdot P(B | A_2) + \ldots + P(A_k) \cdot P(B | A_k) \ldots (3.8)$$

The Rule of Elimination provides a general approach for determining the total probability of the occurrence of an event that can conditionally occur in each of several ways. The total probability of an event is illustrated in Figure 3.9. Following the branches of the tree diagram, the event B can occur either with event A or with event A'.

In the example shown in Figure 3.9 the probabilities associated with each of the events illustrate the application of the rules of probability. In many instances the sample space and the subsets that correspond to the various events must be enumerated to compute probabilities. For example, when sampling without replacement is performed from a finite universe, the probabilities associated with the various events can be determined by use of methods for calculating the number of ways in which a given combination can be obtained. These methods for computing combinations are presented in Chapter 4.

Bayes' Theorem and the Revision of Probabilities

In the example dealing with the awarding of plumbing and heating contracts, there were two ways in which the contractor could receive the heating contract. The probability of receiving the heating contract in each of the two ways is dependent on whether the plumbing contract is received. Suppose the contractor learns that he or she has been awarded the heating contract, but the decision concerning the plumbing contract has not been announced. The contractor now asks, "What is the probability that the plumbing contract will not be received?" This is to ask, "What is $P(A' \mid B)$?"

Bayes' Theorem. Before the announcement of either of the contracts, it was estimated that the probability of the contractor's receiving the plumbing contract is $P(A) = \frac{1}{2}$ and the probability of not receiving the contract is $P(A') = \frac{1}{2}$. These probabilities, determined before any experimental information is obtained, are called *prior* probabilities. The conditional probability associated with each outcome of awarding the plumbing contract is known prior to any contract announcement and is sometimes called the *likelihood*. Once the receipt of the heating contract is learned, that is, experimental data are available, it is possible to estimate whether the plumbing contract was also received. This estimate is expressed as a numerical probability and is called the *posterior* probability, since this probability is determined after the result of an experiment is known. Thus, $P(A' \mid B)$ is the posterior probability estimate that the plumbing contract was not received.

The total probability of receiving the heating contract is the sum of the probabilities on the two corresponding branches of the tree diagram in Figure 3.9, or

$$P(B) = P(A) \cdot P(B \mid A) + P(A') \cdot P(B \mid A') = \tfrac{1}{3} + \tfrac{1}{8} = \tfrac{11}{24}.$$

Event B can occur in more than one way and the total probability of B occurring is the sum of the probabilities of each of the ways in which B can occur. It follows that the probability that B occurred in one *particular* way is the ratio of the probability of B occurring in that particular way to the total probability of B happening at all. Thus the posterior probability

$P(A'|B)$ is determined by calculating what proportion of the total probability of B is attributed to B occurring when A' also occurs. This proportion is

$$P(A'|B) = \frac{P(A') \cdot P(B|A')}{P(A) \cdot P(B|A) + P(A') \cdot P(B|A')} = \frac{(\frac{1}{2})(\frac{1}{4})}{(\frac{1}{2})(\frac{2}{3}) + (\frac{1}{2})(\frac{1}{4})} = \frac{\frac{1}{8}}{\frac{11}{24}}$$

$$= \frac{3}{11}.$$

■ *Example.* In a manufacturing plant, Machine I produces 40% of the output, Machine II produces 25%, and Machine III produces 35%. One and one-half percent of the output of Machine I is defective; Machine II produces 1.2% defective items; and 2.0% of the output of Machine III is defective. A day's output from the machines consists of a large number of items. An item selected randomly from a day's output is found to be defective. A production supervisor wishes to know the respective probabilities that the item was produced by Machine I, Machine II, or Machine III. Let E designate the event of the random selection of a defective item and H_1, H_2, and H_3 denote, respectively, the event of the item having been produced by Machines I, II, and III. The various events and probabilities are shown in Table 3.2.

TABLE 3.2

Calculation of Posterior Probabilities

Event	Prior $P(H_i)$	Conditional $P(E \mid H_i)$	Joint $P(H_i \cap E)$	Posterior $P(H_i \mid E)$
Machine I (H_1)	0.40	0.015	0.006	0.3750
Machine II (H_2)	0.25	0.012	0.003	0.1875
Machine III (H_3)	0.35	0.020	0.007	0.4375
		$P(E)$ =	0.016	

The posterior probability $P(H_1 \mid E)$ that the defective item was produced by Machine I is calculated by dividing the joint probability $P(H_1 \cap E)$ of the event that the item was produced by Machine I *and* defective by the total probability $P(E)$. The probability that the defective item was produced by Machine I is

$$P(H_1 \mid E) = \frac{P(H_1 \cap E)}{P(E)} = \frac{0.006}{0.016} = 0.3750,$$

where $P(H_1 \cap E) = P(H_1) \cdot P(E \mid H_1)$ and $P(E) = P(H_1 \cap E) + P(H_2 \cap E) + P(H_3 \cap E)$. The posterior probabilities for Machines II and III are calculated in a similar manner:

$$P(H_2 \mid E) = \frac{P(H_2 \cap E)}{P(E)} = \frac{0.003}{0.016} = 0.1875$$

and

$$P(H_3 \mid E) = \frac{P(H_3 \cap E)}{P(E)} = \frac{0.007}{0.016} = 0.4375.$$

This example is shown graphically in Figure 3.10 where the rectangle is the set S of a day's output of items; the portions H_1, H_2, and H_3 are the subsets of items produced by Machines I, II, and III, respectively; and the shaded portion E is the subset of defective items.

These results above are expressed in general form by *Bayes' Theorem,* which states:

If H_1, H_2, . . . , H_k are mutually exclusive and collectively exhaustive events with nonzero probabilities, the posterior probability of an event H_i is:

$$P(H_i \mid E) = \frac{P(H_i \cap E)}{P(H_1 \cap E) + P(H_2 \cap E) + \ldots + P(H_k \cap E)}\ldots\ldots(3.9)$$

$$= \frac{P(H_i)\,P(E \mid H_i)}{P(H_1)\,P(E \mid H_1) + \cdots\cdots + P(H_k)\,P(E \mid H_k)}$$

FIGURE 3.10

Diagram of the Output of Three Machines

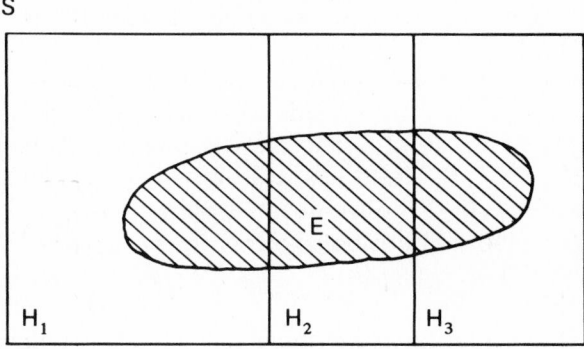

S

H₁   H₂   H₃   E

Revision of Probabilities. The application of Bayes' Theorem provides an important result in that the posterior probabilities constitute modifications of the prior probabilities based on experimental evidence. In the preceding example a defective item was selected, but the three machines differ in the proportion of defective items produced. Therefore, it follows that the probability of selecting a defective item from the production of a given machine should be proportional to the fraction of the total number of defective items produced by that machine. This modification is illustrated by comparing the prior and the posterior probabilities as follows:

	Probability		*Machine*	
		I	II	III
Prior—before the item is known to be defective		0.4000	0.2500	0.3500
Posterior—after the item is known to be defective		0.3750	0.1875	0.4375

On any successive random selection, the probability of obtaining an acceptable *or* defective item from the output of Machine I is the prior probability $P(H_1) = 0.40$; but if an item is selected that is found to be defective, the probability that it belongs to the output of Machine I is $P(H_1 \mid E) = 0.3750$.

The revision of probabilities may also be applied to problems for which repeated experimental trials are possible and successive revisions of prior probabilities are made to verify a hypothesis concerning an event. For each successive revision, the posterior probability of the preceding trial becomes the prior probability of the following trial.

MATHEMATICAL EXPECTATION

In the discussions that follow, the concept of a mathematical expectation will be used frequently and it is important to relate this idea to concepts of probability already presented. The *mathematical expectation,* also called the *expected value,* of a variable is the weighted arithmetic mean of the variable. The weights used to find the mathematical expectation are all the respective probabilities of the values that the variable can possibly assume.

> ■ *Example.* In a game of chance, a player is offered an amount of money in dollars equal to the value that turns up on the toss of a fair die. The sample space of a discrete variable *X* is the set of outcomes {$1, $2, $3, $4, $5, $6} and associated with each sample point is an equal probability of $\frac{1}{6}$. The weighted arithmetic mean or mathematical expectation of the amount paid to the player is $\frac{1}{6}(\$1) + \frac{1}{6}(\$2) + \frac{1}{6}(\$3) + \frac{1}{6}(\$4) + \frac{1}{6}(\$5) + \frac{1}{6}(\$6) = \$3.50$.

Summarizing the results above more formally, let X denote a variable with outcomes $X_1, X_2, \ldots, X_n$ that occur with probabilities $P(X_1)$, $P(X_2)$, $\ldots, P(X_n)$. The mathematical expectation of X is written $E(X)$, and

$$E(X) = X_1P(X_1) + X_2P(X_2) + \ldots + X_nP(X_n)\ldots\ldots\ldots\ldots(3.10)$$

Note that the mathematical expectation of $3.50 in the preceding example is not a value of the variable X that can actually occur. Rather, the expected value of the variable X is the long-run average of payments for many repeated trials of the game expressed as the probability-weighted mean of the values of the variable.

The use of a mathematical expectation was originally applied to games of chance and lotteries, but the notion of an expected value has become more generally applied and is now a common term in everyday parlance. Business situations frequently involve the consideration of expected values.

■ *Example.* A service station operator typically sells an average of $100 of gasoline on rainy days and an average of $300 on clear days. Statistics from the weather bureau indicate that the probability is 0.80 for clear weather and 0.20 for rainy weather. The expected value of gasoline sales is 0.20($100) + 0.80($300) = $260.

■ *Example.* A sporting goods dealer wishes to know how many boats of a particular type can be expected to be sold in the coming season. Based on sales records, the probabilities for the number of boats that may be demanded are as follows:

Demand	Probability
0	0.05
1	0.30
2	0.35
3	0.20
4	0.10

The expected value for the number of boats to be sold in the coming season is 0.05(0) + 0.30(1) + 0.35(2) + 0.20(3) + 0.10(4) = 0 + 0.3 + 0.7 + 0.6 + 0.4 = 2. The dealer can expect to sell two boats, assuming that sales in the coming season will be similar to past seasons for which the records were kept.

STUDY QUESTIONS

3–1. Explain briefly the meaning of each of the following terms:

a. elementary event
b. collectively exhaustive events
c. mutually exclusive event
d. elementary unit
e. universe
f. simple random sampling
g. equiprobable events
h. a priori probability
i. statistical regularity
j. compound event
k. subjective probability
l. set
m. discrete set
n. universal set
o. subset
p. event

q. disjoint set
r. complement
s. stochastic process
t. random variable
u. function
v. domain
w. range
x. point function
y. set function
z. sample space
aa. joint probability
ab. statistically independent events
ac. conditional probability
ad. prior probability
ae. posterior probability
af. mathematical expectation

3–2. What are the mutually exclusive and collectively exhaustive events for the following experiments?
  a. The number of heads in a toss of two coins
  b. The combined value of the faces in a toss of a pair of dice
  c. The number of spades or kings in a hand of five cards dealt from a deck of 52 playing cards

3–3. What assumptions must be made so that the outcomes of each of the following experiments may be considered equiprobable?
  a. Tossing a coin
  b. A salesperson attempting to sell an automobile to a customer
  c. The price of a common stock one month from now

3–4. In an experiment two hands of 12 cards each are dealt from a deck of 52 playing cards. Hand *A* is dealt, with replacement, from the deck and contains five spades. Hand *B* is dealt without replacement and contains four spades. How are the following concepts related to the samples represented by hands *A* and *B?*
  a. statistical regularity   d. compound event
  b. uniform conditions   e. a priori probability
  c. relative frequency   f. conditional probability

3–5. The consumers in a marketing area may be classified by a variety of criteria, such as annual income, occupation, and education. Write a description for each of two subsets that:
  a. Identify consumers with a common characteristic
  b. Are disjoint
  c. Have an intersection
  d. Are the complements of other subsets

3–6. An electronic component of a computer is mass produced by a firm. The component is judged to be of acceptable quality if its voltage rating lies within a specified range. Random samples of components are drawn hourly from the process and, if the sample contains no defective units, production is continued. If a defective component is drawn in the sample, the process is stopped and adjustments are made. Relate the characteristics of this example to each of the following concepts:
  a. discrete random variable   d. sample space
  b. continuous random variable   e. subset
  c. stochastic variable

3–7. A space capsule is to be launched to orbit the planet Jupiter and to transmit data reflecting conditions on the planet. The probability that the capsule will remain on course during the launch period is *A*. The probability that the capsule will drift from the designated course while in flight is designated *B*. Probability *C* denotes the likelihood that corrections can be made in flight to correct any deviations from the desired trajectory and course. Express each of the following probabilities in words:

a. $P(B \mid A)$
b. $P(C \cap B \mid A)$
c. $P(C \mid A')$

d. $P(A \cap B')$
e. $P(A \cup B)$
f. $P(C \mid A \cup B)$

3-8. Draw a tree diagram of the situation described in Question 3–7.

3-9. Considering the situation given in Question 3–7:
a. Which probabilities are independent?
b. How are the rules of addition or multiplication of probabilities related to this situation?

3-10. What is the logical basis of Bayes' Theorem?

PROBLEMS

3-1. If a sportswriter estimates that the odds are five to four that an athletic team will win a championship game, what is the estimate of the probability that the team will win?

3-2. What are the odds of obtaining two heads on two successive tosses of a fair coin?

3-3. What are the odds of obtaining one or more heads on two successive tosses of a fair coin?

3-4. If an investor feels that the chances are one out of three that the price of a security will rise on a given day, what is the investor's estimate of the odds that the security price will rise?

3-5. Perform an experiment by shaking a thumbtack out of a container onto a surface and observing whether the tack lands with its point up or down. Repeat this procedure 50 times. Use the resulting relative frequency to estimate the probability that the tack will land with the point up on a trial.

3-6. Perform an experiment in which random draws, with replacement, are made from a standard deck of playing cards. Remove six spades and six clubs from the deck of cards. Shuffle the remaining 40 cards, deal a card from the deck, and observe whether it is a black card; replace the card and shuffle the deck. Repeat the procedure 50 times. Compare the resulting relative frequency and the probability of drawing a black card on a single random draw from the deck of 40 cards.

3-7. A stockbroker estimates that the probabilities that the prices of three stocks will rise are 0.4, 0.5, and 0.6, respectively. What is the probability that the prices of all three stocks will rise?

3-8. The telephone switchboard of a company is usually busy 30% of the time. If a customer calls at randomly selected times, what is the probability that a busy signal will be obtained on three successive calls?

3-9. How many times must a fair coin be tossed so that the probability of obtaining one or more heads is at least 0.95?

3-10. In an experiment in which two fair dice are tossed:
a. What is the sample space of the experiment?
b. How many sample points correspond to obtaining the number nine?
c. What is the probability of obtaining a nine on one toss of the dice?

3-11. A fair coin is tossed three times in an experiment. Determine the:
a. Sample space of the experiment
b. Number of sample points corresponding to the outcome of two heads
c. Probability of obtaining two heads

3-12. A box contains six red and four green marbles. Two marbles are to be selected randomly without replacement. What is the probability that:
a. Both will be red?
b. Each will be a different color?

3-13. In an extensive study of the effectiveness of a test for detecting a type of disease, the following data for health condition and test results for 10,000 patients were obtained:

	Test result Negative (N)	Positive (P)
Health condition		
Disease confirmed (D)	250	4,750
Healthy (H)	4,800	200

Use the data shown above to evaluate:
a. $P(D \mid P)$
b. $P(P \mid H)$
c. $P(P \mid H \cup D)$
d. $P(N \mid D)$
e. $P(H \cap N)$
f. $P(D \cap P)$

3-14. A survey of voters taken to analyze preferences for candidates and political parties produced the following data:

	Party preference Democrat (D)	Republican (R)	Independent (I)
Candidate preference			
Candidate (A)	100	200	50
Candidate (B)	250	140	90
Undecided (U)	50	60	60

Use the data shown above to evaluate:
a. $P(A \cap R)$
b. $P(B \mid D)$
c. $P(A \cup B)$
d. $P(B \cap R)$
e. $P(U \mid I)$
f. $P(U \cap I)$

3–15. A petroleum company is nearing the completion of drilling an oil well on a new location that the company has leased. On the basis of geological reports, there is a 0.40 probability that a formation of type *A* lies beneath the well site, a 0.35 probability of a formation of type *B,* and a 0.25 probability of a type *C* formation. Company records show that oil is discovered 20% of the time in type *A* formations, 40% in type *B,* and 30% in type *C* formations. What is the probability that:

  a. The well will produce oil?

  b. If the well is dry, a type *C* formation lies beneath the well site?

3–16. A contractor in the building-wrecking business has observed that a major competitor submits bids on about 70% of the jobs on which the contractor bids. The contractor has been awarded jobs about 40% of the time when the major competitor also submitted a bid and about 60% of the time when the competitor did not bid on the job.

  a. What is the probability that the contractor will not be awarded the contract?

  b. If the contractor submits a bid and does not receive the contract, what is the probability that the major competitor also submitted a bid?

3–17. A television repair technician estimates that 70% of house calls are made for service on portable television sets. In addition, 60% of the portable sets are black-and-white receivers and 65% of console television sets are color receivers. If a service call is received and the service is needed for a color set, what is the probability that the set is a console television?

3–18. Records indicate that 40% of all students on a university campus are female. Also, 30% of females are graduate students, and 80% of male students are graduate students. If a graduate student is selected at random, what is the probability that the student is female?

3–19. In anticipating the cash flow from two accounts in the coming month, a manager estimates that there is a 0.60 probability of receiving $5,000 that is due from one account and a 0.70 chance of receiving $3,000 from the other. What is the expected cash flow from these accounts?

3–20. In a fund-raising drive a $2,500 automobile is given as the prize in a drawing. What is the expected value of a ticket if 1,000 tickets are sold?

3–21. Production records indicate that 30% of the transistors produced by a process are defective. From a random sample of four transistors, compute:

  a. The probabilities associated with each of the possible numbers of defective transistors that can be obtained in the sample

  b. The expected number of defectives that will be drawn in the sample

3-22. The market research department of a company estimates the probability that a new product will be successful is 0.70. If the new product is successful, the company will gain $20,000; otherwise, a loss of $10,000 will be incurred. What is the expected value of the product?

3-23. A bakery has studied its records and notices that for the past 200 days the demand for its product has varied as follows:

Demand (units)	Number of days
8,000	12
9,000	60
10,000	80
11,000	40
12,000	8
	200

Using the frequencies in estimating the probabilities for the various levels of demand, compute the expected daily demand for the product.

3-24. The owners of a department store in a desirable downtown business location have an opportunity to sell the business for $400,000. They estimate that if they continue to operate the store and business remains good, they can realize $800,000. If, however, there is a substantial shift of consumer shopping to the suburbs, they will realize only $200,000.
   a. If the probability of continued good business is 0.60, what action do you recommend be taken?
   b. For what probability for continued good business would the building owners be indifferent to selling their business?

Chapter 4
Discrete Probability Distributions

A frequency distribution, as discussed in Chapter 2, is a systematic arrangement of data that shows how often the values of a random variable occurred while the variable was being observed. The data can be arranged into a table or a histogram to organize, summarize, and describe the empirical distribution of the results of an actual experiment. The ratio of each observed frequency to the total number of observations is an approximation of the probability of occurrence of each respective value (or group of values) of the random variable.

In contrast, a theoretical distribution describes the possible outcomes of an experiment on the basis of the probabilities of occurrence of the values of a random variable. The discussions in this chapter principally concern theoretical distributions that can be described by a function with which to calculate *a priori* the probability corresponding to each possible value of a random variable. A systematic arrangement of the probabilities corresponding to the values (or group of values) of a random variable is called a *probability distribution*.

A random variable for which the several possible values differ by clearly defined steps is called a *discrete random variable*. This type of variable can assume only certain values, often integers, and no intermediate values can be taken on. For example, the number of persons arriving at a service counter per hour or the number of microwave ovens sold during periods of a month is a discrete random variable that can be represented by counted data. An arrangement of the probabilities associated with the values of a discrete random variable is called a *discrete probability distribution*.

■ *Example.* The marketing research department of a company believes that customers are evenly divided in their preference for each of two package designs for a product. Half of the customers prefer the blue (*B*) package and the other half prefer a new maroon (*M*) color package. A sample of four customers is to be selected randomly to observe how many prefer the new maroon color. The number of customers in the sample that prefer the maroon package is defined as the discrete random variable X. The elementary events and the probabilities corresponding to the possible outcomes of the experiment are shown in Table 4.1. The theoretical probability distribution for the discrete random variable X is also shown in Figure 4.1.

TABLE 4.1

Probabilities for the Possible Outcomes of an Experiment

X	Elementary events	Probability $P(X)$
0	(B, B, B, B)	$(\frac{1}{2} \cdot \frac{1}{2} \cdot \frac{1}{2} \cdot \frac{1}{2}) = \frac{1}{16}$
1	(M, B, B, B), (B, M, B, B), (B, B, M, B), (B, B, B, M)	$4(\frac{1}{2} \cdot \frac{1}{2} \cdot \frac{1}{2} \cdot \frac{1}{2}) = \frac{4}{16}$
2	(M, M, B, B), (M, B, M, B), (M, B, B, M), (B, M, M, B), (B, M, B, M), (B, B, M, M)	$6(\frac{1}{2} \cdot \frac{1}{2} \cdot \frac{1}{2} \cdot \frac{1}{2}) = \frac{6}{16}$
3	(M, M, M, B), (M, M, B, M), (M, B, M, M), (B, M, M, M)	$4(\frac{1}{2} \cdot \frac{1}{2} \cdot \frac{1}{2} \cdot \frac{1}{2}) = \frac{4}{16}$
4	(M, M, M, M)	$(\frac{1}{2} \cdot \frac{1}{2} \cdot \frac{1}{2} \cdot \frac{1}{2}) = \frac{1}{16}$

FIGURE 4.1

Discrete Probability Distribution of the Sample of Four Customers

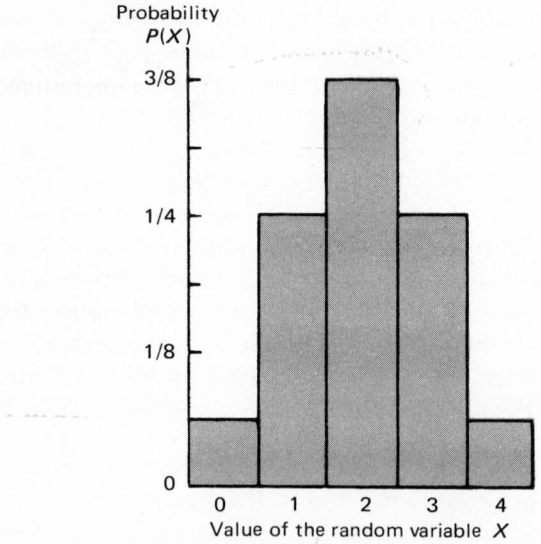

The foregoing example illustrates a theoretical distribution for which the probabilities corresponding to the values of the discrete random variable can be calculated a priori from the likelihoods of the outcomes that make up the elementary events. The probability distribution in this example is an exact model of the distribution of outcomes. In other instances it is not feasible to determine the probability distribution for a variable. It is possible, however, that a theoretical distribution can serve as a suitable model or approximation of a frequency distribution of observed values. This type of relationship is discussed in Chapter 9 in fitting a theoretical distribution to empirical data.

In contrast to a discrete random variable, the values of a *continuous random variable* are obtained by measuring from a continuous scale. Measures such as weight, time, distance, and volume involve measurement on a continuous scale. This type of scale has an infinite number of possible values that need not be whole numbers but which may be carried to as many decimal places as the accuracy of measurement will justify. An arrangement of the probabilities associated with the groups of values in intervals of a continuous random variable, often shown as a table or figure, is called a *continuous probability distribution*. This type of distribution is the subject of Chapter 5.

THE BINOMIAL PROBABILITY DISTRIBUTION

An important class of administrative problems involves random processes for which there are only two possible outcomes. The outcomes occur without any fixed pattern, and the probability of either outcome remains unchanged for each trial. Processes with these characteristics are called *Bernoulli processes*. For example, the parts produced by a machine are classified as being "acceptable" or "defective," and the probability of selecting either type of part remains unchanged for each trial. Similarly, in a survey consumers are asked if they prefer a particular brand of product to other similar brands. The likelihood of obtaining either response remains unchanged, regardless of how many customers are queried.

In order to simplify the expression of the characteristics of Bernoulli processes, a specified or desired outcome of a trial will be termed a *success*. The proportion or fraction of successes obtained from a very large number of trials of a Bernoulli process is called a *parameter*. In some instances the proportion of trials that yields successes is known with certainty. Whatever the results of a finite number of trials, the value of this long-run fraction is constant. The *binomial probability distribution* is a systematic arrangement of the probabilities associated with the possible numbers of successes for a given number of trials of a Bernoulli process, as illustrated in Table 4.1 and Figure 4.1.

Methods of Counting

The application of the binomial distribution to administrative problems often involves an analysis of data obtained from sampling. In drawing samples of outcomes from a Bernoulli process, the results, expressed as numbers of successes and failures, can vary from sample to sample. This possible variation is illustrated by the foregoing example (page 87), for there are 16 different possible sequences of successes and failures (M and B) that are the elementary events. In calculating binomial probabilities it is important to determine how many of the possible sequences correspond to the given value of a discrete random variable. For example, the sequences (M, M, M, B), (M, M, B, M), (M, B, M, M), and (B, M, M, M) are four different ways in which three successes (M) can be obtained in a sample of four customers.

The number of different sequences that can be obtained from sampling becomes large even for moderately sized samples. It is very useful, therefore, to have some generalized methods for counting the number of distinct sequences or elementary events that correspond to different numbers of successes and failures.

An arrangement or sequence of things for which order of occurrence is of importance is called a *permutation. There are $n!$ possible different permutations of n distinct objects if all objects are used.* The term $n!$ is read as "n factorial" and equals $n(n - 1)(n - 2) \ldots (n - n + 1)$. For example, $3! = 3 \cdot 2 \cdot 1 = 6$; $4! = 4 \cdot 3 \cdot 2 \cdot 1 = 24$; and $6! = 6 \cdot 5 \cdot 4 \cdot 3 \cdot 2 \cdot 1 = 720$. The general expression for the number of permutations for n objects with all objects included in each sequence is written $_nP_n = n!$

For some counting problems it is necessary to determine the number of possible permutations of a set of n different objects in which only a portion of the objects is included in each arrangement. Suppose a set has a total of n objects and r of these objects are taken at a time, where r is less than n. *The number of possible permutations of n different things taken r at a time, denoted by $_nP_r$, is*

$$_nP_r = \frac{n!}{(n - r)!} \qquad \qquad (4.1)$$

■ **Example.** The number of different sequences of three letters that can be arranged from the five letters *ABCDE* is

$$_5P_3 = \frac{n!}{(n - r)!} = \frac{5 \cdot 4 \cdot 3 \cdot 2 \cdot 1}{2 \cdot 1} = 60.$$

The permutations of a set of objects are based on the *order* of the arrangements, where each change in order constitutes a different arrangement. However, if one wishes to determine how many different selections of objects can be made, *where order is not of consequence,* a different problem is posed. A selection of objects for which order is not of consequence is called a *combination.* Thus, the number of possible combinations of a set of n objects taken all together is one, since order does not count and there is only one way of including all the objects in the combination. If, however, groups of r objects are taken from a set of n distinct objects, then more than one combination is possible.

■ **Example.** The letters A, B, and C, if taken as a group, constitute just one combination, since order does not matter. However, these letters taken all together can be arranged to form $3! = 6$ permutations.

The number of permutations that correspond to a given combination where n things are taken r at a time is written

$$_nC_r = \binom{n}{r} = \frac{n!}{r!(n-r)!} \dots \dots \dots \dots \dots \dots \dots \dots \dots \dots (4.2)$$

The application of combinations to binomial probability distributions is illustrated by the example shown in Table 4.1 and Figure 4.1. The combinations are the numbers of manufactured parts. The number of permutations per combination is the number of elementary events that correspond to each respective combination. The combination for which no manufactured parts occur in a sample of four items has the one permutation (B, B, B, B). The combination of outcomes that gives three manufactured parts in a sample of four items occurs in each of the permutations (M, M, M, B), (M, M, B, M), (M, B, M, M), (B, M, M, M), and there are four ways to get three manufactured and one bought part in a sample of four items. Similarly, the number of ways in which the combination of two manufactured and two bought parts in a sample of four items can be obtained is computed

$$_4C_2 = \binom{4}{2} = \frac{4!}{2!(4-2)!} = \frac{4 \cdot 3 \cdot 2 \cdot 1}{2 \cdot 1 \cdot 2 \cdot 1} = 6.$$

This result is seen in Table 4.1, for there are six permutations that correspond to the combination of two manufactured and two bought parts.

Binomial Probability Density Function

Consider an experiment in which a die is tossed four times and the number of sixes occurring is recorded. The number of ways in which a given number of sixes can be obtained is found by means of the rule for computing combinations. Thus, the number of ways of getting three sixes in four tosses of the die is

$$\binom{n}{r} = \binom{4}{3} = \frac{4!}{3!(4-3)!} = 4 \text{ ways.}$$

The probability that any one of the four ways will occur is obtained by using the rule for multiplying probabilities. For instance, the probability of obtaining a sequence consisting of three sixes (S) and one nonsix (N) is

$$P(SSSN) = \left(\tfrac{1}{6} \cdot \tfrac{1}{6} \cdot \tfrac{1}{6} \cdot \tfrac{5}{6}\right) = \tfrac{5}{1,296}.$$

The probability of getting three sixes in four tosses of a die is

$$4\left(\tfrac{5}{1,296}\right) = \tfrac{5}{324}.$$

These results can be generalized by viewing the occurrence of a six as a success where the probability of a success is p. Let q denote the probability of a nonsix, or a *failure*, where $q = 1 - p$. The probability that r successes and $n - r$ failures will be obtained in a particular sequence is given by

$$\underset{r \text{ successes}}{(p \cdot p \cdot p \cdot \ldots p)} \underset{n - r \text{ failures.}}{(q \cdot q \cdot q \cdot \ldots q)} = p^r q^{n-r}$$

The number of ways in which r successes can be obtained in n trials is given by $\binom{n}{r}$. The generalized expression of the function describing the probability of obtaining exactly r successes in n trials of an experiment is

$$P(r \,|\, n, p) = \binom{n}{r} p^r q^{n-r} \ldots\ldots\ldots\ldots\ldots\ldots\ldots(4.3)$$

and is called the *binomial probability density function.*

■ *Example.* The probability of obtaining three sixes in four tosses of a die is $P(r = 3 \,|\, n = 4,\ p = 1/6) = \binom{4}{3} (1/6)^3 (5/6)^{4-3} = 4(1/216)(5/6) = 0.0154.$

■ *Example.* A large shipment of purchased parts is received at a warehouse, and 10 parts are randomly selected and checked for quality. The parts are the output of a machine that consistently produces 5% defective items. The probability that the sample of 10 parts will include one defective is equal to the value of the binomial probability density function of the random variable r, where $r = 1, n = 10$, and $p = 0.05$. This probability is expressed by

$$P(r = 1 \,|\, n = 10,\ p = 0.05) = \binom{10}{1} (0.05)^1 (0.95)^9 = \frac{10!}{1!9!} (0.05)(0.63)$$

$$= 0.3151.$$

The general expression, $P(r \,|\, n, p)$, is read "the probability of r successes, given the binomial density function defined by the values of n and p."

The term binomial arises from the fact that the value of Formula 4.3 for specified values of n, r, and p is equivalent to the corresponding term of the expansion of the binomial expression $(p + q)^n$.

■ *Example.* Forty percent of the employees of a large plant are male and a random sample of two employees is taken. The probability that the sample will contain 0, 1, or 2 male employees can be determined by evaluating the terms of the expansion of

$$(0.40 + 0.60)^2 = (0.40)^0(0.60)^2 + 2(0.40)^1(0.60)^1 + (0.40)^2(0.60)^0$$

$$= 0.36 + 0.48 + 0.16.$$

These three terms correspond to the probabilities of zero, one, and two successes. Similarly, the probability of obtaining one male in the sample of two employees is

$$P(r = 1 \mid n = 2, p = 0.40) = \binom{2}{1} (0.40)^1 (0.60)^1 = \frac{2!}{1!1!} (0.40)(0.60)$$

$$= 0.48.$$

This result is identical with the second term of the expansion of the binomial $(0.40 + 0.60)^2$.

Distributions of Binomial Probabilities

The generalized expression of the binomial probability density function $P(r) = \binom{n}{r} p^r q^{n-r}$ provides the means for computing the probability of every possible number of successes in a given number of trials. A systematic arrangement of these probabilities is called a *binomial probability distribution*. The binomial probability density function defines a series of distributions, one for every possible combination of values of n and p, the parameters of the respective distributions.

Some of the binomial probability distributions, presented as histograms in Figure 4.2, illustrate the characteristics of the distributions for selected values of n and p. While only the distributions corresponding to values of $p = 0.50$ are symmetric, the distributions for small values of p are reasonably symmetric, especially for large values of n. This property enables one to employ the symmetric normal curve as a useful approximation, as discussed in the next chapter.

Binomial Probability Tables

Calculating binomial probabilities using the binomial density function (Formula 4.3) can be cumbersome, especially if n is large. Tables of binomial probabilities can be used to obtain desired values in much the same manner as tables of square roots and logarithms are used to save time and effort in computations.

Appendix C presents a table of binomial probabilities for various values of n, p, and r. The values in this table were computed by substituting various values of n, p, and r into Formula 4.3. To find the probability of exactly r successes in n trials and a given value of p, locate in Appendix C: (1) the portion of the table relating to the value of n, (2) the column in this portion of the table corresponding to the value of p, and (3) the desired probability value in the row of the column for the appropriate value of r (read from the left margin).

■ *Example.* In a preceding example (page 92) a sample is selected from a large shipment of items that contains 5% defective items. The

FIGURE 4.2

Binomial Probability Distributions for Selected Values of *n* and *p*

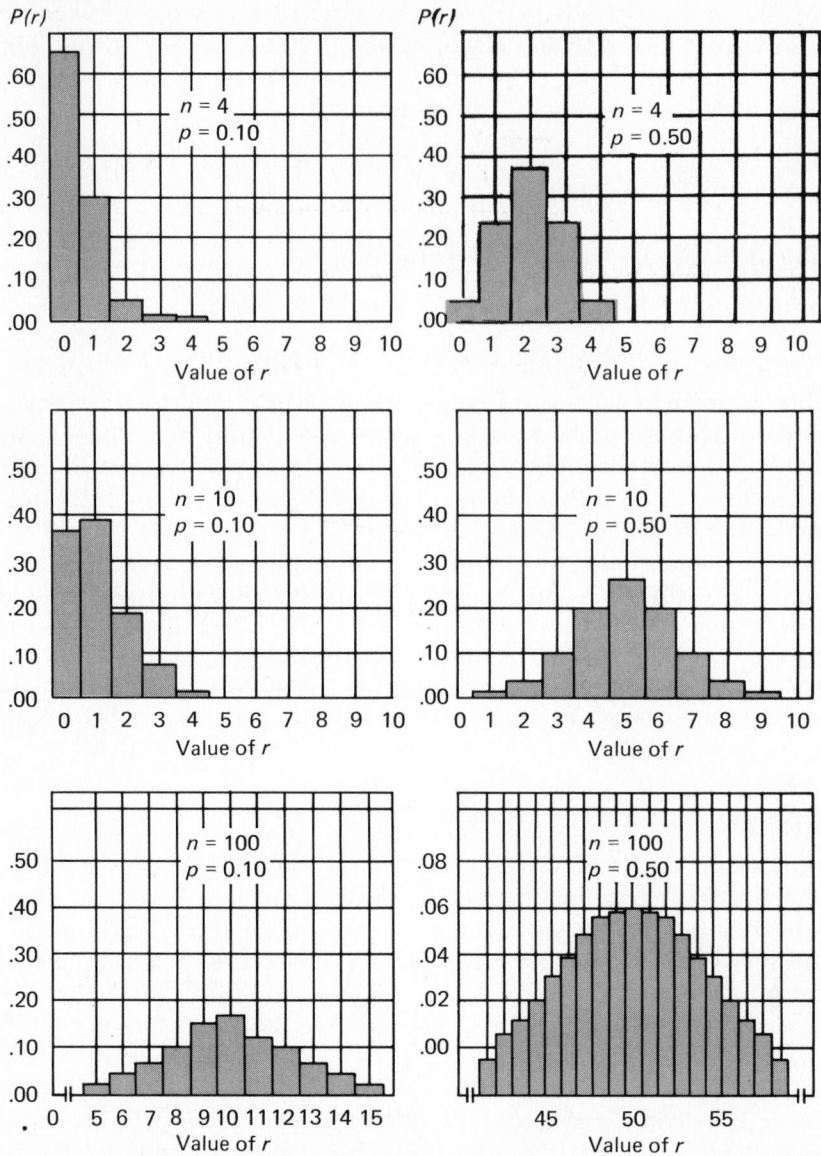

probability of randomly selecting a sample of 10 that contains one defective item is computed to be $P(r = 1 \mid n = 10, p = 0.05) = 0.3151$. This probability is found in the part of Appendix C for $n = 10$ (see page 552). In the column headed 0.05, the value in the second row of the column is the probability 0.3151. This value corresponds to *r* equal to one as seen at the left-hand margin.

In many situations one may wish to determine a cumulative probability such as the probability of r or more successes in a given number of trials. In this case, what is desired is the probability corresponding to the right-hand tail of a binomial distribution. This can be found by adding the probabilities for each of the respective events, and for a large value of n this procedure can be very tedious. Consequently, tables of cumulative binomial probabilities have been prepared to make it easier to determine these probabilities.

Appendix D presents cumulative binomial probabilities for a limited number of distributions. The values in this table correspond to the areas of the right-hand tails of distributions or the probabilities of r or more successes for given values of n and p. Since the total area of any binomial distribution is equal to one, the area of any left-hand tail, or the probability of fewer than r successes, is one minus the probability of r or more successes.

■ *Example.* For a binomial distribution defined by $n = 8$ and $p = 0.40$, the probability of four or more successes $P(r \geq 4 \mid n = 8, p = 0.40)$ is 0.4059 as seen in Appendix D (page 000), opposite the value of r of four. This probability is shown as the right-hand tail (shaded portion) in Figure 4.3. Similarly, the probability of more than four successes, $P(r > 4 \mid n = 8, p = 0.40)$, is 0.1737 and is found opposite $r = 5$ for $n = 8$ and $p = 0.40$. To find $P(r < 4 \mid n = 8, p = 0.40)$, the probability of less than four successes is $1 - P(r \geq 4)$. This is found by reading 0.4059 opposite $r = 4$ and computing $1 - P(r \geq 4) = 1 - 0.4059 = 0.5941$. The probability of exactly four successes $P(r = 4 \mid n = 8, p = 0.40)$ is found by computing $P(r \geq 4) - P(r \geq 5)$; 0.4059 is read opposite $r = 4$, and 0.1737, opposite $r = 5$. The difference is $0.4059 - 0.1737 = 0.2322$.

FIGURE 4.3

Probability Distribution of $P(r \mid n = 8, p = 0.40)$

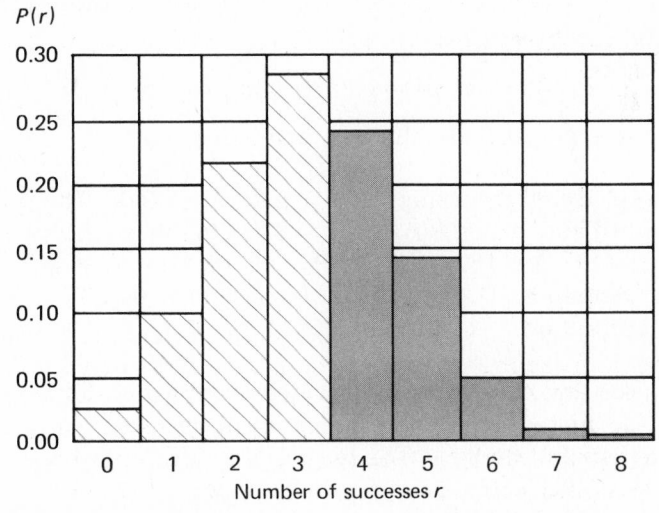

Binomial Probabilities for $p > 0.50$

The problem of determining probabilities for values of $p > 0.50$ is slightly more involved, since Appendix C and Appendix D do not contain probability values for $p > 0.50$. These tables may be used for values of $p > 0.50$, however, by recasting a problem in terms of $q = 1 - p$ and setting $r = n - r$. Restating a problem is possible since the probability of obtaining r successes in n trials for a given value of p is equal to the probability of obtaining $n - r$ failures in n trials with $q = 1 - p$. In other words, if r successes occur in a sample, there must be $n - r$ failures, since the number of successes and failures must total $n = r + (n - r)$. The probability of obtaining exactly r occurrences of an event (usually in terms of successes) in n trials for a value of $p > 0.50$ can be written

$$P(r \mid n, p) = P(r = n - r \mid n, q)\ldots\ldots\ldots\ldots\ldots\ldots\ldots\ldots\ldots\ldots\text{(4.4)}$$

where $q = 1 - p$ and $r = n - r$ is read "define a new value of r that is equal to the value of n minus the old value of r."

■ *Example.* Continuing a preceding example (page 92) and recasting it in terms of the number of acceptable items that are obtained in a sample from a large shipment of items, the probability of getting nine acceptable items in a sample of ten, when 95% of the items in the shipment are acceptable, is $P(r = 9 \mid n = 10, p = 0.95) = P(r = 10 - 9 \mid n = 10, q = 0.05)$. This probability $P(r = 1 \mid n = 10, q = 0.05)$ is read from Appendix C (page 552) in the portion of the table for $n = 10$, $p = 0.05$ (q is read as p), and $r = 1$, and the probability is 0.3151.

Cumulative probabilities for $p > 0.50$ can be determined from Appendix D by recasting problems in a manner similar to that presented in the foregoing discussion. The probability of obtaining r or more successes in n trials with $p > 0.50$ can be written

$$P(\text{r} \geq r' \mid n, p) = 1 - P(r \geq n - r + 1 \mid n, q)\ldots\ldots\ldots\ldots\text{(4.5)}$$

where r' denotes a specified value of r and $q = 1 - p$.

■ *Example.* Given the values of $n = 8$ and $p = 0.60$. The probability of five or more successes $P(r \geq 5 \mid n = 8, p = 0.60)$ is written equivalently as $1 - P(r \geq n - r + 1 \mid n, q) = 1 - P(r \geq 8 - 5 + 1 \mid n = 8, q = 0.40)$. Reading from Appendix D, the appropriate value is 0.4059 and the probability is computed $1 - 0.4059 = 0.5941$.

Formulas 4.3 and 4.4 can be interpreted graphically, for given the same value of n, the histogram for the binomial distribution for q is a mirror image of the distribution for p. The term $n - r$ in Formula 4.4 is computed to locate the bar of the histogram for q that corresponds to the bar for r in the histogram for p. Similarly, the area in the right-hand tail corresponding to the probability of r or more successes in the histogram for q is found by computing the term $n - r + 1$ in Formula 4.5, determining the respective area in the right-hand tail of the histogram for p, and subtracting this area from one to give the desired area or probability, the left-hand tail of the histogram for p.

Descriptive Measures of the Binomial Distribution

The general expression of the binomial distribution describes a series of distributions. Each of these distributions is defined by a unique combination of the parameters n and p. In practice, the value of the long-run fraction of successes is rarely known with certainty, except in a situation where it can be computed *a priori*. More often, n and p are properties of a sample drawn from a universe, and p serves as an estimate of the parameter π, the long-run fraction of successes. Whether the parameters of a binomial distribution are known or estimated, the descriptive measures of the corresponding distribution are of considerable value in the formulation and solution of certain problems.

The nature of the mean and standard deviation of the binomial distribution can be shown by use of an alternate view of Bernoulli trials. Consider an experiment in which items are drawn, with replacement, from a large container in which part of the items are Brand A and the remainder are Brand B. The total number of items in the container is denoted by N. If the number of items that are Brand A is denoted x, the proportion of items that are Brand A is $x/N = \pi$, the universe proportion. The value of π is also the probability of selecting an item of Brand A on a random draw from the container. The probability of obtaining a specified number of successes r in n trials is $P(r \mid n, \pi) = \binom{n}{r} \pi^r (1 - \pi)^{n-r}$.

The derivation of the mean and the standard deviation of a binomial distribution are more readily seen by taking a slightly different view of Bernoulli trials. Assume that a sample of n items is drawn from the container and consider a discrete variable X that takes on a value of one for a success (obtaining a unit of Brand A) and a value of zero for a failure. In this manner, n independent random variables, $X_1, X_2, X_3, \ldots, X_n$ are defined, one for each of the individual trials.

For example, suppose a sample of six items is drawn randomly with the set of outcomes $\{B, B, A, B, A, B\}$. The trials, outcomes, and defined variables are shown in Table 4.2.

The mean or mathematical expectation of the variable X is determined by

$$E(X) = \Sigma XP(X) = (1)(\pi) + (0)(1 - \pi) = \pi.$$

The variance is derived as

$$\text{Var}(X) = E(X - \pi)^2 = \Sigma(X - \pi)^2 P(X) = (1 - \pi)^2 \pi + (0 - \pi)^2(1 - \pi)$$
$$= \pi(1 - \pi).$$

TABLE 4.2

The Results of a Random Sample of Six Items

Trial	Outcome	Value of X	Variable defined
1	B	0	X_1
2	B	0	X_2
3	A	1	X_3
4	B	0	X_4
5	A	1	X_5
6	B	0	X_6

The number of successes for n trials is the sum

$$r = X_1 + X_2 + \ldots + X_n,$$

and it follows[1] that for $n = 6$, the expected value of r is

$$E(r) = E(X_1) + E(X_2) + \ldots + E(X_6) = \pi + \pi + \ldots + \pi$$

or

$$E(r) = n\pi \ldots\ldots\ldots\ldots\ldots\ldots\ldots\ldots\ldots\ldots\ldots\ldots\ldots(4.6)$$

Similarly, the variance of r is given by

$$\mathrm{Var}(r) = \pi(1 - \pi) + \pi(1 - \pi) + \ldots + \pi(1 - \pi)$$

or

$$\mathrm{Var}(r) = n\pi(1 - \pi).$$

The standard deviation of the distribution is written

$$\sigma_r = \sqrt{n\pi(1 - \pi)} \ldots\ldots\ldots\ldots\ldots\ldots\ldots\ldots\ldots\ldots(4.7)$$

■ *Example.* Consider the possible distinct samples of two items that can be drawn from a bin of parts, 10% of which are defective. The selection of a defective part is denoted as S and a value of one is taken on by the variable X. Similarly, F denotes a failure and X takes on the value of zero. The possible outcomes and the corresponding expected values are listed as follows:

---

[1] These relationships are based on a theorem, which is given without proof, that if r is the sum of n independent random variables, all having the same probability distribution, then $E(r)$ is equal to the expected value of the sum, and the variance of r is equal to the variance of the sum.

Sample outcomes	Value of X_i	Probability of the outcomes	Expected value of the sample
SS	1, 1	$(0.10)(0.10) = 0.01$	$2(0.01) = 0.02$
SF	1, 0	$(0.10)(0.90) = 0.09$	$1(0.09) = 0.09$
FS	0, 1	$(0.90)(0.10) = 0.09$	$1(0.09) = 0.09$
FF	0, 0	$(0.90)(0.90) = \underline{0.81}$	$0(0.81) = \underline{0.00}$
Totals		1.00	0.20

The expected value of the number of successes r in a sample of two items is

$$E(r) = n\pi = (2)(0.1) = 0.20.$$

The variance of r for $n = 2$ is

$$\text{Var}(r) = n\pi(1 - \pi) = 2(0.10)(0.90) = 0.18,$$

and the standard deviation is $\sqrt{0.18} = 0.424$.

THE POISSON PROBABILITY DISTRIBUTION

An important class of business problems is characterized by the small probability of a success for any one of many trials of an experiment. Problems of this type include applications in insurance involving the number of deaths in a time period, the analysis of the formation of waiting lines at service facilities, the demand for inventory items, and counting the number of defects in a manufactured item. The *Poisson probability distribution* is a mathematical model with properties suitable for expressing this type of problem. This model can be viewed either as the limiting form of the binomial distribution or as a distribution in its own right, which describes a Poisson process. These approaches and their applications are discussed in the following sections.

The computation of probabilities for a Bernoulli process, where n is large and p is small, can be laborious; but these computations can be simplified by use of a limiting form of the binomial distribution, the Poisson probability distribution. Although, in a strict sense, a Poisson process is not characterized by trials with two possible outcomes and a constant probability of success, by employing suitable definitions, a Poisson process can be viewed as being Bernoulli.

For example, a manufacturing process continuously extrudes metal tubing and the thickness of the tubing wall is occasionally below minimum quality standards. In a sample of 1,000 feet of extruded tubing, 20 defective places were detected, or an average of 2 defects per 100 feet. The defects occur randomly over the tubing. If the probability of finding a specified number of defects in a length of tubing remains constant, this Poisson process may be considered Bernoulli by viewing a very short length of tubing as an independent trial with an outcome of zero or more successes.

Binomial and Poisson Distributions

By definition, a Bernoulli trial has only two possible outcomes, success or failure. For example, this definition is illustrated by viewing a 100-foot length of tubing as being subdivided into 10 pieces. The probability of a defect in a 10-foot segment is 0.20. Now let the 100 feet be divided into one-foot lengths and $p = 0.02$. Note that $np = (10)(0.20) = (100)(0.02) = 2$ for each case. Continuing in this manner, the 100-foot length can be divided into any n number of smaller units so that np is constant for all cases. As n becomes large, the probability of more than one defect per subunit becomes very small. The difference between the binomial probability distribution and its limiting form, the Poisson probability distribution, becomes negligible. This relationship is seen in Figure 4.4, which shows the binomial and the Poisson distributions for a value of $np = 0.50$.

FIGURE 4.4

Binomial Distribution for $P(r|n=10, p=0.05)$
and the Poisson Distribution for $np = \lambda = 0.50$

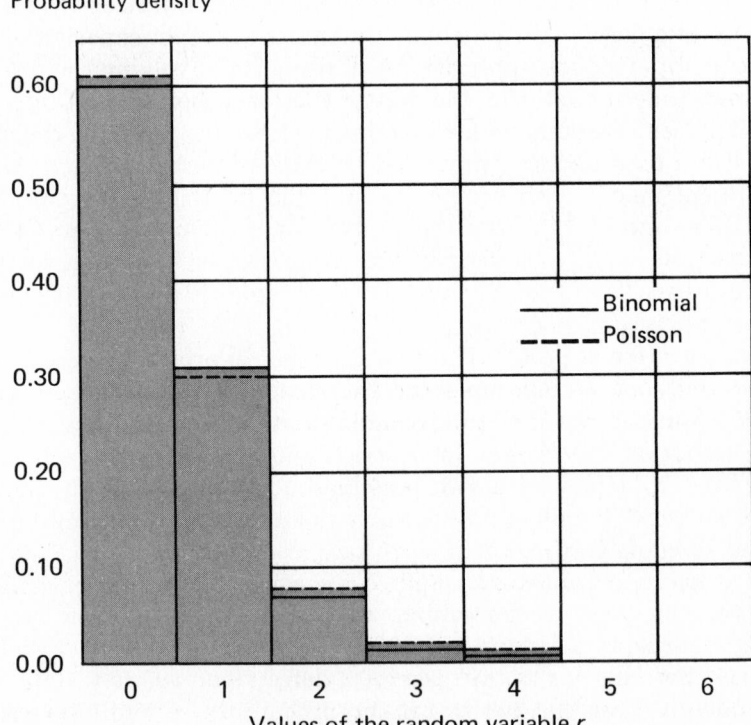

In a Bernoulli process, probabilities are associated with the probability p of a success for each independent trial and r number of successes in n trials. For a Poisson process, probabilities are related to a given number of successes per unit of space (e.g., a small length of tubing) and the number of successes in a given amount of space. The expected number of successes for a Poisson process is

$$np = E(r) = \lambda \dots\dots\dots\dots\dots\dots\dots\dots\dots(4.8)$$

The variance and the standard deviation of a Poisson distribution can be derived from the variance of the binomial $\text{Var}(r) = np(1-p)$. The Poisson distribution is the limit of the binomial distribution, as n increases without limit and the value of p becomes correspondingly small, so that $np = \lambda$ remains constant. Thus, $np(1-p)$ approaches $np = \lambda$ as $(1-p)$ approaches one, the variance is $\text{Var}(r) = \lambda$, and the standard deviation is

$$\sigma_r = \sqrt{\lambda}\dots\dots\dots\dots\dots\dots\dots\dots\dots(4.9)$$

■ *Example.* In a study of the arrivals of trucks at a warehouse, the probability of an arrival during any given minute (a trial) was determined to be $p = 0.04$. The expected number of arrivals per half hour is $np = (30)(0.04) = 1.2$. Viewing a minute as a unit of space and a half hour as the given amount of space, then $\lambda = (30)(0.4) = 1.2$ and $\sigma_r = \sqrt{1.2} = 1.1$.

Binomial probabilities for r successes in n trials are computed by use of the expression $P(r \mid n, p) = \binom{n}{r} p^r (1-p)^{n-r}$. For small values of p, the resulting probability distribution for the possible values of r forms a very skewed distribution. For very small values of p and correspondingly large values of n, so long as np remains constant, the limit of the binomial probability is the Poisson probability, as expressed by

$$\lim_{\substack{n \to \infty \\ p \to 0}} P(r \mid n, p) = \frac{(np)^r}{r!} e^{-np},$$

where e is the base of natural logarithms with the value 2.718282. Expressing the Poisson probability density function in terms of $np = \lambda$,

$$P(r \mid \lambda) = \frac{\lambda^r}{r!} e^{-\lambda}\dots\dots\dots\dots\dots\dots\dots(4.10)$$

From Formula 4.10 it may be seen that the Poisson distribution has one parameter and that the entire distribution can be determined, given the value of λ.

■ *Example.* Cloth is woven continuously in a textile mill, and from experience it is known that an average of 20 defects occur in each 1,000 feet of fabric. A sample of 100 feet of cloth is taken from the output.

The probability that it will contain three defects is found by computing

$$p = \frac{20}{1,000} = 0.02, \lambda = np = 100(0.02) = 2, \text{ and}$$

$$P(r = 3|\lambda = 2) = \frac{2^3}{3!}(2.718282)^{-2} = \frac{8}{(3\cdot2\cdot1)(2.718282)^2} = 0.1804.$$

The binomial approximation of this probability is 0.1823, as read from Appendix C for $n = 100$, $p = 0.02$, and $r = 3$.

Tables of Poisson Probabilities

The time-consuming task of computing Poisson probabilities manually by means of Formula 4.10 can be avoided by use of Appendix F, which presents the probability of r successes for various values of λ. Appendix F is analogous to Appendix C for the binomial distribution. Appendix G presents the probability of r or more successes for various values of λ, and it is a cumulative probability table similar to Appendix D for the binomial distribution.

■ *Example.* From experience it has been determined that, on the average, 3 out of every 100 data cards read into a computer contain a numerical mistake. A sample of 50 data cards is selected at random from a large number of cards on file. The mean of the distribution is $\lambda = np = 50(3/100) = 1.5$. The probability that the sample will include exactly $r = 3$ cards that include a numerical mistake is read from Appendix F (page 611) as 0.1255 for $\lambda = 1.5$ and $r = 3$. The probability that four or more cards in the sample contain a numerical mistake is read from Appendix G (page 617) as 0.0656 for $\lambda = 1.5$ and $r = 4$.

THE HYPERGEOMETRIC PROBABILITY DISTRIBUTION

The binomial probability distribution is an exact model of a Bernoulli process, for which the probabilities of the two possible outcomes remain constant for all trials. In some experiments, however, trials are made so that the sample space is reduced and the corresponding probabilities of a success or failure are changed from trial to trial. A systematic arrangement of the probabilities associated with the two outcomes, success or failure, or a process characterized by the reduction of a finite sample space and a corresponding change in probabilities from trial to trial is defined as a *hypergeometric probability distribution*. For example, if cards are drawn without replacement, the probability of drawing a spade on any given draw is conditional upon the outcomes of previous draws, and the sample space is reduced for each card drawn.

Basic Concepts

Consider a lot of 10 manufactured parts, two of which are defective. A random sample of two items is drawn without replacement from the lot.

The total number of distinct samples of two items that can be drawn is the set of combinations of 10 parts taken two at a time, or

$$\binom{10}{2} = \frac{10!}{2!8!} = 45.$$

Each of the possible combinations has an equal probability of being selected. The set of all combinations is classified into subsets, and the members of each subset consist of a combination with a given number of defective parts.

The probability of selecting a sample with a specified number of defectives is the proportion of all possible samples containing that specified number of defectives. Thus, the probability of selecting a sample with zero defectives is the possible number of samples which can be drawn that include no defectives expressed as a fraction of all possible samples. A sample of two with no defectives must be drawn exclusively from the eight acceptable items in the lot (universe). The number of such samples is the subset of combinations that total

$$\binom{8}{2} = \frac{8!}{2!6!} = 28.$$

The probability of selecting a sample with no defectives is the *a priori* probability

$$\frac{\binom{8}{2}}{\binom{10}{2}} = \frac{28}{45} = 0.622.$$

A sample with one defective will include one of the eight acceptable items and one of the two defective items from the lot. There are $\binom{8}{1} = 8$ ways of selecting an acceptable item, and for each of these ways there are $\binom{2}{1} = 2$ ways of combining a defective item with an acceptable item in a sample of two items. In this manner, the number of possible samples of two items, which include one acceptable and one defective item, is the set of combinations that total

$$\binom{8}{1}\binom{2}{1} = \frac{8!}{1!7!} \cdot \frac{2!}{1!1!} = 16.$$

The probability of drawing a sample with one defective is

$$\frac{\binom{8}{1}\binom{2}{1}}{\binom{10}{2}} = \frac{16}{45} = 0.356.$$

A sample with two defectives can be drawn in only one way since

$$\binom{8}{0}\binom{2}{2} = \frac{8!}{0!8!} \cdot \frac{2!}{0!2!} = 1.$$

The probability of drawing this sample is

$$\frac{\binom{8}{0}\binom{2}{2}}{\binom{10}{2}} = \frac{1}{45} = 0.022.$$

The sample results are mutually exclusive and collectively exhaustive, and for the previous example, the probabilities are $P(c \mid N, r, n)$:

$$P(0 \mid 10, 2, 2) = 0.622$$
$$P(1 \mid 10, 2, 2) = 0.356$$
$$P(2 \mid 10, 2, 2) = \underline{0.022}$$
$$1.000$$

Generalizing these results for two possible outcomes, let N denote the population size, r the total number of defective units, c the number of defectives (successes) in a sample, and n the sample size. The hypergeometric probability of c successes in n trials, given finite values of N and r, is expressed by

$$P(c \mid N, r, n) = \frac{\binom{N-r}{n-c}\binom{r}{c}}{\binom{N}{n}} \quad \dots\dots\dots\dots\dots\dots\dots(4.11)$$

Binomial and Hypergeometric Probabilities

The hypergeometric distribution is an exact model of sampling from a finite universe. Unless N is very small, the binomial distribution provides good approximations of hypergeometric probabilities, since the probability of a success changes only slightly for successive trials.

■ *Example.* A bin of 50 parts contains three defective units. A sample of five units is drawn randomly from the bin. The proportion of defective units in the finite universe is $p = \frac{3}{50} = 0.06$. The value of p is assumed to be constant for all trials, which is equivalent to assuming an infinite lot size. The computation of the binomial approximations of the hypergeometric probabilities is shown in Table 4.3.

The probabilities in Table 4.3 indicate that the binomial distribution provides close approximations of the exact probabilities of the sample results. Calculating exact probabilities for large finite universes is somewhat facilitated by the use of the logarithms of factorials, but even these calculations can be time consuming. For a great many practical problems in statistical quality control, the binomial approximations of exact probabilities are satisfactory. A small sample drawn from a finite universe does not substantially exhaust the universe, and binomial probabilities offer close estimates of exact probabilities. The larger the sample, the greater the tendency to exhaust a finite universe and the greater the disparity between the corresponding exact and approximate probabilities.

TABLE 4.3

Exact and Approximate Probabilities of the Results of a Sample of Five Drawn from a Universe of 50 Items, Three of Which Are Defective

Number of defectives	Hypergeometric probability $P(c \mid N, r, n)$	Binomial probability $P(r \mid n, p)$
0	$\dfrac{\binom{47}{5}\binom{3}{0}}{\binom{50}{5}} = 0.7239$	$\binom{5}{0}(0.06)^0 (0.94)^5 = 0.7339$
1	$\dfrac{\binom{47}{4}\binom{3}{1}}{\binom{50}{5}} = 0.2526$	$\binom{5}{1}(0.06)^1 (0.94)^4 = 0.2342$
2	$\dfrac{\binom{47}{3}\binom{3}{2}}{\binom{50}{5}} = 0.0230$	$\binom{5}{2}(0.06)^2 (0.94)^3 = 0.0299$
3	$\dfrac{\binom{47}{2}\binom{3}{3}}{\binom{50}{5}} = 0.0005$	$\binom{5}{3}(0.06)^3 (0.94)^2 = 0.0019$

THE NEGATIVE BINOMIAL DISTRIBUTION

A binomial probability expresses the likelihood of obtaining a specified number of successes in a given number of Bernoulli trials. There are situations in which one may wish to know the likelihood of what might be called the inverse of the binomial case. One might ask what the probability is that a specified number of Bernoulli trials will be required to obtain a given number of successes. A probability of this type, for which the values of r and p are given, is called a *negative binomial probability* or a *Pascal probability.*

The Nature of Negative Binomial Probabilities

Consider a situation in which two types of metal parts, consisting of shafts and bushings, are fitted together in an assembly operation. Inspection records indicate that if the shafts and bushings are assembled randomly, the assembled clearance between the shaft and the bushing of 10% of the finished assemblies will be too large and the assembly is considered defective. Suppose a production manager wishes to know the probability that of six assemblies selected at random, two will be defective and the second defective unit will be the sixth assembly selected.

Denoting acceptable assemblies as A and defective assemblies as D, one possible sequence that can occur in the random selection is $ADAAAD$. The probability of obtaining this sequence is

$$P = (\tfrac{9}{10})(\tfrac{1}{10})(\tfrac{9}{10})(\tfrac{9}{10})(\tfrac{9}{10})(\tfrac{1}{10}) = \frac{6,561}{1,000,000} = 0.006561.$$

The number of ways in which two defectives can be obtained in a sample of six assemblies is $\binom{6}{2} = 15$ ways. But the problem at hand has the special qualification that the sixth selection yield a defective assembly. In such a case, only five sequences satisfy all the conditions. These sequences are:

Sequence	Probability	
DAAAAD	$(\frac{1}{10})(\frac{9}{10})(\frac{9}{10})(\frac{9}{10})(\frac{9}{10})(\frac{1}{10})$ =	0.006561
ADAAAD	$(\frac{9}{10})(\frac{1}{10})(\frac{9}{10})(\frac{9}{10})(\frac{9}{10})(\frac{1}{10})$ =	0.006561
AADAAD	$(\frac{9}{10})(\frac{9}{10})(\frac{1}{10})(\frac{9}{10})(\frac{9}{10})(\frac{1}{10})$ =	0.006561
AAADAD	$(\frac{9}{10})(\frac{9}{10})(\frac{9}{10})(\frac{1}{10})(\frac{9}{10})(\frac{1}{10})$ =	0.006561
AAAADD	$(\frac{9}{10})(\frac{9}{10})(\frac{9}{10})(\frac{9}{10})(\frac{1}{10})(\frac{1}{10})$ =	0.006561
Total		0.032805

The probability of obtaining any one of the mutually exclusive sequences is 0.006561. The probability of randomly drawing six assemblies, of which two are defective and the second defective assembly is obtained on the sixth draw, is the sum of the probabilities of the five events, which totals 0.032805.

Generalizing in a manner similar to the derivation of binomial probabilities, the probability that n Bernoulli trials will be required to obtain r successes in a particular order is written

$$\underset{r \text{ successes}}{(p \cdot p \cdot p \cdot \ldots \cdot p)} \underset{n - r \text{ failures}}{(q \cdot q \cdot q \cdot \ldots \cdot q)} = p^r q^{n-r}$$

In the type of problem being considered, the rth success must occur on the nth trial. The number of possible sequences that satisfy the conditions of the problem is determined by the number of ways in which $r - 1$ successes can be obtained in $n - 1$ trials. This number is expressed by $\binom{n-1}{r-1}$. The probability that precisely n trials will be required to obtain the rth success is a negative binomial probability written

$$P(n \mid r, p) = \binom{n-1}{r-1} p^r (1 - p)^{n-r} \quad\ldots\ldots\ldots\ldots\ldots(4.12)$$

■ *Example.* A refinery maintains a large inventory of different types of parts for maintenance and repairs. Some types of parts are needed infrequently, and in a typical week, one or more units of only about 30% of the different types of parts are used. The use of these parts is recorded as withdrawals by the accounting department. In making a tabulation of the inventory items used in a given week, a search is made through the inventory accounts to determine whether a type of part was used and to record the number of units withdrawn. The accounts are recorded serially (in order by inventory number) on magnetic tape. The ordering of the sequence of accounts is independent of the frequency of usage of the type of part. The probability that a computer must examine five accounts in order to encounter one which reflects a withdrawal during a week is written

$$P(n = 5 \mid r = 1, p = 0.30) = \binom{5-1}{1-1}(0.30)^1(0.70)^{5-1}$$

$$= \frac{(5-1)!}{0!(5-1)!}(0.30)(0.24)$$

$$= 0.072.$$

Binomial and Negative Binomial Probabilities

Computing negative binomial probabilities by means of Formula 4.12 can become tedious as n becomes large. A table of negative binomial probabilities can be prepared, but the values that would appear in such a table can be obtained by use of a table of binomial probabilities. The relationship between negative binomial and binomial probabilities is

$$P(n \mid r, p) = pP(r - 1 \mid n - 1, p). \qquad \text{....................(4.13)}$$

where the negative binomial probability is equal to p times the binomial probability of $r - 1$ successes given $n - 1$ trials and a probability p.

■ *Example.* The manager of an automobile rental agency in an airport terminal observes that about 25% of customers ask to rent economy cars to take advantage of lower rental rates. The probability that it will take 12 customers to rent three economy cars is

$$\underset{\text{negative binomial}}{P(n = 12 \mid r = 3, p = 0.25)} = \underset{p \text{ times binomial}}{0.25P(r = 2 \mid n = 11, p = 0.25)}$$

The binomial probability may be read from Appendix C as 0.2581, and multiplying this value by $p = 0.25$ gives 0.0645, the negative binomial probability.

STUDY QUESTIONS

4–1. Explain briefly the meaning of each of the following:
a. discrete probability distribution
b. Bernoulli process
c. success
d. parameter
e. permutation
f. combination
g. binomial probability density function
h. binomial probability distribution
i. cumulative binomial probability
j. Poisson probability distribution
k. hypergeometric probability distribution
l. negative binomial probability

4–2. What is the relationship between a frequency distribution and a probability distribution?

4–3. What is the difference between a probability density function and a probability distribution?

4–4. Which of the following can be considered Bernoulli processes?
  a. Tossing a fair coin
  b. Tossing an unfair (biased) coin
  c. Dealing cards from a deck
  d. Determining whether produced parts are acceptable or defective

4–5. What definition is necessary in order to consider a Poisson process as being Bernoulli?

4–6. What is the principal reason for approximating hypergeometric probabilities with binomial probabilities?

4–7. Describe briefly the relationship between binomial and negative binomial probabilities.

PROBLEMS

4–1. Insurance data indicate that 25% of the automobiles in an area are involved in a collision each year. If six insured automobiles are selected at random, what is the probability that two are involved in collisions in the period of a year?

4–2. Records indicate that one in five persons who visit an automobile dealer to look at new models actually purchase new cars. What is the probability that if five persons looking at new cars are selected at random two will purchase new automobiles?

4–3. What is the probability of getting three heads in five tosses of a fair coin?

4–4. If four fair dice are tossed once, what is the probability of obtaining two sixes?

4–5. A machine produces parts that are consistently 6% defective. A sample of 10 items is selected randomly from the output of the machine. What is the probability of getting:
  a. Two defective parts?
  b. Three or more defective parts?

4–6. Using the information in Problem 4–5, find the probability of getting:
  a. Fewer than four defective parts
  b. Two or three defective parts

4–7. Using the information in Problem 4–5, find the mean and standard deviation of the distribution of defective parts.

4-8. Ten items are selected at random from a large inventory of items; 40% are purchased and the remainder are produced by the firm that has the inventory. Compute the mean and standard deviation.

4-9. In controlling the quality of output of a machine, an inspector selects samples of 20 items. If the sample contains one or more defective units, the machine is adjusted. What is the probability that production will be stopped and the machine adjusted if the output is:

a. 80% acceptable?   c. 90% acceptable?
b. 60% acceptable?   d. 99% acceptable?

X **4-10.** From experience it is known that in a given suburb of a city, 60% of the TV viewers watch a particular program on Friday nights. A researcher randomly selects 25 families from the area and calls to ask if the program in question is being viewed. What is the probability that the number of families who respond affirmatively will be:

a. 10 or more?   c. exactly 15?
b. less than 12?   d. either 16 or 17?

4-11. A company purchases manufactured parts in carload lots. The inspection records kept on all incoming lots indicate that carload lots with specified percents of faulty units have been received with the following frequencies:

Proportion of faulty units	Frequency
0.01	0.20
0.02	0.50
0.03	0.20
0.04	0.10
	1.00

Samples of 20 items are drawn from incoming lots. If a sample contains no faulty items, the entire lot is accepted; if it contains one or more faulty items, the lot is inspected in detail.

a. If a sample is drawn from an incoming lot that contains 2% faulty items, what is the probability that the lot will be accepted?
b. If a sample is drawn and contains one faulty item, what is the probability that the lot contains 3% faulty items? Use Bayes' Theorem.

4-12. Production records of a process indicate that the percent of defective items produced has had a stable pattern of variation as follows:

Proportion defective	Frequency
0.01	0.20
0.03	0.50
0.05	0.30
	1.00

These frequencies are assumed to be good estimates of prior probabilities. A sample of 10 items is taken from the process and it contains one defective item. Compute the revised probabilities in view of the sample information. Use Bayes' Theorem. ⟶ posteriors

4–13. The pattern of arrivals of people at a telephone booth was estimated by observing how many people arrived per 15-minute period and counting the number of periods in which various numbers of people arrived to use the telephone. A frequency distribution summarizing the observations for 100 quarter-hour periods is as follows:

People arriving per 15-minute period (r)	Number of periods (observed frequency)
0	14
1	28
2	27
3	19
4	9
5	3
	100

Compute the theoretical Poisson frequencies and compare these with the observed frequencies as the basis for deciding whether the Poisson distribution is a reasonably good model for representing the observed data. *Hint:* Use the value of the mean as the estimate of λ to find the Poisson probabilities.

4–14. A manufacturing company has determined that, on an average, on one in 50 days a machine will experience an equipment failure. Find the exact binomial probability and the Poisson approximation of the probability that in the next 25 days the number of failures will be:
a. Exactly two
b. Less than three
c. More than one
d. Either one or two

4–15. An automatic machine makes paper clips from coils of wire. On the average, one in 200 paper clips is defective. If the paper clips are packed in boxes of 100, what is the probability that any given box of clips will contain:
a. No defectives?
b. One or more defectives?
c. Fewer than two defectives?
d. Fewer than one defective?

4–16. The probability that any single component of the guidance system of a space vehicle will malfunction is 0.001. The system has 400 components.
a. What is the probability that the guidance system will not function properly if activated?
b. What level of reliability of the components must be achieved (by improved design or production methods) to give at least an 0.80

probability that the guidance system will not malfunction when used?

4-17. The number of defects per yard of cotton material produced on a machine is considered a Poisson process. The output of the machine varies in terms of the average number of defects per foot, and the frequency with which various levels of defects have occurred are listed as follows:

Defects per foot	Frequency
0.001	0.50
0.003	0.30
0.005	0.20
	1.00

If a sample of 100 feet of material is inspected and one or more defects is found, the machine is adjusted; otherwise, the machine is allowed to run.
  a. If a sample is taken from the production of the machine as it is averaging 0.003 defects per foot, what is the probability that the machine will be adjusted on the basis of the sample results?
  b. If a sample of 100 feet of material contains two defects, what is the probability that the machine averaged 0.005 defects per foot?

4-18. In an analysis of the time utilization of a manager a record was kept of the date and time of each request by persons wishing to confer with the manager. Data recorded over a period of several weeks indicate that the average number of persons desiring conferences with the manager is five per hour. What is the probability that in a randomly selected hour fewer than four people will request conferences?

4-19. Defective steering mechanisms were mistakenly installed on two of a group of eight new automobiles. It is not known which automobiles have the defective mechanisms, and a sample of four automobiles is selected for testing. What is the probability that the sample will include:
  a. No defective mechanisms?
  b. Both defective mechanisms?

4-20. A poker hand of five cards is dealt from a standard deck of playing cards. What is the probability of its containing:
  a. Two spades?
  b. One or more aces?

4-21. The office staff of a company is comprised of three secretaries and five clerks. If a group of five persons is selected randomly from the office staff, what is the probability that it will include two clerks?

4-22. A random sample of 10 students is selected from the student body of a university consisting of the following groups:

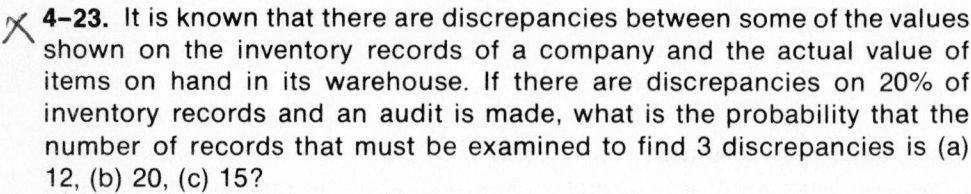

Classification	Percent
Freshman	32
Sophomore	25
Junior	17
Senior	14
Graduate	12
	100

Compute the probability that a sample of five students must be selected to obtain two freshmen.

4–23. It is known that there are discrepancies between some of the values shown on the inventory records of a company and the actual value of items on hand in its warehouse. If there are discrepancies on 20% of inventory records and an audit is made, what is the probability that the number of records that must be examined to find 3 discrepancies is (a) 12, (b) 20, (c) 15?

4–24. Using the data in Problem 4–22, compute the probability that the number of students that must be selected to obtain 2 freshmen is (a) 4, (b) 6, (c) 10.

SELECTED READINGS

Ekeblad, Frederick A. *The Statistical Method, Applications of Probability and Inference to Business and Other Problems.* New York: John Wiley and Sons, Inc., 1962.
    A good discussion of the relationship between the binomial and the Poisson distributions is presented in Chapter 5.
Grant, Eugene L. *Statistical Quality Control,* 4th ed. New York: McGraw-Hill Book Company, Inc., 1972.
    A lucid comparison of the binomial, the Poisson, and the hyper-geometric probability distributions is presented in Chapter 9.
Schlaifer, Robert. *Probability and Statistics for Business Decisions.* New York: McGraw-Hill Book Company, Inc., 1959.
    The revision of probabilities using theoretical distributions of conditional probabilities is clearly presented in Chapters 21 through 23.

Chapter 5
Continuous Probability Distributions

Probability distributions associated with continuous variables are very useful for describing actual and theoretical variables and in the study of statistical inference. The logical basis and practical value of selected continuous distributions are discussed in this chapter.

SAMPLE SPACE, PROBABILITIES, AND CONTINUOUS VARIABLES

A continuous variable, which is defined over a given range, may take on any of the values in the range. In the process of determining the value of a continuous variable, it is rare that measurements can be made on a continuous scale. More often, the precision of measurement is limited, and only a finite number of values can be determined accurately. For example, consider a process in which boxes of sugar are filled. The desired weight is one pound, but the actual weights of the filled boxes vary over a given range. The actual weights of the filled boxes are a continuous variable, defined for all possible weights to the smallest fraction of an ounce. In the process of weighing, the scale is capable of measuring weights to the nearest tenth of an ounce, the minimum interval of measurement. The distribution of the discrete weights of the boxes of sugar recorded in a production run is an approximation of the continuous distribution of the actual weights of the filled boxes.

A distribution of the weights of boxes of sugar filled by the process is shown in Figure 5.1. All the weights are included in the range from 15.5 ounces to 16.5 ounces. For purposes of this discussion, it is assumed that any value in this range is a possible weight of a filled box. Following this approach, it is useful to think of the set of elementary outcomes of an experiment that occur within an interval of the range of a continuous variable, where any point in the interval is a possible outcome. In this manner, the sample space of the variable is the set of points within any interval or union of intervals.

FIGURE 5.1

Probability Distribution of Weights of Boxes of Sugar

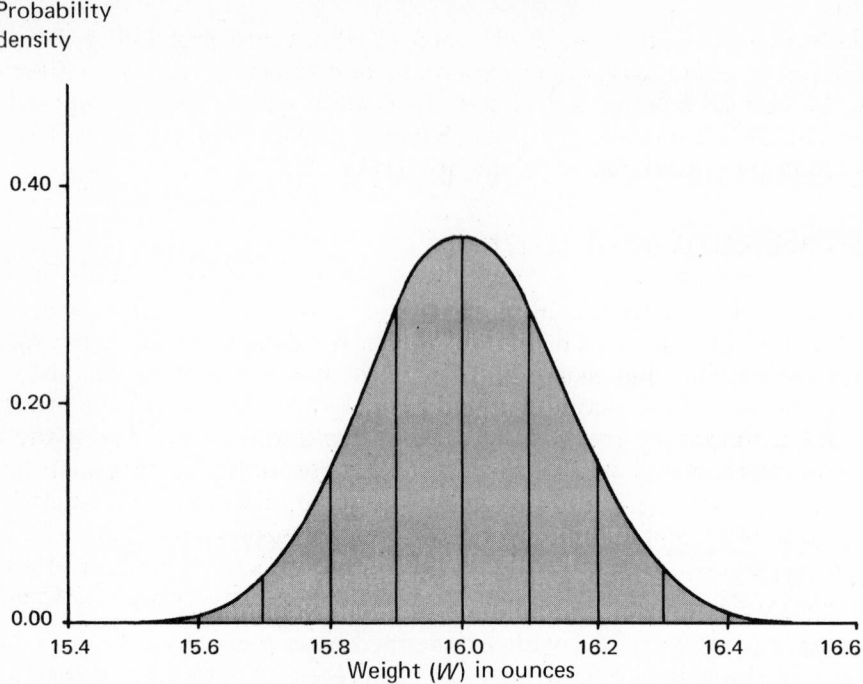

For example, the range of weights of the boxes in Figure 5.1 is divided into intervals of 0.1 ounces. These intervals serve as the basis for the sample space of the variable. The possible outcomes of the variable W are defined as the $S = \{15.5 \leq W \leq 16.5\}$, where any weight from 15.5 ounces to 16.5 ounces can occur. The sample space of the random variable W is all points in the range from 15.5 to 16.5. For any interval of the range, for instance from 16.1 to 16.2, there is a corresponding subset of all possible outcomes and a probability that is assigned by a probability density function. This probability is represented by the area under the curve for the interval.

A grouped frequency distribution can be used as a device for dividing the range of a continuous variable into intervals and associating a frequency with each interval. The intervals are disjoint, but the union of all of them is the set S. The partitioning intervals are usually the same size, and the considerations for determining the number and size of intervals are discussed in Chapter 2.

The probability distribution of a continuous variable is similar to that of a discrete variable. The areas under the curve for selected intervals of the range of a continuous variable are analogous to the areas of the bars of the histogram of a discrete probability distribution. The probability density associated with any single value of a continuous variable is expressed graphically by the height of the curve corresponding to that value.

In practice, a principal application of continuous probability distributions lies in their use as approximations of discrete distributions. Much of the theoretical development of statistical methods has been prompted by a need for approximating methods. Several of the more useful continuous distributions are presented in the discussion that follows.

THE UNIFORM DISTRIBUTION

The simplest distribution for a continuous variable is the *uniform probability distribution* for which the probability density is the same for all values of the variable, as shown in Figure 5.2.

■ *Example.* One thousand tickets are sold in a public lottery and are then placed in a container and mixed thoroughly so that each ticket has an equal opportunity of being selected in a drawing. The uniform probability density is shown by the distribution in Figure 5.2. This distribution is continuous and is used as an approximation of a discrete variable since there is a finite number of possible outcomes.

FIGURE 5.2

Uniform Probability Distribution

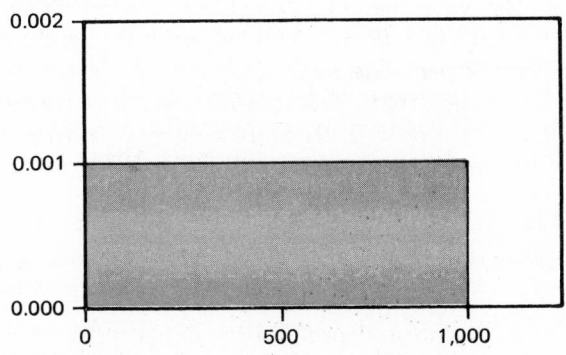

The general expression for the *uniform probability density function* is

$$f(X) = \frac{1}{B - A} \quad \text{................................(5.1)}$$

where A and B are the values at the limits of an interval of the variable X and the value of X is zero outside the interval. For example, the density function for the previous example is $f(X) = 1/(1{,}000 - 0) = 0.001$, and each ticket has one chance in a thousand of being selected in the drawing.

THE NORMAL DISTRIBUTION

Perhaps the best known of the continuous probability distributions is the symmetrical curve called the *normal distribution*. The normal distribution is also known as the *Gaussian curve* or the *normal curve of error*. The normal distribution is significant because it provides close approximations for a number of distributions. Also, the normal distribution has mathematical properties that simplify its application.

The Normal Distribution As the Limit of the Binomial Distribution

The distributions in Figure 5.3 illustrate the significant fact that the histogram of a binomial distribution becomes smoother as n increases. For very large values of n, the binomial distribution approaches its limit, a continuous curve. It can be proved that a sufficiently large value of n can be selected so that the difference between a discrete binomial distribution and its limit, a continuous curve, is less than some arbitrarily selected value, however small. The continuous curve that is the limit of the binomial curve as n increases without limit is called the *normal probability distribution*. The normal curve is symmetrical about the mean and it is the limit of a binomial distribution even for $p \neq 0.50$, as shown in Figure 5.3.

As is true of the binomial distribution, the normal distribution is defined by two parameters. The parameters of the normal distribution are μ, the mean or mathematical expectation, and σ, the standard deviation. Each combination of values of μ and σ defines a different distribution, although all these distributions are normally distributed. The relationship of these distributions is perhaps more easily understood by considering an analogy with circles for which each value of the radius r defines a different circle (the circumference is $2\pi r$ and the area is πr^2), although each circle has the same shape.

The *normal probability density function* is the limit of the binomial probability density function as p is held constant and n increases without limit. The limit of the binomial probability density function $P(r \mid n, p) = \binom{n}{r} p^r (1 - p)^{n-r}$ is the normal probability density function written

$$f(r) = \frac{1}{\sigma_r \sqrt{2\pi}} \, e^{-\frac{1}{2}\left(\frac{r - E(r)}{\sigma_r}\right)^2} \qquad \dots \dots \dots \dots \dots \dots (5.2)$$

where π is the constant 3.1416 and e is 2.7183, the base of natural logarithms. The normal distribution can be also expressed as

FIGURE 5.3

**Binomial Distributions for Selected Values
of *n* and *p* and the Normal Curve as a Limit**

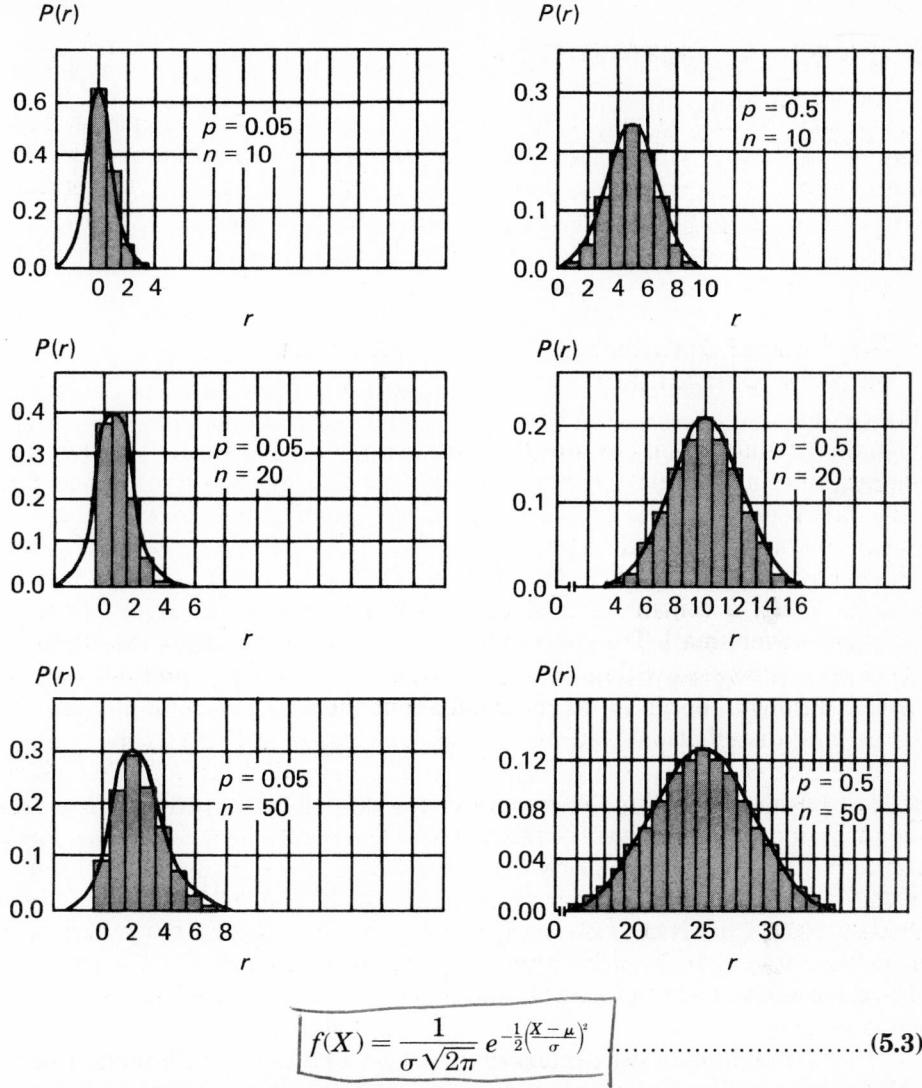

$$f(X) = \frac{1}{\sigma \sqrt{2\pi}}\, e^{-\frac{1}{2}\left(\frac{X-\mu}{\sigma}\right)^2}$$ ....(5.3)

where $f(X)$ is the ordinate of the normal distribution for a given value of X, μ is the mathematical expectation, and σ is the standard deviation. In theory, the range of the normal distribution is infinite and the curve of the density function is asymptotic to the horizontal axis.

Normal Probabilities

Probabilities associated with a normally distributed random variable X can be found by computing the appropriate area under the curve of the density function. The total area under the curve is equal to one and this area represents the set of collectively exhaustive events, the values that can be taken on by the random variable, where some values occur more frequently than others. The probability that a normally distributed random variable X will take on a value in a given range is equal to the area under the normal curve for that range.

Normal probabilities are not easily found by use of the normal density function, but approximations can be computed by numerical methods. Approximations for a wide range of areas are presented in Appendix H. These values correspond to the probability that X will take on a value in a range from μ to some specified value. It is convenient to view the range as a deviation from μ expressed in terms of standard deviations. For example, the range from $\mu = 5$ to $X = 8$ for a normal distribution with $\sigma = 2$ is expressed as a deviation in terms of the standard deviation by $z = \dfrac{X - \mu}{\sigma} = \dfrac{8 - 5}{2} = 1.5\sigma$,

where z is the number of standard deviations.

Areas of the normal distribution are customarily related to deviations from the mean, expressed in terms of standard deviations. For example, the percent of the area of a normal distribution over selected ranges is as follows:

$$\mu \pm 1\sigma = 68.27\%$$
$$\mu \pm 2\sigma = 95.45\%$$
$$\mu \pm 3\sigma = 99.73\%.$$

Values for areas of the normal curve for selected ranges are found in Appendix H. Since a normal distribution is symmetrical, the table reflects values for only one side of the distribution. The area corresponding to $\mu \pm 1\sigma$ is found opposite $z = \dfrac{X - \mu}{\sigma} = 1.0\sigma$. In Appendix H this value is read as 0.34134. Since it corresponds to only one side of the distribution, the desired area is $(2)(0.34134) = 0.68268$. Similarly, the area over the range $\mu \pm 2\sigma$ is read opposite $z = \dfrac{X - \mu}{\sigma} = 2.0\sigma$ in Appendix H as 0.47725, and $(2)(0.47725) = 0.95450$.

■ *Example.* In the past, the demand in the month of March for denim slacks produced by a firm has been normally distributed, with a mean of 10,000 pairs and a standard deviation of 500 pairs. The plant manager wishes to know the probability that demand will be in the range from 8,500 to 10,625 pairs. The range overlaps both sides of the distribution, but not symmetrically. Consequently, the problem must be solved in parts. The area over the portion of the range

$$z = \frac{X - \mu}{\sigma} = \frac{8,500 - 10,000}{500} = -3.00\sigma,$$

where the negative sign denotes direction. Reading from Appendix H, the corresponding value is 0.49865. The area over the partial range

$$z = \frac{X - \mu}{\sigma} = \frac{10,625 - 10,000}{500} = 1.25\sigma$$

is read as 0.39435. The area over the total range is $0.49865 + 0.39435 = 0.89300$, which is shown as the shaded portion of the left-hand curve in Figure 5.4.

Now suppose the plant manager wishes to find the probability that demand will be between 10,350 and 11,150 pairs, as shown in the shaded portion of the right-hand curve in Figure 5.4. The area in question is found by determining the area over the range

$$z = \frac{X - \mu}{\sigma} = \frac{11,150 - 10,000}{500} = 2.3\sigma.$$

The corresponding value in Appendix H is 0.48928.

The area over the range

$$z = \frac{X - \mu}{\sigma} = \frac{10,350 - 10,000}{500} = 0.7\sigma$$

is read as 0.25804. The desired probability is $0.48928 - 0.25804 = 0.23124$.

FIGURE 5.4

Probabilities for Selected Ranges of a Normal Random Variable

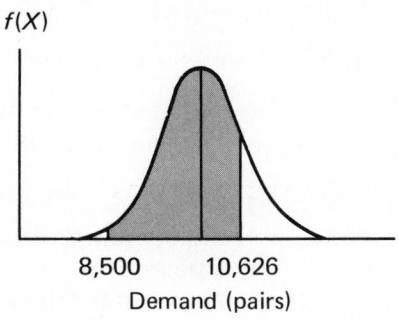

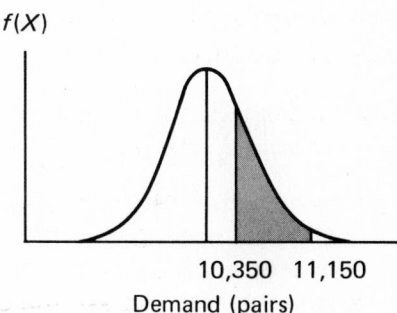

Areas of the normal curve may be used for fitting a normal curve to a frequency distribution.

■ *Example.* A sample of 100 parts of a particular type produced by a machine is taken. The diameters of the parts are measured in terms of deviations in thousandths of an inch from a specified dimension. These deviations are grouped into a frequency distribution, which is used as an estimate of the universe distribution of all parts produced. The distribution and related values are shown in Table 5.1.

TABLE 5.1

**Observed and Expected Frequencies of Diameters
of 100 Parts**

Class limits (deviations in 0.001")	Observed frequency f	m	fm	$f(m - \mu)^2$	Expected normal frequency
Less than 0.5	0	...	0.00	0.00	0.1
0.5 and under 1.0	1	0.75	0.75	3.13	0.7
1.0 and under 1.5	3	1.25	3.75	4.84	4.4
1.5 and under 2.0	16	1.75	28.00	9.49	15.0
2.0 and under 2.5	27	2.25	60.75	1.97	28.2
2.5 and under 3.0	35	2.75	96.25	1.85	28.8
3.0 and under 3.5	12	3.25	39.00	6.40	16.4
3.5 and under 4.0	4	3.75	15.00	6.05	5.5
4.0 and under 4.5	2	4.25	8.50	5.99	0.8
More than 4.5	0	...	0.00	0.00	0.1
Total	100		252.00	39.72	100.0

The descriptive measures computed from the data are:

$$\bar{x} = \frac{\Sigma fm}{n} \qquad\qquad s = \sqrt{\frac{\Sigma f(m - \bar{x})^2}{n}}$$

$$= \frac{252.00}{100} \qquad\qquad = \sqrt{\frac{39.72}{100}}$$

$$= 2.52 \qquad\qquad\qquad = 0.63$$

where

$\bar{x}$ is the sample mean
s is the sample standard deviation.

The expected frequencies are obtained by using the sample statistics $\bar{x}$ and s as estimates of the universe mean and of the standard deviation and applying the normal curve areas. The expected frequency of the interval "2.5 and under 3.0" is computed in two parts, since $\bar{x}$ lies in this interval. The required calculations are:

$$\frac{X - \mu}{\sigma} = \frac{2.50 - 2.52}{0.63} = -0.03\sigma$$

$$\frac{X - \mu}{\sigma} = \frac{3.00 - 2.52}{0.63} = 0.76\sigma.$$

The appropriate normal curve areas read from Appendix H are 0.01197 and 0.27637, respectively. The sum of these values 0.28834 multiplied by $n = 100$ yields the expected normal frequency for the interval shown in Table 5.1. The expected frequency for the interval "3.0 and under 3.5" is computed similarly as follows:

$$\frac{X - \mu}{\sigma} = \frac{3.00 - 2.52}{0.63} = 0.76\sigma$$

$$\frac{X - \mu}{\sigma} = \frac{3.50 - 2.52}{0.63} = 1.56\sigma.$$

The corresponding areas read from Appendix H are 0.27637 and 0.44062, respectively. The desired area is found by subtracting these values, 0.44062 − 0.27637 = 0.16425, and multiplying the result by 100 to give the expected frequency 16.425. The remaining expected frequencies are computed similarly, and the results are shown in Table 5.1. The observed frequencies are shown by a histogram and the expected frequencies are shown by a frequency polygon in Figure 5.5.

FIGURE 5.5

**Observed and Expected Frequencies of Parts
Produced by a Machine**

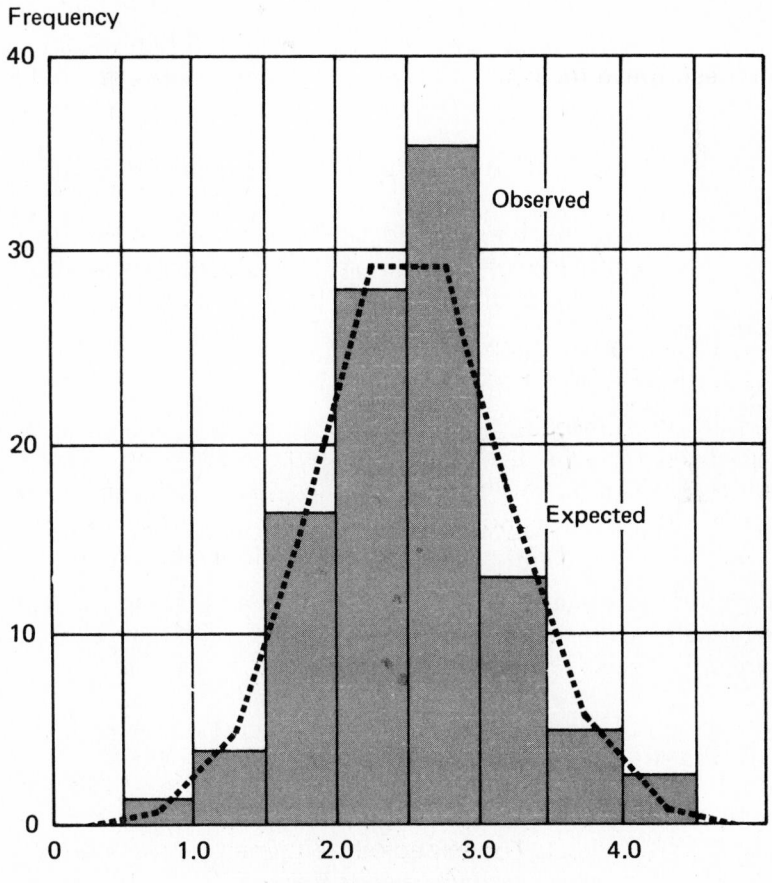

Normal Approximations of Discrete Probability Distributions

Normal and Binomial Probabilities. There is a close correspondence between the binomial and the normal distributions for finite values of n and $p \neq 0.50$, as seen in Figure 5.3. In some problems it is convenient to use normal approximations of binomial probabilities. In this manner, a continuous distribution is employed to represent the histogram of a discrete variable, and the discrete variable is treated as if it were continuous.

A bar of the histogram of a discrete variable corresponds to a single value of the variable. Since only integer (whole number) values are usually defined for this type of variable, the bar is assumed to extend halfway to the integer preceding and the integer following the central value. For example, the bar of a histogram centered on the value 15 of a discrete variable is assumed to extend from 14.5 to 15.5. The extension of the histogram in this manner is called the *continuity correction*. Areas under the normal density function are found in terms of deviations from the mean, and a similar approach is used to find normal areas to approximate binomial probabilities.

■ *Example.* A sample of 20 items is selected randomly from a process for which $p = 0.40$. The probability of obtaining exactly 5 defectives is found by solving

$$P(r = 5 \mid n = 20, p = 0.40) = \binom{20}{5} (0.40)^5 (0.60)^{15} = 0.0746,$$

which is shown as the shaded portion of Figure 5.6. The normal curve approximation of this binomial probability is found by solving for σ_r and $E(r)$ and employing these to obtain the appropriate normal area.

For this example,

$$E(r) = np = (20)(0.40) = 8.00$$

and

$$\sigma_r = \sqrt{npq} = \sqrt{20(0.40)(0.60)} = 2.19.$$

The histogram at $r = 5$ extends from 4.5 to 5.5, and the normal approximation is found by expressing these values as deviations from $E(r)$ in terms of standard deviations. These values are obtained by writing

$$z = \frac{r - E(r)}{\sigma_r} = \frac{4.5 - 8}{2.19} = -1.60\sigma$$

and

$$z = \frac{r - E(r)}{\sigma_r} = \frac{5.5 - 8}{2.19} = -1.14\sigma.$$

FIGURE 5.6

Normal Approximation of Binomial Probabilities

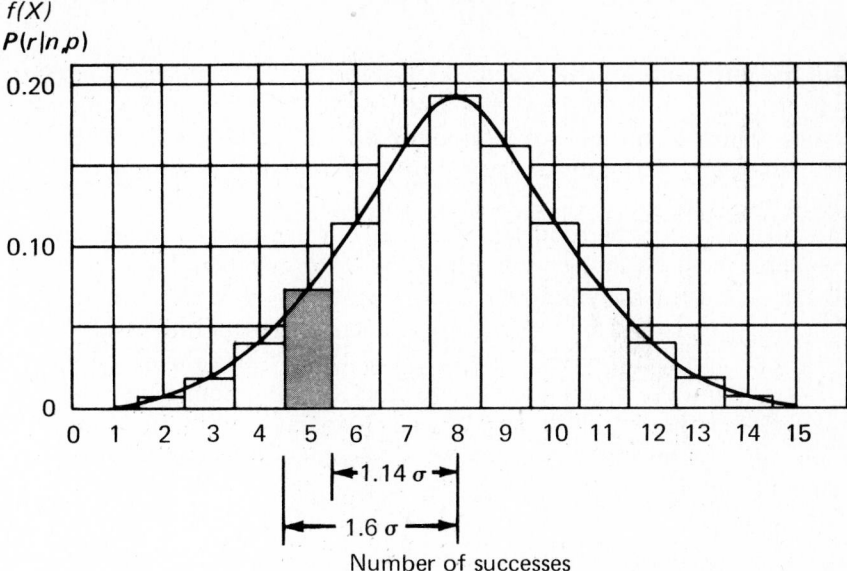

These values of z are read in Appendix H as 0.44520 and 0.37286, respectively. The normal approximation of this binomial probability is $0.44520 - 0.37286 = 0.07234$, which compares very favorably with the exact probability of 0.0746 read from Appendix C.

Normal and Poisson Probabilities. The expected number of successes in a Poisson process is denoted by λ, which is analogous to $E(r)$. Similarly, $\sqrt{\lambda}$ corresponds to σ_r. The normal approximation of a Poisson probability is computed by using the correction and solving for $z = \dfrac{r - \lambda}{\sqrt{\lambda}}$.

■ *Example.* A study of the customer arrivals at the appliance department of a store revealed that the probability of an arrival during the period of one minute is 0.033. The expected number of arrivals every half hour is $np = \lambda = (30)(0.033) = 1$. The Poisson probability of exactly two arrivals during a half-hour period is computed as follows:

$$P(r \mid \lambda) = \frac{\lambda^r}{r!}\, e^{-\lambda} = \left(\frac{1}{2}\right)(e^{-1}) = 0.1839.$$

The normal approximation is computed by solving

$$z = \frac{r - \lambda}{\sqrt{\lambda}} = \frac{2.5 - 1}{1} = 1.5\sigma, \ z = \frac{r - \lambda}{\sqrt{\lambda}} = \frac{1.5 - 1}{1} = 0.5\sigma.$$

Reading the values of the corresponding areas from Appendix H gives 0.43319 and 0.19146, respectively. The normal approximation is the difference $0.43319 - 0.19146 = 0.24173$, which is a fairly good approximation of the exact probability of 0.1839.

The Significance of the Normal Distribution. The normal distribution is dominant among theoretical distributions in the study and application of statistics. The preeminence of this distribution is the result of its mathematical characteristics and its suitability as a mode of expression for many phenomena.

The derivation of the binomial distribution in Chapter 4 uses the notion of a variable X that takes on a value of one or zero, depending upon whether a success or a failure is obtained on a trial. In this fashion, the probability of a success is constant for all trials, and each trial is an independent binary (two-valued) random variable. The sum of these variables is the binomial distribution, and the mean and the variance of the binomial are the sums of the expected values and the variances, respectively, of the independent variables. As the number of variables (n) becomes large, the sum approaches the normal distribution as a limit.

This important result is generalized further by some theorems, which are given without proof. The first theorem states that:

If each of n independent random variables has an identical probability distribution, the sum of these distributions approaches a normal distribution as n becomes large.

It is significant that this is true whatever the nature of the probability distribution, unless a distribution has an infinite mean or standard deviation.

A second theorem states that:

For certain specified conditions, the normal limit extends to sums of independent random variables for which the probability distributions are not all alike.

The importance of the normal distribution in statistical theory is also predicated on the fact that, by proper transformation, any continuous distribution can be converted into a normal distribution. The prominence of the normal distribution also results from the frequent occurrence of variables, in the analysis of practical problems, which are sums of independent random variables with very similar, if not identical, probability distributions. This fact will be expanded in the discussion of the central limit theorem in Chapter 6.

The suitability of the normal distribution as an approximating form of the probability distributions of various random variables is seen in the computation of normal approximations in preceding portions of this chapter. The fact that sums of random variables tend to approach normality as n increases implies that the larger the value of n, the better the normal approximation. For many practical problems, unless exact probabilities are required, normal approximations are used, especially when n is not small.

The theorems described above apply to sums of independent random variables, for which the number of variables and the nature of the identical probability distributions are known. It is fairly common for an administrative problem to involve a variable that is the sum of random variables, the number and the probability distributions of which are unknown and which may or may not be completely independent. While the precise nature and relationship of the component variables may be unknown, many empirical distributions appear reasonably normal when plotted. For these cases the "fitting" of a normal curve to historical data enables one to use the normal curve as a reasonably good model and to take advantage of the considerable amount of information that is known about this model.

Methods for appraising the appropriateness of the fit of a normal curve to empirical data are discussed in Chapter 9.

THE EXPONENTIAL DISTRIBUTION

$$P(t) = M e^{-mt} \quad (density)$$
$$P(x \geqslant t) = e^{-mt}$$
$$P(x \leq t) = 1 - e^{-mt}$$

An important class of problems concerns the probability distribution of the amount of space (or other continuous variables such as time or distance) between events. For example, the length of time that an appliance or a piece of machinery will operate varies, and the distribution of the length of time of operation until failure can often be described by a theoretical probability distribution called the *exponential distribution*.

The Nature of the Exponential Distribution

In introducing the nature of the exponential distribution, it is particularly useful to consider some of the characteristics of Poisson and negative binomial distributions. In contrast to the Poisson distribution, which expresses the probability of obtaining r successes in a given interval t of a continuous variable, where r is a random variable, the exponential distribution expresses the probability that a selected interval length will be required to obtain a success, where r is given and the interval length t is a random variable. The exponential distribution is similar to the Poisson distribution in that each distribution may be viewed as the limit of a discrete distribution. The Poisson distribution is the limit of the binomial distribution as n becomes very large and p approaches zero. The exponential distribution is the limit of the negative binomial distribution for $r = 1$ as n becomes very large and p approaches zero. The limiting curve is called the *exponential probability density function*, which may be written

$$f(t) = me^{-mt} \quad \dots\dots\dots\dots\dots\dots\dots\dots\dots\dots\dots\dots\dots(5.4)$$

where $f(t)$ is the ordinate of the exponential distribution for a given value of the random variable t, m is the mean number of events per unit of space (or other continuous variable), $e = 2.7183$ (the base of natural logarithms), and t is the amount of space measured in intervals and is greater than zero.

■ *Example.* Consider a utility company that maintains standby crews for making emergency repairs and that receives service calls according to a Poisson distribution with a mean of two calls per 24-hour period. If a trial is viewed as an eight-hour interval (one third of a 24-hour day), the probability that eight hours will pass before a call is received is $2(1/3) = 0.67$. The expected number of calls for three eight-hour periods is $np = 3(0.67) = 2$. The probability that n eight-hour periods will be required before a call is received is expressed by the negative binomial probability $P(n \mid r, p) = p^r q^{n-r}$, where $r = 1$ and $p = 0.67$. These probabilities are computed in Table 5.2 and shown in the histogram in Figure 5.7. If a trial is viewed as being a three-hour period (an eighth of a day), the corresponding probabilities are found for a negative binomial distribution for $r = 1$ and $p = 2(1/8) = 0.25$. The probabilities for various values of n are computed in Table 5.2 and are shown respectively as the bars of the histogram in Figure 5.7, where the width of each bar is a fractional part of a 24-hour day and the height of each bar relates to probability density.

The ordinate of the continuous curve shown in the diagrams in Figure 5.7 can be computed for any selected value of t. The ordinate of the curve at $t = 0$ is computed $f(t) = 2(2.7183)^{-2(0)} = 2(1) = 2$, where $m = 2$, as given above. The height of the curve at the end of three eight-hour periods or one 24-hour day is computed $f(t) = 2(2.7183)^{-2(3/3)} = 2(0.13534) = 0.27068$, where an eight-hour period is 1/3 of a day and the value 0.13534 is read from Appendix E for $\lambda = mt = 2(3/3) = 2$ and $e^{-2} = 0.13534$. The ordinate of the curve in the right-hand diagram of Figure 5.7 for $t = 2/8$ or the end of two three-hour periods is computed $f(t) = 2(2.7183)^{-2(0.25)} = 2(0.60653) = 1.21306$. The value 0.60653 is read from Appendix E for $e^{-0.5}$.

Exponential Probabilities

Probabilities associated with a random variable having an exponential distribution may be found by obtaining the appropriate area under the exponential curve. Because of the nature of the exponential distribution, it is simpler to compute the probability that more than t intervals will be required to obtain a success (or failure). The area in the right-hand portion of the exponential distribution from t to ∞ is written

$$P(t) = e^{-mt} \quad \text{...................................(5.5)}$$

where $P(t)$ is the probability that more than t intervals will be required to obtain a success, e is the base for natural logarithms, m is the mean number of events (or successes) per unit space or time, and t is the amount of space measured in intervals and is greater than zero. The probability that t or fewer intervals will be required to obtain a success is $1 - e^{-mt}$, the area in the left-hand portion of the exponential distribution from zero to t.

Probability and Probability Distributions **Part 2**

TABLE 5.2

**Negative Binomial Probabilities for
Selected Values of n and p**

Number of trials n	Probability of n trials to obtain one success $P(n \mid r, p) = p^r q^{n-r}$	Total elapsed time (hours)
	Eight-hour periods $r = 1, p = 0.67$	
1	$(.67)(.33)^0 = 0.667$	8
2	$(.67)(.33)^1 = 0.221$	16
3	$(.67)(.33)^2 = 0.073$	24
4	$(.67)(.33)^3 = 0.024$	32
5	$(.67)(.33)^4 = 0.008$	40
6	$(.67)(.33)^5 = 0.003$	48
	Three-hour periods $r = 1, p = 0.25$	
1	$(.25)(.75)^0 = 0.250$	3
2	$(.25)(.75)^1 = 0.188$	6
3	$(.25)(.75)^2 = 0.141$	9
4	$(.25)(.75)^3 = 0.105$	12
5	$(.25)(.75)^4 = 0.079$	15
6	$(.25)(.75)^5 = 0.059$	18

FIGURE 5.7

**Histograms of Negative Binomial Probabilities
with an Exponential Curve as the Limit**

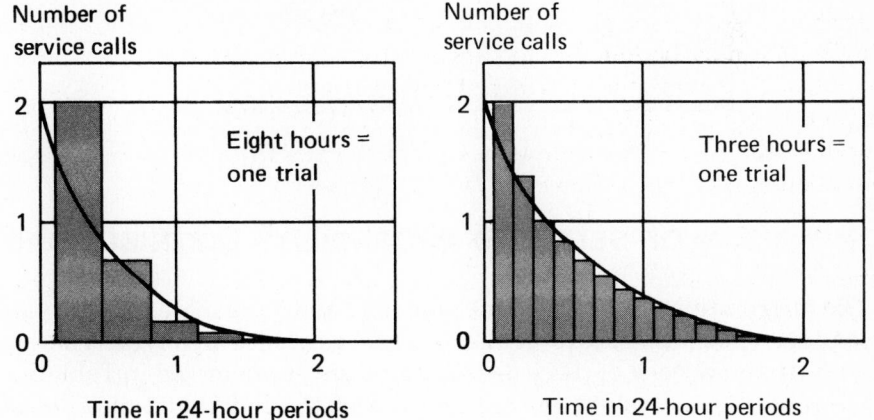

■ *Example.* Tests conducted with a brand of electronic equipment indicate that an average of four failures occur per 100,000 hours of use and the failures are Poisson distributed. A firm that is interested in the purchase of this equipment is interested in the exponential probability distribution of the length of time between failures. The mean of the exponential distribution is $m = 4$ and $t = 25{,}000/100{,}000 = 0.25$. The exponential probability that the equipment will operate more than 25,000 hours without a failure is

$$P(t > 0.25) = e^{-mt} = e^{-4(0.25)} = 0.36788$$

where the value of $e^{-1} = 0.36788$ is read from Appendix E. The exponential probability that the equipment will fail during a 37,500 hour period is

$$P(t \leq 0.375) = 1 - e^{-4(0.375)} = 1 - e^{-1.5} = 1 - 0.22313 = 0.77687$$

where the value of $e^{-1.5} = 0.22313$ is read from Appendix E. These probabilities are illustrated in Figure 5.8. It should be noted that the exponential distribution relates to the interval between successes (failures) as well as to the interval until the first success.

FIGURE 5.8

Exponential Probability Distribution

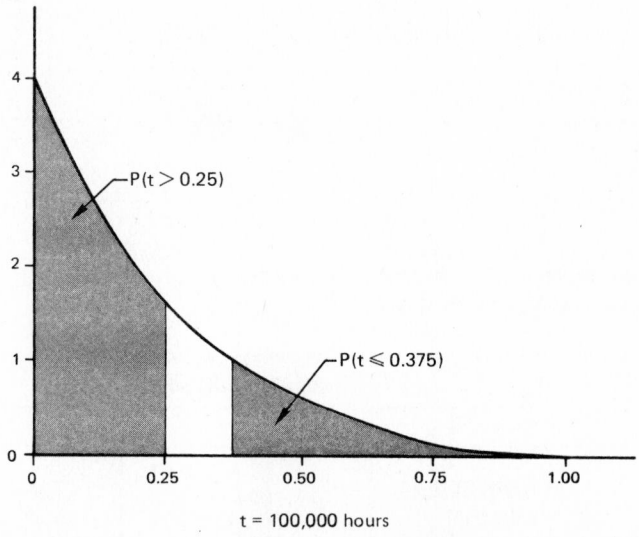

t = 100,000 hours

COMPARISON OF SELECTED PROBABILITY DISTRIBUTIONS

The distributions considered in Chapters 4 and 5 are more or less related, depending upon the nature of the random variables involved. The basic characteristics of each of these distributions are summarized in Table 5.3 to provide additional insight into the nature of the individual distributions and the relationships that exist among distributions.

TABLE 5.3   **Characteristics of Selected Distributions**

DISCRETE DISTRIBUTIONS

Distribution	Density function	Parameters	Probability or frequency	Limiting form or limit of	Approximate or alternate distributions	Applications
Binomial	$\binom{n}{r} p^r (1-p)^{n-r}$	n, p	$P(r \mid n, p)$ = probability of r successes in n Bernoulli trials, given a constant value of p. (Formula 4.3)	Normal and Poisson (if p is small and n is large)	Normal and Poisson	Sampling from a Bernoulli process.
Poisson	$\dfrac{\lambda^r}{r!} e^{-\lambda}$	λ	$P(r \mid \lambda)$ = probability of r successes in many trials, given a constant value of λ. (Formula 4.10)	Poisson	Normal and exponential (if p is small)	Sampling from a process considered Bernoulli, where n is large, p is small, and np is constant.
Hypergeometric	$\dfrac{\binom{N-r}{n-c}\binom{r}{c}}{\binom{N}{n}}$	N, n, c	$P(c \mid N, r, n)$ = probability of r successes in n Bernoulli trials from a finite universe of size N, given the total possible number of successes c. (Formula 4.11)	Hypergeometric	Binomial, Poisson, and normal	Sampling from a finite universe containing a given number of successes and where p changes from trial to trial.
Negative binomial	$\binom{n-1}{r-1} p^r (1-p)^{n-r}$	r, p	$P(n \mid r, p)$ = probability that n Bernoulli trials will be required to obtain r successes, given a constant value of p. (Formula 4.12)	Exponential (for $r = 1$)	Binomial, normal, and exponential (if p is small)	Determining the probability that n Bernoulli trials will be needed to obtain a desired number of successes.

(continued on page 130)

TABLE 5.3 (concluded)

CONTINUOUS DISTRIBUTIONS

Distribution	Density function	Parameters	Probability or frequency	Limiting form or limit of	Approximate or alternate distributions	Applications
Uniform	$\dfrac{1}{B-A}$	None	$P(a \leq X \leq b) =$ the probability that X will take on a value in the interval from a to b. (Formula 5.1)			Primarily of theoretical value.
Normal probability	$\dfrac{1}{\sigma\sqrt{2\pi}}\, e^{-\frac{1}{2}\left(\frac{X-\mu}{\sigma}\right)^2}$	μ, σ	$P(a \leq X \leq b) =$ probability the random variable X will take on a value in the interval from a to b, given μ and σ.	Binomial		Describing continuous and certain discrete variables and sums of random variables that may be considered normal.
Exponential	me^{-mt}	m	$P(t) = e^{-mt} =$ probability that if trials are Bernoulli, t or more intervals will be required to obtain a success. (Formula 5.5)	Negative binomial (for $r = 1$)	Poisson and negative binomial	Determining the probability that a given space or time interval will be required to obtain a success.

STUDY QUESTIONS

5–1. Explain briefly the meaning of each of the following terms:
a. continuous variable
b. uniform probability density function
c. normal distribution
d. normal probability density function
e. continuity correction
f. exponential distribution
g. exponential probability density function

5–2. Relate the following concepts to a continuous random variable:
a. sample space
b. set function
c. probability density function

5–3. Is a continuous probability density function the same thing as a probability distribution? Explain.

5–4. What is the meaning of the term z that relates to areas under the normal curve?

5–5. What is the theoretical and practical significance of the normal distribution?

5–6. Describe the relationship of the exponential distribution to the negative binomial distribution.

PROBLEMS

5–1. If the numerals that appear on auto license plates are uniformly distributed, what is the probability that the last digit of a randomly selected plate will be three or less?

5–2. What is the probability density of the outcomes of three tosses of a fair coin?

5–3. The length of time customers spend shopping in a supermarket is normally distributed, with a mean of 30 minutes and a standard deviation of 10 minutes. What proportion of customers will have shopping times that are between:
a. 20 and 30 minutes?
b. 25 and 35 minutes?
c. 15 and 25 minutes?
d. 37.5 and 45 minutes?

5–4. In a study of the heights of 1,200 male workers, it was found that the average height was 5 feet 7 inches with a standard deviation of 3 inches. If the heights are normally distributed, what is the expected number of workers that are:
a. More than 6 feet tall?
b. Between 5 feet and 6 feet in height?

5–5. The fuel consumption of a fleet of 150 trucks is normally distributed, with a mean of 15 miles per gallon and a standard deviation of 1.2 miles

per gallon. Find the expected number of trucks that average:
   a. 14 but less than 16 miles per gallon
   b. 15.5 but less than 17 miles per gallon

5-6. Electrical power demand in a city is normally distributed, with a mean of 150,000 kilowatts and a standard deviation of 10,000 kilowatts. If the generating capacity of the electrical power plant is 175,000 kilowatts, what percent of the time will demand for power exceed the generating capacity?

5-7. What percent of the area of the normal distribution is in the range of the mean plus and minus 1.6 standard deviations?

5-8. What range of the normal distribution includes the middle 50% of the area under the curve?

5-9. Plastic bags used for packaging produce are received in bulk from a supplier. The breaking strength of the bags averages 5.0 pounds per square inch. If the strength of bags is normally distributed, what is the value of the standard deviation if:
   a. 34% of the bags have a breaking strength between 5.0 and 5.6 pounds per square inch?
   b. Half of the bags have a breaking strength between 4.5 and 5.5 pounds per square inch?
   c. One fourth of the bags have a breaking strength of 4.2 pounds or less?

5-10. A manager estimates that there is a 50–50 chance that the demand for a product will be between 30 and 50 units in the period of a week. If demand is normally distributed, what is the value of the mean and standard deviation of the distribution? Assume that $\mu = 40$.

5-11. A machine produces parts that are boxed in lots of 100 parts. If there has been an average of four defective parts per box:
   a. What is the binomial probability that a box will contain two defective parts?
   b. What is the normal curve approximation of the probability that a box will contain two defective parts?

5-12. Maintenance records indicate that only one in 100 new automobiles of a given brand has a major transmission failure within the warranty period. Records are to be kept on the next 40 new vehicles that are sold. Compute:
   a. The binomial probability that no new automobiles will have a major transmission failure.
   b. The normal curve approximation of the probability that no new automobiles will have a major transmission failure.

5-13. The amount of time to check out customers in a supermarket is exponentially distributed with a mean of five minutes per customer or 0.2 customers per minute. What is the probability that the time to check

out a customer will be:
a. More than two minutes?
b. Less than three minutes?

5-14. Records indicate that the arrivals of aircraft at an airport are exponentially distributed with an average of ten minutes between flight arrivals. What is the probability that the time interval between flights will be:
a. Less than five minutes?
b. More than seven minutes?

5-15. The times required to transact business with patrons at a window in a post office are distributed exponentially with a mean of 3.33 minutes per person. What is the probability that the time required for a transaction will be:
a. More than four minutes?
b. Less than two minutes?

5-16. Telephone calls made from a booth average four minutes in length and are exponentially distributed. What is the probability that the length of a telephone call will be:
a. More than six minutes?
b. Less than two minutes?

5-17. An apartment manager compiled data for the lengths of time that tenants occupied apartments, and the data are as follows:

Time (years)	Number of tenants
1	44
2	17
3	9
4	5
	75

a. Compute the average length of occupancy by tenants.
b. Assuming that length of occupancy is exponentially distributed, what is the probability that an apartment will be occupied by the same tenant for two or more years?

5-18. The processing times of computer programs were recorded as follows:

Time (15-second periods)	Number of programs
1	61
2	29
3	14
4	9
5	2
	115

In terms of processing times, the programs are entered randomly into the computer. Estimate the probability that a program entering the computer will require 30 or more seconds of processing time on the basis of:
  a. Relative frequency.
  b. Negative binomial probability, basing the probability on a five-second interval as one trial.
  c. Exponential probability density.

SELECTED READINGS

Freund, John E. *Mathematical Statistics,* 2d ed. Englewood Cliffs, N.J.: Prentice-Hall, Inc., 1971.
  Chapter 5 presents a description of various density functions.
Schlaifer, Robert. *Probability and Statistics for Business Decisions.* New York: McGraw-Hill Book Company, Inc., 1959.
  Discussion of the exponential distribution is presented in Chapter 14.

Part 3

Sampling

Chapter 6

Sample Distributions
and Estimation

Sampling is a familiar idea; nearly everyone has had occasion to examine a part of an object or a portion of a collection of things in order to make a judgment about the general nature or quality of the entire object or collection. In statistical terms the characteristics of a universe are often expressed by descriptive measures such as the mean or proportion. For example, in examining the accounts receivable of a firm, an auditor may be interested in estimating the mean dollar value of accounts or the proportion of accounts that are delinquent. To obtain the desired estimate, a representative sample of the accounts is selected, the mean or proportion of the sample is computed, and the sample result (statistic) is used as the basis for estimating the corresponding universe parameter. Since all the items in the universe are not examined in taking a sample, estimates based on sample results may vary about the corresponding universe parameters, and some degree of error in estimation is likely.

This chapter relates descriptive statistics, probability, and probability distributions to the conceptual basis of sampling, estimation, and sampling error. Simple random sampling, distributions of sample statistics, properties of estimators, and estimation methods are discussed.

RANDOM SAMPLING AND RANDOM NUMBERS

The objective of sampling is the selection of a representative group of items that constitute a small-scale replica of the universe from which they are drawn. Since such a sample tends to reflect the properties of the universe, statistics computed from the sample data provide estimates of the respective parameters. The larger the sample size, the closer a sample statistic tends to approximate a universe parameter.

135

Simple Random Sampling

A fundamental type of sampling involves the selection of items from a universe in such a way that each item in the universe has an equal probability of being selected as each sample item is drawn. A sample drawn in this manner is called a *simple random sample.* An approach to this type of sampling is illustrated in the shuffling of a deck of cards in an attempt to arrange the cards in random order so that each card has an equal probability of being placed in each position in the deck. Similarly, a die is used in some parlor games to generate random events. The faces tend to turn up with equal likelihoods if the die is tossed fairly and no attempt is made to control or influence which of the faces will turn up on a toss.

Dealing cards from a shuffled deck or tossing a die corresponds to randomly drawing sample items from universes of 52 and 6 items, respectively. If a sample is to be drawn from a universe of many items (such as hundreds, millions, or an unlimited number), then a technique must be used that can generate a large number of random events, one for each item or interval of items in the universe.

Random Numbers

The random selection of sample items is facilitated by the use of *random numbers,* a sequence of numbers generated by a uniformly distributed random variable so that each digit, zero through nine, has an equal probability of occurring in each position in the sequence. Thus, in a long sequence of random numbers, each of the digits will occur with equal frequency, but there is no order or pattern in their occurrence in the sequence. There are a number of techniques for generating random numbers, and some may be used to obtain series of numbers that are random for as many as several million digits.

Table of Random Numbers. A table of six-digit random numbers is presented in Table N in the Appendix. Any series of digits that are read across the rows or down the columns of the table is random.

■ *Example.* A series of five random numbers of three digits each can be obtained by reading down from the upper left-hand part of the first page of Table N to give: 345, 549, 423, 554, and 797. Alternately, five successive groups of three digits read from the first row are the random numbers: 345, 769, 953, 810, and 627.

■ *Example.* A random sample of telephone subscribers can be obtained from the telephone directory of a city by use of six-digit random numbers selected from Table N. The first three digits indicate a randomly selected page. The second three digits correspond to the name on the sample page. Reading under group C on the first page of Table N, the first six-digit number is 627280. It indicates that the name of the first subscriber to be sampled appears on page 627 of the directory and it is the 280th name on that page. The second random number is 059309. The name of the second subscriber to be sampled occurs on page 59 and it is the 309th name on that page. The remainder of the sample can be obtained similarly by continuing to read down the columns until the desired number of names has been obtained. Should a directory have fewer pages than a three-digit random number obtained from the table, omit that number and proceed down to the next random number and obtain another series of digits. This procedure also applies if a three-digit random number is larger than the number of names on a given page.

Monte Carlo Method. Random numbers can be used to obtain a sample of items or events that are distributed according to a frequency distribution or a probability distribution. A process for using random numbers to select a sample of items or events according to a given distribution is called the *Monte Carlo method*. The name of this method is derived from the random outcomes of the roulette wheels observed at the famed gambling casino.

Suppose one wishes to randomly generate events that have a distribution described as follows:

Event	Probability
0	0.3
1	0.5
2	0.2
	1.0

The Monte Carlo method and random numbers can be used to generate the desired sample of events. Equiprobable two-digit random numbers provide the sample space for generating the events. The random numbers are grouped proportionately as follows:

Event	Probability	Cumulative probability	Random numbers
0	0.3	0.3	01–30
1	0.5	0.8	31–80
2	0.2	1.0	81–00

The generation of events by use of random numbers is seen most clearly by the relationship between the number of random numbers in each group and the cumulative probability associated with that group. The group of random numbers (01–30) associated with event "0" includes a total of 30 distinct numbers. This corresponds directly to the probability 0.30. The group of random numbers (31–80) related to event "1" includes 50 different numbers. The probability of event "1" and the increase in the cumulative probability is 0.50. Similarly, the number of random numbers in the third group (81–00) is directly proportional to the probability of event "2" and the increase in the cumulative probability. This proportionality is seen by comparing the 20 random numbers in the third group with the probability of the occurrence of the event "2," which is 0.20.

Simple random sampling from this distribution is achieved artificially, or *simulated*, by selecting a three-digit random number, relating the number to one of the groups, and associating the occurrence of the number with the corresponding event. For example, the random number 24 is between 01 and 30. It is related to the first group and the occurrence of event "0." Similarly, the random number 97, which is between 81 and 00, is associated with the event "2." If many equiprobable two-digit random numbers are related to the groupings and associated events, the events are expected to "occur" with frequencies equal to the theoretical probabilities.

DISTRIBUTIONS OF SAMPLE STATISTICS

The analysis for administrative applications and other scientific research often involves making generalizations or inferences about random variables based on descriptive statistics calculated from sample data. Many different samples can be drawn from a universe as the result of chance in the random selection of sample data. The descriptive statistics computed from sample data, such as the mean or the standard deviation or the proportion of successes, will differ from sample to sample because random selection will produce samples that are made up of different groups of items from a universe. The nature of the distributions of sample statistics is very important in statistical analysis, and this chapter concerns the theoretical and practical importance of some of these distributions.

Distribution of Sample Means

The characteristics of the distribution of sample means are important in making inferences on the basis of sample statistics. These characteristics can be demonstrated empirically by drawing random samples from a known universe.

■ *Example.* A universe is formed from a standard deck of playing cards by removing selected cards with the following distribution:

Universe elements	Frequency	Element value
Ace	4	1
2	4	2
3	4	3
4	3	4
5	3	5
6	3	6
7	2	7
8	2	8
9	2	9
10	1	10

Jack	1	11
Queen	1	12
King	1	13
Total	31	

An experiment is performed by drawing randomly, with replacement, a total of 308 samples of 10 cards each. The frequency distribution of the mean, median, and standard deviation of each of the samples is shown in Table 6.1. The distributions of the sample means and the parent universe are plotted in Figure 6.1 in terms of frequency density. For example, the frequency density of aces in the universe of cards is computed as $\frac{4}{31} = 0.13$. The mean of the sample means is denoted $\bar{\bar{x}}$; the standard deviation of the distribution of sample means is $s_{\bar{x}}$; and μ and σ are the mean and the standard deviation, respectively, of the universe.

TABLE 6.1

Summary of the Sample Statistics of 308 Samples of 10 Items

	Number		
Sample value	Means $\bar{x}$	Medians Md	Standard deviations s
1.0 and under 1.5			4
1.5 and under 2.0			18
2.0 and under 2.5		2	45
2.5 and under 3.0	2	8	74
3.0 and under 3.5	8	23	85
3.5 and under 4.0	23	36	57
4.0 and under 4.5	33	41	21
4.5 and under 5.0	53	49	3
5.0 and under 5.5	65	51	1
5.5 and under 6.0	60	42	
6.0 and under 6.5	36	23	
6.5 and under 7.0	21	16	
7.0 and under 7.5	6	11	
7.5 and under 8.0	1	3	
8.0 and under 8.5		2	
8.5 and under 9.0		1	
Total	308	308	308

Summary:		Empirical	
Average	$\bar{\bar{x}} = 5.25$	$Md_{Md} = 4.95$	$\bar{s} = 3.05$
Standard deviation	$s_{\bar{x}} = 0.94$	$s_{Md} = 1.18$	$s_s = 0.71$

Average	$\mu = 5.26$	$\bar{\bar{x}} = 5.26$
Standard deviation	$\sigma = 3.36$	$\sigma_{\bar{x}} = 1.06$

FIGURE 6.1

Distributions of a Universe of 31 Cards and the Sample Means of 308 Samples

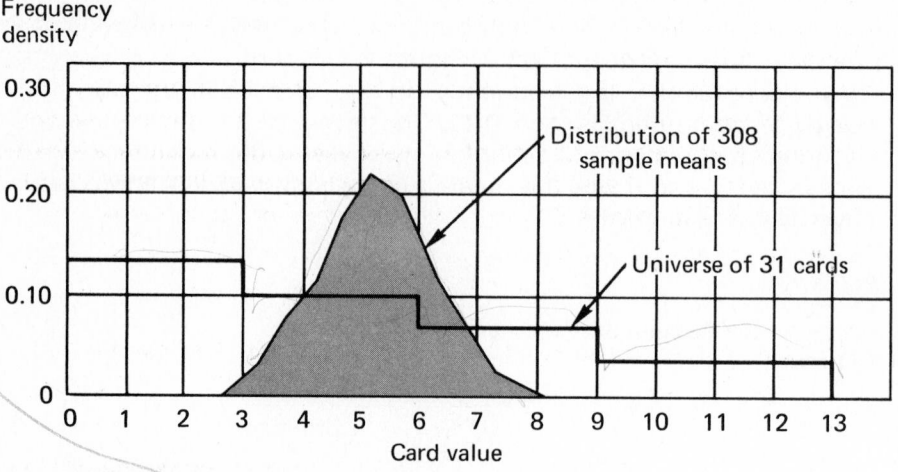

Law of Large Numbers

The distribution of sample means in the foregoing example demonstrates experimentally some important statistical concepts. As shown in Table 6.1, the sample means are approximately centered about the universe mean and are almost normally distributed. The distribution of sample means becomes more concentrated about the universe mean as the sample size becomes larger. These relationships are based on what is called the *law of large numbers*. A statement of the law that is more precise is given by what is called the *central limit theorem*. This very important theorem in statistics states that:

If a universe has a mean μ and a finite standard deviation σ, then the distribution of sample means approaches a normal distribution with a mean μ and a standard deviation $\dfrac{\sigma}{\sqrt{n}}$ as the sample size increases.

Since the distribution of sample means is normally or approximately normally distributed about the universe mean, the expected value of a sample mean is $E(\bar{x}) = \mu$. The standard deviation of sample means, called the *standard error of the mean*, is written

$$\sigma_{\bar{x}} = \frac{\sigma}{\sqrt{n}} \dotfill (6.1)$$

Estimates of parameters based on sample results in the example above tend to confirm two of the relationships in Table 6.1. The mean of the 308 sample means is $\bar{\bar{x}} = 5.25$, a very good estimate of $\mu = 5.26$. The standard deviation of the 308 sample means is $s_{\bar{x}} = 0.94$, a reasonably good estimate of the theoretical value of the standard error of the mean

which?

$$\sigma_{\bar{x}} = \frac{3.36}{\sqrt{10}} = 1.06.$$

The fact that the estimate $s_{\bar{x}}$ is less than $\sigma_{\bar{x}}$ is in part the result of an inherent downward bias in this statistic. This relationship will be discussed in greater detail in a section that follows.

For a constant value of σ, the standard error of the mean varies inversely with sample size. On the average, the mean of a large sample is expected to provide a more reliable estimate of μ than would the mean of a smaller sample. For example, if samples of 25 are drawn with replacement from the universe of cards in Figure 6.1, the standard error of the mean is

$$\sigma_{\bar{x}} = \frac{3.36}{\sqrt{25}} = 0.672.$$

If samples of 100 items are drawn, the standard error of the mean is

$$\sigma_{\bar{x}} = \frac{3.36}{\sqrt{100}} = 0.336.$$

Notice that the standard error for a sample size of 25 is twice the standard error for a sample of 100 items, as shown in Figure 6.2. Thus, if the expected

FIGURE 6.2

Distributions of Sample Means for Selected Sample Sizes

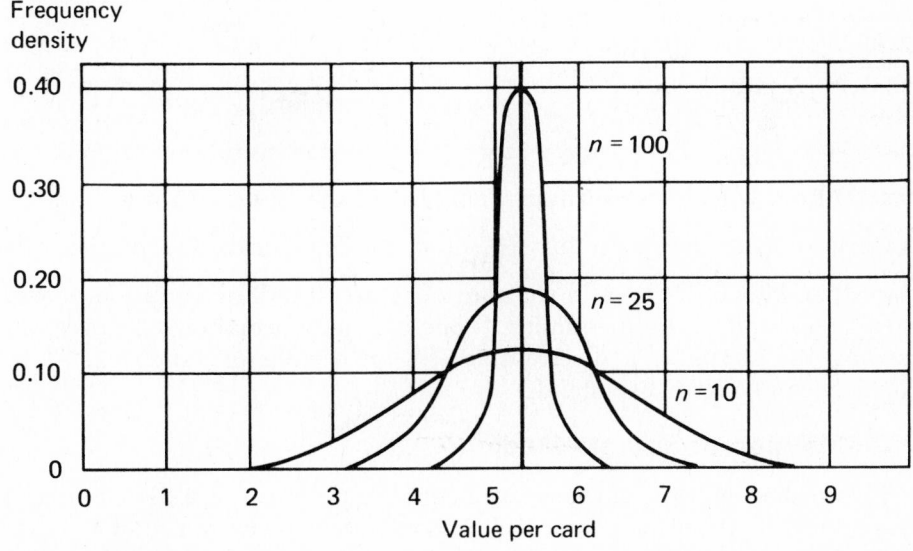

sampling error is to be cut in half, the sample size must be increased four times. For a very large sample, the standard error approaches zero as the sample size n increases without limit.

The distribution of sample means for large samples is approximately normal whatever the shape of the universe, provided σ is finite. Many populations encountered in practice are normal or very nearly so. It can be shown that if the universe standard deviation is known, the distribution of sample means for small sample sizes is normally distributed. Samples of 100 or more are often considered to be large for statistical purposes. The importance of the normal distribution is made clear by the central limit theorem and related theorems.

The law of large numbers also includes the statement of a relationship expressed by what is called *Tchebycheff's inequality*, which may be written

$$P(|x - \mu| \geq k\sigma) \leq \frac{1}{k^2} \quad\dots\dots\dots\dots\dots\dots\dots\dots\dots\dots\text{(6.2)}$$

This relationship states the probability that a randomly selected value which differs from the universe mean by more than k standard deviations will not exceed $\frac{1}{k^2}$. This relationship holds, whatever the form of the distribution of the universe.

■ *Example.* An automatic machine produces ball bearings that vary in diameter, but the distribution of the diameters is unknown. A sample of ball bearings is drawn randomly from the production of the machine and the mean of the sample $\bar{x}$ is computed. The probability that $\bar{x}$ differs from μ, the universe mean diameter, by two standard deviations of sample means or more is written

$$P(|x - \mu| \geq 2\sigma_{\bar{x}}) \leq \frac{1}{(2)^2} = 0.25.$$

The converse implication of Tchebycheff's inequality is also of considerable value. In this manner one might say that the minimum proportion of a distribution included in the range of k standard deviations about the mean is $1 - \left(\frac{1}{k^2}\right)$. For example, for $k = 3$, the minimum proportion of any distribution, whatever its shape, included in the range of three standard deviations about the mean is $1 - \frac{1}{(3)^2} \geq 0.89$. The normal distribution with more than 99% of its area in the range of three standard deviations is well within the limit of the inequality. If one has no information whatever concerning the shape of a distribution, the provisions of Tchebycheff's inequality can be most beneficial.

Distribution of Sample Medians

The median is a position measure equal to the mean if a distribution is symmetric. If samples are drawn randomly from a normally distributed universe, the distribution of sample medians can be described theoretically. This distribution is expressed by a theorem that provides that if samples are drawn from a universe with a mean μ and a standard deviation σ, the medians of random samples of size n are distributed approximately normally with a mean of μ and a standard deviation $1.25\ \sigma/\sqrt{n}$ even if the universe is not normally distributed and the sample is not large.

The relationship between $\sigma_{\bar{x}}$ and σ_{Md} is seen in Figure 6.3, which shows the frequency distributions of the means and medians of 308 samples as presented in Table 6.1. The distribution of these sample medians is more widely dispersed than the distribution of means. The standard deviations of these distributions have a ratio of

$$\frac{s_{Md}}{s_{\bar{x}}} = \frac{1.18}{0.94} = 1.255.$$

This result closely approximates the theoretical result which states that the expected ratio is

$$\frac{\sigma_{Md}}{\sigma_{\bar{x}}} = 1.25.$$

The difference between the experimental and the theoretical results is attributed to random variation in the selection of the samples.

FIGURE 6.3

Frequency Distributions of the Means and the Medians of 308 Samples

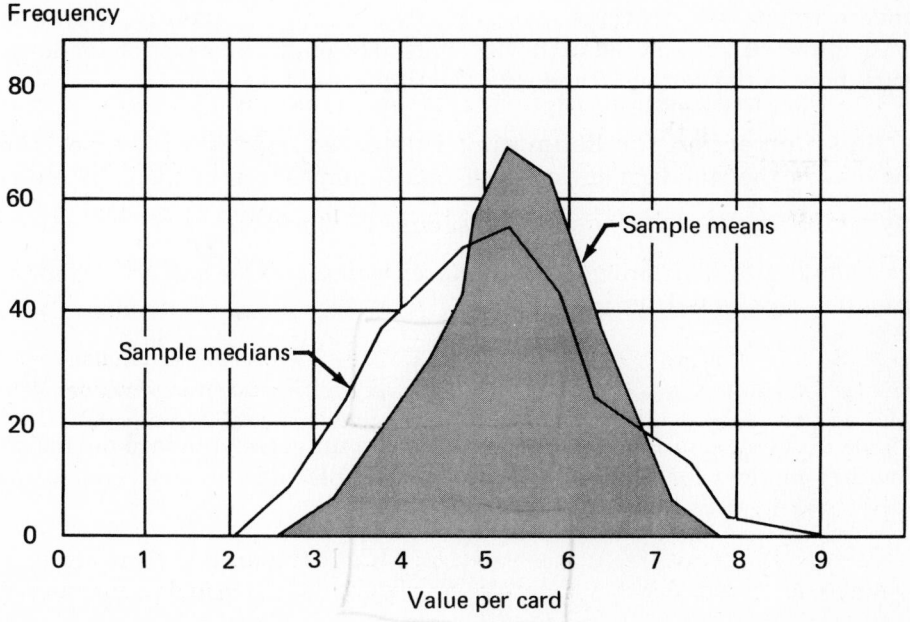

Distribution of Sample Standard Deviations

In the analysis of random variables relevant to business problems, it is common that the standard deviation of the universe is unknown. In such a case σ must be estimated by the sample standard deviation, if a complete enumeration of the universe is infeasible. The distribution of sample standard deviations is of considerable interest, for it provides an insight into the reliability of a sample estimate of universe variation.

The distribution of sample standard deviations is defined by a theorem that states:

If a universe is large and normally distributed with a standard deviation of σ, the standard deviations of random samples of size n, where n is large, are closely approximated by a normal distribution with a standard deviation

$$\frac{\sigma}{\sqrt{2n}}.$$

The provisions of this theorem are also approximately true even if the universe is not large or normally distributed and the sample size is not large. This approximate relationship is shown by the data in Table 6.1. A sample may be considered large if $n > 100$, and in many instances $n > 30$ is viewed to be sufficiently large to assume normality.

The standard deviations of the 308 samples are shown in Table 6.1. This distribution is approximately normal. The average standard deviation, $\bar{s} = 3.05$, indicates the tendency toward downward bias, since $\sigma = 3.36$. The standard deviation of the sample standard deviations $s_s = 0.71$ compares favorably with the theoretical value of $\sigma_s = 0.75$.

This example demonstrates that a sample standard deviation tends to underestimate the universe standard deviation. Consequently, if an estimate of the universe standard deviation is to be made, a correction for downward bias in the sample standard deviation should be applied.

Bias Correction for Estimating Universe Dispersion. A correction for bias in the standard deviation of small samples can be made by multiplying the standard deviation of the sample by the ratio $\sqrt{\dfrac{n}{n-1}}$, where n is the sample size. This provides an *unbiased estimate of the universe standard deviation* that is written

$$\hat{\sigma} = s\sqrt{\frac{n}{n-1}} \quad \dots\dots\dots\dots\dots\dots\dots\dots(6.3)$$

where $\hat{\sigma}$ denotes an unbiased estimate of the universe standard deviation. Another method for correcting for small sample bias involves computing

$$\hat{\sigma} = \sqrt{\frac{\sum\limits_{1}^{n}(x_i - \bar{x})^2}{n-1}} \quad \dots\dots\dots\dots\dots\dots(6.4)$$

■ Example. A sample of five tires of a given type is drawn from the output of a process. The weights of the tires, in pounds, are as follows: 15.2, 14.9, 15.0, 14.8, and 15.1. The mean weight is 15.0 pounds. The sample standard deviation is computed as follows:

$(15.2 - 15.0)^2 = 0.04$
$(14.9 - 15.0)^2 = 0.01$
$(15.0 - 15.0)^2 = 0.00$
$(14.8 - 15.0)^2 = 0.04$
$(15.1 - 15.0)^2 = \underline{0.01}$
Total 0.10

$$s = \sqrt{\dfrac{\sum_1^n (x_i - \bar{x})^2}{n}}$$

$$= \sqrt{\dfrac{0.10}{5}} = 0.14.$$

The unbiased estimate of the universe standard deviation is computed

$$\hat{\sigma} = s\sqrt{\dfrac{n}{n-1}} = 0.14\sqrt{\dfrac{5}{4}} = 0.16$$

and expressed in alternate form by

$$\hat{\sigma} = \sqrt{\dfrac{\sum_1^n (x_i - \bar{x})^2}{n-1}} = \sqrt{\dfrac{0.10}{5-1}} = 0.16.$$

An Unbiased Estimate of the Standard Error of the Mean. If a sample of items is drawn from a universe for which σ is unknown, the standard error of the mean must be estimated from the sample or a complete enumeration of the universe must be made, which is often impractical or impossible. For such a case, the sample standard deviation can be corrected for small sample bias and used as an estimate of σ. Formula 6.2 can be rewritten to utilize the result of Formula 6.4 and to obtain an expression of the desired estimate written

$$\hat{\sigma}_{\bar{x}} = \dfrac{\hat{\sigma}}{\sqrt{n}} \quad \dotfill (6.5)$$

Multiplying the numerator and the denominator of Formula 6.5 by $\sqrt{\dfrac{n-1}{n}}$ provides an alternative expression of an unbiased estimate of $\sigma_{\bar{x}}$. This estimate is given by

$$\hat{\sigma}_{\bar{x}} = \dfrac{s}{\sqrt{n-1}} \quad \dotfill (6.6)$$

■ Example. Four trucks are tested to estimate the average fuel consumption per truck for a fleet of trucks. The fuel consumption for the four trucks, in miles per gallon, for a 5,000-mile test run is: 12.1, 11.8, 12.4, and 11.7. The average consumption rate is 12.0 miles per gallon. An estimate of the standard error of the mean is computed

$$(12.1 - 12.0)^2 = 0.01$$
$$(11.8 - 12.0)^2 = 0.04$$
$$(12.4 - 12.0)^2 = 0.16$$
$$(11.7 - 12.0)^2 = \underline{0.09}$$

Total 0.30

$$\hat{\sigma}_{\bar{x}} = \frac{\hat{\sigma}}{\sqrt{n}} = \frac{\sqrt{\dfrac{0.30}{4-1}}}{\sqrt{4}}$$

$$= \frac{0.316}{2} = 0.158.$$

The estimate of the standard error of the mean is also computed by:

$$\hat{\sigma}_{\bar{x}} = \frac{s}{\sqrt{n-1}} = \frac{\sqrt{\dfrac{0.30}{4}}}{\sqrt{4-1}} = \frac{0.274}{1.732} = 0.158.$$

Distribution of Sample Proportions *; never use t distribution*

Sampling is frequently used to estimate an *attribute* of a universe such as the proportion of items in the universe that have a particular characteristic. For example, an auditor may wish to estimate the proportion of accounts that are incorrect; or a national survey service may wish to estimate the proportion of voters that favors a presidential candidate. The law of large numbers and the central limit theorem apply to sampling involving proportions and provide the basis for estimating universe attributes.

The Characteristics of the Distribution of Sample Proportions. If samples of the same size are drawn from a population, different results can be obtained in terms of the number or proportion of successes per sample. Each of the distinct samples that can be drawn from a population defines a sample point. The probability of a success occurring on any one of the trials of a sample is π. The probability of a failure is $1 - \pi$. The probability associated with a sample point is expressed by the binomial probability $P(r|n, \pi)$.

The fraction of successes in n trials is $p = r/n$ and is defined as the *sample proportion*. Expressing the number of successes r as a fraction of n, the sample size, the corresponding binomial probabilities are unchanged.

Thus, the sampling distribution of p is a binomial distribution. Recalling that $E(r) = n\pi$, the expression of the sample proportion $p = r/n$ may be substituted for r to obtain the mean where $E(p) = \pi$. This mean is an expression of one form of the law of large numbers, for as n becomes large, the expected difference between the sample proportion r/n and the universe proportion π approaches zero. It follows that the sample proportion is an unbiased estimator of the universe proportion and $p = \hat{\pi}$.

The central limit theorem applies to the distribution of sample proportions, for given that the value of π is known, the distribution of sample proportions is approximately normal with a mean of π. Recalling that $\operatorname{var}(r) = n\pi(1 - \pi)$ (the variance of a binomial distribution), and substituting the sample proportion $p = r/n$ for r, the expression for the standard deviation of the sampling distribution of proportions is written

$$\sigma_p = \sqrt{\frac{\pi(1-\pi)}{n}} \qquad \qquad \text{.............................(6.7)}$$

■ *Example.* In a large marketing area 0.40 of the consumers prefer an upright to a chest-type freezer. A sample of $n = 5$ consumers is to be drawn. Let r denote the number of consumers in the sample who prefer an upright freezer. The values of r that can occur in the sample are $r = 0, 1, 2, \ldots, 5$. The number of successes r may be expressed as a sample proportion $p = r/n$, which can take on the values $\frac{0}{5}, \frac{1}{5}, \frac{2}{5}, \ldots, \frac{5}{5}$, each with a corresponding binomial probability $P(p = r/n) = \binom{5}{r}$ $(0.40)^r(0.60)^{5-r}$. These probabilities are listed in Table 6.2.

TABLE 6.2

Values of $P\left(p = \dfrac{r}{5}\right)$ for All Possible Values of r

$$
\begin{aligned}
P(p = \tfrac{0}{5}) &= 0.0778 \\
P(p = \tfrac{1}{5}) &= 0.2592 \\
P(p = \tfrac{2}{5}) &= 0.3456 \\
P(p = \tfrac{3}{5}) &= 0.2304 \\
P(p = \tfrac{4}{5}) &= 0.0768 \\
P(p = \tfrac{5}{5}) &= \underline{0.0102} \\
&\quad\ 1.0000
\end{aligned}
$$

The probability distribution of p is shown in Figure 6.4, where the heights of the bars of the histogram correspond to the probability of drawing a sample with given values of p. The mean, the variance, and the standard deviation of the distribution are computed as

$$E(p) = \pi = 0.40,$$

$$\text{var}(p) = \frac{\pi(1-\pi)}{n} = \frac{0.24}{5} = 0.048$$

$$\sigma_p = \sqrt{\frac{\pi(1-\pi)}{n}} = \sqrt{0.048} = 0.219.$$

Unbiased Estimate of the Standard Error of Proportions. The standard deviation of proportions of samples that can be drawn from a universe with a known value of π is expressed by Formula 6.7. This expression is termed the *standard error of the proportion* and indicates the extent to which a sample proportion can be expected to deviate from the universe proportion. Viewed in this manner, the standard error of the proportion σ_p is analogous to the standard error of the mean $\sigma_{\bar{x}}$.

An unbiased estimate of the standard error of the proportion can be obtained by using Formulas 6.3 and 6.7. The sample value of p is substituted for π in Formula 6.7, and this sample estimate is corrected for bias by use of Formula 6.3 to give

$$\hat{\sigma}_p = \sqrt{\frac{p(1-p)}{n}} \sqrt{\frac{n}{n-1}}$$

FIGURE 6.4

Values of $P\left(p = \dfrac{r}{5}\right)$ for All Possible Values of r

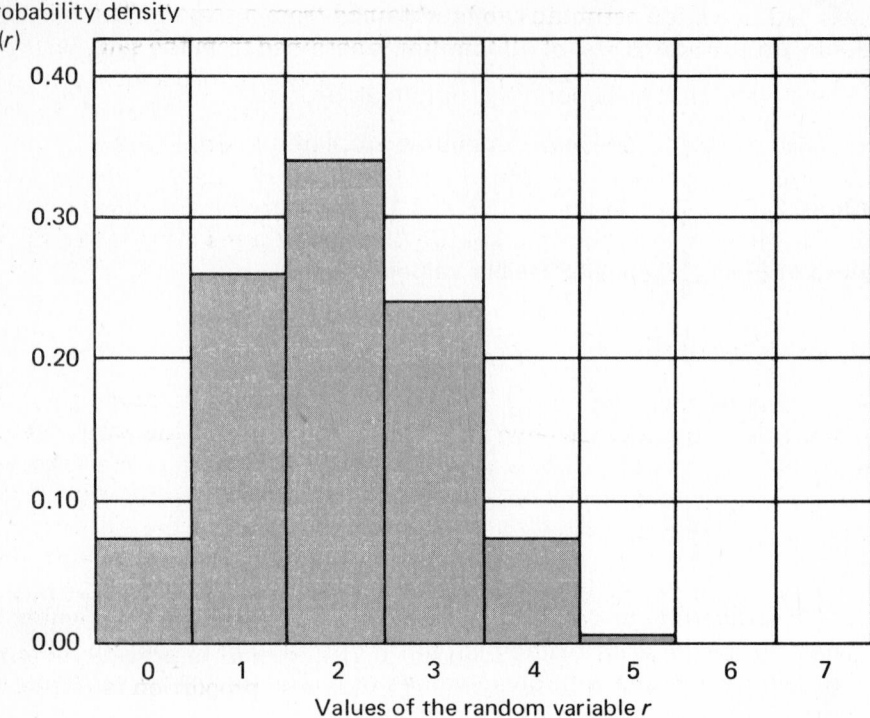

Probability density $P(r)$

Values of the random variable r

$$\hat{\sigma}_p = \sqrt{\frac{p(1-p)}{n-1}} \quad \dotfill \quad (6.8)$$

■ *Example.* A chemical process produces polyethylene containers. It is known that some defective items are produced by the process. A sample of 26 items, selected at random, includes two defective items. Since the value of π is unknown, it is estimated by p, which is computed

$$\hat{\pi} = p = \frac{2}{26} = 0.077.$$

The estimated standard error is computed by use of Formula 6.8 to give

$$\hat{\sigma}_p = \sqrt{\frac{p(1-p)}{n-1}} = \sqrt{\frac{(0.077)(0.923)}{26-1}} = 0.053.$$

ESTIMATION OF INFINITE UNIVERSE PARAMETERS

A number of remarks are made in the discussions of probability and probability distributions that point to the value of these concepts in making estimates of universe parameters on the basis of sample results. Statistical estimation is a part of statistical inference, which is the process of making estimates or inferences concerning universe parameters. For example, if the average annual expenditure for entertainment per family in a geographic area is unknown, an estimate can be obtained from a sample. The estimate of the average expenditure of all families is obtained from the sample mean. This type of estimate that consists of a single value is called a *point estimate*. The concept of the standard error of the mean indicates, however, that the dispersion of sample means about the universe mean can be predicted and a more informative type of estimate called an *interval estimate* can be made. This type of estimate states in terms of probability the likelihood that the universe mean will occur in a specified range expressed in terms of the standard error of the mean.

Point Estimates

If a sample proportion is used to estimate the universe proportion, the statistic p as a random variable is called an *estimator* of the parameter π. The value this variable takes on is called the *point estimate*. While the expected value of a sample proportion is $E(p) = \pi$, the discussion of the distribution of sample proportions indicates that the value of the estimate p is not likely to be precisely the same value as π. While point estimation does have limitations, it is a valuable tool for decision making.

If one must rely on a single value as an estimate of a parameter, it is desirable to select the random variable that is expected to provide the most dependable estimate. For example, if the universe proportion is to be estimated, why not use $\left(\dfrac{m}{n}\right)^2$, $\sqrt{\dfrac{m}{n}}$, or some other statistic as the estimate of π? Any random variable with a range from zero to one could be used as an estimator. The problem is to decide which statistic is the best estimator.

The best estimator is the one that is most suitable to a given problem, most likely to give the desired result, is the least risky, or has other desirable properties. The statistical properties of estimators may be analyzed by four criteria: they should be consistent, efficient, unbiased, and sufficient. These properties are considered in the discussions that follow.

Properties of Good Estimators. Returning to the question concerning the use of $\left(\dfrac{m}{n}\right)^2$, $\sqrt{\dfrac{m}{n}}$, or some other statistic as an estimate of π, consider the case in which one can sample the entire universe. If the entire universe is examined, the sample size is N, the number of items in the universe, and neither $\left(\dfrac{m}{N}\right)^2$ nor $\sqrt{\dfrac{m}{N}}$ is equal to π, unless π is zero or one. However, the value of the variable $\dfrac{m}{n}$, for which $n = N$, is precisely the value of π.

This result demonstrates an important property of a good estimator. If a statistic, viewed as a variable, is a good estimator of a universe parameter, and if a large sample is taken, the estimate should differ only slightly from, if not be precisely equal to, the parameter. An estimate with these properties is said to be *consistent*.

In other words, as the sample size becomes large, the probability that the estimate will differ from the parameter value by even some small amount approaches zero as a limit. On the basis of the foregoing definition, which is based on Tchebycheff's inequality, it follows that $\bar{x}$ is a consistent estimator of μ, where $\bar{x} = \hat{\mu}$, and p is a consistent estimator of π. The median is a consistent estimator of μ for a symmetric universe, but other properties of the median make it a much less desirable estimator than $\bar{x}$.

The second property of a good estimator, efficiency, is illustrated by means of an example. Consider a plant that has two automatic machines which produce identical parts. The machines can be adjusted so that each produces parts with the same average dimension, except that the dispersion of the items produced by the older machine is considerably more than the newer one. Suppose that one day the machines are producing parts with the same but unknown average dimension.

In order to determine the average dimension of the produced parts, a sample is to be taken from the production of one of the machines. Which of the machines is expected to provide the better information? The standard error of the mean is $\sigma_{\bar{x}} = \dfrac{\sigma}{\sqrt{n}}$. The degree to which a sample mean can be expected to deviate from μ is a function of σ, if the sample size is constant. Consequently, the mean of a sample taken from the output of the machine with the smallest degree of dispersion is expected to produce an estimate that is said to be the most *efficient*. It follows from this definition that the mean of a sample is a relatively more efficient estimator of μ than is the sample median. The variance of the mean is less than that of the median since $\sigma_{Md} = 1.25\sigma_{\bar{x}}$.

The discussion of the properties of the distribution of sample standard deviations indicates the bias inherent in estimating universe dispersion on the basis of sample data. A sample standard deviation is a biased estimator of σ. A good estimator must be *unbiased* such that the expected value of the estimator is the value of the parameter for all sample sizes. For example, $\sigma_x = s\sqrt{\dfrac{n}{n-1}}$ is an unbiased estimator of σ for any sample size and all values of σ.

A fourth property required for a good estimator is that the estimator be *sufficient*. Examples of sufficient statistics are $\bar{x}$ and p, which are estimators of μ and π, respectively. These estimators are sufficient since, given the value of these statistics, no additional information can be obtained from a sample that is of any benefit in estimating μ or π. In other words, if the value of the sufficient estimator is known, the individual sample values as such do not provide any additional information about the value of the parameter.

Summary of Distribution Characteristics, Parameters, and Estimators. In the study of sampling distributions and estimation, it is important to distinguish the various distributions of universe, sample, and sample means or proportions. Principal characteristics of the respective distributions are shown in Table 6.3. Note that the distribution of items in a random sample is expected to be like that of the universe from which it was drawn. For example, if the universe shape is rectangular, the shape of the distribution of items in a sample will tend to be rectangular. Also, in the case of attributes, the proportion of items in a sample will tend to be like that of the universe from which it was drawn.

An important difference occurs in the case of sample means or proportions, for the distribution of sample means or proportions tends to be normal or approximately normal whatever the shape of the universe. For example, in the case of measured variables, if many samples of the same size are drawn randomly from a rectangular universe, the means of the samples will

TABLE 6.3

Summary of Distribution Characteristics

Distribution	Distribution shape or expected shape	Expected value	Standard deviation
	Measured variables		
Universe	any distribution with a finite σ	μ	σ
Sample	expected to be like the universe	$\bar{x}$	s
Sample means	normal or approximately normal	$\bar{\bar{x}}$	$\sigma_{\bar{x}}$, estimated by $\hat{\sigma}_x$ if σ is unknown
	Attributes		
Universe	two-valued discrete distribution of a Bernoulli process	π	$\sqrt{\pi(1-\pi)}$
Sample	expected to be like the universe	p	$\sqrt{p(1-p)}$
Sample proportions	binomial and approximately normal	$\bar{p}$	σ_p, estimated by $\hat{\sigma}_p$ if π is unknown

tend to be normally distributed. In the case of attributes, if many samples of the same size are drawn randomly, the distribution of sample proportions will tend to be approximately normally distributed even though the universe will not be normally distributed. These normal distributions of sample means and proportions are the basis for making interval estimates of universe parameters, which are discussed in the next section.

Sampling is frequently employed to estimate the mean value of items in a universe or the proportion of items in a universe that have a particular attribute. The principal parameters and corresponding estimators are as follows:

Parameter	Estimator
μ	$\hat{\mu} = \bar{x}$
σ	$\hat{\sigma} = s\sqrt{\dfrac{n}{n-1}}$
$\sigma_{\bar{x}}$	$\hat{\sigma}_{\bar{x}} = \dfrac{s}{\sqrt{n-1}}$
π	$\hat{\pi} = p$
σ_p	$\hat{\sigma}_p = \sqrt{\dfrac{p(1-p)}{n-1}}$

Each sample statistic (estimator) provides a good point estimate of the respective universe parameter. These estimators are used in making interval estimates of parameters.

Interval Estimates

The process of making point estimates of parameters by the use of good estimators provides valuable information for making judgments concerning the value of a parameter. A moment's reflection on the nature of the distributions of sample statistics enables one to see that even the best point estimate may deviate enough from the parameter value to make the estimate unsatisfactory. For this reason it is common practice to estimate a parameter in terms of an interval.

Interval Estimates for Means. The properties of the distribution of sample means are especially useful in demonstrating the concept of using an interval to estimate a parameter. The central limit theorem provides that the distribution of sample means can be considered normal even if the universe is not normal or symmetric. As a consequence, one can say that if a sample of n items is drawn from a universe with a mean μ and a variance σ^2, the probability is 0.95 that the mean of the sample will have a value in the interval from $\mu - 1.96\sigma_{\bar{x}}$ to $\mu + 1.96\sigma_{\bar{x}}$. This probability may be written as

$$P(\mu - 1.96\sigma_{\bar{x}} \le \bar{x} \le \mu + 1.96\sigma_{\bar{x}}) = 0.95.$$

Note that the likelihood interval is expressed in terms of the standard error of the mean, which is the standard deviation of sample means, and *not* in terms of the standard deviation of either the universe or a sample.

■ Example. The average unit cost of producing a product is $\mu = \$5.00$, with a standard deviation of $\sigma = \$0.10$. The product is produced in batches of 25 units. A batch is selected and is considered to be a random sample. The average unit cost for the 25 items is unknown, but the probability is 0.95 that the sample mean $\bar{x}$ has a value in the interval

$$\mu - 1.96 \frac{\sigma}{\sqrt{n}} \leq \bar{x} \leq \mu + 1.96 \frac{\sigma}{\sqrt{n}}.$$

This is expressed numerically as

$$5.00 - 1.96 \frac{0.10}{\sqrt{25}} \leq \bar{x} \leq 5.00 + 1.96 \frac{0.10}{\sqrt{25}}$$

or

$$\$4.96 \leq \bar{x} \leq \$5.04.$$

The foregoing example illustrates the interval within which the values of $\bar{x}$ are expected to occur, given the values of μ and σ. It is usually true that μ is unknown and must be estimated. The best point estimate of the parameter is $\bar{x}$, but $\bar{x}$ may deviate somewhat from μ. The best estimate of μ therefore consists of the point estimate plus an expression of the interval about $\bar{x}$ within which μ may be expected to occur with a given probability. This type of estimate is called an *interval estimate*.

One of the characteristics of the normal distribution is that it becomes asymptotic for values of the normal variable which differ extensively from the mean. The distribution of sample means tends to be normal and, theoretically, a sample mean may take on *any* value as the result of the random selection of sample items. Consequently, it is not possible to "draw the line" on sampling error, and one cannot say that it is certain that chance in the form of sampling error will not produce a sample mean which is larger than some upper limit or smaller than some lower limit. It is possible to state in terms of probability the likelihood that a mean will take on a value in a specified interval. This type of interval is called a *confidence interval*. The general form of an interval estimate of μ is written

$$\bar{x} - z_{\frac{\alpha}{2}} \sigma_{\bar{x}} \leq \mu \leq \bar{x} + z_{\frac{\alpha}{2}} \sigma_{\bar{x}} \dots\dots\dots\dots\dots\dots(6.9)$$

where z is expressed in standard deviation units and $\frac{\alpha}{2}$ is the probability that μ will exceed a specified limit.

■ Example. From experience, it is known that a grinding machine produces items with a universe standard deviation of 0.100 inches. In the course of a working day, the machine has a breakdown which requires that the machine be reset. With this new setting, it is not certain what the mean dimension of the finished items may be. In order to be sure that the items produced will meet specifications, a sample of 36 items is taken randomly from those produced after the new setting. These items have a mean of 2.100 inches, the point estimate of μ. The probability is 0.95 that μ has a value in the confidence interval

$$2.100 - 1.96 \, \frac{0.100}{\sqrt{36}} \leq \mu \leq 2.100 + 1.96 \, \frac{0.100}{\sqrt{36}}$$

or

$$2.067 \leq \mu \leq 2.133.$$

This interval is seen in Figure 6.5. The halves of two curves are shown in this figure as an alternative way of viewing a confidence interval. In this manner the probability is 95% that $\bar{x}$ will not differ from μ by more than $1.96\sigma_{\bar{x}}$ if μ is as small as 2.067 inches or as large as 2.133 inches.

FIGURE 6.5

A 95% Confidence Interval of μ for Specified Values of σ, n and $\bar{x}$

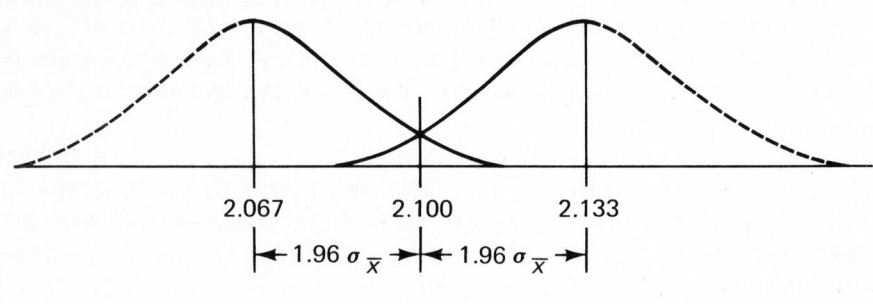

2.067   2.100   2.133

$\leftarrow$ 1.96 $\sigma_{\bar{x}}$ $\rightarrow$$\leftarrow$ 1.96 $\sigma_{\bar{x}}$ $\rightarrow$

Inches

The probability associated with a confidence interval is termed the *level of confidence* or the *confidence coefficient*. From the foregoing discussion, it follows that an interval estimate with a 100% level of confidence is infinitely large. However, one must settle for something less than certainty in making interval estimates. A major point to be considered is that it is impossible to prove that a parameter lies in any finite interval.

A one-sided confidence interval may be computed for the case in which just one limit is desired. Suppose this limit is the lower limit of an interval for estimating μ. The interval is written

$$\bar{x} - z_{\alpha}\sigma_{\bar{x}} \leq \mu \quad \ldots\ldots\ldots\ldots\ldots\ldots\ldots\ldots\ldots\ldots(6.10)$$

where the confidence interval extends to infinity.

■ *Example.* A trucking firm is considering a contract for the purchase of tires for a fleet of trucks. The firm is particularly interested in the average mileage that can be obtained per tire. A sample of 100 tires is tested and the average mileage per sampled tire is 25,000 miles. The standard deviation for all tires is 2,000 miles. The firm is concerned with avoiding the purchase of tires for which the average mileage is low. Consequently, a one-sided interval estimate is to be made. A 95% confidence interval estimate of μ is written

$$X - z_{0.05}\sigma_{\bar{x}} \leq \mu$$

and computed

$$25,000 - 1.64\frac{2,000}{\sqrt{100}} \leq \mu$$

or

$$24,672 \leq \mu.$$

The value of $z = 1.64$ is obtained from Appendix H for a probability of $0.50 - 0.05 = 0.45$.

In this example $z_{0.05}$ implies that the area is in one tail of the curve, since a one-sided interval is computed. This type of problem is illustrated in Figure 6.6. The area to the left of the lower limit is 5%, and the value of z is 1.64. The 95% confidence interval estimate of μ is the unshaded portion of the curve. In other words, it may be stated with 95% confidence that μ is *at least as large* as the lower limit of the interval.

FIGURE 6.6

A One-sided Interval Estimate of μ with a Level of Confidence of 95%

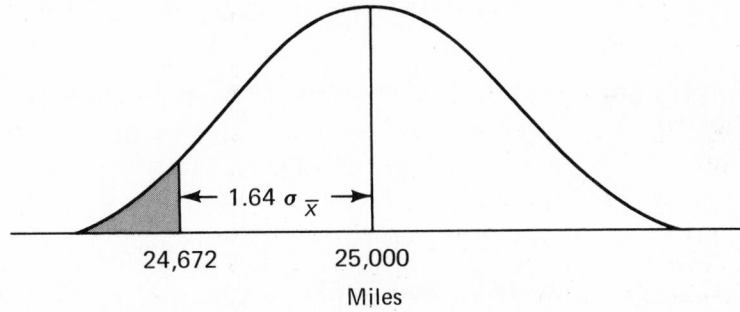

Interval Estimate of the Universe Proportion. The technique of making an interval estimate of the universe percent is applied in much the same fashion as in the case of estimating the universe mean. A confidence interval for a universe proportion is written

$$p - z_{\frac{\alpha}{2}}\hat{\sigma}_p \leq \pi \leq p + z_{\frac{\alpha}{2}}\hat{\sigma}_p \quad \text{.........(6.11)}$$

Ch. 6   Sample Distributions and Estimation

$$\hat{\sigma}_p = \sqrt{\frac{p(1-p)}{n-1}}$$

where p is the point estimate of π, the value of α is related to the level of confidence, and $\hat\sigma_p$ is the estimated standard error of the proportion.

■ **Example.** A sample of 400 sales invoices is drawn randomly from a large number of invoices, and 12 of the invoices have been processed incorrectly. The sample proportion $p = 12/400 = 0.03$ provides a point estimate of the universe proportion, but management wishes to have a confidence interval estimate of π such that the probability is 0.98 that π has a value in the interval. The 98% confidence interval estimate of π is written

$$p - z_{\frac{\alpha}{2}} \hat\sigma_p \le \pi \le p + z_{\frac{\alpha}{2}} \hat\sigma_p$$

and computed

$$0.03 - 2.33 \sqrt{\frac{0.03(1 - 0.03)}{400 - 1}} \le \pi \le 0.03 + 2.33 \sqrt{\frac{0.03(1 - 0.03)}{400 - 1}}$$

to give

$$0.01 \le \pi \le 0.05.$$

Interval Estimate of the Universe Percent. The calculation of interval estimates for proportions involves decimals, which are moderately troublesome computationally if squares or square roots are involved. For this reason, the sample percent is often used in calculations. The conversion from proportion to percent is accomplished by multiplying by a factor of 100. For example, for $p = 0.60$ and $n = 50$, the corresponding estimated values of the universe percent and the standard error of the percent are

$$100p = 100(0.60) = 60\%$$

$$\hat\sigma_{\text{percent}} = \sqrt{\frac{100p(100 - 100p)}{50 - 1}} = \sqrt{\frac{(60)(40)}{49}} = 7\%.$$

The 95% confidence interval based on a percent of 60 and a sample size of 50 is computed

$$60 \pm 1.96 \sqrt{\frac{(60)(40)}{49}}$$

$$60 \pm 1.96(7).$$

The confidence limits are 46.3% and 73.7%.

The corresponding result using a proportion is computed

$$0.60 \pm 1.96 \sqrt{\frac{(0.60)(0.40)}{49}}$$

$$0.60 \pm 1.96(0.07).$$

The confidence limits are 0.463 and 0.737. The two methods give the same results, as long as one is consistent in substituting p or $100p$ in the formulations.

SMALL SAMPLES AND STUDENT'S *t* DISTRIBUTION

In the discussion of the central limit theorem, it was stated that if a universe (with any distribution shape) has a mean, μ, and a finite standard deviation, σ, the distribution of sample means approaches a normal distribution with a mean, μ, and a standard deviation (standard error), $\sigma_{\bar{x}} = \sigma/\sqrt{n}$, as the sample size becomes large. The distribution of sample means can be standardized by the transformation

$$z = \frac{\bar{x} - \mu}{\dfrac{\sigma}{\sqrt{n}}}.$$

The statistic z is normally distributed with a mean of zero and a standard deviation of one. Probabilities corresponding to areas of the normal distribution of z can be determined by use of tables (see Appendix H or I). The statistic z provides an approximation of the transformation for sample proportions written

$$z = \frac{p - \pi}{\sigma_p}.$$

Student's *t* Distribution

In order to compute the statistic z the universe standard deviation must be known. Often the universe standard deviation is not known and must be estimated, as must the standard error of the mean. In that case the appropriate transformation is

$$t = \frac{\bar{x} - \mu}{\dfrac{s}{\sqrt{n-1}}} \quad\dotsfill\text{(6.12)}$$

where $\dfrac{s}{\sqrt{n-1}} = \dfrac{\hat{\sigma}}{\sqrt{n}} = \hat{\sigma}_{\bar{x}}$ is the *estimated standard error of the mean.*

The distribution of the statistic t is called *Student's t distribution* after the pen name "Student," used by W. S. Gosset, who published the pioneer work in 1908.

The statistic z is computed from a ratio that involves one random variable, $\bar{x}$, in the numerator of the ratio; and z is normally distributed. In contrast the statistic t is computed from a ratio that involves two random variables, $\bar{x}$ in the numerator and $\hat{\sigma}_{\bar{x}}$ in the denominator of the ratio, and t is not normally distributed. The t distribution, shown in Figure 6.7, is a symmetrical distribution and approaches normality as the sample size becomes large. More precisely, the t distribution has a different shape for each number of *degrees of freedom,* defined as the sample size minus one $(n-1)$. The abbreviation for degrees of freedom is *d.f.* The smaller the degrees of freedom, the more the t distribution differs from the normal distribution. Thus, if the universe standard deviation is not known and an

FIGURE 6.7

Shape of Student's *t* Distribution

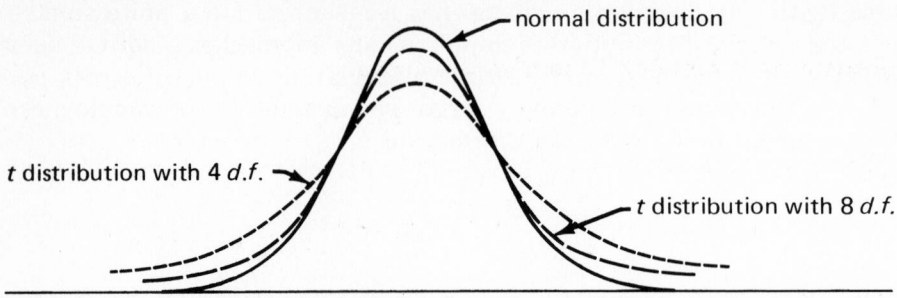

estimate is to be made from a small sample, the statistic *t* should be used in computing interval estimates of μ.

Because the *t* distribution has many different shapes, it is not practical to tabulate the entire distribution as is done for the normal distribution. This would require many tables of *t* values. Instead, only those values of *t* that give certain specified areas in the two tails are shown in the table in Appendix J.

> ■ *Example.* Suppose one wishes to find the value of $\pm t$ which leaves 5% of the total area of the distribution in the two tails when the sample size is 21. Since $n = 21$, $d.f. = 20$, and the appropriate column in the *t* table in Appendix J is 0.05:
>
> $$t_{0.05} \ (20 \ \textit{d.f.}) = \pm 2.086.$$

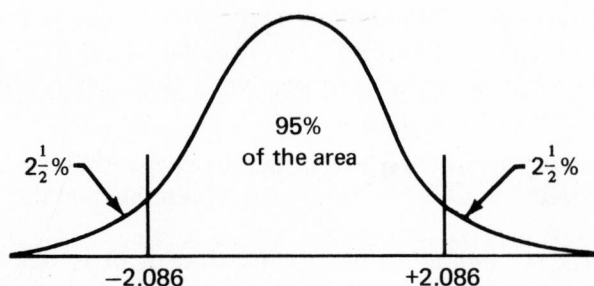

For more than 120 degrees of freedom, the table values of *t* are the same as the comparable value of *z*. For example,

$$z_{\alpha=0.05} = t_{\alpha=0.05}(\infty \, d.f.) = \pm 1.96.$$

Interval Estimates for Means, Small Samples

In the previous example it was shown that 5% of the area of the *t* distribution lies outside $\pm t_{0.05}$ and that 95% of the area lies between $\pm t_{0.05}$. This can be stated another way. There is a 95% probability that any t value computed from a random sample will fall between $\pm t_{0.05}$. This can be expressed as the following inequality:

$$-t_{0.05} \leq t \leq + t_{0.05}.$$

Substituting Formula 6.12 for t in the above,

$$\bar{x} - t_{0.05}\hat{\sigma}_{\bar{x}} \leq \mu \leq \bar{x} + t_{0.05}\hat{\sigma}_{\bar{x}}.$$

This may be written in a more general form to give an interval estimate of μ as

$$\bar{x} - t_\alpha \hat{\sigma}_{\bar{x}} \leq \mu \leq \bar{x} + t_\alpha \hat{\sigma}_{\bar{x}} \quad \dots\dots\dots\dots\dots\dots\dots\text{(6.13)}$$

where
 t is expressed in units of the estimated standard error of the mean, and α is the probability that μ will exceed the limits of the interval.

■ *Example.* Suppose a quality control engineer wishes to estimate the average strength of a particular part being manufactured for an assembly operation. The measure is in terms of pounds per square inch (psi) that can be resisted before the part breaks. Because destructive sampling is costly, the engineer uses a small sample of eight parts. The engineer also decides on an $\alpha = 0.01$. The results of the sample are:

$$\bar{x} = 254 \text{ psi} \qquad\qquad n = 8 \text{ parts}$$
$$s = 24 \text{ psi} \qquad\qquad t_{0.01}\,(7\ d.f.) = \pm 3.499.$$

Then
$$\hat{\sigma}_{\bar{x}} = \frac{s}{\sqrt{n-1}} = \frac{24}{\sqrt{7}} = 9.07 \quad \text{and}$$
$$254 - 3.499(9.07) \leq \mu \leq 254 + 3.499(9.07).$$

It may be stated that there is a 99% probability that μ is not less than 222.3 psi nor greater than 285.7 psi. This may give the engineer all the information needed, in spite of the fact that a very small sample was used.

INTERVAL ESTIMATES AND SAMPLE SIZE

The size of an interval estimate depends on the universe standard deviation, the level of confidence chosen, and the sample size. The effect of each of these factors is introduced in preceding sections. This concept is considered in more detail in this section to provide a basis for determining the sample size needed to produce an interval estimate with a specified range.

Sample Size for an Interval Estimate of μ

If the value of σ is known, a level of confidence is specified, and the allowable error in estimating μ is given, a confidence interval of μ can be produced by selecting a sample of the correct size. For example, the average outstanding balance of signature loans issued by a bank varies from month to month. From experience, it is known that the amounts are normally distributed, with a standard deviation of $500. The bank wishes to compute an interval estimate of μ so that the probability is 0.95 that the point estimate will not differ from μ by more than $60. The fact that the confidence interval is symmetrical simplifies calculations. The above conditions specify that the maximum deviation E, or *allowable error*, of $\bar{x}$ from μ be

$$E = \bar{x} - \mu = \$60.$$

For a level of confidence of 95%,

$$E = \$60 = 1.96\sigma_{\bar{x}}.$$

The sample size for this condition is computed by solving for n as follows:

$$\$60 = 1.96\frac{\$500}{\sqrt{n}}$$

$$(\$60)^2 = \frac{3.84(\$500)^2}{n}$$

$$n = \frac{3.84(\$500)^2}{(\$60)^2}$$

$$n = 267.$$

If a sample of $n = 267$ accounts is selected, the probability is 0.95 that the mean of the sample will not deviate by more than $60 from the universe mean, whatever its value. The formal expression for the general case is written

$$n = \left[\frac{z \cdot \sigma}{E}\right]^2 \quad\text{..(6.14)}$$

■ *Example.* A drug manufacturer wishes to control statistically the production of an antibiotic by taking samples periodically to compute an interval estimate of the process mean. It is especially important that accurate estimates of μ be made, because if there is a substantial shift in the process, the drugs may be hazardous for human consumption. It is known from production records that $\sigma = 10$ milligrams. The maximum allowable error is two milligrams and the level of confidence is specified as 99%. The desired sample size is computed

$$n = \left[\frac{(2.58)(10)}{2}\right]^2 = 166.$$

Sample Size for an Interval Estimate of π

A desired level of precision in estimating a universe proportion can be achieved by selecting an appropriate sample size. If no information is available concerning the universe proportion, a small pilot study can be made to obtain an estimate, or one can assume a value of π of 0.50, for which the standard error is a maximum for any fixed sample size. For example, for a sample size of 100, the standard error for selected values of π are as follows:

Value of π	σ_p
0.10	$\sqrt{\dfrac{(0.10)(0.90)}{100}} = 0.03$
0.25	$\sqrt{\dfrac{(0.25)(0.75)}{100}} = 0.04$
0.50	$\sqrt{\dfrac{(0.50)(0.50)}{100}} = 0.05$
0.75	$\sqrt{\dfrac{(0.75)(0.25)}{100}} = 0.04$
0.90	$\sqrt{\dfrac{(0.90)(0.10)}{100}} = 0.03.$

For a given sample size, the standard error is a maximum for $\pi = 0.50$.

Given a value of E, the allowable error, and a level of confidence, the sample size for making an interval estimate of π is computed by solving

$$p - \pi = E = z_\alpha \sqrt{\frac{\pi(1-\pi)}{n}}$$

for the value of n to obtain

$$n = \pi(1-\pi)\left[\frac{z_\alpha}{E}\right]^2 \quad \text{...............................(6.15)}$$

■ *Example.* A firm wishes to estimate with an error of no more than 0.03 and a level of confidence of 98% the proportion of consumers that prefers its brand of household detergent. Sales reports indicate that about 0.20 of all consumers prefer the firm's brand. The required sample size is computed as

$$n = (0.20)(0.80)\left[\frac{2.33}{0.03}\right]^2$$

$$= 965.$$

■ *Example.* A television station wishes to estimate, within 5%, the percent of viewers in an area that prefer a given program. The estimate is to be made with a level of confidence of 90%. The station has no information concerning the likely value of the percent of viewers preferring the program. The number of items that should be included in the sample is found by substituting percent for proportion in Formula 6.15 and solving

$$n = (50)(50)\left[\frac{1.64}{5}\right]^2$$

$$= 269.$$

ESTIMATION OF FINITE UNIVERSE PARAMETERS

The statistical concepts developed in this chapter to this point are based on the assumption of an infinite universe. Even the selection of a large sample from an infinite universe does not alter the value of the universe parameters. Suppose a universe is finite and consists of 300 items. If a sample of 125 is selected randomly without replacement from the universe, the size and variance of the universe will be steadily reduced as the sample is drawn. For this reason some modification is required in making estimates based on samples drawn from finite universes. As a rule of thumb, this type of modification is required if the sample size is 5% or more of the parent population.

The Finite Multiplier

Where the sample size is a significant proportion of the universe (more than 5%), it is necessary to apply a *finite multiplier*, which is written

$$\frac{N - n}{N - 1}$$

where N is the population size and n is the sample size. The finite multiplier is approximately equal to the proportion of items in the finite universe that is not included in the sample. The fraction or proportion of universe items included in the sample is called the *sampling fraction* and is written

$$f = \frac{n}{N}.$$

The fraction of universe items not in the sample is

$$1 - f = 1 - \frac{n}{N} \dots\dots\dots\dots\dots\dots\dots\dots\dots\dots(6.16)$$

Typically, the size of the universe is sufficiently large so that the difference between N and $N - 1$ is negligible. The fraction of universe items not sampled is very nearly the same value as the finite multiplier. Written symbolically, this relationship is

$$1 - f = \frac{N - n}{N} \cong \frac{N - n}{N - 1}.$$

Because these quantities are very nearly the same, the fraction of items not sampled is very often used as the finite multiplier. This fraction will be used in the remainder of this presentation when a finite correction is indicated. The finite correction is always appropriate in computing interval estimates, but the ratio approaches one for an infinite universe. If sample items are drawn from a finite universe but sampling is done with replacement, the universe is, in effect, infinite.

Interval Estimate of the Mean of a Finite Universe

The foregoing discussion indicates that the formula for the standard error of the mean for samples drawn without replacement from a finite universe must be modified. This modification is accomplished by computing the variance of means by

$$\sigma_{\bar{x}}^2 = \frac{\sigma^2}{n}(1-f).$$

The standard error of the mean for a finite universe is written

$$\sigma_{\bar{x}} = \frac{\sigma}{\sqrt{n}}\sqrt{1-f}\dots\dots\dots\dots\dots\dots\dots\dots\text{(6.17)}$$

The standard error of the mean computed by Formula 6.17 is used to make interval estimates in much the same manner described in the preceding discussion of interval estimation.

■ *Example.* An auditor selects randomly, without replacement, a sample of 36 accounts from the total file of 100 accounts receivable to estimate the mean balance of all accounts. If the standard deviation of the balance of the universe of accounts is $60 and the sample mean is $240, the 95% interval estimate of μ is

$$\bar{x} \pm z_{0.05}\frac{\sigma}{\sqrt{n}}\sqrt{1-f} \qquad \$240 \pm (1.96)\frac{60}{\sqrt{36}}\sqrt{1-\frac{36}{100}}$$

$$\$240 \pm (1.96)(10)\sqrt{0.64}$$

$$\$240 \pm \$15.68.$$

The confidence interval is

$$\$224.32 \text{ to } \$255.68.$$

The use of good estimators applies to finite populations. For example, if σ is unknown, the estimated standard error of the mean of a finite universe is computed

$$\hat{\sigma}_{\bar{x}} = \frac{s}{\sqrt{n-1}}\sqrt{1-f}\dots\dots\dots\dots\dots\dots\dots\text{(6.18)}$$

■ *Example.* A milling machine is used in a manufacturing plant to produce metal parts of different sizes. The machine is adjusted to produce a given number of parts of a specified size. Then the machine must be reset to produce parts of another size. Following a resetting, a sample of production is taken to determine if the parts are, on the average, of the desired size. In such a case the mean and the standard deviation are unknown prior to sampling. After one such adjustment of the machine, a bin of 200 parts is produced and a sample of 25 is selected without replacement. The sample mean is 4.200 inches and the standard deviation is 0.060 inches. The 95% confidence interval estimate of the average dimension of parts being produced is computed as

$$\bar{x} \pm t_{0.05} \frac{s}{\sqrt{n-1}} \sqrt{1-f} \qquad\qquad 4.200 \pm (2.064)\frac{0.060}{\sqrt{25-1}} \sqrt{1 - \frac{25}{200}}$$

$$4.200 \pm (2.064)(0.01225)(0.935)$$

$$4.200 \pm 0.0236$$

where
$t_{0.05} = 2.064$ is read from Appendix J for 24 *d.f.*

The confidence interval is 4.1764 to 4.2236.

Interval Estimate of the Universe Percent

The finite multiplier may be applied to the estimation of the universe percent in a manner analogous to the estimation of a universe mean. If a sufficiently large sample is drawn without replacement from a finite universe, the standard error of the percent should be corrected by application of the finite multiplier. The estimated standard error of the percent of a finite universe is written

$$\hat{\sigma}_p = \sqrt{1-f}(100) \sqrt{\frac{p(1-p)}{n-1}} \qquad\qquad\qquad (6.19)$$

■ *Example.* A salvage dealer purchases 300 used forced-air heaters and wishes to estimate the percent of heaters that are in working condition. A sample of 40 heaters is taken randomly and 32 of the heaters are found to be in working order. The 95% confidence interval estimate of the universe percent is computed

$$100p \pm 1.96 \sqrt{1-f}(100) \sqrt{\frac{p(1-p)}{n-1}}$$

$$80 \pm 1.96 \sqrt{1 - \frac{40}{300}}(100) \sqrt{\frac{0.80(1-0.80)}{40-1}}$$

$$80 \pm (1.96)(0.931)(100)(0.0640)$$

$$80 \pm (1.96)(5.96)$$

$$80 \pm 11.68.$$

The confidence interval is 68.32 to 91.68.

STATISTICAL QUALITY CONTROL CHARTS

The term "mass production" calls to mind the concept of manufacturing large numbers of identical and interchangeable items. In reality, it is impossible to produce two items that are identical. If all dimensions are measured with sufficient precision, it can be determined that the objects differ in some degree. Manufacturing specifications or tolerance limits take into account the variability of "identical" items and allow a tolerance range within which measurements must fall. Manufactured items that fall within the tolerance limits are judged to be of acceptable quality and interchangeable. Items that do not meet specifications must be scrapped or reworked.

It is possible to ensure that all manufactured items or parts meet specifications by inspecting each object for quality. This procedure requires that each object produced be gauged or measured for quality, but 100% inspection of items is expensive. Worker fatigue and other factors also tend to make this type of inspection less than fully reliable. In the majority of instances, statistical quality control techniques can be applied to reduce the total cost of inspection. These techniques take into account the manufactured items and the distributions of sample statistics.

Classes of Variability

The variations in the characteristics of mass-produced items may be classified in terms of the sources of the variations. One class of variations encompasses those that are the result of factors that can be identified. The observed variation can be associated with the source. For example, marked variations in a product dimension may be observed as the result of the adjustment of a machine by an operator, a change in the character of input raw material, or mistakes made by workers. These sources produce variations that tend not to be predictable statistically. Variations of this type are called *assignable variations*. Since the magnitude of these variations tends to be large, the sources of the variations can be assigned and eliminated.

A second class of variation includes variations that result from the interaction of a combination of many random variables that produce slight differences in product characteristics. Individually, these variables induce only slight changes in product dimensions, and it is impossible or uneconomical to identify or eliminate these causes. For example, slight changes in temperature, pressure, friction, metal hardness, and similar factors interact randomly to produce slight variations in product quality. Variations of this type are called *random variations,* are viewed as being characteristic of the production process, and tend to be predictable statistically.

Control Charts for Variables

The identifying of assignable variations is facilitated by describing random variation in terms of probable limits of variation. These limits, called *control limits,* are based on the distributions of sample statistics. The control limits are presented graphically by *control charts* that depict the pattern of variation inherent in a process during a period of observation. Control charts indicate whether variations can be considered to be random or if assignable variations are also indicated. Control charts for variables are based on measured quantities. The most widely used are control charts for sample means and for ranges.

Control Charts for Sample Means. A *control chart for sample means,* or an $\bar{x}$ *chart,* is based on the distribution of sample means. It is used to determine if variations in a product dimension are random and to detect assignable variations. The control chart is based on a series of samples or *subgroups* of items drawn randomly from a process over a period of time. The arithmetic means of samples are computed and the dispersion of these means reflects the pattern of variation of the process. The mean of the sample means $\bar{\bar{x}}$ is computed as an unbiased estimate of the universe or process mean.

The control limits for an $\bar{x}$ chart are the estimated $3\sigma_{\bar{x}}$ limits about the mean of the normal distribution of sample means. Calculating the values of the control limits is made easier by use of sample ranges, for ranges are easy to compute. The ranges of samples are summarized by the average range $\bar{R}$. The value of $3\sigma_{\bar{x}}$ is estimated by $A_2\bar{R}$, where A_2 is a constant for a given sample size and $\bar{R}$ is the mean range for a group of samples. Values of A_2 for selected sample sizes are listed in Table 6.4.

TABLE 6.4

Values of A_2 for Computing Control Limits for $\bar{x}$ Charts

n	A_2
2	1.880
3	1.023
4	0.729
5	0.577
6	0.483
7	0.419
8	0.373
9	0.337
10	0.308

The estimated $3\sigma_{\bar{x}}$ limits about the universe mean are written

$$UCL_{\bar{x}} = \bar{\bar{x}} + A_2\bar{R} \quad\text{......................(6.20)}$$

$$LCL_{\bar{x}} = \bar{\bar{x}} - A_2\bar{R} \quad\text{......................(6.21)}$$

where $UCL_{\bar{x}}$ is called the *upper control limit* and $LCL_{\bar{x}}$ is the *lower control limit* for sample means. These limits reflect the range within which 99.73% of random variations of sample means are expected to occur. Sample means that fall outside these limits, while possibly reflecting random variation, tend to indicate assignable variation. It is expected that only 0.27% of sample means will occur outside the control limits as the result of random or chance variation.

■ *Example.* Samples or subgroups of four items each are drawn randomly from the output of a machine that produces shafts. The machine is one of several identical machines that produce the shafts with a distribution of diameters summarized in Figure 6.8. The sample results are listed in Table 6.5. The mean diameter of all sampled parts is computed

$$\bar{\bar{x}} = \frac{443.00}{15}$$

$$= 29.53.$$

FIGURE 6.8

Control Chart for the Means of Samples of Four Shafts Drawn from the Output of a Machine

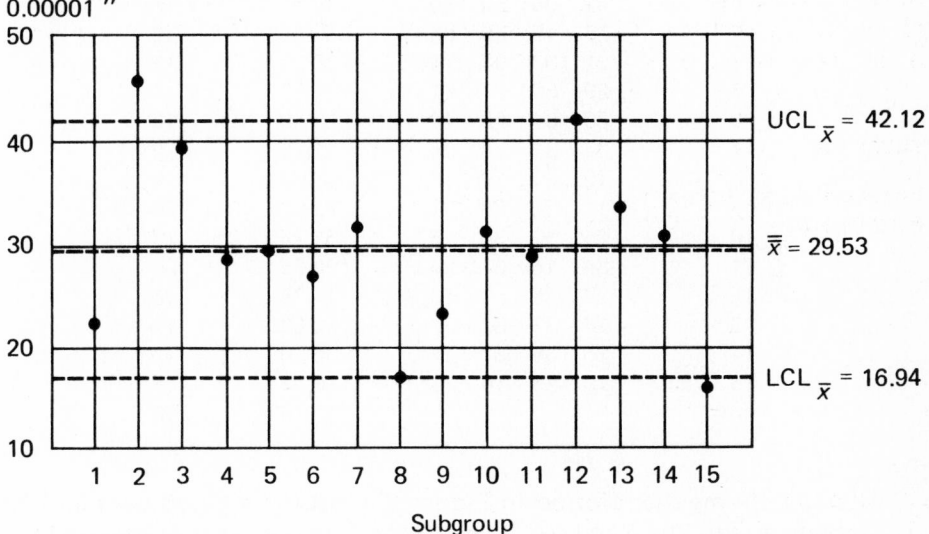

Source: Table 6.5.

The control limits for a control chart for means are computed on the basis of the mean range, which is computed

$$\bar{R} = \frac{259}{15}$$

$$= 17.27.$$

The control limits are found by use of the A_2 factor for $n = 4$ read from Table 6.4 as follows:

$$UCL_{\bar{x}} = \bar{\bar{x}} + A_2\bar{R}$$
$$= 29.53 + (0.729)(17.27)$$
$$= 42.12$$

and

$$LCL_{\bar{x}} = \bar{\bar{x}} - A_2\bar{R}$$
$$= 29.53 - (0.729)(17.27)$$
$$= 16.94.$$

TABLE 6.5

Results of Fifteen Samples of Four Shafts Drawn from the Output of a Machine (Values expressed in 0.00001″ deviations from a nominal dimension)

Subgroup	Observed values				Mean	Range
1	32	20	33	6	22.75	27
2	42	36	52	50	45.00	16
3	25	15	52	63	38.75	48
4	22	33	34	23	28.00	12
5	29	30	27	31	29.25	4
6	30	34	26	16	26.50	18
7	34	31	28	34	31.75	6
8	12	21	19	16	17.00	9
9	11	22	28	31	23.00	20
10	36	30	35	26	31.75	10
11	34	16	37	26	28.25	21
12	27	36	51	53	41.75	26
13	26	35	32	37	32.50	11
14	25	36	37	24	30.50	13
15	10	28	14	13	16.25	18
Total					443.00	259

The sample means, plotted in Figure 6.8, reflect a significant lack of statistical stability. Samples 2 and 15 have means that lie beyond the control limits. The inference is drawn that assignable causes of variation were present as these samples were drawn.

Control Charts for Ranges. The variations in sample dispersion can be presented graphically by a *control chart for ranges* or an *R chart*. The procedure for constructing this type of chart is similar to that for preparing $\bar{x}$ charts. The control limits for ranges are based on an estimate of $3\sigma_R$, or three times the standard deviation of ranges of samples of a given size.

The distribution of sample ranges is neither normal nor symmetrical. Control limits for ranges, however, are assumed to be symmetrical without undue loss of precision. The exception to this rule occurs for a lower control limit for small samples, which is negative in some cases. Since negative ranges cannot occur, the lower limit is taken to be zero rather than some negative value.

Control Charts for Attributes

In contrast to a variable quantity that is a measured characteristic, the quality of a product may be judged also by whether a characteristic is of acceptable quality. For example, the quality of a shaft produced by a machine is dependent on the diameter of the shaft being within specifications. If the shaft diameter is too large or too small, the shaft is judged defective and of unacceptable quality. Only two outcomes can occur in appraising the quality of a shaft diameter, since the diameter is either within or without the specifications. This quality characteristic is called an *attribute*.

Control charts for attributes may be constructed to reflect the pattern of variation and stability of a process in terms of the proportion or fraction of items produced that are defective. Charts may also be based on the number of defects per unit of output.

Control Charts for Fraction Defective. Much of the quality inspection of the output of processes consists of applying a gauge or a standard to an item to determine if it is acceptable or defective. For example, an inspector uses a gauge to test shafts produced by a machine. If the shaft fits within the gauge, it is accepted; otherwise, it is judged to be defective. Similarly, an accountant may examine accounts receivable to determine the fraction of accounts that is delinquent (defective).

Control charts may be constructed to reflect the pattern of random variation in the fraction of items that is defective in the output of a process. A *control chart for fraction defective*, or *p chart*, is based on the distribution of sample proportions. It is assumed that the items are produced by a Bernoulli process. This assumption implies that (1) there are only two possible outcomes (acceptable or defective), (2) the outcomes occur randomly, and (3) the probability of either outcome remains unchanged for each trial.

The control limits of this chart are the estimated $3\sigma_p$ limits about the estimated universe proportion. In the majority of cases, the universe proportion is less than 0.50 and the distribution of sample proportions is skewed. The use of symmetrical control limits is similar to utilizing a normal approximation of a binomial as a suitable approximation. Relatively large samples are used in constructing p charts, because small samples do not provide satisfactory results.

An estimate of the universe proportion denoted p' is found by dividing the total number of defective units in all samples by the total number of items sampled. The control limits are obtained by computing

$$3\hat{\sigma}_p = 3\sqrt{\frac{p'(1-p')}{n}}$$

and

$$UCL_p = p' + 3\hat{\sigma}_p \dots\dots\dots\dots\dots\dots\dots\text{(6.22)}$$

$$LCL_p = p' - 3\hat{\sigma}_p \dots\dots\dots\dots\dots\dots\dots\text{(6.23)}$$

These control limits denote the tolerable range of random variation. A proportion that falls beyond these limits is assumed to be the result of an assignable cause of variation.

■ *Example.* A series of 20 samples of 100 transistors each are drawn randomly from the output of a process that produces several thousand units daily. Sampled items are inspected for quality, and faulty transistors are rejected. The estimated process proportion of defective items is computed by dividing the total number of defective units from all samples by the total number of items sampled to give

$$p' = \frac{220}{2,000} = 0.11.$$

The estimated standard error of the proportion is

$$\hat{\sigma}_p = \sqrt{\frac{(0.11)(0.89)}{100}} = 0.0313.$$

The control limits of a p chart are found as follows:

$$UCL_p = p' + 3\hat{\sigma}_p$$
$$= 0.11 + (3)(0.0313)$$
$$= 0.20$$

and

$$LCL_p = p' - 3\hat{\sigma}_p$$
$$= 0.11 - (3)(0.0313)$$
$$= 0.02.$$

Control Charts for Number of Defects. A control chart for fraction defective is useful for monitoring the quality of units produced by a Bernoulli process. There are applications, however, in which an item may fail to meet specifications in several respects. For example, a length of steel cable may be inspected for flaws and defects may be found in several different places. For this class of quality control problem, the Poisson rather than the binomial distribution is the appropriate theoretical basis. A control chart based on the Poisson distribution is called a *control chart for defects* or *c chart*.

A *defect* is defined as a success obtained in a trial from a Poisson process. It may also be viewed as the failure of a unit to meet specifications in any one of many possible locations. A single unit may contain any number of defects, and the unit may not necessarily be rejected even if one or more defects is present.

The expected number of defects per unit is denoted in the literature of statistical quality control by $\bar{c}$. This quantity corresponds to the value of λ, the mean of a Poisson process. The standard deviation of the process is written

$$\sigma_c = \sqrt{\bar{c}},$$

which is an alternative notation for the standard deviation of a Poisson distribution. The $3\sigma_c$ control limits of a c chart are obtained by computing

$$UCL_{\bar{c}} = \bar{c} + 3\sigma_c \dots\dots\dots\dots\dots\dots\dots\dots\dots\dots\dots\dots(6.24)$$

and

$$LCL_{\bar{c}} = \bar{c} - 3\sigma_c \dots\dots\dots\dots\dots\dots\dots\dots\dots\dots\dots\dots(6.25)$$

■ **Example.** A final inspection is conducted to check for proper adjustment of card readers produced by a computer manufacturer. Inspection records indicate that defects in each of the adjustments of the card reader mechanism occur in a Poisson distributed manner. The total number of defects per card reader, the sum of several Poisson processes, is itself a Poisson process. The results of the inspection of 20 card readers indicate a total of 90 defects. The average number of defects per unit is computed

$$\bar{c} = \frac{90}{20} = 4.5.$$

The standard deviation of the number of defects per unit is computed

$$\sigma_c = \sqrt{\bar{c}} = \sqrt{4.5} = 2.1.$$

The control limits for the number of defects per unit are computed

$$UCL_c = \bar{c} + 3\sigma_c$$
$$= 4.5 + (3)(2.1)$$
$$= 4.5 + 6.3$$
$$= 10.8$$

and

$$LCL_c = \bar{c} - 3\sigma_c$$
$$= 4.5 - 3(2.1)$$
$$= 4.5 - 6.3$$
$$= 0.$$

STUDY QUESTIONS

6-1. Explain briefly the meaning of each of the following terms:
  a. simple random sample
  b. random numbers
  c. Monte Carlo method
  d. Tchebycheff's inequality
  e. central limit theorem
  f. standard error of the mean
  g. standard error of the median
  h. standard error of the standard deviation
  i. standard error of the proportion
  j. point estimate
  k. interval estimate

l. confidence interval
m. level of confidence
n. Student's t distribution
o. degrees of freedom
p. allowable error
q. finite multiplier
r. sampling fraction
s. assignable variation
t. random variation
u. control limits
v. control chart
w. control chart for sample means ($\bar{x}$ chart)
x. attribute
y. control chart for fraction defective (p chart)

6–2. Describe the use of random numbers in sampling and simulation.

6–3. What inference can be made on the basis of Tchebycheff's inequality?

6–4. What are the characteristics of the distribution of sample means that make it significant to statistical inference?

6–5. Compare the distributions of sample means, sample medians, and sample standard deviations.

6–6. Why is it important to correct for bias in making estimates based on sample statistics?

6–7. Describe the properties of good estimators.

6–8. Outline the procedure for computing an interval estimate of the universe mean if:
   a. The universe standard deviation is known.
   b. The universe standard deviation is unknown.

6–9. What is the difference in the nature and application of the z and t statistics?

6–10. Why would a confidence interval of 95% rather than 100% be used in estimating a universe mean?

6–11. What information and assumptions must be given to compute the sample size for an interval estimate of the universe mean?

6–12. In what circumstances should the finite multiplier be used?

6–13. What is meant by statistical stability?

6–14. What is the theoretical basis for control charts for sample means? For sample ranges?

6–15. Contrast the characteristics of p charts and c charts.

PROBLEMS

6-1. The distribution of arrivals of ships at a loading dock is shown as follows:

Number of ships arriving per day	Frequency
0	0.30
1	0.40
2	0.18
3	0.09
4	0.03
	1.00

Select random numbers from Appendix N and use the Monte Carlo method to simulate the arrival of ships for 25 days and estimate the average number of ships arriving per day from the simulated results.

6-2. The service times required to load ships at a dock are summarized by the following distribution:

Service time (days)	Frequency
0.0 and under 0.5	0.63
0.5 and under 1.0	0.27
1.0 and under 1.5	0.08
1.5 and under 2.0	0.02
	1.00

Select random numbers from Appendix N and use the Monte Carlo method to simulate the times required to service 25 ships and estimate the average service time from the simulated results.

6-3. A universe consists of the numbers 2, 3, 4, 5, and 6. Show that the mean of the means of all possible distinct samples containing three numbers is equal to the universe mean.

6-4. A universe consists of the numbers 1, 2, 3, and 4. Show that the mean of the means of all possible distinct samples containing three numbers is equal to the universe mean.

6-5. A customer is selected at random from customers being checked out in a supermarket. The amount of the purchase being made by the customer is computed by the clerk. What is the probability that the computed purchase differs by more than 1.5 standard deviations from the average purchase of all customers?

6-6. The arrivals of automobiles at a municipal parking facility have a mean arrival rate of 30 vehicles per 15-minute period, with a standard deviation of 10 vehicles. A 15-minute period is selected at random and the arriving vehicles are counted.

  a. What is the probability that the number of vehicles arriving in the selected period is within 2.5 standard deviations of the mean arrival rate?

  b. The probability is 0.90 that the number of vehicles arriving in the selected period will be within what range of number of vehicles?

6-7. A freight train makes a regular run between two major cities. Records indicate that the average time required to complete the trip is 10 hours, with a standard deviation of 0.28 hours. If a sample of 49 trips is selected at random, what is the probability that:

  a. The sample mean will be in the range from 9.9 to 10.1 hours?

  b. The sample median will be in the range from 9.9 to 10.1 hours?

6-8. A worker in a shoe factory can attach heels to a type of shoe with an average of 40 per hour, with a standard deviation of three heels per hour. A random sample of 36 hourly periods is selected. What are the probabilities that the following sample statistics will have values greater than 39 heels per hour?

  a. Sample mean.

  b. Sample median.

6-9. A sample of dry-cell batteries is selected at random from the output of a process, and the useful life of each battery (in hours) is 24, 28, 27, 30, 29, 26, 25. Compute an unbiased estimate of the universe standard deviation and the estimated standard error of the mean.

6-10. The length of time required to repair machines in a factory is recorded for a sample of 10 machines. The results (in hours) are: 0.5, 1.3, 0.7, 1.5, 1.1, 0.9, 1.6, 0.7, 0.8, 0.9. Compute an unbiased estimate of the universe standard deviation and an estimate of the standard error of the mean.

6-11. The useful life of a type of automobile tires is known to vary, and the standard deviation has been determined from experience to be 1,500 miles. A sample of 25 tires is tested, and the mean life of the sample tires is 26,000 miles. Compute the 90% confidence interval estimate of the mean life for the type of tires.

6-12. Boxes of cereal are filled by a machine, and samples of boxes periodically are taken at random to estimate the average weight of cereal in filled boxes. The machine is known to vary in the amount of cereal actually put into boxes, with a standard deviation of 0.2 ounces. If a sample of 16 boxes is selected and has a mean weight of 15.9 ounces, what is the 95% confidence interval estimate of the mean weight of boxes filled by the machine?

6-13. Registration records indicate that 40% of voters in an area belong to a particular political party. In a telephone survey, 144 names of voters are selected at random. The probability is 0.90 that the proportion of voters in the sample that belong to the party will be in what range?

6–14. A company that sells detergents has determined from industry sales records that its share of the market is 20%. If a sample of 100 retail stores that sell the product is selected randomly, the probability is 0.95 that the share of the market indicated by the sample will be in what range?

6–15. A new machine is installed in a manufacturing plant and is operated for the first time. A sample of 26 items of the initial output is taken randomly. The sample consists of observations of the diameter of cylindrical metal rods. The sample average is 1.030 inches, and the standard deviation is 0.020 inches.
  a. What is the point estimate of the universe mean diameter? (sample mean)
  b. Find the 98% confidence interval estimate of the universe mean.
  c. Compute the 95% one-sided interval estimate of the upper range of the universe diameter.

6–16. In an audit of inventory accounts in a company, a sample of 17 accounts is selected at random. The mean value of the sampled accounts is $526 and the standard deviation is $132.
  a. What is the point estimate of the mean value of all inventory accounts in the universe?
  b. Compute the 95% confidence interval estimate of the universe mean.

6–17. A random sample of 25 vehicle records is drawn from the files of an automobile insurance company. The selected records indicate that six of the vehicles were involved in a collision within the past year.
  a. What is the point estimate of the universe proportion of vehicles involved in a collision in the period of a year?
  b. Compute the 95% confidence interval estimate of the universe proportion.

6–18. Using the data in Problem 6–17:
  a. Compute the 90% confidence interval estimate of the universe proportion.
  b. Solve Problem 6–17 in terms of universe percent.

6–19. A study is made to estimate the average length of calls made from a telephone booth in an airline terminal. The mean call length is to be estimated within 0.30 minutes with a level of confidence of 98%. Past studies show the standard deviation of call lengths to be approximately 0.90 minutes. If call lengths are distributed normally, what size sample should be taken?

6–20. A new machine (see Problem 6–15) is operated for the first time, and management wishes to obtain a 98% confidence interval estimate of the universe mean with upper and lower limits that differ by 0.012 inches. If the universe standard deviation is estimated to be 0.020 inches, how large a sample should be selected?

6-21. A marketing research department wishes to estimate the useful life of automobile tires in terms of miles driven. It is estimated that 50% of the tires have a useful life that ranges from 18,000 to 20,000 miles per tire. If useful life (miles) is distributed normally, how large a sample should be taken to estimate average useful life so that the probability is 95% that the universe mean does not differ from the sample mean by more than 400 miles?

6-22. A meat-packing firm wishes to determine the proportion of customers who purchase a new brand of dog food distributed by the firm. The estimate is to be computed so that the probability is 95% that the estimate will differ by no more than 0.03 from the universe proportion. What sample size should be used in making the estimate?

6-23. An insurance firm estimates that 18% of passengers purchase flight insurance in a particular airline terminal. An estimate of the true proportion of passengers who purchase flight insurance is to be computed so that the estimated proportion will differ from the universe proportion by no more than 0.05 with a level of confidence of 95%. Compute the sample size required.

6-24. The average time in days required to process orders received by a metal fabrication company is to be estimated. A sample of 20 orders is selected randomly from a total of 200 orders processed over a period of six months. The sample mean is 5.4 days, with a standard deviation of 1.2 days. Compute the 95% interval estimate of the average processing time.

6-25. The maintenance records of digital computers leased to customers by a manufacturer are analyzed to determine the frequency of service calls that involve failures in the input-output equipment. A random sample of 25 calls is drawn from a total of 200 calls recorded over a period of a month. Ten of the sampled service calls involved failures in input-output equipment. Compute the 95% confidence interval estimate of the universe percent.

6-26. A chemical plant produces a plastic material in bulk. Periodically, samples of the plastic material are drawn to monitor the hardness of the material. The tolerance limits for mean hardness are 55 ± 3 hardness units. The results of samples drawn from the process are listed as follows:

Subgroup	Sample values				
1	60.5	55.4	51.2	59.8	56.7
2	71.2	57.3	64.7	50.3	54.4
3	58.1	50.4	55.4	52.7	60.9
4	48.2	54.1	46.2	56.8	58.9
5	47.3	59.7	55.0	48.4	49.6
6	53.7	46.3	57.5	52.0	55.7
7	57.8	56.4	59.6	61.2	54.5

8	62.3	57.2	58.8	50.4	59.7
9	45.8	56.1	52.3	52.2	51.1
10	54.1	42.6	50.1	47.6	43.3
11	63.4	52.1	54.9	49.7	64.9
12	58.7	57.2	53.6	54.3	56.7
13	55.0	48.6	57.4	54.6	55.4
14	53.6	48.2	50.2	50.3	57.2
15	51.2	54.9	57.4	55.3	56.2

a. Compute the control limits and draw a control chart for means.
b. Determine if the process exhibits statistical stability.
c. Is the process capable of meeting the tolerance limits for mean hardness?

6-27. A machine fills boxes with dry cereal. Samples of four boxes are drawn randomly. Draw a control chart for sample means and determine whether the process exhibits statistical stability. The total weights of the sampled boxes are shown as follows:

Subgroup	Sample values			
1	11.02	10.81	10.94	11.07
2	10.98	11.21	11.04	11.26
3	11.04	10.79	10.92	11.01
4	10.97	11.31	11.27	11.25
5	11.15	10.97	10.89	10.91
6	11.34	11.18	11.36	11.40
7	10.87	11.17	10.93	11.03
8	10.82	10.76	11.01	10.85
9	11.60	11.48	11.56	11.52
10	11.43	11.15	11.14	11.56
11	10.54	10.81	10.91	10.78
12	11.59	11.74	11.68	11.95
13	11.23	11.19	11.02	11.04
14	11.67	11.54	11.63	11.60
15	11.72	11.41	11.61	11.46
16	10.81	11.17	11.02	11.08
17	11.24	11.19	11.27	11.34
18	11.23	11.14	11.15	11.12
19	11.45	11.71	11.58	11.82
20	11.47	11.32	11.33	11.60

SELECTED READINGS

Bryant, Edward C. *Statistical Analysis,* 2d ed. New York: McGraw-Hill Book Company, Inc., 1966.

Sampling and estimation are related to probability and the normal distribution in Chapter 4.

Grant, Eugene L. *Statistical Quality Control,* 4th ed. New York: McGraw-Hill Book Company, Inc., 1972.

A thorough development of control charts is presented in Chapters 3 through 12.

McMillan, Claude, and Richard F. Gonzalez. *Systems Analysis: A Computer Approach to Decision Models,* 3rd ed. Homewood, Illinois: Richard D. Irwin, Inc., 1973.

Techniques of generating random numbers for Monte Carlo simulation are presented in Chapter 11.

Chapter 7
Sample Design

In Chapter 6, the student was introduced to the basic theory of simple random sampling. This chapter is devoted to some of the practical problems involved in the application of that theory to sample surveys. Special emphasis is given to stratified and cluster sample designs which permit the researcher to get more precise sample results at a lower cost than would be possible using a pure random sample.

The advantages of using sampling to gather information are both numerous and pervasive. The following list includes only a few of the most important reasons that compel business, industry, government, labor unions, and many others to become heavily involved in using the sampling techniques discussed here.

1. It is less costly to obtain information from a sample than from a complete universe.
2. The information may be secured more quickly from a sample. A complete census of the population of the United States might take an entire year. Much of that information could be secured through sampling in a matter of weeks.
3. Sample information may be more accurate than that obtained by studying all the members of the population because of the factor of boredom. Inspection programs used to inspect the quality of goods by industrial firms and governmental agencies are good examples.
4. Sample data may be secured when a census would be impossible. For example, to test the quality of a television picture tube, it might be necessary to operate it until it burned out. The manufacturer cannot afford to use such destruction tests for all production, but a small sample will provide useful information about the quality of the product.

SAMPLING PRINCIPLES AND TERMS

Before discussing the problems involved in sample design, it is first appropriate to review a few basic sampling principles described in Chapter 6 and to define some additional terms that will be needed.

All sampling described previously has been simple random sampling or probability sampling in which each item in the universe has an equi-probable or known chance of being selected as a member of the sample. There are two advantages to this type of sampling:

1. Probability theory can be used to measure the precision of sample results.
2. Bias which might otherwise result from the exercise of personal judgment in the selection of sample items may be avoided.

Precision and Accuracy

The difference between a sample result and the result of a complete census enumeration taken under the same conditions is referred to as the *precision* of the sample result. This difference is also called *sampling error* or the *reliability* of the sample result. The standard error of a statistic is the measure of the precision of the estimate – the smaller the standard error, the greater the precision of the estimate and the smaller the sampling error. A sample design which is logically correct and properly executed will, never-theless, produce sampling error as long as all the observations in the universe are not included in the sample.

The difference between the sample result and the true state of the universe is called the *accuracy* of the sample result. This difference may include other types of error besides sampling error. For example, the difference may be caused by a clerical error, a computational error, or an incorrect answer to an unclear question used on a survey. Nonsampling error obviously can occur while completing a census as well as while taking a sample.

While it is the accuracy of the survey results with which a business is most concerned, it is the precision of the survey results that the statistician is able to measure. And the precision of the sample can be measured only if proper methods of random selection are used.

■ *Example.* If a random sample of 100 items is drawn from an infinite universe with a standard deviation of 4, the standard error of the mean is computed

$$\sigma_{\bar{x}} = \frac{\sigma}{\sqrt{n}} = \frac{4}{\sqrt{100}} = 0.4.$$

The value of 0.4 is a measure of the precision of the sample, and it can be computed or estimated depending on the information at hand. The accuracy of the sample result will be the closeness of the sample mean to the mean of the universe after considering all other kinds of error. This value is never known and cannot be computed by the statistician.

Definition of the Population

In Chapter 1 a population, or a universe, was defined as each member of some group. A parameter has been defined as a quantity that describes a population. Once the population has been defined carefully, the sample must be drawn from that population and no other. Further, the sample statistic may be used to estimate a parameter of the population from which the sample was drawn and no other.

■ *Example.* Suppose a state highway department establishes tourist information offices on its borders to give travel information to out-of-state visitors who stop to inquire for help. A sample of the visitors who stop at the offices are asked to estimate the number of nights they will stay in the state and an average number of nights per tourist is computed from their answers. Can this sample statistic be used to estimate the average number of nights all tourists will stay in the state? The answer is "no." The reason can be seen in the figure below.

Since the sample was drawn from Universe B, which is a subset of Universe A, the statistic can be used only to estimate the parameter of B, not A. It is quite possible that the characteristics of Universe A are different from those of Universe B. The tourists who stop to ask for help may not be typical of those who do not stop.

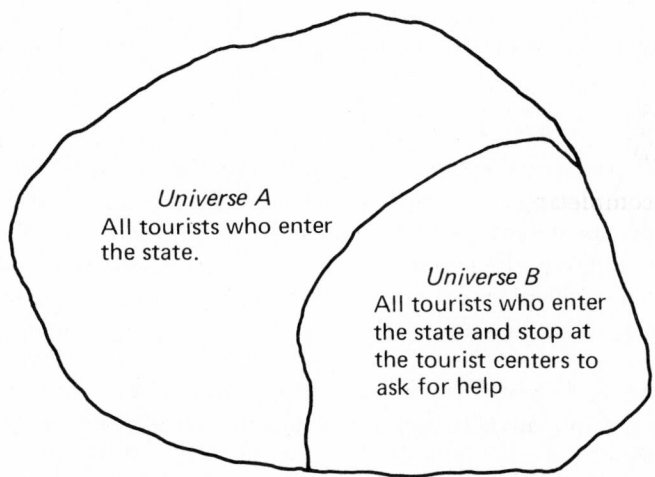

Universe A
All tourists who enter the state.

Universe B
All tourists who enter the state and stop at the tourist centers to ask for help

Some Problems in Simple Random Sampling

While the concept of simple random sampling is readily understood, its execution is often difficult or extremely expensive. A random sample of lottery tickets can be drawn easily from a drum that has been revolved to be sure that the tickets are thoroughly mixed, but it is not possible to select homemakers or personnel folders in this manner to get a random sample. A table of random numbers may be used to select a random sample if each item in the universe has, or can be assigned, a number; but this is not always possible.

In order to be sure that each item in the universe has an equal chance of selection, one needs a list or a *frame* from which to draw the sample. If a sample of households is being drawn from all of those in a large city, there may be no frame available. The universe may be defined as all the households within the city limits so that the survey team knows where the items in the universe are, but it does not know who they are. Any attempt to draw up a frame would be both difficult and very expensive. Families move in and out so rapidly that no list would ever be completely accurate. An approach to this problem will be discussed later in this chapter under the heading, "Cluster Sampling."

INCREASING THE EFFICIENCY OF SAMPLE DESIGN

A discussion of the problems involved in increasing the efficiency of sample design requires both a definition of what is meant by sample design and what is meant by increased efficiency. A *sample design* is a plan for securing a sample from a given universe. This planning takes place before obtaining any sample data, and it involves such considerations as cost, sample size, precision requirements, and the way in which the sample is to be secured.

One sample design is said to be more *efficient* than another when it:

1. Produces a smaller standard error with the same size sample, or
2. Produces the same standard error with a smaller size sample.

Discussions on simple random sampling have shown that the magnitude of the standard error can be reduced in a given sampling distribution only by increasing the size of the sample. It can be demonstrated with an example that if the sample is drawn in a particular way from the universe, the resulting standard error can be reduced without using a larger sample. In other words, by drawing a sample in a particular way and under certain conditions, a more efficient sample can be drawn than is possible with a pure random sample. It should be carefully noted that while the number of possible samples of a given size that can be drawn is reduced by the new sample design, each sample that may be drawn is still a random sample and thus its standard error may be estimated.

■ *Example.* Listed below is a hypothetical universe of seven items. The universe mean and the standard deviation have been computed and also are shown.

Item	Value	Parameters
A	5	
B	15	$\mu = 9$
C	4	$\sigma^2 = 28$
D	16	$\sigma = 5.29$
E	3	
F	6	
G	14	

If all possible simple random samples of $n = 4$ are drawn from this universe of $N = 7$, there are

$$_NC_n = {_7}C_4 = 35 \text{ possible samples.}$$

Table 7.1 shows the 35 samples, the possible values of $\bar{x}$, and the standard error of the mean, which is a measure of how much, on the average, $\bar{x}$ varies from μ.

The standard error of the mean may also be computed as

$$\sigma_{\bar{x}}^2 = \frac{\sigma^2}{n} \cdot \frac{N-n}{N-1} = \frac{28}{4} \cdot \frac{7-4}{7-1} = 3.5$$

$$\sigma_{\bar{x}} = \sqrt{3.5} = 1.87.$$

$$\bar{\bar{x}} = \frac{315.00}{35} = 9 = \mu \qquad\qquad \sigma_{\bar{x}} = \sqrt{\frac{\Sigma(\bar{x} - \bar{\bar{x}})^2}{_NC_n}} = \sqrt{\frac{122.500}{35}}$$

$$= \sqrt{3.5} = 1.87.$$

An examination of the size of the items in the universe shows two distinct groups:

Group	Individuals	Amounts	Totals
I	A, C, E, F	5, 4, 3, 6	18
II	B, D, G	15, 16, 14	45

If, again, all possible samples of $n = 4$ are drawn from this universe of $N = 7$, but with the additional restriction that two of the items in each sample must be drawn from each group, it is possible to have

$$(_4C_2)(_3C_2) = 6 \times 3 = 18 \text{ samples.}$$

Table 7.2 shows the 18 possible samples and the means of each. If the sample means are computed in the same way as those in Table 7.1 (an unweighted $\bar{x}$), the average of the sample means ($\bar{\bar{x}}$) is 9.75 which is greater than the universe mean (μ) of 9. This makes $\bar{x}$ a biased estimate of μ because the larger items in Group II are being given too much weight. Anytime the expected value of a statistic is either greater than or less than its parameter, the statistic is said to be biased. This bias can be overcome by computing a weighted arithmetic mean

$$\bar{x} = \frac{\Sigma w_h x_h}{\Sigma w_h} \text{ or } \frac{\Sigma N_h x_h}{N}$$

where

$w_h = N_h$, the weight assigned to the hth group, which is the number of universe items in the hth group

$N = \Sigma N_h$, the sum of all the weights used in the computation.

The weighted mean of the sample of ACBD in Table 7.1 is computed

TABLE 7.1

**All Possible Simple Random Samples of Size Four
That Might Be Drawn from a Universe of Seven Items**

Samples	Values	Totals	$\bar{x}$ Means	$\bar{x} - \bar{\bar{x}}$	$(x - \bar{\bar{x}})^2$
ABCD	5, 15, 4, 16	40	10.00	1.00	1.0000
ABCE	5, 15, 4, 3	27	6.75	−2.25	5.0625
ABCF	5, 15, 4, 6	30	7.50	−1.50	2.2500
ABCG	5, 15, 4, 14	38	9.50	0.50	0.2500
ABDE	5, 15, 16, 3	39	9.75	0.75	0.5625
ABDF	5, 15, 16, 6	42	10.50	1.50	2.2500
ABDG	5, 15, 16, 14	50	12.50	3.50	12.2500
ABEF	5, 15, 3, 6	29	7.25	−1.75	3.0625
ABEG	5, 15, 3, 14	37	9.25	0.25	0.0625
ABFG	5, 15, 6, 14	40	10.00	1.00	1.0000
ACDE	5, 4, 16, 3	28	7.00	−2.00	4.0000
ACDF	5, 4, 16, 6	31	7.75	−1.25	1.5625
ACDG	5, 4, 16, 14	39	9.75	0.75	0.5625
ACEF	5, 4, 3, 6	18	4.50	−4.50	20.2500
ACEG	5, 4, 3, 14	26	6.50	−2.50	6.2500
ACFG	5, 4, 6, 14	29	7.25	−1.75	3.0625
ADEF	5, 16, 3, 6	30	7.50	−1.50	2.2500
ADEG	5, 16, 3, 14	38	9.50	0.50	0.2500
ADFG	5, 16, 6, 14	41	10.25	1.25	1.5625
AEFG	5, 3, 6, 14	28	7.00	−2.00	4.0000
BCDE	15, 4, 16, 3	38	9.50	0.50	0.2500
BCDF	15, 4, 16, 6	41	10.25	1.25	1.5625
BCDG	15, 4, 16, 14	49	12.25	3.25	10.5625
BCEF	15, 4, 3, 6	28	7.00	−2.00	4.0000
BCEG	15, 4, 3, 14	36	9.00	0	0
BCFG	15, 4, 6, 14	39	9.75	0.75	0.5625
BDEF	15, 16, 3, 6	40	10.00	1.00	1.0000
BDEG	15, 16, 3, 14	48	12.00	3.00	9.0000
BDFG	15, 16, 6, 14	51	12.75	3.75	14.0625
BEFG	15, 3, 6, 14	38	9.50	0.50	0.2500
CDEF	4, 16, 3, 6	29	7.25	−1.75	3.0625
CDEG	4, 16, 3, 14	37	9.25	0.25	0.0625
CDFG	4, 16, 6, 14	40	10.00	1.00	1.0000
CEFG	4, 3, 6, 14	27	6.75	−2.25	5.0625
DEFG	16, 3, 6, 14	39	9.75	0.75	0.5625
	Total		315.00	0	122.5000

TABLE 7.2

All Possible Samples of Size Four That Might Be Drawn from a Universe of Seven When Two Sample Items Are Drawn from Each of Two Universe Groups

Samples	Values	Unweighted means		Weighted means		Deviation of the weighted means	
		Totals	Means $\bar{x}$	$\Sigma N_h x_h$	Means $\bar{x}$	$\bar{x} - \bar{\bar{x}}$	$(\bar{x} - \bar{\bar{x}})^2$
ACBD	5, 4, 15, 16	40	10.00	129	9.2	.2	.04
AEBD	5, 3, 15, 16	39	9.75	125	8.9	−.1	.01
AFBD	5, 6, 15, 16	42	10.50	137	9.8	.8	.64
CEBD	4, 3, 15, 16	38	9.50	121	8.6	−.4	.16
CFBD	4, 6, 15, 16	41	10.25	133	9.5	.5	.25
EFBD	3, 6, 15, 16	40	10.00	129	9.2	.2	.04
ACBG	5, 4, 15, 14	38	9.50	123	8.8	−.2	.04
AEBG	5, 3, 15, 14	37	9.25	119	8.5	−.5	.25
AFBG	5, 6, 15, 14	40	10.00	131	9.4	.4	.16
CEBG	4, 3, 15, 14	36	9.00	115	8.2	−.8	.64
CFBG	4, 6, 15, 14	39	9.75	127	9.1	−.1	.01
EFBG	5, 4, 15, 14	38	9.50	123	8.8	−.2	.04
ACDG	5, 4, 16, 14	39	9.75	126	9.0	.0	.00
AEDG	5, 3, 16, 14	38	9.50	122	8.7	−.3	.09
AFDG	5, 6, 16, 14	41	10.25	134	9.6	.6	.36
CEDG	4, 3, 16, 14	37	9.25	118	8.4	−.6	.36
CFDG	4, 6, 16, 14	40	10.00	130	9.3	.3	.09
EFDG	3, 6, 16, 14	39	9.75	126	9.0	.0	.00
	Total		175.50		162.00	0	3.18

Item	Value x	N_h	$N_h x_h$
A	5	4	20
C	4	4	16
B	15	3	45
D	16	3	48
Total	40	14	129

$$\bar{x} = \frac{129}{14} = 9.2.$$

Note that the value of N_h for item *A* is four because *A* represents a group of four individuals. The value of N_h for item *B* is three because *B* comes from a group of three. When the sample means are computed as weighted arithmetic means, $\bar{x} = \mu$, and $\bar{x}$ is an unbiased estimate of

μ. From Table 7.2 it can be seen that the unweighted mean of the sample means is

$$\bar{\bar{x}} = \frac{175.50}{18} = 9.75 > \mu,$$

whereas the mean of the weighted sample means is

$$\bar{\bar{x}} = \frac{162.0}{18} = 9 = \mu.$$

Computations based on Table 7.2 show the standard error of the mean to be 0.42, as compared with 1.87 for simple random samples of size four drawn from this same universe. In other words, the standard error has been reduced without an increase in sample size but as a result of the way in which the sample was drawn. The standard error of the mean is

$$\sigma_{\bar{x}} = \sqrt{\frac{\Sigma(\bar{x} - \bar{\bar{x}})^2}{(_4C_2)(_3C_2)}} = \sqrt{\frac{3.18}{18}}$$

$$= \sqrt{0.1767} = 0.42.$$

The greater precision of the second sample design can be clearly shown in Table 7.3 which compares the precision of the two sampling methods used in the previous example.

TABLE 7.3

A Comparison of the Precision of Two Sample Designs

Error $\frac{|\bar{x} - \mu|}{\mu} \cdot 100$	Pure random samples		Random samples with two items from each group	
	Number of means	Percent of total	Number of means	Percent of total
Under 5%	3	8.6	12	66.7
5% but under 10%	8	22.9	6	33.3
10% but under 20%	13	37.1	0	0
20% and over	11	31.4	0	0
Totals	35	100.0	18	100.0

STRATIFIED SAMPLING

The stage was set for a discussion of stratified sampling in the previous section where it was shown that under certain circumstances one sample design may be more efficient than another. The example in which the universe was divided into two groups involved stratified sampling. *Stratification* represents an approach to sample design in which available information about the universe can be used to get greater precision from sample estimates.

The Nature of Stratified Sampling

Stratified sampling techniques are based upon the knowledge that a universe which is highly heterogeneous may be divided into several groups or *strata* that are relatively homogeneous. A random sample of items is selected from each stratum, and these samples are then combined to form a single sample of the universe. The problem of determining the optimum number and type of stratum is one of the most difficult of all problems encountered in sampling.

> ■ *Example.* If a researcher were interested in estimating the sales of manufacturers in Texas in 1977, the universe would be made up of 13,679 firms making approximately 3,800 different classes of products. The researcher would almost certainly need to make an estimate from a sample of these firms and could use as the frame the *Directory of Texas Manufacturers,* published by the Bureau of Business Research of The University of Texas at Austin. The listing in this book for each company gives no information on volume of sales, but it does show the employee-size group for each firm. It is logical to assume that a firm with a large number of employees will also have a large volume of sales, while a firm with few employees will have a smaller volume of sales. Thus, the universe of firms might be divided into strata on the basis of a known characteristic—employee-size group—in order to study another characteristic, sales. The second variable is assumed to be correlated with the first. If this correlation is very high, the effects on efficiency will be much better than if the correlation is poor.

The sampling illustration used in the discussion of efficiency of sample design showed that certain samples that were possible under simple random sampling were not possible with stratified sampling. The combinations that were eliminated under stratified sampling were those which contained the extreme samples. For example, the range of sample means in Table 7.1 ran from a low of 4.50 to a high of 12.75 for simple random samples. The range of weighted sample means was only 8.2 to 9.8 in Table 7.2 for the stratified samples.

In stratified sampling, the objective is to reduce the standard error for a given sample size. This can be done where it is possible to stratify the units so that the differences between units within each stratum are as small as possible. At the same time the differences between strata averages should be as large as possible.

Stratification can be most effective when there are extreme values in the universe that can be grouped into one stratum.

■ **Example.** Assume that a large basket of fruit contains lemons, oranges, and grapefruit and that you wish to determine the average weight of the fruit by means of a sample. If you could first sort the fruit by kind into three baskets and draw a random sample of three fruit from each basket, your estimate of the universe mean would probably be more efficient than if you drew a pure random sample of nine fruit from the large basket before it had been sorted.

When the proportion of universe items in each stratum selected for the sample is the same for all strata, the result is called a *proportionate stratified random sample*. It is often more efficient, however, to select a smaller proportion of the items of one stratum than of another. When the sampling fractions are not the same for each stratum, the result is called a *disproportionate stratified random sample*. For example, in the illustration on Texas manufacturers, any manufacturer with 5,000 or more employees might, by virtue of size, be so important to the study that the investigator would want to be sure to include each member of that stratum in the sample. It might be necessary to include only one firm out of every 100 of the small firms with fewer than eight employees.

■ *Example.* The difference between a proportionate and a disproportionate stratified random sample is shown below:

Number of employees	N_h	Proportionate		Disproportionate	
		n_h	f_h	n_h	f_h
Under 8	5,000	200	0.04	180	0.036
8–49	6,150	246	0.04	185	0.030
50–99	675	27	0.04	75	0.111
100–999	150	6	0.04	25	0.167
1,000 and over	25	1	0.04	15	0.600
Total	12,000	480		480	

In this example:
N_h represents the number of firms in each employee group
n_h represents the number of sample firms selected from each employee group
$f_h = \dfrac{n_h}{N_h}$ is the sampling fraction for each employee group

If the proportionate sample is used in this example, no system of weights is required in computing the sample mean. If the disproportionate sample is used, the values of N_h should be used as weights to produce a sample mean which is unbiased.

The final decision as to the exact proportion of the universe to be included in the sample from each stratum is a complex one based on several interrelated factors. This subject is covered later in this chapter under the heading "Optimum Allocation."

If the universe is homogeneous, there is nothing to be gained by stratification. If, on the other hand, little is known about the universe, it may not be possible to arrange the data into strata.

Interval Estimates for Stratified Samples

Interval estimates for means, proportions, totals, and other parameters may be made from stratified samples. In this discussion only the means of large samples will be considered, but the student who wishes to explore sampling theory in greater detail will find a list of selected readings in this field at the end of this chapter.

The problem of dividing the universe into strata is largely a matter of judgment based on the information available about the universe. The problem of how large a sample to draw from each stratum will be considered later. At this point it is assumed that these two problems have already been solved and that the statistician is concerned with analyzing the results of the sample study.

After the universe has been divided into strata and samples have been drawn from each, the means can be combined into an estimate of the universe mean, and the variances of each stratum may be combined to estimate the standard error of the mean. It is then possible to produce an interval estimate of μ using any desired level for α.

Notation and Formulas

Several formulas and computational steps are needed to compute a confidence interval for the universe mean from the results of a stratified sample. Following the presentation of the necessary formulas and an explanation of the meaning of the notation, the formulas and computational steps are illustrated in a simple example to demonstrate how they can be applied.

Mean for a Stratum. The first step is to compute the mean of the sample values selected from each stratum: h

$$stratum \quad \bar{x}_h = \frac{\Sigma x_{hi}}{n_h} \quad \text{...................(7.1)}$$

where
 $\bar{x}_h$ is the mean of the hth stratum
 x_{hi} is the ith observation in the hth stratum
 n_h is the number of sample observations in the hth stratum.

(2) **Variance of a Stratum.** The next step is to compute an unbiased estimate of the variance of the universe items in each stratum:

$$\hat{\sigma}_h^2 = \frac{\Sigma(x_{hi} - \bar{x}_h)^2}{n_h - 1} \quad \dots\dots\dots\dots\dots\dots\dots\dots\dots (7.2)$$

where

$\hat{\sigma}_h^2$ is the variance of the hth stratum.

(3) **Mean of the Stratified Sample.** The sample means for all strata are averaged to get an unbiased point estimate of the universe mean. The averaging is done with a weighted arithmetic mean where the weights are the number of universe items in each stratum:

$$\bar{x}_{st} = \frac{\Sigma N_h \bar{x}_h}{N} \quad \dots\dots\dots\dots\dots\dots\dots\dots\dots (7.3)$$

where

$\bar{x}_{st}$ is the mean of the stratified sample

N_h is the weight or the number of universe items in the hth stratum

N is ΣN_h.

(4) **Variance of Sample Means for a Stratum.** When the variance for each stratum is divided by the number of sample observations taken from the stratum, the result is the square of the standard error of the mean for that stratum:

$$\hat{\sigma}_{\bar{x}_h}^2 = \frac{\hat{\sigma}_h^2}{n_h} (1 - f_h) \quad \dots\dots\dots\dots\dots\dots\dots\dots\dots (7.4)$$

where

$\sigma_{\bar{x}_h}^2$ is the variance of sample means for the hth stratum

f_h is $\dfrac{n_h}{N_h}$ is the sampling fraction for the hth stratum

$1 - f_h$ is the finite population correction for the hth stratum.

Standard Error of the Mean for the Stratified Sample. The variances of the mean for all strata are weighted and combined to give the standard error of the mean for the entire sample. Again, the weights used are the number of universe items in each stratum:

$$\hat{\sigma}_{\bar{x}_{st}} = \frac{1}{N} \sqrt{\Sigma N_h^2 \hat{\sigma}_{\bar{x}_h}^2} \quad \dots\dots\dots\dots\dots\dots\dots\dots\dots (7.5)$$

where

$\bar{x}_{st}$ is the standard error of the mean for the stratified sample.

Confidence Interval for the Universe Mean. The mean of the stratified sample, the estimated standard error of the mean, and a confidence coefficient (selected by the researcher) can now be used to produce a confidence interval for the universe mean:

$$\bar{x}_{st} - a\hat{\sigma}_{\bar{x}_{st}} \le \mu \le \bar{x}_{st} + a\hat{\sigma}_{\bar{x}_{st}} \quad\text{..........................(7.6)}$$

where

a represents a confidence coefficient relating to either the normal or the t distribution. When n is large, a can be represented by a z value; but when n is small, a should be replaced by a t value with degrees of freedom equal to sample size minus one degree of freedom for each stratum.

■ **Example.** A universe of 100 workers is divided into two groups of 60 men and 40 women. Four of the men and three of the women are selected at random and are measured for height. The results are shown in Table 7.4 and are used to estimate the average height of all 100 workers.

TABLE 7.4

Results of a Stratified Sample

Stratum	N_h	n_h	f_h	Values of x_{hi}	$\bar{x}_h$	$\hat{\sigma}_h^2$	$\hat{\sigma}_{\bar{x}h}^2$	$N_h\bar{x}_h$	$N_h^2\sigma_{\bar{x}h}^2$
1 (men)	60	4	0.067	72 70 67 71	70	4.67	1.09	4,200	3,924
2 (women)	40	3	0.075	65 62 68	65	9.00	2.78	2,600	4,448
Total	$N = 100$	$n = 7$	0.070					6,800	8,372

The computed values in Table 7.4 are obtained by the following steps. Using Formulas 7.1 and 7.2:

x_{1i}	$x_{1i} - \bar{x}_1$	$(x_{1i} - \bar{x}_1)^2$	x_{2i}	$x_{2i} - \bar{x}_2$	$(x_{2i} - \bar{x}_2)^2$
72	+2	4	65	0	0
70	0	0	62	−3	9
67	−3	9	68	+3	9
71	+1	1	195	0	18
280	0	14			

$$\bar{x}_1 = \frac{280}{4} = 70 \qquad\qquad \bar{x}_2 = \frac{195}{3} = 65$$

$$\hat{\sigma}_1^2 = \frac{14}{3} = 4.67 \qquad\qquad \hat{\sigma}_2^2 = \frac{18}{2} = 9$$

Using Formula 7.3:

$$\bar{x}_{st} = \frac{6,800}{100} = 68 \text{ inches, which is an unbiased point estimate of } \mu.$$

Using Formula 7.4:

$$\hat{\sigma}^2_{\bar{x}_1} = \frac{4.67}{4}(1 - 0.067) = 1.09$$

$$\hat{\sigma}^2_{\bar{x}_2} = \frac{9}{3}(1 - 0.075) = 2.78$$

Using Formula 7.5:

$$\hat{\sigma}_{\bar{x}_{st}} = \frac{1}{100}\sqrt{8,372} = 0.91.$$

Using Formula 7.6, $\alpha = 0.10$, and t with $7 - 2 = 5$ degrees of freedom:

$$68 - (2.015)(0.91) \le \mu \le 68 + (2.015)(0.91)$$
$$66.2 \le \mu \le 69.8.$$

It can now be said that the probability is 0.90 that the mean height of all 100 workers will not be less than 66.2 inches or greater than 69.8 inches. The width of the confidence interval is large in this example because a very small sample was used to keep the computations as simple as possible.

Optimum Allocation

The problem of how to allocate the sample to the various strata in order to get the most precise results for the money available will be considered under two sets of conditions:

1. Optimum allocation with fixed costs, and
2. Optimum allocation with varying costs.

Optimum Allocation with Fixed Costs. If n has been determined as the total sample size to be used and if the cost per unit is the same for all strata, the size of the sample to be drawn from the hth stratum may be determined as follows:

$$n_h = n\left[\frac{N_h \hat{\sigma}_h}{\Sigma N_h \hat{\sigma}_h}\right] \quad\dots\dots\dots\dots\dots\dots\dots\dots\dots(7.7)$$

where n_h is the number of sample items to be selected from the hth stratum.

This formula, called the _Neyman allocation_, is based on the assumption that something is known about the scatter of the items in each individual stratum and that there is more scatter in some strata than in others. If the standard deviation of each stratum were the same, the sample allocation could be made on the basis of the proportion of the universe total in each stratum. Formula 7.7 provides that the sample size in each stratum shall be proportionate to the product of the size of the stratum and the standard deviation of the stratum.

■ **Example.** The figures in Table 7.5 show a universe of 10,000 items separated into four strata. Estimated standard deviations are available for each stratum. A total sample of 300 is allocated to the four strata on the assumption that it costs exactly the same to sample one unit from Stratum No. 1 as it does to sample one unit from each of the other three strata. The computation of the sample allocation for Stratum No. 1 is shown in detail below Table 7.5.

TABLE 7.5

Optimum Allocation of a Stratified Sample with Fixed Costs (Allocation for a Sample of 300)

Stratum	N_h	$\hat{\sigma}_h$	$N_h \hat{\sigma}_h$	n_h
1	2,000	5	10,000	20
2	3,000	10	30,000	60
3	4,000	20	80,000	160
4	1,000	30	30,000	60
Totals	10,000		150,000	300

Allocation for the first stratum:

$$n_1 = n \left[\frac{N_1 \hat{\sigma}_1}{\Sigma N_h \hat{\sigma}_h} \right] = 300 \left[\frac{10,000}{150,000} \right] = 20.$$

Optimum Allocation with Varying Costs. Often it costs more to draw a sample item from one stratum than from another; thus, an additional factor must be considered in sample allocation. If the total cost of the survey is represented by C, then

$$C = C_1 n_1 + C_2 n_2 + \ldots + C_h n_h + \ldots + C_L n_L, \text{ or}$$

$$C = \Sigma C_h n_h \ \ldots\ldots\ldots\ldots\ldots\ldots\ldots\ldots\ldots\ldots\ldots\ldots\ldots\ldots\ldots(7.8)$$

where

C_h is the cost per sample unit for the hth stratum.

If the total cost, C, is determined first, the size of the sample, n, can be computed by the following formula:

$$n = \frac{C}{\Sigma N_h \hat{\sigma}_h \sqrt{C_h}} \Sigma \left(\frac{N_h \hat{\sigma}_h}{\sqrt{C_h}} \right) \ldots\ldots\ldots\ldots\ldots(7.9)$$

Once the size of n has been determined, the total sample can be allocated to the various strata by the following formula:

$$n_h = \frac{\dfrac{N_h \hat{\sigma}_h}{\sqrt{C_h}}}{\Sigma \left(\dfrac{N_h \hat{\sigma}_h}{\sqrt{C_h}}\right)} n \qquad \qquad \text{(7.10)}$$

■ **Example.** The problem discussed in the previous example is shown again in Table 7.6. This time it is assumed that the cost per sample unit varies with the strata and that a total cost of $1,000 has been set for the survey. The size of the sample total is computed to be 369 using Formula 7.9, and this total is allocated to the four strata using Formula 7.10.

TABLE 7.6

Optimum Allocation of a Stratified Sample with Variable Costs

Stratum	N_h	$\hat{\sigma}_h$	$N_h\hat{\sigma}_h$	C_h	$\sqrt{C_h}$	$\dfrac{N_h\hat{\sigma}_h}{\sqrt{C_h}}$	$N_h\hat{\sigma}_h\sqrt{C_h}$	n_h
1	2,000	5	10,000	$0.50	0.707	14,144	7,070	53
2	3,000	10	30,000	1.00	1.000	30,000	30,000	114
3	4,000	20	80,000	4.00	2.000	40,000	160,000	151
4	1,000	30	30,000	5.00	2.237	13,411	67,110	51
	10,000		150,000			97,555	264,180	369

$$n = \frac{C}{\Sigma N_h \hat{\sigma}_h \sqrt{C_h}} \Sigma \left(\frac{N_h \hat{\sigma}_h}{\sqrt{C_h}}\right)$$

$$n = \frac{1,000}{264,180}(97,555) = 369.$$

With $n = 369$, then

$$n_1 = \frac{\dfrac{N_1 \hat{\sigma}_1}{\sqrt{C_1}}}{\Sigma \left(\dfrac{N_h \hat{\sigma}_h}{\sqrt{C_h}}\right)} n = \frac{14,144}{97,555} 369 \doteq 53.$$

Sample sizes for the remaining strata are computed in the same manner.

CLUSTER SAMPLING

In the previous discussion of stratified sampling, the chief aim was to use a sample design that would provide maximum precision for a given size sample. There are two conditions under which this design will not provide the best approach to sampling:

1. There may not be available a frame or list of universe items from which the sample might be drawn. For example, if one wishes to interview a sample of farmers in a particular state, it might be impossible to find a list of them from which to draw the sample.

2. Even with a frame available, if the units in the universe are widely scattered, it may be cheaper to use a large sample of units that lie close to one another than it would be to use a small sample of widely scattered units. For example, it might be cheaper to interview 50 farmers in 10 counties than 30 farmers in 30 different counties. This might be accomplished with no loss in sample precision.

The Nature of Cluster Sampling

In designing a sample survey, the statistician is always interested in learning something about a universe of items that may be called *listing units* or *elementary units*. It is the characteristics of these elements that the statistician is interested in counting or measuring. In the case of the farm survey, the individual farmer may be thought of as the listing unit.

Listing units may be selected individually, as in simple random sampling, or they may be selected in groups or clusters known as *primary units*. In the example of the farm survey, the counties are considered as the primary units.

When a sample design calls for a random selection of primary units and when a random sample of listing units is selected from each of the sample of primary units, it is called a *cluster sample*. In this case it would be precise to say a *two-stage cluster sample,* since the sampling is done in two stages. A three-stage cluster sample would be one in which the sampling is done in three stages. For example, a city block might be the primary unit; a family, the secondary unit; and an individual person in the family, the listing unit.

In those instances where the population is broken into areas that constitute the primary sampling units, the sample is called an *area sample.* Another variation, in which listing units are taken in groups or chunks from the population, is called *chunk sampling.* This type of sampling is often most convenient in sampling internal records. For example, a chunk may be a box of punched cards taken from a file containing several such boxes. The contents of the sample box might be analyzed on a computer. In this case a very large sample may be inspected at a small cost.

The special advantages of the cluster sample are that it provides a way of selecting a random sample where there is no frame, and it often makes possible cost saving not obtainable with other sample designs.

The formulas for cluster sampling explained in this text are designed for two-stage cluster sampling, in which each primary unit has the same or nearly the same number of listing units as every other primary unit. Formulas to handle more complicated problems may be found in specialized sampling texts such as those listed at the end of this chapter.

Notation

Figure 7.1 shows a hypothetical two-stage cluster (or area) sample drawn from a small city. The primary units are city blocks, and the listing units are houses. The shaded portions represent the sample of primary units (city blocks) selected at the first stage, and the black squares represent the sample of listing units (houses) selected at the second stage. The primary purpose of this figure is to define and to illustrate some of the notation that will be used in formulas for cluster sampling.

FIGURE 7.1

Hypothetical Two-Stage Cluster Sample Drawn from a Universe of 40 City Blocks with Six Houses to Each Block

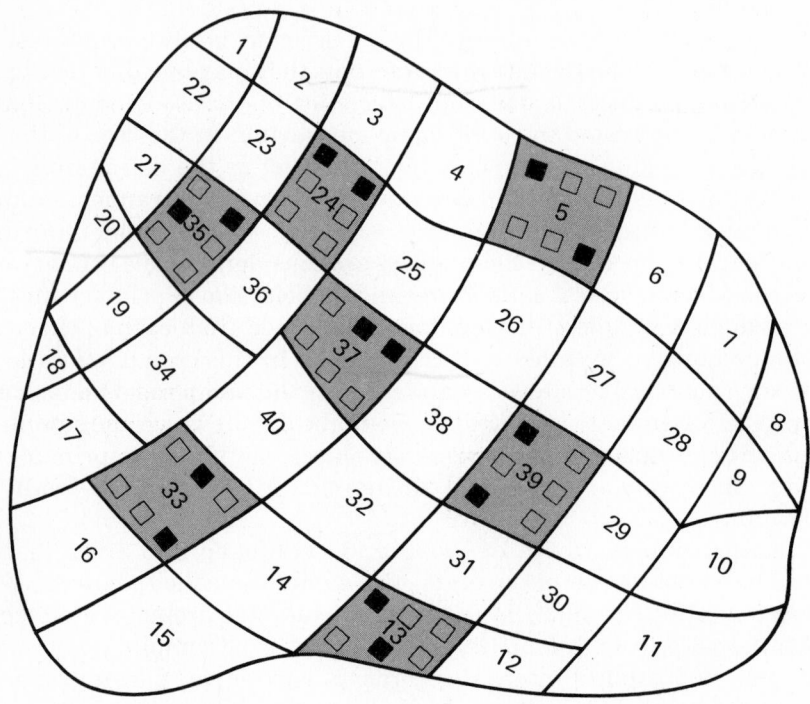

Definition	Notation	In this example
Number of primary units in the universe	M	40 blocks
Number of primary units in the sample	m	7 blocks (shaded)
Number of listing units in each primary unit	$\bar{N}$	6 houses in each block ✓
Number of listing units sampled in each primary unit in the sample	$\bar{n}$	2 houses in each block (black)
Total number of listing units in the universe	$N = \bar{N}M$	240 houses
Total number of listing units in the sample	$n = \bar{n}m$	14 houses

Interval Estimates for Cluster Samples

Just as in stratified sampling, judgment must be exercised in determining how the sample will be designed. However, once the decision has been made as to the number of primary units to be drawn and the number of listing units to be sampled from each of them, the sampling process itself must be random. If each elementary unit has a known chance of selection, it is then possible to estimate the standard error of the mean and to compute a confidence interval based on a given confidence coefficient.

Formulas

Five formulas will be needed to compute an interval estimate for a two-stage cluster sample. These relationships and computational steps are listed below and their use is illustrated by a simple example.

Mean of the Cluster Sample. First the values of the listing units are averaged for each cluster, and then the cluster means are combined to compute the mean of the cluster sample:

$$\bar{\bar{x}} = \frac{\Sigma \bar{x}_i}{m} \dots\dots\dots\dots\dots\dots\dots\dots\dots(7.11)$$

where
  $\bar{\bar{x}}$ is the mean of the cluster sample
  $\bar{x}_i$ is the mean of the ith cluster.

Within-Cluster Variance. This value is the arithmetic mean of cluster variances. The variances of values of the listing units in each cluster are summed and divided by the number of clusters.

$$\hat{\sigma}_w^2 = \frac{\Sigma \hat{\sigma}_i^2}{m} \dots\dots\dots\dots\dots\dots\dots\dots\dots(7.12)$$

where
  $\hat{\sigma}_w^2$ is the estimated within-cluster variance
  $\hat{\sigma}_i^2$ is the estimated variance for the ith cluster.

Between-Cluster Variance. This value is the variance of the cluster means about the average:

$$\hat{\sigma}_b^2 = \frac{\Sigma (\bar{x}_i - \bar{\bar{x}})^2}{m - 1} \dots\dots\dots\dots\dots\dots\dots\dots(7.13)$$

where
  $\hat{\sigma}_b^2$ is the between-cluster variance.

Standard Error of the Mean for the Cluster Sample. The within- and the between-cluster variances are now combined to produce an estimate of the standard error of the mean for the entire sample:

$$\hat{\sigma}_{\bar{x}} = \sqrt{\left(\frac{M-m}{M}\right)\left(\frac{\hat{\sigma}_b^2}{m}\right) + \left(\frac{\bar{N}-\bar{n}}{\bar{N}}\right)\left(\frac{\hat{\sigma}_w^2}{n}\right)} \quad \dots \dots \dots \dots \text{(7.14)}$$

where

$\hat{\sigma}_{\bar{x}}^2$ is the estimated standard error of the mean for the cluster sample

$\dfrac{M-m}{M}$ and $\dfrac{\bar{N}-\bar{n}}{\bar{N}}$ are finite population corrections.

Confidence Interval for the Universe Mean.

$$\bar{\bar{x}} - a\hat{\sigma}_{\bar{\bar{x}}} \leq \mu \leq \bar{\bar{x}} + a\hat{\sigma}_{\bar{\bar{x}}} \dots \dots \dots \dots \dots \text{(7.15)}$$

where

a represents a confidence coefficient. When the sample is small, a should be a t value with degrees of freedom $= n - m - 1$.

■ *Example.* A retailer has on hand 1,000 cartons of infrared heat lamps, each carton containing 24 lamps. The company wishes to estimate the average burning life of these lamps, which have been purchased from several suppliers and at different times. A sample of 9 lamps is drawn from the universe of 24,000 lamps as follows:

1. Three cartons are selected at random.
2. Three lamps are selected at random from each of the three cartons.
3. The test lamps are burned until they burn out. The sample observations, the mean, and the variance of each group of three lamps are shown in Table 7.7.

TABLE 7.7

Results of a Two-Stage Cluster Sample of Heat Lamps (Burning Life in 100's of Hours)

Cluster number	Sample observations	Cluster Mean $\bar{x}_i$	Cluster Variance $\hat{\sigma}_i^2$	$\bar{x}_i - \bar{\bar{x}}$	$(\bar{x}_i - \bar{\bar{x}})^2$
1	24, 26, 25	25	1	0	0
2	20, 20, 23	21	3	−4	16
3	27, 29, 31	29	4	+4	16
Total		75	8	0	32

The sample is a two-stage cluster sample with the following characteristics:

$M = 1,000$ cartons (primary units).
$m = 3$ cartons (number of primary units in the sample).
$\bar{N} = 24$ lamps (number of listing units per primary unit).

$\bar{n} = 3$ lamps (number of listing units sampled in each sample primary unit).

$N = M\bar{N} = 24{,}000$ lamps (total number of listing units in the population).

$n = 9$ lamps.

Mean and variance for the first cluster are:

$$\bar{x}_1 = \frac{24 + 26 + 25}{3} = 25$$

$$\hat{\sigma}_1^2 = \frac{(24 - 25)^2 + (26 - 25)^2 + (25 - 25)^2}{3 - 1} = 1.$$

Using Formula 7.11:

$$\bar{\bar{x}} = \frac{75}{3} = 25.$$

Using Formula 7.12:

$$\hat{\sigma}_w^2 - \frac{8}{3} = 2.67.$$

Using Formula 7.13:

$$\hat{\sigma}_b^2 = \frac{32}{2} = 16.$$

Using Formula 7.14:

$$\hat{\sigma}_{\bar{\bar{x}}} = \sqrt{\left(\frac{1{,}000 - 3}{1{,}000}\right)\left(\frac{16}{3}\right) + \left(\frac{24 - 3}{24}\right)\left(\frac{2.67}{9}\right)} = 2.36.$$

Using Formula 7.15, $\alpha = 0.10$, and t with $9 - 3 - 1 = 5$ degrees of freedom:

$$25 - (2.015)(2.36) \leq \mu \leq 25 + (2.015)(2.36)$$

$$20.2 \leq \mu \leq 29.8$$

and $\qquad P(20.2 \leq \mu \leq 29.8) = 0.90.$

Again it should be pointed out that the example is too simple to be realistic. In actual practice, most cluster samples would include several hundred observations, and the theoretical sampling distribution of $\bar{x}$ would be approximately normal.

Optimum Allocation

The cluster sample with the smallest sampling error would naturally be one that has only one listing unit per primary unit. This, of course, turns out to be a simple random sample and may be much more expensive than one with more than one listing unit per cluster or primary unit. The question is, "How many primary units and how many listing units in each primary unit should be sampled to get the most precision for the money?"

The answer to this question depends on several factors. If the cluster means $(\bar{x}_i)$ are all alike, very few clusters would be needed, but the number of listing units per cluster should be high. On the other hand, if the variance between primary units $(\hat{\sigma}_b^2)$ is large, more primary units should be drawn and fewer listing units sampled per primary unit.

The key measure in this relationship is a value called delta (δ). Delta is the intraclass correlation between elementary units within primary units and can be expressed by the following formula:

$$\delta = \frac{\hat{\sigma}_b^2 - \dfrac{\hat{\sigma}^2}{\overline{N}}}{(\overline{N}-1)\dfrac{\hat{\sigma}^2}{\overline{N}}} \dots\dots\dots\dots\dots\dots\dots\dots\dots\dots\dots\dots(7.16)$$

where

$\hat{\sigma}^2 = \hat{\sigma}_b^2 + \sigma_w^2$ is the estimate of total variance.

The determination of the optimum allocation of the sample must also take into account the total amount of money (exclusive of overhead costs) and the relative cost of drawing a primary unit as compared with that of drawing a listing unit. This cost function in its simplest form may be expressed as follows:

$$C = C_1 m + C_2 m \bar{n} \dots\dots\dots\dots\dots\dots\dots\dots\dots\dots\dots\dots(7.17)$$

where

C is the total cost of the survey, exclusive of overhead costs
C_1 is the cost per primary unit included in the survey
C_2 is the cost per listing unit included in the survey.

The cost of adding one primary unit to the survey, C_1, might include such items as transportation and communications costs that would be incurred in sampling from that cluster. The cost of adding one listing unit, C_2, might include the cost of interviewing and tabulating the data from one listing unit. It must be understood that these cost figures are estimates, and to a large extent the accuracy of the allocation depends on the accuracy of the cost estimates as well as the estimates of the two variances used to compute the value of δ.

In making the actual allocation, it is easiest first to estimate the optimum size of the sample of listing units to be drawn from each primary unit and then to solve for m in the cost function using the optimum $\bar{n}$. The optimum value of n may be computed using the following equation:

$$\text{Opt. } \bar{n} = \sqrt{\frac{C_1}{C_2} \frac{1-\delta}{\delta}} \dots\dots\dots\dots\dots\dots\dots\dots\dots\dots(7.18)$$

An illustration of optimum allocation is given in the following example.

■ *Example.* Prior to making a sample survey using a two-stage cluster sample the following estimates are available:

C = $600 (total amount to be spent, exclusive of overhead)
C_1 = $10 (sampling cost per primary unit)
C_2 = $5 (sampling cost per listing unit)
M = 500 (number of primary units in the universe)
$\bar{N}$ = 10 (average number of listing units per primary unit, assumed in this case to be constant for all clusters)
N = $M\bar{N}$ = 5,000 (total number of listing units in the universe)
$\hat{\sigma}_w^2$ = 20 (estimate of variance of listing units within primary units)
$\hat{\sigma}_b^2$ = 5 (estimate of variance between primary units)
$\hat{\sigma}^2 = \hat{\sigma}_w^2 + \hat{\sigma}_b^2 = 20 + 5 = 25$ (estimate of total variance).

The problem is to estimate m and $\bar{n}$ so as to get maximum precision within the money allocated for the survey.

The first step is to compute δ using Formula 7.16:

$$\delta = \frac{\hat{\sigma}_b^2 - \dfrac{\hat{\sigma}^2}{\bar{N}}}{(\bar{N}-1)\dfrac{\hat{\sigma}^2}{\bar{N}}} = \frac{5 - \dfrac{25}{10}}{(10-1)\left(\dfrac{25}{10}\right)} = \frac{2.5}{22.5} \cong 0.11.$$

and $1 - 0.11 = 0.89$.

The optimum number of listing units to be drawn from each primary unit may be estimated using Formula 7.18:

$$\text{Opt. } \bar{n} = \sqrt{\frac{C_1}{C_2}\frac{1-\delta}{\delta}} = \sqrt{\frac{10}{5}\frac{0.89}{0.11}} = \sqrt{16.18} = 4.02$$

Opt. $\bar{n}$ = 4.

Opt. $\bar{n}$ must always be rounded to an integer.

This value can now be substituted in the cost equation (Formula 7.17) to estimate the optimum size of m.

$$C = C_1 m + C_2 m\bar{n}$$
$$600 = 10m + 5m(4)$$
$$30m = 600$$
$$m = 20.$$

This would mean that the sample should consist of 20 primary units drawn at random from the universe of 500 primary units. From each primary unit in the sample, four listing units would be drawn at random making a total sample size of $n = m\bar{n}$, or 80 listing units.

OTHER SAMPLE DESIGNS

The number of different sample designs from which the researcher may choose is almost limitless. A few of the most common sample designs are discussed briefly in this section.

It should be noted, however, that the theory of sampling has much wider application than just to sample surveys. Sampling theory is basic to many other types of statistical analysis. Some examples are listed below:

1. Monte Carlo methods used in simulation.
2. Measurement of average life of equipment, parts, returnable containers, magazine subscriptions, etc.
3. Statistical quality control.
4. Inventory theory.
5. Estimating totals of moving populations such as itinerate workers or whales in the oceans.
6. Theory of failure as applied to the design and testing of complex equipment.
7. Information theory.
8. Theory of extreme values for design of bridges, roads, and other structures subject to stress.
9. Queueing theory and waiting line models.

Stratified Cluster Sampling

Stratified cluster sampling combines the characteristics of both stratified and cluster sampling. The population is divided into strata which are internally homogeneous but which are heterogeneous with respect to each other. Clusters are then drawn from each stratum. Because the clusters tend to contain items that are not alike, but because the clusters themselves are alike, only a few clusters need be selected from a stratum to represent it adequately. This type of sample is often used in a very large sampling problem and has been used extensively by the United States Department of Agriculture in making crop estimates.

Systematic Sampling

Often it is possible to overcome some of the difficulty and the cost of a pure random sample by using a systematic selection procedure by which every k^{th} item is selected from an ordered universe. This might be every 100th item on an assembly line, every 50th customer entering the main entrance of a department store, or every 250th card in a file of punched cards. If the first unit of the sample is selected at random, then theoretically every item has the same likelihood of selection even though all combinations of items are not possible of selection. Such samples are called *systematic random samples* and are generally considered to be acceptable as long as there is no cyclical or periodic pattern in the universe that might coincide with the size of k. Much marketing research is dependent on systematic samples taken from a telephone book.

Arbitrary Sampling

As a practical matter, not all sampling is done on the basis of random selection. There are other types of samples variously called *judgment samples, representative samples, quota samples,* and *purposive samples.* These samples all involve *arbitrary selection.* For example, a survey firm interested in predicting how the electorate will vote in a state election might send out interviewers with instructions to interview a sample of voters with certain specified characteristics such as age, sex, income, and political registration. The purpose of the survey is to get a sample that is "representative" or "typical" of the universe. This is a quota sample. The design of the sample may be made with meticulous care, following the proportions of each characteristic in the universe as shown by a recent census. As a matter of fact, the sample results may be very accurate. The difficulty with this type of sample, however, lies in the fact that no measure of sampling error can be computed irrespective of the sampling technique used. Consequently, there is absolutely no way of evaluating the reliability of estimates based on samples that are arbitrarily selected. Samples of this type should not be confused with stratified samples in which the selection of sample observations is random and the standard error of the sample statistic can be computed.

Acceptance and Sequential Sampling

Inspection for acceptance purposes is carried out at many stages in manufacturing and by purchasers of large batches of mass-produced items. Much of this acceptance inspection is carried out on a sampling basis. In *acceptance sampling* the number of defective items for a given sample size is specified. This is called an *acceptance number.* When the sample has that number of defective items or fewer, the batch under study is accepted. The plan usually is accompanied by a *rejection number,* which is the number of defectives requiring the rejection of the batch. If the number of defectives at any stage is above the acceptance but below the rejection number, sampling is continued.

The term *sequential sampling* is used when a decision is possible after each item has been inspected and when there is no specified limit on the total number of units to be inspected. The principal advantage of this kind of sampling lies in the fact that many decisions can be made from very small samples. Only the borderline cases require large samples.

Current Population Survey

The Census Bureau's *Current Population Survey* (CPS) is a scientifically selected sample representing the noninstitutional population of the United States. The survey provides monthly statistics on employment, unemployment, and related subjects which are analyzed and published by the Bureau of Labor Statistics of the U.S. Department of Labor. It is the only comprehensive source of information on the personal characteristics of the total population such as age, sex, marital status, veteran status, educational background, and ethnic origin.

The CPS sample is located in 461 sample areas comprising 923 counties and independent cities with coverage in every state and the District of

Columbia. In all, approximately 55,000 listing units containing 100,000 persons 16 years and older are interviewed each month.

Using data from the 1970 Census of Population, the entire U.S. population of 3,146 counties and independent cities was divided into 1,931 primary sampling units. The primary sampling units (PSU) were then grouped into 376 strata. A stratum consisted of PSU's as much alike as possible as to geography, minorities, growth patterns, urban-rural, etc.

Of the 376 strata, 156 had only one PSU and these were automatically selected for the sample. An additional 305 PSU's were selected at random from the remaining 220 strata to give the 461 sample areas. The sampling fraction is about 1 to 1,490.

Within each sample PSU, several stages of sampling are used to select the units to be enumerated. The sampling fraction is determined in such a way that the overall sampling rate for each household included in the survey is equal.

Each month, during the calendar week containing the 19th day, interviewers contact some responsible person in each of the sample households in the CPS. At the first enumeration of a household, the interviewer visits the household and prepares a roster of the household members, including their personal characteristics.

Personal visits are required on the first, second, and fifth months that a household is in the sample. In the other months, the interview may be conducted by telephone.

At each monthly visit, a questionnaire is completed for each household member 16 years of age and over. The primary purpose of the questions is to determine if the person is employed, unemployed, or not in the labor force.

Examples such as the Current Population Survey demonstrate that the basic sampling techniques discussed earlier in this chapter are actually used by business, industry, and government.

STUDY QUESTIONS

7-1. Explain briefly the meaning of each of the following terms:
a. precision of sample result
b. sampling error
c. reliability of the sample result
d. accuracy of the sample result
e. frame
f. sample design
g. efficiency
h. stratified sampling
i. strata
j. proportionate stratified random sample
k. disproportionate stratified random sample
l. Neyman allocation
m. listing unit
n. primary unit
o. cluster sample
p. two-stage cluster sample
q. area sample
r. chunk sampling
s. stratified cluster sample
t. systematic random sample

u. arbitrary sample
v. acceptance sample
w. Current Population Survey

x. acceptance number
y. rejection number
z. sequential sampling

7-2. What are the advantages of using sampling to gather information?

7-3. Why is the business executive more interested in the accuracy than in the precision of the sample results?

7-4. What is the one great weakness in all types of arbitrary sampling?

7-5. Describe how you would take a systematic random sample from the pages of a telephone book. Under what conditions might this be an appropriate sample to use?

7-6. What is the principal advantage in using a sequential sampling plan in an acceptance sampling situation?

7-7. When is a stratified sample more efficient than a simple random sample?

7-8. Describe a situation in which it would be appropriate to use a stratified sample. Explain in your example the criterion you would use to break the universe into strata.

7-9. What factors play a part in the optimum allocation of a stratified sample?

7-10. Give an example of a four-stage cluster sample.

7-11. Under what conditions would you consider using a cluster sample?

7-12. What factors are involved in the optimum allocation of a cluster sample?

7-13. What are some other fields of statistical analysis that use sampling theory?

PROBLEMS

7-1. The values below represent a universe of four:

$$A = 54 \qquad B = 50 \ \bigg| \ C = 12 \qquad D = 8$$

a. If all possible simple random samples of $n = 2$ are drawn from this universe, how many samples would there be? Compute the standard error of the mean for simple random samples.
b. Assume that the universe is divided into the following two strata:

Stratum	Universe items
1	A and B
2	C and D

Draw all possible samples of $n = 2$ with one sample unit drawn from each stratum. Is the mean *unweighted* of the sample means the same as the mean of the universe? How does the standard error of the mean compare with that computed in part a? Discuss any difference you find.

7-2 The values below represent a universe of seven:

$$X_1 = 6 \qquad X_2 = 125 \qquad X_3 = 10 \qquad X_4 = 891$$
$$X_5 = 7 \qquad X_6 = 9 \qquad X_7 = 905$$

a. Compute the universe mean and standard deviation. Compute the standard error of the mean for all possible simple random samples of $n = 3$.

b. Divide the universe into three strata, making the universe values in each stratum as homogeneous as possible.

c. How many different samples of $n = 3$ could you draw from the stratified universe if one sample item comes from each stratum?

d. Draw all possible samples of three as discussed in parts b and c. Compute the standard error of the mean. How does it compare with the standard error computed in part a? Discuss the difference.

7-3. Use the three strata constructed in Problem 7.2 as the data for this problem.

a. How many different samples of five can you draw if two sample items are drawn from the first stratum, one is drawn from the second stratum, and two are drawn from the third stratum?

b. Compute the means of the samples discussed in part a. Is $\bar{\bar{x}} = \mu$?

c. Compute the standard error of the mean for stratified samples of $n = 5$. Use the sample means computed in part b. How does the standard error compare with that computed from samples of $n = 3$ in Problem 7.2d? Discuss.

7-4. A stratified random sample of 10 persons is selected from a county with a population of 2,500. Six members of the sample are drawn from the urban population of the county and four are drawn from the rural population. The results are shown in the table below.

Results of a Stratified Random Sample
(Incomes in $1,000 per Year)

Stratum	Universe N_h	Sample n_h	Values of x_{hi}
Urban	2,000	6	11.5, 12.9, 14.8, 8.5, 10.1, and 14.2
Rural	500	4	7.5, 9.0, 6.6, and 8.9
Total	2,500	10	

a. Compute the mean of the stratified sample.

b. Would you expect the mean of the stratified sample to be an unbiased estimate of the mean of the universe? Explain.

7-5. Use the data from Problem 7.4. Compute the interval estimate of μ from the stratified sample with $\alpha = 0.05$.

7-6. A stratified random sample is drawn from the membership of three locals of a labor union to determine the average number of years workers have been members of that union. The results of the study are shown below:

Local number	Number of members	Number in the sample	Stratum mean	Stratum variance
4	1,629	49	8.2	5.0
32	1,150	62	4.8	4.1
8	1,380	30	7.6	5.6
Total	4,159	141		

a. Make a point estimate of the average tenure of the 4,159 union members. 9.7

b. Make an interval estimate of average tenure using a 95% confidence coefficient. Use t n.b

7-7. A researcher is interested in drawing a stratified random sample of 200 manufacturers from a universe of small firms that has been stratified on the basis of employee size. The researcher is interested in estimating monthly sales for the industry and has done some preliminary work which has produced estimates of the standard deviation in sales for each stratum. Use the data below to compute the optimum allocation of the sample on the assumption that it costs the same amount to sample one unit regardless of the stratum from which it is selected.

Stratum	Number of employees in the firm	Universe N_h	Standard deviation (monthly sales in $1,000) $\hat{\sigma}_h$
1	under 25	4,800	2.5
2	25–49	2,150	4.3
3	50–149	1,130	7.8
4	150–500	150	15.0
5	Over 500	30	35.0
	Total	8,260	

7-8. Use the data in Problem 7.7. Assume that you have $580 to spend on the survey and that the cost of sampling varies with each stratum as shown below:

Stratum	Cost to sample one firm C_h
1	$ 1.00
2	4.00
3	6.00
4	8.00
5	10.00

a. Compute the size of the sample, n.
b. Compute the optimum allocation of n to the five strata.
c. Explain any differences you find in the allocations in this problem with those computed in Problem 7.7.

7-9. In a study to estimate the average value of life insurance policies held by its employees, a large industrial firm stratifies its employee group by annual salary and estimates the scatter in each stratum with the following results:

Stratum	Annual salary (dollars)	Number of employees N_h	$\hat{\sigma}_h$
1	Under 10,000	8,000	1,000
2	10,000–20,000	3,400	1,500
3	Over 20,000	600	3,000
	Total	12,000	

Compute the Neyman allocation for a sample of $n = 300$.

7-10. Suppose that in Problem 7.9, the data on value of life insurance policies was to be gathered differently for each stratum. The costs are shown below:

Stratum	Method used to gather the information	Cost per unit sampled
1	Direct mail	$1.00
2	Telephone	4.00
3	Personal interview	9.00

a. How large a sample could be purchased by spending $636.00 on the survey?
b. Compute the optimum allocation of the sample determined in part a.

7-11. Suppose a universe has 50 primary units with 10 listing units in each. A two-stage cluster sample is drawn with six primary units and four listing units observed in each with the following results:

Code number of the primary unit selected	Values of x_{ij}
13	4 5 5 4
23	4 3 2 3
36	4 4 5 5
41	4 7 5 4
47	2 4 3 7
49	4 3 4 3

a. Determine the values of each of the following:

$$M \qquad n$$
$$m \qquad N$$
$$\bar{n} \qquad \bar{N}$$

b. Compute the values of $\bar{x}_i$ and compute $\bar{\bar{x}}$.

c. Compute the values of $\hat{\sigma}_b^2$ and $\hat{\sigma}_w^2$.

d. Compute an interval estimate of μ with 95 percent confidence co-efficient.

M

$\bar{N}$

7-12. Suppose a universe has 1000 primary sampling units with 60 listing units in each primary unit. A two-stage cluster sample is drawn with the following results:

$$\bar{\bar{x}} = 175 \qquad m = 20$$
$$\hat{\sigma}_b^2 = 25 \qquad \bar{n} = 10$$
$$\hat{\sigma}_w^2 = 10$$

Z

Compute an interval estimate for μ with $\alpha = 0.05$. (7.15)

7-13. A two-stage cluster sample is conducted in a city of 250,000 population to estimate average expenditures a month for entertainment. A random sample of five persons is selected from a sample of 10 blocks. There are approximately 12,500 blocks in the city with an average of 20 persons per block. The results of the study are shown below:

Cluster number	Cluster mean $\bar{x}_i$	Cluster variance $\hat{\sigma}_i$
1	$30.00	$ 5.00
2	32.00	2.00
3	28.00	7.00
4	25.00	3.00
5	35.00	4.00
6	33.00	3.00
7	31.00	4.00
8	19.00	2.00
9	22.00	8.00
10	45.00	12.00

a. Identify each of the following:

$$N = \qquad M = \qquad m =$$
$$\bar{n} = \qquad n = \qquad \bar{N} =$$

b. Compute the cluster mean.

c. Compute the between and the within variances.

d. Compute the total variance.

e. Compute the standard error of the mean.

f. Compute an interval estimate of μ with $\alpha = 0.05$.

7-14. Given the following estimates of the variances in a two-stage cluster sample and the average number of universe items per cluster, compute the value of δ:

$$\hat{\sigma}_b^2 = 50 \qquad \hat{\sigma}_w^2 = 6 \qquad \bar{N} = 14$$

7-15. Compute the value of δ for a two-stage cluster sample, given the following:

$$\hat{\sigma}^2 = 100 \qquad \hat{\sigma}_{\bar{w}}^2 = 30 \qquad \bar{N} = 20$$

7-16. For a two-stage cluster sample with the values shown below, compute the optimum values of m and n:

$$C = \$1,000 \qquad C_1 = \$50.00 \qquad C_2 = \$8.00 \qquad \delta = .25$$

7-17. Given the following estimates for a two-stage cluster sample, how large should the sample be and how should it be allocated?

σ_b^2 Between-cluster variance = 10   Cost per primary unit = $80.00 C_1

σ_w^2 Within-cluster variance   = 20   Cost per listing unit = $5.00 C_2

Average number of listing   Total amount to be spent on the

units per primary unit   survey = $2,000. C

is 10 $\bar{N} = 10$

SELECTED READINGS

Cochran, William G. *Sampling Techniques,* 3d ed. New York: John Wiley & Sons, Inc., 1977.

A comprehensive account of sampling theory as it has been developed for use in sample surveys.

Hansen, Morris H., William N. Hurwitz, and William G. Meadow. *Sample Survey Methods and Theory.* New York: John Wiley & Sons, Inc., 1953.

This book is the most comprehensive presentation of both the theory of sampling and its application to practical problems available at this time. The book is in two volumes. Volume I is *Methods and Applications.* Volume II, *Theory,* contains the derivations of the formulas and proofs of statements made in Volume I.

Yamane, Taro. *Elementary Sampling Theory.* Englewood Cliffs, N.J.: Prentice-Hall, Inc., 1967.

A simple but complete introduction to sampling theory written for the student who is not a professional mathematician or statistician but who needs to understand sampling procedures.

Yates, Frank. *Sampling Methods for Censuses and Surveys,* 3d, revised ed. New York: Hafner Publishing Co., 1965.

A book written primarily for those who have little or no previous training in mathematical statistics but who have some training or experience in the presentation and handling of statistical data.

Concepts and Methods Used in Labor Force Statistics Derived From the Current Population Survey, Bureau of Labor Statistics Report No. 463, Series P-23, No. 62. Washington, D.C.: U.S. Government Printing Office, 1976.

This report describes in detail the Current Population Survey—how it was developed, what it is, and how it is used.

Part 4

Inference

Chapter 8

Tests of Significance for Sample Means and Proportions

One of the most important areas of application of statistical theory is called *tests of significance* or *tests of hypotheses*. It is here that probability theory plays an important role in constructing the criteria on which business decisions are made. In addition to the tests discussed in this chapter, non-parametric tests are discussed in Chapter 9 and tests of significance using the F distribution are explained in Chapter 11.

Because many business decisions must be made on the basis of incomplete information, there is always the risk of making an incorrect decision. Fortunately, there is an extensive body of statistical methods available that makes possible the evaluation of these risks. These methods also provide guidelines that minimize the probability of making wrong decisions.

In previous chapters the discussion of sampling distributions was aimed largely at statistical estimation. A statistic computed from a random sample drawn from a universe was used to estimate a confidence interval within which one could predict, with a given probability, the universe parameter would lie.

The type of problem viewed in this chapter is one in which a decision must be made to take one action or another based on the acceptance or the rejection of a given hypothesis. Hence, the term, "tests of hypotheses." The variety of hypotheses that can be tested is endless.

The hypothesis is made about the value of some parameter, but the only facts available to estimate the parameter are those provided by a sample. If the statistic differs from the hypothesis made about the parameter, a decision must be made as to whether or not this difference is significant. If it is, the hypothesis is rejected. If it is not, it must be accepted. Hence, the term, "tests of significance."

The problem of determining whether the observed difference is significant or not is one of determining whether the difference could be reasonably attributed to random causes or is so large as to make such a conclusion unlikely. It is here that probability and sampling theory play their part in decision making.

■ *Example.* A machine is set to fill boxes of dry cereal with an average of 8 ounces, net weight, per box. While it would be ideal if the operator could be absolutely sure each box would contain exactly the right amount of cereal, this is never possible. There will always be some slight random variation from box to box. The operator must always be alert to the possibility that the machine may get out of adjustment or something may go wrong to change the average amount being put into all the boxes.

As long as the machine is filling the boxes with a universe mean of 8 ounces of cereal and as long as the variation in weight from box to box is random and within specifications, all is well and the process should be allowed to continue. If, however, the universe mean shifts to an amount that is either above or below 8 ounces, the machine should be stopped and proper adjustments made.

While the decision to continue the process or stop the machine is simple in theory, it is made difficult in practice by the fact that the operator never knows what the universe mean really is. It would be far too slow and costly to check the exact weight of every box as it is filled. This means that the operator must rely on the information obtained from studying a random sample of boxes selected periodically from the production line. If a sample of boxes is drawn and the sample mean, $\bar{x}$, is found to be 8.02 ounces, the operator is probably safe in assuming that the difference between that value and a universe mean, μ, of 8.00 ounces is not significant and can be attributed to sampling variation. If, on the other hand, $\bar{x} = 6.5$ ounces, the difference of 1.5 ounces may be much too large to attribute to sampling variation alone, and the operator may conclude that the difference is significant. The machine is out of adjustment. If the difference lies somewhere between 0.02 and 1.5, the decision the operator should make is less clear. A decision rule of some kind is needed to tell the operator the value at which the machine should be stopped or the process continued.

While there are thousands of different kinds of decisions that may be made using tests of significance, the sequence of logic followed is always much the same:

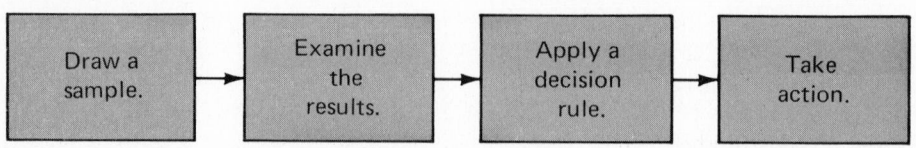

■ *Example.* Suppose in the previous example the operator had been told to follow, once each hour, the procedure outlined below. The operator might not know how the decision rule had been computed but would know how to act in controlling the machine. There would still be times in which the machine would be stopped when it was still in adjustment or would continue operating when it should be stopped and adjusted. These mistakes are inherent in the sampling process. The supervisor who computed the decision rule at least would know the frequency with which mistakes might be expected to occur.

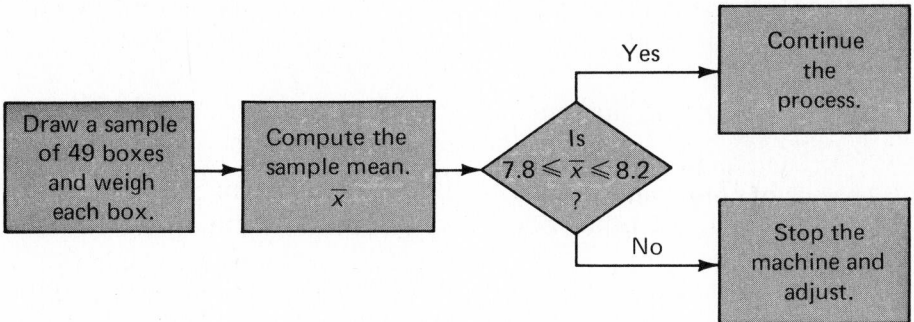

THE STATISTICAL APPROACH TO DECISION MAKING

As with any new subject in statistics, first it is necessary to introduce and define the terminology that will be used. While there are many different kinds of tests of significance that can be made in statistics, all can be systematically approached by following the five-step pattern explained in this chapter. These same steps may be followed in later chapters with other tests of significance involving such techniques as analysis of variance and chi-square.

The State of the World

In any test of significance there are always two possible states of the universe. These are often called *states of the world* or *states of nature*. These states are defined by the statistician in such a way as to be both *exhaustive* and *exclusive*. That is, for a given test, only these two and no other states are possible, and when one exists, the other cannot exist.

The first state of the world will be designated as W_1, and the second state of the world will be designated as W_2.

■ *Example.* In the foregoing discussion of the machine filling boxes of cereal, the two states of the world are:

W_1: The machine is properly adjusted ($\mu = 8$ ounces)
W_2: The machine is not properly adjusted ($\mu \neq 8$ ounces).

■ *Example.* In the case of a marketing executive who is working on a sales campaign, the two states of the world might be:

W_1:   Demand will be sufficient to meet our sales goal ($\pi = 25\%$)
W_2:   Demand will be below expectations ($\pi < 25\%$).

Hypotheses about the State of the World

Unfortunately, the true state of the world is not known in most cases at the time a decision must be made and action taken. One may only set up hypotheses about the two possible states. These hypotheses can then be tested and accepted or rejected, based on the outcome of the test.

■ *Example.* Using the same illustration, it is possible to set up two hypotheses about the machine filling boxes with cereal:

H_o: $\mu = 8$ ounces (W_1 is the true state of the world)
H_a: $\mu \neq 8$ ounces (W_2 is the true state of the world).

The hypothesis H_o is usually called the *null hypothesis.* The word "null" comes from the fact that this hypothesis assumes that there is "no significant difference" between the value of the universe parameter being tested and the value of the statistic computed from a sample drawn from that universe. Stated another way, the null hypothesis assumes that the difference between the parameter designated in the hypothesis and the statistic is a sampling difference.

Hypothesis H_a is called the *alternate hypothesis,* which will be accepted if statistical testing leads to a rejection of H_o.

The fact that H_o is set up and tested first does not necessarily mean that the experimenter believes that it is true. The experimenter must assume that there is no significant difference and reject or not reject this hypothesis first before going on to the alternate hypothesis. If the experimenter begins by testing the hypothesis that there is a significant difference, the question arises, "How much difference?" Therefore, it should be kept in mind that the null hypothesis is the only hypothesis that can be tested.

Decision Rules Determine Action

In spite of the fact that uncertainty always exists when decisions must be made on the basis of samples, action must be taken, nevertheless. *Action A_1* may be defined as that action which is taken if hypothesis H_o is not rejected on the assumption that W_1 is the true state of the world. *Action A_2* is that action which is taken if H_o is rejected, and H_a is accepted on the conclusion that W_2 is the true state of the world. The decision as to whether to take action A_1 or A_2 is made on the basis of a *decision rule.* The calculation of decision rules will be discussed later in this chapter. For the purposes of the present illustration, let the decision rule rest on two key values known as *critical values.* Suppose

$\bar{x}_{c_1}$ is the lower critical value of the sample mean, and
$\bar{x}_{c_2}$ is the upper critical value of the sample mean.

■ *Example.* If the operator of the machine is told to continue the process as long as the mean of the weights of a sample of 49 boxes lies between $\bar{x}_{c_1} = 7.8$ ounces and $\bar{x}_{c_2} = 8.2$ ounces, inclusive, and to stop and adjust the machine if the sample mean falls outside these critical values, the operator has a decision rule.

Hypothesis	State of the world	Decision rule	Action
H_o: $\mu = 8$ ozs.	W_1: Machine is adjusted	$7.8 \le \bar{x} \le 8.2$	A_1: Continue
H_a: $\mu \ne 8$ ozs.	W_2: Machine is not adjusted	$\bar{x} < 7.8$ or $\bar{x} > 8.2$	A_2: Stop and adjust

Types of Error

Because a sample statistic is not always a reliable measure of a universe parameter, there will be times when it will lead to an incorrect decision. If the statistic causes one to reject H_o (and accept H_a), thus taking action A_2 when the true state of the world is W_1, this is defined as a *Type I error,* which is made when one rejects a true null hypothesis. The probability of this error is called *alpha* (α).

If, on the other hand, a decision is made not to reject H_o and to take action A_1 when the true state of the world is W_2, this is a *Type II error.* This error is made when one fails to reject a false null hypothesis. The probability of a Type II error is called *beta* (β).

■ *Example.* This terminology applied to the problem of the machine operator may be shown as follows:

	States of the world	
Action	W_1 (H_o is true)	W_2 (H_o is false)
A_1: Continue	Correct decision	Type II error
A_2: Stop and adjust	Type I error	Correct decision

Probability of Making an Incorrect Decision

While it is recognized that some incorrect decisions are inevitable, it is the job of the statistician to estimate the probability of an incorrect decision so that a business executive can act with a knowledge of the magnitude of the risk that is run.

Probability of a Type I Error. By definition, a Type I error can be made only when the null hypothesis (H_o) is true and W_1 is the true state of the world. Since the central limit theorem states that the distribution of sample means is approximately normal, it is possible by using Formula 8.1 to determine the probability that any given sample mean will fall outside any given set of critical values and thus cause the experimenter to make a decision resulting in a Type I error. Given H_o is true:

$$z = \frac{\bar{x}_c - \mu}{\sigma_{\bar{x}}} \dots\dots\dots\dots\dots\dots\dots\dots\dots\dots\dots\dots\dots\dots\dots\dots(8.1)$$

where
$\quad \bar{x}_c$ is the critical value of the sample mean
$\quad \mu$ is the value designated in H_o
$\quad \sigma_{\bar{x}}$ is the standard error of the mean
$\quad z$ is the distance to the critical value of the sample mean.

The value of z can be used to determine the probability of a Type I error by finding the area in the tail of the normal distribution using either Table H or Table I in the Appendix. For example, if $z = \pm 1.96$, the probability of a Type I error is 0.05.

■ **Example.** Assume that the universe standard deviation of the weights of boxes of cereal filled by the machine under discussion has been determined from long experience to be 0.7 ounces. Further, assume that at the time the operator takes a particular sample of 49 boxes, the universe mean is $\mu = 8$ ounces.

The theoretical sampling distribution shown in Figure 8.1 represents a distribution of the means of all possible samples of 49 boxes that might be drawn by the operator at any one time. The distribution of $\bar{x}$'s is normally distributed with

$$\mu = 8 \text{ ounces,}$$

and the standard deviation of this distribution is the standard error of the mean

$$\sigma_{\bar{x}} = \frac{\sigma}{\sqrt{n}} = \frac{0.7}{\sqrt{49}} = \frac{0.7}{7} = 0.1 \text{ ounce.}$$

The student should take particular note of the fact that the distributions shown in Figure 8.1 are distributions of sample means, not the items in a sample. Also, the mean of those distributions is the mean of the universe from which the samples were drawn.

If the decision rule is to reject H_o and take action A_2 when $\bar{x} < 7.8$ or $\bar{x} > 8.2$, the probability of a Type I error may be seen in the top distribution (Example A) in Figure 8.1 as the shaded area in each tail. The shaded area represents the probability that the sample mean of a sample of 49 drawn from the universe with a mean of 8 will be smaller than 7.8 or greater than 8.2, causing the decision-maker to reject the null hypothesis and make a Type I error.

FIGURE 8.1

**Probability of Making a Type 1 Error Given
H_o Is True**

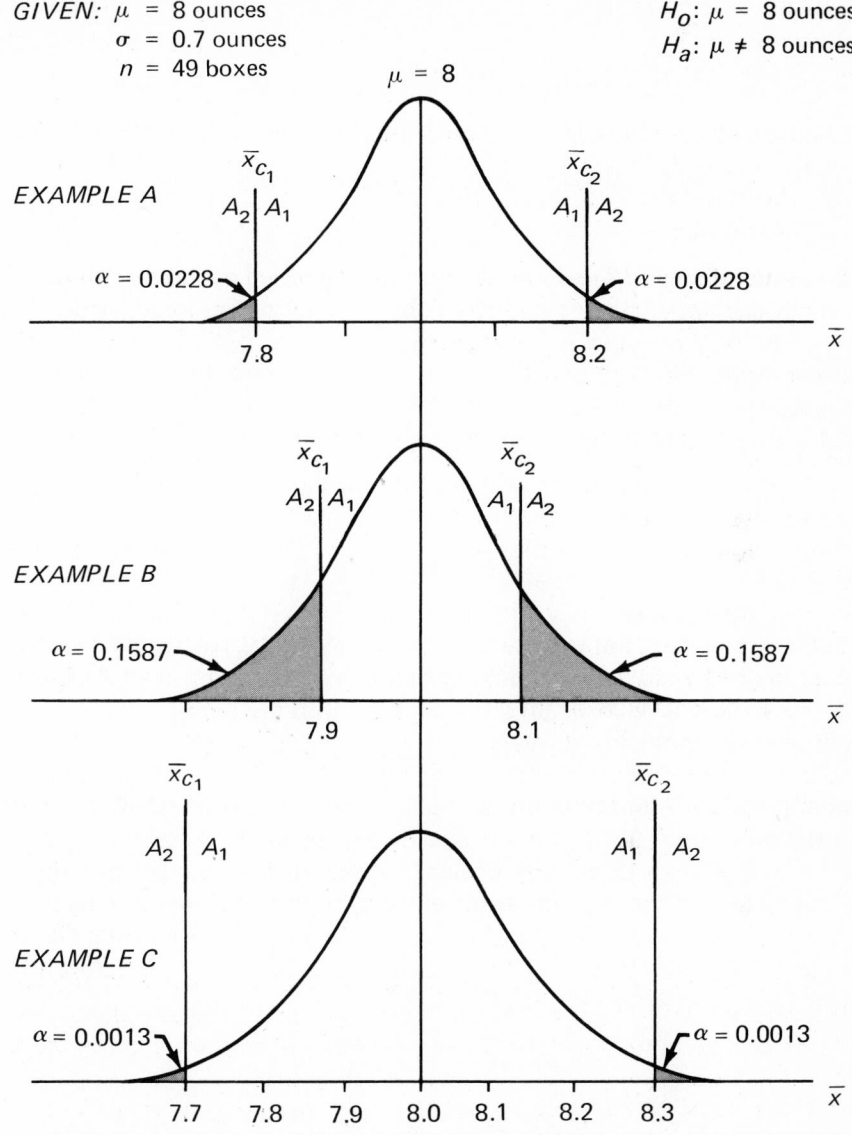

GIVEN: μ = 8 ounces
σ = 0.7 ounces
n = 49 boxes

H_o: μ = 8 ounces
H_a: $\mu \neq$ 8 ounces

Since the theoretical sampling distribution is known to be normal,
the z distances from μ to the critical values may be computed as

$$z_1 = \frac{\overline{x}_{c_1} - \mu}{\dfrac{\sigma}{\sqrt{n}}} = \frac{7.8 - 8}{0.1} = \frac{-0.2}{0.1} = -2$$

$$z_2 = \frac{\overline{X}_{c_2} - \mu}{\frac{\sigma}{\sqrt{n}}} = \frac{8.2 - 8}{0.1} = \frac{0.2}{0.1} = 2.$$

Using the table in Appendix I, the area in each tail is found to be 0.0228, or a combined area in both tails of 0.0456. This may be interpreted as

$$P(A_2 \mid W_1) = 0.0456 \text{ or } 4.56\%.$$

Also, the probability of a correct decision under these conditions is

$$P(A_1 \mid W_1) = 1 - P(A_2 \mid W_1) = 1 - 0.0456 = 0.9544,$$

or just over 95%.

The probability of a Type I error may be controlled by moving the critical values closer to or farther away from the parameter assumed in H_o.

■ *Example.* An examination of the second distribution (Example B) in Figure 8.1 shows that when the critical values are changed to 7.9 and 8.1 ounces, respectively, the new z distances are

$$z_1 = \frac{7.9 - 8.0}{0.1} = \frac{-0.1}{0.1} = -1$$

$$z_2 = \frac{8.1 - 8.0}{0.1} = \frac{0.1}{0.1} = 1.$$

The area in each tail is now 0.1587, and $P(A_2 \mid W_1) = 0.1587 + 0.1587 = 0.3174$ or 31.74%. The probability of a correct decision is $1 - P(A_2 \mid W_1) = 1 - 0.3174 = 0.6826$ or 68.26%. This probability is represented by the white area under the curve.

If, as seen in Example C in this same figure, the critical values are changed to 7.7 and 8.3 ounces, respectively, the probability of a Type I error drops to 0.0013 in each tail, or 0.0026 for both tails.

If one wishes to set the critical values so that the probability of a Type I error is some given amount, say 5%, this may be done by finding the $\pm z$ value in the Table of Area in One Tail of the Normal Curve in Appendix I, which gives 2.5% in each tail. This value is 1.96 and the critical values are computed:

$$\pm z = \frac{\overline{X}_c - \mu}{\sigma_{\overline{x}}}$$

$$-1.96 = \frac{\overline{X}_{c_1} - \mu}{\sigma_{\overline{x}}} = \frac{\overline{X}_{c_1} - 8}{0.1}$$

$$-0.196 = \overline{X}_{c_1} - 8$$

$$\overline{X}_{c_1} = 8 - 0.196 = 7.804, \text{ and}$$

$$1.96 = \frac{\overline{X}_{c_2} - \mu}{\sigma_{\overline{x}}} = \frac{\overline{X}_{c_2} - 8}{0.1}$$

$$0.196 = \bar{x}_{c_2} - 8$$
$$\bar{x}_{c_2} = 8 + 0.196 = 8.196.$$

Probability of a Type II Error. By definition, a Type II error can be made only when the null hypothesis (H_o) is false, and W_2 is the true state of the world. In such a case the sample is drawn from a theoretical sampling distribution which is centered at a value other than the value stated in the null hypothesis. For example, if the universe mean (μ) is 8.2, the null hypothesis is false, and the distribution of sample mean is centered on the value 8.2, not 8.

The probability of a Type II error is difficult to determine because it can occur whenever the true parameter is different from that stated in H_o, and the probability varies with the magnitude of that difference. For example, if $\mu = 8.2$, the probability of a Type II error is different from what it would be if $\mu = 8.3$ because the critical values are the same in both cases. The null hypothesis is false, but in neither case does the experimenter know the true value of μ when making a decision.

■ *Example.* Suppose in the previous example the universe mean, μ, is not 8 ounces but is 7.7 ounces, and H_o is false. The only kind of error the machine operator can make is to fail to stop the machine and adjust it. It has already been decided, on the basis of the value of α, not to reject H_o (that is, not to stop and adjust) if the sample mean falls between 7.9 and 8.1 ounces.

$$z = \frac{\bar{x}_c - \mu}{\sigma_{\bar{x}}} = \frac{7.9 - 7.7}{0.1} = 2.$$

The probability of a Type II error is the probability that the sample mean will lie between 7.9 and 8.1 causing the operator to fail to reject H_o, which is false. The probability is

$$P(A_1 \mid W_2, \text{ where } \mu = 7.7) = 0.0228.$$

This may be seen as Example A in Figure 8.2. The probability of 0.0228 is the area in the right tail of the distribution which lies between the critical values of 7.9 and 8.1. In Example B, Figure 8.2, the probability is

$$P(A_1 \mid W_2, \text{ where } \mu = 7.9) = 0.4773.$$

In Example C, Figure 8.2, H_o is correct, so the only type of error that can be made is a Type I error; and the probability of making this error is $P(A_2 \mid W_1, \text{ where } \mu = 8) = 0.1587 + 0.1587 = 0.3174$. The value 0.1587 comes from Table I of the Appendix for:

$$z = \frac{8.1 - 8}{0.1} = 1 \text{ (area in right-hand tail is 0.1587)}$$

$$z = \frac{7.9 - 8}{0.1} = -1 \text{ (area in left-hand tail is 0.1587)}$$

FIGURE 8.2

**Probability of Making an Error for a Given Value
of the Parameter**

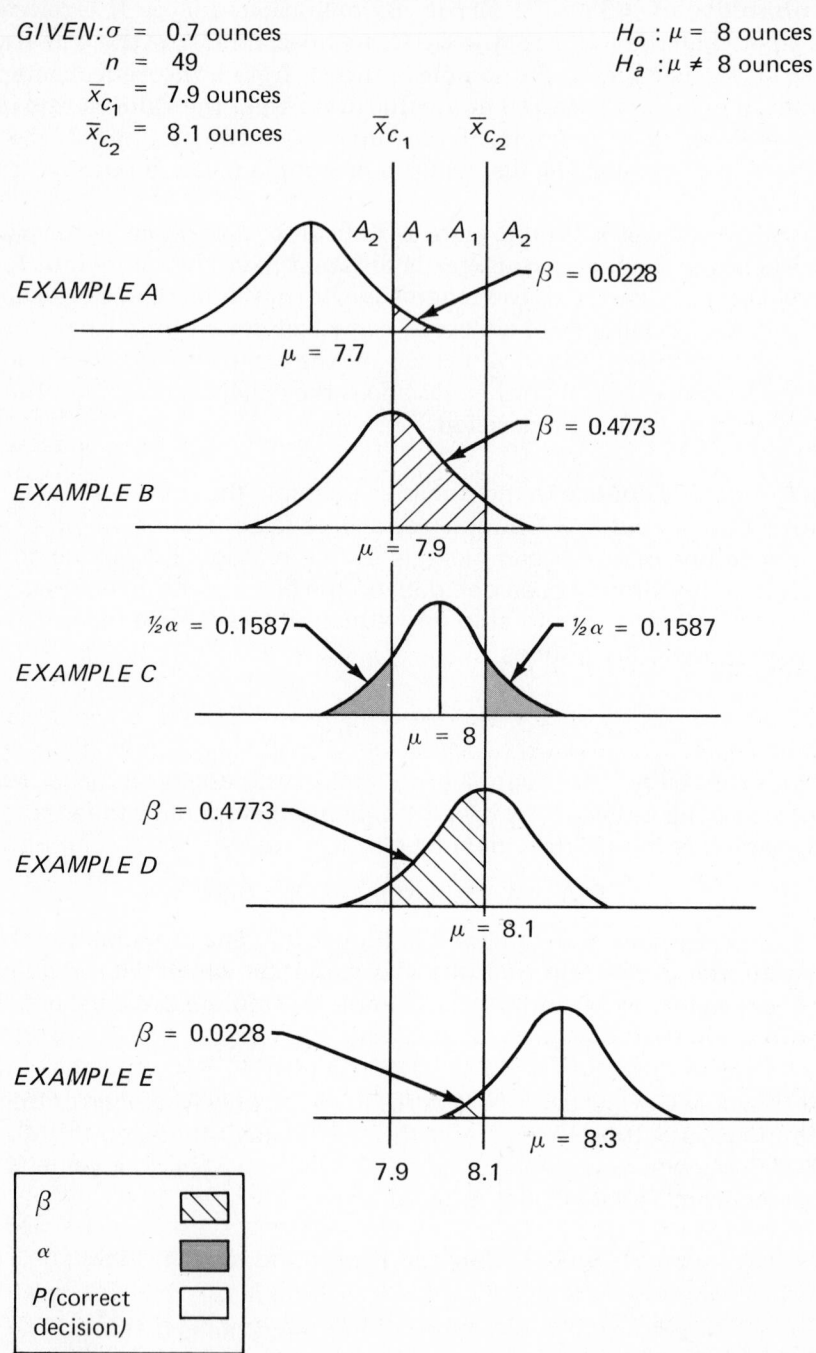

$GIVEN:\sigma$ = 0.7 ounces

n = 49

$\overline{x}_{C_1}$ = 7.9 ounces

$\overline{x}_{C_2}$ = 8.1 ounces

$H_o : \mu$ = 8 ounces

$H_a : \mu \neq$ 8 ounces

$\overline{x}_{C_1}$ $\overline{x}_{C_2}$

A_2 | A_1 | A_1 | A_2

EXAMPLE A

β = 0.0228

μ = 7.7

EXAMPLE B

β = 0.4773

μ = 7.9

$\frac{1}{2}\alpha$ = 0.1587

$\frac{1}{2}\alpha$ = 0.1587

EXAMPLE C

μ = 8

β = 0.4773

EXAMPLE D

μ = 8.1

β = 0.0228

EXAMPLE E

μ = 8.3

7.9   8.1

β

α

P(correct
decision)

In Example D, H_o is false and $P(A_1 \mid W_2$, where $\mu = 8.1)$ is 0.4773.
In Example E, H_o is false and $P(A_1 \mid W_2$, where $\mu = 8.3)$ is 0.0228.

In general, it can be stated that if H_o is true:

1. Probability of a correct decision is that area of the theoretical sampling distribution which lies between $\bar{x}_{c_1}$ and $\bar{x}_{c_2}$, and
2. Probability of a Type I error is that area of the distribution which lies outside $\bar{x}_{c_1}$ and $\bar{x}_{c_2}$.

But if H_o is false:

1. Probability of a correct decision is that area of the theoretical sampling distribution which lies outside $\bar{x}_{c_1}$ and $\bar{x}_{c_2}$, and
2. Probability of a Type II error is that area of the distribution which lies between $\bar{x}_{c_1}$ and $\bar{x}_{c_2}$.

Another point which should be emphasized is that as the critical values are changed to decrease the probability of a Type I error, these changes automatically increase the probability of a Type II error if H_o is false.

It is easy to control the probability of a Type I error through the selection of the critical values. The probability of a Type II error cannot be determined for a particular decision because that probability is determined by the value of the parameter when that parameter is not the same as that stated in the null hypothesis.

One- and Two-Tail Tests

The test of significance examples discussed so far have concerned the problem of adjusting a machine whenever it was filling boxes with either too much or too little cereal. The region in which H_o might be rejected lay in both tails of the sampling distribution. This is called a *two-tail test.*

In many other problems, one is concerned with a rejection area in only one tail of the sampling distribution. Tests of significance in such cases are called *one-tail tests.*

■ *Example.* Two service station co-operators have kept careful records of sales for a two-year period and know the average sale (μ) to be $4.00 with a standard deviation (σ) of $1.60. The operators start giving a free car wash with each fill-up of gasoline in the hope of improving the average size of sales. After trying the new promotional scheme for a few days, they draw a random sample of 100 sales slips and compute a sample mean.

To justify the cost of giving the car wash, the service station operators are looking for a significant increase in sales. They set their critical value at some figure greater than $4.00 and conduct a one-tail test of significance. If they choose a critical value of $4.36, the null hypothesis will be rejected only if a sample mean is equal to or greater than $4.36. The selection of the value $4.36 is a judgmental decision of the operators and could just as well have been based on a given value of α.

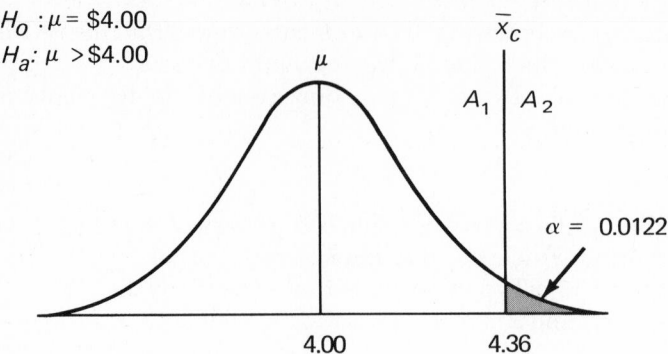

$H_o : \mu = \$4.00$
$H_a: \mu > \$4.00$

$\bar{x}_C$

μ

A_1 A_2

$\alpha = 0.0122$

4.00   4.36

$$z = \frac{\bar{x}_c - \mu}{\sigma_{\bar{x}}} = \frac{4.36 - 4.00}{\dfrac{1.60}{\sqrt{100}}} = \frac{0.36}{0.16} = 2.25$$

and $P(A_2 \mid W_1) = 0.0122$ if H_o is true. $P(A_1 \mid W_2)$ is H_o is false would depend on the new value of μ. The smaller the increase in μ, the greater β; the greater the increase in μ, the smaller β.

STEPS TO FOLLOW IN MAKING A TEST OF SIGNIFICANCE

At this point it is possible to state a general procedure that may be followed in making any test of significance. In this section the tests are stated in terms of the technical notation that has just been discussed. The five steps listed below may be used in conducting systematically any test of significance:

STEP 1. Set up a null hypothesis (H_o) to be tested.

STEP 2. Set up an alternate hypothesis (H_a) that can be accepted if H_o is rejected.

STEP 3. Determine the probability of a Type I error that management is prepared to risk (α). Select the proper probability distribution for the test.

STEP 4. Use statistical theory to write a criterion stating the conditions under which H_o will be rejected.

STEP 5. Apply the information provided by the sample to make a decision and to determine the action to be taken.

In the sections of this chapter that follow, these rules will be applied under a series of different test conditions.

TESTING THE MEAN OF A SINGLE SAMPLE

If a single random sample is drawn from a universe, and if one wishes to test a hypothesis concerning the universe mean based on the information from that sample, there are two basic types of problems to be considered:

1. The universe standard deviation is known, and
2. The universe standard deviation is not known.

Universe Standard Deviation Is Known

When the standard deviation of the universe is known, the theoretical sampling distribution of sample means from which a particular sample mean, $\bar{x}$, is drawn is a normal distribution with a mean, μ, and a standard deviation, $\sigma_{\bar{x}}$. For a given value of α, it is not necessary to compute critical values, $\bar{x}_{c_1}$ and $\bar{x}_{c_2}$, when making a single test since a table value of z will perform the same function. To distinguish this table value from another z value that will be computed using the sample data, the table value will be designated as z_α. This approach is illustrated in the following example. Values are stated for $\bar{x}_{c_1}$, and $\bar{x}_{c_2}$, but the values z_α take their place. The value of z computed from the sample data is -2.33, and that value is compared to the -1.96 to reach a decision.

■ **Example.** A manufacturer produces television tubes that are intended to have an average life (μ) of 580 hours and a standard deviation (σ) of 30 hours. Random samples of 100 tubes are regularly drawn from the production line to test for any significant change in μ. If a particular sample of 100 tubes shows a sample mean ($\bar{x}$) of 573 hours, test at an α level of 0.05 to determine if there has been a significant change.

STEPS:
1. H_o: $\mu = 580$ hours
2. H_a: $\mu \neq 580$ hours
3. An α level of 0.05 (two-tail test) requires z_α values $= \pm 1.96$.

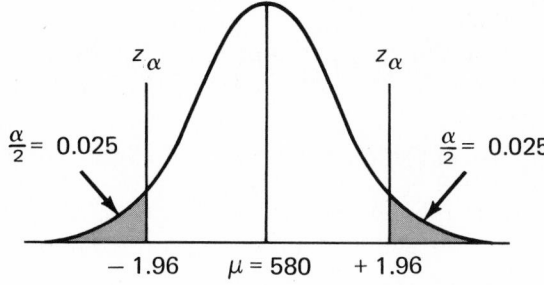

4. Criterion: Reject H_o (accept H_a) if $z < -1.96$ or if $z > +1.96$; do not reject H_o if $-1.96 \leq z \leq +1.96$ where

$$z = \frac{\bar{x} - \mu}{\sigma_{\bar{x}}} \quad\dots\dots\dots\dots\dots\dots\dots\dots\dots\dots\dots\dots\dots(8.2)$$

5. Using the sample data and the assumptions about the universe:

$$z = \frac{573 - 580}{3} = \frac{-7}{3} = -2.33$$

where

$$\sigma_{\bar{x}} = \frac{30}{\sqrt{100}} = 3.$$

Since $z(-2.33) < z_\alpha(-1.96)$, H_o should be rejected and H_a accepted. There has been a significant change in μ as indicated by this sample. When H_o is rejected, the only type of error that can be made is Type I, and the probability of having made such an error is something less than 2.5%. The probability of a correct decision in this case is 97.5% or greater.

■ **Example.** Suppose that in the previous example the sample mean had been 576 hours with a random sample of 225 tubes, and one wished to test for a significant decrease in μ at an α level of 0.01 with a one-tail test.

STEPS:
    1. H_o: $\mu = 580$ hours
    2. H_a: $\mu < 580$ hours
    3. An α level of 0.01 (one-tail test) requires a z_α value of -2.33.

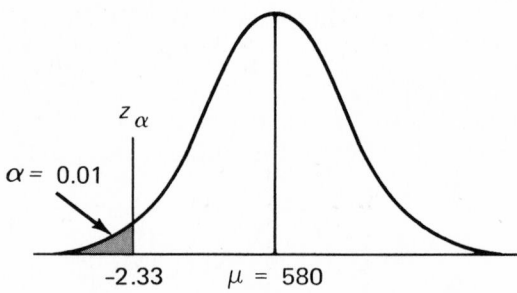

4. Criterion: Reject H_o (accept H_a) if $z < -2.33$; do not reject H_o if $z \geq -2.33$, where

$$z = \frac{\bar{x} - \mu}{\sigma_{\bar{x}}}.$$

5. Using the sample data

$$z = \frac{576 - 580}{\frac{30}{\sqrt{225}}} = \frac{-4}{2} = -2.$$

Since $z(-2) > z_\alpha$ (-2.33), do not reject H_o. A significant change in μ cannot be shown from the sample. In making this decision, it is possible that a Type II error has been made, but there is no way to measure this probability.

Universe Standard Deviation Is Not Known

In many situations the universe standard deviation is not known, but it must be estimated from the sample. In such cases the distribution of sample means is not normal but is distributed as Student's t distribution with a mean, μ, and a standard deviation, $\hat{\sigma}_{\bar{x}}$.

■ **Example.** If a manufacturer of television sets does not make tubes but buys them from another manufacturer, tests of significance may be used in determining whether to accept or to reject a particular shipment based on an inspection of a random sample of tubes drawn from the shipment. Suppose that the contract between the manufacturer of the tubes and the buyer calls for an average life of 550 hours. The firm receiving the shipment tests a sample of 25 tubes and finds $\bar{x} =$ 530 hours, and $s = 37$ hours. If a one-tail test is made at an α level of 0.05, should the shipment be accepted or rejected?

STEPS:
1. H_o: $\mu = 550$ hours
2. H_a: $\mu < 550$ hours
3. An α level of 0.05 (one-tail test) requires a t_α value of -1.711. (Use $t_{0.10}$ with $n - 1$ or 24 degrees of freedom in the table in Appendix J to get t_α since the t table is two-tailed. The level of significance of 0.10 represents a total area of 10% in both tails or 5% in one tail.)

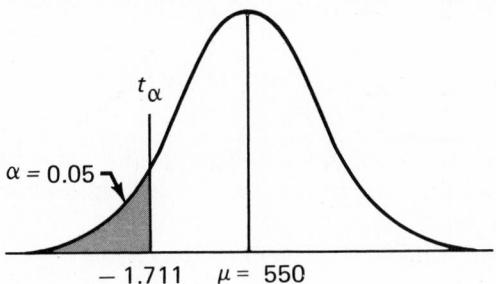

4. Criterion: Reject H_o (accept H_a) if $t < -1.711$; do not reject H_o if $t \geq -1.711$, where

$$t = \frac{\bar{x} - \mu}{\hat{\sigma}_{\bar{x}}} \quad \dots\dots\dots\dots\dots\dots\dots\dots\dots\dots\dots(8.3)$$

$$\text{and } \hat{\sigma}_{\bar{x}} = \frac{s}{\sqrt{n-1}}$$

5. Using the sample data

$$t = \frac{530 - 550}{7.55} = \frac{-20}{7.55} = -2.65$$

where

$$\hat{\sigma}_{\bar{x}} = \frac{37}{\sqrt{24}} = 7.55.$$

Since $t(-2.65) < t_\alpha(-1.711)$, reject H_o and accept H_a. The shipment would be rejected as not meeting the contract requirements for average length of life of the tubes.

TESTING THE DIFFERENCE BETWEEN THE MEANS OF TWO SAMPLES

A very common problem encountered in tests of significance is one in which it is necessary to determine if the means of two samples indicate that the samples were drawn from the same universe or from universes with identical values of μ.

If the two samples of sizes n_1 and n_2 have means $\bar{x}_1$ and $\bar{x}_2$, the null hypothesis may be stated as follows:

$$H_o: \mu_1 = \mu_2.$$

If this hypothesis is not rejected, a decision has been made that the two samples were drawn from a single universe with a mean, μ, and that any difference in the sample means is a sampling difference and is not significant.

If H_o is rejected, and H_a is accepted, the conclusion reached is that the difference between $\bar{x}_1$ and $\bar{x}_2$ is too large to be explained as a sampling difference and, therefore, the samples were drawn from two universes with different means.

In approaching tests of this nature, three basic types of problems will be considered:

1. The universe standard deviations, σ_1 and σ_2, are known,
2. The universe standard deviations are not known but are assumed to be the same, and
3. The pairing of dependent observations.

Universe Standard Deviations Are Known

Since the assumption in H_o is that $\mu_1 = \mu_2$, then $\mu_1 - \mu_2 = 0$. When σ_1 and σ_2 are known, the theoretical sampling distribution the statistics,

$\bar{x}_1 - \bar{x}_2$, is assumed to be normal with a mean of zero and a standard deviation

$$\sigma_{\bar{x}_1 - \bar{x}_2} = \sqrt{\frac{\sigma_1^2}{n_1} + \frac{\sigma_2^2}{n_2}} \dots \dots \dots \dots \dots (8.4)$$

where

$\sigma_{\bar{x}_1 - \bar{x}_2}$ is the standard error of the difference between the two sample means.

As with any theoretical sampling distribution that is normal, a z_α value can be established by use of a table of areas under the normal curve, and data supplied by the sample can be used to compute the z value to be compared with z_α. This value will always be

$$z = \frac{\text{statistic} - \text{parameter}}{\text{standard error}}.$$

The statistic is supplied by the sample data, in this case, $\bar{x}_1 - \bar{x}_2$. The parameter is that assumed in H_o, in this case, $\mu_1 - \mu_2$, which is zero. The standard error is the standard deviation of the theoretical sampling distribution, in this case, $\sigma_{\bar{x}_1 - \bar{x}_2}$. Thus, the formula to be used here for z is

$$z = \frac{(\bar{x}_1 - \bar{x}_2) - (\mu_1 - \mu_2)}{\sigma_{\bar{x}_1 - \bar{x}_2}} \quad \text{or} \quad \frac{\bar{x}_1 - \bar{x}_2}{\sigma_{\bar{x}_1 - \bar{x}_2}} \dots \dots \dots \dots (8.5)$$

since it is hypothesized that $\mu_1 - \mu_2 = 0$.

■ **Example.** In a manufacturing plant there are two machines used to cut steel bars. While each machine can be adjusted to control the average length of the bars cut, there will always be some slight variation in the length of the individual bars. Over a period of time the variation in the production of each machine has been carefully measured and is shown in terms of standard deviations:

Machine I: $\sigma_1 = 0.10$ inches
Machine II: $\sigma_2 = 0.12$ inches.

A machinist is asked to set the two machines so that they will cut bars with equal average lengths. The worker sets the two machines as carefully as possible and then cuts a sample of 50 bars on each machine. The sample results are shown below:

Machine	Sample size	Sample mean
I	$n_1 = 50$	$\bar{x}_1 = 27.80$ inches
II	$n_2 = 50$	$\bar{x}_2 = 27.70$ inches.

The problem is to test at an α level of 0.01 with a two-tail test to see if the machines are set to cut bars of equal average lengths.

STEPS:
1. $H_o : \mu_1 = \mu_2$

2. $H_a: \mu_1 \neq \mu_2$
3. An α level of 0.01 (two-tail test) requires a z_α value of ± 2.58.

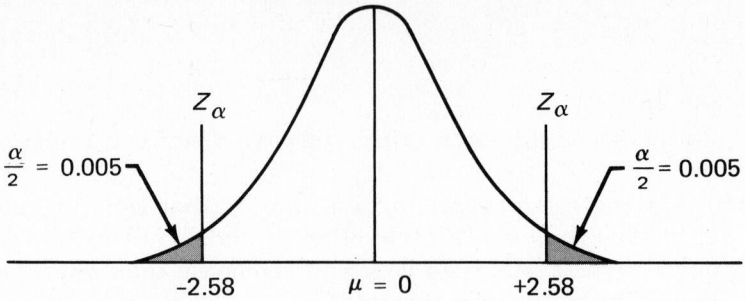

4. Criterion: Reject H_o (accept H_a) if $z > 2.58$ or $z < -2.58$; do not reject H_o if $-2.58 \leq z \leq 2.58$, where

$$z = \frac{\bar{X}_1 - \bar{X}_2}{\sigma_{\bar{x}_1 - \bar{x}_2}}$$

5. Using the sample data

$$z = \frac{27.80 - 27.70}{0.022} = \frac{0.10}{0.022} = 4.54$$

where

$$\sigma_{\bar{x}_1 - \bar{x}_2} = \sqrt{\frac{(0.10)^2}{50} + \frac{(0.12)^2}{50}} = 0.022.$$

Since $z(4.54) > z_\alpha(2.58)$, reject H_o and accept H_a. The machines are not adjusted to cut bars of equal average lengths.

Universe Standard Deviations Are Not Known

Tests of significance involving two sample means are often made under conditions where the universe standard deviations are not known but are assumed to be equal. The sample standard deviations must be used as estimates. In such cases the theoretical sampling distribution of differences $\mu_1 - \mu$ is assumed to be a t distribution with a mean equal to zero and a standard deviation that is the estimated standard error of the difference

$$\hat{\sigma}_{\bar{x}_1 - \bar{x}_2} = \sqrt{\frac{n_1 s_1^2 + n_2 s_2^2}{n_1 + n_2 - 2}} \sqrt{\frac{n_1 + n_2}{n_1 n_2}} \quad \dotsb (8.6)$$

The t value can then be computed as

$$t = \frac{(\bar{x}_1 - \bar{x}_2) - (\mu_1 - \mu_2)}{\hat{\sigma}_{\bar{x}_1 - \bar{x}_2}} \quad \text{or} \quad \frac{\bar{x}_1 - \bar{x}_2}{\hat{\sigma}_{\bar{x}_1 - \bar{x}_2}} \quad \dotsb (8.7)$$

where

degrees of freedom are $n_1 + n_2 - 2$.

■ *Example*. Assume that two types of precast concrete beams are being considered for manufacture and sale. The only difference in the two beams is the type of coarse material used. A sample of each type is made and tested for strength, with the following results:

	Material A	Material B
Sample size	$n_1 = 12$	$n_2 = 10$
Sample mean	$\bar{x}_1 = 5{,}000$ psi	$\bar{x}_2 = 4{,}975$ psi
Sample standard deviation	$s_1 = 50$ psi	$s_2 = 60$ psi.

The problem is to test at an α level of 0.05 to determine if the beams made with Material *A* are stronger than the beams made with Material *B*.

STEPS:

1. $H_o: \mu_1 = \mu_2$
2. $H_a: \mu_1 > \mu_2$
3. An α level of 0.05 (one-tail test) requires a t_α value of 1.725 ($t_{0.10}$ with $n_1 + n_2 - 2$ degrees of freedom).
4. Criterion: Reject H_o (accept H_a) if $t > 1.725$; do not reject H_o if $t \leq 1.725$, where

$$t = \frac{\bar{X}_1 - \bar{X}_2}{\hat{\sigma}_{\bar{x}_1 - \bar{x}_2}}$$

5. Using the sample data

$$t = \frac{5{,}000 - 4{,}975}{24.59} = \frac{25}{24.59} = 1.02$$

where

$$\hat{\sigma}_{\bar{x}_1 - \bar{x}_2} = \sqrt{\frac{12(50)^2 + 10(60)^2}{20}} \sqrt{\frac{12 + 10}{(12)(10)}} = 24.59.$$

Since $t(1.02) < t_\alpha(1.725)$, do not reject H_o. It is not possible to show a significant difference in the strength of the two types of beams.

It is possible, of course, to make two-tail tests for differences in two means. If the two universe standard deviations, σ_1^2 and σ_2^2, are known but unequal, there is no problem with using Formula 8.4 to compute the standard error of the difference in the two sample means. If the two universe standard deviations are not known and cannot be assumed to be equal, a nonparametric test, such as the Kruskal-Wallis *H* test, should be used. This test is discussed in Chapter 9.

Pairing of Dependent Observations

In the two previous sections in which comparisons were made between two sample means, it was assumed that the samples were independent. *Independent samples* are those in which individuals (or items) in one sample cannot be related to, or associated with, individuals (or items) in the other sample.

There are cases in which two measurements are made on a single individual, say, before and after treatment. When this is done, the two groups of observations cannot be treated as independent samples.

If the assumption can be made that $\sigma_1^2 = \sigma_2^2$,[1] the theoretical sampling distribution of differences $(\bar{x}_1 - \bar{x}_2)$ is assumed to be a t distribution with a mean of zero and a standard deviation that is the estimated standard error of the difference written

$$\hat{\sigma}_{\bar{D}} = \frac{\hat{\sigma}_D}{\sqrt{n}} \dots\dots\dots\dots\dots\dots\dots\dots\dots\dots\dots(8.8)$$

where
  D is the difference between each pair of observations
  $\bar{D}$ is the mean of D

$\hat{\sigma}_D = \sqrt{\dfrac{n\Sigma D^2 - (\Sigma D)^2}{n(n-1)}}$ is the standard deviation of the difference, and n is

the number of pairs of observations.

The appropriate statistic t for a test of significance is written

$$t = \frac{\bar{D} - 0}{\hat{\sigma}_{\bar{D}}} = \frac{\bar{D}}{\hat{\sigma}_{\bar{D}}} \dots\dots\dots\dots\dots\dots\dots\dots\dots\dots(8.9)$$

where
  degrees of freedom for t are $n - 1$.

■ **Example.** A random sample of 20 workers is observed both before and after installation of a new device to be used for holding an electronic part being assembled. The number of parts assembled in a 10-minute period is shown in Table 8.1. The problem is to test at an α level of 0.01 to determine whether there has been a significant increase in the average number of parts assembled after the installation of the new device.

STEPS:
  1. H_o: $\Delta = 0$ (Let Δ represent the universe difference.)
  2. H_a: $\Delta < 0$
  3. An α level of 0.01 (one-tail test) requires a t_α value of -2.539 ($t_{0.02}$ with $n - 1$ degrees of freedom).
  4. Criterion: Reject H_o (accept H_a) if $t < -2.539$; do not reject H_o if $t \geq -2.539$, where

$$t = \frac{\bar{D}}{\hat{\sigma}_{\bar{D}}}$$

  5. Using the sample data

---

[1] A test for this hypothesis is discussed in Chapter 11, page 326.

TABLE 8.1

**Number of Parts Assembled By 20 Employees Before
and After Installation of a New Holding Frame**

Employee Number	Before	After	Difference D	D^2
1	12	15	−3	9
2	10	10	0	0
3	11	14	−3	9
4	13	11	2	4
5	15	17	−2	4
6	9	13	−4	16
7	14	18	−4	16
8	15	18	−3	9
9	12	10	2	4
10	10	11	−1	1
11	11	13	−2	4
12	15	17	−2	4
13	13	16	−3	9
14	12	14	−2	4
15	10	15	−5	25
16	14	14	0	0
17	14	12	2	4
18	13	17	−4	16
19	15	18	−3	9
20	10	12	−2	4
Total	248	285	−37	151

$$\bar{D} = \frac{-37}{20} = -1.85$$

$$\hat{\sigma}_D = \sqrt{\frac{20(151) - (-37)^2}{(20)(19)}} = 2.084$$

$$\hat{\sigma}_{\bar{D}} = \frac{2.084}{\sqrt{20}} = 0.466$$

$$t = \frac{-1.85}{0.466} = -3.97.$$

Since t (−3.97) $< t_\alpha$ (−2.539), reject H_o. There has been a significant increase in the average number of parts assembled when using the new holding frame.

TESTING THE PROPORTION OF A SINGLE SAMPLE

In Chapter 4 it was noted that the binomial probability distribution is the appropriate model for a sampling distribution when the population is split into two qualitative categories. One group has a particular characteristic and the other group does not. For example, a shipment of parts can be divided into two groups, defective and nondefective. In one group the parts are all defective and in the other group no part has the characteristic of being defective.

When the proportion of occurrence of some characteristic of sample items is used to test a hypothesis concerning a universe proportion of the same characteristic, there are two basic types of approaches to be considered:

1. The size of the sample is small, and
2. The size of the sample is large.

Significance Tests with Small Samples

While the proper theoretical sampling distribution to use when dealing with a proportion characteristic is always the binomial distribution, it can be used in practice only when the sample is small. In writing the criterion, it is not always possible to set up an α value that is exactly 0.05 or 0.01 as normally used. It is possible, however, to choose from those values available one that satisfactorily controls the probability of a Type I error. This is demonstrated in the following example.

■ *Example.* During World War II a recruiter for a large West Coast shipbuilder traveled about the country searching for qualified machinists, who were in short supply and in great demand. A large number of applicants were interviewed, and the interviewer tried to hire those who were qualified and to reject those who were not.

The interviewer, J. B. Jones, used as the basis of selection a multiple-choice quiz with 10 questions, each of which had four choices. An applicant who was an experienced machinist could usually pick the correct answer to a question. If the applicant was not qualified and had to guess at an answer, the chances of selecting the correct one was only one out of four.

While interviewing in Central City, Jones gave the quiz to 10 applicants. Five made very low grades and were eliminated. The top five applicants made the grades shown below:

Applicant	Number of correct answers out of 10 questions
A	5
B	8
C	9
D	4
E	7

If Jones had to select those applicants who demonstrated through their answers to the questions a knowledge of the subject rather than just a series of lucky guesses, which ones should be hired? Assume that the company would be satisfied with an α level of no more than 0.05.

STEPS:
1. H_o: $\pi \leq 0.25$ (applicant is not qualified, reject)[2]
2. H_a: $\pi > 0.25$ (applicant is qualified, hire)
3. To determine the critical value, it is necessary to look at the following table of binomial probabilities: (see Appendix C)

Number of correct answers r	Probability $P(r \mid n = 10, \pi = 0.25)$		
0	0.0563		
1	0.1877		
2	0.2816		
3	0.2503		
4	0.1460		
5	0.0584	0.0584	
6	0.0162	0.0162	0.0162
7	0.0031	0.0031	0.0031
8	0.0004	0.0004	0.0004
9	0.0000	0.0000	0.0000
10	0.0000	0.0000	0.0000
	1.0000	0.0781	0.0197

If Jones accepts an applicant who has five or more correct answers, the probability of accepting an unqualified applicant is $\alpha = P(A_2 \mid W_1) = 0.0781$ or 7.81%, which is too large a value for α. A_2 represents the action of hiring the applicant, and W_1 represents the state of the world in which the applicant is guessing at answers and is not qualified. If Jones accepts an applicant who has six or more correct answers, the value of α is 0.0197. Since this probability is well under the 0.05 required, six correct answers was taken as the critical value.

4. Criterion: If the applicant has six or more correct answers, reject H_o and accept H_a. If the applicant has less than six correct answers, do not reject H_o.
5. Applying the criterion to the scores of the top five applicants, Jones would hire Applicants B, C, and E, and would reject Applicants A and D.

One must recognize in looking at this example that the use of the binomial distribution is based on the validity of the following assumptions:

1. Each question has only two possible answers: right or wrong.
2. The location of the correct answer in each question is random.

---

[2] The value of 0.25 is used here since the applicant who is guessing has one chance in four of getting the correct answer.

3. When the applicant does not know the correct answer to a question, he or she guesses at random.

■ *Example.* Assume that in the previous example Jones had used a true-false test with 20 questions to determine if an applicant was a qualified machinist. The probability of a correct answer based on a pure guess is 0.5. If the top five applicants made the scores listed below, which ones should be hired without exceeding an α of 0.05?

Applicant	Number of correct answers out of 20 questions
A	14
B	17
C	19
D	13
E	15

STEPS:
1. H_o: $\pi = 0.50$
2. H_a: $\pi > 0.50$
3. The following partial table shows the binomial probabilities needed to determine the critical value:

Number of correct answers r	Probability $P(r \mid n = 20, \pi = 0.50)$		
.	.		
.	.		
.	.		
13	0.0739		
14	0.0370	0.0370	
15	0.0148	0.0148	0.0148
16	0.0046	0.0046	0.0046
17	0.0011	0.0011	0.0011
18	0.0002	0.0002	0.0002
19	0.0000	0.0000	0.0000
20	0.0000	0.0000	0.0000
	1.0000	0.0577	0.0207

If the critical value is taken as 14 correct answers, $\alpha = 0.0577$, which is too large. If the critical value is taken as 15, $\alpha = 0.0207$, which meets the company requirements.
4. Applying this criterion to the scores of the top five applicants, Jones, again, would hire Applicants *B, C,* and *E,* and would reject Applicants *A* and *D.*

Significance Tests With Large Samples

When the sample size is large, it is necessary to approximate the binomial distribution with the normal distribution because of the difficulties involved in solving the binomial formula for large values of n. Appendix C gives the binomial values up to and including $n = 100$. Other tables seldom go beyond that number.

As the size of the sample continues to increase, the normal distribution can be used as an approximation of the binomial even in cases where $p \neq 0.5$. As a general rule of thumb, if $n\pi \geq 25$, the normal curve approximation is appropriate. Also, as n increases, the importance of the continuity correction becomes negligible, and the formula for z may be written

$$z = \frac{p - \pi}{\sigma_p} \quad\quad\quad\quad\quad\quad\quad\quad (8.10)$$

where
p is the sample proportion
π is the universe proportion in H_o
σ_p is the standard error of the proportion.

■ Example. A mail-order house that sells men's shirts has learned from long experience that 15% of all shirts sold are returned to the firm by customers who complain that the shirts do not fit properly. In an attempt to correct this situation, the firm redesigns the order blank that it sends its customers and finds that of the next 500 sales using the new blank, there are 60 returns. Test at an α level of 0.05 to see if there has been a significant change in the universe proportion of returns.

STEPS:
 1. $H_o: \pi = 0.15$
 2. $H_a: \pi < 0.15$
 3. An α level of 0.05 (one-tail test) requires a z_α value of -1.64.
 4. Criterion: Reject H_o (accept H_a) if $z < -1.64$; do not reject H_o if $z \geq -1.64$, where

$$z = \frac{p - \pi}{\sigma_p}.$$

 5. Using the sample data
$$z = \frac{0.12 - 0.15}{0.0160} = -1.875$$

where

$$\sigma_p = \sqrt{\frac{\pi(1 - \pi)}{n}} = \sqrt{\frac{(0.15)(0.85)}{500}} = 0.0160, \text{ and}$$

$$p = \frac{60}{500} = 0.12.$$

Since $z(-1.875) < z_\alpha(-1.64)$, reject H_o and accept H_a. There has been a significant change in the universe proportion of returns as a result of the changes made in the order blank.

A two-tail test can also be made of a sample percent by using a two-tail alternate hypothesis and by setting the decision limits so as to divide the value of α equally in the two tails of the sampling distribution.

TESTING THE DIFFERENCE BETWEEN THE PROPORTIONS OF TWO LARGE SAMPLES

Testing the difference between proportions of two samples is much the same as testing the difference between the means of two samples. The null hypothesis assumes that there is no difference in the parameters and that the difference observed between the sample percents is due to chance. The theoretical sampling distribution of differences is assumed to be normal, with a mean of zero ($\pi_1 - \pi_2 = 0$) and a standard deviation which is the standard error of the difference between the sample proportions

$$\hat{\sigma}_{p_1 - p_2} = \sqrt{\frac{\hat{\pi}(1 - \hat{\pi})}{n_1} + \frac{\hat{\pi}(1 - \hat{\pi})}{n_2}} \quad \ldots\ldots\ldots\ldots\ldots\ldots (8.11)$$

where

$$\hat{\pi} = \frac{x_1 + x_2}{n_1 + n_2} \quad \ldots\ldots\ldots\ldots\ldots\ldots\ldots\ldots\ldots\ldots\ldots\ldots\ldots (8.12)$$

and x_1 and x_2 represent the number of occurrences in the two samples.

Since π is not known, it is estimated by combining the data from both samples to give $\hat{\pi}$.

Thus, the value of z can be computed as

$$z = \frac{(p_1 - p_2) - (\pi_1 - \pi_2)}{\hat{\sigma}_{p_1 - p_2}} \quad \ldots\ldots\ldots\ldots\ldots\ldots\ldots (8.13)$$

where it is hypothesized that $\pi_1 - \pi_2 = 0$.

■ *Example.* An importer of fine cheeses, who sells a product by direct-mail advertising, has developed an extensive mailing list of people to whom brochures announcing new assortments of cheeses are regularly sent. In developing an announcement of Christmas offerings, the importer has designed two radically different layouts and would like to know if one is better than the other. The importer decides to test them on samples of customers drawn at random from the total mailing list before sending the final mailing to all the names on the list. The test is made with the following results:

	Layout 1	Layout 2
Sample size:	$n_1 = 400$	$n_2 = 200$
Number of orders:	$x_1 = 100$	$x_2 = 44$
Sample percent:	$p_1 = \dfrac{x_1}{n_1} = \dfrac{100}{400} = 0.25$	$p_2 = \dfrac{x_2}{n_2} = \dfrac{44}{200} = 0.22.$

The problem is to test at an α level of 0.05 to see if Layout 1 is significantly better than Layout 2.

STEPS:
1. H_o: $\pi_1 = \pi_2$
2. H_a: $\pi_1 > \pi_2$
3. An α of 0.05 requires a z_α value of 1.64 for a one-tail test.
4. Criterion: Reject H_o (accept H_a) if $z > 1.64$; do not reject H_o if $z \leq 1.64$, when

$$z = \frac{(p_1 - p_2) - (\pi_1 - \pi_2)}{\hat{\sigma}_{p_1 - p_2}}.$$

5. Using the sample data

$$z = \frac{(0.25 - 0.22) - 0}{0.037} = \frac{0.03}{0.037} = 0.81$$

when

$$\hat{\pi} = \frac{100 + 44}{400 + 200} = 0.24, \text{ and}$$

$$\hat{\sigma}_{p_1 - p_2} = \sqrt{\frac{(0.24)(0.76)}{400} + \frac{(0.24)(0.76)}{200}} = 0.037.$$

Since $z(0.81) < z_\alpha(1.64)$, do not reject H_o. The test does not show that Layout 1 is significantly better than Layout 2.

■ *Example.* In order to carry out the test in the previous example as a two-tail test, only a few changes in the procedure are necessary.

STEPS:
1. H_o: $\pi_1 = \pi_2$
2. H_a: $\pi_1 \neq \pi_2$
3. An $\alpha = 0.05$ would require z_α values of ± 1.96.
4. Criterion: Reject H_o (accept H_a) if $z < -1.96$ or $z > +1.96$; do not reject H_o if $-1.96 \leq z \leq 1.96$.
5. The computed value of $z = 0.81$ and H_o cannot be rejected.

STUDY QUESTIONS

8-1. Explain briefly the meaning of each of the following terms:
a. test of significance
b. test of hypothesis
c. state of the world
d. state of nature
e. null hypothesis
f. alternate hypothesis
g. action
h. decision rule
i. critical value
j. Type I error
k. Type II error
l. two-tail test
m. one-tail test
n. independent samples.

8-2. Why is the null hypothesis the one normally set up to be tested?

8-3. Why is the criterion written to control the probability of a Type I error rather than the probability of a Type II error?

8-4. In what way can the probability of a Type I error be reduced?

8-5. If the decision maker is able to reduce the probability of making a Type I error, what effect does this action have on the probability of making a Type II error?

8-6. What are the steps to be followed in making a test of significance?

8-7. If a test of significance is made that involves a sample mean, what will be the shape of the theoretical sampling distribution of means in each of the following cases:
  a. When the universe standard deviation is known?
  b. When the universe standard deviation is not known?

8-8. In testing the difference between two sample means:
  a. What is the value of the mean of the theoretical sampling distribution of differences assumed in H_o?
  b. What is the shape of the sampling distribution? Explain the two cases.
  c. What is the standard deviation of the theoretical sampling distribution called? What is its importance in the test of significance?

8-9. How do you determine degrees of freedom for t when testing for the difference in means of two samples that are not independent? How does this computation differ for tests where the samples are independent?

8-10. In a test of significance involving the proportion of a single sample:
  a. What is the theoretical sampling distribution involved?
  b. What are the mean and the standard deviation of this distribution?
  c. What effect does an increase in sample size have on the testing procedure?

8-11. In testing the difference between two sample proportions:
  a. What kind of theoretical sampling distribution is involved?
  b. What are the mean and the standard deviation of this distribution?

8-12. Is it possible to make both a Type I and a Type II error on the same decision? Explain.

8-13. What is the relationship between tests of significance and the theory of sampling distribution (discussed in Chapter 6)?

PROBLEMS

8-1. A firm that manufactures small electric motors plans to purchase some plastic parts from a supplier if the parts will withstand pressure of

350 pounds or more per square inch without breaking. If the parts are not that strong, the manufacturer will not buy them. If tests are made on a random sample of 100 parts, find a decision rule for this firm. Assume $\alpha = 0.05$, and the universe standard deviation is known to be 18 psi.

a. Assume the hypotheses are:
$H_o: \mu = 350$ (buy)
$H_a: \mu < 350$ (do not buy)

b. Assume the hypotheses are:
$H_o: \mu = 350$ (do not buy)
$H_a: \mu > 350$ (buy)

8-2. An oil company will build a new self-service station on a given corner lot if an average of more than 1,800 cars a day passes the lot. If it is assumed that the universe standard deviation is 126 cars, find a decision rule for the company using an α value of 0.01, a random sample of 36 days, and the following hypotheses:

$$H_o: \mu = 1,800 \text{ cars (do not build)}$$
$$H_a: \mu > 1,800 \text{ cars (build)}$$

8-3. An automatic machine is used to fill sacks of seed with an average of 50 pounds a sack. The universe standard deviation is known to be 1.2 pounds a sack. A sample of 25 sacks is checked each hour to determine if the machine is in adjustment. Using an α value of 0.05, compute the two critical values of the sample mean and write the instructions to tell the operator when the machine should be stopped and adjusted.

8-4. The average time required for a worker to assemble an electric chain saw is 30 minutes, with a universe standard deviation of 6 minutes. From time to time the supervisor takes a sample of the average time required for a particular worker to assemble 16 of these units to see if performance is above or below average. Use an α level of 0.01 and set up a decision rule that would allow the supervisor to decide when a worker is above or below standard.

8-5. The following decision rules have been determined to show when a machine, which cuts rods to a specified length, is out of adjustment. The value of α used in determining the rules was 0.05, and the universe standard deviation was 0.02 inches.

$$\bar{x}_{c_1} = 26.9951 \text{ inches and } \bar{x}_{c_2} = 27.0049 \text{ inches.}$$

a. What is the null hypothesis concerning μ?
b. How large a sample should be drawn when using the decision rules?

8-6. If in Problem 8.1 a random sample of 625 parts is drawn but all other facts are the same, recompute the decision rules and discuss the effect of the change in sample size.

8–7. Use a one-tail test and an α level of 0.01 to determine which of the following samples are likely to have come from a universe with a mean of 447 and a standard deviation of 6.

Sample	Sample Mean	Sample Size
1	450	36
2	446	81
3	446	256
4	446.5	900
5	447.2	1,764

8–8. Entrance examinations given by a city college in the past have produced a mean grade of 78.4 and a standard deviation of 7.5. A random sample of 49 grades from one high school shows an average grade of 80.2.
   a. Are the students who apply from that high school significantly better than the students who usually apply to that college? Use an α level of 0.05 and a one-tail test. *Use 5 steps on p222 → eg.(8.2)*
   b. Would your answer to (a) be the same if you used a two-tail test with an α level of 0.05? How would you have to restate the alternate hypothesis for such a test?
   c. Would your answer to (a) be the same if you used an α level of 0.01 and a one-tail test?

8–9. A manufacturer of light bulbs states that the average life of a bulb is 1,200 hours. Make a test of significance to determine whether to accept or reject a large shipment of these bulbs if a random sample of 10 bulbs has a sample mean life of 1,116 hours and a sample standard deviation of 180 hours. Use an α value of 0.05 and a one-tail test. *(8.3)*

8–10. A business college makes a claim in its advertising that its graduates can type 30 words a minute after a 10-week course in typewriting. Test this claim using a one-tail test, an α value of 0.05, and the sample data below gathered on eight of the school's graduates.

Student	Words a minute	
1	28	*(8.3)*
2	29	
3	33	
4	25	
5	26	
6	30	
7	26	
8	27	

8–11. An automatic painting machine is designed to spray metal desks with an average of 4.5 ounces of paint. The universe standard deviation is 0.32 ounces. Sample observations of the output of the machine on successive days show the following results:

	Wednesday	*Thursday*
Sample size	$n_1 = 25$ desks	$n_2 = 25$ desks
Sample mean	$\bar{x}_1 = 4.52$ ozs.	$\bar{x}_2 = 4.30$ ozs.

If the value of α is 0.01, test the hypothesis that the machine was adjusted to spray the same average amount of paint on both days against the alternative hypothesis that the averages were different (two-tail test).

8–12. Recompute the answer to Problem 8.11 using samples of 250 desks on each of the two days. If all other data are the same, would your decision be different?

8–13. Two randomly selected groups, each containing six machine operators, are taught to operate milling machines using two different methods. After two weeks of training, each group is tested to determine the number of parts each worker can produce in an hour. The results are shown below:

Group 1	*Group 2*
48	33
52	18
60	70
20	30
56	40
64	25

Using a value of α of 0.05, test the hypothesis that the two groups are equally well trained against the alternate hypothesis that group 1 is better than group 2.

8–14. A manufacturer wishes to increase the strength of a metal part used in farm tractors through a change in the manufacturing process. A sample of 30 parts is tested before the change takes place and another sample of 32 parts produced after the change is tested later. Analyze the results of the study shown below and write up your findings. Is the new process better?

	Before	*After*
Sample size	$n_1 = 30$	$n_2 = 32$
Sample mean	$\bar{x}_1 = 300$	$\bar{x}_2 = 320$
Sample standard deviation	$s_1 = 15$	$s_2 = 17$

8–15. An oil company develops an additive for gasoline which it claims will increase car mileage significantly when used. An experiment is conducted on seven cars both with and without the gasoline additive. The results of the experiment are shown below and indicate an average increase in miles per gallon with the use of the additive. Is this increase significant at the 0.01 level?

	Miles per gallon	
Car	Without additive	With additive
1	12	13.5
2	18	17.9
3	15	17.8
4	16	19.0
5	20	18.8
6	27	32.0
7	13	14.7

8–16. In an effort to improve employee morale and reduce the number of sick leave days taken, a personnel director tries a new sick leave policy on a small sample of employees selected at random from a large work force. These employees are told they will be paid in cash at the end of the year for unused sick leave. After one year the sick leave records are compared for the sample group with records for the same employees for the year before the new policy went into effect. Test the following results for significant difference at a value of α of 0.05:

Number of sick leave days taken

Employee	Before the new policy	After the new policy
1	12	4
2	3	1
3	8	10
4	10	5
5	4	5
6	2	0
7	9	2
8	7	2
9	11	3

8–17. A manufacturer of plastic water guns checks the production process every two hours. If the proportion of defective guns is more than 0.10, the machine is stopped and adjusted. Use the table of the cumulative binomial probability distribution to determine how many defective guns the manufacturer would have to find in a random sample of 100 to decide to stop the machine with an $\alpha \leq 0.05$. (8.10) p.116, then (8.3)

8–18. Use the normal approximation of the binomial distribution to solve Problem 8.17. Is the answer the same for $\alpha = 0.05$?

8–19. In a large university, experience has shown that it is normal for 0.38 of the students registered for the regular school term to return in the summer. The registrar, however, is alert to changes in student habits and makes a sample study each spring to determine student plans for the summer. If $\alpha = 0.05$ and it is important to detect either an increase or a decrease in the universe proportion:

a. Compute a decision rule to reject the H_o that $\pi = 0.38$ if a sample of 225 is used in the study. Use a two-tail alternate hypothesis.
b. Compute a decision rule for the following hypotheses if a sample of 900 students is used in the study:

$$H_o: \pi = 0.38$$
$$H_a: \pi \neq 0.38$$

8-20. If you toss a coin 25 times, how many heads would you have to get to decide that the coin is unfair (balanced to favor heads)? The value of α is ≤ 0.05.
a. Do the above computation using the binomial distribution.
b. Do the above computation using the normal curve approximation.

8-21. A manufacturer claims that only 3% of the items in a large shipment will fail to meet specifications. A random sample of 320 parts from the shipment shows that 16 are faulty. Test the manufacturer's claim with a one-tail test when:
a. The value of $\alpha = 0.01$
b. The value of $\alpha = 0.05$.

8-22. Credit records in a large retail store show that 87% of all charge accounts are paid, at least in part, by the 10th of the month. An additional service charge is announced as a penalty for those who fail to pay the minimum amount required in the hope of improving payments. After a trial period, a sample of 500 accounts shows that 460 paid the minimum required amount by the 10th of the month. Using an α level of 0.01, test the hypothesis that the new service charge has not increased the proportion of accounts paid on time against the alternate hypothesis that it has influenced payment on time. $H_o: p_1 = p_2$ $H_A: p_2 > p_1$ use (8.13)

8-23. A random sample of 225 shoppers taken during daytime hours at a shopping center shows that 72% are women. A sample of 300 shoppers taken at night shows that 64% are women. Is there a significant difference in the proportion of women shoppers at the two times? Test the hypothesis using an α level of 0.01 and a two-tail test.

8-24. Two manufacturing processes produce 18 and 24 defective parts in samples of 225 and 320, respectively. Use $\alpha = 0.05$ to test the hypothesis that the proportion of defective pieces is the same for both processes. Use a one-tail test.

8-25. A headache pill is tested on 400 hospital patients who complain of mild headaches. This sample is accumulated over a two-month period. To provide a control group for the experiment every other patient is given a sugar pill instead of the headache pill without being told the difference. The results of the test follow.

	Headache pill	*Sugar pill*
Sample size	200	200
Number who report headache gone one-half hour later	140	130

Test at $\alpha = 0.05$ the hypothesis that the two pills are equally good at relieving a headache. Use a one-tail alternate hypothesis. ~~Use (8.9)~~

same as prob 8-22.

SELECTED READINGS

Duncan, Acheson J. *Quality Control and Industrial Statistics,* 4th ed. Homewood, Illinois: Richard D. Irwin, Inc., 1974.

Chapters 25 through 31 cover a wide variety of tests of hypotheses in considerable detail, including tests of means, proportions, and variances.

Hays, William L., and Robert L. Winkler. *Statistics: Probability, Inference, and Decision.* Vol. 1. New York: Holt, Rinehart and Winston, Inc., 1972.

Chapter 7 gives a complete and clear, basic discussion of hypothesis testing, with explanatory illustrations.

Leabo, Dick A. *Basic Statistics,* 5th ed. Homewood, Illinois: Richard D. Irwin, Inc., 1976.

Chapter 10 gives an unusually clear presentation of the concept of the null hypothesis, Type I and Type II errors, and tests of hypothesis for means and proportions for one and two samples.

Yamane, Taro. *Statistics, An Introductory Analysis,* 3d ed. New York: Harper & Row, Publishers, 1973.

This text has a very good introductory approach to hypothesis testing in Chapter 9.

Chapter 9
Some Nonparametric Methods

In Chapter 8 tests of significance concerning sample means were made under the following assumptions:

1. The data were measured on either an interval or a ratio scale.
2. The distribution of means for samples of a given size was approximately normal if the universe standard deviation was known. (See central limit theorem.)
3. The distribution of means for small samples could be described by a t distribution when the universe standard deviation was not known.
4. In comparing the means of two samples, the universe variances either had to be known or were assumed to be equal.

In Chapter 11 the student will find that a rigid set of assumptions is necessary to compare the means of two or more samples using the F distribution.

These approaches to inferential statistics may be called *parametric methods* because there are assumptions made about the value of a parameter and the nature of the distribution from which the sample is drawn.

There is a useful group of tests that can be applied to nominal and ordinal level data which require no assumptions concerning the distribution from which the sample is drawn or any specific values of any parameters of that distribution. These tests are called *nonparametric* or *distribution-free tests*. The two terms are not exactly synonymous, but as a practical matter, the entire group of tests is usually referred to as *nonparametric methods*. A selected group of nonparametric methods is presented in this chapter.

Not only do nonparametric methods make it possible to work with data that do not meet the assumptions required for parametric methods, but they also have certain other advantages:

1. Many nonparametric methods provide easy, "shortcut" tests that involve much less mathematical detail and are simpler to understand.
2. Many nonparametric methods may be used to test data that are not exact in any numerical sense but which, in effect, are simply rankings.

3. Some nonparametric methods make it possible to work with very small samples, where parametric methods can be used only if the population distribution is known exactly. This is particularly helpful to the researcher collecting pilot study data or to the medical researcher working with a rare disease.

If all the assumptions of the parametric statistical model can be met in the data, the classical methods are generally preferred to the nonparametric methods because they are more precise, and for that reason they are more efficient.

In preceding chapters emphasis was placed on the four levels of measurement of data: nominal, ordinal, interval, and ratio. To review, parametric statistical methods cannot be used validly with nominal and ordinal data. Nonparametric tests may be applied to all four levels of measurement, but the researcher would normally prefer the more powerful parametric tests when they can be appropriately used.

While nonparametric tests have been used for some years in the behavioral sciences, there has been an increased interest in their use in business research in recent years. Areas of application include accounting, marketing, industrial relations, management science, and organizational theory.

THE CHI-SQUARE DISTRIBUTION

The most important of all distribution-free tests is the chi-square (χ^2) test introduced in 1900 by Karl Pearson. While the test is distribution free, since it makes no assumptions about the population from which the sample is drawn, there is a rigidly defined chi-square distribution with a mathematically expressed frequency function. The *chi-square distribution* may be defined as the sum of the squares of independent, normally distributed variables with zero means and unit variances.

If $Y_1, Y_2, \ldots, Y_n$ are normally distributed variables with mean, μ, and variance, σ^2, these variables may be standardized by the transformation

$$X_i = \frac{Y_i - \mu}{\sigma}.$$

The variable X_i will also be normally distributed with a mean of zero and a variance of one. The statistic χ^2, which is $\sum_{i=1}^{n} X_i^2$, has a chi-square distribution.

Even though chi-square is a statistic, it is represented by a Greek letter since it has no parameter. The chi-square distribution can be best applied to the solution of practical problems when expressed in the following form

$$\chi^2 = \sum \frac{(f_o - f_e)^2}{f_e} \dots\dots\dots\dots\dots\dots\dots\dots\dots\dots\dots\dots(9.1)$$

where
    f_o is an observed frequency, and
    f_e is an expected or theoretical frequency.

The characteristics of this distribution are completely defined by the number of degrees of freedom:

$$E(\chi^2) = d.f.$$
$$\mathrm{Var}(\chi^2) = 2\ d.f.$$
$$\mathrm{Mode} = d.f. - 2.$$

The number of degrees of freedom may be described as the number of observations that are free to vary after certain restrictions have been placed on the data. These restrictions are inherent in the organization of the data. For example, if a sample of 50 items is classified as "effective" or "defective," the determination that 40 are effective automatically means that the remaining group of 10 is defective. For this example, $d.f. = 2 - 1 = 1$. Since the number of parts is known, when the total in one category is ascertained, the total in the other category is determined.

The use of the chi-square table (see Appendix K) is illustrated in Figure 9.1.

FIGURE 9.1

Distribution of Chi-Square for Five Degrees of Freedom

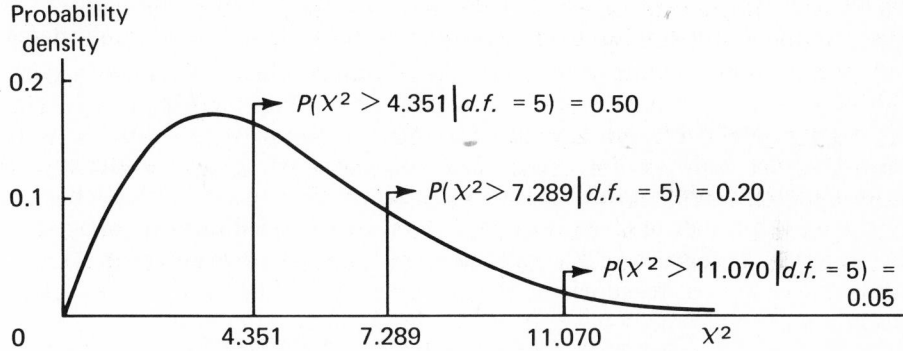

As with Student's t distribution, the chi-square distribution is a different distribution with each change in the number of degrees of freedom. It is badly skewed (to the right) for a few degrees of freedom and approaches the shape of the normal distribution when the number of degrees of freedom is approximately 30. The table of chi-square values in Appendix K lists the values of chi-square that give a specified area in the right-hand tail of the distribution. For example, in Figure 9.1 with five degrees of freedom, the area in the tail to the right of $\chi^2 = 11.070$ is 0.05 or 5%. The area to the right of $\chi^2 = 7.289$ is 0.20 or 20%.

There are several ways in which chi-square tests may be classified, for they may be used for many different purposes. In this chapter three main types of tests are considered: tests of goodness of fit, independence of classification, and homogeneity.

In addition, there are four conditions which should be met before a valid chi-square analysis can be applied to any kind of test.

1. The sample of observations should be independent of one another and drawn from the target population.
2. The data are usually of nominal measurement but may be higher for some kinds of tests.
3. The sample should contain at least 50 observations.
4. There should be no fewer than five observations in any expected cell.

It should be noted that while statisticians generally agree on these conditions, there is some difference of opinion on the exact numbers stated in conditions three and four.

Tests of Goodness of Fit

An observed sample distribution of any type may be compared with a theoretical distribution assumed to be the population distribution from which the sample was drawn. If there is a high degree of conformity between the two distributions, any slight difference may be assumed to be the result of sampling variation. On the other hand, any large discrepancy between the two distributions may lead to the conclusion that the sample was drawn from some theoretical distribution other than the one proposed. The null hypothesis usually states that the sample is drawn from the theoretical population distribution, and the alternate hypothesis usually states that it is not.

Uniform Distribution. One of the simplest tests is one in which the observed sample distribution is assumed to come from a population with a uniform distribution. In this instance the expected values (f_e) for each class are the total number of observations divided by the total number of classes. The number of degrees of freedom are the number of groups (or classes) minus one degree of freedom for the requirement of the total for the distribution.

■ *Example.* A personnel director is interested in trying to determine if the season of the year has any effect on the number of employees who resign. The records give the following information:

Season	Number of resignations
Winter	10
Spring	22
Summer	19
Fall	9
Total	60

The problem is to test at an α level of 0.05 to determine if there is a significant deviation between the observed distribution and a uniform distribution.

STEPS:

1. H_o: The observed distribution is drawn from a population that is a uniform distribution. (This is to say that the proportion of resignations is independent of the season of the year.)
2. H_a: The observed distribution is drawn from a population that is not uniformly distributed.
3. An α of 0.05 (one-tail test) requires a χ^2 value of 7.815 (column in the chi-square table headed 0.05 with three degrees of freedom).
4. Criterion: Reject H_o (accept H_a) if $\chi^2 > 7.815$; do not reject H_o if $\chi^2 \leq 7.815$, where $\chi^2 = \sum \dfrac{(f_o - f_e)^2}{f_e}$.
5. Using the sample data, chi-square is computed in Table 9.1.

TABLE 9.1

Computation of Chi-Square for a Goodness of Fit to a Uniform Distribution

Season	f_o	f_e	$(f_o - f_e)$	$(f_o - f_e)^2$	$\dfrac{(f_o - f_e)^2}{f_e}$
Winter	10	15	−5	25	1.67
Spring	22	15	7	49	3.27
Summer	19	15	4	16	1.07
Fall	9	15	−6	36	2.40
Total	60	60	0		$\chi^2 = 8.41$

Since $\chi^2(8.41) > \chi_\alpha^2(7.815)$, reject H_o and accept H_a. The number of resignations does vary significantly from a uniform distribution. The season of the year has a significant effect on the number of employees who resign.

Poisson Distribution. In Chapter 4 it was pointed out that the Poisson distribution applies to many situations in which one is concerned with the analysis of the formation of waiting lines at service facilities. When an observed sample distribution is thought to come from a parent population that is Poisson distributed, this can be tested using chi-square.

■ *Example.* A study is conducted of the volume of calls received on the switchboard of an insurance firm. A count is made of the number of incoming calls per minute for a sample of 100 minutes, with the following results:

Number of calls per minute r	Number of minutes f_o
none	40
1	35
2	14
3	8
4	2
5	1
Total	100

The statistician making the study believes that the incoming calls are distributed according to the Poisson distribution and uses a chi-square test to check the hypothesis at an α of 0.05.

STEPS:

1. H_o: The universe distribution of incoming calls is Poisson distributed.
2. H_a: The universe distribution of incoming calls is not Poisson distributed.
3. Before the α value can be translated into a table value for chi-square, it is necessary to determine the number of degrees of freedom. This will be the number of classes being compared minus one degree of freedom for each restriction placed on the expected distribution. Since a Poisson distribution can be completely determined by λ (which is the mean of the distribution) and the total frequency, there will be two restrictions. The theoretical Poisson distribution is computed in Table 9.2.

   Because of the general rule which states that there should be at least five items in each theoretical frequency class, it is necessary to group the last several classes of both the observed and the expected distributions into a class of "3 or more." This leaves a total of four classes minus two degrees of freedom for the requirements (mean and total) of the Poisson distribution, or two degrees of freedom for chi-square. The table value for $\chi^2_{\alpha=0.05}$ (2 *d.f.*) = 5.991.
4. Criterion: Reject H_o (accept H_a) if $\chi^2 > 5.991$; do not reject H_o if $\chi^2 \leq 5.991$, when χ^2 is computed using Formula 9.1.
5. Using the sample data, the value of chi-square is computed in Table 9.3.

From the last column in Table 9.3, it can be seen that the computed value of chi-square is 3.13. Therefore, since $\chi^2 (3.13) < \chi^2_\alpha (5.991)$, do not reject H_o. The observed distribution is drawn from a parent population that is Poisson distributed.

TABLE 9.2

Computation of a Poisson Distribution with the Same Mean and Total Frequency as An Observed Distribution

Observed distribution			Poisson distribution		
r	f_o	$f_o r$	r	$P(r\mid\lambda = 1.1)$	f_e
0	32	0	0	0.3329	33.29
1	42	42	1	0.3662	36.62
2	14	28	2	0.2014	20.14
3	9	27	3	0.0738	7.38
4	2	8	4	0.0203	2.03
5	1	5	5	0.0045	0.45
	100	110	6	0.0008	0.08
			7	0.0001	0.01
				1.0000	100.00

$$\text{Mean} = \frac{\Sigma f_o r}{\Sigma f_o} = \frac{110}{100} = 1.1 = \lambda$$

TABLE 9.3

Computation of Chi-Square for a Test of Goodness of Fit to a Poisson Distribution

Number of calls per minute (r)	f_o	f_e	$(f_o - f_e)$	$(f_o - f_e)^2$	$\dfrac{(f_o - f_e)^2}{f_e}$
0	32	33.29	−1.29	1.6641	0.05
1	42	36.62	5.38	28.9444	0.79
2	14	20.14	−6.14	37.6996	1.87
3 or more	12	9.95	2.05	4.2025	0.42
Total	100	100.00	0		$\chi^2 = 3.13$

Normal Distribution. Since the normal distribution is one of the most useful distributions in statistics, it is often important to be able to use a chi-square test to see whether it is likely that an observed distribution is drawn from a population that is normally distributed. This is done in the following example.

■ *Example.* The supervisor of an assembly department that hires several hundred workers is anxious to know if the distribution of times required to perform a particular assembly operation is normal. The supervisor times a sample of 100 workers doing this job and records the results in the distribution shown below.

Time required to make one assembly (in minutes)	Number of workers f_o
20 and under 25	7
25 and under 30	25
30 and under 35	33
35 and under 40	27
40 and under 45	8
Total	100

The mean of the observed distribution is 32.7 minutes, and the standard deviation is 5.3 minutes.

The problem is to use chi-square to test, at an $\alpha = 0.05$, the hypothesis that the distributions of worker times comes from a population that is normally distributed.

STEPS:

1. H_o: The population distribution of worker times is normal.
2. H_a: The population distribution of worker times is not normal.
3. In Chapter 5 it is shown that if the mean, standard deviation, and total frequency are known, a normal distribution can be constructed to fit any given frequency distribution. Using a mean of 32.7, a standard deviation of 5.3, and a total frequency of 100, the following expected normal distribution has been constructed using normal curve areas.

Time required (minutes)	Expected normal curve frequencies
Under 20 minutes	0.8
20 and under 25	6.5
25 and under 30	23.2
30 and under 35	36.1
35 and under 40	25.0
40 and under 45	7.4
45 and over	1.0
Total	100.0

Because the first and the last classes are too small, they are combined in each case with the adjoining class to give a theoretical frequency in each class of at least five. After combining the first two and the last two classes, the number of degrees of freedom for chi-square is the number of classes (five) minus one degree of freedom for each of the three parameters (μ, σ, and Σf_o) of the expected distribution. Therefore, the table value of $\chi^2_{\alpha=0.05}$ (2 *d.f.*) $= 5.991$.

4. Criterion: Reject H_o (accept H_a) if $\chi^2 > 5.991$; do not reject H_o if $\chi^2 \leq 5.991$, when chi-square is computed using Formula 9.1.
5. Using the sample data, the value of chi-square is computed in Table 9.4.

TABLE 9.4

**Computation of Chi-Square for a Test of Goodness of
Fit to a Normal Distribution**

Time required (minutes)	f_o	f_e	$(f_o - f_e)$	$(f_o - f_e)^2$	$\dfrac{(f_o - f_e)^2}{f_e}$
Under 25 minutes	7	7.3	−0.3	0.09	0.012
25 and under 30	25	23.2	1.8	3.24	0.140
30 and under 35	33	36.1	−3.1	9.61	0.266
35 and under 40	27	25.0	2.0	4.00	0.160
40 and over	8	8.4	−0.4	0.16	0.019
Totals	100	100.0	0		$\chi^2 = 0.597$

Since $\chi^2(0.597) < \chi^2_\alpha(5.991)$, do not reject H_o. The population from which the sample of worker times was drawn is normal.

Tests of Independence of Classification

In tests of *independence of classification,* sample data drawn from a single universe are classified according to several attributes. Chi-square is used to determine if the principles or criteria used for cross classification are meaningful. As a test of independence of classification, chi-square is not a measure of the degree or form of relationship but only a help in determining if the relationship is significant. The tables of values that result from the cross classification of data are often called *contingency tables.* These may vary in size from a 2×2 table to the general form with r rows and c columns, known as an $r \times c$ table.

This type of test gets its name from the fact that the hypothesis to be tested is the hypothesis that the principles of classification are independent.

The number of degrees of freedom in a test of independence of classification is always the product of the number of rows minus one times the number of columns minus one, *i.e.,* $d.f. = (r - 1)(c - 1)$.

2×2 **Contingency Table.** The simplest type of contingency table to test with chi-square is one with only two rows and two columns.

■ *Example.* The manager of a chamber of commerce in a small town in the Lower Rio Grande Valley in Texas is interested in learning more about the tourists who spend part of each winter in the Valley. From the local hotel and motel association, a list of the tourists from the past season is secured. The manager plans to send questionnaires to the people on the list to find out why they came to the Valley, how much they spent, how long they stayed, and what their future plans are. The manager speculates that an offer to send each respondent a free can of grapefruit juice will increase the percentage of questionnaires returned. To test this theory, questionnaires are sent to a random sample of 30 persons on the list with the offer of the premium. The manager sends another sample of 30 with no premium offer. The results of the experiment are shown in Table 9.5.

TABLE 9.5

Results of a Random Sample of 60 Questionnaires in Which Half Received the Offer of a Premium to Encourage Response

Premium	Questionnaire		Totals
	Returned	Not returned	
Offered	22	8	30
Not offered	14	16	30
Total	36	24	60

The problem is to test at $\alpha = 0.05$ to see if there is a significant difference in the proportion of returns when the premium is offered.

STEPS:
1. H_o: The universe proportion of returns is independent of the promise of a premium.
2. H_a: The universe proportion is affected by the promise of a premium.
3. An α of 0.05 requires a chi-square value of 3.841 (column 0.05 with $(r - 1)(c - 1)$ or one degree of freedom).
4. Criterion: Reject H_o (accept H_a) if $\chi^2 > 3.841$; do not reject H_o if $\chi^2 \leq 3.841$, where chi-square is computed using Formula 9.1.
5. Using the sample data, the chi-square value is computed in Table 9.6 in this manner. Cells are numbered as shown below:

Row	Column	
	I	II
I	1	2
II	3	4

I: $30 \times 36 / 60 = 18$

II: $30 \times 24 / 60 = 12$

The expected frequencies (f_e) for those who returned the questionnaires are computed as:

Cell 1: $\frac{30}{60} \times 36 = 18$ for premium offered, questionnaire returned.

Cell 3: $\frac{30}{60} \times 36 = 18$ for premium not offered, questionnaire returned.

The expected frequencies for those who did not return the questionnaires are computed as:

Cell 2: $\dfrac{24}{60} \times 30 = 12$ for premium offered, questionnaire not returned.

Cell 4: $\dfrac{24}{60} \times 30 = 12$ for premium not offered, questionnaire not returned.

TABLE 9.6

Computation of Chi-Square for a Test of Independence of Classification for a 2 × 2 Contingency Table

Cell	f_o	f_e	$(f_o - f_e)$	$(f_o - f_e)^2$	$\dfrac{(f_o - f_e)^2}{f_e}$
1. Premium, returned	22	18	4	16	0.89
2. Premium, not returned	8	12	−4	16	1.33
3. No premium, returned	14	18	−4	16	0.89
4. No premium, not returned	16	12	4	16	1.33
Total	60	60	0		$\chi^2 = 4.44$

Since $\chi^2(4.44) > \chi^2_\alpha(3.841)$, reject H_o and accept H_a. The universe proportion of returns is influenced by the premium offer.

An $r \times c$ Contingency Table. Another useful characteristic of the chi-square distribution is that it can be used to test any number of cross classifications. Tables of chi-square values are normally given for 30 degrees of freedom. If the number of degrees of freedom exceeds 30, the quantity $\sqrt{2\chi^2}$ is approximately normally distributed with a mean of $\sqrt{2(d.f.) - 1}$, and a standard deviation of one. This may be expressed as

$$z = \frac{\sqrt{2\chi^2} - \sqrt{2(d.f.) - 1}}{1} \quad \text{or}$$

$$z = \sqrt{2\chi^2} - \sqrt{2(d.f.) - 1} \dots\dots\dots\dots\dots\dots(9.2)$$

■ *Example.* If in a chi-square test involving 60 degrees of freedom the computed value of $\chi^2 = 98$, then using Formula 9.2,

$$z = \sqrt{2(98)} - \sqrt{(2)(60) - 1}$$
$$z = \sqrt{196} - \sqrt{119} = 14 - 10.9 = 3.1.$$

The probability of a deviation of more than three standard deviations from the mean of a normal distribution is so remote as to cause one to reject the null hypothesis.

An example of an $r \times c$ table with three rows and two columns is shown below.

■ *Example.* Changing the previous example, suppose that three different kinds of premiums were offered to three randomly selected groups of 20 in the sample of 60 as shown in Table 9.7.

TABLE 9.7

Results of a Random Sample of 60 Questionnaires in which Three Different Premium Offers Are Made

	Questionnaires		
Premium	Returned	Not returned	Total
A	15	5	20
B	12	8	20
C	8	12	20
Total	35	25	60

The criterion for this test will be written to reject H_o when $\chi^2 > 5.991$. Degrees of freedom are $(r - 1)(c - 1) = 2$.

The computations for the chi-square test are shown in Table 9.8.

TABLE 9.8

Computation of Chi-Square for a Test of Independence of Classification for a 3 × 2 Contingency Table

Cell	f_o	f_e	$f_o - f_e$	$(f_o - f_e)^2$	$\dfrac{(f_o - f_c)^2}{f_e}$
Premium A, returned	15	11.67	3.33	11.09	0.95
Premium A, not returned	5	8.33	−3.33	11.09	1.33
Premium B, returned	12	11.67	0.33	0.11	0.01
Premium B, not returned	8	8.33	−0.33	0.11	0.01
Premium C, returned	8	11.67	−3.67	13.47	1.15
Premium C, not returned	12	8.33	3.67	13.47	1.62
Total	60	60.00	0.00	. . .	$\chi^2 = 5.07$

Since $\chi^2(5.07) < \chi_\alpha^2(5.991)$, do not reject H_o.

Tests of Homogeneity

Tests of homogeneity are much like tests of independence in that both deal with the cross classification of nominal data, that is $r \times c$ tables. The mechanics of computing chi-square is the same for both tests.

The two tests differ, however, in the following respects. Tests of independence are made on data drawn from a single random sample where one is concerned with whether one set of attributes is independent of another set. Tests of homogeneity, on the other hand, are designed to test whether two or more random samples are drawn from the same population or from different populations.

■ **Example.** The board of directors of a labor union wishes to sample the opinion of its members before submitting a change in its constitution at a forthcoming annual meeting. Questionnaires are sent to a random sample of members in three union locals. The results of the survey are shown in Table 9.9.

TABLE 9.9

Reactions of a Sample of Union Members to a Proposed Change in the Union Constitution

Reaction	Union local			Totals
	A	B	C	
Favor change	18	22	10	50
Against change	7	14	9	30
No response	5	4	11	20
Total	30	40	30	100.

The problem here is not to try to determine whether the union members are in favor of the change. The problem is to test at $\alpha = 0.05$ to see if there is a significant difference in the proportions of opinion of the three universes of members concerning the proposed change.

STEPS:
1. H_o: The true universe proportions of reactions of the members of the three locals are the same.
2. H_a: The true universe proportions of reactions of the members of the three locals are not the same.
3. An α of 0.05 requires a chi-square value of 9.488 (column 0.05 with $(r-1)(c-1)$ or four degrees of freedom).
4. Criterion: Reject H_o (accept H_a) if $\chi^2 > 9.488$; do not reject H_o if $\chi^2 \leq 9.488$, where chi-square is computed using Formula 9.1.
5. Using the sample data, the chi-square value is computed in Table

9.10. The expected values are computed based on the assumptions in the null hypothesis. For example, for row one, column one, the value of f_e is computed as:

$$\frac{50}{100} \times 30 = 15, \text{ members of Local } A \text{ who favor the change.}$$

For row two, column one, the value of f_e is computed as:

$$\frac{30}{100} \times 30 = 9, \text{ members of Local } A \text{ who do not favor the change.}$$

Since $\chi^2(9.58) > \chi_a^2(9.488)$, reject H_o and accept H_a. There is a significant difference in the reactions of the memberships of the three locals to the proposed change. No local has a majority either in favor of or against the change. Members of Locals A and B are about equally divided, but members of Local C had a 55 percent no response rate, indicating that they don't care.

TABLE 9.10

Computation of Chi-Square for a Test of Independence of Classification for an $r \times c$ Contingency Table

r	c	Cell Reaction	Local	f_o	f_e	$f_o - f_e$	$(f_o - f_e)^2$	$\dfrac{(f_o - f_e)^2}{f_e}$
1	1	In favor	A	18	15	3	9	0.60
1	2	of	B	22	20	2	4	0.20
1	3	change	C	10	15	−5	25	1.67
2	1	Against	A	7	9	−2	4	0.44
2	2	the	B	14	12	2	4	0.33
2	3	change	C	9	9	0	0	0
3	1	No	A	5	6	−1	1	0.17
3	2	response	B	4	8	−4	16	2.00
3	3		C	11	6	5	25	4.17
		Total		100	100	0		$\chi^2 = 9.58$

THE KOLMOGOROV-SMIRNOV ONE-SAMPLE TEST

The Kolmogorov-Smirnov one-sample test may be used as an alternative to a chi-square test for goodness of fit when one is concerned with the hypothesis that an observed sample distribution is drawn from a population with a given theoretical distribution. It has two advantages over chi-square:

1. The Kolmogorov-Smirnov test treats individual observations separately. Thus, it is not necessary to lose information by combining categories as is often required in chi-square. This makes it a more powerful test than chi-square.

2. When samples are very small, it may be possible to use the Kolmo-gorov-Smirnov test when chi-square would be impractical because of the requirement that each expected frequency be at least five and that the sample be at least 50.

The Kolmogorov-Smirnov test involves working with two cumulative frequency distributions. One is an observed cumulative frequency distribution secured from the sample, and the other is a theoretical cumulative frequency distribution assumed in the null hypothesis. The point at which these two distributions show the greatest divergence is determined, and a decision is made to accept or reject the null hypothesis depending on the probability that the observed difference would occur if the observations were really a random sample from the theoretical distribution.

If F_o represents the cumulative values of f_o (the same observed distribution used in chi-square) expressed as a proportion of the total, and if F_e represents the cumulative values of f_e (the expected distribution) shown as a proportion of the total, then D can be defined as the maximum absolute difference between F_o and F_e.

$$D = \text{maximum} \, | \, F_o - F_e \, | \quad \text{.............................(9.3)}$$

This maximum difference, D, can be compared with a known theoretical sampling distribution of D that is determined by the assumptions in H_o. Certain critical values of this known distribution are shown in Table 9.11. The table gives values of D for five different levels of significance for samples as large as 35. For samples larger than 35, the value of D can be computed using the fractions shown in the bottom row of the table. For example, if the sample size, n, is 49, $D = \dfrac{1.36}{\sqrt{49}} = 0.19$ for $\alpha = 0.05$ (two-tail test).

■ *Example.* A baker who plans to add fruitcake to the line of baked goods wishes to test a statement made by a competitor to the effect that, "If you want a popular fruitcake that will sell, put in lots of nuts."

The baker makes one fruitcake from each of six different recipes, differing only in the proportion of nuts. Cake A has the smallest proportion of nuts and Cake F has the largest proportion. The baker gives a slice of each of the cakes to each of 12 homemakers. The women taste the slices and designate the cake that each likes best and would be most likely to buy. The following shows the test results.

Fruitcake ranked by the proportion of nuts (A has the fewest nuts)	Number of homemakers selecting each cake
A	0
B	1
C	1
D	1
E	5
F	4
Total	12

TABLE 9.11

Table of Critical Values of D in the Kolmogorov-Smirnov One-Sample Test*

Sample size (n)	Level of significance for D = maximum $\mid F_o - F_e \mid$				
	.20	.15	.10	.05	.01
1	.900	.925	.950	.975	.995
2	.684	.726	.776	.842	.929
3	.565	.597	.642	.708	.828
4	.494	.525	.564	.624	.733
5	.446	.474	.510	.565	.669
6	.410	.436	.470	.521	.618
7	.381	.405	.438	.486	.577
8	.358	.381	.411	.457	.543
9	.339	.360	.388	.432	.514
10	.322	.342	.368	.410	.490
11	.307	.326	.352	.391	.468
12	.295	.313	.338	.375	.450
13	.284	.302	.325	.361	.433
14	.274	.292	.314	.349	.418
15	.266	.283	.304	.338	.404
16	.258	.274	.295	.328	.392
17	.250	.266	.286	.318	.381
18	.244	.259	.278	.309	.371
19	.237	.252	.272	.301	.363
20	.231	.246	.264	.294	.356
25	.21	.22	.24	.27	.32
30	.19	.20	.22	.24	.29
35	.18	.19	.21	.23	.27
Over 35	$\dfrac{1.07}{\sqrt{n}}$	$\dfrac{1.14}{\sqrt{n}}$	$\dfrac{1.22}{\sqrt{n}}$	$\dfrac{1.36}{\sqrt{n}}$	$\dfrac{1.63}{\sqrt{n}}$

* Adapted from Massey, F. J., Jr., 1951. The Kolmogorov-Smirnov test for goodness of fit. *Journal of the American Statistical Association*, pp. 46, 70, with the kind permission of the author and publisher.

The problem is to test at $\alpha = 0.05$ the hypothesis that the proportion of nuts is not important to the popularity of the fruitcake.

STEPS:
1. H_o: The observed distribution comes from a population that has a uniform distribution (*i.e.*, the proportion of nuts is not important).

2. H_a: The observed distribution comes from a population that does not have a uniform distribution (*i.e.*, the proportion of nuts is important).
3. An $\alpha = 0.05$ requires a value of $D = 0.375$ ($D_{\alpha=0.05}$ for $n = 12$).
4. Criterion: Reject H_o (accept H_a) if $D > 0.375$; do not reject H_o if $D \le 0.375$, when $D =$ maximum $|F_o - F_e|$.
5. Using the sample results, the value of D is computed in Table 9.12. The assumption underlying the expected distribution is that if the proportion of nuts is not important, each recipe for fruitcake should be chosen by two homemakers.

TABLE 9.12

Computation of D for a Kolmogorov-Smirnov One-Sample Test

Fruitcake ranked by proportion of nuts (A has fewest nuts)	Number chosen f_o	f_e	F_o	F_e	$\mid F_o - F_e \mid$
A	0	2	$\frac{0}{12}$	$\frac{2}{12}$	$\frac{2}{12}$
B	1	2	$\frac{1}{12}$	$\frac{4}{12}$	$\frac{3}{12}$
C	1	2	$\frac{2}{12}$	$\frac{6}{12}$	$\frac{4}{12}$
D	1	2	$\frac{3}{12}$	$\frac{8}{12}$	$\frac{5}{12} = D$
E	5	2	$\frac{8}{12}$	$\frac{10}{12}$	$\frac{2}{12}$
F	4	2	$\frac{12}{12}$	$\frac{12}{12}$	0
Total	12	12			

Since $D(\frac{5}{12} = 0.417) > D_\alpha(0.375)$, reject H_o and accept H_a. The proportion of nuts in the fruitcake does make a difference in its acceptance.

In the example on page 251, a chi-square test of goodness of fit was made to determine if it was probable that an observed distribution of assembly times of 100 workers was drawn from a universe that was normally distributed. The Kolmogorov-Smirnov test could also be used for this purpose.

■ *Example.* The observed and expected distributions of workers' times are shown below:

Time (minutes)	f_o	f_e
Under 20	0	0.8
20 and under 25	7	6.5
25 and under 30	25	23.2
30 and under 35	33	36.1
35 and under 40	27	25.0
40 and under 45	8	7.4
45 and over	0	1.0
Total	100	100.0

Each distribution can be shown as a "less than" percentage distribution to permit the computation of $D = \text{maximum} \, |F_o - F_e|$.

For $\alpha = 0.05$, the critical value of D found in Table 9.11 is $D = \dfrac{1.36}{\sqrt{100}} = 0.136$. Since the value of $D(0.016) < D_\alpha(0.136)$, it is still appropriate to decide that the sample distribution is drawn from a population which is normally distributed. In this particular example the decision has been the same when using both the chi-square and the Kolmogorov-Smirnov tests; thus, the outcome is conclusive.

	Percent of total		
Time (minutes)	F_o	F_e	$|F_o - F_e|$
Less than 20	0.000	0.008	0.008
Less than 25	0.070	0.073	0.003
Less than 30	0.320	0.305	0.015
Less than 35	0.650	0.666	0.016 = D
Less than 40	0.920	0.916	0.004
Less than 45	1.000	0.990	0.010

TESTS USING SIGNS AND RANKS

There are a number of very useful nonparametric tests based on the signs of differences and on ranks of data. Often experimental data are easier to collect in this form; the methods are quick and easy to apply; and the tests do not require that the underlying distribution be specified. In market research it is possible to rank products according to consumer preference when no quantitative measurement of preference is possible.

Four of the most common tests of this type are discussed in this section: (1) the sign test, (2) the Wilcoxon matched-pairs signed-ranks test, (3) the Mann-Whitney U test, and (4) the Kruskal-Wallis H test. Chapter 12 has a discussion on rank correlation techniques. In each case the size of the sample used is sufficiently large to obviate the need for special tables of critical values. The selected readings at the end of this chapter provide sources of additional information on small sample techniques requiring special tables and on additional tests using signs and ranks of data.

The Sign Test

The *sign test* is so called because it uses plus and minus signs as its data rather than quantitative measures. The test is based on the signs of the differences between pairs of observations, and it does not take into consideration the magnitudes of the differences. Magnitudes will be considered in a later test. The sign test has particular application when dealing with two samples that are not independent.

If the first observation in each pair is designated x_i and the second observation is designated y_i, the value of the term $x_i - y_i$ will be +, −, or 0. All cases in which $x_i - y_i = 0$ will be ignored, and the total of the remaining pairs of observations will constitute the sample, n. The null hypothesis assumes that

$$P(x_i > y_i) = P(x_i < y_i) = \tfrac{1}{2} = \pi.$$

Since there are only two possible outcomes, + or −, the probability of a given number of +'s or −'s can be determined as $P(r \mid n; p = \tfrac{1}{2})$, which is the binomial probability distribution. It is also known that in a binomial distribution

$$E(r) = n\pi \quad \text{(Formula 4.6)}$$

$$\text{and } \sigma_r = \sqrt{n\pi(1 - \pi)} \quad \text{(Formula 4.7)}$$

For samples of more than 25, it can be assumed that the theoretical sampling distribution of r is normally distributed and

$$z = \frac{r - \tfrac{1}{2} - E(r)}{\sigma_r}$$

where
r is the number of +'s (or the number of −'s, if there are more of them).

■ **Example.** The general manager of a chain of 30 food stores is interested in determining whether packages of paper cartons to be used for storing food in home freezers will sell best when located in the store next to the frozen foods or located with the paper goods. Each of the local managers is asked to try a display of the cartons for one week in the first location and then for one week in the second location. The results of the study are shown in Table 9.13.

The problem is to use the sign test and an $\alpha = 0.05$ to determine if there are significantly more −'s than +'s. If there are, this would mean that the best location for the cartons is with the paper goods.

STEPS:
1. H_o: $P(x_i > y_i) = P(x_i < y_i)$. The universe proportions of +'s and −'s are the same. It makes no difference in which place the cartons are located.
2. H_a: $P(x_i > y_i) < P(x_i < y_i)$. There are significantly more −'s than +'s. The paper goods location is the better.
3. An $\alpha = 0.05$ requires a $z = 1.64$ if r represents the number of −'s.
4. Criterion: Reject H_o (accept H_a) if $z > 1.64$; do not reject H_o if $z \leq 1.64$ when z is computed using Formulas 4.6 and 4.7.

5. The sample data in Table 9.13 show 10 +'s, 18 −'s, and two 0's. When the observations for stores 10 and 21 are eliminated from the study, the following measures are available:

$$n = 28 \text{ (number of pairs of observations)}$$
$$r = 18 \text{ (number of −'s)}$$
$$E(r) = n\pi = 28(0.5) = 14$$
$$\sigma_r = \sqrt{n\pi(1 - \pi)} = \sqrt{28(0.5)(0.5)} = 2.65$$
$$z = \frac{17.5 - 14}{2.65} = 1.32.$$

Since $z(1.32) < z_\alpha(1.64)$, the decision would be not to reject H_o. The sign test does not show a significant difference.

TABLE 9.13

Sales of Frozen Food Cartons at Two Different Locations in Each of 30 Different Stores

	Number of cartons sold				Number of cartons sold		
Store	Frozen foods	Paper goods	Sign	Store	Frozen foods	Paper goods	Sign
1	40	65	−	16	20	29	−
2	75	60	+	17	49	60	−
3	24	36	−	18	32	22	+
4	21	15	+	19	15	32	−
5	8	12	−	20	80	120	−
6	10	15	−	21	30	30	0
7	15	12	+	22	16	32	−
8	30	48	−	23	41	20	+
9	22	21	+	24	35	11	+
10	16	16	0	25	24	50	−
11	15	8	+	26	18	49	−
12	56	85	−	27	16	58	−
13	12	20	−	28	10	8	+
14	4	18	−	29	37	18	+
15	32	45	−	30	50	70	−

Wilcoxon Matched-Pairs Signed-Ranks Test

The *Wilcoxon test* is a more powerful test than the sign test since it gives more weight to a large difference than to a small one. It considers both the sign of the difference within pairs of observations and the magnitude of that difference.

If d_i represents the absolute difference between x_i and y_i, then each pair of observations will have a value for d_i. If $d_i = 0$, that pair of observations is again dropped from the study. After the values of d_i are computed, they are ranked in order of magnitude from the smallest to the largest without regard to sign. If there are ties in ranks, all the tied values of d_i are given the same rank. For example, if $+4$ and -4 are tied for rank two, both would be listed as 2.5.

After the values of d_i are ranked, each rank is then given the sign of the original difference between x_i and y_i. The value T is the sum either of the positive ranks or of the negative ranks, whichever sum is smaller. The null hypothesis assumes that for the universe, the sum of the liked-sign ranks is equal. For samples of more than 25 observations, the theoretical sampling distribution of T is approximately normal and

$$\mu_T = \frac{n(n + 1)}{4} \dots\dots\dots\dots\dots\dots\dots\dots\dots\dots\dots(9.4)$$

$$\sigma_T = \sqrt{\frac{n(n + 1)(2n + 1)}{24}} \dots\dots\dots\dots\dots\dots(9.5)$$

$$\text{and } z = \frac{T - \mu_T}{\sigma_T} \dots\dots\dots\dots\dots\dots\dots\dots\dots\dots(9.6)$$

■ *Example.* To show the greater discriminatory power of this test over the sign test, the example of the frozen food cartons is repeated, but the test is made using the Wilcoxon matched-pairs signed-ranks test.[1]

STEPS:
1. H_o: For the universe, the sum of the positive-sign ranks is the same as the sum of the negative-sign ranks. The two locations are equally good.
2. H_a: For the universe, the sum of the positive-sign ranks is less than the sum of the negative-sign ranks. The paper goods location is the better.
3. An $\alpha = 0.05$ requires a $z = -1.64$.
4. Criterion: Reject H_o (accept H_a) if $z < -1.64$; do not reject H_o if $z \geq -1.64$, when z is computed using Formulas 9.4, 9.5, and 9.6.
5. The computation of T is shown in Table 9.14. The figures shown in the column headed d_i are the absolute differences between the values of x_i and y_i in Table 9.13. After the rank of each value of d_i is determined, it is given the sign of the original difference. The sum of the negative ranks is -300, and the sum of the positive ranks is 106. Since the absolute value of 106 is less than the absolute value of -300, T is taken as 106. Stores 10 and 21 are eliminated since they have values of $d_i = 0$. The value of n is 28.

$$\mu_T = \frac{n(n + 1)}{4} = \frac{(28)(29)}{4} = 203$$

$$\sigma_T = \sqrt{\frac{n(n + 1)(2n + 1)}{24}} = \sqrt{\frac{(28)(29)(57)}{24}} = 43.9$$

$$z = \frac{T - \mu_T}{\sigma_T} = \frac{106 - 203}{43.9} = -2.21.$$

---

[1] The *power of a test* is defined as the probability of making a correct decision when H_o is false. Power $= 1 - \beta$.

Since $z(-2.21) < z_\alpha(-1.64)$, reject H_o and accept H_a. The location of the frozen food cartons with the paper goods will lead to greater sales than in a location near the frozen foods.

TABLE 9.14

Computation of T for a Wilcoxon Matched-Pairs Signed-Ranks Test

Store	d_i	Rank of d_i	Rank with less frequent sign (+)
1	25	−23	
2	15	+15	15
3	12	−12	
4	6	+6	6
5	4	−4	
6	5	−5	
7	3	+3	3
8	18	−18	
9	1	+1	1
10	0	(This store was eliminated)	
11	7	+7	7
12	29	−25	
13	8	−8	
14	14	−14	
15	13	−13	
16	9	−9	
17	11	−11	
18	10	+10	10
19	17	−17	
20	40	−27	
21	0	(This store was eliminated)	
22	16	−16	
23	21	+21	21
24	24	+22	22
25	26	−24	
26	31	−26	
27	42	−28	
28	2	+2	2
29	19	+19	19
30	20	−20	
			$T = 106$

Mann-Whitney U Test

The *Mann-Whitney U test* may be used to test whether two independent samples are drawn from the same universe when the data are measured on at least an ordinal scale. When the level of measurement is interval or ratio, this test is a good substitute for the parametric tests of the difference between two sample means discussed in Chapter 8. The U test can be used by the statistician who wishes to avoid the assumptions that must be made in a parametric test or who wishes a shortcut method.

Suppose that n_1 represents the number of items in the first sample, and n_2 represents the number of items in the second sample. The first step in the U test is to combine the two samples into one group and to rank the values from smallest to largest, keeping track of the sample to which each value belongs. The value R_1 represents the total of the ranks assigned to values of the first sample. The statistic U is defined as

$$U = n_1 n_2 + \frac{n_1(n_1 + 1)}{2} - R_1 \quad \dots\dots\dots\dots\dots\dots (9.7)$$

If n_1 and n_2 are each ≥ 10, the theoretical sampling distribution of U is approximately normal and

$$\mu_U = \frac{n_1 n_2}{2} \quad \dots\dots\dots\dots\dots\dots\dots\dots\dots\dots\dots\dots\dots\dots\dots (9.8)$$

$$\sigma_U = \sqrt{\frac{n_1 n_2 (n_1 + n_2 + 1)}{12}} \quad \dots\dots\dots\dots\dots\dots (9.9)$$

■ *Example.* Two mixes, *A* and *B*, are used to make concrete beams. A sample of 12 beams made from Mix *A* is tested and found to have an average strength of 5,094 psi (pounds per square inch). A sample of 10 beams made from Mix *B* is tested and found to have an average strength of 5,745 psi. The problem is to determine at an $\alpha = 0.05$ whether Mix *B* produces stronger beams than Mix *A*. The sample results are shown below:

	Mix A	Mix B
	5,050	4,280
	6,120	5,920
	5,000	5,500
	4,650	4,988
	5,100	6,700
	4,800	6,000
	5,120	4,320
	4,900	7,100
	5,210	6,040
	5,020	6,602
	5,041	
	5,117	
Total	61,128	57,450
Mean	5,094	5,745

STEPS:
1. H_o: $\mu_A = \mu_B$.
2. H_a: $\mu_A \neq \mu_B$.
3. An $\alpha = 0.05$ requires a z value of ± 1.96.

4. Criterion: Reject H_o (accept H_a) if $z < -1.96$ or if $z > 1.96$; do not reject H_o if $-1.96 \leq z \leq 1.96$, when z is computed using Formulas 9.7, 9.8, and 9.9.

5. The computation of R_1 using the sample values is shown in Table 9.15.

TABLE 9.15

Computation of R_1 for a Mann-Whitney U Test

Array of the sample values (in psi)	Mix	Rank	Ranks assigned to values of Mix A
4,280	B	1	
4,320	B	2	
4,650	A	3	3
4,800	A	4	4
4,900	A	5	5
4,988	B	6	
5,000	A	7	7
5,020	A	8	8
5,041	A	9	9
5,050	A	10	10
5,100	A	11	11
5,117	A	12	12
5,120	A	13	13
5,210	A	14	14
5,500	B	15	
5,920	B	16	
6,000	B	17	
6,040	B	18	
6,120	A	19	19
6,602	B	20	
6,700	B	21	
7,100	B	22	
			$R_1 = \overline{115}$

$n_1 = 12$ (number with Mix A) $n_2 = 10$ (number with Mix B)

$$U = n_1 n_2 + \frac{n_1(n_1 + 1)}{2} - R_1 = 120 + \frac{156}{2} - 115 = 83$$

$$\mu_U = \frac{n_1 n_2}{2} = \frac{120}{2} = 60$$

$$\sigma_U = \sqrt{\frac{n_1 n_2 (n_1 + n_2 + 1)}{12}} = \sqrt{\frac{(120)(23)}{12}} = 15.17$$

$$z = \frac{U - \mu_U}{\sigma_U} = \frac{83 - 60}{15.17} = 1.52.$$

Since $z(1.52)$ is $< z_\alpha(1.96)$, do not reject H_o.

It should be noted that this test is always a two-tail test and can be applied without making the assumption that the samples come from normal universes with the same variances. Such assumptions would be necessary if the t distribution were used to test for significant differences in two sample means.

Kruskal-Wallis *H* Test

The Mann-Whitney U test is a nonparametric test used to decide if two independent samples are drawn from the same universe where the data are ranked or ordinal. The *Kruskal-Wallis H Test* goes one step further and permits the researcher to test the hypothesis that two or more independent samples are drawn from the same universe when the data are measured on at least an ordinal scale. This test is often referred to as a nonparametric test of analysis of variance, but it does not require the assumptions necessary to make the kinds of analysis of variance tests discussed in Chapter 11. No assumptions need to be made about the distribution of the populations from which the samples are drawn except that they are continuous.

To make the H test, samples are first arranged by columns and the letter "c" is used to represent the number of columns, which is also the number of samples. The notation n_j represents the number of observations in the jth sample, so the total number of observations is $n_1 + n_2 + \ldots + n_j + \ldots + n_c = n$.

Each of the n observations is represented by a rank. A rank value of 1 is assigned to the largest value (if ranked in descending order); a rank value of 2 goes to the second largest value; and so on. The smallest observation is given the rank value equal to that of n. The values can also be ranked in ascending order, and the final outcome of the test will be the same.

The statistic H is computed as follows:

$$H = \frac{12}{n(n+1)} \sum_{j=1}^{c} \frac{R_j^2}{n_j} - 3(n+1) \ldots\ldots\ldots\ldots\ldots\ldots(9.10)$$

where

n_j is the total number of observations in the jth sample
n is the total number of observations in all of the samples
R_j is the sum of the ranks in the jth sample.

The statistic H is chi-square distributed with $c - 1$ degrees of freedom when each of the samples contains at least six observations. When any sample is less than six, special tables are needed to interpret H.

■ *Example.* Suppose that three mixes, *A*, *B*, and *C*, are used to make concrete beams. Samples of beams from each mix are tested for strength in psi and the results are shown in Table 9.16. The problem is to determine at an α value of 0.05 if there is a significant difference in the three sample means. A nonparametric test is used to avoid the assumptions necessary to use the *F* distribution.

STEPS:
  1. H_o: $\mu_1 = \mu_2 = \mu_3$

2. H_a: μ's are not all the same
3. An $\alpha = 0.05$ requires a chi-square value of 5.991 since the degrees of freedom are $c - 1 = 2$.
4. Criterion: Reject H_o (accept H_a) if $H > 5.991$; do not reject H_o if $H \leq 5.991$, when H is computed using Formula 9.10.
5. The computation of H is shown following Table 9.16.

TABLE 9.16

Computation of Kruskal-Wallis H (Sample values given in psi)

| Mix A | | Mix B | | Mix C | |
Sample value	Rank	Sample value	Rank	Sample value	Rank
6,748	17	7,050	2	6,732	18
6,900	9	6,975	5	6,782	13
6,725	19	6,927	8	6,990	4
6,775	15	6,950	7	6,780	14
6,790	12	7,099	1	6,770	16
6,970	6	6,880	10	6,800	11
		7,000	3		
$R_j =$	78		36		76
$R_j^2 =$	6,084		1,296		5,776
$n_j =$	6		7		6
$\dfrac{R_j^2}{n_j} =$	1,014		185.14		962.67

$$\sum_{j=1}^{c} \frac{R_j^2}{n_j} = 1{,}014 + 185.14 + 962.67 = 2{,}161.81$$

$$n = 6 + 7 + 6 = 19$$

$$H = \frac{12}{19(20)}(2{,}161.81) - 3(20) = 8.27.$$

Since H (8.27) is $> \chi_\alpha^2$(5.991), reject H_o and accept H_a.

When two or more scores are tied, each score is given the arithmetic mean of the ranks for which it is tied. To correct for the effect of ties, H is computed as before using Formula 9.10, but the value is divided by a correction factor written as follows:

$$1 - \frac{\Sigma T}{n^3 - n} \quad\quad\quad\quad\quad\quad\quad (9.11)$$

where
$T = t^3 - 1$
t = the number of tied observations in a tied group of scores.

■ *Example.* Suppose that in the previous example, the sample values one, five, and seven for Mix B had all been 7,000 psi. Those three values would have all been tied for first, second and third places, so all would have been given the rank of 2. The value of H would be the same, 8.27. The value of T would be

$$T = t^3 - 1 = 3^3 - 1 = 26$$

where $t = 3$ (number of tied values). The correction factor would be

$$1 - \frac{26}{19^3 - 19} = 0.996.$$

The value of H can now be modified by dividing it by the correction factor as shown below:

$$H = \frac{H}{\text{correction factor}} = \frac{8.27}{0.996} = 8.30.$$

The decision to reject the null hypothesis would be the same.

TEST OF RANDOMNESS

Anytime researchers use a sample statistic to make an estimate about a universe parameter, they can make probability statements about the accuracy of their estimates only if they are dealing with a random sample. While the concept of a random sample is simple, the execution of the concept is often difficult.

For example, suppose a merchant wishes to take a random sample of shoppers leaving the store in order to learn what customers think about the store's pricing policies. The merchant instructs an interviewer to stand outside the store and to stop every 10th person who leaves to ask for an opinion. If the interviewer's records show the following sequence of the sex of the person interviewed, it is clear the interviewer talked only to women: $F\,F\,F\,F\,F\,F\,F\,F\,F\,F\,F\,F\,F\,F$. If the sequence is $F\,F\,F\,F\,F\,F\,F\,F\,M\,M\,M\,M\,M\,M$, the interviewer talked first only to women and then only to men. The sequence $M\,F\,M\,F\,M\,F\,M\,F\,M\,F\,M\,F\,M\,F$ is also obviously not random. The question is, "How can one test a sequence to see if it is random?" The test presented here is called a *one-sample runs test*. Such a test is based on the order in which the individual sample observations were obtained. A *run* is defined as a series of identical occurrences that are preceded and followed by different occurrences or by none at all. For example, suppose a coin is tossed 12 times and lands with heads (H) or tails (T) in the following sequence:

$$\underbrace{H\,H}_{1}\ \underbrace{T}_{2}\ \underbrace{H}_{3}\ \underbrace{T\,T}_{4}\ \underbrace{H\,H\,H\,H}_{5}\ \underbrace{T\,T}_{6}.$$

If R represents the number of runs, $R = 6$ in this example. Also, if n_1 represents the number of heads, $n_1 = 7$; and if n_2 represents the number of tails, $n_2 = 5$.

If either n_1 or n_2 is greater than 20, the theoretical sampling distribution of R is approximately normal with

$$\mu_R = \frac{2n_1n_2}{n_1 + n_2} + 1 \dots\dots\dots\dots\dots\dots\dots\dots\dots\dots\dots (9.12)$$

$$\sigma_R = \sqrt{\frac{2n_1n_2(2n_1n_2 - n_1 - n_2)}{(n_1 + n_2)^2(n_1 + n_2 - 1)}} \dots\dots\dots\dots (9.13)$$

The test will always be two-tail.

■*Example.* Assume that in the example of the persons being interviewed as they left the department store, the interviewer recorded the sex of 64 persons interviewed in the order in which they were stopped. The records are presented in Table 9.17. The problem is to determine at $\alpha = 0.05$ whether the sample was random with respect to male and female.

TABLE 9.17

Order and Sex of 64 Persons Interviewed While Leaving a Department Store

Row	Sex of person interviewed*
1	F M F F M F F F
2	M M F M F F M M
3	F M F F F M M M
4	F F M F M F F M
5	F M M F F M F F
6	M F F F F M M M
7	F M F M F F M F
8	M F F F M F M M

* *M* represents male and *F* represents female.
Note: Order is from left to right by row.
Runs have been underlined for emphasis.

STEPS:
1. H_o: The order of males and females is random.
2. H_a: The order of males and females is not random.
3. An $\alpha = 0.05$ requires a $z = \pm 1.96$.
4. Criterion: Reject H_o (accept H_a) if $z < -1.96$ or if $z > 1.96$; do not reject H_o if $-1.96 \leq z \leq 1.96$, when z is computed using Formulas 9.12 and 9.13.
5. If n_1 represents the number of females, $n_1 = 36$. If n_2 represents the number of males, $n_2 = 28$. Since there is a total of 40 runs, $R = 40$.

$$\mu_R = \frac{2n_1n_2}{n_1 + n_2} + 1 = \frac{2(36)(28)}{36 + 28} + 1 = 32.5$$

$$\sigma_R = \sqrt{\frac{2n_1 n_2 (2n_1 n_2 - n_1 - n_2)}{(n_1 + n_2)^2 (n_1 + n_2 - 1)}} = \sqrt{\frac{2(36)(28)(2,016 - 36 - 28)}{64^2(63)}}$$

$$= 3.91$$

$$z = \frac{R - \mu_R}{\sigma_R} = \frac{40 - 32.5}{3.91} = 1.92.$$

Since $z(1.92) < z_\alpha(1.96)$, do not reject H_0. The order of the males and females in the sample is random.

STUDY QUESTIONS

9-1. Explain briefly the meaning of each of the following terms:

a. parametric method
b. nonparametric method
c. distribution-free test
d. chi-square distribution
e. test of goodness of fit
f. test of independence of classification
g. contingency table
h. test of homogeneity
i. sign test
j. Wilcoxon test
k. Mann-Whitney U test
l. Kruskal-Wallis H test
m. one-sample runs test
n. run

9-2. What advantages do nonparametric or distribution-free tests have over parametric tests?

9-3. Discuss the shape of the chi-square distribution. What are its mean and standard deviation?

9-4. How would you describe the number of degrees of freedom of a chi-square distribution? Give an example.

9-5. What type of null hypothesis is made in chi-square tests of goodness of fit? What type of alternate hypothesis is made?

9-6. In a test of goodness of fit to a normal distribution, what are the requirements of the expected distribution?

9-7. What type of null hypothesis is made in chi-square tests of independence of classification? What type of alternate hypothesis is made?

9-8. Explain how ties in ranks can be handled in a Kruskal-Wallis H test.

9-9. In what ways are tests of homogeneity similar to tests of independence? In what ways do they differ?

9-10. In what ways is the Kolmogorov-Smirnov one-sample test superior to the chi-square test?

9-11. When is it possible to use tests of signs and ranks when parametric tests cannot be used? Give an example.

9–12. What probability distribution is basic to the development of the sign test? What other probability distribution is used to approximate it and why?

9–13. What makes the Wilcoxon test a more powerful test than the sign test?

9–14. What kind of test is the Mann-Whitney U test? What type of parametric test may it be used to replace?

9–15. What kind of test is the one-sample runs test? Why is this kind of test important?

PROBLEMS

9–1. Four different machines doing the same job are used for a trial period of six months in a plant that bottles hand lotion. A careful record is kept of the number of times each machine requires maintenance to determine which make of machine is the most reliable.

Machine code number	Number of repair calls
K27	17
L15	20
B219	30
MK6	13
Total	80

Use a chi-square test of goodness of fit to test, at $\alpha = 0.05$, the hypothesis that the four machines are equally reliable.

9–2. Six plots of land of equal size are all planted in corn. The number of bushels of corn produced on each plot is shown below:

Plot	Bushels of corn
A	78
B	68
C	60
D	75
E	51
F	40

Use a chi-square test of goodness of fit to test at $\alpha = 0.01$ the hypothesis that the six plots are equally good for growing corn.

9–3. The number of customers in a supermarket who arrive at the check-out stations each minute on a Saturday are shown below. Use a chi-square test of goodness of fit and $\alpha = 0.01$ to test the observed sample distribution to see if it is drawn from a universe that is Poisson distributed. *Note:* Use the table value for λ that comes closest to the mean of the observed distribution.

Number of customers per minute	Number of minutes
r	f_o
0	82
1	165
2	88
3	46
4	15
5	3
6	1
Total	400

9-4. The number of emergency calls coming into a police switchboard in a large city are tabulated to show the number of calls that come in each hour for a total of 120 hours, or five days.

Number of calls per hour	Number of hours
r	f
0	6
1	17
2	26
3	28
4	22
5	12
6	5
7	3
8	1
Total	120

Fit a Poisson distribution to the observed distribution and test for goodness of fit using chi-square and an $\alpha = 0.05$.

9-5. Use a Kolmogorov-Smirnov test of goodness of fit on the distribution in Problem 9.3 to test if the sample of 400 observations becomes a universe which is Poisson distributed. Use $\alpha = 0.05$.

9-6. The following table shows an observed distribution of the length of running time of 100 computer programs and a normal distribution with the same mean, standard deviation, and total frequency.
   a. Use a chi-square test of goodness of fit and $\alpha = 0.05$ to test the hypothesis that the observed distribution is drawn from a normally distributed population.
   b. Use a Kolmogorov-Smirnov test and $\alpha = 0.05$ to make the same test.

Time (octal seconds)	Observed distribution f_o	Normal distribution f_e
Under 1	0	2
1 and under 2	6	7
2 and under 3	25	19
3 and under 4	32	38
4 and under 5	23	17
5 and under 6	7	12
6 and under 7	5	4
7 and over	2	1
Total	100	100

9-7. The following distribution shows expenses as a percent of earnings for 300 mortgage loan companies. The mean of this distribution is 65.4% and the standard deviation is 8.8%.

a. Use a chi-square test of goodness of fit and $\alpha = 0.05$ to test the hypothesis that the observed distribution is drawn from a normally distributed universe.

b. Use a Kolmogorov-Smirnov test and $\alpha = 0.05$.

Expenses as a percent of earnings	Number of mortgage loan companies
40 and under 45	3
45 and under 50	9
50 and under 55	24
55 and under 60	45
60 and under 65	60
65 and under 70	66
70 and under 75	51
75 and under 80	30
80 and under 85	9
85 and under 90	3
Total	300

9-8. The following table shows how a random sample of 120 voters cast their ballots in a local election.

Age of voter	Candidate A	Candidate B	Total
Under 30	20	30	50
30 and older	50	20	70
Total	70	50	120

Can you conclude from this sample information that age of the voter in that election was independent of the voter's choice of a candidate at $\alpha = 0.05$?

9-9. A credit union manager is interested in whether the credit union's married members are more or less likely to save than its single members. The manager designs an experiment and draws a random sample of 200 of the members to give the values in the table below:

	Single members	Married members
Share accounts greater than loan accounts	20	82
Share accounts less than loan accounts	48	50
Total	68	132

If you were the manager of the credit union, what conclusions could you draw from the results of this study? Use $\alpha = 0.01$.

9–10. Two salesclerks working in the same department of a department store make a total of 100 sales in one week selected at random from the store records. The first clerk, Johnson, made 58 of the sales, and the other clerk, Wilson, made the other 42 sales.

    a. Make a chi-square test of goodness of fit, with $\alpha = 0.05$, to test the hypothesis that the two are equally good salesclerks.

    b. If you could not reject the null hypothesis in part a, use the cumulative binomial (Table D) to determine how many of the 100 sales Johnson would have to make to be able to reject the null hypothesis.

9–11. A random sample of 142 college professors were asked their opinion on whether more or less emphasis should be placed on a teacher's research as a basis for promotion. The survey produced the following results.

Emphasis on research	Teaching field			Total
	Liberal arts	Sciences	Professional	
More	28	20	12	60
Less	15	5	27	47
Same	15	5	15	35
Total	58	30	54	142

Use a chi-square test of independence with $\alpha = 0.05$ to test the hypothesis that opinions on research are independent of a professor's teaching field.

9–12. A morale survey, shown below, was made of four random samples drawn from different employee groups of a large manufacturing company.

Feelings about employee morale	Employee group			
	Office	Sales	Shop	Management
Better than average	15	20	5	12
Average	10	10	10	5
Below average	5	5	25	3

Use a chi-square test with $\alpha = 0.01$ to test the hypothesis that the universe distribution of proportions of opinion is the same for all employee groups.

9–13. The personnel director of a large company is interested in determining whether marriage is a factor in the frequency of absence from work of female employees. A random sample of the absence records of 385 women reveals the following:

Married	Often absent	Seldom absent	Totals
Yes	75	100	175
No	60	150	210
Total	135	250	385

Use a chi-square test and $\alpha = 0.05$ to determine if the universe proportion of the "often absent" group is independent of marriage.

9–14. Use a Kolmogorov-Smirnov one-sample test and $\alpha = 0.05$ to test the hypothesis that the following sample distribution comes from a universe that is a uniform distribution:

Category	f_o	f_e
A	8	5
B	10	5
C	4	5
D	3	5
E	2	5
F	3	5
Total	30	30

9–15. Four coins are placed in a cup, shaken well, and then tossed onto a hard surface so that the number of heads can be counted. This experiment is conducted 25 times with the following results:

Number of heads on one trial	Number of trials
0	1
1	5
2	10
3	6
4	3
Total	25

Use a Kolmogorov-Smirnov one-sample test and $\alpha = 0.05$ to test the hypothesis that the sample distribution comes from a universe that is a binomial distribution with value of $\pi = \frac{1}{2}$.

9–16. Given the following observations in which the differences between pairs of values are shown as +'s and −'s, use the sign test and $\alpha = 0.05$ to test the hypothesis that the universe proportion of +'s and −'s is the same.

Observation number	Sign	Observation number	Sign
1	+	6	+
2	+	7	+
3	−	8	−
4	+	9	+
5	−	10	−

Observation number	Sign	Observation number	Sign
11	−	21	−
12	+	22	−
13	+	23	−
14	+	24	+
15	+	25	+
16	+	26	−
17	+	27	+
18	+	28	−
19	−	29	+
20	+	30	+

9-17. A random sample of 11 clerical employees from each of two departments in a company is given clerical aptitude tests. The test scores are shown below. Use a Mann-Whitney U test and $\alpha = 0.05$ to test the hypothesis that $\mu_A = \mu_B$.

Department A		Department B	
70	75	75	107
63	100	92	120
76	85	60	61
91	93	96	82
65	65	110	110
60		90	

9-18. The weights of 25 children are checked at the beginning and again at the end of summer camp to determine if each child gained or lost weight during the season. The recorded weights are shown below:

	Weight (pounds)		
	Beginning	Ending	Sign
Name	X	Y	X − Y
Bill	119	121	−
Jane	73	89	−
Sam	60	64	−
Joe	119	115	+
Cathy	80	75	+
Harry	140	141	−
Jesus	93	102	−
Linda	95	102	−
Norman	82	81	+
Sidney	102	103	−
Anita	100	105	−
Carlos	75	72	+
Sandy	115	118	−
Jason	111	115	−
Rhonda	85	90	−
Edward	130	133	−

| | Weight (pounds) | | |
Name	Beginning X	Ending Y	Sign X − Y
Debbie	97	103	−
Ronald	110	105	+
Martha	96	105	−
Wilson	95	98	−
Andy	115	120	−
Carol	77	76	+
Boynton	160	154	+
Maria	72	80	−
Douglas	99	102	−

Use a sign test and $\alpha = 0.05$ to test the hypothesis that the universe proportion of +'s and −'s is the same.

9–19. Use a Wilcoxon matched-pairs signed-ranks test and $\alpha = 0.05$ to test the hypothesis that in Problem 9.18 the universe sum of positive signed ranks is the same as the universe sum of negative signed ranks.

9–20. A firm with several hundred salespersons on the road uses two brands of automobiles. A random sample of 10 repair bills for Brand I cars and a random sample of 15 repair bills for Brand II cars are shown below. Use a Mann-Whitney U test and an $\alpha = 0.05$ to test the hypothesis that the universe average cost of maintaining Brand I cars is the same as the universe average cost of maintaining Brand II cars.

Brand I		Brand II		
$ 26.00	$ 5.20	$17.82	$ 72.27	$26.50
63.00	527.00	6.80	28.25	16.22
25.19	30.57	25.10	6.27	29.97
32.00	105.00	45.00	26.50	12.32
225.00	16.18	22.00	314.00	55.60

9–21. The table below shows the dollar weekly sales for three salesclerks for a random sample of weeks selected from the records of each. The numbers in parentheses represent the ranks for the entire group from largest (1) to smallest (21).

Weekly sales in dollars (rank)		
Franklin	Moore	Galvan
$ 982 (12)	$1,000 (10)	$1,208 (1)
1,149 (5)	995 (11)	1,119 (8)
937 (18)	967 (14)	1,200 (2)
958 (15)	1,198 (3)	1,007 (9)
878 (20)	950 (16)	1,150 (4)
935 (19)	970 (13)	1,140 (6)
750 (21)	1,132 (7)	
945 (17)		

Test the hypothesis that the three samples come from identical universes. Use the Kruskal-Wallis H test and an $\alpha = 0.05$.

9-22. To determine if the distributions of three brands of paints are identically distributed in terms of square feet covered, the following random observations were obtained through tests on different kinds of surfaces.

Brand	Square feet covered per gallon of paint					
Ajax	625	600	622	582	625	627
Bright	578	600	625	630	580	590
Colorfirm	575	570	772	579	590	588

Use the Kruskal-Wallis H test to test the hypothesis that the three samples come from identical universes. Use an $\alpha = 0.05$.

9-23. Use a Wilcoxon matched-pairs signed-ranks test and $\alpha = 0.05$ to test the hypothesis that the universe sum of positive signed ranks is the same as the universe sum of negative signed ranks. Use the sample of 25 observations shown.

Observation number	Value of X	Value of Y
1	50	49
2	65	67
3	72	75
4	61	78
5	74	68
6	52	76
7	84	92
8	72	76
9	59	58
10	82	63
11	90	96
12	51	58
13	90	95
14	58	73
15	80	62
16	88	87
17	62	47
18	66	55
19	56	78
20	69	59
21	86	63
22	70	79
23	68	52
24	75	63
25	54	39

9-24. Test the sequence of 0's and 1's shown below with a one-sample runs test to see if the sequence is random. Use $\alpha = 0.05$.

0 0 1 1 0 1 1 1 0 0 1 0 0 0 1 1 1 1 0 1 0 1 0 0 1 1 0 0 0 1 0 0 0 1
0 0 0 0 0 0 1 1 1 0 1 0 0 1 1 0 0 0 1 0 1 1 0 0 0 0 1 1 0 1 1 1 0 1

9-25. A professor making up a true-false test is interested in arranging the questions so that the sequence of true and false answers is random. If the key to the test follows the pattern shown below, has the professor achieved the objective? Use $\alpha = 0.05$.

T T F T F T F T T F F T F T F T T F T T F T T T T F
T T T F T F F T F T F T F T T F T F T F F T F F F F

SELECTED READINGS

Chou, Ya-lun. *Statistical Analysis With Business and Economic Applications,* 2d ed. New York: Holt, Rinehart and Winston, Inc., 1975.
> Chapter 16 has a very clear, concise description of some of the most commonly used nonparametric statistical methods.

Gibbons, Jean Dickinson. *Nonparametric Statistical Inference.* New York: McGraw-Hill Book Company, Inc., 1971.
> This book stresses the theory of nonparametric statistics. The material is organized with regard to the type of statistical information collected and the type of questions answered by the inference procedure. The book is at an intermediate level of difficulty.

Handbook of Tables for Probability and Statistics. Cleveland: The Chemical Rubber Company, 1965.
> Part X of this handbook gives complete tables of critical values to be used in nonparametric tests such as the sign test, Mann-Whitney *U* test, Kolmogorov-Smirnov one-sample test, Spearman's Rank Correlation Coefficient, and the matched-pairs signed-ranks test. These tables make it possible to apply these tests to very small samples.

Siegel, Sidney. *Nonparametric Statistics for the Behavioral Sciences.* New York: McGraw-Hill Book Company, Inc., 1956.
> This book pulls together into one source a wide variety of nonparametric tests. It is particularly useful to the researcher who is in need of nonparametric tests in the analysis of research data but who lacks an extensive background in mathematics and classical statistics.

Chapter 10
Statistical Decision Theory

Decision making is familiar to individuals and groups who choose among alternative courses of action on the basis of what they know or think they know about the consequences of each decision option. Economic or other value considerations are important to decisions, and decision makers may estimate the value or utility of the outcomes associated with each course of action. In some decision situations prior information about the probabilities with which possible states of the world can occur is incomplete or not available at all. When prior information is available about possible states of the world, these probabilities can be combined with monetary or utility values to determine the best action on the basis of expected values. In situations where sampling is possible, the value of sample information can be assessed and the sample information can be used to reduce risk in making decisions.

In recent years classical statistics has been augmented to provide a more comprehensive theory for decision making. These additions encompass what is called *statistical decision theory*, the study of decisions involving uncertainty and risk, where monetary or utility values are explicitly incorporated into the determination of the best decision. The term "Bayesian decision theory" is also used when Bayes' theorem and subjective probabilities are used in decision analysis. This chapter contains a presentation of some of the principal concepts of statistical decision theory that provide prescriptive criteria for making decisions under given circumstances. This theory is not descriptive in that it does not purport to describe how decisions are actually made by decision makers.

ELEMENTS OF DECISION PROBLEMS

Before discussing classes of decision problems, certain basic concepts are defined to provide a general description of decision problems and a framework for obtaining solutions.

Actions, Decisions, and States of Nature

In the context of human choice, every decision situation involves a *decision maker,* an individual or group that has the need or responsibility for making a choice. If a choice is to be made, two or more *actions* or alternative options must be available from which the decision maker can choose. Choosing among alternative actions is called a *decision.* The objective in deciding among available actions is the selection of the action that provides the best expected return or benefit.

A problem in choosing among actions can arise because it is usually not known for certain what the *state of nature* will be. These states are viewed as environmental conditions or external states of the world that determine the outcome that will result from a given choice. For example, if it is decided to hold a sales promotion outdoors, weather conditions will affect the number of persons who attend the promotion.

Payoff and Loss

Associated with each combination of an action and a state of nature is a *payoff,* a consequence or outcome that is usually expressed in monetary terms (gain or loss). An outcome may also be expressed in terms of utility, that is, the subjective evaluation of the monetary outcome by the decision maker. A payoff is also called a *conditional value,* since it is the value corresponding to an action, given the occurrence of a particular state of nature. A tabular arrangement that summarizes these conditional values is called a *payoff matrix.*

Uncertainty and Risk

In some decision situations no prior information is available concerning the likelihoods with which states of nature are expected to occur. This condition is called *uncertainty.* In other cases it is possible to obtain prior information about the probabilities of occurrence of states of nature. Decisions made with the benefit of such information, whether obtained objectively from data analysis or subjectively from feelings or experience, are made under a condition called *risk.* Where complete information is available about which state of nature will occur, a decision can be made under *certainty.*

The discussion in this chapter focuses on decisions made under uncertainty and risk; although decision making under certainty can be very complex, it does not involve probabilities and is not considered further in this presentation.

Decision Criteria

In the process of choosing among available actions, a decision maker uses a rationale, an objectively or subjectively reasoned basis or rule for selecting the best of alternatives. Such rules are called *decision criteria.* Some examples of decision rules include maximizing utility, minimizing regret, maximizing expected gain, and minimizing expected loss. Selected decision criteria for conditions of uncertainty and risk are discussed in a later section of this chapter.

■ *Example.* An automobile manufacturer (decision maker) must choose among available types of engines (actions) for use in a new model of automobile. The choice (decision) is among the actions using a new injection engine (a_1), a modified piston engine (a_2), or a standard piston engine (a_3). The monetary return (payoff) for each action depends on whether the level of acceptance by consumers (state of nature) is high (n_1), moderate (n_2), or low (n_3). The conditional outcomes in monetary terms are summarized in Table 10.1.

TABLE 10.1

Payoff Matrix

| Action | State of nature (level of acceptance) | | |
	High n_1	Moderate n_2	Low n_3
a_1 Injection	9	6	−2
a_2 Modified piston	7	5	2
a_3 Standard piston	5	3	1

If the manufacturer has no prior information about the likelihood with which each level of acceptance will occur, a decision is made under uncertainty. If prior information is available from objective data or subjective evaluation, the decision is made under risk. Decision criteria or prescriptive rules for making decisions under these respective conditions are discussed in later sections of this chapter.

Dominance and Optimal Action

A comparison of the payoffs for actions a_2 and a_3 in Table 10.1 indicates that the gains are greater for action a_2 than for a_3 whatever the state of nature. This illustrates the concept of *dominance*. The manufacturer will be better off not giving further consideration to a_3, for a_2 is a *dominating action*. Action a_2 does not dominate action a_1, for a_1 is the best action given states of nature n_1 and n_2; but action a_2 has the best payoff if n_3 occurs. The decision in this case involves the selection of only one of the acts, a_1 or a_2. Since the payoff for one of the actions is not superior to that of the other action for all possible states of nature, the approach is to choose the *optimal action;* i.e., the action with the best overall payoff as determined by a decision criterion. Choosing optimal actions under conditions of uncertainty and risk is discussed in later sections of this chapter.

Loss Matrix

For some types of decision problems it is helpful to express the payoffs for each combination of an action and a state of nature as a *loss*, the opportunity cost resulting from not having taken the best action for a given state of nature. A tabular arrangement of these losses is called a *loss matrix*.

■ *Example.* The loss matrix for the example on page 285 is obtained by locating the best payoff for a given state of nature (reading down a column) and subtracting the payoffs for all actions from this value. The best payoff for n_1 is 9 (action a_1). Subtracting this value from all the payoffs in column n_1 gives the opportunity loss L for each action as follows: $L(a_1 | n_1) = 9 - 9 = 0$, $L(a_2 | n_1) = 9 - 7 = 2$, and $L(a_3 | n_1) = 9 - 5 = 4$. Other values obtained similarly are summarized in Table 10.2.

TABLE 10.2

Loss Matrix

Action	State of nature (level of acceptance)		
	High n_1	Moderate n_2	Low n_3
a_1 Injection	0	0	4
a_2 Modified piston	2	1	0
a_3 Standard piston	4	3	1

The application of the concept of a loss matrix is considered in the sections on decision making under uncertainty and risk.

Utility of Money

The subjective assessment of the value of a quantity of money by a decision maker when risk is involved is called the *utility of money*. A payoff or loss matrix is frequently expressed in terms of monetary value. The use of monetary value as the basis for decisions assumes that the utility of money is directly proportional to the quantity of money, and utility is a linear function of monetary value. The use of monetary values in a payoff or loss matrix is not always appropriate, for human decisions are made in terms of utility and the value of money for a decision maker may not be a linear function of money because of attitudes toward risk, financial position, or other factors. It is important to consider briefly the nature of a utility function, although monetary value is used in the remaining sections of this chapter to simplify the presentation.

Utility Function. In general, a utility function increases over a relevant range of monetary amounts, for most people prefer more money to less money. Many individuals are inclined to gamble if relatively small amounts of money are involved, but they also tend to insure against the loss of large monetary amounts. This case is illustrated in Figure 10.1, where the slope of the utility function corresponds to marginal utility. The slope increases for small dollar amounts and it decreases for larger monetary values, reflecting the gambling and risk aversion ranges, respectively. The gambling range corresponds to increasing marginal utility and the tendency to assume risks for which the expected value is negative. An example of such a risk is betting a dollar in a sweepstakes with a very small chance of winning a large amount of money and the expected value of the bet is less than a dollar. For relatively large amounts of money, the subjective worth of each additional dollar decreases but is never zero. Over this range of decreasing marginal utility, the person tends to exhibit conservative behavior by seeking to avoid losses by purchasing insurance even though the cost of insurance is greater than the expected value of the loss. For some types of insurance, the premium cost is two or more times the actuarial or expected value of a loss.

FIGURE 10.1

Utility Function

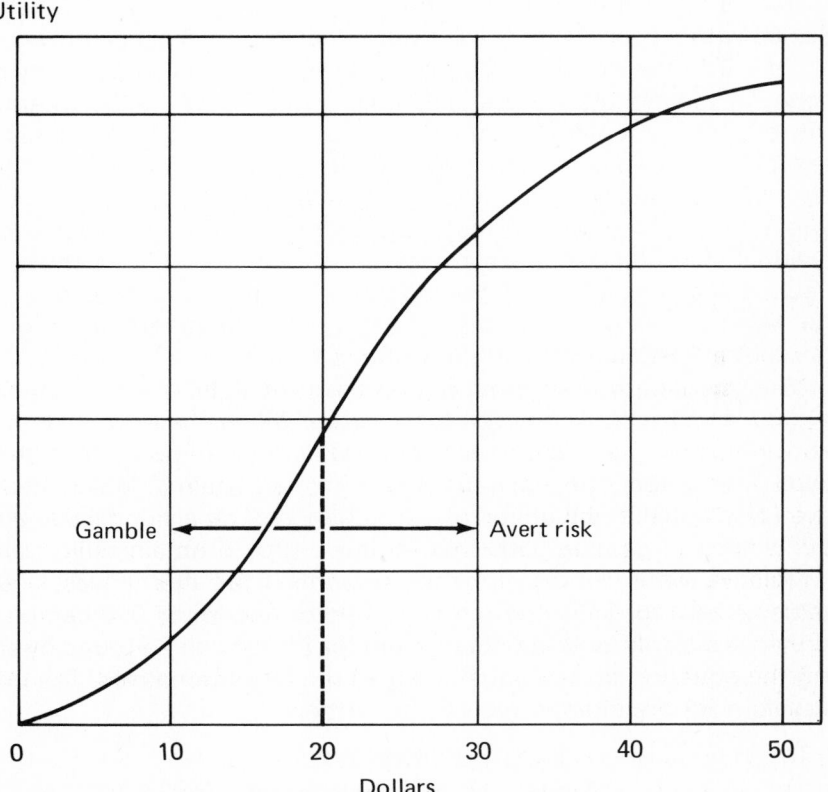

If an individual does not gamble, the utility function is convex from above for all dollar amounts. The specific shape of a utility function tends to vary with the individual, and a technique for deriving the utility function for a person is described in the following section.

Standard Gamble. An individual utility function for monetary values can be derived by determining the preferences of a decision maker for a series of choices that involve risk. This method is called the *standard gamble*. In applying this method a decision maker is asked to choose between (1) the certainty of receiving a sum of money or (2) a lottery in which there is a chance of receiving or, in some cases, losing one of two sums of money in which risk is expressed in terms of the probabilities associated with winning each amount. If the decision maker expresses a preference for one of the alternatives, the probabilities are changed successively until the alternatives appear as equally desirable to the decision maker. At this point of indifference the alternatives are equal in terms of utility. Since a utility function reflects subjective evaluations of amounts of money in relative terms, the utilities for two of the dollar amounts in the initial lottery can be chosen arbitrarily, and the utilities of other dollar amounts can be determined in relation to these utility values.

■ *Example.* An individual is asked to choose between (1) the certainty of receiving $1,000 or (2) a lottery with the outcomes of receiving $5,000 with a probability $p = 0.1$ and receiving $500 with a probability $1 - p = 0.9$. The individual chooses alternative (1) as would many persons, for the monetary value of $1,000 for alternative (1) is greater than the expected monetary value of $0.1(\$5,000) + 0.9(\$500) = \$950$ for alternative (2). To determine the point at which the individual finds the alternatives equally desirable, the probabilities are changed to $p = 0.2$ and $1 - p = 0.8$. Suppose that with the changed probabilities the individual still indicates a preference for alternative (1). This choice reflects risk aversion by the individual, for the monetary value of $1,000 for alternative (1) is less than the expected monetary value of $0.2 (\$5,000) + 0.8(\$500) = \$1,400$ for alternative (2).

This procedure is continued, and the probabilities are changed to $p = 0.3$ and $1 - p = 0.7$. Given these probabilities, the individual might now indicate equal preference for or indifference between the alternatives. At this point the individual's utility for a certain $1,000 in alternative (1) is equal to the utility for a 0.3 chance of receiving $5,000 and a 0.7 chance of gaining $500 in alternative (2). To obtain utility values (in relative terms) for the monetary amounts in the alternatives, a utility value of zero for $500 and a utility value of one for $5,000 can be assigned arbitrarily, and the utility value for $1,000 can be found by solving the equation for the equal utility of the two alternatives. The utility equation for the alternatives can be written:

$$\text{Utility of (1)} = \text{Utility of (2)}$$
$$U(\$1,000) = 0.3U(\$5,000) + 0.7U(\$500),$$

where U designates utility of a monetary amount. Substituting the value of one for the utility of $5,000 and the value of zero for the utility of $500, solving the utility equation gives:

$$U(\$1,000) = 0.3(1) + 0.7(0)$$
$$= 0.3.$$

Since U($500) = 0, U($1,000) = 0.3, and U($5,000) = 1, the utility function for the individual is not linear over the range of monetary amounts from $500 to $5,000, for the utility values are not precisely proportional to the respective dollar amounts. The utility function U(M) for these utility and monetary values is shown in Figure 10.2.

The utility of a negative monetary amount (loss) can be computed by the procedure used previously. For instance, if the decision maker is indifferent between (1) receiving $500 for certain and (2) a 0.8 chance of receiving $1,000 and a 0.2 probability of losing $250, the utility of −$250 is computed:

FIGURE 10.2

Derived Utility Function

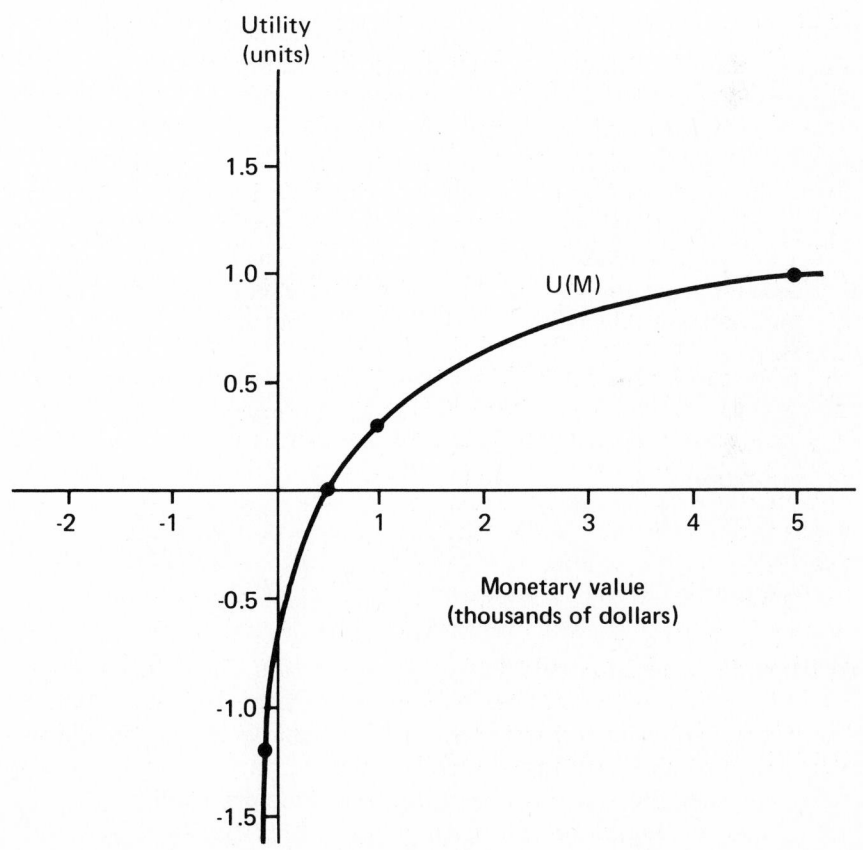

$$0.8U(\$1,000) + 0.2U(-\$250) = U(\$500)$$
$$0.8(0.3) + 0.2U(-\$250) = 0$$
$$U(-\$250) = -1.2.$$

The utility of -1.2 for $-\$250$ is shown in Figure 10.2. The utility function $U(M)$ is convex from above over the range of monetary amounts from $-\$250$ to \$5,000, indicating risk aversion by the decision maker. Risk aversion is also reflected by the fact that the decision maker is indifferent between alternatives only when the expected monetary value of the risky alternative is greater than the monetary value of the certain amount. These values are summarized as follows:

Certain amount	Expected value of the risky alternative
\$500	$0.8(\$1,000) + 0.2(-\$250) = \$750$
\$1,000	$0.2(\$5,000) + 0.8(\$500) = \$1,400$

The excess of expected monetary value over certain value may be viewed as the amount required to offset the riskiness of the alternative.

Classical Statistical Inference and Statistical Decision Theory

Basic concepts of the classical approach to statistical inference are presented in Chapters 6 and 8. This approach is characterized by the logical sequence of formulating a hypothesis, determining a decision rule, and testing the hypothesis by use of sample evidence. Accepting or rejecting a hypothesis involves the risk of making either a Type I or a Type II error. For instance, in testing a hypothesis about μ, a Type I error results from rejecting a null hypothesis ($\mu = \mu_o$) that is true, and the risk of making this incorrect decision is α. Accepting a false null hypothesis results in an incorrect decision, and the risk of this Type II error is β. The probabilities of correct and incorrect decisions for the states of nature can be summarized as follows:

	State of nature	
	n_1	n_2
Action	($\mu = \mu_o$)	($\mu \neq \mu_o$)
a_1 (accept H_o)	$P(a_1 \mid n_1) = 1 - \alpha$ (correct)	$P(a_1 \mid n_2) = \beta$ (incorrect)
a_2 (reject H_o)	$P(a_2 \mid n_1) = \alpha$ (incorrect)	$P(a_2 \mid n_2) = 1 - \beta$ (correct)

To determine a decision rule for hypothesis testing, the classical approach is to select a value of α and then to choose a critical decision value or criterion that will tend to minimize β, but this approach does not provide a specific procedure for selecting values of α and β. Statistical decision theory provides a method for explicitly including available prior information about the likelihoods of the states of nature, information from sampling, and the consequences (losses in utility or monetary terms) of making either a Type I or a Type II error in the determination of a decision rule for choosing an action. If n_1 (H_o is true) is estimated to be more probable than n_2 (H_o is false), the tendency is to decrease α and reduce the risk of a Type I error. If the probability of n_2 is estimated to be greater than that of n_1, α tends to be increased and β is decreased. The consequences or losses resulting from the respective types of errors also influence the choice of α and β. If the loss from a Type I error is greater than that for a Type II error, α tends to be decreased and β increased. Conversely, if the loss from a Type II error is the greater, the value of α would be increased and the value of β decreased. The optimal decision rule is based on the combination of α and β values that minimize total expected loss. The expected loss for a decision rule for action a_1 (accept H_o) and action a_2 (reject H_o) is illustrated in the following diagram:

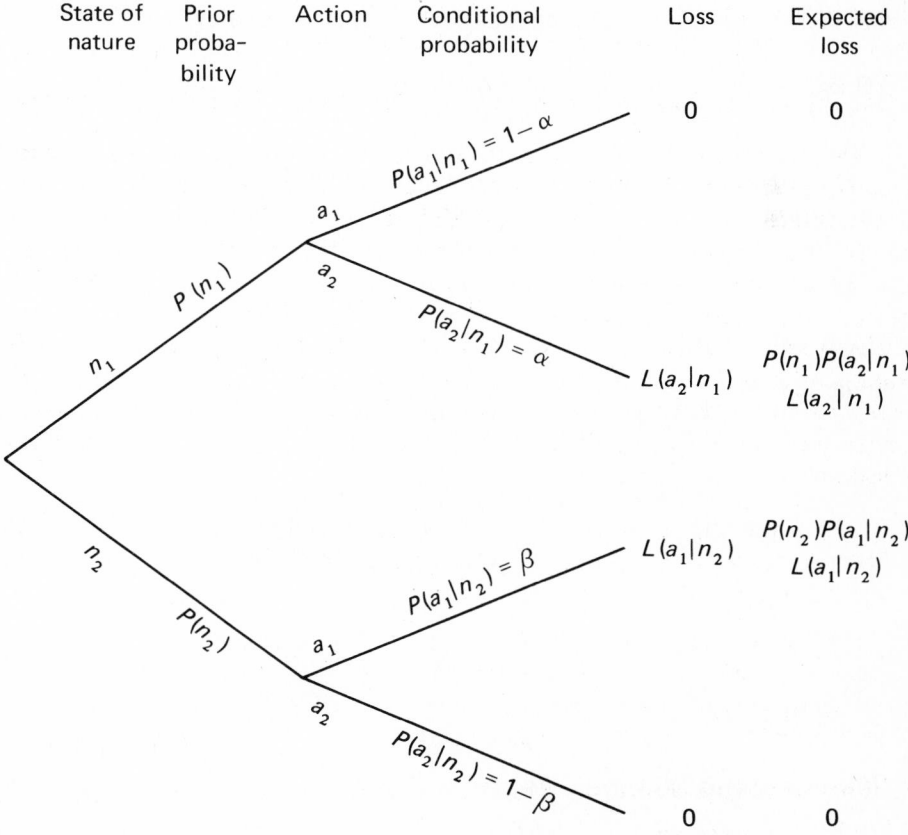

The procedure for determining optimal decision rules by use of the relationships in the preceding diagram is discussed in later sections of this chapter.

CRITERIA FOR MAKING DECISIONS UNDER UNCERTAINTY

Decisions are made under uncertainty when the state of nature is unknown and it is not possible to obtain prior information about the state of nature by experimentation. Various prescriptive criteria for evaluating actions have been proposed and some of these are considered briefly.

Maximin and Maximax

A decision rule for determining the minimum gain for each action and for selecting the action with the largest of the minimum gains is called the *maximin criterion*. This criterion, suggested by decision theorist Abraham Wald, is pessimistic, for it is based on the best of the worst payoffs for available actions.

An alternative is an optimistic decision rule, the *maximax criterion,* that is based on choosing the largest of the maximum payoffs for available actions. It is assumed that the payoffs are in terms of utility.

■ *Example.* The maximin and maximax criteria are illustrated by continuing the example from an earlier section. The payoff matrix in Table 10.3 includes columns showing the minimum and maximum for each action (row). The value 2 is the maximum of the row minima and action a_2 is the optimal choice under the maximin criterion. Similarly, the optimal action under the maximax criterion is a_1 since 9 is the largest of the row maxima.

TABLE 10.3

Payoff Matrix

| Action | State of nature (level of acceptance) | | | Row minimum | Row maximum |
	High n_1	Moderate n_2	Low n_3		
a_1	9	6	−2	−2	9* maximax
a_2	7	5	2	2* maximin	7
a_3	5	3	1	1	5

* optimal action

Minimax and Minimax Regret

If the payoffs are losses or opportunity losses expressed in terms of utility, a rule for choosing the optimal action on the basis of minimizing the maximum loss is called the *minimax criterion.* In applying this rule the maximum loss is determined for each action, and the action with the smallest of these losses is selected.

A similar concept, suggested by statistician L. J. Savage, involves transforming gains into a regret or opportunity loss matrix and applying the minimax criterion. This decision rule is called *minimax regret.*

■ *Example.* A regret or opportunity loss matrix is determined from the payoff matrix in Table 10.3 by subtracting each of the values in a column from the largest value in that column. This procedure is discussed in more detail in the derivation of Table 10.2. The maximum regret or opportunity loss for each action is shown in Table 10.4 in the column at the right. The optimal action is a_2, for the maximum regret for this action is the smallest of those for all actions.

TABLE 10.4

Regret Matrix

| Action | State of nature (level of acceptance) | | | Row maximum |
	High n_1	Moderate n_2	Low n_3	
a_1	0	0	4	4
a_2	2	1	0	2* minimax regret
a_3	4	3	1	4

*optimal action

Hurwicz Criterion

A decision rule called the *Hurwicz criterion,* after the decision theorist Leonid Hurwicz, involves computing a weighted average of the largest and smallest payoffs (utilities) for each action and choosing the action with the largest average. The weights represent subjective evaluations that reflect the degree of optimism or pessimism of the decision maker.

■ *Example.* In a continuation of the foregoing example, a weight of $\frac{3}{5}$ is applied to the minimum payoff in Table 10.3 and the maximum payoff is weighted by $\frac{2}{5}$. The results are:

$$
\begin{array}{ccl}
 & n_1 & n_2 \\
a_1 & \frac{2}{5}(9) + \frac{3}{5}(-2) & = 2.4 \\
a_2 & \frac{2}{5}(7) + \frac{3}{5}(2) & = 4.0^* \text{ optimal} \\
a_3 & \frac{2}{5}(5) + \frac{3}{5}(1) & = 2.6
\end{array}
$$

* The weighted average is greatest for action a_2, the optimal action under the Hurwicz criterion.

Laplace Criterion

An alternate decision rule is based on the assumption that if one is completely ignorant of the likelihoods with which states of nature will occur, then the states should be looked upon as being equally likely. Equal probabilities are assigned to the states, and the optimal action is that with the largest expected gain (utility). This decision rule is called the *Laplace criterion,* after the noted mathematician Pierre Laplace. This criterion is also called the principle of insufficient reason.

■ *Example.* The Laplace criterion is applied to the foregoing example by assigning equal probabilities or weights to the payoffs in Table 10.3 and then multiplying and summing as follows:

$$
\begin{array}{cccc}
 & n_1 & n_2 & n_3 \\
a_1 & \tfrac{1}{3}(9) + \tfrac{1}{3}(6) + \tfrac{1}{3}(-2) = 4.33 \\
a_2 & \tfrac{1}{3}(7) + \tfrac{1}{3}(5) + \tfrac{1}{3}(2) & = 4.67^* \text{ Laplace optimal} \\
a_3 & \tfrac{1}{3}(5) + \tfrac{1}{3}(3) + \tfrac{1}{3}(1) & = 3.00
\end{array}
$$

* The optimal action is a_2, for the expected value is the largest of the actions.

DECISIONS UNDER RISK WITHOUT SAMPLING

In many decision situations information can be obtained about the prior probability distribution of the states of the world from the analysis of historical data, or from experience and judgment. The following sections present models for making decisions under risk that incorporate prior probability distributions into the procedure for determining optimal actions.

Bayesian Criterion

It is seldom that a decision maker is totally ignorant of the likelihoods with which states of nature are expected to occur. In the absence of objective information, probabilities of occurrence of states of nature can be assigned subjectively. By use of a subjective prior probability distribution, the action with the largest expected gain (utility) is optimal. This decision rule is called the *Bayesian criterion* because of the use of subjective probabilities, although no revision of probabilities is involved.

■ *Example.* The Bayesian criterion is applied to the payoff matrix in Table 10.3 by assuming that a decision maker assigns a subjective probability distribution to the states of nature as follows:

$$
\begin{array}{cccc}
 & n_1 & n_2 & n_3 \\
a_1 & 0.5(9) + 0.3(6) + 0.2(-2) = 5.9^* \text{ Bayesian optimal} \\
a_2 & 0.5(7) + 0.3(5) + 0.2(2) & = 5.4 \\
a_3 & 0.5(5) + 0.3(3) + 0.2(1) & = 3.6
\end{array}
$$

* Action a_1 has the largest expected value and is the optimal action according to the Bayesian criterion.

Several criteria for decision making under uncertainty are discussed in foregoing sections of this chapter. Each of these criteria can be shown to be equivalent to assuming a subjective probability distribution of the likelihoods of the states of nature, using these probabilities to compute expected values and selecting the action that is best according to the respective criteria. This procedure is equivalent to the application of the Bayesian criterion. It is usually the case that a decision maker is able to assign a subjective probability distribution of the states of nature, and maximizing expected value frequently serves adequately as the basis for selecting the optimal action.

Models with Discrete Prior Probabilities

The optimal choice, as defined by the Bayesian criterion, is the action with the largest expected value. The expected value for each action is the sum of the probability-weighted conditional values for the possible states of nature.

■ *Example.* A department store buyer must decide how many high fashion dresses of a given type to stock for the coming season. The profit per dress is $100, but there is a loss of $80 for each dress not sold by the end of the season. The buyer estimates the prior probability distribution of demand from experience during past seasons. The conditional values are found by calculating the profit for dresses sold less any loss resulting from overstocking. For instance, suppose three dresses are stocked and only two are demanded. The profit from selling two dresses is $200, but there is a loss of $80 for the third dress not sold during the season. The conditional value for action a_4 (stock three dresses) and state of nature n_3 (demand for two) is $120 as seen in Table 10.5. The expected value is 0.4($120) = $48.

The optimal action is a_3 which has the largest expected value under risk of the three actions.

Expected Value of Perfect Information. The foregoing example illustrates the Bayesian criterion for determining the optimal action under risk. It is often of interest to ascertain how much profit is expected to be foregone because one does not have complete knowledge of when each state of nature will occur. If this perfect information were available, the best action could always be taken, conditional losses could be avoided, and expected value could be maximized. The expected value under these particular conditions is called the *expected value under certainty*. The difference between the expected value under certainty and the expected value of the optimal action under risk is called the *expected value of perfect information* (EVPI).

■ *Example.* The expected value of perfect information for the preceding example is found by summing the expected conditional values

TABLE 10.5

Conditional and Expected Values

			Action							
			Stock 0 a_1		Stock 1 a_2		Stock 2 a_3		Stock 3 a_4	
State of nature	De-mand	Prior proba-bility	Condi-tional value	Ex-pected value	Condi-tional value	Ex-pected value	Condi-tional value	Ex-pected value	Condi-tional value	Ex-pected value
n_1	0	0.1	$0	$0	$-80	$-8	$-160	$-16	$-240	$-24
n_2	1	0.3	0	0	100	30	20	6	-60	-18
n_3	2	0.4	0	0	100	40	200	80	120	48
n_4	3	0.2	0	0	100	20	200	40	300	60
Expected value under risk				$0		$82		$110		$66

for the best action for each state of nature. For instance, if demand is two (n_3), the best action is a_3. The probability of n_3 times the conditional value for a_2 is 0.4($200) = $80. The expected value certainty is computed as follows:

Condition	Conditional value	Prior probability	Expected value
$(a_1 \mid n_1)$	0	0.1	0
$(a_2 \mid n_2)$	$100	0.3	$30
$(a_3 \mid n_3)$	200	0.4	80
$(a_4 \mid n_4)$	300	0.2	60
Expected value under certainty			$170

The value of EVPI = $170 − $110 = $60.

In computing EVPI, it is assumed the buyer can select actions in a sequence of choices; and although demand does vary, the buyer knows in advance which state of nature will occur each time. The concept of EVPI is interpreted as the amount one would be willing to spend to obtain additional information in order to reduce risk. In the previous example this amount is EVPI = $60. The cost of sampling should be considered, and this is discussed in a later section.

Incremental Analysis. An alternative approach for determining an optimal action under risk, called *incremental analysis,* involves an iterative procedure for evaluating the expected marginal value of additional units. For instance, in the previous example the expected marginal value of stocking an additional dress is

$$pMP + (1 - p)ML$$

where

p is the probability of an incremental or additional dress being sold, MP is the marginal profit of $100 for selling the incremental dress, $(1 - p)$ is the probability of not selling the incremental unit, and ML is the marginal loss of $80 for not selling the additional dress during the season.

The net expected marginal value of stocking the first dress (a_2) is shown as follows:

	State of nature	Demand	Prior probability	Conditional value	Expected value
First unit not sold	n_1	$D < 1$	0.1	$-80	$-8
First unit sold	n_2, n_3, n_4	$D \geq 1$	0.9	100	90
					$82

The expected value of $82 is the same value as that computed for a_2 in Table 10.5. The expected marginal value of adding a second dress is

	State of nature	Demand	Prior probability	Conditional value	Expected value
Second unit not sold	n_1, n_2	$D < 2$	0.4	$-80	$-32
Second unit sold	n_3, n_4	$D \geq 2$	0.6	100	60
					$ 28

The addition of the expected marginal values for stocking the first and second dresses is $82 + $28 = $110, the expected value for a_3 in Table 10.5. The expected marginal value of adding a third dress is

	State of nature	Demand	Prior probability	Conditional value	Expected value
Third unit not sold	n_1, n_2, n_3	$D < 3$	0.8	$-80	$-64
Third unit sold	n_4	$D \geq 3$	0.2	100	20
					$-44

The expected marginal value of the third dress is negative and it should not be stocked. The optimal action is a_3 since the third one is the last dress added that has a positive expected marginal value.

The foregoing procedure can be shortened considerably by using a modification of a concept from microeconomics. Total expected value is a maximum for a scale of operation where expected marginal profit is equal to the expected marginal loss. This relationship is written

$$pMP = (1 - p)ML \dots\dots\dots\dots\dots\dots\dots\dots(10.1)$$

Solving this expression gives

$$p_c = \frac{ML}{ML + MP}\dots\dots\dots\dots\dots\dots\dots(10.2)$$

where p_c is called the *critical probability*.

In the foregoing example the value of p_c is computed

$$p_c = \frac{80}{80 + 100} = 0.44.$$

The interpretation of this value of p_c is that the number of dresses should be increased successively as long as each additional dress has a probability of at least 0.44 of being sold. In general, the procedure is to form a decreasing cumulative prior distribution of the probability that D or more units will be demanded and compare the calculated value of p_c with the cumulative probabilities. Since the cumulative distribution is discrete, the optimal action corresponds to the interval with a probability that includes the value of p_c. For this example the cumulative probabilities and optimal action are as follows:

Demand (D)	Probability that D or more units are demanded	
0	1.0	
1	0.9	$p_c = 0.44$ is in this interval and the
2	0.6	optimal action is to stock two units.
3	0.2	

An alternate procedure can also be used in which the marginal values are expressed as opportunity costs. The opportunity cost of understocking or foregone profit is written k_u, the opportunity cost of overstocking is written k_o, and p_c corresponds to the probability of incurring the cost of underage. The value of p_c is found by writing $pk_u = (1-p)k_o$ and solving for p_c to give

$$p_c = \frac{k_o}{k_o + k_u} \quad\dots\dots\dots\dots\dots\dots\dots\dots\dots\dots\dots\dots\dots\dots(10.3)$$

This value of p_c corresponds to the probability that demand will be D or more units. In general, a decreasing cumulative prior probability distribution is formed, the value of p_c is compared with the interval values, and the stocking level is increased to the point that the value of the cumulative probability for p_c occurs in the interval corresponding to the optimal action. For the foregoing example $p_c = \dfrac{80}{80 + 100} = 0.44$. The cumulative probability distribution and optimal action are as follows:

Demand (D)	Probability that D or more units are demanded	
0	1.0	
1	0.9	$p_c = 0.44$ is in this interval and the
2	0.6	optimal action is to stock two units.
3	0.2	

Linear Payoff Functions. An important class of decision problems is characterized by states of nature that are values taken on by a random variable, payoffs that are a linear function of the variable, and a defined *payoff function, P,* for each action. Problems of this type usually have a break-even point between the payoff functions for the actions, but it is not certain what value will be taken on by the variable. The optimal action is determined on the basis of expected values.

■ **Example.** A decision is to be made by the executive committee of a company whether to market a proposed new product. Cost studies project a fixed cost of $10,000 and a variable cost of $300 per unit of product. The proposed price is $500 per unit. The market research staff estimates the probability distribution of demand to be as follows:

Demand	Probability
40	0.2
50	0.4
60	0.3
70	0.1

The payoff for action a_1 (market the product) is a linear function of the quantity, q, of units sold, where q is a random variable. This function, P_1, is written

$$P_1 = \text{Total sales} - \text{Total cost} = \$500q - (\$10{,}000 + \$300q)$$
$$= -\$10{,}000 + \$200q.$$

The payoff function for action a_2 (do not market the product) is $P_2 = \$0 + \$0q$, since no costs or sales are involved. These functions and the probability distribution of demand are shown in Figure 10.3. The break-even quantity, q_b, is found by equating the payoff functions and solving for q_b as follows:

$$-\$10{,}000 + \$200q = \$0 + \$0q$$
$$\$200q = \$10{,}000$$
$$q_b = 50.$$

The optimal action can be determined by comparing the expected values of the payoff functions for the actions that are written

$$E(P_1) = E(-\$10{,}000) + E(\$200q)$$
$$= -\$10{,}000 + \$200E(q)$$
$$E(P_2) = E(\$0) + E(\$0) = \$0.$$

The term $E(q)$ is the sum of the probability-weighted quantities and is computed

$$E(q) = 0.2(40) + 0.4(50) + 0.3(60) + 0.1(70) = 53.$$

The expected payoff for action a_1 is

$$E(P_1) = -\$10{,}000 + \$200(53) = \$600,$$

and $E(P_2) = \$0$. The optimal action is a_1, since $E(P_1) > E(P_2)$.

The optimal action can also be determined by comparing $E(q)$ and q_b. The profitable region in this example corresponds to values of $q > q_b$. Since $E(q) > q_b$, the optimal action is a_1.

FIGURE 10.3

**Payoff Functions and Prior Probability
Distribution of Demand**

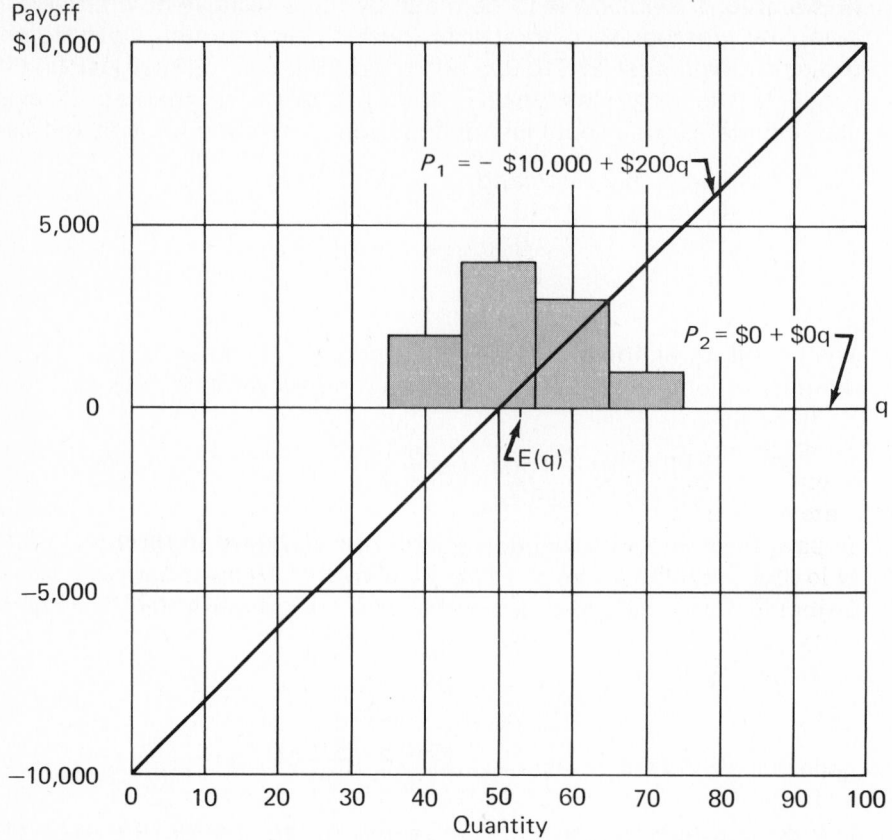

In general terms, the payoff and expected payoff functions can be written

Action	Payoff	Expected payoff
a_1	$P_1 = A_1 + B_1 q$	$E(P_1) = A_1 + B_1 E(q)$
a_2	$P_2 = A_2 + B_2 q$	$E(P_2) = A_2 + B_2 E(q)$

The optimal action can be determined by comparing $E(q)$ with q_b and comparing B_1 with B_2, the slopes of the functions, or by comparing the expected values of the functions, as summarized in Table 10.6. The terms A_1 and A_2 are the intercepts of the respective functions but are not involved in determining the optimal action. These rules for selecting the optimal action also apply to problems for which the slopes of both payoff functions are negative.

Loss Functions. The optimal action for a problem with linear payoff functions can be obtained by expressing the payoffs in terms of opportunity

TABLE 10.6

Criteria for Optimal Actions

Conditions	Optimal action
Payoff functions	
$E(q) > q_b$ and $B_1 > B_2$	a_1
$E(q) < q_b$ and $B_1 < B_2$	a_1
$E(q) < q_b$ and $B_1 > B_2$	a_2
$E(q) > q_b$ and $B_1 < B_2$	a_2
$E(q) = q_b$	a_1 or a_2
Expected payoff functions	
$E(P_1) > E(P_2)$	a_1
$E(P_1) < E(P_2)$	a_2
$E(P_1) = E(P_2)$	a_1 or a_2

losses and selecting the action with the smallest expected opportunity loss. Other problems may involve losses directly, and loss functions are the appropriate expressions of the outcomes of actions.

The payoffs in the previous example can be expressed in terms of opportunity losses. For instance, if the quantity of sales is 40 units, the best action is a_2, since 40 units is less than the break-even point of 50 units. The opportunity loss for taking action a_1 given $q = 40$ is

$$L_1(a_1 \mid q = 40) = P_2 - P_1 = 0 - [-\$10{,}000 + \$200(40)]$$
$$= \$2{,}000.$$

The opportunity losses for other quantities and actions (Table 10.7) can be found similarly, remembering that the opportunity loss for taking the correct action is zero. The loss functions L_1 and L_2 are shown as continuous functions in Figure 10.4. Note that these functions are not linear, for each has a horizontal portion equal to zero over the range for which each action is the best choice. Each function changes direction at the break-even point, q_b.

The expected value of $L_1(a_1 \mid q = 40)$ is

$$P(40) L_1(a_1 \mid q = 40) = 0.2(\$2{,}000) = \$400.$$

The expected values of the other losses are found similarly and are summarized in Table 10.7. The smallest total expected loss is $400. The optimal action is a_1. The expected opportunity loss for a_1 is equal to the expected value of perfect information (EVPI) associated with the decision.

Models Involving Normal Prior Distributions

Payoff and loss functions, EVPI, and other concepts introduced in the previous sections concerning discrete prior probabilities also apply to decisions for problems with continuous prior probability distributions. This

TABLE 10.7

Expected Loss Matrix

State of nature (q)	Prior probability	Opportunity loss		Expected loss	
		a_1	a_2	a_1	a_2
40	0.2	$2,000	$ 0	$400	$ 0
50	0.4	0	0	0	0
60	0.3	0	2,000	0	600
70	0.1	0	4,000	0	400
				$400	$1,000

FIGURE 10.4

Loss Functions

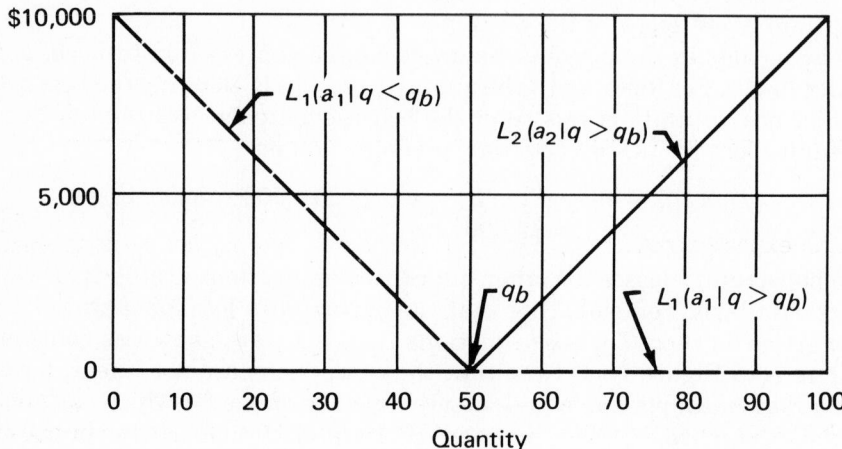

presentation is limited, however, to applications with normal prior distributions. In applying these concepts to the continuous case it is assumed that a state of nature is a value of a continuous variable.

Criteria for Optimal Actions. The payoff and loss functions associated with continuous probabilities are expressed in a similar form, with the exception that the population mean μ is viewed as a random variable and payoff or loss is a function of μ. For a two-action problem the payoff functions may be written

Action	Payoff function
a_1	$P_1 = A_1 + B_1 \mu$
a_2	$P_2 = A_2 + B_2 \mu.$

If B_1 and B_2 are both positive, the break-even point, μ_b, is found by equating $P_1 = P_2 = A_1 + B_1\mu = A_2 + B_2\mu$, and solving for μ gives

$$\mu = \frac{A_2 - A_1}{B_1 - B_2} = \mu_b.$$

The payoff functions and the break-even point are shown in general form in Figure 10.5.

FIGURE 10.5

Payoff Functions

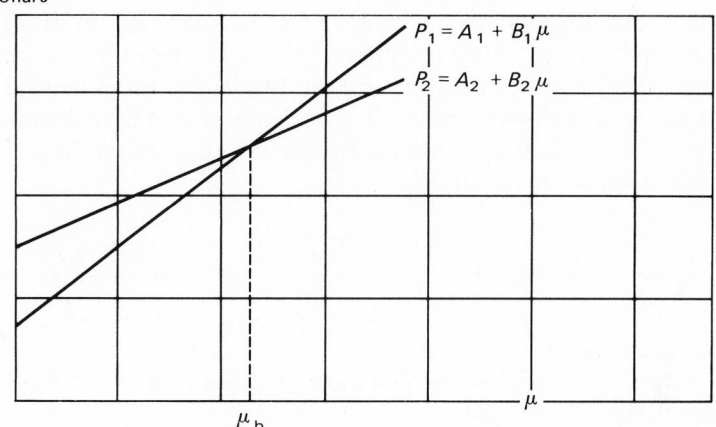

Values of μ

The expected payoff functions for actions a_1 and a_2 are written, respectively,

$$E(P_1) = E(A_1) + E(B_1\mu) = A_1 + B_1E(\mu)$$
$$E(P_2) = E(A_1) + E(B_2\mu) = A_2 + B_2E(\mu)$$

where μ is a random variable. If both B_1 and B_2 have values > 0, and μ is substituted for q in Table 10.6, the criteria for determining the optimal action in this table can be applied to problems involving normal prior distributions and linear payoff functions.

■ *Example.* Continuing the example in the preceding section, assume that the demand for the product is estimated to be normally distributed with a mean of 53 and a standard deviation of 9 units. The payoff functions are

$$a_1: \text{market} \qquad P_1 = -\$10,000 + 200\mu$$
$$a_2: \text{do not market} \qquad P_2 = \$0 + \$0\mu$$

The value of $E(\mu) = 53$ and $\mu_b = (\$10,000/\$200) = 50$. Since $E(\mu) > \mu_b$ and $B_1 > B_2$ the optimal action is a_1. The expected payoff for the actions are $E(P_1) = -\$10,000 + \$200\,E(\mu) = -\$10,000 + \$10,600 = \$600$ and $E(P_2) = \$0$. The optimal action is a_1, since $E(P_1) > E(P_2)$.

Expected Value of Perfect Information. For the discrete case, EVPI is the sum of the conditional opportunity losses for the optimal action weighted by the respective prior probabilities. The concept of EVPI for the continuous case can be viewed intuitively in a similar manner. The continuous prior distribution is viewed as being approximated by a histogram with a large number of bars of equal width and heights equal to the ordinate of the normal density function at the midpoint of each bar. This view is similar to the relationship between the binomial and normal distribution as the sample size becomes large. The area of each bar, width times height, approximates the probability associated with the interval on the μ (horizontal) scale. If each probability is multiplied times the corresponding value of the opportunity loss function at the midpoint of the bar and the interval width on the μ scale becomes small to approach zero, the limit of the sum of these products is EVPI for the continuous case. Often the loss function is zero to the right of the break-even point, μ_b, and the probability-weighted opportunity losses are effectively summed from minus infinity to μ_b. This sum can be expressed symbolically by

$$\sum_{i=1}^{n} L(\mu_i) P'(z_i) \frac{\Delta\mu}{\sigma}$$

where
n is the number of intervals
$L(\mu_i)$ is the value of the loss function for the optimal action at the midpoint of the ith interval
$P'(z_i)$ is the ordinate of the unit normal distribution at the midpoint of the ith interval
$\Delta\mu$ is the interval width on the μ scale
σ is the standard deviation of the normal prior probability distribution.

As n becomes very large and $\Delta\mu$ approaches zero, this sum approaches EVPI. Ordinates of the unit normal distribution are used to provide a general expression which can be related to a particular normal distribution by the use of σ, the standard deviation of that distribution.

To facilitate calculations the expression for EVPI can be written

$$\text{EVPI} = L\sigma N(D) \dots\dots\dots\dots\dots\dots\dots\dots\text{(10.4)}$$

where
$L = |B_1 - B_2|$ is the absolute value of the difference of the slopes of the payoff functions for the actions
σ is the standard deviation of the prior distribution
$N(D)$ is the *unit normal loss function,* also called the normal loss integral.

The value of the term D is the absolute value of the deviation of μ_b from $E(\mu)$ expressed in number of standard deviations and written

$$D = \frac{|\mu_b - E(\mu)|}{\sigma} \dots\dots\dots\dots\dots\dots\dots\text{(10.5)}$$

The term $N(D)$ can be shown to be equal to

$$P'(D) - \mu_b P(\mu < \mu_b)$$

where

$P'(D)$ is the unit normal ordinate at D standard deviations

μ_b is the break-even value of μ

$P(\mu < \mu_b)$ is the area of the normal distribution to the left of μ_b.

Values of $N(D)$ have been computed and are presented in Appendix O.

■ **Example.** Continuing the previous example, the data with which to determine EVPI are:

$$E(\mu) = 53 \qquad \mu_b = 50$$
$$\sigma = 9 \qquad L = |\$200 - 0| = \$200$$

These data are illustrated in Figure 10.6. The normal loss function is computed

$$D = \frac{|50 - 53|}{9} = 0.33$$

and $N(D = 0.33) = 0.2555$ as read from Appendix O. The desired value is

$$EVPI = \$200(9)(0.2555) = \$460.$$

FIGURE 10.6

Loss Function and Normal Prior Distribution

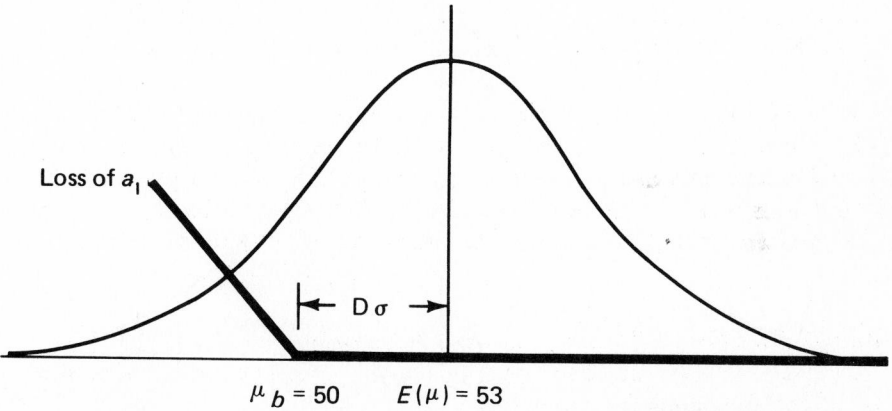

$\mu_b = 50 \qquad E(\mu) = 53$

Decision Problems with Many Actions. The optimal action for problems with many actions and discrete prior probabilities can be determined by use of p_c (Formula 10.2). This approach can be extended to problems with many possible actions, a continuous prior probability distribution of the state of nature, and a linear loss function. The optimal action is identified by computing p_c and determining the action that corresponds to this critical probability.

■Example. A bakery must decide how many loaves of a type of bread to make on a particular day. The bread costs 20 cents per loaf to produce and sells for 30 cents per loaf if sold the day it is baked. Bread that is not sold the same day must be sold at a reduced price of 15 cents. Sales records indicate that the demand for the given day has a normal distribution with a mean of 1,200 and a standard deviation of 150 loaves, written $N(1,200, 150)$. The cost of overage is $k_o = 20 - 15 = 5$ cents for each unit, and the cost of underage is $k_u = 30 - 20 = 10$ cents. The critical probability computed by Formula 10.2 is

$$p_c = \frac{k_o}{k_o + k_u} = \frac{5}{5 + 10} = 0.33.$$

The optimal action is found by determining the number of loaves that corresponds to $p_c = 0.33$, the area in the right-hand portion of the normal prior distribution as shown in Figure 10.7. The value of $p_c = 0.33$ is interpolated from the body of Appendix I. The number of standard deviations is 0.4317. The optimal number of loaves to bake is

$$E(\mu) + 0.4317\sigma = 1,200 + 0.4317(150) = 1,264.755$$

or 1,265 loaves.

FIGURE 10.7

Normal Distribution and p_c

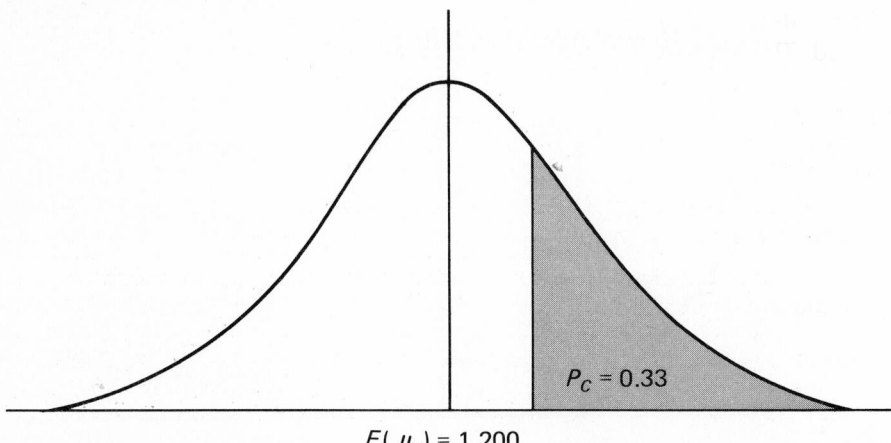

$E(\mu) = 1,200$

DECISIONS UNDER RISK WITH SAMPLING

In some decision situations it is possible to sample to obtain additional information concerning the state of nature. This information can be combined with that provided by prior probabilities to determine the optimal action. This approach also provides the basis for deciding if sampling is worthwhile in view of the benefit and cost of sampling.

Decision Rules with Binomial Sampling

In decision problems where a state of nature is an attribute, such as a proportion, it is often possible to obtain information about the existing state through binomial sampling. In two-action problems with binomial sampling, the decision maker chooses between actions on the basis of c, a critical number of successes (failures) that can be obtained in a sample. For a sample of n items, the optimal value of c is determined on the basis of minimum expected loss.

■ *Example.* A company is considering the bulk purchase of a lot of 1,000 transistors for making toys. The proportion of defective transistors in such lots has been either 0.20 or 0.60 because of the nature of the manufacturing process. The prior probabilities for these states are 0.4 and 0.6, respectively. It is estimated that a profit of 25 cents can be made with each acceptable transistor, but a loss of 20 cents will result from each defective transistor. A sample of three transistors is taken, and it contains one defective item. Should the lot be purchased?

The profit function for action a_1 (purchase the lot) is $P_1 = \$0.25$ $(1,000)(1 - p) - \$0.20(1,000)p = \$250 - \$450p$. The break-even point is $p_b = \$250/\$450 = 0.56$. If $p < p_b$, the optimal action is a_1; otherwise, a_2 (do not purchase) is the best action. The opportunity loss for taking action a_1 is zero if the state of nature is $n_1 (p = 0.20)$, but the opportunity loss for a_2 is $P_1 - P_2 = [\$250 - \$450(0.20)] - \$0 = \$160$. The opportunity loss for a_2 is zero if the state of nature is n_2 ($p = 0.60$), but the opportunity loss for taking action a_1 is $P_2 - P_1 = \$0 - [\$250 - \$450(0.60)] = \$20$. The opportunity losses are shown in Table 10.8.

TABLE 10.8

Loss Matrix

State of nature	Proportion defective	Action Purchase a_1	Action Not purchase a_2
n_1	0.2	$L_1(a_1 \mid n_1) = \$0$	$L_2(a_2 \mid n_1) = \$160$
n_2	0.6	$L_1(a_1 \mid n_2) = \$20$	$L_2(a_2 \mid n_2) = \$0$

The optimal decision rule is determined by computing the expected loss for each number of successes (failures) that can be obtained in a sample of n items and choosing the number of successes for which expected loss is a minimum. This critical number is designated c and is called the *criterion number*. In the example in this section, the sample size is three and the possible values of c are 0, 1, 2, and 3. A choice is to be made between a_1 and a_2 on the basis of the number of successes obtained in the sample. In this example the decision rule is to take action a_1 if the number of defectives, d, in the sample is less than c, and choose a_2 if greater than or equal to c. For instance, decision rule (3, 2) for $n = 3$ and $c = 2$ is illustrated by the tree diagram in Figure 10.8. The branches depict the states of nature, actions based on sample outcomes, respective probabilities, and corresponding losses and expected losses.

The expected losses for $n = 3$ and various values of c are computed in Table 10.9. The conditional probabilities in column (3) for each decision rule are obtained from Appendix D for $n = 3$ and $r = 1$. The probability of a loss is found by multiplying the prior probability for each state times the conditional probability for the respective action that would result in a loss. The product is a joint probability that is multiplied by the conditional loss to give the expected loss. Conditional probabilities for optimal actions are not shown since the corresponding losses are zero. The losses for the states are summed to give the total expected loss for the decision rule.

FIGURE 10.8

Tree Diagram for Decision Rule (3,2)

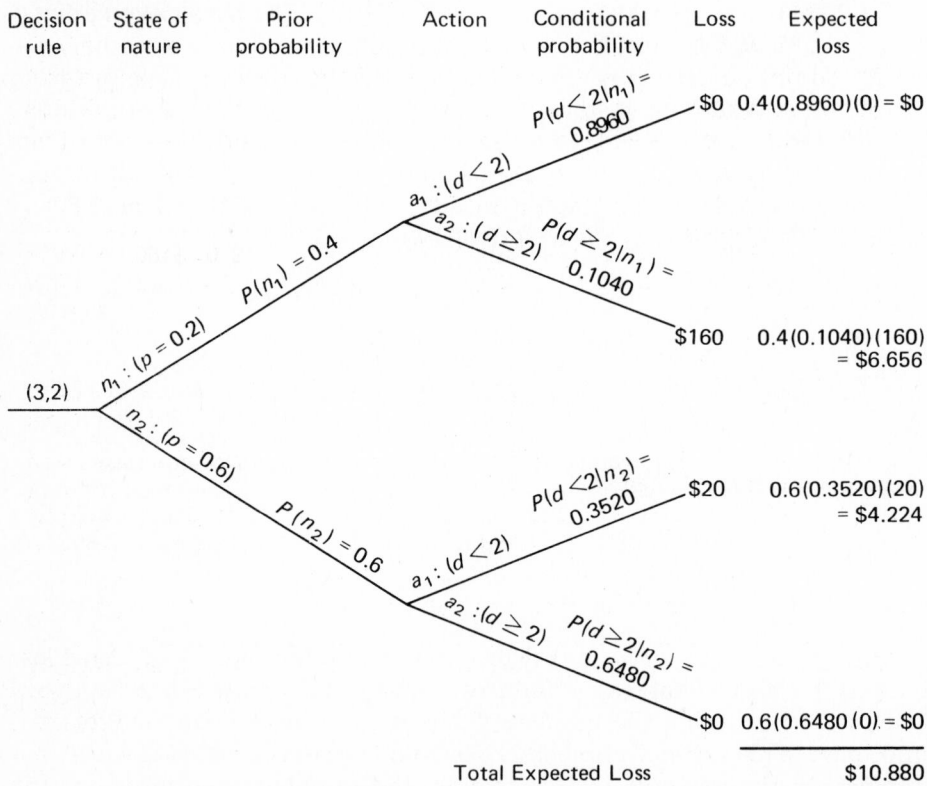

From Table 10.9 it is seen that expected loss is a minimum for decision rule (3, 3), which is interpreted that the lot is accepted (purchased) if the

TABLE 10.9

Expected Loss for Decision Rules

(1)	(2)	(3) Conditional probability given state and incorrect action		(4) Joint probability for state and incorrect action	(5) Loss for action		(6) Expected loss
State of nature	Prior probability	a_1	a_2		a_1	a_2	
		(3,0)					
		$P(c < 0)$	$P(c \geq 0)$				
0.2	0.4		1.0000	0.4000	$ 0	$160	$64.000
0.6	0.6	0.0000		0.0000	20	0	0.000
							$64.000
		(3,1)					
		$P(c < 1)$	$P(c \geq 1)$				
0.2	0.4		0.4880	0.1952	$ 0	$160	$31.232
0.6	0.6	0.0640		0.0384	20	0	0.768
							$32.000
		(3,2)					
		$P(c < 2)$	$P(c \geq 2)$				
0.2	0.4		0.1040	0.0416	$ 0	$160	$ 6.656
0.6	0.6	0.3520		0.2112	20	0	4.224
							$10.880
		(3,3)					
		$P(c < 3)$	$P(c \geq 3)$				
0.2	0.4		0.0080	0.0032	$ 0	$160	$ 0.512
0.6	0.6	0.7840		0.4704	20	0	9.408
							$9.920*
		(3, $\geq$4)					
		$P(c < 4)$	$P(c \geq 4)$				
0.2	0.4		0.0000	0.0000	$ 0	$160	$ 0.000
0.6	0.6	1.0000		0.6000	20	0	12.000
							$12.000

* minimum

number of defectives in the sample is less than three and rejected (not purchased) if it is equal to three. In the example one defective was obtained in the sample, and the optimal action is a_1 (purchase the lot).

A sample size of three is used in the previous example to illustrate the procedure for determining the optimal decision rule and action. The procedure applies to various sample sizes, and before a sample is taken it is desirable to determine the optimal sample size that should be taken and the optimal criterion number to use in determining the optimal action. The basis for determining an optimal sample size is presented in the following section.

Optimal Sample Size

The foregoing section describes the logic for determining the optimal rejection number for a given binomial sample size. Expected loss decreases as the sample size is increased, and it approaches zero as the sample size becomes large. This relationship is seen in column (2) of Table 10.10, which presents the expected loss for selected sample sizes and optimal criterion numbers related to the foregoing example. On the basis of sample size alone, one could conclude that the best approach is to take a very large sample to reduce risk. If costs are incurred in taking a sample, the total expected loss should include the cost of sampling. Suppose the cost of sampling is 50 cents per sample item in the transistor example. This cost is shown in column (3) of Table 10.10. The total expected loss in column (4) is the sum of the two types of cost. The optimal sample size and criterion number is (10, 5), for the corresponding total loss is a minimum. The determination of the optimal sample size and criterion number is usually found by trial and error and this requires the computation of expected losses for combinations of values of n and c. A computer, using the proper computational routine, will enable many combinations of n and c to be examined with only minimal effort.

TABLE 10.10

Total Expected Loss for Selected Decision Rules

Decision rule (n,c) (1)	Expected loss (2)	Cost of sampling (3)	Total expected loss (4)
(1,1)	$17.60	$0.50	$18.10
(3,3)	9.92	1.50	11.42
(5,3)	7.52	2.50	10.02
(7,4)	5.61	3.50	9.11
(10,5)	4.09	5.00	9.09*
(11,6)	3.71	5.50	9.21
(20,9)	1.32	10.00	11.32
(50,21)	0.06	25.00	25.06
(100,39)	0.00	50.00	50.00

* minimum

Sampling and the Revision of Prior Probabilities

The discussion in the preceding section presents the procedure for determining the optimal sample size. This analysis is performed prior to sampling. After a sample of optimal size has been taken, the information obtained can be utilized in revising prior probabilities. The revision of prior probabilities is based on Bayes' theorem (Chapter 3).

■ *Example.* In the example on page 307 the proportion of defectives (states of nature) are 0.2 and 0.6, $B_1 = -\$450$, and $B_2 = \$0$. The respective prior probabilities are 0.4 and 0.6. The break-even proportion is $p_b = 0.56$, and $E(p) = 0.2(0.4) + 0.6(0.6) = 0.44$. The optimal action prior to sampling is a_1, purchase the lot, since $E(p) < p_b$ and $B_1 < B_2$ (slopes of the respective loss functions). A sample of three items was taken and contained one defective. What action should be taken in view of the sample information?

The prior probabilities are revised by (1) finding the conditional probabilities of obtaining the sample result given each state of nature, (2) computing the respective joint probabilities, and (3) determining the posterior or revised prior probabilities. The data for these calculations are summarized in Table 10.11.

TABLE 10.11

Revision of Prior Probabilities

State of nature	Percent defective	Prior probability	Conditional probability	Joint probability	Posterior probability
n_1	0.2	0.4	0.3840	0.1536	0.4706
n_2	0.6	0.6	0.2880	0.1728	0.5294
				0.3264	

The conditional probabilities are obtained from Appendix C, where $P(r=1 \mid n=3, p=0.2) = 0.3840$ and $P(r=2 \mid n=3, q=1-0.6) = 0.2880$. The posterior probabilities are found by dividing the total of the joint probabilities into its components, to obtain the revised prior probability for each of the states of nature. The posterior probabilities are the best estimates of the likelihoods of the states of nature. The expected value of the proportion of defectives in the lot is now computed to be $E(p) = 0.2(0.4706) + 0.6(0.5294) = 0.41$. Since $E(p) < p_b$ and $B_1 < B_2$, the optimal action is a_1 (purchase the lot).

Decisions with Posterior Normal Distributions

The revision of probabilities by use of Bayes' theorem can be applied to normal distributions by extending the approach presented in the preceding section. This extension involves the revision of a normal prior distribution of the universe mean by use of sample information. To illustrate the revision procedure, consider a random variable x, such as the demand for a product, that is normally distributed with a mean μ, a standard deviation σ, and written $N(\mu, \sigma)$. Assume that the universe mean is not known but its likelihood is estimated by a prior distribution that is normally distributed with a mean μ_o, a standard deviation σ_o, and written $N(\mu_o, \sigma_o)$. In contrast to the universe of values of x which correspond to numbers of units demanded, the prior distribution expresses the likelihood of the mean number of units that will be demanded. To obtain the best estimate of the mean demand, a sample of n observations of demand is taken, and the sample information is combined with the prior distribution to obtain the revised distribution of the likelihood of the mean of the universe of values of x. From the joint likelihood of a particular sample and the prior probability distribution it can be shown that the mean $E_1(\mu)$ and standard deviation σ_1 of the revised or *posterior distribution* of μ are

$$E_1(\mu) = \frac{\mu_o \sigma_{\bar{x}}^2 + \bar{x} \sigma_o^2}{\sigma_o^2 + \sigma_{\bar{x}}^2} \dots\dots\dots\dots\dots\dots\dots\text{(10.6)}$$

and

$$\sigma_1 = \sqrt{\frac{\sigma_o^2 \sigma_{\bar{x}}^2}{\sigma_o^2 + \sigma_{\bar{x}}^2}} \dots\dots\dots\dots\dots\dots\dots\text{(10.7)}$$

where μ_o and σ_o^2 are the mean and variance of the prior distribution, $\sigma_{\bar{x}}^2 = \dfrac{\sigma^2}{n}$ is the square of the standard error of the mean, and $\bar{x}$ the sample mean. The posterior distribution is normally distributed and has a standard deviation that is smaller than the prior distribution of μ. From Formula 10.6 it can be seen that as the sample size n becomes very large, $E_1(\mu)$ approaches $\bar{x}$. In Formula 10.7, $\sigma_{\bar{x}}^2$ approaches zero as n becomes large, and consequently σ_1 also approaches zero. These results are consistent with the concepts of sampling presented in Chapter 6.

Note that it is necessary to know or estimate σ, the standard deviation of the universe, to be able to compute the posterior distribution.

■ *Example.* A preceding example concerning the marketing of a new product (page 299) is continued to illustrate the application of the posterior distribution. The data given previously are summarized as follows:

$\mu_o = E(\mu) = 53$	$\mu_b = 50$	$B_1 = \$200$
$\sigma_o = 9$	EVPI $= \$460$	$B_2 = \$0$

Assume that the universe standard deviation is estimated to be $\sigma = 12$. A sample of 10 observations of demand at different geographic locations is taken to estimate mean demand, producing a mean $\bar{x} = 52$.

The square of the standard error of the mean is $\sigma_{\bar{x}}^2 = \dfrac{\sigma^2}{n} = \dfrac{(12)^2}{10} = 14.4$.

The posterior mean and standard deviation are

$$E_1(\mu) = \frac{53(14.4) + 52(9)^2}{(9)^2 + 14.4} = \frac{4{,}975.2}{95.4} = 52.15$$

and

$$\sigma_1 = \sqrt{\frac{(9)^2(14.4)}{(9)^2 + 14.4}} = \sqrt{12.23} = 3.50.$$

The posterior distribution is written $N(52.15, 3.50)$. The expected pay-offs for the actions based on the posterior distributions are

$$E(P_1) = -\$10{,}000 + \$200(52.15) = \$430$$
$$E(P_2) = \$0.$$

Since $E(P_1) > E(P_2)$, the optimal action is a_1 (market the product). The value of EVPI for the posterior distribution is computed as follows

$$D_1 = \frac{|50 - 52.15|}{3.50} = 0.61$$

and

$$\text{EVPI} = L\sigma_1 N(D_1) = \$200(3.50)(0.1659) = \$116$$

where the subscripts for D_1 and $N(D_1)$ designate the posterior distribution. The value of EVPI for the posterior distribution is less than the EVPI for the prior distribution, indicating a gain of $\$460 - \$116 = \$344$ as the result of sampling.

This example is simplified to illustrate the application of the posterior distribution and does not consider the cost of sampling. If costs are incurred by sampling, a decision maker would want to know prior to sampling if the expected benefit of sampling is greater than the sampling cost. Otherwise, it would not be worthwhile to sample. The following section presents an approach to this determination.

Optimal Sampling with Normal Distributions

It is known from sampling distributions (Chapter 6) that if a sample of a given size is taken from a universe, any one of many values from the normal distribution of sample means could be obtained (central limit theorem). For each possible sample mean there is a corresponding posterior distribution (Formulas 10.6 and 10.7). In this sense, the posterior distribution is a random variable and its probability distribution is called the *preposterior distribution*. It can be shown that the mean of this distribution is equal to the prior mean and the standard deviation is

$$\sigma_{E_1} = \sqrt{\frac{\sigma_0^4}{\sigma_0^2 + \sigma_{\bar{x}}^2}} \quad \dots\dots\dots\dots\dots\dots\dots\dots(10.8)$$

The preposterior distribution is normally distributed. The expected loss due to risk for this distribution is called the *expected value of sample information* or EVSI, for it expresses the likely benefit of taking a sample of a given size. EVSI is analogous to EVPI and is computed

$$\text{EVSI} = L\sigma_{E_1} N(D_E) \qquad \textbf{(10.9)}$$

If EVSI is greater than the cost of sampling, it is worthwhile to sample. The amount by which EVSI exceeds the cost of sampling is sometimes called ENGS, the *expected net gain from sampling.*

■ ***Example.*** The preceding example is continued by computing EVSI for a sample of 10. The mean of the preposterior distribution is equal to $\mu_o = E(\mu) = 53$, the mean of the prior distribution. The standard deviation is

$$\sigma_{E_1} = \sqrt{\frac{(9)^4}{(9)^2 + \frac{(12)^2}{10}}} = \sqrt{68.77} = 8.29.$$

EVSI is computed as follows

$$D_E = \frac{|\mu_b - \mu_o|}{\sigma_{E_1}} = \frac{|50 - 53|}{8.29} = 0.36$$

and

$$\text{EVSI} = L\sigma_{E_1} N(D_E) = \$200(8.29)(0.2445) = \$405$$

where $L = |B_1 - B_2| = |\$200 - \$0| = \$200$ and $N(D_E)$ is the loss function for the preposterior distribution read from Appendix O.

Suppose that the cost per sample item is \$20, and the total cost of the sample of 10 is \$200. The expected net gain from sampling, which is determined prior to taking the sample, is

$$\text{ENGS} = \text{EVSI} - \text{Sampling cost} = \$405 - \$200 = \$205.$$

The value of EVSI and the cost of sampling tend to increase with sample size. The optimal sample size is that for which ENGS is a maximum. These relationships are illustrated in Table 10.12 and by Figure 10.9. The data for these illustrations are based on the example in this section. Figure 10.9 shows that EVSI increases with sample size n and it approaches EVPI as a limit as n becomes very large. ENGS has a maximum value for $n = 4$, the optimal sample size. At approximately $n = 22$, EVSI equals the cost of sampling and ENGS is zero.

In practice, the optimal sample size is found by trial and error by computing ENGS for selected sample sizes.

Termination of Sampling

Although a sample of optimal size may be taken and the results used to obtain the posterior distribution, a value of ENGS > 0 based on the posterior

TABLE 10.12

ENGS for Selected Sample Sizes

Sample size	$\dfrac{\sigma^2}{n} = \dfrac{12^2}{n}$	σ_{E_1}	$D_E = \dfrac{\lvert 50 - 53 \rvert}{\sigma_{E_1}}$	$L(D_E)$	EVSI	Sample cost	ENGS
1	144.0	5.40	0.556	0.181	$195	$ 20	$175
2	72.0	6.55	0.458	0.211	276	40	236
3	48.0	7.13	0.421	0.223	318	60	258
4	36.0	7.49	0.401	0.230	345	80	265*
5	28.8	7.73	0.388	0.235	363	100	263
7	20.6	8.04	0.373	0.240	386	140	246
10	14.4	8.29	0.362	0.244	405	200	205
15	9.6	8.51	0.353	0.247	420	300	120
20	7.2	8.62	0.348	0.249	429	400	29
25	5.8	8.70	0.345	0.250	435	500	−65
30	4.8	8.74	0.343	0.251	439	600	−161

*maximum

FIGURE 10.9

Relationship of Value and Cost of Sampling to Sample Size

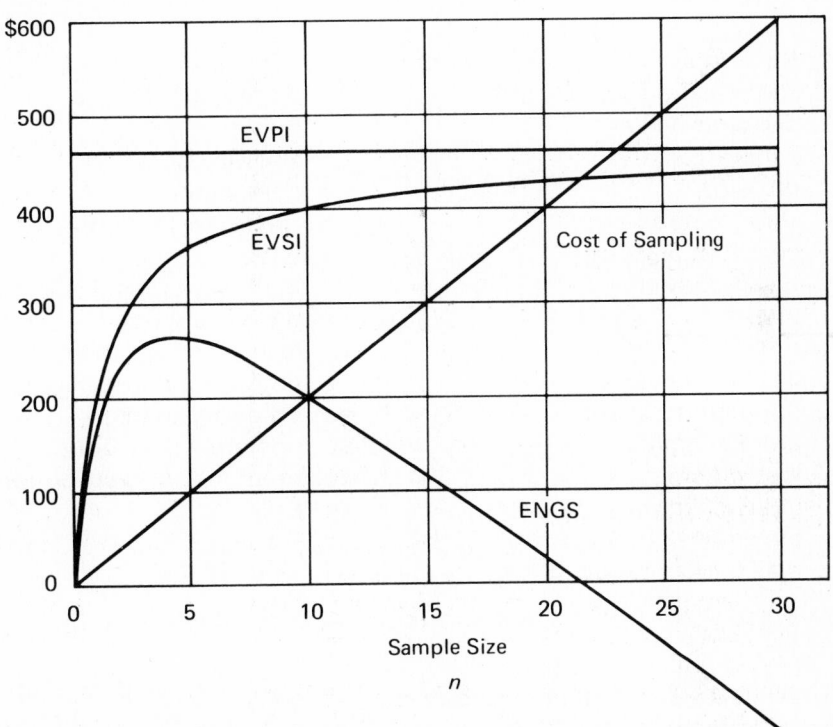

distribution might indicate that additional sampling would be beneficial. As a consequence, an action would not be taken until after it is determined whether additional sampling would be worthwhile.

■ *Example.* The posterior distribution in the preceding new product example (page 312) was determined to be $N(52.15, 3.50)$. To determine EVSI at this point, the posterior distribution is viewed as being the new prior distribution. The value of ENGS for a sample of one is based on the following calculations:

$$\sigma_{E_1} = \sqrt{\frac{(3.5)^4}{(3.5)^2 + (12)^2/1}} = \sqrt{0.96} = 0.98$$

$$D_E = \frac{|50 - 52.15|}{0.98} = 2.19$$

$$\text{EVSI} = L\sigma_{E_1}N(D_E) = \$200(0.98)(0.00503) = \$0.99$$

$$\text{ENGS} = \$0.99 - (1)(\$20) = -\$19.01.$$

Since the value of ENGS for a sample of one is negative, as are the values of ENGS for larger sample sizes, further sampling would not be beneficial. Sampling is terminated, and the optimal action is a_1 (market the product).

STUDY QUESTIONS

10–1. Explain briefly the meaning of the following terms:

a. statistical decision theory
b. decision maker
c. action
d. decision
e. state of nature
f. conditional value
g. payoff matrix
h. uncertainty
i. risk
j. decision criteria
k. dominating action
l. optimal action
m. loss matrix
n. utility of money
o. maximin criterion
p. maximax criterion

q. minimax criterion
r. minimax regret
s. Hurwicz criterion
t. Laplace criterion
u. Bayesian criterion
v. EVPI
w. incremental analysis
x. payoff function
y. loss function
z. unit normal loss function
aa. criterion number
ab. posterior distribution
ac. preposterior distribution
ad. EVSI
ae. ENGS

10–2. What does a utility function indicate about one's attitude toward risk?

10–3. What is the relationship between statistical decision theory and classical statistics?

10-4. Why are there different criteria for making decisions under uncertainty?

10-5. Explain what is meant by a critical probability.

10-6. What is the relationship between the payoff functions and the loss functions for a decision problem?

10-7. Explain the meaning of each of the terms in the following expression: $P_1 = A_1 + B_1 \mu$.

10-8. What determines the optimal decision rule for binomial sampling?

10-9. Contrast the posterior and preposterior distributions for normal sampling.

10-10. How is the decision to terminate normal sampling determined?

PROBLEMS

10-1. The alternatives of (1) receiving \$3,000 with a probability $p = 0.2$ and \$500 with a probability $1 - p = 0.8$ or (2) receiving \$1,000 for certain are equally desirable to an individual. What is the utility of \$3,000 if the utility of \$500 is five and the utility of \$1,000 is 10?

10-2. An individual is indifferent between (1) receiving \$500 with certainty or (2) receiving \$2,000 with a probability $p = 0.4$ and receiving \$100 with a probability $1 - p = 0.6$. If the utility for \$500 is one and the utility of \$2,000 is two, what is the utility of \$100?

10-3. If the alternatives of (1) receiving \$1,000 for certain or (2) receiving \$2,000 with a probability $p = 0.3$ and losing \$100 with a probability $1 - p = 0.7$ are equally desirable, what is the utility of a loss of \$100 if the utility of \$100 is 5 and the utility of \$2,000 is 20?

10-4. The alternatives of (1) receiving \$1,500 with a probability $p = 0.8$ and losing \$500 with a probability $1 - p = 0.2$ or (2) receiving \$1,000 for certain are preferred equally. What is the utility of a loss of \$500 if the utility for \$1,500 is 10 and the utility for \$1,000 is 7?

10-5. What does the utility function for Problem 10-3 indicate about the attitude toward risk over the range of dollar amounts?

10-6. Given the data and results of Problem 10-4 and if the utility of \$0 is zero, what can be said about the attitude toward risk over the range of amounts?

10-7. Determine the optimal actions for the maximin and maximax criteria for the following matrix:

	n_1	n_2	n_3	n_4
a_1	7	2	−1	4
a_2	4	3	4	6
a_3	3	4	2	5
a_4	5	1	0	4

10-8. Given the following payoff matrix, what is the optimal action using maximin and maximax criteria?

	n_1	n_2	n_3
a_1	2	−1	4
a_2	6	1	3
a_3	3	2	5

10-9. Find the optimal action by use of the minimax regret criterion for the matrix in Problem 10-7.

10-10. Determine the minimax regret action for the matrix in Problem 10-8.

10-11. Determine the optimal action by the Hurwicz criterion by using weights of 0.6 for maximum and 0.4 minimum payoffs in Problem 10-7.

10-12. Using weights of 2/5 for maximum and 3/5 for minimum payoffs in Problem 10-8, determine the optimal action by the Hurwicz criterion.

10-13. Use the Laplace criterion to determine the optimal action for Problem 10-7.

10-14. Find the optimal action for Problem 10-8 by use of the Laplace criterion.

10-15. If an individual assigns weights of 0.3, 0.1, 0.4, and 0.2 to states n_1, n_2, n_3, and n_4, respectively, for the matrix in Problem 10-7, what is the optimal action in terms of the Bayesian criterion?

10-16. If subjective weights of 0.2, 0.3, and 0.5 are assigned to states n_1, n_2, and n_3, respectively, for the matrix in Problem 10-8, what is the optimal action according to the Bayesian criterion?

10-17. For the matrix in Problem 10-7, determine if there are dominated actions.

10-18. Determine why action a_1 is not the optimal action for the matrix in Problem 10-8 for any of the decision criteria.

10-19. A bookstore manager must decide how many copies of the current edition of a tax law book should be stocked. Since some of the tax laws change from year to year, a new edition of the book is published each year and old editions become obsolete. The bookstore purchases the books for $8 per copy and the books retail at $10 per copy. Books not sold in the year while the edition is current must be sold for $3 per copy. Sales records indicate that the probability of demand for tax books is as follows:

Demand (units)	Probability
10	0.05
11	0.15
12	0.35
13	0.25
14	0.15
15	0.05

a. Determine the optimal action on the basis of expected value under risk.
b. What is the expected marginal value of stocking the 13th unit?
c. Find p_c and the optimal action.
d. Compute EVPI.

10–20. The probability distribution of the demand for a product is estimated to be:

Demand	Probability
0	0.2
1	0.4
2	0.3
3	0.1

The product costs $10 and sells for $30 per unit. If the product is not sold it is worthless.
a. Determine the action with the maximum expected value under risk.
b. Compute the expected marginal value of stocking the second unit.
c. Compute p_c and determine the optimal action.
d. What is the value of EVPI?

10–21. Determine the optimal action for Problem 10–19 by use of overage and underage costs in computing p_c.

10–22. Find the optimal action for Problem 10–20 by use of overage and underage costs in computing p_c.

10–23. A leasing company is considering the purchase of a piece of heavy equipment at a fixed cost of $18,000. The equipment is leased to customers for $15 per hour. The variable cost to the company for operating the equipment, including the operator, fuel, maintenance, and other costs, is $9 per hour. The probability distribution of the number of days the equipment is expected to be leased is as follows:

Number of days	Probability
1,500	0.2
3,500	0.5
4,000	0.3

Determine the optimal action by comparing:
a. Payoff functions.
b. Expected payoff functions.

10–24. A company has an opportunity to market a product (a_1) for a fixed cost of $5,000. The variable cost is $5 and the sales price is $9 per unit. It is estimated that there is a 0.6 probability that economic conditions will be favorable and the demand will be 1,500 units, but there is a 0.4 probability that demand will be 800 units because of less favorable conditions. Determine the optimal action by comparing:

   a. Payoff functions.
   b. Expected payoff functions.

10–25. Compute the expected loss matrix for Problem 10–23 and determine the optimal action.

10–26. Compute the expected loss matrix for Problem 10–24 and determine the optimal action.

10–27. In Problem 10–23, assume that the number of days of equipment lease is estimated to be distributed $N(3111, 740)$. Determine the:

   a. Optimal action by use of payoff and expected payoff functions.
   b. Value of EVPI.

10–28. Assume in Problem 10–24 that demand is estimated to be normally distributed with $N(1306, 400)$. Determine the:

   a. Optimal action by use of payoff and expected payoff functions.
   b. Value of EVPI.

10–29. The produce department of a supermarket stocks avocados that cost 25 cents and sell for 33 cents each. Avocados not sold become over-ripe and cannot be sold. It is estimated that the weekly demand is distributed $N(90, 10)$. How many should be stocked?

10–30. A newsstand wishes to determine how many copies of a monthly issue of a magazine to stock. The cost per copy is 40 cents and the sales price is 75 cents per copy. Magazines not sold within a month are worthless. If demand for the magazine is estimated to be distributed $N(30, 4)$, how many copies should be stocked?

10–31. A mail-order company is considering mailing 5,000 circulars to advertise a product. A profit of $1.40 is expected from each order received in response to the circular, but a loss of $0.50 will be incurred for each circular that does not produce an order. The prior distribution of response proportions is as follows:

Proportion of responses	Probability
0.20	0.1
0.25	0.5
0.35	0.4

   a. Determine the optimal action without sampling.
   b. Compute the expected loss for decision rule (20, 2).
   c. If the cost of sampling is $1 per observation, determine if a sample of 10 or 20 observations provides the better decision rule.

d. If a sample of ten is taken and it contains two circulars that produced orders, compute the revised prior probabilities.

10–32. A salvage dealer has the opportunity to purchase a lot of 200 surplus parts. It is expected that a profit of $7.50 can be made from each part in working condition, but a loss of $3 will result from each defective part. From experience with similar lots, the prior probability distribution of the proportion of defective parts is estimated to be:

Proportion defective	Probability
0.2	0.3
0.5	0.5
0.8	0.2

a. Determine the optimal action without sampling.
b. Compute the expected loss for decision rule (10, 2).
c. If the sampling cost is $2 per observation, determine if a sample of five or ten provides the better decision rule.
d. If a sample of five is taken and it contains two defective parts, compute the revised prior probabilities.

10–33. Assume in Problem 10–27 that the universe standard deviation is 750.
a. Determine the optimal sample size if the cost of sampling is $20 per observation.
b. If a sample of seven items has a mean of 3,200, compute the parameters of the posterior distribution, optimal action, and EVPI.
c. Determine if additional sampling is warranted.

10–34. In Problem 10–28, assume that the universe standard deviation is 425.
a. Find the optimal sample size if the cost of sampling is $20 per observation.
b. If a sample of three items produces a mean of 1,350, compute the parameters of the posterior distribution, optimal action, and EVPI.
c. Would additional sampling be worthwhile? Explain.

Chapter 11
Analysis of Variance and the Design of Experiments

The concept of tests of significance is introduced in Chapter 8, but problems involving only one or two samples are discussed. In testing means, both the normal and t distributions are used; and in testing percentages, the binomial and normal distributions are found to be appropriate.

In Chapter 9 on nonparametric methods, stress was placed on the importance of the level of measurement in determining the appropriate statistical test to use. The very useful chi-square distribution was introduced in Chapter 9.

In this chapter further emphasis will be placed on the need for careful planning in the collection and analysis of data. In addition, the following three new areas of analysis will be explored:

1. Tests of significance for variances of one and two samples using the chi-square and F distributions.
2. Tests of significance of means of more than two samples using analysis of variance and the F distribution.
3. The relationship between the normal, t, chi-square, and F distributions.

THE PROBLEM OF DESIGN

An *experimental design* is a plan for the orderly collection and analysis of data. The chief objective of a good design is to obtain more information for less cost than normally can be obtained by traditional sampling methods.

Many investigators gather data under the assumption that statistical problems must be faced only when the task of analysis begins. The need for careful planning well in advance of a statistical study is as important as the detailed blueprints and specifications that must precede the construction of a house. In a statistical study bad planning or no planning at all can lead to poor results or exorbitant costs, or both.

SIGNIFICANCE TEST AND CONFIDENCE LIMITS OF A SAMPLE VARIANCE

The means of samples drawn randomly from a normal universe are distributed normally. However, the variances of random samples drawn from a normal universe have a distribution that is skewed positively. The distribution of a sample variance is a function of sample size and the universe variance. Because the distribution of variances is neither normal nor symmetrical, a separate table of areas would have to be derived for each combination of n and σ^2 in order to determine if a significant difference exists between a sample and a universe variance.

A significance test involving a sample variance and the corresponding universe variance is simplified because of a fortuitous relationship. This relationship is expressed by

$$\chi^2 = \frac{(n-1)\hat{\sigma}^2}{\sigma^2} \quad\dots\dots\dots\dots\dots\dots\dots\dots\dots\dots\dots\text{(11.1)}$$

where the ratio of the unbiased estimator times the number of degrees of freedom (based on the sample size) to the universe variance has a chi-square distribution for $d.f. = n - 1$. Since the unbiased estimator of the universe variance has the relationship

$$\hat{\sigma}^2 = \frac{n}{n-1}s^2$$

by Formula 6.3, Formula 11.1 may be written alternatively as

$$\chi^2 = \frac{(n-1)\dfrac{n}{n-1}s^2}{\sigma^2}$$

or

$$\chi^2 = \frac{ns^2}{\sigma^2} \quad\dots\dots\dots\dots\dots\dots\dots\dots\dots\dots\dots\text{(11.2)}$$

Significance Test for a Sample Variance

A sample variance may be tested for significance by use of the chi-square distribution.

■ *Example.* A tire manufacturing process is designed to produce tires with a standard deviation in weight of 0.30 ounces. A sample of 15 tires is taken and the sample standard deviation is 0.35 ounces. The problem is to test at $\alpha = 0.05$ to determine if the universe standard deviation is 0.30.

STEPS:
  1. H_0: $\sigma^2 = (0.30)^2 = 0.09$

2. H_a: $\sigma^2 > 0.09$
3. $\alpha = 0.05$ requires a $\chi^2_{0.05}$ $(d.f. = 15 - 1 = 14) = 23.685$
4. Criterion: Reject H_0 (accept H_a) if $\chi^2 > 23.685$.
5. Using the sample data and Formula 11.2:

$$\chi^2 = \frac{15(0.35)^2}{(0.30)^2} = 20.417.$$

Since $\chi^2(20.417) < \chi^2_\alpha(23.685)$, the null hypothesis cannot be rejected.

Confidence Interval of a Universe Variance

The confidence interval for estimating the universe variance can be computed by use of Formula 11.2 and the appropriate values read from Appendix K. The 96% confidence limits for σ^2 are found by reading the $\chi^2_{0.02}$ and $\chi^2_{0.98}$ values from Appendix K, substituting these values into Formula 11.2, and solving for the value of σ^2 at the upper and lower limits. The value for $\chi^2_{0.02}$ gives 2% of the distribution in the right-hand tail; $\chi^2_{0.98}$ gives 2% of the distribution in the left-hand tail; and the remaining 96% of the distribution lies between these two values.

■ *Example.* A random sample of 25 observations is drawn from a normal universe. The sample standard deviation is six. The values of σ^2 at the 96% confidence limits are computed by reading $\chi^2_{0.02} = 40.270$ and $\chi^2_{0.98} = 11.992$ from Appendix K and solving

$$\chi^2_{0.02} = \frac{ns^2}{\sigma^2}$$

$$40.270 = \frac{25(6)^2}{\sigma^2}$$

$$40.270\sigma^2 = 900$$

$$\sigma^2 = 22.3$$

$$\chi^2_{0.98} = \frac{ns^2}{\sigma^2}$$

$$11.992 = \frac{25(6)^2}{\sigma^2}$$

$$11.992\sigma^2 = 900$$

$$\sigma^2 = 75.1.$$

The lower and upper 96% confidence limits of σ^2 are, respectively, 22.3 and 75.1.

THE *F* DISTRIBUTION

Before it is possible to consider a significant difference in two sample variances, it is first necessary to discuss the *F* distribution. The *F* distribution is so called in honor of the statistical theorist R. A. Fisher and is one of the most useful distributions in statistical analysis. As will be demonstrated later in this chapter, the normal, t, and chi-square distributions are all special cases of the F distribution.

A test of significance concerning two sample variances is based on the ratio rather than on the difference between these variances. The *statistic F* is the ratio of unbiased estimates of the universe variance. The distribution of F describes the frequency of the ratio of two unbiased estimates of the universe variance that can be obtained by chance in drawing two samples randomly from a normal universe.

The Distribution of the Statistic *F*

Formula 11.2 shows that the ratio of ns^2 to σ^2 has a chi-square distribution for $n - 1$ degrees of freedom. Consider two samples drawn randomly from a normally distributed universe with sample sizes n_1 and n_2 and sample variances s_1^2 and s_2^2, respectively. For each sample, the ratio given by Formula 11.2 is computed

$$\chi_1^2 = \frac{n_1 s_1^2}{\sigma^2}, \qquad \text{for } d.f._1 = n_1 - 1$$

and

$$\chi_2^2 = \frac{n_2 s_2^2}{\sigma^2}, \qquad \text{for } d.f._2 = n_2 - 1.$$

The statistic F is the ratio

$$F = \frac{\dfrac{n_1 s_1^2}{(n_1 - 1)}}{\dfrac{n_2 s_2^2}{(n_2 - 1)}} \dotfill (11.3)$$

and is called the *variance ratio*. Since

$$\sigma^2 = \frac{n}{n - 1} s^2,$$

Formula 11.3 may be written

$$F = \frac{\hat{\sigma}_1^2}{\hat{\sigma}_2^2} \dotfill (11.4)$$

The range of values of F is from zero to positive infinity, since F is the ratio of two positive quantities. The distribution of F is a function of $d.f._1$ and $d.f._2$, and there is a different distribution for each pair of values of $d.f._1$ and $d.f._2$. The distribution of F is skewed positively for small values of $d.f._1$ and $d.f._2$ but approaches normality as the values of the degrees of freedom become large. The F distribution for selected values of $d.f._1$ and $d.f._2$ is shown in Figure 11.1.

Table of Critical Values of F

In making a significance test of the ratio of two unbiased estimates of the universe variance, it is necessary to determine if it is likely that the value of F obtained from sample data could be the result of chance. The expression for the density function of F is complex, and calculating critical values of F is very tedious. To facilitate making significance tests, critical values of F at the 0.05 and 0.01 levels of significance have been computed and are shown in Appendix L. These values correspond to the respective areas in the right tail of the F distribution for specified values of $d.f._1$ and $d.f._2$.

> ■ *Example.* The distribution of F for $d.f._1 = 9$ and $d.f._2 = 11$ is shown in Figure 11.1. The critical values of F at the 0.05 and 0.01 levels (areas in the right tail) are read from Appendix L at the intersection of the column for $d.f._1 = 9$ and the row for $d.f._2 = 11$. The 0.05 critical values in Appendix L are shown in Roman type and the 0.01 values are in bold-face type.

FIGURE 11.1

Distribution of F for $d.f._1 = 9$ and $d.f._2 = 11$, Showing the 0.05 and 0.01 Critical Values of F

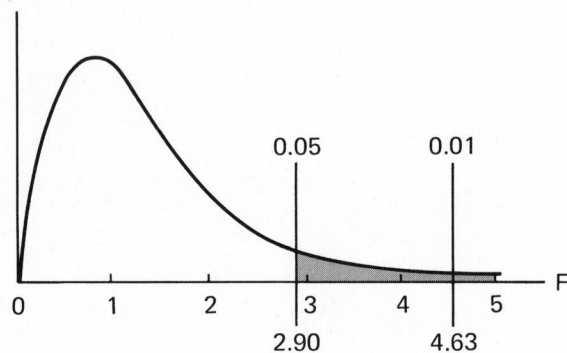

SIGNIFICANCE TESTS FOR TWO VARIANCES

There are situations in which it is of interest to compare the variances of two universes. If there are two universes with known variances σ_1^2 and σ_2^2, respectively, the variances can be compared directly to determine if they are equal. Most often the universe variances are not known and must be estimated from sample data. In this case it is assumed that the universes are normally distributed and that the two samples, one from each universe, are independent. A comparison is made by forming the ratio of the variance estimates (Formula 11.4), where the larger of the variance estimates is the numerator. A two-tail test of the null hypothesis $\sigma_1^2 = \sigma_2^2$ or the alternate hypothesis $\sigma^2 \neq \sigma^2$ can be made by use of the F distribution.

Typically, it is expected that one of the universe variances is greater than the other. In such a case a one-tail test of the alternate hypothesis is appropriate, and the numerator of the F ratio is $\hat{\sigma}_1^2$ if $\sigma_1^2 > \sigma_2^2$, and $\hat{\sigma}_2^2$ if $\sigma_2^2 > \sigma_1^2$.

■ **Example.** The purchasing agent of a company wishes to test whether the variances in the bursting strength (pounds per square inch) of two brands of plastic bags for packaging food products can be considered equal. A sample of each brand is taken and the results are as follows:

Sample 1	Sample 2
(Brand A)	(Brand B)
$n_1 = 21$	$n_2 = 16$
$s = 2.5$ psi	$s = 1.5$ psi

The problem is to test at $\alpha = 0.10$ to determine if the two universe variances are the same. (Note: Since this is a two-tail test, the table value is for $\alpha = 0.05$, and the larger of the two sample variances will be used as the numerator for F.)

STEPS:
1. $H_0: \sigma_1^2 = \sigma_2^2$
2. $H_a: \sigma_1^2 \neq \sigma_2^2$
3. $\alpha = 0.10$ requires $F_{0.05}$ ($d.f._1 = n_1 = 1 = 20$, $d.f._2 = n_2 - 1 = 15) = 2.33$.
4. Criterion: Reject H_0 (accept H_a) if $F > 2.33$.
5. Using the sample data and Formula 11.3:

$$F = \frac{\hat{\sigma}_1^2}{\hat{\sigma}_2^2} = \frac{\dfrac{n_1 s_1^2}{(n_1 - 1)}}{\dfrac{n_2 s_2^2}{(n_2 - 1)}} = \frac{\dfrac{(21)(2.5)^2}{(21 - 1)}}{\dfrac{(16)(1.5)^2}{(16 - 1)}} = \frac{6.562}{2.400} = 2.73.$$

Since $F(2.73) > F_\alpha(2.33)$, reject H_0 and accept H_a.

■ **Example.** If in the previous example the purchasing agent wished to test the hypothesis that the variance of Brand A is greater than that of Brand B, the alternate hypothesis $\sigma_1^2 > \sigma_2^2$ would be tested. Since this is a one-tail test, the comparison of the critical and computed values of F for $d.f._1 = 20$ and $d.f._2 = 15$ is $F(2.73) > F_\alpha(2.33)$, so the null hypothesis is rejected at the 0.05 level of significance.

A special problem arises when one wishes a one-tail test where the alternate hypothesis is $\sigma_1^2 < \sigma_2^2$ and the variance of the first sample is less than the variance of the second. Of course, if one wishes to use a two-tail alternate hypothesis, there must be a decision limit in the left-hand tail of the F distribution. The calculated value in this case would typically be less than one, and critical values in the left tail of the F distribution would be needed for the significance test. The F distribution has the fortunate property that the distribution of F for $d.f._1, d.f._2$ is the same as that of $1/F$ for $d.f._2, d.f._1$. This relationship is known as the *reciprocal property*. By use of this property it is possible to obtain critical values in the left tail of the F distribution from a table of the critical values in the right tail of F distributions. For example, the 0.95 critical value in the left tail of the distribution of F for $d.f._1, d.f._2$ is equal to the reciprocal of the 0.05 critical value for the distribution of F for $d.f._2, d.f._1$.

■ **Example.** Assume from the two preceding examples that $\hat{\sigma}_1^2 = 2.400$ and $\hat{\sigma}_2^2 = 6.562$, and the alternate hypothesis is $\sigma_1^2 < \sigma_2^2$. The calculated ratio of $F = 2.400/6.562 = 0.366$, where $d.f._1 = 15$ and $d.f._2 = 20$. The 0.05 critical value in the right tail of the distribution of $F_\alpha(20,15)$ is 2.33. The reciprocal of this critical value is 0.95 in the left tail of the distribution of $F_\alpha(15,20)$. The reciprocal is $1/2.33 = 0.429$. Since $F(0.366) < F_\alpha(0.429)$, the null hypothesis can be rejected at the 0.05 level of significance.

METHOD OF PRESENTATION

In order to provide an orderly approach to the complex problems involved in looking at a whole series of analysis of variance designs, the following plan of presentation has been adopted for this chapter:

1. The organization of the data to be analyzed will be shown and the notation to be used will be defined.
2. The model to be used and the hypotheses to be tested will be established.
3. An analysis of variance table will be shown to make it possible to see at a glance the type of variation being studied, the degrees of freedom involved, the mean square variation, and the F ratios to be computed.
4. Computational formulas, which may be used for solution either on a computer or with the help of an electronic calculator, will be shown.
5. An example will be shown to illustrate the application of the particular design to a practical problem.

ONE-WAY ANALYSIS OF VARIANCE, SAMPLE SIZE EQUAL

The technique of analysis of variance is one of the most powerful of statistical methods. This method provides the basis for determining whether several sample means differ significantly. A test of significance for two sample means, presented in Chapter 8, is the simplest case of analysis of variance. The technique of analysis of variance is sometimes referred to as ANOVA.

In this section a model for analyzing the dispersion of the means of several samples of the same size is discussed.

Organization of the Data

	Sample 1	Sample 2		Sample j		Sample c
	x_{11}	x_{12}	$\cdots$	x_{1j}	$\cdots$	x_{1c}
	x_{21}	x_{22}	$\cdots$	x_{2j}	$\cdots$	x_{2c}
	$\vdots$	$\vdots$		$\vdots$		$\vdots$
	x_{i1}	x_{i2}	$\cdots$	x_{ij}	$\cdots$	x_{ic}
	$\vdots$	$\vdots$		$\vdots$		$\vdots$
	x_{r1}	x_{r2}	$\cdots$	x_{rj}	$\cdots$	x_{rc}
Total	$T_{.1}$	$T_{.2}$		$T_{.j}$		$T_{.c}$

$$\sum_{j=1}^{c} T_j = T$$

Observation x_{ij} is the ith observation of the jth sample where the samples are arranged in columns. The samples are assumed to be random and independent and must be all the same size. The total $T_{.j}$ is the total of the n_j observations of the jth sample, and T is the grand total of all c samples.

The Model

A test of significance of several sample means is based on the following basic assumptions:

1. Each sample is drawn randomly and independently from a different class or treatment population.
2. The variances of the class or treatment populations are all equal.
3. The class or treatment populations are normally distributed.

A statistical model that is equivalent to these three basic assumptions and includes some additional assumptions for a one-way analysis of variance can be written

$$x_{ij} = \mu + \theta_j + \epsilon_{ij} \ (j = 1, 2, \cdots, c)$$

where
   x_{ij} is the ith observation of the jth class or treatment population, where x_{ij} consists of three components that are additive
   μ is the overall or grand mean of x_{ij} values for all populations in the analysis
   θ_j is the extent to which x_{ij} values reflect consistent deviation (class or treatment effect) from the overall mean
   ϵ_{ij} is the experimental chance error of the ith observation of the jth class or treatment population, where ϵ_{ij} is independently and normally distributed with a mean of zero.

The model assumes that the sum of the deviations (class or treatment effects) of the x_{ij} values from the overall mean is zero or $\Sigma \theta_j = 0$. It is also assumed that the deviations are consistent or fixed. In the example which follows, the x_{ij} are the observations of quality rating for the ith row and jth column of the data table. The term θ_j designates the consistent amount by which the observations of the jth class or treatment population (service station) deviate from the overall mean of quality ratings. The experimental chance error present in the ith observation of quality rating in the jth column is ϵ_{ij}.

An alternate model can be formulated in which the θ_j are assumed to be independently and normally distributed, and the sum of the θ_j is not assumed to be zero. The discussion of this model is beyond the scope of this presentation, but it is described in references listed at the end of this chapter.

The Hypotheses

The hypotheses may be expressed in either of two ways:
$H_0: \mu_1 = \mu_2 = \ldots = \mu_j = \ldots = \mu_c$
H_a: At least two of the universe means are unequal, or
$H_0: \theta_j = 0$ for all j samples
$H_a: \theta_j$ are not all $= 0$.

The null hypothesis asserts that there is no significant difference between column (class or treatment population) means. The alternate hypothesis states that there is a significant class or treatment effect in one or more of the populations.

An Estimate of Universe Variance Based on the Dispersion of Sample Means

The standard error of the mean, as described in Chapter 6, is the standard deviation of the means of samples of a given size, drawn from a universe of values. The estimated standard error of the mean is computed by Formula 6.1 to be

$$\hat{\sigma}_x = \frac{\hat{\sigma}}{\sqrt{n}}.$$

An expression of the estimated universe variance is written

$$\hat{\sigma}^2 = n\hat{\sigma}_{\bar{x}}^2 \dots\dots\dots\dots\dots\dots\dots\dots\dots\dots\dots\dots\dots\dots(11.5)$$

The standard error of the mean may be estimated by computing the standard deviation of the sample means and correcting for small sample bias. This unbiased estimator (free of bias due to smallness in sample size) expressed as a variance is written

$$\sigma_{\bar{x}}^2 = \frac{\sum\limits_{j}(\bar{x}_j - \bar{\bar{x}})^2}{c - 1} \dots\dots\dots\dots\dots\dots\dots\dots\dots\dots\dots(11.6)$$

where j designates columns, $\bar{x}_j$ denotes a sample mean, $\bar{\bar{x}}$ is the mean of the observed values in all samples taken together, c (for columns) is the number of samples, and $c - 1$ is the number of degrees of freedom.

An estimate of the universe variance based on the estimate of the variance of sample means is found by writing Formula 11.5 in terms of estimated values to give

$$\hat{\sigma}^2 = r\sigma_{\bar{x}}^2$$

where r is the number of rows in the table of observed data and $r = n$, the sample size. The estimated variance of sample means is substituted into the expression for the estimated universe variance by writing

$$\hat{\sigma}_c^2 = \frac{r\Sigma(\bar{x}_j - \bar{\bar{x}})^2}{c - 1} \quad\ldots\ldots\ldots\ldots\ldots\ldots\ldots\ldots\ldots\ldots(\mathbf{11.7})$$

The value obtained from Formula 11.7 is the estimated variance based on the variation between sample (column) means, as denoted by the subscript c. This variance is abbreviated *MSC* (Mean Square Column).

If bias is present in one or more sample means, it will tend to be reflected in the relative magnitude of $\hat{\sigma}_c^2$. Should the dispersion of sample means be greater than that expected as the result of random sampling error (chance), $\hat{\sigma}_c^2$ will be too large and will overstate the value of σ^2 significantly.

Whether $\hat{\sigma}_c^2$ is significantly greater than σ^2 can be tested by use of Formula 11.4, where $\hat{\sigma}_c^2$ is the numerator of the F ratio. The value of F can be obtained if a second estimator of σ^2 can be computed as the denominator of the F ratio. The denominator must be another estimate of the universe variance that is inherently free of any bias (θ_j) which may be present in sample values of the random variable x_{ij}. The method for computing a second estimate of the universe variance is described in the discussion that follows.

An Estimate of Universe Variance Based on the Dispersion of Sample Observations

The standard deviation of a sample tends to reflect the dispersion of the universe from which the sample is drawn. An estimate of the universe variance can be obtained from the dispersion of sample data about the sample mean. Sample data, expressed as deviations, are free from bias (θ_j), for any consistent bias that may be present in the data is eliminated by subtracting $x_{ij} - \bar{x}_j$. In other words, since the extent of this consistent bias is reflected in the value of the sample mean $\bar{x}_j$, and since $\bar{x}_j$ is subtracted from each observation of that sample, the bias is eliminated from the sample observations.

By subtracting the sample mean from the respective sample observations, a residual ϵ is obtained. The distribution of ϵ is assumed to be normal. This residual results from random sampling error and therefore is unbiased. The estimate of the universe variance computed from the sum of the squared error values is the required term for the denominator of the F ratio.

An unbiased (free from small sample bias) estimate of the universe variance is obtained by combining the squared deviations of all samples. An unbiased estimate of the universe variance based on a single sample may be written

$$\hat{\sigma}^2 = \frac{\Sigma(x_{ij} - \bar{x}_j)^2}{(r - 1)}$$

where r is the number of rows (sample size). An unbiased estimate of the universe variance is obtained by summing the deviations of all samples and averaging accordingly. The sum of the squared deviations of the observations in all samples is written

$$\left[\frac{\sum_i (x_{i1} - \bar{x}_1)^2}{r-1} + \frac{\sum_i (x_{i2} - \bar{x}_2)^2}{r-1} + \ldots + \frac{\sum_i (x_{ic} - \bar{x}_c)^2}{r-1} \right] = \frac{\sum_i \sum_j (x_{ij} - \bar{x}_j)^2}{r-1}.$$

The desired variance estimate is the mean sum of squared deviations, written

$$\hat{\sigma}_\epsilon^2 = \frac{\sum_i \sum_j (x_{ij} - \bar{x}_j)^2}{c(r-1)} \dots\dots\dots\dots\dots\dots\dots\dots\dots (11.8)$$

This estimate is called the variance estimate based on variation *within* the samples or the residual *error* values; hence, the subscript ϵ. This variance is abbreviated *MSE* (Mean Square Error).

Analysis of variance is applied to the one-way classification model by computing the F ratio of the two estimates of the universe variance. This ratio is expressed by

$$F = \frac{\hat{\sigma}_c^2}{\hat{\sigma}_\epsilon^2} \dots\dots\dots\dots\dots\dots\dots\dots\dots\dots\dots\dots\dots (11.9)$$

where $d.f._1 = c - 1$ and $d.f._2 = c(r-1)$. The value of $d.f._1 = c - 1$ results from the fact that only $c - 1$ of the column (sample) means $\bar{x}_j$ can be chosen arbitrarily without affecting the value of the mean of all items $\bar{\bar{x}}$. Similarly, $d.f._2 = c(r-1)$ since $r - 1$ sample values may be chosen without affecting a column (sample) mean, and there is a total of c samples.

Analysis of Variance Table

The analysis of variance table is the key to every analysis of variance problem. It always shows the source of variation, the sum of squares, degrees of freedom, mean square (variance), and the formula(s) for the F ratio. Table 11.1 is the appropriate table to use for one-way analysis when the samples are all the same size.

Computational Formulas

There are two ways to secure the sums of squares necessary to solve an analysis of variance problem. The first method involves the use of the sample means, and the second method uses only sample totals. Both techniques will be used here to demonstrate that they give the same answer, but only the second approach will be used for other problems in this chapter. There are computational advantages inherent in the second method.

$$SSC = r \sum_j (\bar{x}_j - \bar{\bar{x}})^2 \dots\dots\dots\dots\dots\dots\dots\dots\dots (11.10)$$

TABLE 11.1

Table of Analysis of Variance for a One-Way Classification (sample sizes equal)

Source of variation	Sum of squares	Degrees of freedom	Mean square	F
Between samples (column means)	SSC	$d.f._1 = c - 1$	$MSC = \dfrac{SSC}{c - 1}$	
				$F = \dfrac{MSC}{MSE}$
Within samples (error)	SSE	$d.f._2 = c(r - 1)$	$MSE = \dfrac{SSE}{c(r - 1)}$	
Total	SST	$cr - 1$		

where
  SSC is the sum of squares for columns
  r is the number of rows (size of each sample)
  $\bar{x}_j$ is the mean of the jth sample
  $\bar{x}$ is the mean of the sample (column) means.

$$SSE = \sum_i \sum_j (x_{ij} - \bar{x}_j)^2 \quad \ldots\ldots\ldots\ldots\ldots\ldots\ldots\ldots(11.11)$$

where
  SSE is the error sum of squares
  x_{ij} is the ith observation in the jth sample
  $\bar{x}_j$ is the mean of the jth sample.

■ **Example.** Three service stations in a large city are rated in terms of overall quality and effectiveness. More than 20 factors are considered in computing the rating score. A sample of four ratings is made for each station, and the results are shown in Table 11.2. The distributor of petroleum products to these service stations wishes to determine if the stations differ significantly in their average ratings or whether the variation in the sample means can be attributed to chance.

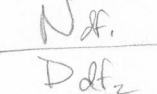

STEPS:

  1. H_0: $\theta_j = 0$ for all values of j
  2. H_a: $\theta_j \neq 0$ for all values of j
  3. $\alpha = 0.05$ gives a table value for $F = 4.26$ with $d.f._1 = c - 1 = 2$, and $d.f._2 = c(r - 1) = 3 \times 3 = 9$.
  4. Criterion: Reject H_0 (accept H_a) if $F > 4.26$, where $F = \dfrac{MSC}{MSE}$.

  5. The sample data are now used to compute F:

TABLE 11.2

Quality Ratings of Three Service Stations

	Stations			
	A	B	C	Total
	72	72	75	
	73	74	78	
	71	75	79	
	76	75	80	
Total	292	296	312	900
Mean	73	74	78	75

The mean of the three sample means is computed as

$$\bar{\bar{x}} = \frac{73 + 74 + 78}{3} = 75.$$

The sum of squares for columns is computed using Formula 11.5

$$SSC = r \sum_j (\bar{x}_j - \bar{\bar{x}})^2 = 4 \left[(73 - 75)^2 + (74 - 75)^2 + (78 - 75)^2 \right]$$
$$= 56.$$

The mean square for columns is computed as

$$MSC = \frac{SSC}{c - 1} = \frac{56}{2} = 28.$$

The sum of squares for the error can be computed using Formula 11.6

$$SSE = (72 - 73)^2 + (73 - 73)^2 + (71 - 73)^2 + (76 - 73)^2 = 14$$
$$(72 - 74)^2 + (74 - 74)^2 + (75 - 74)^2 + (75 - 74)^2 = 6$$
$$(75 - 78)^2 + (78 - 78)^2 + (79 - 78)^2 + (80 - 78)^2 = 14$$
$$SSE = 34.$$

$$MSE = \frac{SSE}{c(r - 1)} = \frac{34}{9} = 3.78$$

$$F = \frac{MSC}{MSE} = \frac{28}{3.78} = 7.41.$$

Since $F(7.41) > F_\alpha (4.26)$, reject H_0 and accept H_a. There is a significant difference in the average ratings of the three service stations.

In the example the observations of quality ratings are grouped so that each service station may be viewed as a class. The classes for grouping or classifying data are sometimes called *treatments*. This term reflects the early use of analysis of variance in agriculture. For instance, experiments were designed to test for significant effects of different treatments of plants where treatments might be various soil types, extent of fertilization, levels of irrigation, and similar factor levels.

The problem in this example is to test at an α level of 0.05 to determine if there is a significant difference in the average ratings of the three stations.

Alternate Computational Methods

The sums of squares necessary to solve one-way analysis of variance problems with equal sample sizes can also be computed using the following shortcut formulas:

Correction Factor.

$$C = \frac{T^2}{rc} \dots\dots\dots\dots\dots\dots\dots\dots\dots\dots\dots\dots\dots (11.12)$$

where
  C corrects for the fact that sample totals are used rather than sample means.
  T is the grand total of the values in all of the samples.

Between Columns (Samples) Sum of Squares.

$$SSC = \frac{\sum_j T_j^2}{r} - C \dots\dots\dots\dots\dots\dots\dots\dots\dots (11.13)$$

Total Sum of Squares.

$$SST = \sum_i \sum_j x_{ij}^2 - C \dots\dots\dots\dots\dots\dots\dots\dots\dots (11.14)$$

Error Sum of Squares.

$$SSE = SST - SSC \dots\dots\dots\dots\dots\dots\dots\dots (11.15)$$

■ *Example.* Formulas 11.12 through 11.15 are used to compute the sums of squares for the previous example using the data in Table 11.2.

$$C = \frac{900^2}{3 \times 4} = 67,500$$

$$SSC = \frac{292^2 + 296^2 + 312^2}{4} - 67,500 = 67,556 - 67,500 = 56$$

$$SST = 72^2 + 73^2 + \ldots + 80^2 - 67,500 = 67,590 - 67,500 = 90$$

$$SSE = 90 - 56 = 34.$$

The rest of the problem is the same as the previous example.

ONE-WAY ANALYSIS OF VARIANCE, SAMPLE SIZES UNEQUAL

Often it is desired to test the hypothesis that the means of c normal populations are equal when the sample size n_j is not the same for all samples. In this type of problem the organization of the data, the model, and the hypotheses to be tested are the same as for one-way analysis with equal sample sizes. There are some differences, however, as noted below.

Analysis of Variance Table

Table 11.3 is similar to Table 11.1, but it does provide for samples of different sizes.

TABLE 11.3

Table for Analysis of Variance for a One-Way Classification (sample sizes unequal)

Source of variation	Sum of squares	d.f.	Mean square	Variance ratio
Between samples (Column means)	SSC	$d.f._1 = c - 1$	$MSC = \dfrac{SSC}{c-1}$	$F = \dfrac{MSC}{MSE}$
Within samples (Error)	SSE	$d.f._2 = N - c$	$MSE = \dfrac{SSE}{N-c}$	
Total	SST	$N - 1$		

Computational Formulas

Earlier in this chapter shortcut formulas for computing variation were discussed under the heading, "Alternate Computational Methods." These formulas were shown to give the same results as the more conventional ones, but with simpler computations. In the remainder of this chapter short-cut computational formulas will be used throughout, since they are particularly well-adapted to computer solution.

Correction Factor.

$$C = \frac{T^2}{N} \dots\dots\dots\dots\dots\dots\dots\dots\dots\dots\dots\dots\dots\dots(11.16)$$

where

$N = n_1 + n_2 + \ldots + n_j + \ldots + n_c$ is the total number of observations in all the samples.

Between Columns (Samples) Sum of Squares.

$$SSC = \sum_{j=1}^{c} \frac{T_j^2}{n_j} - C \dots\dots\dots\dots\dots\dots\dots\dots\dots\dots(11.17)$$

The total sum of squares and the error sum of squares can be computed using Formulas 11.14 and 11.15.

Example. Table 11.4 shows quality ratings of five service stations, with the number of observations in each sample varying from a minimum of two to a maximum of five. There is a total of 18 observations.

TABLE 11.4

Quality Ratings of Five Service Stations

Ratings	Service station 1	2	3	4	5	Total
1	72	82	86	70	80	
2	80	80	83	73	80	
3	78	84	82	70	. . .	
4	70	. . .	80	75	. . .	
5	. . .	. . .	79	. . .	. . .	
Total	300	246	410	288	160	1,404
Mean	75	82	82	72	80	

The problem is to test at an α level of 0.05 to determine if there is a significant difference in the average ratings of the five service stations.

STEPS:
1. $H_0: \mu_1 = \mu_2 = \mu_3 = \mu_4 = \mu_5$
2. H_a: At least two of the μ's are not equal.
3. An $\alpha = 0.05$ requires an F value of 3.18, from the table in Appendix L, using the following degrees of freedom:

$$d.f._1 = c - 1 = 4$$
$$d.f._2 = N - c = 18 - 5 = 13.$$

4. Criterion: Reject H_0 (accept H_a) if $F > 3.18$; do not reject H_0 if $F \leq 3.18$, where

$$F = \frac{MSC}{MSE}.$$

5. The sample data are now used to compute F using Formulas 11.16, 11.17, 11.14, and 11.15.

$$C = \frac{T^2}{N} = \frac{(1,404)^2}{18} = \frac{1,971,216}{18}$$

$$C = 109,512.$$

$$SSC = \sum_{j=1}^{c} \frac{T_{.j}^2}{n_j} - C$$

$$SSC = \frac{300^2}{4} + \frac{246^2}{3} + \frac{410^2}{5} + \frac{288^2}{4} + \frac{160^2}{2} - 109,512$$

$$SSC = 22{,}500 + 20{,}172 + 33{,}620 + 20{,}736 + 12{,}800 - 109{,}512$$

$$SSC = 316.$$

$$SST = \sum_{i=1}^{r} \sum_{j=1}^{c} x_{ij}^2 - C$$

$$SST = (72)^2 + (80)^2 + (78)^2 + \ldots + (80)^2 - C$$

$$SST = 5{,}184 + 6{,}400 + 6{,}084 + 4{,}900 + 6{,}724 + 6{,}400 + 7{,}056 + 7{,}396 + 6{,}889 + 6{,}724 + 6{,}400 + 6{,}241 + 4{,}900 + 5{,}329 + 4{,}900 + 5{,}625 + 6{,}400 + 6{,}400 - C$$

$$SST = 109{,}952 - 109{,}512 = 440.$$

$$SSE = SST - SSC = 440 - 316 = 124.$$

$$MSC = \frac{SSC}{c-1} = \frac{316}{4} = 79.$$

$$MSE = \frac{SSE}{N-c} = \frac{124}{18-5} = 9.54.$$

$$F = \frac{MSC}{MSE} = \frac{79}{9.54} = 8.28.$$

Since $F(8.28) > F_\alpha(3.18)$, reject H_0 and accept H_a. There is a significant difference in the average ratings.

TWO-WAY ANALYSIS OF VARIANCE, ONE OBSERVATION PER CELL

Often it is desirable to test hypotheses concerning two variables. These two variables may be referred to as *row effects* and *column effects*.

In the previous example on the rating of service stations, the question was whether or not there were significant differences between stations. Since the samples were arranged by columns, the concern was with column effects. To carry this example a step further, assume there were five raters who rated each of the service stations. The investigator might be interested also in testing to see if there was a significant difference in the average scores of the raters. If the ratings of each rater were arranged in rows, the concern would be with row effects.

Organization of the Data

	c_1	c_2		c_j		c_c	Totals
r_1	x_{11}	x_{12}	$\cdots$	x_{1j}	$\cdots$	x_{1c}	$T_{1.}$
r_2	x_{21}	x_{22}	$\cdots$	x_{2j}	$\cdots$	x_{2c}	$T_{2.}$
	$\vdots$	$\vdots$		$\vdots$		$\vdots$	$\vdots$
r_i	x_{i1}	x_{i2}	$\cdots$	x_{ij}	$\cdots$	x_{ic}	$T_{i.}$
	$\vdots$	$\vdots$		$\vdots$		$\vdots$	$\vdots$
r_r	x_{r1}	x_{r2}	$\cdots$	x_{rj}	$\cdots$	x_{rc}	$T_{r.}$
Total	$T_{.1}$	$T_{.2}$		$T_{.j}$		$T_{.c}$	$T_{..}$

The observation x_{ij} is the value for the ith row and the jth column. The value $T_{i.}$ is the total of the ith row, and the value $T_{.j}$ is the total of the jth column. The value $T_{..}$ is the grand total of all observations.

The Model

The model may be expressed as

$$x_{ij} = \mu + \tau_i + \theta_j + \epsilon_{ij} \begin{cases} i = 1, 2, \ldots, r \\ j = 1, 2, \ldots, c \end{cases}$$

where
τ_i is the effect of the ith row
θ_j is the effect of the jth column, with the restrictions

$$\sum_{i=1}^{r} \tau_i = 0 \text{ and } \sum_{j=1}^{c} \theta_j = 0.$$

The Hypotheses

In two-way analysis of variance with one observation per cell, there are two sets of hypotheses to be tested.

For row means:
H_0: $\tau_i = 0$ for all i
H_a: τ_i are not all equal to zero.

The null hypothesis has the effect of saying that there is no significant difference in the row means.

For column means:
H_0: $\theta_j = 0$ for all j
H_a: θ_j are not all equal to zero.

Here the null hypothesis is saying that there is no significant difference in the column means. This is the same hypothesis that was tested in the one-way analysis of variance case.

Analysis of Variance Table

Table 11.5 is the analysis of variance table for two-way analysis with one observation per cell. Total variation is now defined as that which results from column differences, from row differences, and from residual random (error) differences. Two F ratios are computed. The first, F_C, is used to test for significant differences between column means; the second, F_R, is used to test for significant differences between row means.

Computational Formulas

Correction Factor.

$$C = \frac{T_{..}^2}{r \cdot c} \quad \text{...(11.18)}$$

TABLE 11.5

Table for Analysis of Variance for a Two-Way Classification (one observation per cell)

Source of variation	Sum of squares	d.f.	Mean square	Variance ratio
Between columns	SSC	$d.f._1 = c - 1$	$MSC = \dfrac{SSC}{c - 1}$	$F_C = \dfrac{MSC}{MSE}$
Between rows	SSR	$d.f._1 = r - 1$	$MSR = \dfrac{SSR}{r - 1}$	$F_R = \dfrac{MSR}{MSE}$
Error	SSE	$d.f._2 = (c - 1)(r - 1)$	$MSE = \dfrac{SSE}{(r - 1)(c - 1)}$	
Total	SST	$cr - 1$		

where
  r is the number of rows, and c is the number of columns.

Between Rows Sum of Squares.

$$SSR = \frac{\sum\limits_{i=1}^{r} T_{i.}^2}{c} - C \dots\dots\dots\dots\dots\dots\dots(11.19)$$

Between Columns Sum of Squares.

$$SSC = \frac{\sum\limits_{j=1}^{c} T_{.j}^2}{r} - C \dots\dots\dots\dots\dots\dots\dots(11.20)$$

Total Sum of Squares.

$$SST = \sum_{i=1}^{r} \sum_{j=1}^{c} x_{ij}^2 - C \dots\text{(Same as Formula 11.14)}$$

Error Sum of Squares.

$$SSE = SST - SSR - SSC \dots\dots\dots\dots(11.21)$$

■ *Example.* Table 11.6 shows the same data presented in Table 11.2 except that the row values have been identified as the ratings of four professional raters.

TABLE 11.6

**Quality Ratings of Three Service Stations by Four
Professional Raters**

Rater	Service Station			Total	Mean
	A	B	C		
I	72	72	75	219	73
II	73	74	78	225	75
III	71	75	79	225	75
IV	76	75	80	231	77
Total	292	296	312	900	300
Mean	73	74	78	225	75

The problem is to test at an α level of 0.05 to determine if there is a significant difference in the average ratings of the three service stations or in the average ratings given by the four professional raters. A significant difference in the row means would show that some raters tend to be more lenient or stricter than others in their ratings.

STEPS:

For row means
1. H_0: $\tau_i = 0$ for all i
2. H_a: τ_i are not all equal to zero
3. $\alpha = 0.05$ gives a table value for $F = 4.76$ with $d.f._1 = r - 1 = 3$ and $d.f._2 = (r-1)(c-1) = 6$
4. Criterion: Reject H_0 (accept H_a) if $F_R > 4.76$; do not reject H_0 if $F_R \leq 4.76$, when

$$F_R = \frac{MSR}{MSE}$$

For column means
H_0: $\theta_j = 0$ for all j
H_a: θ_j are not all equal to zero
$\alpha = 0.05$ gives a table value for $F = 5.14$ with $d.f._1 = c - 1 = 2$ and $d.f._2 = (r-1)(c-1) = 6$
Reject H_0 (accept H_a) if $F_C > 5.14$; do not reject H_0 if $F_C \leq 5.14$, when

$$F_C = \frac{MSC}{MSE}$$

5. The sample data are now used to compute F_R and F_C using Formulas 11.18 through 11.21:

$$C = \frac{T_{..}^2}{r \cdot c} = \frac{900^2}{(3)(4)} = 67,500$$

$$SSR = \frac{\sum_{i=1}^{r} T_{i.}^2}{c} - C$$

$$SSR = \frac{219^2 + 225^2 + 225^2 + 231^2}{3} - C$$

$$SSR = 67,524 - 67,500 = 24$$

$$SSC = \frac{\sum_{j=1}^{c} T_{.j}^2}{r} - C$$

$$SSC = \frac{292^2 + 296^2 + 312^2}{4} - C$$

$$SSC = 67{,}556 - 67{,}500 = 56$$

$$SST = \sum_{i=1}^{c} \sum_{j=1}^{r} x_{ij}^2 - C$$

$$SST = 72^2 + 73^2 + \cdots + 80^2 - C$$

$$SST = 67{,}590 - 67{,}500 = 90$$

$$SSE = 90 - 24 - 56 = 10.$$

$$MSC = \frac{SSC}{c-1} = \frac{56}{2} = 28$$

$$MSR = \frac{SSR}{r-1} = \frac{24}{3} = 8$$

$$MSE = \frac{SSE}{(r-1)(c-1)} = \frac{10}{6} = 1.67$$

$$F_R = \frac{MSR}{MSE} = \frac{8}{1.67} = 4.79$$

$$F_C = \frac{MSC}{MSE} = \frac{28}{1.67} = 16.77$$

Since $F_R(4.79) > F_\alpha(4.76)$, reject H_0 and decide that there is significant difference (bias) between raters.

Since $F_C(16.77) > F_\alpha(5.14)$, reject H_0 and accept H_a. There are significant differences between stations.

TWO-WAY ANALYSIS OF VARIANCE, n OBSERVATIONS PER CELL

In testing hypotheses concerning two variables, two possible models may be considered. First, in the previous model in which there was only one observation per cell, the column and row effects, θ_j and τ_i, were assumed to be independent and additive. That is to say, the brand of oil carried by the service station was independent of the rater who rated the station. It was assumed that the rater exercised no bias either for or against a particular brand but made a completely objective rating based on what was found at the station.

Second, in the model to be considered in this section, where the number of observations in each cell is two or more, it is possible that θ_j and τ_i are not completely independent and the variables may *interact* on one another. For example, in the rating of service stations by professional raters, each rater might rate each service station several times, making it possible to test for any interaction between raters and stations.

Organization of the Data

The observation x_{ijk} is the kth observation of the ith row and the jth column. The value $T_{i..}$ is the total of all observations in the ith row, and $T_{.j.}$ is the total of all the observations in the jth column. The value $T_{...}$ is the grand total of all the observations. The value of n is the number of observations per cell and must be the same for all cells.

	c_1	c_2		c_j		c_c	
r_1	x_{111} x_{112} $\vdots$ x_{11n}	x_{121} x_{122} $\vdots$ x_{12n}	$\cdots$ $\cdots$ $\cdots$	x_{1j1} x_{1j2} $\vdots$ x_{1jn}	$\cdots$ $\cdots$ $\cdots$	x_{1c1} x_{1c2} $\vdots$ x_{1cn}	$T_{1..}$
r_2	x_{211} x_{212} $\vdots$ x_{21n}	x_{221} x_{222} $\vdots$ x_{22n}	$\cdots$ $\cdots$ $\cdots$	x_{2j1} x_{2j2} $\vdots$ x_{2jn}	$\cdots$ $\cdots$ $\cdots$	x_{2c1} x_{2c2} $\vdots$ x_{2cn}	$T_{2..}$
	$\vdots$	$\vdots$		$\vdots$		$\vdots$	
r_i	x_{i11} x_{i12} $\vdots$ x_{i1n}	x_{i21} x_{i22} $\vdots$ x_{i2n}	$\cdots$ $\cdots$ $\cdots$	x_{ij1} x_{ij2} $\vdots$ x_{ijn}	$\cdots$ $\cdots$ $\cdots$	x_{ic1} x_{ic2} $\vdots$ x_{icn}	$T_{i..}$
	$\vdots$	$\vdots$		$\vdots$		$\vdots$	
r_r	x_{r11} x_{r12} $\vdots$ x_{r1n}	x_{r21} x_{r22} $\vdots$ x_{r2n}	$\cdots$ $\cdots$ $\cdots$	x_{rj1} x_{rj2} $\vdots$ x_{rjn}	$\cdots$ $\cdots$ $\cdots$	x_{rc1} x_{rc2} $\vdots$ x_{rcn}	$T_{r..}$
	$T_{.1.}$	$T_{.2.}$		$T_{.j.}$		$T_{.c.}$	$T_{...}$

The Model

The model may be expressed as

$$x_{ijk} = \mu + \tau_i + \theta_j + \gamma_{ij} + \epsilon_{ijk} \begin{cases} i = 1, 2, \ldots, r \\ j = 1, 2, \ldots, c \\ k = 1, 2, \ldots, n \end{cases}$$

where

τ_i is the effect of the ith row

θ_j is the effect of the jth column

γ_{ij} is the interaction of the ith row with the jth column, with the restrictions

$$\sum_{i=1}^{r} \tau_i = 0, \ \sum_{j=1}^{c} \theta_j = 0, \text{ and } \sum_{i=1}^{r} \sum_{j=1}^{c} \gamma_{ij} = 0.$$

The Hypotheses

When the two-way classification has more than one observation per cell, there are three sets of hypotheses to be tested.

For row means:
H_0: $\tau_i = 0$ for all i
H_a: τ_i are not all equal to zero.

For column means:
H_0: $\theta_j = 0$ for all j
H_a: θ_j are not all equal to zero.

For interaction between rows and columns:
H_0: $\gamma_{ij} = 0$ for all i and j
H_a: γ_{ij} are not all equal to zero.

Analysis of Variance Table

Table 11.7 is the analysis of variance table for two-way analysis with n observations per cell. The total variation is defined as the sum of that which results from row differences, from column differences, from interaction between rows and columns, and from residual random (error) differences. Three F ratios are used to test the three sets of hypotheses described above.

TABLE 11.7

Table for Analysis of Variance for a Two-Way Classification (n observations per cell)

Source of variation	Sum of squares	d.f.	Mean square	Variance ratio
Between columns	SSC	$d.f._1 = c - 1$	$MSC = \dfrac{SSC}{c - 1}$	$F_C = \dfrac{MSC}{MSE}$
Between rows	SSR	$d.f._1 = r - 1$	$MSR = \dfrac{SSR}{r - 1}$	$F_R = \dfrac{MSR}{MSE}$
Interaction	SSI	$d.f._1 = (c - 1)(r - 1)$	$MSI = \dfrac{SSI}{(c - 1)(r - 1)}$	$F_I = \dfrac{MSI}{MSE}$
Error	SSE	$d.f._2 = rc(n - 1)$	$MSE = \dfrac{SSE}{rc(n - 1)}$	
Total	SST	$rcn - 1$		

Computational Formulas

Correction Factor.

$$C = \frac{T_{...}^2}{r \cdot c \cdot n} \quad\dotfill(11.22)$$

where
  r is the number of rows
  c is the number of columns
  n is the number of observations per cell and is the same for all cells.

Between Rows Sum of Squares.

$$SSR = \frac{\sum_{i=1}^{r} T_{i..}^2}{c \cdot n} - C \quad\dotfill(11.23)$$

Between Columns Sum of Squares.

$$SSC = \frac{\sum_{j=1}^{c} T_{.j.}^2}{r \cdot n} - C \quad\dotfill(11.24)$$

Between Means Sum of Squares.

$$SSM = \frac{\sum_{i=1}^{r} \sum_{j=1}^{c} T_{ij}^2}{n} - C \quad\dotfill(11.25)$$

where T_{ij} is the total for the cell in the ith row and j^{th} column.

Interaction Sum of Squares.

$$SSI = SSM - SSR - SSC \quad\dotfill(11.26)$$

Total Sum of Squares.

$$SST = \sum_{i=1}^{r} \sum_{j=1}^{c} \sum_{k=1}^{n} x_{ijk}^2 - C \quad\dotfill(11.27)$$

Error Sum of Squares.

$$SSE = SST - SSM \quad\dotfill(11.28)$$

■ *Example.* In the ratings of the service stations, imagine that each of four raters rated each of three stations twice. The results of the ratings are shown in Table 11.8.

The problem is to test at an α level of 0.05 to determine if there is a significant difference between the average ratings of the three stations or between the average ratings of the four raters, and if there is a significant interaction between raters and stations. An interaction might be the bias of one rater (either favorable or unfavorable) for a particular oil company or a particular station because of some previous experience that will unknowingly influence the ratings.

TABLE 11.8

Quality Ratings of Three Service Stations by Four Raters with Each Rater Rating Each Station Twice

Raters	Stations			Total	Means
	c_1	c_2	c_3		
r_1	72	66	80		
	76	72	84	450	75
r_2	71	69	97		
	75	73	95	480	80
r_3	81	75	100		
	83	75	96	510	85
r_4	70	64	95		
	72	66	89	456	76
Total	600	560	736	1,896	
Mean	75	70	92		

STEPS:

	Row means	Column means	Interaction
1. H_0:	$\tau_i = 0$ for all i	$\theta_j = 0$ for all j	$\gamma_{ij} = 0$ for all i and j
2. H_a:	τ_i not all $= 0$	θ_j not all $= 0$	γ_{ij} not all $= 0$
3. $d.f._1$:	$r - 1 = 3$	$c - 1 = 2$	$(c-1)(r-1) = 6$
$d.f._2$:	$rc(n-1) = 12$	$= 12$	$= 12$
Table value for F:	$F_{\alpha=0.05} = 3.49$	$= 3.89$	$= 3.00$

4. Criterion:

Reject H_0 (Accept H_a)	If $F_R > 3.49$	If $F_C > 3.89$	If $F_I > 3.00$
Do not reject H_0	If $F_R \leq 3.49$	If $F_C \leq 3.89$	If $F_I \leq 3.00$

5. The sample data are now used to compute F_R, F_C, and F_I using Formulas 11.22 through 11.28.

$$C = \frac{T_{...}^2}{r \cdot c \cdot n} = \frac{1,896^2}{(4)(3)(2)} = \frac{3,594,816}{24} = 149,784.$$

$$SSR = \frac{\sum_{i=1}^{r} T_{i..}^2}{c \cdot n} - C$$

$$SSR = \frac{450^2 + 480^2 + 510^2 + 456^2}{(3)(2)} - C$$

$$SSR = 150{,}156 - 149{,}784 = 372.$$

$$SSC = \frac{\sum_{j=1}^{c} T_{.j.}^2}{r \cdot n} - C$$

$$SSC = \frac{600^2 + 560^2 + 736^2}{(4)(2)} - C = 151{,}912 - 149{,}784 = 2{,}128$$

$$SSM = \frac{\sum_{i=1}^{r} \sum_{j=1}^{c} T_{ij}^2}{n} - C.$$

Table 11.9 shows the totals for each cell (T_{ij}).

TABLE 11.9

Table of Cell Totals (T_{ij})

Raters	Service Stations		
	c_1	c_2	c_3
r_1	148	138	164
r_2	146	142	192
r_3	164	150	196
r_4	142	130	184

$$SSM = \frac{148^2 + 146^2 + \cdots + 184^2}{2} - C$$

$$SSM = 152{,}460 - 149{,}784 = 2{,}676.$$

$$SSI = SSM - SSR - SSC$$

$$SSI = 2{,}676 - 372 - 2{,}128 = 176.$$

$$SST = \sum_{i=1}^{r} \sum_{j=1}^{c} \sum_{k=1}^{n} x_{ijk}^2 - C$$

$$SST = 72^2 + 76^2 + \cdots + 89^2 - C$$

$$SST = 152{,}544 - 149{,}784 = 2{,}760.$$

$$SSE = SST - SSM$$

$$SSE = 2{,}760 - 2{,}676 = 84.$$

$$MSC = \frac{SSC}{c - 1} = \frac{2{,}128}{2} = 1{,}064.$$

$$MSR = \frac{SSR}{r-1} = \frac{372}{3} = 124.$$

$$MSI = \frac{SSI}{(c-1)(r-1)} = \frac{176}{6} = 29.33.$$

$$MSE = \frac{SSE}{rc(n-1)} = \frac{84}{12} = 7.0.$$

$$F_R = \frac{MSR}{MSE} = \frac{124}{7.0} = 17.71.$$

$$F_C = \frac{MSC}{MSE} = \frac{1,064}{7.0} = 152.00.$$

$$F_I = \frac{MSI}{MSE} = \frac{29.33}{7.0} = 4.19.$$

The null hypotheses would be rejected in all three cases. There are significant differences between stations and between raters, and there is significant interaction between raters and stations. It should be noted, however, that at an $\alpha = 0.01$ it would not be possible to show significant interaction.

LATIN SQUARES

When experimenters wish to study the effects of three variables on the basis of relatively few observations, they may turn to the use of a Latin-square design. The experiment is performed by arranging the levels of one factor which are denoted by the letters A, B, C, etc., into an array so that every letter appears once and only once in every row and column. One Latin square with four levels for one variable is shown below:

$$\begin{array}{cccc}
B & A & C & D \\
D & B & A & C \\
C & D & B & A \\
A & C & D & B
\end{array}$$

For example, the study group engaged in rating service stations might be concerned with another variable, the time of day when the rating was made. The group may feel that during very busy times of the day the service station operator is not able to give as good service as at other times and that this factor might influence the rating of the station. The letters A, B, C, and D might be used to refer to four different times with different levels of business activity. These different levels are commonly called *treatments*.

Organization of the Data

The size of the Latin square is determined by the number of treatments. The observations $x_{ij(k)}$ are r^2 in number in a Latin square of r rows and r columns. The subscript i refers to the row; the subscript j refers to the column; and the subscript k refers to the treatment. The number of rows and columns will always be the same as the number of treatments. The totals are denoted as

$T_{i.}$ is the total for the ith row
$T_{.j}$ is the total for the jth column
T_k is the total of the observations for the kth treatment
$T_{..}$ is the grand total of all the observations.

The Model

The model may be expressed as

$$x_{ij(k)} = \mu + \tau_i + \theta_j + \gamma_k + \epsilon_{ij(k)} \quad \begin{cases} i = 1, 2, \ldots, r \\ j = 1, 2, \ldots, r \\ k = 1, 2, \ldots, r \end{cases}$$

where
τ_i is the effect of the ith row
θ_j is the effect of the jth column
γ_k is the effect of the kth treatment, with the restrictions

$$\sum_{i=1}^{r} \tau_i = 0, \ \sum_{j=1}^{r} \theta_j = 0, \text{ and } \sum_{k=1}^{r} \gamma_k = 0.$$

The Hypotheses

There are three sets of hypotheses to be tested in a Latin square, regardless of the number of treatments.

For row means:
H_0: $\tau_i = 0$ for all i
H_a: τ_i are not all equal to zero.
For column means:
H_0: $\theta_j = 0$ for all j
H_a: θ_j are not all equal to zero.
For treatments:
H_0: $\gamma_k = 0$ for all k
H_a: γ_k are not all equal to zero.

Analysis of Variance Table

Table 11.10 is the analysis of variance table for a Latin square. The total variation is the sum of the row variation, the column variation, the treatment variation, and the error variation. Three F ratios are used to test the three sets of hypotheses described above.

Computational Formulas

Correction Factor.

$$C = \frac{T_{..}^2}{r^2} \dots\dots\dots\dots\dots\dots\dots\dots\dots\dots\dots(11.29)$$

where r is the number of rows.

Between Rows Sum of Squares.

$$SSR = \frac{\sum\limits_{i=1}^{r} T_{i.}^2}{r} - C \dots\dots\dots\dots\dots\dots\dots\dots\dots\dots\dots\dots\dots\dots(11.30)$$

Between Columns Sum of Squares.

$$SSC = \frac{\sum\limits_{j=1}^{r} T_j^2}{r} - C \dots\dots\dots\dots\dots\dots\dots\dots\dots\dots\dots\dots\dots\dots(11.31)$$

Between Treatments Sum of Squares.

$$SS(Tr) = \frac{\sum\limits_{k=1}^{r} T_k^2}{r} - C \dots\dots\dots\dots\dots\dots\dots\dots\dots\dots\dots\dots(11.32)$$

Total Sum of Squares.

$$SST = \sum\limits_{i=1}^{r} \sum\limits_{j=1}^{r} x_{ij(k)}^2 - C \dots\dots\dots\dots\dots\dots\dots\dots\dots\dots\dots(11.33)$$

Error Sum of Squares.

$$SSE = SST - SSR - SSC - SS(Tr) \dots\dots\dots\dots(11.34)$$

TABLE 11.10

Table for Analysis of Variance for a Latin Square

Source of variation	Sum of squares	d.f.	Mean square	Variance ratio
Rows	SSR	$d.f._1 = r - 1$	$MSR = \dfrac{SSR}{r-1}$	$F_R = \dfrac{MSR}{MSE}$
Columns	SSC	$d.f._1 = r - 1$	$MSC = \dfrac{SSC}{r-1}$	$F_C = \dfrac{MSC}{MSE}$
Treatments	$SS(Tr)$	$d.f._1 = r - 1$	$MS(Tr) = \dfrac{SS(Tr)}{r-1}$	$F_{Tr} = \dfrac{MS(Tr)}{MSE}$
Error	SSE	$d.f._2 = (r-1)(r-2)$	$MSE = \dfrac{SSE}{(r-1)(r-2)}$	
Total	SST	$r^2 - 1$		

■ Example. Suppose that four raters rate the same four service stations, following carefully the time pattern shown below as treatments:

Treatment	Time of rating	Latin square
A	7:45 a.m.	B A C D
B	12:00 noon	D B A C
C	5:15 p.m.	C D B A
D	9:00 p.m.	A C D B

The results of the ratings are shown in Table 11.11.

TABLE 11.11

Quality Ratings of Service Stations with Four Raters Rating Each of Four Stations at Four Different Times (A four-by-four Latin square)

Raters	Stations				Totals
	c_1	c_2	c_3	c_4	
r_1	85	79	76	78	318
r_2	73	81	84	75	313
r_3	75	78	92	83	328
r_4	82	70	79	90	321
Total	315	308	331	326	1,280

The problem is to test at an α of 0.05 to determine if there is a significant difference in raters, stations, and treatments (time of day the rating is made).

STEPS:

	Row means	*Column means*	*Treatments*
1. H_0:	$\tau_i = 0$ for all i	$\theta_j = 0$ for all j	$\gamma_k = 0$ for all k
2. H_a:	τ_i not all $= 0$	θ_j not all $= 0$	γ_k not all $= 0$
3. $d.f._1$:	$r - 1 = 3$	$r - 1 = 3$	$r - 1 = 3$
$d.f._2$:	$(r-1)(r-2) = 6$	$(r-1)(r-2) = 6$	$(r-1)(r-2) = 6$
Table value for F	$F_{\alpha=0.05} = 4.76$	$F_{\alpha=0.05} = 4.76$	$F_{\alpha=0.05} = 4.76$
4. Criterion: Reject H_0 (Accept H_a)	If $F_R > 4.76$	If $F_C > 4.76$	If $F_{Tr} > 4.76$
Do not reject H_0	If $F_R \leq 4.76$	If $F_C \leq 4.76$	If $F_{Tr} \leq 4.76$

5. The sample data are now used to compute F_R, F_C, and F_{Tr} using Formulas 11.29 through 11.34.

Table 11.12 shows the treatment totals, T_k.

Ch. 11 Analysis of Variance and the Design of Experiments

TABLE 11.12

Table of Treatment Totals T_k

Treatment	Service station ratings				Totals
A: 7:45 a.m.	79	84	83	82	328
B: 12:00 noon	92	90	85	81	348
C: 5:15 p.m.	76	70	75	75	296
D: 9:00 p.m.	79	78	73	78	308
					1,280

Source: Table 11.11.

$$C = \frac{T_{..}^2}{r^2} = \frac{1{,}280^2}{4^2} = \frac{1{,}638{,}400}{16} = 102{,}400.$$

$$SSR = \frac{\sum\limits_{i=1}^{r} T_{i.}^2}{r} - C$$

$$SSR = \frac{318^2 + \cdots + 321^2}{4} - C$$

$$SSR = 102{,}430 - 102{,}400 = 30.$$

$$SSC = \frac{\sum\limits_{j=1}^{r} T_{.j}^2}{r} - C$$

$$SSC = \frac{315^2 + \cdots + 326^2}{4} - C$$

$$SSC = 102{,}482 - 102{,}400 = 82.$$

$$SS(Tr) = \frac{\sum\limits_{k=1}^{r} T_{k}^2}{r} - C$$

$$SS(Tr) = \frac{328^2 + \cdots + 308^2}{4} - C$$

$$SS(Tr) = 102{,}792 - 102{,}400 = 392.$$

$$SST = \sum\limits_{i=1}^{r}\sum\limits_{j=1}^{r} x_{ij(k)}^2 - C$$

$$SST = 85^2 + 73^2 + \cdots + 90^2 - C$$

$$SST = 102{,}924 - 102{,}400 = 524.$$

$$SSE = SST - SSR - SSC - SS(Tr)$$

$$SSE = 524 - 30 - 82 - 392 = 20.$$

$$MSR = \frac{SSR}{r-1} = \frac{30}{3} = 10.$$

$$MSC = \frac{SSC}{r-1} = \frac{82}{3} = 27.33.$$

$$MS(Tr) = \frac{SS(Tr)}{r-1} = \frac{392}{3} = 130.67.$$

$$MSE = \frac{SSE}{(r-1)(r-2)} = \frac{20}{6} = 3.33.$$

$$F_R = \frac{MSR}{MSE} = \frac{10}{3.33} = 3.00.$$

$$F_C = \frac{MSC}{MSE} = \frac{27.33}{3.33} = 8.21.$$

$$F_{Tr} = \frac{MS(Tr)}{MSE} = \frac{130.67}{3.33} = 39.24.$$

The null hypothesis on rater (row) differences would be accepted. There is no rater bias. The other two null hypotheses would be rejected; there are significant differences in stations and in treatments.

THE RELATIONSHIP OF THE NORMAL, t, CHI-SQUARE, AND F DISTRIBUTIONS

Because the normal, t, chi-square, and F distributions are treated separately in different chapters of this text, the beginning student of statistics tends to think of them as completely unrelated topics. The fact is that F is an inclusive distribution, and that the other three distributions are special cases of F, discovered by different mathematicians at different times in the history of statistics. An understanding of this relationship can be very helpful in understanding many of the topics already discussed and some more advanced topics yet to come.

It can be demonstrated that over the range of probability values used most commonly for making significance tests, the F distribution is equivalent to the normal, t, and chi-square distributions. A comparison of the assumptions implicit in the use of each of the distributions is summarized in Table 11.13. Note that the F distribution is appropriate for every combination of assumptions. The relationship of the values of F with the corresponding characteristics of each of the other three distributions is summarized in Table 11.14.

A Comparison of Values of z and F

The tail values of normal deviates can be obtained from the F table by taking the square root of the F values for $d.f._1 = 1$ and $d.f._2 = \infty$.

■ *Example.* The F values for $d.f._1 = 1$ and $d.f._2 = \infty$ read from Appendix L and the corresponding normal curve deviates read from Appendix I are as follows:

Probability	Normal deviate z	F Value* $F = z^2$
0.100	1.65	$2.71 = (1.65)^2$
0.050	1.96	$3.84 = (1.96)^2$

* Some precision is lost in comparing F and z^2 due to rounding error.

The equivalence of z^2 and F holds for the right tails of the respective distributions, but not for the entire distributions. For example, the value of z for a probability of 0.500 is zero, but the F value for $d.f._1 = 1$ and $d.f._2 = \infty$ is 0.455.

TABLE 11.13

Assumptions in the Use of Selected Distributions

Distribution	Basis of inference		Source of the value of the variance used in the test
	Number of observations	Number of parameters or estimates	
Normal	Infinite	Two	Known
t	Finite	Two	Estimated
Chi-square	Infinite	Two or more	Known
F	Finite or infinite	Two or more	Known or estimated

TABLE 11.14

The Relationship of the F Distribution with Tail Values of the Normal, t, and Chi-Square Distributions for a Probability of 0.10 or less

Distribution	Equivalent F value	Corresponding degrees of freedom
Normal	$F = z^2$	$d.f._1 = 1$, $d.f._2 = \infty$
t	$F = t^2$	$d.f._1 = 1$, $d.f._2 = $ Any finite integer greater than zero
Chi-square	$F = \dfrac{\chi^2}{d.f._1}$	$d.f._1 = $ Any finite integer greater than zero $d.f._2 = \infty$

The Relationship of the *t* and *F* Distributions

Values of the *t* distribution for relatively small probabilities can be obtained from the *F* table by taking the square root of the value of F for $d.f._1 = 1$ and $d.f._2$ equal to the degrees of freedom used in selecting a value of *t*.

■ *Example.* The values of *t* for selected degrees of freedom and probabilities read from Appendix J and the corresponding *F* values for $d.f._1 = 1$ in the *F* table for selected values of $d.f._2$, which correspond to the degrees of freedom in the *t* table.

Probability	Value of t d.f. = 5	Value of F $F = t^2$ $d.f._1 = 1, d.f._2 = 5$
0.050	2.57	$6.61 = (2.57)^2$
0.010	4.03	$16.3 = (4.03)^2$
	d.f. = 15	$d.f._1 = 1, d.f._2 = 15$
0.050	2.13	$4.54 = (2.13)^2$
0.010	2.95	$8.68 = (2.95)^2$
	d.f. = ∞	$d.f._1 = 1, d.f._2 = ∞$
0.050	1.96	$3.84 = (1.96)^2$
0.010	2.58	$6.64 = (2.58)^2$

Note that for $d.f._1 = 1$ and $d.f._2 = ∞$, the values of *t* and *z* are equal and $F = t^2 = z^2$. The values of t^2 are found in the column denoted $d.f._1 = 1$ in the *F* table for selected values of $d.f._2$, which correspond to the degrees of freedom in the *t* table.

The Relationship of Values of Chi-Square and *F*

The tail values of χ^2 for selected probabilities can be obtained from the *F* table for selected values of $d.f._1$ and for $d.f._2 = ∞$. The relationship between χ^2 and *F* is obtained from the relationship

$$F = \frac{\chi^2}{d.f.} = \frac{\hat{\sigma}^2}{\sigma^2},$$

where *d.f.* corresponds to the degrees of freedom in applying the chi-square distribution and $d.f._1$ of the *F* distribution.

■ *Example.* The equivalence of the values of *F* (Appendix L) and the values of chi-square (Appendix K) for selected degrees of freedom and selected tail probabilities is shown as follows:

Probability	Value of chi-square	Value of F $F = \dfrac{\chi^2}{d.f.}$
	$d.f. = 1$	$d.f._1 = 1,\ d.f._2 = \infty$
0.050	3.84	$3.84 = \dfrac{3.84}{1}$
0.010	6.63	$6.64 = \dfrac{6.64}{1}$
	$d.f. = 5$	$d.f._1 = 5,\ d.f._2 = \infty$
0.050	11.07	$2.21 = \dfrac{11.07}{5}$
0.010	15.09	$3.02 = \dfrac{15.09}{5}$
	$d.f. = 15$	$d.f._1 = 15,\ d.f._2 = \infty$
0.050	25.00	$1.67 = \dfrac{25.00}{15}$
0.010	30.58	$2.04 = \dfrac{30.58}{15}$

Note that for $d.f._1 = 1$ and $d.f._2 = \infty$, the value of F corresponds to

$$F = z^2 = t^2 = \chi^2.$$

This relationship between the F distribution and values of t^2, z^2, and χ^2 is shown in Table 11.15. This table demonstrates that the F distribution may be viewed as the general case, while the normal, t, and chi-square distributions may be viewed as special cases of F.

A MEASURE OF LEAST SIGNIFICANT DIFFERENCE

When the null hypothesis is rejected in a test of hypothesis that employs analysis of variance, the researcher can conclude that there are significant differences between at least some of the sample means. The test does not reveal, however, where the differences lie. When the sample sizes are the same, the significant differences can be located with the help of a measure called the *least significant difference*.

The reader will recall that for only two samples, the test for differences in the means was computed as:

$$t = \frac{\bar{x}_1 - \bar{x}_2}{\hat{\sigma}_{\bar{x}_1 - \bar{x}_2}}$$

When the difference between $\bar{x}_1$ and $\bar{x}_2$ exceeded some given value for t, the null hypothesis ($H_0\!: \mu_1 = \mu_2$) was rejected, and it was decided that the

TABLE 11.15

An Illustration of the Relationship Between Values of z, t, z^2 and F

$d.f._{.2}$	P	$d.f._{.1} = 1$	2	3	$\cdots$	∞
1	0.050	161	200	216	$\cdots$	254
	0.010	4,050	5,000	5,400		3,370
2	0.050	18.5	19.0	19.2	$\cdots$	19.5
	0.010	98.5	99.0	99.2		99.5
3	0.050	10.1	9.55	9.28	$\cdots$	8.53
	0.010	34.1	30.8	29.5		26.1
$\vdots$	$\vdots$	$\vdots$	$\vdots$	$\vdots$		$\vdots$
$\dfrac{\chi^2}{d.f._1} \rightarrow \infty$	0.050	3.84	3.00	2.60	$\cdots$	1.00
	0.010	6.63	4.61	3.78		1.00

z^2 $\uparrow$ t^2

means were significantly different. This relationship can be stated as:

$$LSD = t\hat{\sigma}_{\bar{x}_1 - \bar{x}_2}$$

where LSD is least significant difference, and the value of t is determined by the level of significance (α) and the degrees of freedom. Further, if $n_1 = n_2 = n$, and $\sigma_1^2 = \sigma_2^2$ is assumed,

$$\hat{\sigma}_{\bar{x}_1 - \bar{x}_2} = \sqrt{\frac{\hat{\sigma}_1^2}{n_1} + \frac{\hat{\sigma}_2^2}{n_2}} = \sqrt{\frac{2}{n}\hat{\sigma}^2}$$

In analysis of variance $\hat{\sigma}^2$ was represented by mean square error, MSE. This gives:

$$LSD = t\sqrt{\frac{2}{n}MSE} \quad \text{or} \quad \sqrt{\frac{2}{n}MSE\,t^2}.$$

In the previous section relating the normal, t, χ^2, and F distributions, it was shown that:

$$t^2\,(d.f._2) = F\,(d.f._1 = 1, d.f._2)$$

If $d.f._2$ represents the degrees of freedom for MSE, then

$$LSD = \sqrt{\frac{2}{n}} \; MSE \; F(d.f._1 = 1, \; d.f._2 \; \text{for } MSE, \; \alpha) \; \text{..........}(\textbf{11.35})$$

■ *Example.* In the example on page 333, the three sample means were 73, 74, and 78. The null hypothesis was rejected at $\alpha = 0.05$, MSE was 3.78, $d.f._2$ was $c(r-1) = 9$, and all samples contained 4 observations.

$$LSD = \sqrt{\frac{2}{4}} \; (3.78) \; F \; (1, \; 9, \; 0.05)$$

$$= \sqrt{(0.5)(3.78)(5.12)} = \sqrt{9.6768} = 3.11$$

Any difference between two sample means greater than 3.11 is significant.

Sample means	Difference	
73 and 74	1	not significant
73 and 78	5	is significant
74 and 78	4	is significant

Stations A and B are not significantly different, but station C is different from the other two.

■ *Example.* In the example on page 345, the row means were 75, 80, 85, and 76. The null hypothesis was rejected at $\alpha = 0.05$, MSE was 7.0, $d.f._2$ was $rc(n-1) = 12$, and all samples contained 6 observations.

$$LSD = \sqrt{\frac{2}{n}} \; (7.0) \; F \; (1, \; 12, \; 0.05)$$

$$= \sqrt{\frac{2}{6} \; (7.0) \; (4.75)} = \sqrt{11.08} = 3.33.$$

Row pairs	Sample means	Difference	
1–2	75 and 76	1	not significant
1–3	75 and 80	5	is significant
1–4	75 and 85	10	is significant
2–3	76 and 80	4	is significant
2–4	76 and 85	9	is significant
3–4	80 and 85	5	is significant

The difference between raters 1 and 4 is not significant, but all other differences are significant at $\alpha = 0.05$.

STUDY QUESTIONS

11–1. Explain briefly the meaning of each of the following terms:
   a. analysis of variance   b. experimental design

c. the statistic F
d. reciprocal property of F
e. ANOVA
f. treatments
g. correction factor

h. row effects
i. column effects
j. interaction
k. Latin square

11-2. Distinguish between the types of problems for which the normal, t, and chi-square distributions are appropriate.

11-3. Why is a good experimental design important to the success of a research project?

11-4. For whom was the F distribution named?

11-5. Of what value is a significance test for a sample variance?

11-6. Discuss the shape of the F distribution.

11-7. What assumptions are implicit in the analysis of variance for a one-way classification problem?

11-8. In a one-way analysis of variance problem, is it always necessary to have samples all the same size?

11-9. What are the sources of variation in one-way analysis of variance?

11-10. What are the sources of variation in a two-way analysis of variance problem:
a. When there is only one observation per cell?
b. When there are n observations per cell?

11-11. Why are there more null hypotheses to be tested in a two-way analysis of variance when there is more than one observation per cell?

11-12. Explain the meaning of the following notation for totals:
a. $T_{i.}$ c. $T_{.j}$ e. $T_{..}$ g. $T_{...}$
b. $T_{i..}$ d. $T_{.j.}$ f. T_k

11-13. If you wish to use a Latin-square design to study the effect on sales of the amount of shelf space used to display a food product in a supermarket, how could this be done? Explain how you would set up such an experiment using five different sizes of shelf space.

11-14. Summarize briefly the relationship between the normal, t, chi-square, and F distributions.

PROBLEMS

11-1. An automatic stamping machine is designed to stamp parts with a standard deviation in a critical dimension of 0.005 centimeters provided the machine is adjusted properly. A random sample of 25 parts has a standard deviation of 0.008 centimeters. Test at $\alpha = 0.05$ to determine if the machine is adjusted properly.

$H_0: \mu_1 = \mu_2$

11-2. A machine is designed to fill No. 2 cans with vegetables so that the weight of the contents of a can has a variance of no more than 0.0625 ounces. The weight of filled cans is checked periodically to determine if the machine is adjusted properly. If a sample of 28 cans has a variance in weight of 0.080, is it likely that the machine is in need of adjustment? Use $\alpha = 0.05$.

11-3. Compute the 98% confidence limits of the universe variance based on the sample data in Problem 11-1.

11-4. Compute the 96% confidence limits of the universe variance based on the sample data in Problem 11-2.

11-5. Two machines are used to fill sacks of fertilizer. A random sample of 21 sacks filled by Machine A has a standard deviation of 4.7 cubic centimeters. A random sample of 15 sacks filled by Machine B has a standard deviation of 3.8 cubic centimeters. Can the dispersion in weight of sacks filled by the two machines be considered equal at $\alpha = 0.05$?

11-6. A claim is made that a new type of process manufactures products that are of more consistent quality than those produced with a standard process. A sample of 25 items from the new process has a variance of 200, and a sample of 31 items from a standard process has a variance of 280. Test the claim that the new process is more consistent at $\alpha = 0.05$.

11-7. A trucking firm is considering two brands of tires, X and Y, for use on a fleet of trucks. The two brands of tires are essentially alike in average number of miles of service life. The manufacturer of Brand Y asserts that his tires are more consistent in terms of miles of service than Brand X. Samples are taken of each type of tire, and the results are as follows:

Brand X	Brand Y
$n_1 = 25$	$n_2 = 21$
$s_1 = 620$	$s_2 = 354$

Is the assertion supported by the sample results? Use $\alpha = 0.01$.

11-8. A manufacturer develops three different work designs to try to increase the number of electronic components that can be produced in an hour. A sample of five measurements is taken on each design with the following results:

$X_{ij} = \mu_G + \epsilon_{ij}$

Design I	Design II	Design III
17	18	19
16	20	19
18	21	22
15	19	23
20	22	21

$X_i \approx N(\mu, \sigma)$

$X_i = \mu + \epsilon_i$

$\epsilon_i \sim N(0, \sigma)$

360

$H_0: \mu_1 = \mu_2 = \mu_3$

μ_G

Inference   **Part 4**

$X_{i2} = \mu_G + \epsilon_{ij} + \theta_2$

Determine if the sample means differ significantly at $\alpha = 0.05$.

11-9. The weekly earnings of four salesclerks for a sample of four weeks are as follows:

Edmonds	Schultz	Herbert	Gonzales
233	414	350	399
367	409	372	406
275	388	396	319
350	375	288	335

Test at $\alpha = 0.01$ to determine if the average earnings of the salesclerks differ significantly.

11-10. A manufacturer has four identical machines that are used in a production process. Each machine is operated by a different operator. A sample of the production (expressed as deviations in thousandths of an inch from a given dimension) is taken from each machine. The results are as follows:

	MACHINES		
A	B	C	D
10	6	10	10
8	7	9	11
5	7	12	11
11	8	9	11

Test the hypothesis that the average dimension of parts produced by each of the four machines is identical. Use $\alpha = 0.05$.

11-11. Three spray machines are used to paint automobile fenders. The data below represent random samples of fenders for which the amount of paint used was measured in ounces. Test at $\alpha = 0.05$ to determine if there is a significant difference in the average amount of paint required by each spray machine to paint one fender.

Machine I	Machine II	Machine III
4.92	5.01	4.98
4.77	5.03	4.88
4.97	5.02	
	4.99	

11-12. The following table shows the average weekly salary paid typists in a sample of cities of various sizes. Test at $\alpha = 0.01$ to determine if there is a significant difference in typists' salaries based on city size.

Under 25,000	25,000 and under 250,000	250,000 and under 500,000	500,000 and over
104	117	98	123
110	119	101	127
109	123	97	
115		85	
		92	

11–13. The following table shows the times required by four operators to mill a part using each of three machines twice. Test at an $\alpha = 0.05$ to see if there are significant differences in machines, in operators, and in interactions between operators and machines.

	Machine		
Operator	1	2	3
Gill	4.2	5.1	3.8
	5.6	6.2	4.6
Kennamer	6.0	5.3	4.7
	7.1	4.3	5.2
Benney	4.5	3.2	4.4
	4.3	4.2	5.0
Rogers	8.2	7.7	7.2
	8.0	7.5	7.0

11–14. The table below shows the life of a mold, in units produced, based on the type of metal poured and the level of heat. There are two observations per cell.

	Metal		
Heat	A	B	C
Medium	22	18	14
	23	19	15
High	17	19	19
	19	21	19
Very high	13	15	20
	14	17	21

Test at an $\alpha = 0.01$ to determine if there are significant differences in metals, in heat, and in interaction between amount of heat and type of metal.

11–15. The table below shows the results of an experiment in which four different production methods, A, B, C, and D, are used in a manufacturing operation. The time required to perform the operation is the variable being studied. Use the Latin-square design below to test at $\alpha = 0.05$ the hypothesis that there is no significant difference in the times the methods require.

Machine	Operator			
	I	II	III	IV
1	A = 20	B = 15	C = 30	D = 29
2	D = 30	A = 21	B = 18	C = 31
3	C = 28	D = 31	A = 20	B = 16
4	B = 27	C = 32	D = 29	A = 20

11-16. The table below gives all the information needed for a simple Latin-square design in which $r = 3$. Test at $\alpha = 0.05$ for significant differences in rows, in columns, and in treatments (designated as A, B, and C).

Row	Column		
	I	II	III
1	A = 17	B = 24	C = 29
2	C = 30	A = 16	B = 25
3	B = 25	C = 31	A = 18

SELECTED READINGS

Campbell, Donald T., and Julian C. Stanley. *Experimental and Quasi-Experimental Design for Research.* Chicago: Rand McNally & Company, 1966.

> This booklet provides excellent background reading for anyone working in the area of experimental design. Examples are taken mostly from the social sciences, but the methodological recommendations apply to any subject area.

Freund, John E., Paul E. Livermore, and Irwin Miller. *Manual of Experimental Statistics.* Englewood Cliffs, New Jersey: Prentice-Hall, Inc., 1960.

> An excellent manual on the most frequently used statistical techniques, including complete examples. It is not complete enough to be used as a text.

Hicks, Charles R. *Fundamental Concepts in the Design of Experiments.* 2d ed. New York: Holt, Rinehart, and Winston, Inc., 1973.

> A text presenting the fundamental concepts in the design of experiments. It uses simple numerical problems, many from actual research work.

Natrella, Mary Gibbons. *Experimental Statistics,* National Bureau of Standards Handbook 91. Washington: U.S. Government Printing Office, 1966.

A very complete reference book going from basic statistical concepts to many specialized types of experimental designs. This handbook is also keyed to match the statistical analysis that can be accomplished using the computer program, OMNITAB, available on many large computer systems.

Winer, B. J., *Statistical Principles in Experimental Design,* 2d ed. New York: McGraw-Hill Book Company, Inc., 1971.

A comprehensive reference source on the statistical principles underlying experimental design for research workers in the area of behavioral sciences.

Part 5

Regression and Correlation

Chapter 12

Regression and Correlation— Linear Bivariate Analysis

The process of observing two variables and deciding if they vary together is a familiar experience, for much of human learning involves drawing conclusions based on associating the variation in one set of events with that of another. The analysis of data in the search for cause-and-effect or any other kind of relationship between variables is a basic type of research activity. Mathematical expressions derived from this kind of analysis are frequently used in applications in administration, industry, and science. For example, an analyst may seek to forecast the need for health services by use of a mathematical expression that relates variations in level of demand with those in income of residents in different geographic areas. In an effort to obtain more consistent quality, a production manager studies the effects of changes in temperature and pressure on properties of a petrochemical product to derive an equation to account for variations in product quality. The personnel director of a company uses test results to match personal characteristics with job requirements for the most effective placement of employees. The loan officer of a bank screens loan applicants on the basis of the results of studies that correlate the quality of a credit risk with personal and financial characteristics of the applicants. In an experimental study, the amount of food additives given to laboratory animals is varied and the effects are analyzed as the basis for deciding if the additives can possibly cause harm to human beings. In other studies, physical laws, such as those for gravity and electricity, have been verified by observing variables, analyzing data, and deriving mathematical expressions of the relationships between the variables.

The foregoing examples illustrate the use of regression and correlation, which are based on *analysis by association. Regression* involves the analysis of the variation of variables to (1) derive a mathematical expression of the joint variation of the variables, (2) provide some information that can be used for deciding if the variables are related, (3) explain or account for the variations of a variable, and (4) furnish an equation with which to forecast or predict values of a variable. *Correlation* concerns the analysis of the mutual variation of variables to (1) obtain a measure of their interrelatedness, expressed as a coefficient rather than an equation, and (2) provide a basis for testing the degree or extent of association between the variables.

Regression and correlation are powerful statistical tools that provide quantitative expressions or models of the manner or extent to which events are related mathematically. The application of these statistical methods cannot offer proof of the existence of a relationship between selected variables. Statistical analysis with these methods can, however, provide valuable information that the analyst can employ to support a judgment concerning the existence of a relationship between the variables selected for analysis.

This chapter is concerned principally with the simplest case, *linear bivariate analysis* — the application of linear regression and correlation methods to two variables, one dependent and one independent. Chapter 13 takes up more complex cases in which a nonlinear bivariate relation exists and in which the variations of a dependent variable are related to those of two or more independent variables.

ANALYSIS BY ASSOCIATION

An associative method that makes use of the statistical features of variations of variables can be illustrated by a realistic example adapted from an actual industrial situation.

A petrochemical manufacturer operates an experimental pilot plant with which to study the effects of varying manufacturing conditions, such as temperature, on the hardness of a type of plastic material. The principal component of the pilot plant is a steel pressure vessel, called a reactor. A hydrocarbon gas is pumped into the reactor, and during its passage through the reactor, the molecular structure of the entering gas is changed. This transformation results in the formation of a plastic material. The quality of the plastic produced in the reactor is measured in terms of the hardness of the material. The relationship between plastic hardness (presumably the dependent variable) and the corresponding temperature in the reactor (assumed to be an independent variable) is the focus of the statistical analysis.

The analysis is begun by observing sets of events — the hardness of the plastic material and the temperature of the reactor as the plastic is produced. The plastic is produced in a batch of several hundred pounds of material. The temperature and hardness are recorded as each batch is produced. A plot of pairs of these values is shown in the *scatter diagram* in

Figure 12.1, where the coordinates of each point are the temperature and hardness recorded for each of 194 batches of plastic material. The hardness of all batches ranges from approximately 30 to 80.

FIGURE 12.1

**Scatter Diagram of the Joint Distribution of
Observations of Plastic Hardness and Reactor
Temperature for 194 Batches of Material**

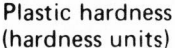
Plastic hardness
(hardness units)

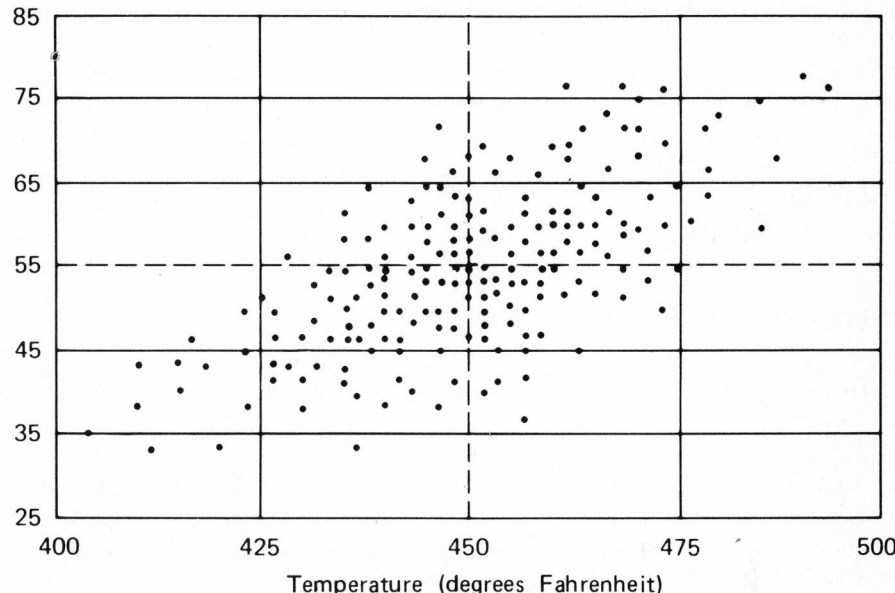

Temperature (degrees Fahrenheit)

The mean hardness of all batches selected is 55 units and the standard deviation is 10 units. The expected value of a batch chosen randomly is 55 units, but the degree of error associated with the estimate of hardness of the batch is expressed by the standard deviation of 10 units. The likely error in estimating the hardness of the batch is relatively large. How can the degree of error associated with estimating the hardness of a batch be reduced? Perhaps if the variations in the independent variable, temperature, can be associated with variations in hardness of batches, the reliability of estimation can be improved. An analysis of the variations in hardness associated with temperature can be approached by classifying batches in terms of temperature.

Association Analysis by Classification

Reactor temperature is a continuous variable; and for the sake of simplicity in presenting the associative method, the range of recorded temperatures is divided into two groups. The lower half of temperatures corresponds to the event denoted T_I, and the upper half, the event T_{II}. This simple classification provides an insight into the general way in which hardness and temperature are related. An examination of Table 12.1 and Figure 12.2 indicates that low hardness tends to be associated with lower temperatures (T_I) and the converse is true for higher temperatures (T_{II}).

TABLE 12.1

Hardness Characteristics of Selected Subsets of Batches of Plastic Material

Characteristics of hardness of groups	Designation of batch groupings		
	Set of all batches produced	Subset of batches produced with temperature I (T_I)	Subset of batches produced with temperature II (T_{II})
Range	30–80	30–70	40–80
Mean value $E(H)$	55	50	60
Standard deviation σ_H	10	8	8

Source: Company records of the firm.

More precisely, the subset of batches produced with condition T_I has a mean of 50 and a standard deviation of 8. The corresponding statistical measures for the subset of batches produced with condition T_{II} are 60 and 8, respectively. The information derived from classifying or structuring the batches by temperature permits a relative reduction in the error of estimating batch hardness (in terms of the respective standard deviations) of one fifth, which is computed

$$\frac{10 - 8}{10} = 0.20.$$

This ratio can be viewed as a measure of the degree of association that exists

FIGURE 12.2

**Range of Hardness of Batches of Plastic Material
Produced by a Reactor**

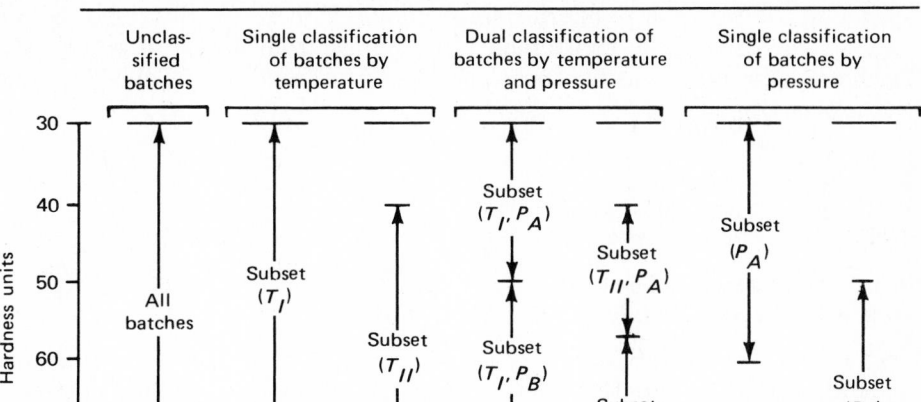

between hardness and temperature. The larger the absolute value of the ratio, the greater the degree of association.

The estimate of batch hardness is more precise if temperature is known, because the smaller standard deviation of the subset can be associated with the mean of the subset. For example, if a batch is selected randomly from the subset produced with T_I, the expected value of hardness denoted (H) is the conditional value.

$$E(H \mid T_I) = 50,$$

which is read "the expected value of hardness, given T_I, is equal to 50." Similarly, the standard deviation for this subset is written

$$\sigma(H \mid T_I) = 8.$$

The range of hardness for this subset of batches is

$$\text{Range } (H \mid T_I) = 30 \text{ to } 70.$$

The corresponding values for the subset of batches produced with T_{II} are

$$E(H \mid T_{II}) = 60$$
$$\sigma(H \mid T_{II}) = 8$$
$$\text{Range } (H \mid T_{II}) = 40 \text{ to } 80.$$

The classification of batches by temperature setting in this example is valuable in providing information for estimating plastic hardness.

The Line of Average Relationship

Analysis by association may be extended to provide information about the functional relationship that exists between variables. This extension is illustrated by means of the temperature-hardness relationship in the plastic material example. Temperature condition T_I in Table 12.1 corresponds to the range of temperatures from 400°F to 450°F. Similarly, condition T_{II} corresponds to the temperature range from 450°F to 500°F. The hardness characteristics for these conditions are read from Table 12.1 and written as follows:

Batch hardness characteristic	Subset	
	T_I (400°F–450°F)	T_{II} (450°F–500°F)
Range	30–70	40–80
Expected value $E(H)$	50	60
Standard deviation σ_{II}	8	8

These data provide the basis for an approximation of the functional relationship between hardness and temperature. Suppose a batch of material is selected at random from the subset of batches T_I. The expected hardness of the batch is $E(H) = 50$, and the expected temperature at which the material was produced is 425°F, the midpoint or mean of the temperature range. Continuing in this manner, the mean hardness and mean temperature of subset T_{II} are 60 and 475°F, respectively. These average data are indicated in Figure 12.3. The line drawn through the points is called the *line of average relationship* and is an approximation of the functional relationship between the variables. The dotted lines above and below the line of average relationship correspond to the limits of the range of batch hardness for each temperature. A prediction of batch hardness can be made from this crude approximation of the functional relationship. Reading vertically upward from a temperature of 450°F to the line of average relationship and then across horizontally to the scale of hardness on the left, it is seen that a hardness of 55 is the expected value corresponding to this temperature.

The value of hardness of 55 may be viewed as a conditional mean written

$$E(\text{Hardness} \mid \text{Temperature} = 450) = 55.$$

Conditional means can be determined for other values of temperature; thus, the line of average relationship may be called the *line of conditional means*. In this sense, the mean of the subset of values of hardness that corresponds to a given temperature lies on the line of conditional means.

In order to make more precise estimates, the approximation of the functional relationship must be refined. This modification is accomplished by use of an analytical technique called the *method of least squares*. This method is described in the following discussion of regression and in Technical Note No. 1 at the end of this chapter.

FIGURE 12.3

Line of Average Relationship Between Hardness and Temperature

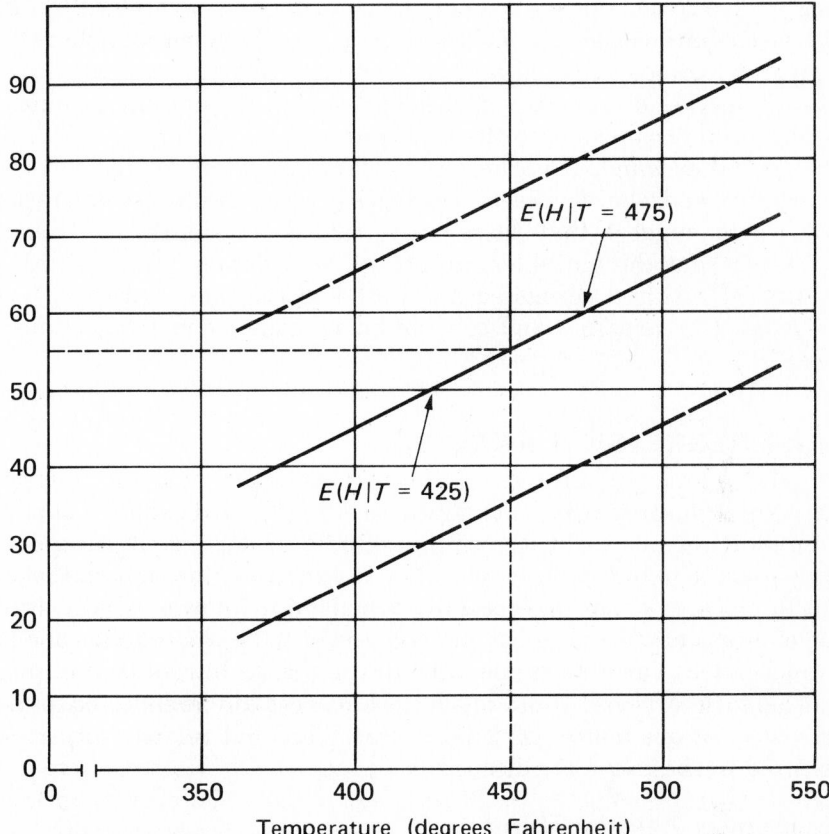

Plastic hardness
(hardness units)

Temperature (degrees Fahrenheit)

The Relationship of Association and Causation

In the analysis of administrative problems, there is a strong motivation to identify cause-and-effect relationships that may exist between variables. On the basis of the results obtained in the foregoing example, one might be inclined toward the opinion that plastic hardness is at least partially determined by temperature settings. However, these results only indicate that the hardness of selected batches tends to vary directly with temperature.

The choice of hardness as the dependent variable involves a judgment on the part of the analyst, and this choice cannot be determined strictly by associative analysis. For example, one could associate temperature (as being dependent) with hardness (assumed to be an independent variable). If this seems illogical, it is because one makes a judgment concerning the most appropriate designation of the variables as being dependent or independent. Measures of the degree of association of temperature variations with those of hardness can be computed in a way similar to that illustrated previously. If variations in temperature are associated with those in hardness, should one conclude that plastic hardness is a causal factor which determines reactor temperature? Common sense suggests that the reverse is true in this example. This conclusion concerning which is the causal variable and which is the dependent variable is based on judgment rather than the result of statistical outcomes. It could also be, however, that the two variables are both the function of a third variable, and a causal relationship exists between the two variables with the third variable.

On the other hand, if variations in hardness were related to those of temperature and the degree of association were minute, this statistical result would suggest that there is no causal relationship between the variables or that the variables are not related. The appraisal of this type of statistical result is discussed more fully in the presentation of tests of significance of regression and correlation coefficients in the sections that follow.

LINEAR REGRESSION ANALYSIS

In many administrative situations it is highly desirable to be able to make predictions or estimates of the value of a dependent variable from given values of an independent variable. In experimentation or in the operation of a process, it may be especially beneficial to know to what extent the value of a dependent variable can be expected to be altered by a change in the independent variable of one unit. In the plastic hardness example, one may wish to determine by how much the hardness can be expected to change with a shift of one degree of temperature. This and related questions are considered in the following discussion.

Functional Relationships

The problem of making a prediction or an estimate of the value of a dependent variable corresponding to a given value of an independent variable requires that a mathematical expression in equation form be derived to express the relationship between the two variables. This equation is an expression of the functional relationship between the assumed dependent variable and the independent variable. In the discussions that follow, the dependent variable is denoted Y, and the independent variable is designated by X.

The relationship in which a dependent variable can be determined exactly from a selected value of the independent variable X is described by the functional expression

$$Y = f(X),$$

which is read "Y is a function of X." The dependent variable involved in many problems is a function of more than one independent variable, and this case is considered in detail in Chapter 13. In most applications the dependent variable cannot be determined exactly from a set of specified values of the independent variable(s), even if these values are determined without error. Consequently, the best relationship that can be derived is an *average* value of Y associated with a specified value of the independent variable(s).

The mean value of Y associated with a value of an independent variable X is denoted Y_c, where the subscript c is used to indicate a "calculated value of Y." The case in which the mean value of the dependent variable Y has a linear relationship with an independent variable X is of particular interest in this discussion. The general form of this relationship is written

$$Y_c = \alpha + \beta X \dots\dots\dots\dots\dots\dots\dots\dots\dots(12.1)$$

where
  Y_c is the average value of Y
  α and β are parameters or constants
  X is the independent variable.

This expression states that for any specified value of X, there exists a corresponding value of Y_c, and the value of Y_c is equal to the transformed value of X. The transformation is accomplished by adding the value of the parameter α to the product of the parameter β times a specified value of X.

■ *Example.* In a study of the annual income of the salaried personnel of an electronics firm, the personnel director analyzed the relationship between annual income and age for employees between 25 and 65 years of age. The analysis revealed that the average annual income of employees tends to vary directly with age in a straight-line or linear manner. A functional expression of the relationship is written

$$Y_c = f(X, \alpha, \beta) = \alpha + \beta X$$

where
  Y_c is the average annual income
  X is the age in years
  α and β are constants.

This functional expression describes the relationship between average income and age since the income of one employee may differ from that of another employee of the same age. The exact income of a randomly selected employee cannot ordinarily be computed by use of the equation derived in this example. The values of the constants of the functional expression are found to be $\alpha = \$2,000$ and $\beta = \$500$. In order to compute the average annual income for a given age, the functional expression is

$$Y_c = \alpha + \beta X$$

and

$$Y_c = \$2,000 + \$500X.$$

The average annual income for a male employee 30 years of age is computed

$$Y_c = \$2,000 + (\$500)(30)$$
$$= \$17,000.$$

Similarly, the average annual income of a male employee 60 years of age is computed

$$Y_c = \$2,000 + (\$500)(60)$$
$$= \$32,000.$$

Bivariate Distributions

Graphic Presentation Methods. Regression analysis is concerned primarily with the derivation of an equation that describes mathematically the manner in which selected variables vary jointly or covary. The choice of the most appropriate form of descriptive equation, whether linear or curvilinear, may be facilitated by plotting the observed values of the variables. This technique is illustrated in Figure 12.4, which shows the data presented in the scatter diagram in Figure 12.1. The ordinate of each point is an observed value of plastic hardness (Y), and the abcissa is the temperature (X) at which the batch of material was manufactured.

The distribution of points in a scatter diagram provides a clue to the functional relationship that exists between two variables, especially if limited information is available concerning this relationship. The line drawn through the points in Figure 12.4 is a geometric representation of the best estimate of a linear equation of the general form $Y_c = \alpha + \beta X$ fitted by visual inspection. This is the line of average relationship between hardness and temperature, because all points do not lie on the line. While the information provided by the scatter diagram may be quite useful for discovering whether the general form of an appropriate equation is linear or curvilinear, it is of limited value for calculating expected values of hardness on the basis of temperature. The calculation of expected values of the dependent variable requires an explicit statement of the parameters of the equation of average relationship. Before considering the methods for deriving an explicit statement of the relationship, it is well to consider some of the theoretical assumptions implicit in bivariate analysis.

If the variables to be analyzed are continuous, the range of the variables to be considered may be viewed as being divided into intervals. The points that appear vertically above each interval of the independent variable X reflect the variation of a subset of observed values of the dependent variable Y. If the number of paired observations becomes very large, the width of intervals approaches zero, and the density of points can be represented as a continuous surface called a *bivariate regression surface*. A surface of this type is shown in Figure 12.5.

FIGURE 12.4

**Scatter Diagram of the Joint Distribution of
Observations of Plastic Hardness and Reactor
Temperature for 194 Batches of Material**

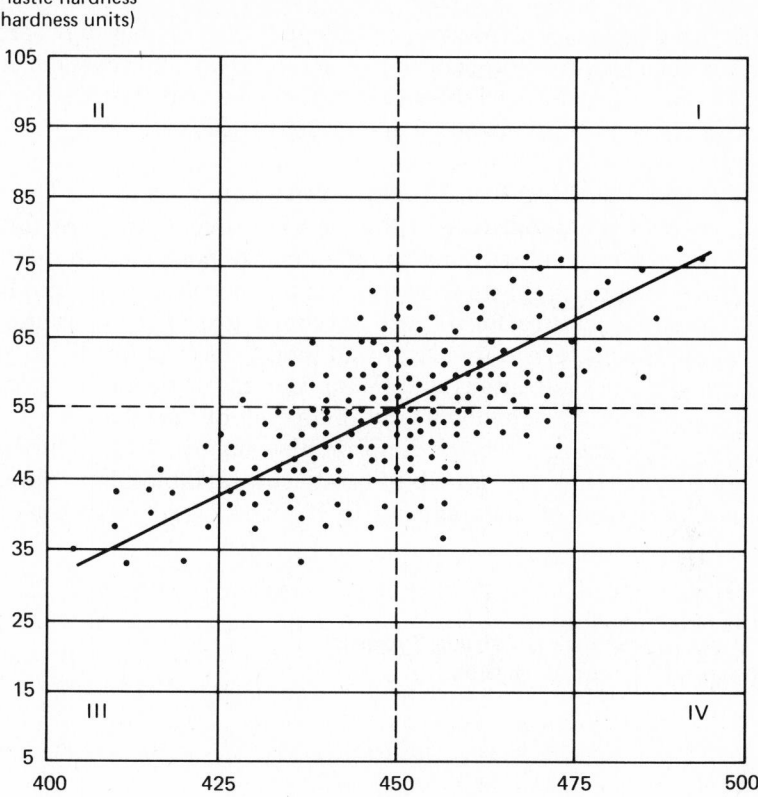

FIGURE 12.5

Bivariate Regression Surface

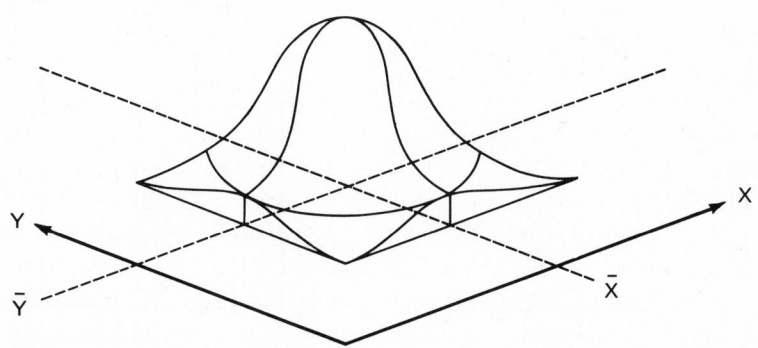

The maximum height of the surface lies above the intersection of $\overline{Y}$ and $\overline{X}$, the expected values of the respective variables. The volume under the surface corresponds to probability. The probability that a point selected at random occurs in a selected area or interval in the Y, X plane is represented by the portion of the volume under the regression surface that lies above the chosen area.

Regression analysis is always applied to a finite number of observations of the variables. The technique of regression analysis, however, is based on the assumption that the variables are continuous and that the regression surface is an appropriate model of the values of the variables.

Point Scatter and the Relationship Between Variables. The locus of points in each of the quadrants in Figure 12.4 reveals that the pattern of scatter is shaped like an oval and the majority of points lie in quadrants I and III. This pattern suggests that there is a positive relationship between hardness and temperature; for if there were no degree of association between the variables, the pattern of scatter would tend to be circular. If the majority of points occurs in quadrants II and IV, an inverse or negative relationship is implied between the dependent and independent variables.

The locus of points in a scatter diagram also suggests the nature of a line of average relationship with which to relate the variables. For example, the locus of points in each of the diagrams in Figure 12.6 suggests the presence

FIGURE 12.6

Scatter Diagrams Showing Various Types of Relationships Between Variables

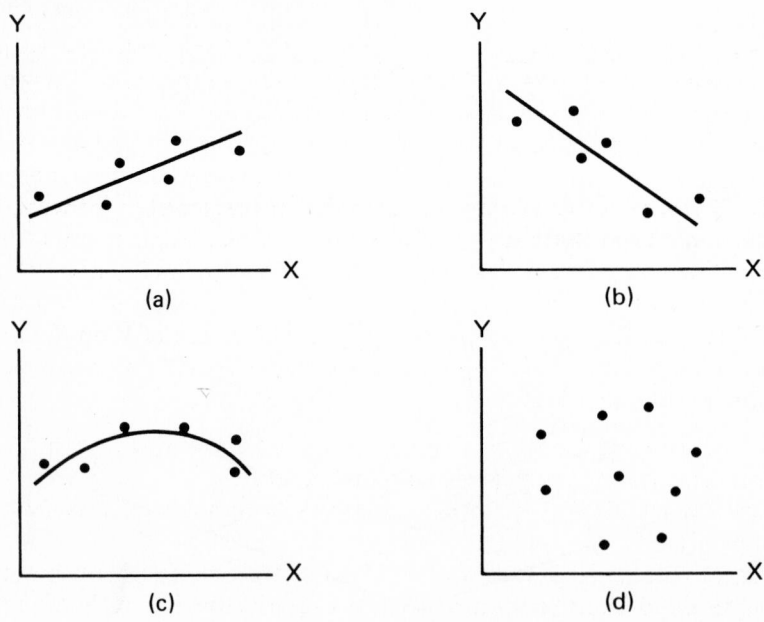

or absence of functional relationships. Diagram (a) suggests a positive linear relationship; the relationship in (b) is negative linear; distinct curvilinearity is reflected by (c); and in (d) a causal relationship between the variables is not indicated because of the circular pattern.

If the relationship between the variables can be represented properly with a linear function, the slope of the line can be derived by making use of the cross products of the data. This method is considered in the discussion that follows.

Line of Regression

In fitting visually a line of average relationship to a series of points, the objective is to position the line so that it lies at the center of the range of points. This type of approach can be stated explicitly by specifying the conditions that define the line which best fits the data. Since the equation of a line of averages is to be derived, the properties of the arithmetic mean are used to specify the desired conditions. One of these properties states that the sum of the deviations of a random variable about its mean is zero and is written

$$\Sigma(Y - \bar{Y}) = 0.$$

A second property of the arithmetic mean is that the sum of the squared deviations about the mean is a minimum and is written

$$\text{Minimum Sum of Squares} = \Sigma(Y - \bar{Y})^2.$$

If the deviations are squared and summed about any value of the random variable other than the mean, the sum of the squared deviations about that value of the random variable will exceed the least squares sum obtained about the mean.

Each point on the line of conditional means represents the mean of a subset of values of the dependent variable that corresponds to a specified value of the independent variable. Each of these mean values is a least squares value. The composite of these averages is the *least squares regression line*. The functional expression of the mean value of a vector of a bivariate universe with a linear relationship is denoted by Formula 12.1 as $Y_c = \alpha + \beta X$. The coefficient α represents the intercept of the regression line at the origin $(X = 0)$. The coefficient β is the rate of change of Y with respect to X, or the amount of change in Y for a change of one unit in X. Formula 12.1 is also referred to as the true regression of Y on X, since it is based on a bivariate universe of values. This regression model is based on the following assumptions:

1. A linear functional expression is an appropriate model of the relationship that exists between variables Y and X.
2. The subset of Y values that corresponds to a given X is distributed normally.
3. The standard deviation of the Y values that corresponds to a given X is the same for all X values. A bivariate distribution with this property

is said to be *homoscedastic*. The converse of this property is termed *heteroscedastic*.

4. The X values do not have a distribution and are considered to be fixed. This implies that X is a mathematical variable and not a random variable.

Given a line of regression defined by Formula 12.1, a value of Y is expressed in general form by

$$Y = \alpha + \beta X + \epsilon \dots\dots\dots\dots\dots\dots\dots\dots\dots\dots\dots(12.2)$$

where ϵ is the *residual* or error of estimating Y with Y_c. Since Y_c is the expected value of Y for a given value of X, Formula 12.2 may be written

$$Y = E(Y \mid X) + \epsilon \dots\dots\dots\dots\dots\dots\dots\dots\dots\dots\dots(12.3)$$

The error term for a single observation of Y is $\epsilon = Y - Y_c$. The values of ϵ are assumed to be distributed normally about the line of regression so that $E(\epsilon) = 0$. The variance of ϵ is written

$$\mathrm{Var}\,(\epsilon) = \sigma_{YX}^2 = E\,[Y - E(Y \mid X)]^2$$

where the subscript $_{YX}$ of the variance term denotes the regression of Y on X.

Parameter Estimates from Sample Data. In many administrative problems it is impossible or impractical to obtain all the observations of a bivariate universe and, consequently, the analysis must be based on a sample of paired observations. The use of sample data in regression analysis presents the problems of sampling error similar to those considered in the discussions of inference. The sample observations are used to estimate the relationship between the variables. For a bivariate distribution, the estimate of the functional relationship is written

$$y_c = a + bx \dots\dots\dots\dots\dots\dots\dots\dots\dots\dots\dots(12.4)$$

Formula 12.4 is called the *estimated regression of Y on X* and is used to make a point estimate of the dependent variable, given a specified value of the independent variable. Given an estimated line of regression defined by Formula 12.4, the error of predicting y with y_c is $\epsilon = y - y_c$ and $\epsilon = y - E(y \mid x)$. An individual sample value of the dependent variable is written

$$y = a + bx + \epsilon \dots\dots\dots\dots\dots\dots\dots\dots\dots\dots\dots(12.5)$$

and $y = E(y \mid x) + \epsilon$. As in the case of the true line of regression derived from a universe of data, $E(\epsilon) = E\,[y - E(y \mid x)] = 0$.

The method of least squares provides estimates of α and β that are both efficient and unbiased. A subset of observations of the dependent variable is assumed to correspond to each value of the independent variable. If the values of each vector are normally distributed, it can be demonstrated that the parameter estimates a and b are efficient and unbiased. The method of least squares, therefore, is a technique for deriving the estimators of the parameters α and β which minimize the sum of squared deviations.

The sum of squared deviations, $\Sigma(y - y_c)^2$, is a function of the estimators a and b. This sum is a minimum about a line defined by the estimators

$$b = \frac{n\Sigma xy - (\Sigma x)(\Sigma y)}{n\Sigma x^2 - (\Sigma x)^2} \quad \dots\dots\dots\dots\dots\dots\dots(12.6)$$

and

$$a = \bar{y} - b\bar{x} \dots\dots\dots\dots\dots\dots\dots\dots(12.7)$$

where

b reflects the change in y for a unit change in x, and
a is the intercept of estimated regression line at the origin $(x = 0)$.

These relationships for computing a and b are derived by the method of least squares presented in Technical Note No. 1 at the end of this chapter.

■ **Example.** A sample of five paired observations of the number of surfaces cut by a milling machine (x) and processing time (in hours) (y) on metal parts produced in a machine shop are as follows:

x	y	xy	x^2	y^2
3	5	15	9	25
4	8	32	16	64
5	9	45	25	81
2	6	12	4	36
1	2	2	1	4
15	30	106	55	210

The least squares estimators a and b are computed as follows:

$$b = \frac{n\Sigma xy - (\Sigma x)(\Sigma y)}{n\Sigma x^2 - (\Sigma x)^2}$$

$$= \frac{5(106) - (15)(30)}{5(55) - (15)^2}$$

$$= \frac{530 - 450}{275 - 225}$$

$$= \frac{80}{50}$$

$$= 1.6.$$

$$a = \bar{y} - b\bar{x}$$
$$= 6 - 1.6(3)$$
$$= 6 - 4.8$$
$$= 1.2.$$

The estimated regression of processing time on number of surfaces cut is expressed by

$$y_c = 1.2 + 1.6x$$

where

$a = 1.2$ is the height of the estimated regression line for $x = 0$
$b = 1.6$ is the change in y for a change of one unit in x.

The estimated processing time for three cuts is computed

$$y_c = E(y \mid x = 3)$$
$$= 1.2 + 1.6(3)$$
$$= 6.0$$

as indicated by the regression line in Figure 12.7. The value of five hours observed for three cuts deviates from the estimate by

$$\epsilon = y - E(y \mid x = 3) = 5.0 - 6.0 = -1.0.$$

The error of estimation for each of the observed values of the dependent variable is shown in the following table.

y	a	b	x	a + bx	$\epsilon = y - (a + bx)$
5	1.2	1.6	3	6.0	−1.0
8	1.2	1.6	4	7.6	0.4
9	1.2	1.6	5	9.2	−0.2
6	1.2	1.6	2	4.4	1.6
2	1.2	1.6	1	2.8	−0.8
				$\Sigma\epsilon =$	0.0

FIGURE 12.7

Estimated Regression of Processing Time on Number of Surfaces Cut by a Milling Machine

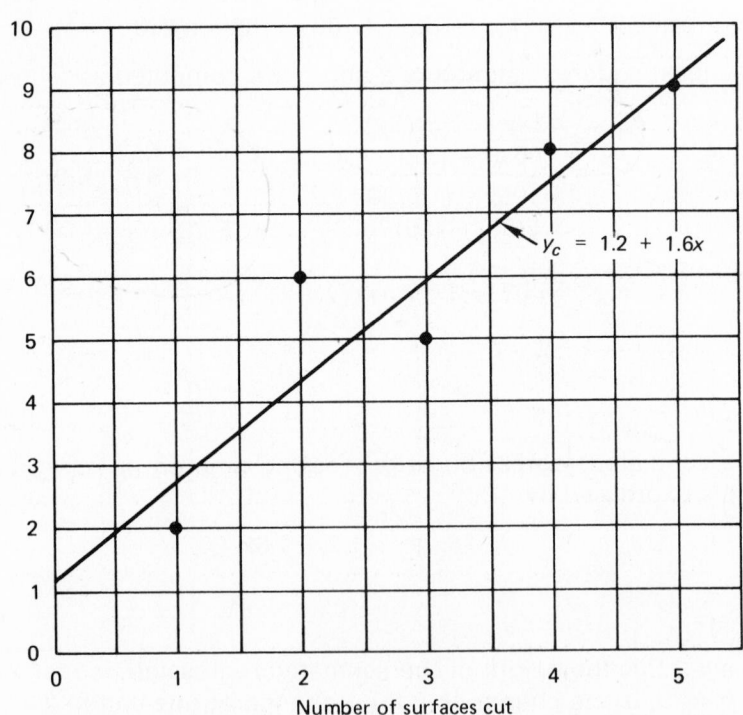

Regression and Correlation   **Part 5**

The sum of the error terms is zero, which reflects the fact that the estimated line of regression is a line of average relationship obtained by use of unbiased estimators *a* and *b*.

The Standard Error of the Estimate. The deviations of pairs of values of two variables from a line of regression reflect the goodness of fit of the line with the data. If it can be assumed that the residuals or prediction errors are independent and distributed normally about the line of regression, a numeric measure of these variations can be computed. This measure is called the *standard error of the estimate*. For a universe of values, this measure is written

$$\sigma_{YX} = \sqrt{\frac{\Sigma(Y - Y_c)^2}{N}} \quad \dots \dots \dots \dots \dots \dots \dots \dots \dots \dots (12.8)$$

This formula is based on the assumption that the error values are distributed normally and homoscedastically (the standard error is the same for all values of X) about the line of regression. This type of error distribution is illustrated in Figure 12.8, which shows the relationship between plastic hardness and temperature (based on data shown in Figure 12.4) that is

FIGURE 12.8

Confidence Limits About a Line of Regression

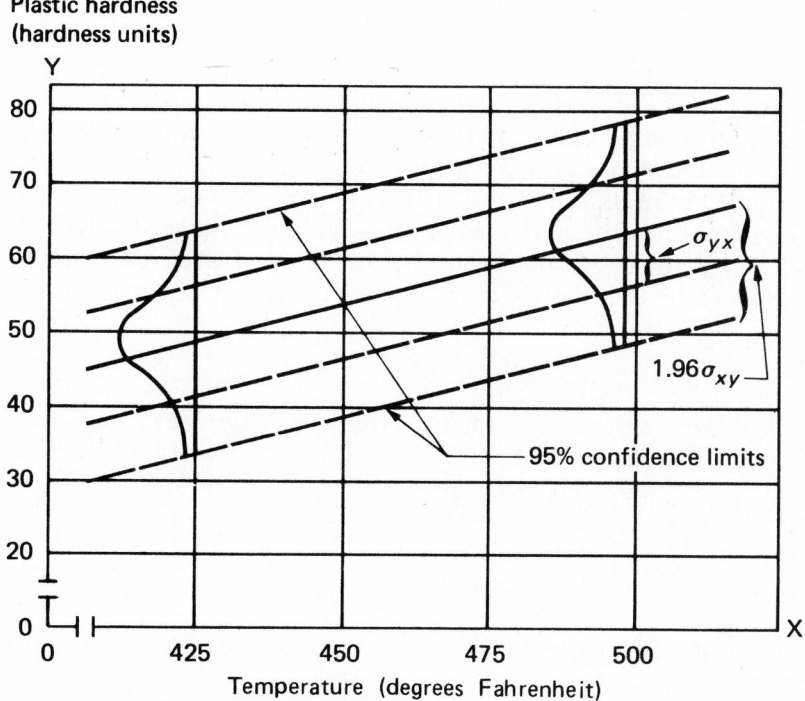

Plastic hardness
(hardness units)

Temperature (degrees Fahrenheit)

assumed to be homoscedastic for purposes of this illustration. Normal curve properties are used in making an interval estimate of Y.

■ *Example.* The relationship between the universe of plastic hardness and temperature values shown in Figure 12.8 is described by the true line of regression computed from the data to be

$$Y_c = -35.0 + 0.2X$$

and the normal distribution of estimation errors with the standard error of estimate computed to be

$$\sigma_{YX} = 7.0.$$

A point estimate of plastic hardness for a temperature setting of 425°F is computed

$$\begin{aligned}
Y_c &= \alpha + \beta X \\
&= -35.0 + 0.2(425) \\
&= -35.0 + 85.0 \\
&= 50.0.
\end{aligned}$$

The 95% interval estimate of plastic hardness, given $X = 425°F$, is computed

$$\begin{aligned}
E(Y \mid X) &\pm z_{0.05}\sigma_{YX} \\
E(Y \mid X = 425) &\pm 1.96(7) \\
50 &\pm 13.72 \\
36.28 &\text{ to } 63.72.
\end{aligned}$$

An Unbiased Estimate of the Standard Error of Estimate. If regression analysis is based on sample data, the standard error of estimate must be approximated from the sample observations. Recalling that the variance of a sample is a biased estimator of the universe variance, it follows that a sample estimate of the standard error of estimate must also be corrected for bias. An unbiased estimator of the universe standard error of the estimate obtained by the method of maximum likelihood is written

$$\hat{\sigma}_{YX} = \sqrt{\frac{\Sigma(y - y_c)^2}{n - 2}} \quad\ldots\ldots\ldots\ldots\ldots\ldots\ldots\ldots\ldots(12.9)$$

The loss of two degrees of freedom in this expression reflects the use of a and b as estimates of α and β in computing the estimate of the standard error of the estimate. Manual computation of $\hat{\sigma}_{YX}$ is facilitated by using an alternate expression obtained by writing Formula 12.9 as

$$\hat{\sigma}_{YX} = \sqrt{\frac{\Sigma(y - a - bx)^2}{n - 2}}.$$

Squaring and substituting terms in the numerator gives the alternate expression

$$\hat{\sigma}_{YX} = \sqrt{\frac{\Sigma y^2 - a\Sigma y - b\Sigma xy}{n-2}} \quad\ldots\ldots\ldots\ldots\ldots\ldots\ldots(12.10)$$

where n is the sample size. Formula 12.10 permits one to avoid the tedious task of computing the error terms required by Formula 12.9.

■ **Example.** The estimated standard error of the estimate obtained from the machine shop data on page 379 is computed as follows:

$$\hat{\sigma}_{YX} = \sqrt{\frac{\Sigma y^2 - a\Sigma y - b\Sigma xy}{n-2}}$$

$$= \sqrt{\frac{210 - 1.2(30) - 1.6(106)}{5-2}}$$

$$= \sqrt{\frac{4.4}{3}}$$

$$= 1.21.$$

This result is verified by computing the unbiased estimate of the standard deviation of the estimation errors, shown on page 380, by means of Formula 12.9.

$$\hat{\sigma}_{YX} = \sqrt{\frac{\Sigma(y - y_c)^2}{n-2}}$$

$$= \sqrt{\frac{(-1.0)^2 + (0.4)^2 + (-0.2)^2 + (1.6)^2 + (-0.8)^2}{5-2}}$$

$$= \sqrt{\frac{4.4}{3}}$$

$$= 1.21.$$

Sampling Error Associated with the Es̶timated Line of Regression

An estimate of the true line of regressio̶ ̶̶ ̶̶om sample data in order to predict the value of a depende̶ ̶ given value of an independent variable. The statistics a a̶ ̶d estimators of the parameters α and β, but the values c̶ ̶ are subject to sampling error. It follows that predictio̶ ̶of an estimated line of regression are subject to sampling ̶ error may arise in the estimate of α, the intercept of t̶ ̶e at the origin, and of β, the slope of the line of regressi̶

The Sampling Error of ̶ d slope of the line of regression b is a random variable wi̶ ̶

̶β.

The sampling distrib̶ ̶tistic b is distributed normally about β. An example of t̶' ̶ is shown in Figure 12.9. The standard

FIGURE 12.9

Normal Distribution of the Statistic *b* About the Parameter β

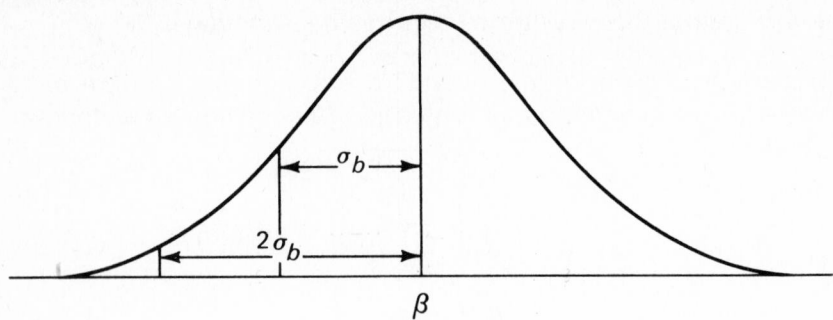

Values of the statistic *b*

deviation of the distribution of *b* is called the *standard error of b*. This parameter is written

$$\sigma_b = \frac{\sigma_{YX}}{\sqrt{\Sigma(x - \bar{x})^2}} \quad \ldots\ldots\ldots\ldots\ldots\ldots\ldots(12.11)$$

The magnitude of σ_b varies directly with the standard error of the estimate but inversely with the number of sample observations and the variability of the independent variable. An unbiased estimator of σ_b is written

$$\hat{\sigma}_b = \frac{\hat{\sigma}_{YX}}{\sqrt{\Sigma(x - \bar{x})^2}} \quad \ldots\ldots\ldots\ldots\ldots\ldots\ldots(12.12)$$

An equivalent algebraic form is written

$$\hat{\sigma}_b = \frac{\hat{\sigma}_{YX}}{\sqrt{\Sigma x^2 - \dfrac{(\Sigma x)^2}{n}}} \quad \ldots\ldots\ldots\ldots\ldots\ldots(12.13)$$

A value of *b* obtained from a sample of observations does not necessarily lead to the conclusion that the slope of the universe line of regression has a value other than zero. It is possible to obtain a nonzero value of *b* even if $\beta = 0$. This type of result arises from sampling error and creates the need for a test of significance of the value of *b*.

A sample value of *b* can be tested for significance by testing the hypothesis that $\beta = 0$, which implies that the dependent and the independent variables are not related. A sample value of *b* must differ significantly from zero before it supports the conclusion that a functional relationship does exist between the variables. A test of significance is made by computing the statistic

$$t = \frac{b - \beta}{\hat{\sigma}_b} \quad \ldots\ldots\ldots\ldots\ldots\ldots\ldots(12.14)$$

and comparing the result with the value of t for $n - 2$ degrees of freedom. The t distribution is used because $\hat{\sigma}_{YX}$ is used in the calculation.

■ **Example.** The slope of the estimated line of regression for the data in the example on page 379 is tested for significance in the following steps. The results computed from these data in preceding examples are:

$$n = 5$$
$$b = 1.6$$

and

$$\hat{\sigma}_{YX} = 1.21.$$

The statistic t for these data is obtained by computing

$$t = \frac{b - \beta}{\hat{\sigma}_b} = \frac{1.6 - 0.0}{\dfrac{1.21}{\sqrt{55 - \dfrac{(15)^2}{5}}}} = 4.18.$$

STEPS:
1. H_0: $\beta = 0$
2. H_a: $\beta \neq 0$
3. An α level of 0.05 requires a t value of ± 3.182.
4. Criterion: Reject H_0 (accept H_a) if $t < -3.182$ or if $t > +3.182$; do not reject H_0 if $t \leq 3.182$.

Since $t(4.18) > t_\alpha(3.182)$, reject H_0. The value of b is significant, and the regression is not likely to be due to chance.

The Standard Error of an Estimated Value of Y. The principal objective of most regression analysis applications is the derivation of an expression with which to predict values of Y for specified values of X. The prediction of values of Y is subject to two types of error. The first occurs if a less than perfect relationship exists between the variables. In this case, even if all the universe data were known, some degree of error would occur in predicting Y.

The second source of prediction error is sampling, and the standard error of the estimate is partially a function of the sample size. If the scatter diagram of sample points is not uniformly dense over the range of values of X, then the standard error of the estimate varies inversely with the number of joint observations of Y and X. In Figure 12.4 it can be seen that the density of points is greatest near the mean of X or 450°F and least toward each extreme end of the range of X. The *standard error of an estimated value of Y* is the standard error of the estimate adjusted for the sample size corresponding to a given value of X and is written

$$\hat{\sigma}_{(Y \mid X)} = \hat{\sigma}_{YX} \sqrt{1 + \frac{1}{n} + \frac{(X - \bar{x})^2}{\Sigma x^2 - \dfrac{(\Sigma x)^2}{n}}} \quad \ldots\ldots\ldots\ldots\ldots(12.15)$$

The statistic $\hat{\sigma}_{(Y|X)}$ approaches $\hat{\sigma}_{YX}$ as a limit for $X = \bar{x}$ as the sample size n becomes very large.

■ *Example.* The value of $\hat{\sigma}_{(Y|X)}$ is computed from the data in the foregoing example. Given $n = 5$, $\hat{\sigma}_{YX} = 1.21$, $X = 4$, and $\Sigma x^2 - \dfrac{(\Sigma x)^2}{n} = 10.0$, the value of $\hat{\sigma}_{(Y|X)}$ is computed

$$\hat{\sigma}_{(Y|X)} = \hat{\sigma}_{YX} \sqrt{1 + \frac{1}{n} + \frac{(X - \bar{x})^2}{\Sigma x^2 - \dfrac{(\Sigma x)^2}{n}}}$$

$$\hat{\sigma}_{(Y|X=4)} = 1.21 \sqrt{1 + \frac{1}{5} + \frac{(4 - 3)^2}{10}}$$

$$= 1.38 \text{ for } X = 4.$$

The point estimate of Y is $E(Y|X = 4)$ and is computed

$$Y = y_c = a + bx = 1.2 + 1.6(4) = 7.6.$$

The 95% interval estimate of $Y = y_c = E(Y|X = 4)$ is computed as follows:

Lower limit	Upper limit
$y_c - t_{0.05}\hat{\sigma}_{(Y|X)}$	$y_c + t_{0.05}\hat{\sigma}_{(y|X)}$
$7.6 - 3.18(1.38) = 3.21$	$7.6 + 3.18(1.38) = 11.99$

The value of $\hat{\sigma}_{(Y|X)}$ is a minimum for $X = \bar{x}$ and increases as X deviates from $\bar{x}$. The 95% confidence limits of predicted values of Y vary in the same manner.

CORRELATION ANALYSIS

Regression analysis is concerned with the derivation of an appropriate mathematical expression of the functional relationship between variables. This expression is derived for the express purpose of predicting values of a dependent variable on the basis of independent variables. Situations as described in the first paragraph of this chapter occur in the analysis of administrative problems in which an expression of the degree of association between variables is desired. The ability to predict values of the dependent variable may or may not be of particular value. It is in this type of situation that *correlation analysis* is applicable. Regression analysis and correlation analysis of two variables as presented in this discussion are contrasted as follows:

Regression analysis model	*Correlation analysis model*
Y is a normally distributed random variable and X is a mathematical or fixed variable.	Y and X are normally distributed random variables.

A functional relationship $Y = f(X)$ is known or assumed and the variables are identified as dependent and independent.

The analysis is appropriate for either $Y = f(X)$ or $X = f(Y)$.

An analysis of one variable as being dependent upon another.

An analysis of interrelationship and mutual variation.

A model for estimating and predicting Y on the basis of X.

A model for testing and verifying the degree of association between variables.

The extent of relationship is indicated principally by the regression coefficient β.

The degree of association is reflected by the correlation coefficient ρ.

The results obtained from sample data are subject to sampling error.

The result obtained from sample data is subject to sampling error.

UNIVERSE COEFFICIENT OF CORRELATION

The extent of joint variation between two variables can be expressed by a coefficient of correlation denoted ρ. The pattern of mutual variation can be expressed by an algebraic statement of the scatter of paired observations of the variables. This is accomplished by expressing each point in terms of the product of its coordinates, where each coordinate is stated as a deviation from the respective mean. In this manner, a paired data point has an abcissa written $(X - \overline{X})$ and an ordinate written $(Y - \overline{Y})$. A point in quadrant I (see Figure 12.4 on page 375) has coordinates that are positive values, since the expression is in terms of deviations. Similarly, a point in quadrant II has a positive ordinate $(Y - \overline{Y})$ and a negative abcissa $(X - \overline{X})$. In quadrant III the coordinates are both negative, and in quadrant IV the ordinate is negative and the abcissa is positive.

The extent of the relationship between two variables is reflected in the scatter of paired data points. An expression of the position of a point in its respective quadrant is obtained by computing the product of its coordinates as deviations. The result of the multiplication of $(X - \overline{X})(Y - \overline{Y})$ is called a *cross product*. The cross products of points in quadrants I and III are all positive, since both coordinates (deviations) are positive in quadrant I and both negative in quadrant III. The cross products in quadrants II and IV are negative since one coordinate is positive and the other is negative.

■ *Example.* The temperature (X) and hardness (Y) for a batch of material are 490 and 68, respectively. The cross product of the point in quadrant I in Figure 12.4 is computed

$$(X - \overline{X})(Y - \overline{Y}) = (490 - 450)(68 - 55)$$
$$= (40)(13)$$
$$= 520.$$

A point in quadrant IV that corresponds to a batch of plastic material with temperature of 465 and hardness of 48 has a cross product of

$$(X - \bar{X})(Y - \bar{Y}) = (465 - 450)(48 - 55)$$
$$= (15)(-7)$$
$$= -105.$$

The arithmetic mean or expected value of the cross products is called the *covariance*, which is denoted $cov(X, Y)$. The value of the covariance is influenced by the units in which the deviations are expressed and the number of points involved. For example, a deviation in degrees Fahrenheit in Figure 12.4 has a larger numerical value than the same temperature expressed in degrees centigrade, although the condition is qualitatively the same in each case. The covariance would be smaller if temperature were measured in degrees centigrade as the result of the unit of measurement. The influence of unit of measurement can be eliminated by standardizing the covariance. This is accomplished by expressing the covariance in standard deviation units, which is written

$$\rho = \frac{E(X - \bar{X})(Y - \bar{Y})}{\sigma_X \sigma_Y} = \frac{\frac{1}{N}\Sigma(X - \bar{X})(Y - \bar{Y})}{\sigma_X \sigma_Y} \quad\ldots\ldots\ldots(12.16)$$

and is called the *universe coefficient of correlation*. This coefficient is a measure of the extent to which two variables are related linearly. It is an abstract measure since it is divorced from the units of X and Y. The range of this measure is $(-1 \leq \rho \leq +1)$. The algebraic sign denotes an inverse (negative) or direct (positive) relationship between the variables. A positive standardized covariance reflects a direct relationship between the variables, and a negative standardized covariance indicates an inverse relationship. The covariance (sum of cross products) for a circular scatter of points is zero and $\rho = 0$. This is interpreted to mean that the variables are independent and are not related linearly. A value of ρ that approaches (-1) reflects a very close inverse linear relationship. As ρ approaches $(+1)$, the indication is that a linear regression line with a positive slope is an excellent expression of the relationship between the variables.

■ *Example.* The percentage of acid concentration (X) and the amount of impurity in water (Y) (in parts per million) in the water system of each of five cities are recorded as follows:

City	Acid concentration X	Amount of impurity Y	
A	7	20	
B	3	27	
C	8	10	$\bar{X} = 5$
D	2	36	
E	5	22	$\bar{Y} = 23$
	25	115	

Regression and Correlation   **Part 5**

The universe coefficient of correlation (standardized covariance) is computed

$$\rho = \frac{E(X - \bar{X})(Y - \bar{Y})}{\sigma_X \, \sigma_Y} = \frac{\begin{array}{l} \frac{1}{5}[(7-5)(20-23) + (3-5)(27-23) \\ + (8-5)(10-23) + (2-5)(36-23) \\ + (5-5)(22-23)] \end{array}}{(2.28)(8.53)}$$

$$= \frac{-18.4}{19.4} = -0.95.$$

The coefficient is negative and quite close to (-1), indicating an almost perfect inverse relationship between the variables, as shown in Figure 12.10. The scatter of points and the negative slope of the line of average relationship in this figure indicate the inverse relationship. This relationship indicates that by increasing the acid concentration, the purity of water can be improved; and this information can be used in the management of city water systems and other types of applications.

FIGURE 12.10

Scatter Diagram of Impurity and Acid Concentration

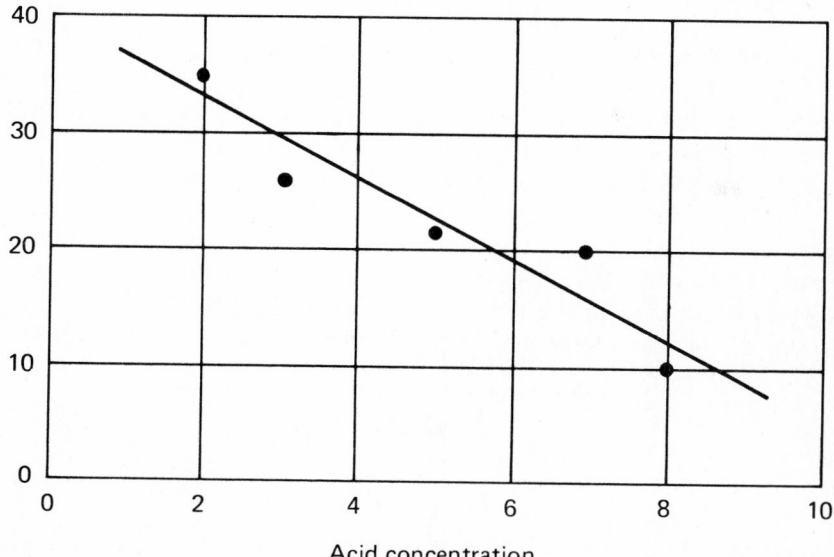

The concept of correlation can also be developed by examining the variations in the dependent variable that are associated with those of the independent variable. The regression equation reflects the functional relationship between the variables, and ρ^2 indicates the percentage of dispersion of the dependent variable that is associated with the independent variable. The *total variation* of the dependent variable is the sum of the squared deviations, written

$$SST = \text{total sum of squares} = \Sigma(Y - \overline{Y})^2.$$

If there is a perfect linear relationship between X and Y, then $(Y|X) = E(Y|X)$ for all X, and all the Y values lie on the regression line. It follows that if there is a perfect linear relationship between X and Y, the

$$SSA = \text{associated sum of squares} = \Sigma(Y_c - \overline{Y})^2$$

is equal to the total sum of squares and the

$$SSU = \text{unassociated sum of squares} = \Sigma(Y - Y_c)^2$$

is equal to zero.

If the regression of Y on X is not perfect, some values of $(Y|X)$ differ from $E(Y|X)$ for some or all values of X, and the unassociated sum of squares is greater than zero. The sum of squares has the relationship

$$\text{total} = \text{associated} + \text{unassociated}.$$

A measure of the degree to which X and Y are related linearly is written

$$\rho^2 = \frac{\text{associated sum of squares}}{\text{total sum of squares}}$$

and

$$\rho^2 = \frac{\Sigma(Y_c - \overline{Y})^2}{\Sigma(Y - \overline{Y})^2} \quad \dots\dots\dots\dots\dots\dots\dots\dots(12.17)$$

The term ρ^2 is called the *universe coefficient of determination* and is the ratio of the variation of Y associated with the variation of X to the total variation of Y. The range of this ratio is $(0 \leq \rho^2 \leq 1)$ since the numerator of Formula 12.17 cannot be less than zero or greater than the denominator. The square root of ρ^2 is the universe coefficient of correlation.

A related measure written

$$1 - \rho^2 = \frac{\text{unassociated sum of squares}}{\text{total sum of squares}}$$

$$k^2 = \frac{\Sigma(Y - Y_c)^2}{\Sigma(Y - \overline{Y})^2} \quad \dots\dots\dots\dots\dots\dots\dots\dots\dots(12.18)$$

is called the *universe coefficient of nondetermination*. The square root of this term is called the *coefficient of alienation*.

■Example. A member of the staff of the personnel department of a firm recorded scores made on an apitude test (X) and corresponding performance ratings (Y) for a universe of five employees in a specialized section of the firm. The observed data and related computations are shown in the following table.

	Employee					Total
	A	B	C	D	E	
(1) X	50	70	55	60	65	300
(2) Y	75	100	85	95	85	440
(3) X^2	2,500	4,900	3,025	3,600	4,225	18,250
(4) Y^2	5,625	10,000	7,225	9,025	7,225	39,100
(5) XY	3,750	7,000	4,675	5,700	5,525	26,650
(6) Y_c	78	98	83	88	93	440
(7) $(Y - \bar{Y})$	-13	12	-3	7	-3	0
(8) $(Y - \bar{Y})^2$	169	144	9	49	9	380
(9) $(Y_c - \bar{Y})$	-10	10	-5	0	5	0
(10) $(Y_c - \bar{Y})^2$	100	100	25	0	25	250
(11) $(Y - Y_c)$	-3	2	2	7	-8	0
(12) $(Y - Y_c)^2$	9	4	4	49	64	130

The coefficients for the line of regression for the data are $\alpha = 28$ and $\beta = 1$. The value of Y_c for each value of X is shown in row (6). The total deviations, associated deviation, and unassociated deviation for each value of X are found in rows (7), (9), and (11), respectively. These values for $X = 70$ are shown in Figure 12.11. The total squared deviations, associated squared deviations, and unassociated squared deviations are shown in rows (8), (10), and (12), respectively. The totals of these rows demonstrate that the relationship between total and component sums of squares is

$$\text{total} = \text{associated} + \text{unassociated}$$
$$380 = 250 + 130.$$

The coefficient of determination is computed

$$\rho^2 = \frac{\Sigma(Y_c - \bar{Y})^2}{\Sigma(Y - \bar{Y})^2}$$

$$= \frac{250}{380} = 0.658.$$

This result indicates that more than 65% of the variation in performance ratings is associated with the variations in aptitude test scores. The coefficient of correlation is computed

$$\rho = \sqrt{\rho^2}$$
$$= \sqrt{0.658}$$
$$= 0.811.$$

FIGURE 12.11

**A Scatter Diagram Illustrating Total,
Associated, and Unassociated Deviation**

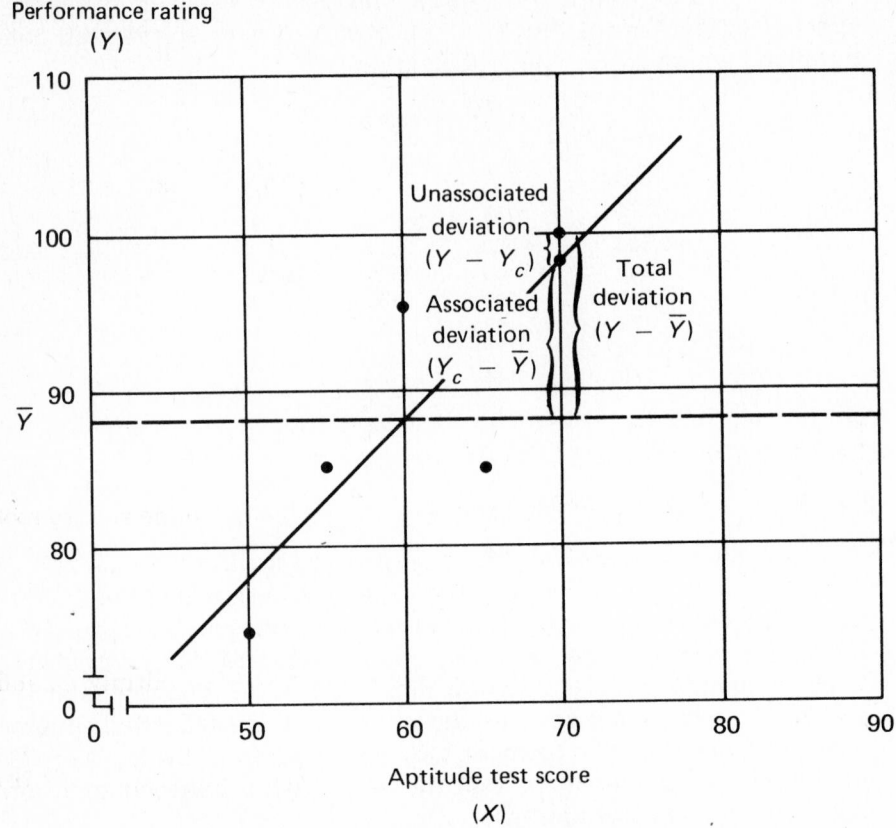

This result indicates that a linear model is a rather good representation of the relationship between variables X and Y. The coefficient of nondetermination is

$$\kappa^2 = 1 - \rho^2 = \frac{\Sigma(Y - Y_c)^2}{\Sigma(Y - \bar{Y})^2}$$

$$= \frac{130}{380} = 0.342,$$

and the coefficient of alienation is

$$\kappa = \sqrt{1 - \rho^2} = \sqrt{1 - 0.658} = 0.585.$$

CORRELATION AND SAMPLING THEORY

The coefficient of determination for a sample of data is the ratio of the associated to the total sum of squares

$$r^2 = \frac{\Sigma(y_c - \bar{y})^2}{\Sigma(y - \bar{y})^2}.$$

Computing r^2 by use of this expression is tedious, for one must compute the deviations about $\bar{y}$ and find the ratio of the corresponding sums of squares. The computation can be facilitated by use of an expression derived from that given above. An equivalent form of r^2 is written

$$r^2 = \frac{b^2 \Sigma(x - \bar{x})^2}{\Sigma(y - \bar{y})^2}.$$

Substituting the algebraic form of b into this alternate expression of r^2 and simplifying gives

$$r^2 = \left[\frac{\Sigma(x - \bar{x})(y - \bar{y})}{\Sigma(x - \bar{x})}\right]^2 \left[\frac{\Sigma(x - \bar{x})^2}{\Sigma(y - \bar{y})^2}\right]$$

$$= \frac{[\Sigma(x - \bar{x})(y - \bar{y})]^2}{\Sigma(x - \bar{x})^2 \Sigma(y - \bar{y})^2}.$$

Sample Coefficient of Correlation

The sample coefficient of correlation is found by taking the square root of the second expression above to give

$$r = \frac{\Sigma(x - \bar{x})(y - \bar{y})}{\sqrt{\Sigma(x - \bar{x})^2 \Sigma(y - \bar{y})^2}}.$$

This expression is simplified for computation purposes by multiplying and collecting terms to give

$$r = \frac{n\Sigma xy - (\Sigma x)(\Sigma y)}{\sqrt{[n\Sigma x^2 - (\Sigma x)^2][n\Sigma y^2 - (\Sigma y)^2]}} \quad\ldots\ldots\ldots\ldots\ldots(12.19)$$

where r is called the *sample coefficient of correlation*. Formula 12.19 is called the *product-moment* formula for the sample correlation coefficient.

The sample coefficient of correlation is a biased estimator of ρ, since the tendency is for r to be greater than ρ for small samples. An unbiased estimator of the universe coefficient of determination is written

$$\hat{\rho}^2 = 1 - (1 - r^2)\left(\frac{n - 1}{n - 2}\right)\ldots\ldots\ldots\ldots\ldots\ldots(12.20)$$

An unbiased estimator of the universe coefficient of correlation is obtained by taking the square root of the expression in Formula 12.20.

■ *Example.* The sample coefficient of correlation is computed for five paired observations of number of surfaces machined, *x*, and processing time in hours, *y*, on metal parts (see page 379). The sample data are given as follows:

x	y	xy	x^2	y^2
3	5	15	9	25
4	8	32	16	64
5	9	45	25	81
2	6	12	4	36
1	2	2	1	4
15	30	106	55	210

The sample coefficient of correlation is

$$r = \frac{n\Sigma xy - (\Sigma x)(\Sigma y)}{\sqrt{[n\Sigma x^2 - (\Sigma x)^2][n\Sigma y^2 - (\Sigma y)^2]}}$$

$$= \frac{5(106) - (15)(30)}{\sqrt{[5(55) - (15)^2][5(210) - (30)^2]}}$$

$$= 0.924.$$

The unbiased estimate of the universe coefficient of correlation is found by the use of Formula 12.20 where

$$\hat{\rho}^2 = 1 - (1 - 0.854)\left(\frac{5-1}{5-2}\right) = 0.805$$

and

$$\hat{\rho} = \sqrt{0.805} = 0.897.$$

Note that the unbiased estimator $\hat{\rho}$ is smaller than r, for the sample coefficient of correlation tends to be larger than the universe coefficient of correlation for small samples. For large sample sizes the bias correction becomes insignificant.

The Relationship Between r and b

The regression coefficient b and the correlation coefficient r computed from a set of data both reflect the degree of association in the variation of the two variables. Consequently, b and r are related and vary together in a precise mathematical manner.

The sample coefficient of correlation is the geometric mean of the slopes of the lines of regression of Y on X and X on Y written

$$r^2 = b_{yx} \cdot b_{xy}$$
$$r = \sqrt{b_{yx} \cdot b_{xy}}.$$

This relationship assumes that regression analysis is applied to a bivariate distribution in which the regressions of Y on X and X on Y are computed. In a causal relationship both regressions may not have operational meaning. The value of r does not indicate which variable is dependent and which is independent.

The relationship between r and b is also shown by the expression

$$r = b_{yx}\frac{\hat{\sigma}_X}{\hat{\sigma}_Y}.$$

Stated in this manner, r is the standardized slope of the regression line in which the values of Y and X are expressed in standard deviation units.

■ **Example.** The relationship between r and b_{yx} is demonstrated by using the data for a sample of five paired observations of number of surfaces machined (x) and processing time in hours (y) on parts (see page 379).

$$b_{yx} = \frac{n\Sigma xy - (\Sigma x)(\Sigma y)}{n\Sigma x^2 - (\Sigma x)^2}$$

$$= \frac{5(106) - (15)(30)}{5(55) - (15)^2}$$

$$= \frac{80}{50} = 1.6.$$

$$b_{xy} = \frac{n\Sigma xy - (\Sigma x)(\Sigma y)}{n\Sigma y^2 - (\Sigma y)^2}$$

$$= \frac{5(106) - (15)(30)}{5(210) - (30)^2}$$

$$= \frac{80}{150} = 0.533.$$

$$r = \sqrt{b_{yx} \cdot b_{xy}}$$

$$= \sqrt{(1.6)(0.533)}$$

$$= 0.924.$$

This is the correlation coefficient obtained previously (page 394). The relationship between r and b_{yx} is also demonstrated by

$$r = b_{yx} \frac{\hat{\sigma}_X}{\hat{\sigma}_Y}$$

$$= (b_{yx}) \frac{\sqrt{\dfrac{n}{n-1}} \sqrt{\dfrac{\Sigma x^2}{n} - \left[\dfrac{\Sigma x}{n}\right]^2}}{\sqrt{\dfrac{n}{n-1}} \sqrt{\dfrac{\Sigma y^2}{n} - \left[\dfrac{\Sigma y}{n}\right]^2}}$$

$$= (1.6) \frac{\sqrt{\dfrac{5}{4}} \sqrt{\dfrac{55}{5} - (3)^2}}{\sqrt{\dfrac{5}{4}} \sqrt{\dfrac{210}{5} - (6)^2}}$$

$$= 0.924.$$

Test of Significance for r

A value of the statistic r is subject to sampling error. If ρ is actually zero and X and Y vary independently, a value of r other than zero can be obtained due to sampling error. Before the judgment is made whether there is correlation between variables, a test of significance should be made to determine the likelihood that the sample result could have been obtained by chance. This is accomplished by testing the hypothesis that $\rho = 0$; for unless the value of r is significantly different from zero, there is little support for the judgment that X and Y are correlated.

A significance test of r can be performed by computing the statistic

$$t = \frac{r - \rho}{\sigma_r}.$$

The distribution of r is symmetric about $\rho = 0$, but the distribution becomes increasingly skewed as ρ approaches plus or minus one. The standard error of r for the null hypothesis $\rho = 0$ is written

$$\hat{\sigma}_r = \sqrt{\frac{1 - r^2}{n - 2}}.$$

The ratio for testing the null hypothesis is

$$t = \frac{r - 0}{\hat{\sigma}_r}$$

$$= \frac{r}{\sqrt{\dfrac{1 - r^2}{n - 2}}},$$

which may be written

$$t = r \sqrt{\frac{n - 2}{1 - r^2}} \quad\quad\quad\quad\quad\quad\quad\quad\quad (12.21)$$

This statistic has a t distribution with $n - 2$ degrees of freedom.

■ *Example.* The sample correlation coefficient for five paired observations of surfaces machined (*x*) and processing time in hours (*y*) shown in the foregoing example is tested for significance. Assuming the null hypothesis

$$t = r \sqrt{\frac{n - 2}{1 - r^2}}$$

$$= 0.924 \sqrt{\frac{5 - 2}{1 - 0.854}} = 4.19.$$

STEPS:
1. $H_0: \rho = 0$
2. $H_a: \rho \neq 0$
3. An α level of 0.05 requires a t value of ± 3.182.
4. Criterion: Reject H_0 (accept H_a) if $t < -3.182$ or if $t > +3.182$; do not reject H_0 if $t \leq 3.182$.

Since $t(4.19) > t_\alpha(3.182)$, reject H_0; and r is judged to be significant at the 0.05 level.

Appendix M is designed especially for facilitating a test of significance of r assuming the null hypothesis. In the foregoing example the value of $r = 0.924$ is compared with the values in Appendix M for $d.f. = 3$. This comparison shows the sample coefficient of correlation is significant at the 0.05 level, but not at the 0.02 level of significance. This is the same result obtained by the use of t.

RANK CORRELATION

The correlation coefficient r is based on the assumption that the two variables being analyzed are distributed normally. If neither of the variables is normally distributed, correlation analysis can be applied if the variables are expressed as ranked data. In other instances data may be recorded originally in terms of ranks. The ranking of collegiate football teams is familiar to sports fans, and the consistency of the rankings is of interest. As another example, a marketing analyst may wish to determine if the brand preferences of two groups of consumers are consistent. Ranked data are measured on an ordinal scale, and the appropriate measure of the degree of association between variables is obtained from a nonparametric (or distribution-free) method called *rank correlation*. A widely used measure of the correlation between ranked series is a *coefficient of rank correlation* developed by C. Spearman in 1904. This measure is expressed by

$$r_s = 1 - \frac{6\Sigma d^2}{n(n^2 - 1)} \dots\dots\dots\dots\dots\dots\dots(12.22)$$

where
  d is the difference in rank between paired items in a series
  n is the number of pairs of ranked items in a series.

As in the case of the coefficient r, the range of this coefficient is $-1 \le r_s \le 1$.

■ *Example.* Two groups of consumers, each in a different marketing area, were asked to rank brands of coffee in order of preference. The results are as follows:

Brand of coffee	Ranking Group I	Ranking Group II	Difference d	Difference d²
A	2	1	1	1
B	1	3	-2	4
C	3	2	1	1
D	4	4	0	0
E	5	5	0	0
F	6	7	-1	1
G	7	6	1	1
			$\Sigma d = 0$	$\Sigma d^2 = 8$

$$r_s = 1 - \frac{6\Sigma d^2}{n(n^2 - 1)}$$

$$= 1 - \frac{6(8)}{7(49 - 1)} = 1 - \frac{48}{336} = 0.857.$$

The coefficient r_s computed from sample data should be tested for significance, since it is subject to sampling error. The computations for a significance test for small samples are intricate, but testing the null hypothesis is facilitated by use of Table 12.2. This table is similar to Appendix M, and it shows the 0.05 and 0.01 significance levels for r_s for sample sizes of 30 or less.

■ *Example.* The value of $r_s = 0.857$ obtained from the sample of seven paired observations in the previous example is tested for significance by use of Table 12.2. By comparing the computed value of r_s with values in Table 12.2 for a sample size of $n = 7$, it is seen that the value of r_s is significant at the 0.05 level but not at the 0.01 level of significance for a one-tail test.

TABLE 12.2

Significant Levels of r_s for Small Samples*

Sample size n	Significance level (one-tail test)	
	0.05	0.01
4	1.000	
5	.900	1.000
6	.829	.943
7	.714	.893
8	.643	.833
9	.600	.783
10	.564	.746
12	.506	.712
14	.456	.645
16	.425	.601
18	.399	.564
20	.377	.534
22	359	.508
24	.343	.485
26	.329	.465
28	.317	.448
30	.306	.432

* This table is adapted from the work of E. G. Olds, *Annals of Mathematical Statistics*, Vol. 9, pp. 133–48 and Vol. 20, pp. 117–18.

In the preceding example the data are given as ranks. When data are given or recorded in terms of interval or ratio scale measurements (e.g., distance, dollars, enumerations, etc.), the procedure is to rank the items in each set of data according to ascending or descending order of magnitude. The coefficient of rank correlation is then computed on the basis of the ranks of the sets of data.

The derivation of r_s assumes that there are no ties in either or both sets of data. If there are ties in the data, these should be reflected appropriately in the ranks; otherwise, the value of r_s will be overstated. A widely used method for treating ties is to average the ranks that would have occurred had there been no ties and assign these mean values as the ranks for the tied items. This method is appropriate if the number of ties is small. For example, the effect of two or three ties on the value of r_s is usually negligible.

■ **Example.** Scores on an aptitude test and performance rates are recorded for a sample of workers. The original data include a tie in point scores, and a mean value of $(2 + 3)/2 = 2.5$ is assigned to the tied items in the ranked data shown below. The quantity $\Sigma d^2 = 5.5$ is computed for use in Formula 12.22 to obtain $r_s = 1 - 6(5.5)/5(25 - 1) = 0.725$. If r_s were computed without this method for treating ties, the result would be $r_s = 1 - 6(5)/5(25 - 1) = 0.750$, indicating the overstatement of the coefficient.

Original data			Ranked data			Difference	
Worker	Score	Rate	Worker	Score	Rate	d	d^2
A	12	6	A	1	2	−1	1
B	14	5	B	2.5	1	1.5	2.25
C	14	7	C	2.5	3	−0.5	0.25
D	17	10	D	4	5	−1	1
E	18	9	E	5	4	1	1
						$\Sigma d = 0$	$\Sigma d^2 = 5.5$

The sampling distribution of r_s is symmetrical about 0, but it is not normal for small samples. For samples of 10 or more, a significance test can be made using a variation of Formula 12.20

$$t = r_s \sqrt{\frac{n - 2}{1 - r_s^2}} \quad \dots\dots\dots\dots\dots\dots\dots\dots\dots(12.23)$$

where t is distributed with a Student's t for $d.f. = n - 2$.

The sampling distribution of r_s approaches normality as the sample size becomes large. For samples of 20 or more, r_s can be tested for significance by use of the normal distribution and computing the ratio for the null hypothesis

$$z = \frac{r_s - 0}{\sigma_{r_s}} \quad\dots\dots\dots\dots\dots\dots\dots\dots\dots\dots\dots\dots(12.24)$$

where the standard error of r_s is

$$\sigma_{r_s} = \frac{1}{\sqrt{n - 1}}.$$

The necessity for computing the statistics t and z by Formulas 12.23 and 12.24 in a significance test for r_s for samples of 10 or more can be avoided by use of Appendix M. The values in this table correspond to the values of r_s at the 0.05, 0.02, and 0.01 levels of significance. To make a significance test, assuming the null hypothesis, compute r_s by means of Formula 12.22 and compare the result with the values in Appendix M for $d.f. = n - 2$. The procedure for using Appendix M is illustrated in the last example in the previous section on a significance test for r.

TECHNICAL NOTE NO. 1: THE METHOD OF LEAST SQUARES

The *method of least squares* is a method for deriving a linear expression that best fits a series of paired observations. The coefficients a and b derived by this method are maximum likelihood estimators of α and β, the parameters of the true line of regression. There are many lines that could be fitted to a series of data, but the one that fits the data best is that for which the sum of squared estimation errors between the observed values of the dependent variable (y) and the corresponding values of the linear equation (y_c) is a minimum.

Let S denote the sum of squared estimation error for all values of y so that

$$S = \Sigma\epsilon^2$$

where $\epsilon^2 = (y - y_c)^2$. The estimated value of y is written $y_c = a + bx$, and values of a and b are to be derived so that

$$S = \Sigma\epsilon^2 = \Sigma(y - y_c)^2$$
$$= \Sigma(y - a - bx)^2$$

is a minimum. Since there are many lines that could be fitted to a series of data, and each line is defined by particular values of a and b, assume that a and b are variables and that S is a function of these variables, or $S = f(a, b)$. Values of a and b are to be found which jointly make S a minimum. These values are found by minimizing S with respect to a and b, setting the partial derivatives equal to zero, and solving the equations simultaneously. The expression for S can be written

$$S = \Sigma(y - a - bx)^2$$
$$= \Sigma(y^2 - 2ya - 2bxy + a^2 + 2abx + b^2x^2).$$

Minimizing S with respect to a and b gives

$$\frac{\partial S}{\partial a} = -2\Sigma(y - a - bx)$$

and

$$\frac{\partial S}{\partial b} = -2\Sigma(xy - ax - bx^2),$$

respectively. Equating these partials to zero and rearranging terms, the expressions give the *normal equations* for estimating α and β. These equations are

$$\Sigma y = na + b\Sigma x$$
$$\Sigma xy = a\Sigma x + b\Sigma x^2.$$

If x and y are expressed as deviations from the respective means $\bar{x}$ and $\bar{y}$, then $\Sigma x = 0$ and $\Sigma y = 0$. Substituting these expressions into the normal equations and solving for b gives

$$b = \frac{\Sigma(x - \bar{x})(y - \bar{y})}{\Sigma(x - \bar{x})^2}.$$

Performing the multiplications and collecting terms gives

$$b = \frac{n\Sigma xy - (\Sigma x)(\Sigma y)}{n\Sigma x^2 - (\Sigma x)^2}.$$

This expression for b can be substituted into the first normal equation, and solving for a gives

$$a = \frac{\Sigma y}{n} - b\frac{\Sigma x}{n}$$
$$= \bar{y} - b\bar{x}.$$

■ *Example.* The estimators of a and b are derived by the least squares method for five paired observations as follows:

x	y	$(y - a - bx)$	$(y - a - bx)^2$	xy
2	1	$1 - a - 2b$	$1 - 2a - 4b + a^2 + 4ab + 4b^2$	2
4	2	$2 - a - 4b$	$4 - 4a - 16b + a^2 + 8ab + 16b^2$	8
5	3	$3 - a - 5b$	$9 - 6a - 30b + a^2 + 10ab + 25b^2$	15
6	4	$4 - a - 6b$	$16 - 8a - 48b + a^2 + 12ab + 36b^2$	24
8	5	$5 - a - 8b$	$25 - 10a - 80b + a^2 + 16ab + 64b^2$	40
25	15	$15 - 5a - 25b$	$55 - 30a - 178b + 5a^2 + 50ab + 145b^2$	89

$$\frac{\partial S}{\partial a} = -2\Sigma(y - a - bx) = 0$$
$$= -2(\Sigma y - na - b\Sigma x) = 0$$
$$= -30 + 10a + 50b = 0$$
$$= 15 - 5a - 25b = 0$$

$$\frac{\partial S}{\partial b} = -2\Sigma(xy - ax - bx^2) = 0$$
$$= -2(\Sigma xy - a\Sigma x - b\Sigma x^2) = 0$$
$$= -178 + 50a + 290b = 0$$
$$= 89 - 25a - 145b = 0.$$

Solving the last expressions of the partials (the normal equations) simultaneously for b gives

$$b = \frac{n\Sigma xy - (\Sigma x)(\Sigma y)}{n\Sigma x^2 - (\Sigma x)^2}$$
$$= \frac{(5)(89) - (25)(15)}{(5)(145) - (25)^2}$$
$$= \frac{70}{100}$$
$$= 0.7,$$

and

$$a = \bar{y} - b\bar{x}$$
$$= 3 - 0.7(5)$$
$$= -0.5.$$

STUDY QUESTIONS

12-1. Explain briefly the meaning of each of the following terms:
- a. regression
- b. correlation
- c. analysis by association
- d. scatter diagram
- e. line of average relationship
- f. line of conditional means
- g. bivariate regression surface
- h. least squares regression line
- i. homoscedastic
- j. heteroscedastic
- k. estimated regression of Y on X
- l. standard error of the estimate
- m. cross product
- n. covariance
- o. universe coefficient of correlation
- p. universe coefficient of determination
- q. universe coefficient of nondetermination
- r. sample coefficient of correlation
- s. rank correlation

12-2. What is meant by analysis by association?

12-3. How can statistics be used in deciding whether a causal relationship exists between two variables?

12-4. Why is a line of regression called a line of conditional means?

12-5. What is the purpose of a scatter diagram?

12-6. Describe what is meant by the method of least squares.

12-7. Upon what assumptions is the linear regression model based?

12-8. Describe the sampling problems in regression analysis.

12-9. Why should a test of significance be used in interpreting sample regression results?

12-10. Contrast regression analysis and correlation analysis.

12-11. What is the relationship between the correlation coefficient r and the regression coefficient b?

12-12. Describe the problem of sampling in correlation analysis.

12-13. Why is rank correlation called a nonparametric method?

PROBLEMS

12-1. The following data for work force size and production output was taken for a sample period:

Work force size x	Production output y
1	5
1	6
2	6
2	7
2	8
3	7
3	8
4	8
4	9
5	9

a. Plot a scatter diagram of the data.
b. Compute the least squares line of regression for the sample data.
c. Compute a point estimate of production output for a work force size of seven.
d. What is the 95% interval estimate of production output if the work force size is six and the data are homoscedastic?
e. Test the regression coefficient b for significance at the 0.01 level.

12-2. A department store chain collected data on advertising expenditure and sales volume from a sample of its stores. The sample data are as follows:

Advertising expenditure ($10,000)	Sales volume ($100,000)
x	y
3.8	3.4
4.4	3.9
4.6	4.5
2.5	2.9
6.2	5.4
4.2	4.4
3.0	3.6
5.1	4.7

a. Plot a scatter diagram of the data.
b. Compute the least squares line of regression for the data.
c. Compute a point estimate of sales if advertising expenditure is $38,000.
d. What is the 95% interval estimate of sales if advertising expenditure is $67,000 and the data are homoscedastic?
e. Test the regression coefficient b for significance at the 0.05 level.

12-3. Compute the correlation coefficient for Problem 12–1 and test it for significance at the 0.01 level.

12-4. Compute the correlation coefficient for Problem 12–2 and test it for significance at the 0.05 level.

12-5. In a study of the effectiveness of a disinfectant, the following sample data for percent of disinfectant in a water solution and bacteria count on surfaces cleaned with each solution were taken:

Solution percent	Bacteria count
x	y
1	31
2	25
3	28
4	22
5	14
5	24
6	23
6	15
7	18
8	13

a. Plot a scatter diagram of the data.
b. Estimate the regression of bacteria count on solution percent.
c. Use a 0.05 level of significance to test b.
d. Compute the 95% interval estimate of bacteria count for a solution percent of 9%. Assume homoscedasticity.

12–6. A time-study analyst observes a packaging operation and collects data of package volume and time required for the operation. A sample of observations recorded during the packaging operation is as follows:

Volume (*in cubic feet*)	Time (*in seconds*)
x	*y*
1.42	23.6
0.75	11.1
0.82	13.5
1.20	19.4
0.64	10.9
1.12	18.1
1.08	15.4
0.49	7.9
1.05	14.4

a. Plot a scatter diagram of the data.
b. Estimate the regression of operation time on package volume.
c. Compute the estimated standard error of the estimate.
d. Use a 0.05 level of significance to test the significance of *b*.
e. Compute the 95% interval estimate of the operation time for a package volume of 1.15 cubic feet. Assume homoscedasticity.

12–7. Using the results obtained for Problem 12–5 and assuming the data are heteroscedastic, compute the 95% confidence interval estimate of bacteria count for a 1% solution.

12–8. Using the results obtained for Problem 12–6 and assuming that the sample data are heteroscedastic, compute:
a. The 95% confidence interval estimate of the mean value of operation time for a package volume of 1.15 cubic feet.
b. The 95% confidence interval estimate of operation time for a package volume of 1.15 cubic feet.

12–9. A sample of data is taken from the maintenance records of nearly identical machines in a study of the relationship that may exist between the age of machines and maintenance cost during the period of time. The results are as follows:

Age (*years*)	Maintenance cost (*dollars*)	Age (*years*)	Maintenance cost (*dollars*)
x	*y*	*x*	*y*
3	39	6	90
1	24	9	140
5	115	3	112
8	105	5	70
1	50	7	186
4	86	2	43
2	67	6	126

a. Plot a scatter diagram of the data.
b. Fit a least squares line of regression to the data.
c. Compute a point estimate of maintenance cost for a machine four years of age.
d. Find the 95% interval estimate of maintenance cost for a machine six years of age, assuming the data are homoscedastic.
e. Test the regression coefficient b for significance at the 0.05 level.

12-10. A statistician interested in a possible relationship between the population and total employment of cities of 10,000 or more in a certain section of the country collected a sample of data as follows:

Employment (thousands)	Population (thousands)
x	y
38.2	107.1
35.0	94.0
35.3	98.7
68.9	185.6
23.0	55.2
41.4	112.9
186.5	582.8
57.5	166.3
28.2	61.4
284.7	680.2
5.1	15.2
89.1	296.4
28.9	83.0
183.6	386.5
47.8	127.8
24.5	62.7
366.3	958.3
16.1	51.6

a. Determine if the regression of population on total employment is significant.
b. Is there a significant degree of correlation between the variables?
c. Are the regression and correlation models appropriate representations of the relationship between the variables? (Consider the assumptions of each of the models.)

12-11. Compute the correlation coefficient for Problem 12-5 and test it for significance at the 0.05 level.

12-12. Compute the correlation coefficient for Problem 12-6 and test it for significance at the 0.05 level.

12-13. The number of employees and sales for a sample of eight retail stores are as follows:

Store	Number of employees	Sales
1	15	21
2	12	22
3	10	17
4	9	20
5	12	18
6	10	19
7	19	35
8	8	15

Compute the coefficient of rank correlation and determine if it is significant.

12-14. Using the data for Problem 12–13, compute the coefficient of rank correlation without adjusting for ties and compare the result with that of Problem 12–13.

12-15. Two managers are asked to rank a group of employees in order of potential for eventually becoming top managers. The rankings are as follows:

Employee	Ranking by Manager I	Ranking by Manager II
Rogers	1	4
Black	2	5
Jones	3	7
Rivera	4	2
Smith	5	3
Edwards	6	1
Ling	7	6
Evans	8	8
Roberts	9	9
Goldberg	10	13
Brown	11	17
Thomas	12	19
Gray	13	18
Clark	14	10
James	15	14
Martin	16	20
Diaz	17	11
Richards	18	15
West	19	12
Short	20	16

Compute the coefficient of rank correlation and determine if it is significant.

12-16. Five contestants are ranked by two judges with these results:

Contestant	Judge I	Judge II
A	1	2
B	2	4
C	4	1
D	3	5
E	5	3

Determine if there is a significant degree of correlation between the rankings of the judges.

12-17. The rankings of collegiate basketball teams are as follows:

College	Panel I	Panel II
UCLA	1	1
Maryland	2	3
Marquette	3	2
Long Beach State	4	5
North Carolina State	5	6
Minnesota	6	4
Missouri	7	8
North Carolina	8	9
Southwestern Louisiana	9	12
Houston	10	7
Vanderbilt	11	10
San Francisco	12	11
Providence	13	17
New Mexico	14	14
Alabama	15	16
Brigham Young	16	13
Pennsylvania	17	20
Kansas State	18	15
Florida State	19	19
Indiana	20	18

a. Compute r_s.
b. Compute the standard error of r_s and use it to test r_s for significance.

SELECTED READINGS

Hamburg, Morris. *Statistical Analysis for Decision Making.* New York: Harcourt, Brace and World, Inc., 1970.

    Concepts of regression and correlation are presented in Chapter 10.

Richmond, Samuel B. *Statistical Analysis,* 2d ed. New York: The Ronald Press Company, 1964.

    An introductory treatment of regression and correlation is presented in Chapter 19.

Stockton, John R., and Charles T. Clark. *Introduction to Business and Economic Statistics,* 5th ed. Cincinnati: South-Western Publishing Co., 1975. Chapter 11 introduces regression and correlation.

Chapter 13
Regression and Correlation— Curvilinear and Multivariate Analysis

The bivariate relationship of variables can be approximated by a line drawn on a scatter diagram that represents the average relationship of paired observations. In many instances the average relationship may be represented appropriately by a straight line. In other cases the scatter of paired observations suggests a curvilinear (nonlinear) average relationship that is not well represented by a straight line. The greater the degree to which a bivariate relationship differs from linearity, the more inappropriate are linear regression and correlation models for representing the relationship. If the average relationship of two variables is distinctly curvilinear, the application of linear regression and correlation models will yield poor results.

The variation of a dependent variable, in most instances, however, results from the interaction and effects of two or more independent variables. This type of relationship is best described by *multivariate* (several variables) rather than bivariate regression and correlation models. A much higher portion of the variation of the dependent variable may be associated (explained) if this variation is analyzed jointly with that of two or more independent variables.

Regression and correlation models for analyzing nonlinear bivariate and multivariate relationships are derived by means of the method of least squares. The rationale used in the derivation of the linear models in the foregoing chapter is used in this chapter in the derivation of curvilinear and multivariate regression and correlation models.

CURVILINEAR BIVARIATE REGRESSION

An expression that has the functional form such as that of a linear bivariate regression equation is called a *first-order polynomial* equation. The term, first-order, refers to a linear expression such as

$$y_c = a + bx$$

where x is of the first degree or order. A curvilinear (nonlinear) expression may take the form of a higher order polynomial such as

$$y_c = a + bx + cx^2$$

where x^2 is of the second degree or order. This equation expresses the nonlinear relationship between the variables x and y.

Nonlinear relationships may also be expressed by equations involving transformations, such as with logarithms or reciprocals. These transformations are used to convert data into a form in which the relationship between two series of data may be considered linear. The techniques for using polynomials and transformations in nonlinear regression analysis are considered in the discussions that follow.

Polynomial Regression

In many applications of regression analysis, the relationship between two variables is curvilinear and is assumed to be a polynomial function. The general form of a polynomial expression of the estimated nonlinear regression of y on x obtained from sample data is written

$$y_c = a + bx + cx^2 + \ldots + rx^q$$

where q indicates the order or degree of the polynomial. The coefficients in this expression are maximum likelihood estimators of the respective parameters. The values of these estimators are obtained by the method of least squares.

Second-Order Polynomial Regression

A scatter diagram of paired sample observations of two variables may indicate that a parabola is a more appropriate expression of the relationship between the variables than a straight line.

■ *Example.* A sample of observations of the volume of production and the size of work force in a small manufacturing firm is taken. The data are shown in Table 13.1 and are plotted in Figure 13.1, page 412. The linear regression of production volume (y) on work force size (x) is computed as follows:

$$b = \frac{n\Sigma xy - (\Sigma x)(\Sigma y)}{n\Sigma x^2 - (\Sigma x)^2}$$

$$a = \bar{y} - b\bar{x}$$
$$= 7.83 - 0.17(5.21)$$
$$= 6.94.$$

$$= \frac{(24)(1,007) - (125)(188)}{(24)(815) - (125)^2}$$

$$= \frac{668}{3,935} = 0.17.$$

$$\hat{\sigma}_{yx} = \sqrt{\frac{\Sigma y^2 - a\Sigma y - b\Sigma xy}{n - 2}}$$

$$= \sqrt{\frac{1{,}508 - (6.94)(188) - (0.17)(1{,}007)}{24 - 2}} = \sqrt{\frac{32.1}{22}} = 1.21.$$

$$r = \frac{n\Sigma xy - (\Sigma x)(\Sigma y)}{\sqrt{[n\Sigma x^2 - (\Sigma x)^2][n\Sigma y^2 - (\Sigma y)^2]}}$$

$$= \frac{24(1{,}007) - (125)(188)}{\sqrt{[(24)(815) - (125)^2\,[(24)(1{,}508) - (188)^2]}}$$

$$= 0.37.$$

TABLE 13.1

Data for Curvilinear Regression of Production Volume(y) on Work Force Size(x)

x	y	x^2	y^2	xy	x^2y	x^3	x^4
1	5	1	25	5	5	1	1
1	6	1	36	6	6	1	1
2	6	4	36	12	24	8	16
2	7	4	49	14	28	8	16
2	8	4	64	16	32	8	16
3	7	9	49	21	63	27	81
3	8	9	64	24	72	27	81
4	7	16	49	28	112	64	256
4	8	16	64	32	128	64	256
4	9	16	81	36	144	64	256
5	8	25	64	40	200	125	625
5	9	25	81	45	225	125	625
5	10	25	100	50	250	125	625
6	8	36	64	48	288	216	1,296
6	9	36	81	54	324	216	1,296
6	10	36	100	60	360	216	1,296
7	8	49	64	56	392	343	2,401
7	9	49	81	63	441	343	2,401
8	7	64	49	56	448	512	4,096
8	8	64	64	64	512	512	4,096
8	9	64	81	72	576	512	4,096
9	7	81	49	63	567	729	6,561
9	8	81	64	72	648	729	6,561
10	7	100	49	70	700	1,000	10,000
125	188	815	1,508	1,007	6,545	5,975	46,955

The estimated line of regression is plotted in Figure 13.1. The fit of the linear regression line to the data is poor. A second-order polynomial fitted to the data provides a more appropriate model. In a later section of this chapter the hypothesis that the second-order model provides a better fit is tested for significance.

FIGURE 13.1

**First- and Second-Order Polynomial Regression
Equations Fitted to Data of Production Volume (y)
and Work Force Size (x)**

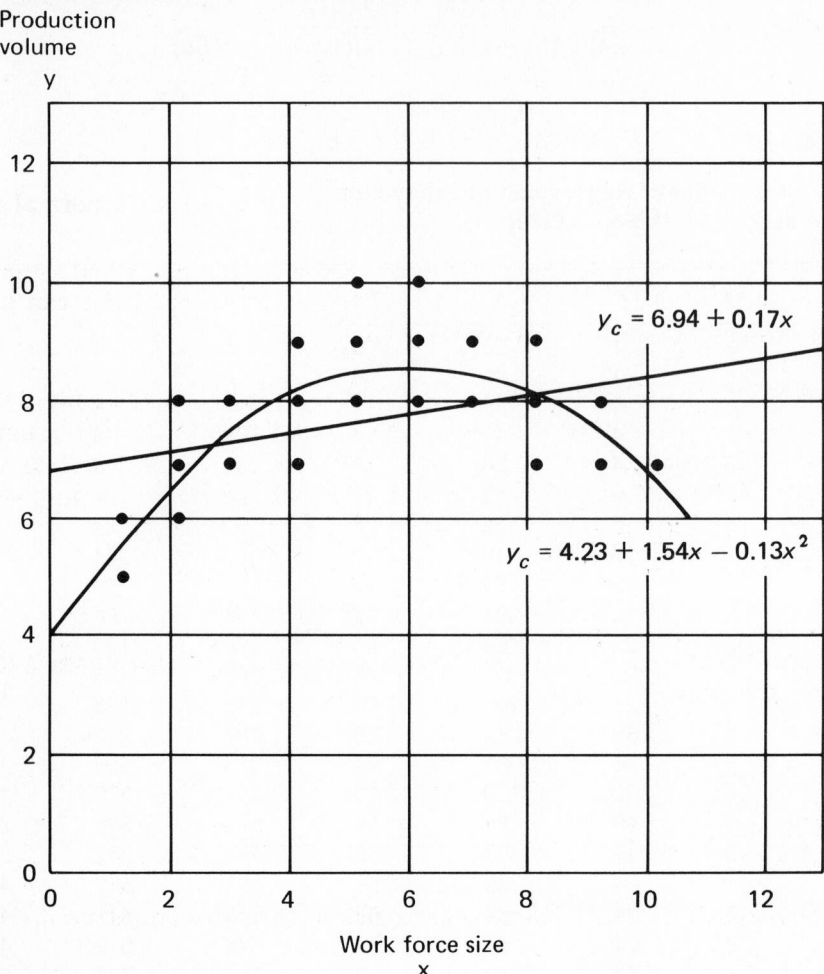

Production
volume
y

$y_c = 6.94 + 0.17x$

$y_c = 4.23 + 1.54x - 0.13x^2$

Work force size
x

The Method of Least Squares and Polynomial Regression. The simplest parabola is a second-order polynomial regression equation, which is written

$$y_c = a + bx + cx^2 \dots\dots\dots\dots\dots\dots\dots\dots\dots(13.1)$$

The coefficients of this expression are estimators which are found by solving a set of simultaneous equations. These equations are obtained by the method of least squares in a manner similar to that presented in Technical Note No. 1 of Chapter 12. The simultaneous normal equations are derived by expressing the sum of squared deviations of the dependent variable about a regression line as a function of the coefficients a, b, and c. First-order partial derivatives of the function (sum of squared deviations) with respect to a, b, and c are taken and set equal to zero. The three resulting expressions are the normal equations for the second-order polynomial case, and are written

$$\begin{aligned}
\text{I.} \quad & \Sigma y = na + b\Sigma x + c\Sigma x^2 \\
\text{II.} \quad & \Sigma xy = a\Sigma x + b\Sigma x^2 + c\Sigma x^3 \\
\text{III.} \quad & \Sigma x^2 y = a\Sigma x^2 + b\Sigma x^3 + c\Sigma x^4.
\end{aligned}$$

Note that these equations are related in form to the first-order normal equations.

The estimators a, b, and c are found by solving the normal equations simultaneously. The simultaneous solution of these equations can be accomplished by the method of elimination.

■ *Example.* A second-order polynomial or parabola can be fitted to the sample data plotted in Figure 13.1 by solving the normal equations simultaneously for the estimators a, b, and c. The appropriate totals from Table 13.1 are substituted into the normal equations to give

$$\begin{aligned}
\text{I.} \quad & 188 = 24a + 125b + 815c \\
\text{II.} \quad & 1{,}007 = 125a + 815b + 5{,}975c \\
\text{III.} \quad & 6{,}545 = 815a + 5{,}975b + 46{,}955c.
\end{aligned}$$

Equations I and II are solved simultaneously by eliminating the a terms as follows:

$\left(-\dfrac{125}{24} \text{ times I}\right)$ $\qquad -979.17 = -125a - 651.04b - 4{,}244.79c$

(Equation II) $\qquad\qquad\qquad 1{,}007.00 = \quad 125a + 815.00b + 5{,}975.00c$

(Equations I + II) $\qquad\qquad\quad 27.83 = \qquad\qquad\quad 163.96b + 1{,}730.21c$

Similarly, Equations II and III are solved simultaneously as follows:

$\left(-\dfrac{815}{125} \text{ times II}\right)$ $\qquad -6{,}565.64 = -815a - 5{,}313.80b - 38{,}957.00c$

(Equation III) $\qquad\qquad\qquad 6{,}545.00 = \quad 815a + 5{,}975.00b + 46{,}955.00c$

(Equations II + III) $\qquad\qquad -20.64 = \qquad\qquad\quad 661.20b + \quad 7{,}998.00c$

The equations that result from the elimination of the a terms are solved for the value of b as follows:

(Equations II + III) $\qquad\qquad\qquad\qquad -20.64 = \quad 661.20b + 7{,}998.00c$

$\left(-\dfrac{7{,}998.00}{1{,}730.21} \text{ times I + II}\right)$ $\qquad -128.64 = -757.91b - 7{,}998.00c$

$\qquad\qquad\qquad\qquad\qquad\qquad\qquad -149.28 = \quad -96.71b$

$\qquad\qquad\qquad\qquad\qquad\qquad\qquad\qquad\qquad\quad b = 1.54.$

The value of b is substituted into Equation (I + II) to give

$$27.83 = (163.96)(1.54) + 1{,}730.21c$$
$$c = -0.13.$$

Finally, the value of a is found by substituting b and c into Equation I to give

$$188.00 = 24.00a + (125.00)(1.54) + (815.00)(-0.13)$$
$$a = 4.23.$$

The second-order polynomial regression equation is written

$$y_c = 4.23 + 1.54x - 0.13x^2.$$

This equation is plotted in Figure 13.1, and visual inspection suggests that the second-order polynomial regression equation is a more appropriate model than the first-order (linear) model.

Estimated Standard Error of the Estimate. The universe standard error of the estimate for the second-order polynomial regression equation can be estimated from sample data. An unbiased estimator of the universe standard error of the estimate is written

$$\hat{\sigma}_{y.xx^2} = \sqrt{\frac{\Sigma(y - y_c)^2}{n - 3}} \quad\text{.............................(13.2)}$$

where $n - 3$ represents the number of degrees of freedom. The loss of three degrees of freedom results from the use of a, b, and c as estimators of the respective universe parameters. An alternative form of Formula 13.2, which is better suited to manual computation, is written

$$\hat{\sigma}_{y.xx^2} = \sqrt{\frac{\Sigma y^2 - a\Sigma y - b\Sigma xy - c\Sigma x^2 y}{n - 3}} \quad\text{.................(13.3)}$$

where the subscript $y.xx^2$ denotes the regression of y on x and x^2.

■ *Example.* The estimated standard error of the estimate for the data in Table 13.1 is computed by use of Formula 13.3 as

$$\hat{\sigma}_{y.xx^2} = \sqrt{\frac{1{,}508 - (4.23)(188) - (1.54)(1{,}007) - (-0.13)(6{,}545)}{24 - 3}}$$

$$= \sqrt{\frac{12.8}{21}} = 0.78.$$

This value, when compared with $\hat{\sigma}_{yx} = 1.21$ for the linear regression model, indicates that the second-order regression model provides more reliable estimates of the dependent variable.

Computers and Polynomial Regression

The selection of the polynomial expression that provides the most suitable representation of the regression between two variables can be obtained by:

(1) computing successively higher order polynomial regression equations (first order, second order, third order, etc.) for the data, (2) obtaining the standard error of the estimate for each regression equation, and (3) selecting the equation for which the standard error is a minimum. If approached manually, the calculations required for applying this technique can be prohibitive. The computational capability of a computer, however, makes this technique feasible for most problems.

Normal Equations for Higher Order Polynomials. The normal equations for a second-order polynomial regression equation can be obtained from the normal equations of the first-order (linear) polynomial. The normal equations for the second-order polynomial are

$$
\begin{array}{ll}
\text{I.} & \Sigma y \ \ = na \ \ + b\Sigma x \ + c\Sigma x^2 \\
\text{II.} & \Sigma xy = a\Sigma x \ + b\Sigma x^2 + c\Sigma x^3 \\
\text{III.} & \Sigma x^2 y = a\Sigma x^2 + b\Sigma x^3 + c\Sigma x^4
\end{array}
$$

The terms within the rectangle are the normal equations for the first-order polynomial. The normal equations for the second-degree polynomial are obtained in the following manner. Add the $c\Sigma x^2$ term to the first normal equation for the linear case to obtain Equation I. Increase by one degree the power of x in each summation in Equation I to give Equation II. Similarly, increase the power of x in each summation in Equation I by two degrees to obtain Equation III.

The normal equations for the third-order polynomial are derived from those of the second-order case as follows. Add the terms $d\Sigma x^3$ to Equation I, $d\Sigma x^4$ to Equation II, and $d\Sigma x^5$ to Equation III. Since these equations involve four unknowns, a fourth normal equation is required to obtain the solution. This equation is obtained by increasing the power of x in each of the summations in Equation III. The equations that result from these modifications are written

$$
\begin{array}{ll}
\text{I.} & \Sigma y \ \ = na \ \ + b\Sigma x \ + c\Sigma x^2 + d\Sigma x^3 \\
\text{II.} & \Sigma xy = a\Sigma x \ + b\Sigma x^2 + c\Sigma x^3 + d\Sigma x^4 \\
\text{III.} & \Sigma x^2 y = a\Sigma x^2 + b\Sigma x^3 + c\Sigma x^4 + d\Sigma x^5 \\
\text{IV.} & \Sigma x^3 y = a\Sigma x^3 + b\Sigma x^4 + c\Sigma x^5 + d\Sigma x^6
\end{array}
$$

The second-order normal equations are shown within the rectangle. The four equations can be solved simultaneously to obtain the third-order polynomial regression coefficients. The normal equations for higher order polynomials can be obtained in a similar manner.

An Approach to the Selection of a Polynomial Regression Equation. One approach to the selection of the most suitable polynomial regression equation for observations of two variables consists of computing the regression equation and standard error of the estimate for several polynomial cases. The most appropriate regression equation is that for which the standard error is a minimum.

This type of algorithm is sometimes called a polynomial curve fit program. Programs of this type are commonly available in computer program libraries.

Transformations in Bivariate Regression

If the regression of one variable on another is curvilinear, the values of one or both of the variables may be changed to a form that is linear. This change is accomplished by transforming the data. The most commonly used transformations are logarithms in exponential regression and reciprocals in hyperbolic regression. The transformation converts the data into such form that the relationship between a converted series and an original series may be considered linear.

■ *Example.* A sample of observations of the total cost of production and number of units produced in a manufacturing firm is taken. The data are shown in Table 13.2 and are plotted in Figure 13.2. The plot of the original data in Figure 13.2 reflects the curvilinear relationship of the variables. The total cost data are transformed by use of logarithms, and the plot of this converted series with the original output data is shown in Figure 13.3, page 418. The scatter of the points is approximately linear.

TABLE 13.2

Seven Observations of Total Cost and Total Output of a Manufacturing Firm

Observation number	Total output (units) x	Total cost (thousands) y
1	27	$ 62
2	58	68
3	106	102
4	124	127
5	153	184
6	172	217
7	194	264

The transformation of the total cost (y) values in the foregoing example yields the data required for the use of the normal equations. The relationship of the logarithms of the y values to the original values of x is approximately linear, as shown in Figure 13.3. These series of data provide the data for substitution into the linear normal equations to solve for the coefficients of the estimated regression equation.

FIGURE 13.2

**A Sample of Observations of Volume of Output
and Corresponding Total Cost of Production**

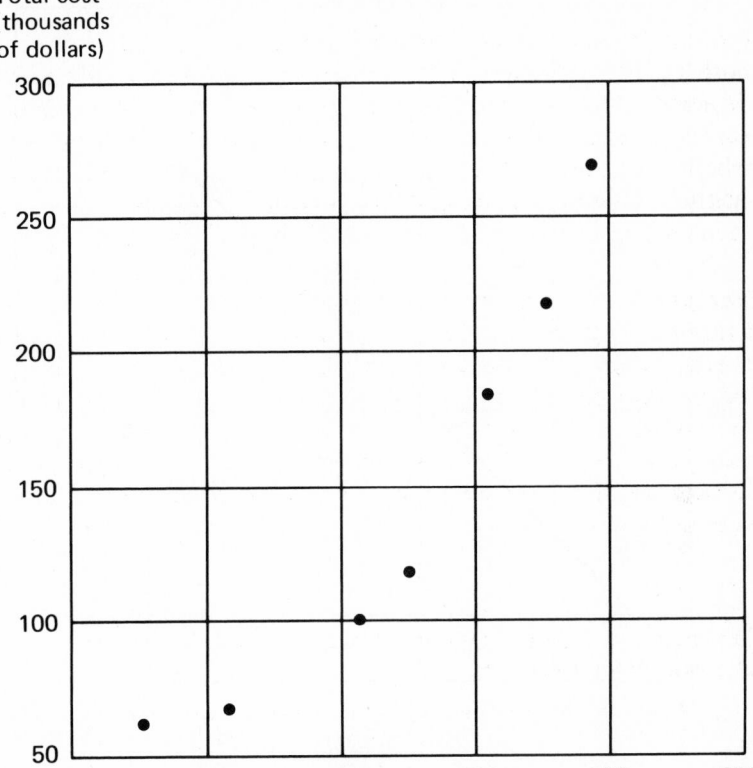

Exponential Regression. The simplest case, *first-degree exponential regression,* involves two series of data, one of which is transformed by use of logarithms. For example, the dependent variable, transformed by logarithms, may be regressed on the untransformed independent variable to give a regression equation with the functional form

$$y_c = ab^x.$$

The linear form of the regression equation is written

$$\log y_c = \log a + x \log b \ldots\ldots\ldots\ldots\ldots\ldots(13.4)$$

The estimators of the regression coefficients are found by solving simultaneously the normal equations

FIGURE 13.3

A Plot of the Logarithms of Total Cost and Volume of Output

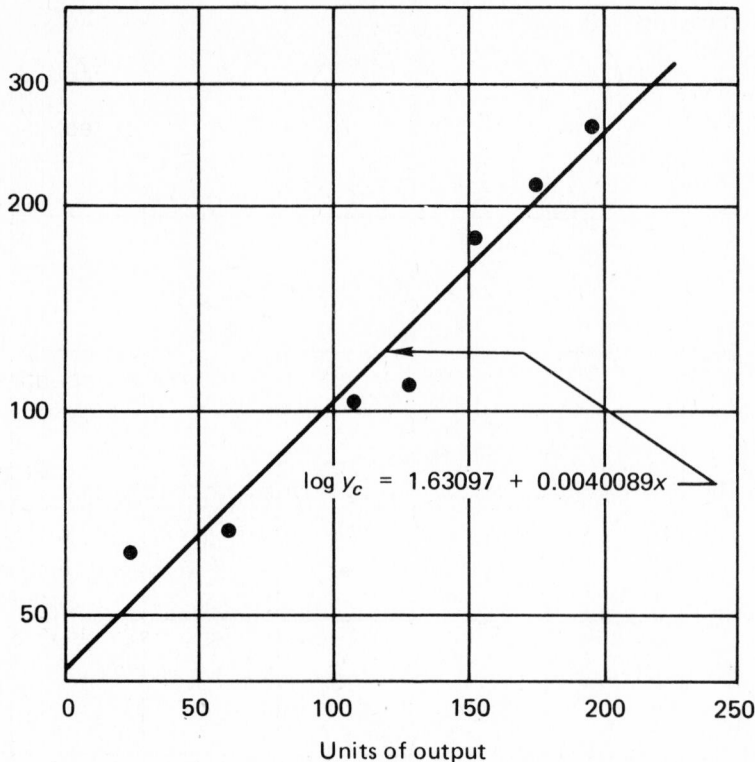

Total cost
(log scale)

$\log y_c = 1.63097 + 0.0040089x$

Units of output

I. $\Sigma(\log y) = n \log a + \log b \Sigma x$

II. $\Sigma(x \log y) = \log a \Sigma x + \log b \Sigma x^2$.

An unbiased estimator of the standard error of the estimate is written

$$\hat{\sigma}_{\log y.x} = \sqrt{\frac{\Sigma(\log y - \log y_c)^2}{n-2}} \dots\dots\dots\dots\dots(13.5)$$

■ *Example.* An exponential regression equation is fitted to the data in Table 13.2 by transforming the observed values of total cost (*y*) by the use of logarithms and by solving the normal equations. The data substituted into these equations are shown in Table 13.3. The equations are solved as follows:

I. $14.76018 = 7 \log a + 834 \log b$

II. $1{,}846.64189 = 834 \log a + 121{,}334 \log b$

$$\left(-\frac{834}{7} \text{ times I}\right) -1{,}758.57002 = -834 \log a - 99{,}365 \log b$$

$$\text{(II)} \quad \underline{1{,}846.64189 = 834 \log a + 121{,}334 \log b}$$
$$88.07187 = \qquad\qquad 21{,}969 \log b$$

$$\log b = \frac{88.07187}{21{,}969} = 0.0040089$$

$$\log a = \frac{14.76018 - 834(0.0040089)}{7} = 1.63097.$$

The estimated standard error of the estimate is computed

$$\hat{\sigma}_{\log\, y.x} = \sqrt{\frac{0.007456}{7-2}} = 0.03862.$$

The regression equation

$$\log y_c = \log a \quad + x \log b$$
$$= 1.63097 + 0.0040089x$$

is plotted in Figure 13.3. The exponential regression equation provides a very good representation of the relationship between x and y.

It is important to note that the minimum sum of squared deviations obtained by use of the normal equations relates to the deviations of the *logarithms* of total cost (y) about the regression line and not to the minimum sum of squared deviations of the actual data (y) about the regression line. Expected values of y are obtained by computing $\log y_c$ for given values of x and taking the antilog of the result. The expected value of y, given $x = 150$, in the foregoing example, is computed

$$E(\log y \mid x = 150) = 1.63097 + (0.0040089)(150)$$
$$= 2.23230$$

TABLE 13.3

**Calculations for the Exponential Regression
of Total Cost on Total Output**

Total output x	Total cost y	log y	x log y	x^2	log y_c	$(\log y - \log y_c)^2$
27	62	1.79239	48.39453	729	1.73921	0.002828
58	68	1.83251	106.28558	3,364	1.86349	0.000960
106	102	2.00860	212.91160	11,236	2.05591	0.002238
124	127	2.10380	260.87120	15,376	2.12807	0.000589
153	184	2.26482	346.51746	23,409	2,24433	0.000420
172	217	2.33646	401.87112	29,584	2.32050	0.000255
194	264	2.42160	469.79040	37,636	2.40870	0.000166
834	1,024	14.76018	1,846.64189	121,334	...	0.007456

$$E(y \mid x = 150) = \text{antilog } 2.23230$$
$$= 170.7.$$

Other Transformations. Exponential regression may also involve the regression of the logarithmic transformation of both variables. The regression equation for this case has the functional form $y_c = ax^b$. The linear form of the regression of the regression equation is written $\log y_c = \log a + b \log x$. The coefficients for this equation are found by solving simultaneously the normal equations in the logarithms of the data of both variables. The standard error of the estimate is found in a manner analogous to that described in the previous section.

A wide variety of other transformations can be used to obtain regression equations that best fit bivariate relationships. Some examples of these transformations include complex exponential forms, reciprocals, trigonometric functions, and product forms. In each case, the coefficients of the regression equation are found by solving appropriate normal equations.

CURVILINEAR BIVARIATE CORRELATION

The coefficient of correlation is a measure of the extent to which two variables are related linearly. If the relationship of two variables is distinctly curvilinear (nonlinear), the application of linear correlation methods is not likely to yield a good representation of the extent to which the variables are related. The appropriate measure of the correlation of two variables that are related curvilinearly is called the *index of correlation*. Similarly, the coefficient that reflects the degree of nonlinear determination is called the *index of determination*. These two measures are analogous to the coefficients of correlation and determination for bivariate linear correlation analysis.

The indexes of correlation and determination are based on the ratio of the associated sum of squared deviations to the total sum of squared deviations. The derivation of these indexes is similar to that presented in Chapter 12, which described the derivation of the correlation and determination coefficients for the linear case. Indexes of correlation and determination for bivariate curvilinear relationships, including polynomial and exponential functions, are presented in this chapter.

Polynomial Correlation

Second-Order Polynomial Correlation. The index of determination for the second-order polynomial case is the ratio

$$I^2_{y.xx^2} = \frac{\text{total sum of squares} - \text{unassociated sum of squares}}{\text{total sum of squares}}$$

$$= \frac{\Sigma(y - \bar{y})^2 - \Sigma(y - y_c)^2}{\Sigma(y - \bar{y})^2}.$$

An algebraically equivalent expression of this statement is obtained by completing the squares and collecting terms to give

$$I^2_{y.xx^2} = \frac{a\Sigma y + b\Sigma xy + c\Sigma x^2 y - n\bar{y}^2}{\Sigma y^2 - n\bar{y}^2} \dots\dots\dots\dots\dots(13.6)$$

The index of correlation is the square root of the index of determination.

■ **Example.** The index of determination for the data in Table 13.1 is obtained by substituting the appropriate values into Formula 13.6 and solving to give

$$I^2_{y.xx^2} = \frac{4.227(188) + 1.544(1,007) - 0.130(6,545) - 24(7.833)^2}{1,508.000 - 1,472.541}$$

$$= 0.736.$$

The values of *a*, *b*, and *c* used in the preceding computation include three decimal digits to provide greater accuracy in computing the value of the index. The index of correlation is found by solving for

$$I_{y.xx^2} = \sqrt{I^2_{y.xx^2}}$$

$$= \sqrt{0.736} = 0.858.$$

The value of this index is somewhat larger than the value $r = 0.37$ obtained in the linear correlation analysis of the data in Table 13.1. This result indicates that the second-degree polynomial regression model is a better representation of the bivariate relationship than is the linear model.

Higher Order Polynomial Correlation. The index of determination for polynomials of orders greater than two can be obtained by extending Formula 13.6.

■ **Example.** The index of determination for the third-order polynomial case is written

$$I^2_{y.xx^2x^3} = \frac{a\Sigma y + b\Sigma xy + c\Sigma x^2 y + d\ \Sigma x^3 y - n\bar{y}}{\Sigma y^2 - n\bar{y}^2}.$$

Significance Test for an Index of Determination. The selection of a polynomial regression equation may be approached by making a test of significance to determine if an index of determination is significantly greater than that obtained for a polynomial of the next lower order. For example, suppose one wishes to determine if the associated sum of squares for a second-order polynomial is significantly greater than the associated sum of squares for the first-order polynomial. One would test to see if the addition of the x^2 term in the regression increases the associated sum of squares by a greater amount than that which is expected to be obtained by chance.

This test is made by computing the proportion of unassociated sum of squares for the first-order polynomial regression that is associated with the addition of x^2 in the second-order regression and determining whether the proportion is significantly greater than that which could be obtained by chance. The proportionate increase in associated sum of squares is written

$$
\begin{bmatrix} \text{proportion of total sum of squares} \\ \text{not associated with linear regression} \\ \text{which is associated with the} \\ \text{addition of } x^2. \end{bmatrix} = \frac{\begin{bmatrix} \text{second-order associated} \\ \text{sum of squares} \end{bmatrix} - \begin{bmatrix} \text{first-order associated} \\ \text{sum of squares} \end{bmatrix}}{\begin{bmatrix} \text{total sum of} \\ \text{squares} \end{bmatrix} - \begin{bmatrix} \text{first-order associated} \\ \text{sum of squares} \end{bmatrix}}.
$$

The sum of squares may be expressed as a ratio to the total sum of squares by writing

$$
r^2_{y.x^2.x} = \frac{I^2_{y.xx^2} - r^2}{1 - r^2} \quad\dots\dots\dots\dots\dots\dots\dots\dots(13.7)
$$

where $r^2_{y.x^2.x}$ is the proportion of the unassociated sum of squares for the first-order polynomial that is associated with the addition of x^2 as an independent variable. This proportion is called the *index of partial determination.*

The index of partial determination can be tested for significance by computing the statistic

$$
t = \sqrt{\frac{r^2_{y.x^2.x}(n-3)}{1 - r^2_{y.x^2.x}}} \quad\dots\dots\dots\dots\dots\dots\dots\dots(13.8)
$$

This statistic has a t distribution with $n - 3$ degrees of freedom and is analogous to the statistic expressed by Formula 12.21.

■ *Example.* The data in Table 13.1 are used to compute the coefficient of correlation for the linear regression (Figure 13.1). This value is used in conjunction with the index of determination computed previously to test the coefficient of partial determination for significance. The coefficient r^2 is computed by use of Formula 12.19 to be

$$
r = \frac{24(1{,}007) - (125)(188)}{\sqrt{[24(815) - (125)^2][24(1{,}508) - (188)^2]}}
$$
$$
= 0.366, \text{ and squaring the result to give}
$$
$$
r^2 = 0.134.
$$

The index of partial determination is computed by Formula 13.7 to be

$$
r^2_{y.x^2.x} = \frac{0.736 - 0.134}{1 - 0.134}
$$
$$
= \frac{0.602}{0.866} = 0.695.
$$

The statistic t is computed by Formula 13.8 to yield

$$t = \sqrt{\frac{0.695(24 - 3)}{1 - 0.695}}$$

$$= \sqrt{\frac{14.60}{0.305}}$$

$$= 6.92.$$

The computed value of $t = 6.92$ for 21 degrees of freedom exceeds the value of 3.819 at the 0.001 level, as seen in Appendix J. The conclusion is that x^2 has a significant relationship with y.

The test of significance of an index of partial determination can be computed by substituting the appropriate values into Formula 13.7 to compute the desired partial determination index and computing the necessary value of t by the corresponding substitution into Formula 13.8.

An Alternative Method for Selecting a Polynomial Regression Equation. The significance test provides an alternative approach to the selection of a polynomial regression equation to express the relationship between two variables. The statistic t for the index of partial determination associated with each successive higher order polynomial regression equation can be computed. A test can be made to determine if the additional term in the next higher order polynomial reduces significantly the residual unassociated sum of squares related to the next lower polynomial regression. Successively higher polynomials can be computed until additional terms are not significant in reducing the unassociated sum of squares.

Exponential Correlation

The index of correlation for the first-degree exponential case involving the logarithms of the dependent variable is found readily by use of the product-moment formulation. The product-moment formulation for the linear case is given by Formula 12.19. The corresponding expression for the first-degree exponential case is obtained by substituting log y for y in Formula 12.19 and writing

$$I_{\log y.x} = \frac{n\Sigma(x \log y) - (\Sigma x)(\Sigma\log y)}{\sqrt{[n\Sigma x^2 - (\Sigma x)^2][n\Sigma(\log y)^2 - (\Sigma\log y)^2]}} \quad\ldots\ldots\ldots(13.9)$$

■ *Example.* The index of correlation for the exponential relationship of total cost and total output data shown in Table 13.3 is computed by use of Formula 13.9 as follows:

$$I_{\log y.x} = \frac{(7)(1,846.64189) - (834)(14.76018)}{\sqrt{[(7)(121,334) - (834)^2][(7)(31.48380) - (14.76018)^2]}}$$

$$= 0.99.$$

The index of correlation is very close to unity, indicating that the exponential correlation model is an excellent representation of the relationship between the variables.

The index of correlation for the first-degree exponential case involving the logarithms of both variables is found by use of the product-moment formula

$$I_{\log y \,\cdot\, \log x} = \frac{n\Sigma(\log x \, \log y) - (\Sigma \log x)(\log y)}{\sqrt{[n\Sigma(\log x)^2 - (\Sigma \log x)^2][n\Sigma(\log y)^2 - (\Sigma \log y)^2]}} \dots\dots(13.10)$$

MULTIVARIATE ANALYSIS BY ASSOCIATION

The regression and correlation methods presented in Chapter 12 are used to derive mathematical models of the relationship between two variables. If there is a high degree of association between the variations of the dependent variable and one independent variable, a bivariate regression or correlation model provides a good approximation of this relationship. The variation of a dependent variable, in most instances, however, results from the effects of two or more independent variables.

For instance, refer to the example described on page 382 in the first portion of Chapter 12. Suppose that plastic hardness is related to the pressure as well as the temperature of the reactor. This relationship is multivariate (several variables) rather than bivariate (two variables). The variation in plastic hardness is related to the two independent variables that are observed (and perhaps more that were not observed). The degree of association of the variation of the dependent variable with either of the independent variables taken individually is significant. A much higher portion of the variation is associated (explained), however, if the variations of the dependent variable and the two independent variables are analyzed jointly.

The multivariate analysis of variations in plastic hardness, temperature, and pressure is presented in an example on page 428 in this chapter. The regression and correlation methods for multivariate analysis are extensions of the bivariate methods and are derived by the method of least squares.

Regression analysis is concerned with the derivation of a mathematical model with which to relate quantitatively the variation of a dependent variable with the variations of one or more independent variables. Since multivariate regression and correlation analysis involve more than one independent variable, the notation is changed slightly from that used in bivariate analysis.

Notation for Multivariate Analysis

In the presentation of bivariate regression and correlation analysis in Chapter 12, the dependent variable is denoted Y and the independent variable X. In analyses involving multiple independent variables, a widely used statistical notation refers to all independent variables in terms of X

with a subscript. In this manner the first independent variable is X_1, the second independent variable is X_2, and so forth. This difference in notation results in some slight changes in some formulas.

Analysis by Association

The degree to which the dependent variable (Y) and the independent variables $(X_1, X_2, X_3, \ldots, X_n)$ covary is reflected by the proportion of the total variation of the dependent variable that is associated with the variations of the independent variables. The regression and correlation coefficients derived in the analysis reflect the extent of covariation of the variables.

Multivariate analysis by association may be viewed as a stepwise procedure in which the dependent variable is regressed or correlated successively on the independent variables. The dependent variable is regressed on an independent variable and the degree of covariation is computed. Next, the variation of the dependent variable not associated with this independent variable is related by regression to the variation of a second independent variable. The extent to which this residual variation is related to the second independent variable is computed. The process is continued in this manner until the variation of the last of the independent variables is related to the residual variation from the previous step. This process for a universe of data is illustrated in Figure 13.4.

The variation of Y is shown as the bar at the top of Figure 13.4 and the corresponding variance of Y is shown in the right-hand column. The variation of Y associated with the variation of X_1 as the result of the regression of Y on X_1 is represented by the unshaded portion of the second bar and is denoted A_{Y1}. The corresponding portion of the variation of Y not associated with the variation of X_1 is the residual or unassociated variation denoted $U_{Y.1}$. The variance of estimating Y is $\sigma_{Y.1}^2 = 0.55 \, \sigma_Y^2$ since 55% of the variation of Y is not associated with the variation of X_1, where σ_Y^2 and $\sigma_{Y.1}^2$ are measures of average variation.

Only a portion of the variation of Y is associated with that of X_1 and, in a sense, accounted for or explained. Therefore, only the unassociated variation $U_{Y.1}$ is related to the variation of the second independent variable X_2 to determine if this residual variation can be reduced. The portion of the unassociated variation $U_{Y.1}$ that is associated with the variation of X_2 is the portion of the third bar denoted $A_{Y2.1}$. The subscript $Y2.1$ denotes the associated variation derived from the regression of Y on X_2 with the variation of Y associated with that of X_1 excluded. The variance of estimating Y that results from the multiple regression of Y on X_1 and X_2 is $\sigma_{Y.12}^2 = 0.18 \, \sigma_Y^2$, since 18% of the variation of Y is not associated with that of X_1 or X_2.

The final step in this example consists of relating the variation of Y not associated with X_1 or X_2, denoted $U_{Y2.1}$, with the variation of the third independent variable X_3. The portion of the residual variation $U_{Y2.1}$ associated with the variation of X_3 is denoted $A_{Y3.12}$. The subscript indicates

FIGURE 13.4

An Illustration of the Stepwise Multivariate Analysis of a Dependent Variable with Three Independent Variables

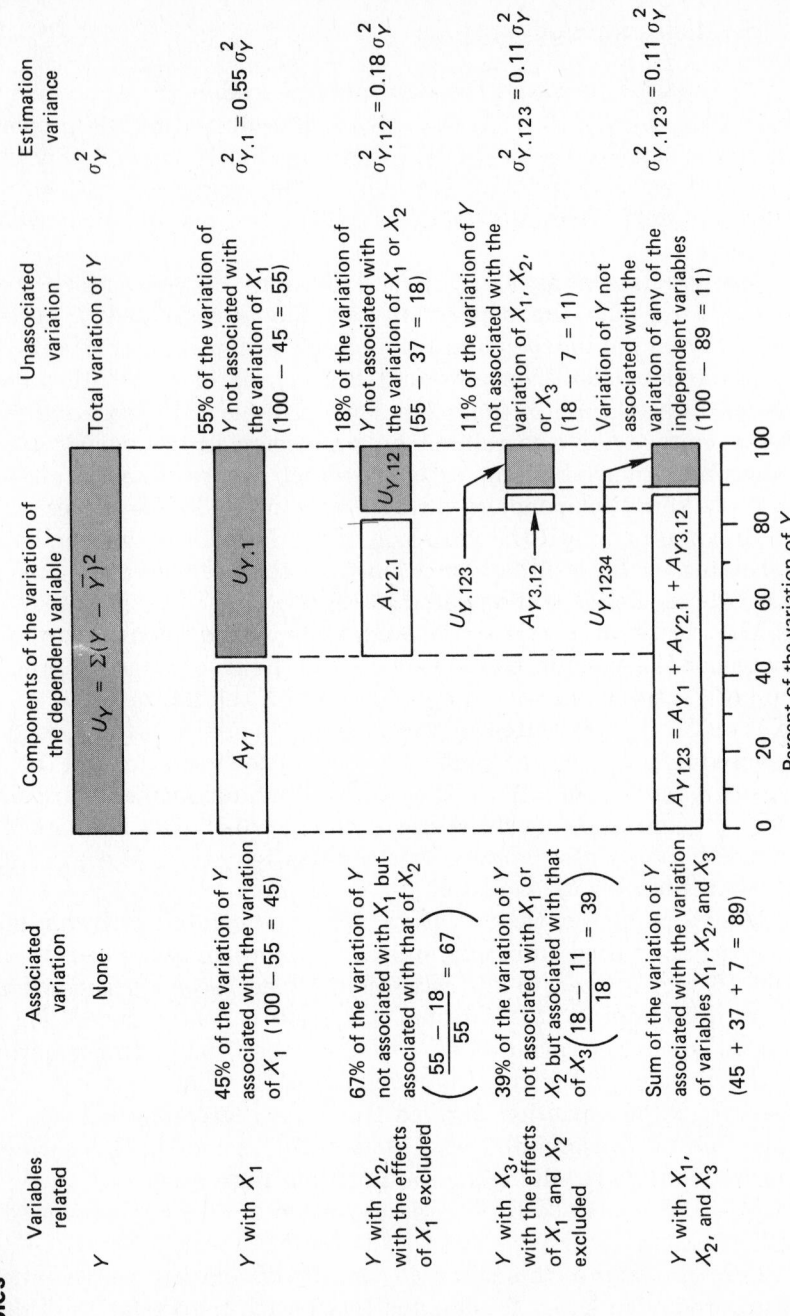

the regression of Y on X_3 with the variation of Y associated with X_1 and X_2 excluded. The variance of estimating Y based on the regression of Y on X_1, X_2, and X_3 is $\sigma^2_{Y.123} = 0.11\ \sigma^2_Y$, for 11% of the variation of Y is not associated with that of X_1, X_2, or X_3.

The portion of the variation of Y associated with that of the independent variables X_1, X_2, and X_3 is $A_{Y.123} = 0.89\ [\Sigma(Y-\overline{Y})^2]$, for 89% of the variation of Y is associated with the variation of X_1, X_2, or X_3. This result indicates that a rather precise estimate of Y can be obtained by use of a regression equation derived from the regression of the four variables.

TRIVARIATE REGRESSION

The linear regression of a dependent variable Y on two independent variables X_1 and X_2 produces an estimating equation written

$$Y_c = \alpha + \beta_1 X_1 + \beta_2 X_2.$$

The parameter α is the intercept of the plane of regression (in three dimensions) with the Y axis. The term β_1 is called the *coefficient of partial regression* and is the expected increase (decrease) in Y for a change of one unit in X_1. The term β_2 is a coefficient of partial regression that indicates the expected change in Y for a unit change in X_2. For example, a value of $\beta_1 = 1.2$ indicates an expected increase of 1.2 units in Y for an increase of one unit (1.0) in X_1. Similarly, a value of $\beta_2 = -34.2$ indicates the expected decrease in Y for an increase of one unit of X_2. An unbiased estimate of the trivariate regression equation obtained from sample data is denoted in lowercase by

$$y_c = a + b_1 x_1 + b_2 x_2 \dots\dots\dots\dots\dots\dots\dots(13.11)$$

where y_c is the calculated value of the dependent variable. For purposes of this discussion, multiple regression is based on the following assumptions:

1. The dependent variable is a normally distributed random variable.
2. The independent variables are mathematical or fixed (not random) variables.
3. The variance of the estimation of the dependent variable is homoscedastic.
4. The coefficients $a, b_1, b_2, \dots, b_r$ are maximum likelihood estimators of the parameters $\alpha, \beta_1, \beta_2, \dots, \beta_r$.
5. The error term ϵ is normally distributed and $E(\epsilon) = E[\Sigma(y - y_c)] = 0$.

Trivariate Regression Equation

The estimators of the regression coefficients can be obtained by use of normal equations derived by the method of least squares. The equations are derived in a manner similar to that demonstrated in Technical Note No. 1 of Chapter 12. The normal equations for trivariate regression (for which $\Sigma\epsilon^2$ is a minimum) are based on the method of least squares:

$$
\begin{aligned}
\text{I. } & na && + b_1\Sigma x_1 && + b_2\Sigma x_2 && = \Sigma y \\
\text{II. } & a\Sigma x_1 + b_1\Sigma x_1^2 && + b_2\Sigma x_1 x_2 && = \Sigma x_1 y \\
\text{III. } & a\Sigma x_2 + b_1\Sigma x_1 x_2 + b_2\Sigma x_2^2 && && = \Sigma x_2 y
\end{aligned}
$$

The number of normal equations can be reduced and other calculations simplified if the sampled values of the three variables are expressed as deviations about the respective means. Written in this manner, the values as deviations are denoted by subscripted d terms. The first-order sums $\Sigma d_1 = \Sigma(x_1 - \bar{x}_1)$, $\Sigma d_2 = \Sigma(x_2 - \bar{x}_2)$, and $\Sigma d_y = \Sigma(y - \bar{y})$ are all equal to zero and, consequently, a is also zero. The three normal equations reduce to the two following equations:

$$
\begin{aligned}
\text{II. } & b_1\Sigma d_1^2 + b_2\Sigma d_{12} = \Sigma d_{1y} \\
\text{III. } & b_1\Sigma d_{12} + b_2\Sigma d_2^2 = \Sigma d_{2y}
\end{aligned} \quad \text{........................(13.12)}
$$

where the sums of squares and cross products of the deviations for use in the normal equations and other calculations are obtained by the relationships:

$$
\begin{aligned}
\Sigma d_1^2 &= \Sigma(x_1 - \bar{x}_1)^2 = \Sigma x_1^2 - n\bar{x}_1^2 \\
\Sigma d_2^2 &= \Sigma(x_2 - \bar{x}_2)^2 = \Sigma x_2^2 - n\bar{x}_2^2 \\
\Sigma d_y^2 &= \Sigma(y - \bar{y})^2 = \Sigma y^2 - n\bar{y}^2 \\
\Sigma d_{1y} &= \Sigma(x_1 - \bar{x}_1)(y - \bar{y}) = \Sigma x_1 y - n\bar{x}_1\bar{y} \\
\Sigma d_{2y} &= \Sigma(x_2 - \bar{x}_2)(y - \bar{y}) = \Sigma x_2 y - n\bar{x}_2\bar{y} \\
\Sigma d_{12} &= \Sigma(x_1 - \bar{x}_1)(x_2 - \bar{x}_2) = \Sigma x_1 x_2 - n\bar{x}_1\bar{x}_2
\end{aligned}
$$

The values of the estimators b_1 and b_2 are found by solving the normal equations in Formula 13.12 simultaneously. An unbiased estimate of the intercept is found by computing

$$
a = \bar{y} - b_1\bar{x}_1 - b_2\bar{x}_2 \quad \text{.............................(13.13)}
$$

The unbiased estimate of the standard error of the estimate is written

$$
\hat{\sigma}_{y.12} = \sqrt{\frac{\Sigma d_y^2 - b_1\Sigma d_{1y} - b_2\Sigma d_{2y}}{n - 3}} \quad \text{....................(13.14)}
$$

where the loss of three degrees of freedom results from the estimation of three parameters in the regression equation.

■ *Example.* A sample of 25 observations of plastic hardness (y), temperature (x_1), and reactor pressure (x_2) is taken from a chemical process. Multiple regression analysis is to be applied to derive an expression for predicting plastic hardness on the basis of the observed operating conditions. The sample data shown in Table 13.4, page 430, are taken from a process similar to that discussed in Chapter 12. The observations of the variable percent additive (x_3) are used in the next portion of the chapter, which presents the regression of four variables. The required means and sums of squares and cross products are given below.

$$
\bar{y} = \frac{1{,}389}{25} = 55.56 \qquad\qquad \bar{x}_2 = \frac{562.5}{25} = 22.50
$$

Regression and Correlation   Part 5

$$\bar{x}_1 = \frac{11,200}{25} = 448.00$$

$$\Sigma d_1^2 = \Sigma(x_1 - \bar{x}_1)^2 = \Sigma x_1^2 - n\bar{x}_1^2 = 5,040.284 - 25(448.00)^2$$
$$= 5,040,284 - 5,017,600 = 22,684$$

$$\Sigma d_2^2 = \Sigma(x_2 - \bar{x}_2)^2 = \Sigma x_2^2 - n\bar{x}_2^2 = 12,702.63 - 25(22.5)^2$$
$$= 12,702.63 - 12,656.25 = 46.38$$

$$\Sigma d_y^2 = \Sigma(y - \bar{y})^2 = \Sigma y^2 - n\bar{y}^2 = 80,319 - 25(55.56)^2$$
$$= 80,319 - 77,172.84 = 3,146.16$$

$$\Sigma d_{1y} = \Sigma(x_1 - \bar{x}_1)(y - \bar{y}) = \Sigma x_1 y - n\bar{x}_1\bar{y}$$
$$= 627,910 - 25(448.00)(55.56) = 627,910 - 622,272$$
$$= 5,638$$

$$\Sigma x_2 y = \Sigma(x_2 - \bar{x}_2)(y - \bar{y}) = \Sigma x_2 y - n\bar{x}_2\bar{y}$$
$$= 31,569.0 - 25(22.50)(55.56) = 31,569.0 - 31,252.5$$
$$= 316.5$$

$$\Sigma x_1 x_2 = \Sigma(x_1 - \bar{x}_1)(x_2 - \bar{x}_2) = \Sigma x_1 x_2 - n\bar{x}_1\bar{x}_2$$
$$= 252,270.8 - 25(448.00)(22.50) = 252,270.8 - 252,000.0$$
$$= 270.8$$

The normal equations are

II. $22,684b_1 + 270.8b_2 = 5,638$

III. $270.8b_1 + 46.38b_2 = 316.5$

These equations are solved by the method of elimination as follows:

(Equation II) $\qquad\qquad\qquad\qquad 22,684b_1 + 270.8b_2 = 5,638.0$

$\left(-\dfrac{22,684}{270.8} \text{ times Equation III}\right)$ $\dfrac{-22,684b_1 - 3,885.1b_2 = -26,512.1}{}$

$\qquad\qquad\qquad\qquad\qquad\qquad\qquad\qquad -3,614.3b_2 = -20,874.1$

(Equation II + III) $\qquad\qquad\qquad\qquad\qquad\quad b_2 = 5.7754.$

The value of b_2 is substituted into Equation II, and solving for b_1 gives

(Equation II) $22,684b_1 + 270.8(5.7754) = 5,638.0$

$\qquad\qquad\quad 22,684b_1 + 1,564.0 \qquad\quad = 5,638.0$

$\qquad\qquad\quad 22,684b_1 \qquad\qquad\qquad\quad = 4,074$

$\qquad\qquad\qquad\qquad\qquad\qquad\quad b_1 = 0.179598.$

Substituting the partial regression coefficients into Formula 13.13 gives

$$a = \bar{y} - b_1\bar{x}_1 - b_2\bar{x}_2$$
$$= 55.56 - 0.179598(448.00) - 5.775436(22.50)$$
$$= 55.56 - 80.4599 - 129.94731$$
$$= -154.84721.$$

The unbiased estimate of the trivariate regression equation is

$$y_c = -154.84721 + 0.179598x_1 + 5.775436x_2.$$

An unbiased estimate of the standard error of the estimate is computed

TABLE 13.4

Sample Data of 25 Observations of Plastic Hardness(y), Temperature(x₁), Reactor Pressure(x₂), and Percent Additive(x₃)

y	x_1	x_2	x_3	y^2	x_1^2	x_2^2	x_3^2	x_1y	x_2y	x_3y	x_1x_2	x_1x_3	x_2x_3
44	410	22.1	4.9	1,936	168,100	488.41	24.01	18,040	972.4	215.6	9,061.0	2,009.0	108.29
47	419	22.5	3.0	2,209	175,561	506.25	9.00	19,693	1,057.5	141.0	9,427.5	1,257.0	67.50
60	427	23.1	1.5	3,600	182,329	533.61	2.25	25,620	1,386.0	90.0	9,863.7	640.5	34.65
71	431	24.0	0.6	5,041	185,761	576.00	0.36	30,601	1,704.0	42.6	10,344.0	258.6	14.40
61	464	22.6	1.8	3,721	215,296	510.76	3.24	28,304	1,378.6	109.8	10,486.4	835.2	40.68
60	481	21.7	3.3	3,600	231,361	470.89	10.89	28,860	1,302.0	198.0	10,437.7	1,587.3	71.61
56	467	22.0	2.1	3,136	218,089	484.00	4.41	26,152	1,232.0	117.6	10,274.0	980.7	46.20
66	482	24.6	0.2	4,356	232,324	605.16	0.04	31,812	1,623.6	13.2	11,857.2	96.4	4.92
51	457	21.1	3.8	2,601	208,849	445.21	14.44	23,307	1,076.1	193.8	9,642.7	1,736.6	80.18
53	448	22.2	4.5	2,809	200,704	492.84	20.25	23,744	1,176.6	238.5	9,945.6	2,016.0	99.90
74	496	24.8	0.1	5,476	246,016	615.04	0.01	36,704	1,835.2	7.4	12,300.8	49.6	2.48
33	412	20.5	4.8	1,089	169,744	420.25	23.04	13,596	676.5	158.4	8,446.0	1,977.6	98.40
54	447	21.9	2.3	2,916	199,809	479.61	5.29	24,138	1,182.6	124.2	9,789.3	1,028.1	50.37
52	473	20.8	0.3	2,704	223,729	432.64	0.09	24,596	1,081.6	15.6	9,838.4	141.9	6.24
30	404	20.0	2.7	900	163,216	400.00	7.29	12,120	600.0	81.0	8,080.0	1,090.8	54.00
58	409	23.3	4.4	3,364	167,281	542.89	19.36	23,722	1,351.4	255.2	9,529.7	1,799.6	102.52
59	498	21.3	3.9	3,481	248,004	453.69	15.21	29,382	1,256.7	230.1	10,607.4	1,942.2	83.07
52	427	22.9	1.4	2,704	182,329	524.41	1.96	22,204	1,190.8	72.8	9,778.3	597.8	32.06
56	459	22.3	2.7	3,136	210,681	497.29	7.29	25,704	1,248.8	151.2	10,235.7	1,239.3	60.21
49	423	22.6	2.7	2,401	178,929	510.76	7.29	20,727	1,107.4	132.3	9,559.8	1,142.1	61.02
63	490	22.4	2.2	3,969	240,100	501.76	4.84	30,870	1,411.2	138.6	10,976.0	1,078.0	49.28
61	434	23.8	0.7	3,721	188,356	566.44	0.49	26,474	1,451.8	42.7	10,329.2	303.8	16.66
39	416	20.6	3.1	1,521	173,056	424.36	9.61	16,224	803.4	120.9	8,569.6	1,289.6	63.86
62	432	24.4	0.6	3,844	186,624	595.36	0.36	26,784	1,512.8	37.2	10,540.8	259.2	14.64
78	494	25.0	4.6	6,084	244,036	625.00	21.16	38,532	1,950.0	358.8	12,350.0	2,272.4	115.00
1,389	11,200	562.5	62.2	80,319	5,040,284	12,702.63	212.18	627,910	31,569.0	3,286.5	252,270.8	27,629.3	1,378.14

Source: Company records.

by use of Formula 13.14 to give

$$\hat{\sigma}_{y.12} = \sqrt{\frac{3{,}146.16 - 0.179598(5{,}638) - 5.775436(316.5)}{25 - 3}}$$

$$= 3.727.$$

Estimation with Trivariate Regression

The computation of point and interval estimates for trivariate regression is similar to that presented in Chapter 12.

■ **Example.** Continuing the preceding example, a point estimate of plastic hardness (*y*) for a temperature (x_1) of 471 and a pressure (x_2) of 23.8 is computed as follows:

$$y_c = -154.84721 + 0.179598(471) + 5.775436(23.8)$$
$$= \quad 67.19881.$$

The 95% confidence interval estimate of plastic hardness corresponding to this point estimate is

$$y_c \pm t_{0.05}\,\hat{\sigma}_{y.12} = 67.19881 \pm 2.074(3.727)$$

where the confidence limits are 59.47 and 74.93. The value of $t_{0.05} = 2.074$ is read from Appendix J for *d.f.* $= 25 - 3 = 22$.

Comparison of Bivariate and Trivariate Regression

The reduction in the expected variance in estimating *y* by the addition of a third variable x_2 is demonstrated by comparing the results of the foregoing example with those of the regression of *y* on x_1 and *y* on x_2. The variance of the estimate of *y* for the trivariate and bivariate (using Formula 12.9) regression equations are:

$$\sigma_{y.123}^2 = 13.7$$
$$\sigma_{y.1}^2 \;\; = 75.9$$
$$\sigma_{y.2}^2 \;\; = 42.9$$

The variance based on the trivariate regression is less than either of the two bivariate regression results. The addition of the third variable aids in reducing the variance of estimating *y* since x_1 and x_2 are not correlated perfectly. If x_1 and x_2 were correlated perfectly, the addition of x_2 in the trivariate regression would not reduce the variance of the estimate since the variations of x_1 and x_2 would be, in effect, identical. The bivariate regressions indicate that x_2 is more highly related with *y* than x_1, for $\hat{\sigma}_{y.2}^2$ is less than $\hat{\sigma}_{y.1}^2$. In general, the addition of an independent variable in multiple regression will reduce the unassociated variation of the dependent variable and thereby produce more precise estimates of *y*. The exception to this general statement arises when the addition of an independent variable does not reduce the residual variation sufficiently to offset the loss of an additional degree of freedom. In such a case, the variance of the estimate of y may increase, but this would be interpreted to mean that the additional independent variable does not aid in making more precise estimates of y.

The situation in which there is a very high degree of correlation (approximately 0.90 or higher) between independent variables is called *multicollinearity*. Regression coefficients become less valuable for predictive purposes as the correlation between independent variables approaches unity. Conversely, the lower the correlation between independent variables, the greater the "effectiveness" of the regression equation for prediction, provided there is a significant multiple relationship between dependent and independent variables. The problem of multicollinearity can be remedied by combining highly correlated variables into a single variable or by eliminating all but one of the independent variables that are highly correlated with one another.

Sampling Error in Trivariate Regression

The coefficients of the multiple regression equation obtained from sample data are unbiased estimators of the parameters α, β_1, and β_2. Sample estimates of these parameters are distributed normally about the respective parameters. An unbiased estimate of the standard of the estimate of α is written

$$\hat{\sigma}_{a_{y.12}} = \frac{\hat{\sigma}_{y.12}}{\sqrt{n}}$$

An unbiased estimate of the standard error of the estimate of β_1 is expressed by

$$\hat{\sigma}_{b_1} = \frac{\hat{\sigma}_{y.12}}{\sqrt{\Sigma d_1^2 - \frac{(\Sigma d_{12})^2}{\Sigma d_2^2}}} \quad \dots\dots\dots\dots\dots(13.15)$$

A test of significance can be applied to b_1 as the basis for judging whether the coefficient is significantly different from zero. The value of $\beta_1 = 0$ if the variables are not related. The same type of test can be applied to b_2 by computing

$$\hat{\sigma}_{b_2} = \frac{\hat{\sigma}_{y.12}}{\sqrt{\Sigma d_2^2 - \frac{(\Sigma d_{12})^2}{\Sigma d_1^2}}} \quad \dots\dots\dots\dots\dots(13.16)$$

and utilizing the result in a test of significance.

■ *Example.* The partial regression coefficients obtained in the trivariate regression of plastic hardness (y), temperature (x_1), and pressure (x_2) are tested for significance by computing the required standard errors and the ratio needed for the significance test. The standard errors are computed

$$\hat{\sigma}_{b_1} = \frac{3.727}{\sqrt{22,684 - \dfrac{(270.8)^2}{46.38}}}$$

$$= \frac{3.727}{\sqrt{21,102.87}}$$

$$= \frac{3.727}{145.27} = 0.02566,$$

and

$$\hat{\sigma}_{b_2} = \frac{3.727}{\sqrt{46.38 - \dfrac{(270.8)^2}{22,684}}}$$

$$= \frac{3.727}{\sqrt{43.15}} = \frac{3.727}{6.569} = 0.5674.$$

The ratios for the significance tests are computed

$$t = \frac{b_1 - 0}{\hat{\sigma}_{b_1}}$$

$$= \frac{0.1796}{0.02566} = 6.999,$$

and

$$t = \frac{b_2 - 0}{\hat{\sigma}_{b_2}}$$

$$= \frac{5.775}{0.5674} = 10.18.$$

The value of $t = 6.999$ for $25 - 3 = 22$ degrees of freedom exceeds $t_{0.001} = 3.792$, as read from Appendix J. The difference $b_1 - 0$ is judged to be significant. Similarly, the value $t = 10.18$ exceeds $t_{0.001} = 3.792$ for a significance test of b_2. The regression of y on x_2, with the effects of x_1 held constant, is judged to be significant.

TRIVARIATE CORRELATION

The degree of association between the variables in a trivariate regression can be determined by *multiple correlation* analysis.

Coefficient of Multiple Determination

The extent to which a linear multiple regression equation fits the observed data can be indicated by the ratio of the associated variation to the total variation of the dependent variable. A maximum likelihood estimator of the universe *coefficient of determination* for the trivariate case is written

$$R^2_{y.12} = \frac{\text{associated sum of squares}}{\text{total sum of squares}} = \frac{\Sigma(y_c - \bar{y})^2}{\Sigma(y - \bar{y})^2} \cdots\cdots\cdots(13.17)$$

where $R^2_{y.12}$ is an estimator of the universe determination coefficient. Formula 13.17 can be expressed in a more convenient form by writing

$$R^2_{y.12} = \frac{b_1 \Sigma d_{1y} + b_2 \Sigma d_{2y}}{\Sigma d^2_y} \cdots\cdots\cdots\cdots\cdots(13.18)$$

The *coefficient of multiple correlation* $R_{y.12}$ is the square root of the multiple determination coefficient.

■ *Example.* The coefficients of multiple determination and correlation are computed for the data on plastic hardness, temperature, and pressure given in the trivariate regression example. The multiple determination coefficient is computed

$$R^2_{y.12} = \frac{0.179598(5,638) + 5.775436(316.5)}{3,146.16}$$

$$= \frac{2,840.50}{3,146.16} = 0.90285.$$

The coefficient of multiple correlation is

$$R_{y.12} = \sqrt{0.90285} = 0.950.$$

The value of $R^2_{y.12} = 0.90285$ obtained in the foregoing example may be interpreted by stating that 90.285% of the total variation of the dependent variable is associated with or explained by the regression of y on x_1 and x_2.

Significance Test for a Multiple Determination Coefficient

Multiple correlation results obtained from sample data are subject to sampling error. A test of significance can be applied to the multiple determination coefficient by application of analysis of variance. This test is equivalent to testing whether the joint regression of the dependent variable on the independent variables is significant. The test is applied by computing the ratio of the mean associated sum of squares to the mean unassociated sum of squares. This ratio has an F distribution for degrees of freedom $d.f._1 = r - 1$ and $d.f._2 = n - r$. The components of this ratio for the trivariate case are summarized in Table 13.5. This ratio is expressed in terms of the multiple determination coefficient by the general expression

$$F = \frac{\dfrac{(R^2_{y.12...r})}{(r - 1)}}{\dfrac{(1 - R^2_{y.12...r})}{(n - r)}} \cdots\cdots\cdots\cdots\cdots(13.19)$$

where r represents the total number of variables in the correlation.

TABLE 13.5

Analysis of Variance for Trivariate Linear Regression

Source of variation	Sum of squares	Degrees of freedom	Mean sum of squares
Regression of y on x_1 and x_2	associated	$d.f._1 = r - 1$	$\dfrac{\text{associated}}{r - 1}$
Residual	unassociated	$d.f._2 = n - r$	$\dfrac{\text{unassociated}}{n - r}$
Total	associated + unassociated	$d.f. = n - 1$	...

■ *Example.* A test of significance is applied to the trivariate regression of plastic hardness on temperature and pressure and the resulting multiple determination coefficient. The necessary data are summarized below.

Source of variation	Sum of squares	Degrees of freedom	Mean sum of squares
Regression of y on x_1 and x_2	2,840.50	$d.f._1 = 3 - 1 - 2$	1,420.25
Residual	305.66	$d.f._2 = 25 - 3 = 22$	13.90
Total	3,146.16	$d.f. = 25 - 1 = 24$	...

The F ratio is computed

$$F = \frac{\text{mean associated sum of squares}}{\text{mean unassociated sum of squares}}$$

$$= \frac{1{,}420.25}{13.90} = 102.18.$$

An alternative derivation of the F ratio is found by use of Formula 13.18 and computing

$$F = \frac{\dfrac{(R^2_{y.12})}{(r - 1)}}{\dfrac{(1 - R^2_{y.12})}{(n - r)}}$$

$$= \frac{\dfrac{(0.90285)}{(3 - 1)}}{\dfrac{(1 - 0.90285)}{(25 - 3)}} = \frac{0.4514}{0.004416} = 102.22.$$

The slight difference in this computed value of F from the ratio computed above is due to rounding error. Since $F_{0.01}$ for $d.f._1 = 2$ and $d.f._2 = 22$ read from Appendix L is 5.72, and $F = 102.22$ in this example, the multiple determination coefficient is highly significant. The hypothesis that the universe determination coefficient is zero is rejected. The same conclusion applies to the multiple correlation coefficient.

PARTIAL CORRELATION

The degree to which the residual variation of a dependent variable is correlated with the variation of an independent variable can be expressed by the *coefficient of partial determination*. This coefficient may be interpreted as the percent of residual variation associated with or explained by an independent variable.

Zero- and First-Order Partial Coefficients

The order of a partial determination coefficient corresponds to the number of independent variables regressed as a particular residual was obtained. Zero- and first-order partial determination coefficients can be computed from trivariate regression results.

■ *Example.* The zero- and first-order partial determination coefficients for the regression of plastic hardness (y) on temperature (x_1) and pressure (x_2) are computed from the trivariate regression and correlation results. The zero-order coefficients are computed

$$r_{y1}^2 = \frac{b_1 \Sigma d_{1y}}{\Sigma d_y^2} \qquad\qquad r_{y2}^2 = \frac{b_2 \Sigma d_{2y}}{\Sigma d_y^2}$$

$$= \frac{0.2485(5,638)}{3,146.16} \qquad\qquad = \frac{6.8240(316.5)}{3,146.16}$$

$$= \frac{1,401.04}{3,146.16} = 0.4453 \qquad\qquad = \frac{2,159.80}{3,146.16} = 0.6865.$$

The first-order partial determination coefficients are computed as follows:

$$r_{y1.2}^2 = \frac{R_{y.12}^2 - r_y^2}{1 - r_{y2}^2} \quad\dots\dots\dots\dots\dots\dots\dots\dots\dots\text{(13.20)}$$

$$= \frac{0.9028 - 0.6865}{1 - 0.6865}$$

$$= \frac{0.2163}{0.3135} = 0.6900.$$

$$r_{y2.1}^2 = \frac{R_{y.12}^2 - r_{y1}^2}{1 - r_{y1}^2} \quad\dots\dots\dots\dots\dots\dots\dots\dots\text{(13.21)}$$

$$= \frac{0.9028 - 0.4453}{1 - 0.4453}$$

$$= \frac{0.4575}{0.5547} = 0.8248.$$

Comparison of Partial and Multiple Determination Coefficients

The partial determination coefficients computed in the foregoing example may be interpreted as follows:

Coefficient	Interpretation
$r_{y1}^2 = 0.4453$	About 45% of the variation of plastic hardness is explained by variations in temperature, with pressure not considered.
$r_{y2}^2 = 0.6865$	Approximately 69% of the variation of plastic hardness is explained by variations in pressure, with temperature not considered.
$r_{y1.2}^2 = 0.6901$	About 69% of the variation in plastic hardness not explained by variations in pressure is explained by variations in temperature.
$r_{y2.1}^2 = 0.8248$	More than 82% of the variation in plastic hardness not explained by variations in temperature is explained by variations in pressure.

The relationship of partial determination coefficients to the multiple determination coefficient is illustrated by use of the plastic hardness example shown below.

Percent of the variation of y associated with the variation of x_1 and x_2		Percent of the variation of y associated with the variation of x_1		Percent of the variation of y not associated with the variation of x_1		Percent of the variation of y, not associated with x_1 that is associated with the variation of x_2
	=		+		$\cdot$	

$$R_{y.12}^2 = r_{y1}^2 + (1 - r_{y1}^2) \cdot (r_{y2.1}^2)$$

Substituting the values for the coefficients gives

$$R_{y.12}^2 = r_{y1}^2 + (1 - r_{y1}^2)(r_{y2.1}^2)$$

$$= 0.4453 + (1 - 0.4453)(0.8248)$$
$$= 0.4453 + (0.5547)(0.8248)$$
$$= 0.4453 + 0.4575 = 0.9028.$$

The multiple determination coefficient is also related to partial determination coefficients based on x_2. The relationship is written

$$R_{y.12}^2 = r_{y2}^2 + (1 - r_{y2}^2)(r_{y1.2}^2)$$
$$= 0.6865 + (1 - 0.6865)(0.6901)$$

$$= 0.6865 + (0.3135)(0.6901)$$
$$= 0.6865 + 0.2163 = 0.9028.$$

This result is precisely that obtained in the foregoing illustration.

It should be noted that the value of $R^2_{y.12}$ is obtained from the joint regression of y, x_1, and x_2. The partial determination coefficients, in contrast, reflect with what might be viewed as the order or sequence in which the variables are regressed. But, as seen in the foregoing illustrations, the same value of $R^2_{y.12}$ is obtained *regardless of the order used* in regressing the variables.

REGRESSION AND CORRELATION OF MORE THAN THREE VARIABLES

Multiple regression or correlation problems may involve more than three variables. The following discussion concerning the regression and correlation of four variables is designed to provide insight into the analysis of complex multivariate relationships. The regression and correlation of four variables is an extension of the basic concepts introduced in the discussion of trivariate analysis.

Regression of Four Variables

The regression equation that expresses the linear relationship of a dependent variable with three independent variables can be written

$$y_c = a + b_1 x_1 + b_2 x_2 + b_3 x_3 \quad \dots \dots \dots \dots \dots \dots (13.22)$$

The assumptions implicit in Formula 13.11 also apply to the four-variable regression case. The parameter estimators are obtained by solving the normal equations

$$\text{II. } b_1 \Sigma d^2_1 + b_2 \Sigma d_{12} + b_3 \Sigma d_{13} = \Sigma d_{1y}$$
$$\text{III. } b_1 \Sigma d_{12} + b_2 \Sigma d^2_2 + b_3 \Sigma d_{23} = \Sigma d_{2y}$$
$$\text{IV. } b_1 \Sigma d_{13} + b_2 \Sigma d_{23} + b_3 \Sigma d^2_3 = \Sigma d_{3y}$$

for the partial regression coefficients and by solving

$$a = \bar{y} - b_1 \bar{x}_1 - b_2 \bar{x}_2 - b_3 \bar{x}_3 \quad \dots \dots \dots \dots \dots \dots (13.23)$$

for the intercept. The estimated variance of the error of estimating y_c is obtained by solving

$$\hat{\sigma}_{y.123} = \sqrt{\frac{\Sigma d^2_y - b_1 \Sigma d_{1y} - b_2 \Sigma d_{2y} - b_3 \Sigma d_{3y}}{n-4}} \quad \dots \dots \dots \dots (13.24)$$

where the loss of four degrees of freedom results from the estimation of four parameters in the regression equation.

■ *Example.* A sample of 25 observations of plastic hardness (y), temperature (x_1), pressure (x_2), and percent additive (x_3) is taken from a chemical process. The four variables are regressed to derive an expression for predicting plastic hardness on the basis of the observed operating conditions. The sample data are shown in Table 13.4, a portion of which was used in the trivariate regression example. The regression equation and estimated standard error of the estimate computed for the data by use of the normal equations, Formula 13.23, and Formula 13.24 are

$$y_c = -153.76 + 0.179205x_1 + 5.743450x_2 - 0.074443x_3$$

and

$$\hat{\sigma}_{y.123} = \sqrt{\frac{3,146.16 - 0.179205(5,638) - 5.743450(316.5) - 0.074443(169.3)}{25 - 4}} = 3.813.$$

A comparison of $\hat{\sigma}_{y.12} = 3.727$ and $\hat{\sigma}_{y.123} = 3.813$ indicates that the addition of the third independent variable increases rather than decreases the expected error of estimating values of y. This results from the fact that the reduction in unassociated variation of the dependent variable is more than offset by the loss of an additional degree of freedom.

A test of significance can be applied to each regression coefficient to determine if each of the independent variables is related significantly to the dependent variable in the joint regression of four variables.

■ **Example.** The partial regression coefficients obtained in the regression of the four variables—plastic hardness, temperature, pressure, and percent additive—are tested for significance by use of an extension of Formulas 13.15 and 13.16. It can be shown that the denominator of each formula is the reciprocal of the square root of the respective element on the principal diagonal of the inverse of the matrix of sums of squares and products of the normal equations. The values of the required estimates are, respectively,

$$\hat{\sigma}_{b_1} = 3.813 \sqrt{0.0000479818} = 0.02641$$
$$\hat{\sigma}_{b_2} = 3.813 \sqrt{0.0272750234} = 0.6295$$
$$\hat{\sigma}_{b_3} = 3.813 \sqrt{0.0212798680} = 0.5563.$$

The t values for the significance tests are, respectively,

$$t = \frac{b_1 - 0}{\hat{\sigma}_{b_1}} = \frac{0.179205}{0.02641} = 6.785$$

$$t = \frac{b_2 - 0}{\hat{\sigma}_{b_2}} = \frac{5.743450}{0.6296} = 9.123$$

$$t = \frac{b_3 - 0}{\hat{\sigma}_{b_3}} = \frac{-0.074443}{0.5563} = -0.1338.$$

The value $t_{0.001} = 3.819$ for $25 - 4 = 21$ degrees of freedom is read from Appendix J. The coefficients b_1 and b_2 differ significantly from zero. The coefficient b_3 is not significant since $t = -0.1338$ is greater than $t_{0.80} = -0.257$ for $25 - 4 = 21$ degrees of freedom, as read from Appendix J.

Multiple Correlation of More Than Three Variables

Determination Coefficient. The multiple determination coefficient for the correlation of four variables is computed by the general expression

$$R^2_{y.123} = \frac{b_1 \Sigma d_{1y} + b_2 \Sigma d_{2y} + b_3 \Sigma d_{3y}}{\Sigma d^2_y} \dots\dots\dots\dots(13.25)$$

■ *Example.* The multiple determination coefficient for the four variable regression example presented previously is computed

$$R^2_{y.123} = \frac{0.179205(5,638) + 5.743450(316.5) + (-0.074443)(-169.3)}{3,146.16}$$

$$= 0.9029.$$

The difference between $R^2_{y.123} = 0.9029$ and $R^2_{y.12} = 0.9028$ indicates that the addition of variable x_3 increases the associated variation by an insignificant amount.

Significance Test for the Coefficient of Multiple Determination. A test of significance for the coefficient of multiple determination is made by the application of analysis of variance.

■ *Example.* Analysis of variance is applied to the regression of plastic hardness on temperature, pressure, and percent additive by use of the following data:

Source of variation	Sum of squares	Degrees of freedom	Mean sum of squares
Regression of y on x_1, x_2, and x_3	2,840.76	$d.f._1 = \ 4 - 1 = \ 3$	946.92
Residual	305.40	$d.f._2 = 25 - 4 = 21$	14.54
Total	3,146.16	$d.f. \ = 25 - 1 = 24$	...

The F ratio is computed

$$F = \frac{\text{mean associated sum of squares}}{\text{mean unassociated sum of squares}}$$

$$= \frac{946.92}{14.54}$$

$$= 65.13.$$

The value $F_{0.01} = 4.87$ for $d.f._1 = 3$ and $d.f._2 = 21$ is read from Appendix L. Since $F = 65.13$, the coefficient is highly significant. The significance of this coefficient reflects the joint correlation of the four variables rather than the significance of any one variable. This significance does not mean that all of the independent variables are significantly related to the dependent variable.

USING COMPUTERS IN MULTIPLE REGRESSION AND CORRELATION ANALYSIS

The application of multiple regression and correlation analysis requires extensive, highly precise computations. Consequently, it is no surprise that computers are used widely in the application of these techniques. A large number of computer installations have one or more multiple regression and correlation programs in the program library that are available to users.

The availability of these programs enables many an analyst to obtain the desired regression and correlation results without the analyst having to spend time writing a computer program. The suitability of a given library program for use in a particular problem depends upon the input requirements, operating procedure, and results computed by the program. Many library programs are sufficiently general and comprehensive to fulfill the requirements of a wide variety of users.

The flexibility of some general-purpose multiple regression and correlation programs is such as to give the user the matrix of sums of squares, the inverse of the matrix of sums of squares, constant term, partial regression coefficients, determination and correlation coefficients, t or F ratios for significance tests, and a variety of other results that the analyst may desire. With the benefit of this type of versatile program, one can concentrate on the analysis of results and avoid the time-consuming task of computing the results manually.

■ *Example.* The multiple regression and correlation of plastic hardness with temperature, pressure, and percent additive is computed by use of a library program. The output of the program is shown in Table 13.6. This program includes a deletion feature which provides that the total number of variables is regressed initially. Then, the variable with the smallest F or t^2 ratio for the corresponding partial regression coefficient is deleted, and the remaining variables are regressed. The deletion operation is repeated, a second independent variable is deleted, and the remaining variables are regressed. The process continues until the dependent variable is regressed on a single independent variable. This deletion feature provides excellent diagnostic information in the selection of variables that are related significantly with the dependent variable. The values in Table 13.6 differ slightly from those in the examples in this chapter because of rounding error. The computer program carries computations to eight significant digits.

TABLE 13.6

**Computer Output of a Multiple Regression Program
with Deletion Features**

Variable	Average	Variance
x_1	55.559999	131.090080
x_2	447.999990	945.174990
x_3	22.499999	1.932541
x_4	2.487999	2.392767

Variables		Correlation
x_1	x_1	1.000000
x_1	x_2	0.667381
x_1	x_3	0.828544
x_1	x_4	−0.398375
x_2	x_2	1.000000
x_2	x_3	0.264017
x_2	x_4	−0.207035
x_3	x_3	1.000000
x_3	x_4	−0.413878
x_4	x_4	1.000000

Independent variables	Regression coefficient	F or t^2 ratio		
x_1	0.179199	46.016362		
x_2	5.743030	83.669138	Delete variable x_3	
x_3	−0.07169	0.018259		

Error variance	Constant term	Multiple F	$d.f._1$	$d.f._2$	R^2
14.544052	−153.752330	65.106497	3	21	0.902921

Independent variables	Regression coefficient	F or t^2 ratio		
x_1	0.179596	48.986952	Delete variable x_1	
x_2	5.775327	103.574860		

Error variance	Constant term	Multiple F	$d.f._1$	$d.f._2$	R^2
13.895029	−154.844090	102.211770	2	22	0.902836

Independent variable	Regression coefficient	F or t^2 ratio
x_2	6.823957	50.361954

Error variance	Constant term	Multiple F	$d.f._1$	$d.f._2$	R^2
42.885468	−97.979040	50.361959	1	23	0.686486

STUDY QUESTIONS

13–1. Explain briefly the meaning of each of the following terms:

a. first-order polynomial equation
b. polynomial regression
c. exponential regression
d. index of correlation
e. index of determination
f. index of partial determination
g. multiple regression
h. coefficient of partial regression
i. multiple correlation
j. coefficient of partial determination
k. zero-order partial correlation coefficient
l. first-order partial correlation coefficient

13-2. What techniques may be used to determine if a nonlinear regression equation is a more suitable bivariate model than a linear regression equation?

13-3. Describe the relationship between the normal equations for first-order polynomial and higher order polynomial regression.

13-4. When should a significance test be applied to the index of determination computed in regression analysis?

13-5. How can the most appropriate polynomial regression for a bivariate relationship be selected?

13-6. Describe the rationale of multiple regression.

13-7. Give a brief description of each of the terms in the trivariate regression equation in Formula 13.11.

13-8. When should a significance test be applied to the partial regression coefficients in multiple regression?

13-9. Why is an F test required for a significance test for a multiple determination coefficient?

13-10. Distinguish between multiple determination coefficients and partial determination coefficients.

PROBLEMS

13-1. The advertising expense and monthly sales of a brand of candy for a month are shown as follows:

Advertising expense (hundreds of dollars)	Sales volume (thousands of units)
x	y
1.95	229
1.39	152
1.80	225
1.62	206
1.28	131
2.52	247
1.42	183
1.58	198
2.26	241

a. Plot a scatter diagram of the data.
b. Compute a second-order polynomial regression equation and plot the result.
c. Compute a point estimate of sales volume if advertising expense is $2.10 (hundred dollars).
d. Compute an estimate of the standard error of the estimate.

13-2. The price of a product and the corresponding sales volumes are recorded as follows:

Price (dollars)	Sales volume (thousands of units)
x	y
52.0	1.67
63.9	1.29
47.1	1.94
56.2	1.52
54.1	1.43
85.3	1.19
44.9	1.64
51.5	1.73
66.0	1.39

a. Plot a scatter diagram of the data.
b. Compute a second-order polynomial regression of sales volume on price and plot the result.
c. Compute a point estimate of sales volume for a price of $1.60.
d. Compute an estimate of the standard error of estimate.

13-3. A market analyst is interested in a possible relationship between the consistency with which a brand of product is purchased and the average length of time between purchases. A sample of data is taken with the following results:

Average length of time between purchases (days)	Frequency of purchase of a given brand (percent)
x	y
62	43
31	56
270	12
13	69
8	82
139	16
345	8
15	60
190	15
91	22

a. Plot a scatter diagram of the data.
b. Compute a second-order polynomial regression equation. Plot the result.
c. What is the expected percent of repeat purchases for an average length of time between purchases of 80 days?
d. Compute the estimated standard error of the estimate.

13-4. The values of purchases by customers and the corresponding times required to check out customers in a supermarket are as follows:

Value of purchase (dollars)	Time required (minutes)
x	y
6.4	1.7
16.1	2.7
42.1	4.9
2.1	0.3
30.7	3.9
32.1	4.1
7.2	1.2
3.4	0.5
20.8	3.3
38.2	4.4

a. Plot a scatter diagram of the data.
b. Compute a second-order polynomial regression equation. Plot the result.
c. What is the expected time to be required to check out a customer with a purchase of $25.40?
d. Compute the estimated standard error of the estimate.

13-5. Use the data in Problem 13-1 to:
a. Compute the index of determination.
b. Test the index of partial determination for significance.

13-6. Use the data in Problem 13-2 to:
a. Compute the index of determination.
b. Test the index of partial determination for significance.

13-7. Use the data in Problem 13-3 to:
a. Compute the index of determination.
b. Test the index of partial determination for significance.

13-8. Use the data in Problem 13-4 to:
a. Compute the index of determination.
b. Test the index of partial determination for significance.

13-9. A sample of observations of price and per capita consumption of natural gas in selected cities is summarized as follows:

Average price (dollars)	Per capita consumption (thousands of cubic feet)
x	y
0.88	48
0.43	107
0.46	86
0.96	35
0.62	59
0.27	136
0.58	56
0.31	112
1.02	41
0.73	49
0.42	109
0.92	35
0.57	51
0.35	99
1.18	37

a. Plot a scatter diagram of the data using an arithmetic chart.
b. Plot a scatter diagram of the data using a semilogarithmic chart.
c. Compute the first-degree exponential regression equation and the corresponding standard error of the estimate.
d. What is the point estimate of per capita consumption, given a price of $0.80?

13-10. Compute the index of correlation for the first-degree exponential case applied to the data of Problem 13-9.

13-11. Sales volume of a product (y), price per unit (x_1), and advertising expense (x_2) are recorded as follows:

Sales volume (thousands of units)	Price per unit (dollars)	Advertising expense (hundreds of dollars)
y	x_1	x_2
14.4	1.2	9.6
4.8	1.6	6.3
6.4	1.9	7.0
12.0	1.4	10.0
9.9	1.3	8.6
5.0	1.7	5.4
9.7	1.6	18.1
11.6	1.5	13.5

a. Compute the equation for the linear regression of sales volume on price per unit and advertising expense.
b. Compute the 95% confidence limits of sales volume for a price of $1.80 per unit and an advertising expense of $12.2 hundred dollars.
c. Test the partial regression coefficients for significance.

13–12. In a study of water consumption in an industrial plant, a sample of data was taken of monthly water usage (y), average monthly temperature (x_1), and number of days of plant operation in a month (x_2). The data are as follows:

Water usage (thousands of gallons)	Average temperature (°F)	Days of operation per month
y	x_1	x_2
2.8	64	22
3.9	72	21
3.9	80	23
4.4	88	21
3.1	81	25
3.1	45	19
3.5	46	22
3.6	69	20
3.0	54	22
3.3	39	20

a. Compute the linear regression equation.
b. Compute the 95% confidence limits of water usage for an average temperature of 60°F and 24 days of operation.
c. Test the partial regression coefficients for significance.

13–13. A sample of data for output (y), labor input (x_1), and overhead cost per unit (x_2) are as follows:

Output (units)	Labor (hours)	Overhead (dollars)
y	x_1	x_2
8	8	18
3	2	24
11	10	19
7	8	21
6	7	23
9	10	24
5	6	25
2	3	22
10	9	21
4	5	23

a. Compute the equation for the linear regression of output on labor input and overhead cost per unit.
b. Compute the 95% confidence limits of the expected value of output for a labor input of seven units and an overhead cost per unit of $20.
c. Test the partial regression coefficients for significance.

13-14. Observations of strength of fiberboard (y), length of fibers in raw material (x_1), and processing temperature (x_2) of a process are taken. The results are listed as follows:

Fiberboard strength (psi)	Fiber length (mm.)	Processing temperature (°F)
y	x_1	x_2
81.4	2.72	295
150.3	3.17	301
122.2	3.12	279
64.8	2.55	284
101.7	3.08	305
92.1	2.75	310
175.6	3.22	304
113.8	3.02	309

a. Compute the equation for the linear regression of fiberboard strength on fiber length and processing temperature.
b. Compute the 95% confidence limits of the expected value of fiberboard strength for a fiber length of 3.20 mm. and a processing temperature of 290°F.
c. Test the partial regression coefficients for significance.

13-15. Compute the multiple determination coefficient for the data in Problem 13-11 and test it for significance.

13-16. Compute the multiple determination coefficient for the data in Problem 13-12 and test it for significance.

13-17. Using the data in Problem 13-13:
a. Compute the multiple determination coefficient and test it for significance.
b. Compute the zero- and first-order determination coefficients.

13-18. Using the data in Problem 13-14:
a. Compute the multiple determination coefficient and test it for significance.
b. Compute the zero- and first-order determination coefficients.

13-19. In an effort to estimate the number of man-hours required for engineers to design aircraft, a study was made of the relationship design effort (y) with aircraft speed (x_1), weight (x_2), and the percent of parts of an aircraft that are common to one or more other models of aircraft (x_3). The sample data are as follows:

Design effort (millions of man-hours)	Speed (mach number)	Weight (tons)	Common parts (percent)
y	x_1	x_2	x_3
1.1	0.8	8.5	40
0.8	0.6	7.0	35
1.6	1.6	9.1	32
0.5	0.5	7.1	48
0.8	0.8	7.0	36
1.0	1.4	8.9	56
0.9	0.5	6.9	20
0.4	0.4	4.8	45
1.6	1.2	7.9	28

a. Compute the linear multiple regression equation for the data.
b. Determine the 95% confidence limits of the estimate of design effort for an aircraft with a speed of 2.0 (mach), a weight of 9.5 tons, and 25% common parts.
c. Test the partial regression coefficients for significance.
d. Compute the multiple determination coefficient and test it for significance.
e. Compute the second-order determination coefficients.

Chapter 14

Time Series—Measurement
and Forecasting

A set of ordered observations of a quantitative variable taken at successive points in time is called a *time series*. Time, in terms of years, months, days, or hours, is a device that enables one to relate phenomena to a set of common, stable reference points.

The statistical analysis of time-series data is of particular interest to an administrator because a large proportion of the basic statistical data with which one must deal are time-series data. The quantitative measurement of inventories, sales, costs, prices, and many other business and economic variables is recorded on the basis of intervals of time. Since one of the chief responsibilities of management is to forecast the future, the careful, detailed study of time series data is a prerequisite of survival. The chief aim in analyzing statistical information about the past is the desire to gain an understanding of the forces at work and to use that understanding to predict the future. Every administrator must forecast, and success or failure may depend on the accuracy of the predictions.

PROBLEMS OF ANALYSIS

The analysis of time-series data presents its own unique set of problems and pitfalls. The very fact that economic data exist in such vast quantities and in such complex surroundings is enough to discourage all but the most determined investigator. Further, the application of many conventional statistical methods is difficult because it cannot be assumed that successive observations are statistically independent. A sample of data ordered in time is not the same as a random sample of observations drawn from a population, and it cannot be treated in the same fashion in analysis. For example, the cost of operating an organization in one month is not independent of the cost of operating the organization the month before. It is true that costs may change from one time period to another, but these changes are not entirely independent. They are part of a changing pattern over time.

Another complexity of time-series analysis arises from the fact that the individual observations in the time series are a composite of several forces which may be pulling together or in opposite directions at any particular time. An attempt to separate the time-series model into its component parts will assist in an understanding of the historical past and may give some insight into the future. This process of dividing the series into its component parts is called the *decomposition* of time series.

THE CLASSICAL APPROACH

The classical approach to time-series analysis holds that any given observation is made up of trend, seasonal, cyclical, and erratic components. The fact is that this is probably an oversimplification of the true state of affairs, for the art of time-series analysis is not as well developed as some other branches of statistics. Not all analysts agree on the classification of the components used here or on the manner in which they are related. Some argue that there are more than four components, and some think that trend and cyclical movements are produced by the same set of forces.

During the past two or three decades the attempt to make forecasting more scientific has led to the development of alternate approaches such as econometrics. *Econometrics* attempts to express economic theories in mathematical models that can be tested and verified by statistical methods. It tries to measure the impact of one economic variable upon another in the hope of being able to predict future events.

The approach in this chapter is to present the classical statistical approach to time-series analysis, but at the same time to point out that many other possible models exist which are based on different assumptions and which may lead to different results.

Time-Series Components

A typical time series may be thought of as being made up of four types of fluctuations:

1. A *trend* component, which may be defined as long-term growth or decay.
2. A *seasonal* component, which may be defined as a regularly recurring periodic fluctuation.
3. A *cyclical* component, which may be defined as a wavelike fluctuation about trend. The length and the amplitude of the cycle are not constant, as in the seasonal component, but may vary from one cycle to the next.
4. An *erratic* or random component, which is completely unsystematic.

The Time-Series Model

If the letters T, S, C, and E are used to represent the four components of trend, seasonal, cyclical, and erratic fluctuations, respectively, the time series, y, may be written as

$$y = T \times S \times C \times E \quad\text{................................(14.1)}$$

This normally is called the *multiplicative model* and is the most commonly used model in the decomposition of time series.

Many econometricians and others prefer the *additive model,* in which

$$y = T + S + C + E \quad\text{................................(14.2)}$$

To prevent confusion between the two models, it should be pointed out that in the multiplicative model (Formula 14.1) S, C, and E are indexes expressed as decimal percents. In the additive model (Formula 14.2) S, C, and E are quantitative deviations about trend that can be expressed as seasonal, cyclical, and erratic in nature.

■ *Example.* If in the multiplicative model, $T = 500$, $S = 1.20$, $C = 1.05$, and $E = 0.90$, then

$$y = (500)(1.20)(1.05)(0.90) = 567.$$

If in the additive model, $T = 500$, $S = +100$, $C = +25$, and $E = -45$, then

$$y = 500 + 100 + 25 - 45 = 580.$$

The additive model assumes that all the components of the time series are independent of one another. For example, it assumes that trend has no effect on the seasonal component no matter how high or how low this value may become. Further, it assumes that the business cycle has no effect on the seasonal component. If the index for December is typically 1.50 or 150%, this percent will not be affected by either prosperity or recession. While the additive model may work well within limits, it is doubtful if one always can rely on the independence of components that it assumes.

In the multiplicative model, it is assumed that the four components are due to different causes but they are not necessarily independent and they can affect one another. This model is also much easier to use and makes possible the isolation of the components.

The manipulation of these models will be considered after first examining in more detail the four basic types of fluctuations.

TREND

The trend in a time series may be represented graphically by a straight line or by one of many types of smooth curves. It can be represented algebraically by an equation. If the vertical axis of the graph is taken as the Y axis and if the horizontal axis is taken as the X axis, then Y, which is the variable being measured, may be shown as a function of X, which represents time. The general form of this equation is

$$Y = f(X).$$

If the functional relationship is that of a straight line, the equation may be written

$$y_c = a + bx \dots\dots\dots\dots\dots\dots\dots\dots\dots\dots(14.3)$$

where

    a is the Y intercept
    b is the slope of the line
    y_c values are the computed values of Y on the trend line.

Linear Trend

When the amount of increase (or decrease) is fairly constant from one time period to another, a straight line may be appropriate as a trend line. While such a line might be drawn by inspection, a more objective method of computing the equation for such a line is generally preferred.

The most common method employed to compute a straight-line trend is the *method of least squares*. The mathematics of this method are described in Technical Note No. 1 at the end of Chapter 12. In Chapter 12 the least squares line was used as a regression equation to describe the relationship between two variables, x and y. In time-series analysis the same line may be used to define trend, with the x variable representing time, and the y variable, the value of the series under study, such as sales, inventories, prices, or some other time series.

The traditional notation in the literature on time series is somewhat different from that used in Chapter 12 on regression and correlation, but the principles involved are the same. For example, Formula 12.5

$$y = a + bx + \epsilon$$

is the same as Formula 14.3,

$$y_c = a + bx.$$

The normal equations discussed in the technical note are written as

$$\Sigma y = na + b\Sigma x$$
$$\Sigma xy = a\Sigma x + b\Sigma x^2.$$

Since the values of x are coded values representing time, it is always possible to set them up so that $\Sigma x = 0$. When this is done, one term in each of the normal equations is equal to zero and the equations become

$$a = \frac{\Sigma y}{n} \dots\dots\dots\dots\dots\dots\dots\dots\dots\dots(14.4)$$

$$b = \frac{\Sigma xy}{\Sigma x^2} \dots\dots\dots\dots\dots\dots\dots\dots\dots\dots(14.5)$$

where
    n is the number of time periods.

The coding of x is done in the following manner:

If n is odd:		*If n is even:*	
Year	*x*	*Year*	*x*
1	−2	1	−3
2	−1	2	−1
3	0	3	1
4	1	4	3
5	2	Total	0
Total	0		
x unit is one year		*x* unit is one-half year	

■ *Example.* The computation of a least-squares trend line for annual earnings of the United Technologies Corporation from 1972 through 1976 is shown in Table 14.1, and the trend line is shown in Figure 14.1. Because there is an odd number of years, the x unit is taken as one year.

TABLE 14.1

Annual Earnings of United Technologies Corporation, 1972–1976 (Computation of trend by method of least squares)

Year	Earnings in $ millions y	x	x^2	xy	Trend values y_c
1972	50.6	−2	4	−101.2	43.06
1973	58.1	−1	1	− 58.1	70.36
1974	104.7	0	0	0	97.66
1975	117.5	1	1	117.5	124.96
1976	157.4	2	4	314.8	152.26
Total	488.3	0	10	273.0	488.30

Source: The Wall Street Journal, 25 March, 1977.

$$a = \frac{\Sigma y}{n} = \frac{488.3}{5} = 97.66$$

$$b = \frac{\Sigma xy}{\Sigma x^2} = \frac{273.0}{10} = 27.3$$

$y_c = 97.66 + 27.3x$
    origin: July 1, 1974
    x unit: one year
    y unit: earnings in millions of dollars.

FIGURE 14.1

Annual Earnings of United Technologies Corporation, 1972–1976

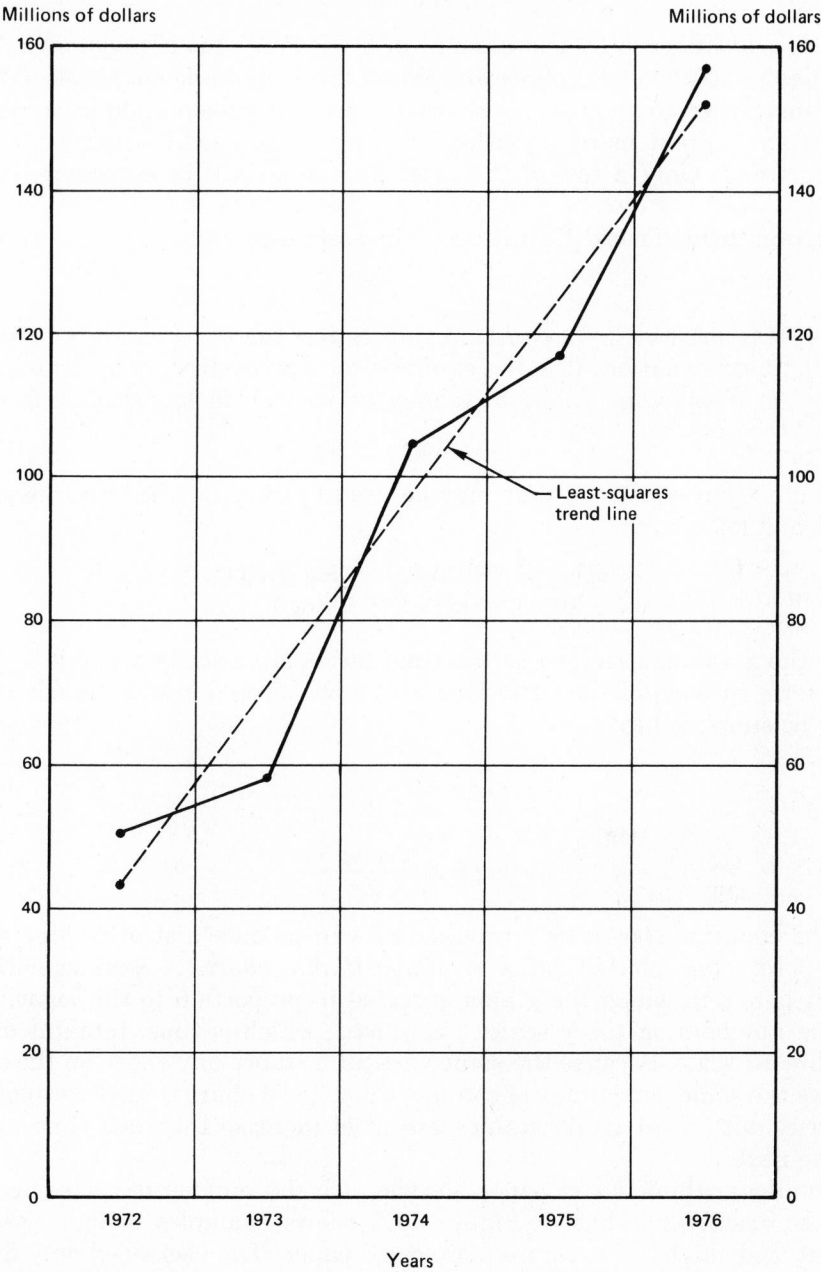

Source: Table 14.1.

Nonlinear Trend

In the discussion of linear trend, it was assumed that a straight line would best describe the trend in the time series when plotted on an arithmetic chart. The trend equation

$$y_c = a + bx$$

causes y to increase by the amount of b for each unit increase in x. This is called an *arithmetic progression.* When the increase is not constant from one time period to another, some other kind of trend equation is called for. There are a great many equations that might be used to describe a nonlinear trend. Only a few of the most important will be considered here.

Exponential Trend Equations. The trend equation

$$y_c = ab^x$$

causes y to increase by a constant rate rather than a constant amount as in the linear equation. It is the equation for a *geometric progression* and is called an *exponential equation.* It may be written in logarithmic form as

$$\log y_c = \log a + \log bx \dots\dots\dots\dots\dots\dots\dots(14.6)$$

The normal equations that may be used to compute the two constants, $\log a$ and $\log b$, are:

$$\Sigma(\log y) = n(\log a) + (\log b)\Sigma x$$
$$\Sigma(x \log y) = (\log a)\Sigma x + (\log b)\Sigma x^2.$$

If the x values assigned to the time series are selected so that $\Sigma x = 0$, one term in each of the equations above will drop out and the equations may be simplified to:

$$\log a = \frac{\Sigma(\log y)}{n} \dots\dots\dots\dots\dots\dots\dots\dots(14.7)$$

$$\log b = \frac{\Sigma(x \log y)}{\Sigma x^2} \dots\dots\dots\dots\dots\dots\dots\dots(14.8)$$

The equation shown by Formula 14.6 will produce a straight line when the points are plotted on a *semilogarithmic chart.* A semilogarithmic chart is one in which the y axis is scaled in proportion to the logarithms of the numbers on the y scale. The x axis, which is time, remains on an arithmetic scale. Because the same vertical distance anywhere on the chart shows the same percentage of change, this type of chart is ideal for plotting a series with a relatively stable percent of increase from one time period to the next.

Semilogarithmic chart paper, drawn with the number of cycles needed, can be readily purchased. Figure 14.2 shows examples of four possible scales that might be set up on two-cycle paper. The user need only follow these rules in setting up the scale for the y axis:

1. The first numbered line (in the first cycle) may be labeled with any positive value that is convenient to show the data. The value cannot be zero.
2. The second numbered line is double the value of the first.
3. For each additional numbered line in that cycle, add the difference between the values of the first and second lines.
4. The value of the top line in a cycle is always 10 times the value of the bottom line in that cycle.
5. No part of the vertical scale may be omitted.

FIGURE 14.2

Sample Logarithmic Scales, Two-Cycle Paper

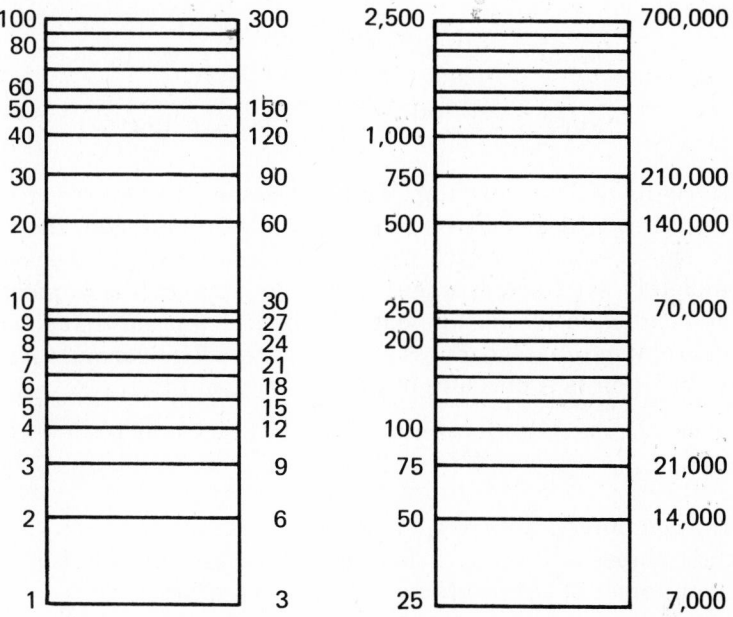

■ *Example.* If one wished to use a trend line to describe the growth in earnings of the United Technologies Corporation from 1972 through 1976 based on the average rate of increase during the period, the exponential equation below might be used:

$$\log y_c = 1.9510634 + 0.129157x$$

origin: July 1, 1974
x unit: one year
y unit: earnings in millions of dollars.

The constants in this equation are computed from the data in Table 14.2, using Formulas 14.7 and 14.8.

TABLE 14.2

Annual Earnings of United Technologies Corporation, 1972–1976 (Computation of exponential trend)

Year	Earnings* y	log y	x	x^2	x log y	log y_c	y_c
1972	50.6	1.704151	−2	4	−3.408302	1.6927494	49.29
1973	58.1	1.764176	−1	1	−1.764176	1.8219064	66.36
1974	104.7	2.019947	0	0	0	1.9510634	89.34
1975	117.5	2.070038	1	1	2.070038	2.0802204	120.29
1976	157.4	2.197005	2	4	4.394010	2.2093774	161.95
Total	448.3	9.755317	0	10	1.291570	9.7553170	

* Millions of dollars
Source: Table 14.1

$$\log a = \frac{\Sigma(\log y)}{n} = \frac{9.755317}{5} = 1.9510634$$

$$\log b = \frac{\Sigma(x \log y)}{x^2} = \frac{1.291570}{10} = 0.129157.$$

Comparison of Forecasting Models. Having fit two trend equations to the annual earnings of United Technologies Corporation, the forecaster might ask the question, "Which model provides the better forecast?" There is no completely satisfactory answer, but one approach is to measure how well each trend equation fits the data on the assumption that the goodness of the fit is related to the goodness of the forecast. This formula for *residual standard deviation* is a measure of the goodness of fit:

$$\hat{\sigma}_{y.x} = \sqrt{\frac{\Sigma(y - y_c)^2}{n - k}} \quad \dots\dots\dots\dots\dots\dots\dots\dots\text{(14.9)}$$

where
  y_c is the computed value of y
  n is the number of time periods used to compute the equation
  k is the number of constants in the trend equation.

■ *Example.* Using the data for United Technologies from 1972 through 1976, the least squares straight line and the exponential trend equations may be evaluated as follows:

Year	Earnings* y	Least Squares y_c	$y - y_c$	$(y - y_c)^2$	Exponential y_c	$y - y_c$	$(y - y_c)^2$
1972	50.6	43.06	7.54	56.8516	49.29	1.31	1.7161
1973	58.1	70.36	−12.26	150.3076	66.36	−8.26	68.2276
1974	104.7	97.66	7.04	49.5616	89.34	15.36	235.9296
1975	117.5	124.96	−7.46	55.6516	120.29	−2.79	7.7841
1976	157.4	152.26	5.14	26.4196	161.95	−4.55	20.7025
Total				338.7920			334.3599

* Millions of dollars

Since both equations have two constants, degrees of freedom are $5 - 2$ for each residual standard deviation. For the least squares straight line:

$$\hat{\sigma}_{y.x} = \sqrt{\frac{338.7920}{3}} = 10.627$$

For the exponential:

$$\hat{\sigma}_{y.x} = \sqrt{\frac{334.3599}{3}} = 10.557.$$

The exponential equation is a slightly better fit to the data.

It should be pointed out that while the more complicated equations (those with the most constants) may provide the best short-term forecast, the simpler models, such as the straight line, are often best for long-term forecasts.

Polynomial Trend Equations. Polynomial trend equations take the form

$$y_c = a + bx + cx^2 + dx^3 + \cdots + jx^n \,\ldots\ldots\ldots\ldots\ldots(14.10)$$

where
a is the value of y_c when $x = 0$
b is the slope of the line at the origin
c is the rate of change in the slope at the origin
d is the change in the rate of change, etc.
n is a positive integer.

The straight line is a special case in which the value of c is zero, which means there is no change in the slope and the only two terms to the right of the equality sign are a and bx. It is said to be a *first-degree curve*.

When the term cx^2 is added, the equation will produce a curved trend line such as that shown in Figure 14.4. Since x is carried to the second power, this is a *second-degree curve*. A *third-degree curve* tends to change direction twice and a *fourth-degree curve* three times.

While it may be possible to have a polynomial trend equation fit the data quite closely by increasing the degree of the curve, there is no advantage in doing this since the equation will no longer be describing trend but will also be describing other fluctuations such as cyclical or even erratic. As a practical matter, curves more complex than the third degree are seldom used to describe trend.

All polynomial trend equations may be fitted by the method of least squares. An nth degree polynomial requires $n + 1$ equations, such as these:

Equation

$$\text{I.} \quad \Sigma y = na \quad + b\Sigma x \quad + c\Sigma x^2 \quad + \cdots + j\Sigma x^n$$
$$\text{II.} \quad \Sigma xy = a\Sigma x \quad + b\Sigma x^2 \quad + c\Sigma x^3 \quad + \cdots + j\Sigma x^{n+1}$$
$$\text{III.} \quad \Sigma x^2y = a\Sigma x^2 + b\Sigma x^3 \quad + c\Sigma x^4 \quad + \cdots + j\Sigma x^{n+2}$$

$$\cdots$$

$$n + 1 \, \Sigma x^n y = a\Sigma x^n + b\Sigma x^{n+1} + c\Sigma x^{n+2} + \cdots + j\Sigma x^{2n}.$$

Excellent computer programs are available in most computer libraries for polynomial curve fitting.

FIGURE 14.3

Annual Earnings of United Technologies Corporation, 1972–1976

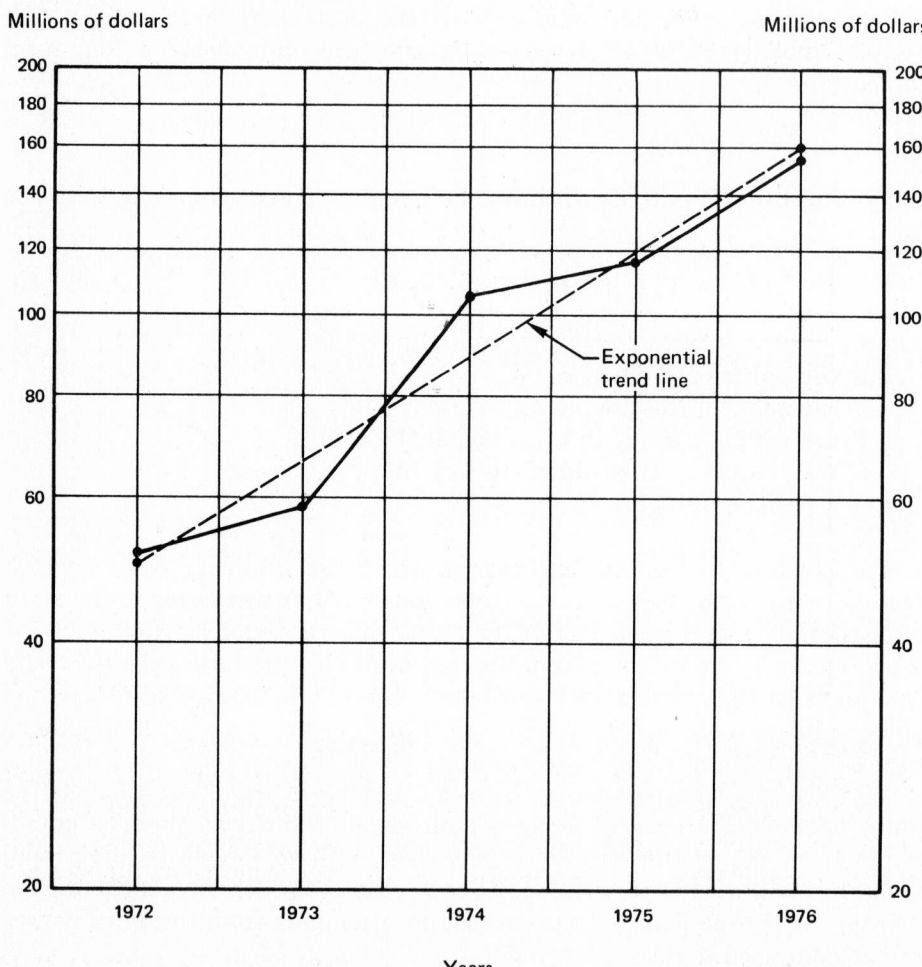

Source: Table 14.2

Time Series and Index Numbers   **Part 6**

FIGURE 14.4

Typical Forms of Polynomial Trend Lines

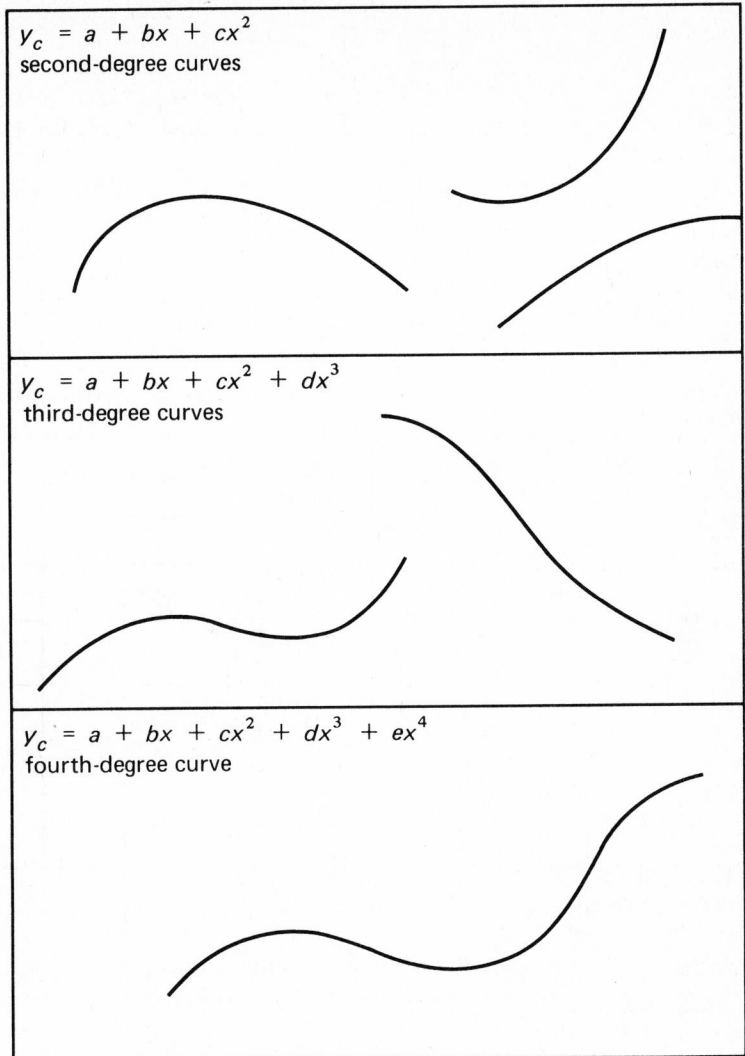

$y_c = a + bx + cx^2$
second-degree curves

$y_c = a + bx + cx^2 + dx^3$
third-degree curves

$y_c = a + bx + cx^2 + dx^3 + ex^4$
fourth-degree curve

■ *Example.* The number of amendments to the Texas Constitution submitted to the voters by the Texas Legislature from 1947 through 1975 is shown in Table 14.3. A plot of the data is shown in Figure 14.5. A computer program was used to fit first- through sixth-degree polynomial trend equations for the 15 observations in the series.[1] The results were:

---

[1] Davis Hogben, Sally T. Peavy, and Ruth N. Varner. *OMNITAB II User's Reference Manual*, National Bureau of Standards Technical Report 552. (Washington: U.S. Government Printing Office, 1971), pp. 138–45.

Degree of curve	Equation
First	$y_c = 7.94 + 0.51x$
Second	$y_c = 5.35 + 1.42x - 0.057x^2$
Third	$y_c = 16.65 - 5.90x + 1.05x^2 - 0.046x^3$
Fourth	$y_c = 8.56 + 1.96x - 0.999x^2 + 0.149x^3 - 0.006x^4$
Fifth	$y_c = -7.98 + 23.37x - 9.21x^2 + 1.45x^3 - 0.096x^4 + 0.02x^5$
Sixth	$y_c = 18.54 - 18.98x + 12.51x^2 - 3.70x^3 + 0.46x^4 - 0.028x^5 + 0.0006x^6$

origin: July 1, 1947

x unit: two years

y unit: number of amendments

TABLE 14.3

Number of Amendments to the Texas Constitution Submitted to the Voters by the Texas Legislature, 1947–1975

Year	Number of amendments	Year	Number of amendments
1947	9	1963	7
1949	10	1965	27
1951	7	1967	20
1953	14	1969	16
1955	9	1971	18
1957	6	1973	9
1959	4	1975	10
1961	14		

Source: Unpublished report of Texas Legislative Council, Austin, Texas.

The first-, third-, and fifth-degree curves are shown in Figure 14.5.

The residual standard deviation for each of the polynomial equations is shown below:

Degree of polynomial	Number of constants	Degrees of freedom	Residual standard deviation
First	2	13	5.96
Second	3	12	6.11
Third	4	11	5.45
Fourth	5	10	5.46
Fifth	6	9	5.27
Sixth	7	8	5.06

The sixth-order equation has the smallest residual standard deviation and is the best fit.

FIGURE 14.5

**Number of Amendments to the Texas Constitution
Submitted to the Voters by the Texas Legislature,
1947–1975**

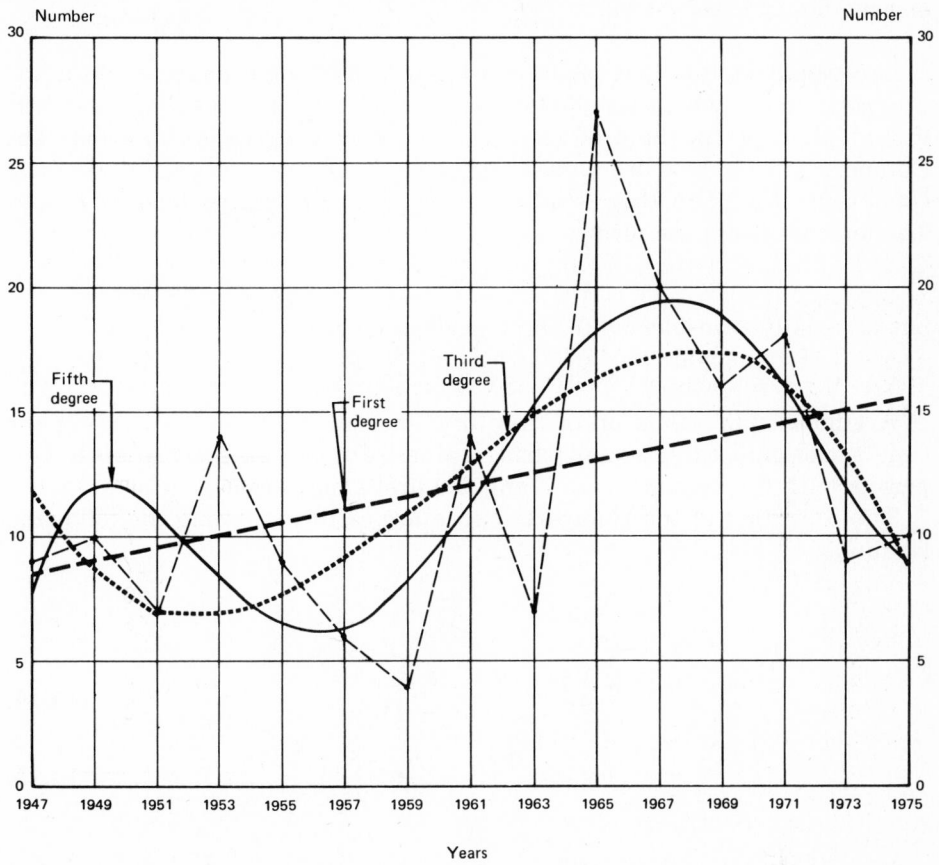

Source: Table 14.3

Growth Curves. The linear and nonlinear trends just described frequently will give excellent fits to time series that do not exceed about 25 or 30 years in length. However, such trend equations may be inadequate to describe growth for longer time series. There is considerable evidence to show that many of the so-called *growth curves* that have an upper limit are frequently more appropriate to describe the trends in long time series. Three of the more important types of curves are mentioned here, with examples given for the latter two.

MODIFIED EXPONENTIAL. The formula for the *modified exponential trend* is written as follows:

$$y_c = a + bc^x \dots\dots\dots\dots\dots\dots\dots\dots\dots(14.11)$$

This formula will be recognized as a modification of the exponential trend equation $y_c = ab^x$ to which a constant has been added. For this curve the amount of growth (or decline) decreases by a constant percentage per unit of time. The constant, a, is either the upper or the lower limit, or asymptote, of the curve.

GOMPERTZ CURVE. One of the most common of the growth curves is the *Gompertz curve*, which was developed for use in actuarial science and was first applied to the field of economics by Ray B. Prescott in 1922. The Gompertz curve has been used extensively by the National Industrial Conference Board in their studies of long time-growth patterns of states. The formula takes the form

$$y_c = ab^{c^x}$$

but is usually transformed to the logarithmic form

$$\log y_c = \log a + (\log b)c^x \dots\dots\dots\dots\dots\dots(14.12)$$

A simple approximation of this function can be made by dividing the time series into three equal parts. Values of x are assigned to each time period, with the origin $(x = 0)$ being the first time period.

The constants of the Gompertz curve are estimated using the following formulas:

$$c^n = \frac{S_3 - S_2}{S_2 - S_1} \dots\dots\dots\dots\dots\dots\dots\dots\dots(14.13)$$

$$\log b = \frac{(S_2 - S_1)(c - 1)}{(c^n - 1)^2} \dots\dots\dots\dots\dots\dots\dots(14.14)$$

$$\log a = \frac{1}{n}\left(S_1 - \frac{S_2 - S_1}{c^n - 1}\right) \dots\dots\dots\dots\dots\dots(14.15)$$

where
   $\log a$ is the logarithm of the maximum value that the curve approaches
   $(\log b)c^x$ measures the amount by which the trend value falls short of the maximum at a given point in time
S_1, S_2, and S_3 are the subtotals of $\log y$ for each of the three subperiods
n is the number of time periods in each subperiod.

■ *Example.* In Table 14.4 a Gompertz curve is fitted to annual sales of the Burton Manufacturing Company from 1962 through 1976. The constants of the equation are computed below:

$$c^n = \frac{S_3 - S_2}{S_2 - S_1} = \frac{9.12060 - 8.62493}{8.62493 - 6.80015} = 0.27163$$

$$c = \text{antilog}\left[\frac{\log 0.27163}{5}\right] = 0.770541$$

$$\log b = \frac{(S_2 - S_1)(c-1)}{(c^n - 1)^2} = \frac{(1.82479)(-0.229459)}{(0.770541^5 - 1)^2} = -0.789249$$

$$\log a = \frac{1}{n}\left[S_1 - \frac{S_2 - S_1}{c^n - 1}\right] = \frac{1}{5}\left[6.80015 - \frac{1.82479}{0.77054^5 - 1}\right] = 1.86109.$$

The trend values, y_c, computed using the constants above are shown in Figure 14.6 to display the shape of the curve. It is apparent from the figure that the rate of growth in sales is constantly decreasing with time.

The equation is

$$\log y_c = 1.86109 + (-0.789249)(0.770541^x)$$
origin: July 1, 1962
x unit: one year
y unit: sales in millions of dollars.

TABLE 14.4

Annual Sales of the Burton Manufacturing Company, 1962–1976 (millions of dollars)

Year	x	y	$\log y$	Subperiod totals	c^x	$(\log b)c^x$	$\log y_c =$ $(\log b)c^x +$ $\log a$	y_c
1962	0	13	1.11394		1.000000	−0.78925	1.07184	11.80
1963	1	17	1.23045		0.770541	−0.60815	1.25294	17.90
1964	2	21	1.32222	$S_1 = 6.80015$	0.593734	−0.46860	1.39249	24.69
1965	3	34	1.53148		0.457497	−0.36107	1.50001	31.62
1966	4	40	1.60206		0.352520	−0.27822	1.58286	38.27
1967	5	44	1.64345		0.271631	−0.21438	1.64670	44.33
1968	6	52	1.71600		0.209303	−0.16519	1.69590	49.65
1969	7	53	1.72428	$S_2 = 8.62493$	0.161277	−0.12729	1.73380	54.18
1970	8	57	1.75587		0.124270	−0.09808	1.76301	57.94
1971	9	61	1.78533		0.095756	−0.07558	1.78551	61.03
1972	10	63	1.79934		0.073784	−0.05823	1.80286	63.51
1973	11	65	1.81291		0.056853	−0.04487	1.81622	65.50
1974	12	64	1.80618	$S_3 = 9.12060$	0.043808	−0.03458	1.82651	67.07
1975	13	69	1.83885		0.033756	−0.02664	1.83445	68.30
1976	14	73	1.86332		0.026010	−0.02053	1.84056	69.27

Source: Company records.

The data are plotted on a semilog chart to show that the series is increasing at a decreasing rate. A Gompertz curve should not be fit to a series with a constant or increasing rate of growth.

SEASONAL VARIATION

While there are many techniques available for computing an index of seasonal variation, many of the simpler methods were devised prior to

FIGURE 14.6

Annual Sales of the Burton Manufacturing Company, 1962–1976

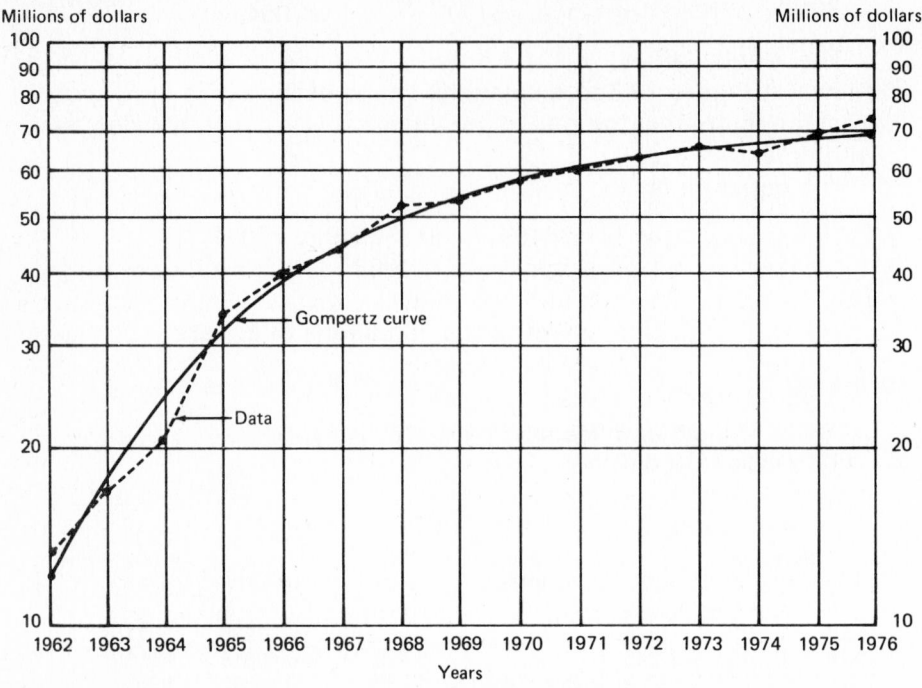

the development of computers and were designed for manual computation. Any method for computing such an index can be programmed for a computer solution. The method should be designed to meet the following criteria:

1. It should measure only the seasonal forces in the data. It should not be influenced by the forces of trend or cycle that may be present.
2. It should modify the erratic fluctuations in the data with an acceptable system of averaging.
3. It should recognize slowly changing seasonal patterns that may be be present and modify the index to keep up with these changes.

One method that meets the criteria above is called the *ratio of two-item average of a 12-month moving average*. The ratios computed by this method are called *specific seasonals*. In terms of the multiplicative time-series model, $y = T \times S \times C \times E$, a specific seasonal is a measure of the seasonal and the erratic components in the series.

$$SS = \frac{y}{\text{moving average}} = \frac{T \times S \times C \times E}{T \times C} = S \times E$$

where

SS is used to represent a specific seasonal.

The moving average technique eliminates the effects of the trend and the cyclical components by comparing the y value for each month with the year in which that month is centered. A two-item average is necessary to adjust for the awkward fact that a year has an even rather than an odd number of months.

An arithmetic mean of the specific seasonals for each month would be one way to eliminate much of the erratic component still left in the data and to get a measure of the seasonal importance of that month. An even better device is to compute a least squares trend line for the specific seasonals for each month. This means a total of 12 trend equations, one for each month. The value of y_c on the trend line for January at any particular time (x) will be a measure of the seasonal importance of January at that time. The use of a trend line takes care both of the problem of smoothing (averaging) the erratic component and at the same time adjusting for any long-term shifts in the seasonal pattern. If the importance of a particular month in the seasonal pattern is not changing, the b value of the trend equation of specific seasonals for that month will be zero.

If, for a given year, the total of the trend values (Σy_c) for each month is 1,200, these 12 trend values constitute the index of seasonal variation for that year. If the total is not equal to 1,200, each of the trend values should be modified by multiplying it by a *leveling factor*, which is computed as follows:

$$\text{leveling factor} = \frac{1,200}{\text{total of the 12 trend values}}.$$

■ *Example.* The Bureau of Business Research of The University of Texas at Austin collects and publishes figures monthly on residential construction authorized in Texas. These figures come from building permits issued for building within incorporated areas of Texas cities. Because there is a distinct seasonal pattern in these data, an index of seasonal variation is computed using the method of ratio of two-item average of a 12-month moving average.

Table 14.5 demonstrates how the specific seasonals might be computed using an electronic calculator. The specific seasonal of 98.19 for July, 1976, was computed as follows:

1. The y values for all 12 months in 1976 were totaled, and the sum of 1,548.0 was centered between June and July, 1976. The next 12-month total of 1,627.9 was secured by subtracting the value 84.8 (January, 1976) from the old total and adding the value 164.7 (January, 1977).
2. The two-year moving total of 3,175.9 is the sum of 1,548.0 and 1,627.9.
3. The 12-month moving average of 132.3 is $\dfrac{3,175.9}{24}$.
4. The specific seasonal for July, 1976, is found by dividing the y

value 129.9 for July, 1976, by the corresponding 12-month moving average of 132.3 and multiplying by 100. This value is $\frac{129.9}{132.3}100 = 98.17$.

The bureau always works with 10 years of data at a time and more significant digits than are shown here when computing an index of seasonal variation. This example has been simplified to show only a small part of the series.

TABLE 14.5

Residential Construction Authorized in Texas:
Work Sheet for the Computation of Specific Seasonals
for an Index of Seasonal Variation

Year and month	Construction (thousands of dollars) y	12-month moving total, centered	Two-year moving total	12-month moving average, centered	Ratio to 12-month moving average, SS
1976 Jan.	84.8				
Feb.	93.6				
Mar.	115.6				
Apr.	144.3				
May	124.1				
June	130.8				
July	129.9	1,548.0 / 1,627.9	3,175.9	132.3	98.19
Aug.	142.9				
Sept.	148.0				
Oct.	156.6				
Nov.	123.6				
Dec.	153.8				
1977 Jan.	164.7				

Source: Bureau of Business Research, The University of Texas at Austin.

Table 14.6 shows the specific seasonals for July from 1968 through 1976. A least-squares trend equation is fit to the nine values and is then used to produce an estimate of the seasonal index for July of 1977.

$$a = \frac{\Sigma y}{n} = \frac{896.75}{9} = 99.64 \quad \text{and} \quad b = \frac{\Sigma xy}{\Sigma x^2} = \frac{-65.62}{60} = -1.094$$

Estimate for July, 1977:

$$y_c = 99.64 - 1.094 (5) = 94.17.$$

Specific seasonals and trend estimates for each month are computed in the same manner as for July, and these values are shown in Table 14.7. Since the total of the 12 estimates is greater than 1,200, a leveling factor is computed and applied to the value for each month to give the final index of seasonal variation for that month. The total of the 12 indexes is now 1,200.

TABLE 14.6

Residential Construction Authorized in Texas:
Work Sheet for the Computation of the Index of
Seasonal Variation for the Month of July, 1977

Year	Specific seasonals for July y	x	x^2	xy
1968	102.76	−4	16	−411.04
1969	104.52	−3	9	−313.56
1970	103.66	−2	4	−207.32
1971	100.07	−1	1	−100.07
1972	99.16	0	0	0
1973	97.30	1	1	97.30
1974	96.96	2	4	193.92
1975	94.13	3	9	282.39
1976	98.19*	4	16	392.76
Total	896.75	0	60	−65.62

Source: Bureau of Business Research, The University of Texas at Austin.
* The computation of this value is shown in Table 14.5

TABLE 14.7

Residential Construction Authorized in Texas:
Work Sheet for the Computation of the Index of
Seasonal Variation for 1977

Month	Trend estimate for month	Leveling factor	Index of seasonal variation
January	96.40	0.9978	96.19
February	106.57	0.9978	106.34
March	118.79	0.9978	118.53
April	121.56	0.9978	121.29
May	113.85	0.9978	113.60
June	105.28	0.9978	105.05
July	94.17*	0.9978	93.96
August	101.09	0.9978	100.87
September	75.56	0.9978	75.39
October	88.32	0.9978	88.13
November	92.83	0.9978	92.63
December	88.21	0.9978	88.02
Total	1,202.63		1,200.00

Source: Bureau of Business Research, The University of Texas at Austin.
* This value was computed in Table 14.6.

The leveling factor $= \dfrac{1,200.00}{1,202.63} = 0.9978$.

Finally, data on residential construction for 1977 are shown in Table 14.8 and are adjusted for seasonal variation using the index computed in Table 14.7.

TABLE 14.8

Residential Construction Authorized in Texas in 1977, Adjusted for Seasonal Variation (millions of dollars)

Month	Data	Seasonal index*	Seasonally adjusted data
January	164.7	96.19	171.2
February	169.0	106.34	158.9
March	193.9	118.53	163.6
Apri!	182.3	121.29	150.3
May	182.3	113.60	160.5
June	185.7	105.05	176.8
July	168.8	93.96	179.7
August	189.3	100.87	187.7
September	178.1	75.39	236.2
October	175.2	88.13	198.8
November	161.8	92.63	174.7
December	181.2	88.02	205.9

Source: Bureau of Business Research, The University of Texas at Austin.
* This index was computed in Table 14.7.

CYCLICAL FLUCTUATIONS

Cyclical fluctuations, which have been defined as wavelike fluctuations about trend, are more difficult to measure than either the trend or the seasonal components. The very fact that the length and the amplitude of the cycle may vary substantially from one cycle to the next makes any kind of direct measurement hazardous. While it is possible to compute averages both of length and of amplitude, the dispersion about these averages is so great as to render them virtually useless. Nevertheless, business executives are vitally concerned with the measurement of cyclical fluctuations, particularly as they affect their own businesses. Such measurements are usually made indirectly, as may be seen from the discussion that follows.

The classical approach to measuring cyclical fluctuations has been to measure and remove the forces exerted by the trend and the seasonal components, thus leaving a measure of cyclical and erratic components. Erratic fluctuations probably cannot be removed altogether, but they can be modified by a moving average. The decomposition of the multiplicative time-series model may be shown as follows:

Original data $(y) = T \times S \times C \times E$

Data adjusted for seasonal $= \dfrac{T \times S \times C \times E}{S} = T \times C \times E$

Data adjusted for seasonal and trend $= \dfrac{T \times C \times E}{T} = C \times E$

A moving average of the values of $C \times E$ gives an estimate of C.

■ *Example.* To demonstrate the technique of decomposition of a time series, the theoretical data shown in Table 14.9 are first deseasonalized, then detrended, and finally smoothed with a three-period moving average to give an index of cycle. Columns (2), (4), and (5) are in the original units of the data. The values in Columns (3), (6), and (8) are index numbers with a base = 100.00. In the example it is assumed that an index of seasonal variation is available on a quarterly basis and that a least-squares trend equation for a straight line has already been computed to give the trend values by quarters. The data in Table 14.9 are shown also in Figure 14.7. Graph A in that figure shows the original series; graph B shows the trend line and the series after adjustment for seasonal variation; graph C shows the series after adjustment for both trend and seasonal; and graph D shows the estimate of cycle. The shading in graph D is intended to emphasize the swings above and below 100%, which represents normal for cycle.

TABLE 14.9

Computation of a Measure of Cycle by Eliminating Seasonal and Trend and by Modifying Erratic Fluctuations

Year and quarter (1)	Original data $y =$ $T \times S \times C \times E$ (2)	I.S.V. S (3)	$T \times C \times E$ (4)	Trend T (5)	$C \times E$ (6)	3-qr. moving total (7)	3-qr. moving average C (8)
1973 1	274.4	108	254.1	242	105.0	...	...
2	262.4	96	273.3	244	112.0	328.5	109.5
3	224.9	82	274.3	246	111.5	324.0	108.0
4	284.1	114	249.2	248	100.5	309.0	103.0
1974 1	261.9	108	242.5	250	97.0	294.0	98.0
2	233.5	96	243.2	252	96.5	285.0	95.0
3	190.6	82	232.4	254	91.5	282.0	94.0
4	274.3	114	240.6	256	94.0	286.5	95.5
1975 1	281.4	108	260.6	258	101.0	292.5	97.5
2	243.4	96	253.5	260	97.5	300.0	100.0
3	218.0	82	265.9	262	101.5	310.5	103.5
4	335.6	114	294.4	264	111.5	321.0	107.0
1976 1	310.3	108	287.3	266	108.0	330.0	110.0
2	284.3	96	296.1	268	110.5	342.0	114.0
3	273.5	82	333.5	270	123.5	354.0	118.0
4	372.1	114	326.4	272	120.0	...	...

FIGURE 14.7

**Computation of Cycle by Eliminating Seasonal
and Trend and Modifying Erratic Fluctuations**

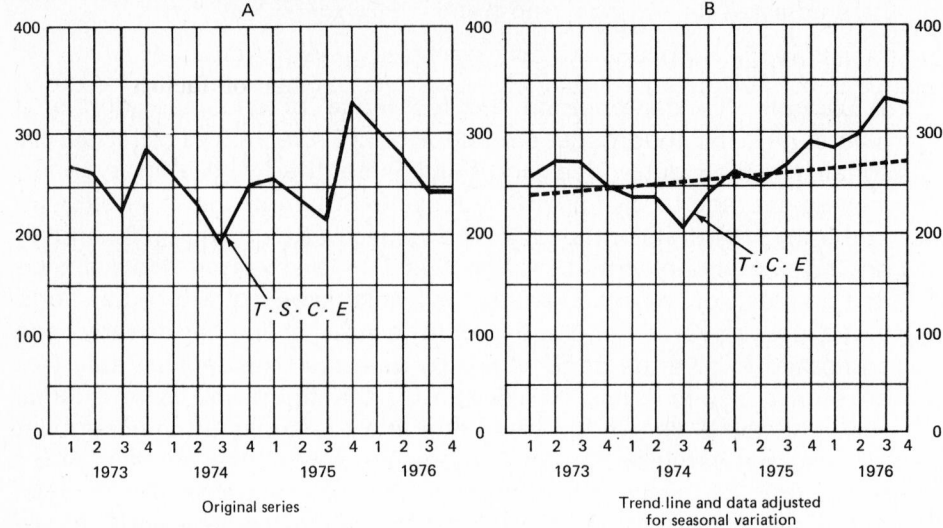

A

Original series

B

Trend line and data adjusted
for seasonal variation

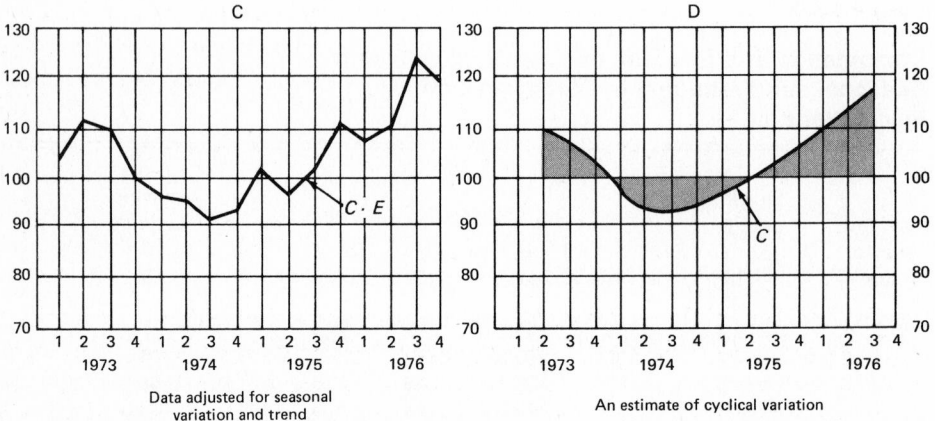

C

Data adjusted for seasonal
variation and trend

D

An estimate of cyclical variation

One of the greatest uncertainties in the decomposition approach lies in the choice of the equation to represent trend. A good example is found in the data shown in Figure 14.5 on page 463. Here, three possible trend lines have been plotted on a time series representing number of amendments to the Texas Constitution. Quite obviously, any measure of cycle computed for these data based on one trend equation would vary substantially from any other based on a different trend equation. A high-degree polynomial would be measuring both trend and cycle, so one could not measure cycle by taking out trend.

The problem of forecasting the critical turns in the business cycle is discussed briefly in the discussion of a diffusion index later in this chapter.

ERRATIC FLUCTUATIONS

Earlier in this chapter erratic fluctuations were defined as a random component. This category includes a great number of factors, some of which can be identified and others cannot. For example, unusual increases or decreases in sales due to strikes, fire, weather, or special promotions can all be classed as erratic. A very pronounced erratic fluctuation produced by a national emergency such as a war may be difficult to distinguish from the trend component if the war lasts long enough. Many small erratic fluctuations have no known cause.

FORECASTING TIME SERIES

The future is always filled with uncertainty, and no statistical technique exists that can enable one to forecast the future state of events with certainty. Even so, one of the most compelling reasons for studying past events is to allow the forecaster to use an understanding of the past to predict the future.

The management of every organization has no choice but to make forecasts and to use those forecasts to plan for the future. The greatest single hazard in forecasting lies in the fact that unforeseen events can always occur and invalidate a forecast. The likelihood of a serious forecast error increases with the length of the forecast.

Since the manager must forecast, the problem is to determine the most accurate ways to make the forecast. The techniques available are many and varied, but only a few of the most common ones are discussed here.

Judgment Forecasting

The administrator who does not forecast is admitting that decisions concerning the future of the organization are based on hunches and intuition, assisted by whatever facts may be available at the time. Judgment forecasts made by experienced administrators may be very good, but like judgment samples, they may be very poor; and there is no way to determine the quality of the forecast in advance.

In making forecasts or in deciding which of several forecasts may be best, judgment based on past experience will play an important role regardless of the quantitative methods used to make the forecast.

Trend Forecasting

Frequently the researcher will study the past pattern of the trend in a series in order to obtain a clue about the future direction that series may take. The forecast can be made mechanically by merely extrapolating the trend equation into any future time period for which a forecast is desired. This process can be complicated, however, by the need to choose from among many different trend models that may be fitted to any given time series. Judgment plays an important role in this decision, and it can be enhanced by plotting the data and observing the type of trend the pattern of the series suggests.

The researcher must also take into consideration the nature of the forecast desired. For example, trend forecasting is more useful in long-term forecasts than in short-term forecasts. Short-term forecasts may be more influenced by seasonal, cyclical, and erratic forces than by trend.

Finally, the researcher must make a decision as to whether the forces that were at work in the past to produce a trend will continue to work in the same way in the future. If not, there is no statistical basis for the trend extrapolation.

Cycle Forecasting

Measuring the past effects of the business cycle can be accomplished by decomposing a time series as described earlier in this chapter. Forecasting future changes in the cycle is a much more difficult undertaking.

Analysis by the National Bureau of Economic Research has shown that certain statistical time series may be useful as indicators of cyclical patterns of revivals and recessions of business activity.

The business cycle is a loosely coordinated movement whose net effect is that of cyclical expansion or contraction in the economy over time. It tends to follow closely a measure such as the Federal Reserve Board Index of Industrial Production or Gross National Product. A study of individual economic time series has shown that some series tend to increase or decrease ahead of the same kinds of swings of the business cycle. Some tend to be roughly coincident, some tend to lag the cycle, and in the remaining series there seems to be no measurable relationship at all. It is that group of *leading indicators* that provides a method of forecasting changes in direction of the business cycle as a whole.

The U.S. Department of Commerce uses the 12 leading indicators shown below to compute a measure called a *diffusion index*.

1. Average workweek of production workers in manufacturing
2. Index of net business formation
3. Index of 500 common stock prices
4. Layoff rate in manufacturing (inverted)
5. New orders for consumer goods and materials (1967 dollars)
6. Index of new building permits for private housing units
7. Contract and orders for plant and equipment (1967 dollars)
8. Net change in inventories on hand and on order (1967 dollars)
9. Percent change in sensitive prices in Wholesale Price Index (smoothed)

10. Percent of vendor companies reporting slower deliveries
11. Money balance (1967 dollars)
12. Percent change in total liquid assets (smoothed).

A diffusion index is a simple measure that summarizes changes in the group of leading indicators. It expresses the percent of the series that have risen over a given span of time. For example, if eight of the indicators were higher than they were in the previous month, the index would be $\frac{8}{12} = .67$ or 67 percent. The turning points of the diffusion index tend to lead turning points in the aggregate business cycle, and the index suggests how widespread the change may be.

Regression Forecasting

Some of the unique problems connected with time-series analysis were mentioned at the beginning of this chapter. One of these problems centers on the correlation of time series and forecasts using regression.

Because time-series data consist of observations of a variable at different points in time, there is usually a mutual dependence of successive observations. It is this lack of independence that may seriously affect the interpretation of the least squares estimates of population parameters. In the regression equation (Formula 12.5), $y_c = a + bx + \epsilon$, y and ϵ are assumed to be random variables, but not x. The validity of traditional statistical tests is dependent on the assumption that the successive values of ϵ are independent of one another and are normally distributed. If this is not true, the sample cannot be treated as a random sample, and the traditional tests of significance are not applicable.

An observed value of y in an economic time series is usually correlated with, and not independent of, the value of that same variable in the previous time period. This type of correlation is called *autocorrelation*. This term is used to describe the lead or lag correlation of a particular time series with itself. When there is a lead or lag correlation between two different time series, this is usually referred to as *serial correlation*.

One way in which the researcher may remove autocorrelation in order to make the observations mutually independent is to eliminate trend from the original data and work with the deviations about trend. If strong cyclical or seasonal components are present in the data, they may also cause autocorrelation. Adjustment for these forces may be necessary.

A lengthy discussion of the problems with and the techniques for handling autocorrelation is not presented here, but the reader can find additional material in specialized books on regression and correlation, time-series analysis, and econometrics.

Box-Jenkins Method of Forecasting

All forecasting methods assume that there is a basic underlying pattern represented by the historical data plus some randomness. The focus of the forecasting method is always to isolate that basic pattern as accurately as possible and then to use it as the basis for future forecasts.

The *Box-Jenkins forecasting method* developed by Professors Box and Jenkins has been described as a philosophy for approaching forecasting situations. It differs from other methods in that it recognizes that any one of many forecasting models may be the correct one to use and that a great deal of experimentation is necessary to select the proper model.

The method divides the forecasting problem into four stages, as shown in Figure 14.8. The approach is for the manager to specify tentatively a forecasting pattern, which may or may not be correct, and then to test it

FIGURE 14.8

The Box-Jenkins Forecasting Method

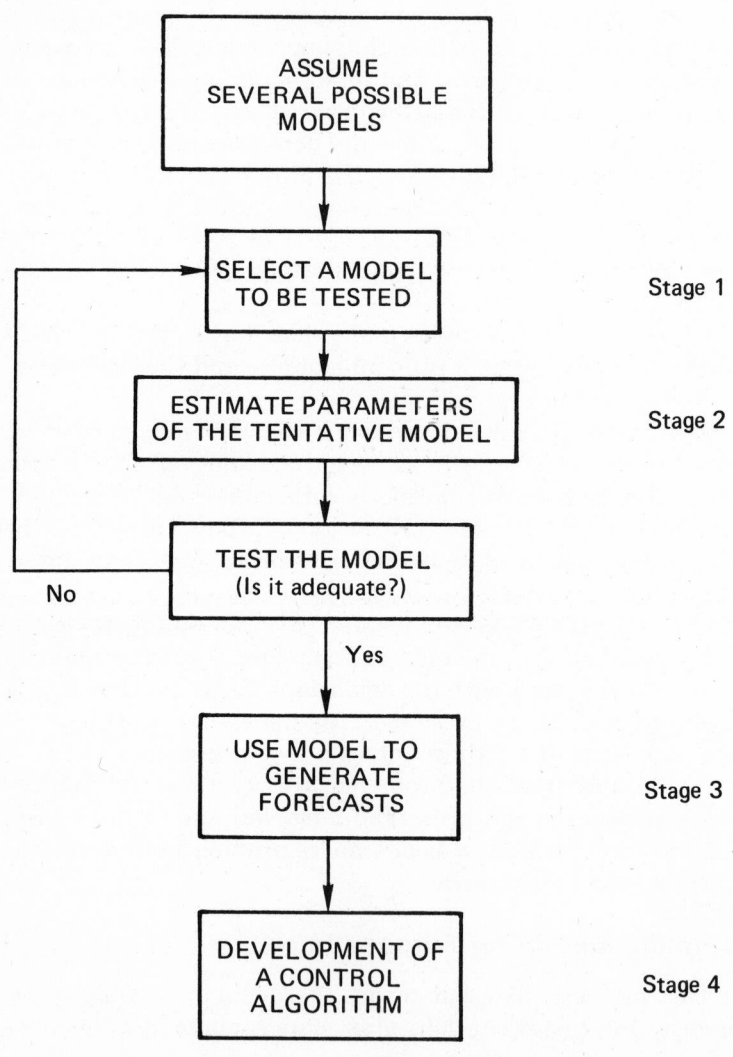

and improve it until the model which gives the most reliable forecast can be identified. The stages can be summarized as follows:

Stage 1 — This stage involves the tentative selection of a model to be tested. This process is a combination of theory and practice.

Stage 2 — This stage consists of fitting that model to the available historical data and then checking to determine if the fit is adequate. If it is not, the forecaster returns to stage 1 and an alternative model is identified.

Stage 3 — At this stage a forecast is developed for some future time period.

Stage 4 — A control algorithm is developed for a situation in which the forecasting method is used for control purposes.

The Box-Jenkins method of forecasting is particularly well suited to handling complex time series and other forecasting situations in which the basic pattern is not readily apparent. With the help of a computer, the power and attractiveness of this forecasting approach is that it can handle complex patterns of data with very little effort on the part of the manager.

Exponential Smoothing

Another forecasting technique with broad application is *exponential smoothing,* which is a term applied to a special type of weighted moving average useful in sales and inventory forecasting.[2]

The chief advantage of this technique lies in the simplicity of using the model in a digital computer. Only five computer instructions are necessary and can be used repeatedly for each degree of smoothing. The data to be stored are quite brief, the computations are quick and simple, and the smoothing constant can be adjusted at will as current information indicates a need for a change. In brief, exponential smoothing overcomes almost all the problems connected with forecasting with a moving average.

The Nature of Exponential Smoothing. One of the fundamental problems in using a moving average is the cumbersome job of keeping track of past observations in order to adjust the moving totals. It is also not possible to forecast with a moving average.

■ *Example.* In the case of a three-month moving average:

Time period (t)	Value (x)	Moving average ($\bar{x}$)
1	10	
2	8	
3	12	$\bar{x}_{t=3} = \dfrac{10 + 8 + 12}{3} = 10$
4	13	$\bar{x}_{t=4} = \dfrac{8 + 12 + 13}{3} = 11.$

---

[2] Robert G. Brown and Richard F. Meyer, "The Fundamental Theorem of Exponential Smoothing," *Operations Research,* Volume 9, No. 5 (September–October, 1961), pp. 673–687.

In order to compute the moving average for time period four, it was necessary to use data for time periods two, three, and four. Even if the new average had been computed as

$$\bar{x}_{t=4} = \bar{x}_{t=3} + \tfrac{1}{3}(13 - 10) = 11,$$

it is still necessary to remember the value of x for time period one. The moving average produces no trend equation to make possible a forecast.

In exponential smoothing, only the old average is retained and the new average is estimated as

new average $= \alpha$ (new value) $+ (1 - \alpha)$ old average,

or, the simple exponential smoothing equation is

$$S_t(x) = \alpha x_t + (1 - \alpha)S_{t-1}(x) \dots\dots\dots\dots\dots\dots(14.16)$$

where
x_t is the value of the series in time period t
$S_t(x)$ is the smoothed value (moving average) of the series in time period t
$S_{t-1}(x)$ is the smoothed value (moving average) of the series in time period just previous to period t
α is the smoothing constant, $0 < \alpha < 1$.

The value $S_{t-1}(x)$ represents the average experience to date for a series. In time period t a new observation x_t becomes available. If S_t is greater than the old average, the new average will be greater than the old, and conversely. The function $S_t(x)$ is a linear combination of all past observations, and the weight given to all previous observations decreases geometrically with time.

■ *Example.* If the value of the smoothing constant is $\alpha = 0.4$, then

Time period	Weight
t	0.4
$t - 1$	0.24
$t - 2$	0.144
$t - 3$	0.0864
etc.	0.1296 (all other).

The weight given to the most recent observation is 0.4 and the weight given to all previous observations is 0.6, which is $1 - \alpha$.

For higher degrees of smoothing, the nth order function may be defined as

$$S_t^n(x) = \alpha S_t^{n-1}(x) + (1 - \alpha)S_{t-1}^n(x) \dots\dots\dots\dots\dots(14.17)$$

Applications have been found in industry for the first three degrees of smoothing, but only simple exponential smoothing will be illustrated here.

Exponential smoothing deals with equally spaced observations in a time series. The time span between successive observations is the *sampling interval*. The appropriate length of the sampling interval depends on the individual series being forecast. It may vary from a few hours in forecasting stock market prices to quarterly data in estimating inventory demands in a very stable industry. If the interval chosen is too short, the cost of making the projections may be excessive; and if the interval is too long, changes in the data pattern will not be reflected as quickly as might be desirable.

Value of the Smoothing Constant. The value of the smoothing constant determines in large part the responsiveness of the smoothing process to changes in current demand. A large smoothing constant will cause the process to adjust rapidly to a change in trend. However, the very fact that it is so sensitive to change will also cause it to react to some of the erratic fluctuations in the data. A small smoothing constant will be less sensitive to important changes in the data but will be influenced less by random changes also. If a significant change in trend is anticipated, the value of the smoothing constant may be increased without difficulty in the computer program. Management need not predict the direction or the magnitude of the change but only the fact that one may take place.

The value of α affects the smoothed estimate or forecast in the same way that the length of the averaging period affects a moving average. The relationship between the smoothing constant and the number of time periods represented by the average is shown in the following formulas and by example in Table 14.10:

$$N = \frac{2}{\alpha} - 1$$

$$\alpha = \frac{2}{N+1}$$

where
N is the number of observations in a moving average.

TABLE 14.10

Smoothing Constants and Equivalent Moving Averages

N	α
3	0.500
4	0.400
5	0.333
7	0.250
9	0.200
19	0.100
199	0.010

Adjustment for Trend. Since exponential smoothing, like any other moving average, lags behind a systematic trend in the data, it is necessary to correct the system for a steadily rising or falling demand. A simple procedure is available to use information stored in the computer to measure a trend and to compensate for it. This procedure uses the differences between successive forecasts as estimates of trend. Exponential smoothing is used on successive differences to compute an average trend. The estimate of trend is adjusted by the smoothing constant and the adjusted value is then added to each new forecast to correct the forecast for trend. The three steps to be taken to adjust for trend are:

1. Change in average = new average − old average or

$$C_t = S_t(x) - S_{t-1}(x) \quad\ldots\ldots\ldots\ldots\ldots\ldots\ldots\ldots\ldots\text{(14.18)}$$

where
C_t is the change in the smoothed value between time period t and the previous time period.

2. New trend = α (change in average) + $(1 - \alpha)$ old trend or

$$T_t = \alpha C_t + (1 - \alpha)T_{t-1} \quad\ldots\ldots\ldots\ldots\ldots\text{(14.19)}$$

where
T_t is the estimated trend for time period t
T_{t-1} is the estimate of trend for the previous time period.

3. Expected demand (forecast) = new average + $\dfrac{(1 - \alpha)}{\alpha}$ (new trend) or

$$D_{t+1} = S_t(x) + \frac{(1 - \alpha)}{\alpha} T_t \quad\ldots\ldots\ldots\ldots\text{(14.20)}$$

where
D_{t+1} is the expected demand or the forecast for the next time period.

This method of correcting for trend still has some lag and requires several sampling intervals to compensate fully for a rise or fall in demand resulting from trend. The number of sampling intervals required is dependent upon the smoothing constant. For this reason the smoothing constant should be increased in anticipation of a change in trend.

Adjustment for Seasonal Variation. Before any steps are taken to apply exponential smoothing for seasonal variation, one must make certain a definite seasonal pattern exists and has been measured by computing an index of seasonal variation. Adjustment for seasonal variation should be made only if the seasonal variation exceeds in magnitude the erratic fluctuations in the data.

Once the index of seasonal variation is at hand, the forecast can be adjusted as follows:

adjusted expected demand = expected demand times the index of seasonal variation for the month of the forecast or

$$AD_{t+1} = D_{t+1}(I.S.V._{t+1}) \dots\dots\dots\dots\dots\dots\dots\dots(14.21)$$

where

AD_{t+1} is the expected demand for period $t + 1$ adjusted for seasonal variation

$I.S.V._{t+1}$ is the index of seasonal variation for period $t + 1$.

The adjusted forecast is not stored in the computer or used in any subsequent computations. To prevent distortion in future forecasts, the adjusting process should be kept outside the exponential smoothing system.

Estimating Initial Conditions. Before exponential smoothing can begin, the initial values for the average and for trend must be estimated in some fashion. The most common method used to get the estimate for the average is to use an average of past demand. If a trend equation has been fitted to past observations, the slope of this trend line will provide an initial estimate of trend. Often, a value of $\alpha = 0.50$ is used for the first three time periods forecast to correct automatically the system for any larger error in estimates of appropriate starting conditions.

Forecast Errors. The multiplicity of unpredictable influences on demand means that actual demand will fluctuate around the average, creating errors in the forecast of demand. Assuming that these errors are serially independent and normally distributed, the probability that an error of any given magnitude will occur can be calculated once the mean and the standard deviation of the error have been estimated. Error may be expressed as

$$e = D_{t+1} - x_{t+1} \dots\dots\dots\dots\dots\dots\dots\dots\dots\dots(14.22)$$

where

e is the error in the forecast.

■ *Example.* Table 14.11 shows the exponential smoothing of the U.S. production of primary aluminum from 1969 through 1974. The initial value of the average was taken as the average for the five-year period, 1964–1968. The initial value of trend was set at zero. Both beginning estimates were too small, which accounts for the fact that the expected production was too small for the first four forecasts. This situation was corrected by the sixth forecast, which is more accurate. More realistic initial estimates and a large value of α would have made the adjustment possible much more quickly.

TABLE 14.11

**U.S. Production of Primary Aluminum, 1969–1974
(millions of short tons)**

Year (1)	Production x (2)	Average $S(x)$ (3)	Change in average C (4)	Trend T (5)	Expected demand D (6)	Error in estimate e (7)
Initial estimates	...	3.50	...	0	...	...
1969	3.79	3.572	.072	.018	...	...
1970	3.89	3.652	.079	.033	3.627	−.263
1971	3.93	3.721	.070	.042	3.752	−.178
1972	4.53	3.924	.202	.082	3.849	−.681
1973	4.90	4.168	.244	.123	4.171	−.729
1974	3.88	4.096	−.072	.074	4.536	.656
1975	...	...	...	...	4.318	...

Source: Commodity Yearbook, 1976.

$$\alpha = 0.25 \qquad 1 - \alpha = 0.75 \qquad \frac{1-\alpha}{\alpha} = 3$$

To compute the expected value for 1970:

1. $S_{t=1969}(x) = \alpha x_{t=1969} + (1 - \alpha)S_{t-1=1968}(x)$
   $3.572 \quad = (0.25)(3.79) + (0.75)(3.50)$

2. $C_{t=1969} \quad = S_{t=1969}(x) - S_{t-1=1968}(x)$
   $.072 \quad = 3.572 - 3.50$

3. $T_{t=1969} \quad = \alpha C_{t=1969} + (1 - \alpha)T_{t-1=1968}$
   $.018 \quad = (0.25)(0.072) + (0.75)(0)$

4. $D_{t+1=1970} = S_{t=1969}(x) + \dfrac{(1-\alpha)}{\alpha} T_{t=1969}$
   $3.627 \quad = 3.572 + 3(0.018)$

5. $e_{t+1=1970} \quad = D_{t+1=1970} - x_{t+1=1970}$
   $-.263 \quad = 3.627 - 3.89$

Making the Forecast

Making a forecast using the techniques discussed in this chapter is an art, not a science. It requires a thorough knowledge of the series being forecast and judgment acquired through experience. There is no one correct mathematical answer. The fact that several experienced forecasters may make different forecasts using the same data emphasizes the subjective nature of forecasting.

In spite of the difficulties, forecasts must be made; they must be constantly monitored; and they must be updated and revised frequently as new data become available.

■ *Example.* Suppose the Vice-President for Research of a large corporation has the following data and other estimates available and wishes to forecast sales for July, 1979.

Year	Sales (millions of dollars)
1971	16
1972	18
1973	23
1974	21
1975	25
1976	29

Index of seasonal variation for July is 86.72.

Estimate of cycle for July, 1979 = 112.23.

STEPS IN THE FORECAST:

1. *Estimate of annual sales for 1979.*
   Four different trend equations are fit to the historical data and are used to forecast annual sales for 1979.

Trend equation	Sales forecast for 1979*	$\Sigma(y - y_c)^2$	Constants in equation	Residual standard deviation*
Linear	35.20	11.20	2	1.67
Exponential	39.62	10.67	2	1.63
Second-order polynomial	38.19	10.77	3	1.89
Gompertz	34.82	11.54	3	1.96

* millions of dollars

The forecaster selects the annual forecast of $39,620,000 made by the exponential equation since it has the lowest residual standard deviation and experience suggests sales will continue to grow at a constant rate.

2. *Estimate of average monthly sales.*
   The simplest estimate of monthly sales is to divide annual sales by 12. For months at the beginning or the end of the year, more accurate estimates can be made by computing monthly trend values. Since July is in the middle of the year, the estimate is made as: $\frac{39.62}{12} = 3.30$ million dollars.

3. *Estimate for July, 1979.*
   Since July is traditionally a slow month, this factor must be

considered in the forecast. The estimate for July, 1979, after adjustment for seasonal variation is $\dfrac{3.30 \times 86.72}{100} = 2.86176$ million dollars.

4. *Revised estimate for July, 1979.*

Since business in that month is expected to be better than normal due to an upswing in the business cycle, a revised estimate for July, 1979, can be made as $\dfrac{2.86176 \times 112.23}{100} = 3.211753$ or $3,211,753.

STUDY QUESTIONS

14-1. Explain briefly the meaning of each of the following terms:

a. time series
b. decomposition
c. econometrics
d. trend
e. seasonal variation
f. cyclical variation
g. erratic variation
h. multiplicative time-series model
i. additive time-series model
j. arithmetic progression
k. geometric progression
l. exponential equation
m. semilogarithmic chart
n. first-degree curve
o. second-degree curve
p. growth curve
q. modified exponential curve
r. Gompertz curve
s. index of seasonal variation
t. specific seasonal
u. leveling factor
v. leading indicator
w. diffusion index
x. autocorrelation
y. serial correlation
z. exponential smoothing
aa. sampling interval.

14-2. Why is the administrator interested in the analysis of time-series data?

14-3. What are some of the unique problems that arise when dealing with the analysis of time-series data?

14-4. What are the four types of fluctuations in a time series? Give an example of each.

14-5. Distinguish between the ways of expressing the four types of fluctuations in the multiplicative and the additive time-series models.

14-6. How does a least-squares trend line differ from a least-squares regression equation for two variables? What do these two equations have in common?

14-7. When would you use an exponential equation to describe the trend in a time series?

14-8. How many times can a fifth-degree polynomial equation change direction? What danger lies in using such an equation to describe trend?

14-9. When is a growth curve a good measure of trend?

14-10. What is residual standard deviation? How can it be used?

14-11. How are degrees of freedom computed for a residual standard deviation?

14-12. In what way does a modified exponential trend equation differ from an exponential equation?

14-13. If a Gompertz curve is plotted on a semilogarithmic chart, will the curve be rising or falling? Explain.

14-14. What are the criteria that should be met in an acceptable method of computing an index of seasonal variation?

14-15. What is meant by the term, "decomposition of time series"?

14-16. If you wish to correlate two time series, both of which have positive trend, how would you handle the problem of serial correlation?

14-17. How can a diffusion index be used to predict changes in the business cycle?

14-18. What are the four stages in the Box-Jenkins forecasting method?

14-19. In what ways does exponential smoothing overcome the difficulties involved in using a moving average as a measure of trend?

14-20. When is it appropriate to use a large value of α in exponential smoothing?

14-21. In what ways does exponential smoothing correct for trend and seasonal variation when forecasting a time series?

PROBLEMS

14-1. Plot the following trend equations on graph paper for the years 1968 through 1976. All have an origin at July 1, 1972, with an x unit of one year.
   a. $y_c = 14.75 + 2.37x$
   b. $y_c = 193.6 - 1.5x$
   c. $y_c = 14.75 + 2.37x - 0.52x^2$
   d. $\log y_c = 2.109579 + 0.00484x$
   e. $\log y_c = 0.866843 + (-1.383198)(0.8094796^x)$
   f. $y_c = 14.75 + 2.37x - 0.52x^2 + 0.15x^3$

14-2. Use each of the equations given in Problem 14–1 to forecast *y* for 1978.

14-3. Table 14.A shows life insurance carried per family in the United States from 1965 through 1974.

TABLE 14.A

Life Insurance Per Family in the United States, 1965–1974

Year	Average amount (in dollars)
1965	14,600
1966	15,800
1967	17,100
1968	18,300
1969	19,400
1970	20,700
1971	21,700
1972	22,900
1973	24,400
1974	26,500

Source: Institute of Life Insurance, 1975. *Life Insurance Fact Book*, p. 21.

a. Fit a straight line to the data using the method of least squares.
b. Fit an exponential equation to the data. Can this time series be described best by an average amount of increase or by an average rate of increase? What is the difference?
c. Fit a second-degree parabola to the data. Is the trend line curving up or down? What is the danger of using this equation to forecast too far into the future?
d. Which of the three trend equations seems to fit the data best? Why?

14-4. Use the data in Table 14.B to compute the following trend equations and use each to forecast deposits in saving and loan associations in 1980. Compare the forecasts and explain the relative merits and dangers in using each.

a. Straight line by the method of least squares.
b. Second-degree polynomial.
c. Exponential curve.
d. Gompertz curve.

TABLE 14.B

**Over-the-counter Deposits in Savings and Loan
Associations in the United States, 1949–1975
(billions of dollars)**

Year	Amount	Year	Amount	Year	Amount
1949	12.5	1958	48.0	1967	124.5
1950	14.0	1959	54.6	1968	131.6
1951	16.1	1960	62.1	1969	135.5
1952	19.2	1961	70.9	1970	146.4
1953	22.3	1962	80.2	1971	174.2
1954	27.3	1963	91.3	1972	206.8
1955	32.1	1964	101.9	1973	227.0
1956	37.1	1965	110.4	1974	243.0
1957	41.9	1966	114.0	1975	286.0

Source: United Savings and Loan League, *1976 Savings and Loan Fact Book,* p. 14.

14-5. Table 14.C shows book value of U.S. investments in Japan and Latin America.

TABLE 14.C

**Book Value of U.S. Investments in Japan and Latin
America, 1964–1971 (millions of dollars)**

Year	Japan	Latin America
1964	598	10,254
1965	675	10,886
1966	756	11,498
1967	870	12,049
1968	1,050	13,101
1969	1,244	13,858
1970	1,483	14,760
1971	1,818	15,765

Source: U.S. Department of Commerce. *Survey of Current Business,* October, 1972, p. 28.

a. Plot both series on the same semilogarithmic chart. Use two scales to bring the two series as close together as possible. On inspection of the two series, which would you say is growing at the faster rate?

b. Compute an exponential trend equation for Japan and plot it on the graph drawn in part a.

c. Compute an exponential trend equation for Latin America and plot it on the graph drawn in part a. Can the rate of growth in the two series be more clearly seen by comparing the trend lines than by comparing the plots of the raw data? Explain.

d. Use the antilogs of the "b" values of the two trend equations to discuss relative rates of growth.

14-6. Compute the residual standard deviation for the following series. The trend equation is:

$$y_c = 43.8095 - 0.25x - 0.988095x^2$$
Origin is July 1, 1975
x unit is one year.

Year	Value of y	Year	Value of y
1972	36	1976	42
1973	39	1977	38
1974	44	1978	35
1975	45		

14-7. Four polynomial trend equations were fit to a time series covering a 10-year period. Given the following information, which equation has the best fit?

Degree of polynomial	$\Sigma(y - y_c)^2$
First	20.88
Second	17.50
Third	13.92
Fourth	12.20

14-8. The table below shows sales, index of seasonal variation, and monthly trend values for a four-month period. Adjust sales for the other two components and estimate the effects of the business cycle on the series for the period.

Month	Sales*	Index of seasonal variation	Monthly* trend
January	137.09	132	132.7
February	128.22	125	133.4
March	136.70	117	134.1
April	130.80	105	134.8

* Millions of dollars

14-9.

Month	Sales (millions of dollars)	Index of seasonal variation
January	5.3	88.11
February	6.2	106.25
March	6.2	112.44
April	8.4	101.16
May	7.8	105.22
June	9.5	98.21
July	7.5	99.61
August	6.6	95.94
September	8.2	99.17
October	7.1	92.59
November	8.3	99.04
December	9.2	102.28

a. Compute sales for each month after adjustment for seasonal variation.
b. If total sales for the coming year are estimated to be $120 million, what would you expect sales to be in March and in August?
c. If sales next September are $9.1 million, use this figure to estimate total sales for the year.

14-10.

Month	Actual sales (thousands of dollars)	Sales adjusted for seasonal variation (thousands of dollars)
January	33.9	30.0
February	29.7	30.3
March	32.0	29.1
April	33.6	30.3
May	34.3	29.8
June	38.5	32.1
July	24.6	30.7
August	10.0	32.3
September	26.4	30.0
October	32.6	29.6
November	33.2	29.6
December	34.2	29.2

a. Assume that the actual sales figures shown above have no trend or cyclical influences in them and estimate the index of seasonal variation used to compute the adjusted figures.
b. If sales in the next year are $38,000 in April, what would sales be after adjustment for seasonal variation?
c. If total sales in the following year are $450,000, what would you expect actual sales for June to be?

14–11.

TABLE 14.D
Aluminum Exports from the United States
(thousands of short tons)

Month	1971	1972	1973	1974	1975
January	15.8	13.4	12.4	22.0	4.8
February	14.3	3.5	11.5	20.9	4.9
March	11.0	6.7	10.6	30.4	3.6
April	11.3	6.4	12.4	22.8	4.5
May	8.0	7.5	11.1	17.7	13.4
June	10.3	8.4	10.3	13.6	8.6
July	3.6	7.7	14.1	15.0	4.8
August	5.6	7.3	16.4	14.4	20.9
September	12.6	9.1	29.8	12.3	13.7
October	4.0	14.2	31.2	16.7	25.2
November	7.7	10.0	47.0	9.2	36.8
December	6.9	14.0	22.8	12.8	44.9

Source: 1976 Commodity Yearbook, p. 64.

a. Plot the data above on an arithmetic chart. What kinds of fluctuations can be seen from a study of the chart?
b. Compute a least-squares straight line trend equation and use the trend values to detrend the series.
c. Compute an index of seasonal variation and use the index to de-seasonalize the detrended series computed in part b.
d. Use a three-month moving average of the detrended and deseasonalized series computed in part c. Describe and interpret what you have found.

14–12.

TABLE 14.E
Stocks of Oats on United States Farms (millions
of bushels)

Year	Quarter*			
	1	2	3	4
1970	738.9	541.0	352.8	859.1
1971	711.6	509.8	316.2	812.5
1972	692.6	507.3	336.5	679.2
1973	556.1	337.2	229.0	609.1
1974	475.2	288.9	151.3	495.9
1975	384.1	235.9	120.4	496.1

* Value recorded at the beginning of the quarter.
Source: 1976 Commodity Yearbook, p. 237.

a. Plot the series on an arithmetic chart. Does there appear to be trend in the data? Can you see any quarterly seasonal pattern from looking at the chart?
b. Compute an index of seasonal variation using the method of ratio of two-item average of a four-quarter moving average. Use a straight arithmetic mean of specific seasonals and a leveling factor in computing the index.
c. Deseasonalize the data using the index computed in part b.
d. Fit a straight-line trend to the data using the method of least squares. Use the quarterly trend values to detrend the series computed in part c to produce an index of cyclical and erratic forces.

14–13.

TABLE 14.F
**Imports of Crude Oil into the United States
(millions of 42 gallon barrels)**

Year	Amount
1965	452.0
1966	447.1
1967	411.6
1968	472.3
1969	514.1
1970	483.3
1971	613.4
1972	811.1
1973	1,183.9
1974	1,269.2
1975	1,498.2

*Source: 1976 Commodity
Yearbook, p. 260.*

a. Use exponential smoothing to forecast imports of crude oil into the United States in 1966 using $\alpha = 0.30$. Use 460.0 and a trend value of 0 as your initial estimates of amount and trend.
b. Repeat the steps in part a using $\alpha = 0.50$ and compare the results.

14–14. Use the data in Problem 14–13 and a computer program to forecast imports of crude oil into the United States. Use an α value of your own selection. (Hint: Many computer centers will already have a library program for exponential smoothing. If they do not, you should be able to write one using BASIC, FORTRAN, COBOL, or some other computer language.)

SELECTED READINGS

Brennan, Michael J., Jr. *Preface to Econometrics,* 3d ed. Cincinnati: South-Western Publishing Co., 1973.
> The author introduces the student to the subject of econometrics as the application of modern statistical methods to economic theory expressed in mathematical terms.

Brown, Robert Goodell. *Smoothing, Forecasting and Prediction.* Englewood Cliffs, N.J.: Prentice-Hall, Inc., 1963.
> Section III, Smoothing Techniques, develops the techniques of exponential smoothing, including multiple smoothing for higher order polynomials.

Croxton, Frederick E., Dudley J. Cowden, and Sidney Klein. *Applied General Statistics,* 3d ed. Englewood Cliffs, N.J.: Prentice-Hall, Inc., 1967.
> Chapters 11 through 16 give an excellent discussion of the classical approach to time-series analysis. Chapter 22 discusses the correlation of time series.

Dauten, Carl A., and Lloyd M. Valentine. *Business Cycles and Forecasting,* 5th ed. Cincinnati: South-Western Publishing Co., 1978.
> This book covers the factors which contribute to economic growth and stability and to the level of national income. It surveys the techniques which may be used to analyze current economic conditions and to forecast future levels of activity.

Chapter 15
Index Numbers of Business Change

Index numbers are statistical measures of how much something has changed from one time period to another. Index numbers associated with business and economics are often described as barometers of business change. Every economic variable that affects the business manager, whether it is sales, prices, costs, or the purchasing power of the dollar, changes over time. These changes can be expressed as index numbers.

The use of index numbers is not confined to business and economics. They are widely used in many other fields, and they are not always related to changes over time in some fields. For example, the National Weather Service has a *Discomfort Index* that measures the combined effects of heat or cold, wind, and humidity on individuals. The psychologist's measure of intelligence (IQ) is essentially an index number comparing a person's intelligence with that of an average for others of the same age. State boards of education compute indexes to measures of effectiveness of school systems; health officials have measures of the efficiency of hospitals; and so on.

In its simplest form an index number is a ratio of two numbers, expressed as a percent. When changes in only one variable are involved, such as the number of automobiles produced in the United States each year, it is a simple matter to express the number produced each year as a percent of the number produced in some given base year. On the other hand, to compute a cost of living index can be a complex, costly, and difficult task involving many technical decisions. Such an index must consider all the important goods and services bought by thousands of consumers in dozens of cities and communities. In both of these cases, the purpose of the index is to give a quick, overall picture of changes taking place.

The purpose of this chapter is to summarize briefly the basic techniques and theory of index numbers and to examine a few of the more important indexes produced by private and governmental agencies to see how these indexes are put together and what they measure.

An *index number* is a percentage relative that compares economic measures in a given period with those same measures at a fixed time period in the past.

KINDS OF INDEX NUMBERS

The usefulness of any index number lies in the types of questions it can answer. Each index number is designed for a particular purpose, and it is this specific purpose that determines its method of construction. In this chapter, three basic types of index numbers will be considered. These are the value index, price index, and quantity index.

Value Index

The simplest kind of index number is the *value index*. It compares total value in some period with total value in the base period. For example, an index of department store sales would be a value index. Total value would be the sum of the price of each item times the number sold. This type of index is seldom used because it is difficult to determine just what changes it measures. If the index rises, one is not sure whether it has risen because of an increase in prices or because of an increase in volume. It may be the result of both.

Price Index

Emphasis in this chapter is on *indexes of prices*. Most of the classic formulas will be discussed, as well as such well-known indexes as the Index of Consumer Prices, Wholesale Price Index, Dow-Jones Stock Averages, and Standard & Poor's Price Indexes. All of these are designed to measure changes in prices while holding measures of quantity constant.

Quantity Index

A *quantity index* measures changes in volume of goods produced, bought, or consumed. For almost every formula for a price index, there is a corresponding index to measure changes in quantities. For this reason, the discussion of quantity indexes here will be limited to the Index of Industrial Production.

DECISIONS ON INDEX-NUMBER CONSTRUCTION

Just as a builder spends a great deal of time and effort designing and planning a building before the first spade of dirt is turned, so the statistician must carefully design an index number to meet the need that originally called for its creation. The design must first take into account the intended uses of the index. If it is a price index, it may be concerned with measuring prices of only a few commodities or of a great many. It may be concerned with price changes on a nationwide basis or with changes in a restricted area only.

Once the basic decisions are made concerning how the index number will be used, it is possible to decide what data are to be used, how they are to be collected, and how often. While sampling techniques are seldom used to determine which items should be priced, random samples of prices of selected items may be called for. Other decisions that must be made include the choice of a base period, a method of weighting the components for the index, and finally the actual method of construction. These critical decision areas and several others not yet mentioned are discussed in greater detail as some of the classic formulas of index number construction are discussed in later sections of this chapter.

HOW INDEX NUMBERS ARE USED

Index numbers have a great many uses and new ones are being added constantly as managers and the general public become more familiar with them. A quick review of four of the more common uses will help to put later discussions in a more understandable context. These uses are:

1. *Measure changes that have taken place from one time period to an-other.* Measuring economic changes over time is basic to success in business. Such a barometer tells what has happened in the past, and its careful study may foretell much of the future.
2. *Combine changes in several series.* A builder concerned with price changes in several commodities used for construction may wish to summarize changes in costs of lumber, glass, steel, and many other materials. Since these materials are measured in many different kinds of units for pricing, such as board feet, pounds, and gallons, they cannot be added and compared directly. An index number can be designed, however, that combines relative changes in all the series into a single measure of overall change.
3. *Devalue a time series in terms of constant dollars.* The purchasing power of the dollar is constantly changing. Over the short run these changes may be small, but over a long period of time they can be substantial. If a series such as wage rates is divided by its equivalent cost of living index for each period, the resulting series is said to be expressed in *constant dollars.*
4. *Measure consumer attitudes.* The Survey Research Center at the University of Michigan has devised an *Index of Consumer Confidence* which is watched closely by executives in many businesses. The staff of the center uses scientifically designed sample interviews to measure consumer attitudes and expectations and to predict future consumer behavior.

CONSTRUCTING INDEX NUMBERS OF PRICES

There are dozens of ways to construct a price index. The approach here is to begin with the simplest methods and to proceed to the more complicated methods in an attempt to overcome the limitations of each method just discussed.

Simple Relatives

If an index of prices is wanted for a single series such as wheat, it is necessary only to express each price as a fixed-base relative. Such an index would be expressed as

$$P = \frac{p_i}{p_0} 100 \dots\dots\dots\dots\dots\dots\dots\dots\dots\dots\dots(15.1)$$

where
  P is a price index
  p_0 is a price in the base year
  p_i is a price in the given year (i.e., p_{76} is a price in 1976).

■ *Example.* The price of spring wheat in the United States was $11.887 per 100 pound sack in 1974, $10.552 in 1975, and $9.509 in 1976. The following price index for wheat might be constructed using 1975 as the base year:

$$P(1974) = \frac{p_{74}}{p_0} 100 = \frac{11.887}{10.552} 100 = 112.65$$

$$P(1975) = \frac{p_0}{p_0} 100 = \frac{10.552}{10.552} 100 = 100.00$$

$$P(1976) = \frac{p_{76}}{p_0} 100 = \frac{9.509}{10.552} 100 = 90.12.$$

The price index for 1976 indicates that the price of wheat in 1976 was 90.12 percent of the price in 1975.

The principal limitation to the technique shown above is that it can be used when only one commodity or class of items is being considered. When more than one series or class is involved, an average of price relatives must be considered.

Simple Averages of Price Relatives

If the assumption is made that all the series being considered are of equal importance, the only problem is the selection of a method of averaging the price relatives. While, theoretically, any average might be used, the choice usually narrows to the arithmetic mean, the geometric mean, or the harmonic mean. It should be noted, however, that each average gives a different answer; the appropriate one to use will be determined by the nature of the problem. The formulas are given below.

An Arithmetic Mean of Price Relatives.

$$P = \frac{\sum \frac{p_i}{p_0} 100}{n} \dots\dots\dots\dots\dots\dots\dots\dots(15.2)$$

A Geometric Mean of Price Relatives.

$$P = \text{antilog} \; \frac{\sum \log \frac{p_i}{p_0} 100}{n} \quad \text{.........................(15.3)}$$

A Harmonic Mean of Price Relatives.

$$P = \frac{n}{\sum \dfrac{1}{\dfrac{p_i}{p_0} 100}} \quad \text{...............................(15.4)}$$

where

n is the number of different series in the index.

Weighted Averages of Price Relatives

The assumption made in the previous section that all the series being averaged are of equal importance is one which can seldom be made in actual practice. Some of the series are almost always more important than others, and their relative positions need to be recognized with an appropriate system of weighting when their respective price changes are combined into an index.

The decision to use some system of weights in averaging price ratios is a next logical step. In taking such a step, the statistician wants to be sure that the system of weights accurately represents the relative importance of each series to be included in the index; and, of course, the weights must be in units that can be added.

While it is possible to assign weights to each series arbitrarily, this action involves judgment and is usually avoided as being too subjective. Some system that uses the relative values of the products in some given period is most commonly used.

Laspeyres' Price Index. One logical system of weights is to use the value of each series in the base year as the weight for that series in the index. *Value* is the product of price times quantity. If one product has twice the value of another in the base year, it is given twice as much weight in computing the index. If the index is computed as an arithmetic mean of price relatives weighted with base-year values, the formula can be expressed as

$$P = \frac{\sum p_0 q_0 \dfrac{p_i}{p_0} 100}{\sum p_0 q_0}$$

where

$p_0 q_0$ is price times quantity (value) for each series in the base year.

The formula can be simplified by cancelling the values of p_0 in the numerator of the fraction to give the formula for what is commonly called *Laspeyres' price index*

$$P_L = \frac{\Sigma p_i q_0}{\Sigma p_0 q_0} \; 100 \dots\dots\dots\dots\dots\dots\dots\dots\dots(15.5)$$

Paasche's Price Index. Another well-known but less used price index is *Paasche's price index*. This index corresponds to the harmonic mean of price relatives weighted with given-year values. The fact that Paasche's formula requires that new weights, q_i, be found for each new year of the index presents some practical problems. Not only is it difficult and costly to secure the quantity information required for weights, but the index when computed can only be compared with the base period and not with other years of the index.

The formula for Paasche's price index is

$$P_P = \frac{\Sigma p_i q_i}{\Sigma p_0 q_i} \; 100 \dots\dots\dots\dots\dots\dots\dots\dots\dots(15.6)$$

■ *Example.* Laspeyres' and Paasche's price indexes are computed for three grains for 1976 with 1975 used as the base year. The data are shown in Table 15.1.

TABLE 15.1

Laspeyres' and Paasche's Price Indexes for Three Grains, 1976 (1975 = 100.0)

Product	p_0	p_{76}	q_0	q_{76}	$p_0 q_0$	$p_{76} q_0$	$p_{76} q_{76}$	$p_0 q_{76}$
Barley	3.60	3.06	383.0	377.0	1,378.80	1,171.98	1,153.62	1,357.20
Corn	2.88	2.56	5,767.0	6,216.0	16,608.96	14,763.52	15,912.96	17,902.08
Oats	1.67	1.74	656.9	562.5	1,097.02	1,143.01	978.75	939.38
Total					19,084.78	17,078.51	18,045.33	20,198.66

Source: Survey of Current Business
Note: Prices are in dollars per bushel and quantities are in millions of bushels.

$$P_L = \frac{\Sigma(p_{76} q_0)}{\Sigma(p_0 q_0)} \; 100 = \frac{17,078.51}{19,084.78} \; 100 = 89.49$$

$$P_P = \frac{\Sigma(p_{76} q_{76})}{\Sigma(p_0 q_{76})} \; 100 = \frac{18,045.33}{20,198.66} \; 100 = 89.34.$$

The two index numbers are nearly the same because there was very little shift in the relative importance of the three series between 1975 and 1976.

Chain Index Numbers

All the index-number formulas just discussed use a fixed-base period. In each case, the price index for a given period made it possible to compare prices in that period with prices in some fixed period. It is often more convenient and practical to compute an index that has as its base the time period just past. This is particularly true with such indexes as the Consumer Price Index or the Wholesale Price Index published by the Bureau of Labor Statistics of the United States Department of Labor. The samples of information will vary from one month to another and even the products being priced may change over time. It is much easier to get information that is strictly comparable for two adjoining time periods than it is to get comparable information over longer periods of time. A *chain index* is one that has a moving base, which is the period immediately preceding the period of the index.

The formula for a chain price index for a current period, i, based on prices in the previous period, $i - 1$, may be written

$$P_{i-1,i} = \frac{\Sigma p_i q_a}{\Sigma p_{i-1} q_a} \, 100 \, \dots \dots \dots \dots \dots \dots \dots (15.7)$$

where

p_i is the price in a current period

p_{i-1} is the price in a period immediately preceding period p_i

q_a is a quantity in a fixed-weight period.

This formula is a modified Laspeyres'-type index formula.

■ *Example.* The data in Table 15.2 are used to compute a chain index number for three grains for 1975 using 1974 as the base. Then a chain index number for 1976 is computed using 1975 as the base. The weights (q_a values) have been arbitrarily selected to represent the relative importance of the three grains in the index.

TABLE 15.2

Chain Index Numbers for Three Grains for 1975 and 1976 Using an Arbitrary System of Weights

Product	p_{74}	p_{75}	p_{76}	q_a	$p_{74}q_a$	$p_{75}q_a$	$p_{76}q_a$
Barley	3.40	3.60	3.06	1	3.40	3.60	3.06
Corn	3.14	2.88	2.56	7	21.98	20.16	17.92
Oats	1.66	1.67	1.74	2	3.32	3.34	3.48
Total					28.70	27.10	24.46

Source of price data: *Survey of Current Business.*
Note: Prices are in dollars per bushel and q_a values were arbitrarily selected.

$$P_{74,75} = \frac{\Sigma(p_{75}q_a)}{\Sigma(p_{74}q_a)} 100 = \frac{27.10}{28.70} 100 = 94.43$$

$$P_{75,76} = \frac{\Sigma(p_{76}q_a)}{\Sigma(p_{75}q_a)} 100 = \frac{24.46}{27.10} 100 = 90.26.$$

To convert a chain index to a fixed-base index, the index for period i is computed in this fashion:

$$P_i = P_{i-1} \frac{\Sigma p_i q_a}{\Sigma p_{i-1} q_a}$$

Since
$$\frac{\Sigma p_i q_a}{\Sigma p_{i-1} q_a} \quad \text{is} \quad \frac{p_{i-1, i}}{100},$$

then

$$P_i = \frac{[P_{i-1}] \cdot [P_{i-1, i}]}{100} \ldots\ldots\ldots\ldots\ldots\ldots(15.8)$$

■ **Example.** Using the data in the previous example it can be shown that the price index for 1976 with 1974 as a base is

$$P_{74,75} = \frac{(P_{74,75})(P_{75,76})}{100} = \frac{94.43 \times 90.26}{100} = 85.23.$$

This value is the same as would be an index for 1976 with 1974 as the base computed as an arithmetic mean of price relatives using the same system of arbitrary weights. If base-year values had been used as weights, the index number would be the same as Laspeyres' price index for the same period.

While only two chain index numbers were used in the example above, a chain series of any length can be converted to a series of price index numbers with a common base by the same procedure. Since both the Consumer Price Index and the Wholesale Price Index are chain index numbers converted to a fixed base, it is important to understand this kind of index number construction in order to understand those two important index numbers.

SOME IMPORTANT INDEX NUMBERS

There is seldom an issue of any news magazine that does not contain a discussion of business conditions and forecasts of future conditions. The articles in these magazines quote liberally from important government and private indexes. Many newspaper headlines scream the latest index measures of food prices, stock prices, energy prices, and so on. Of the many important indexes published, five of the most widely used indexes are described briefly in the following sections.

Consumer Price Index

The full title for this index is the *Consumer Price Index for Urban Wage Earners and Clerical Workers,* and it is constructed and published by the Bureau of Labor Statistics of the U.S. Department of Labor. The index is designed to measure the effect of price changes of about 400 consumption items called a "market basket" of goods and services purchased by urban wage earners and clerical workers. The index measures what that market basket costs this month as compared to a month ago, a year ago, or ten years ago.

The importance of this index is reflected by the fact that the incomes of about half of the U.S. population are pegged to the Consumer Price Index. Collective bargaining contracts covering more than 8.5 million workers tie wages to the Consumer Price Index. Pensions and other incomes are adjusted to changes in this index for about 50 million social security beneficiaries, retired military and federal civil service employees and survivors, and food stamp recipients.

The index covers prices of almost everything consumers buy for living, including food, clothing, transportation, medical and personal care, and many other goods and services.

The market basket was developed from detailed expenditure information provided by families and single individuals on what they actually buy. In a consumer expenditure survey conducted in 1972 and 1973, about 20,000 families provided information on spending habits in a series of quarterly interviews. In a second independent study 18,000 families kept diaries listing everything they bought during a two-week period.

Beginning in April, 1977, the bureau began publishing the new revised index and also began the publication of a new index called the *Consumer Price Index for all Urban Households.* The second index is intended to be a more comprehensive measure of consumer prices covering about 80 percent of the population.

Price information for both indexes is now being gathered monthly from 85 different urban areas in the United States, selected by probability methods, on the basis of the 1970 Census of Population. The index for the nation as a whole and the indexes for the five largest areas (New York, Los Angeles, Chicago, Detroit, and Philadelphia) are published monthly. For 23 other metropolitan areas the index is published every other month.

The base period of the index is taken as 1967. This is changed from time to time, but the index is also still published regularly using the old bases of 1939, 1947–1949, and 1957–1959.

A standard chain index formula such as Formula 15.7 is used to calculate the Consumer Price Index from prices for the market-basket items. The weights are represented by the q_a values in the formula. Average price changes from the previous pricing period to the current month are expressed in percentage terms for each item. The percentage changes of all goods and services are combined using the formula. The chain index number thus produced is multiplied by the index number for the previous month and divided by 100 to secure a fixed-base index number with 1967 as the base.

Producer Price Index

This index (previously the Wholesale Price Index) is also published by the Bureau of Labor Statistics of the United States Department of Labor and is designed to measure average changes in prices of all commodities sold in the primary markets of the United States. The goods priced for the index include 2,800 items representing manufacturing, agriculture, forestry, fishing, mining, quarrying, well operation, and gas and electric public utilities. Prices are at the wholesale rather than the retail level.

The index is computed using the formula

$$P_i = P_{i-1} \left[\frac{\sum q_a p_{i-1} \frac{p_i}{p_{i-1}}}{\sum q_a p_{i-1}} \right] \text{ which simplifies to}$$

$$P_i = P_{i-1} \left[\frac{\sum p_i q_a}{\sum p_{i-1} q_a} \right] \text{ which is Formula 15.7.}$$

The reference base for the index is $1967 = 100.0$. The weights $(q_a p_{i-1})$ are computed as the amounts (q_a) of these goods sold in 1972 times the prices (p_{i-1}) in the previous period.

Dow-Jones Stock Averages

Dow-Jones & Company computes four price indexes. One is for 30 industrial common stocks, one is for 20 transportation stocks, one is for 15 utility common stocks, and the fourth is a composite of the first three.

When the company first began publishing its index of closing industrial stock prices in 1897, there were only 12 stocks used, and the index was computed as:

$$P = \frac{\Sigma(12 \text{ closing prices})}{12}.$$

As stocks were added to the list, the formula for the index was changed by increasing the size of the denominator so that it was always the same as the total number of stocks whose prices were being averaged.

Serious problems began to arise with the index when some of the corporations whose stocks were included in the average had stock splits.

■ *Example.* Imagine a simplified example with only two stocks: Stock A is worth $8 a share and Stock B is worth $10. The index is

$$P = \frac{\$8 + \$10}{2} = \$9.$$

If Stock B splits two for one so that a share now sells for $5, the index when next computed drops to

$$P = \frac{\$8 + \$5}{2} = \$6.50$$

even though the total market value of the two stocks is the same.

The method first used to overcome this distortion was to multiply the price of each split share by the amount of the split so that the index was

$$P = \frac{\$8 + 2(\$5)}{2} = \$9.$$

This method became too cumbersome to use in time, and in 1928 a new method was adopted to handle stock splits. This method is still in use and works as follows. The evening before the split takes place, two calculations are made:

1. The index for that day is computed as before.
2. The total value of all stock prices is calculated as if the split had taken place (i.e., using the new price of the split stock). This new total is divided by the index computed in 1 above. The quotient is the new divisor that will be used to compute the index the next night.

■ **Example.** In the previous example, the index before the stock split is

$$P = \frac{\$8 + \$10}{2} = \$9.$$

The divisor for the index after the stock split is computed as the sum of $8 and $5 divided by the old index of $9. The new divisor is $\frac{13}{9} = 1.44$. The next day, if there is no other change in prices,

$$P = \frac{\$13}{1.44} = \$9.$$

While the industrial index includes 30 stocks, the divisor for the index has shrunk from 30 to 1.443 (July, 1978) as a result of numerous stock splits. This fact explains why the Dow-Jones Industrial Common Stock Average is much higher than the average price of the stocks used to compute the index.

Standard & Poor's Price Index

A more scientifically constructed index of common stock prices is computed by Standard & Poor's Corporation. This index covers 425 stocks representing 93 individual categories that comprise the four main groups of industrials, rails, utilities, and the 425-stock composite.

The formula used to compute the index is a modified Paasche's formula with a base period of 1941–1943 = 10.0. A system of weights is used to reflect the relative market importance of each stock in the index. The price of each stock multiplied by the number of shares outstanding gives the current market value of that particular issue. This market value determines the relative importance of each stock. The formula used is

$$P = \frac{\Sigma p_i q_i}{\Sigma p_0 q_0} \, 10 \dots\dots\dots\dots\dots\dots\dots\dots\dots\dots\text{(15.9)}$$

where
  p_i is current market price
  p_0 is average price in the base period
  q_i is number of shares currently outstanding
  q_0 is number of shares outstanding in the base period.

The problem of stock dividends and stock splits is handled by simply changing the weighting factor to equal the number of shares of stock outstanding after the dividend or stock split has become effective.

The Standard & Poor's index has three distinct advantages over the Dow-Jones index:

1. It weights the price changes in stock based on their relative importance in the market.
2. It results in an index level that is more in line with the average value of the stock included.
3. It includes a much larger sample of stock prices.

Index of Industrial Production

Unlike the indexes measuring changes in prices, the *Federal Reserve Board Index of Industrial Production* measures changes in physical volume of output from the nation's factories, mines, and utilities. This index is constructed by combining 235 individual monthly series for manufactured goods and mineral products representing about 80 percent of the nation's output of goods and products. Major revisions in the index were made in 1940, 1953, 1959, and, most recently, 1971. Since the base of the index is 1967, the formula is written

$$Q = \frac{\Sigma q_n p_{67}}{\Sigma q_0 p_{67}} \, 100 \dots\dots\dots\dots\dots\dots\dots\dots\text{(15.10)}$$

where
  Q is the quantity index
  q_n is the quantity in the period of the index
  q_0 is the quantity in the base period (1967), and
  p_{67} is the price in 1967.

This very complete measure of business activity is often used (along with Gross National Product) as a measure of the general swings in the business cycle.

SOME PROBLEMS OF INDEX NUMBER CONSTRUCTION

The imposing array of index number formulas just discussed may leave the student somewhat confused as to their relative merits. Certainly the formulas themselves give little indication of the many practical problems involved in their use. The very fact that there are many formulas suggests that there is no best one to use. The one selected for a particular index will depend on the particular problems associated with that index.

Commodities To Be Included

The purpose for which the index is being computed is basic in determining the commodities to be included. However, it may be said without reservation that a sufficiently large number of relevant items must be selected to obtain a reliable index. Among other things, the Dow-Jones Stock Average suffers as an index because it measures price changes in only 30 stocks. It is doubtful that the group of stocks is sufficiently large for the index to be representative of what is happening to the prices of industrial stocks in general. This is in contrast to the Standard & Poor's Price Index, which is computed from considerably more data.

The vast amount of data going into index numbers produced by the federal government can be judged by the figures already given for the Consumer Price Index and the Wholesale Price Index. These involve hundreds of commodities priced at thousands of locations.

Quality and Price

To ensure that a price index reflects only changes in price and not changes in quality, detailed specifications are required to describe the items to be priced. For example, in the Consumer Price Index the specifications for a man's shirt to be priced carefully describe the style, fabric, yarn, thread count, finish, construction, and size range, and require that the shirt be a nationally advertised brand. When an agent prices a shirt in a store, that person must first examine it carefully to make sure the price recorded is for a shirt that meets the specifications fully.

In spite of the use of specifications to try to ensure against the confusing of quality changes with price changes, certain quality changes take place that cannot be handled in this manner. For example, a product that has been priced in the past may be taken off the market and replaced with a new product of different quality.

Problems of changing quality are handled in one of three basic ways:

1. *Direct comparison.* This method assumes that qualities are identical and that quality differences are insignificant.
2. *Linking.* This method requires prices for both qualities for at least one date. The old quality product measures price change up to the date of introduction, and the new quality product from that date forward.
3. *Adjustment for quality difference.* This method reduces or increases the price in the current period by the value of the quality difference and then compares the adjusted current price directly with the price of the former item in the preceding period.

These three methods can best be further explained by an example showing how the three methods are employed by the Bureau of Labor Statistics in constructing the Consumer Price Index.[1]

■ *Example.* The three methods of computing price changes are illustrated in the following tabulation:

Method	Base period	Period 1	Period 2
1. *Direct comparison*			
reported price	$1.25	$1.60	$1.75
price relative	...	$\frac{1.60}{1.25}100 = 128.0$	$\frac{1.75}{1.60}100 = 109.4$
price index	100.0	128.0	$\frac{128.0 \times 109.4}{100} = 140.0$
2. *Linking*			
reported price			
quality I	$1.00	$1.30	$...
quality II	...	0.80	0.92
price relative	...	$\frac{1.30}{1.00}100 = 130.0$	$\frac{0.92}{0.80}100 = 115.0$
price index	100.0	130.0	$\frac{130.0 \times 115.0}{100} = 149.5$
3. *Adjustment for quality difference*			
reported price			
quality I	$1.00	$...	$...
quality II	...	1.50	1.80
value of quality difference between I and II	...	0.25	...
price relative	...	$\frac{1.50 - 0.25}{1.00}100 = 125.0$	$\frac{1.80}{1.50}100 = 120.0$
price index	100.0	125.0	$\frac{125.0 \times 120.0}{100} = 150.0$

The Base Period

The selection of a *base period* for an index involves one overriding consideration—it should be a period in the past that is considered to be relatively "normal." The year 1967 was considered to be such a period. In the

[1] Ethel D. Hoover, "The CPI and Problems of Quality Change," *Monthly Labor Review* (Washington, D.C.: Bureau of Labor Statistics), Vol. 84 (November, 1961), pp. 1175–1185.

past it has often been difficult to find any one year thought to be entirely normal. For this reason the periods 1957–1959 and 1947–1949 have been used as base periods. It is now necessary to shift the base period for most index numbers about every 10 years to keep pace with our rapidly changing economy.

When the base for an index number is shifted from one period to another, the change can be made by dividing the index number for each year of the old index by the value of that index at the time of the new base.

■ *Example.* The conversion from an index with a base 1971 = 100.0 to an index with a base of 1974 = 100.0 can be accomplished as follows:

Year	Old index (1971 = 100.0)	New index (1974 = 100.0)
1971	100.0	$\frac{100.0}{125.0}100 = 80.0$
1972	115.0	$\frac{115.0}{125.0}100 = 92.0$
1973	122.0	$\frac{122.0}{125.0}100 = 97.6$
1974	125.0	$\frac{125.0}{125.0}100 = 100.0$
1975	130.2	$\frac{130.2}{125.0}100 = 104.2$
1976	132.1	$\frac{132.1}{125.0}100 = 105.7$

The Selection of an Average

Statisticians have several averages they can use in computing an index number. In selecting one to use, they should strive to choose an average that is both accurate and simple. The median and the mode are generally unsatisfactory since they are highly unstable unless the items being averaged are very numerous. It is the arithmetic, harmonic, and geometric means that are most often considered.

Arithmetic Mean. It can be shown that if an arithmetic mean and constant weights are used to compute two index numbers, computing forward and backward between two dates, the resulting indexes are not reciprocals of each other, and their product is always greater than 100.0. For this reason the arithmetic mean is said to have an upward bias.

■ *Example.* The upward bias of the arithmetic mean in averaging price relatives is shown in the following computations in which only two commodities are used and in which each product is assumed to have the same weight:

	Price		Price relatives: $\frac{p_i}{p_0} 100$	
Product	1972	1976	1972 = 100.0	1976 = 100.0
A	$0.20	$0.22	110.00	90.91
B	0.60	0.50	83.33	120.00
			193.33	210.91

$$P(1972 = 100.0) = \frac{193.33}{2} = 96.7 \text{ (Formula 15.2)}$$

$$P(1976 = 100.0) = \frac{210.91}{2} = 105.5 \text{ (Formula 15.2)}$$

$$\frac{96.7 \times 105.5}{100} = 102 > 100.0.$$

Harmonic Mean. It can further be shown that if the harmonic mean is used to compute the same two index numbers, their product is always less than 100. Thus, the harmonic mean has a downward bias.

■ *Example.* Using the data in the previous example and averaging the price relatives using the harmonic mean produce the results shown below:

	$\frac{p_i}{p_0} 100$		$\frac{1}{\frac{p_i}{p_0} 100}$	
Product	1972 = 100.0	1976 = 100.0	1972 = 100.0	1976 = 100.0
A	110.0	90.91	0.0090909	0.0109999
B	83.33	120.00	0.0120005	0.0083333
			0.0210914	0.0193332

$$P(1972 = 100.0) = \frac{2}{0.0210914} = 94.8 \text{ (Formula 15.4)}$$

$$P(1976 = 100.0) = \frac{2}{0.0193332} = 103.4 \text{ (Formula 15.4)}$$

$$\frac{94.8 \times 103.4}{100} = 98.0 < 100.0.$$

Geometric Mean. The geometric mean gives consistent results. The product of geometric means with constant weights, computed forward and backward, always equals 100.0.

■ *Example.* For the same data just used, the geometric mean of price relatives reveals the following:

Time Series and Index Numbers   **Part 6**

Product	$\dfrac{p_i}{p_0}100$		$\log\dfrac{p_i}{p_0}100$	
	1972 = 100.0	1976 = 100.0	1972 = 100.0	1976 = 100.0
A	110.00	90.91	2.041393	1.958612
B	83.33	120.00	1.920801	2.079181
			3.962194	4.037793

$$P(1972 = 100.0) = \text{antilog}\,\frac{3.962194}{2} = \text{antilog}\,1.981097$$

$$= 95.74 \text{ (Formula 15.3)}$$

$$P(1976 = 100.0) = \text{antilog}\,\frac{4.037793}{2} = \text{antilog}\,2.018896$$

$$= 104.45 \text{ (Formula 15.3)}$$

$$\frac{95.74 \times 104.45}{100} = 100.00.$$

Since the geometric mean alone is free of bias, one might conclude that it is the only appropriate average to use in computing index numbers. However, there is still another problem to be considered along with the type of average when one speaks of bias. This is the problem of weights, which is considered next.

Weights

It has already been recognized that it is seldom possible to obtain a useful average of price relatives without weighting the relatives in proportion to the quantities they represent. In other words, a realistic price index must be a weighted index; and since the only unit that is common to all commodities is value, it is necessary to use weights based on values.

Values in the Base Period as Weights. Values in the base period are often used as weights. This is logical since the base period is selected as a normal period, and the value relationship should be normal. This system of weights has the added advantage of being a fixed period in the past so that index numbers computed in the future can be compared with one another.

There is one disadvantage to this system of weights. As time passes, values change; and in a price index too much weight will be given to those items that have the smallest rise in price or the largest drop when prices are falling. Generally, base-year weights have a downward bias.

■ *Example.* If the prices of two products, A and B, are recorded for two years as shown below, the 1972 values are equal. In this example, it is assumed that the price for A increases much faster than that for *B* but that the quantities remain constant. By 1976 the value of *A* is much greater than the value of *B*. If values for 1972 are used as weights to compute a price index for 1976, the index is 310. If, on the other hand, values for 1976 are used as weights for the price index for 1976, the index is 426.5. The difference in the two index numbers (each with the same base period of 1972 = 100.0) lies in the weights used.

Product	Price 1972 p_0	Price 1976 p_i	$q_0 = q_i$	Value 1972 $p_0 q_0$	Value 1976 $p_i q_i$	$\dfrac{p_i}{p_0}100$	$p_0 q_0 \dfrac{p_i}{p_0}100$	$p_i q_i \dfrac{p_i}{p_0}100$
A	$1.	$5.00	10	$10.	$50.	500.0	5,000	25,000
B	1.	1.20	10	10.	12.	120.0	1,200	1,440
				20.	62.		6,200	26,440

$$P(1972 = 100.0; \text{ base-year weights}) = \frac{6,200}{20} = 310.0$$

$$P(1976 = 100.0; \text{ given-year weights}) = \frac{26,440}{62} = 426.5.$$

Values in the Year of the Index as Weights. If values in the given years are used as weights, it is possible to overcome the bias discussed in connection with base-year weights. But other problems result. Since new quantities as well as new prices must be secured each year, many more data are needed, and the computation of the index becomes more costly. Further, each index number when computed may be compared only with the base period.

Arbitrary Values as Weights. Some indexes use values that are neither base-year nor given-year values but are determined by averaging several years or by otherwise establishing weights. For example, the weights for the Consumer Price Index were established by a consumer expenditures survey in 1972–1973, while the base period of the index is 1967.

Weight Correlation Bias. Another problem of bias is encountered in index number construction. This one, which is highly complex in nature, is the bias that is introduced because of correlation between weights and the relatives to which they are applied. This type of bias is called *weight correlation bias*. An intensive study on weight correlation bias was made by Dr. Warren M. Persons and the results were published in 1928.[2]

Persons found that if there is no correlation between prices and quantities or if there is positive correlation, base-year weights produce a downward bias and given-year weights produce an upward bias. If there is negative correlation between prices and quantities, the bias may be either upward or downward or offsetting, depending on the relative strength of each series.

---

[2] Warren M. Persons, *The Construction of Index Numbers* (Boston: Houghton-Mifflin Company, 1928).

STUDY QUESTIONS

15-1. Explain briefly each of the following terms:

a. index number
b. value index
c. price index
d. quantity index
e. constant dollars
f. index of consumer confidence
g. price relative

h. chain index number
i. market basket of goods and services
j. linking
k. base period
l. weight correlation bias

15-2. List and describe four uses of index numbers.

15-3. What kinds of averages may be used to combine price relatives into a price index?

15-4. What weights are normally used to compute Laspeyres' price index?

15-5. Why is Paasche's price index used less frequently than Laspeyres' price index?

15-6. What type formula is used to compute the Wholesale Price Index?

15-7. What system of weights is used to compute the Consumer Price Index?

15-8. If you were to compare the formulas for Standard & Poor's Price Index with that used for the Dow-Jones Stock Averages, which would you consider to be the better measure of changes in stock prices? Why?

15-9. What things need to be considered in determining the commodities to be used in a price index?

15-10. What does the Federal Reserve Board Index measure?

15-11. Under what conditions would it be necessary to use the "adjustment for quality difference" method rather than the "linking" method to handle a substantial change in quality of an item included in a price index? If you could use either method, which would you prefer? Why?

15-12. What base period is currently used for most federally constructed index numbers? Why is this a logical base?

15-13. What kind of bias might you expect in an index number computed using an arithmetic mean of price relatives? A harmonic mean? A geometric mean?

15-14. What kind of bias can result from using base-year values as weights in a price index?

15-15. What are some of the disadvantages of using given-year values as weights in a price index?

PROBLEMS

15–1.

TABLE 15.A

Total Value of All Cattle Produced on Farms in the United States, 1971–1976

Year	Value (billions of dollars)
1971	21.1
1972	24.5
1973	30.6
1974	37.4
1975	21.0
1976	24.3

Source: Commodity Yearbook, 1976

a. Compute a value index for the series using 1971 = 100.0.
b. Can the fact that the value of cattle is fluctuating from one year to the next be explained by changes in the number of cattle raised or because cattle prices fluctuate? Explain.

15–2.

TABLE 15.B

Price Per Gallon and Sales in Gallons for Three Petroleum Products, 1972 and 1976

Product	Price per gallon		Sales in gallons	
	1972	1976	1972	1976
Fuel oil	$0.21	$0.44	8,000	8,150
Gasoline	0.34	0.63	11,620	12,040
Lubricants	0.35	0.51	580	610

Compute the following indexes of petroleum products for 1976 with 1972 = 100.0.
a. Price index computed as an unweighted arithmetic mean of price relatives.
b. Price index computed as an unweighted geometric mean of price relatives.
c. Price index computed as an unweighted harmonic mean of quantity relatives.

15–3. Use the data in Problem 15–2 on petroleum products to compute the following index numbers for 1976 with 1972 = 100.0.
  a. Laspeyres' price index.
  b. Paasche's price index.

15–4.

TABLE 15.C

**Number and Price of Three Models of Lawn Mowers
Sold by a Hardware Store, 1972 and 1975**

| Model of | 1972 | | 1975 | |
lawn mower	Number sold	Price	Number sold	Price
Model I	225	$77	315	$92
Model II	300	83	420	112
Self-propelled	75	162	95	185

Using 1972 as the base period, compute the following indexes of prices for 1975:
  a. Laspeyres' price index.
  b. Paasche's price index.

15–5.

TABLE 15.D

**Prices and Slaughter of Livestock in the United
States, 1972 and 1975**

| | 1972 | | 1975 | |
Livestock	Price (per 100 lbs)	Slaughter (thousands)	Price (per 100 lbs)	Slaughter (thousands)
Cattle and calves	$32.03	38,830	$41.20	46,110
Hogs and pigs	26.58	59,180	47.65	49,602
Sheep and lambs	30.13	18,700	44.68	14,500

  a. Compute Laspreyes' price index for 1975 with 1972 = 100.0.
  b. Compute Paasche's price index for 1975 with 1972 = 100.0.

15–6. For the series in Table 15.E, compute the values of the new index using 1975 as the base year from the old index that has 1970 as its base.

TABLE 15.E

Index for the Years 1968–1976

Year	Old index (1970 = 100.0)	New index (1975 = 100.0)
1968	79.2	
1969	84.6	
1970	100.0	
1971	109.7	
1972	111.2	
1973	116.7	
1974	123.8	
1975	163.8	100.0
1976	180.5	

15–7. In the series in Table 15.F, the values of the new index with a base of 1975 are given. Compute the values of the old index with 1970 as the base.

TABLE 15.F

Index for the Years 1969–1976

Year	Old index (1970 = 100.0)	New index (1975 = 100.0)
1969		133.5
1970	100.0	131.7
1971		127.2
1972		120.0
1973		118.6
1974		105.3
1975		100.0
1976		88.5

15–8. Judging from Table 15.G, at the top of page 515, are the real wages of the employees of Company A keeping pace with the cost of living? What is the exact situation in 1976?

15–9. In March, 1977, the consumer price index for Detroit stood at 177.4 (1967 = 100.0). On the same date the index for San Francisco was 182.1. What does this tell you about the relative cost of living in the two cities?

TABLE 15.G

**Consumer Price Index and Average Weekly Earnings
in Company A, 1972–1976**

Year	Consumer price index 1967 = 100.0	Average weekly earnings in Company A
1972	142.8	$61.50
1973	150.5	61.75
1974	162.8	62.20
1975	168.7	63.20
1976	174.3	64.75

15–10.

TABLE 15.H

Prices of Four Commodities, 1970–1975

Commodity	Weights q_a	Prices					
		1970	1971	1972	1973	1974	1975
A	0.3	$1.00	$1.10	$1.05	$1.11	$1.18	$1.20
B	0.2	0.26	0.30	0.35	0.42	0.55	0.60
C	0.2	0.58	0.56	0.52	0.50	0.50	0.45
D	0.3	2.00	2.05	2.10	2.25	2.50	2.65

Using the values of q_a as weights:
  a. Compute chain index numbers 1971 through 1975.
  b. Use the values computed in part a to compute $P_{70\text{-}75}$.
  c. Compute an arithmetic mean of price relatives using 1970 = 100.0.
  d. Compare the answers to parts b and c. Are they the same?

15–11. Given the following price index: (1971 = 100.0)

1968	1969	1970	1971	1972	1973	1974	1975	1976
87.2	93.2	97.3	100.0	107.8	112.6	118.6	133.4	142.0

  a. Shift the base to 1969 = 100.0
  b. Shift the base to 1973 = 100.0.

15–12.

TABLE 15.I

Prices of Three Dairy Products, 1973–1976

Product	Unit	Weights q_a	Prices			
			1973	1974	1975	1976
Milk	Fluid pound	0.5	$0.66	$0.69	$0.71	$0.72
Butter	Pound	0.2	0.66	0.68	0.70	0.68
Eggs	Dozen	0.3	0.49	0.61	0.37	0.30

Using the values of q_a as weights:
   a. Compute chain price index numbers for 1974 through 1976.
   b. Using 1973 = 100.0, compute $P_{73,74}$, $P_{74,75}$, $P_{75,76}$.
   c. Compute $P_{73,76}$.

15–13. Assume that one of the products selected for a price index has a substantial change in quality.
   a. If you have the following information, compute the index using the "linking" method:

Reported price	Base period	Period 1	Period 2
Quality I	$5.00	$6.00	$ ...
Quality II	...	9.00	10.00

   b. If you have the following information, compute the index using the "adjustment of quality difference" method:

Price for:	Base period	Period 1	Period 2
Quality I	$5.00	...	...
Quality II	...	$9.00	$10.00
Value of the difference between I & II	...	3.00	...

SELECTED READINGS

Fisher, Irving. *The Making of Index Numbers.* Boston: Houghton Mifflin Company, 1927.
   A definitive work on index numbers. In this book Professor Fisher examines and tests for reliability many different formulas for computing index numbers.
Persons, Warren Milton. *The Construction of Index Numbers.* Boston: Houghton Mifflin Company, 1928.

A short but highly instructive book on the construction of index numbers of prices. Special attention is given to the problems of bias resulting from the type of average used and from correlation between quantities and prices.

Stockton, John R., and Charles T. Clark. *Introduction to Business & Economic Statistics,* 5th ed. Cincinnati: South-Western Publishing Co., 1975.

Chapter 17 gives an introductory look at index numbers.

U.S. Department of Labor, Bureau of Labor Statistics. *BLS Handbook of Methods.* Bulletin 1910. Washington, D.C.: U.S. Government Printing Office, 1976.

This handbook explains the methods employed by the Bureau of Labor Statistics in the many surveys and studies it conducts. It gives a brief but clear explanation of how it measures changes in consumer and wholesale prices.

APPENDIX

SQUARES — SQUARE ROOTS — RECIPROCALS

n	n^2	$\sqrt{n}$	$\sqrt{10n}$	$1/n$	n	n^2	$\sqrt{n}$	$\sqrt{10n}$	$1/n$
1.00	1.0000	1.00000	3.16228	1.000000	**1.50**	2.2500	1.22474	3.87298	.666667
1.01	1.0201	1.00499	3.17805	.990099	1.51	2.2801	1.22882	3.88587	.662252
1.02	1.0404	1.00995	3.19374	.980392	1.52	2.3104	1.23288	3.89872	.657895
1.03	1.0609	1.01489	3.20936	.970874	1.53	2.3409	1.23693	3.91152	.653595
1.04	1.0816	1.01980	3.22490	.961538	1.54	2.3716	1.24097	3.92428	.649351
1.05	1.1025	1.02470	3.24037	.952381	1.55	2.4025	1.24499	3.93700	.645161
1.06	1.1236	1.02956	3.25576	.943396	1.56	2.4336	1.24900	3.94968	.641026
1.07	1.1449	1.03441	3.27109	.934579	1.57	2.4649	1.25300	3.96232	.636943
1.08	1.1664	1.03923	3.28634	.925926	1.58	2.4964	1.25698	3.97492	.632911
1.09	1.1881	1.04403	3.30151	.917431	1.59	2.5281	1.26095	3.98748	.628931
1.10	1.2100	1.04881	3.31662	.909091	**1.60**	2.5600	1.26491	4.00000	.625000
1.11	1.2321	1.05357	3.33167	.900901	1.61	2.5921	1.26886	4.01248	.621118
1.12	1.2544	1.05830	3.34664	.892857	1.62	2.6244	1.27279	4.02492	.617284
1.13	1.2769	1.06301	3.36155	.884956	1.63	2.6569	1.27671	4.03733	.613497
1.14	1.2996	1.06771	3.37639	.877193	1.64	2.6896	1.28062	4.04969	.609756
1.15	1.3225	1.07238	3.39116	.869565	1.65	2.7225	1.28452	4.06202	.606061
1.16	1.3456	1.07703	3.40588	.862069	1.66	2.7556	1.28841	4.07431	.602410
1.17	1.3689	1.08167	3.42053	.854701	1.67	2.7889	1.29228	4.08656	.598802
1.18	1.3924	1.08628	3.43511	.847458	1.68	2.8224	1.29615	4.09878	.595238
1.19	1.4161	1.09087	3.44964	.840336	1.69	2.8561	1.30000	4.11096	.591716
1.20	1.4400	1.09545	3.46410	.833333	**1.70**	2.8900	1.30384	4.12311	.588235
1.21	1.4641	1.10000	3.47851	.826446	1.71	2.9241	1.30767	4.13521	.584795
1.22	1.4884	1.10454	3.49285	.819672	1.72	2.9584	1.31149	4.14729	.581395
1.23	1.5129	1.10905	3.50714	.813008	1.73	2.9929	1.31529	4.15933	.578035
1.24	1.5376	1.11355	3.52136	.806452	1.74	3.0276	1.31909	4.17133	.574713
1.25	1.5625	1.11803	3.53553	.800000	1.75	3.0625	1.32288	4.18330	.571429
1.26	1.5876	1.12250	3.54965	.793651	1.76	3.0976	1.32665	4.19524	.568182
1.27	1.6129	1.12694	3.56371	.787402	1.77	3.1329	1.33041	4.20714	.564972
1.28	1.6384	1.13137	3.57771	.781250	1.78	3.1684	1.33417	4.21900	.561798
1.29	1.6641	1.13578	3.59166	.775194	1.79	3.2041	1.33791	4.23084	.558659
1.30	1.6900	1.14018	3.60555	.769231	**1.80**	3.2400	1.34164	4.24264	.555556
1.31	1.7161	1.14455	3.61939	.763359	1.81	3.2761	1.34536	4.25441	.552486
1.32	1.7424	1.14891	3.63318	.757576	1.82	3.3124	1.34907	4.26615	.549451
1.33	1.7689	1.15326	3.64692	.751880	1.83	3.3489	1.35277	4.27785	.546448
1.34	1.7956	1.15758	3.66060	.746269	1.84	3.3856	1.35647	4.28952	.543478
1.35	1.8225	1.16190	3.67423	.740741	1.85	3.4225	1.36015	4.30116	.540541
1.36	1.8496	1.16619	3.68782	.735294	1.86	3.4596	1.36382	4.31277	.537634
1.37	1.8769	1.17047	3.70135	.729927	1.87	3.4969	1.36748	4.32435	.534759
1.38	1.9044	1.17473	3.71484	.724638	1.88	3.5344	1.37113	4.33590	.531915
1.39	1.9321	1.17898	3.72827	.719424	1.89	3.5721	1.37477	4.34741	.529101
1.40	1.9600	1.18322	3.74166	.714286	**1.90**	3.6100	1.37840	4.35890	.526316
1.41	1.9881	1.18743	3.75500	.709220	1.91	3.6481	1.38203	4.37035	.523560
1.42	2.0164	1.19164	3.76829	.704225	1.92	3.6864	1.38564	4.38178	.520833
1.43	2.0449	1.19583	3.78153	.699301	1.93	3.7249	1.38924	4.39318	.518135
1.44	2.0736	1.20000	3.79473	.694444	1.94	3.7636	1.39284	4.40454	.515464
1.45	2.1025	1.20416	3.80789	.689655	1.95	3.8025	1.39642	4.41588	.512821
1.46	2.1316	1.20830	3.82099	.684932	1.96	3.8416	1.40000	4.42719	.510204
1.47	2.1609	1.21244	3.83406	.680272	1.97	3.8809	1.40357	4.43847	.507614
1.48	2.1904	1.21655	3.84708	.675676	1.98	3.9204	1.40712	4.44972	.505051
1.49	2.2201	1.22066	3.86005	.671141	1.99	3.9601	1.41067	4.46094	.502513
1.50	2.2500	1.22474	3.87298	.666667	**2.00**	4.0000	1.41421	4.47214	.500000
n	n^2	$\sqrt{n}$	$\sqrt{10n}$	$1/n$	n	n^2	$\sqrt{n}$	$\sqrt{10n}$	$1/n$

Table A

n	n²	√n	√10n	1/n	n	n²	√n	√10n	1/n
2.00	4.0000	1.41421	4.47214	.500000	**2.50**	6.2500	1.58114	5.00000	.400000
2.01	4.0401	1.41774	4.48330	.497512	2.51	6.3001	1.58430	5.00999	.398406
2.02	4.0804	1.42127	4.49444	.495050	2.52	6.3504	1.58745	5.01996	.396825
2.03	4.1209	1.42478	4.50555	.492611	2.53	6.4009	1.59060	5.02991	.395257
2.04	4.1616	1.42829	4.51664	.490196	2.54	6.4516	1.59374	5.03984	.393701
2.05	4.2025	1.43178	4.52769	.487805	2.55	6.5025	1.59687	5.04975	.392157
2.06	4.2436	1.43527	4.53872	.485437	2.56	6.5536	1.60000	5.05964	.390625
2.07	4.2849	1.43875	4.54973	.483092	2.57	6.6049	1.60312	5.06952	.389105
2.08	4.3264	1.44222	4.56070	.480769	2.58	6.6564	1.60624	5.07937	.387597
2.09	4.3681	1.44568	4.57165	.478469	2.59	6.7081	1.60935	5.08920	.386100
2.10	4.4100	1.44914	4.58258	.476190	**2.60**	6.7600	1.61245	5.09902	.384615
2.11	4.4521	1.45258	4.59347	.473934	2.61	6.8121	1.61555	5.10882	.383142
2.12	4.4944	1.45602	4.60435	.471698	2.62	6.8644	1.61864	5.11859	.381679
2.13	4.5369	1.45945	4.61519	.469484	2.63	6.9169	1.62173	5.12835	.380228
2.14	4.5796	1.46287	4.62601	.467290	2.64	6.9696	1.62481	5.13809	.378788
2.15	4.6225	1.46629	4.63681	.465116	2.65	7.0225	1.62788	5.14782	.377358
2.16	4.6656	1.46969	4.64758	.462963	2.66	7.0756	1.63095	5.15752	.375940
2.17	4.7089	1.47309	4.65833	.460829	2.67	7.1289	1.63401	5.16720	.374532
2.18	4.7524	1.47648	4.66905	.458716	2.68	7.1824	1.63707	5.17687	.373134
2.19	4.7961	1,47986	4.67974	.456621	2.69	7.2361	1.64012	5.18652	.371747
2.20	4.8400	1.48324	4.69042	.454545	**2.70**	7.2900	1.64317	5.19615	.370370
2.21	4.8841	1.48661	4.70106	.452489	2.71	7.3441	1.64621	5.20577	.369004
2.22	4.9284	1.48997	4.71169	.450450	2.72	7.3984	1.64924	5.21536	.367647
2.23	4.9729	1.49332	4.72229	.448430	2.73	7.4529	1.65227	5.22494	.366300
2.24	5.0176	1.49666	4.73286	.446429	2.74	7.5076	1.65529	5.23450	.364964
2.25	5.0625	1.50000	4.74342	.444444	2.75	7.5625	1.65831	5.24404	.363636
2.26	5.1076	1.50333	4.75395	.442478	2.76	7.6176	1.66132	5.25357	.362319
2.27	5.1529	1.50665	4.76445	.440529	2.77	7.6729	1.66433	5.26308	.361011
2.28	5.1984	1.50997	4.77493	.438596	2.78	7.7284	1.66733	5.27257	.359712
2.29	5.2441	1.51327	4.78539	.436681	2.79	7.7841	1.67033	5.28205	.358423
2.30	5.2900	1.51658	4.79583	.434783	**2.80**	7.8400	1.67332	5.29150	.357143
2.31	5.3361	1.51987	4.80625	.432900	2.81	7.8961	1.67631	5.30094	.355872
2.32	5.3824	1.52315	4.81664	.431034	2.82	7.9524	1.67929	5.31037	.354610
2.33	5.4289	1.52643	4.82701	.429185	2.83	8.0089	1.68226	5.31977	.353357
2.34	5.4756	1.52971	4.83735	.427350	2.84	8.0656	1.68523	5.32917	.352113
2.35	5.5225	1.53297	4.84768	.425532	2.85	8.1225	1.68819	5.33854	.350877
2.36	5.5696	1.53623	4.85798	.423729	2.86	8.1796	1.69115	5.34790	.349650
2.37	5.6169	1.53948	4.86826	.421941	2.87	8.2369	1.69411	5.35724	.348432
2.38	5.6644	1.54272	4.87852	.420168	2.88	8.2944	1.69706	5.36656	.347222
2.39	5.7121	1.54596	4.88876	.418410	2.89	8.3521	1.70000	5.37587	.346021
2.40	5.7600	1.54919	4.89898	.416667	**2.90**	8.4100	1.70294	5.38516	.344828
2.41	5.8081	1.55242	4.90918	.414938	2.91	8.4681	1.70587	5.39444	.343643
2.42	5.8564	1.55563	4.91935	.413223	2.92	8.5264	1.70880	5.40370	.342466
2.43	5.9049	1.55885	4.92950	.411523	2.93	8.5849	1.71172	5.41295	.341297
2.44	5.9536	1.56205	4.93964	.409836	2.94	8.6436	1.71464	5.42218	.340136
2.45	6.0025	1.56525	4.94975	.408163	2.95	8.7025	1.71756	5.43139	.338983
2.46	6.0516	1.56844	4.95984	.406504	2.96	8.7616	1.72047	5.44059	.337838
2.47	6.1009	1.57162	4.96991	.404858	2.97	8.8209	1.72337	5.44977	.336700
2.48	6.1504	1.57480	4.97996	.403226	2.98	8.8804	1.72627	5.45894	.335570
2.49	6.2001	1.57797	4.98999	.401606	2.99	8.9401	1.72916	5.46809	.334448
2.50	6.2500	1.58114	5.00000	.400000	**3.00**	9.0000	1.73205	5.47723	.333333
n	n²	√n	√10n	1/n	n	n²	√n	√10n	1/n

SQUARES — SQUARE ROOTS — RECIPROCALS (*Continued*)

n	n^2	$\sqrt{n}$	$\sqrt{10n}$	$1/n$	n	n^2	$\sqrt{n}$	$\sqrt{10n}$	$1/n$
3.00	9.0000	1.73205	5.47723	.333333	**3.50**	12.2500	1.87083	5.91608	.285714
3.01	9.0601	1.73494	5.48635	.332226	3.51	12.3201	1.87350	5.92453	.284900
3.02	9.1204	1.73781	5.49545	.331126	3.52	12.3904	1.87617	5.93296	.284091
3.03	9.1809	1.74069	5.50454	.330033	3.53	12.4609	1.87883	5.94138	.283286
3.04	9.2416	1.74356	5.51362	.328947	3.54	12.5316	1.88149	5.94979	.282486
3.05	9.3025	1.74642	5.52268	.327869	3.55	12.6025	1.88414	5.95819	.281690
3.06	9.3636	1.74929	5.53173	.326797	3.56	12.6736	1.88680	5.96657	.280899
3.07	9.4249	1.75214	5.54076	.325733	3.57	12.7449	1.88944	5.97495	.280112
3.08	9.4864	1.75499	5.54977	.324675	3.58	12.8164	1.89209	5.98331	.279330
3.09	9.5481	1.75784	5.55878	.323625	3.59	12.8881	1.89473	5.99166	.278552
3.10	9.6100	1.76068	5.56776	.322581	**3.60**	12.9600	1.89737	6.00000	.277778
3.11	9.6721	1.76352	5.57674	.321543	3.61	13.0321	1.90000	6.00833	.277008
3.12	9.7344	1.76635	5.58570	.320513	3.62	13.1044	1.90263	6.01664	.276243
3.13	9.7969	1.76918	5.59464	.319489	3.63	13.1769	1.90526	6.02495	.275482
3.14	9.8596	1.77200	5.60357	.318471	3.64	13.2496	1.90788	6.03324	.274725
3.15	9.9225	1.77482	5.61249	.317460	3.65	13.3225	1.91050	6.04152	.273973
3.16	9.9856	1.77764	5.62139	.316456	3.66	13.3956	1.91311	6.04979	.273224
3.17	10.0489	1.78045	5.63028	.315457	3.67	13.4689	1.91572	6.05805	.272480
3.18	10.1124	1.78326	5.63915	.314465	3.68	13.5424	1.91833	6.06630	.271739
3.19	10.1761	1.78606	5.64801	.313480	3.69	13.6161	1.92094	6.07454	.271003
3.20	10.2400	1.78885	5.65685	.312500	**3.70**	13.6900	1.92354	6.08276	.270270
3.21	10.3041	1.79165	5.66569	.311526	3.71	13.7641	1.92614	6.09098	.269542
3.22	10.3684	1.79444	5.67450	.310559	3.72	13.8384	1.92873	6.09918	.268817
3.23	10.4329	1.79722	5.68331	.309598	3.73	13.9129	1.93132	6.10737	.268097
3.24	10.4976	1.80000	5.69210	.308642	3.74	13.9876	1.93391	6.11555	.267380
3.25	10.5625	1.80278	5.70088	.307692	3.75	14.0625	1.93649	6.12372	.266667
3.26	10.6276	1.80555	5.70964	.306748	3.76	14.1376	1.93907	6.13188	.265957
3.27	10.6929	1.80831	5.71839	.305810	3.77	14.2129	1.94165	6.14003	.265252
3.28	10.7584	1.81108	5.72713	.304878	3.78	14.2884	1.94422	6.14817	.264550
3.29	10.8241	1.81384	5.73585	.303951	3.79	14.3641	1.94679	6.15630	.263852
3.30	10.8900	1.81659	5.74456	.303030	**3.80**	14.4400	1.94936	6.16441	.263158
3.31	10.9561	1.81934	5.75326	.302115	3.81	14.5161	1.95192	6.17252	.262467
3.32	11.0224	1.82209	5.76194	.301205	3.82	14.5924	1.95448	6.18061	.261780
3.33	11.0889	1.82483	5.77062	.300300	3.83	14.6689	1.95704	6.18870	.261097
3.34	11.1556	1.82757	5.77927	.299401	3.84	14.7456	1.95959	6.19677	.260417
3.35	11.2225	1.83030	5.78792	.298507	3.85	14.8225	1.96214	6.20484	.259740
3.36	11.2896	1.83303	5.79655	.297619	3.86	14.8996	1.96469	6.21289	.259067
3.37	11.3569	1.83576	5.80517	.296736	3.87	14.9769	1.96723	6.22093	.258398
3.38	11.4244	1.83848	5.81378	.295858	3.88	15.0544	1.96977	6.22896	.257732
3.39	11.4921	1.84120	5.82237	.294985	3.89	15.1321	1.97231	6.23699	.257069
3.40	11.5600	1.84391	5.83095	.294118	**3.90**	15.2100	1.97484	6.24500	.256410
3.41	11.6281	1.84662	5.83952	.293255	3.91	15.2881	1.97737	6.25300	.255754
3.42	11.6964	1.84932	5.84808	.292398	3.92	15.3664	1.97990	6.26099	.255102
3.43	11.7649	1.85203	5.85662	.291545	3.93	15.4449	1.98242	6.26897	.254453
3.44	11.8336	1.85472	5.86515	.290698	3.94	15.5236	1.98494	6.27694	.253807
3.45	11.9025	1.85742	5.87367	.289855	3.95	15.6025	1.98746	6.28490	.253165
3.46	11.9716	1.86011	5.88218	.289017	3.96	15.6816	1.98997	6.29285	.252525
3.47	12.0409	1.86279	5.89067	.288184	3.97	15.7609	1.99249	6.30079	.251889
3.48	12.1104	1.86548	5.89915	.287356	3.98	15.8408	1.99499	6.30872	.251256
3.49	12.1801	1.86815	5.90762	.286533	3.99	15.9201	1.99750	6.31664	.250627
3.50	12.2500	1.87083	5.91608	.285714	**4.00**	16.0000	2.00000	6.32456	.250000
n	n^2	$\sqrt{n}$	$\sqrt{10n}$	$1/n$	n	n^2	$\sqrt{n}$	$\sqrt{10n}$	$1/n$

Table A

n	n²	√n	√10n	1/n	n	n²	√n	√10n	1/n
4.00	16.0000	2.00000	6.32456	.250000	**4.50**	20.2500	2.12132	6.70820	.222222
4.01	16.0801	2.00250	6.33246	.249377	4.51	20.3401	2.12368	6.71565	.221729
4.02	16.1604	2.00499	6.34035	.248756	4.52	20.4304	2.12603	6.72309	.221239
4.03	16.2409	2.00749	6.34823	.248139	4.53	20.5209	2.12838	6.73053	.220751
4.04	16.3216	2.00998	6.35610	.247525	4.54	20.6116	2.13073	6.73795	.220264
4.05	16.4025	2.01246	6.36396	.246914	4.55	20.7025	2.13307	6.74537	.219780
4.06	16.4836	2.01494	6.37181	.246305	4.56	20.7936	2.13542	6.75278	.219298
4.07	16.5649	2.01742	6.37966	.245700	4.57	20.8849	2.13776	6.76018	.218818
4.08	16.6464	2.01990	6.38749	.245098	4.58	20.9764	2.14009	6.76757	.218341
4.09	16.7281	2.02237	6.39531	.244499	4.59	21.0681	2.14243	6.77495	.217865
4.10	16.8100	2.02485	6.40312	.243902	**4.60**	21.1600	2.14476	6.78233	.217391
4.11	16.8921	2.02731	6.41093	.243309	4.61	21.2521	2.14709	6.78970	.216920
4.12	16.9744	2.02978	6.41872	.242718	4.62	21.3444	2.14942	6.79706	.216450
4.13	17.0569	2.03224	6.42651	.242131	4.63	21.4369	2.15174	6.80441	.215983
4.14	17.1396	2.03470	6.43428	.241546	4.64	21.5296	2.15407	6.81175	.215517
4.15	17.2225	2.03715	6.44205	.240964	4.65	21.6225	2.15639	6.81909	.215054
4.16	17.3056	2.03961	6.44981	.240385	4.66	21.7156	2.15870	6.82642	.214592
4.17	17.3889	2.04206	6.45755	.239808	4.67	21.8089	2.16102	6.83374	.214133
4.18	17.4724	2.04450	6.46529	.239234	4.68	21.9024	2.16333	6.84105	.213675
4.19	17.5561	2.04695	6.47302	.238663	4.69	21.9961	2.16564	6.84836	.213220
4.20	17.6400	2.04939	6.48074	.238095	**4.70**	22.0900	2.16795	6.85565	.212766
4.21	17.7241	2.05183	6.48845	.237530	4.71	22.1841	2.17025	6.86294	.212314
4.22	17.8084	2.05426	6.49615	.236967	4.72	22.2784	2.17256	6.87023	.211864
4.23	17.8929	2.05670	6.50384	.236407	4.73	22.3729	2.17486	6.87750	.211416
4.24	17.9776	2.05913	6.51153	.235849	4.74	22.4676	2.17715	6.88477	.210970
4.25	18.0625	2.06155	6.51920	.235294	4.75	22.5625	2.17945	6.89202	.210526
4.26	18.1476	2.06398	6.52687	.234742	4.76	22.6576	2.18174	6.89928	.210084
4.27	18.2329	2.06640	6.53452	.234192	4.77	22.7529	2.18403	6.90652	.209644
4.28	18.3184	2.06882	6.54217	.233645	4.78	22.8484	2.18632	6.91375	.209205
4.29	18.4041	2.07123	6.54981	.233100	4.79	22.9441	2.18861	6.92098	.208768
4.30	18.4900	2.07364	6.55744	.232558	**4.80**	23.0400	2.19089	6.92820	.208333
4.31	18.5761	2.07605	6.56506	.232019	4.81	23.1361	2.19317	6.93542	.207900
4.32	18.6624	2.07846	6.57267	.231481	4.82	23.2324	2.19545	6.94262	.207469
4.33	18.7489	2.08087	6.58027	.230947	4.83	23.3289	2.19773	6.94982	.207039
4.34	18.8356	2.08327	6.58787	.230415	4.84	23.4256	2.20000	6.95701	.206612
4.35	18.9225	2.08567	6.59545	.229885	4.85	23.5225	2.20227	6.96419	.206186
4.36	19.0096	2.08806	6.60303	.229358	4.86	23.6196	2.20454	6.97137	.205761
4.37	19.0969	2.09045	6.61060	.228833	4.87	23.7169	2.20681	6.97854	.205339
4.38	19.1844	2.09284	6.61816	.228311	4.88	23.8144	2.20907	6.98570	.204918
4.39	19.2721	2.09523	6.62571	.227790	4.89	23.9121	2.21133	6.99285	.204499
4.40	19.3600	2.09762	6.63325	.227273	**4.90**	24.0100	2.21359	7.00000	.204082
4.41	19.4481	2.10000	6.64078	.226757	4.91	24.1081	2.21585	7.00714	.203666
4.42	19.5364	2.10238	6.64831	.226244	4.92	24.2064	2.21811	7.01427	.203252
4.43	19.6249	2.10476	6.65582	.225734	4.93	24.3049	2.22036	7.02140	.202840
4.44	19.7136	2.10713	6.66333	.225225	4.94	24.4036	2.22261	7.02851	.202429
4.45	19.8025	2.10950	6.67083	.224719	4.95	24.5025	2.22486	7.03562	.202020
4.46	19.8916	2.11187	6.67832	.224215	4.96	24.6016	2.22711	7.04273	.201613
4.47	19.9809	2.11424	6.68581	.223714	4.97	24.7009	2.22935	7.04982	.201207
4.48	20.0704	2.11660	6.69328	.223214	4.98	24.8004	2.23159	7.05691	.200803
4.49	20.1601	2.11896	6.70075	.222717	4.99	24.9001	2.23383	7.06399	.200401
4.50	20.2500	2.12132	6.70820	.222222	**5.00**	25.0000	2.23607	7.07107	.200000
n	n²	√n	√10n	1/n	n	n²	√n	√10n	1/n

SQUARES — SQUARE ROOTS — RECIPROCALS (*Continued*)

n	n^2	$\sqrt{n}$	$\sqrt{10n}$	$1/n$	n	n^2	$\sqrt{n}$	$\sqrt{10n}$	$1/n$
5.00	25.0000	2.23607	7.07107	.200000	**5.50**	30.2500	2.34521	7.41620	.181818
5.01	25.1001	2.23830	7.07814	.199601	5.51	30.3601	2.34734	7.42294	.181488
5.02	25.2004	2.24054	7.08520	.199203	5.52	30.4704	2.34947	7.42967	.181159
5.03	25.3009	2.24277	7.09225	.198807	5.53	30.5809	2.35160	7.43640	.180832
5.04	25.4016	2.24499	7.09930	.198413	5.54	30.6916	2.35372	7.44312	.180505
5.05	25.5025	2.24722	7.10634	.198020	5.55	30.8025	2.35584	7.44983	.180180
5.06	25.6036	2.24944	7.11337	.197628	5.56	30.9136	2.35797	7.45654	.179856
5.07	25.7049	2.25167	7.12039	.197239	5.57	31.0249	2.36008	7.46324	.179533
5.08	25.8064	2.25389	7.12741	.196850	5.58	31.1364	2.36220	7.46994	.179211
5.09	25.9081	2.25610	7.13442	.196464	5.59	31.2481	2.36432	7.47663	.178891
5.10	26.0100	2.25832	7.14143	.196078	**5.60**	31.3600	2.36643	7.48331	.178571
5.11	26.1121	2.26053	7.14843	.195695	5.61	31.4721	2.36854	7.48999	.178253
5.12	26.2144	2.26274	7.15542	.195312	5.62	31.5844	2.37065	7.49667	.177936
5.13	26.3169	2.26495	7.16240	.194932	5.63	31.6969	2.37276	7.50333	.177620
5.14	26.4196	2.26716	7.16938	.194553	5.64	31.8096	2.37487	7.50999	.177305
5.15	26.5225	2.26936	7.17635	.194175	5.65	31.9225	2.37697	7.51665	.176991
5.16	26.6256	2.27156	7.18331	.193798	5.66	32.0356	2.37908	7.52330	.176678
5.17	26.7289	2.27376	7.19027	.193424	5.67	32.1489	2.38118	7.52994	.176367
5.18	26.8324	2.27596	7.19722	.193050	5.68	32.2624	2.38328	7.53658	.176056
5.19	26.9361	2.27816	7.20417	.192678	5.69	32.3761	2.38537	7.54321	.175747
5.20	27.0400	2.28035	7.21110	.192308	**5.70**	32.4900	2.38747	7.54983	.175439
5.21	27.1441	2.28254	7.21803	.191939	5.71	32.6041	2.38956	7.55645	.175131
5.22	27.2484	2.28473	7.22496	.191571	5.72	32.7184	2.39165	7.56307	.174825
5.23	27.3529	2.28692	7.23187	.191205	5.73	32.8329	2.39374	7.56968	.174520
5.24	27.4576	2.28910	7.23878	.190840	5.74	32.9476	2.39583	7.57628	.174216
5.25	27.5625	2.29129	7.24569	.190476	5.75	33.0625	2.39792	7.58288	.173913
5.26	27.6676	2.29347	7.25259	.190114	5.76	33.1776	2.40000	7.58947	.173611
5.27	27.7729	2.29565	7.25948	.189753	5.77	33.2929	2.40208	7.59605	.173310
5.28	27.8784	2.29783	7.26636	.189394	5.78	33.4084	2.40416	7.60263	.173010
5.29	27.9841	2.30000	7.27324	.189036	5.79	33.5241	2.40624	7.60920	.172712
5.30	28.0900	2.30217	7.28011	.188679	**5.80**	33.6400	2.40832	7.61577	.172414
5.31	28.1961	2.30434	7.28697	.188324	5.81	33.7561	2.41039	7.62234	.172117
5.32	28.3024	2.30651	7.29383	.187970	5.82	33.8724	2.41247	7.62889	.171821
5.33	28.4089	2.30868	7.30068	.187617	5.83	33.9889	2.41454	7.63544	.171527
5.34	28.5156	2.31084	7.30753	.187266	5.84	34.1056	2.41661	7.64199	.171233
5.35	28.6225	2.31301	7.31437	.186916	5.85	34.2225	2.41868	7.64853	.170940
5.36	28.7296	2.31517	7.32120	.186567	5.86	34.3396	2.42074	7.65506	.170649
5.37	28.8369	2.31733	7.32803	.186220	5.87	34.4569	2.42281	7.66159	.170358
5.38	28.9444	2.31948	7.33485	.185874	5.88	34.5744	2.42487	7.66812	.170068
5.39	29.0521	2.32164	7.34166	.185529	5.89	34.6921	2.42693	7.67463	.169779
5.40	29.1600	2.32379	7.34847	.185185	**5.90**	34.8100	2.42899	7.68115	.169492
5.41	29.2681	2.32594	7.35527	.184843	5.91	34.9281	2.43105	7.68765	.169205
5.42	29.3764	2.32809	7.36206	.184502	5.92	35.0464	2.43311	7.69415	.168919
5.43	29.4849	2.33024	7.36885	.184162	5.93	35.1649	2.43516	7.70065	.168634
5.44	29.5936	2.33238	7.37564	.183824	5.94	35.2836	2.43721	7.70714	.168350
5.45	29.7025	2.33452	7.38241	.183486	5.95	35.4025	2.43926	7.71362	.168067
5.46	29.8116	2.33666	7.38918	.183150	5.96	35.5216	2.44131	7.72010	.167785
5.47	29.9209	2.33880	7.39594	.182815	5.97	35.6409	2.44336	7.72658	.167504
5.48	30.0304	2.34094	7.40270	.182482	5.98	35.7604	2.44540	7.73305	.167224
5.49	30.1401	2.34307	7.40945	.182149	5.99	35.8801	2.44745	7.73951	.166945
5.50	30.2500	2.34521	7.41620	.181818	**6.00**	36.0000	2.44949	7.74597	.166667
n	n^2	$\sqrt{n}$	$\sqrt{10n}$	$1/n$	n	n^2	$\sqrt{n}$	$\sqrt{10n}$	$1/n$

Table A

SQUARES — SQUARE ROOTS — RECIPROCALS (Continued)

n	n²	√n	√10n	1/n	n	n²	√n	√10n	1/n
6.00	36.0000	2.44949	7.74597	.166667	6.50	42.2500	2.54951	8.06226	.153846
6.01	36.1201	2.45153	7.75242	.166389	6.51	42.3801	2.55147	8.06846	.153610
6.02	36.2404	2.45357	7.75887	.166113	6.52	42.5104	2.55343	8.07465	.153374
6.03	36.3609	2.45561	7.76531	.165837	6.53	42.6409	2.55539	8.08084	.153139
6.04	36.4816	2.45764	7.77174	.165563	6.54	42.7716	2.55734	8.08703	.152905
6.05	36.6025	2.45967	7.77817	.165289	6.55	42.9025	2.55930	8.09321	.152672
6.06	36.7236	2.46171	7.78460	.165017	6.56	43.0336	2.56125	8.09938	.152439
6.07	36.8449	2.46374	7.79102	.164745	6.57	43.1649	2.56320	8.10555	.152207
6.08	36.9664	2.46577	7.79744	.164474	6.58	43.2964	2.56515	8.11172	.151976
6.09	37.0881	2.46779	7.80385	.164204	6.59	43.4281	2.56710	8.11788	.151745
6.10	37.2100	2.46982	7.81025	.163934	6.60	43.5600	2.56905	8.12404	.151515
6.11	37.3321	2.47184	7.81665	.163666	6.61	43.6921	2.57099	8.13019	.151286
6.12	37.4544	2.47386	7.82304	.163399	6.62	43.8244	2.57294	8.13634	.151057
6.13	37.5769	2.47588	7.82943	.163132	6.63	43.9569	2.57488	8.14248	.150830
6.14	37.6996	2.47790	7.83582	.162866	6.64	44.0896	2.57682	8.14862	.150602
6.15	37.8225	2.47992	7.84219	.162602	6.65	44.2225	2.57876	8.15475	.150376
6.16	37.9456	2.48193	7.84857	.162338	6.66	44.3556	2.58070	8.16088	.150150
6.17	38.0689	2.48395	7.85493	.162075	6.67	44.4889	2.58263	8.16701	.149925
6.18	38.1924	2.48596	7.86130	.161812	6.68	44.6224	2.58457	8.17313	.149701
6.19	38.3161	2.48797	7.86766	.161551	6.69	44.7561	2.58650	8.17924	.149477
6.20	38.4400	2.48998	7.87401	.161290	6.70	44.8900	2.58844	8.18535	.149254
6.21	38.5641	2.49199	7.88036	.161031	6.71	45.0241	2.59037	8.19146	.149031
6.22	38.6884	2.49399	7.88670	.160772	6.72	45.1584	2.59230	8.19756	.148810
6.23	38.8129	2.49600	7.89303	.160514	6.73	45.2929	2.59422	8.20366	.148588
6.24	38.9376	2.49800	7.89937	.160256	6.74	45.4276	2.59615	8.20975	.148368
6.25	39.0625	2.50000	7.90569	.160000	6.75	45.5625	2.59808	8.21584	.148148
6.26	39.1876	2.50200	7.91202	.159744	6.76	45.6976	2.60000	8.22192	.147929
6.27	39.3129	2.50400	7.91833	.159490	6.77	45.8329	2.60192	8.22800	.147710
6.28	39.4384	2.50599	7.92465	.159236	6.78	45.9684	2.60384	8.23408	.147493
6.29	39.5641	2.50799	7.93095	.158983	6.79	46.1041	2.60576	8.24015	.147275
6.30	39.6900	2.50998	7.93725	.158730	6.80	46.2400	2.60768	8.24621	.147059
6.31	39.8161	2.51197	7.94355	.158479	6.81	46.3761	2.60960	8.25227	.146843
6.32	39.9424	2.51396	7.94984	.158228	6.82	46.5124	2.61151	8.25833	.146628
6.33	40.0689	2.51595	7.95613	.157978	6.83	46.6489	2.61343	8.26438	.146413
6.34	40.1956	2.51794	7.96241	.157729	6.84	46.7856	2.61534	8.27043	.146199
6.35	40.3225	2.51992	7.96869	.157480	6.85	46.9225	2.61725	8.27647	.145985
6.36	40.4496	2.52190	7.97496	.157233	6.86	47.0596	2.61916	8.28251	.145773
6.37	40.5769	2.52389	7.98123	.156986	6.87	47.1969	2.62107	8.28855	.145560
6.38	40.7044	2.52587	7.98749	.156740	6.88	47.3344	2.62298	8.29458	.145349
6.39	40.8321	2.52784	7.99375	.156495	6.89	47.4721	2.62488	8.30060	.145138
6.40	40.9600	2.52982	8.00000	.156250	6.90	47.6100	2.62679	8.30662	.144928
6.41	41.0881	2.53180	8.00625	.156006	6.91	47.7481	2.62869	8.31264	.144718
6.42	41.2164	2.53377	8.01249	.155763	6.92	47.8864	2.63059	8.31865	.144509
6.43	41.3449	2.53574	8.01873	.155521	6.93	48.0249	2.63249	8.32466	.144300
6.44	41.4736	2.53772	8.02496	.155280	6.94	48.1636	2.63439	8.33067	.144092
6.45	41.6025	2.53969	8.03119	.155039	6.95	48.3025	2.63629	8.33667	.143885
6.46	41.7316	2.54165	8.03741	.154799	6.96	48.4416	2.63818	8.34266	.143678
6.47	41.8609	2.54362	8.04363	.154560	6.97	48.5809	2.64008	8.34865	.143472
6.48	41.9904	2.54558	8.04984	.154321	6.98	48.7204	2.64197	8.35464	.143266
6.49	42.1201	2.54755	8.05605	.154083	6.99	48.8601	2.64386	8.36062	.143062
6.50	42.2500	2.54951	8.06226	.153846	7.00	49.0000	2.64575	8.36660	.142857
n	n²	√n	√10n	1/n	n	n²	√n	√10n	1/n

Table A

SQUARES — SQUARE ROOTS — RECIPROCALS (*Continued*)

n	n^2	$\sqrt{n}$	$\sqrt{10n}$	$1/n$	n	n^2	$\sqrt{n}$	$\sqrt{10n}$	$1/n$
7.00	49.0000	2.64575	8.36660	.142857	**7.50**	56.2500	2.73861	8.66025	.133333
7.01	49.1401	2.64764	8.37257	.142653	7.51	56.4001	2.74044	8.66603	.133156
7.02	49.2804	2.64953	8.37854	.142450	7.52	56.5504	2.74226	8.67179	.132979
7.03	49.4209	2.65141	8.38451	.142248	7.53	56.7009	2.74408	8.67756	.132802
7.04	49.5616	2.65330	8.39047	.142045	7.54	56.8516	2.74591	8.68332	.132626
7.05	49.7025	2.65518	8.39643	.141844	7.55	57.0025	2.74773	8.68907	.132450
7.06	49.8436	2.65707	8.40238	.141643	7.56	57.1536	2.74955	8.69483	.132275
7.07	49.9849	2.65895	8.40833	.141443	7.57	57.3049	2.75136	8.70057	.132100
7.08	50.1264	2.66083	8.41427	.141243	7.58	57.4564	2.75318	8.70632	.131926
7.09	50.2681	2.66271	8.42021	.141044	7.59	57.6081	2.75500	8.71206	.131752
7.10	50.4100	2.66458	8.42615	.140845	**7.60**	57.7600	2.75681	8.71780	.131579
7.11	50.5521	2.66646	8.43208	.140647	7.61	57.9121	2.75862	8.72353	.131406
7.12	50.6944	2.66833	8.43801	.140449	7.62	58.0644	2.76043	8.72926	.131234
7.13	50.8369	2.67021	8.44393	.140252	7.63	58.2169	2.76225	8.73499	.131062
7.14	50.9796	2.67208	8.44985	.140056	7.64	58.3696	2.76405	8.74071	.130890
7.15	51.1225	2.67395	8.45577	.139860	7.65	58.5225	2.76586	8.74643	.130719
7.16	51.2656	2.67582	8.46168	.139665	7.66	58.6756	2.76767	8.75214	.130548
7.17	51.4089	2.67769	8.46759	.139470	7.67	58.8289	2.76948	8.75785	.130378
7.18	51.5524	2.67955	8.47349	.139276	7.68	58.9824	2.77128	8.76356	.130208
7.19	51.6961	2.68142	8.47939	.139082	7.69	59.1361	2.77308	8.76926	.130039
7.20	51.8400	2.68328	8.48528	.138889	**7.70**	59.2900	2.77489	8.77496	.129870
7.21	51.9841	2.68514	8.49117	.138696	7.71	59.4441	2.77669	8.78066	.129702
7.22	52.1284	2.68701	8.49706	.138504	7.72	59.5984	2.77849	8.78635	.129534
7.23	52.2729	2.68887	8.50294	.138313	7.73	59.7529	2.78029	8.79204	.129366
7.24	52.4176	2.69072	8.50882	.138122	7.74	59.9076	2.78209	8.79773	.129199
7.25	52.5625	2.69258	8.51469	.137931	7.75	60.0625	2.78388	8.80341	.129032
7.26	52.7076	2.69444	8.52056	.137741	7.76	60.2176	2.78568	8.80909	.128866
7.27	52.8529	2.69629	8.52643	.137552	7.77	60.3729	2.78747	8.81476	.128700
7.28	52.9984	2.69815	8.53229	.137363	7.78	60.5284	2.78927	8.82043	.128535
7.29	53.1441	2.70000	8.53815	.137174	7.79	60.6841	2.79106	8.82610	.128370
7.30	53.2900	2.70185	8.54400	.136986	**7.80**	60.8400	2.79285	8.83176	.128205
7.31	53.4361	2.70370	8.54985	.136799	7.81	60.9961	2.79464	8.83742	.128041
7.32	53.5824	2.70555	8.55570	.136612	7.82	61.1524	2.79643	8.84308	.127877
7.33	53.7289	2.70740	8.56154	.136426	7.83	61.3089	2.79821	8.84873	.127714
7.34	53.8756	2.70924	8.56738	.136240	7.84	61.4656	2.80000	8.85438	.127551
7.35	54.0225	2.71109	8.57321	.136054	7.85	61.6225	2.80179	8.86002	.127389
7.36	54.1696	2.71293	8.57904	.135870	7.86	61.7796	2.80357	8.86566	.127226
7.37	54.3169	2.71477	8.58487	.135685	7.87	61 9369	2.80535	8.87130	.127065
7.38	54.4644	2.71662	8.59069	.135501	7.88	62.0944	2.80713	8.87694	.126904
7.39	54.6121	2.71846	8.59651	.135318	7.89	62.2521	2.80891	8.88257	.126743
7.40	54.7600	2.72029	8.60233	.135135	**7.90**	62.4100	2.81069	8.88819	.126582
7.41	54.9081	2.72213	8.60814	.134953	7.91	62.5681	2.81247	8.89382	.126422
7.42	55.0564	2.72397	8.61394	.134771	7.92	62.7264	2.81425	8.89944	.126263
7.43	55.2049	2.72580	8.61974	.134590	7.93	62.8849	2.81603	8.90505	.126103
7.44	55.3536	2.72764	8.62554	.134409	7.94	63.0436	2.81780	8.91067	.125945
7.45	55.5025	2.72947	8.63134	.134228	7.95	63.2025	2.81957	8.91628	.125786
7.46	55.6516	2.73130	8.63713	.134048	7.96	63.3616	2.82135	8.92188	.125628
7.47	55.8009	2.73313	8.64292	.133869	7.97	63.5209	2.82312	8.92749	.125471
7.48	55.9504	2.73496	8.64870	.133690	7.98	63.6804	2.82489	8.93308	.125313
7.49	56.1001	2.73679	8.65448	.133511	7.99	63.8401	2.82666	8.93868	.125156
7.50	56.2500	2.73861	8.66025	.133333	**8.00**	64.0000	2.82843	8.94427	.125000
n	n^2	$\sqrt{n}$	$\sqrt{10n}$	$1/n$	n	n^2	$\sqrt{n}$	$\sqrt{10n}$	$1/n$

Table A

n	n^2	$\sqrt{n}$	$\sqrt{10n}$	$1/n$	n	n^2	$\sqrt{n}$	$\sqrt{10n}$	$1/n$
8.00	64.0000	2.82843	8.94427	.125000	**8.50**	72.2500	2.91548	9.21954	.117647
8.01	64.1601	2.83019	8.94986	.124844	8.51	72.4201	2.91719	9.22497	.117509
8.02	64.3204	2.83196	8.95545	.124688	8.52	72.5904	2.91890	9.23038	.117371
8.03	64.4809	2.83373	8.96103	.124533	8.53	72.7609	2.92062	9.23580	.117233
8.04	64.6416	2.83549	8.96660	.124378	8.54	72.9316	2.92233	9.24121	.117096
8.05	64.8025	2.83725	8.97218	.124224	8.55	73.1025	2.92404	9.24662	.116959
8.06	64.9636	2.83901	8.97775	.124069	8.56	73.2736	2.92575	9.25203	.116822
8.07	65.1249	2.84077	8.98332	.123916	8.57	73.4449	2.92746	9.25743	.116686
8.08	65.2864	2.84253	8.98888	.123762	8.58	73.6164	2.92916	9.26283	.116550
8.09	65.4481	2.84429	8.99444	.123609	8.59	73.7881	2.93087	9.26823	.116414
8.10	65.6100	2.84605	9.00000	.123457	**8.60**	73.9600	2.93258	9.27362	.116279
8.11	65.7721	2.84781	9.00555	.123305	8.61	74.1321	2.93428	9.27901	.116144
8.12	65.9344	2.84956	9.01110	.123153	8.62	74.3044	2.93598	9.28440	.116009
8.13	66.0969	2.85132	9.01665	.123001	8.63	74.4769	2.93769	9.28978	.115875
8.14	66.2596	2.85307	9.02219	.122850	8.64	74.6496	2.93939	9.29516	.115741
8.15	66.4225	2.85482	9.02774	.122699	8.65	74.8225	2.94109	9.30054	.115607
8.16	66.5856	2.85657	9.03327	.122549	8.66	74.9956	2.94279	9.30591	.115473
8.17	66.7489	2.85832	9.03881	.122399	8.67	75.1689	2.94449	9.31128	.115340
8.18	66.9124	2.86007	9.04434	.122249	8.68	75.3424	2.94618	9.31665	.115207
8.19	67.0761	2.86182	9.04986	.122100	8.69	75.5161	2.94788	9.32202	.115075
8.20	67.2400	2.86356	9.05539	.121951	**8.70**	75.6900	2.94958	9.32738	.114943
8.21	67.4041	2.86531	9.06091	.121803	8.71	75.8641	2.95127	9.33274	.114811
8.22	67.5684	2.86705	9.06642	.121655	8.72	76.0384	2.95296	9.33809	.114679
8.23	67.7329	2.86880	9.07193	.121507	8.73	76.2129	2.95466	9.34345	.114548
8.24	67.8976	2.87054	9.07744	.121359	8.74	76.3876	2.95635	9.34880	.114416
8.25	68.0625	2.87228	9.08295	.121212	8.75	76.5625	2.95804	9.35414	.114286
8.26	68.2276	2.87402	9.08845	.121065	8.76	76.7376	2.95973	9.35949	.114155
8.27	68.3929	2.87576	9.09395	.120919	8.77	76.9129	2.96142	9.36483	.114025
8.28	68.5584	2.87750	9.09945	.120773	8.78	77.0884	2.96311	9.37017	.113895
8.29	68.7241	2.87924	9.10494	.120627	8.79	77.2641	2.96479	9.37550	.113766
8.30	68.8900	2.88097	9.11043	.120482	**8.80**	77.4400	2.96648	9.38083	.113636
8.31	69.0561	2.88271	9.11592	.120337	8.81	77.6161	2.96816	9.38616	.113507
8.32	69.2224	2.88444	9.12140	.120192	8.82	77.7924	2.96985	9.39149	.113379
8.33	69.3889	2.88617	9.12688	.120048	8.83	77.9689	2.97153	9.39681	.113250
8.34	69.5556	2.88791	9.13236	.119904	8.84	78.1456	2.97321	9.40213	.113122
8.35	69.7225	2.88964	9.13783	.119760	8.85	78.3225	2.97489	9.40744	.112994
8.36	69.8896	2.89137	9.14330	.119617	8.86	78.4996	2.97658	9.41276	.112867
8.37	70.0569	2.89310	9.14877	.119474	8.87	78.6769	2.97825	9.41807	.112740
8.38	70.2244	2.89482	9.15423	.119332	8.88	78.8544	2.97993	9.42338	.112613
8.39	70.3921	2.89655	9.15969	.119190	8.89	79.0321	2.98161	9.42868	.112486
8.40	70.5600	2.89828	9.16515	.119048	**8.90**	79.2100	2.98329	9.43398	.112360
8.41	70.7281	2.90000	9.17061	.118906	8.91	79.3881	2.98496	9.43928	.112233
8.42	70.8964	2.90172	9.17606	.118765	8.92	79.5664	2.98664	9.44458	.112108
8.43	71.0649	2.90345	9.18150	.118624	8.93	79.7449	2.98831	9.44987	.111982
8.44	71.2336	2.90517	9.18695	.118483	8.94	79.9236	2.98998	9.45516	.111857
8.45	71.4025	2.90689	9.19239	.118343	8.95	80.1025	2.99166	9.46044	.111732
8.46	71.5716	2.90861	9.19783	.118203	8.96	80.2816	2.99333	9.46573	.111607
8.47	71.7409	2.91033	9.20326	.118064	8.97	80.4609	2.99500	9.47101	.111483
8.48	71.9104	2.91204	9.20869	.117925	8.98	80.6404	2.99666	9.47629	.111359
8.49	72.0801	2.91376	9.21412	.117786	8.99	80.8201	2.99833	9.48156	.111235
8.50	72.2500	2.91548	9.21954	.117647	**9.00**	81.0000	3.00000	9.48683	.111111
n	n^2	$\sqrt{n}$	$\sqrt{10n}$	$1/n$	n	n^2	$\sqrt{n}$	$\sqrt{10n}$	$1/n$

SQUARES — SQUARE ROOTS — RECIPROCALS (*Concluded*)

n	n^2	$\sqrt{n}$	$\sqrt{10n}$	$1/n$	n	n^2	$\sqrt{n}$	$\sqrt{10n}$	$1/n$
9.00	81.0000	3.00000	9.48683	.111111	**9.50**	90.2500	3.08221	9.74679	.105263
9.01	81.1801	3.00167	9.49210	.110988	9.51	90.4401	3.08383	9.75192	.105152
9.02	81.3604	3.00333	9.49737	.110865	9.52	90.6304	3.08545	9.75705	.105042
9.03	81.5409	3.00500	9.50263	.110742	9.53	90.8209	3.08707	9.76217	.104932
9.04	81.7216	3.00666	9.50789	.110619	9.54	91.0116	3.08869	9.76729	.104822
9.05	81.9025	3.00832	9.51315	.110497	9.55	91.2025	3.09031	9.77241	.104712
9.06	82.0836	3.00998	9.51840	.110375	9.56	91.3936	3.09192	9.77753	.104603
9.07	82.2649	3.01164	9.52365	.110254	9.57	91.5849	3.09354	9.78264	.104493
9.08	82.4464	3.01330	9.52890	.110132	9.58	91.7764	3.09516	9.78775	.104384
9.09	82.6281	3.01496	9.53415	.110011	9.59	91.9681	3.09677	9.79285	.104275
9.10	82.8100	3.01662	9.53939	.109890	**9.60**	92.1600	3.09839	9.79796	.104167
9.11	82.9921	3.01828	9.54463	.109769	9.61	92.3521	3.10000	9.80306	.104058
9.12	83.1744	3.01993	9.54987	.109649	9.62	92.5444	3.10161	9.80816	.103950
9.13	83.3569	3.02159	9.55510	.109529	9.63	92.7369	3.10322	9.81326	.103842
9.14	83.5396	3.02324	9.56033	.109409	9.64	92.9296	3.10483	9.81835	.103734
9.15	83.7225	3.02490	9.56556	.109290	9.65	93.1225	3.10644	9.82344	.103627
9.16	83.9056	3.02655	9.57079	.109170	9.66	93.3156	3.10805	9.82853	.103520
9.17	84.0889	3.02820	9.57601	.109051	9.67	93.5089	3.10966	9.83362	.103413
9.18	84.2724	3.02985	9.58123	.108932	9.68	93.7024	3.11127	9.83870	.103306
9.19	84.4561	3.03150	9.58645	.108814	9.69	93.8961	3.11288	9.84378	.103199
9.20	84.6400	3.03315	9.59166	.108696	**9.70**	94.0900	3.11448	9.84886	.103093
9.21	84.8241	3.03480	9.59687	.108578	9.71	94.2841	3.11609	9.85393	.102987
9.22	85.0084	3.03645	9.60208	.108460	9.72	94.4784	3.11769	9.85901	.102881
9.23	85.1929	3.03809	9.60729	.108342	9.73	94.6729	3.11929	9.86408	.102775
9.24	85.3776	3.03974	9.61249	.108225	9.74	94.8676	3.12090	9.86914	.102669
9.25	85.5625	3.04138	9.61769	.108108	9.75	95.0625	3.12250	9.87421	.102564
9.26	85.7476	3.04302	9.62289	.107991	9.76	95.2576	3.12410	9.87927	.102459
9.27	85.9329	3.04467	9.62808	.107875	9.77	95.4529	3.12570	9.88433	.102354
9.28	86.1184	3.04631	9.63328	.107759	9.78	95.6484	3.12730	9.88939	.102249
9.29	86.3041	3.04795	9.63846	.107643	9.79	95.8441	3.12890	9.89444	.102145
9.30	86.4900	3.04959	9.64365	.107527	**9.80**	96.0400	3.13050	9.89949	.102041
9.31	86.6761	3.05123	9.64883	.107411	9.81	96.2361	3.13209	9.90454	.101937
9.32	86.8624	3.05287	9.65401	.107296	9.82	96.4324	3.13369	9.90959	.101833
9.33	87.0489	3.05450	9.65919	.107181	9.83	96.6289	3.13528	9.91464	.101729
9.34	87.2356	3.05614	9.66437	.107066	9.84	96.8256	3.13688	9.91968	.101626
9.35	87.4225	3.05778	9.66954	.106952	9.85	97.0225	3.13847	9.92472	.101523
9.36	87.6096	3.05941	9.67471	.106838	9.86	97.2196	3.14006	9.92975	.101420
9.37	87.7969	3.06105	9.67988	.106724	9.87	97.4169	3.14166	9.93479	.101317
9.38	87.9844	3.06268	9.68504	.106610	9.88	97.6144	3.14325	9.93982	.101215
9.39	88.1721	3.06431	9.69020	.106496	9.89	97.8121	3.14484	9.94485	.101112
9.40	88.3600	3.06594	9.69536	.106383	**9.90**	98.0100	3.14643	9.94987	.101010
9.41	88.5481	3.06757	9.70052	.106270	9.91	98.2081	3.14802	9.95490	.100908
9.42	88.7364	3.06920	9.70567	.106157	9.92	98.4064	3.14960	9.95992	.100806
9.43	88.9249	3.07083	9.71082	.106045	9.93	98.6049	3.15119	9.96494	.100705
9.44	89.1136	3.07246	9.71597	.105932	9.94	98.8036	3.15278	9.96995	.100604
9.45	89.3025	3.07409	9.72111	.105820	9.95	99.0025	3.15436	9.97497	.100503
9.46	89.4916	3.07571	9.72625	.105708	9.96	99.2016	3.15595	9.97998	.100402
9.47	89.6809	3.07734	9.73139	.105597	9.97	99.4009	3.15753	9.98499	.100301
9.48	89.8704	3.07896	9.73653	.105485	9.98	99.6004	3.15911	9.98999	.100200
9.49	90.0601	3.08058	9.74166	.105374	9.99	99.8001	3.16070	9.99500	.100100
9.50	90.2500	3.08221	9.74679	.105263	**10.00**	100.000	3.16228	10.0000	.100000
n	n^2	$\sqrt{n}$	$\sqrt{10n}$	$1/n$	n	n^2	$\sqrt{n}$	$\sqrt{10n}$	$1/n$

Table A

LOGARITHMS OF NUMBERS 1,000–1,499†
Six-Place Mantissas

N	0	1	2	3	4	5	6	7	8	9	D#
100	00 0000	0434	0868	1301	1734	2166	2598	3029	3461	3891	434
01	4321	4751	5181	5609	6038	6466	6894	7321	7748	8174	430
02	00 8600	9026	9451	9876	*0300	*0724	*1147	*1570	*1993	*2415	426
03	01 2837	3259	3680	4100	4521	4940	5360	5779	6197	6616	422
04	01 7033	7451	7868	8284	8700	9116	9532	9947	*0361	*0775	418
05	02 1189	1603	2016	2428	2841	3252	3664	4075	4486	4896	414
06	5306	5715	6125	6533	6942	7350	7757	8164	8571	8978	410
07	02 9384	9789	*0195	*0600	*1004	*1408	*1812	*2216	*2619	*3021	406
08	03 3424	3826	4227	4628	5029	5430	5830	6230	6629	7028	402
09	03 7426	7825	8223	8620	9017	9414	9811	*0207	*0602	*0998	399
110	04 1393	1787	2182	2576	2969	3362	3755	4148	4540	4932	395
11	5323	5714	6105	6495	6885	7275	7664	8053	8442	8830	391
12	04 9218	9606	9993	*0380	*0766	*1153	*1538	*1924	*2309	*2694	388
13	05 3078	3463	3846	4230	4613	4996	5378	5760	6142	6524	385
14	05 6905	7286	7666	8046	8426	8805	9185	9563	9942	*0320	381
15	06 0698	1075	1452	1829	2206	2582	2958	3333	3709	4083	377
16	4458	4832	5206	5580	5953	6326	6699	7071	7443	7815	374
17	06 8186	8557	8928	.9298	9668	*0038	*0407	*0776	*1145	*1514	371
18	07 1882	2250	2617	2985	3352	3718	4085	4451	4816	5182	368
19	5547	5912	6276	6640	7004	7368	7731	8094	8457	8819	365
120	07 9181	9543	9904	*0266	*0626	*0987	1347	*1707	*2067	*2426	362
21	08. 2785	3144	3503	3861	4219	4576	4934	5291	5647	6004	359
22	6360	6716	7071	7426	7781	8136	8490	8845	9198	9552	356
23	08 9905	*0258	*0611	*0963	*1315	*1667	*2018	*2370	*2721	*3071	353
24	09 3422	3772	4122	4471	4820	5169	5518	5866	6215	6562	350
25	09 6910	7257	7604	7951	8298	8644	8990	9335	9681	*0026	347
26	10 0371	0715	1059	1403	1747	2091	2434	2777	3119	3462	344
27	3804	4146	4487	4828	5169	5510	5851	6191	6531	6871	342
28	10 7210	7549	7888	8227	8565	8903	9241	9579	9916	*0253	339
29	11 0590	0926	1263	1599	1934	2270	2605	2940	3275	3609	337
130	3943	4277	4611	4944	5278	5611	5943	6276	6608	6940	334
31	11 7271	7603	7934	8265	8595	8926	9256	9586	9915	*0245	332
32	12 0574	0903	1231	1560	1888	2216	2544	2871	3198	3525	329
33	3852	4178	4504	4830	5156	5481	5806	6131	6456	6781	326
34	12 7105	7429	7753	8076	8399	8722	9045	9368	9690	*0012	324
35	13 0334	0655	0977	1298	1619	1939	2260	2580	2900	3219	322
36	3539	3858	4177	4496	4814	5133	5451	5769	6086	6403	319
37	6721	7037	7354	7671	7987	8303	8618	8934	9249	9564	317
38	13 9879	*0194	*0508	*0822	*1136	*1450	*1763	*2076	*2389	*2702	315
39	14 3015	3327	3639	3951	4263	4574	4885	5196	5507	5818	312
140	6128	6438	6748	7058	7367	7676	7985	8294	8603	8911	310
41	14 9219	9527	9835	*0142	*0449	*0756	*1063	*1370	*1676	*1982	308
42	15 2288	2594	2900	3205	3510	3815	4120	4424	4728	5032	306
43	5336	5640	5943	6246	6549	6852	7154	7457	7759	8061	304
44	15 8362	8664	8965	9266	9567	9868	*0168	*0469	*0769	*1068	302
45	16 1368	1667	1967	2266	2564	2863	3161	3460	3758	4055	300
46	4353	4650	4947	5244	5541	5838	6134	6430	6726	7022	297
47	16 7317	7613	7908	8203	8497	8792	9086	9380	9674	9968	296
48	17 0262	0555	0848	1141	1434	1726	2019	2311	2603	2895	293
49	3186	3478	3769	4060	4351	4641	4932	5222	5512	5802	292
N	0	1	2	3	4	5	6	7	8	9	D

*Prefix first two places on next line.
Example: The mantissa for number (N) 1072 is 03 0195.

#The *bighest difference* between adjacent mantissas on the *individual line*. It is also the *lowest difference* between adjacent mantissas on the *preceding line* in many cases.
†With permission of Stephen P. Shao, MATHEMATICS OF FINANCE, (Cincinnati: South-Western Publishing Co., 1962).

Table B

N	0	1	2	3	4	5	6	7	8	9	D
150	17 6091	6381	6670	6959	7248	7536	7825	8113	8401	8689	290
51	17 8977	9264	9552	9839	*0126	*0413	*0699	*0986	*1272	*1558	288
52	18 1844	2129	2415	2700	2985	3270	3555	3839	4123	4407	286
53	4691	4975	5259	5542	5825	6108	6391	6674	6956	7239	284
54	18 7521	7803	8084	8366	8647	8928	9209	9490	9771	*0051	282
55	19 0332	0612	0892	1171	1451	1730	2010	2289	2567	2846	280
56	3125	3403	3681	3959	4237	4514	4792	5069	5346	5623	278
57	5900	6176	6453	6729	7005	7281	7556	7832	8107	8382	277
58	19 8657	8932	9206	9481	9755	*0029	*0303	*0577	*0850	*1124	275
59	20 1397	1670	1943	2216	2488	2761	3033	3305	3577	3848	273
160	4120	4391	4663	4934	5204	5475	5746	6016	6286	6556	272
61	6826	7096	7365	7634	7904	8173	8441	8710	8979	9247	270
62	20 9515	9783	*0051	*0319	*0586	*0853	*1121	*1388	*1654	*1921	268
63	21 2188	2454	2720	2986	3252	3518	3783	4049	4314	4579	266
64	4844	5109	5373	5638	5902	6166	6430	6694	6957	7221	265
65	21 7484	7747	8010	8273	8536	8798	9060	9323	9585	9846	263
66	22 0108	0370	0631	0892	1153	1414	1675	1936	2196	2456	262
67	2716	2976	3236	3496	3755	4015	4274	4533	4792	5051	260
68	5309	5568	5826	6084	6342	6600	6858	7115	7372	7630	259
69	22 7887	8144	8400	8657	8913	9170	9426	9682	9938	*0193	257
170	23 0449	0704	0960	1215	1470	1724	1979	2234	2488	2742	256
71	2996	3250	3504	3757	4011	4264	4517	4770	5023	5276	254
72	5528	5781	6033	6285	6537	6789	7041	7292	7544	7795	253
73	23 8046	8297	8548	8799	9049	9299	9550	9800	*0050	*0300	251
74	24 0549	0799	1048	1297	1546	1795	2044	2293	2541	2790	250
75	3038	3286	3534	3782	4030	4277	4525	4772	5019	5266	248
76	5513	5759	6006	6252	6499	6745	6991	7237	7482	7728	247
77	24 7973	8219	8464	8709	8954	9198	9443	9687	9932	*0176	246
78	25 0420	0664	0908	1151	1395	1638	1881	2125	2368	2610	244
79	2853	3096	3338	3580	3822	4064	4306	4548	4790	5031	243
180	5273	5514	5755	5996	6237	6477	6718	6958	7198	7439	241
81	25 7679	7918	8158	8398	8637	8877	9116	9355	9594	9833	240
82	26 0071	0310	0548	0787	1025	1263	1501	1739	1976	2214	239
83	2451	2688	2925	3162	3399	3636	3873	4109	4346	4582	237
84	4818	5054	5290	5525	5761	5996	6232	6467	6702	6937	236
85	7172	7406	7641	7875	8110	8344	8578	8812	9046	9279	235
86	26 9513	9746	9980	*0213	*0446	*0679	*0912	*1144	*1377	*1609	234
87	27 1842	2074	2306	2538	2770	3001	3233	3464	3696	3927	232
88	4158	4389	4620	4850	5081	5311	5542	5772	6002	6232	231
89	6462	6692	6921	7151	7380	7609	7838	8067	8296	8525	230
190	27 8754	8982	9211	9439	9667	9895	*0123	*0351	*0578	*0806	229
91	28 1033	1261	1488	1715	1942	2169	2396	2622	2849	3075	228
92	3301	3527	3753	3979	4205	4431	4656	4882	5107	5332	226
93	5557	5782	6007	6232	6456	6681	6905	7130	7354	7578	225
94	28 7802	8026	8249	8473	8696	8920	9143	9366	9589	9812	224
95	29 0035	0257	0480	0702	0925	1147	1369	1591	1813	2034	223
96	2256	2478	2699	2920	3141	3363	3584	3804	4025	4246	222
97	4466	4687	4907	5127	5347	5567	5787	6007	6226	6446	221
98	6665	6884	7104	7323	7542	7761	7979	8198	8416	8635	220
99	29 8853	9071	9289	9507	9725	9943	*0161	*0378	*0595	*0813	218
N	0	1	2	3	4	5	6	7	8	9	D

N	0	1	2	3	4	5	6	7	8	9	D
200	30 1030	1247	1464	1681	1898	2114	2331	2547	2764	2980	217
01	3196	3412	3628	3844	4059	4275	4491	4706	4921	5136	216
02	5351	5566	5781	5996	6211	6425	6639	6854	7068	7282	215
03	7496	7710	7924	8137	8351	8564	8778	8991	9204	9417	214
04	30 9630	9843	*0056	*0268	*0481	*0693	*0906	*1118	*1330	*1542	213
05	31 1754	1966	2177	2389	2600	2812	3023	3234	3445	3656	212
06	3867	4078	4289	4499	4710	4920	5130	5340	5551	5760	211
07	5970	6180	6390	6599	6809	7018	7227	7436	7646	7854	210
08	31 8063	8272	8481	8689	8898	9106	9314	9522	9730	9938	209
09	32 0146	0354	0562	0769	0977	1184	1391	1598	1805	2012	208
210	2219	2426	2633	2839	3046	3252	3458	3665	3871	4077	207
11	4282	4488	4694	4899	5105	5310	5516	5721	5926	6131	206
12	6336	6541	6745	6950	7155	7359	7563	7767	7972	8176	205
13	32 8380	8583	8787	8991	9194	9398	9601	9805	*0008	*0211	204
14	33 0414	0617	0819	1022	1225	1427	1630	1832	2034	2236	203
15	2438	2640	2842	3044	3246	3447	3649	3850	4051	4253	202
16	4454	4655	4856	5057	5257	5458	5658	5859	6059	6260	201
17	6460	6660	6860	7060	7260	7459	7659	7858	8058	8257	200
18	33 8456	8656	8855	9054	9253	9451	9650	9849	*0047	*0246	200
19	34 0444	0642	0841	1039	1237	1435	1632	1830	2028	2225	199
220	2423	2620	2817	3014	3212	3409	3606	3802	3999	4196	198
21	4392	4589	4785	4981	5178	5374	5570	5766	5962	6157	197
22	6353	6549	6744	6939	7135	7330	7525	7720	7915	8110	196
23	34 8305	8500	8694	8889	9083	9278	9472	9666	9860	*0054	195
24	35 0248	0442	0636	0829	1023	1216	1410	1603	1796	1989	194
25	2183	2375	2568	2761	2954	3147	3339	3532	3724	3916	193
26	4108	4301	4493	4685	4876	5068	5260	5452	5643	5834	192
27	6026	6217	6408	6599	6790	6981	7172	7363	7554	7744	191
28	7935	8125	8316	8506	8696	8886	9076	9266	9456	9646	191
29	35 9835	*0025	*0215	*0404	*0593	*0783	*0972	*1161	*1350	*1539	190
230	36 1728	1917	2105	2294	2482	2671	2859	3048	3236	3424	189
31	3612	3800	3988	4176	4363	4551	4739	4926	5113	5301	188
32	5488	5675	5862	6049	6236	6423	6610	6796	6983	7169	187
33	7356	7542	7729	7915	8101	8287	8473	8659	8845	9030	187
34	36 9216	9401	9587	9772	9958	*0143	*0328	*0513	*0698	*0883	186
35	37 1068	1253	1437	1622	1806	1991	2175	2360	2544	2728	185
36	2912	3096	3280	3464	3647	3831	4015	4198	4382	4565	184
37	4748	4932	5115	5298	5481	5664	5846	6029	6212	6394	184
38	6577	6759	6942	7124	7306	7488	7670	7852	8034	8216	183
39	37 8398	8580	8761	8943	9124	9306	9487	9668	9849	*0030	182
240	38 0211	0392	0573	0754	0934	1115	1296	1476	1656	1837	181
41	2017	2197	2377	2557	2737	2917	3097	3277	3456	3636	180
42	3815	3995	4174	4353	4533	4712	4891	5070	5249	5428	180
43	5606	5785	5964	6142	6321	6499	6677	6856	7034	7212	179
44	7390	7568	7746	7923	8101	8279	8456	8634	8811	8989	178
45	38 9166	9343	9520	9698	9875	*0051	*0228	*0405	*0582	*0759	178
46	39 0935	1112	1288	1464	1641	1817	1993	2169	2345	2521	177
47	2697	2873	3048	3224	3400	3575	3751	3926	4101	4277	176
48	4452	4627	4802	4977	5152	5326	5501	5676	5850	6025	175
49	6199	6374	6548	6722	6896	7071	7245	7419	7592	7766	175
N	0	1	2	3	4	5	6	7	8	9	D

Table B

N	0	1	2	3	4	5	6	7	8	9	D
250	39 7940	8114	8287	8461	8634	8808	8981	9154	9328	9501	174
51	39 9674	9847	*0020	*0192	*0365	*0538	*0711	*0883	*1056	*1228	173
52	40 1401	1573	1745	1917	2089	2261	2433	2605	2777	2949	172
53	3121	3292	3464	3635	3807	3978	4149	4320	4492	4663	172
54	4834	5005	5176	5346	5517	5688	5858	6029	6199	6370	171
55	6540	6710	6881	7051	7221	7391	7561	7731	7901	8070	171
56	8240	8410	8579	8749	8918	9087	9257	9426	9595	9764	170
57	40 9933	*0102	*0271	*0440	*0609	*0777	*0946	*1114	*1283	*1451	169
58	41 1620	1788	1956	2124	2293	2461	2629	2796	2964	3132	169
59	3300	3467	3635	3803	3970	4137	4305	4472	4639	4806	168
260	4973	5140	5307	5474	5641	5808	5974	6141	6308	6474	167
61	6641	6807	6973	7139	7306	7472	7638	7804	7970	8135	167
62	8301	8467	8633	8798	8964	9129	9295	9460	9625	9791	166
63	41 9956	*0121	*0286	*0451	*0616	*0781	*0945	*1110	*1275	*1439	165
64	42 1604	1768	1933	2097	2261	2426	2590	2754	2918	3082	165
65	3246	3410	3574	3737	3901	4065	4228	4392	4555	4718	164
66	4882	5045	5208	5371	5534	5697	5860	6023	6186	6349	163
67	6511	6674	6836	6999	7161	7324	7486	7648	7811	7973	163
68	8135	8297	8459	8621	8783	8944	9106	9268	9429	9591	162
69	42 9752	9914	*0075	*0236	*0398	*0559	*0720	*0881	*1042	*1203	162
270	43 1364	1525	1685	1846	2007	2167	2328	2488	2649	2809	161
71	2969	3130	3290	3450	3610	3770	3930	4090	4249	4409	161
72	4569	4729	4888	5048	5207	5367	5526	5685	5844	6004	160
73	6163	6322	6481	6640	6799	6957	7116	7275	7433	7592	159
74	7751	7909	8067	8226	8384	8542	8701	8859	9017	9175	159
75	43 9333	9491	9648	9806	9964	*0122	*0279	*0437	*0594	*0752	158
76	44 0909	1066	1224	1381	1538	1695	1852	2009	2166	2323	158
77	2480	2637	2793	2950	3106	3263	3419	3576	3732	3889	157
78	4045	4201	4357	4513	4669	4825	4981	5137	5293	5449	156
79	5604	5760	5915	6071	6226	6382	6537	6692	6848	7003	156
280	7158	7313	7468	7623	7778	7933	8088	8242	8397	8552	155
81	44 8706	8861	9015	9170	9324	9478	9633	9787	9941	*0095	155
82	45 0249	0403	0557	0711	0865	1018	1172	1326	1479	1633	154
83	1786	1940	2093	2247	2400	2553	2706	2859	3012	3165	154
84	3318	3471	3624	3777	3930	4082	4235	4387	4540	4692	153
85	4845	4997	5150	5302	5454	5606	5758	5910	6062	6214	153
86	6366	6518	6670	6821	6973	7125	7276	7428	7579	7731	152
87	7882	8033	8184	8336	8487	8638	8789	8940	9091	9242	152
88	45 9392	9543	9694	9845	9995	*0146	*0296	*0447	*0597	*0748	151
89	46 0898	1048	1198	1348	1499	1649	1799	1948	2098	2248	151
290	2398	2548	2697	2847	2997	3146	3296	3445	3594	3744	150
91	3893	4042	4191	4340	4490	4639	4788	4936	5085	5234	149
92	5383	5532	5680	5829	5977	6126	6274	6423	6571	6719	149
93	6868	7016	7164	7312	7460	7608	7756	7904	8052	8200	148
94	8347	8495	8643	8790	8938	9085	9233	9380	9527	9675	148
95	46 9822	9969	*0116	*0263	*0410	*0557	*0704	*0851	*0998	*1145	147
96	47 1292	1438	1585	1732	1878	2025	2171	2318	2464	2610	147
97	2756	2903	3049	3195	3341	3487	3633	3779	3925	4071	147
98	4216	4362	4508	4653	4799	4944	5090	5235	5381	5526	146
99	5671	5816	5962	6107	6252	6397	6542	6687	6832	6976	146
N	0	1	2	3	4	5	6	7	8	9	D

N	0	1	2	3	4	5	6	7	8	9	D
300	47 7121	7266	7411	7555	7700	7844	7989	8133	8278	8422	145
01	47 8566	8711	8855	8999	9143	9287	9431	9575	9719	9863	145
02	48 0007	0151	0294	0438	0582	0725	0869	1012	1156	1299	144
03	1443	1586	1729	1872	2016	2159	2302	2445	2588	2731	144
04	2874	3016	3159	3302	3445	3587	3730	3872	4015	4157	143
05	4300	4442	4585	4727	4869	5011	5153	5295	5437	5579	143
06	5721	5863	6005	6147	6289	6430	6572	6714	6855	6997	142
07	7138	7280	7421	7563	7704	7845	7986	8127	8269	8410	142
08	8551	8692	8833	8974	9114	9255	9396	9537	9677	9818	141
09	48 9958	*0099	*0239	*0380	*0520	*0661	*0801	*0941	*1081	*1222	141
310	49 1362	1502	1642	1782	1922	2062	2201	2341	2481	2621	140
11	2760	2900	3040	3179	3319	3458	3597	3737	3876	4015	140
12	4155	4294	4433	4572	4711	4850	4989	5128	5267	5406	139
13	5544	5683	5822	5960	6099	6238	6376	6515	6653	6791	139
14	6930	7068	7206	7344	7483	7621	7759	7897	8035	8173	139
15	8311	8448	8586	8724	8862	8999	9137	9275	9412	9550	138
16	49 9687	9824	9962	*0099	*0236	*0374	*0511	*0648	*0785	*0922	138
17	50 1059	1196	1333	1470	1607	1744	1880	2017	2154	2291	137
18	2427	2564	2700	2837	2973	3109	3246	3382	3518	3655	137
19	3791	3927	4063	4199	4335	4471	4607	4743	4878	5014	136
320	5150	5286	5421	5557	5693	5828	5964	6099	6234	6370	136
21	6505	6640	6776	6911	7046	7181	7316	7451	7586	7721	136
22	7856	7991	8126	8260	8395	8530	8664	8799	8934	9068	135
23	50 9203	9337	9471	9606	9740	9874	*0009	*0143	*0277	*0411	135
24	51 0545	0679	0813	0947	1081	1215	1349	1482	1616	1750	134
25	1883	2017	2151	2284	2418	2551	2684	2818	2951	3084	134
26	3218	3351	3484	3617	3750	3883	4016	4149	4282	4415	133
27	4548	4681	4813	4946	5079	5211	5344	5476	5609	5741	133
28	5874	6006	6139	6271	6403	6535	6668	6800	6932	7064	133
29	7196	7328	7460	7592	7724	7855	7987	8119	8251	8382	132
330	8514	8646	8777	8909	9040	9171	9303	9434	9566	9697	132
31	51 9828	9959	*0090	*0221	*0353	*0484	*0615	*0745	*0876	*1007	132
32	52 1138	1269	1400	1530	1661	1792	1922	2053	2183	2314	131
33	2444	2575	2705	2835	2966	3096	3226	3356	3486	3616	131
34	3746	3876	4006	4136	4266	4396	4526	4656	4785	4915	130
35	5045	5174	5304	5434	5563	5693	5822	5951	6081	6210	130
36	6339	6469	6598	6727	6856	6985	7114	7243	7372	7501	130
37	7630	7759	7888	8016	8145	8274	8402	8531	8660	8788	129
38	52 8917	9045	9174	9302	9430	9559	9687	9815	9943	*0072	129
39	53 0200	0328	0456	0584	0712	0840	0968	1096	1223	1351	128
340	1479	1607	1734	1862	1990	2117	2245	2372	2500	2627	128
41	2754	2882	3009	3136	3264	3391	3518	3645	3772	3899	128
42	4026	4153	4280	4407	4534	4661	4787	4914	5041	5167	127
43	5294	5421	5547	5674	5800	5927	6053	6180	6306	6432	127
44	6558	6685	6811	6937	7063	7189	7315	7441	7567	7693	127
45	7819	7945	8071	8197	8322	8448	8574	8699	8825	8951	126
46	53 9076	9202	9327	9452	9578	9703	9829	9954	*0079	*0204	126
47	54 0329	0455	0580	0705	0830	0955	1080	1205	1330	1454	126
48	1579	1704	1829	1953	2078	2203	2327	2452	2576	2701	125
49	2825	2950	3074	3199	3323	3447	3571	3696	3820	3944	125
N	0	1	2	3	4	5	6	7	8	9	D

N	0	1	2	3	4	5	6	7	8	9	D
350	54 4068	4192	4316	4440	4564	4688	4812	4936	5060	5183	124
51	5307	5431	5555	5678	5802	5925	6049	6172	6296	6419	124
52	6543	6666	6789	6913	7036	7159	7282	7405	7529	7652	124
53	7775	7898	8021	8144	8267	8389	8512	8635	8758	8881	123
54	54 9003	9126	9249	9371	9494	9616	9739	9861	9984	*0106	123
55	55 0228	0351	0473	0595	0717	0840	0962	1084	1206	1328	123
56	1450	1572	1694	1816	1938	2060	2181	2303	2425	2547	122
57	2668	2790	2911	3033	3155	3276	3398	3519	3640	3762	122
58	3883	4004	4126	4247	4368	4489	4610	4731	4852	4973	122
59	5094	5215	5336	5457	5578	5699	5820	5940	6061	6182	121
360	6303	6423	6544	6664	6785	6905	7026	7146	7267	7387	121
61	7507	7627	7748	7868	7988	8108	8228	8349	8469	8589	121
62	8709	8829	8948	9068	9188	9308	9428	9548	9667	9787	120
63	55 9907	*0026	*0146	*0265	*0385	*0504	*0624	*0743	*0863	*0982	120
64	56 1101	1221	1340	1459	1578	1698	1817	1936	2055	2174	120
65	2293	2412	2531	2650	2769	2887	3006	3125	3244	3362	119
66	3481	3600	3718	3837	3955	4074	4192	4311	4429	4548	119
67	4666	4784	4903	5021	5139	5257	5376	5494	5612	5730	119
68	5848	5966	6084	6202	6320	6437	6555	6673	6791	6909	118
69	7026	7144	7262	7379	7497	7614	7732	7849	7967	8084	118
370	8202	8319	8436	8554	8671	8788	8905	9023	9140	9257	118
71	56 9374	9491	9608	9725	9842	9959	*0076	*0193	*0309	*0426	117
72	57 0543	0660	0776	0893	1010	1126	1243	1359	1476	1592	117
73	1709	1825	1942	2058	2174	2291	2407	2523	2639	2755	117
74	2872	2988	3104	3220	3336	3452	3568	3684	3800	3915	116
75	4031	4147	4263	4379	4494	4610	4726	4841	4957	5072	116
76	5188	5303	5419	5534	5650	5765	5880	5996	6111	6226	116
77	6341	6457	6572	6687	6802	6917	7032	7147	7262	7377	116
78	7492	7607	7722	7836	7951	8066	8181	8295	8410	8525	115
79	8639	8754	8868	8983	9097	9212	9326	9441	9555	9669	115
380	57 9784	9898	*0012	*0126	*0241	*0355	*0469	*0583	*0697	*0811	115
81	58 0925	1039	1153	1267	1381	1495	1608	1722	1836	1950	114
82	2063	2177	2291	2404	2518	2631	2745	2858	2972	3085	114
83	3199	3312	3426	3539	3652	3765	3879	3992	4105	4218	114
84	4331	4444	4557	4670	4783	4896	5009	5122	5235	5348	113
85	5461	5574	5686	5799	5912	6024	6137	6250	6362	6475	113
86	6587	6700	6812	6925	7037	7149	7262	7374	7486	7599	113
87	7711	7823	7935	8047	8160	8272	8384	8496	8608	8720	113
88	8832	8944	9056	9167	9279	9391	9503	9615	9726	9838	112
89	58 9950	*0061	*0173	*0284	*0396	*0507	*0619	*0730	*0842	*0953	112
390	59 1065	1176	1287	1399	1510	1621	1732	1843	1955	2066	112
91	2177	2288	2399	2510	2621	2732	2843	2954	3064	3175	111
92	3286	3397	3508	3618	3729	3840	3950	4061	4171	4282	111
93	4393	4503	4614	4724	4834	4945	5055	5165	5276	5386	111
94	5496	5606	5717	5827	5937	6047	6157	6267	6377	6487	111
95	6597	6707	6817	6927	7037	7146	7256	7366	7476	7586	110
96	7695	7805	7914	8024	8134	8243	8353	8462	8572	8681	110
97	8791	8900	9009	9119	9228	9337	9446	9556	9665	9774	110
98	9883	9992	*0101	*0210	*0319	*0428	*0537	*0646	*0755	*0864	109
99	60 0973	1082	1191	1299	1408	1517	1625	1734	1843	1951	109
N	0	1	2	3	4	5	6	7	8	9	D

Table B

N	0	1	2	3	4	5	6	7	8	9	D
400	60 2060	2169	2277	2386	2494	2603	2711	2819	2928	3036	109
01	3144	3253	3361	3469	3577	3686	3794	3902	4010	4118	109
02	4226	4334	4442	4550	4658	4766	4874	4982	5089	5197	108
03	5305	5413	5521	5628	5736	5844	5951	6059	6166	6274	108
04	6381	6489	6596	6704	6811	6919	7026	7133	7241	7348	108
05	7455	7562	7669	7777	7884	7991	8098	8205	8312	8419	108
06	8526	8633	8740	8847	8954	9061	9167	9274	9381	9488	107
07	60 9594	9701	9808	9914	*0021	*0128	*0234	*0341	*0447	*0554	107
08	61 0660	0767	0873	0979	1086	1192	1298	1405	1511	1617	107
09	1723	1829	1936	2042	2148	2254	2360	2466	2572	2678	107
410	2784	2890	2996	3102	3207	3313	3419	3525	3630	3736	106
11	3842	3947	4053	4159	4264	4370	4475	4581	4686	4792	106
12	4897	5003	5108	5213	5319	5424	5529	5634	5740	5845	106
13	5950	6055	6160	6265	6370	6476	6581	6686	6790	6895	106
14	7000	7105	7210	7315	7420	7525	7629	7734	7839	7943	105
15	8048	8153	8257	8362	8466	8571	8676	8780	8884	8989	105
16	61 9093	9198	9302	9406	9511	9615	9719	9824	9928	*0032	105
17	62 0136	0240	0344	0448	0552	0656	0760	0864	0968	1072	104
18	1176	1280	1384	1488	1592	1695	1799	1903	2007	2110	104
19	2214	2318	2421	2525	2628	2732	2835	2939	3042	3146	104
420	3249	3353	3456	3559	3663	3766	3869	3973	4076	4179	104
21	4282	4385	4488	4591	4695	4798	4901	5004	5107	5210	104
22	5312	5415	5518	5621	5724	5827	5929	6032	6135	6238	103
23	6340	6443	6546	6648	6751	6853	6956	7058	7161	7263	103
24	7366	7468	7571	7673	7775	7878	7980	8082	8185	8287	103
25	8389	8491	8593	8695	8797	8900	9002	9104	9206	9308	103
26	62 9410	9512	9613	9715	9817	9919	*0021	*0123	*0224	*0326	102
27	63 0428	0530	0631	0733	0835	0936	1038	1139	1241	1342	102
28	1444	1545	1647	1748	1849	1951	2052	2153	2255	2356	102
29	2457	2559	2660	2761	2862	2963	3064	3165	3266	3367	102
430	3468	3569	3670	3771	3872	3973	4074	4175	4276	4376	101
31	4477	4578	4679	4779	4880	4981	5081	5182	5283	5383	101
32	5484	5584	5685	5785	5886	5986	6087	6187	6287	6388	101
33	6488	6588	6688	6789	6889	6989	7089	7189	7290	7390	101
34	7490	7590	7690	7790	7890	7990	8090	8190	8290	8389	100
35	8489	8589	8689	8789	8888	8988	9088	9188	9287	9387	100
36	63 9486	9586	9686	9785	9885	9984	*0084	*0183	*0283	*0382	100
37	64 0481	0581	0680	0779	0879	0978	1077	1177	1276	1375	100
38	1474	1573	1672	1771	1871	1970	2069	2168	2267	2366	100
39	2465	2563	2662	2761	2860	2959	3058	3156	3255	3354	99
440	3453	3551	3650	3749	3847	3946	4044	4143	4242	4340	99
41	4439	4537	4636	4734	4832	4931	5029	5127	5226	5324	99
42	5422	5521	5619	5717	5815	5913	6011	6110	6208	6306	99
43	6404	6502	6600	6698	6796	6894	6992	7089	7187	7285	98
44	7383	7481	7579	7676	7774	7872	7969	8067	8165	8262	98
45	8360	8458	8555	8653	8750	8848	8945	9043	9140	9237	98
46	64 9335	9432	9530	9627	9724	9821	9919	*0016	*0113	*0210	98
47	65 0308	0405	0502	0599	0696	0793	0890	0987	1084	1181	97
48	1278	1375	1472	1569	1666	1762	1859	1956	2053	2150	97
49	2246	2343	2440	2536	2633	2730	2826	2923	3019	3116	97
N	0	1	2	3	4	5	6	7	8	9	D

Table B

N	0	1	2	3	4	5	6	7	8	9	D
450	65 3213	3309	3405	3502	3598	3695	3791	3888	3984	4080	97
51	4177	4273	4369	4465	4562	4658	4754	4850	4946	5042	97
52	5138	5235	5331	5427	5523	5619	5715	5810	5906	6002	97
53	6098	6194	6290	6386	6482	6577	6673	6769	6864	6960	96
54	7056	7152	7247	7343	7438	7534	7629	7725	7820	7916	96
55	8011	8107	8202	8298	8393	8488	8584	8679	8774	8870	96
56	8965	9060	9155	9250	9346	9441	9536	9631	9726	9821	96
57	65 9916	*0011	*0106	*0201	*0296	*0391	*0486	*0581	*0676	*0771	95
58	66 0865	0960	1055	1150	1245	1339	1434	1529	1623	1718	95
59	1813	1907	2002	2096	2191	2286	2380	2475	2569	2663	95
460	2758	2852	2947	3041	3135	3230	3324	3418	3512	3607	95
61	3701	3795	3889	3983	4078	4172	4266	4360	4454	4548	95
62	4642	4736	4830	4924	5018	5112	5206	5299	5393	5487	94
63	5581	5675	5769	5862	5956	6050	6143	6237	6331	6424	94
64	6518	6612	6705	6799	6892	6986	7079	7173	7266	7360	94
65	7453	7546	7640	7733	7826	7920	8013	8106	8199	8293	94
66	8386	8479	8572	8665	8759	8852	8945	9038	9131	9224	94
67	66 9317	9410	9503	9596	9689	9782	9875	9967	*0060	*0153	93
68	67 0246	0339	0431	0524	0617	0710	0802	0895	0988	1080	93
69	1173	1265	1358	1451	1543	1636	1728	1821	1913	2005	93
470	2098	2190	2283	2375	2467	2560	2652	2744	2836	2929	93
71	3021	3113	3205	3297	3390	3482	3574	3666	3758	3850	93
72	3942	4034	4126	4218	4310	4402	4494	4586	4677	4769	92
73	4861	4953	5045	5137	5228	5320	5412	5503	5595	5687	92
74	5778	5870	5962	6053	6145	6236	6328	6419	6511	6602	92
75	6694	6785	6876	6968	7059	7151	7242	7333	7424	7516	92
76	7607	7698	7789	7881	7972	8063	8154	8245	8336	8427	92
77	8518	8609	8700	8791	8882	8973	9064	9155	9246	9337	91
78	67 9428	9519	9610	9700	9791	9882	9973	*0063	*0154	*0245	91
79	68 0336	0426	0517	0607	0698	0789	0879	0970	1060	1151	91
480	1241	1332	1422	1513	1603	1693	1784	1874	1964	2055	91
81	2145	2235	2326	2416	2506	2596	2686	2777	2867	2957	91
82	3047	3137	3227	3317	3407	3497	3587	3677	3767	3857	90
83	3947	4037	4127	4217	4307	4396	4486	4576	4666	4756	90
84	4845	4935	5025	5114	5204	5294	5383	5473	5563	5652	90
85	5742	5831	5921	6010	6100	6189	6279	6368	6458	6547	90
86	6636	6726	6815	6904	6994	7083	7172	7261	7351	7440	90
87	7529	7618	7707	7796	7886	7975	8064	8153	8242	8331	90
88	8420	8509	8598	8687	8776	8865	8953	9042	9131	9220	89
89	68 9309	9398	9486	9575	9664	9753	9841	9930	*0019	*0107	89
490	69 0196	0285	0373	0462	0550	0639	0728	0816	0905	0993	89
91	1081	1170	1258	1347	1435	1524	1612	1700	1789	1877	89
92	1965	2053	2142	2230	2318	2406	2494	2583	2671	2759	89
93	2847	2935	3023	3111	3199	3287	3375	3463	3551	3639	88
94	3727	3815	3903	3991	4078	4166	4254	4342	4430	4517	88
95	4605	4693	4781	4868	4956	5044	5131	5219	5307	5394	88
96	5482	5569	5657	5744	5832	5919	6007	6094	6182	6269	88
97	6356	6444	6531	6618	6706	6793	6880	6968	7055	7142	88
98	7229	7317	7404	7491	7578	7665	7752	7839	7926	8014	88
99	8101	8188	8275	8362	8449	8535	8622	8709	8796	8883	87
N	0	1	2	3	4	5	6	7	8	9	D

Table B

LOGARITHMS OF NUMBERS 5,000–5,499
Six-Place Mantissas

N	0	1	2	3	4	5	6	7	8	9	D
500	69 8970	9057	9144	9231	9317	9404	9491	9578	9664	9751	87
01	69 9838	9924	*0011	*0098	*0184	*0271	*0358	*0444	*0531	*0617	87
02	70 0704	0790	0877	0963	1050	1136	1222	1309	1395	1482	87
03	1568	1654	1741	1827	1913	1999	2086	2172	2258	2344	87
04	2431	2517	2603	2689	2775	2861	2947	3033	3119	3205	86
05	3291	3377	3463	3549	3635	3721	3807	3893	3979	4065	86
06	4151	4236	4322	4408	4494	4579	4665	4751	4837	4922	86
07	5008	5094	5179	5265	5350	5436	5522	5607	5693	5778	86
08	5864	5949	6035	6120	6206	6291	6376	6462	6547	6632	86
09	6718	6803	6888	6974	7059	7144	7229	7315	7400	7485	86
510	7570	7655	7740	7826	7911	7996	8081	8166	8251	8336	86
11	8421	8506	8591	8676	8761	8846	8931	9015	9100	9185	85
12	70 9270	9355	9440	9524	9609	9694	9779	9863	9948	*0033	85
13	71 0117	0202	0287	0371	0456	0540	0625	0710	0794	0879	85
14	0963	1048	1132	1217	1301	1385	1470	1554	1639	1723	85
15	1807	1892	1976	2060	2144	2229	2313	2397	2481	2566	85
16	2650	2734	2818	2902	2986	3070	3154	3238	3323	3407	85
17	3491	3575	3659	3742	3826	3910	3994	4078	4162	4246	84
18	4330	4414	4497	4581	4665	4749	4833	4916	5000	5084	84
19	5167	5251	5335	5418	5502	5586	5669	5753	5836	5920	84
520	6003	6087	6170	6254	6337	6421	6504	6588	6671	6754	84
21	6838	6921	7004	7088	7171	7254	7338	7421	7504	7587	84
22	7671	7754	7837	7920	8003	8086	8169	8253	8336	8419	84
23	8502	8585	8668	8751	8834	8917	9000	9083	9165	9248	83
24	71 9331	9414	9497	9580	9663	9745	9828	9911	9994	*0077	83
25	72 0159	0242	0325	0407	0490	0573	0655	0738	0821	0903	83
26	0986	1068	1151	1233	1316	1398	1481	1563	1646	1728	83
27	1811	1893	1975	2058	2140	2222	2305	2387	2469	2552	83
28	2634	2716	2798	2881	2963	3045	3127	3209	3291	3374	83
29	3456	3538	3620	3702	3784	3866	3948	4030	4112	4194	82
530	4276	4358	4440	4522	4604	4685	4767	4849	4931	5013	82
31	5095	5176	5258	5340	5422	5503	5585	5667	5748	5830	82
32	5912	5993	6075	6156	6238	6320	6401	6483	6564	6646	82
33	6727	6809	6890	6972	7053	7134	7216	7297	7379	7460	82
34	7541	7623	7704	7785	7866	7948	8029	8110	8191	8273	82
35	8354	8435	8516	8597	8678	8759	8841	8922	9003	9084	82
36	9165	9246	9327	9408	9489	9570	9651	9732	9813	9893	81
37	72 9974	*0055	*0136	*0217	*0298	*0378	*0459	*0540	*0621	*0702	81
38	73 0782	0863	0944	1024	1105	1186	1266	1347	1428	1508	81
39	1589	1669	1750	1830	1911	1991	2072	2152	2233	2313	81
540	2394	2474	2555	2635	2715	2796	2876	2956	3037	3117	81
41	3197	3278	3358	3438	3518	3598	3679	3759	3839	3919	81
42	3999	4079	4160	4240	4320	4400	4480	4560	4640	4720	81
43	4800	4880	4960	5040	5120	5200	5279	5359	5439	5519	80
44	5599	5679	5759	5838	5918	5998	6078	6157	6237	6317	80
45	6397	6476	6556	6635	6715	6795	6874	6954	7034	7113	80
46	7193	7272	7352	7431	7511	7590	7670	7749	7829	7908	80
47	7987	8067	8146	8225	8305	8384	8463	8543	8622	8701	80
48	8781	8860	8939	9018	9097	9177	9256	9335	9414	9493	80
49	73 9572	9651	9731	9810	9889	9968	*0047	*0126	*0205	*0284	80
N	0	1	2	3	4	5	6	7	8	9	D

LOGARITHMS OF NUMBERS 5,500–5,999
Six-Place Mantissas

N	0	1	2	3	4	5	6	7	8	9	D
550	74 0363	0442	0521	0600	0678	0757	0836	0915	0994	1073	79
51	1152	1230	1309	1388	1467	1546	1624	1703	1782	1860	79
52	1939	2018	2096	2175	2254	2332	2411	2489	2568	2647	79
53	2725	2804	2882	2961	3039	3118	3196	3275	3353	3431	79
54	3510	3588	3667	3745	3823	3902	3980	4058	4136	4215	79
55	4293	4371	4449	4528	4606	4684	4762	4840	4919	4997	79
56	5075	5153	5231	5309	5387	5465	5543	5621	5699	5777	78
57	5855	5933	6011	6089	6167	6245	6323	6401	6479	6556	78
58	6634	6712	6790	6868	6945	7023	7101	7179	7256	7334	78
59	7412	7489	7567	7645	7722	7800	7878	7955	8033	8110	78
560	8188	8266	8343	8421	8498	8576	8653	8731	8808	8885	78
61	8963	9040	9118	9195	9272	9350	9427	9504	9582	9659	78
62	74 9736	9814	9891	9968	*0045	*0123	*0200	*0277	*0354	*0431	78
63	75 0508	0586	0663	0740	0817	0894	0971	1048	1125	1202	78
64	1279	1356	1433	1510	1587	1664	1741	1818	1895	1972	77
65	2048	2125	2202	2279	2356	2433	2509	2586	2663	2740	77
66	2816	2893	2970	3047	3123	3200	3277	3353	3430	3506	77
67	3583	3660	3736	3813	3889	3966	4042	4119	4195	4272	77
68	4348	4425	4501	4578	4654	4730	4807	4883	4960	5036	77
69	5112	5189	5265	5341	5417	5494	5570	5646	5722	5799	77
570	5875	5951	6027	6103	6180	6256	6332	6408	6484	6560	77
71	6636	6712	6788	6864	6940	7016	7092	7168	7244	7320	76
72	7396	7472	7548	7624	7700	7775	7851	7927	8003	8079	76
73	8155	8230	8306	8382	8458	8533	8609	8685	8761	8836	76
74	8912	8988	9063	9139	9214	9290	9366	9441	9517	9592	76
75	75 9668	9743	9819	9894	9970	*0045	*0121	*0196	*0272	*0347	76
76	76 0422	0498	0573	0649	0724	0799	0875	0950	1025	1101	76
77	1176	1251	1326	1402	1477	1552	1627	1702	1778	1853	76
78	1928	2003	2078	2153	2228	2303	2378	2453	2529	2604	76
79	2679	2754	2829	2904	2978	3053	3128	3203	3278	3353	75
580	3428	3503	3578	3653	3727	3802	3877	3952	4027	4101	75
81	4176	4251	4326	4400	4475	4550	4624	4699	4774	4848	75
82	4923	4998	5072	5147	5221	5296	5370	5445	5520	5594	75
83	5669	5743	5818	5892	5966	6041	6115	6190	6264	6338	75
84	6413	6487	6562	6636	6710	6785	6859	6933	7007	7082	75
85	7156	7230	7304	7379	7453	7527	7601	7675	7749	7823	75
86	7898	7972	8046	8120	8194	8268	8342	8416	8490	8564	74
87	8638	8712	8786	8860	8934	9008	9082	9156	9230	9303	74
88	76 9377	9451	9525	9599	9673	9746	9820	9894	9968	*0042	74
89	77 0115	0189	0263	0336	0410	0484	0557	0631	0705	0778	74
590	0852	0926	0999	1073	1146	1220	1293	1367	1440	1514	74
91	1587	1661	1734	1808	1881	1955	2028	2102	2175	2248	74
92	2322	2395	2468	2542	2615	2688	2762	2835	2908	2981	74
93	3055	3128	3201	3274	3348	3421	3494	3567	3640	3713	74
94	3786	3860	3933	4006	4079	4152	4225	4298	4371	4444	74
95	4517	4590	4663	4736	4809	4882	4955	5028	5100	5173	73
96	5246	5319	5392	5465	5538	5610	5683	5756	5829	5902	73
97	5974	6047	6120	6193	6265	6338	6411	6483	6556	6629	73
98	6701	6774	6846	6919	6992	7064	7137	7209	7282	7354	73
99	7427	7499	7572	7644	7717	7789	7862	7934	8006	8079	73
N	0	1	2	3	4	5	6	7	8	9	D

Table B

N	0	1	2	3	4	5	6	7	8	9	D
600	77 8151	8224	8296	8368	8441	8513	8585	8658	8730	8802	73
01	8874	8947	9019	9091	9163	9236	9308	9380	9452	9524	73
02	77 9596	9669	9741	9813	9885	9957	*0029	*0101	*0173	*0245	73
03	78 0317	0389	0461	0533	0605	0677	0749	0821	0893	0965	72
04	1037	1109	1181	1253	1324	1396	1468	1540	1612	1684	72
05	1755	1827	1899	1971	2042	2114	2186	2258	2329	2401	72
06	2473	2544	2616	2688	2759	2831	2902	2974	3046	3117	72
07	3189	3260	3332	3403	3475	3546	3618	3689	3761	3832	72
08	3904	3975	4046	4118	4189	4261	4332	4403	4475	4546	72
09	4617	4689	4760	4831	4902	4974	5045	5116	5187	5259	72
610	5330	5401	5472	5543	5615	5686	5757	5828	5899	5970	72
11	6041	6112	6183	6254	6325	6396	6467	6538	6609	6680	71
12	6751	6822	6893	6964	7035	7106	7177	7248	7319	7390	71
13	7460	7531	7602	7673	7744	7815	7885	7956	8027	8098	71
14	8168	8239	8310	8381	8451	8522	8593	8663	8734	8804	71
15	8875	8946	9016	9087	9157	9228	9299	9369	9440	9510	71
16	78 9581	9651	9722	9792	9863	9933	*0004	*0074	*0144	*0215	71
17	79 0285	0356	0426	0496	0567	0637	0707	0778	0848	0918	71
18	0988	1059	1129	1199	1269	1340	1410	1480	1550	1620	71
19	1691	1761	1831	1901	1971	2041	2111	2181	2252	2322	71
620	2392	2462	2532	2602	2672	2742	2812	2882	2952	3022	70
21	3092	3162	3231	3301	3371	3441	3511	3581	3651	3721	70
22	3790	3860	3930	4000	4070	4139	4209	4279	4349	4418	70
23	4488	4558	4627	4697	4767	4836	4906	4976	5045	5115	70
24	5185	5254	5324	5393	5463	5532	5602	5672	5741	5811	70
25	5880	5949	6019	6088	6158	6227	6297	6366	6436	6505	70
26	6574	6644	6713	6782	6852	6921	6990	7060	7129	7198	70
27	7268	7337	7406	7475	7545	7614	7683	7752	7821	7890	70
28	7960	8029	8098	8167	8236	8305	8374	8443	8513	8582	70
29	8651	8720	8789	8858	8927	8996	9065	9134	9203	9272	69
630	79 9341	9409	9478	9547	9616	9685	9754	9823	9892	9961	69
31	80 0029	0098	0167	0236	0305	0373	0442	0511	0580	0648	69
32	0717	0786	0854	0923	0992	1061	1129	1198	1266	1335	69
33	1404	1472	1541	1609	1678	1747	1815	1884	1952	2021	69
34	2089	2158	2226	2295	2363	2432	2500	2568	2637	2705	69
35	2774	2842	2910	2979	3047	3116	3184	3252	3321	3389	69
36	3457	3525	3594	3662	3730	3798	3867	3935	4003	4071	69
37	4139	4208	4276	4344	4412	4480	4548	4616	4685	4753	69
38	4821	4889	4957	5025	5093	5161	5229	5297	5365	5433	68
39	5501	5569	5637	5705	5773	5841	5908	5976	6044	6112	68
640	6180	6248	6316	6384	6451	6519	6587	6655	6723	6790	68
41	6858	6926	6994	7061	7129	7197	7264	7332	7400	7467	68
42	7535	7603	7670	7738	7806	7873	7941	8008	8076	8143	68
43	8211	8279	8346	8414	8481	8549	8616	8684	8751	8818	68
44	8886	8953	9021	9088	9156	9223	9290	9358	9425	9492	68
45	80 9560	9627	9694	9762	9829	9896	9964	*0031	*0098	*0165	68
46	81 0233	0300	0367	0434	0501	0569	0636	0703	0770	0837	68
47	0904	0971	1039	1106	1173	1240	1307	1374	1441	1508	68
48	1575	1642	1709	1776	1843	1910	1977	2044	2111	2178	67
49	2245	2312	2379	2445	2512	2579	2646	2713	2780	2847	67
N	0	1	2	3	4	5	6	7	8	9	D

N	0	1	2	3	4	5	6	7	8	9	D
650	81 2913	2980	3047	3114	3181	3247	3314	3381	3448	3514	67
51	3581	3648	3714	3781	3848	3914	3981	4048	4114	4181	67
52	4248	4314	4381	4447	4514	4581	4647	4714	4780	4847	67
53	4913	4980	5046	5113	5179	5246	5312	5378	5445	5511	67
54	5578	5644	5711	5777	5843	5910	5976	6042	6109	6175	67
55	6241	6308	6374	6440	6506	6573	6639	6705	6771	6838	67
56	6904	6970	7036	7102	7169	7235	7301	7367	7433	7499	67
57	7565	7631	7698	7764	7830	7896	7962	8028	8094	8160	67
58	8226	8292	8358	8424	8490	8556	8622	8688	8754	8820	66
59	8885	8951	9017	9083	9149	9215	9281	9346	9412	9478	66
660	81 9544	9610	9676	9741	9807	9873	9939	*0004	*0070	*0136	66
61	82 0201	0267	0333	0399	0464	0530	0595	0661	0727	0792	66
62	0858	0924	0989	1055	1120	1186	1251	1317	1382	1448	66
63	1514	1579	1645	1710	1775	1841	1906	1972	2037	2103	66
64	2168	2233	2299	2364	2430	2495	2560	2626	2691	2756	66
65	2822	2887	2952	3018	3083	3148	3213	3279	3344	3409	66
66	3474	3539	3605	3670	3735	3800	3865	3930	3996	4061	66
67	4126	4191	4256	4321	4386	4451	4516	4581	4646	4711	65
68	4776	4841	4906	4971	5036	5101	5166	5231	5296	5361	65
69	5426	5491	5556	5621	5686	5751	5815	5880	5945	6010	65
670	6075	6140	6204	6269	6334	6399	6464	6528	6593	6658	65
71	6723	6787	6852	6917	6981	7046	7111	7175	7240	7305	65
72	7369	7434	7499	7563	7628	7692	7757	7821	7886	7951	65
73	8015	8080	8144	8209	8273	8338	8402	8467	8531	8595	65
74	8660	8724	8789	8853	8918	8982	9046	9111	9175	9239	65
75	9304	9368	9432	9497	9561	9625	9690	9754	9818	9882	65
76	82 9947	*0011	*0075	*0139	*0204	*0268	*0332	*0396	*0460	*0525	65
77	83 0589	0653	0717	0781	0845	0909	0973	1037	1102	1166	65
78	1230	1294	1358	1422	1486	1550	1614	1678	1742	1806	64
79	1870	1934	1998	2062	2126	2189	2253	2317	2381	2445	64
680	2509	2573	2637	2700	2764	2828	2892	2956	3020	3083	64
81	3147	3211	3275	3338	3402	3466	3530	3593	3657	3721	64
82	3784	3848	3912	3975	4039	4103	4166	4230	4294	4357	64
83	4421	4484	4548	4611	4675	4739	4802	4866	4929	4993	64
84	5056	5120	5183	5247	5310	5373	5437	5500	5564	5627	64
85	5691	5754	5817	5881	5944	6007	6071	6134	6197	6261	64
86	6324	6387	6451	6514	6577	6641	6704	6767	6830	6894	64
87	6957	7020	7083	7146	7210	7273	7336	7399	7462	7525	64
88	7588	7652	7715	7778	7841	7904	7967	8030	8093	8156	64
89	8219	8282	8345	8408	8471	8534	8597	8660	8723	8786	63
690	8849	8912	8975	9038	9101	9164	9227	9289	9352	9415	63
91	83 9478	9541	9604	9667	9729	9792	9855	9918	9981	*0043	63
92	84 0106	0169	0232	0294	0357	0420	0482	0545	0608	0671	63
93	0733	0796	0859	0921	0984	1046	1109	1172	1234	1297	63
94	1359	1422	1485	1547	1610	1672	1735	1797	1860	1922	63
95	1985	2047	2110	2172	2235	2297	2360	2422	2484	2547	63
96	2609	2672	2734	2796	2859	2921	2983	3046	3108	3170	63
97	3233	3295	3357	3420	3482	3544	3606	3669	3731	3793	63
98	3855	3918	3980	4042	4104	4166	4229	4291	4353	4415	63
99	4477	4539	4601	4664	4726	4788	4850	4912	4974	5036	63
N	0	1	2	3	4	5	6	7	8	9	D

Table B

LOGARITHMS OF NUMBERS 7,000–7,499
Six-Place Mantissas

N	0	1	2	3	4	5	6	7	8	9	D
700	84 5098	5160	5222	5284	5346	5408	5470	5532	5594	5656	62
01	5718	5780	5842	5904	5966	6028	6090	6151	6213	6275	62
02	6337	6399	6461	6523	6585	6646	6708	6770	6832	6894	62
03	6955	7017	7079	7141	7202	7264	7326	7388	7449	7511	62
04	7573	7634	7696	7758	7819	7881	7943	8004	8066	8128	62
05	8189	8251	8312	8374	8435	8497	8559	8620	8682	8743	62
06	8805	8866	8928	8989	9051	9112	9174	9235	9297	9358	62
07	84 9419	9481	9542	9604	9665	9726	9788	9849	9911	9972	62
08	85 0033	0095	0156	0217	0279	0340	0401	0462	0524	0585	62
09	0646	0707	0769	0830	0891	0952	1014	1075	1136	1197	62
710	1258	1320	1381	1442	1503	1564	1625	1686	1747	1809	62
11	1870	1931	1992	2053	2114	2175	2236	2297	2358	2419	61
12	2480	2541	2602	2663	2724	2785	2846	2907	2968	3029	61
13	3090	3150	3211	3272	3333	3394	3455	3516	3577	3637	61
14	3698	3759	3820	3881	3941	4002	4063	4124	4185	4245	61
15	4306	4367	4428	4488	4549	4610	4670	4731	4792	4852	61
16	4913	4974	5034	5095	5156	5216	5277	5337	5398	5459	61
17	5519	5580	5640	5701	5761	5822	5882	5943	6003	6064	61
18	6124	6185	6245	6306	6366	6427	6487	6548	6608	6668	61
19	6729	6789	6850	6910	6970	7031	7091	7152	7212	7272	61
720	7332	7393	7453	7513	7574	7634	7694	7755	7815	7875	61
21	7935	7995	8056	8116	8176	8236	8297	8357	8417	8477	61
22	8537	8597	8657	8718	8778	8838	8898	8958	9018	9078	61
23	9138	9198	9258	9318	9379	9439	9499	9559	9619	9679	61
24	85 9739	9799	9859	9918	9978	*0038	*0098	*0158	*0218	*0278	60
25	86 0338	0398	0458	0518	0578	0637	0697	0757	0817	0877	60
26	0937	0996	1056	1116	1176	1236	1295	1355	1415	1475	60
27	1534	1594	1654	1714	1773	1833	1893	1952	2012	2072	60
28	2131	2191	2251	2310	2370	2430	2489	2549	2608	2668	60
29	2728	2787	2847	2906	2966	3025	3085	3144	3204	3263	60
730	3323	3382	3442	3501	3561	3620	3680	3739	3799	3858	60
31	3917	3977	4036	4096	4155	4214	4274	4333	4392	4452	60
32	4511	4570	4630	4689	4748	4808	4867	4926	4985	5045	60
33	5104	5163	5222	5282	5341	5400	5459	5519	5578	5637	60
34	5696	5755	5814	5874	5933	5992	6051	6110	6169	6228	60
35	6287	6346	6405	6465	6524	6583	6642	6701	6760	6819	60
36	6878	6937	6996	7055	7114	7173	7232	7291	7350	7409	59
37	7467	7526	7585	7644	7703	7762	7821	7880	7939	7998	59
38	8056	8115	8174	8233	8292	8350	8409	8468	8527	8586	59
39	8644	8703	8762	8821	8879	8938	8997	9056	9114	9173	59
740	9232	9290	9349	9408	9466	9525	9584	9642	9701	9760	59
41	86 9818	9877	9935	9994	*0053	*0111	*0170	*0228	*0287	*0345	59
42	87 0404	0462	0521	0579	0638	0696	0755	0813	0872	0930	59
43	0989	1047	1106	1164	1223	1281	1339	1398	1456	1515	59
44	1573	1631	1690	1748	1806	1865	1923	1981	2040	2098	59
45	2156	2215	2273	2331	2389	2448	2506	2564	2622	2681	59
46	2739	2797	2855	2913	2972	3030	3088	3146	3204	3262	59
47	3321	3379	3437	3495	3553	3611	3669	3727	3785	3844	59
48	3902	3960	4018	4076	4134	4192	4250	4308	4366	4424	58
49	4482	4540	4598	4656	4714	4772	4830	4888	4945	5003	58
N	0	1	2	3	4	5	6	7	8	9	D

Table B

LOGARITHMS OF NUMBERS 7,500-7,999
Six-Place Mantissas

N	0	1	2	3	4	5	6	7	8	9	D
750	87 5061	5119	5177	5235	5293	5351	5409	5466	5524	5582	58
51	5640	5698	5756	5813	5871	5929	5987	6045	6102	6160	58
52	6218	6276	6333	6391	6449	6507	6564	6622	6680	6737	58
53	6795	6853	6910	6968	7026	7083	7141	7199	7256	7314	58
54	7371	7429	7487	7544	7602	7659	7717	7774	7832	7889	58
55	7947	8004	8062	8119	8177	8234	8292	8349	8407	8464	58
56	8522	8579	8637	8694	8752	8809	8866	8924	8981	9039	58
57	9096	9153	9211	9268	9325	9383	9440	9497	9555	9612	58
58	87 9669	9726	9784	9841	9898	9956	*0013	*0070	*0127	*0185	58
59	88 0242	0299	0356	0413	0471	0528	0585	0642	0699	0756	58
760	0814	0871	0928	0985	1042	1099	1156	1213	1271	1328	58
61	1385	1442	1499	1556	1613	1670	1727	1784	1841	1898	57
62	1955	2012	2069	2126	2183	2240	2297	2354	2411	2468	57
63	2525	2581	2638	2695	2752	2809	2866	2923	2980	3037	57
64	3093	3150	3207	3264	3321	3377	3434	3491	3548	3605	57
65	3661	3718	3775	3832	3888	3945	4002	4059	4115	4172	57
66	4229	4285	4342	4399	4455	4512	4569	4625	4682	4739	57
67	4795	4852	4909	4965	5022	5078	5135	5192	5248	5305	57
68	5361	5418	5474	5531	5587	5644	5700	5757	5813	5870	57
69	5926	5983	6039	6096	6152	6209	6265	6321	6378	6434	57
770	6491	6547	6604	6660	6716	6773	6829	6885	6942	6998	57
71	7054	7111	7167	7223	7280	7336	7392	7449	7505	7561	57
72	7617	7674	7730	7786	7842	7898	7955	8011	8067	8123	57
73	8179	8236	8292	8348	8404	8460	8516	8573	8629	8685	57
74	8741	8797	8853	8909	8965	9021	9077	9134	9190	9246	57
75	9302	9358	9414	9470	9526	9582	9638	9694	9750	9806	56
76	88 9862	9918	9974	*0030	*0086	*0141	*0197	*0253	*0309	*0365	56
77	89 0421	0477	0533	0589	0645	0700	0756	0812	0868	0924	56
78	0980	1035	1091	1147	1203	1259	1314	1370	1426	1482	56
79	1537	1593	1649	1705	1760	1816	1872	1928	1983	2039	56
780	2095	2150	2206	2262	2317	2373	2429	2484	2540	2595	56
81	2651	2707	2762	2818	2873	2929	2985	3040	3096	3151	56
82	3207	3262	3318	3373	3429	3484	3540	3595	3651	3706	56
83	3762	3817	3873	3928	3984	4039	4094	4150	4205	4261	56
84	4316	4371	4427	4482	4538	4593	4648	4704	4759	4814	56
85	4870	4925	4980	5036	5091	5146	5201	5257	5312	5367	56
86	5423	5478	5533	5588	5644	5699	5754	5809	5864	5920	56
87	5975	6030	6085	6140	6195	6251	6306	6361	6416	6471	56
88	6526	6581	6636	6692	6747	6802	6857	6912	6967	7022	56
89	7077	7132	7187	7242	7297	7352	7407	7462	7517	7572	55
790	7627	7682	7737	7792	7847	7902	7957	8012	8067	8122	55
91	8176	8231	8286	8341	8396	8451	8506	8561	8615	8670	55
92	8725	8780	8835	8890	8944	8999	9054	9109	9164	9218	55
93	9273	9328	9383	9437	9492	9547	9602	9656	9711	9766	55
94	89 9821	9875	9930	9985	*0039	*0094	*0149	*0203	*0258	*0312	55
95	90 0367	0422	0476	0531	0586	0640	0695	0749	0804	0859	55
96	0913	0968	1022	1077	1131	1186	1240	1295	1349	1404	55
97	1458	1513	1567	1622	1676	1731	1785	1840	1894	1948	55
98	2003	2057	2112	2166	2221	2275	2329	2384	2438	2492	55
99	2547	2601	2655	2710	2764	2818	2873	2927	2981	3036	55
N	0	1	2	3	4	5	6	7	8	9	D

Table B

LOGARITHMS OF NUMBERS 8,000–8,499
Six-Place Mantissas

N	0	1	2	3	4	5	6	7	8	9	D
800	90 3090	3144	3199	3253	3307	3361	3416	3470	3524	3578	55
01	3633	3687	3741	3795	3849	3904	3958	4012	4066	4120	55
02	4174	4229	4283	4337	4391	4445	4499	4553	4607	4661	55
03	4716	4770	4824	4878	4932	4986	5040	5094	5148	5202	54
04	5256	5310	5364	5418	5472	5526	5580	5634	5688	5742	54
05	5796	5850	5904	5958	6012	6066	6119	6173	6227	6281	54
06	6335	6389	6443	6497	6551	6604	6658	6712	6766	6820	54
07	6874	6927	6981	7035	7089	7143	7196	7250	7304	7358	54
08	7411	7465	7519	7573	7626	7680	7734	7787	7841	7895	54
09	7949	8002	8056	8110	8163	8217	8270	8324	8378	8431	54
810	8485	8539	8592	8646	8699	8753	8807	8860	8914	8967	54
11	9021	9074	9128	9181	9235	9289	9342	9396	9449	9503	54
12	90 9556	9610	9663	9716	9770	9823	9877	9930	9984	*0037	54
13	91 0091	0144	0197	0251	0304	0358	0411	0464	0518	0571	54
14	0624	0678	0731	0784	0838	0891	0944	0998	1051	1104	54
15	1158	1211	1264	1317	1371	1424	1477	1530	1584	1637	54
16	1690	1743	1797	1850	1903	1956	2009	2063	2116	2169	54
17	2222	2275	2328	2381	2435	2488	2541	2594	2647	2700	54
18	2753	2806	2859	2913	2966	3019	3072	3125	3178	3231	54
19	3284	3337	3390	3443	3496	3549	3602	3655	3708	3761	53
820	3814	3867	3920	3973	4026	4079	4132	4184	4237	4290	53
21	4343	4396	4449	4502	4555	4608	4660	4713	4766	4819	53
22	4872	4925	4977	5030	5083	5136	5189	5241	5294	5347	53
23	5400	5453	5505	5558	5611	5664	5716	5769	5822	5875	53
24	5927	5980	6033	6085	6138	6191	6243	6296	6349	6401	53
25	6454	6507	6559	6612	6664	6717	6770	6822	6875	6927	53
26	6980	7033	7085	7138	7190	7243	7295	7348	7400	7453	53
27	7506	7558	7611	7663	7716	7768	7820	7873	7925	7978	53
28	8030	8083	8135	8188	8240	8293	8345	8397	8450	8502	53
29	8555	8607	8659	8712	8764	8816	8869	8921	8973	9026	53
830	9078	9130	9183	9235	9287	9340	9392	9444	9496	9549	53
31	91 9601	9653	9706	9758	9810	9862	9914	9967	*0019	*0071	53
32	92 0123	0176	0228	0280	0332	0384	0436	0489	0541	0593	53
33	0645	0697	0749	0801	0853	0906	0958	1010	1062	1114	53
34	1166	1218	1270	1322	1374	1426	1478	1530	1582	1634	52
35	1686	1738	1790	1842	1894	1946	1998	2050	2102	2154	52
36	2206	2258	2310	2362	2414	2466	2518	2570	2622	2674	52
37	2725	2777	2829	2881	2933	2985	3037	3089	3140	3192	52
38	3244	3296	3348	3399	3451	3503	3555	3607	3658	3710	52
39	3762	3814	3865	3917	3969	4021	4072	4124	4176	4228	52
840	4279	4331	4383	4434	4486	4538	4589	4641	4693	4744	52
41	4796	4848	4899	4951	5003	5054	5106	5157	5209	5261	52
42	5312	5364	5415	5467	5518	5570	5621	5673	5725	5776	52
43	5828	5879	5931	5982	6034	6085	6137	6188	6240	6291	52
44	6342	6394	6445	6497	6548	6600	6651	6702	6754	6805	52
45	6857	6908	6959	7011	7062	7114	7165	7216	7268	7319	52
46	7370	7422	7473	7524	7576	7627	7678	7730	7781	7832	52
47	7883	7935	7986	8037	8088	8140	8191	8242	8293	8345	52
48	8396	8447	8498	8549	8601	8652	8703	8754	8805	8857	52
49	8908	8959	9010	9061	9112	9163	9215	9266	9317	9368	52
N	0	1	2	3	4	5	6	7	8	9	D

Table B

N	0	1	2	3	4	5	6	7	8	9	D
850	92 9419	9470	9521	9572	9623	9674	9725	9776	9827	9879	52
51	92 9930	9981	*0032	*0083	*0134	*0185	*0236	*0287	*0338	*0389	51
52	93 0440	0491	0542	0592	0643	0694	0745	0796	0847	0898	51
53	0949	1000	1051	1102	1153	1204	1254	1305	1356	1407	51
54	1458	1509	1560	1610	1661	1712	1763	1814	1865	1915	51
55	1966	2017	2068	2118	2169	2220	2271	2322	2372	2423	51
56	2474	2524	2575	2626	2677	2727	2778	2829	2879	2930	51
57	2981	3031	3082	3133	3183	3234	3285	3335	3386	3437	51
58	3487	3538	3589	3639	3690	3740	3791	3841	3892	3943	51
59	3993	4044	4094	4145	4195	4246	4296	4347	4397	4448	51
860	4498	4549	4599	4650	4700	4751	4801	4852	4902	4953	51
61	5003	5054	5104	5154	5205	5255	5306	5356	5406	5457	51
62	5507	5558	5608	5658	5709	5759	5809	5860	5910	5960	51
63	6011	6061	6111	6162	6212	6262	6313	6363	6413	6463	51
64	6514	6564	6614	6665	6715	6765	6815	6865	6916	6966	51
65	7016	7066	7117	7167	7217	7267	7317	7367	7418	7468	51
66	7518	7568	7618	7668	7718	7769	7819	7869	7919	7969	51
67	8019	8069	8119	8169	8219	8269	8320	8370	8420	8470	51
68	8520	8570	8620	8670	8720	8770	8820	8870	8920	8970	50
69	9020	9070	9120	9170	9220	9270	9320	9369	9419	9469	50
870	93 9519	9569	9619	9669	9719	9769	9819	9869	9918	9968	50
71	94 0018	0068	0118	0168	0218	0267	0317	0367	0417	0467	50
72	0516	0566	0616	0666	0716	0765	0815	0865	0915	0964	50
73	1014	1064	1114	1163	1213	1263	1313	1362	1412	1462	50
74	1511	1561	1611	1660	1710	1760	1809	1859	1909	1958	50
75	2008	2058	2107	2157	2207	2256	2306	2355	2405	2455	50
76	2504	2554	2603	2653	2702	2752	2801	2851	2901	2950	50
77	3000	3049	3099	3148	3198	3247	3297	3346	3396	3445	50
78	3495	3544	3593	3643	3692	3742	3791	3841	3890	3939	50
79	3989	4038	4088	4137	4186	4236	4285	4335	4384	4433	50
880	4483	4532	4581	4631	4680	4729	4779	4828	4877	4927	50
81	4976	5025	5074	5124	5173	5222	5272	5321	5370	5419	50
82	5469	5518	5567	5616	5665	5715	5764	5813	5862	5912	50
83	5961	6010	6059	6108	6157	6207	6256	6305	6354	6403	50
84	6452	6501	6551	6600	6649	6698	6747	6796	6845	6894	50
85	6943	6992	7041	7090	7140	7189	7238	7287	7336	7385	50
86	7434	7483	7532	7581	7630	7679	7728	7777	7826	7875	49
87	7924	7973	8022	8070	8119	8168	8217	8266	8315	8364	49
88	8413	8462	8511	8560	8609	8657	8706	8755	8804	8853	49
89	8902	8951	8999	9048	9097	9146	9195	9244	9292	9341	49
890	9390	9439	9488	9536	9585	9634	9683	9731	9780	9829	49
91	94 9878	9926	9975	*0024	*0073	*0121	*0170	*0219	*0267	*0316	49
92	95 0365	0414	0462	0511	0560	0608	0657	0706	0754	0803	49
93	0851	0900	0949	0997	1046	1095	1143	1192	1240	1289	49
94	1338	1386	1435	1483	1532	1580	1629	1677	1726	1775	49
95	1823	1872	1920	1969	2017	2066	2114	2163	2211	2260	49
96	2308	2356	2405	2453	2502	2550	2599	2647	2696	2744	49
97	2792	2841	2889	2938	2986	3034	3083	3131	3180	3228	49
98	3276	3325	3373	3421	3470	3518	3566	3615	3663	3711	49
99	3760	3808	3856	3905	3953	4001	4049	4098	4146	4194	49
N	0	1	2	3	4	5	6	7	8	9	D

N	0	1	2	3	4	5	6	7	8	9	D
900	95 4243	4291	4339	4387	4435	4484	4532	4580	4628	4677	49
01	4725	4773	4821	4869	4918	4966	5014	5062	5110	5158	49
02	5207	5255	5303	5351	5399	5447	5495	5543	5592	5640	49
03	5688	5736	5784	5832	5880	5928	5976	6024	6072	6120	48
04	6168	6216	6265	6313	6361	6409	6457	6505	6553	6601	48
05	6649	6697	6745	6793	6840	6888	6936	6984	7032	7080	48
06	7128	7176	7224	7272	7320	7368	7416	7464	7512	7559	48
07	7607	7655	7703	7751	7799	7847	7894	7942	7990	8038	48
08	8086	8134	8181	8229	8277	8325	8373	8421	8468	8516	48
09	8564	8612	8659	8707	8755	8803	8850	8898	8946	8994	48
910	9041	9089	9137	9185	9232	9280	9328	9375	9423	9471	48
11	9518	9566	9614	9661	9709	9757	9804	9852	9900	9947	48
12	95 9995	*0042	*0090	*0138	*0185	*0233	*0280	*0328	*0376	*0423	48
13	96 0471	0518	0566	0613	0661	0709	0756	0804	0851	0899	48
14	0946	0994	1041	1089	1136	1184	1231	1279	1326	1374	48
15	1421	1469	1516	1563	1611	1658	1706	1753	1801	1848	48
16	1895	1943	1990	2038	2085	2132	2180	2227	2275	2322	48
17	2369	2417	2464	2511	2559	2606	2653	2701	2748	2795	48
18	2843	2890	2937	2985	3032	3079	3126	3174	3221	3268	48
19	3316	3363	3410	3457	3504	3552	3599	3646	3693	3741	48
920	3788	3835	3882	3929	3977	4024	4071	4118	4165	4212	48
21	4260	4307	4354	4401	4448	4495	4542	4590	4637	4684	48
22	4731	4778	4825	4872	4919	4966	5013	5061	5108	5155	48
23	5202	5249	5296	5343	5390	5437	5484	5531	5578	5625	47
24	5672	5719	5766	5813	5860	5907	5954	6001	6048	6095	47
25	6142	6189	6236	6283	6329	6376	6423	6470	6517	6564	47
26	6611	6658	6705	6752	6799	6845	6892	6939	6986	7033	47
27	7080	7127	7173	7220	7267	7314	7361	7408	7454	7501	47
28	7548	7595	7642	7688	7735	7782	7829	7875	7922	7969	47
29	8016	8062	8109	8156	8203	8249	8296	8343	8390	8436	47
930	8483	8530	8576	8623	8670	8716	8763	8810	8856	8903	47
31	8950	8996	9043	9090	9136	9183	9229	9276	9323	9369	47
32	9416	9463	9509	9556	9602	9649	9695	9742	9789	9835	47
33	96 9882	9928	9975	*0021	*0068	*0114	*0161	*0207	*0254	*0300	47
34	97 0347	0393	0440	0486	0533	0579	0626	0672	0719	0765	47
35	0812	0858	0904	0951	0997	1044	1090	1137	1183	1229	47
36	1276	1322	1369	1415	1461	1508	1554	1601	1647	1693	47
37	1740	1786	1832	1879	1925	1971	2018	2064	2110	2157	47
38	2203	2249	2295	2342	2388	2434	2481	2527	2573	2619	47
39	2666	2712	2758	2804	2851	2897	2943	2989	3035	3082	47
940	3128	3174	3220	3266	3313	3359	3405	3451	3497	3543	47
41	3590	3636	3682	3728	3774	3820	3866	3913	3959	4005	47
42	4051	4097	4143	4189	4235	4281	4327	4374	4420	4466	47
43	4512	4558	4604	4650	4696	4742	4788	4834	4880	4926	46
44	4972	5018	5064	5110	5156	5202	5248	5294	5340	5386	46
45	5432	5478	5524	5570	5616	5662	5707	5753	5799	5845	46
46	5891	5937	5983	6029	6075	6121	6167	6212	6258	6304	46
47	6350	6396	6442	6488	6533	6579	6625	6671	6717	6763	46
48	6808	6854	6900	6946	6992	7037	7083	7129	7175	7220	46
49	7266	7312	7358	7403	7449	7495	7541	7586	7632	7678	46
N	0	1	2	3	4	5	6	7	8	9	D

Table B

Six-Place Mantissas

N	0	1	2	3	4	5	6	7	8	9	D
950	97 7724	7769	7815	7861	7906	7952	7998	8043	8089	8135	46
51	8181	8226	8272	8317	8363	8409	8454	8500	8546	8591	46
52	8637	8683	8728	8774	8819	8865	8911	8956	9002	9047	46
53	9093	9138	9184	9230	9275	9321	9366	9412	9457	9503	46
54	97 9548	9594	9639	9685	9730	9776	9821	9867	9912	9958	46
55	98 0003	0049	0094	0140	0185	0231	0276	0322	0367	0412	46
56	0458	0503	0549	0594	0640	0685	0730	0776	0821	0867	46
57	0912	0957	1003	1048	1093	1139	1184	1229	1275	1320	46
58	1366	1411	1456	1501	1547	1592	1637	1683	1728	1773	46
59	1819	1864	1909	1954	2000	2045	2090	2135	2181	2226	46
960	2271	2316	2362	2407	2452	2497	2543	2588	2633	2678	46
61	2723	2769	2814	2859	2904	2949	2994	3040	3085	3130	46
62	3175	3220	3265	3310	3356	3401	3446	3491	3536	3581	46
63	3626	3671	3716	3762	3807	3852	3897	3942	3987	4032	46
64	4077	4122	4167	4212	4257	4302	4347	4392	4437	4482	45
65	4527	4572	4617	4662	4707	4752	4797	4842	4887	4932	45
66	4977	5022	5067	5112	5157	5202	5247	5292	5337	5382	45
67	5426	5471	5516	5561	5606	5651	5696	5741	5786	5830	45
68	5875	5920	5965	6010	6055	6100	6144	6189	6234	6279	45
69	6324	6369	6413	6458	6503	6548	6593	6637	6682	6727	45
970	6772	6817	6861	6906	6951	6996	7040	7085	7130	7175	45
71	7219	7264	7309	7353	7398	7443	7488	7532	7577	7622	45
72	7666	7711	7756	7800	7845	7890	7934	7979	8024	8068	45
73	8113	8157	8202	8247	8291	8336	8381	8425	8470	8514	45
74	8559	8604	8648	8693	8737	8782	8826	8871	8916	8960	45
75	9005	9049	9094	9138	9183	9227	9272	9316	9361	9405	45
76	9450	9494	9539	9583	9628	9672	9717	9761	9806	9850	45
77	98 9895	9939	9983	*0028	*0072	*0117	*0161	*0206	*0250	*0294	45
78	99 0339	0383	0428	0472	0516	0561	0605	0650	0694	0738	45
79	0783	0827	0871	0916	0960	1004	1049	1093	1137	1182	45
980	1226	1270	1315	1359	1403	1448	1492	1536	1580	1625	45
81	1669	1713	1758	1802	1846	1890	1935	1979	2023	2067	45
82	2111	2156	2200	2244	2288	2333	2377	2421	2465	2509	45
83	2554	2598	2642	2686	2730	2774	2819	2863	2907	2951	45
84	2995	3039	3083	3127	3172	3216	3260	3304	3348	3392	45
85	3436	3480	3524	3568	3613	3657	3701	3745	3789	3833	45
86	3877	3921	3965	4009	4053	4097	4141	4185	4229	4273	44
87	4317	4361	4405	4449	4493	4537	4581	4625	4669	4713	44
88	4757	4801	4845	4889	4933	4977	5021	5065	5108	5152	44
89	5196	5240	5284	5328	5372	5416	5460	5504	5547	5591	44
990	5635	5679	5723	5767	5811	5854	5898	5942	5986	6030	44
91	6074	6117	6161	6205	6249	6293	6337	6380	6424	6468	44
92	6512	6555	6599	6643	6687	6731	6774	6818	6862	6906	44
93	6949	6993	7037	7080	7124	7168	7212	7255	7299	7343	44
94	7386	7430	7474	7517	7561	7605	7648	7692	7736	7779	44
95	7823	7867	7910	7954	7998	8041	8085	8129	8172	8216	44
96	8259	8303	8347	8390	8434	8477	8521	8564	8608	8652	44
97	8695	8739	8782	8826	8869	8913	8956	9000	9043	9087	44
98	9131	9174	9218	9261	9305	9348	9392	9435	9479	9522	44
99	99 9565	9609	9652	9696	9739	9783	9826	9870	9913	9957	44
N	0	1	2	3	4	5	6	7	8	9	D

Table B

BINOMIAL PROBABILITY DISTRIBUTION

$$P(r \mid n, p) = \binom{n}{r} p^r q^{n-r}$$

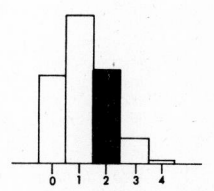

$P(r = 2 \mid n = 4, p = 0.3) = 0.2646$

n = 1

r\p	.01	.02	.03	.04	.05	.06	.07	.08	.09	.10
0	.9900	.9800	.9700	.9600	.9500	.9400	.9300	.9200	.9100	.9000
1	.0100	.0200	.0300	.0400	.0500	.0600	.0700	.0800	.0900	.1000

	.11	.12	.13	.14	.15	.16	.17	.18	.19	.20
0	.8900	.8800	.8700	.8600	.8500	.8400	.8300	.8200	.8100	.8000
1	.1100	.1200	.1300	.1400	.1500	.1600	.1700	.1800	.1900	.2000

	.21	.22	.23	.24	.25	.26	.27	.28	.29	.30
0	.7900	.7800	.7700	.7600	.7500	.7400	.7300	.7200	.7100	.7000
1	.2100	.2200	.2300	.2400	.2500	.2600	.2700	.2800	.2900	.3000

	.31	.32	.33	.34	.35	.36	.37	.38	.39	.40
0	.6900	.6800	.6700	.6600	.6500	.6400	.6300	.6200	.6100	.6000
1	.3100	.3200	.3300	.3400	.3500	.3600	.3700	.3800	.3900	.4000

	.41	.42	.43	.44	.45	.46	.47	.48	.49	.50
0	.5900	.5800	.5700	.5600	.5500	.5400	.5300	.5200	.5100	.5000
1	.4100	.4200	.4300	.4400	.4500	.4600	.4700	.4800	.4900	.5000

n = 2

r\p	.01	.02	.03	.04	.05	.06	.07	.08	.09	.10
0	.9801	.9604	.9409	.9216	.9025	.8836	.8649	.8464	.8281	.8100
1	.0198	.0392	.0582	.0768	.0950	.1128	.1302	.1472	.1638	.1800
2	.0001	.0004	.0009	.0016	.0025	.0036	.0049	.0064	.0081	.0100

	.11	.12	.13	.14	.15	.16	.17	.18	.19	.20
0	.7921	.7744	.7569	.7396	.7225	.7056	.6889	.6724	.6561	.6400
1	.1958	.2112	.2262	.2408	.2550	.2688	.2822	.2952	.3078	.3200
2	.0121	.0144	.0169	.0196	.0225	.0256	.0289	.0324	.0361	.0400

	.21	.22	.23	.24	.25	.26	.27	.28	.29	.30
0	.6241	.6084	.5929	.5776	.5625	.5476	.5329	.5184	.5041	.4900
1	.3318	.3432	.3542	.3648	.3750	.3848	.3942	.4032	.4118	.4200
2	.0441	.0484	.0529	.0576	.0625	.0676	.0729	.0784	.0841	.0900

	.31	.32	.33	.34	.35	.36	.37	.38	.39	.40
0	.4761	.4624	.4489	.4356	.4225	.4096	.3969	.3844	.3721	.3600
1	.4278	.4352	.4422	.4488	.4550	.4608	.4662	.4712	.4758	.4800
2	.0961	.1024	.1089	.1156	.1225	.1296	.1369	.1444	.1521	.1600

	.41	.42	.43	.44	.45	.46	.47	.48	.49	.50
0	.3481	.3364	.3249	.3136	.3025	.2916	.2809	.2704	.2601	.2500
1	.4838	.4872	.4902	.4928	.4950	.4968	.4982	.4992	.4998	.5000
2	.1681	.1764	.1849	.1936	.2025	.2116	.2209	.2304	.2401	.2500

Table C 547

	n = 3									
r \ p	.01	.02	.03	.04	.05	.06	.07	.08	.09	.10
0	.9704	.9412	.9127	.8847	.8574	.8306	.8044	.7787	.7536	.7290
1	.0294	.0576	.0847	.1106	.1354	.1590	.1816	.2031	.2236	.2430
2	.0003	.0012	.0026	.0046	.0071	.0102	.0137	.0177	.0221	.0270
3	.0000	.0000	.0000	.0001	.0001	.0002	.0003	.0005	.0007	.0010
	.11	.12	.13	.14	.15	.16	.17	.18	.19	.20
0	.7050	.6815	.6585	.6361	.6141	.5927	.5718	.5514	.5314	.5120
1	.2614	.2788	.2952	.3106	.3251	.3387	.3513	.3631	.3740	.3840
2	.0323	.0380	.0441	.0506	.0574	.0645	.0720	.0797	.0877	.0960
3	.0013	.0017	.0022	.0027	.0034	.0041	.0049	.0058	.0069	.0080
	.21	.22	.23	.24	.25	.26	.27	.28	.29	.30
0	.4930	.4746	.4565	.4390	.4219	.4052	.3890	.3732	.3579	.3430
1	.3932	.4015	.4091	.4159	.4219	.4271	.4316	.4355	.4386	.4410
2	.1045	.1133	.1222	.1313	.1406	.1501	.1597	.1693	.1791	.1890
3	.0093	.0106	.0122	.0138	.0156	.0176	.0197	.0220	.0244	.0270
	.31	.32	.33	.34	.35	.36	.37	.38	.39	.40
0	.3285	.3144	.3008	.2875	.2746	.2621	.2500	.2383	.2270	.2160
1	.4428	.4439	.4444	.4443	.4436	.4424	.4406	.4382	.4354	.4320
2	.1989	.2089	.2189	.2289	.2389	.2488	.2587	.2686	.2783	.2880
3	.0298	.0328	.0359	.0393	.0429	.0467	.0507	.0549	.0593	.0640
	.41	.42	.43	.44	.45	.46	.47	.48	.49	.50
0	.2054	.1951	.1852	.1756	.1664	.1575	.1489	.1406	.1327	.1250
1	.4282	.4239	.4191	.4140	.4084	.4024	.3961	.3894	.3823	.3750
2	.2975	.3069	.3162	.3252	.3341	.3428	.3512	.3594	.3674	.3750
3	.0689	.0741	.0795	.0852	.0911	.0973	.1038	.1106	.1176	.1250

	n = 4									
r \ p	.01	.02	.03	.04	.05	.06	.07	.08	.09	.10
0	.9606	.9224	.8853	.8493	.8145	.7807	.7481	.7164	.6857	.6561
1	.0388	.0753	.1095	.1416	.1715	.1993	.2252	.2492	.2713	.2916
2	.0006	.0023	.0051	.0088	.0135	.0191	.0254	.0325	.0402	.0486
3	.0000	.0000	.0001	.0002	.0005	.0008	.0013	.0019	.0027	.0036
4	.0000	.0000	.0000	.0000	.0000	.0000	.0000	.0000	.0001	.0001
	.11	.12	.13	.14	.15	.16	.17	.18	.19	.20
0	.6274	.5997	.5729	.5470	.5220	.4979	.4746	.4521	.4305	.4096
1	.3102	.3271	.3424	.3562	.3685	.3793	.3888	.3970	.4039	.4096
2	.0575	.0669	.0767	.0870	.0975	.1084	.1195	.1307	.1421	.1536
3	.0047	.0061	.0076	.0094	.0115	.0138	.0163	.0191	.0222	.0256
4	.0001	.0002	.0003	.0004	.0005	.0007	.0008	.0010	.0013	.0016
	.21	.22	.23	.24	.25	.26	.27	.28	.29	.30
0	.3895	.3702	.3515	.3336	.3164	.2999	.2840	.2687	.2541	.2401
1	.4142	.4176	.4200	.4214	.4219	.4214	.4201	.4180	.4152	.4116
2	.1651	.1767	.1882	.1996	.2109	.2221	.2331	.2439	.2544	.2646
3	.0293	.0332	.0375	.0420	.0469	.0520	.0575	.0632	.0693	.0756
4	.0019	.0023	.0028	.0033	.0039	.0046	.0053	.0061	.0071	.0081
	.31	.32	.33	.34	.35	.36	.37	.38	.39	.40
0	.2267	.2138	.2015	.1897	.1785	.1678	.1575	.1478	.1385	.1296
1	.4074	.4025	.3970	.3910	.3845	.3775	.3701	.3623	.3541	.3456
2	.2745	.2841	.2933	.3021	.3105	.3185	.3260	.3330	.3396	.3456
3	.0822	.0891	.0963	.1038	.1115	.1194	.1276	.1361	.1447	.1536
4	.0092	.0105	.0119	.0134	.0150	.0168	.0187	.0209	.0231	.0256
	.41	.42	.43	.44	.45	.46	.47	.48	.49	.50
0	.1212	.1132	.1056	.0983	.0915	.0850	.0789	.0731	.0677	.0625
1	.3368	.3278	.3185	.3091	.2995	.2897	.2799	.2700	.2600	.2500
2	.3511	.3560	.3604	.3643	.3675	.3702	.3723	.3738	.3747	.3750
3	.1627	.1719	.1813	.1908	.2005	.2102	.2201	.2300	.2400	.2500
4	.0283	.0311	.0342	.0375	.0410	.0448	.0488	.0531	.0576	.0625

 Table C

r \ p	.01	.02	.03	.04	.05	.06	.07	.08	.09	.10
0	.9510	.9039	.8587	.8154	.7738	.7339	.6957	.6591	.6240	.5905
1	.0480	.0922	.1328	.1699	.2036	.2342	.2618	.2866	.3086	.3280
2	.0010	.0038	.0082	.0142	.0214	.0299	.0394	.0498	.0610	.0729
3	.0000	.0001	.0003	.0006	.0011	.0019	.0030	.0043	.0060	.0081
4	.0000	.0000	.0000	.0000	.0000	.0001	.0001	.0002	.0003	.0004

r \ p	.11	.12	.13	.14	.15	.16	.17	.18	.19	.20
0	.5584	.5277	.4984	.4704	.4437	.4182	.3939	.3707	.3487	.3277
1	.3451	.3598	.3724	.3829	.3915	.3983	.4034	.4069	.4089	.4096
2	.0853	.0981	.1113	.1247	.1382	.1517	.1652	.1786	.1919	.2048
3	.0105	.0134	.0166	.0203	.0244	.0289	.0338	.0392	.0450	.0512
4	.0007	.0009	.0012	.0017	.0022	.0028	.0035	.0043	.0053	.0064
5	.0000	.0000	.0000	.0001	.0001	.0001	.0001	.0002	.0002	.0003

r \ p	.21	.22	.23	.24	.25	.26	.27	.28	.29	.30
0	.3077	.2887	.2707	.2536	.2373	.2219	.2073	.1935	.1804	.1681
1	.4090	.4072	.4043	.4003	.3955	.3898	.3834	.3762	.3685	.3602
2	.2174	.2297	.2415	.2529	.2637	.2739	.2836	.2926	.3010	.3087
3	.0578	.0648	.0721	.0798	.0879	.0962	.1049	.1138	.1229	.1323
4	.0077	.0091	.0108	.0126	.0146	.0169	.0194	.0221	.0251	.0284
5	.0004	.0005	.0006	.0008	.0010	.0012	.0014	.0017	.0021	.0024

r \ p	.31	.32	.33	.34	.35	.36	.37	.38	.39	.40
0	.1564	.1454	.1350	.1252	.1160	.1074	.0992	.0916	.0845	.0778
1	.3513	.3421	.3325	.3226	.3124	.3020	.2914	.2808	.2700	.2592
2	.3157	.3220	.3275	.3323	.3364	.3397	.3423	.3441	.3452	.3456
3	.1418	.1515	.1613	.1712	.1811	.1911	.2010	.2109	.2207	.2304
4	.0319	.0357	.0397	.0441	.0488	.0537	.0590	.0646	.0706	.0768
5	.0029	.0034	.0039	.0045	.0053	.0060	.0069	.0079	.0090	.0102

r \ p	.41	.42	.43	.44	.45	.46	.47	.48	.49	.50
0	.0715	.0656	.0602	.0551	.0503	.0459	.0418	.0380	.0345	.0312
1	.2484	.2376	.2270	.2164	.2059	.1956	.1854	.1755	.1657	.1562
2	.3452	.3442	.3424	.3400	.3369	.3332	.3289	.3240	.3185	.3125
3	.2399	.2492	.2583	.2671	.2757	.2838	.2916	.2990	.3060	.3125
4	.0834	.0902	.0974	.1049	.1128	.1209	.1293	.1380	.1470	.1562
5	.0116	.0131	.0147	.0165	.0185	.0206	.0229	.0255	.0282	.0312

r \ p	.01	.02	.03	.04	.05	.06	.07	.08	.09	.10
0	.9415	.8858	.8330	.7828	.7351	.6899	.6470	.6064	.5679	.5314
1	.0571	.1085	.1546	.1957	.2321	.2642	.2922	.3164	.3370	.3543
2	.0014	.0055	.0120	.0204	.0305	.0422	.0550	.0688	.0833	.0984
3	.0000	.0002	.0005	.0011	.0021	.0036	.0055	.0080	.0110	.0146
4	.0000	.0000	.0000	.0000	.0001	.0002	.0003	.0005	.0008	.0012
5	.0000	.0000	.0000	.0000	.0000	.0000	.0000	.0000	.0000	.0001

r \ p	.11	.12	.13	.14	.15	.16	.17	.18	.19	.20
0	.4970	.4644	.4336	.4046	.3771	.3513	.3269	.3040	.2824	.2621
1	.3685	.3800	.3888	.3952	.3993	.4015	.4018	.4004	.3975	.3932
2	.1139	.1295	.1452	.1608	.1762	.1912	.2057	.2197	.2331	.2458
3	.0188	.0236	.0289	.0349	.0415	.0486	.0562	.0643	.0729	.0819
4	.0017	.0024	.0032	.0043	.0055	.0069	.0086	.0106	.0128	.0154
5	.0001	.0001	.0002	.0003	.0004	.0005	.0007	.0009	.0012	.0015
6	.0000	.0000	.0000	.0000	.0000	.0000	.0000	.0000	.0000	.0001

r \ p	.21	.22	.23	.24	.25	.26	.27	.28	.29	.30
0	.2431	.2252	.2084	.1927	.1780	.1642	.1513	.1393	.1281	.1176
1	.3877	.3811	.3735	.3651	.3560	.3462	.3358	.3251	.3139	.3025
2	.2577	.2687	.2789	.2882	.2966	.3041	.3105	.3160	.3206	.3241
3	.0913	.1011	.1111	.1214	.1318	.1424	.1531	.1639	.1746	.1852
4	.0182	.0214	.0249	.0287	.0330	.0375	.0425	.0478	.0535	.0595
5	.0019	.0024	.0030	.0036	.0044	.0053	.0063	.0074	.0087	.0102
6	.0001	.0001	.0001	.0002	.0002	.0003	.0004	.0005	.0006	.0007

Table C 549

n = 6 (Continued)

r \ p	.31	.32	.33	.34	.35	.36	.37	.38	.39	.40
0	.1079	.0989	.0905	.0827	.0754	.0687	.0625	.0568	.0515	.0467
1	.2909	.2792	.2673	.2555	.2437	.2319	.2203	.2089	.1976	.1866
2	.3267	.3284	.3292	.3290	.3280	.3261	.3235	.3201	.3159	.3110
3	.1957	.2061	.2162	.2260	.2355	.2446	.2533	.2616	.2693	.2765
4	.0660	.0727	.0799	.0873	.0951	.1032	.1116	.1202	.1291	.1382
5	.0119	.0137	.0157	.0180	.0205	.0232	.0262	.0295	.0330	.0369
6	.0009	.0011	.0013	.0015	.0018	.0022	.0026	.0030	.0035	.0041

r \ p	.41	.42	.43	.44	.45	.46	.47	.48	.49	.50
0	.0422	.0381	.0343	.0308	.0277	.0248	.0222	.0198	.0176	.0156
1	.1759	.1654	.1552	.1454	.1359	.1267	.1179	.1095	.1014	.0938
2	.3055	.2994	.2928	.2856	.2780	.2699	.2615	.2527	.2436	.2344
3	.2831	.2891	.2945	.2992	.3032	.3065	.3091	.3110	.3121	.3125
4	.1475	.1570	.1666	.1763	.1861	.1958	.2056	.2153	.2249	.2344
5	.0410	.0455	.0503	.0554	.0609	.0667	.0729	.0795	.0864	.0938
6	.0048	.0055	.0063	.0073	.0083	.0095	.0108	.0122	.0138	.0156

n = 7

r \ p	.01	.02	.03	.04	.05	.06	.07	.08	.09	.10
0	.9321	.8681	.8080	.7514	.6983	.6485	.6017	.5578	.5168	.4783
1	.0659	.1240	.1749	.2192	.2573	.2897	.3170	.3396	.3578	.3720
2	.0020	.0076	.0162	.0274	.0406	.0555	.0716	.0886	.1061	.1240
3	.0000	.0003	.0008	.0019	.0036	.0059	.0090	.0128	.0175	.0230
4	.0000	.0000	.0000	.0001	.0002	.0004	.0007	.0011	.0017	.0026
5	.0000	.0000	.0000	.0000	.0000	.0000	.0000	.0001	.0001	.0002

r \ p	.11	.12	.13	.14	.15	.16	.17	.18	.19	.20
0	.4423	.4087	.3773	.3479	.3206	.2951	.2714	.2493	.2288	.2097
1	.3827	.3901	.3946	.3965	.3960	.3935	.3891	.3830	.3756	.3670
2	.1419	.1596	.1769	.1936	.2097	.2248	.2391	.2523	.2643	.2753
3	.0292	.0363	.0441	.0525	.0617	.0714	.0816	.0923	.1033	.1147
4	.0036	.0049	.0066	.0086	.0109	.0136	.0167	.0203	.0242	.0287
5	.0003	.0004	.0006	.0008	.0012	.0016	.0021	.0027	.0034	.0043
6	.0000	.0000	.0000	.0000	.0001	.0001	.0001	.0002	.0003	.0004

r \ p	.21	.22	.23	.24	.25	.26	.27	.28	.29	.30
0	.1920	.1757	.1605	.1465	.1335	.1215	.1105	.1003	.0910	.0824
1	.3573	.3468	.3356	.3237	.3115	.2989	.2860	.2731	.2600	.2471
2	.2850	.2935	.3007	.3067	.3115	.3150	.3174	.3186	.3186	.3177
3	.1263	.1379	.1497	.1614	.1730	.1845	.1956	.2065	.2169	.2269
4	.0336	.0389	.0447	.0510	.0577	.0648	.0724	.0803	.0886	.0972
5	.0054	.0066	.0080	.0097	.0115	.0137	.0161	.0187	.0217	.0250
6	.0005	.0006	.0008	.0010	.0013	.0016	.0020	.0024	.0030	.0036
7	.0000	.0000	.0000	.0000	.0001	.0001	.0001	.0001	.0002	.0002

r \ p	.31	.32	.33	.34	.35	.36	.37	.38	.39	.40
0	.0745	.0672	.0606	.0546	.0490	.0440	.0394	.0352	.0314	.0280
1	.2342	.2215	.2090	.1967	.1848	.1732	.1619	.1511	.1407	.1306
2	.3156	.3127	.3088	.3040	.2985	.2922	.2853	.2778	.2698	.2613
3	.2363	.2452	.2535	.2610	.2679	.2740	.2793	.2838	.2875	.2903
4	.1062	.1154	.1248	.1345	.1442	.1541	.1640	.1739	.1838	.1935
5	.0286	.0326	.0369	.0416	.0466	.0520	.0578	.0640	.0705	.0774
6	.0043	.0051	.0061	.0071	.0084	.0098	.0113	.0131	.0150	.0172
7	.0003	.0003	.0004	.0005	.0006	.0008	.0009	.0011	.0014	.0016

r \ p	.41	.42	.43	.44	.45	.46	.47	.48	.49	.50
0	.0249	.0221	.0195	.0173	.0152	.0134	.0117	.0103	.0090	.0078
1	.1211	.1119	.1032	.0950	.0872	.0798	.0729	.0664	.0604	.0547
2	.2524	.2431	.2336	.2239	.2140	.2040	.1940	.1840	.1740	.1641
3	.2923	.2934	.2937	.2932	.2918	.2897	.2867	.2830	.2786	.2734
4	.2031	.2125	.2216	.2304	.2388	.2468	.2543	.2612	.2676	.2734
5	.0847	.0923	.1003	.1086	.1172	.1261	.1353	.1447	.1543	.1641
6	.0196	.0223	.0252	.0284	.0320	.0358	.0400	.0445	.0494	.0547
7	.0019	.0023	.0027	.0032	.0037	.0044	.0051	.0059	.0068	.0078

r \ p	.01	.02	.03	.04	.05	.06	.07	.08	.09	.10
0	.9227	.8508	.7837	.7214	.6634	.6096	.5596	.5132	.4703	.4305
1	.0746	.1389	.1939	.2405	.2793	.3113	.3370	.3570	.3721	.3826
2	.0026	.0099	.0210	.0351	.0515	.0695	.0888	.1087	.1288	.1488
3	.0001	.0004	.0013	.0029	.0054	.0089	.0134	.0189	.0255	.0331
4	.0000	.0000	.0001	.0002	.0004	.0007	.0013	.0021	.0031	.0046
5	.0000	.0000	.0000	.0000	.0000	.0000	.0001	.0001	.0002	.0004

r \ p	.11	.12	.13	.14	.15	.16	.17	.18	.19	.20
0	.3937	.3596	.3282	.2992	.2725	.2479	.2252	.2044	.1853	.1678
1	.3892	.3923	.3923	.3897	.3847	.3777	.3691	.3590	.3477	.3355
2	.1684	.1872	.2052	.2220	.2376	.2518	.2646	.2758	.2855	.2936
3	.0416	.0511	.0613	.0723	.0839	.0959	.1084	.1211	.1339	.1468
4	.0064	.0087	.0115	.0147	.0185	.0228	.0277	.0332	.0393	.0459
5	.0006	.0009	.0014	.0019	.0026	.0035	.0045	.0058	.0074	.0092
6	.0000	.0001	.0001	.0002	.0002	.0003	.0005	.0006	.0009	.0011
7	.0000	.0000	.0000	.0000	.0000	.0000	.0000	.0000	.0001	.0001

r \ p	.21	.22	.23	.24	.25	.26	.27	.28	.29	.30
0	.1517	.1370	.1236	.1113	.1001	.0899	.0806	.0722	.0646	.0576
1	.3226	.3092	.2953	.2812	.2670	.2527	.2386	.2247	.2110	.1977
2	.3002	.3052	.3087	.3108	.3115	.3108	.3089	.3058	.3017	.2965
3	.1596	.1722	.1844	.1963	.2076	.2184	.2285	.2379	.2464	.2541
4	.0530	.0607	.0689	.0775	.0865	.0959	.1056	.1156	.1258	.1361
5	.0113	.0137	.0165	.0196	.0231	.0270	.0313	.0360	.0411	.0467
6	.0015	.0019	.0025	.0031	.0038	.0047	.0058	.0070	.0084	.0100
7	.0001	.0002	.0002	.0003	.0004	.0005	.0006	.0008	.0010	.0012
8	.0000	.0000	.0000	.0000	.0000	.0000	.0000	.0000	.0001	.0001

r \ p	.31	.32	.33	.34	.35	.36	.37	.38	.39	.40
0	.0514	.0457	.0406	.0360	.0319	.0281	.0248	.0218	.0192	.0168
1	.1847	.1721	.1600	.1484	.1373	.1267	.1166	.1071	.0981	.0896
2	.2904	.2835	.2758	.2675	.2587	.2494	.2397	.2297	.2194	.2090
3	.2609	.2668	.2717	.2756	.2786	.2805	.2815	.2815	.2806	.2787
4	.1465	.1569	.1673	.1775	.1875	.1973	.2067	.2157	.2242	.2322
5	.0527	.0591	.0659	.0732	.0808	.0888	.0971	.1058	.1147	.1239
6	.0118	.0139	.0162	.0188	.0217	.0250	.0285	.0324	.0367	.0413
7	.0015	.0019	.0023	.0028	.0033	.0040	.0048	.0057	.0067	.0079
8	.0001	.0001	.0001	.0002	.0002	.0003	.0004	.0004	.0005	.0007

r \ p	.41	.42	.43	.44	.45	.46	.47	.48	.49	.50
0	.0147	.0128	.0111	.0097	.0084	.0072	.0062	.0053	.0046	.0039
1	.0816	.0742	.0672	.0608	.0548	.0493	.0442	.0395	.0352	.0312
2	.1985	.1880	.1776	.1672	.1569	.1469	.1371	.1275	.1183	.1094
3	.2759	.2723	.2679	.2627	.2568	.2503	.2431	.2355	.2273	.2188
4	.2397	.2465	.2526	.2580	.2627	.2665	.2695	.2717	.2730	.2734
5	.1332	.1428	.1525	.1622	.1719	.1816	.1912	.2006	.2098	.2188
6	.0463	.0517	.0575	.0637	.0703	.0774	.0848	.0926	.1008	.1094
7	.0092	.0107	.0124	.0143	.0164	.0188	.0215	.0244	.0277	.0312
8	.0008	.0010	.0012	.0014	.0017	.0020	.0024	.0028	.0033	.0039

r \ p	.01	.02	.03	.04	.05	.06	.07	.08	.09	.10
0	.9135	.8337	.7602	.6925	.6302	.5730	.5204	.4722	.4279	.3874
1	.0830	.1531	.2116	.2597	.2985	.3292	.3525	.3695	.3809	.3874
2	.0034	.0125	.0262	.0433	.0629	.0840	.1061	.1285	.1507	.1722
3	.0001	.0006	.0019	.0042	.0077	.0125	.0186	.0261	.0348	.0446
4	.0000	.0000	.0001	.0003	.0006	.0012	.0021	.0034	.0052	.0074
5	.0000	.0000	.0000	.0000	.0000	.0001	.0002	.0003	.0005	.0008
6	.0000	.0000	.0000	.0000	.0000	.0000	.0000	.0000	.0000	.0001

Table C   551

p r	.11	.12	.13	.14	.15	.16	.17	.18	.19	.20
0	.3504	.3165	.2855	.2573	.2316	.2082	.1869	.1676	.1501	.1342
1	.3897	.3884	.3840	.3770	.3679	.3569	.3446	.3312	.3169	.3020
2	.1927	.2119	.2295	.2455	.2597	.2720	.2823	.2908	.2973	.3020
3	.0556	.0674	.0800	.0933	.1069	.1209	.1349	.1489	.1627	.1762
4	.0103	.0138	.0179	.0228	.0283	.0345	.0415	.0490	.0573	.0661
5	.0013	.0019	.0027	.0037	.0050	.0066	.0085	.0108	.0134	.0165
6	.0001	.0002	.0003	.0004	.0006	.0008	.0012	.0016	.0021	.0028
7	.0000	.0000	.0000	.0000	.0000	.0001	.0001	.0001	.0002	.0003

p r	.21	.22	.23	.24	.25	.26	.27	.28	.29	.30
0	.1199	.1069	.0952	.0846	.0751	.0665	.0589	.0520	.0458	.0404
1	.2867	.2713	.2558	.2404	.2253	.2104	.1960	.1820	.1685	.1556
2	.3049	.3061	.3056	.3037	.3003	.2957	.2899	.2831	.2754	.2668
3	.1891	.2014	.2130	.2238	.2336	.2424	.2502	.2569	.2624	.2668
4	.0754	.0852	.0954	.1060	.1168	.1278	.1388	.1499	.1608	.1715
5	.0200	.0240	.0285	.0335	.0389	.0449	.0513	.0583	.0657	.0735
6	.0036	.0045	.0057	.0070	.0087	.0105	.0127	.0151	.0179	.0210
7	.0004	.0005	.0007	.0010	.0012	.0016	.0020	.0025	.0031	.0039
8	.0000	.0000	.0001	.0001	.0001	.0001	.0002	.0002	.0003	.0004

p r	.31	.32	.33	.34	.35	.36	.37	.38	.39	.40
0	.0355	.0311	.0272	.0238	.0207	.0180	.0156	.0135	.0117	.0101
1	.1433	.1317	.1206	.1102	.1004	.0912	.0826	.0747	.0673	.0605
2	.2576	.2478	.2376	.2270	.2162	.2052	.1941	.1831	.1721	.1612
3	.2701	.2721	.2731	.2729	.2716	.2693	.2660	.2618	.2567	.2508
4	.1820	.1921	.2017	.2109	.2194	.2272	.2344	.2407	.2462	.2508
5	.0818	.0904	.0994	.1086	.1181	.1278	.1376	.1475	.1574	.1672
6	.0245	.0284	.0326	.0373	.0424	.0479	.0539	.0603	.0671	.0743
7	.0047	.0057	.0069	.0082	.0098	.0116	.0136	.0158	.0184	.0212
8	.0005	.0007	.0008	.0011	.0013	.0016	.0020	.0024	.0029	.0035
9	.0000	.0000	.0000	.0001	.0001	.0001	.0001	.0002	.0002	.0003

p r	.41	.42	.43	.44	.45	.46	.47	.48	.49	.50
0	.0087	.0074	.0064	.0054	.0046	.0039	.0033	.0028	.0023	.0020
1	.0542	.0484	.0431	.0383	.0339	.0299	.0263	.0231	.0202	.0176
2	.1506	.1402	.1301	.1204	.1110	.1020	.0934	.0853	.0776	.0703
3	.2442	.2369	.2291	.2207	.2119	.2027	.1933	.1837	.1739	.1641
4	.2545	.2573	.2592	.2601	.2600	.2590	.2571	.2543	.2506	.2461
5	.1769	.1863	.1955	.2044	.2128	.2207	.2280	.2347	.2408	.2461
6	.0819	.0900	.0983	.1070	.1160	.1253	.1348	.1445	.1542	.1641
7	.0244	.0279	.0318	.0360	.0407	.0458	.0512	.0571	.0635	.0703
8	.0042	.0051	.0060	.0071	.0083	.0097	.0114	.0132	.0153	.0176
9	.0003	.0004	.0005	.0006	.0008	.0009	.0011	.0014	.0016	.0020

p r	.01	.02	.03	.04	.05	.06	.07	.08	.09	.10
0	.9044	.8171	.7374	.6648	.5987	.5386	.4840	.4344	.3894	.3487
1	.0914	.1667	.2281	.2770	.3151	.3438	.3643	.3777	.3851	.3874
2	.0042	.0153	.0317	.0519	.0746	.0988	.1234	.1478	.1714	.1937
3	.0001	.0008	.0026	.0058	.0105	.0168	.0248	.0343	.0452	.0574
4	.0000	.0000	.0001	.0004	.0010	.0019	.0033	.0052	.0078	.0112
5	.0000	.0000	.0000	.0000	.0001	.0001	.0003	.0005	.0009	.0015
6	.0000	.0000	.0000	.0000	.0000	.0000	.0000	.0000	.0001	.0001

p r	.11	.12	.13	.14	.15	.16	.17	.18	.19	.20
0	.3118	.2785	.2484	.2213	.1969	.1749	.1552	.1374	.1216	.1074
1	.3854	.3798	.3712	.3603	.3474	.3331	.3178	.3017	.2852	.2684
2	.2143	.2330	.2496	.2639	.2759	.2856	.2929	.2980	.3010	.3020
3	.0706	.0847	.0995	.1146	.1298	.1450	.1600	.1745	.1883	.2013
4	.0153	.0202	.0260	.0326	.0401	.0483	.0573	.0670	.0773	.0881
5	.0023	.0033	.0047	.0064	.0085	.0111	.0141	.0177	.0218	.0264
6	.0002	.0004	.0006	.0009.	.0012	.0018	.0024	.0032	.0043	.0055
7	.0000	.0000	.0000	.0001	.0001	.0002	.0003	.0004	.0006	.0008
8	.0000	.0000	.0000	.0000	.0000	.0000	.0000	.0000	.0001	.0001

Table C

r \ p	.21	.22	.23	.24	.25	.26	.27	.28	.29	.30
0	.0947	.0834	.0733	.0643	.0563	.0492	.0430	.0374	.0326	.0282
1	.2517	.2351	.2188	.2030	.1877	.1730	.1590	.1456	.1330	.1211
2	.3011	.2984	.2942	.2885	.2816	.2735	.2646	.2548	.2444	.2335
3	.2134	.2244	.2343	.2429	.2503	.2563	.2609	.2642	.2662	.2668
4	.0993	.1108	.1225	.1343	.1460	.1576	.1689	.1798	.1903	.2001
5	.0317	.0375	.0439	.0509	.0584	.0664	.0750	.0839	.0933	.1029
6	.0070	.0088	.0109	.0134	.0162	.0195	.0231	.0272	.0317	.0368
7	.0011	.0014	.0019	.0024	.0031	.0039	.0049	.0060	.0074	.0090
8	.0001	.0002	.0002	.0003	.0004	.0005	.0007	.0009	.0011	.0014
9	.0000	.0000	.0000	.0000	.0000	.0000	.0001	.0001	.0001	.0001

r \ p	.31	.32	.33	.34	.35	.36	.37	.38	.39	.40
0	.0245	.0211	.0182	.0157	.0135	.0115	.0098	.0084	.0071	.0060
1	.1099	.0995	.0898	.0808	.0725	.0649	.0578	.0514	.0456	.0403
2	.2222	.2107	.1990	.0873	.1757	.1642	.1529	.1419	.1312	.1209
3	.2662	.2644	.2614	.2573	.2522	.2462	.2394	.2319	.2237	.2150
4	.2093	.2177	.2253	.2320	.2377	.2424	.2461	.2487	.2503	.2508
5	.1128	.1229	.1332	.1434	.1536	.1636	.1734	.1829	.1920	.2007
6	.0422	.0482	.0547	.0616	.0689	.0767	.0849	.0934	.1023	.1115
7	.0108	.0130	.0154	.0181	.0212	.0247	.0285	.0327	.0374	.0425
8	.0018	.0023	.0028	.0035	.0043	.0052	.0063	.0075	.0090	.0106
9	.0002	.0002	.0003	.0004	.0005	.0006	.0008	.0010	.0013	.0016
10	.0000	.0000	.0000	.0000	.0000	.0000	.0000	.0001	.0001	.0001

r \ p	.41	.42	.43	.44	.45	.46	.47	.48	.49	.50
0	.0051	.0043	.0036	.0030	.0025	.0021	.0017	.0014	.0012	.0010
1	.0355	.0312	.0273	.0238	.0207	.0180	.0155	.0133	.0114	.0098
2	.1111	.1017	.0927	.0843	.0763	.0688	.0619	.0554	.0494	.0439
3	.2058	.1963	.1865	.1765	.1665	.1564	.1464	.1364	.1267	.1172
4	.2503	.2488	.2462	.2427	.2384	.2331	.2271	.2204	.2130	.2051
5	.2087	.2162	.2229	.2289	.2340	.2383	.2417	.2441	.2456	.2461
6	.1209	.1304	.1401	.1499	.1596	.1692	.1786	.1878	.1966	.2051
7	.0480	.0540	.0604	.0673	.0746	.0824	.0905	.0991	.1080	.1172
8	.0125	.0147	.0171	.0198	.0229	.0263	.0301	.0343	.0389	.0439
9	.0019	.0024	.0029	.0035	.0042	.0050	.0059	.0070	.0083	.0098
10	.0001	.0002	.0002	.0003	.0003	.0004	.0005	.0006	.0008	.0010

r \ p	.01	.02	.03	.04	.05	.06	.07	.08	.09	.10
0	.8953	.8007	.7153	.6382	.5688	.5063	.4501	.3996	.3544	.3138
1	.0995	.1798	.2433	.2925	.3293	.3555	.3727	.3823	.3855	.3835
2	.0050	.0183	.0376	.0609	.0867	.1135	.1403	.1662	.1906	.2131
3	.0002	.0011	.0035	.0076	.0137	.0217	.0317	.0434	.0566	.0710
4	.0000	.0000	.0002	.0006	.0014	.0028	.0048	.0075	.0112	.0158
5	.0000	.0000	.0000	.0000	.0001	.0002	.0005	.0009	.0015	.0025
6	.0000	.0000	.0000	.0000	.0000	.0000	.0000	.0001	.0002	.0003

r \ p	.11	.12	.13	.14	.15	.16	.17	.18	.19	.20
0	.2775	.2451	.2161	.1903	.1673	.1469	.1288	.1127	.0985	.0859
1	.3773	.3676	.3552	.3408	.3248	.3078	.2901	.2721	.2541	.2362
2	.2332	.2507	.2654	.2774	.2866	.2932	.2971	.2987	.2980	.2953
3	.0865	.1025	.1190	.1355	.1517	.1675	.1826	.1967	.2097	.2215
4	.0214	.0280	.0356	.0441	.0536	.0638	.0748	.0864	.0984	.1107
5	.0037	.0053	.0074	.0101	.0132	.0170	.0214	.0265	.0323	.0388
6	.0005	.0007	.0011	.0016	.0023	.0032	.0044	.0058	.0076	.0097
7	.0000	.0001	.0001	.0002	.0003	.0004	.0006	.0009	.0013	.0017
8	.0000	.0000	.0000	.0000	.0000	.0000	.0001	.0001	.0001	.0002

Table C 553

r\p	.21	.22	.23	.24	.25	.26	.27	.28	.29	.30
0	.0748	.0650	.0564	.0489	.0422	.0364	.0314	.0270	.0231	.0198
1	.2187	.2017	.1854	.1697	.1549	.1408	.1276	.1153	.1038	.0932
2	.2907	.2845	.2768	.2680	.2581	.2474	.2360	.2242	.2121	.1998
3	.2318	.2407	.2481	.2539	.2581	.2608	.2619	.2616	.2599	.2568
4	.1232	.1358	.1482	.1603	.1721	.1832	.1937	.2035	.2123	.2201
5	.0459	.0536	.0620	.0709	.0803	.0901	.1003	.1108	.1214	.1321
6	.0122	.0151	.0185	.0224	.0268	.0317	.0371	.0431	.0496	.0566
7	.0023	.0030	.0039	.0050	.0064	.0079	.0098	.0120	.0145	.0173
8	.0003	.0004	.0006	.0008	.0011	.0014	.0018	.0023	.0030	.0037
9	.0000	.0000	.0001	.0001	.0001	.0002	.0002	.0003	.0004	.0005

r\p	.31	.32	.33	.34	.35	.36	.37	.38	.39	.40
0	.0169	.0144	.0122	.0104	.0088	.0074	.0062	.0052	.0044	.0036
1	.0834	.0744	.0662	.0587	.0518	.0457	.0401	.0351	.0306	.0266
2	.1874	.1751	.1630	.1511	.1395	.1284	.1177	.1075	.0978	.0887
3	.2526	.2472	.2408	.2335	.2254	.2167	.2074	.1977	.1876	.1774
4	.2269	.2326	.2372	.2406	.2428	.2438	.2436	.2423	.2399	.2365
5	.1427	.1533	.1636	.1735	.1830	.1920	.2003	.2079	.2148	.2207
6	.0641	.0721	.0806	.0894	.0985	.1080	.1176	.1274	.1373	.1471
7	.0206	.0242	.0283	.0329	.0379	.0434	.0494	.0558	.0627	.0701
8	.0046	.0057	.0070	.0085	.0102	.0122	.0145	.0171	.0200	.0234
9	.0007	.0009	.0011	.0015	.0018	.0023	.0028	.0035	.0043	.0052
10	.0001	.0001	.0001	.0001	.0002	.0003	.0003	.0004	.0005	.0007

r\p	.41	.42	.43	.44	.45	.46	.47	.48	.49	.50
0	.0030	.0025	.0021	.0017	.0014	.0011	.0009	.0008	.0006	.0005
1	.0231	.0199	.0171	.0147	.0125	.0107	.0090	.0076	.0064	.0054
2	.0801	.0721	.0646	.0577	.0513	.0454	.0401	.0352	.0308	.0269
3	.1670	.1566	.1462	.1359	.1259	.1161	.1067	.0976	.0888	.0806
4	.2321	.2267	.2206	.2136	.2060	.1978	.1892	.1801	.1707	.1611
5	.2258	.2299	.2329	.2350	.2360	.2359	.2348	.2327	.2296	.2256
6	.1569	.1664	.1757	.1846	.1931	.2010	.2083	.2148	.2206	.2256
7	.0779	.0861	.0947	.1036	.1128	.1223	.1319	.1416	.1514	.1611
8	.0271	.0312	.0357	.0407	.0462	.0521	.0585	.0654	.0727	.0806
9	.0063	.0075	.0090	.0107	.0126	.0148	.0173	.0201	.0233	.0269
10	.0009	.0011	.0014	.0017	.0021	.0025	.0031	.0037	.0045	.0054
11	.0001	.0001	.0001	.0001	.0002	.0002	.0002	.0003	.0004	.0005

r\p	.01	.02	.03	.04	.05	.06	.07	.08	.09	.10
0	.8864	.7847	.6938	.6127	.5404	.4759	.4186	.3677	.3225	.2824
1	.1074	.1922	.2575	.3064	.3413	.3645	.3781	.3837	.3827	.3766
2	.0060	.0216	.0438	.0702	.0988	.1280	.1565	.1835	.2082	.2301
3	.0002	.0015	.0045	.0098	.0173	.0272	.0393	.0532	.0686	.0852
4	.0000	.0001	.0003	.0009	.0021	.0039	.0067	.0104	.0153	.0213
5	.0000	.0000	.0000	.0001	.0002	.0004	.0008	.0014	.0024	.0038
6	.0000	.0000	.0000	.0000	.0000	.0000	.0001	.0001	.0003	.0005

r\p	.11	.12	.13	.14	.15	.16	.17	.18	.19	.20
0	.2470	.2157	.1880	.1637	.1422	.1234	.1069	.0924	.0798	.0687
1	.3663	.3529	.3372	.3197	.3012	.2821	.2627	.2434	.2245	.2062
2	.2490	.2647	.2771	.2863	.2924	.2955	.2960	.2939	.2897	.2835
3	.1026	.1203	.1380	.1553	.1720	.1876	.2021	.2151	.2265	.2362
4	.0285	.0369	.0464	.0569	.0683	.0804	.0931	.1062	.1195	.1329
5	.0056	.0081	.0111	.0148	.0193	.0245	.0305	.0373	.0449	.0532
6	.0008	.0013	.0019	.0028	.0040	.0054	.0073	.0096	.0123	.0155
7	.0001	.0001	.0002	.0004	.0006	.0009	.0013	.0018	.0025	.0033
8	.0000	.0000	.0000	.0000	.0001	.0001	.0002	.0002	.0004	.0005
9	.0000	.0000	.0000	.0000	.0000	.00000	.0000	.0000	.0000	.0001

r \ p	.21	.22	.23	.24	.25	.26	.27	.28	.29	.30
0	.0591	.0507	.0434	.0371	.0317	.0270	.0229	.0194	.0164	.0138
1	.1885	.1717	.1557	.1407	.1267	.1137	.1016	.0906	.0804	.0712
2	.2756	.2663	.2558	.2444	.2323	.2197	.2068	.1937	.1807	.1678
3	.2442	.2503	.2547	.2573	.2581	.2573	.2549	.2511	.2460	.2397
4	.1460	.1589	.1712	.1828	.1936	.2034	.2122	.2197	.2261	.2311
5	.0621	.0717	.0818	.0924	.1032	.1143	.1255	.1367	.1477	.1585
6	.0193	.0236	.0285	.0340	.0401	.0469	.0542	.0620	.0704	.0792
7	.0044	.0057	.0073	.0092	.0115	.0141	.0172	.0207	.0246	.0291
8	.0007	.0010	.0014	.0018	.0024	.0031	.0040	.0050	.0063	.0078
9	.0001	.0001	.0002	.0003	.0004	.0005	.0007	.0009	.0011	.0015
10	.0000	.0000	.0000	.0000	.0000	.0001	.0001	.0001	.0001	.0002

r \ p	.31	.32	.33	.34	.35	.36	.37	.38	.39	.40
0	.0116	.0098	.0082	.0068	.0057	.0047	.0039	.0032	.0027	.0022
1	.0628	.0552	.0484	.0422	.0368	.0319	.0276	.0237	.0204	.0174
2	.1552	.1429	.1310	.1197	.1088	.0986	.0890	.0800	.0716	.0639
3	.2324	.2241	.2151	.2055	.1954	.1849	.1742	.1634	.1526	.1419
4	.2349	.2373	.2384	.2382	.2367	.2340	.2302	.2254	.2195	.2128
5	.1688	.1787	.1879	.1963	.2039	.2106	.2163	.2210	.2246	.2270
6	.0885	.0981	.1079	.1180	.1281	.1382	.1482	.1580	.1675	.1766
7	.0341	.0396	.0456	.0521	.0591	.0666	.0746	.0830	.0918	.1009
8	.0096	.0116	.0140	.0168	.0199	.0234	.0274	.0318	.0367	.0420
9	.0019	.0024	.0031	.0038	.0048	.0059	.0071	.0087	.0104	.0125
10	.0003	.0003	.0005	.0006	.0008	.0010	.0013	.0016	.0020	.0025
11	.0000	.0000	.0000	.0001	.0001	.0001	.0001	.0002	.0002	.0003

r \ p	.41	.42	.43	.44	.45	.46	.47	.48	.49	.50
0	.0018	.0014	.0012	.0010	.0008	.0006	.0005	.0004	.0003	.0002
1	.0148	.0126	.0106	.0090	.0075	.0063	.0052	.0043	.0036	.0029
2	.0567	.0502	.0442	.0388	.0339	.0294	.0255	.0220	.0189	.0161
3	.1314	.1211	.1111	.1015	.0923	.0836	.0754	.0676	.0604	.0537
4	.2054	.1973	.1886	.1794	.1700	.1602	.1504	.1405	.1306	.1208
5	.2284	.2285	.2276	.2256	.2225	.2184	.2134	.2075	.2008	.1934
6	.1851	.1931	.2003	.2068	.2124	.2171	.2208	.2234	.2250	.2256
7	.1103	.1198	.1295	.1393	.1489	.1585	.1678	.1768	.1853	.1934
8	.0479	.0542	.0611	.0684	.0762	.0844	.0930	.1020	.1113	.1208
9	.0148	.0175	.0205	.0239	.0277	.0319	.0367	.0418	.0475	.0537
10	.0031	.0038	.0046	.0056	.0068	.0082	.0098	.0116	.0137	.0161
11	.0004	.0005	.0006	.0008	.0010	.0013	.0016	.0019	.0024	.0029
12	.0000	.0000	.0000	.0001	.0001	.0001	.0001	.0001	.0002	.0002

n = 13

r \ p	.01	.02	.03	.04	.05	.06	.07	.08	.09	.10
0	.8775	.7690	.6730	.5882	.5133	.4474	.3893	.3383	.2935	.2542
1	.1152	.2040	.2706	.3186	.3512	.3712	.3809	.3824	.3773	.3672
2	.0070	.0250	.0502	.0797	.1109	.1422	.1720	.1995	.2239	.2448
3	.0003	.0019	.0057	.0122	.0214	.0333	.0475	.0636	.0812	.0997
4	.0000	.0001	.0004	.0013	.0028	.0053	.0089	.0138	.0201	.0277
5	.0000	.0000	.0000	.0001	.0003	.0006	.0012	.0022	.0036	.0055
6	.0000	.0000	.0000	.0000	.0000	.0001	.0001	.0003	.0005	.0008
7	.0000	.0000	.0000	.0000	.0000	.0000	.0000	.0000	.0000	.0001

r \ p	.11	.12	.13	.14	.15	.16	.17	.18	.19	.20
0	.2198	.1898	.1636	.1408	.1209	.1037	.0887	.0758	.0646	.0550
1	.3532	.3364	.3178	.2979	.2774	.2567	.2362	.2163	.1970	.1787
2	.2619	.2753	.2849	.2910	.2937	.2934	.2903	.2848	.2773	.2680
3	.1187	.1376	.1561	.1737	.1900	.2049	.2180	.2293	.2385	.2457
4	.0367	.0469	.0583	.0707	.0838	.0976	.1116	.1258	.1399	.1535
5	.0082	.0115	.0157	.0207	.0266	.0335	.0412	.0497	.0591	.0691
6	.0013	.0021	.0031	.0045	.0063	.0085	.0112	.0145	.0185	.0230
7	.0002	.0003	.0005	.0007	.0011	.0016	.0023	.0032	.0043	.0058
8	.0000	.0000	.0001	.0001	.0001	.0002	.0004	.0005	.0008	.0011
9	.0000	.0000	.0000	.0000	.0000	.0000	.0000	.0001	.0001	.0001

Table C 555

r \ p	.21	.22	.23	.24	.25	.26	.27	.28	.29	.30
0	.0467	.0396	.0334	.0282	.0238	.0200	.0167	.0140	.0117	.0097
1	.1613	.1450	.1299	.1159	.1029	.0911	.0804	.0706	.0619	.0540
2	.2573	.2455	.2328	.2195	.2059	.1921	.1784	.1648	.1516	.1388
3	.2508	.2539	.2550	.2542	.2517	.2475	.2419	.2351	.2271	.2181
4	.1667	.1790	.1904	.2007	.2097	.2174	.2237	.2285	.2319	.2337
5	.0797	.0909	.1024	.1141	.1258	.1375	.1489	.1600	.1705	.1803
6	.0283	.0342	.0408	.0480	.0559	.0644	.0734	.0829	.0928	.1030
7	.0075	.0096	.0122	.0152	.0186	.0226	.0272	.0323	.0379	.0442
8	.0015	.0020	.0027	.0036	.0047	.0060	.0075	.0094	.0116	.0142
9	.0002	.0003	.0005	.0006	.0009	.0012	.0015	.0020	.0026	.0034
10	.0000	.0000	.0001	.0001	.0001	.0002	.0002	.0003	.0004	.0006
11	.0000	.0000	.0000	.0000	.0000	.0000	.0000	.0000	.0000	.0001

r \ p	.31	.32	.33	.34	.35	.36	.37	.38	.39	.40
0	.0080	.0066	.0055	.0045	.0037	.0030	.0025	.0020	.0016	.0013
1	.0469	.0407	.0351	.0302	.0259	.0221	.0188	.0159	.0135	.0113
2	.1265	.1148	.1037	.0933	.0836	.0746	.0663	.0586	.0516	.0453
3	.2084	.1981	.1874	.1763	.1651	.1538	.1427	.1317	.1210	.1107
4	.2341	.2331	.2307	.2270	.2222	.2163	.2095	.2018	.1934	.1845
5	.1893	.1974	.2045	.2105	.2154	.2190	.2215	.2227	.2226	.2214
6	.1134	.1239	.1343	.1446	.1546	.1643	.1734	.1820	.1898	.1968
7	.0509	.0583	.0662	.0745	.0833	.0924	.1019	.1115	.1213	.1312
8	.0172	.0206	.0244	.0288	.0336	.0390	.0449	.0513	.0582	.0656
9	.0043	.0054	.0067	.0082	.0101	.0122	.0146	.0175	.0207	.0243
10	.0008	.0010	.0013	.0017	.0022	.0027	.0034	.0043	.0053	.0065
11	.0001	.0001	.0002	.0002	.0003	.0004	.0006	.0007	.0009	.0012
12	.0000	.0000	.0000	.0000	.0000	.0000	.0001	.0001	.0001	.0001

r \ p	.41	.42	.43	.44	.45	.46	.47	.48	.49	.50
0	.0010	.0008	.0007	.0005	.0004	.0003	.0003	.0002	.0002	.0001
1	.0095	.0079	.0066	.0054	.0045	.0037	.0030	.0024	.0020	.0016
2	.0395	.0344	.0298	.0256	.0220	.0188	.0160	.0135	.0114	.0095
3	.1007	.0913	.0823	.0739	.0660	.0587	.0519	.0457	.0401	.0349
4	.1750	.1653	.1553	.1451	.1350	.1250	.1151	.1055	.0962	.0873
5	.2189	.2154	.2108	.2053	.1989	.1917	.1838	.1753	.1664	.1571
6	.2029	.2080	.2121	.2151	.2169	.2177	.2173	.2158	.2131	.2095
7	.1410	.1506	.1600	.1690	.1775	.1854	.1927	.1992	.2048	.2095
8	.0735	.0818	.0905	.0996	.1089	.1185	.1282	.1379	.1476	.1571
9	.0284	.0329	.0379	.0435	.0495	.0561	.0631	.0707	.0788	.0873
10	.0079	.0095	.0114	.0137	.0162	.0191	.0224	.0261	.0303	.0349
11	.0015	.0019	.0024	.0029	.0036	.0044	.0054	.0066	.0079	.0095
12	.0002	.0002	.0003	.0004	.0005	.0006	.0008	.0010	.0013	.0016
13	.0000	.0000	.0000	.0000	.0000	.0000	.0001	.0001	.0001	.0001

n = 14

r \ p	.01	.02	.03	.04	.05	.06	.07	.08	.09	.10
0	.8687	.7536	.6528	.5647	.4877	.4205	.3620	.3112	.2670	.2288
1	.1229	.2153	.2827	.3294	.3593	.3758	.3815	.3788	.3698	.3559
2	.0081	.0286	.0568	.0892	.1229	.1559	.1867	.2141	.2377	.2570
3	.0003	.0023	.0070	.0149	.0259	.0398	.0562	.0745	.0940	.1142
4	.0000	.0001	.0006	.0017	.0037	.0070	.0116	.0178	.0256	.0349
5	.0000	.0000	.0000	.0001	.0004	.0009	.0018	.0031	.0051	.0078
6	.0000	.0000	.0000	.0000	.0000	.0001	.0002	.0004	.0008	.0013
7	.0000	.0000	.0000	.0000	.0000	.0000	.0000	.0000	.0001	.0002

r \ p	.11	.12	.13	.14	.15	.16	.17	.18	.19	.20
0	.1956	.1670	.1423	.1211	.1028	.0871	.0736	.0621	.0523	.0440
1	.3385	.3188	.2977	.2759	.2539	.2322	.2112	.1910	.1719	.1539
2	.2720	.2826	.2892	.2919	.2912	.2875	.2811	.2725	.2620	.2501
3	.1345	.1542	.1728	.1901	.2056	.2190	.2303	.2393	.2459	.2501
4	.0457	.0578	.0710	.0851	.0998	.1147	.1297	.1444	.1586	.1720
5	.0113	.0158	.0212	.0277	.0352	.0437	.0531	.0634	.0744	.0860
6	.0021	.0032	.0048	.0068	.0093	.0125	.0163	.0209	.0262	.0322
7	.0003	.0005	.0008	.0013	.0019	.0027	.0038	.0052	.0070	.0092
8	.0000	.0001	.0001	.0002	.0003	.0005	.0007	.0010	.0014	.0020
9	.0000	.0000	.0000	.0000	.0000	.0001	.0001	.0001	.0002	.0003

 Table C

r \ p	.21	.22	.23	.24	.25	.26	.27	.28	.29	.30
0	.0369	.0309	.0258	.0214	.0178	.0148	.0122	.0101	.0083	.0068
1	.1372	.1218	.1077	.0948	.0832	.0726	.0632	.0548	.0473	.0407
2	.2371	.2234	.2091	.1946	.1802	.1659	.1519	.1385	.1256	.1134
3	.2521	.2520	.2499	.2459	.2402	.2331	.2248	.2154	.2052	.1943
4	.1843	.1955	.2052	.2135	.2202	.2252	.2286	.2304	.2305	.2290
5	.0980	.1103	.1226	.1348	.1468	.1583	.1691	.1792	.1883	.1963
6	.0391	.0466	.0549	.0639	.0734	.0834	.0938	.1045	.1153	.1262
7	.0119	.0150	.0188	.0231	.0280	.0335	.0397	.0464	.0538	.0618
8	.0028	.0037	.0049	.0064	.0082	.0103	.0128	.0158	.0192	.0232
9	.0005	.0007	.0010	.0013	.0018	.0024	.0032	.0041	.0052	.0066
10	.0001	.0001	.0001	.0002	.0003	.0004	.0006	.0008	.0011	.0014
11	.0000	.0000	.0000	.0000	.0000	.0001	.0001	.0001	.0002	.0002

r \ p	.31	.32	.33	.34	.35	.36	.37	.38	.39	.40
0	.0055	.0045	.0037	.0030	.0024	.0019	.0016	.0012	.0010	.0008
1	.0349	.0298	.0253	.0215	.0181	.0152	.0128	.0106	.0088	.0073
2	.1018	.0911	.0811	.0719	.0634	.0557	.0487	.0424	.0367	.0317
3	.1830	.1715	.1598	.1481	.1366	.1253	.1144	.1039	.0940	.0845
4	.2261	.2219	.2164	.2098	.2022	.1938	.1848	.1752	.1652	.1549
5	.2032	.2088	.2132	.2161	.2178	.2181	.2170	.2147	.2112	.2066
6	.1369	.1474	.1575	.1670	.1759	.1840	.1912	.1974	.2026	.2066
7	.0703	.0793	.0886	.0983	.1082	.1183	.1283	.1383	.1480	.1574
8	.0276	.0326	.0382	.0443	.0510	.0582	.0659	.0742	.0828	.0918
9	.0083	.0102	.0125	.0152	.0183	.0218	.0258	.0303	.0353	.0408
10	.0019	.0024	.0031	.0039	.0049	.0061	.0076	.0093	.0113	.0136
11	.0003	.0004	.0006	.0007	.0010	.0013	.0016	.0021	.0026	.0033
12	.0000	.0000	.0001	.0001	.0001	.0002	.0002	.0003	.0004	.0005
13	.0000	.0000	.0000	.0000	.0000	.0000	.0000	.0000	.0000	.0001

r \ p	.41	.42	.43	.44	.45	.46	.47	.48	.49	.50
0	.0006	.0005	.0004	.0003	.0002	.0002	.0001	.0001	.0001	.0001
1	.0060	.0049	.0040	.0033	.0027	.0021	.0017	.0014	.0011	.0009
2	.0272	.0233	.0198	.0168	.0141	.0118	.0099	.0082	.0068	.0056
3	.0757	.0674	.0597	.0527	.0462	.0403	.0350	.0303	.0260	.0222
4	.1446	.1342	.1239	.1138	.1040	.0945	.0854	.0768	.0687	.0611
5	.2009	.1943	.1869	.1788	.1701	.1610	.1515	.1418	.1320	.1222
6	.2094	.2111	.2115	.2108	.2088	.2057	.2015	.1963	.1902	.1833
7	.1663	.1747	.1824	.1892	.1952	.2003	.2043	.2071	.2089	.2095
8	.1011	.1107	.1204	.1301	.1398	.1493	.1585	.1673	.1756	.1833
9	.0469	.0534	.0605	.0682	.0762	.0848	.0937	.1030	.1125	.1222
10	.0163	.0193	.0228	.0268	.0312	.0361	.0415	.0475	.0540	.0611
11	.0041	.0051	.0063	.0076	.0093	.0112	.0134	.0160	.0189	.0222
12	.0007	.0009	.0012	.0015	.0019	.0024	.0030	.0037	.0045	.0056
13	.0001	.0001	.0001	.0002	.0002	.0003	.0004	.0005	.0007	.0009
14	.0000	.0000	.0000	.0000	.0000	.0000	.0000	.0000	.0000	.0001

n = 15

r \ p	.01	.02	.03	.04	.05	.06	.07	.08	.09	.10
0	.8601	.7386	.6333	.5421	.4633	.3953	.3367	.2863	.2430	.2059
1	.1303	.2261	.2938	.3388	.3658	.3785	.3801	.3734	.3605	.3432
2	.0092	.0323	.0636	.0988	.1348	.1691	.2003	.2273	.2496	.2669
3	.0004	.0029	.0085	.0178	.0307	.0468	.0653	.0857	.1070	.1285
4	.0000	.0002	.0008	.0022	.0049	.0090	.0148	.0223	.0317	.0428
5	.0000	.0000	.0001	.0002	.0006	.0013	.0024	.0043	.0069	.0105
6	.0000	.0000	.0000	.0000	.0000	.0001	.0003	.0006	.0011	.0019
7	.0000	.0000	.0000	.0000	.0000	.0000	.0000	.0001	.0001	.0003

Table C 557

p r	.11	.12	.13	.14	.15	.16	.17	.18	.19	.20
0	.1741	.1470	.1238	.1041	.0874	.0731	.0611	.0510	.0424	.0352
1	.3228	.3006	.2775	.2542	.2312	.2090	.1878	.1678	.1492	.1319
2	.2793	.2870	.2903	.2897	.2856	.2787	.2692	.2578	.2449	.2309
3	.1496	.1696	.1880	.2044	.2184	.2300	.2389	.2452	.2489	.2501
4	.0555	.0694	.0843	.0998	.1156	.1314	.1468	.1615	.1752	.1876
5	.0151	.0208	.0277	.0357	.0449	.0551	.0662	.0780	.0904	.1032
6	.0031	.0047	.0069	.0097	.0132	.0175	.0226	.0285	.0353	.0430
7	.0005	.0008	.0013	.0020	.0030	.0043	.0059	.0081	.0107	.0138
8	.0001	.0001	.0002	.0003	.0005	.0008	.0012	.0018	.0025	.0035
9	.0000	.0000	.0000	.0000	.0001	.0001	.0002	.0003	.0005	.0007
10	.0000	.0000	.0000	.0000	.0000	.0000	.0000	.0000	.0001	.0001

	.21	.22	.23	.24	.25	.26	.27	.28	.29	.30
0	.0291	.0241	.0198	.0163	.0134	.0109	.0089	.0072	.0059	.0047
1	.1162	.1018	.0889	.0772	.0668	.0576	.0494	.0423	.0360	.0305
2	.2162	.2010	.1858	.1707	.1559	.1416	.1280	.1150	.1029	.0916
3	.2490	.2457	.2405	.2336	.2252	.2156	.2051	.1939	.1821	.1700
4	.1986	.2079	.2155	.2213	.2252	.2273	.2276	.2262	.2231	.2186
5	.1161	.1290	.1416	.1537	.1651	.1757	.1852	.1935	.2005	.2061
6	.0514	.0606	.0705	.0809	.0917	.1029	.1142	.1254	.1365	.1472
7	.0176	.0220	.0271	.0329	.0393	.0465	.0543	.0627	.0717	.0811
8	.0047	.0062	.0081	.0104	.0131	.0163	.0201	.0244	.0293	.0348
9	.0010	.0014	.0019	.0025	.0034	.0045	.0058	.0074	.0093	.0116
10	.0002	.0002	.0003	.0005	.0007	.0009	.0013	.0017	.0023	.0030
11	.0000	.0000	.0000	.0001	.0001	.0002	.0002	.0003	.0004	.0006
12	.0000	.0000	.0000	.0000	.0000	.0000	.0000	.0000	.0001	.0001

	.31	.32	.33	.34	.35	.36	.37	.38	.39	.40
0	.0038	.0031	.0025	.0020	.0016	.0012	.0010	.0008	.0006	.0005
1	.0258	.0217	.0182	.0152	.0126	.0104	.0086	.0071	.0058	.0047
2	.0811	.0715	.0627	.0547	.0476	.0411	.0354	.0303	.0259	.0219
3	.1579	.1457	.1338	.1222	.1110	.1002	.0901	.0805	.0716	.0634
4	.2128	.2057	.1977	.1888	.1792	.1692	.1587	.1481	.1374	.1268
5	.210	.2130	.2142	.2140	.2123	.2093	.2051	.1997	.1933	.1859
6	.1575	.1671	.1759	.1837	.1906	.1963	.2008	.2040	.2059	.2066
7	.0910	.1011	.1114	.1217	.1319	.1419	.1516	.1608	.1693	.1771
8	.0409	.0476	.0549	.0627	.0710	.0798	.0890	.0985	.1082	.1181
9	.0143	.0174	.0210	.0251	.0298	.0349	.0407	.0470	.0538	.0612
10	.0038	.0049	.0062	.0078	.0096	.0118	.0143	.0173	.0206	.0245
11	.0008	.0011	.0014	.0018	.0024	.0030	.0038	.0048	.0060	.0074
12	.0001	.0002	.0002	.0003	.0004	.0006	.0007	.0010	.0013	.0016
13	.0000	.0000	.0000	.0000	.0001	.0001	.0001	.0001	.0002	.0003

	.41	.42	.43	.44	.45	.46	.47	.48	.49	.50
0	.0004	.0003	.0002	.0002	.0001	.0001	.0001	.0001	.0000	.0000
1	.0038	.0031	.0025	.0020	.0016	.0012	.0010	.0008	.0006	.0005
2	.0185	.0156	.0130	.0108	.0090	.0074	.0060	.0049	.0040	.0032
3	.0558	.0489	.0426	.0369	.0318	.0272	.0232	.0197	.0166	.0139
4	.1163	.1061	.0963	.0869	.0780	.0696	.0617	.0545	.0478	.0417
5	.1778	.1691	.1598	.1502	.1404	.1304	.1204	.1106	.1010	.0916
6	.2060	.2041	.2010	.1967	.1914	.1851	.1780	.1702	.1617	.1527
7	.1840	.1900	.1949	.1987	.2013	.2028	.2030	.2020	.1997	.1964
8	.1279	.1376	.1470	.1561	.1647	.1727	.1800	.1864	.1919	.1964
9	.0691	.0775	.0863	.0954	.1048	.1144	.1241	.1338	.1434	.1527
10	.0288	.0337	.0390	.0450	.0515	.0585	.0661	.0741	.0827	.0916
11	.0091	.0111	.0134	.0161	.0191	.0226	.0266	.0311	.0361	.0417
12	.0021	.0027	.0034	.0042	.0052	.0064	.0079	.0096	.0116	.0139
13	.0003	.0004	.0006	.0008	.0010	.0013	.0016	.0020	.0026	.0032
14	.0000	.0000	.0001	.0001	.0001	.0002	.0002	.0003	.0004	.0005

Table C

r \ p	.01	.02	.03	.04	.05	.06	.07	.08	.09	.10
0	.8515	.7238	.6143	.5204	.4401	.3716	.3131	.2634	.2211	.1853
1	.1376	.2363	.3040	.3469	.3706	.3795	.3771	.3665	.3499	.3294
2	.0104	.0362	.0705	.1084	.1463	.1817	.2129	.2390	.2596	.2745
3	.0005	.0034	.0102	.0211	.0359	.0541	.0748	.0970	.1198	.1423
4	.0000	.0002	.0010	.0029	.0061	.0112	.0183	.0274	.0385	.0514
5	.0000	.0000	.0001	.0003	.0008	.0017	.0033	.0057	.0091	.0137
6	.0000	.0000	.0000	.0000	.0001	.0002	.0005	.0009	.0017	.0028
7	.0000	.0000	.0000	.0000	.0000	.0000	.0000	.0001	.0002	.0004
8	.0000	.0000	.0000	.0000	.0000	.0000	.0000	.0000	.0000	.0001

r \ p	.11	.12	.13	.14	.15	.16	.17	.18	.19	.20
0	.1550	.1293	.1077	.0895	.0743	.0614	.0507	.0418	.0343	.0281
1	.3065	.2822	.2575	.2332	.2097	.1873	.1662	.1468	.1289	.1126
2	.2841	.2886	.2886	.2847	.2775	.2675	.2554	.2416	.2267	.2111
3	.1638	.1837	.2013	.2163	.2285	.2378	.2441	.2475	.2482	.2463
4	.0658	.0814	.0977	.1144	.1311	.1472	.1625	.1766	.1892	.2001
5	.0195	.0266	.0351	.0447	.0555	.0673	.0799	.0930	.1065	.1201
6	.0044	.0067	.0096	.0133	.0180	.0235	.0300	.0374	.0458	.0550
7	.0008	.0013	.0020	.0031	.0045	.0064	.0088	.0117	.0153	.0197
8	.0001	.0002	.0003	.0006	.0009	.0014	.0020	.0029	.0041	.0055
9	.0000	.0000	.0000	.0001	.0001	.0002	.0004	.0006	.0008	.0012
10	.0000	.0000	.0000	.0000	.0000	.0000	.0001	.0001	.0001	.0002

r \ p	.21	.22	.23	.24	.25	.26	.27	.28	.29	.30
0	.0230	.0188	.0153	.0124	.0100	.0081	.0065	.0052	.0042	.0033
1	.0979	.0847	.0730	.0626	.0535	.0455	.0385	.0325	.0273	.0228
2	.1952	.1792	.1635	.1482	.1336	.1198	.1068	.0947	.0835	.0732
3	.2421	.2359	.2279	.2185	.2079	.1964	.1843	.1718	.1591	.1465
4	.2092	.2162	.2212	.2242	.2252	.2243	.2215	.2171	.2112	.2040
5	.1334	.1464	.1586	.1699	.1802	.1891	.1966	.2026	.2071	.2099
6	.0650	.0757	.0869	.0984	.1101	.1218	.1333	.1445	.1551	.1649
7	.0247	.0305	.0371	.0444	.0524	.0611	.0704	.0803	.0905	.1010
8	.0074	.0097	.0125	.0158	.0197	.0242	.0293	.0351	.0416	.0487
9	.0017	.0024	.0033	.0044	.0058	.0075	.0096	.0121	.0151	.0185
10	.0003	.0005	.0007	.0010	.0014	.0019	.0025	.0033	.0043	.0056
11	.0000	.0001	.0001	.0002	.0002	.0004	.0005	.0007	.0010	.0013
12	.0000	.0000	.0000	.0000	.0000	.0001	.0001	.0001	.0002	.0002

r \ p	.31	.32	.33	.34	.35	.36	.37	.38	.39	.40
0	.0026	.0021	.0016	.0013	.0010	.0008	.0006	.0005	.0004	.0003
1	.0190	.0157	.0130	.0107	.0087	.0071	.0058	.0047	.0038	.0030
2	.0639	.0555	.0480	.0413	.0353	.0301	.0255	.0215	.0180	.0150
3	.1341	.1220	.1103	.0992	.0888	.0790	.0699	.0615	.0538	.0468
4	.1958	.1865	.1766	.1662	.1553	.1444	.1333	.1224	.1118	.1014
5	.2111	.2107	.2088	.2054	.2008	.1949	.1879	.1801	.1715	.1623
6	.1739	.1818	.1885	.1940	.1982	.2010	.2024	.2024	.2010	.1983
7	.1116	.1222	.1326	.1428	.1524	.1615	.1698	.1772	.1836	.1889
8	.0564	.0647	.0735	.0827	.0923	.1022	.1122	.1222	.1320	.1417
9	.0225	.0271	.0322	.0379	.0442	.1511	.0586	.0666	.0750	.0840
10	.0071	.0089	.0111	.0137	.0167	.0201	.0241	.0286	.0336	.0392
11	.0017	.0023	.0030	.0038	.0049	.0062	.0077	.0095	.0117	.0142
12	.0003	.0004	.0006	.0008	.0011	.0014	.0019	.0024	.0031	.0040
13	.0000	.0001	.0001	.0001	.0002	.0003	.0003	.0005	.0006	.0008
14	.0000	.0000	.0000	.0000	.0000	.0000	.0000	.0001	.0001	.0001

r \ p	.41	.42	.43	.44	.45	.46	.47	.48	.49	.50
0	.0002	.0002	.0001	.0001	.0001	.0001	.0000	.0000	.0000	.0000
1	.0024	.0019	.0015	.0012	.0009	.0007	.0005	.0004	.0003	.0002
2	.0125	.0103	.0085	.0069	.0056	.0046	.0037	.0029	.0023	.0018
3	.0405	.0349	.0299	.0254	.0215	.0181	.0151	.0126	.0104	.0085
4	.0915	.0821	.0732	.0649	.0572	.0501	.0436	.0378	.0325	.0278
5	.1526	.1426	.1325	.1224	.1123	.1024	.0929	.0837	.0749	.0667
6	.1944	.1894	.1833	.1762	.1684	.1600	.1510	.1416	.1319	.1222
7	.1930	.1959	.1975	.1978	.1969	.1947	.1912	.1867	.1811	.1746
8	.1509	.1596	.1676	.1749	.1812	.1865	.1908	.1939	.1958	.1964
9	.0932	.1027	.1124	.1221	.1318	.1413	.1504	.1591	.1672	.1746
10	.0453	.0521	.0594	.0672	.0755	.0842	.0934	.1028	.1124	.1222
11	.0172	.0206	.0244	.0288	.0337	.0391	.0452	.0518	.0589	.0667
12	.0050	.0062	.0077	.0094	.0115	.0139	.0167	.0199	.0236	.0278
13	.0011	.0014	.0018	.0023	.0029	.0036	.0046	.0057	.0070	.0085
14	.0002	.0002	.0003	.0004	.0005	.0007	.0009	.0011	.0014	.0018
15	.0000	.0000	.0000	.0000	.0001	.0001	.0001	.0001	.0002	.0002

Table C

					n = 17					

r\p	.01	.02	.03	.04	.05	.06	.07	.08	.09	.10
0	.8429	.7093	.5958	.4996	.4181	.3493	.2912	.2423	.2012	.1668
1	.1447	.2461	.3133	.3539	.3741	.3790	.3726	.3582	.3383	.3150
2	.0117	.0402	.0775	.1180	.1575	.1935	.2244	.2492	.2677	.2800
3	.0006	.0041	.0120	.0246	.0415	.0618	.0844	.1083	.1324	.1556
4	.0000	.0003	.0013	.0036	.0076	.0138	.0222	.0330	.0458	.0605
5	.0000	.0000	.0001	.0004	.0010	.0023	.0044	.0075	.0118	.0175
6	.0000	.0000	.0000	.0000	.0001	.0003	.0007	.0013	.0023	.0039
7	.0000	.0000	.0000	.0000	.0000	.0000	.0001	.0002	.0004	.0007
8	.0000	.0000	.0000	.0000	.0000	.0000	.0000	.0000	.0000	.0001

r\p	.11	.12	.13	.14	.15	.16	.17	.18	.19	.20
0	.1379	.1138	.0937	.0770	.0631	.0516	.0421	.0343	.0278	.0225
1	.2898	.2638	.2381	.2131	.1893	.1671	.1466	.1279	.1109	.0957
2	.2865	.2878	.2846	.2775	.2673	.2547	.2402	.2245	.2081	.1914
3	.1771	.1963	.2126	.2259	.2359	.2425	.2460	.2464	.2441	.2393
4	.0766	.0937	.1112	.1287	.1457	.1617	.1764	.1893	.2004	.2093
5	.0246	.0332	.0432	.0545	.0668	.0801	.0939	.1081	.1222	.1361
6	.0061	.0091	.0129	.0177	.0236	.0305	.0385	.0474	.0573	.0680
7	.0012	.0019	.0030	.0045	.0065	.0091	.0124	.0164	.0211	.0267
8	.0002	.0003	.0006	.0009	.0014	.0022	.0032	.0045	.0062	.0084
9	.0000	.0000	.0001	.0002	.0003	.0004	.0006	.0010	.0015	.0021
10	.0000	.0000	.0000	.0000	.0000	.0001	.0001	.0002	.0003	.0004
11	.0000	.0000	.0000	.0000	.0000	.0000	.0000	.0000	.0000	.0001

r\p	.21	.22	.23	.24	.25	.26	.27	.28	.29	.30
0	.0182	.0146	.0118	.0094	.0075	.0060	.0047	.0038	.0030	.0023
1	.0822	.0702	.0597	.0505	.0426	.0357	.0299	.0248	.0206	.0169
2	.1747	.1584	.1427	.1277	.1136	.1005	.0883	.0772	.0672	.0581
3	.2322	.2234	.2131	.2016	.1893	.1765	.1634	.1502	.1372	.1245
4	.2161	.2205	.2228	.2228	.2209	.2170	.2115	.2044	.1961	.1868
5	.1493	.1617	.1730	.1830	.1914	.1982	.2033	.2067	.2083	.2081
6	.0794	.0912	.1034	.1156	.1276	.1393	.1504	.1608	.1701	.1784
7	.0332	.0404	.0485	.0573	.0668	.0769	.0874	.0982	.1092	.1201
8	.0110	.0143	.0181	.0226	.0279	.0338	.0404	.0478	.0558	.0644
9	.0029	.0040	.0054	.0071	.0093	.0119	.0150	.0186	.0228	.0276
10	.0006	.0009	.0013	.0018	.0025	.0033	.0044	.0058	.0074	.0095
11	.0001	.0002	.0002	.0004	.0005	.0007	.0010	.0014	.0019	.0026
12	.0000	.0000	.0000	.0001	.0001	.0001	.0002	.0003	.0004	.0006
13	.0000	.0000	.0000	.0000	.0000	.0000	.0000	.0000	.0001	.0001

r\p	.31	.32	.33	.34	.35	.36	.37	.38	.39	.40
0	.0018	.0014	.0011	.0009	.0007	.0005	.0004	.0003	.0002	.0002
1	.0139	.0114	.0093	.0075	.0060	.0048	.0039	.0031	.0024	.0019
2	.0500	.0428	.0364	.0309	.0260	.0218	.0182	.0151	.0125	.0102
3	.1123	.1007	.0898	.0795	.0701	.0614	.0534	.0463	.0398	.0341
4	.1766	.1659	.1547	.1434	.1320	.1208	.1099	.0993	.0892	.0796
5	.2063	.2030	.1982	.1921	.1849	.1767	.1677	.1582	.1482	.1379
6	.1854	.1910	.1952	.1979	.1991	.1988	.1970	.1939	.1895	.1839
7	.1309	.1413	.1511	.1602	.1685	.1757	.1818	.1868	.1904	.1927
8	.0735	.0831	.0930	.1032	.1134	.1235	.1335	.1431	.1521	.1606
9	.0330	.0391	.0458	.0531	.0611	.0695	.0784	.0877	.0973	.1070
10	.0119	.0147	.0181	.0219	.0263	.0313	.0368	.0430	.0498	.0571
11	.0034	.0044	.0057	.0072	.0090	.0112	.0138	.0168	.0202	.0242
12	.0008	.0010	.0014	.0018	.0024	.0031	.0040	.0051	.0065	.0081
13	.0001	.0002	.0003	.0004	.0005	.0007	.0009	.0012	.0016	.0021
14	.0000	.0000	.0000	.0001	.0001	.0001	.0002	.0002	.0003	.0004
15	.0000	.0000	.0000	.0000	.0000	.0000	.0000	.0000	.0000	.0001

r \ p	.41	.42	.43	.44	.45	.46	.47	.48	.49	.50
0	.0001	.0001	.0001	.0001	.0000	.0000	.0000	.0000	.0000	.0000
1	.0015	.0012	.0009	.0007	.0005	.0004	.0003	.0002	.0002	.0001
2	.0084	.0068	.0055	.0044	.0035	.0028	.0022	.0017	.0013	.0010
3	.0290	.0246	.0207	.0173	.0144	.0119	.0097	.0079	.0064	.0052
4	.0706	.0622	.0546	.0475	.0411	.0354	.0302	.0257	.0217	.0182
5	.1276	.1172	.1070	.0971	.0875	.0784	.0697	.0616	.0541	.0472
6	.1773	.1697	.1614	.1525	.1432	.1335	.1237	.1138	.1040	.0944
7	.1936	.1932	.1914	.1883	.1841	.1787	.1723	.1650	.1570	.1484
8	.1682	.1748	.1805	.1850	.1883	.1903	.1910	.1904	.1886	.1855
9	.1169	.1266	.1361	.1453	.1540	.1621	.1694	.1758	.1812	.1855
10	.0650	.0733	.0822	.0914	.1008	.1105	.1202	.1298	.1393	.1484
11	.0287	.0338	.0394	.0457	.0525	.0599	.0678	.0763	.0851	.0944
12	.0100	.0122	.0149	.0179	.0215	.0255	.0301	.0352	.0409	.0472
13	.0027	.0034	.0043	.0054	.0068	.0084	.0103	.0125	.0151	.0182
14	.0005	.0007	.0009	.0012	.0016	.0020	.0026	.0033	.0041	.0052
15	.0001	.0001	.0001	.0002	.0003	.0003	.0005	.0006	.0008	.0010
16	.0000	.0000	.0000	.0000	.0000	.0000	.0001	.0001	.0001	.0001

r \ p	.01	.02	.03	.04	.05	.06	.07	.08	.09	.10
0	.8345	.6951	.5780	.4796	.3972	.3283	.2708	.2229	.1831	.1501
1	.1517	.2554	.3217	.3597	.3763	.3772	.3669	.3489	.3260	.3002
2	.0130	.0443	.0846	.1274	.1683	.2047	.2348	.2579	.2741	.2835
3	.0007	.0048	.0140	.0283	.0473	.0697	.0942	.1196	.1446	.1680
4	.0000	.0004	.0016	.0044	.0093	.0167	.0266	.0390	.0536	.0700
5	.0000	.0000	.0001	.0005	.0014	.0030	.0056	.0095	.0148	.0218
6	.0000	.0000	.0000	.0000	.0002	.0004	.0009	.0018	.0032	.0052
7	.0000	.0000	.0000	.0000	.0000	.0000	.0001	.0003	.0005	.0010
8	.0000	.0000	.0000	.0000	.0000	.0000	.0000	.0000	.0001	.0002

r \ p	.11	.12	.13	.14	.15	.16	.17	.18	.19	.20
0	.1227	.1002	.0815	.0662	.0536	.0434	.0349	.0281	.0225	.0180
1	.2731	.2458	.2193	.1940	.1704	.1486	.1288	.1110	.0951	.0811
2	.2869	.2850	.2785	.2685	.2556	.2407	.2243	.2071	.1897	.1723
3	.1891	.2072	.2220	.2331	.2406	.2445	.2450	.2425	.2373	.2297
4	.0877	.1060	.1244	.1423	.1592	.1746	.1882	.1996	.2087	.2153
5	.0303	.0405	.0520	.0649	.0787	.0931	.1079	.1227	.1371	.1507
6	.0081	.0120	.0168	.0229	.0301	.0384	.0479	.0584	.0697	.0816
7	.0017	.0028	.0043	.0064	.0091	.0126	.0168	.0220	.0280	.0350
8	.0003	.0005	.0009	.0014	.0022	.0033	.0047	.0066	.0090	.0120
9	.0000	.0001	.0001	.0003	.0004	.0007	.0011	.0016	.0024	.0033
10	.0000	.0000	.0000	.0000	.0001	.0001	.0002	.0003	.0005	.0008
11	.0000	.0000	.0000	.0000	.0000	.0000	.0000	.0001	.0001	.0001

r \ p	.21	.22	.23	.24	.25	.26	.27	.28	.29	.30
0	.0144	.0114	.0091	.0072	.0056	.0044	.0035	.0027	.0021	.0016
1	.0687	.0580	.0487	.0407	.0338	.0280	.0231	.0189	.0155	.0126
2	.1553	.1390	.1236	.1092	.0958	.0836	.0725	.0626	.0537	.0458
3	.2202	.2091	.1969	.1839	.1704	.1567	.1431	.1298	.1169	.1046
4	.2195	.2212	.2205	.2177	.2130	.2065	.1985	.1892	.1790	.1681
5	.1634	.1747	.1845	.1925	.1988	.2031	.2055	.2061	.2048	.2017
6	.0941	.1067	.1194	.1317	.1436	.1546	.1647	.1736	.1812	.1873
7	.0429	.0516	.0611	.0713	.0820	.0931	.1044	.1157	.1269	.1376
8	.0157	.0200	.0251	.0310	.0376	.0450	.0531	.0619	.0713	.0811
9	.0046	.0063	.0083	.0109	.0139	.0176	.0218	.0267	.0323	.0386
10	.0011	.0016	.0022	.0031	.0042	.0056	.0073	.0094	.0119	.0149
11	.0002	.0003	.0005	.0007	.0010	.0014	.0020	.0026	.0035	.0046
12	.0000	.0001	.0001	.0001	.0002	.0003	.0004	.0006	.0008	.0012
13	.0000	.0000	.0000	.0000	.0000	.0000	.0001	.0001	.0002	.0002

Table C   561

r \ p	.31	.32	.33	.34	.35	.36	.37	.38	.39	.40
0	.0013	.0010	.0007	.0006	.0004	.0003	.0002	.0002	.0001	.0001
1	.0102	.0082	.0066	.0052	.0042	.0033	.0026	.0020	.0016	.0012
2	.0388	.0327	.0275	.0229	.0190	.0157	.0129	.0105	.0086	.0069
3	.0930	.0822	.0722	.0630	.0547	.0471	.0404	.0344	.0292	.0246
4	.1567	.1450	.1333	.1217	.1104	.0994	.0890	.0791	.0699	.0614
5	.1971	.1911	.1838	.1755	.1664	.1566	.1463	.1358	.1252	.1146
6	.1919	.1948	.1962	.1959	.1941	.1908	.1862	.1803	.1734	.1655
7	.1478	.1572	.1656	.1730	.1792	.1840	.1875	.1895	.1900	.1892
8	.0913	.1017	.1122	.1226	.1327	.1423	.1514	.1597	.1671	.1734
9	.0456	.0532	.0614	.0701	.0794	.0890	.0988	.1087	.1187	.1284
10	.0184	.0225	.0272	.0325	.0385	.0450	.0522	.0600	.0683	.0771
11	.0060	.0077	.0097	.0122	.0151	.0184	.0223	.0267	.0318	.0374
12	.0016	.0021	.0028	.0037	.0047	.0060	.0076	.0096	.0118	.0145
13	.0003	.0005	.0006	.0009	.0012	.0016	.0021	.0027	.0035	.0045
14	.0001	.0001	.0001	.0002	.0002	.0003	.0004	.0006	.0008	.0011
15	.0000	.0000	.0000	.0000	.0000	.0000	.0001	.0001	.0001	.0002

r \ p	.41	.42	.43	.44	.45	.46	.47	.48	.49	.50
0	.0001	.0001	.0000	.0000	.0000	.0000	.0000	.0000	.0000	.0000
1	.0009	.0007	.0005	.0004	.0003	.0002	.0002	.0001	.0001	.0001
2	.0055	.0044	.0035	.0028	.0022	.0017	.0013	.0010	.0008	.0006
3	.0206	.0171	.0141	.0116	.0095	.0077	.0062	.0050	.0039	.0031
4	.0536	.0464	.0400	.0342	.0291	.0246	.0206	.0172	.0142	.0117
5	.1042	.0941	.0844	.0753	.0666	.0586	.0512	.0444	.0382	.0327
6	.1569	.1477	.1380	.1281	.1181	.1081	.0983	.0887	.0796	.0708
7	.1869	.1833	.1785	.1726	.1657	.1579	.1494	.1404	.1310	.1214
8	.1786	.1825	.1852	.1864	.1864	.1850	.1822	.1782	.1731	.1669
9	.1379	.1469	.1552	.1628	.1694	.1751	.1795	.1828	.1848	.1855
10	.0862	.0957	.1054	.1151	.1248	.1342	.1433	.1519	.1598	.1669
11	.0436	.0504	.0578	.0658	.0742	.0831	.0924	.1020	.1117	.1214
12	.0177	.0213	.0254	.0301	.0354	.0413	.0478	.1549	.0626	.0708
13	.0057	.0071	.0089	.0109	.0134	.0162	.0196	.0234	.0278	.0327
14	.0014	.0018	.0024	.0031	.0039	.0049	.0062	.0077	.0095	.0117
15	.0003	.0004	.0005	.0006	.0009	.0011	.0015	.0019	.0024	.0031
16	.0000	.0000	.0001	.0001	.0001	.0002	.0002	.0003	.0004	.0006
17	.0000	.0000	.0000	.0000	.0000	.0000	.0000	.0000	.0000	.0001

n = 19

r \ p	.01	.02	.03	.04	.05	.06	.07	.08	.09	.10
0	.8262	.6812	.5606	.4604	.3774	.3086	.2519	.2051	.1666	.1351
1	.1586	.2642	.3294	.3645	.3774	.3743	.3602	.3389	.3131	.2852
2	.0144	.0485	.0917	.1367	.1787	.2150	.2440	.2652	.2787	.2852
3	.0008	.0056	.0161	.0323	.0533	.0778	.1041	.1307	.1562	.1796
4	.0000	.0005	.0020	.0054	.0112	.0199	.0313	.0455	.0618	.0798
5	.0000	.0000	.0002	.0007	.0018	.0038	.0071	.0119	.0183	.0266
6	.0000	.0000	.0000	.0001	.0002	.0006	.0012	.0024	.0042	.0069
7	.0000	.0000	.0000	.0000	.0000	.0001	.0002	.0004	.0008	.0014
8	.0000	.0000	.0000	.0000	.0000	.0000	.0000	.0001	.0001	.0002

r \ p	.11	.12	.13	.14	.15	.16	.17	.18	.19	.20
0	.1092	.0881	.0709	.0569	.0456	.0364	.0290	.0230	.0182	.0144
1	.2565	.2284	.2014	.1761	.1529	.1318	.1129	.0961	.0813	.0685
2	.2854	.2803	.2708	.2581	.2428	.2259	.2081	.1898	.1717	.1540
3	.1999	.2166	.2293	.2381	.2428	.2439	.2415	.2361	.2282	.2182
4	.0988	.1181	.1371	.1550	.1714	.1858	.1979	.2073	.2141	.2182
5	.0366	.0483	.0614	.0757	.0907	.1062	.1216	.1365	.1507	.1636
6	.0106	.0154	.0214	.0288	.0374	.0472	.0581	.0699	.0825	.0955
7	.0024	.0039	.0059	.0087	.0122	.0167	.0221	.0285	.0359	.0443
8	.0004	.0008	.0013	.0021	.0032	.0048	.0068	.0094	.0126	.0166
9	.0001	.0001	.0002	.0004	.0007	.0011	.0017	.0025	.0036	.0051
10	.0000	.0000	.0000	.0001	.0001	.0002	.0003	.0006	.0009	.0013
11	.0000	.0000	.0000	.0000	.0000	.0000	.0001	.0001	.0002	.0003

 Table C

r \ p	.21	.22	.23	.24	.25	.26	.27	.28	.29	.30
0	.0113	.0089	.0070	.0054	.0042	.0033	.0025	.0019	.0015	.0011
1	.0573	.0477	.0396	.0326	.0268	.0219	.0178	.0144	.0116	.0093
2	.1371	.1212	.1064	.0927	.0803	.0692	.0592	.0503	.0426	.0358
3	.2065	.1937	.1800	.1659	.1517	.1377	.1240	.1109	.0985	.0869
4	.2196	.2185	.2151	.2096	.2023	.1935	.1835	.1726	.1610	.1491
5	.1751	.1849	.1928	.1986	.2023	.2040	.2036	.2013	.1973	.1916
6	.1086	.1217	.1343	.1463	.1574	.1672	.1757	.1827	.1880	.1916
7	.0536	.0637	.0745	.0858	.0974	.1091	.1207	.1320	.1426	.1525
8	.0214	.0270	.0334	.0406	.0487	.0575	.0670	.0770	.0874	.0981
9	.0069	.0093	.0122	.0157	.0198	.0247	.0303	.0366	.0436	.0514
10	.0018	.0026	.0036	.0050	.0066	.0087	.0112	.0142	.0178	.0220
11	.0004	.0006	.0009	.0013	.0018	.0025	.0034	.0045	.0060	.0077
12	.0001	.0001	.0002	.0003	.0004	.0006	.0008	.0012	.0016	.0022
13	.0000	.0000	.0000	.0000	.0001	.0001	.0002	.0002	.0004	.0005
14	.0000	.0000	.0000	.0000	.0000	.0000	.0000	.0000	.0001	.0001

r \ p	.31	.32	.33	.34	.35	.36	.37	.38	.39	.40
0	.0009	.0007	.0005	.0004	.0003	.0002	.0002	.0001	.0001	.0001
1	.0074	.0059	.0046	.0036	.0029	.0022	.0017	.0013	.0010	.0008
2	.0299	.0249	.0206	.0169	.0138	.0112	.0091	.0073	.0058	.0046
3	.0762	.0664	.0574	.0494	.0422	.0358	.0302	.0253	.0211	.0175
4	.1370	.1249	.1131	.1017	.0909	.0806	.0710	.0621	.0540	.0467
5	.1846	.1764	.1672	.1572	.1468	.1360	.1251	.1143	.1036	.0933
6	.1935	.1936	.1921	.1890	.1844	.1785	.1714	.1634	.1546	.1451
7	.1615	.1692	.1757	.1808	.1844	.1865	.1870	.1860	.1835	.1797
8	.1088	.1195	.1298	.1397	.1489	.1573	.1647	.1710	.1760	.1797
9	.0597	.0687	.0782	.0880	.0980	.1082	.1182	.1281	.1375	.1464
10	.0268	.0323	.0385	.0453	.0528	.0608	.0694	.0785	.0879	.0976
11	.0099	.0124	.0155	.0191	.0233	.0280	.0334	.0394	.0460	.0532
12	.0030	.0039	.0051	.0066	.0083	.0105	.0131	.0161	.0196	.0237
13	.0007	.0010	.0014	.0018	.0024	.0032	.0041	.0053	.0067	.0085
14	.0001	.0002	.0003	.0004	.0006	.0008	.0010	.0014	.0018	.0024
15	.0000	.0000	.0000	.0001	.0001	.0001	.0002	.0003	.0004	.0005
16	.0000	.0000	.0000	.0000	.0000	.0000	.0000	.0000	.0001	.0001

r \ p	.41	.42	.43	.44	.45	.46	.47	.48	.49	.50
0	.0000	.0000	.0000	.0000	.0000	.0000	.0000	.0000	.0000	.0000
1	.0006	.0004	.0003	.0002	.0002	.0001	.0001	.0001	.0001	.0000
2	.0037	.0029	.0022	.0017	.0013	.0010	.0008	.0006	.0004	.0003
3	.0144	.0118	.0096	.0077	.0062	.0049	.0039	.0031	.0024	.0018
4	.0400	.0341	.0289	.0243	.0203	.0168	.0138	.0113	.0092	.0074
5	.0834	.0741	.0653	.0572	.0497	.0429	.0368	.0313	.0265	.0222
6	.1353	.1252	.1150	.1049	.0949	.0853	.0751	.0674	.0593	.0518
7	.1746	.1683	.1611	.1530	.1443	.1350	.1254	.1156	.1058	.0961
8	.1820	.1829	.1823	.1803	.1771	.1725	.1668	.1601	.1525	.1442
9	.1546	.1618	.1681	.1732	.1771	.1796	.1808	.1806	.1791	.1762
10	.1074	.1172	.1268	.1361	.1449	.1530	.1603	.1667	.1721	.1762
11	.0611	.0694	.0783	.0875	.0970	.1066	.1163	.1259	.1352	.1442
12	.0283	.0335	.0394	.0458	.0529	.0606	.0688	.0775	.0866	.0961
13	.0106	.0131	.0160	.0194	.0233	.0278	.0328	.0385	.0448	.0518
14	.0032	.0041	.0052	.0065	.0082	.0101	.0125	.0152	.0185	.0222
15	.0007	.0010	.0013	.0017	.0022	.0029	.0037	.0047	.0059	.0074
16	.0001	.0002	.0002	.0003	.0005	.0006	.0008	.0011	.0014	.0018
17	.0000	.0000	.0000	.0000	.0001	.0001	.0001	.0002	.0002	.0003

n = 20

r \ p	.01	.02	.03	.04	.05	.06	.07	.08	.09	.10
0	.8179	.6676	.5438	.4420	.3585	.2901	.2342	.1887	.1516	.1216
1	.1652	.2725	.3364	.3683	.3774	.3703	.3526	.3282	.3000	.2702
2	.0159	.0528	.0988	.1458	.1887	.2246	.2521	.2711	.2818	.2852
3	.0010	.0065	.0183	.0364	.0596	.0860	.1139	.1414	.1672	.1901
4	.0000	.0006	.0024	.0065	.0133	.0233	.0364	.0523	.0703	.0898
5	.0000	.0000	.0002	.0009	.0022	.0048	.0088	.0145	.0222	.0319
6	.0000	.0000	.0000	.0001	.0003	.0008	.0017	.0032	.0055	.0089
7	.0000	.0000	.0000	.0000	.0000	.0001	.0002	.0005	.0011	.0020
8	.0000	.0000	.0000	.0000	.0000	.0000	.0000	.0001	.0002	.0004
9	.0000	.0000	.0000	.0000	.0000	.0000	.0000	.0000	.0000	.0001

Table C 563

r \ p	.11	.12	.13	.14	.15	.16	.17	.18	.19	.20
0	.0972	.0776	.0617	.0490	.0388	.0306	.0241	.0189	.0148	.0115
1	.2403	.2115	.1844	.1595	.1368	.1165	.0986	.0829	.0693	.0576
2	.2822	.2740	.2618	.2466	.2293	.2109	.1919	.1730	.1545	.1369
3	.2093	.2242	.2347	.2409	.2428	.2410	.2358	.2278	.2175	.2054
4	.1099	.1299	.1491	.1666	.1821	.1951	.2053	.2125	.2168	.2182
5	.0435	.0567	.0713	.1868	.1028	.1189	.1345	.1493	.1627	.1746
6	.0134	.0193	.0266	.0353	.0454	.0566	.0689	.0819	.0954	.1091
7	.0033	.0053	.0080	.0115	.0160	.0216	.0282	.0360	.0448	.0545
8	.0007	.0012	.0019	.0030	.0046	.0067	.0094	.0128	.0171	.0222
9	.0001	.0002	.0004	.0007	.0011	.0017	.0026	.0038	.0053	.0074
10	.0000	.0000	.0001	.0001	.0002	.0004	.0006	.0009	.0014	.0020
11	.0000	.0000	.0000	.0000	.0000	.0001	.0001	.0002	.0003	.0005
12	.0000	.0000	.0000	.0000	.0000	.0000	.0000	.0000	.0001	.0001

r \ p	.21	.22	.23	.24	.25	.26	.27	.28	.29	.30
0	.0090	.0069	.0054	.0041	.0032	.0024	.0018	.0014	.0011	.0008
1	.0477	.0392	.0321	.0261	.0211	.0170	.0137	.0109	.0087	.0068
2	.1204	.1050	.0910	.0783	.0669	.0569	.0480	.0403	.0336	.0278
3	.1920	.1777	.1631	.1484	.1339	.1199	.1065	.0940	.0823	.0716
4	.2169	.2131	.2070	.1991	.1897	.1790	.1675	.1553	.1429	.1304
5	.1845	.1923	.1979	.2012	.2023	.2013	.1982	.1933	.1868	.1789
6	.1226	.1356	.1478	.1589	.1686	.1768	.1833	.1879	.1907	.1916
7	.0652	.0765	.0883	.1003	.1124	.1242	.1356	.1462	.1558	.1643
8	.0282	.0351	.0429	.0515	.0609	.0709	.0815	.0924	.1034	.1144
9	.0100	.0132	.0171	.0217	.0271	.0332	.0402	.0479	.0563	.0654
10	.0029	.0041	.0056	.0075	.0099	.0128	.0163	.0205	.0253	.0308
11	.0007	.0010	.0015	.0022	.0030	.0041	.0055	.0072	.0094	.0120
12	.0001	.0002	.0003	.0005	.0008	.0011	.0015	.0021	.0029	.0039
13	.0000	.0000	.0001	.0001	.0002	.0002	.0003	.0005	.0007	.0010
14	.0000	.0000	.0000	.0000	.0000	.0000	.0001	.0001	.0001	.0002

r \ p	.31	.32	.33	.34	.35	.36	.37	.38	.39	.40
0	.0006	.0004	.0003	.0002	.0002	.0001	.0001	.0001	.0001	.0000
1	.0054	.0042	.0033	.0025	.0020	.0015	.0011	.0009	.0007	.0005
2	.0229	.0188	.0153	.0124	.0100	.0080	.0064	.0050	.0040	.0031
3	.0619	.0531	.0453	.0383	.0323	.0270	.0224	.0185	.0152	.0123
4	.1181	.1062	.0947	.0839	.0738	.0645	.0559	.0482	.0412	.0350
5	.1698	.1599	.1493	.1384	.1272	.1161	.1051	.0945	.0843	.0746
6	.1907	.1881	.1839	.1782	.1712	.1632	.1543	.1447	.1347	.1244
7	.1714	.1770	.1811	.1836	.1844	.1836	.1812	.1774	.1722	.1659
8	.1251	.1354	.1450	.1537	.1614	.1678	.1730	.1767	.1790	.1797
9	.0750	.0849	.0952	.1056	.1158	.1259	.1354	.1444	.1526	.1597
10	.0370	.0440	.0516	.0598	.0686	.0779	.0875	.0974	.1073	.1171
11	.0151	.0188	.0231	.0280	.0336	.0398	.0467	.0542	.0624	.0710
12	.0051	.0066	.0085	.0108	.0136	.0168	.0206	.0249	.0299	.0355
13	.0014	.0019	.0026	.0034	.0045	.0058	.0074	.0094	.0118	.0146
14	.0003	.0005	.0006	.0009	.0012	.0016	.0022	.0029	.0038	.0049
15	.0001	.0001	.0001	.0002	.0003	.0004	.0005	.0007	.0010	.0013
16	.0000	.0000	.0000	.0000	.0000	.0001	.0001	.0001	.0002	.0003

r \ p	.41	.42	.43	.44	.45	.46	.47	.48	.49	.50
0	.0000	.0000	.0000	.0000	.0000	.0000	.0000	.0000	.0000	.0000
1	.0004	.0003	.0002	.0001	.0001	.0001	.0001	.0000	.0000	.0000
2	.0024	.0018	.0014	.0011	.0008	.0006	.0005	.0003	.0002	.0002
3	.0100	.0080	.0064	.0051	.0040	.0031	.0024	.0019	.0014	.0011
4	.0295	.0247	.0206	.0170	.0139	.0113	.0092	.0074	.0059	.0046
5	.0656	.0573	.0496	.0427	.0365	.0309	.0260	.0217	.0180	.0148
6	.1140	.1037	.0936	.0839	.0746	.0658	.0577	.0501	.0432	.0370
7	.1585	.1502	.1413	.1318	.1221	.1122	.1023	.0925	.0830	.0739
8	.1790	.1768	.1732	.1683	.1623	.1553	.1474	.1388	.1296	.1201
9	.1658	.1707	.1742	.1763	.1771	.1763	.1742	.1708	.1661	.1602
10	.1268	.1359	.1446	.1524	.1593	.1652	.1700	.1734	.1755	.1762
11	.0801	.0895	.0991	.1089	.1185	.1280	.1370	.1455	.1533	.1602
12	.0417	.0486	.0561	.0642	.0727	.0818	.0911	.1007	.1105	.1201
13	.0178	.0217	.0260	.0310	.0366	.0429	.0497	.0572	.0653	.0739
14	.0062	.0078	.0098	.0122	.0150	.0183	.0221	.0264	.0314	.0370
15	.0017	.0023	.0030	.0038	.0049	.0062	.0078	.0098	.0121	.0148
16	.0004	.0005	.0007	.0009	.0013	.0017	.0022	.0028	.0036	.0046
17	.0001	.0001	.0001	.0002	.0002	.0003	.0005	.0006	.0008	.0011
18	.0000	.0000	.0000	.0000	.0000	.0000	.0001	.0001	.0001	.0002

Table C

r \ p	.01	.02	.03	.04	.05	.06	.07	.08	.09	.10
0	.7778	.6035	.4670	.3604	.2774	.2129	.1630	.1244	.0946	.0718
1	.1964	.3079	.3611	.3754	.3650	.3398	.3066	.2704	.2340	.1994
2	.0238	.0754	.1340	.1877	.2305	.2602	.2770	.2821	.2777	.2659
3	.0018	.0118	.0318	.0600	.0930	.1273	.1598	.1881	.2106	.2265
4	.0001	.0013	.0054	.0137	.0269	.0447	.0662	.0899	.1145	.1384
5	.0000	.0001	.0007	.0024	.0060	.0120	.0209	.0329	.0476	.0646
6	.0000	.0000	.0001	.0003	.0010	.0026	.0052	.0095	.0157	.0239
7	.0000	.0000	.0000	.0000	.0001	.0004	.0011	.0022	.0042	.0072
8	.0000	.0000	.0000	.0000	.0000	.0001	.0002	.0004	.0009	.0018
9	0	.0000	.0000	.0000	.0000	.0000	.0000	.0001	.0002	.0004
10	0	.0000	.0000	.0000	.0000	.0000	.0000	.0000	.0000	.0001

r \ p	.11	.12	.13	.14	.15	.16	.17	.18	.19	.20
0	.0543	.0409	.0308	.0230	.0172	.0128	.0095	.0070	.0052	.0038
1	.1678	.1395	.1149	.0938	.0759	.0609	.0486	.0384	.0302	.0236
2	.2488	.2283	.2060	.1832	.1607	.1392	.1193	.1012	.0851	.0708
3	.2358	.2387	.2360	.2286	.2174	.2033	.1874	.1704	.1530	.1358
4	.1603	.1790	.1940	.2047	.2110	.2130	.2111	.2057	.1974	.1867
5	.0832	.1025	.1217	.1399	.1564	.1704	.1816	.1897	.1945	.1960
6	.0343	.0466	.0606	.0759	.0920	.1082	.1240	.1388	.1520	.1633
7	.0115	.0173	.0246	.0336	.0441	.0559	.0689	.0827	.0968	.1108
8	.0032	.0053	.0083	.0123	.0175	.0240	.0318	.0408	.0511	.0623
9	.0007	.0014	.0023	.0038	.0058	.0086	.0123	.0169	.0226	.0294
10	.0001	.0003	.0006	.0010	.0016	.0026	.0040	.0059	.0085	.0118
11	.0000	.0001	.0001	.0002	.0004	.0007	.0011	.0018	.0027	.0040
12	.0000	.0000	.0000	.0000	.0001	.0002	.0003	.0005	.0007	.0012
13	.0000	.0000	.0000	.0000	.0000	.0000	.0001	.0001	.0002	.0003
14	.0000	.0000	.0000	.0000	.0000	.0000	.0000	.0000	.0000	.0001

r \ p	.21	.22	.23	.24	.25	.26	.27	.28	.29	.30
0	.0028	.0020	.0015	.0010	.0008	.0005	.0004	.0003	.0002	.0001
1	.0183	.0141	.0109	.0083	.0063	.0047	.0035	.0026	.0020	.0014
2	.0585	.0479	.0389	.0314	.0251	.0199	.0157	.0123	.0096	.0074
3	.1192	.1035	.0891	.0759	.0641	.0537	.0446	.0367	.0300	.0243
4	.1742	.1606	.1463	.1318	.1175	.1037	.0906	.0785	.0673	.0572
5	.1945	.1903	.1836	.1749	.1645	.1531	.1408	.1282	.1155	.1030
6	.1724	.1789	.1828	.1841	.1828	.1793	.1736	.1661	.1572	.1472
7	.1244	.1369	.1482	.1578	.1654	.1709	.1743	.1754	.1743	.1712
8	.0744	.0869	.0996	.1121	.1241	.1351	.1450	.1535	.1602	.1651
9	.0373	.0463	.0562	.0669	.0781	.0897	.1013	.1127	.1236	.1336
10	.0159	.0209	.0269	.0338	.0417	.0504	.0600	.0701	.0808	.0916
11	.0058	.0080	.0109	.0145	.0189	.0242	.0302	.0372	.0450	.0536
12	.0018	.0026	.0038	.0054	.0074	.0099	.0130	.0169	.0214	.0268
13	.0005	.0007	.0011	.0017	.0025	.0035	.0048	.0066	.0088	.0115
14	.0001	.0002	.0003	.0005	.0007	.0010	.0015	.0022	.0031	.0042
15	.0000	.0000	.0001	.0001	.0002	.0003	.0004	.0006	.0009	.0013
16	.0000	.0000	.0000	.0000	.0000	.0001	.0001	.0002	.0002	.0004
17	.0000	.0000	.0000	.0000	.0000	.0000	.0000	.0000	.0001	.0001

r \ p	.31	.32	.33	.34	.35	.36	.37	.38	.39	.40
0	.0001	.0001	.0000	.0000	.0000	.0000	.0000	.0000	.0000	.0000
1	.0011	.0008	.0006	.0004	.0003	.0002	.0001	.0001	.0001	.0000
2	.0057	.0043	.0033	.0025	.0018	.0014	.0010	.0007	.0005	.0004
3	.0195	.0156	.0123	.0097	.0076	.0058	.0045	.0034	.0026	.0019
4	.0482	.0403	.0334	.0274	.0224	.0181	.0145	.0115	.0091	.0071
5	.0910	.0797	.0691	.0594	.0506	.0427	.0357	.0297	.0244	.0199
6	.1363	.1250	.1134	.1020	.0908	.0801	.0700	.0606	.0520	.0442
7	.1662	.1596	.1516	.1426	.1327	.1222	.1115	.1008	.0902	.0800
8	.1680	.1690	.1681	.1652	.1607	.1547	.1474	.1390	.1298	.1200
9	.1426	.1502	.1563	.1608	.1635	.1644	.1635	.1609	.1567	.1511
10	.1025	.1131	.1232	.1325	.1409	.1479	.1536	.1578	.1603	.1612
11	.0628	.0726	.0828	.0931	.1034	.1135	.1230	.1319	.1398	.1465
12	.0329	.0399	.0476	.0560	.0650	.0745	.0843	.0943	.1043	.1140
13	.0148	.0188	.0234	.0288	.0350	.0419	.0495	.0578	.0667	.0760
14	.0057	.0076	.0099	.0127	.0161	.0202	.0249	.0304	.0365	.0434
15	.0019	.0026	.0036	.0048	.0064	.0083	.0107	.0136	.0171	.0212
16	.0005	.0008	.0011	.0015	.0021	.0029	.0039	.0052	.0068	.0088
17	.0001	.0002	.0003	.0004	.0006	.0009	.0012	.0017	.0023	.0031
18	.0000	.0000	.0001	.0001	.0001	.0002	.0003	.0005	.0007	.0009
19	.0000	.0000	.0000	.0000	.0000	.0000	.0001	.0001	.0002	.0002

Table C 565

					n = 25 (Continued)					
r \ p	.41	.42	.43	.44	.45	.46	.47	.48	.49	.50
0	.0000	.0000	.0000	.0000	.0000	.0000	.0000	.0000	.0000	.0000
1	.0000	.0000	.0000	.0000	.0000	.0000	.0000	.0000	.0000	.0000
2	.0003	.0002	.0001	.0001	.0001	.0000	.0000	.0000	.0000	.0000
3	.0014	.0011	.0008	.0006	.0004	.0003	.0002	.0001	.0001	.0001
4	.0055	.0042	.0032	.0024	.0018	.0014	.0010	.0007	.0005	.0004
5	.0161	.0129	.0102	.0081	.0063	.0049	.0037	.0028	.0021	.0016
6	.0372	.0311	.0257	.0211	.0172	.0138	.0110	.0087	.0068	.0053
7	.0703	.0611	.0527	.0450	.0381	.0319	.0265	.0218	.0178	.0143
8	.1099	.0996	.0895	.0796	.0701	.0612	.0529	.0453	.0384	.0322
9	.1442	.1363	.1275	.1181	.1084	.0985	.0886	.0790	.0697	.0609
10	.1603	.1579	.1539	.1485	.1419	.1342	.1257	.1166	.1071	.0974
11	.1519	.1559	.1583	.1591	.1583	.1559	.1521	.1468	.1404	.1328
12	.1232	.1317	.1393	.1458	.1511	.1550	.1573	.1581	.1573	.1550
13	.0856	.0954	.1051	.1146	.1236	.1320	.1395	.1460	.1512	.1550
14	.0510	.0592	.0680	.0772	.0867	.0964	.1060	.1155	.1245	.1328
15	.0260	.0314	.0376	.0445	.0520	.0602	.0690	.0782	.0877	.0974
16	.0113	.0142	.0177	.0218	.0266	.0321	.0382	.0451	.0527	.0609
17	.0042	.0055	.0071	.0091	.0115	.0145	.0179	.0220	.0268	.0322
18	.0013	.0018	.0024	.0032	.0042	.0055	.0071	.0090	.0114	.0143
19	.0003	.0005	.0007	.0009	.0013	.0017	.0023	.0031	.0040	.0053
20	.0001	.0001	.0001	.0002	.0003	.0004	.0006	.0009	.0012	.0016
21	.0000	.0000	.0000	.0000	.0001	.0001	.0001	.0002	.0003	.0004
22	.0000	.0000	.0000	.0000	.0000	.0000	.0000	.0000	.0000	.0001

					n = 30					
r \ p	.01	.02	.03	.04	.05	.06	.07	.08	.09	.10
0	.7397	.5455	.4010	.2939	.2146	.1563	.1134	.0820	.0591	.0424
1	.2242	.3340	.3721	.3673	.3389	.2992	.2560	.2138	.1752	.1413
2	.0328	.0988	.1669	.2219	.2586	.2769	.2794	.2696	.2513	.2277
3	.0031	.0188	.0482	.0863	.1270	.1650	.1963	.2188	.2319	.2361
4	.0002	.0026	.0101	.0243	.0451	.0711	.0997	.1284	.1548	.1771
5	.0000	.0003	.0016	.0053	.0124	.0236	.0390	.0581	.0796	.1023
6	.0000	.0000	.0002	.0009	.0027	.0063	.0122	.0210	.0328	.0474
7	.0000	.0000	.0000	.0001	.0005	.0014	.0032	.0063	.0111	.0180
8	.0000	.0000	.0000	.0000	.0001	.0003	.0007	.0016	.0032	.0058
9	0	.0000	.0000	.0000	.0000	.0000	.0001	.0003	.0008	.0016
10	0	.0000	.0000	.0000	.0000	.0000	.0000	.0001	.0002	.0004
11	0	0	.0000	.0000	.0000	.0000	.0000	.0000	.0000	.0001
12	0	0	.0000	.0000	.0000	.0000	.0000	.0000	.0000	.0000
13	0	0	0	.0000	.0000	.0000	.0000	.0000	.0000	.0000

	.11	.12	.13	.14	.15	.16	.17	.18	.19	.20
0	.0303	.0216	.0153	.0108	.0076	.0054	.0037	.0026	.0018	.0012
1	.1124	.0884	.0687	.0529	.0404	.0306	.0230	.0171	.0126	.0093
2	.2015	.1747	.1489	.1249	.1034	.0844	.0682	.0544	.0430	.0337
3	.2324	.2224	.2077	.1898	.1703	.1501	.1303	.1115	.0942	.0785
4	.1939	.2047	.2095	.2086	.2028	.1930	.1802	.1652	.1491	.1325
5	.1246	.1451	.1628	.1766	.1861	.1912	.1919	.1886	.1819	.1723
6	.0642	.0825	.1013	.1198	.1368	.1517	.1638	.1725	.1777	.1795
7	.0272	.0386	.0519	.0668	.0828	.0991	.1150	.1298	.1429	.1538
8	.0097	.0151	.0223	.0313	.0420	.0543	.0677	.0819	.0964	.1106
9	.0029	.0050	.0081	.0125	.0181	.0253	.0339	.0440	.0553	.0676
10	.0008	.0014	.0026	.0043	.0067	.0101	.0146	.0203	.0272	.0355
11	.0002	.0004	.0007	.0013	.0022	.0035	.0054	.0081	.0116	.0161
12	.0000	.0001	.0002	.0003	.0006	.0011	.0018	.0028	.0043	.0064
13	.0000	.0000	.0000	.0001	.0001	.0003	.0005	.0009	.0014	.0022
14	.0000	.0000	.0000	.0000	.0000	.0001	.0001	.0002	.0004	.0007
15	.0000	.0000	.0000	.0000	.0000	.0000	.0000	.0001	.0001	.0002

Table C

r \ p	.21	.22	.23	.24	.25	.26	.27	.28	.29	.30
0	.0008	.0006	.0004	.0003	.0002	.0001	.0001	.0001	.0000	.0000
1	.0068	.0049	.0035	.0025	.0018	.0013	.0009	.0006	.0004	.0003
2	.0261	.0200	.0153	.0115	.0086	.0064	.0047	.0035	.0025	.0018
3	.0647	.0528	.0426	.0340	.0269	.0210	.0163	.0125	.0095	.0072
4	.1161	.1005	.0858	.0724	.0604	.0499	.0407	.0329	.0263	.0208
5	.1605	.1473	.1333	.1189	.1047	.0911	.0783	.0665	.0559	.0464
6	.1778	.1732	.1659	.1565	.1455	.1334	.1207	.1078	.0951	.0829
7	.1621	.1674	.1699	.1694	.1662	.1606	.1530	.1437	.1332	.1219
8	.1239	.1358	.1459	.1538	.1593	.1623	.1627	.1607	.1564	.1501
9	.0805	.0936	.1065	.1187	.1298	.1394	.1471	.1527	.1562	.1573
10	.0449	.0554	.0668	.0787	.0909	.1028	.1143	.1247	.1339	.1416
11	.0217	.0284	.0363	.0452	.0551	.0657	.0768	.0882	.0995	.1103
12	.0091	.0127	.0172	.0226	.0291	.0365	.0450	.0543	.0643	.0749
13	.0034	.0050	.0071	.0099	.0134	.0178	.0230	.0292	.0364	.0444
14	.0011	.0017	.0026	.0038	.0054	.0076	.0103	.0138	.0180	.0231
15	.0003	.0005	.0008	.0013	.0019	.0028	.0041	.0057	.0079	.0106
16	.0001	.0001	.0002	.0004	.0006	.0009	.0014	.0021	.0030	.0042
17	.0000	.0000	.0001	.0001	.0002	.0003	.0004	.0007	.0010	.0015
18	.0000	.0000	.0000	.0000	.0000	.0001	.0001	.0002	.0003	.0005
19	.0000	.0000	.0000	.0000	.0000	.0000	.0000	.0000	.0001	.0001

r \ p	.31	.32	.33	.34	.35	.36	.37	.38	.39	.40
0	.0000	.0000	.0000	.0000	.0000	.0000	.0000	.0000	.0000	.0000
1	.0002	.0001	.0001	.0001	.0000	.0000	.0000	.0000	.0000	.0000
2	.0013	.0009	.0006	.0004	.0003	.0002	.0001	.0001	.0001	.0000
3	.0054	.0040	.0029	.0021	.0015	.0011	.0008	.0006	.0004	.0003
4	.0163	.0127	.0098	.0074	.0056	.0042	.0031	.0023	.0017	.0012
5	.0382	.0311	.0250	.0199	.0157	.0123	.0095	.0073	.0055	.0041
6	.0715	.0609	.0513	.0428	.0353	.0288	.0233	.0186	.0147	.0115
7	.1101	.0983	.0867	.0756	.0652	.0556	.0469	.0391	.0323	.0263
8	.1422	.1330	.1228	.1120	.1009	.0899	.0792	.0689	.0593	.0505
9	.1562	.1530	.1478	.1410	.1328	.1236	.1136	.1032	.0927	.0823
10	.1474	.1512	.1529	.1526	.1502	.1460	.1402	.1329	.1245	.1152
11	.1204	.1293	.1369	.1429	.1471	.1493	.1497	.1481	.1447	.1396
12	.0856	.0964	.1068	.1166	.1254	.1330	.1392	.1437	.1465	.1474
13	.0533	.1628	.1728	.0831	.0935	.1036	.1132	.1219	.1296	.1360
14	.0291	.0359	.0436	.0520	.0611	.0708	.0807	.0908	.1007	.1101
15	.0139	.0180	.0229	.0286	.0351	.0425	.0506	.0593	.0686	.0783
16	.0059	.0079	.0106	.0138	.0177	.0224	.0278	.0341	.0411	.0489
17	.0022	.0031	.0043	.0059	.0079	.0104	.0135	.0172	.0217	.0269
18	.0007	.0010	.0015	.0022	.0031	.0042	.0057	.0076	.0100	.0129
19	.0002	.0003	.0005	.0007	.0010	.0015	.0021	.0029	.0040	.0054
20	.0000	.0001	.0001	.0002	.0003	.0005	.0007	.0010	.0014	.0020
21	.0000	.0000	.0000	.0000	.0001	.0001	.0002	.0003	.0004	.0006
22	.0000	.0000	.0000	.0000	.0000	.0000	.0000	.0001	.0001	.0002

r \ p	.41	.42	.43	.44	.45	.46	.47	.48	.49	.50
0	.0000	.0000	.0000	.0000	.0000	.0000	.0000	.0000	.0000	.0000
1	.0000	.0000	.0000	.0000	.0000	.0000	.0000	.0000	.0000	.0000
2	.0000	.0000	.0000	.0000	.0000	.0000	.0000	.0000	.0000	.0000
3	.0002	.0001	.0001	.0001	.0000	.0000	.0000	.0000	.0000	.0000
4	.0009	.0006	.0004	.0003	.0002	.0001	.0001	.0001	.0000	.0000
5	.0031	.0023	.0017	.0012	.0008	.0006	.0004	.0003	.0002	.0001
6	.0089	.0068	.0052	.0039	.0029	.0021	.0015	.0011	.0008	.0006
7	.0213	.0170	.0134	.0105	.0081	.0062	.0047	.0035	.0026	.0019
8	.0425	.0354	.0291	.0237	.0191	.0152	.0120	.0093	.0072	.0055
9	.0722	.0626	.0537	.0456	.0382	.0317	.0260	.0210	.0168	.0133
10	.1054	.0952	.0851	.0752	.0656	.0567	.0483	.0408	.0340	.0280
11	.1331	.1254	.1167	.1074	.0976	.0877	.0779	.0684	.0593	.0509
12	.1465	.1438	.1394	.1336	.1265	.1183	.1094	.1000	.0903	.0806
13	.1409	.1442	.1456	.1453	.1433	.1396	.1344	.1278	.1201	.1115
14	.1189	.1268	.1334	.1387	.1424	.1444	.1447	.1432	.1401	.1354
15	.0881	.0979	.1074	.1162	.1242	.1312	.1369	.1410	.1436	.1445
16	.0574	.0665	.0759	.0856	.0953	.1048	.1138	.1221	.1293	.1354
17	.0329	.0396	.0472	.0554	.0642	.0735	.0831	.0928	.1023	.1115
18	.0165	.0207	.0257	.0314	.0379	.0452	.0532	.0619	.0710	.0806
19	.0072	.0095	.0122	.0156	.0196	.0243	.0298	.0361	.0431	.0509
20	.0028	.0038	.0051	.0067	.0088	.0114	.0145	.0183	.0228	.0280
21	.0009	.0013	.0018	.0025	.0034	.0046	.0061	.0080	.0104	.0133
22	.0003	.0004	.0006	.0008	.0012	.0016	.0022	.0030	.0041	.0055
23	.0001	.0001	.0001	.0002	.0003	.0005	.0007	.0010	.0014	.0019
24	.0000	.0000	.0000	.0001	.0001	.0001	.0002	.0003	.0004	.0006
25	.0000	.0000	.0000	.0000	.0000	.0000	.0000	.0001	.0001	.0001

Table C

p r	.01	.02	.03	.04	.05	.06	.07	.08	.09	.10
0	.6690	.4457	.2957	.1954	.1285	.0842	.0549	.0356	.0230	.0148
1	.2703	.3638	.3658	.3256	.2706	.2149	.1652	.1238	.0910	.0657
2	.0532	.1448	.2206	.2646	.2777	.2675	.2425	.2100	.1754	.1423
3	.0068	.0374	.0864	.1396	.1851	.2162	.2312	.2313	.2198	.2003
4	.0006	.0071	.0247	.0538	.0901	.1277	.1609	.1860	.2011	.2059
5	.0000	.0010	.0055	.0161	.0342	.0587	.0872	.1165	.1432	.1647
6	.0000	.0001	.0010	.0039	.0105	.0218	.0383	.0591	.0826	.1068
7	.0000	.0000	.0001	.0008	.0027	.0068	.0140	.0250	.0397	.0576
8	.0000	.0000	.0000	.0001	.0006	.0018	.0043	.0090	.0162	.0264
9	.0000	.0000	.0000	.0000	.0001	.0004	.0012	.0028	.0057	.0104
10	0	.0000	.0000	.0000	.0000	.0001	.0003	.0007	.0017	.0036
11	0	.0000	.0000	.0000	.0000	.0000	.0001	.0002	.0005	.0011
12	0	0	.0000	.0000	.0000	.0000	.0000	.0000	.0001	.0003
13	0	0	.0000	.0000	.0000	.0000	.0000	.0000	.0000	.0001
14	0	0	0	.0000	.0000	.0000	.0000	.0000	.0000	.0000
15	0	0	0	.0000	.0000	.0000	.0000	.0000	.0000	.0000
16	0	0	0	0	.0000	.0000	.0000	.0000	.0000	.0000
17	0	0	0	0	0	.0000	.0000	.0000	.0000	.0000
18	0	0	0	0	0	0	.0000	.0000	.0000	.0000

p r	.11	.12	.13	.14	.15	.16	.17	.18	.19	.20
0	.0095	.0060	.0038	.0024	.0015	.0009	.0006	.0004	.0002	.0001
1	.0467	.0328	.0228	.0156	.0106	.0071	.0047	.0031	.0020	.0013
2	.1126	.0873	.0663	.0496	.0365	.0265	.0190	.0134	.0094	.0065
3	.1763	.1507	.1255	.1022	.0816	.0639	.0492	.0373	.0279	.0205
4	.2016	.1901	.1735	.1539	.1332	.1126	.0932	.0757	.0604	.0475
5	.1794	.1867	.1867	.1804	.1692	.1544	.1375	.1197	.1021	.0854
6	.1293	.1485	.1627	.1713	.1742	.1715	.1642	.1533	.1397	.1246
7	.0777	.0983	.1181	.1355	.1493	.1587	.1634	.1634	.1592	.1513
8	.0396	.0553	.0728	.0910	.1087	.1247	.1381	.1480	.1540	.1560
9	.0174	.0268	.0387	.0527	.0682	.0844	.1005	.1155	.1284	.1386
10	.0067	.0113	.0179	.0266	.0373	.0499	.0638	.0786	.0934	.1075
11	.0022	.0042	.0073	.0118	.0180	.0259	.0357	.0470	.0597	.0733
12	.0007	.0014	.0026	.0046	.0077	.0119	.0176	.0250	.0339	.0443
13	.0002	.0004	.0008	.0016	.0029	.0049	.0078	.0118	.0171	.0238
14	.0000	.0001	.0002	.0005	.0010	.0018	.0031	.0050	.0077	.0115
15	.0000	.0000	.0001	.0001	.0003	.0006	.0011	.0019	.0031	.0050
16	.0000	.0000	.0000	.0000	.0001	.0002	.0003	.0007	.0012	.0019
17	.0000	.0000	.0000	.0000	.0000	.0000	.0001	.0002	.0004	.0007
18	.0000	.0000	.0000	.0000	.0000	.0000	.0000	.0001	.0001	.0002
19	.0000	.0000	.0000	.0000	.0000	.0000	.0000	.0000	.0000	.0001

p r	.21	.22	.23	.24	.25	.26	.27	.28	.29	.30
0	.0001	.0000	.0000	.0000	.0000	.0000	.0000	.0000	.0000	.0000
1	.0009	.0005	.0003	.0002	.0001	.0001	.0001	.0000	.0000	.0000
2	.0044	.0030	.0020	.0013	.0009	.0006	.0004	.0002	.0001	.0001
3	.0149	.0107	.0076	.0053	.0037	.0025	.0017	.0011	.0008	.0005
4	.0367	.0279	.0210	.0155	.0113	.0082	.0058	.0041	.0029	.0020
5	.0702	.0567	.0451	.0353	.0272	.0207	.0155	.0115	.0084	.0061
6	.1088	.0933	.0786	.0650	.0530	.0424	.0335	.0261	.0200	.0151
7	.1405	.1278	.1140	.0997	.0857	.0724	.0602	.0493	.0397	.0315
8	.1541	.1487	.1404	.1299	.1179	.1050	.0919	.0790	.0669	.0557
9	.1456	.1491	.1492	.1459	.1397	.1312	.1208	.1093	.0972	.0849
10	.1200	.1304	.1381	.1428	.1444	.1429	.1385	.1318	.1230	.1128
11	.0870	.1003	.1125	.1230	.1312	.1369	.1397	.1397	.1370	.1319
12	.0559	.0684	.0812	.0939	.1057	.1162	.1249	.1313	.1353	.1366
13	.0320	.0415	.0523	.0638	.0759	.0880	.0995	.1100	.1190	.1261
14	.0164	.0226	.0301	.0389	.0488	.0596	.0710	.0825	.0937	.1042
15	.0076	.0110	.0156	.0213	.0282	.0363	.0455	.0556	.0664	.0774
16	.0031	.0049	.0073	.0105	.0147	.0199	.0263	.0338	.0424	.0518
17	.0012	.0019	.0031	.0047	.0069	.0099	.0137	.0186	.0244	.0314
18	.0004	.0007	.0012	.0019	.0029	.0044	.0065	.0092	.0127	.0172
19	.0001	.0002	.0004	.0007	.0011	.0018	.0028	.0042	.0060	.0085
20	.0000	.0001	.0001	.0002	.0004	.0007	.0011	.0017	.0026	.0038
21	.0000	.0000	.0000	.0001	.0001	.0002	.0004	.0006	.0010	.0016
22	.0000	.0000	.0000	.0000	.0000	.0001	.0001	.0002	.0004	.0006
23	.0000	.0000	.0000	.0000	.0000	.0000	.0000	.0001	.0001	.0002
24	.0000	.0000	.0000	.0000	.0000	.0000	.0000	.0000	.0000	.0001

Table C

p \ r	.31	.32	.33	.34	.35	.36	.37	.38	.39	.40
0	.0000	.0000	.0000	.0000	.0000	.0000	.0000	.0000	.0000	.0000
1	.0000	.0000	.0000	.0000	.0000	.0000	.0000	.0000	.0000	.0000
2	.0001	.0000	.0000	.0000	.0000	.0000	.0000	.0000	.0000	.0000
3	.0003	.0002	.0001	.0001	.0001	.0000	.0000	.0000	.0000	.0000
4	.0013	.0009	.0006	.0004	.0003	.0002	.0001	.0001	.0000	.0000
5	.0043	.0030	.0021	.0014	.0010	.0007	.0004	.0003	.0002	.0001
6	.0113	.0083	.0061	.0043	.0031	.0021	.0015	.0010	.0007	.0005
7	.0247	.0190	.0145	.0109	.0080	.0059	.0042	.0030	.0021	.0015
8	.0457	.0369	.0294	.0231	.0179	.0136	.0102	.0076	.0056	.0040
9	.0730	.0618	.0515	.0423	.0342	.0272	.0214	.0166	.0126	.0095
10	.1017	.0902	.0786	.0675	.0571	.0475	.0389	.0315	.0250	.0196
11	.1246	.1157	.1056	.0948	.0838	.0729	.0624	.0526	.0437	.0357
12	.1353	.1316	.1257	.1181	.1090	.0990	.0885	.0779	.0675	.0576
13	.1309	.1334	.1334	.1310	.1265	.1200	.1120	.1028	.0929	.0827
14	.1134	.1210	.1267	.1302	.1313	.1302	.1269	.1216	.1146	.1063
15	.0883	.0987	.1082	.1162	.1226	.1269	.1291	.1291	.1270	.1228
16	.0620	.0726	.0832	.0935	.1031	.1116	.1185	.1237	.1268	.1279
17	.0393	.0482	.0579	.0680	.0784	.0886	.0983	.1070	.1145	.1204
18	.0226	.0290	.0364	.0448	.0539	.0637	.0737	.0838	.0935	.1026
19	.0117	.0158	.0208	.0267	.0336	.0415	.0501	.0595	.0692	.0792
20	.0055	.0078	.0107	.0144	.0190	.0245	.0309	.0383	.0465	.0554
21	.0024	.0035	.0050	.0071	.0097	.0131	.0173	.0223	.0283	.0352
22	.0009	.0014	.0021	.0032	.0045	.0064	.0088	.0118	.0156	.0203
23	.0003	.0005	.0008	.0013	.0019	.0028	.0040	.0057	.0078	.0106
24	.0001	.0002	.0003	.0005	.0007	.0011	.0017	.0025	.0035	.0050
25	.0000	.0001	.0001	.0002	.0003	.0004	.0006	.0010	.0014	.0021
26	.0000	.0000	.0000	.0000	.0001	.0001	.0002	.0003	.0005	.0008
27	.0000	.0000	.0000	.0000	.0000	.0000	.0001	.0001	.0002	.0003
28	.0000	.0000	.0000	.0000	.0000	.0000	.0000	.0000	.0001	.0001

p \ r	.41	.42	.43	.44	.45	.46	.47	.48	.49	.50
0	.0000	.0000	.0000	.0000	.0000	.0000	0	0	0	0
1	.0000	.0000	.0000	.0000	.0000	.0000	.0000	.0000	.0000	.0000
2	.0000	.0000	.0000	.0000	.0000	.0000	.0000	.0000	.0000	.0000
3	.0000	.0000	.0000	.0000	.0000	.0000	.0000	.0000	.0000	.0000
4	.0000	.0000	.0000	.0000	.0000	.0000	.0000	.0000	.0000	.0000
5	.0001	.0000	.0000	.0000	.0000	.0000	.0000	.0000	.0000	.0000
6	.0003	.0002	.0001	.0001	.0000	.0000	.0000	.0000	.0000	.0000
7	.0010	.0007	.0004	.0003	.0002	.0001	.0001	.0000	.0000	.0000
8	.0029	.0020	.0014	.0009	.0006	.0004	.0003	.0002	.0001	.0001
9	.0071	.0052	.0037	.0026	.0018	.0013	.0009	.0006	.0004	.0002
10	.0152	.0116	.0087	.0064	.0047	.0034	.0024	.0017	.0011	.0008
11	.0288	.0229	.0179	.0138	.0105	.0078	.0058	.0042	.0030	.0021
12	.0484	.0400	.0326	.0262	.0207	.0161	.0124	.0093	.0069	.0051
13	.0724	.0624	.0530	.0443	.0365	.0296	.0236	.0186	.0144	.0109
14	.0970	.0871	.0771	.0671	.0575	.0486	.0404	.0330	.0266	.0211
15	.1168	.1094	.1008	.0914	.0816	.0717	.0621	.0529	.0443	.0366
16	.1269	.1238	.1188	.1122	.1043	.0955	.0860	.0763	.0665	.0572
17	.1245	.1265	.1265	.1245	.1205	.1148	.1077	.0994	.0903	.0807
18	.1105	.1171	.1220	.1250	.1260	.1250	.1220	.1172	.1108	.1031
19	.0889	.0982	.1065	.1137	.1194	.1233	.1253	.1253	.1233	.1194
20	.0649	.0746	.0844	.0938	.1025	.1103	.1166	.1214	.1244	.1254
21	.0429	.0515	.0606	.0702	.0799	.0895	.0985	.1067	.1138	.1194
22	.0258	.0322	.0395	.0476	.0565	.0658	.0754	.0851	.0944	.1031
23	.0140	.0182	.0233	.0293	.0362	.0439	.0524	.0615	.0710	.0807
24	.0069	.0094	.0125	.0163	.0210	.0265	.0329	.0402	.0483	.0572
25	.0031	.0043	.0060	.0082	.0110	.0144	.0187	.0237	.0297	.0366
26	.0012	.0018	.0026	.0037	.0052	.0071	.0096	.0126	.0165	.0211
27	.0004	.0007	.0010	.0015	.0022	.0031	.0044	.0061	.0082	.0109
28	.0001	.0002	.0004	.0006	.0008	.0012	.0018	.0026	.0037	.0051
29	.0000	.0001	.0001	.0002	.0003	.0004	.0007	.0010	.0015	.0021
30	.0000	.0000	.0000	.0001	.0001	.0001	.0002	.0003	.0005	.0008
31	.0000	.0000	.0000	.0000	.0000	.0000	.0001	.0001	.0002	.0002
32	.0000	.0000	.0000	.0000	.0000	.0000	.0000	.0000	.0000	.0001

Table C

r \ p	.01	.02	.03	.04	.05	.06	.07	.08	.09	.10
0	.6050	.3642	.2181	.1299	.0769	.0453	.0266	.0155	.0090	.0052
1	.3056	.3716	.3372	.2706	.2025	.1447	.0999	.0672	.0443	.0286
2	.0756	.1858	.2555	.2762	.2611	.2262	.1843	.1433	.1073	.0779
3	.0122	.0607	.1264	.1842	.2199	.2311	.2219	.1993	.1698	.1386
4	.0015	.0145	.0459	.0902	.1360	.1733	.1963	.2037	.1973	.1809
5	.0001	.0027	.0131	.0346	.0658	.1018	.1359	.1629	.1795	.1849
6	.0000	.0004	.0030	.0108	.0260	.0487	.0767	.1063	.1332	.1541
7	.0000	.0001	.0006	.0028	.0086	.0195	.0363	.0581	.0828	.1076
8	.0000	.0000	.0001	.0006	.0024	.0067	.0147	.0271	.0440	.0643
9	.0000	.0000	.0000	.0001	.0006	.0020	.0052	.0110	.0203	.0333
10	.0000	.0000	.0000	.0000	.0001	.0005	.0016	.0039	.0082	.0152
11	0	.0000	.0000	.0000	.0000	.0001	.0004	.0012	.0030	.0061
12	0	.0000	.0000	.0000	.0000	.0000	.0001	.0004	.0010	.0022
13	0	0	.0000	.0000	.0000	.0000	.0000	.0001	.0003	.0007
14	0	0	.0000	.0000	.0000	.0000	.0000	.0000	.0001	.0002
15	0	0	0	.0000	.0000	.0000	.0000	.0000	.0000	.0001
16	0	0	0	.0000	.0000	.0000	.0000	.0000	.0000	.0000
17	0	0	0	0	.0000	.0000	.0000	.0000	.0000	.0000
18	0	0	0	0	0	.0000	.0000	.0000	.0000	.0000
19	0	0	0	0	0	.0000	.0000	.0000	.0000	.0000
20	0	0	0	0	0	0	.0000	.0000	.0000	.0000
21	0	0	0	0	0	0	0	.0000	.0000	.0000
22	0	0	0	0	0	0	0	0	.0000	.0000
23	0	0	0	0	0	0	0	0	0	.0000

r	.11	.12	.13	.14	.15	.16	.17	.18	.19	.20
0	.0029	.0017	.0009	.0005	.0003	.0002	.0001	.0000	.0000	.0000
1	.0182	.0114	.0071	.0043	.0026	.0016	.0009	.0005	.0003	.0002
2	.0552	.0382	.0259	.0172	.0113	.0073	.0046	.0029	.0018	.0011
3	.1091	.0833	.0619	.0449	.0319	.0222	.0151	.0102	.0067	.0044
4	.1584	.1334	.1086	.0858	.0661	.0496	.0364	.0262	.0185	.0128
5	.1801	.1674	.1493	.1286	.1072	.0869	.0687	.0530	.0400	.0295
6	.1670	.1712	.1674	.1570	.1419	.1242	.1055	.0872	.0703	.0554
7	.1297	.1467	.1572	.1606	.1575	.1487	.1358	.1203	.1037	.0870
8	.0862	.1075	.1263	.1406	.1493	.1523	.1495	.1420	.1307	.1169
9	.0497	.0684	.0880	.1068	.1230	.1353	.1429	.1454	.1431	.1364
10	.0252	.0383	.0539	.0713	.0890	.1057	.1200	.1309	.1376	.1398
11	.0113	.0190	.0293	.0422	.0571	.0732	.0894	.1045	.1174	.1271
12	.0045	.0084	.0142	.0223	.0328	.0453	.0595	.0745	.0895	.1033
13	.0016	.0034	.0062	.0106	.0169	.0252	.0356	.0478	.0613	.0755
14	.0005	.0012	.0025	.0046	.0079	.0127	.0193	.0277	.0380	.0499
15	.0002	.0004	.0009	.0018	.0033	.0058	.0095	.0146	.0214	.0299
16	.0000	.0001	.0003	.0006	.00p3	.0024	.0042	.0070	.0110	.0164
17	.0000	.0000	.0001	.0002	.0005	.0009	.0017	.0031	.0052	.0082
18	.0000	.0000	.0000	.0001	.0001	.0003	.0007	.0012	.0022	.0037
19	.0000	.0000	.0000	.0000	.0000	.0001	.0002	.0005	.0009	.0016
20	.0000	.0000	.0000	.0000	.0000	.0000	.0001	.0002	.0003	.0006
21	.0000	.0000	.0000	.0000	.0000	.0000	.0000	.0000	.0001	.0002
22	.0000	.0000	.0000	.0000	.0000	.0000	.0000	.0000	.0000	.0001
23	.0000	.0000	.0000	.0000	.0000	.0000	.0000	.0000	.0000	.0000

r	.21	.22	.23	.24	.25	.26	.27	.28	.29	.30
0	.0000	.0000	.0000	.0000	.0000	.0000	.0000	.0000	.0000	.0000
1	.0001	.0001	.0000	.0000	.0000	.0000	.0000	.0000	.0000	.0000
2	.0007	.0004	.0002	.0001	.0001	.0000	.0000	.0000	.0000	.0000
3	.0028	.0018	.0011	.0007	.0004	.0002	.0001	.0001	.0000	.0000
4	.0088	.0059	.0039	.0025	.0016	.0010	.0006	.0004	.0002	.0001
5	.0214	.0152	.0106	.0073	.0049	.0033	.0021	.0014	.0009	.0006
6	.0427	.0322	.0238	.0173	.0123	.0087	.0060	.0040	.0027	.0018
7	.0713	.0571	.0447	.0344	.0259	.0191	.0139	.0099	.0069	.0048
8	.1019	.0865	.0718	.0583	.0463	.0361	.0276	.0207	.0152	.0110
9	.1263	.1139	.1001	.0859	.0721	.0592	.0476	.0375	.0290	.0220
10	.1377	.1317	.1226	.1113	.0985	.0852	.0721	.0598	.0485	.0386
11	.1331	.1351	.1332	.1278	.1194	.1089	.0970	.0845	.0721	.0602
12	.1150	.1238	.1293	.1311	.1294	.1244	.1166	.1068	.0957	.0838
13	.0894	.1021	.1129	.1210	.1261	.1277	.1261	.1215	.1142	.1050
14	.0628	.0761	.0891	.1010	.1110	.1186	.1233	.1248	.1233	.1189

Table C

r \ p	.21	.22	.23	.24	.25	.26	.27	.28	.29	.30
15	.0400	.0515	.0639	.0766	.0888	.1000	.1094	.1165	.1209	.1223
16	.0233	.0318	.0417	.0529	.0648	.0769	.0885	.0991	.1080	.1147
17	.0124	.0179	.0249	.0334	.0432	.0540	.0655	.0771	.0882	.0983
18	.0060	.0093	.0137	.0193	.0264	.0348	.0444	.0550	.0661	.0772
19	.0027	.0044	.0069	.0103	.0148	.0206	.0277	.0360	.0454	.0558
20	.0011	.0019	.0032	.0050	.0077	.0112	.0159	.0217	.0288	.0370
21	.0004	.0008	.0014	.0023	.0036	.0056	.0084	.0121	.0168	.0227
22	.0001	.0003	.0005	.0009	.0016	.0026	.0041	.0062	.0090	.0128
23	.0000	.0001	.0002	.0004	.0006	.0011	.0018	.0029	.0045	.0067
24	.0000	.0000	.0001	.0001	.0002	.0004	.0008	.0013	.0021	.0032
25	.0000	.0000	.0000	.0000	.0001	.0002	.0003	.0005	.0009	.0014
26	.0000	.0000	.0000	.0000	.0000	.0001	.0001	.0002	.0003	.0006
27	.0000	.0000	.0000	.0000	.0000	.0000	.0000	.0001	.0001	.0002
28	.0000	.0000	.0000	.0000	.0000	.0000	.0000	.0000	.0000	.0001

r \ p	.31	.32	.33	.34	.35	.36	.37	.38	.39	.40
0	.0000	.0000	.0000	.0000	.0000	.0000	.0000	.0000	.0000	0
1	.0000	.0000	.0000	.0000	.0000	.0000	.0000	.0000	.0000	.0000
2	.0000	.0000	.0000	.0000	.0000	.0000	.0000	.0000	.0000	.0000
3	.0000	.0000	.0000	.0000	.0000	.0000	.0000	.0000	.0000	.0000
4	.0001	.0000	.0000	.0000	.0000	.0000	.0000	.0000	.0000	.0000
5	.0003	.0002	.0001	.0001	.0000	.0000	.0000	.0000	.0000	.0000
6	.0011	.0007	.0005	.0003	.0002	.0001	.0001	.0000	.0000	.0000
7	.0032	.0022	.0014	.0009	.0006	.0004	.0002	.0001	.0001	.0000
8	.0078	.0055	.0037	.0025	.0017	.0011	.0007	.0004	.0003	.0002
9	.0164	.0120	.0086	.0061	.0042	.0029	.0019	.0013	.0008	.0005
10	.0301	.0231	.0174	.0128	.0093	.0066	.0046	.0032	.0022	.0014
11	.0493	.0395	.0311	.0240	.0182	.0136	.0099	.0071	.0050	.0035
12	.0719	.0604	.0498	.0402	.0319	.0248	.0189	.0142	.0105	.0076
13	.0944	.0831	.0717	.0606	.0502	.0408	.0325	.0255	.0195	.0147
14	.1121	.1034	.0933	.0825	.0714	.0607	.0505	.0412	.0330	.0260
15	.1209	.1168	.1103	.1020	.0923	.0819	.0712	.0606	.0507	.0415
16	.1188	.1202	.1189	.1149	.1088	.1008	.0914	.0813	.0709	.0606
17	.1068	.1132	.1171	.1184	.1171	.1133	.1074	.0997	.0906	.0808
18	.0880	.0976	.1057	.1118	.1156	.1169	.1156	.1120	.1062	.0987
19	.0666	.0774	.0877	.0970	.1048	.1107	.1144	.1156	.1144	.1109
20	.0463	.0564	.0670	.0775	.0875	.0965	.1041	.1098	.1134	.1146
21	.0297	.0379	.0471	.0570	.0673	.0776	.0874	.0962	.1035	.1091
22	.0176	.0235	.0306	.0387	.0478	.0575	.0676	.0777	.0873	.0959
23	.0096	.0135	.0183	.0243	.0313	.0394	.0484	.0580	.0679	.0778
24	.0049	.0071	.0102	.0141	.0190	.0249	.0319	.0400	.0489	.0584
25	.0023	.0035	.0052	.0075	.0106	.0146	.0195	.0255	.0325	.0405
26	.0010	.0016	.0025	.0037	.0055	.0079	.0110	.0150	.0200	.0259
27	.0004	.0007	.0011	.0017	.0026	.0039	.0058	.0082	.0113	.0154
28	.0001	.0003	.0004	.0007	.0012	.0018	.0028	.0041	.0060	.0084
29	.0000	.0001	.0002	.0003	.0005	.0008	.0012	.0019	.0029	.0043
30	.0000	.0000	.0001	.0001	.0002	.0003	.0005	.0008	.0013	.0020
31	.0000	.0000	.0000	.0000	.0001	.0001	.0002	.0003	.0005	.0009
32	.0000	.0000	.0000	.0000	.0000	.0000	.0001	.0001	.0002	.0003
33	.0000	.0000	.0000	.0000	.0000	.0000	.0000	.0000	.0001	.0001

r \ p	.41	.42	.43	.44	.45	.46	.47	.48	.49	.50
0	0	0	0	0	0	0	0	0	0	0
1	.0000	.0000	.0000	0	0	0	0	0	0	0
2	.0000	.0000	.0000	.0000	.0000	.0000	.0000	0	0	0
3	.0000	.0000	.0000	.0000	.0000	.0000	.0000	.0000	.0000	.0000
4	.0000	.0000	.0000	.0000	.0000	.0000	.0000	.0000	.0000	.0000
5	.0000	.0000	.0000	.0000	.0000	.0000	.0000	.0000	.0000	.0000
6	.0000	.0000	.0000	.0000	.0000	.0000	.0000	.0000	.0000	.0000
7	.0000	.0000	.0000	.0000	.0000	.0000	.0000	.0000	.0000	.0000
8	.0001	.0001	.0000	.0000	.0000	.0000	.0000	.0000	.0000	.0000
9	.0003	.0002	.0001	.0001	.0000	.0000	.0000	.0000	.0000	.0000
10	.0009	.0006	.0004	.0002	.0001	.0001	.0001	.0000	.0000	.0000
11	.0024	.0016	.0010	.0007	.0004	.0003	.0002	.0001	.0001	.0000
12	.0054	.0037	.0026	.0017	.0011	.0007	.0005	.0003	.0002	.0001
13	.0109	.0079	.0057	.0040	.0027	.0018	.0012	.0008	.0005	.0003
14	.0200	.0152	.0113	.0082	.0059	.0041	.0029	.0019	.0013	.0008

Table C 571

n = 50 (Continued)									
p r	.41	.42	.43	.44	.45	.46	.47	.48	.49	.50
15	.0334	.0264	.0204	.0155	.0116	.0085	.0061	.0043	.0030	.0020
16	.0508	.0418	.0337	.0267	.0207	.0158	.0118	.0086	.0062	.0044
17	.0706	.0605	.0508	.0419	.0339	.0269	.0209	.0159	.0119	.0087
18	.0899	.0803	.0703	.0604	.0508	.0420	.0340	.0270	.0210	.0160
19	.1053	.0979	.0893	.0799	.0700	.0602	.0507	.0419	.0340	.0270
20	.1134	.1099	.1044	.0973	.0888	.0795	.0697	.0600	.0506	.0419
21	.1126	.1137	.1126	.1092	.1038	.0967	.0884	.0791	.0695	.0598
22	.1031	.1086	.1119	.1131	.1119	.1086	.1033	.0963	.0880	.0788
23	.0872	.0957	.1028	.1082	.1115	.1126	.1115	.1082	.1029	.0960
24	.0682	.0780	.0872	.0956	.1026	.1079	.1112	.1124	.1112	.1080
25	.0493	.0587	.0684	.0781	.0873	.0956	.1026	.1079	.1112	.1123
26	.0329	.0409	.0497	.0590	.0687	.0783	.0875	.0957	.1027	.1080
27	.0203	.0263	.0333	.0412	.0500	.0593	.0690	.0786	.0877	.0960
28	.0116	.0157	.0206	.0266	.0336	.0415	.0502	.0596	.0692	.0788
29	.0061	.0086	.0118	.0159	.0208	.0268	.0338	.0417	.0504	.0598
30	.0030	.0044	.0062	.0087	.0119	.0160	.0210	.0270	.0339	.0419
31	.0013	.0020	.0030	.0044	.0063	.0088	.0120	.0161	.0210	.0270
32	.0006	.0009	.0014	.0021	.0031	.0044	.0063	.0088	.0120	.0160
33	.0002	.0003	.0006	.0009	.0014	.0021	.0031	.0044	.0063	.0087
34	.0001	.0001	.0002	.0003	.0006	.0009	.0014	.0020	.0030	.0044
35	.0000	.0000	.0001	.0001	.0002	.0003	.0005	.0009	.0013	.0020
36	.0000	.0000	.0000	.0000	.0001	.0001	.0002	.0003	.0005	.0008
37	.0000	.0000	.0000	.0000	.0000	.0000	.0001	.0001	.0002	.0003
38	.0000	.0000	.0000	.0000	.0000	.0000	.0000	.0000	.0001	.0001

n = 75									
p r	.01	.02	.03	.04	.05	.06	.07	.08	.09	.10
0	.4706	.2198	.1018	.0468	.0213	.0097	.0043	.0019	.0008	.0004
1	.3565	.3364	.2362	.1463	.0843	.0462	.0244	.0125	.0063	.0031
2	.1332	.2540	.2703	.2255	.1641	.1091	.0680	.0404	.0230	.0127
3	.0327	.1261	.2034	.2287	.2101	.1695	.1246	.0854	.0554	.0343
4	.0060	.0463	.1132	.1715	.1991	.1947	.1688	.1337	.0985	.0685
5	.0009	.0134	.0497	.1015	.1488	.1765	.1804	.1651	.1384	.1081
6	.0001	.0032	.0179	.0493	.0914	.1314	.1584	.1674	.1597	.1402
7	.0000	.0006	.0055	.0203	.0474	.0827	.1176	.1435	.1557	.1535
8	.0000	.0001	.0014	.0072	.0212	.0449	.0752	.1061	.1309	.1450
9	.0000	.0000	.0003	.0022	.0083	.0213	.0421	.0687	.0964	.1199
10	.0000	.0000	.0001	.0006	.0029	.0090	.0209	.0394	.0629	.0880
11	.0000	.0000	.0000	.0002	.0009	.0034	.0093	.0203	.0368	.0578
12	0	.0000	.0000	.0000	.0003	.0012	.0037	.0094	.0194	.0342
13	0	.0000	.0000	.0000	.0001	.0004	.0014	.0040	.0093	.0184
14	0	.0000	.0000	.0000	.0000	.0001	.0005	.0015	.0041	.0091
15	0	.0000	.0000	.0000	.0000	.0000	.0001	.0005	.0016	.0041
16	0	0	.0000	.0000	.0000	.0000	.0000	.0002	.0006	.0017
17	0	0	.0000	.0000	.0000	.0000	.0000	.0001	.0002	.0007
18	0	0	0	.0000	.0000	.0000	.0000	.0000	.0001	.0002
19	0	0	0	.0000	.0000	.0000	.0000	.0000	.0000	.0001
20	0	0	0	0	.0000	.0000	.0000	.0000	.0000	.0000
21	0	0	0	0	.0000	.0000	.0000	.0000	.0000	.0000
22	0	0	0	0	0	.0000	.0000	.0000	.0000	.0000
23	0	0	0	0	0	.0000	.0000	.0000	.0000	.0000
24	0	0	0	0	0	0	.0000	.0000	.0000	.0000
25	0	0	0	0	0	0	.0000	.0000	.0000	.0000
26	0	0	0	0	0	0	0	.0000	.0000	.0000
27	0	0	0	0	0	0	0	0	.0000	.0000
28	0	0	0	0	0	0	0	0	.0000	.0000
29	0	0	0	0	0	0	0	0	0	.0000
30	0	0	0	0	0	0	0	0	0	0
31	0	0	0	0	0	0	0	0	0	0
32	0	0	0	0	0	0	0	0	0	0
33	0	0	0	0	0	0	0	0	0	0
34	0	0	0	0	0	0	0	0	0	0
35	0	0	0	0	0	0	0	0	0	0

Table C

p \ r	.11	.12	.13	.14	.15	.16	.17	.18	.19	.20
0	.0002	.0001	.0000	.0000	.0000	.0000	.0000	.0000	.0000	.0000
1	.0015	.0007	.0003	.0001	.0001	.0000	.0000	.0000	.0000	.0000
2	.0068	.0035	.0018	.0009	.0004	.0002	.0001	.0000	.0000	.0000
3	.0204	.0117	.0066	.0036	.0019	.0010	.0005	.0002	.0001	.0001
4	.0454	.0288	.0176	.0104	.0060	.0034	.0018	.0010	.0005	.0003
5	.0797	.0558	.0374	.0241	.0150	.0091	.0053	.0030	.0017	.0009
6	.1149	.0888	.0652	.0458	.0309	.0201	.0127	.0077	.0046	.0027
7	.1400	.1193	.0961	.0735	.0538	.0378	.0256	.0167	.0106	.0065
8	.1470	.1383	.1220	.1018	.0807	.0612	.0446	.0313	.0212	.0139
9	.1353	.1404	.1357	.1233	.1060	.0868	.0679	.0511	.0370	.0258
10	.1104	.1264	.1339	.1325	.1235	.1091	.0919	.0740	.0572	.0426
11	.0806	.1018	.1182	.1275	.1288	.1228	.1112	.0960	.0793	.0630
12	.0531	.0741	.0942	.1107	.1212	.1248	.1214	.1124	.0992	.0840
13	.0318	.0489	.0682	.0873	.1037	.1152	.1205	.1195	.1128	.1017
14	.0174	.0296	.0451	.0629	.0810	.0971	.1093	.1162	.1172	.1126
15	.0088	.0164	.0274	.0417	.0581	.0752	.0911	.1037	.1118	.1145
16	.0041	.0084	.0154	.0254	.0385	.0537	.0699	.0854	.0983	.1073
17	.0017	.0040	.0080	.0144	.0236	.0355	.0497	.0650	.0800	.0931
18	.0007	.0017	.0038	.0075	.0134	.0218	.0328	.0460	.0605	.0750
19	.0003	.0007	.0017	.0037	.0071	.0125	.0202	.0303	.0426	.0563
20	.0001	.0003	.0007	.0017	.0035	.0066	.0116	.0186	.0280	.0394
21	.0000	.0001	.0003	.0007	.0016	.0033	.0062	.0107	.0172	.0258
22	.0000	.0000	.0001	.0003	.0007	.0016	.0031	.0058	.0099	.0158
23	.0000	.0000	.0000	.0001	.0003	.0007	.0015	.0029	.0053	.0091
24	.0000	.0000	.0000	.0000	.0001	.0003	.0007	.0014	.0027	.0049
25	.0000	.0000	.0000	.0000	.0000	.0001	.0003	.0006	.0013	.0025
26	.0000	.0000	.0000	.0000	.0000	.0000	.0001	.0003	.0006	.0012
27	.0000	.0000	.0000	.0000	.0000	.0000	.0000	.0001	.0002	.0005
28	.0000	.0000	.0000	.0000	.0000	.0000	.0000	.0000	.0001	.0002
29	.0000	.0000	.0000	.0000	.0000	.0000	.0000	.0000	.0000	.0001
30	.0000	.0000	.0000	.0000	.0000	.0000	.0000	.0000	.0000	.0000
31	0	.0000	.0000	.0000	.0000	.0000	.0000	.0000	.0000	.0000
32	0	.0000	.0000	.0000	.0000	.0000	.0000	.0000	.0000	.0000
33	0	0	.0000	.0000	.0000	.0000	.0000	.0000	.0000	.0000
34	0	0	0	.0000	.0000	.0000	.0000	.0000	.0000	.0000
35	0	0	0	0	.0000	.0000	.0000	.0000	.0000	.0000

p \ r	.21	.22	.23	.24	.25	.26	.27	.28	.29	.30
0	.0000	.0000	.0000	.0000	.0000	.0000	.0000	.0000	0	0
1	.0000	.0000	.0000	.0000	.0000	.0000	.0000	.0000	.0000	.0000
2	.0000	.0000	.0000	.0000	.0000	.0000	.0000	.0000	.0000	.0000
3	.0000	.0000	.0000	.0000	.0000	.0000	.0000	.0000	.0000	.0000
4	.0001	.0001	.0000	.0000	.0000	.0000	.0000	.0000	.0000	.0000
5	.0005	.0002	.0001	.0001	.0000	.0000	.0000	.0000	.0000	.0000
6	.0015	.0008	.0004	.0002	.0001	.0001	.0000	.0000	.0000	.0000
7	.0039	.0023	.0013	.0007	.0004	.0002	.0001	.0001	.0000	.0000
8	.0088	.0055	.0033	.0019	.0011	.0006	.0003	.0002	.0001	.0000
9	.0175	.0115	.0073	.0045	.0027	.0016	.0009	.0005	.0003	.0001
10	.0307	.0213	.0144	.0094	.0060	.0037	.0022	.0013	.0007	.0004
11	.0481	.0355	.0254	.0176	.0118	.0077	.0049	.0030	.0018	.0011
12	.0683	.0535	.0404	.0296	.0209	.0144	.0096	.0062	.0039	.0024
13	.0879	.0731	.0585	.0453	.0338	.0245	.0172	.0118	.0078	.0050
14	.1035	.0913	.0774	.0633	.0500	.0381	.0282	.0202	.0141	.0095
15	.1119	.1047	.0940	.0813	.0677	.0545	.0424	.0320	.0234	.0166
16	.1116	.1107	.1053	.0962	.0846	.0718	.0589	.0467	.0359	.0267
17	.1029	.1084	.1092	.1055	.0979	.0876	.0756	.0630	.0508	.0397
18	.0881	.0985	.1051	.1073	.1052	.0991	.0900	.0789	.0669	.0549
19	.0703	.0834	.0942	.1017	.1052	.1045	.0999	.0921	.0820	.0705
20	.0523	.0658	.0788	.0899	.0982	.1028	.1035	.1003	.0938	.0846
21	.0364	.0486	.0616	.0744	.0857	.0946	.1002	.1021	.1003	.0950
22	.0238	.0337	.0452	.0576	.0701	.0816	.0910	.0975	.1005	.1000
23	.0146	.0219	.0311	.0419	.0539	.0661	.0776	.0874	.0946	.0987
24	.0084	.0134	.0201	.0287	.0389	.0503	.0622	.0736	.0838	.0917
25	.0045	.0077	.0123	.0185	.0265	.0360	.0469	.0584	.0698	.0801
26	.0023	.0042	.0070	.0112	.0170	.0244	.0334	.0437	.0548	.0660
27	.0011	.0021	.0038	.0064	.0103	.0155	.0224	.0308	.0406	.0514
28	.0005	.0010	.0020	.0035	.0059	.0094	.0142	.0206	.0285	.0377
29	.0002	.0005	.0009	.0018	.0032	.0053	.0085	.0130	.0188	.0262

Table C   573

r \ p	.21	.22	.23	.24	.25	.26	.27	.28	.29	.30
30	.0001	.0002	.0004	.0009	.0016	.0029	.0048	.0077	.0118	.0172
31	.0000	.0001	.0002	.0004	.0008	.0015	.0026	.0044	.0070	.0107
32	.0000	.0000	.0001	.0002	.0004	.0007	.0013	.0023	.0039	.0063
33	.0000	.0000	.0000	.0001	.0002	.0003	.0006	.0012	.0021	.0035
34	.0000	.0000	.0000	.0000	.0001	.0001	.0003	.0006	.0011	.0019
35	.0000	.0000	.0000	.0000	.0000	.0001	.0001	.0003	.0005	.0009
36	.0000	.0000	.0000	.0000	.0000	.0000	.0001	.0001	.0002	.0004
37	.0000	.0000	.0000	.0000	.0000	.0000	.0000	.0000	.0001	.0002
38	.0000	.0000	.0000	.0000	.0000	.0000	.0000	.0000	.0000	.0001

r	.31	.32	.33	.34	.35	.36	.37	.38	.39	.40
0	0	0	0	0	0	0	0	0	0	0
1	.0000	0	0	0	0	0	0	0	0	0
2	.0000	.0000	.0000	.0000	0	0	0	0	0	0
3	.0000	.0000	.0000	.0000	.0000	.0000	0	0	0	0
4	.0000	.0000	.0000	.0000	.0000	.0000	.0000	.0000	.0000	0
5	.0000	.0000	.0000	.0000	.0000	.0000	.0000	.0000	.0000	.0000
6	.0000	.0000	.0000	.0000	.0000	.0000	.0000	.0000	.0000	.0000
7	.0000	.0000	.0000	.0000	.0000	.0000	.0000	.0000	.0000	.0000
8	.0000	.0000	.0000	.0000	.0000	.0000	.0000	.0000	.0000	.0000
9	.0001	.0000	.0000	.0000	.0000	.0000	.0000	.0000	.0000	.0000
10	.0002	.0001	.0001	.0000	.0000	.0000	.0000	.0000	.0000	.0000
11	.0006	.0003	.0002	.0001	.0001	.0000	.0000	.0000	.0000	.0000
12	.0014	.0008	.0005	.0003	.0001	.0001	.0000	.0000	.0000	.0000
13	.0032	.0019	.0011	.0007	.0004	.0002	.0001	.0001	.0000	.0000
14	.0063	.0040	.0025	.0015	.0009	.0005	.0003	.0002	.0001	.0000
15	.0115	.0077	.0050	.0032	.0020	.0012	.0007	.0004	.0002	.0001
16	.0193	.0136	.0093	.0061	.0040	.0025	.0015	.0009	.0005	.0003
17	.0301	.0222	.0158	.0110	.0074	.0049	.0031	.0019	.0012	.0007
18	.0436	.0336	.0251	.0182	.0129	.0088	.0059	.0038	.0024	.0015
19	.0588	.0474	.0371	.0282	.0208	.0149	.0104	.0070	.0046	.0030
20	.0739	.0625	.0512	.0407	.0314	.0235	.0171	.0121	.0083	.0056
21	.0870	.0770	.0660	.0549	.0442	.0346	.0263	.0194	.0139	.0097
22	.0959	.0890	.0798	.0694	.0585	.0478	.0379	.0292	.0218	.0159
23	.0993	.0965	.0906	.0824	.0725	.0619	.0513	.0412	.0321	.0244
24	.0967	.0984	.0967	.0919	.0846	.0755	.0652	.0547	.0445	.0352
25	.0886	.0944	.0972	.0966	.0930	.0866	.0782	.0684	.0581	.0479
26	.0765	.0855	.0920	.0957	.0963	.0937	.0883	.0806	.0714	.0614
27	.0624	.0730	.0823	.0895	.0941	.0956	.0941	.0897	.0829	.0742
28	.0481	.0589	.0695	.0790	.0868	.0922	.0947	.0942	.0908	.0848
29	.0350	.0449	.0554	.0660	.0758	.0841	.0902	.0936	.0941	.0917
30	.0241	.0324	.0419	.0521	.0626	.0725	.0812	.0880	.0922	.0937
31	.0157	.0221	.0299	.0390	.0489	.0592	.0692	.0783	.0856	.0907
32	.0097	.0143	.0203	.0276	.0362	.0458	.0559	.0659	.0753	.0831
33	.0057	.0088	.0130	.0185	.0254	.0336	.0428	.0527	.0627	.0722
34	.0032	.0051	.0079	.0118	.0169	.0233	.0310	.0399	.0495	.0595
35	.0017	.0028	.0046	.0071	.0107	.0154	.0214	.0286	.0371	.0464
36	.0008	.0015	.0025	.0041	.0064	.0096	.0139	.0195	.0263	.0344
37	.0004	.0007	.0013	.0022	.0036	.0057	.0086	.0126	.0178	.0242
38	.0002	.0003	.0006	.0011	.0019	.0032	.0051	.0077	.0114	.0161
39	.0001	.0002	.0003	.0006	.0010	.0017	.0028	.0045	.0069	.0102
40	.0000	.0001	.0001	.0003	.0005	.0009	.0015	.0025	.0040	.0061
41	.0000	.0000	.0001	.0001	.0002	.0004	.0007	.0013	.0022	.0035
42	.0000	.0000	.0000	.0000	.0001	.0002	.0004	.0006	.0011	.0019
43	.0000	.0000	.0000	.0000	.0000	.0001	.0002	.0003	.0005	.0010
44	.0000	.0000	.0000	.0000	.0000	.0000	.0001	.0001	.0003	.0005
45	.0000	.0000	.0000	.0000	.0000	.0000	.0000	.0001	.0001	.0002
46	.0000	.0000	.0000	.0000	.0000	.0000	.0000	.0000	.0000	.0001

r	.41	.42	.43	.44	.45	.46	.47	.48	.49	.50
0	0	0	0	0	0	0	0	0	0	0
1	0	0	0	0	0	0	0	0	0	0
2	0	0	0	0	0	0	0	0	0	0
3	0	0	0	0	0	0	0	0	0	0
4	0	0	0	0	0	0	0	0	0	0
5	.0000	0	0	0	0	0	0	0	0	0
6	.0000	.0000	.0000	0	0	0	0	0	0	0
7	.0000	.0000	.0000	.0000	.0000	0	0	0	0	0
8	.0000	.0000	.0000	.0000	.0000	.0000	0	0	0	0
9	.0000	.0000	.0000	.0000	.0000	.0000	.0000	.0000	0	0

Table C

p \ r	.41	.42	.43	.44	.45	.46	.47	.48	.49	.50
10	.0000	.0000	.0000	.0000	.0000	.0000	.0000	.0000	.0000	.0000
11	.0000	.0000	.0000	.0000	.0000	.0000	.0000	.0000	.0000	.0000
12	.0000	.0000	.0000	.0000	.0000	.0000	.0000	.0000	.0000	.0000
13	.0000	.0000	.0000	.0000	.0000	.0000	.0000	.0000	.0000	.0000
14	.0000	.0000	.0000	.0000	.0000	.0000	.0000	.0000	.0000	.0000
15	.0001	.0000	.0000	.0000	.0000	.0000	.0000	.0000	.0000	.0000
16	.0002	.0001	.0000	.0000	.0000	.0000	.0000	.0000	.0000	.0000
17	.0004	.0002	.0001	.0001	.0000	.0000	.0000	.0000	.0000	.0000
18	.0009	.0005	.0003	.0002	.0001	.0000	.0000	.0000	.0000	.0000
19	.0019	.0011	.0007	.0004	.0002	.0001	.0001	.0000	.0000	.0000
20	.0036	.0023	.0014	.0008	.0005	.0003	.0002	.0001	.0000	.0000
21	.0066	.0043	.0028	.0017	.0010	.0006	.0004	.0002	.0001	.0001
22	.0112	.0077	.0051	.0033	.0021	.0013	.0008	.0004	.0003	.0001
23	.0179	.0128	.0089	.0060	.0040	.0025	.0016	.0009	.0006	.0003
24	.0270	.0201	.0146	.0103	.0070	.0047	.0030	.0019	.0012	.0007
25	.0383	.0298	.0225	.0165	.0117	.0081	.0055	.0036	.0023	.0014
26	.0512	.0414	.0326	.0249	.0185	.0133	.0093	.0063	.0042	.0027
27	.0645	.0544	.0446	.0355	.0274	.0206	.0150	.0106	.0073	.0049
28	.0769	.0676	.0577	.0478	.0384	.0300	.0228	.0168	.0120	.0083
29	.0866	.0793	.0705	.0609	.0510	.0415	.0327	.0251	.0187	.0135
30	.0923	.0881	.0816	.0733	.0639	.0541	.0445	.0355	.0275	.0207
31	.0931	.0926	.0893	.0836	.0760	.0670	.0573	.0476	.0384	.0300
32	.0889	.0922	.0927	.0903	.0854	.0784	.0699	.0604	.0507	.0413
33	.0805	.0870	.0911	.0925	.0911	.0871	.0807	.0727	.0635	.0538
34	.0691	.0778	.0849	.0898	.0921	.0916	.0884	.0829	.0753	.0665
35	.0563	.0660	.0750	.0826	.0882	.0914	.0919	.0896	.0848	.0779
36	.0434	.0531	.0629	.0721	.0802	.0865	.0905	.0919	.0905	.0865
37	.0318	.0405	.0500	.0597	.0692	.0777	.0846	.0894	.0917	.0912
38	.0221	.0294	.0377	.0469	.0566	.0662	.0750	.0825	.0881	.0912
39	.0146	.0202	.0270	.0350	.0439	.0535	.0631	.0723	.0803	.0865
40	.0091	.0131	.0183	.0247	.0324	.0410	.0504	.0600	.0694	.0779
41	.0054	.0081	.0118	.0166	.0226	.0298	.0381	.0473	.0569	.0665
42	.0030	.0048	.0072	.0106	.0150	.0206	.0274	.0354	.0443	.0538
43	.0016	.0026	.0042	.0064	.0094	.0134	.0186	.0250	.0327	.0413
44	.0008	.0014	.0023	.0036	.0056	.0083	.0120	.0168	.0228	.0300
45	.0004	.0007	.0012	.0020	.0032	.0049	.0073	.0107	.0151	.0207
46	.0002	.0003	.0006	.0010	.0017	.0027	.0042	.0064	.0095	.0135
47	.0001	.0001	.0003	.0005	.0008	.0014	.0023	.0037	.0056	.0083
48	.0000	.0001	.0001	.0002	.0004	.0007	.0012	.0020	.0031	.0049
49	.0000	.0000	.0000	.0001	.0002	.0003	.0006	.0010	.0017	.0027
50	.0000	.0000	.0000	.0000	.0001	.0001	.0003	.0005	.0008	.0014
51	.0000	.0000	.0000	.0000	.0000	.0001	.0001	.0002	.0004	.0007
52	.0000	.0000	.0000	.0000	.0000	.0000	.0000	.0001	.0002	.0003
53	.0000	.0000	.0000	.0000	.0000	.0000	.0000	.0000	.0001	.0001
54	.0000	.0000	.0000	.0000	.0000	.0000	.0000	.0000	.0000	.0001

p \ r	.01	.02	.03	.04	.05	.06	.07	.08	.09	.10
0	.3660	.1326	.0476	.0169	.0059	.0021	.0007	.0002	.0001	.0000
1	.3697	.2707	.1471	.0703	.0312	.0131	.0053	.0021	.0008	.0003
2	.1849	.2734	.2252	.1450	.0812	.0414	.0198	.0090	.0039	.0016
3	.0610	.1823	.2275	.1973	.1396	.0864	.0486	.0254	.0125	.0059
4	.0149	.0902	.1706	.1994	.1781	.1338	.0888	.0536	.0301	.0159
5	.0029	.0353	.1013	.1595	.1800	.1639	.1283	.0895	.0571	.0339
6	.0005	.0114	.0496	.1052	.1500	.1657	.1529	.1233	.0895	.0596
7	.0001	.0031	.0206	.0589	.1060	.1420	.1545	.1440	.1188	.0889
8	.0000	.0007	.0074	.0285	.0649	.1054	.1352	.1455	.1366	.1148
9	.0000	.0002	.0023	.0121	.0349	.0687	.1040	.1293	.1381	.1304
10	.0000	.0000	.0007	.0046	.0167	.0399	.0712	.1024	.1243	.1319
11	.0000	.0000	.0002	.0016	.0072	.0209	.0439	.0728	.1006	.1199
12	.0000	.0000	.0000	.0005	.0028	.0099	.0245	.0470	.0738	.0988
13	.0000	.0000	.0000	.0001	.0010	.0043	.0125	.0276	.0494	.0743
14	0	.0000	.0000	.0000	.0003	.0017	.0058	.0149	.0304	.0513
15	0	.0000	.0000	.0000	.0001	.0006	.0025	.0074	.0172	.0327
16	0	.0000	.0000	.0000	.0000	.0002	.0010	.0034	.0090	.0193
17	0	.0000	.0000	.0000	.0000	.0001	.0004	.0015	.0044	.0106
18	0	0	.0000	.0000	.0000	.0000	.0001	.0006	.0020	.0054
19	0	0	.0000	.0000	.0000	.0000	.0000	.0002	.0009	.0026

Table C   575

r \ p	.01	.02	.03	.04	.05	.06	.07	.08	.09	.10
20	0	0	.0000	.0000	.0000	.0000	.0000	.0001	.0003	.0012
21	0	0	0	.0000	.0000	.0000	.0000	.0000	.0001	.0005
22	0	0	0	.0000	.0000	.0000	.0000	.0000	.0000	.0002
23	0	0	0	0	.0000	.0000	.0000	.0000	.0000	.0001
24	0	0	0	0	.0000	.0000	.0000	.0000	.0000	.0000
25	0	0	0	0	0	.0000	.0000	.0000	.0000	.0000
26	0	0	0	0	0	0	.0000	.0000	.0000	.0000
27	0	0	0	0	0	0	.0000	.0000	.0000	.0000
28	0	0	0	0	0	0	0	.0000	.0000	.0000
29	0	0	0	0	0	0	0	.0000	.0000	.0000
30	0	0	0	0	0	0	0	.0000	.0000	.0000
31	0	0	0	0	0	0	0	.0000	.0000	.0000
32	0	0	0	0	0	0	0	0	.0000	.0000
33	0	0	0	0	0	0	0	0	.0000	.0000
34	0	0	0	0	0	0	0	0	0	.0000
35	0	0	0	0	0	0	0	0	0	0
36	0	0	0	0	0	0	0	0	0	0
37	0	0	0	0	0	0	0	0	0	0
38	0	0	0	0	0	0	0	0	0	0
39	0	0	0	0	0	0	0	0	0	0
40	0	0	0	0	0	0	0	0	0	0
41	0	0	0	0	0	0	0	0	0	0
42	0	0	0	0	0	0	0	0	0	0
43	0	0	0	0	0	0	0	0	0	0
44	0	0	0	0	0	0	0	0	0	0
45	0	0	0	0	0	0	0	0	0	0
46	0	0	0	0	0	0	0	0	0	0
47	0	0	0	0	0	0	0	0	0	0
48	0	0	0	0	0	0	0	0	0	0

r	.11	.12	.13	.14	.15	.16	.17	.18	.19	.20
0	.0000	.0000	.0000	.0000	.0000	.0000	.0000	.0000	.0000	.0000
1	.0001	.0000	.0000	.0000	.0000	.0000	.0000	.0000	.0000	.0000
2	.0007	.0003	.0001	.0000	.0000	.0000	.0000	.0000	.0000	.0000
3	.0027	.0012	.0005	.0002	.0001	.0000	.0000	.0000	.0000	.0000
4	.0080	.0038	.0018	.0008	.0003	.0001	.0001	.0000	.0000	.0000
5	.0189	.0100	.0050	.0024	.0011	.0005	.0002	.0001	.0000	.0000
6	.0369	.0215	.0119	.0063	.0031	.0015	.0007	.0003	.0001	.0001
7	.0613	.0394	.0238	.0137	.0075	.0039	.0020	.0009	.0004	.0002
8	.0881	.0625	.0414	.0259	.0153	.0086	.0047	.0024	.0012	.0006
9	.1112	.0871	.0632	.0430	.0276	.0168	.0098	.0054	.0029	.0015
10	.1251	.1080	.0860	.0637	.0444	.0292	.0182	.0108	.0062	.0034
11	.1265	.1205	.1051	.0849	.0640	.0454	.0305	.0194	.0118	.0069
12	.1160	.1219	.1165	.1025	.0838	.0642	.0463	.0316	.0206	.0128
13	.0970	.1125	.1179	.1130	.1001	.0827	.0642	.0470	.0327	.0216
14	.0745	.0954	.1094	.1143	.1098	.0979	.0817	.0641	.0476	.0335
15	.0528	.0745	.0938	.1067	.1111	.1070	.0960	.0807	.0640	.0481
16	.0347	.0540	.0744	.0922	.1041	.1082	.1044	.0941	.0798	.0638
17	.0212	.0364	.0549	.0742	.0908	.1019	.1057	.1021	.0924	.0789
18	.0121	.0229	.0379	.0557	.0739	.0895	.0998	.1033	.1000	.0909
19	.0064	.0135	.0244	.0391	.0563	.0736	.0882	.0979	.1012	.0981
20	.0032	.0074	.0148	.0258	.0402	.0567	.0732	.0870	.0962	.0993
21	.0015	.0039	.0084	.0160	.0270	.0412	.0571	.0728	.0859	.0946
22	.0007	.0019	.0045	.0094	.0171	.0282	.0420	.0574	.0724	.0849
23	.0003	.0009	.0023	.0052	.0103	.0182	.0292	.0427	.0576	.0720
24	.0001	.0004	.0011	.0027	.0058	.0111	.0192	.0301	.0433	.0577
25	.0000	.0002	.0005	.0013	.0031	.0064	.0119	.0201	.0309	.0439
26	.0000	.0001	.0002	.0006	.0016	.0035	.0071	.0127	.0209	.0316
27	.0000	.0000	.0001	.0003	.0008	.0018	.0040	.0076	.0134	.0217
28	.0000	.0000	.0000	.0001	.0004	.0009	.0021	.0044	.0082	.0141
29	.0000	.0000	.0000	.0000	.0002	.0004	.0011	.0024	.0048	.0088
30	.0000	.0000	.0000	.0000	.0001	.0002	.0005	.0012	.0027	.0052
31	.0000	.0000	.0000	.0000	.0000	.0001	.0002	.0006	.0014	.0029
32	.0000	.0000	.0000	.0000	.0000	.0000	.0001	.0003	.0007	.0016
33	.0000	.0000	.0000	.0000	.0000	.0000	.0000	.0001	.0003	.0008
34	.0000	.0000	.0000	.0000	.0000	.0000	.0000	.0001	.0002	.0004
35	.0000	.0000	.0000	.0000	.0000	.0000	.0000	.0000	.0001	.0002
36	.0000	.0000	.0000	.0000	.0000	.0000	.0000	.0000	.0000	.0001
37	0	.0000	.0000	.0000	.0000	.0000	.0000	.0000	.0000	.0000
38	0	.0000	.0000	.0000	.0000	.0000	.0000	.0000	.0000	.0000
39	0	0	.0000	.0000	.0000	.0000	.0000	.0000	.0000	.0000

Table C

r \ p	.11	.12	.13	.14	.15	.16	.17	.18	.19	.20
40	0	0	0	.0000	.0000	.0000	.0000	.0000	.0000	.0000
41	0	0	0	.0000	.0000	.0000	.0000	.0000	.0000	.0000
42	0	0	0	0	.0000	.0000	.0000	.0000	.0000	.0000
43	0	0	0	0	0	.0000	.0000	.0000	.0000	.0000
44	0	0	0	0	0	0	.0000	.0000	.0000	.0000
45	0	0	0	0	0	0	.0000	.0000	.0000	.0000
46	0	0	0	0	0	0	0	.0000	.0000	.0000
47	0	0	0	0	0	0	0	.0000	.0000	.0000
48	0	0	0	0	0	0	0	0	.0000	.0000

r	.21	.22	.23	.24	.25	.26	.27	.28	.29	.30
0	.0000	.0000	0	0	0	0	0	0	0	0
1	.0000	.0000	.0000	.0000	0	0	0	0	0	0
2	.0000	.0000	.0000	.0000	.0000	.0000	.0000	0	0	0
3	.0000	.0000	.0000	.0000	.0000	.0000	.0000	.0000	.0000	0
4	.0000	.0000	.0000	.0000	.0000	.0000	.0000	.0000	.0000	.0000
5	.0000	.0000	.0000	.0000	.0000	.0000	.0000	.0000	.0000	.0000
6	.0000	.0000	.0000	.0000	.0000	.0000	.0000	.0000	.0000	.0000
7	.0001	.0000	.0000	.0000	.0000	.0000	.0000	.0000	.0000	.0000
8	.0003	.0001	.0000	.0000	.0000	.0000	.0000	.0000	.0000	.0000
9	.0007	.0003	.0002	.0001	.0000	.0000	.0000	.0000	.0000	.0000
10	.0018	.0009	.0004	.0002	.0001	.0000	.0000	.0000	.0000	.0000
11	.0038	.0021	.0011	.0005	.0003	.0001	.0001	.0000	.0000	.0000
12	.0076	.0043	.0024	.0012	.0006	.0003	.0001	.0001	.0000	.0000
13	.0136	.0082	.0048	.0027	.0014	.0007	.0004	.0002	.0001	.0000
14	.0225	.0144	.0089	.0052	.0030	.0016	.0009	.0004	.0002	.0001
15	.0343	.0233	.0152	.0095	.0057	.0033	.0018	.0010	.0005	.0002
16	.0484	.0350	.0241	.0159	.0100	.0061	.0035	.0020	.0011	.0006
17	.0636	.0487	.0356	.0248	.0165	.0106	.0065	.0038	.0022	.0012
18	.0780	.0634	.0490	.0361	.0254	.0171	.0111	.0069	.0041	.0024
19	.0895	.0772	.0631	.0492	.0365	.0259	.0177	.0115	.0072	.0044
20	.0963	.0881	.0764	.0629	.0493	.0369	.0264	.0182	.0120	.0076
21	.0975	.0947	.0869	.0756	.0626	.0494	.0373	.0269	.0186	.0124
22	.0931	.0959	.0932	.0858	.0749	.0623	.0495	.0376	.0273	.0190
23	.0839	.0917	.0944	.0919	.0847	.0743	.0621	.0495	.0378	.0277
24	.0716	.0830	.0905	.0931	.0906	.0837	.0736	.0618	.0496	.0380
25	.0578	.0712	.0822	.0893	.0918	.0894	.0828	.0731	.0615	.0496
26	.0444	.0579	.0708	.0814	.0883	.0906	.0883	.0819	.0725	.0613
27	.0323	.0448	.0580	.0704	.0806	.0873	.0896	.0873	.0812	.0720
28	.0224	.0329	.0451	.0580	.0701	.0799	.0864	.0886	.0864	.0804
29	.0148	.0231	.0335	.0455	.0580	.0697	.0793	.0855	.0876	.0856
30	.0093	.0154	.0237	.0340	.0458	.0580	.0694	.0787	.0847	.0868
31	.0056	.0098	.0160	.0242	.0344	.0460	.0580	.0691	.0781	.0840
32	.0032	.0060	.0103	.0165	.0248	.0349	.0462	.0579	.0688	.0776
33	.0018	.0035	.0063	.0107	.0170	.0252	.0352	.0464	.0579	.0685
34	.0009	.0019	.0037	.0067	.0112	.0175	.0257	.0356	.0466	.0579
35	.0005	.0010	.0021	.0040	.0070	.0116	.0179	.0261	.0359	.0468
36	.0002	.0005	.0011	.0023	.0042	.0073	.0120	.0183	.0265	.0362
37	.0001	.0003	.0006	.0012	.0024	.0045	.0077	.0123	.0187	.0268
38	.0000	.0001	.0003	.0006	.0013	.0026	.0047	.0079	.0127	.0191
39	.0000	.0001	.0001	.0003	.0007	.0015	.0028	.0049	.0082	.0130
40	.0000	.0000	.0001	.0002	.0004	.0008	.0016	.0029	.0051	.0085
41	.0000	.0000	.0000	.0001	.0002	.0004	.0008	.0017	.0031	.0053
42	.0000	.0000	.0000	.0000	.0001	.0002	.0004	.0009	.0018	.0032
43	.0000	.0000	.0000	.0000	.0000	.0001	.0002	.0005	.0010	.0019
44	.0000	.0000	.0000	.0000	.0000	.0000	.0001	.0002	.0005	.0010
45	.0000	.0000	.0000	.0000	.0000	.0000	.0000	.0001	.0003	.0005
46	.0000	.0000	.0000	.0000	.0000	.0000	.0000	.0001	.0001	.0003
47	.0000	.0000	.0000	.0000	.0000	.0000	.0000	.0000	.0001	.0001
48	.0000	.0000	.0000	.0000	.0000	.0000	.0000	.0000	.0000	.0001

r	.31	.32	.33	.34	.35	.36	.37	.38	.39	.40
0	0	0	0	0	0	0	0	0	0	0
1	0	0	0	0	0	0	0	0	0	0
2	0	0	0	0	0	0	0	0	0	0
3	0	0	0	0	0	0	0	0	0	0
4	0	0	0	0	0	0	0	0	0	0
5	.0000	.0000	0	0	0	0	0	0	0	0
6	.0000	.0000	.0000	.0000	0	0	0	0	0	0
7	.0000	.0000	.0000	.0000	.0000	0	0	0	0	0
8	.0000	.0000	.0000	.0000	.0000	.0000	.0000	0	0	0
9	.0000	.0000	.0000	.0000	.0000	.0000	.0000	.0000	0	0

Table C

p r	.31	.32	.33	.34	.35	.36	.37	.38	.39	.40
10	.0000	.0000	.0000	.0000	.0000	.0000	.0000	.0000	.0000	.0000
11	.0000	.0000	.0000	.0000	.0000	.0000	.0000	.0000	.0000	.0000
12	.0000	.0000	.0000	.0000	.0000	.0000	.0000	.0000	.0000	.0000
13	.0000	.0000	.0000	.0000	.0000	.0000	.0000	.0000	.0000	.0000
14	.0000	.0000	.0000	.0000	.0000	.0000	.0000	.0000	.0000	.0000
15	.0001	.0001	.0000	.0000	.0000	.0000	.0000	.0000	.0000	.0000
16	.0003	.0001	.0001	.0000	.0000	.0000	.0000	.0000	.0000	.0000
17	.0006	.0003	.0002	.0001	.0000	.0000	.0000	.0000	.0000	.0000
18	.0013	.0007	.0004	.0002	.0001	.0000	.0000	.0000	.0000	.0000
19	.0025	.0014	.0008	.0004	.0002	.0001	.0000	.0000	.0000	.0000
20	.0046	.0027	.0015	.0008	.0004	.0002	.0001	.0001	.0000	.0000
21	.0079	.0049	.0029	.0016	.0009	.0005	.0002	.0001	.0001	.0000
22	.0127	.0082	.0051	.0030	.0017	.0010	.0005	.0003	.0001	.0001
23	.0194	.0131	.0085	.0053	.0032	.0018	.0010	.0006	.0003	.0001
24	.0280	.0198	.0134	.0088	.0055	.0033	.0019	.0011	.0006	.0003
25	.0382	.0283	.0201	.0137	.0090	.0057	.0035	.0020	.0012	.0006
26	.0496	.0384	.0286	.0204	.0140	.0092	.0059	.0036	.0021	.0012
27	.0610	.0495	.0386	.0288	.0207	.0143	.0095	.0060	.0037	.0022
28	.0715	.0608	.0495	.0387	.0290	.0209	.0145	.0097	.0062	.0038
29	.0797	.0710	.0605	.0495	.0388	.0292	.0211	.0147	.0098	.0063
30	.0848	.0791	.0706	.0603	.0494	.0389	.0294	.0213	.0149	.0100
31	.0860	.0840	.0785	.0702	.0601	.0494	.0389	.0295	.0215	.0151
32	.0833	.0853	.0834	.0779	.0698	.0599	.0493	.0390	.0296	.0217
33	.0771	.0827	.0846	.0827	.0774	.0694	.0597	.0493	.0390	.0297
34	.0683	.0767	.0821	.0840	.0821	.0769	.0691	.0595	.0492	.0391
35	.0578	.0680	.0763	.0816	.0834	.0816	.0765	.0688	.0593	.0491
36	.0469	.0578	.0678	.0759	.0811	.0829	.0811	.0761	.0685	.0591
37	.0365	.0471	.0578	.0676	.0755	.0806	.0824	.0807	.0757	.0682
38	.0272	.0367	.0472	.0577	.0674	.0752	.0802	.0820	.0803	.0754
39	.0194	.0275	.0369	.0473	.0577	.0672	.0749	.0799	.0816	.0799
40	.0133	.0197	.0277	.0372	.0474	.0577	.0671	.0746	.0795	.0812
41	.0087	.0136	.0200	.0280	.0373	.0475	.0577	.0670	.0744	.0792
42	.0055	.0090	.0138	.0203	.0282	.0375	.0476	.0576	.0668	.0742
43	.0033	.0057	.0092	.0141	.0205	.0285	.0377	.0477	.0576	.0667
44	.0019	.0035	.0059	.0094	.0143	.0207	.0287	.0378	.0477	.0576
45	.0011	.0020	.0036	.0060	.0096	.0145	.0210	.0289	.0380	.0478
46	.0006	.0011	.0021	.0037	.0062	.0098	.0147	.0212	.0290	.0381
47	.0003	.0006	.0012	.0022	.0038	.0063	.0099	.0149	.0213	.0292
48	.0001	.0003	.0007	.0012	.0023	.0039	.0064	.0101	.0151	.0215
49	.0001	.0002	.0003	.0007	.0013	.0023	.0040	.0066	.0102	.0152
50	.0000	.0001	.0002	.0004	.0007	.0013	.0024	.0041	.0067	.0103
51	.0000	.0000	.0001	.0002	.0004	.0007	.0014	.0025	.0042	.0068
52	.0000	.0000	.0000	.0001	.0002	.0004	.0008	.0014	.0025	.0042
53	.0000	.0000	.0000	.0000	.0001	.0002	.0004	.0008	.0015	.0026
54	.0000	.0000	.0000	.0000	.0000	.0001	.0002	.0004	.0008	.0015
55	.0000	.0000	.0000	.0000	.0000	.0000	.0001	.0002	.0004	.0008
56	.0000	.0000	.0000	.0000	.0000	.0000	.0000	.0001	.0002	.0004
57	.0000	.0000	.0000	.0000	.0000	.0000	.0000	.0000	.0001	.0002
58	.0000	.0000	.0000	.0000	.0000	.0000	.0000	.0000	.0001	.0001
59	.0000	.0000	.0000	.0000	.0000	.0000	.0000	.0000	.0000	.0001

r	.41	.42	.43	.44	.45	.46	.47	.48	.49	.50
0	0	0	0	0	0	0	0	0	0	0
1	0	0	0	0	0	0	0	0	0	0
2	0	0	0	0	0	0	0	0	0	0
3	0	0	0	0	0	0	0	0	0	0
4	0	0	0	0	0	0	0	0	0	0
5	0	0	0	0	0	0	0	0	0	0
6	0	0	0	0	0	0	0	0	0	0
7	0	0	0	0	0	0	0	0	0	0
8	0	0	0	0	0	0	0	0	0	0
9	0	0	0	0	0	0	0	0	0	0
10	0	0	0	0	0	0	0	0	0	0
11	.0000	0	0	0	0	0	0	0	0	0
12	.0000	.0000	0	0	0	0	0	0	0	0
13	.0000	.0000	.0000	.0000	0	0	0	0	0	0
14	.0000	.0000	.0000	.0000	.0000	0	0	0	0	0

Table C

						n = 100 (Continued)				
r \ p	.41	.42	.43	.44	.45	.46	.47	.48	.49	.50
15	.0000	.0000	.0000	.0000	.0000	.0000	. 0	0	0	0
16	.0000	.0000	.0000	.0000	.0000	.0000	.0000	.0000	0	0
17	.0000	.0000	.0000	.0000	.0000	.0000	.0000	.0000	.0000	0
18	.0000	.0000	.0000	.0000	.0000	.0000	.0000	.0000	.0000	.0000
19	.0000	.0000	.0000	.0000	.0000	.0000	.0000	.0000	.0000	.0000
20	.0000	.0000	.0000	.0000	.0000	.0000	.0000	.0000	.0000	.0000
21	.0000	.0000	.0000	.0000	.0000	.0000	.0000	.0000	.0000	.0000
22	.0000	.0000	.0000	.0000	.0000	.0000	.0000	.0000	.0000	.0000
23	.0001	.0000	.0000	.0000	.0000	.0000	.0000	.0000	.0000	.0000
24	.0002	.0001	.0000	.0000	.0000	.0000	.0000	.0000	.0000	.0000
25	.0003	.0002	.0001	.0000	.0000	.0000	.0000	.0000	.0000	.0000
26	.0007	.0003	.0002	.0001	.0000	.0000	.0000	.0000	.0000	.0000
27	.0013	.0007	.0004	.0002	.0001	.0000	.0000	.0000	.0000	.0000
28	.0023	.0013	.0007	.0004	.0002	.0001	.0000	.0000	.0000	.0000
29	.0039	.0024	.0014	.0008	.0004	.0002	.0001	.0000	.0000	.0000
30	.0065	.0040	.0024	.0014	.0008	.0004	.0002	.0001	.0001	.0000
31	.0102	.0066	0041	.0025	.0014	.0008	.0004	.0002	.0001	.0001
32	.0152	.0103	0067	.0042	.0025	.0015	.0008	.0004	.0002	.0001
33	.0218	.0154	0104	.0068	.0043	.0026	.0015	.0008	.0004	.0002
34	.0298	.0219	.0155	.0105	.0069	.0043	.0026	.0015	.0009	.0005
35	.0391	.0299	.0220	.0156	.0106	.0069	.0044	.0026	.0015	.0009
36	.0491	.0391	.0300	.0221	.0157	.0107	.0070	.0044	.0027	.0016
37	.0590	.0490	.0391	.0300	.0222	.0157	.0107	.0070	.0044	.0027
38	.0680	.0588	.0489	.0391	.0301	.0222	.0158	.0108	.0071	.0045
39	.0751	.0677	.0587	.0489	.0391	.0301	.0223	.0158	.0108	.0071
40	.0796	.0748	.0675	.0586	.0488	.0391	.0301	.0223	.0159	.0108
41	.0809	.0793	.0745	.0673	.0584	.0487	.0391	.0301	.0223	.0159
42	.0790	.0806	.0790	.0743	.0672	.0583	.0487	.0390	.0301	.0223
43	.0740	.0787	.0804	.0788	.0741	.0670	.0582	.0486	.0390	.0301
44	.0666	.0739	.0785	.0802	.0786	.0739	.0669	.0581	.0485	.0390
45	.0576	.0666	.0737	.0784	.0800	.0784	.0738	.0668	.0580	.0485
46	.0479	.0576	.0665	.0736	.0782	.0798	.0783	.0737	.0667	.0580
47	.0382	.0480	.0576	.0665	.0736	.0781	.0797	.0781	.0736	.0666
48	.0293	.0383	.0480	.0577	.0665	.0735	.0781	.0797	.0781	.0735
49	.0216	.0295	.0384	.0481	.0577	.0664	.0735	.0780	.0796	.0780
50	.0153	.0218	.0296	.0385	.0482	.0577	.0665	.0735	.0780	.0796
51	.0104	.0155	.0219	.0297	.0386	.0482	.0578	.0665	.0735	.0780
52	.0068	.0105	.0156	.0220	.0298	.0387	.0483	.0578	.0665	.0735
53	.0043	.0069	.0106	.0156	.0221	.0299	.0388	.0483	.0579	.0666
54	.0026	.0044	.0070	.0107	.0157	.0221	.0299	.0388	.0484	.0580
55	.0015	.0026	.0044	.0070	.0108	.0158	.0222	.0300	.0389	.0485
56	.0008	.0015	.0027	.0044	.0071	.0108	.0158	.0222	.0300	.0390
57	.0005	.0009	.0016	.0027	.0045	.0071	.0108	.0158	.0223	.0301
58	.0002	.0005	.0009	.0016	.0027	.0045	.0071	.0108	.0159	.0223
59	.0001	.0002	.0005	.0009	.0016	.0027	.0045	.0071	.0109	.0159
60	.0001	.0001	.0002	.0005	.0009	.0016	.0027	.0045	.0071	.0108
61	.0000	.0001	.0001	.0002	.0005	.0009	.0016	.0027	.0045	.0071
62	.0000	.0000	.0001	.0001	.0002	.0005	.0009	.0016	.0027	.0045
63	.0000	.0000	.0000	.0001	.0001	.0002	.0005	.0009	.0016	.0027
64	.0000	.0000	.0000	.0000	.0001	.0001	.0002	.0005	.0009	.0016
65	.0000	.0000	.0000	.0000	.0000	.0001	.0001	.0002	.0005	.0009
66	.0000	.0000	.0000	.0000	.0000	.0000	.0001	.0001	.0002	.0005
67	.0000	.0000	.0000	.0000	.0000	.0000	.0000	.0001	.0001	.0002
68	.0000	.0000	.0000	.0000	.0000	.0000	.0000	.0000	.0001	.0001
69	.0000	.0000	.0000	.0000	.0000	.0000	.0000	.0000	.0000	.0001

Table C 579

CUMULATIVE BINOMIAL PROBABILITY DISTRIBUTION

$$P\left(r \geq \tilde{r} \mid n, p\right) = \sum_{r=\tilde{r}}^{n} \binom{n}{r} p^{r} q^{n-r}$$

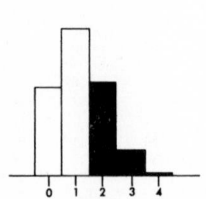

$$P\left(r \geq 2 \mid n = 4, p = 0.30\right) = 0.3483$$

n = 1									

r \\ p	.01	.02	.03	.04	.05	.06	.07	.08	.09	.10
1	.0100	.0200	.0300	.0400	.0500	.0600	.0700	.0800	.0900	.1000
	.11	.12	.13	.14	.15	.16	.17	.18	.19	.20
1	.1100	.1200	.1300	.1400	.1500	.1600	.1700	.1800	.1900	.2000
	.21	.22	.23	.24	.25	.26	.27	.28	.29	.30
1	.2100	.2200	.2300	.2400	.2500	.2600	.2700	.2800	.2900	.3000
	.31	.32	.33	.34	.35	.36	.37	.38	.39	.40
1	.3100	.3200	.3300	.3400	.3500	.3600	.3700	.3800	.3900	.4000
	.41	.42	.43	.44	.45	.46	.47	.48	.49	.50
1	.4100	.4200	.4300	.4400	.4500	.4600	.4700	.4800	.4900	.5000

n = 2									

r \\ p	.01	.02	.03	.04	.05	.06	.07	.08	.09	.10
1	.0199	.0396	.0591	.0784	.0975	.1164	.1351	.1536	.1719	.1900
2	.0001	.0004	.0009	.0016	.0025	.0036	.0049	.0064	.0081	.0100
	.11	.12	.13	.14	.15	.16	.17	..18	.19	.20
1	.2079	.2256	.2431	.2604	.2775	.2944	.3111	.3276	.3439	.3600
2	.0121	.0144	.0169	.0196	.0225	.0256	.0289	.0324	.0361	.0400
	.21	.22	.23	.24	.25	.26	.27	.28	.29	.30
1	.3759	.3916	.4071	.4224	.4375	.4524	.4671	.4816	.4959	.5100
2	.0441	.0484	.0529	.0576	.0625	.0676	.0729	.0784	.0841	.0900
	.31	.32	.33	.34	.35	.36	.37	.38	.39	.40
1	.5239	.5376	.5511	.5644	.5775	.5904	.6031	.6156	.6279	.6400
2	.0961	.1024	.1089	.1156	.1225	.1296	.1369	.1444	.1521	.1600
	.41	.42	.43	.44	.45	.46	.47	.48	.49	.50
1	.6519	.6636	.6751	.6864	.6975	.7084	.7191	.7296	.7399	.7500
2	.1681	.1764	.1849	.1936	.2025	.2116	.2209	.2304	.2401	.2500

n = 3									

r \\ p	.01	.02	.03	.04	.05	.06	.07	.08	.09	.10
1	.0297	.0588	.0873	.1153	.1426	.1694	.1956	.2213	.2264	.2710
2	.0003	.0012	.0026	.0047	.0072	.0104	.0140	.0182	.0228	.0280
3	.0000	.0000	.0000	.0001	.0001	.0002	.0003	.0005	.0007	.0010

p \ r	.11	.12	.13	.14	.15	.16	.17	.18	.19	.20
1	.2950	.3185	.3415	.3639	.3859	.4073	.4282	.4486	.4686	.4880
2	.0336	.0397	.0463	.0533	.0608	.0686	.0769	.0855	.0946	.1040
3	.0013	.0017	.0022	.0027	.0034	.0041	.0049	.0058	.0069	.0080

r	.21	.22	.23	.24	.25	.26	.27	.28	.29	.30
1	.5070	.5254	.5435	.5610	.5781	.5948	.6110	.6268	.6421	.6570
2	.1138	.1239	.1344	.1452	.1562	.1676	.1793	.1913	.2035	.2160
3	.0093	.0106	.0122	.0138	.0156	.0176	.0197	.0220	.0244	.0270

r	.31	.32	.33	.34	.35	.36	.37	.38	.39	.40
1	.6715	.6856	.6992	.7125	.7254	.7379	.7500	.7617	.7730	.7840
2	.2287	.2417	.2548	.2682	.2818	.2955	.3094	.3235	.3377	.3520
3	.0298	.0328	.0359	.0393	.0429	.0467	.0507	.0549	.0593	.0640

r	.41	.42	.43	.44	.45	.46	.47	.48	.49	.50
1	.7946	.8049	.8148	.8244	.8336	.8425	.8511	.8594	.8673	.8750
2	.3665	.3810	.3957	.4104	.4252	.4401	.4551	.4700	.4850	.5000
3	.0689	.0741	.0797	.0852	.0911	.0973	.1038	.1106	.1176	.1250

n = 4

p \ r	.01	.02	.03	.04	.05	.06	.07	.08	.09	.10
1	.0394	.0776	.1147	.1507	.1855	.2193	.2519	.2836	.3143	.3439
2	.0006	.0023	.0052	.0091	.0140	.0199	.0267	.0344	.0430	.0523
3	.0000	.0000	.0001	.0002	.0005	.0008	.0013	.0019	.0027	.0037
4	.0000	.0000	.0000	.0000	.0000	.0000	.0000	.0000	.0001	.0001

r	.11	.12	.13	.14	.15	.16	.17	.18	.19	.20
1	.3726	.4003	.4271	.4530	.4780	.5021	.5254	.5479	.5695	.5904
2	.0624	.0732	.0847	.0968	.1095	.1228	.1366	.1509	.1656	.1808
3	.0049	.0063	.0079	.0098	.0120	.0144	.0171	.0202	.0235	.0272
4	.0001	.0002	.0003	.0004	.0005	.0007	.0008	.0010	.0013	.0016

r	.21	.22	.23	.24	.25	.26	.27	.28	.29	.30
1	.6105	.6298	.6485	.6664	.6836	.7001	.7160	.7313	.7459	.7599
2	.1963	.2122	.2285	.2450	.2617	.2787	.2959	.3132	.3307	.3483
3	.0312	.0356	.0403	.0453	.0508	.0566	.0628	.0694	.0763	.0837
4	.0019	.0023	.0028	.0033	.0039	.0046	.0053	.0061	.0071	.0081

r	.31	.32	.33	.34	.35	.36	.37	.38	.39	.40
1	.7733	.7862	.7985	.8103	.8215	.8322	.8425	.8522	.8615	.8704
2	.3660	.3837	.4015	.4193	.4370	.4547	.4724	.4900	.5075	.5248
3	.0915	.0996	.1082	.1171	.1265	.1362	.1464	.1569	.1679	.1792
4	.0092	.0105	.0119	.0134	.0150	.0168	.0187	.0209	.0231	.0256

r	.41	.42	.43	.44	.45	.46	.47	.48	.49	.50
1	.8788	.8868	.8944	.9017	.9085	.9150	.9211	.9269	.9323	.9375
2	.5420	.5590	.5759	.5926	.6090	.6252	.6412	.6569	.6724	.6875
3	.1909	.2030q	.2155	.2283	.2415	.2550	.2689	.2831	.2977	.3125
4	.0283	.0311	.0342	.0375	.0410	.0448	.0488	.0531	.0576	.0625

n = 5

p \ r	.01	.02	.03	.04	.05	.06	.07	.08	.09	.10
1	.0490	.0961	.1413	.1846	.2262	.2661	.3043	.3409	.3760	.4095
2	.0010	.0038	.0085	.0148	.0226	.0319	.0425	.0544	.0674	.0815
3	.0000	.0001	.0003	.0006	.0012	.0020	.0031	.0045	.0063	.0086
4	.0000	.0000	.0000	.0000	.0000	.0001	.0001	.0002	.0003	.0005

r	.11	.12	.13	.14	.15	.16	.17	.18	.19	.20
1	.4416	.4723	.5016	.5296	.5563	.5818	.6061	.6293	.6513	.6723
2	.0965	.1125	.1292	.1467	.1648	.1835	.2027	.2224	.2424	.2627
3	.0112	.0143	.0179	.0220	.0266	.0318	.0375	.0437	.0505	.0579
4	.0007	.0009	.0013	.0017	.0022	.0029	.0036	.0045	.0055	.0067
5	.0000	.0000	.0000	.0001	.0001	.0001	.0001	.0002	.0002	.0003

Table D

r\p	.21	.22	.23	.24	.25	.26	.27	.28	.29	.30
1	.6923	.7113	.7293	.7464	.7627	.7781	.7927	.8065	.8196	.8319
2	.2833	.3041	.3251	.3461	.3672	.3883	.4093	.4303	.4511	.4718
3	.0659	.0744	.0836	.0933	.1035	.1143	.1257	.1376	.1501	.1631
4	.0081	.0097	.0114	.0134	.0156	.0181	.0208	.0238	.0272	.0308
5	.0004	.0005	.0006	.0008	.0010	.0012	.0014	.0017	.0021	.0024

	.31	.32	.33	.34	.35	.36	.37	.38	.39	.40
1	.8436	.8546	.8650	.8748	.8840	.8926	.9008	.9084	.9155	.9222
2	.4923	.5125	.5325	.5522	.5716	.5906	.6093	.6276	.6455	.6630
3	.1766	.1905	.2050	.2199	.2352	.2509	.2670	.2835	.3003	.3174
4	.0347	.0390	.0436	.0486	.0540	.0598	.0660	.0726	.0796	.0870
5	.0029	.0034	.0039	.0045	.0053	.0060	.0069	.0079	.0090	.0102

	.41	.42	.43	.44	.45	.46	.47	.48	.49	.50
1	.9285	.9344	.9398	.9449	.9497	.9541	.9582	.9620	.9655	.9688
2	.6801	.6967	.7129	.7286	.7438	.7585	.7728	.7865	.7998	.8125
3	.3349	.3525	.3705	.3886	.4069	.4253	.4439	.4625	.4813	.5000
4	.0949	.1033	.1121	.1214	.1312	.1415	.1522	.1635	.1752	.1875
5	.0116	.0131	.0147	.0165	.0185	.0206	.0229	.0255	.0282	.0312

r\p	.01	.02	.03	.04	.05	.06	.07	.08	.09	.10
1	.0585	.1142	.1670	.2172	.2649	.3101	.3530	.3936	.4321	.4686
2	.0015	.0057	.0125	.0216	.0328	.0459	.0608	.0773	.0952	.1143
3	.0000	.0002	.0005	.0012	.0022	.0038	.0058	.0085	.0118	.0158
4	.0000	.0000	.0000	.0000	.0001	.0002	.0003	.0005	.0008	.0013
5	.0000	.0000	.0000	.0000	.0000	.0000	.0000	.0000	.0000	.0001

	.11	.12	.13	.14	.15	.16	.17	.18	.19	.20
1	.5030	.5356	.5664	.5954	.6229	.6487	.6731	.6960	.7176	.7379
2	.1345	.1556	.1776	.2003	.2235	.2472	.2713	.2956	.3201	.3446
3	.0206	.0261	.0324	.0395	.0476	.0560	.0655	.0759	.0870	.0989
4	.0018	.0025	.0034	.0045	.0059	.0075	.0094	.0116	.0141	.0170
5	.0001	.0001	.0002	.0003	.0004	.0005	.0007	.0010	.0013	.0016
6	.0000	.0000	.0000	.0000	.0000	.0000	.0000	.0000	.0000	.0001

	.21	.22	.23	.24	.25	.26	.27	.28	.29	.30
1	.7569	.7748	.7916	.8073	.8220	.8358	.8487	.8607	.8719	.8824
2	.3692	.3937	.4180	.4422	.4661	.4896	.5128	.5356	.5580	.5798
3	.1115	.1250	.1391	.1539	.1694	.1856	.2023	.2196	.2374	.2557
4	.0202	.0239	.0280	.0326	.0376	.0431	.0492	.0557	.0628	.0705
5	.0020	.0025	.0031	.0038	.0046	.0056	.0067	.0079	.0093	.0109
6	.0001	.0001	.0001	.0002	.0002	.0003	.0004	.0005	.0006	.0007

	.31	.32	.33	.34	.35	.36	.37	.38	.39	.40
1	.8921	.9011	.9095	.9173	.9246	.9313	.9375	.9432	.9485	.9533
2	.6012	.6220	.6422	.6619	.6809	.6994	.7172	.7343	.7508	.7667
3	.2744	.2936	.3130	.3328	.3529	.3732	.3937	.4143	.4350	.4557
4	.0787	.0875	.0969	.1069	.1174	.1286	.1404	.1527	.1657	.1792
5	.0127	.0148	.0170	.0195	.0223	.0254	.0288	.0325	.0365	.0410
6	.0009	.0011	.0013	.0015	.0018	.0022	.0026	.0030	.0035	.0041

	.41	.42	.43	.44	.45	.46	.47	.48	.49	.50
1	.9578	.9619	.9657	.9692	.9723	.9752	.9778	.9802	.9824	.9844
2	.7819	.7965	.8105	.8238	.8364	.8485	.8599	.8707	.8810	.8906
3	.4764	.4971	.5177	.5382	.5585	.5786	.5985	.6180	.6373	.6562
4	.1933	.2080	.2232	.2390	.2553	.2721	.2893	.3070	.3252	.3438
5	.0458	.0510	.0566	.0627	.0692	.0762	.0837	.0917	.1003	.1094
6	.0048	.0055	.0063	.0073	.0083	.0095	.0108	.0122	.0138	.0156

r\p	.01	.02	.03	.04	.05	.06	.07	.08	.09	.10
1	.0679	.1319	.1920	.2486	.3017	.3515	.3983	.4422	.4832	.5217
2	.0020	.0079	.0171	.0294	.0444	.0618	.0813	.1026	.1255	.1497
3	.0000	.0003	.0009	.0020	.0038	.0063	.0097	.0140	.0193	.0257
4	.0000	.0000	.0000	.0001	.0002	.0004	.0007	.0012	.0018	.0027
5	.0000	.0000	.0000	.0000	.0000	.0000	.0000	.0001	.0001	.0002

n = 7 (Continued)

r \ p	.11	.12	.13	.14	.15	.16	.17	.18	.19	.20
1	.5577	.5913	.6227	.6521	.6794	.7049	.7286	.7507	.7712	.7903
2	.1750	.2012	.2281	.2556	.2834	.3115	.3396	.3677	.3956	.4233
3	.0331	.0416	.0513	.0620	.0738	.0866	.1005	.1154	.1313	.1480
4	.0039	.0054	.0072	.0094	.0121	.0153	.0189	.0231	.0279	.0333
5	.0003	.0004	.0006	.0009	.0012	.0017	.0022	.0029	.0037	.0047
6	.0000	.0000	.0000	.0000	.0001	.0001	.0001	.0002	.0003	.0004

r \ p	.21	.22	.23	.24	.25	.26	.27	.28	.29	.30
1	.8080	.8243	.8395	.8535	.8665	.8785	.8895	.8997	.9090	.9176
2	.4506	.4775	.5040	.5298	.5551	.5796	.6035	.6266	.6490	.6706
3	.1657	.1841	.2033	.2231	.2436	.2646	.2861	.3081	.3304	.3529
4	.0394	.0461	.0536	.0617	.0706	.0802	.0905	.1016	.1134	.1260
5	.0058	.0072	.0088	.0107	.0129	.0153	.0181	.0213	.0248	.0288
6	.0005	.0006	.0008	.0011	.0013	.0017	.0021	.0026	.0031	.0038
7	.0000	.0000	.0000	.0000	.0001	.0001	.0001	.0001	.0002	.0002

r \ p	.31	.32	.33	.34	.35	.36	.37	.38	.39	.40
1	.9255	.9328	.9394	.9454	.9510	.9560	.9606	.9648	.9686	.9720
2	.6914	.7113	.7304	.7487	.7662	.7828	.7987	.8137	.8279	.8414
3	.3757	.3987	.4217	.4447	.4677	.4906	.5134	.5359	.5581	.5801
4	.1394	.1534	.1682	.1837	.1998	.2167	.2341	.2521	.2707	.2898
5	.0332	.0380	.0434	.0492	.0556	.0625	.0701	.0782	.0869	.0963
6	.0046	.0055	.0065	.0077	.0090	.0105	.0123	.0142	.0164	.0188
7	.0003	.0003	.0004	.0005	.0006	.0008	.0009	.0011	.0014	.0016

r \ p	.41	.42	.43	.44	.45	.46	.47	.48	.49	.50
1	.9751	.9779	.9805	.9827	.9848	.9866	.9883	.9897	.9910	.9922
2	.8541	.8660	.8772	.8877	.8976	.9068	.9153	.9233	.9307	.9375
3	.6017	.6229	.6436	.6638	.6836	.7027	.7213	.7393	.7567	.7734
4	.3094	.3294	.3498	.3706	.3917	.4131	.4346	.4563	.4781	.5000
5	.1063	.1169	.1282	.1402	.1529	.1663	.1803	.1951	.2105	.2266
6	.0216	.0246	.0279	.0316	.0357	.0402	.0451	.0504	.0562	.0625
7	.0019	.0023	.0027	.0032	.0037	.0044	.0051	.0059	.0068	.0078

n = 8

r \ p	.01	.02	.03	.04	.05	.06	.07	.08	.09	.10
1	.0773	.1492	.2163	.2786	.3366	.3904	.4404	.4868	.5297	.5695
2	.0027	.0103	.0223	.0381	.0572	.0792	.1035	.1298	.1577	.1869
3	.0001	.0004	.0013	.0031	.0058	.0096	.0147	.0211	.0289	.0381
4	.0000	.0000	.0001	.0002	.0004	.0007	.0013	.0022	.0034	.0050
5	.0000	.0000	.0000	.0000	.0000	.0000	.0001	.0001	.0003	.0004

r \ p	.11	.12	.13	.14	.15	.16	.17	.18	.19	.20
1	.6063	.6404	.6718	.7008	.7275	.7521	.7748	.7956	.8147	.8322
2	.2171	.2480	.2794	.3111	.3428	.3744	.4057	.4366	.4670	.4967
3	.0487	.0608	.0743	.0891	.1052	.1226	.1412	.1608	.1815	.2031
4	.0071	.0097	.0129	.0168	.0214	.0267	.0328	.0397	.0476	.0563
5	.0007	.0010	.0015	.0021	.0029	.0038	.0050	.0065	.0083	.0104
6	.0000	.0001	.0001	.0002	.0002	.0004	.0005	.0007	.0009	.0012
7	.0000	.0000	.0000	.0000	.0000	.0000	.0000	.0000	.0001	.0001

r \ p	.21	.22	.23	.24	.25	.26	.27	.28	.29	.30
1	.8483	.8630	.8764	.8887	.8999	.9101	.9194	.9278	.9354	.9424
2	.5257	.5538	.5811	.6075	.6329	.6573	.6807	.7031	.7244	.7447
3	.2255	.2486	.2724	.2967	.3215	.3465	.3718	.3973	.4228	.4482
4	.0659	.0765	.0880	.1004	.1138	.1281	.1433	.1594	.1763	.1941
5	.0129	.0158	.0191	.0230	.0273	.0322	.0377	.0438	.0505	.0580
6	.0016	.0021	.0027	.0034	.0042	.0052	.0064	.0078	.0094	.0113
7	.0001	.0002	.0002	.0003	.0004	.0005	.0006	.0008	.0010	.0013
8	.0000	.0000	.0000	.0000	.0000	.0000	.0000	.0000	.0001	.0001

r \ p	.31	.32	.33	.34	.35	.36	.37	.38	.39	.40
1	.9486	.9543	.9594	.9640	.9681	.9719	.9752	.9782	.9808	.9832
2	.7640	.7822	.7994	.8156	.8309	.8452	.8586	.8711	.8828	.8936
3	.4736	.4987	.5236	.5481	.5722	.5958	.6189	.6415	.6634	.6846
4	.2126	.2319	.2519	.2724	.2936	.3153	.3374	.3599	.3828	.4059
5	.0661	.0750	.0846	.0949	.1061	.1180	.1307	.1443	.1586	.1737
6	.0134	.0159	.0187	.9218	.0253	.0293	.0336	.0385	.0439	.0498
7	.0016	.0020	.0024	.0030	.0036	.0043	.0051	.0061	.0072	.0085
8	.0001	.0001	.0001	.0002	.0002	.0003	.0004	.0004	.0005	.0007

r \ p	.41	.42	.43	.44	.45	.46	.47	.48	.49	.50
1	.9853	.9872	.9889	.9903	.9916	.9928	.9938	.9947	.9954	.9961
2	.9037	.9130	.9216	.9295	.9368	.9435	.9496	.9552	.9602	.9648
3	.7052	.7250	.7440	.7624	.7799	.7966	.8125	.8276	.8419	.8555
4	.4292	.4527	.4762	.4996	.5230	.5463	.5694	.5922	.6146	.6367
5	.1895	.2062	.2235	.2416	.2604	.2798	.2999	.3205	.3416	.3633
6	.0563	.0634	.0711	.0794	.0885	.0982	.1086	.1198	.1318	.1445
7	.0100	.0117	.0136	.0157	.0181	.0208	.0239	.0272	.0310	.0352
8	.0008	.0010	.0012	.0014	.0017	.0020	.0024	.0028	.0033	.0039

n = 9

r \ p	.01	.02	.03	.04	.05	.06	.07	.08	.09	.10
1	.0865	.1663	.2398	.3075	.3698	.4270	.4796	.5278	.5721	.6126
2	.0034	.0131	.0282	.0478	.0712	.0978	.1271	.1583	.1912	.2252
3	.0001	.0006	.0020	.0045	.0084	.0138	.0209	.0298	.0405	.0530
4	.0000	.0000	.0001	.0003	.0006	.0013	.0023	.0037	.0057	.0083
5	.0000	.0000	.0000	.0000	.0000	.0001	.0002	.0003	.0005	.0009
6	.0000	.0000	.0000	.0000	.0000	.0000	.0000	.0000	.0000	.0001

r \ p	.11	.12	.13	.14	.15	.16	.17	.18	.19	.20
1	.6496	.6835	.7145	.7427	.7684	.7918	.8131	.8324	.8499	.8658
2	.2599	.2951	.3304	.3657	.4005	.4348	.4685	.5012	.5330	.5638
3	.0672	.0833	.1009	.1202	.1409	.1629	.1861	.2105	.2357	.2618
4	.0117	.0158	.0209	.0269	.0339	.0420	.0512	.0615	.0730	.0856
5	.0014	.0021	.0030	.0041	.0056	.0075	.0098	.0125	.0158	.0196
6	.0001	.0002	.0003	.0004	.0006	.0009	.0013	.0017	.0023	.0031
7	.0000	.0000	.0000	.0000	.0000	.0001	.0001	.0002	.0002	.0003

r \ p	.21	.22	.23	.24	.25	.26	.27	.28	.29	.30
1	.8801	.8931	.9048	.9154	.9249	.9335	.9411	.9480	.9542	.9596
2	.5934	.6218	.6491	.6750	.6997	.7230	.7452	.7660	.7856	.8040
3	.2885	.3158	.3434	.3713	.3993	.4273	.4552	.4829	.5102	.5372
4	.0994	.0114	.1304	.1475	.1657	.1849	.2050	.2260	.2478	.2703
5	.0240	.0291	.0350	.0416	.0489	.0571	.0662	.0762	.0870	.0988
6	.0040	.0051	.0065	.0081	.0100	.0122	.0149	.0179	.0213	.0253
7	.0004	.0006	.0008	.0010	.0013	.0017	.0022	.0028	.0035	.0043
8	.0000	.0000	.0001	.0001	.0001	.0001	.0002	.0003	.0003	.0004

r \ p	.31	.32	.33	.34	.35	.36	.37	.38	.39	.40
1	.9645	.9689	.9728	.9762	.9793	.9820	.9844	.9865	.9883	.9899
2	.8212	.8372	.8522	.8661	.8789	.8908	.9017	.9118	.9210	.9295
3	.5636	.5894	.6146	.6390	.6627	.6856	.7076	.7287	.7489	.7682
4	.2935	.3173	.3415	.3662	.3911	.4163	.4416	.4669	.4922	.5174
5	.1115	.1252	.1398	.1553	.1717	.1890	.2072	.2262	.2460	.2666
6	.0298	.0348	.0404	.0467	.0536	.0612	.0696	.0787	.0886	.0994
7	.0053	.0064	.0078	.0094	.0112	.0133	.0157	.0184	.0215	.0250
8	.0006	.0007	.0009	.0011	.0014	.0017	.0021	.0026	.0031	.0038
9	.0000	.0000	.0000	.0001	.0001	.0001	.0001	.0002	.0002	.0003

r \ p	.41	.42	.43	.44	.45	.46	.47	.48	.49	.50
1	.9913	.9926	.9936	.9946	.9954	.9961	.9967	.9972	.9977	.9980
2	.9372	.9442	.9505	.0563	.9615	.9662	.9704	.9741	.9775	.9805
3	.7866	.8039	.8204	.8359	.8505	.8642	.8769	.8889	.8999	.9102
4	.5424	.5670	.5913	.6152	.6386	.6614	.6836	.7052	.7260	.7461
5	.2878	.3097	.3322	.3551	.3786	.4024	.4265	.4509	.4754	.5000
6	.1109	.1233	.1366	.1508	.1658	.1817	.1985	.2161	.2346	.2539
7	.0290	.0334	.0383	.0437	.0498	.0564	.0637	.0717	.0804	.0898
8	.0046	.0055	.0065	.0077	.0091	.0107	.0125	.0145	.0169	.0195
9	.0003	.0004	.0005	.0006	.0008	.0009	.0011	.0014	.0016	.0020

Table D

p / r	.01	.02	.03	.04	.05	.06	.07	.08	.09	.10
1	.0956	.1829	.2626	.3352	.4013	.4614	.5160	.5656	.6106	.6513
2	.0043	.0162	.0345	.0582	.0861	.1176	.1517	.1879	.2254	.2639
3	.0001	.0009	.0028	.0062	.0115	.0188	.0283	.0401	.0540	.0702
4	.0000	.0000	.0001	.0004	.0010	.0020	.0036	.0058	.0088	.0128
5	.0000	.0000	.0000	.0000	.0001	.0002	.0003	.0006	.0010	.0016
6	.0000	.0000	.0000	.0000	.0000	.0000	.0000	.0000	.0001	.0001

p / r	.11	.12	.13	.14	.15	.16	.17	.18	.19	.20
1	.6882	.7215	.7516	.7787	.8031	.8251	.8448	.8626	.8784	.8926
2	.3028	.3417	.3804	.4184	.4557	.4920	.5270	.5608	.5932	.6242
3	.0884	.1087	.1308	.1545	.1798	.2064	.2341	.2628	.2922	.3222
4	.0178	.0239	.0313	.0400	.0500	.0614	.0741	.0883	.1039	.1209
5	.0025	.0037	.0053	.0073	.0099	.0130	.0168	.0213	.0266	.0328
6	.0003	.0004	.0006	.0010	.0014	.0020	.0027	.0037	.0049	.0064
7	.0000	.0000	.0001	.0001	.0001	.0002	.0003	.0004	.0006	.0009
8	.0000	.0000	.0000	.0000	.0000	.0000	.0000	.0000	.0001	.0001

p / r	.21	.22	.23	.24	.25	.26	.27	.28	.29	.30
1	.9053	.9166	.9267	.9357	.9437	.9508	.9570	.9626	.9674	.9718
2	.6536	.6815	.7079	.7327	.7560	.7778	.7981	.8170	.8345	.8507
3	.3526	.3831	.4137	.4442	.4744	.5042	.5335	.5622	.5901	.6172
4	.1391	.1587	.1794	.2012	.2241	.2479	.2726	.2979	.3239	.3504
5	.0399	.0479	.0569	.0670	.0781	.0904	.1037	.1181	.1337	.1503
6	.0082	.0104	.0130	.0161	.0197	.0239	.0287	.0342	.0404	.0473
7	.0012	.0016	.0021	.0027	.0035	.0045	.0056	.0070	.0087	.0106
8	.0001	.0002	.0002	.0003	.0004	.0006	.0007	.0010	.0012	.0016
9	.0000	.0000	.0000	.0000	.0000	.0000	0001	.0001	.0001	.0001

p / r	.31	.32	.33	.34	.35	.36	.37	.38	.39	.40
1	.9755	.9789	.9818	.9843	.9865	.9885	.9902	.9916	.9929	.9940
2	.8656	.8794	.8920	.9035	.9140	.9236	.9323	.9402	.9473	.9536
3	.6434	.6687	.6930	.7162	.7384	.7595	.7794	.7983	.8160	.8327
4	.3772	.4044	.4316	.4589	.4862	.5132	.5400	.5664	.5923	.6177
5	.1679	.1867	.2064	.2270	.2485	.2708	.2939	.3177	.3420	.3669
6	.0551	.0637	.0732	.0836	.0949	.1072	.1205	.1348	.1500	.1662
7	.0129	.0155	.0185	.0220	.0260	.0305	.0356	.0413	.0477	.0548
8	.0020	.0025	.0032	.0039	.0048	.0059	.0071	.0086	.0103	.0123
9	.0002	.0003	.0003	.0004	.0005	.0007	.0009	.0011	.0014	.0017
10	.0000	.0000	.0000	.0000	.0000	.0000	.0000	.0001	.0001	.0001

p / r	.41	.42	.43	.44	.45	.46	.47	.48	.49	.50
1	.9949	.9957	.9964	.9970	.9975	.9979	.9983	.9986	.9988	.9990
2	.9594	.9645	.9691	.9731	.9767	.9799	.9827	.9852	.9874	.9892
3	.8483	.8628	.8764	.8889	.9004	.9111	.9209	.9298	.9379	.9453
4	.6425	.6665	.6898	.7123	.7340	.7547	.7745	.7933	.8112	.8281
5	.3922	.4178	.4436	.4696	.4956	.5216	.5474	.5730	.5982	.6230
6	.1834	.2016	.2207	.2407	.2616	.2832	.3057	.3288	.3526	.3770
7	.0626	.0712	.0806	.0908	.1020	.1141	.1271	.1410	.1560	.1719
8	.0146	.0172	.0202	.0236	.0274	.0317	.0366	.0420	.0480	.0547
9	.0021	.0025	.0031	.0037	.0045	.0054	.0065	.0077	.0091	.0107
10	.0001	.0002	.0002	.0003	.0003	.0004	.0005	.0006	.0008	.0010

p / r	.01	.02	.03	.04	.05	.06	.07	.08	.09	.10
1	.1047	.1993	.2847	.3618	.4312	.4937	.5499	.6004	.6456	.6862
2	.0052	.0195	.0413	.0692	.1019	.1382	.1772	.2181	.2601	.3026
3	.0002	.0012	.0037	.0083	.0152	.0248	.0370	.0519	.0695	.0896
4	.0000	.0000	.0002	.0007	.0016	.0030	.0053	.0085	.0129	.0185
5	.0000	.0000	.0000	.0000	.0001	.0003	.0005	.0010	.0017	.0028
6	.0000	.0000	.0000	.0000	.0000	.0000	.0000	.0001	.0002	.0003

p / r	.11	.12	.13	.14	.15	.16	.17	.18	.19	.20
1	.7225	.7549	.7839	.8097	.8327	.8531	.8712	.8873	.9015	.9141
2	.3452	.3873	.4286	.4689	.5078	.5453	.5811	.6151	.6474	.6779
3	.1120	.1366	.1632	.1915	.2212	.2521	.2839	.3164	.3494	.3826
4	.0256	.0341	.0442	.0560	.0694	.0846	.1013	.1197	.1397	.1611
5	.0042	.0061	.0087	.0119	.0159	.0207	.0266	.0334	.0413	.0504
6	.0005	.0008	.0012	.0018	.0027	.0037	.0051	.0068	.0090	.0117
7	.0000	.0001	.0001	.0002	.0003	.0005	.0007	.0010	.0014	.0020
8	.0000	.0000	.0000	.0000	.0000	.0000	.0001	.0001	.0002	.0002

n = 11 (Continued)

r \ p	.21	.22	.23	.24	.25	.26	.27	.28	.29	.30
1	.9252	.9350	.9436	.9511	.9578	.9636	.9686	.9730	.9769	.9802
2	.7065	.7333	.7582	.7814	.8029	.8227	.8410	.8577	.8730	.8870
3	.4158	.4488	.4814	.5134	.5448	.5753	.6049	.6335	.6610	.6873
4	.1840	.2081	.2333	.2596	.2867	.3146	.3430	.3719	.4011	.4304
5	.0607	.0723	.0851	.0992	.1146	.1313	.1493	.1685	.1888	.2103
6	.0148	.0186	.0231	.0283	.0343	.0412	.0490	.0577	.0674	.0782
7	.0027	.0035	.0046	.0059	.0076	.0095	.0119	.0146	.0179	.0216
8	.0003	.0005	.0007	.0009	.0012	.0016	.0021	.0027	.0034	.0043
9	.0000	.0000	.0001	.0001	.0001	.0002	.0002	.0003	.0004	.0006

r \ p	.31	.32	.33	.34	.35	.36	.37	.38	.39	.40
1	.9831	.9856	.9878	.9896	.9912	.9926	.9938	.9948	.9956	.9964
2	.8997	.9112	.9216	.9310	.9394	.9470	.9537	.9597	.9650	.9698
3	.7123	.7361	.7587	.7799	.7999	.8186	.8360	.8522	.8672	.8811
4	.4598	.4890	.5179	.5464	.5744	.6019	.6286	.6545	.6796	.7037
5	.2328	.2563	.2807	.3059	.3317	.3581	.3850	.4122	.4397	.4672
6	.0901	.1031	.1171	.1324	.1487	.1661	.1847	.2043	.2249	.2465
7	.0260	.0309	.0366	.0430	.0501	.0581	.0670	.0768	.0876	.0994
8	.0054	.0067	.0082	.0101	.0122	.0148	.0177	.0210	.0249	.0293
9	.0008	.0010	.0013	.0016	.0020	.0026	.0032	.0039	.0048	.0059
10	.0001	.0001	.0001	.0002	.0002	.0003	.0004	.0005	.0006	.0007

r \ p	.41	.42	.43	.44	.45	.46	.47	.48	.49	.50
1	.9970	.9975	.9979	.9983	.9986	.9989	.9991	.9992	.9994	.9995
2	.9739	.9776	.9808	.9836	.9861	.9882	.9900	.9916	.9930	.9941
3	.8938	.9055	.9162	.9260	.9348	.9428	.9499	.9564	.9622	.9673
4	.7269	.7490	.7700	.7900	.8089	.8266	.8433	.8588	.8733	.8867
5	.4948	.5223	.5495	.5764	.6029	.6288	.6541	.6787	.7026	.7256
6	.2690	.2924	.3166	.3414	.3669	.3929	.4193	.4460	.4729	.5000
7	.1121	.1260	.1408	.1568	.1738	.1919	.2110	.2312	.2523	.2744
8	.0343	.0399	.0461	.0532	.0610	.0696	.0791	.0895	.1009	.1133
9	.0072	.0087	.0104	.0125	.0148	.0175	.0206	.0241	.0282	.0327
10	.0009	.0012	.0014	.0018	.0022	.0027	.0033	.0040	.0049	.0059
11	.0001	.0001	.0001	.0001	.0002	.0002	.0002	.0003	.0004	.0005

n = 12

r \ p	.01	.02	.03	.04	.05	.06	.07	.08	.09	.10
1	.1136	.2153	.3062	.3873	.4596	.5241	.5814	.6323	.6775	.7176
2	.0062	.0231	.0486	.0809	.1184	.1595	.2033	.2487	.2948	.3410
3	.0002	.0015	.0048	.0107	.0196	.0316	.0468	.0652	.0866	.1109
4	.0000	.0001	.0003	.0010	.0022	.0043	.0075	.0120	.0180	.0256
5	.0000	.0000	.0000	.0001	.0002	.0004	.0009	.0016	.0027	.0043
6	.0000	.0000	.0000	.0000	.0000	.0000	.0001	.0002	.0003	.0005
7	.0000	.0000	.0000	.0000	.0000	.0000	.0000	.0000	.0000	.0001

r \ p	.11	.12	.13	.14	.15	.16	.17	.18	.19	.20
1	.7530	.7843	.8120	.8363	.8578	.8766	.8931	.9076	.9202	.9313
2	.3867	.4314	.4748	.5166	.5565	.5945	.6304	.6641	.6957	.7251
3	.1377	.1667	.1977	.2303	.2642	.2990	.3344	.3702	.4060	.4417
4	.0351	.0464	.0597	.0750	.0922	.1114	.1324	.1552	.1795	.2054
5	.0065	.0095	.0133	.0181	.0239	.0310	.0393	.0489	.0600	.0726
6	.0009	.0014	.0022	.0033	.0046	.0065	.0088	.0116	.0151	.0194
7	.0001	.0002	.0003	.0004	.0007	.0010	.0015	.0021	.0029	.0039
8	.0000	.0000	.0000	.0000	.0001	.0001	.0002	.0003	.0004	.0006
9	.0000	.0000	.0000	.0000	.0000	.0000	.0000	.0000	.0000	.0001

r \ p	.21	.22	.23	.24	.25	.26	.27	.28	.29	.30
1	.9409	.9493	.9566	.9629	.9683	.9730	.9771	.9806	.9836	.9862
2	.7524	.7776	.8009	.8222	.8416	.8594	.8755	.8900	.9032	.9150
3	.4768	.5114	.5450	.5778	.6093	.6397	.6687	.6963	.7225	.7472
4	.2326	.2610	.2904	.3205	.3512	.3824	.4137	.4452	.4765	.5075
5	.0866	.1021	.1192	.1377	.1576	.1790	.2016	.2254	.2504	.2763
6	.0245	.0304	.0374	.0453	.0544	.0646	.0760	.0887	.1026	.1178
7	.0052	.0068	.0089	.0113	.0143	.0178	.0219	.0267	.0322	.0386
8	.0008	.0011	.0016	.0021	.0028	.0036	.0047	.0060	.0076	.0095
9	.0001	.0001	.0002	.0003	.0004	.0005	.0007	.0010	.0013	.0017
10	.0000	.0000	.0000	.0000	.0000	.0001	.0001	.0001	.0002	.0002

Table D

r \ p	.31	.32	.33	.34	.35	.36	.37	.38	.39	.40
1	.9884	.9902	.9918	.9932	.9943	.9953	.9961	.9968	.9973	.9978
2	.9256	.9350	.9435	.9509	.9576	.9634	.9685	.9730	.9770	.9804
3	.7704	.7922	.8124	.8313	.8487	.8648	.9795	.8931	.9054	.9166
4	.5381	.5681	.5973	.6258	.6533	.6799	.7053	.7296	.7528	.7747
5	.3032	.3308	.3590	.3876	.4167	.4459	.4751	.5043	.5332	.5618
6	.1343	.1521	.1711	.1913	.2127	.2352	.2588	.2833	.3087	.3348
7	.0458	.0540	.0632	.0734	.0846	.0970	.1106	.1253	.1411	.1582
8	.0118	.0144	.0176	.0213	.0255	.0304	.0359	.0422	.0493	.0573
9	.0022	.0028	.0036	.0045	.0056	.0070	.0086	.0104	.0127	.0153
10	.0003	.0004	.0005	.0007	.0008	.0011	.0014	.0018	.0022	.0028
11	.0000	.0000	.0000	.0001	.0001	.0001	.0001	.0002	.0002	.0003

r \ p	.41	.42	.43	.44	.45	.46	.47	.48	.49	.50
1	.9982	.9986	.9988	.9990	.9992	.9994	.9995	.9996	.9997	.9998
2	.9834	.9860	.9882	.9901	.9917	.9931	.9943	.9953	.9961	.9968
3	.9267	.9358	.9440	.9513	.9579	.9637	.9688	.9733	.9773	.9807
4	.7953	.8147	.8329	.8498	.7555	.8801	.8934	.9057	.9168	.9270
5	.5899	.6175	.6443	.6704	.6956	.7198	.7430	.7652	.7862	.8062
6	.3616	.3889	.4167	.4448	.4731	.5014	.5297	.5577	.5855	.6128
7	.1765	.1959	.2164	.2380	.2607	.2843	.3089	.3343	.3604	.3872
8	.0662	.0760	.0869	.0988	.1117	.1258	.1411	.1575	.1751	.1938
9	.0183	.0218	.0258	.0304	.0356	.0415	.0481	.0555	.0638	.0730
10	.0035	.0043	.0053	.0065	.0079	.0095	.0114	.0137	.0163	.0193
11	.0004	.0005	.0007	.0009	.0011	.0014	.0017	.0021	.0026	.0032
12	.0000	.0000	.0000	.0001	.0001	.0001	.0001	.0001	.0002	.0002

r \ p	.01	.02	.03	.04	.05	.06	.07	.08	.09	.10
1	.1225	.2310	.3270	.4118	.4867	.5526	.6107	.6617	.7065	.7458
2	.0072	.0270	.0564	.0932	.1354	.1814	.2298	.2794	.3293	.3787
3	.0003	.0020	.0062	.0135	.0245	.0392	.0578	.0799	.1054	.1339
4	.0000	.0001	.0005	.0014	.0031	.0060	.0103	.0163	.0242	.0342
5	.0000	.0000	.0000	.0001	.0003	.0007	.0013	.0024	.0041	.0065
6	.0000	.0000	.0000	.0000	.0000	.0001	.0001	.0003	.0005	.0009
7	.0000	.0000	.0000	.0000	.0000	.0000	.0000	.0000	.0001	.0001

r \ p	.11	.12	.13	.14	.15	.16	.17	.18	.19	.20
1	.7802	.8102	.8364	.8592	.8791	.8963	.9113	.9242	.9354	.9450
2	.4270	.4738	.5186	.5614	.6017	.6396	.6751	.7080	.7384	.7664
3	.1651	.1985	.2337	.2704	.3080	.3463	.3848	.4231	.4611	.4983
4	.0464	.0609	.0776	.0967	.1180	.1414	.1667	.1939	.2226	.2527
5	.0097	.0139	.0193	.0260	.0342	.0438	.0551	.0681	.0827	.0991
6	.0015	.0024	.0036	.0053	.0075	.0104	.0139	.0183	.0237	.0300
7	.0002	.0003	.0005	.0008	.0013	.0019	.0027	.0038	.0052	.0070
8	.0000	.0000	.0001	.0001	.0002	.0003	.0004	.0006	.0009	.0012
9	.0000	.0000	.0000	.0000	.0000	.0000	.0000	.0001	.0001	.0002

r \ p	.21	.22	.23	.24	.25	.26	.27	.28	.29	.30
1	.9533	.9604	.9666	.9718	.9762	.9800	.9833	.9860	.9883	.9903
2	.7920	.8154	.8367	.8559	.8733	.8889	.9029	.9154	.9265	.9363
3	.5347	.5699	.6039	.6364	.6674	.6968	.7245	.7505	.7749	.7975
4	.2839	.3161	.3489	.3822	.4157	.4493	.4826	.5155	.5478	.5794
5	.1173	.1371	.1585	.1816	.2060	.2319	.2589	.2870	.3160	.3457
6	.0375	.0462	.0562	.0675	.0802	.0944	.1099	.1270	.1455	.1654
7	.0093	.0120	.0154	.0195	.0243	.0299	.0365	.0440	.0527	.0624
8	.0017	.0024	.0032	.0043	.0056	.0073	.0093	.0118	.0147	.0182
9	.0002	.0004	.0005	.0007	.0010	.0013	.0018	.0024	.0031	.0040
10	.0000	.0000	.0001	.0001	.0001	.0002	.0003	.0004	.0005	.0007
11	.0000	.0000	.0000	.0000	.0000	.0000	.0000	.0000	.0001	.0001

r \ p	.31	.32	.33	.34	.35	.36	.37	.38	.39	.40
1	.9920	.9934	.9945	.9955	.9963	.9970	.9975	.9980	.9984	.9987
2	.9450	.9527	.9594	.9653	.9704	.0749	.9787	.9821	.9849	.9874
3	.8185	.8379	.8557	.8720	.8868	.9003	.9125	.9235	.9333	.9421
4	.6101	.6398	.6683	.6957	.7217	.7464	.7698	.7917	.8123	.8314
5	.3760	.4067	.4376	.4686	.4995	.5301	.5603	.5899	.6188	.6470

n = 13 (Continued)

p / r	.31	.32	.33	.34	.35	.36	.37	.38	.39	.40
6	.1867	.2093	.2331	.2581	.2841	.3111	.3388	.3673	.3962	.4256
7	.0733	.0854	.0988	.1135	.1295	.1468	.1654	.1853	.2065	.2288
8	.0223	.0271	.0326	.0390	.0462	.0544	.0635	.0738	.0851	.0977
9	.0052	.0065	.0082	.0102	.0126	.0154	.0187	.0225	.0270	.0321
10	.0009	.0012	.0015	.0020	.0025	.0032	.0040	.0051	.0063	.0078
11	.0001	.0001	.0002	.0003	.0003	.0005	.0006	.0008	.0010	.0013
12	.0000	.0000	.0000	.0000	.0000	.0000	.0001	.0001	.0001	.0001

p / r	.41	.42	.43	.44	.45	.46	.47	.48	.49	.50
1	.9990	.9992	.9993	.9995	.9996	.9997	.9997	.9998	.9998	.9999
2	.9895	.9912	.9928	.9940	.9951	.9960	.9967	.9974	.9979	.9983
3	.9499	.9569	.9630	.9684	.9731	.9772	.9808	.9838	.9865	.9888
4	.8492	.8656	.8807	.8945	.9071	.9185	.9288	.9381	.9464	.9539
5	.6742	.7003	.7254	.7493	.7721	.7935	.8137	.8326	.8502	.8666
6	.4552	.4849	.5146	.5441	.5732	.6019	.6299	.6573	.6838	.7095
7	.2524	.2770	.3025	.3290	.3563	.3842	.4127	.4415	.4707	.5000
8	.1114	.1264	.1426	.1600	.1788	.1988	.2200	.2424	.2659	.2905
9	.0379	.0446	.0520	.0605	.0698	.0803	.0918	.1045	.1183	.1334
10	.0096	.0117	.0141	.0170	.0203	.0242	.0287	.0338	.0396	.0461
11	.0017	.0021	.0027	.0033	.0041	.0051	.0063	.0077	.0093	.0112
12	.0002	.0002	.0003	.0004	.0005	.0007	.0009	.0011	.0014	.0017
13	.0000	.0000	.0000	.0000	.0000	.0000	.0001	.0001	.0001	.0001

n = 14

p / r	.01	.02	.03	.04	.05	.06	.07	.08	.09	.10
1	.1313	.2464	.3472	.4353	.5123	.5795	.6380	.6888	.7330	.7712
2	.0084	.0310	.0645	.1059	.1530	.2037	.2564	.3100	.3632	.4154
3	.0003	.0025	.0077	.0167	.0301	.0478	.0698	.0958	.1255	.1584
4	.0000	.0001	.0006	.0019	.0042	.0080	.0136	.0214	.0315	.0441
5	.0000	.0000	.0000	.0002	.0004	.0010	.0020	.0035	.0059	.0092
6	.0000	.0000	.0000	.0000	.0000	.0001	.0002	.0004	.0008	.0015
7	.0000	.0000	.0000	.0000	.0000	.0000	.0000	.0000	.0001	.0002

p / r	.11	.12	.13	.14	.15	.16	.17	.18	.19	.20
1	.8044	.8330	.8577	.8789	.8972	.9129	.9264	.9379	.9477	.9560
2	.4658	.5141	.5599	.6031	.6433	.6807	.7152	.7469	.7758	.8021
3	.1938	.2315	.2708	.3111	.3521	.3932	.4341	.4744	.5138	.5519
4	.0594	.0774	.0979	.1210	.1465	.1742	.2038	.2351	.2679	.3018
5	.0137	.0196	.0269	.0359	.0467	.0594	.0741	.0907	.1093	.1298
6	.0024	.0038	.0057	.0082	.0115	.0157	.0209	.0273	.0349	.0439
7	.0003	.0006	.0009	.0015	.0022	.0032	.0046	.0064	.0087	.0116
8	.0000	.0001	.0001	.0002	.0003	.0005	.0008	.0012	.0017	.0024
9	.0000	.0000	.0000	.0000	.0000	.0001	.0001	.0002	.0003	.0004

p / r	.21	.22	.23	.24	.25	.26	.27	.28	.29	.30
1	.9631	.9691	.9742	.9786	.9822	.9852	.9878	.9899	.9917	.9932
2	.8259	.8473	.8665	.8837	.8990	.9126	.9246	.9352	.9444	.9525
3	.5887	.6239	.6574	.6891	.7189	.7467	.7727	.7967	.8188	.8392
4	.3366	.3719	.4076	.4432	.4787	.5136	.5479	.5813	.6137	.6448
5	.1523	.1765	.2023	.2297	.2585	.2884	.3193	.3509	.3832	.4158
6	.0543	.0662	.0797	.0949	.1117	.1301	.1502	.1718	.1949	.2195
7	.0152	.0196	.0248	.0310	.0383	.0467	.0563	.0673	.0796	.0933
8	.0033	.0045	.0060	.0079	.0103	.0132	.0167	.0208	.0257	.0315
9	.0006	.0008	.0011	.0016	.0022	.0029	.0038	.0050	.0065	.0083
10	.0001	.0001	.0002	.0002	.0003	.0005	.0007	.0009	.0012	.0017
11	.0000	.0000	.0000	.0000	.0000	.0001	.0001	.0001	.0002	.0002

p / r	.31	.32	.33	.34	.35	.36	.37	.38	.39	.40
1	.9945	.9955	.9963	.9970	.9976	.9981	.9984	.9988	.9990	.9992
2	.9596	.9657	.9710	.9756	.9795	.9828	.9857	.9881	.9902	.9919
3	.8577	.8746	.8899	.9037	.9161	.9271	.9370	.9457	.9534	.9602
4	.6747	.7032	.7301	.7556	.7795	.8018	.8226	.8418	.8595	.8757
5	.4486	.4813	.5138	.5458	.5773	.6080	.6378	.6666	.6943	.7207
6	.2454	.2724	.3006	.3297	.3595	.3899	.4208	.4519	.4831	.5141
7	.1084	.1250	.1431	.1626	.1836	.2059	.2296	.2545	.2805	.3075
8	.0381	.0458	.0545	.0643	.0753	.0876	.1012	.1162	.1325	.1501
9	.0105	.0131	.0163	.0200	.0243	.0294	.0353	.0420	.0497	.0583
10	.0022	.0029	.0037	.0048	.0060	.0076	.0095	.0117	.0144	.0175

Table D

n = 14 (Continued)

r\p	.31	.32	.33	.34	.35	.36	.37	.38	.39	.40
11	.0003	.0005	.0006	.0008	.0011	.0014	.0019	.0024	.0031	.0039
12	.0000	.0001	.0001	.0001	.0001	.0002	.0003	.0003	.0005	.0006
13	.0000	.0000	.0000	.0000	.0000	.0000	.0000	.0000	.0000	.0001

r\p	.41	.42	.43	.44	.45	.46	.47	.48	.49	.50
1	.9994	.9995	.9996	.9997	.9998	.9998	.9999	.9999	.9999	.9999
2	.9934	.9946	.9956	.9964	.9971	.9977	.9981	.9985	.9988	.9991
3	.9661	.9713	.9758	.9797	.9830	.9858	.9883	.9903	.9921	.9935
4	.8905	.9039	.9161	.9270	.9368	.9455	.9532	.9601	.9661	.9713
5	.7459	.7697	.7922	.8132	.8328	.8510	.8678	.8833	.8974	.9102
6	.5450	.5754	.6052	.6344	.6627	.6900	.7163	.7415	.7654	.7880
7	.3355	.3643	.3937	.4236	.4539	.4843	.5148	.5451	.5751	.6047
8	.1692	.1896	.2113	.2344	.2586	.2840	.3105	.3380	.3663	.3953
9	.0680	.0789	.0910	.1043	.1189	.1348	.1520	.1707	.1906	.2120
10	.0212	.0255	.0304	.0361	.0426	.0500	.0583	.0677	.0782	.0898
11	.0049	.0061	.0076	.0093	.0114	.0139	.0168	.0202	.0241	.0287
12	.0008	.0010	.0013	.0017	.0022	.0027	.0034	.0042	.0053	.0065
13	.0001	.0001	.0001	.0002	.0003	.0003	.0004	.0006	.0007	.0009
14	.0000	.0000	.0000	.0000	.0000	.0000	.0000	.0000	.0000	.0001

n = 15

r\p	.01	.02	.03	.04	.05	.06	.07	.08	.09	.10
1	.1399	.2614	.3667	.4579	.5367	.6047	.6633	.7137	.7570	.7941
2	.0096	.0353	.0730	.1191	.1710	.2262	.2832	.3403	.3965	.4510
3	.0004	.0030	.0094	.0203	.0362	.0571	.0829	.1130	.1469	.1841
4	.0000	.0002	.0008	.0024	.0055	.0104	.0175	.0273	.0399	.0556
5	.0000	.0000	.0001	.0002	.0006	.0014	.0028	.0050	.0082	.0127
6	.0000	.0000	.0000	.0000	.0001	.0001	.0003	.0007	.0013	.0022
7	.0000	.0000	.0000	.0000	.0000	.0000	.0000	.0001	.0002	.0003

r\p	.11	.12	.13	.14	.15	.16	.17	.18	.19	.20
1	.8259	.8530	.8762	.8959	.9126	.9269	.9389	.9490	.9576	.9648
2	.5031	.5524	.5987	.6417	.6814	.7179	.7511	.7813	.8085	.8329
3	.2238	.2654	.3084	.3520	.3958	.4392	.4819	.5234	.5635	.6020
4	.0742	.0959	.1204	.1476	.1773	.2092	.2429	.2782	.3146	.3518
5	.0187	.0265	.0361	.0478	.0617	.0778	.0961	.1167	.1394	.1642
6	.0037	.0057	.0084	.0121	.0168	.0227	.0300	.0387	.0490	.0611
7	.0006	.0010	.0015	.0024	.0036	.0052	.0074	.0102	.0137	.0181
8	.0001	.0001	.0002	.0004	.0006	.0010	.0014	.0021	.0030	.0042
9	.0000	.0000	.0000	.0000	.0001	.0001	.0002	.0003	.0005	.0008
10	.0000	.0000	.0000	.0000	.0000	.0000	.0000	.0000	.0001	.0001

r\p	.21	.22	.23	.24	.25	.26	.27	.28	.29	.30
1	.9709	.9759	.9802	.9837	.9866	.9891	.9911	.9928	.9941	.9953
2	.8547	.8741	.8913	.9065	.9198	.9315	.9417	.9505	.9581	.9647
3	.6385	.6731	.7055	.7358	.7639	.7899	.8137	.8355	.8553	.8732
4	.3895	.4274	.4650	.5022	.5387	.5742	.6086	.6416	.6732	.7031
5	.1910	.2195	.2495	.2810	.3135	.3469	.3810	.4154	.4500	.4845
6	.0748	.0905	.1079	.1272	.1484	.1713	.1958	.2220	.2495	.2784
7	.0234	.0298	.0374	.0463	.0566	.0684	.0817	.0965	.1130	.1311
8	.0058	.0078	.0104	.0135	.0173	.0219	.0274	.0338	.0413	.0500
9	.0011	.0016	.0023	.0031	.0042	.0056	.0073	.0094	.0121	.0152
10	.0002	.0003	.0004	.0006	.0008	.0011	.0015	.0021	.0028	.0037
11	.0000	.0000	.0001	.0001	.0001	.0002	.0002	.0003	.0005	.0007
12	.0000	.0000	.0000	.0000	.0000	.0000	.0000	.0000	.0001	.0001

r\p	.31	.32	.33	.34	.35	.36	.37	.38	.39	.40
1	.9962	.9969	.9975	.9980	.9984	.9988	.9990	.9992	.9994	.9995
2	.9704	.9752	.9794	.9829	.9858	.9883	.9904	.9922	.9936	.9948
3	.8893	.9038	.9167	.9281	.9383	.9472	.9550	.9618	.9678	.9729
4	.7314	.7580	.7829	.8060	.8273	.8469	.8649	.8813	.8961	.9095
5	.5187	.5523	.5852	.6171	.6481	.6778	.7062	.7332	.7587	.7827
6	.3084	.3393	.3709	.4032	.4357	.4684	.5011	.5335	.5654	.5968
7	.1509	.1722	.1951	.2194	.2452	.2722	.3003	.3295	.3595	.3902
8	.0599	.0711	.0837	.0977	.1132	.1302	.1487	.1687	.1902	.2131
9	.0190	.0236	.0289	.0351	.0422	.0504	.0597	.0702	.0820	.0950
10	.0048	.0062	.0079	.0099	.0124	.0154	.0190	.0232	.0281	.0338
11	.0009	.0012	.0016	.0022	.0028	.0037	.0047	.0059	.0075	.0093
12	.0001	.0002	.0003	.0004	.0005	.0006	.0009	.0011	.0015	.0019
13	.0000	.0000	.0000	.0000	.0001	.0001	.0001	.0002	.0002	.0003

n = 15 (Continued)

r\p	.41	.42	.43	.44	.45	.46	.47	.48	.49	.50
1	.9996	.9997	.9998	.9998	.9999	.9999	.9999	.9999	1.0000	1.0000
2	.9958	.9966	.9973	.9979	.9983	.9987	.9990	.9992	.9994	.9995
3	.9773	.9811	.9843	.9870	.9893	.9913	.9929	.9943	.9954	.9963
4	.9215	.9322	.9417	.9502	.9576	.9641	.9697	.9746	.9788	.9824
5	.8052	.8261	.8454	.8633	.8796	.8945	.9080	.9201	.9310	.9408
6	.6274	.6570	.6856	.7131	.7392	.7641	.7875	.8095	.8301	.8491
7	.4214	.4530	.4847	.5164	.5478	.5789	.6095	.6394	.6684	.6964
8	.2374	.2630	.2898	.3176	.3465	.3762	.4065	.4374	.4686	.5000
9	.1095	.1254	.1427	.1615	.1818	.2034	.2265	.2510	.2767	.3036
10	.0404	.0479	.0565	.0661	.0769	.0890	.1024	.1171	.1333	.1509
11	.0116	.0143	.0174	.0211	.0255	.0305	.0363	.0430	.0506	.0592
12	.0025	.0032	.0040	.0051	.0063	.0079	.0097	.0119	.0145	.0176
13	.0004	.0005	.0007	.0009	.0011	.00p4	.0018	.0023	.0029	.0037
14	.0000	.0000	.0001	.0001	.0001	.0002	.0002	.0003	.0004	.0005

n = 16

r\p	.01	.02	.03	.04	.05	.06	.07	.08	.09	.10
1	.1485	.2762	.3857	.4796	.5599	.6284	.6869	.7366	.7789	.8147
2	.0109	.0399	.0818	.1327	.1892	.2489	.3098	.3701	.4289	.4853
3	.0005	.0037	.0113	.0242	.0429	.0673	.0969	.1311	.1694	.2108
4	.0000	.0002	.0011	.0032	.0070	.0132	.0221	.0342	.0496	.0684
5	.0000	.0000	.0001	.0003	.0009	.0019	.0038	.0068	.0111	.0170
6	.0000	.0000	.0000	.0000	.0001	.0002	.0005	.0010	.0019	.0033
7	.0000	.0000	.0000	.0000	.0000	.0000	.0001	.0001	.0003	.0005
8	.0000	.0000	.0000	.0000	.0000	.0000	.0000	.0000	.0000	.0001

r\p	.11	.12	.13	.14	.15	.16	.17	.18	.19	.20
1	.8450	.8707	.8923	.9105	.9257	.9386	.9493	.9582	.9657	.9719
2	.5386	.5885	.6347	.6773	.7161	.7513	.7830	.8115	.8368	.8593
3	.2545	.2999	.3461	.3926	.4386	.4838	.5277	.5698	.6101	.6482
4	.0907	.1162	.1448	.1763	.2101	.2460	.2836	.3223	.3619	.4019
5	.0248	.0348	.0471	.0618	.0791	.0988	.1211	.1458	.1727	.2018
6	.0053	.0082	.0120	.0171	.0235	.0315	.0412	.0527	.0662	.0817
7	.0009	.0015	.0024	.0038	.0056	.0080	.0112	.0153	.0204	.0267
8	.0001	.0002	.0004	.0007	.0011	.0016	.0024	.0036	.0051	.0070
9	.0000	.0000	.0001	.0001	.0002	.0003	.0004	.0007	.0010	.0015
10	.0000	.0000	.0000	.0000	.0000	.0000	.0001	.0001	.0002	.0002

r\p	.21	.22	.23	.24	.25	.26	.27	.28	.29	.30
1	.9770	.9812	.9847	.9876	.9900	.9919	.9935	.9948	.9958	.9967
2	.8791	.8965	.9117	.9250	.9365	.9465	.9550	.9623	.9686	.9739
3	.6839	.7173	.7483	.7768	.8029	.8267	.8482	.8677	.8851	.9006
4	.4418	.4814	.5203	.5583	.5950	.6303	.6640	.6959	.7260	.7541
5	.2327	.2652	.2991	.3341	.3698	.4060	.4425	.4788	.5147	.5501
6	.0992	.1188	.1405	.1641	.1897	.2169	.2458	.2761	.3077	.3402
7	.0342	.0432	.0536	.0658	.0796	.0951	.1125	.1317	.1526	.1753
8	.0095	.0127	.0166	.0214	.0271	.0340	.0420	.0514	.0621	.0744
9	.0021	.0030	.0041	.0056	.0075	.0098	.0127	.0163	.0206	.0257
10	.0004	.0006	.0008	.0012	.0016	.0023	.0031	.0041	.0055	.0071
11	.0001	.0001	.0001	.0002	.0003	.0004	.0006	.0008	.0011	.0016
12	.0000	.0000	.0000	.0000	.0000	.0001	.0001	.0001	.0002	.0003

r\p	.31	.32	.33	.34	.35	.36	.37	.38	.39	.40
1	.9974	.9979	.9984	.9987	.9990	.9992	.9994	.9995	.9996	.9997
2	.9784	.9822	.9854	.9880	.9902	.9921	.9936	.9948	.9959	.9967
3	.9144	.9266	.9374	.9467	.9549	.9620	.9681	.9734	.9778	.9817
4	.7804	.8047	.8270	.8475	.8661	.8830	.8982	.9119	.9241	.9349
5	.5846	.6181	.6504	.6813	.7108	.7387	.7649	.7895	.8123	.8334
6	.3736	.4074	.4416	.4759	.5100	.5438	.5770	.6094	.6408	.6712
7	.1997	.2257	.2531	.2819	.3119	.3428	.3746	.4070	.4398	.4728
8	.0881	.1035	.1205	.1391	.1594	.1813	.2048	.2298	.2562	.2839
9	.0317	.0388	.0470	.0564	.0671	.0791	.0926	.1076	.1242	.1423
10	.0092	.0117	.0148	.0185	.0229	.0280	.0341	.0411	.0491	.0583
11	.0021	.0028	.0037	.0048	.0062	.0079	.0100	.0125	.0155	.0191
12	.0004	.0005	.0007	.0010	.0013	.0017	.0023	.0030	.0038	.0049
13	.0001	.0001	.0001	.0001	.0002	.0003	.0004	.0005	.0007	.0009
14	.0000	.0000	.0000	.0000	.0000	.0000	.0000	.0001	.0001	.0001

n = 16 (Continued)

r \ p	.41	.42	.43	.44	.45	.46	.47	.48	.49	.50
1	.9998	.9998	.9999	.9999	.9999	.9999	1.0000	1.0000	1.0000	1.0000
2	.9974	.9979	.9984	.9987	.9990	.9992	.9994	.9995	.9997	.9997
3	.9849	.9876	.9899	.9918	.9934	.9947	.9958	.9966	.9973	.9979
4	.9444	.9527	.9600	.9664	.9719	.9766	.9806	.9840	.9869	.9894
5	.8529	.8707	.8869	.9015	.9147	.9265	.9370	.9463	.9544	.9616
6	.7003	.7280	.7543	.7792	.8024	.8241	.8441	.8626	.8795	.8949
7	.5058	.5387	.5711	.6029	.6340	.6641	.6932	.7210	.7476	.7728
8	.3128	.3428	.3736	.4051	.4371	.4694	.5019	.5343	.5665	.5982
9	.1619	.1832	.2060	.2302	.2559	.2829	.3111	.3405	.3707	.4018
10	.0687	.0805	.0936	.1081	.1241	.1416	.1607	.1814	.2036	.2272
11	.0234	.0284	.0342	.0409	.0486	.0574	.0674	.0786	.0911	.1051
12	.0062	.0078	.0098	.0121	.0149	.0183	.0222	.0268	.0322	.0384
13	.0012	.0016	.0021	.0027	.0035	.0044	.0055	.0069	.0086	.0106
14	.0002	.0002	.0003	.0004	.0006	.0007	.0010	.0013	.0016	.0021
15	.0000	.0000	.0000	.0000	.0001	.0001	.0001	.0001	.0002	.0003

n = 17

r \ p	.01	.02	.03	.04	.05	.06	.07	.08	.09	.10
1	.1571	.2907	.4042	.5004	.5819	.6507	.7088	.7577	.7988	.8332
2	.0123	.0446	.0909	.1465	.2078	.2717	.3362	.3995	.4604	.5182
3	.0006	.0044	.0134	.0286	.0503	.0782	.1118	.1503	.1927	.2382
4	.0000	.0003	.0014	.0040	.0088	.0164	.0273	.0419	.0603	.0826
5	.0000	.0000	.0001	.0004	.0012	.0026	.0051	.0090	.0145	.0221
6	.0000	.0000	.0000	.0000	.0001	.0003	.0007	.0015	.0027	.0047
7	.0000	.0000	.0000	.0000	.0000	.0000	.0001	.0002	.0004	.0008
8	.0000	.0000	.0000	.0000	.0000	.0000	.0000	.0000	.0000	.0001

r \ p	.11	.12	.13	.14	.15	.16	.17	.18	.19	.20
1	.8621	.8862	.9063	.9230	.9369	.9484	.9579	.9657	.9722	.9775
2	.5723	.6223	.6682	.7099	.7475	.7813	.8113	.8379	.8613	.8818
3	.2858	.3345	.3836	.4324	.4802	.5266	.5711	.6133	.6532	.6904
4	.1087	.1383	.1710	.2065	.2444	.2841	.3251	.3669	.4091	.4511
5	.0321	.0446	.0598	.0778	.0987	.1224	.1487	.1775	.2087	.2418
6	.0075	.0114	.0166	.0234	.0319	.0423	.0548	.0695	.0864	.1057
7	.0014	.0023	.0037	.0056	.0083	.0118	.0163	.0220	.0291	.0377
8	.0002	.0004	.0007	.0011	.0017	.0027	.0039	.0057	.0080	.0109
9	.0000	.0001	.0001	.0002	.0003	.0005	.0008	.0012	.0018	.0026
10	.0000	.0000	.0000	.0000	.0000	.0001	.0001	.0002	.0003	.0005
11	.0000	.0000	.0000	.0000	.0000	.0000	.0000	.0000	.0000	.0001

r \ p	.21	.22	.23	.24	.25	.26	.27	.28	.29	.30
1	.9818	.9854	.9882	.9906	.9925	.9940	.9953	.9962	.9970	.9977
2	.8996	.9152	.9285	.9400	.9499	.9583	.9654	.9714	.9765	.9807
3	.7249	.7567	.7859	.8123	.8363	.8578	.8771	.8942	.9093	.9226
4	.4927	.5333	.5728	.6107	.6470	.6814	.7137	.7440	.7721	.7981
5	.2766	.3128	.3500	.3879	.4261	.4643	.5023	.5396	.5760	.6113
6	.1273	.1510	.1770	.2049	.2347	.2661	.2989	.3329	.3677	.4032
7	.0479	.0598	.0736	.0894	.1071	.1268	.1485	.1721	.1976	.2248
8	.0147	.0194	.0251	.0320	.0402	.0499	.0611	.0739	.0884	.1046
9	.0037	.0051	.0070	.0094	.0124	.0161	.0206	.0261	.0326	.0403
10	.0007	.0011	.0016	.0022	.0031	.0042	.0057	.0075	.0098	.0127
11	.0001	.0002	.0003	.0004	.0006	.0009	.0013	.0018	.0024	.0032
12	.0000	.0000	.0000	.0001	.0001	.0002	.0002	.0003	.0005	.0007
13	.0000	.0000	.0000	.0000	.0000	.0000	.0000	.0000	.0001	.0001

r \ p	.31	.32	.33	.34	.35	.36	.37	.38	.39	.40
1	.9982	.9986	.9989	.9991	.9993	.9995	.9996	.9997	.9998	.9998
2	.9843	.9872	.9896	.9917	.9933	.9946	.9957	.9966	.9973	.9979
3	.9343	.9444	.9532	.9608	.9673	.9728	.9775	.9815	.9849	.9877
4	.8219	.8437	.8634	.8812	.8972	.9115	.9241	.9353	.9450	.9536
5	.6453	.6778	.7087	.7378	.7652	.7906	.8142	.8360	.8559	.8740
6	.4390	.4749	.5105	.5458	.5803	.6139	.6465	.6778	.7077	.7361
7	.2536	.2838	.3153	.3479	.3812	.4152	.4495	.4839	.5182	.5522
8	.1227	.1426	.1642	.1877	.2128	.2395	.2676	.2971	.3278	.3595
9	.0492	.0595	.0712	.0845	.0994	.1159	.1341	.1541	.1757	.1989
10	.0162	.0204	.0254	.0314	.0383	.0464	.0557	.0664	.0784	.0919

Table D

r \ p	.31	.32	.33	.34	.35	.36	.37	.38	.39	.40
11	.0043	.0057	.0074	.0095	.0120	.0151	.0189	.0234	.0286	.0348
12	.0009	.0013	.0017	.0023	.0030	.0040	.0051	.0066	.0084	.0106
13	.0002	.0002	.0003	.0004	.0006	.0008	.0011	.0015	.0019	.0025
14	.0000	.0000	.0000	.0001	.0001	.0001	.0002	.0002	.0003	.0005
15	.0000	.0000	.0000	.0000	.0000	.0000	.0000	.0000	.0000	.0001

r \ p	.41	.42	.43	.44	.45	.46	.47	.48	.49	.50
1	.9999	.9999	.9999	.9999	1.0000	1.0000	1.0000	1.0000	1.0000	1.0000
2	.9984	.9987	.9990	.9992	.9994	.9996	.9997	.9998	.9998	.9999
3	.9900	.9920	.9935	.9948	.9959	.9968	.9975	.9980	.9985	.9988
4	.9610	.9674	.9729	.9776	.9816	.9849	.9877	.9901	.9920	.9936
5	.8904	.9051	.9183	.9301	.9404	.9495	.9575	.9644	.9704	.9755
6	.7628	.7879	.8113	.8330	.8529	.8712	.8878	.9028	.9162	.9283
7	.5856	.6182	.6499	.6805	.7098	.7377	.7641	.7890	.8122	.8338
8	.3920	.4250	.4585	.4921	.5257	.5590	.5918	.6239	.6552	.6855
9	.2238	.2502	.2780	.3072	.3374	.3687	.4008	.4335	.4667	.5000
10	.1070	.1236	.1419	.1618	.1834	.2066	.2314	.2577	.2855	.3145
11	.0420	.0503	.0597	.0705	.0826	.0962	.1112	.1279	.1462	.1662
12	.0133	.0165	.0203	.0248	.0301	.0363	.0434	.0517	.0611	.0717
13	.0033	.0042	.0054	.0069	.0086	.0108	.0134	.0165	.0202	.0245
14	.0006	.0008	.0011	.0014	.0019	.0024	.0031	.0040	.0050	.0064
15	.0001	.0001	.0002	.0002	.0003	.0004	.0005	.0007	.0009	.0012
16	.0000	.0000	.0000	.0000	.0000	.0000	.0001	.0001	.0001	.0001

n = 18

r \ p	.01	.02	.03	.04	.05	.06	.07	.08	.09	.10
1	.1655	.3049	.4220	.5204	.6028	.6717	.7292	.7771	.8169	.8499
2	.0138	.0495	.1003	.1607	.2265	.2945	.3622	.4281	.4909	.5497
3	.0007	.0052	.0157	.0333	.0581	.0898	.1275	.1702	.2168	.2662
4	.0000	.0004	.0018	.0050	.0109	.0201	.0333	.0506	.0723	.0982
5	.0000	.0000	.0002	.0006	.0015	.0034	.0067	.0116	.0187	.0282
6	.0000	.0000	.0000	.0001	.0002	.0005	.0010	.0021	.0038	.0064
7	.0000	.0000	.0000	.0000	.0000	.0000	.0001	.0003	.0006	.0012
8	.0000	.0000	.0000	.0000	.0000	.0000	.0000	.0000	.0001	.0002

r \ p	.11	.12	.13	.14	.15	.16	.17	.18	.19	.20
1	.8773	.8998	.9185	.9338	.9464	.9566	.9651	.9719	.9775	.9820
2	.6042	.6540	.6992	.7398	.7759	.8080	.8362	.8609	.8824	.9009
3	.3173	.3690	.4206	.4713	.5203	.5673	.6119	.6538	.6927	.7287
4	.1282	.1618	.1986	.2382	.2798	.3229	.3669	.4112	.4554	.4990
5	.0405	.0558	.0743	.0959	.1206	.1482	.1787	.2116	.2467	.2836
6	.0102	.0154	.0222	.0310	.0419	.0551	.0708	.0889	.1097	.1329
7	.0021	.0034	.0054	.0081	.0118	.0167	.0229	.0306	.0400	.0513
8	.0003	.0006	.0011	.0017	.0027	.0041	.0060	.0086	.0120	.0163
9	.0000	.0001	.0002	.0003	.0005	.0008	.0013	.0020	.0030	.0043
10	.0000	.0000	.0000	.0000	.0001	.0001	.0002	.0004	.0006	.0009
11	.0000	.0000	.0000	.0000	.0000	.0000	.0000	.0001	.0001	.0002

r \ p	.21	.22	.23	.24	.25	.26	.27	.28	.29	.30
1	.9856	.9886	.9909	.9928	.9944	.9956	.9965	.9973	.9979	.9984
2	.9169	.9306	.9423	.9522	.9605	.9676	.9735	.9784	.9824	.9858
3	.7616	.7916	.8187	.8430	.8647	.8839	.9009	.9158	.9288	.9400
4	.5414	.5825	.6218	.6591	.6943	.7272	.7578	.7860	.8119	.8354
5	.3220	.3613	.4012	.4414	.4813	.5208	.5594	.5968	.6329	.6673
6	.1586	.1866	.2168	.2488	.2825	.3176	.3538	.3907	.4281	.4656
7	.0645	.0799	.0974	.1171	.1390	.1630	.1891	.2171	.2469	.2783
8	.0217	.0283	.0363	.0458	.0569	.0699	.0847	.1014	.1200	.1407
9	.0060	.0083	.0112	.0148	.0193	.0249	.0316	.0395	.0488	.0596
10	.0014	.0020	.0028	.0039	.0054	.0073	.0097	.0127	.0164	.0210
11	.0003	.0004	.0006	.0009	.0012	.0018	.0025	.0034	.0046	.0061
12	.0000	.0001	.0001	.0002	.0002	.0003	.0005	.0007	.0010	.0014
13	.0000	.0000	.0000	.0000	.0000	.0001	.0001	.0001	.0002	.0003

r \ p	.31	.32	.33	.34	.35	.36	.37	.38	.39	.40
1	.9987	.9990	.9993	.9994	.9996	.9997	.9998	.9998	.9999	.9999
2	.9886	.9908	.9927	.9942	.9954	.9964	.9972	.9978	.9983	.9987
3	.9498	.9581	.9652	.9713	.9764	.9807	.9843	.9873	.9897	.9918
4	.8568	.8759	.8931	.9083	.9217	.9335	.9439	.9528	.9606	.9672
5	.7001	.7309	.7598	.7866	.8114	.8341	.8549	.8737	.8907	.9058

n = 18 (Continued)

r \ p	.31	.32	.33	.34	.35	.36	.37	.38	.39	.40
6	.5029	.5398	.5759	.6111	.6450	.6776	.7086	.7379	.7655	.7912
7	.3111	.3450	.3797	.4151	.4509	.4867	.5224	.5576	.5921	.6257
8	.1633	.1878	.2141	.2421	.2717	.3027	.3349	.3681	.4021	.4366
9	.0720	.0861	.1019	.1196	.1391	.1604	.1835	.2084	.2350	.2632
10	.0264	.0329	.0405	.0494	.0597	.0714	.0847	.0997	.1163	.1347
11	.0080	.0104	.0133	.0169	.0212	.0264	.0325	.0397	.0480	.0576
12	.0020	.0027	.0036	.0047	.0062	.0080	.0102	.0130	.0163	.0203
13	.0004	.0005	.0008	.0011	.0014	.0019	.0026	.0034	.0044	.0058
14	.0001	.0001	.0001	.0002	.0003	.0004	.0005	.0007	.0010	.0013
15	.0000	.0000	.0000	.0000	.0000	.0001	.0001	.0001	.0002	.0002

r \ p	.41	.42	.43	.44	.45	.46	.47	.48	.49	.50
1	.9999	.9999	1.0000	1.0000	1.0000	1.0000	1.0000	1.0000	1.0000	1.0000
2	.9990	.9992	.9994	.9996	.9997	.9998	.9998	.9999	.9999	.9999
3	.9934	.9948	.9959	.9968	.9975	.9981	.9985	.9989	.9991	.9993
4	.9729	.9777	.9818	.9852	.9880	.9904	.9923	.9939	.9952	.9962
5	.9193	.9313	.9418	.9510	.9589	.9658	.9717	.9767	.9810	.9846
6	.8151	.8372	.8573	.8757	.8923	.9072	.9205	.9324	.9428	.9519
7	.6582	.6895	.7193	.7476	.7742	.7991	.8222	.8436	.8632	.8811
8	.4713	.5062	.5408	.5750	.6085	.6412	.6728	.7032	.7322	.7597
9	.2928	.3236	.3556	.3885	.4222	.4562	.4906	.5249	.5591	.5927
10	.1549	.1768	.2004	.2258	.2527	.2812	.3110	.3421	.3742	.4073
11	.0686	.0811	.0951	.1107	.1280	.1470	.1677	.1902	.2144	.2403
12	.0250	.0307	.0372	.0449	.0537	.0638	.0753	.0883	.1028	.1189
13	.0074	.0094	.0118	.0147	.0183	.0225	.0275	.0334	.0402	.0481
14	.0017	.0022	.0029	.0038	.0049	.0063	.0079	.0100	.0125	.0154
15	.0003	.0004	.0006	.0007	.0010	.0013	.0017	.0023	.0029	.0038
16	.0000	.0001	.0001	.0001	.0001	.0002	.0003	.0004	.0005	.0007
17	.0000	.0000	.0000	.0000	.0000	.0000	.0000	.0000	.0001	.0001

n = 19

r \ p	.01	.02	.03	.04	.05	.06	.07	.08	.09	.10
1	.1738	.3188	.4394	.5396	.6226	.6914	.7481	.7949	.8334	.8649
2	.0153	.0546	.1100	.1751	.2453	.3171	.3879	.4560	.5202	.5797
3	.0009	.0061	.0083	.0384	.0665	.1021	.1439	.1908	.2415	.2946
4	.0000	.0005	.0002	.0061	.0132	.0243	.0398	.0602	.0853	.1150
5	.0000	.0000	.0002	.0007	.0020	.0044	.0085	.0147	.0235	.0352
6	.0000	.0000	.0000	.0001	.0002	.0006	.0014	.0029	.0051	.0086
7	.0000	.0000	.0000	.0000	.0000	.0001	.0002	.0004	.0009	.0017
8	.0000	.0000	.0000	.0000	.0000	.0000	.0000	.0001	.0001	.0003

r \ p	.11	.12	.13	.14	.15	.16	.17	.18	.19	.20
1	.8908	.9119	.9291	.9431	.9544	.9636	.9710	.9770	.9818	.9856
2	.6342	.6835	.7277	.7669	.8015	.8318	.8581	.8809	.9004	.9171
3	.3488	.4032	.4568	.5089	.5587	.6059	.6500	.6910	.7287	.7631
4	.1490	.1867	.2275	.2708	.3159	.3620	.4085	.4549	.5005	.5449
5	.0502	.0685	.0904	.1158	.1444	.1762	.2107	.2476	.2864	.3267
6	.0135	.0202	.0290	.0401	.0537	.0700	.0891	.1110	.1357	.1631
7	.0030	.0048	.0076	.0113	.0163	.0228	.0310	.0411	.0532	.0676
8	.0005	.0009	.0016	.0026	.0041	.0061	.0089	.0126	.0173	.0233
9	.0001	.0002	.0003	.0005	.0008	.0014	.0021	.0032	.0047	.0067
10	.0000	.0000	.0000	.0001	.0001	.0002	.0004	.0007	.0010	.0016
11	.0000	.0000	.0000	.0000	.0000	.0000	.0001	.0001	.0002	.0003
12	.0000	.0000	.0000	.0000	.0000	.0000	.0000	.0000	.0000	.0001

r \ p	.21	.22	.23	.24	.25	.26	.27	.28	.29	.30
1	.9887	.9911	.9930	.9946	.9958	.9967	.9975	.9981	.9985	.9989
2	.9313	.9434	.9535	.9619	.9690	.9749	.9797	.9837	.9869	.9896
3	.7942	.8222	.8471	.8692	.8887	.9057	.9205	.9333	.9443	.9538
4	.5877	.6285	.6671	.7032	.7369	.7680	.7965	.8224	.8458	.8668
5	.3681	.4100	.4520	.4936	.5346	.5744	.6129	.6498	.6848	.7178
6	.1929	.2251	.2592	.2950	.3322	.3705	.4093	.4484	.4875	.5261
7	.0843	.1034	.1249	.1487	.1749	.2032	.2336	.2657	.2995	.3345
8	.0307	.0396	.0503	.0629	.0775	.0941	.1129	.1338	.1568	.1820
9	.0093	.0127	.0169	.0222	.0287	.0366	.0459	.0568	.0694	.0839
10	.0023	.0034	.0047	.0066	.0089	.0119	.0156	.0202	.0258	.0326

| | | | | n = 19 (Continued) | | | | | | |

r \ p	.21	.22	.23	.24	.25	.26	.27	.28	.29	.30
11	.0005	.0007	.0011	.0016	.0023	.0032	.0044	.0060	.0080	.0105
12	.0001	.0001	.0002	.0003	.0005	.0007	.0010	.0015	.0021	.0028
13	.0000	.0000	.0000	.0001	.0001	.0001	.0002	.0003	.0004	.0006
14	.0000	.0000	.0000	.0000	.0000	.0000	.0000	.0000	.0001	.0001

r	.31	.32	.33	.34	.35	.36	.37	.38	.39	.40
1	.9991	.9993	.9995	.9996	.9997	.9998	.9998	.9999	.9999	.9999
2	.9917	.9935	.9949	.9960	.9969	.9976	.9981	.9986	.9989	.9992
3	.9618	.9686	.9743	.9791	.9830	.9863	.9890	.9913	.9931	.9945
4	.8856	.9022	.9169	.9297	.9409	.9505	.9588	.9659	.9719	.9770
5	.7486	.7773	.8037	.8280	.8500	.8699	.8878	.9038	.9179	.9304
6	.5641	.6010	.6366	.6707	.7032	.7339	.7627	.7895	.8143	.8371
7	.3705	.4073	.4445	.4818	.5188	.5554	.5913	.6261	.6597	.6919
8	.2091	.2381	.2688	.3010	.3344	.3690	.4043	.4401	.4762	.5122
9	.1003	.1186	.1389	.1612	.1855	.2116	.2395	.2691	.3002	.3325
10	.0405	.0499	.0608	.0733	.0875	.1035	.1213	.1410	.1626	.1861
11	.0137	.0176	.0223	.0280	.0347	.0426	.0518	.0625	.0747	.0885
12	.0038	.0051	.0068	.0089	.0114	.0146	.0185	.0231	.0287	.0352
13	.0009	.0012	.0017	.0023	.0031	.0041	.0054	.0070	.0091	.0116
14	.0002	.0002	.0003	.0005	.0007	.0009	.0013	.0017	.0023	.0031
15	.0000	.0000	.0001	.0001	.0001	.0002	.0002	.0003	.0005	.0006
16	.0000	.0000	.0000	.0000	.0000	.0000	.0000	.0000	.0001	.0001

r	.41	.42	.43	.44	.45	.46	.47	.48	.49	.50
1	1.0000	1.0000	1.0000	1.0000	1.0000	1.0000	1.0000	1.0000	1.0000	1.0000
2	.9994	.9995	.9996	.9997	.9998	.9999	.9999	.9999	.9999	1.0000
3	.9957	.9967	.9974	.9980	.9985	.9988	.9991	.9993	.9995	.9996
4	.9813	.9849	.9878	.9903	.9923	.9939	.9952	.9963	.9971	.9978
5	.9413	.9518	.9590	.9660	.9720	.9771	.9814	.9850	.9879	.9904
6	.8579	.8767	.8937	.9088	.9223	.9342	.9446	.9537	.9615	.9682
7	.7226	.7515	.7787	.8039	.8273	.8488	.8684	.8862	.9022	.9165
8	.5480	.5832	.6176	.6509	.6831	.7138	.7430	.7706	.7964	.8204
9	.3660	.4003	.4353	.4706	.5060	.5413	.5762	.6105	.6439	.6762
10	.2114	.2385	.2672	.2974	.3290	.3617	.3954	.4299	.4648	.5000
11	.1040	.1213	.1404	.1613	.1841	.2087	.2351	.2631	.2928	.3238
12	.0429	.0518	.0621	.0738	.0871	.1021	.1187	.1372	.1575	.1796
13	.0146	.0183	.0227	.0280	.0342	.0415	.0500	.0597	.0709	.0835
14	.0040	.0052	.0068	.0086	.0109	.0137	.0171	.0212	.0261	.0318
15	.0009	.0012	.0016	.0021	.0028	.0036	.0046	.0060	.0076	.0096
16	.0001	.0002	.0003	.0004	.0005	.0007	.0010	.0013	.0017	.0022
17	.0000	.0000	.0000	.0001	.0001	.0001	.0001	.0002	.0003	.0004

| | | | | n = 20 | | | | | | |

r \ p	.01	.02	.03	.04	.05	.06	.07	.08	.09	.10
1	.1821	.3324	.4562	.5580	.6415	.7099	.7658	.8113	.8484	.8784
2	.0169	.0599	.1198	.1897	.2642	.3395	.4131	.4831	.5484	.6083
3	.0010	.0071	.0210	.0439	.0755	.1150	.1610	.2121	.2666	.3231
4	.0000	.0006	.0027	.0074	.0159	.0290	.0471	.0706	.0993	.1330
5	.0000	.0000	.0003	.0010	.0026	.0056	.0107	.0183	.0290	.0432
6	.0000	.0000	.0000	.0001	.0003	.0009	.0019	.0038	.0068	.0113
7	.0000	.0000	.0000	.0000	.0000	.0001	.0003	.0006	.0013	.0024
8	.0000	.0000	.0000	.0000	.0000	.0000	.0000	.0001	.0002	.0004
9	.0000	.0000	.0000	.0000	.0000	.0000	.0000	.0000	.0000	.0001

r	.11	.12	.13	.14	.15	.16	.17	.18	.19	.20
1	.9028	.9224	.9383	.9510	.9612	.9694	.9759	.9811	.9852	.9885
2	.6624	.7109	.7539	.7916	.8244	.8529	.8773	.8982	.9159	.9308
3	.3802	.4369	.4920	.5450	.5951	.6420	.6854	.7252	.7614	.7939
4	.1710	.2127	.2573	.3041	.3523	.4010	.4496	.4974	.5439	.5886
5	.0610	.0827	.1083	.1375	.1702	.2059	.2443	.2849	.3271	.3704
6	.0175	.0260	.0370	.0507	.0673	.0870	.1098	.1356	.1643	.1958
7	.0041	.0067	.0103	.0153	.0219	.0304	.0409	.0537	.0689	.0867
8	.0008	.0014	.0024	.0038	.0059	.0088	.0127	.0177	.0241	.0321
9	.0001	.0002	.0005	.0008	.0013	.0021	.0033	.0049	.0071	.0100
10	.0000	.0000	.0001	.0001	.0002	.0004	.0007	.0011	.0017	.0026
11	.0000	.0000	.0000	.0000	.0000	.0001	.0001	.0002	.0004	.0006
12	.0000	.0000	.0000	.0000	.0000	.0000	.0000	.0000	.0001	.0001

Table D

r \ p	.21	.22	.23	.24	.25	.26	.27	.28	.29	.30
1	.9910	.9931	.9946	.9959	.9968	.9976	.9982	.9986	.9989	.9992
2	.9434	.9539	.9626	.9698	.9757	.9805	.9845	.9877	.9903	.9924
3	.8230	.8488	.8716	.8915	.9087	.9237	.9365	.9474	.9567	.9645
4	.6310	.6711	.7085	.7431	.7748	.8038	.8300	.8534	.8744	.8929
5	.4142	.4580	.5014	.5439	.5852	.6248	.6625	.6981	.7315	.7625
6	.2297	.2657	.3035	.3427	.3828	.4235	.4643	.5048	.5447	.5836
7	.1071	.1301	.1558	.1838	.2142	.2467	.2810	.3169	.3540	.3920
8	.0419	.0536	.0675	.0835	.1018	.1225	.1455	.1707	.1982	.2277
9	.0138	.0186	.0246	.0320	.0409	.0515	.0640	.0784	.0948	.1133
10	.0038	.0054	.0075	.0103	.0139	.0183	.0238	.0305	.0385	.0480
11	.0009	.0013	.0019	.0028	.0039	.0055	.0074	.0100	.0132	.0171
12	.0002	.0003	.0004	.0006	.0009	.0014	.0019	.0027	.0038	.0051
13	.0000	.0000	.0001	.0001	.0002	.0003	.0004	.0006	.0009	.0013
14	.0000	.0000	.0000	.0000	.0000	.0000	.0000	.0001	.0001	.0003

r \ p	.31	.32	.33	.34	.35	.36	.37	.38	.39	.40
1	.9994	.9996	.9997	.9998	.9998	.9999	.9999	.9999	.9999	1.0000
2	.9940	.9953	.9964	.9972	.9979	.9984	.9988	.9991	.9993	.9995
3	.9711	.9765	.9811	.9848	.9879	.9904	.9924	.9940	.9953	.9964
4	.9092	.9235	.9358	.9465	.9556	.9634	.9700	.9755	.9802	.9840
5	.7911	.8173	.8411	.8626	.8818	.8989	.9141	.9274	.9390	.9490
6	.6213	.6574	.6918	.7242	.7546	.7829	.8090	.8329	.8547	.8744
7	.4305	.4693	.5079	.5460	.5834	.6197	.6547	.6882	.7200	.7500
8	.2591	.2922	.3268	.3624	.3990	.4361	.4735	.5108	.5478	.5841
9	.1340	.1568	.1818	.2087	.2376	.2683	.3005	.3341	.3688	.4044
10	.0591	.0719	.0866	.1032	.1218	.1424	.1650	.1897	.2163	.2447
11	.0220	.0279	.0350	.0434	.0532	.0645	.0775	.0923	.1090	.1275
12	.0069	.0091	.0119	.0154	.0196	.0247	.0308	.0381	.0466	.0565
13	.0018	.0025	.0034	.0045	.0060	.0079	.0102	.0132	.0167	.0210
14	.0004	.0006	.0008	.0011	.0015	.0021	.0028	.0037	.0049	.0065
15	.0001	.0001	.0001	.0002	.0003	.0004	.0006	.0009	.0012	.0016
16	.0000	.0000	.0000	.0000	.0001	.0001	.0001	.0002	.0002	.0003

r \ p	.41	.42	.43	.44	.45	.46	.47	.48	.49	.50
1	1.0000	1.0000	1.0000	1.0000	1.0000	1.0000	1.0000	1.0000	1.0000	1.0000
2	.9996	.9997	.9998	.9998	.9999	.9999	.9999	1.0000	1.0000	1.0000
3	.9972	.9979	.9984	.9988	.9991	.9993	.9995	.9996	.9997	.9998
4	.9872	.9898	.9920	.9937	.9951	.9962	.9971	.9977	.9983	.9987
5	.9577	.9651	.9714	.9767	.9811	.9848	.9879	.9904	.9924	.9941
6	.8921	.9078	.9217	.9340	.9447	.9539	.9619	.9687	.9745	.9793
7	.7780	.8041	.8281	.8501	.8701	.8881	.9042	.9186	.9312	.9423
8	.6196	.6539	.6868	.7183	.7480	.7759	.8020	.8261	.8482	.8684
9	.4406	.4771	.5136	.5499	.5847	.6207	.6546	.6873	.7186	.7483
10	.2748	.3064	.3394	.3736	.4086	.4443	.4804	.5166	.5525	.5881
11	.1480	.1705	.1949	.2212	.2493	.2791	.3104	.3432	.3771	.4119
12	.0679	.0810	.0958	.1123	.1308	.1511	.1734	.1977	.2238	.2517
13	.0262	.0324	.0397	.0482	.0580	.0694	.0823	.0969	.1133	.1316
14	.0084	.0107	.0136	.0172	.0214	.0265	.0326	.0397	.0480	.0577
15	.0022	.0029	.0038	.0050	.0064	.0083	.0105	.0133	.0166	.0207
16	.0004	.0006	.0008	.0011	.0015	.0020	.0027	.0035	.0046	.0059
17	.0001	.0001	.0001	.0002	.0003	.0004	.0005	.0007	.0010	.0013
18	.0000	.0000	.0000	.0000	.0000	.0001	.0001	.0001	.0001	.0002

n = 25

r \ p	.01	.02	.03	.04	.05	.06	.07	.08	.09	.10
1	.2222	.3965	.5330	.6396	.7226	.7871	.8370	.8756	.9054	.9282
2	.0258	.0886	.1720	.2642	.3576	.4473	.5304	.6053	.6714	.7288
3	.0020	.0132	.0380	.0765	.1271	.1871	.2534	.3232	.3937	.4629
4	.0001	.0014	.0062	.0165	.0341	.0598	.0936	.1351	.1831	.2364
5	.0000	.0001	.0008	.0028	.0072	.0150	.0274	.0451	.0686	.0980
6	.0000	.0000	.0001	.0004	.0012	.0031	.0065	.0123	.0210	.0334
7	.0000	.0000	.0000	.0000	.0002	.0005	.0013	.0028	.0054	.0095
8	.0000	.0000	.0000	.0000	.0000	.0001	.0002	.0005	.0011	.0023
9	.0000	.0000	.0000	.0000	.0000	.0000	.0000	.0001	.0002	.0005
10	.0000	.0000	.0000	.0000	.0000	.0000	.0000	.0000	.0000	.0001

p r	.11	.12	.13	.14	.15	.16	.17	.18	.19	.20
1	.9457	.9591	.9692	.9770	.9828	.9872	.9905	.9930	.9948	.9962
2	.7779	.8195	.8543	.8832	.9069	.9263	.9420	.9546	.9646	.9726
3	.5291	.5912	.6483	.7000	.7463	.7870	.8226	.8533	.8796	.9018
4	.2934	.3525	.4123	.4714	.5289	.5837	.6352	.6829	.7266	.7660
5	.1331	.1734	.1283	.2668	.3179	.3707	.4241	.4772	.5292	.5793
6	.0499	.0709	.0965	.1268	.1615	.2002	.2425	.2875	.3347	.3833
7	.0156	.0243	.0359	.0509	.0695	.0920	.1185	.1488	.1827	.2200
8	.0041	.0070	.0113	.0173	.0255	.0361	.0495	.0661	.0859	.1091
9	.0009	.0017	.0030	.0050	.0080	.0121	.0178	.0252	.0348	.0468
10	.0002	.0004	.0007	.0013	.0021	.0035	.0055	.0083	.0122	.0173
11	.0000	.0001	.0001	.0003	.0005	.0009	.0015	.0024	.0037	.0056
12	.0000	.0000	.0000	.0000	.0001	.0002	.0003	.0006	.0010	.0015
13	.0000	.0000	.0000	.0000	.0000	.0000	.0001	.0001	.0002	.0004
14	.0000	.0000	.0000	.0000	.0000	.0000	.0000	.0000	.0000	.0001

	.21	.22	.23	.24	.25	.26	.27	.28	.29	.30
1	.9972	.9980	.9985	.9990	.9992	.9995	.9996	.9997	.9998	.9999
2	.9789	.9838	.9877	.9907	.9930	.9947	.9961	.9971	.9979	.9984
3	.9204	.9360	.9488	.9593	.9679	.9748	.9804	.9848	.9883	.9910
4	.8013	.8324	.8597	.8834	.9038	.9211	.9358	.9481	.9583	.9668
5	.6270	.6718	.7134	.7516	.7863	.8174	.8452	.8696	.8910	.9095
6	.4325	.4816	.5299	.5767	.6217	.6644	.7044	.7415	.7755	.8065
7	.2601	.3027	.3471	.3927	.4389	.4851	.5308	.5753	.6183	.6593
8	.1358	.1658	.1989	.2349	.2735	.3142	.3565	.3999	.4440	.4882
9	.0614	.0788	.0993	.1228	.1494	.1790	.2115	.2465	.2838	.3231
10	.0240	.0325	.0431	.0560	.0713	.0893	.1101	.1338	.1602	.1894
11	.0082	.0117	.0163	.0222	.0297	.0389	.0502	.0636	.0795	.0978
12	.0024	.0036	.0053	.0076	.0107	.0148	.0199	.0264	.0345	.0442
13	.0006	.0010	.0015	.0023	.0034	.0049	.0069	.0096	.0130	.0175
14	.0001	.0002	.0004	.0006	.0009	.0014	.0021	.0030	.0043	.0060
15	.0000	.0000	.0001	.0001	.0002	.0003	.0005	.0008	.0012	.0018
16	.0000	.0000	.0000	.0000	.0000	.0001	.0001	.0002	.0003	.0005
17	.0000	.0000	.0000	.0000	.0000	.0000	.0000	.0000	.0001	.0001

	.31	.32	.33	.34	.35	.36	.37	.38	.39	.40
1	.9999	.9999	1.0000	1.0000	1.0000	1.0000	1.0000	1.0000	1.0000	1.0000
2	.9989	.9992	.9994	.9996	.9997	.9998	.9998	.9999	.9999	.9999
3	.9932	.9949	.9961	.9971	.9979	.9984	.9989	.9992	.9994	.9996
4	.9737	.9793	.9838	.9874	.9903	.9926	.9944	.9958	.9968	.9976
5	.9254	.9390	.9504	.9600	.9680	.9745	.9799	.9842	.9877	.9905
6	.8344	.8593	.8813	.9006	.9174	.9318	.9441	.9546	.9633	.9706
7	.6981	.7343	.7679	.7987	.8266	.8517	.8742	.8940	.9114	.9264
8	.5319	.5747	.6163	.6561	.6939	.7295	.7626	.7932	.8211	.8464
9	.3639	.4057	.4482	.4908	.5332	.5748	.6152	.6542	.6914	.7265
10	.2213	.2555	.2919	.3300	.3697	.4104	.4517	.4933	.5347	.5754
11	.1188	.1424	.1686	.1975	.2288	.2624	.2981	.3355	.3743	.4142
12	.0560	.0698	.0859	.1044	.1254	.1490	.1751	.2036	.2346	.2677
13	.0230	.0299	.0383	.0485	.0604	.0745	.0907	.1093	.1303	.1538
14	.0083	.0112	.0149	.0196	.0255	.0326	.0412	.0515	.0637	.0778
15	.0026	.0036	.0050	.0069	.0093	.0124	.0163	.0212	.0271	.0344
16	.0007	.0010	.0015	.0021	.0029	.0041	.0056	.0075	.0100	.0132
17	.0002	.0002	.0004	.0005	.0008	.0011	.0016	.0023	.0032	.0043
18	.0000	.0000	.0001	.0001	.0002	.0003	.0004	.0006	.0008	.0012
19	.0000	.0000	.0000	.0000	.0000	.0001	.0001	.0001	.0002	.0003
20	.0000	.0000	.0000	.0000	.0000	.0000	.0000	.0000	.0000	.0001

	.41	.42	.43	.44	.45	.46	.47	.48	.49	.50
1	1.0000	1.0000	1.0000	1.0000	1.0000	1.0000	1.0000	1.0000	1.0000	1.0000
2	1.0000	1.0000	1.0000	1.0000	1.0000	1.0000	1.0000	1.0000	1.0000	1.0000
3	.9997	.9998	.9998	.9999	.9999	1.0000	1.0000	1.0000	1.0000	1.0000
4	.9983	.9987	.9991	.9993	.9995	.9997	.9998	.9998	.9999	.9999
5	.9927	.9945	.9958	.9969	.9977	.9983	.9988	.9991	.9994	.9995
6	.9767	.9816	.9856	.9888	.9914	.9934	.9950	.9963	.9972	.9980
7	.9394	.9505	.9599	.9677	.9742	.9796	.9840	.9876	.9904	.9927
8	.8692	.8894	.9071	.9227	.9361	.9477	.9575	.9658	.9727	.9784
9	.7593	.7897	.8177	.8431	.8660	.8865	.9046	.9205	.9343	.9461
10	.6151	.6535	.6902	.7250	.7576	.7880	.8160	.8415	.8646	.8852

n = 25 (Continued)

r \ p	.41	.42	.43	.44	.45	.46	.47	.48	.49	.50
11	.4548	.4956	.5363	.5765	.6157	.6538	.6902	.7249	.7574	.7878
12	.3029	.3397	.3780	.4174	.4574	.4978	.5382	.5780	.6171	.6550
13	.1797	.2080	.2387	.2715	.3063	.3429	.3808	.4199	.4598	.5000
14	.0941	.1127	.1336	.1569	.1827	.2109	.2413	.2740	.3086	.3450
15	.0431	.0535	.0656	.0797	.0960	.1145	.1353	.1585	.1841	.2122
16	.0171	.0220	.0280	.0353	.0440	.0543	.0663	.0803	.0964	.1148
17	.0058	.0078	.0103	.0134	.0174	.0222	.0281	.0352	.0438	.0539
18	.0017	.0023	.0032	.0044	.0058	.0077	.0102	.0132	.0170	.0216
19	.0004	.0006	.0008	.0012	.0016	.0023	.0031	.0041	.0055	.0073
20	.0001	.0001	.0002	.0003	.0004	.0005	.0008	.0011	.0015	.0020
21	.0000	.0000	.0000	.0000	.0001	.0001	.0002	.0002	.0003	.0005
22	.0000	.0000	.0000	.0000	.0000	.0000	.0000	.0000	.0001	.0001

n = 30

r \ p	.01	.02	.03	.04	.05	.06	.07	.08	.09	.10
1	.2603	.4545	.4990	.7061	.7854	.8437	.8866	.9180	.9409	.9576
2	.0361	.1205	.2269	.3388	.4465	.5445	.6306	.7042	.7657	.8163
3	.0033	.0217	.0601	.1169	.1878	.2676	.3513	.4346	.5145	.5886
4	.0002	.0029	.0119	.0306	.0608	.1026	.1550	.2158	.2825	.3526
5	.0000	.0003	.0019	.0063	.0156	.0315	.0553	.0874	.1277	.1755
6	.0000	.0000	.0002	.0011	.0033	.0079	.0162	.0293	.0481	.0732
7	.0000	.0000	.0000	.0001	.0006	.0017	.0040	.0082	.0152	.0258
8	.0000	.0000	.0000	.0000	.0001	.0003	.0008	.0020	.0041	.0078
9	.0000	.0000	.0000	.0000	.0000	.0000	.0001	.0004	.0010	.0020
10	.0000	.0000	.0000	.0000	.0000	.0000	.0000	.0001	.0002	.0005
11	.0000	.0000	.0000	.0000	.0000	.0000	.0000	.0000	.0000	.0001

r \ p	.11	.12	.13	.14	.15	.16	.17	.18	.19	.20
1	.9697	.9784	.9847	.9892	.9924	.9946	.9963	.9974	.9982	.9988
2	.8573	.8900	.9159	.9362	.9520	.9641	.9733	.9803	.9856	.9895
3	.6558	.7153	.7670	.8113	.8486	.8796	.9051	.9259	.9425	.9558
4	.4234	.4929	.5594	.6215	.6783	.7295	.7748	.8144	.8484	.8773
5	.2295	.2882	.3499	.4129	.4755	.5365	.5947	.6491	.6993	.7448
6	.1049	.1431	.1871	.2363	.2894	.3453	.4028	.4605	.5174	.5725
7	.0407	.0606	.0858	.1165	.1526	.1936	.2390	.2880	.3397	.3930
8	.0136	.0221	.0339	.0497	.0698	.0945	.1240	.1582	.1968	.2392
9	.0039	.0069	.0116	.0184	.0278	.0403	.0563	.0763	.1004	.1287
10	.0010	.0019	.0035	.0059	.0097	.0150	.0224	.0323	.0451	.0611
11	.0002	.0005	.0009	.0017	.0029	.0049	.0078	.0120	.0179	.0256
12	.0000	.0001	.0002	.0004	.0008	.0014	.0024	.0040	.0062	.0095
13	.0000	.0000	.0000	.0001	.0002	.0004	.0007	.0011	.0019	.0031
14	.0000	.0000	.0000	.0000	.0000	.0001	.0002	.0003	.0005	.0009
15	.0000	.0000	.0000	.0000	.0000	.0000	.0000	.0001	.0001	.0002
16	.0000	.0000	.0000	.0000	.0000	.0000	.0000	.0000	.0000	.0001

r \ p	.21	.22	.23	.24	.25	.26	.27	.28	.29	.30
1	.9992	.9994	.9996	.9997	.9998	.9999	.9999	.9999	1.0000	1.0000
2	.9924	.9945	.9961	.9972	.9980	.9986	.9990	.9993	.9995	.9997
3	.9663	.9745	.9808	.9857	.9894	.9922	.9943	.9959	.9970	.9979
4	.9016	.9217	.9383	.9517	.9626	.9712	.9780	.9834	.9875	.9907
5	.7854	.8213	.8525	.8793	.9021	.9213	.9373	.9505	.9612	.9698
6	.6249	.6739	.7192	.7604	.7974	.8302	.8590	.8839	.9053	.9234
7	.4470	.5008	.5533	.6039	.6519	.6969	.7384	.7762	.8102	.8405
8	.2850	.3333	.3834	.4345	.4857	.5362	.5853	.6324	.6770	.7186
9	.1611	.1975	.2376	.2807	.3264	.3739	.4226	.4718	.5206	.5685
10	.0806	.1039	.1311	.1620	.1966	.2346	.2756	.3190	.3645	.4112
11	.0357	.0485	.0642	.0833	.1057	.1317	.1613	.1943	.2305	.2696
12	.0140	.0200	.0280	.0381	.0507	.0660	.0845	.1061	.1310	.1593
13	.0049	.0073	.0108	.0155	.0216	.0295	.0395	.0518	.0667	.0845
14	.0015	.0024	.0037	.0056	.0082	.0117	.0164	.0225	.0303	.0401
15	.0004	.0007	.0011	.0018	.0028	.0041	.0061	.0087	.0123	.0169
16	.0001	.0002	.0003	.0005	.0008	.0013	.0020	.0030	.0044	.0064
17	.0000	.0000	.0001	.0001	.0002	.0004	.0006	.0009	.0014	.0021
18	.0000	.0000	.0000	.0000	.0001	.0001	.0001	.0002	.0004	.0006
19	.0000	.0000	.0000	.0000	.0000	.0000	.0000	.0001	.0001	.0002

| | n = 30 (Continued) | | | | | | | | | |
r \ p	.31	.32	.33	.34	.35	.36	.37	.38	.39	.40
1	1.0000	1.0000	1.0000	1.0000	1.0000	1.0000	1.0000	1.0000	1.0000	1.0000
2	.9998	.9999	.9999	.9999	1.0000	1.0000	1.0000	1.0000	1.0000	1.0000
3	.9985	.9989	.9993	.9995	.9997	.9998	.9998	.9999	.9999	1.0000
4	.9931	.9950	.9963	.9974	.9981	.9987	.9991	.9993	.9995	.9997
5	.9768	.9823	.9866	.9899	.9925	.9944	.9959	.9971	.9979	.9985
6	.9386	.9512	.9615	.9700	.9767	.9822	.9864	.9898	.9924	.9943
7	.8671	.8903	.9102	.9271	.9414	.9533	.9631	.9712	.9776	.9828
8	.7570	.7920	.8235	.8515	.8762	.8977	.9163	.9321	.9454	.9565
9	.6148	.6590	.7007	.7395	.7753	.8078	.8371	.8631	.8861	.9060
10	.4586	.5060	.5529	.5985	.6425	.6842	.7235	.7599	.7934	.8237
11	.3112	.3549	.4000	.4460	.4922	.5382	.5833	.6270	.6689	.7085
12	.1909	.2255	.2631	.3031	.3452	.3889	.4337	.4790	.5242	.5689
13	.1053	.1292	.1563	.1865	.2198	.2559	.2945	.3353	.3778	.4215
14	.0520	.0664	.0835	.1034	.1263	.1523	.1813	.2133	.2481	.2855
15	.0229	.0305	.0399	.0514	.0652	.0815	.1006	.1226	.1475	.1754
16	.0090	.0125	.0170	.0228	.0301	.0391	.0501	.0632	.0788	.0971
17	.0031	.0045	.0065	.0090	.0124	.0167	.0222	.0291	.0377	.0481
18	.0010	.0015	.0022	.0032	.0045	.0063	.0088	.0119	.0160	.0212
19	.0003	.0004	.0006	.0010	.0014	.0021	.0031	.0043	.0060	.0083
20	.0001	.0001	.0002	.0003	.0004	.0006	.0009	.0014	.0020	.0029
21	.0000	.0000	.0000	.0001	.0001	.0002	.0002	.0004	.0006	.0009
22	.0000	.0000	.0000	.0000	.0000	.0000	.0001	.0001	.0001	.0002

r \ p	.41	.42	.43	.44	.45	.46	.47	.48	.49	.50
1	1.0000	1.0000	1.0000	1.0000	1.0000	1.0000	1.0000	1.0000	1.0000	1.0000
2	1.0000	1.0000	1.0000	1.0000	1.0000	1.0000	1.0000	1.0000	1.0000	1.0000
3	1.0000	1.0000	1.0000	1.0000	1.0000	1.0000	1.0000	1.0000	1.0000	1.0000
4	.9998	.9999	.9999	.9999	1.0000	1.0000	1.0000	1.0000	1.0000	1.0000
5	.9989	.9993	.9995	.9996	.9998	.9998	.9999	.9999	1.0000	1.0000
6	.9959	.9970	.9978	.9985	.9989	.9992	.9995	.9996	.9998	.9998
7	.9869	.9901	.9926	.9946	.9960	.9971	.9979	.9985	.9990	.9993
8	.9656	.9731	.9792	.9841	.9879	.9909	.9932	.9950	.9964	.9974
9	.9231	.9378	.9501	.9603	.9688	.9757	.9813	.9857	.9892	.9919
10	.8510	.8751	.8964	.9148	.9306	.9440	.9553	.9647	.9724	.9786
11	.7456	.7799	.8112	.8396	.8650	.8874	.9070	.9239	.9384	.9506
12	.6125	.6545	.6945	.7322	.7673	.7996	.8290	.8555	.8790	.8998
13	.4660	.5107	.5551	.5986	.6408	.6813	.7196	.7555	.7888	.8192
14	.3251	.3666	.4095	.4533	.4975	.5417	.5852	.6277	.6687	.7077
15	.2062	.2398	.2760	.3146	.3552	.3973	.4406	.4845	.5285	.5722
16	.1180	.1419	.1687	.1984	.2309	.2661	.3037	.3434	.3849	.4278
17	.0606	.0754	.0928	.1128	.1356	.1613	.1899	.2214	.2556	.2923
18	.0278	.0358	.0456	.0574	.0714	.0878	.1068	.1286	.1533	.1808
19	.0113	.0151	.0199	.0260	.0334	.0426	.0536	.0668	.0822	.1002
20	.0040	.0056	.0077	.0104	.0138	.0183	.0238	.0307	.0391	.0494
21	.0013	.0018	.0026	.0036	.0050	.0069	.0093	.0124	.0164	.0214
22	.0003	.0005	.0008	.0011	.0016	.0022	.0031	.0043	.0060	.0081
23	.0001	.0001	.0002	.0003	.0004	.0006	.0009	.0013	.0019	.0026
24	.0000	.0000	.0000	.0001	.0001	.0001	.0002	.0003	.0005	.0007
25	.0000	.0000	.0000	.0000	.0000	.0000	.0000	.0001	.0001	.0002

| | n = 40 | | | | | | | | | |
r \ p	.01	.02	.03	.04	.05	.06	.07	.08	.09	.10
1	.3310	.5543	.7043	.8046	.8715	.9158	.9451	.9644	.9770	.9852
2	.0607	.1905	.3385	.4790	.6009	.7010	.7799	.8406	.8860	.9195
3	.0075	.0457	.1178	.2145	.3233	.4335	.5375	.6306	.7106	.7772
4	.0007	.0082	.0314	.0748	.1382	.2173	.3063	.3993	.4908	.5769
5	.0000	.0012	.0067	.0210	.0480	.0896	.1454	.2132	.2897	.3710
6	.0000	.0001	.0012	.0049	.0139	.0309	.0581	.0967	.1465	.2063
7	.0000	.0000	.0002	.0010	.0034	.0091	.0199	.0376	.0639	.0995
8	.0000	.0000	.0000	.0002	.0007	.0023	.0059	.0127	.0242	.0419
9	.0000	.0000	.0000	.0000	.0001	.0005	.0015	.0037	.0081	.0155
10	.0000	.0000	.0000	.0000	.0000	.0001	.0003	.0010	.0024	.0051
11	.0000	.0000	.0000	.0000	.0000	.0000	.0001	.0002	.0006	.0015
12	.0000	.0000	.0000	.0000	.0000	.0000	.0000	.0000	.0001	.0004
13	.0000	.0000	.0000	.0000	.0000	.0000	.0000	.0000	.0000	.0001

r \ p	.11	.12	.13	.14	.15	.16	.17	.18	.19	.20
1	.9905	.9940	.9962	.9976	.9985	.9991	.9994	.9996	.9998	.9999
2	.9438	.9612	.9734	.9820	.9879	.9919	.9947	.9965	.9977	.9985
3	.8312	.8739	.9071	.9324	.9514	.9655	.9757	.9831	.9884	.9921
4	.6548	.7232	.7816	.8302	.8698	.9016	.9265	.9458	.9605	.9715
5	.4532	.5331	.6080	.6762	.7367	.7890	.8333	.8701	.9000	.9241
6	.2738	.3464	.4213	.4958	.5675	.6346	.6958	.7504	.7980	.8387
7	.1445	.1980	.2586	.3245	.3933	.4631	.5316	.5971	.6583	.7141
8	.0668	.0996	.1405	.1890	.2441	.3044	.3682	.4337	.4991	.5629
9	.0272	.0443	.0677	.0980	.1354	.1797	.2301	.2857	.3451	.4069
10	.0098	.0175	.0290	.0453	.0672	.0952	.1296	.1702	.2167	.2682
11	.0032	.0062	.0111	.0188	.0299	.0454	.0657	.0916	.1233	.1608
12	.0009	.0019	.0038	.0070	.0120	.0194	.0301	.0446	.0636	.0875
13	.0002	.0005	.0012	.0023	.0043	.0075	.0124	.0196	.0297	.0432
14	.0001	.0001	.0003	.0007	.0014	.0026	.0047	.0078	.0126	.0194
15	.0000	.0000	.0001	.0002	.0004	.0008	.0016	.0028	.0048	.0079
16	.0000	.0000	.0000	.0000	.0001	.0002	.0005	.0009	.0017	.0029
17	.0000	.0000	.0000	.0000	.0000	.0001	.0001	.0003	.0005	.0010
18	.0000	.0000	.0000	.0000	.0000	.0000	.0000	.0001	.0002	.0003
19	.0000	.0000	.0000	.0000	.0000	.0000	.0000	.0000	.0000	.0001

r	.21	.22	.23	.24	.25	.26	.27	.28	.29	.30
1	.9999	1.0000	1.0000	1.0000	1.0000	1.0000	1.0000	1.0000	1.0000	1.0000
2	.9991	.9994	.9996	.9998	.9999	.9999	.9999	1.0000	1.0000	1.0000
3	.9946	.9964	.9976	.9984	.9990	.9993	.9996	.9997	.9998	.9999
4	.9797	.9857	.9900	.9931	.9953	.9968	.9979	.9986	.9991	.9994
5	.9430	.9578	.9691	.9776	.9840	.9886	.9920	.9945	.9962	.9974
6	.8729	.9011	.9240	.9423	.9567	.9679	.9765	.9830	.9878	.9914
7	.7640	.8078	.8454	.8773	.9038	.9255	.9430	.9569	.9678	.9762
8	.6235	.6799	.7314	.7775	.8180	.8530	.8828	.9076	.9281	.9447
9	.4694	.5312	.5910	.6476	.7002	.7480	.7909	.8286	.8612	.8890
10	.3238	.3821	.4419	.5017	.5605	.6169	.6701	.7193	.7641	.8041
11	.2038	.2517	.3038	.3589	.4161	.4740	.5315	.5875	.6410	.6913
12	.1167	.1514	.1912	.2359	.2849	.3371	.3918	.4478	.5040	.5594
13	.0609	.0830	.1100	.1421	.1791	.2209	.2669	.3165	.3687	.4228
14	.0289	.0415	.0578	.0782	.1032	.1329	.1674	.2065	.2498	.2968
15	.0124	.0189	.0277	.0394	.0544	.0733	.0964	.1240	.1560	.1926
16	.0049	.0078	.0121	.0181	.0262	.0370	.0509	.0683	.0897	.1151
17	.0017	.0030	.0048	.0076	.0116	.0171	.0246	.0345	.0473	.0633
18	.0006	.0010	.0018	.0029	.0047	.0072	.0109	.0160	.0229	.0320
19	.0002	.0003	.0006	.0010	.0017	.0028	.0044	.0068	.0101	.0148
20	.0000	.0001	.0002	.0003	.0006	.0010	.0016	.0026	.0041	.0063
21	.0000	.0000	.0000	.0001	.0002	.0003	.0005	.0009	.0015	.0024
22	.0000	.0000	.0000	.0000	.0000	.0001	.0002	.0003	.0005	.0009
23	.0000	.0000	.0000	.0000	.0000	.0000	.0000	.0001	.0002	.0003
24	.0000	.0000	.0000	.0000	.0000	.0000	.0000	.0000	.0000	.0001

r	.31	.32	.33	.34	.35	.36	.37	.38	.39	.40
1	1.0000	1.0000	1.0000	1.0000	1.0000	1.0000	1.0000	1.0000	1.0000	1.0000
2	1.0000	1.0000	1.0000	1.0000	1.0000	1.0000	1.0000	1.0000	1.0000	1.0000
3	.9999	1.0000	1.0000	1.0000	1.0000	1.0000	1.0000	1.0000	1.0000	1.0000
4	.9996	.9998	.9998	.9999	.9999	1.0000	1.0000	1.0000	1.0000	1.0000
5	.9983	.9989	.9993	.9995	.9997	.9998	.9999	.9999	1.0000	1.0000
6	.9940	.9958	.9971	.9981	.9987	.9991	.9994	.9996	.9998	.9999
7	.9827	.9875	.9911	.9937	.9956	.9970	.9980	.9986	.9991	.9994
8	.9580	.9685	.9766	.9829	.9876	.9911	.9937	.9956	.9970	.9979
9	.9123	.9315	.9472	.9598	.9697	.9775	.9835	.9880	.9914	.9939
10	.8393	.8697	.8957	.9175	.9356	.9503	.9621	.9715	.9788	.9844
11	.7376	.7796	.8171	.8500	.8785	.9028	.9232	.9400	.9537	.9648
12	.6130	.6639	.7115	.7552	.7947	.8299	.8608	.8874	.9101	.9291
13	.4777	.5323	.5857	.6371	.6857	.7309	.7722	.8095	.8426	.8715
14	.3467	.3989	.4524	.5061	.5592	.6109	.6602	.7067	.7497	.7888
15	.2333	.2779	.3257	.3759	.4279	.4807	.5334	.5851	.6351	.6826
16	.1450	.1791	.2175	.2597	.3054	.3538	.4043	.4560	.5081	.5598
17	.0830	.1065	.1343	.1662	.2022	.2422	.2858	.3323	.3813	.4319
18	.0436	.0583	.0764	.0981	.1239	.1536	.1875	.2253	.2668	.3115
19	.0210	.0293	.0399	.0534	.0699	.0900	.1138	.1415	.1732	.2089
20	.0093	.0135	.0192	.0266	.0363	.0485	.0636	.0820	.1040	.1298

Table D

p r	.31	.32	.33	.34	.35	.36	.37	.38	.39	.40
21	.0038	.0057	.0084	.0122	.0173	.0240	.0327	.0438	.0575	.0744
22	.0014	.0022	.0034	.0051	.0075	.0109	.0154	.0214	.0292	.0392
23	.0005	.0008	.0012	.0020	.0030	.0045	.0066	.0096	.0136	.0189
24	.0001	.0002	.0004	.0007	.0011	.0017	.0026	.0039	.0058	.0083
25	.0000	.0001	.0001	.0002	.0004	.0006	.0009	.0015	.0022	.0034
26	.0000	.0000	.0000	.0001	.0001	.0002	.0003	.0005	.0008	.0012
27	.0000	.0000	.0000	.0000	.0000	.0001	.0001	.0002	.0002	.0004
28	.0000	.0000	.0000	.0000	.0000	.0000	.0000	.0000	.0001	.0001

p r	.41	.42	.43	.44	.45	.46	.47	.48	.49	.50
1	1.0000	1.0000	1.0000	1.0000	1.0000	1.0000	1.0000	1.0000	1.0000	1.0000
2	1.0000	1.0000	1.0000	1.0000	1.0000	1.0000	1.0000	1.0000	1.0000	1.0000
3	1.0000	1.0000	1.0000	1.0000	1.0000	1.0000	1.0000	1.0000	1.0000	1.0000
4	1.0000	1.0000	1.0000	1.0000	1.0000	1.0000	1.0000	1.0000	1.0000	1.0000
5	1.0000	1.0000	1.0000	1.0000	1.0000	1.0000	1.0000	1.0000	1.0000	1.0000
6	.9999	.9999	1.0000	1.0000	1.0000	1.0000	1.0000	1.0000	1.0000	1.0000
7	.9996	.9998	.9998	.9999	.9999	1.0000	1.0000	1.0000	1.0000	1.0000
8	.9986	.9991	.9994	.9996	.9998	.9998	.9999	.9999	1.0000	1.0000
9	.9958	.9971	.9980	.9987	.9991	.9994	.9996	.9998	.9999	.9999
10	.9887	.9919	.9943	.9960	.9973	.9981	.9988	.9992	.9995	.9997
11	.9735	.9803	.9856	.9896	.9926	.9948	.9964	.9975	.9983	.9989
12	.9447	.9575	.9677	.9758	.9821	.9869	.9906	.9933	.9953	.9968
13	.8964	.9175	.9351	.9496	.9614	.9708	.9782	.9840	.9884	.9917
14	.8240	.8551	.8821	.9053	.9249	.9413	.9546	.9654	.9740	.9808
15	.7270	.7679	.8051	.8382	.8674	.8927	.9143	.9324	.9474	.9597
16	.6102	.6586	.7043	.7468	.7858	.8209	.8522	.8795	.9031	.9231
17	.4833	.5348	.5855	.6346	.6815	.7255	.7662	.8033	.8365	.8659
18	.3589	.4083	.4590	.5101	.5609	.6107	.6585	.7039	.7463	.7852
19	.2484	.2912	.3370	.3851	.4349	.4857	.5365	.5867	.6354	.6821
20	.1594	.1930	.2305	.2714	.3156	.3624	.4112	.4614	.5122	.5627
21	.0946	.1184	.1461	.1776	.2130	.2521	.2946	.3400	.3878	.4373
22	.0516	.0669	.0855	.1074	.1331	.1627	.1961	.2333	.2740	.3179
23	.0259	.0348	.0460	.0598	.0767	.0969	.1206	.1482	.1796	.2148
24	.0118	.0165	.0226	.0305	.0405	.0530	.0683	.0867	.1086	.1341
25	.0049	.0072	.0102	.0142	.0196	.0265	.0354	.0465	.0602	.0769
26	.0019	.0028	.0042	.0060	.0086	.0121	.0167	.0228	.0305	.0403
27	.0006	.0010	.0015	.0023	.0034	.0050	.0072	.0101	.0140	.0192
28	.0002	.0003	.0005	.0008	.0012	.0019	.0028	.0041	.0058	.0083
29	.0001	.0001	.0002	.0002	.0004	.0006	.0010	.0015	.0022	.0032
30	.0000	.0000	.0000	.0001	.0001	.0002	.0003	.0005	.0007	.0011
31	.0000	.0000	.0000	.0000	.0000	.0000	.0001	.0001	.0002	.0003
32	.0000	.0000	.0000	.0000	.0000	.0000	.0000	.0000	.0001	.0001

p r	.01	.02	.03	.04	.05	.06	.07	.08	.09	.10
1	.3950	.6358	.7819	.8701	.9231	.9547	.9734	.9845	.9910	.9948
2	.0894	.2642	.4447	.5995	.7206	.8100	.8735	.9173	.9468	.9662
3	.0138	.0784	.1892	.3233	.4595	.5838	.6892	.7740	.8395	.8883
4	.0016	.0178	.0628	.1391	.2396	.3527	.4673	.5747	.6697	.7497
5	.0001	.0032	.0168	.0490	.1036	.1794	.2710	.3711	.4723	.5688
6	.0000	.0005	.0037	.0144	.0378	.0776	.1350	.2081	.2928	.3839
7	.0000	.0001	.0007	.0036	.0118	.0289	.0583	.1019	.1596	.2298
8	.0000	.0000	.0001	.0008	.0032	.0094	.0220	.0438	.0768	.1221
9	.0000	.0000	.0000	.0001	.0008	.0027	.0073	.0167	.0328	.0579
10	.0000	.0000	.0000	.0000	.0002	.0007	.0022	.0056	.0125	.0245
11	.0000	.0000	.0000	.0000	.0000	.0002	.0006	.0017	.0043	.0094
12	.0000	.0000	.0000	.0000	.0000	.0000	.0001	.0005	.0013	.0032
13	.0000	.0000	.0000	.0000	.0000	.0000	.0000	.0001	.0004	.0010
14	.0000	.0000	.0000	.0000	.0000	.0000	.0000	.0000	.0001	.0003
15	.0000	.0000	.0000	.0000	.0000	.0000	.0000	.0000	.0000	.0001

p r	.11	.12	.13	.14	.15	.16	.17	.18	.19	.20
1	.9971	.9983	.9991	.9995	.9997	.9998	.9999	1.0000	1.0000	1.0000
2	.9788	.9869	.9920	.9951	.9971	.9983	.9990	.9994	.9997	.9998
3	.9237	.9487	.9661	.9779	.9858	.9910	.9944	.9965	.9979	.9987
4	.8146	.8655	.9042	.9330	.9540	.9688	.9792	.9863	.9912	.9943
5	.6562	.7320	.7956	.8472	.8879	.9192	.9428	.9601	.9726	.9815

r \ p	.11	.12	.13	.14	.15	.16	.17	.18	.19	.20
6	.4760	.5647	.6463	.7186	.7806	.8323	.8741	.9071	.9327	.9520
7	.3091	.3935	.4789	.5616	.6387	.7081	.7686	.8199	.8624	.8966
8	.1793	.2467	.3217	.4010	.4812	.5594	.6328	.6996	.7587	.8096
9	.0932	.1392	.1955	.2605	.3319	.4071	.4832	.5576	.6280	.6927
10	.0435	.0708	.1074	.1537	.2089	.2718	.3403	.4122	.4849	.5563
11	.0183	.0325	.0535	.0824	.1199	.1661	.2203	.2813	.3473	.4164
12	.0069	.0135	.0242	.0402	.0628	.0929	.1309	.1768	.2300	.2893
13	.0024	.0051	.0100	.0179	.0301	.0475	.0714	.1022	.1405	.1861
14	.0008	.0018	.0037	.0073	.0132	.0223	.0357	.0544	.0791	.1106
15	.0002	.0006	.0013	.0027	.0053	.0096	.0164	.0266	.0411	.0607
16	.0001	.0002	.0004	.0009	.0020	.0038	.0070	.0120	.0197	.0308
17	.0000	.0000	.0001	.0003	.0007	.0014	.0027	.0050	.0087	.0144
18	.0000	.0000	.0000	.0001	.0002	.0005	.0010	.0019	.0036	.0063
19	.0000	.0000	.0000	.0000	.0001	.0001	.0003	.0007	.0013	.0025
20	.0000	.0000	.0000	.0000	.0000	.0000	.0001	.0002	.0005	.0009
21	.0000	.0000	.0000	.0000	.0000	.0000	.0000	.0001	.0002	.0003
22	.0000	.0000	.0000	.0000	.0000	.0000	.0000	.0000	.0000	.0001

r	.21	.22	.23	.24	.25	.26	.27	.28	.29	.30
1	1.0000	1.0000	1.0000	1.0000	1.0000	1.0000	1.0000	1.0000	1.0000	1.0000
2	.9999	.9999	1.0000	1.0000	1.0000	1.0000	1.0000	1.0000	1.0000	1.0000
3	.9992	.9995	.9997	.9998	.9999	1.0000	1.0000	1.0000	1.0000	1.0000
4	.9964	.9978	.9986	.9992	.9995	.9997	.9998	.9999	.9999	1.0000
5	.9877	.9919	.9948	.9967	.9979	.9987	.9992	.9995	.9997	.9998
6	.9963	.9767	.9841	.9893	.9930	.9954	.9970	.9981	.9988	.9993
7	.9236	.9445	.9603	.9720	.9806	.9868	.9911	.9941	.9961	.9975
8	.8523	.8874	.9156	.9377	.9547	.9676	.9772	.9842	.9892	.9927
9	.7505	.8009	.8437	.8794	.9084	.9316	.9497	.9635	.9740	.9817
10	.6241	.6870	.7436	.7934	.8363	.8724	.9021	.9260	.9450	.9598
11	.4864	.5552	.6210	.6822	.7378	.7871	.8299	.8663	.8965	.9211
12	.3533	.4201	.4878	.5544	.6184	.6782	.7329	.7817	.8244	.8610
13	.2383	.2963	.3585	.4233	.4890	.5539	.6163	.6749	.7287	.7771
14	.1490	.1942	.2456	.3023	.3630	.4261	.4901	.5534	.6145	.6721
15	.0862	.1181	.1565	.2013	.2519	.3075	.3669	.4286	.4912	.5532
16	.0462	.0665	.0926	.1247	.1631	.2075	.2575	.3121	.3703	.4308
17	.0229	.0347	.0508	.0718	.0983	.1306	.1689	.2130	.2623	.3161
18	.0105	.0168	.0259	.0384	.0551	.0766	.1034	.1359	.1741	.2178
19	.0045	.0075	.0122	.0191	.0287	.0418	.0590	.0809	.1080	.1406
20	.0018	.0031	.0054	.0088	.0139	.0212	.0314	.0449	.0626	.0848
21	.0006	.0012	.0022	.0038	.0063	.0100	.0155	.0232	.0338	.0478
22	.0002	.0004	.0008	.0015	.0026	.0044	.0071	.0112	.0170	.0251
23	.0001	.0001	.0003	.0006	.0010	.0018	.0031	.0050	.0080	.0123
24	.0000	.0000	.0001	.0002	.0004	.0007	.0012	.0021	.0035	.0056
25	.0000	.0000	.0000	.0001	.0001	.0002	.0004	.0008	.0014	.0024
26	.0000	.0000	.0000	.0000	.0000	.0001	.0002	.0003	.0005	.0009
27	.0000	.0000	.0000	.0000	.0000	.0000	.0001	.0001	.0002	.0003
28	.0000	.0000	.0000	.0000	.0000	.0000	.0000	.0000	.0001	.0001

r	.31	.32	.33	.34	.35	.36	.37	.38	.39	.40
1	1.0000	1.0000	1.0000	1.0000	1.0000	1.0000	1.0000	1.0000	1.0000	1.0000
2	1.0000	1.0000	1.0000	1.0000	1.0000	1.0000	1.0000	1.0000	1.0000	1.0000
3	1.0000	1.0000	1.0000	1.0000	1.0000	1.0000	1.0000	1.0000	1.0000	1.0000
4	1.0000	1.0000	1.0000	1.0000	1.0000	1.0000	1.0000	1.0000	1.0000	1.0000
5	.9999	.9999	1.0000	1.0000	1.0000	1.0000	1.0000	1.0000	1.0000	1.0000
6	.9996	.9997	.9998	.9999	.9999	1.0000	1.0000	1.0000	1.0000	1.0000
7	.9984	.9990	.9994	.9996	.9998	.9999	.9999	1.0000	1.0000	1.0000
8	.9952	.9969	.9980	.9987	.9992	.9995	.9997	.9998	.9999	.9999
9	.9874	.9914	.9942	.9962	.9975	.9984	.9990	.9994	.9996	.9998
10	.9710	.9794	.9856	.9901	.9933	.9955	.9971	.9981	.9988	.9992
11	.9409	.9563	.9683	.9773	.9840	.9889	.9924	.9949	.9966	.9978
12	.8916	.9168	.9371	.9533	.9658	.9753	.9825	.9878	.9916	.9943
13	.8197	.8564	.8874	.9130	.9339	.9505	.9635	.9736	.9811	.9867
14	.7253	.7732	.8157	.8524	.8837	.9097	.9310	.9481	.9616	.9720
15	.6131	.6698	.7223	.7699	.8122	.8491	.8805	.9069	.9286	.9460
16	.4922	.5530	.6120	.6679	.7199	.7672	.8094	.8462	.8779	.9045
17	.3734	.4328	.4931	.5530	.6111	.6664	.7179	.7649	.8070	.8439
18	.2666	.3197	.3760	.4346	.4940	.5531	.6105	.6653	.7164	.7631
19	.1786	.2220	.2703	.3227	.3784	.4362	.4949	.5533	.6101	.6644
20	.1121	.1447	.1826	.2257	.2736	.3255	.3805	.4376	.4957	.5535

r \ p	.31	.32	.33	.34	.35	.36	.37	.38	.39	.40
21	.0657	.0882	.1156	.1482	.1861	.2289	.2764	.3278	.3824	.4390
22	.0360	.0503	.0685	.0912	.1187	.1513	.1890	.2317	.2788	.3299
23	.0184	.0267	.0379	.0525	.0710	.0938	.1214	.1540	.1916	.2340
24	.0087	.0133	.0196	.0282	.0396	.0544	.0730	.0960	.1236	.1562
25	.0039	.0061	.0094	.0141	.0207	.0295	.0411	.0560	.0748	.0978
26	.0016	.0026	.0042	.0066	.0100	.0149	.0216	.0306	.0423	.0573
27	.0006	.0011	.0018	.0029	.0045	.0070	.0106	.0155	.0223	.0314
28	.0002	.0004	.0007	.0012	.0019	.0031	.0048	.0074	.0110	.0160
29	.0001	.0001	.0002	.0004	.0007	.0012	.0020	.0032	.0050	.0076
30	.0000	.0000	.0001	.0002	.0003	.0005	.0008	.0013	.0021	.0034
31	.0000	.0000	.0000	.0000	.0001	.0002	.0003	.0005	.0008	.0014
32	.0000	.0000	.0000	.0000	.0000	.0001	.0001	.0002	.0003	.0005
33	.0000	.0000	.0000	.0000	.0000	.0000	.0000	.0001	.0001	.0002
34	.0000	.0000	.0000	.0000	.0000	.0000	.0000	.0000	.0000	.0001

r \ p	.41	.42	.43	.44	.45	.46	.47	.48	.49	.50
1	1.0000	1.0000	1.0000	1.0000	1.0000	1.0000	1.0000	1.0000	1.0000	1.0000
2	1.0000	1.0000	1.0000	1.0000	1.0000	1.0000	1.0000	1.0000	1.0000	1.0000
3	1.0000	1.0000	1.0000	1.0000	1.0000	1.0000	1.0000	1.0000	1.0000	1.0000
4	1.0000	1.0000	1.0000	1.0000	1.0000	1.0000	1.0000	1.0000	1.0000	1.0000
5	1.0000	1.0000	1.0000	1.0000	1.0000	1.0000	1.0000	1.0000	1.0000	1.0000
6	1.0000	1.0000	1.0000	1.0000	1.0000	1.0000	1.0000	1.0000	1.0000	1.0000
7	1.0000	1.0000	1.0000	1.0000	1.0000	1.0000	1.0000	1.0000	1.0000	1.0000
8	1.0000	1.0000	1.0000	1.0000	1.0000	1.0000	1.0000	1.0000	1.0000	1.0000
9	.9999	.9999	1.0000	1.0000	1.0000	1.0000	1.0000	1.0000	1.0000	1.0000
10	.9995	.9997	.9998	.9999	.9999	1.0000	1.0000	1.0000	1.0000	1.0000
11	.9986	.9991	.9994	.9997	.9998	.9999	.9999	.9999	1.0000	1.0000
12	.9962	.9975	.9984	.9990	.9994	.9996	.9998	.9999	.9999	1.0000
13	.9908	.9938	.9958	.9973	.9982	.9989	.9993	.9996	.9997	.9998
14	.9799	.9858	.9902	.9933	.9955	.9970	.9981	.9988	.9992	.9995
15	.9599	.9707	.9789	.9851	.9896	.9929	.9952	.9968	.9980	.9987
16	.9265	.9443	.9585	.9696	.9780	.9844	.9892	.9926	.9950	.9967
17	.8757	.9025	.9248	.9429	.9573	.9687	.9774	.9839	.9888	.9923
18	.8051	.8421	.8740	.9010	.9235	.9418	.9565	.9680	.9769	.9836
19	.7151	.7617	.8037	.8406	.8727	.8998	.9225	.9410	.9559	.9675
20	.6099	.6638	.7143	.7608	.8026	.8396	.8718	.8991	.9219	.9405
21	.4965	.5539	.6099	.6635	.7138	.7602	.8020	.8391	.8713	.8987
22	.3840	.4402	.4973	.5543	.6100	.6634	.7137	.7599	.8018	.8389
23	.2807	.3316	.3854	.4412	.4981	.5548	.6104	.6636	.7138	.7601
24	.1936	.2359	.2826	.3331	.3866	.4422	.4989	.5554	.6109	.6641
25	.1255	.1580	.1953	.2375	.2840	.3343	.3876	.4431	.4996	.5561
26	.0762	.0992	.1269	.1593	.1966	.2386	.2850	.3352	.3885	.4439
27	.0432	.0584	.0772	.1003	.1279	.1603	.1975	.2395	.2858	.3359
28	.0229	.0321	.0439	.0591	.0780	.1010	.1286	.1609	.1981	.2399
29	.0113	.0164	.0233	.0325	.0444	.0595	.0784	.1013	.1289	.1611
30	.0052	.0078	.0115	.0166	.0235	.0327	.0446	.0596	.0784	.1013
31	.0022	.0034	.0053	.0079	.0116	.0167	.0236	.0327	.0445	.0595
32	.0009	.0014	.0022	.0035	.0053	.0079	.0116	.0166	.0234	.0325
33	.0003	.0005	.0009	.0014	.0022	.0035	.0053	.0078	.0114	.0164
34	.0001	.0002	.0003	.0005	.0009	.0014	.0022	.0034	.0052	.0077
35	.0000	.0001	.0001	.0002	.0003	.0005	.0009	.0014	.0021	.0033
36	.0000	.0000	.0000	.0001	.0001	.0002	.0003	.0005	.0008	.0013
37	.0000	.0000	.0000	.0000	.0000	.0001	.0001	.0002	.0003	.0005
38	.0000	.0000	.0000	.0000	.0000	.0000	.0000	.0001	.0001	.0002

n = 75

r \ p	.01	.02	.03	.04	.05	.06	.07	.08	.09	.10
1	.5294	.7802	.8982	.9532	.9787	.9903	.9957	.9981	.9992	.9996
2	.1729	.4439	.6620	.8069	.8944	.9441	.9712	.9855	.9929	.9965
3	.0397	.1899	.3917	.5814	.7303	.8350	.9032	.9452	.9699	.9839
4	.0069	.0637	.1882	.3527	.5202	.6655	.7786	.8598	.9145	.9496
5	.0010	.0174	.0750	.1812	.3211	.4708	.6098	.7261	.8160	.8811
6	.0001	.0040	.0253	.0798	.1724	.2943	.4294	.5610	.6776	.7729
7	.0000	.0008	.0073	.0305	.0810	.1629	.2709	.3936	.5179	.6327
8	.0000	.0001	.0019	.0102	.0336	.0802	.1534	.2501	.3622	.4792
9	.0000	.0000	.0004	.0030	.0124	.0353	.0781	.1440	.2313	.3342
10	.0000	.0000	.0001	.0008	.0041	.0140	.0360	.0753	.1350	.2142

Table D

r \ p	.01	.02	.03	.04	.05	.06	.07	.08	.09	.10
11	.0000	.0000	.0000	.0002	.0012	.0050	.0151	.0359	.0721	.1263
12	.0000	.0000	.0000	.0000	.0003	.0016	.0057	.0157	.0353	.0685
13	.0000	.0000	.0000	.0000	.0001	.0005	.0020	.0063	.0159	.0343
14	.0000	.0000	.0000	.0000	.0000	.0001	.0006	.0023	.0066	.0159
15	.0000	.0000	.0000	.0000	.0000	.0000	.0002	.0008	.0025	.0068
16	.0000	.0000	.0000	.0000	.0000	.0000	.0001	.0002	.0009	.0027
17	.0000	.0000	.0000	.0000	.0000	.0000	.0000	.0001	.0003	.0010
18	.0000	.0000	.0000	.0000	.0000	.0000	.0000	.0000	.0001	.0003
19	.0000	.0000	.0000	.0000	.0000	.0000	.0000	.0000	.0000	.0001

r \ p	.11	.12	.13	.14	.15	.16	.17	.18	.19	.20
1	.9998	.9999	1.0000	1.0000	1.0000	1.0000	1.0000	1.0000	1.0000	1.0000
2	.9984	.9992	.9996	.9998	.9999	1.0000	1.0000	1.0000	1.0000	1.0000
3	.9916	.9957	.9978	.9989	.9995	.9998	.9999	.9999	1.0000	1.0000
4	.9712	.9839	.9913	.9954	.9976	.9988	.9994	.9997	.9999	.9999
5	.9258	.9551	.9736	.9849	.9916	.9954	.9976	.9987	.9994	.9997
6	.8461	.8993	.9362	.9608	.9766	.9864	.9923	.9957	.9977	.9988
7	.7312	.8105	.8710	.9150	.9456	.9662	.9796	.9880	.9931	.9961
8	.5913	.6912	.7749	.8414	.8918	.9284	.9540	.9712	.9825	.9896
9	.4442	.5528	.6529	.7397	.8111	.8672	.9094	.9400	.9613	.9757
10	.3090	.4124	.5171	.6164	.7051	.7804	.8415	.8889	.9243	.9499
11	.1986	.2860	.3833	.4839	.5816	.6713	.7496	.8149	.8671	.9072
12	.1180	.1842	.2651	.3564	.4528	.5485	.6385	.7190	.7878	.8443
13	.0649	.1101	.1708	.2458	.3316	.4237	.5170	.6066	.6886	.7603
14	.0330	.0612	.1026	.1585	.2279	.3086	.3965	.4871	.5758	.6586
15	.0156	.0316	.0575	.0955	.1469	.2114	.2872	.3709	.4586	.5460
16	.0069	.0152	.0301	.0539	.0888	.1362	.1961	.2672	.3468	.4315
17	.0028	.0068	.0147	.0284	.0503	.0824	.1261	.1818	.2485	.3241
18	.0011	.0029	.0067	.0141	.0268	.0469	.0764	.1168	.1685	.2310
19	.0004	.0011	.0029	.0065	.0134	.0251	.0436	.0707	.1080	.1560
20	.0001	.0004	.0012	.0028	.0063	.0126	.0235	.0404	.0654	.0997
21	.0000	.0001	.0004	.0012	.0028	.0060	.0119	.0218	.0374	.0603
22	.0000	.0000	.0002	.0004	.0012	.0027	.0057	.0111	.0202	.0345
23	.0000	.0000	.0001	.0002	.0005	.0011	.0026	.0054	.0104	.0187
24	.0000	.0000	.0000	.0001	.0002	.0005	.0011	.0024	.0050	.0096
25	.0000	.0000	.0000	.0000	.0001	.0002	.0004	.0010	.0023	.0047
26	.0000	.0000	.0000	.0000	.0000	.0001	.0002	.0004	.0010	.0021
27	.0000	.0000	.0000	.0000	.0000	.0000	.0001	.0002	.0004	.0009
28	.0000	.0000	.0000	.0000	.0000	.0000	.0000	.0001	.0002	.0004
29	.0000	.0000	.0000	.0000	.0000	.0000	.0000	.0000	.0001	.0002
30	.0000	.0000	.0000	.0000	.0000	.0000	.0000	.0000	.0000	.0001

r \ p	.21	.22	.23	.24	.25	.26	.27	.28	.29	.30
1	1.0000	1.0000	1.0000	1.0000	1.0000	1.0000	1.0000	1.0000	1.0000	1.0000
2	1.0000	1.0000	1.0000	1.0000	1.0000	1.0000	1.0000	1.0000	1.0000	1.0000
3	1.0000	1.0000	1.0000	1.0000	1.0000	1.0000	1.0000	1.0000	1.0000	1.0000
4	1.0000	1.0000	1.0000	1.0000	1.0000	1.0000	1.0000	1.0000	1.0000	1.0000
5	.9998	.9999	1.0000	1.0000	1.0000	1.0000	1.0000	1.0000	1.0000	1.0000
6	.9994	.9997	.9998	.9999	1.0000	1.0000	1.0000	1.0000	1.0000	1.0000
7	.9979	.9989	.9994	.9997	.9998	.9999	1.0000	1.0000	1.0000	1.0000
8	.9940	.9966	.9981	.9990	.9995	.9997	.9999	.9999	1.0000	1.0000
9	.9851	.9911	.9948	.9971	.9984	.9991	.9995	.9998	.9999	.9999
10	.9677	.9797	.9875	.9925	.9956	.9975	.9986	.9992	.9996	.9998
11	.9370	.9583	.9732	.9831	.9897	.9938	.9964	.9979	.9988	.9994
12	.8889	.9228	.9478	.9656	.9779	.9861	.9915	.9949	.9970	.9983
13	.8206	.8693	.9074	.9360	.9569	.9717	.9819	.9887	.9931	.9959
14	.7327	.7963	.8488	.8908	.9231	.9472	.9647	.9769	.9853	.9909
15	.6291	.7050	.7714	.8275	.8731	.9091	.9365	.9567	.9712	.9813
16	.5172	.6003	.6774	.7462	.8054	.8546	.8940	.9247	.9478	.9647
17	.4057	.4895	.5720	.6500	.7208	.7827	.8352	.8780	.9120	.9380
18	.3028	.3811	.4628	.5445	.6228	.6952	.7596	.8150	.8611	.8983
19	.2146	.2826	.3577	.4372	.5176	.5960	.6696	.7361	.7942	.8434
20	.1443	.1992	.2636	.3355	.4125	.4915	.5696	.6440	.7122	.7729
21	.0920	.1334	.1848	.2456	.3143	.3887	.4662	.5437	.6185	.6882
22	.0556	.0848	.1232	.1712	.2286	.2941	.3659	.4415	.5182	.5932
23	.0318	.0511	.0780	.1136	.1585	.2125	.2749	.3440	.4177	.4933
24	.0173	.0292	.0469	.0717	.1046	.1465	.1974	.2567	.3230	.3945
25	.0089	.0158	.0268	.0430	.0657	.0962	.1352	.1830	.2393	.3029

Table D

p\r	.21	.22	.23	.24	.25	.26	.27	.28	.29	.30
26	.0043	.0082	.0145	.0245	.0393	.0602	.0883	.1246	.1695	.2227
27	.0020	.0040	.0075	.0132	.0223	.0358	.0550	.0809	.1147	.1567
28	.0009	.0018	.0036	.0068	.0120	.0203	.0326	.0501	.0740	.1053
29	.0004	.0008	.0017	.0033	.0062	.0109	.0184	.0296	.0456	.0676
30	.0001	.0003	.0007	.0015	.0030	.0056	.0099	.0166	.0268	.0414
31	.0001	.0001	.0003	.0007	.0014	.0027	.0050	.0089	.0150	.0242
32	.0000	.0001	.0001	.0003	.0006	.0013	.0025	.0045	.0080	.0134
33	.0000	.0000	.0000	.0001	.0003	.0006	.0011	.0022	.0040	.0071
34	.0000	.0000	.0000	.0000	.0001	.0002	.0005	.0010	.0020	.0036
35	.0000	.0000	.0000	.0000	.0000	.0001	.0002	.0004	.0009	.0017
36	.0000	.0000	.0000	.0000	.0000	.0000	.0001	.0002	.0004	.0008
37	.0000	.0000	.0000	.0000	.0000	.0000	.0000	.0001	.0002	.0003
38	.0000	.0000	.0000	.0000	.0000	.0000	.0000	.0000	.0001	.0001
39	.0000	.0000	.0000	.0000	.0000	.0000	.0000	.0000	.0000	.0001

r	.31	.32	.33	.34	.35	.36	.37	.38	.39	.40
1	1.0000	1.0000	1.0000	1.0000	1.0000	1.0000	1.0000	1.0000	1.0000	1.0000
2	1.0000	1.0000	1.0000	1.0000	1.0000	1.0000	1.0000	1.0000	1.0000	1.0000
3	1.0000	1.0000	1.0000	1.0000	1.0000	1.0000	1.0000	1.0000	1.0000	1.0000
4	1.0000	1.0000	1.0000	1.0000	1.0000	1.0000	1.0000	1.0000	1.0000	1.0000
5	1.0000	1.0000	1.0000	1.0000	1.0000	1.0000	1.0000	1.0000	1.0000	1.0000
6	1.0000	1.0000	1.0000	1.0000	1.0000	1.0000	1.0000	1.0000	1.0000	1.0000
7	1.0000	1.0000	1.0000	1.0000	1.0000	1.0000	1.0000	1.0000	1.0000	1.0000
8	1.0000	1.0000	1.0000	1.0000	1.0000	1.0000	1.0000	1.0000	1.0000	1.0000
9	1.0000	1.0000	1.0000	1.0000	1.0000	1.0000	1.0000	1.0000	1.0000	1.0000
10	.9999	.9999	1.0000	1.0000	1.0000	1.0000	1.0000	1.0000	1.0000	1.0000
11	.9997	.9998	.9999	1.0000	1.0000	1.0000	1.0000	1.0000	1.0000	1.0000
12	.9991	.9995	.9997	.9999	.9999	1.0000	1.0000	1.0000	1.0000	1.0000
13	.9976	.9986	.9992	.9996	.9998	.9999	.9999	1.0000	1.0000	1.0000
14	.9945	.9967	.9981	.9989	.9994	.9997	.9998	.9999	1.0000	1.0000
15	.9882	.9927	.9956	.9974	.9985	.9992	.9995	.9998	.9999	.9999
16	.9767	.9850	.9906	.9942	.9965	.9980	.9988	.9994	.9997	.9998
17	.9574	.9714	.9813	.9881	.9926	.9955	.9973	.9984	.9991	.9995
18	.9273	.9493	.9655	.9771	.9851	.9906	.9942	.9965	.9979	.9988
19	.8837	.9157	.9404	.9588	.9723	.9818	.9883	.9927	.9955	.9973
20	.8249	.8683	.9033	.9306	.9515	.9669	.9779	.9856	.9909	.9944
21	.7510	.8058	.8521	.8900	.9201	.9434	.9608	.9736	.9826	.9888
22	.6640	.7288	.7860	.8351	.8759	.9088	.9346	.9542	.9687	.9791
23	.5681	.6398	.7062	.7657	.8174	.8610	.8967	.9250	.9469	.9633
24	.4688	.5433	.6156	.6833	.7449	.7991	.8454	.8838	.9147	.9389
25	.3722	.4450	.5189	.5914	.6603	.7236	.7802	.8291	.8702	.9037
26	.2836	.3506	.4217	.4948	.5673	.6371	.7020	.7607	.8121	.8559
27	.2070	.2651	.3297	.3991	.4711	.5434	.6138	.6801	.7407	.7945
28	.1446	.1921	.2474	.3096	.3770	.4478	.5197	.5904	.6579	.7203
29	.0966	.1333	.1780	.2305	.2902	.3556	.4249	.4962	.5671	.6354
30	.0616	.0884	.1225	.1646	.2144	.2715	.3348	.4026	.4730	.5438
31	.0375	.0560	.0807	.1124	.1519	.1990	.2536	.3146	.3807	.4501
32	.0217	.0338	.0507	.0735	.1030	.1398	.1844	.2364	.2951	.3594
33	.0120	.0195	.0305	.0459	.0668	.0941	.1285	.1704	.2199	.2763
34	.0063	.0107	.0174	.0273	.0414	.0605	.0857	.1178	.1572	.2041
35	.0032	.0056	.0095	.0155	.0245	.0372	.0547	.0779	.1077	.1446
36	.0015	.0028	.0050	.0084	.0138	.0218	.0333	.0492	.0706	.0981
37	.0007	.0013	.0025	.0044	.0074	.0122	.0194	.0297	.0442	.0637
38	.0003	.0006	.0012	.0021	.0038	.0065	.0108	.0172	.0265	.0396
39	.0001	.0003	.0005	.0010	.0019	.0033	.0057	.0094	.0151	.0235
40	.0000	.0001	.0002	.0004	.0009	.0016	.0029	.0049	.0082	.0133
41	.0000	.0000	.0001	.0002	.0004	.0007	.0014	.0025	.0043	.0072
42	.0000	.0000	.0000	.0001	.0002	.0003	.0006	.0012	.0021	.0037
43	.0000	.0000	.0000	.0000	.0001	.0001	.0003	.0005	.0010	.0018
44	.0000	.0000	.0000	.0000	.0000	.0001	.0001	.0002	.0004	.0008
45	.0000	.0000	.0000	.0000	.0000	.0000	.0000	.0001	.0002	.0004
46	.0000	.0000	.0000	.0000	.0000	.0000	.0000	.0000	.0001	.0002
47	.0000	.0000	.0000	.0000	.0000	.0000	.0000	.0000	.0000	.0001

r	.41	.42	.43	.44	.45	.46	.47	.48	.49	.50
1	1.0000	1.0000	1.0000	1.0000	1.0000	1.0000	1.0000	1.0000	1.0000	1.0000
2	1.0000	1.0000	1.0000	1.0000	1.0000	1.0000	1.0000	1.0000	1.0000	1.0000
3	1.0000	1.0000	1.0000	1.0000	1.0000	1.0000	1.0000	1.0000	1.0000	1.0000
4	1.0000	1.0000	1.0000	1.0000	1.0000	1.0000	1.0000	1.0000	1.0000	1.0000
5	1.0000	1.0000	1.0000	1.0000	1.0000	1.0000	1.0000	1.0000	1.0000	1.0000

r \ p	.41	.42	.43	.44	.45	.46	.47	.48	.49	.50
6	1.0000	1.0000	1.0000	1.0000	1.0000	1.0000	1.0000	1.0000	1.0000	1.0000
7	1.0000	1.0000	1.0000	1.0000	1.0000	1.0000	1.0000	1.0000	1.0000	1.0000
8	1.0000	1.0000	1.0000	1.0000	1.0000	1.0000	1.0000	1.0000	1.0000	1.0000
9	1.0000	1.0000	1.0000	1.0000	1.0000	1.0000	1.0000	1.0000	1.0000	1.0000
10	1.0000	1.0000	1.0000	1.0000	1.0000	1.0000	1.0000	1.0000	1.0000	1.0000
11	1.0000	1.0000	1.0000	1.0000	1.0000	1.0000	1.0000	1.0000	1.0000	1.0000
12	1.0000	1.0000	1.0000	1.0000	1.0000	1.0000	1.0000	1.0000	1.0000	1.0000
13	1.0000	1.0000	1.0000	1.0000	1.0000	1.0000	1.0000	1.0000	1.0000	1.0000
14	1.0000	1.0000	1.0000	1.0000	1.0000	1.0000	1.0000	1.0000	1.0000	1.0000
15	1.0000	1.0000	1.0000	1.0000	1.0000	1.0000	1.0000	1.0000	1.0000	1.0000
16	.9999	1.0000	1.0000	1.0000	1.0000	1.0000	1.0000	1.0000	1.0000	1.0000
17	.9997	.9999	.9999	1.0000	1.0000	1.0000	1.0000	1.0000	1.0000	1.0000
18	.9993	.9996	.9998	.9999	1.0000	1.0000	1.0000	1.0000	1.0000	1.0000
19	.9985	.9991	.9995	.9997	.9999	.9999	1.0000	1.0000	1.0000	1.0000
20	.9966	.9980	.9989	.9994	.9996	.9998	.9999	1.0000	1.0000	1.0000
21	.9930	.9957	.9974	.9985	.9992	.9995	.9998	.9999	.9999	1.0000
22	.9864	.9914	.9947	.9968	.9981	.9989	.9994	.9997	.9998	.9999
23	.9752	.9837	.9895	.9935	.9960	.9976	.9986	.9992	.9996	.9998
24	.9573	.9709	.9806	.9874	.9920	.9951	.9971	.9983	.9990	.9995
25	.9303	.9507	.9660	.9771	.9850	.9904	.9940	.9964	.9979	.9988
26	.8920	.9210	.9436	.9607	.9733	.9823	.9886	.9928	.9956	.9974
27	.8408	.8795	.9110	.9358	.9548	.9690	.9793	.9865	.9914	.9947
28	.7763	.8251	.8664	.9003	.9274	.9484	.9643	.9759	.9841	.9899
29	.6994	.7575	.8087	.8525	.8890	.9184	.9415	.9591	.9721	.9815
30	.6128	.6782	.7382	.7917	.8380	.8770	.9088	.9340	.9535	.9680
31	.5206	.5901	.6566	.7184	.7741	.8228	.8643	.8985	.9259	.9473
32	.4275	.4975	.5673	.6348	.6981	.7559	.8070	.8509	.8876	.9173
33	.3386	.4053	.4746	.5444	.6127	.6774	.7371	.7905	.8369	.8760
34	.2581	.3183	.3835	.4519	.5216	.5904	.6564	.7178	.7734	.8222
35	.1889	.2405	.2986	.3622	.4295	.4988	.5679	.6349	.6980	.7557
36	.1327	.1745	.2236	.2795	.3413	.4073	.4760	.5453	.6132	.6778
37	.0892	.1214	.1608	.2074	.2610	.3208	.3855	.4534	.5227	.5912
38	.0574	.0809	.1108	.1477	.1918	.2431	.3009	.3640	.4310	.5000
39	.0353	.0515	.0730	.1007	.1352	.1770	.2259	.2815	.3429	.4088
40	.0207	.0313	.0460	.0657	.0913	.1235	.1627	.2092	.2626	.3222
41	.0116	.0182	.0277	.0410	.0590	.0825	.1123	.1492	.1932	.2443
42	.0062	.0101	.0159	.0244	.0364	.0527	.0742	.1018	.1363	.1778
43	.0031	.0053	.0087	.0139	.0214	.0321	.0468	.0665	.0920	.1240
44	.0015	.0027	.0045	.0075	.0120	.0186	.0282	.0414	.0593	.0827
45	.0007	.0013	.0022	.0039	.0064	.0103	.0162	.0246	.0365	.0527
46	.0003	.0006	.0011	.0019	.0032	.0054	.0088	.0139	.0214	.0320
47	.0001	.0002	.0005	.0009	.0016	.0027	.0046	.0075	.0119	.0185
48	.0000	.0001	.0002	.0004	.0007	.0013	.0023	.0038	.0063	.0101
49	.0000	.0000	.0001	.0002	.0003	.0006	.0011	.0019	.0032	.0053
50	.0000	.0000	.0000	.0001	.0001	.0002	.0005	.0009	.0015	.0026
51	.0000	.0000	.0000	.0000	.0000	.0001	.0002	.0004	.0007	.0012
52	.0000	.0000	.0000	.0000	.0000	.0000	.0001	.0002	.0003	.0005
53	.0000	.0000	.0000	.0000	.0000	.0000	.0000	.0001	.0001	.0002
54	.0000	.0000	.0000	.0000	.0000	.0000	.0000	.0000	.0000	.0001

n = 100

r \ p	.01	.02	.03	.04	.05	.06	.07	.08	.09	.10
1	.6340	.8674	.9524	.9831	.9941	.9979	.9993	.9998	.9999	1.0000
2	.2642	.5967	.8054	.9128	.9629	.9848	.9940	.9977	.9991	.9997
3	.0794	.3233	.5802	.7679	.8817	.9434	.9742	.9887	.9952	.9981
4	.0184	.1410	.3528	.5705	.7422	.8570	.9256	.9633	.9827	.9922
5	.0034	.0508	.1821	.3711	.5640	.7232	.8368	.9097	.9526	.9763
6	.0005	.0155	.0808	.2116	.3840	.5593	.7086	.8201	.8955	.9424
7	.0001	.0041	.0312	.1064	.2340	.3936	.5557	.6968	.8060	.8828
8	.0000	.0009	.0106	.0475	.1280	.2517	.4012	.5529	.6872	.7939
9	.0000	.0002	.0032	.0190	.0631	.1463	.2660	.4074	.5506	.6791
10	.0000	.0000	.0009	.0068	.0282	.0775	.1620	.2780	.4125	.5487
11	.0000	.0000	.0002	.0022	.0115	.0376	.0908	.1757	.2882	.4168
12	.0000	.0000	.0000	.0007	.0043	.0168	.0469	.1028	.1876	.2970
13	.0000	.0000	.0000	.0002	.0015	.0069	.0224	.0559	.1138	.1982
14	.0000	.0000	.0000	.0000	.0005	.0026	.0099	.0282	.0645	.1239
15	.0000	.0000	.0000	.0000	.0001	.0009	.0041	.0133	.0341	.0726

Table D 605

p / r	.01	.02	.03	.04	.05	.06	.07	.08	.09	.10
16	.0000	.0000	.0000	.0000	.0000	.0003	.0016	.0058	.0169	.0399
17	.0000	.0000	.0000	.0000	.0000	.0001	.0006	.0024	.0078	.0206
18	.0000	.0000	.0000	.0000	.0000	.0000	.0002	.0009	.0034	.0100
19	.0000	.0000	.0000	.0000	.0000	.0000	.0001	.0003	.0014	.0046
20	.0000	.0000	.0000	.0000	.0000	.0000	.0000	.0001	.0005	.0020
21	.0000	.0000	.0000	.0000	.0000	.0000	.0000	.0000	.0002	.0008
22	.0000	.0000	.0000	.0000	.0000	.0000	.0000	.0000	.0001	.0003
23	.0000	.0000	.0000	.0000	.0000	.0000	.0000	.0000	.0000	.0001

p / r	.11	.12	.13	.14	.15	.16	.17	.18	.19	.20
1	1.0000	1.0000	1.0000	1.0000	1.0000	1.0000	1.0000	1.0000	1.0000	1.0000
2	.9999	1.0000	1.0000	1.0000	1.0000	1.0000	1.0000	1.0000	1.0000	1.0000
3	.9992	.9997	.9999	1.0000	1.0000	1.0000	1.0000	1.0000	1.0000	1.0000
4	.9966	.9985	.9994	.9998	.9999	1.0000	1.0000	1.0000	1.0000	1.0000
5	.9886	.9947	.9977	.9990	.9996	.9998	.9999	1.0000	1.0000	1.0000
6	.9698	.9848	.9926	.9966	.9984	.9993	.9997	.9999	1.0000	1.0000
7	.9328	.9633	.9808	.9903	.9953	.9978	.9990	.9996	.9998	.9999
8	.8715	.9239	.9569	.9766	.9878	.9939	.9970	.9986	.9994	.9997
9	.7835	.8614	.9155	.9508	.9725	.9853	.9924	.9962	.9982	.9991
10	.6722	.7743	.8523	.9078	.9449	.9684	.9826	.9908	.9953	.9977
11	.5471	.6663	.7663	.8440	.9006	.9393	.9644	.9800	.9891	.9943
12	.4206	.5458	.6611	.7591	.8365	.8939	.9340	.9605	.9773	.9874
13	.3046	.4239	.5446	.6566	.7527	.8297	.8876	.9289	.9567	.9747
14	.2076	.3114	.4268	.5436	.6526	.7469	.8234	.8819	.9241	.9531
15	.1330	.2160	.3173	.4294	.5428	.6490	.7417	.8177	.8765	.9196
16	.0802	.1414	.2236	.3227	.4317	.5420	.6458	.7370	.8125	.8715
17	.0456	.0874	.1492	.2305	.3275	.4338	.5414	.6429	.7327	.8077
18	.0244	.0511	.0942	.1563	.2367	.3319	.4357	.5408	.6403	.7288
19	.0123	.0282	.0564	.1006	.1628	.2424	.3359	.4374	.5403	.6379
20	.0059	.0147	.0319	.0614	.1065	.1689	.2477	.3395	.4391	.5398
21	.0026	.0073	.0172	.0356	.0663	.1121	.1745	.2525	.3429	.4405
22	.0011	.0034	.0088	.0196	.0393	.0710	.1174	.1797	.2570	.3460
23	.0005	.0015	.0042	.0103	.0221	.0428	.0754	.1223	.1846	.2611
24	.0002	.0006	.0020	.0051	.0119	.0246	.0462	.0796	.1270	.1891
25	.0001	.0003	.0009	.0024	.0061	.0135	.0271	.0496	.0837	.1314
26	.0000	.0001	.0004	.0011	.0030	.0071	.0151	.0295	.0528	.0875
27	.0000	.0000	.0001	.0005	.0014	.0035	.0081	.0168	.0318	.0558
28	.0000	.0000	.0001	.0002	.0006	.0017	.0041	.0091	.0184	.0342
29	.0000	.0000	.0000	.0001	.0003	.0008	.0020	.0048	.0102	.0200
30	.0000	.0000	.0000	.0000	.0001	.0003	.0009	.0024	.0054	.0112
31	.0000	.0000	.0000	.0000	.0000	.0001	.0004	.0011	.0027	.0061
32	.0000	.0000	.0000	.0000	.0000	.0001	.0002	.0005	.0013	.0031
33	.0000	.0000	.0000	.0000	.0000	.0000	.0001	.0002	.0006	.0016
34	.0000	.0000	.0000	.0000	.0000	.0000	.0000	.0001	.0003	.0007
35	.0000	.0000	.0000	.0000	.0000	.0000	.0000	.0000	.0001	.0003
36	.0000	.0000	.0000	.0000	.0000	.0000	.0000	.0000	.0000	.0001
37	.0000	.0000	.0000	.0000	.0000	.0000	.0000	.0000	.0000	.0001

p / r	.21	.22	.23	.24	.25	.26	.27	.28	.29	.30
1	1.0000	1.0000	1.0000	1.0000	1.0000	1.0000	1.0000	1.0000	1.0000	1.0000
2	1.0000	1.0000	1.0000	1.0000	1.0000	1.0000	1.0000	1.0000	1.0000	1.0000
3	1.0000	1.0000	1.0000	1.0000	1.0000	1.0000	1.0000	1.0000	1.0000	1.0000
4	1.0000	1.0000	1.0000	1.0000	1.0000	1.0000	1.0000	1.0000	1.0000	1.0000
5	1.0000	1.0000	1.0000	1.0000	1.0000	1.0000	1.0000	1.0000	1.0000	1.0000
6	1.0000	1.0000	1.0000	1.0000	1.0000	1.0000	1.0000	1.0000	1.0000	1.0000
7	1.0000	1.0000	1.0000	1.0000	1.0000	1.0000	1.0000	1.0000	1.0000	1.0000
8	.9999	1.0000	1.0000	1.0000	1.0000	1.0000	1.0000	1.0000	1.0000	1.0000
9	.9996	1.9998	1.9999	1.0000	1.0000	1.0000	1.0000	1.0000	1.0000	1.0000
10	.9989	.9995	.9998	.9999	1.0000	1.0000	1.0000	1.0000	1.0000	1.0000
11	.9971	.9986	.9993	.9997	.9999	.9999	1.0000	1.0000	1.0000	1.0000
12	.9933	.9965	.9983	.9992	.9996	.9998	.9999	1.0000	1.0000	1.0000
13	.9857	.9922	.9959	.9979	.9990	.9995	.9998	.9999	1.0000	1.0000
14	.9721	.9840	.9911	.9953	.9975	.9988	.9994	.9997	.9999	.9999
15	.9496	.9695	.9823	.9900	.9946	.9972	.9986	.9993	.9997	.9998
16	.9153	.9462	.9671	.9806	.9889	.9939	.9967	.9983	.9992	.9996
17	.8668	.9112	.9430	.9647	.9789	.9878	.9932	.9963	.9981	.9990
18	.8032	.8625	.9074	.9399	.9624	.9773	.9867	.9925	.9959	.9978
19	.7252	.7991	.8585	.9038	.9370	.9601	.9757	.9856	.9918	.9955
20	.6358	.7220	.7953	.8547	.9005	.9342	.9580	.9741	.9846	.9911

p \ r	.21	.22	.23	.24	.25	.26	.27	.28	.29	.30
21	.5394	.6338	.7189	.7918	.8512	.8973	.9316	.9560	.9726	.9835
22	.4419	.5391	.6320	.7162	.7886	.8479	.8943	.9291	.9540	.9712
23	.3488	.4432	.5388	.6304	.7136	.7856	.8448	.8915	.9267	.9521
24	.2649	.3514	.4444	.5386	.6289	.7113	.7828	.8420	.8889	.9245
25	.1933	.2684	.3539	.4455	.5383	.6276	.7091	.7802	.8393	.8864
26	.1355	.1972	.2717	.3561	.4465	.5381	.6263	.7071	.7778	.8369
27	.0911	.1393	.2009	.2748	.3583	.4475	.5380	.6252	.7053	.7756
28	.0588	.0945	.1429	.2043	.2776	.3602	.4484	.5378	.6242	.7036
29	.0364	.0616	.0978	.1463	.2075	.2803	.3621	.4493	.5377	.6232
30	.0216	.0386	.0643	.1009	.1495	.2105	.2828	.3638	.4501	.5377
31	.0123	.0232	.0406	.0669	.1038	.1526	.2134	.2851	.3654	.4509
32	.0067	.0134	.0247	.0427	.0693	.1065	.1554	.2160	.2873	.3669
33	.0035	.0074	.0144	.0262	.0446	.0717	.1091	.1580	.2184	.2893
34	.0018	.0039	.0081	.0154	.0276	.0465	.0739	.1116	.1605	.2207
35	.0009	.0020	.0044	.0087	.0164	.0290	.0482	.0760	.1139	.1629
36	.0004	.0010	.0023	.0048	.0094	.0174	.0303	.0499	.0780	.1161
37	.0002	.0005	.0011	.0025	.0052	.0101	.0183	.0316	.0515	.0799
38	.0001	.0002	.0005	.0013	.0027	.0056	.0107	.0193	.0328	.0530
39	.0000	.0001	.0002	.0006	.0014	.0030	.0060	.0113	.0201	.0340
40	.0000	.0000	.0001	.0003	.0007	.0015	.0032	.0064	.0119	.0210
41	.0000	.0000	.0000	.0001	.0003	.0008	.0017	.0035	.0068	.0125
42	.0000	.0000	.0000	.0001	.0001	.0004	.0008	.0018	.0037	.0072
43	.0000	.0000	.0000	.0000	.0001	.0002	.0004	.0009	.0020	.0040
44	.0000	.0000	.0000	.0000	.0000	.0001	.0002	.0005	.0010	.0021
45	.0000	.0000	.0000	.0000	.0000	.0000	.0001	.0002	.0005	.0011
46	.0000	.0000	.0000	.0000	.0000	.0000	.0000	.0001	.0002	.0005
47	.0000	.0000	.0000	.0000	.0000	.0000	.0000	.0000	.0001	.0003
48	.0000	.0000	.0000	.0000	.0000	.0000	.0000	.0000	.0000	.0001
49	.0000	.0000	.0000	.0000	.0000	.0000	.0000	.0000	.0000	.0001

	.31	.32	.33	.34	.35	.36	.37	.38	.39	.40
1	1.0000	1.0000	1.0000	1.0000	1.0000	1.0000	1.0000	1.0000	1.0000	1.0000
2	1.0000	1.0000	1.0000	1.0000	1.0000	1.0000	1.0000	1.0000	1.0000	1.0000
3	1.0000	1.0000	1.0000	1.0000	1.0000	1.0000	1.0000	1.0000	1.0000	1.0000
4	1.0000	1.0000	1.0000	1.0000	1.0000	1.0000	1.0000	1.0000	1.0000	1.0000
5	1.0000	1.0000	1.0000	1.0000	1.0000	1.0000	1.0000	1.0000	1.0000	1.0000
6	1.0000	1.0000	1.0000	1.0000	1.0000	1.0000	1.0000	1.0000	1.0000	1.0000
7	1.0000	1.0000	1.0000	1.0000	1.0000	1.0000	1.0000	1.0000	1.0000	1.0000
8	1.0000	1.0000	1.0000	1.0000	1.0000	1.0000	1.0000	1.0000	1.0000	1.0000
9	1.0000	1.0000	1.0000	1.0000	1.0000	1.0000	1.0000	1.0000	1.0000	1.0000
10	1.0000	1.0000	1.0000	1.0000	1.0000	1.0000	1.0000	1.0000	1.0000	1.0000
11	1.0000	1.0000	1.0000	1.0000	1.0000	1.0000	1.0000	1.0000	1.0000	1.0000
12	1.0000	1.0000	1.0000	1.0000	1.0000	1.0000	1.0000	1.0000	1.0000	1.0000
13	1.0000	1.0000	1.0000	1.0000	1.0000	1.0000	1.0000	1.0000	1.0000	1.0000
14	1.0000	1.0000	1.0000	1.0000	1.0000	1.0000	1.0000	1.0000	1.0000	1.0000
15	.9999	1.0000	1.0000	1.0000	1.0000	1.0000	1.0000	1.0000	1.0000	1.0000
16	.9998	.9999	1.0000	1.0000	1.0000	1.0000	1.0000	1.0000	1.0000	1.0000
17	.9995	.9998	.9999	1.0000	1.0000	1.0000	1.0000	1.0000	1.0000	1.0000
18	.9989	.9995	.9997	.9999	.9999	1.0000	1.0000	1.0000	1.0000	1.0000
19	.9976	.9988	.9994	.9997	.9999	.9999	1.0000	1.0000	1.0000	1.0000
20	.9950	.9973	.9986	.9993	.9997	.9998	.9999	1.0000	1.0000	1.0000
21	.9904	.9946	.9971	.9985	.9992	.9996	.9998	.9999	1.0000	1.0000
22	.9825	.9898	.9942	.9968	.9983	.9991	.9996	.9998	.9999	1.0000
23	.9698	.9816	.9891	.9938	.9966	.9982	.9991	.9995	.9998	.9999
24	.9504	.9685	.9806	.9885	.9934	.9963	.9980	.9990	.9995	.9997
25	.9224	.9487	.9672	.9797	.9879	.9930	.9961	.9979	.9989	.9994
26	.8841	.9204	.9471	.9660	.9789	.9873	.9926	.9958	.9977	.9988
27	.8346	.8820	.9185	.9456	.9649	.9780	.9867	.9922	.9956	.9976
28	.7736	.8325	.8800	.9168	.9442	.9638	.9773	.9862	.9919	.9954
29	.7021	.7717	.8305	.8781	.9152	.9429	.9628	.9765	.9857	.9916
30	.6224	.7007	.7699	.8287	.8764	.9137	.9417	.9618	.9759	.9852
31	.5376	.6216	.6994	.7684	.8270	.8748	.9123	.9405	.9610	.9752
32	.4516	.5376	.6209	.6982	.7669	.8254	.8733	.9110	.9395	.9602
33	.3683	.4523	.5375	.6203	.6971	.7656	.8240	.8720	.9098	.9385
34	.2912	.3696	.4530	.5375	.6197	.6961	.7643	.8227	.8708	.9087
35	.2229	.2929	.3708	.4536	.5376	.6192	.6953	.7632	.8216	.8697
36	.1650	.2249	.2946	.3720	.4542	.5376	.6188	.6945	.7623	.8205
37	.1181	.1671	.2268	.2961	.3731	.4547	.5377	.6184	.6938	.7614
38	.0816	.1200	.1690	.2285	.2976	.3741	.4553	.5377	.6181	.6932
39	.0545	.0833	.1218	.1708	.2301	.2989	.3750	.4558	.5378	.6178
49	.0351	.0558	.0849	.1235	.1724	.2316	.3001	.3759	.4562	.5379

Table D

p / r	.31	.32	.33	.34	.35	.36	.37	.38	.39	.40
41	.0218	.0361	.0571	.0863	.1250	.1739	.2330	.3012	.3767	.4567
42	.0131	.0226	.0371	.0583	.0877	.1265	.1753	.2343	.3023	.3775
43	.0075	.0136	.0233	.0380	.0594	.0889	.1278	.1766	.2355	.3033
44	.0042	.0079	.0141	.0240	.0389	.0605	.0901	.1290	.1778	.2365
45	.0023	.0044	.0082	.0146	.0246	.0397	.0614	.0911	.1301	.1789
46	.0012	.0024	.0046	.0085	.0150	.0252	.0405	.0623	.0921	.1311
47	.0006	.0012	.0025	.0048	.0088	.0154	.0257	.0411	.0631	.0930
48	.0003	.0006	.0013	.0026	.0050	.0091	.0158	.0262	.0417	.0638
49	.0001	.0003	.0007	.0014	.0027	.0052	.0094	.0162	.0267	.0423
50	.0001	.0001	.0003	.0007	.0015	.0029	.0054	.0096	.0165	.0271
51	.0000	.0001	.0002	.0003	.0007	.0015	.0030	.0055	.0098	.0168
52	.0000	.0000	.0001	.0002	.0004	.0008	.0016	.0030	.0056	.0100
53	.0000	.0000	.0000	.0001	.0002	.0004	.0008	.0016	.0031	.0058
54	.0000	.0000	.0000	.0000	.0001	.0002	.0004	.0008	.0017	.0032
55	.0000	.0000	.0000	.0000	.0000	.0001	.0002	.0004	.0009	.0017
56	.0000	.0000	.0000	.0000	.0000	.0000	.0001	.0002	.0004	.0009
57	.0000	.0000	.0000	.0000	.0000	.0000	.0000	.0001	.0002	.0004
58	.0000	.0000	.0000	.0000	.0000	.0000	.0000	.0000	.0001	.0002
59	.0000	.0000	.0000	.0000	.0000	.0000	.0000	.0000	.0000	.0001

r	.41	.42	.43	.44	.45	.46	.47	.48	.49	.50
1	1.0000	1.0000	1.0000	1.0000	1.0000	1.0000	1.0000	1.0000	1.0000	1.0000
2	1.0000	1.0000	1.0000	1.0000	1.0000	1.0000	1.0000	1.0000	1.0000	1.0000
3	1.0000	1.0000	1.0000	1.0000	1.0000	1.0000	1.0000	1.0000	1.0000	1.0000
4	1.0000	1.0000	1.0000	1.0000	1.0000	1.0000	1.0000	1.0000	1.0000	1.0000
5	1.0000	1.0000	1.0000	1.0000	1.0000	1.0000	1.0000	1.0000	1.0000	1.0000
6	1.0000	1.0000	1.0000	1.0000	1.0000	1.0000	1.0000	1.0000	1.0000	1.0000
7	1.0000	1.0000	1.0000	1.0000	1.0000	1.0000	1.0000	1.0000	1.0000	1.0000
8	1.0000	1.0000	1.0000	1.0000	1.0000	1.0000	1.0000	1.0000	1.0000	1.0000
9	1.0000	1.0000	1.0000	1.0000	1.0000	1.0000	1.0000	1.0000	1.0000	1.0000
10	1.0000	1.0000	1.0000	1.0000	1.0000	1.0000	1.0000	1.0000	1.0000	1.0000
11	1.0000	1.0000	1.0000	1.0000	1.0000	1.0000	1.0000	1.0000	1.0000	1.0000
12	1.0000	1.0000	1.0000	1.0000	1.0000	1.0000	1.0000	1.0000	1.0000	1.0000
13	1.0000	1.0000	1.0000	1.0000	1.0000	1.0000	1.0000	1.0000	1.0000	1.0000
14	1.0000	1.0000	1.0000	1.0000	1.0000	1.0000	1.0000	1.0000	1.0000	1.0000
15	1.0000	1.0000	1.0000	1.0000	1.0000	1.0000	1.0000	1.0000	1.0000	1.0000
16	1.0000	1.0000	1.0000	1.0000	1.0000	1.0000	1.0000	1.0000	1.0000	1.0000
17	1.0000	1.0000	1.0000	1.0000	1.0000	1.0000	1.0000	1.0000	1.0000	1.0000
18	1.0000	1.0000	1.0000	1.0000	1.0000	1.0000	1.0000	1.0000	1.0000	1.0000
19	1.0000	1.0000	1.0000	1.0000	1.0000	1.0000	1.0000	1.0000	1.0000	1.0000
20	1.0000	1.0000	1.0000	1.0000	1.0000	1.0000	1.0000	1.0000	1.0000	1.0000
21	1.0000	1.0000	1.0000	1.0000	1.0000	1.0000	1.0000	1.0000	1.0000	1.0000
22	1.0000	1.0000	1.0000	1.0000	1.0000	1.0000	1.0000	1.0000	1.0000	1.0000
23	1.0000	1.0000	1.0000	1.0000	1.0000	1.0000	1.0000	1.0000	1.0000	1.0000
24	.9999	.9999	.9999	1.0000	1.0000	1.0000	1.0000	1.0000	1.0000	1.0000
25	.9997	.9999	.9999	1.0000	1.0000	1.0000	1.0000	1.0000	1.0000	1.0000
26	.9994	.9997	.9999	.9999	1.0000	1.0000	1.0000	1.0000	1.0000	1.0000
27	.9987	.9994	.9997	.9998	.9999	1.0000	1.0000	1.0000	1.0000	1.0000
28	.9975	.9987	.9993	.9997	.9998	.9999	1.0000	1.0000	1.0000	1.0000
29	.9952	.9974	.9986	.9993	.9996	.9998	.9999	1.0000	1.0000	1.0000
30	.9913	.9950	.9972	.9985	.9992	.9996	.9998	.9999	1.0000	1.0000
31	.9848	.9910	.9948	.9971	.9985	.9992	.9996	.9998	.9999	1.0000
32	.9746	.9844	.9907	.9947	.9970	.9984	.9992	.9996	.9998	.9999
33	.9594	.9741	.9840	.9905	.9945	.9969	.9984	.9991	.9996	.9998
34	.9376	.9587	.9736	.9837	.9902	.9944	.9969	.9983	.9991	.9996
35	.9078	.9368	.9581	.9732	.9834	.9900	.9942	.9968	.9983	.9991
36	.8687	.9069	.9361	.9576	.9728	.9831	.9899	.9941	.9967	.9982
37	.8196	.8678	.9061	.9355	.9571	.9724	.9829	.9897	.9941	.9967
38	.7606	.8188	.8670	.9054	.9349	.9567	.9721	.9827	.9896	.9940
39	.6927	.7599	.8181	.8663	.9049	.9345	.9563	.9719	.9825	.9895
40	.6176	.6922	.7594	.8174	.8657	.9044	.9341	.9561	.9717	.9824
41	.5380	.6174	.6919	.7589	.8169	.8653	.9040	.9338	.9558	.9716
42	.4571	.5382	.6173	.6916	.7585	.8165	.8649	.9037	.9335	.9557
43	.3782	.4576	.5383	.6173	.6913	.7582	.8162	.8646	.9035	.9334
44	.3041	.3788	.4580	.5385	.6172	.6912	.7580	.8160	.8645	.9033
45	.2375	.3049	.3794	.4583	.5387	.6173	.6911	.7579	.8159	.8644

r \ p	.41	.42	.43	.44	.45	.46	.47	.48	.49	.50
46	.1799	.2384	.3057	.3799	.4587	.5389	.6173	.6911	.7579	.8159
47	.1320	.1807	.2391	.3063	.3804	.4590	.5391	.6174	.6912	.7579
48	.0938	.1328	.1815	.2398	.3069	.3809	.4593	.5393	.6176	.6914
49	.0644	.0944	.1335	.1822	.2404	.3074	.3813	.4596	.5395	.6178
50	.0428	.0650	.0950	.1341	.1827	.2409	.3078	.3816	.4599	.5398
51	.0275	.0432	.0655	.0955	.1346	.1832	.2413	.3082	.3819	.4602
52	.0170	.0278	.0436	.0659	.0960	.1350	.1836	.2417	.3084	.3822
53	.0102	.0172	.0280	.0439	.0662	0963	.1353	.1838	.2419	.3086
54	.0059	.0103	.0174	.0282	.0441	.0664	.0965	.1355	.1840	.2421
55	.0033	.0059	.0104	.0175	.0284	.0443	.0666	.0967	.1356	.1841
56	.0017	.0033	.0060	.0105	.0176	.0285	.0444	.0667	.0967	.1356
57	.0009	.0018	.0034	.0061	.0106	.0177	.0286	.0444	.0667	.0967
58	.0004	.0009	.0018	.0034	.0061	.0106	.0177	.0286	.0444	.0666
59	.0002	.0005	.0009	.0018	.0034	.0061	.0106	.0177	.0285	.0443
60	.0001	.0002	.0005	.0009	.0018	.0034	.0061	.0106	.0177	.0284
61	.0000	.0001	.0002	.0005	.0009	.0018	.0034	.0061	.0106	.0176
62	.0000	.0000	.0001	.0002	.0005	.0009	.0018	.0034	.0061	.0105
63	.0000	.0000	.0000	.0001	.0002	.0005	.0009	.0018	.0034	.0060
64	.0000	.0000	.0000	.0000	.0001	.0002	.0005	.0009	.0018	.0033
65	.0000	.0000	.0000	.0000	.0000	.0001	.0002	.0005	.0009	.0018
66	.0000	.0000	.0000	.0000	.0000	.0000	.0001	.0002	.0004	.0009
67	.0000	.0000	.0000	.0000	.0000	.0000	.0000	.0001	.0002	.0004
68	.0000	.0000	.0000	.0000	.0000	.0000	.0000	.0000	.0001	.0002
69	.0000	.0000	.0000	.0000	.0000	.0000	.0000	.0000	.0000	.0001

Table D

With permission of Samuel B. Richmond, STATISTICAL ANALYSIS
Second Edition, Copyright ©, 1964
The Ronald Press Company, New York

λ	$e^{-\lambda}$	λ	$e^{-\lambda}$
0.0	1.00000	2.5	.08208
0.1	.90484	2.6	.07427
0.2	.81873	2.7	.06721
0.3	.74082	2.8	.06081
0.4	.67032	2.9	.05502
0.5	.60653	3.0	.04979
0.6	.54881	3.2	.04076
0.7	.49659	3.4	.03337
0.8	.44933	3.6	.02732
0.9	.40657	3.8	.02237
1.0	.36788	4.0	.01832
1.1	.33287	4.2	.01500
1.2	.30119	4.4	.01228
1.3	.27253	4.6	.01005
1.4	.24660	4.8	.00823
1.5	.22313	5.0	.00674
1.6	.20190	5.5	.00409
1.7	.18268	6.0	.00248
1.8	.16530	6.5	.00150
1.9	.14957	7.0	.00091
2.0	.13534	7.5	.00055
2.1	.12246	8.0	.00034
2.2	.11080	8.5	.00020
2.3	.10026	9.0	.00012
2.4	.09072	10.0	.00005

POISSON PROBABILITY DISTRIBUTION

$$P(r \mid \lambda) = \frac{\lambda^r}{r!} e^{-\lambda}$$

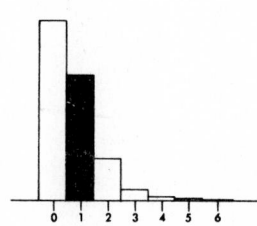

$$P(r = 1 \mid \lambda = 0.7) = 0.3476$$

r	0.10	0.20	0.30	0.40	λ 0.50	0.60	0.70	0.80	0.90	1.00
0	.9048	.8187	.7408	.6703	.6065	.5488	.4966	.4493	.4066	.3679
1	.0905	.1637	.2222	.2681	.3033	.3293	.3476	.3595	.3659	.3679
2	.0045	.0164	.0333	.0536	.0758	.0988	.1217	.1438	.1647	.1839
3	.0002	.0011	.0033	.0072	.0126	.0198	.0284	.0383	.0494	.0613
4	.0000	.0001	.0003	.0007	.0016	.0030	.0050	.0077	.0111	.0153
5	.0000	.0000	.0000	.0001	.0002	.0004	.0007	.0012	.0020	.0031
6	.0000	.0000	.0000	.0000	.0000	.0000	.0001	.0002	.0003	.0005
7	.0000	.0000	.0000	.0000	.0000	.0000	.0000	.0000	.0000	.0001

r	1.10	1.20	1.30	1.40	λ 1.50	1.60	1.70	1.80	1.90	2.00
0	.3329	.3012	.2725	.2466	.2231	.2019	.1827	.1653	.1496	.1353
1	.3662	.3614	.3543	.3452	.3347	.3230	.3106	.2975	.2842	.2707
2	.2014	.2169	.2303	.2417	.2510	.2584	.2640	.2678	.2700	.2707
3	.0738	.0867	.0998	.1128	.1255	.1378	.1496	.1607	.1710	.1804
4	.0203	.0260	.0324	.0395	.0471	.0551	.0636	.0723	.0812	.0902
5	.0045	.0062	.0084	.0111	.0141	.0176	.0216	.0260	.0309	.0361
6	.0008	.0012	.0018	.0026	.0035	.0047	.0061	.0078	.0098	.0120
7	.0001	.0002	.0003	.0005	.0008	.0011	.0015	.0020	.0027	.0034
8	.0000	.0000	.0001	.0001	.0001	.0002	.0003	.0005	.0006	.0009
9	.0000	.0000	.0000	.0000	.0000	.0000	.0001	.0001	.0001	.0002

r	2.10	2.20	2.30	2.40	λ 2.50	2.60	2.70	2.80	2.90	3.00
0	.1225	.1108	.1003	.0907	.0821	.0743	.0672	.0608	.0550	.0498
1	.2572	.2438	.2306	.2177	.2052	.1931	.1815	.1703	.1596	.1494
2	.2700	.2681	.2652	.2613	.2565	.2510	.2450	.2384	.2314	.2240
3	.1890	.1966	.2033	.2090	.2138	.2176	.2205	.2225	.2237	.2240
4	.0992	.1082	.1169	.1254	.1336	.1414	.1488	.1557	.1622	.1680
5	.0417	.0476	.0538	.0602	.0668	.0735	.0804	.0872	.0940	.1008
6	.0146	.0174	.0206	.0241	.0278	.0319	.0362	.0407	.0455	.0504
7	.0044	.0055	.0068	.0083	.0099	.0118	.0139	.0163	.0188	.0216
8	.0011	.0015	.0019	.0025	.0031	.0038	.0047	.0057	.0068	.0081
9	.0003	.0004	.0005	.0007	.0009	.0011	.0014	.0018	.0022	.0027
10	.0001	.0001	.0001	.0002	.0002	.0003	.0004	.0005	.0006	.0008
11	.0000	.0000	.0000	.0000	.0000	.0001	.0001	.0001	.0002	.0002
12	.0000	.0000	.0000	.0000	.0000	.0000	.0000	.0000	.0000	.0001

r	3.10	3.20	3.30	3.40	λ 3.50	3.60	3.70	3.80	3.90	4.00
0	.0450	.0408	.0369	.0334	.0302	.0273	.0247	.0224	.0202	.0183
1	.1397	.1304	.1217	.1135	.1057	.0984	.0915	.0850	.0789	.0733
2	.2165	.2087	.2008	.1929	.1850	.1771	.1692	.1615	.1539	.1465
3	.2237	.2226	.2209	.2186	.2158	.2125	.2087	.2046	.2001	.1954
4	.1733	.1781	.1823	.1858	.1888	.1912	.1931	.1944	.1951	.1954

r	3.10	3.20	3.30	3.40	λ 3.50	3.60	3.70	3.80	3.90	4.00
5	.1075	.1140	.1203	.1264	.1322	.1377	.1429	.1477	.1522	.1563
6	.0555	.0608	.0662	.0716	.0771	.0826	.0881	.0936	.0989	.1042
7	.0246	.0278	.0312	.0348	.0385	.0425	.0466	.0508	.0551	.0595
8	.0095	.0111	.0129	.0148	.0169	.0191	.0215	.0241	.0269	.0298
9	.0033	.0040	.0047	.0056	.0066	.0076	.0089	.0102	.0116	.0132
10	.0010	.0013	0016	.0019	.0023	.0028	.0033	.0039	.0045	.0053
11	.0003	.0004	.0005	.0006	.0007	.0009	.0011	.0013	.0016	.0019
12	.0001	.0001	.0001	.0002	.0002	.0003	.0003	.0004	.0005	.0006
13	.0000	.0000	.0000	.0000	.0001	.0001	.0001	.0001	.0002	.0002
14	.0000	.0000	.0000	.0000	.0000	.0000	.0000	.0000	.0000	.0001

r	4.10	4.20	4.30	4.40	λ 4.50	4.60	4.70	4.80	4.90	5.00
0	.0166	.0150	.0136	.0123	.0111	.0101	.0091	.0082	.0074	.0067
1	.0679	.0630	.0583	.0540	.0500	.0462	.0427	.0395	.0365	.0337
2	.1393	.1323	.1254	.1188	.1125	.1063	.1005	.0948	.0894	.0842
3	.1904	.1852	.1798	.1743	.1687	.1631	.1574	.1517	.1460	.1404
4	.1951	.1944	.1933	.1917	.1898	.1875	.1849	.1820	.1789	.1755
5	.1600	.1633	.1662	.1687	.1708	.1725	.1738	.1747	.1753	.1755
6	.1093	.1143	.1191	.1237	.1281	.1323	.1362	.1398	.1432	.1462
7	.0640	.0686	.0732	.0778	.0824	.0869	.0914	.0959	.1002	.1044
8	.0328	.0360	.0393	.0428	.0463	.0500	.0537	.0575	.0614	.0653
9	.0150	.0168	.0188	.0209	.0232	.0255	.0281	.0307	.0334	.0363
10	.0061	.0071	.0081	.0092	.0104	.0118	.0132	.0147	.0164	.0181
11	.0023	.0027	.0032	.0037	.0043	.0049	.0056	.0064	.0073	.0082
12	.0008	.0009	.0011	.0013	.0016	.0019	.0022	.0026	.0030	.0034
13	.0002	.0003	.0004	.0005	.0006	.0007	.0008	.0009	.0011	.0013
14	.0001	.0001	.0001	.0001	.0002	.0002	.0003	.0003	.0004	.0005
15	.0000	.0000	.0000	.0000	.0001	.0001	.0001	.0001	.0001	.0002

r	5.10	5.20	5.30	5.40	λ 5.50	5.60	5.70	5.80	5.90	6.00
0	.0061	.0055	.0050	.0045	.0041	.0037	.0033	.0030	.0027	.0025
1	.0311	.0287	.0265	.0244	.0225	.0207	.0191	.0176	.0162	.0149
2	.0793	.0746	.0701	.0659	.0618	.0580	.0544	.0509	.0477	.0446
3	.1348	.1293	.1239	.1185	.1133	.1082	.1033	.0985	.0938	.0892
4	.1719	.1681	.1641	.1600	.1558	.1515	.1472	.1428	.1383	.1339
5	.1753	.1748	.1740	.1728	.1714	.1697	.1678	.1656	.1632	.1606
6	.1490	.1515	.1537	.1555	.1571	.1584	.1594	.1601	.1605	.1606
7	.1086	.1125	.1163	.1200	.1234	.1267	.1298	.1326	.1353	.1377
8	.0692	.0731	.0771	.0810	.0849	.0887	.0925	.0962	.0998	.1033
9	.0392	.0423	.0454	.0486	.0519	.0552	.0586	.0620	.0654	.0688
10	.0200	.0220	.0241	.0262	.0285	.0309	.0334	.0359	.0386	.0413
11	.0093	.0104	.0116	.0129	.0143	.0157	.0173	.0190	.0207	.0225
12	.0039	.0045	.0051	.0058	.0065	.0073	.0082	.0092	.0102	.0113
13	.0015	.0018	.0021	.0024	.0028	.0032	.0036	.0041	.0046	.0052
14	.0006	.0007	.0008	.0009	.0011	.0013	.0015	.0017	.0019	.0022
15	.0002	.0002	.0003	.0003	.0004	.0005	.0006	.0007	.0008	.0009
16	.0001	.0001	.0001	.0001	.0001	.0002	.0002	.0002	.0003	.0003
17	.0000	.0000	.0000	.0000	.0000	.0001	.0001	.0001	.0001	.0001

r	6.10	6.20	6.30	6.40	λ 6.50	6.60	6.70	6.80	6.90	7.00
0	.0022	.0020	.0018	.0017	.0015	.0014	.0012	.0011	.0010	.0009
1	.0137	.0126	.0116	.0106	.0098	.0090	.0082	.0076	.0070	.0064
2	.0417	.0390	.0364	.0340	.0318	.0296	.0276	.0258	.0240	.0223
3	.0848	.0806	.0765	.0726	.0688	.0652	.0617	.0584	.0552	.0521
4	.1294	.1249	.1205	.1161	.1118	.1076	.1034	.0992	.0952	.0912
5	.1579	.1549	.1519	.1487	.1454	.1420	.1385	.1349	.1314	.1277
6	.1605	.1601	.1595	.1586	.1575	.1562	.1546	.1529	.1511	.1490
7	.1399	.1418	.1435	.1450	.1462	.1472	.1480	.1486	.1489	.1490
8	.1066	.1099	.1130	.1160	.1188	.1215	.1240	.1263	.1284	.1304
9	.0723	.0757	.0791	.0825	.0858	.0891	.0923	.0954	.0985	.1014
10	.0441	.0469	.0498	.0528	.0558	.0588	.0618	.0649	.0679	.0710
11	.0244	.0265	.0285	.0307	.0330	.0353	.0377	.0401	.0426	.0452
12	.0124	.0137	.0150	.0164	.0179	.0194	.0210	.0227	.0245	.0263
13	.0058	.0065	.0073	.0081	.0089	.0099	.0108	.0119	.0130	.0142
14	.0025	.0029	.0033	.0037	.0041	.0046	.0052	.0058	.0064	.0071

r	6.10	6.20	6.30	6.40	λ 6.50	6.60	6.70	6.80	6.90	7.00
15	.0010	.0012	.0014	.0016	.0018	.0020	.0023	.0026	.0029	.0033
16	.0004	.0005	.0005	.0006	.0007	.0008	.0010	.0011	.0013	.0014
17	.0001	.0002	.0002	.0002	.0003	.0003	.0004	.0004	.0005	.0006
18	.0000	.0001	.0001	.0001	.0001	.0001	.0001	.0002	.0002	.0002
19	.0000	.0000	.0000	.0000	.0000	.0000	.0001	.0001	.0001	.0001

r	7.10	7.20	7.30	7.40	λ 7.50	7.60	7.70	7.80	7.90	8.00
0	.0008	.0007	.0007	.0006	.0006	.0005	.0005	.0004	.0004	.0003
1	.0059	.0054	.0049	.0045	.0041	.0038	.0035	.0032	.0029	.0027
2	.0208	.0194	.0180	.0167	.0156	.0145	.0134	.0125	.0116	.0107
3	.0492	.0464	.0438	.0413	.0389	.0366	.0345	.0324	.0305	.0286
4	.0874	.0836	.0799	.0764	.0729	.0696	.0663	.0632	.0602	.0573
5	.1241	.1204	.1167	.1130	.1094	.1057	.1021	.0986	.0951	.0916
6	.1468	.1445	.1420	.1394	.1367	.1339	.1311	.1282	.1252	.1221
7	.1489	.1486	.1481	.1474	.1465	.1454	.1442	.1428	.1413	.1396
8	.1321	.1337	.1351	.1363	.1373	.1381	.1388	.1392	.1395	.1396
9	.1042	.1070	.1096	.1121	.1144	.1167	.1187	.1207	.1224	.1241
10	.0740	.0770	.0800	.0829	.0858	.0887	.0914	.0941	.0967	.0993
11	.0478	.0504	.0531	.0558	.0585	.0613	.0640	.0667	.0695	.0722
12	.0283	.0303	.0323	.0344	.0366	.0388	.0411	.0434	.0457	.0481
13	.0154	.0168	.0181	.0196	.0211	.0227	.0243	.0260	.0278	.0296
14	.0078	.0086	.0095	.0104	.0113	.0123	.0134	.0145	.0157	.0169
15	.0037	.0041	.0046	.0051	.0057	.0062	.0069	.0075	.0083	.0090
16	.0016	.0019	.0021	.0024	.0026	.0030	.0033	.0037	.0041	.0045
17	.0007	.0008	.0009	.0010	.0012	.0013	.0015	.0017	.0019	.0021
18	.0003	.0003	.0004	.0004	.0005	.0006	.0006	.0007	.0008	.0009
19	.0001	.0001	.0001	.0002	.0002	.0002	.0003	.0003	.0003	.0004
20	.0000	.0000	.0001	.0001	.0001	.0001	.0001	.0001	.0001	.0002
21	.0000	.0000	.0000	.0000	.0000	.0000	.0000	.0000	.0001	.0001

r	8.10	8.20	8.30	8.40	λ 8.50	8.60	8.70	8.80	8.90	9.00
0	.0003	.0003	.0002	.0002	.0002	.0002	.0002	.0002	.0001	.0001
1	.0025	.0023	.0021	.0019	.0017	.0016	.0014	.0013	.0012	.0011
2	.0100	.0092	.0086	.0079	.0074	.0068	.0063	.0058	.0054	.0050
3	.0269	.0252	.0237	.0222	.0208	.0195	.0183	.0171	.0160	.0150
4	.0544	.0517	.0491	.0466	.0443	.0420	.0398	.0377	.0357	.0337
5	.0882	.0849	.0816	.0784	.0752	.0722	.0692	.0663	.0635	.0607
6	.1191	.1160	.1128	.1097	.1066	.1034	.1003	.0972	.0941	.0911
7	.1378	.1358	.1338	.1317	.1294	.1271	.1247	.1222	.1197	.1171
8	.1395	.1392	.1388	.1382	.1375	.1366	.1356	.1344	.1332	.1318
9	.1256	.1269	.1280	.1290	.1299	.1306	.1311	.1315	.1317	.1318
10	.1017	.1040	.1063	.1084	.1104	.1123	.1140	.1157	.1172	.1186
11	.0749	.0776	.0802	.0828	.0853	.0878	.0902	.0925	.0948	.0970
12	.0505	.0530	.0555	.0579	.0604	.0629	.0654	.0679	.0703	.0728
13	.0315	.0334	.0354	.0374	.0395	.0416	.0438	.0459	.0481	.0504
14	.0182	.0196	.0210	.0225	.0240	.0256	.0272	.0289	.0306	.0324
15	.0098	.0107	.0116	.0126	.0136	.0147	.0158	.0169	.0182	.0194
16	.0050	.0055	.0060	.0066	.0072	.0079	.0086	.0093	.0101	.0109
17	.0024	.0026	.0029	.0033	.0036	.0040	.0044	.0048	.0053	.0058
18	.0011	.0012	.0014	.0015	.0017	.0019	.0021	.0024	.0026	.0029
19	.0005	.0005	.0006	.0007	.0008	.0009	.0010	.0011	.0012	.0014
20	.0002	.0002	.0002	.0003	.0003	.0004	.0004	.0005	.0005	.0006
21	.0001	.0001	.0001	.0001	.0001	.0002	.0002	.0002	.0002	.0003
22	.0000	.0000	.0000	.0000	.0001	.0001	.0001	.0001	.0001	.0001

r	9.10	9.20	9.30	9.40	λ 9.50	9.60	9.70	9.80	9.90	10.00
0	.0001	.0001	.0001	.0001	.0001	.0001	.0001	.0001	.0001	.0000
1	.0010	.0009	.0009	.0008	.0007	.0007	.0006	.0005	.0005	.0005
2	.0046	.0043	.0040	.0037	.0034	.0031	.0029	.0027	.0025	.0023
3	.0140	.0131	.0123	.0115	.0107	.0100	.0093	.0087	.0081	.0076
4	.0319	.0302	.0285	.0269	.0254	.0240	.0226	.0213	.0201	.0189
5	.0581	.0555	.0530	.0506	.0483	.0460	.0439	.0418	.0398	.0378
6	.0881	.0851	.0822	.0793	.0764	.0736	.0709	.0682	.0656	.0631
7	.1145	.1118	.1091	.1064	.1037	.1010	.0982	.0955	.0928	.0901
8	.1302	.1286	.1269	.1251	.1232	.1212	.1191	.1170	.1148	.1126
9	.1317	.1315	.1311	.1306	.1300	.1293	.1284	.1274	.1263	.1251

r	9.10	9.20	9.30	9.40	λ 9.50	9.60	9.70	9.80	9.90	10.00
10	.1198	.1210	.1219	.1228	.1235	.1241	.1245	.1249	.1250	.1251
11	.0991	.1012	.1031	.1049	.1067	.1083	.1098	.1112	.1125	.1137
12	.0752	.0776	.0799	.0822	.0844	.0866	.0888	.0908	.0928	.0948
13	.0526	.0549	.0572	.0594	.0617	.0640	.0662	.0685	.0707	.0729
14	.0342	.0361	.0380	.0399	.0419	.0439	.0459	.0479	.0500	.0521
15	.0208	.0221	.0235	.0250	.0265	.0281	.0297	.0313	.0330	.0347
16	.0118	.0127	.0137	.0147	.0157	.0168	.0180	.0192	.0204	.0217
17	.0063	.0069	.0075	.0081	.0088	.0095	.0103	.0111	.0119	.0128
18	.0032	.0035	.0039	.0042	.0046	.0051	.0055	.0060	.0065	.0071
19	.0015	.0017	.0019	.0021	.0023	.0026	.0028	.0031	.0034	.0037
20	.0007	.0008	.0009	.0010	.0011	.0012	.0014	.0015	.0017	.0019
21	.0003	.0003	.0004	.0004	.0005	.0006	.0006	.0007	.0008	.0009
22	.0001	.0001	.0002	.0002	.0002	.0002	.0003	.0003	.0004	.0004
23	.0000	.0001	.0001	.0001	.0001	.0001	.0001	.0001	.0002	.0002
24	.0000	.0000	.0000	.0000	.0000	.0000	.0000	.0001	.0001	.0001

r	11.	12.	13.	14.	λ 15.	16.	17.	18.	19.	20.
0	.0000	.0000	.0000	.0000	.0000	.0000	.0000	.0000	.0000	.0000
1	.0002	.0001	.0000	.0000	.0000	.0000	.0000	.0000	.0000	.0000
2	.0010	.0004	.0002	.0001	.0000	.0000	.0000	.0000	.0000	.0000
3	.0037	.0018	.0008	.0004	.0002	.0001	.0000	.0000	.0000	.0000
4	.0102	.0053	.0027	.0013	.0006	.0003	.0001	.0001	.0000	.0000
5	.0224	.0127	.0070	.0037	.0019	.0010	.0005	.0002	.0001	.0001
6	.0411	.0255	.0152	.0087	.0048	.0026	.0014	.0007	.0004	.0002
7	.0646	.0437	.0281	.0174	.0104	.0060	.0034	.0019	.0010	.0005
8	.0888	.0655	.0457	.0304	.0194	.0120	.0072	.0042	.0024	.0013
9	.1085	.0874	.0661	.0473	.0324	.0213	.0135	.0083	.0050	.0029
10	.1194	.1048	.0859	.0663	.0486	.0341	.0230	.0150	.0095	.0058
11	.1194	.1144	.1015	.0844	.0663	.0496	.0355	.0245	.0164	.0106
12	.1094	.1144	.1099	.0984	.0829	.0661	.0504	.0368	.0259	.0176
13	.0926	.1056	.1099	.1060	.0956	.0814	.0658	.0509	.0378	.0271
14	.0728	.0905	.1021	.1060	.1024	.0930	.0800	.0655	.0514	.0387
15	.0534	.0724	.0885	.0989	.1024	.0992	.0906	.0786	.0650	.0516
16	.0367	.0543	.0719	.0866	.0960	.0992	.0963	.0884	.0772	.0646
17	.0237	.0383	.0550	.0713	.0847	.0934	.0963	.0936	.0863	.0760
18	.0145	.0256	.0397	.0554	.0706	.0830	.0909	.0936	.0911	.0844
19	.0084	.0161	.0272	.0409	.0557	.0699	.0814	.0887	.0911	.0888
20	.0046	.0097	.0177	.0286	.0418	.0559	.0692	.0798	.0866	.0888
21	.0024	.0055	.0109	.0191	.0299	.0426	.0560	.0684	.0783	.0846
22	.0012	.0030	.0065	.0121	.0204	.0310	.0433	.0560	.0676	.0769
23	.0006	.0016	.0037	.0074	.0133	.0216	.0320	.0438	.0559	.0669
24	.0003	.0008	.0020	.0043	.0083	.0144	.0226	.0329	.0442	.0557
25	.0001	.0004	.0010	.0024	.0050	.0092	.0154	.0237	.0336	.0446
26	.0000	.0002	.0005	.0013	.0029	.0057	.0101	.0164	.0246	.0343
27	.0000	.0001	.0002	.0007	.0016	.0034	.0063	.0109	.0173	.0254
28	.0000	.0000	.0001	.0003	.0009	.0019	.0038	.0070	.0117	.0181
29	.0000	.0000	.0001	.0002	.0004	.0011	.0023	.0044	.0077	.0125
30	.0000	.0000	.0000	.0001	.0002	.0006	.0013	.0026	.0049	.0083
31	.0000	.0000	.0000	.0000	.0001	.0003	.0007	.0015	.0030	.0054
32	.0000	.0000	.0000	.0000	.0001	.0001	.0004	.0009	.0018	.0034
33	.0000	.0000	.0000	.0000	.0000	.0001	.0002	.0005	.0010	.0020
34	.0000	.0000	.0000	.0000	.0000	.0000	.0001	.0002	.0006	.0012
35	.0000	.0000	.0000	.0000	.0000	.0000	.0000	.0001	.0003	.0007
36	.0000	.0000	.0000	.0000	.0000	.0000	.0000	.0001	.0002	.0004
37	.0000	.0000	.0000	.0000	.0000	.0000	.0000	.0000	.0001	.0002
38	.0000	.0000	.0000	.0000	.0000	.0000	.0000	.0000	.0000	.0001
39	.0000	.0000	.0000	.0000	.0000	.0000	.0000	.0000	.0000	.0001

Table F

r	25.0	30.0	40.0	50.0	λ 75.0	100.0
0	.0000	.0000	0	0	0	0
1	.0000	.0000	0	0	0	0
2	.0000	.0000	0	0	0	0
3	.0000	.0000	0	0	0	0
4	.0000	.0000	0	0	0	0
5	.0000	.0000	0	0	0	0
6	.0000	.0000	.0000	0	0	0
7	.0000	.0000	.0000	0	0	0
8	.0001	.0000	.0000	0	0	0
9	.0001	.0000	.0000	0	0	0
10	.0004	.0000	.0000	0	0	0
11	.0008	.0000	.0000	.0000	0	0
12	.0017	.0001	.0000	.0000	0	0
13	.0033	.0002	.0000	.0000	0	0
14	.0059	.0005	.0000	.0000	0	0
15	.0099	.0010	.0000	.0000	0	0
16	.0155	.0019	.0000	.0000	0	0
17	.0227	.0034	.0000	.0000	0	0
18	.0316	.0057	.0000	.0000	0	0
19	.0415	.0089	.0001	.0000	0	0
20	.0519	.0134	.0002	.0000	0	0
21	.0618	.0192	.0004	.0000	0	0
22	.0702	.0261	.0007	.0000	0	0
23	.0763	.0341	.0012	.0000	0	0
24	.0795	.0426	.0019	.0000	0	0
25	.0795	.0511	.0031	.0000	0	0
26	.0765	.0590	.0047	.0001	.0000	0
27	.0708	.0655	.0070	.0001	.0000	0
28	.0632	.0702	.0100	.0002	.0000	0
29	.0545	.0726	.0138	.0004	.0000	0
30	.0454	.0726	.0185	.0007	.0000	0
31	.0366	.0703	.0238	.0011	.0000	0
32	.0286	.0659	.0298	.0017	.0000	0
33	.0217	.0599	.0361	.0026	.0000	0
34	.0159	.0529	.0425	.0038	.0000	0
35	.0114	.0453	.0485	.0054	.0000	0
36	.0079	.0378	.0539	.0075	.0000	0
37	.0053	.0306	.0583	.0102	.0000	0
38	.0035	.0242	.0614	.0134	.0000	0
39	.0023	.0186	.0629	.0172	.0000	0
40	.0014	.0139	.0629	.0215	.0000	0
41	.0009	.0102	.0614	.0262	.0000	0
42	.0005	.0073	.0585	.0312	.0000	.0000
43	.0003	.0051	.0544	.0363	.0000	.0000
44	.0002	.0035	.0495	.0412	.0000	.0000
45	.0001	.0023	.0440	.0458	.0001	.0000
46	.0001	.0015	.0382	.0498	.0001	.0000
47	.0000	.0010	.0325	.0530	.0001	.0000
48	.0000	.0006	.0271	.0552	.0002	.0000
49	.0000	.0004	.0221	.0563	.0003	.0000
50	.0000	.0002	.0177	.0563	.0005	.0000
51	.0000	.0001	.0139	.0552	.0007	.0000
52	.0000	.0001	.0107	.0531	.0011	.0000
53	.0000	.0000	.0081	.0501	.0015	.0000
54	.0000	.0000	.0060	.0464	.0021	.0000
55	.0000	.0000	.0043	.0422	.0028	.0000
56	.0000	.0000	.0031	.0376	.0038	.0000
57	.0000	.0000	.0022	.0330	.0050	.0000
58	.0000	.0000	.0015	.0285	.0065	.0000
59	.0000	.0000	.0010	.0241	.0082	.0000
60	.0000	.0000	.0007	.0201	.0103	.0000
61	.0000	.0000	.0004	.0165	.0126	.0000
62	.0000	.0000	.0003	.0133	.0153	.0000
63	.0000	.0000	.0002	.0105	.0182	.0000
64	.0000	.0000	.0001	.0082	.0213	.0000
65	0	.0000	.0001	.0063	.0246	.0000
66	0	.0000	.0000	.0048	.0279	.0001
67	0	.0000	.0000	.0036	.0313	.0001
68	0	.0000	.0000	.0026	.0345	.0002
69	0	.0000	.0000	.0019	.0375	.0002

r	25.0	30.0	40.0	50.0	λ 75.0	100.0
70	.000	.0000	.0000	.0014	.0402	.0003
71	0	.0000	.0000	.0010	.0424	.0004
72	0	.0000	.0000	.0007	.0442	.0006
73	0	0	.0000	.0005	.0454	.0008
74	0	0	.0000	.0003	.0460	.0011
75	0	0	.0000	.0002	.0460	.0015
76	0	0	.0000	.0001	.0454	.0020
77	0	0	.0000	.0001	.0442	.0026
78	0	0	.0000	.0001	.0425	.0033
79	0	0	.0000	.0000	.0404	.0042
80	0	0	.0000	.0000	.0379	.0052
81	0	0	.0000	.0000	.0350	.0064
82	0	0	.0000	.0000	.0321	.0078
83	0	0	.0000	.0000	.0290	.0094
84	0	0	.0000	.0000	.0259	.0112
85	0	0	.0000	.0000	.0228	.0132
86	0	0	.0000	.0000	.0199	.0154
87	0	0	.0000	.0000	.0172	.0176
88	0	0	.0000	.0000	.0146	.0201
89	0	0	0	.0000	.0123	.0225
90	0	0	0	.0000	.0103	.0250
91	0	0	0	.0000	.0085	.0275
92	0	0	0	.0000	.0069	.0299
93	0	0	0	.0000	.0056	.0322
94	0	0	0	.0000	.0044	.0342
95	0	0	0	.0000	.0035	.0360
96	0	0	0	.0000	.0027	.0375
97	0	0	0	.0000	.0021	.0387
98	0	0	0	.0000	.0016	.0395
99	0	0	0	.0000	.0012	.0399
100	0	0	0	.0000	.0009	.0399
101	0	0	0	.0000	.0007	.0395
102	0	0	0	.0000	.0005	.0387
103	0	0	0	.0000	.0004	.0376
104	0	0	0	0	.0003	.0361
105	0	0	0	0	.0002	.0344
106	0	0	0	0	.0001	.0325
107	0	0	0	0	.0001	.0303
108	0	0	0	0	.0001	.0281
109	0	0	0	0	.0000	.0258
110	0	0	0	0	.0000	.0234
111	0	0	0	0	.0000	.0211
112	0	0	0	0	.0000	.0188
113	0	0	0	0	.0000	.0167
114	0	0	0	0	.0000	.0146
115	0	0	0	0	.0000	.0127
116	0	0	0	0	.0000	.0110
117	0	0	0	0	.0000	.0094
118	0	0	0	0	.0000	.0079
119	0	0	0	0	.0000	.0067
120	0	0	0	0	.0000	.0056
121	0	0	0	0	.0000	.0046
122	0	0	0	0	.0000	.0038
123	0	0	0	0	.0000	.0031
124	0	0	0	0	.0000	.0025
125	0	0	0	0	.0000	.0020
126	0	0	0	0	.0000	.0016
127	0	0	0	0	.0000	.0012
128	0	0	0	0	.0000	.0010
129	0	0	0	0	.0000	.0007
130	0	0	0	0	.0000	.0006
131	0	0	0	0	.0000	.0004
132	0	0	0	0	.0000	.0003
133	0	0	0	0	.0000	.0003
134	0	0	0	0	.0000	.0002
135	0	0	0	0	.0000	.0001
136	0	0	0	0	.0000	.0001
137	0	0	0	0	.0000	.0001
138	0	0	0	0	.0000	.0001

Table F

CUMULATIVE POISSON PROBABILITY DISTRIBUTION

$$P(r \geq \tilde{r} \mid \lambda) = \sum_{r = \tilde{r}}^{\infty} \frac{\lambda^r}{r!} e^{-\lambda}$$

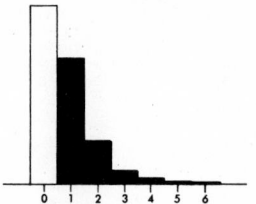

$$P(r \geq 1 \mid \lambda = 0.70) = 0.5034$$

r	0.1	0.2	0.3	0.4	λ 0.5	0.6	0.7	0.8	0.9	1.0
1	.0952	.1813	.2592	.3297	.3935	.4512	.5034	.5507	.5934	.6321
2	.0047	.0175	.0369	.0616	.0902	.1219	.1558	.1912	.2275	.2642
3	.0002	.0011	.0036	.0079	.0144	.0231	.0341	.0474	.0629	.0803
4	.0000	.0001	.0003	.0008	.0018	.0034	.0058	.0091	.0135	.0190
5	.0000	.0000	.0000	.0001	.0002	.0004	.0008	.0014	.0023	.0037
6	.0000	.0000	.0000	.0000	.0000	.0000	.0001	.0002	.0003	.0006
7	.0000	.0000	.0000	.0000	.0000	.0000	.0000	.0000	.0000	.0001

r	1.1	1.2	1.3	1.4	λ 1.5	1.6	1.7	1.8	1.9	2.0
1	.6671	.6988	.7275	.7534	.7769	.7981	.8173	.8347	.8504	.8647
2	.3010	.3374	.3732	.4082	.4422	.4751	.5068	.5372	.5663	.5940
3	.0996	.1205	.1429	.1665	.1912	.2166	.2428	.2694	.2963	.3233
4	.0257	.0338	.0431	.0537	.0656	.0788	.0932	.1087	.1253	.1429
5	.0054	.0077	.0107	.0143	.0186	.0237	.0296	.0364	.0441	.0527
6	.0010	.0015	.0022	.0032	.0045	.0060	.0080	.0104	.0132	.0166
7	.0001	.0003	.0004	.0006	.0009	.0013	.0019	.0026	.0034	.0045
8	.0000	.0000	.0001	.0001	.0002	.0003	.0004	.0006	.0008	.0011
9	.0000	.0000	.0000	.0000	.0000	.0000	.0001	.0001	.0002	.0002

r	2.1	2.2	2.3	2.4	λ 2.5	2.6	2.7	2.8	2.9	3.0
1	.8775	.8892	.8997	.9093	.9179	.9257	.9328	.9392	.9450	.9502
2	.6204	.6454	.6691	.6916	.7127	.7326	.7513	.7689	.7854	.8009
3	.3504	.3773	.4040	.4303	.4562	.4816	.5064	.5305	.5540	.5768
4	.1614	.1806	.2007	.2213	.2424	.2640	.2859	.3081	.3304	.3528
5	.0621	.0725	.0838	.0959	.1088	.1226	.1371	.1523	.1682	.1847
6	.0204	.0249	.0300	.0357	.0420	.0490	.0567	.0651	.0742	.0839
7	.0059	.0075	.0094	.0116	.0142	.0172	.0206	.0244	.0287	.0335
8	.0015	.0020	.0026	.0033	.0042	.0053	.0066	.0081	.0099	.0119
9	.0003	.0005	.0006	.0009	.0011	.0015	.0019	.0024	.0031	.0038
10	.0001	.0001	.0001	.0002	.0003	.0004	.0005	.0007	.0009	.0011
11	.0000	.0000	.0000	.0000	.0001	.0001	.0001	.0002	.0002	.0003
12	.0000	.0000	.0000	.0000	.0000	.0000	.0000	.0000	.0001	.0001

r	3.1	3.2	3.3	3.4	λ 3.5	3.6	3.7	3.8	3.9	4.0
1	.9550	.9592	.9631	.9666	.9698	.9727	.9753	.9776	.9798	.9817
2	.8153	.8288	.8414	.8532	.8641	.8743	.8838	.8926	.9008	.9084
3	.5988	.6201	.6406	.6603	.6792	.6973	.7146	.7311	.7469	.7619
4	.3752	.3975	.4197	.4416	.4634	.4848	.5058	.5265	.5468	.5665
5	.2018	.2194	.2374	.2558	.2746	.2936	.3128	.3322	.3516	.3712
6	.0943	.1054	.1171	.1295	.1424	.1559	.1699	.1844	.1994	.2149
7	.0388	.0446	.0510	.0579	.0653	.0733	.0818	.0909	.1005	.1107
8	.0142	.0168	.0198	.0231	.0267	.0308	.0352	.0401	.0454	.0511
9	.0047	.0057	.0069	.0083	.0099	.0117	.0137	.0160	.0185	.0214
10	.0014	.0018	.0022	.0027	.0033	.0040	.0048	.0058	.0069	.0081

Table G

r	3.1	3.2	3.3	3.4	λ 3.5	3.6	3.7	3.8	3.9	4.0
11	.0004	.0005	.0006	.0008	.0010	.0013	.0016	.0019	.0023	.0028
12	.0001	.0001	.0002	.0002	.0003	.0004	.0005	.0006	.0007	.0009
13	.0000	.0000	.0000	.0001	.0001	.0001	.0001	.0002	.0002	.0003
14	.0000	.0000	.0000	.0000	.0000	.0000	.0000	.0000	.0001	.0001

r	4.1	4.2	4.3	4.4	λ 4.5	4.6	4.7	4.8	4.9	5.0
1	.9834	.9850	.9864	.9877	.9889	.9899	.9909	.9918	.9926	.9933
2	.9155	.9220	.9281	.9337	.9389	.9437	.9482	.9523	.9561	.9596
3	.7762	.7898	.8026	.8149	.8264	.8374	.8477	.8575	.8667	.8753
4	.5858	.6046	.6228	.6406	.6577	.6743	.6903	.7058	.7207	.7350
5	.3907	.4102	.4296	.4488	.4679	.4868	.5054	.5237	.5418	.5595
6	.2307	.2469	.2633	.2801	.2971	.3142	.3316	.3490	.3665	.3840
7	.1214	.1325	.1442	.1564	.1689	.1820	.1954	.2092	.2233	.2378
8	.0573	.0639	.0710	.0786	.0866	.0951	.1040	.1133	.1231	.1334
9	.0245	.0279	.0317	.0358	.0403	.0451	.0503	.0558	.0618	.0681
10	.0095	.0111	.0129	.0149	.0171	.0195	.0222	.0251	.0283	.0318
11	.0034	.0041	.0048	.0057	.0067	.0078	.0090	.0104	.0120	.0137
12	.0011	.0014	.0017	.0020	.0024	.0029	.0034	.0040	.0047	.0055
13	.0003	.0004	.0005	.0007	.0008	.0010	.0012	.0014	.0017	.0020
14	.0001	.0001	.0002	.0002	.0003	.0003	.0004	.0005	.0006	.0007
15	.0000	.0000	.0000	.0001	.0001	.0001	.0001	.0001	.0002	.0002
16	.0000	.0000	.0000	.0000	.0000	.0000	.0000	.0000	.0001	.0001

r	5.1	5.2	5.3	5.4	λ 5.5	5.6	5.7	5.8	5.9	6.0
1	.9939	.9945	.9950	.9955	.9959	.9963	.9967	.9970	.9973	.9975
2	.9628	.9658	.9686	.9711	.9734	.9756	.9776	.9794	.9811	.9826
3	.8835	.8912	.8984	.9052	.9116	.9176	.9232	.9285	.9334	.9380
4	.7487	.7619	.7746	.7867	.7983	.8094	.8200	.8300	.8396	.8488
5	.5769	.5939	.6105	.6267	.6425	.6578	.6728	.6873	.7013	.7149
6	.4016	.4191	.4365	.4539	.4711	.4881	.5050	.5217	.5381	.5543
7	.2526	.2676	.2829	.2983	.3140	.3297	.3456	.3616	.3776	.3937
8	.1440	.1551	.1665	.1783	.1905	.2030	.2159	.2290	.2424	.2560
9	.0748	.0819	.0894	.0973	.1056	.1143	.1234	.1328	.1426	.1528
10	.0356	.0397	.0441	.0488	.0538	.0591	.0648	.0708	.0772	.0839
11	.0156	.0177	.0200	.0225	.0253	.0282	.0314	.0349	.0386	.0426
12	.0063	.0073	.0084	.0096	.0110	.0125	.0141	.0159	.0179	.0201
13	.0024	.0028	.0033	.0038	.0044	.0051	.0059	.0068	.0078	.0088
14	.0008	.0010	.0012	.0014	.0017	.0020	.0023	.0027	.0031	.0036
15	.0003	.0003	.0004	.0005	.0006	.0007	.0009	.0010	.0012	.0014
16	.0001	.0001	.0001	.0002	.0002	.0002	.0003	.0004	.0004	.0005
17	.0000	.0000	.0000	.0000	.0001	.0001	.0001	.0001	.0001	.0002
18	.0000	.0000	.0000	.0000	.0000	.0000	.0000	.0000	.0000	.0001

r	6.1	6.2	6.3	6.4	λ 6.5	6.6	6.7	6.8	6.9	7.0
1	.9978	.9980	.9982	.9983	.9985	.9986	.9988	.9989	.9990	.9991
2	.9841	.9854	.9866	.9877	.9887	.9897	.9905	.9913	.9920	.9927
3	.9423	.9464	.9502	.9537	.9570	.9600	.9629	.9656	.9680	.9704
4	.8575	.8658	.8736	.8811	.8882	.8948	.9012	.9072	.9129	.9182
5	.7281	.7408	.7531	.7649	.7763	.7873	.7978	.8080	.8177	.8270
6	.5702	.5859	.6012	.6163	.6310	.6453	.6594	.6730	.6863	.6993
7	.4098	.4258	.4418	.4577	.4735	.4892	.5047	.5201	.5353	.5503
8	.2699	.2840	.2983	.3127	.3272	.3419	.3567	.3715	.3864	.4013
9	.1633	.1741	.1852	.1967	.2084	.2204	.2327	.2452	.2580	.2709
10	.0910	.0984	.1061	.1142	.1226	.1314	.1404	.1498	.1595	.1695
11	.0469	.0514	.0563	.0614	.0668	.0726	.0786	.0849	.0916	.0985
12	.0224	.0250	.0277	.0307	.0339	.0373	.0409	.0448	.0490	.0533
13	.0100	.0113	.0127	.0143	.0160	.0179	.0199	.0221	.0245	.0270
14	.0042	.0048	.0055	.0062	.0071	.0080	.0091	.0102	.0115	.0128
15	.0016	.0019	.0022	.0026	.0030	.0034	.0039	.0044	.0050	.0057
16	.0006	.0007	.0008	.0010	.0012	.0014	.0016	.0018	.0021	.0024
17	.0002	.0003	.0003	.0004	.0004	.0005	.0006	.0007	.0008	.0010
18	.0001	.0001	.0001	.0001	.0002	.0002	.0002	.0003	.0003	.0004
19	.0000	.0000	.0000	.0000	.0000	.0001	.0001	.0001	.0001	.0001

Table G

r	7.1	7.2	7.3	7.4	λ 7.5	7.6	7.7	7.8	7.9	8.0
1	.9992	.9993	.9993	.9994	.9994	.9995	.9995	.9996	.9996	.9997
2	.9933	.9939	.9944	.9949	.9953	.9957	.9961	.9964	.9967	.9970
3	.9725	.9745	.9764	.9781	.9797	.9812	.9826	.9835	.9851	.9862
4	.9233	.9281	.9326	.9368	.9409	.9446	.9482	.9515	.9547	.9576
5	.8359	.8445	.8527	.8605	.8679	.8751	.8819	.8883	.8945	.9004
6	.7119	.7241	.7360	.7474	.7586	.7693	.7797	.7897	.7994	.8088
7	.5651	.5796	.5940	.6080	.6218	.6354	.6486	.6616	.6743	.6866
8	.4162	.4311	.4459	.4607	.4754	.4900	.5044	.5188	.5330	.5470
9	.2840	.2973	.3108	.3243	.3380	.3518	.3657	.3796	.3935	.4075
10	.1798	.1903	.2012	.2123	.2236	.2351	.2469	.2589	.2710	.2834
11	.1058	.1133	.1212	.1293	.1378	.1465	.1555	.1648	.1743	.1841
12	.0580	.0629	.0681	.0735	.0792	.0852	.0915	.0980	.1048	.1119
13	.0297	.0327	.0358	.0391	.0427	.0464	.0504	.0546	.0591	.0638
14	.0143	.0159	.0176	.0195	.0216	.0238	.0261	.0286	.0313	.0342
15	.0065	.0073	.0082	.0092	.0103	.0114	.0127	.0141	.0156	.0173
16	.0028	.0031	.0036	.0041	.0046	.0052	.0059	.0066	.0074	.0082
17	.0011	.0013	.0015	.0017	.0020	.0022	.0026	.0029	.0033	.0037
18	.0004	.0005	.0006	.0007	.0008	.0009	.0011	.0012	.0014	.0016
19	.0002	.0002	.0002	.0003	.0003	.0004	.0004	.0005	.0006	.0006
20	.0001	.0001	.0001	.0001	.0001	.0001	.0002	.0002	.0002	.0003
21	.0000	.0000	.0000	.0000	.0000	.0000	.0001	.0001	.0001	.0001

r	8.1	8.2	8.3	8.4	λ 8.5	8.6	8.7	8.8	8.9	9.0
1	.9997	.9997	.9998	.9998	.9998	.9998	.9998	.9998	.9999	.9999
2	.9972	.9975	.9977	.9979	.9981	.9982	.9984	.9985	.9986	.9988
3	.9873	.9882	.9891	.9900	.9907	.9914	.9921	.9927	.9932	.9938
4	.9604	.9630	.9654	.9677	.9699	.9719	.9738	.9756	.9772	.9788
5	.9060	.9113	.9163	.9211	.9256	.9299	.9340	.9379	.9416	.9450
6	.8178	.8264	.8347	.8427	.8504	.8578	.8648	.8716	.8781	.8843
7	.6987	.7104	.7219	.7330	.7438	.7543	.7645	.7744	.7840	.7932
8	.5609	.5746	.5881	.6013	.6144	.6272	.6398	.6522	.6643	.6761
9	.4214	.4353	.4493	.4631	.4769	.4906	.5042	.5177	.5311	.5443
10	.2959	.3085	.3212	.3341	.3470	.3600	.3731	.3863	.3994	.4126
11	.1942	.2044	.2150	.2257	.2366	.2478	.2591	.2706	.2822	.2940
12	.1193	.1269	.1348	.1429	.1513	.1600	.1689	.1780	.1874	.1970
13	.0687	.0739	.0793	.0850	.0909	.0971	.1035	.1102	.1171	.1242
14	.0372	.0405	.0439	.0476	.0514	.0555	.0597	.0642	.0689	.0738
15	.0190	.0209	.0229	.0251	.0274	.0299	.0325	.0353	.0383	.0415
16	.0092	.0102	.0113	.0125	.0138	.0152	.0168	.0184	.0202	.0220
17	.0042	.0047	.0053	.0059	.0066	.0074	.0082	.0091	.0101	.0111
18	.0018	.0021	.0023	.0027	.0030	.0034	.0038	.0043	.0048	.0053
19	.0007	.0009	.0010	.0011	.0013	.0015	.0017	.0019	.0021	.0024
20	.0003	.0003	.0004	.0005	.0005	.0006	.0007	.0008	.0009	.0011
21	.0001	.0001	.0002	.0002	.0002	.0002	.0003	.0003	.0004	.0004
22	.0000	.0000	.0001	.0001	.0001	.0001	.0001	.0001	.0001	.0002
23	.0000	.0000	.0000	.0000	.0000	.0000	.0000	.0000	.0001	.0001

r	9.1	9.2	9.3	9.4	λ 9.5	9.6	9.7	9.8	9.9	10.0
1	.9999	.9999	.9999	.9999	.9999	.9999	.9999	.9999	.9999	1.0000
2	.9989	.9990	.9991	.9991	.9992	.9993	.9993	.9994	.9995	.9995
3	.9942	.9947	.9951	.9955	.9958	.9962	.9965	.9967	.9970	.9972
4	.9802	.9816	.9828	.9840	.9851	.9862	.9871	.9880	.9889	.9897
5	.9483	.9514	.9544	.9571	.9597	.9622	.9645	.9667	.9688	.9707
6	.8902	.8959	.9014	.9065	.9115	.9162	.9207	.9250	.9290	.9329
7	.8022	.8108	.8192	.8273	.8351	.8426	.8498	.8567	.8634	.8699
8	.6877	.6990	.7100	.7208	.7313	.7416	.7515	.7612	.7706	.7798
9	.5574	.5704	.5832	.5958	.6082	.6204	.6324	.6442	.6558	.6672
10	.4258	.4389	.4521	.4651	.4782	.4911	.5040	.5168	.5295	.5421
11	.3059	.3180	.3301	.3424	.3547	.3671	.3795	.3920	.4045	.4170
12	.2068	.2168	.2270	.2374	.2480	.2588	.2697	.2807	.2919	.3032
13	.1316	.1393	.1471	.1552	.1636	.1721	.1809	.1899	.1991	.2084
14	.0790	.0844	.0900	.0958	.1019	.1081	.1147	.1214	.1284	.1355
15	.0448	.0483	.0520	.0559	.0600	.0643	.0688	.0735	.0784	.0835

Table G

r	9.1	9.2	9.3	9.4	λ 9.5	9.6	9.7	9.8	9.9	10.0
16	.0240	.0262	.0285	.0309	.0335	.0362	.0391	.0421	.0454	.0487
17	.0122	.0135	.0148	.0162	.0177	.0194	.0211	.0230	.0249	.0270
18	.0059	.0066	.0073	.0081	.0089	.0098	.0108	.0119	.0130	.0143
19	.0027	.0031	.0034	.0038	.0043	.0048	.0053	.0059	.0065	.0072
20	.0012	.0014	.0015	.0017	.0020	.0022	.0025	.0028	.0031	.0035
21	.0005	.0006	.0007	.0008	.0009	.0010	.0011	.0012	.0014	.0016
22	.0002	.0002	.0003	.0003	.0004	.0004	.0005	.0005	.0006	.0007
23	.0001	.0001	.0001	.0001	.0001	.0002	.0002	.0002	.0003	.0003
24	.0000	.0000	.0000	.0000	.0001	.0001	.0001	.0001	.0001	.0001

r	11.0	12.0	13.0	14.0	λ 15.0	16.0	17.0	18.0	19.0	20.0
1	1.0000	1.0000	1.0000	1.0000	1.0000	1.0000	1.0000	1.0000	1.0000	1.0000
2	.9998	.9999	1.0000	1.0000	1.0000	1.0000	1.0000	1.0000	1.0000	1.0000
3	.9988	.9995	.9998	.9999	1.0000	1.0000	1.0000	1.0000	1.0000	1.0000
4	.9951	.9977	.9989	.9995	.9998	.9999	1.0000	1.0000	1.0000	1.0000
5	.9849	.9924	.9963	.9982	.9991	.9996	.9998	.9999	1.0000	1.0000
6	.9625	.9797	.9893	.9945	.9972	.9986	.9993	.9997	.9998	.9999
7	.9214	.9542	.9741	.9858	.9924	.9960	.9979	.9990	.9995	.9997
8	.8568	.9105	.9460	.9684	.9820	.9900	.9946	.9971	.9985	.9992
9	.7680	.8450	.9002	.9379	.9626	.9780	.9874	.9929	.9961	.9979
10	.6595	.7576	.8342	.8906	.9301	.9567	.9739	.9846	.9911	.9950
11	.5401	.6528	.7483	.8243	.8815	.9226	.9509	.9696	.9817	.9892
12	.4207	.5384	.6468	.7400	.8152	.8730	.9153	.9451	.9653	.9786
13	.3113	.4240	.5369	.6415	.7324	.8069	.8650	.9083	.9394	.9610
14	.2187	.3185	.4270	.5356	.6368	.7255	.7991	.8574	.9016	.9339
15	.1460	.2280	.3249	.4296	.5343	.6325	.7192	.7919	.8502	.8951
16	.0926	.1556	.2364	.3306	.4319	.5333	.6285	.7133	.7852	.8435
17	.0559	.1013	.1645	.2441	.3359	.4340	.5323	.6249	.7080	.7789
18	.0322	.0630	.1095	.1728	.2511	.3407	.4360	.5314	.6216	.7030
19	.0177	.0374	.0698	.1174	.1805	.2576	.3450	.4378	.5305	.6186
20	.0093	.0213	.0427	.0765	.1248	.1877	.2637	.3491	.4394	.5297
21	.0047	.0116	.0250	.0479	.0830	.1318	.1945	.2693	.3528	.4409
22	.0022	.0061	.0141	.0288	.0531	.0892	.1385	.2009	.2745	.3563
23	.0010	.0030	.0076	.0167	.0327	.0582	.0953	.1449	.2069	.2794
24	.0005	.0015	.0040	.0093	.0195	.0367	.0633	.1011	.1510	.2125
25	.0002	.0007	.0020	.0050	.0112	.0223	.0406	.0683	.1067	.1568
26	.0001	.0003	.0010	.0026	.0062	.0131	.0252	.0446	.0731	.1122
27	.0000	.0001	.0004	.0013	.0033	.0075	.0152	.0282	.0486	.0779
28	.0000	.0001	.0002	.0006	.0017	.0041	.0088	.0173	.0313	.0525
29	.0000	.0000	.0001	.0003	.0009	.0022	.0050	.0103	.0195	.0343
30	.0000	.0000	.0000	.0001	.0004	.0011	.0027	.0059	.0118	.0218
31	.0000	.0000	.0000	.0001	.0002	.0006	.0014	.0033	.0070	.0135
32	.0000	.0000	.0000	.0000	.0001	.0003	.0007	.0018	.0040	.0081
33	.0000	.0000	.0000	.0000	.0000	.0001	.0004	.0010	.0022	.0047
34	.0000	.0000	.0000	.0000	.0000	.0001	.0002	.0005	.0012	.0027
35	.0000	.0000	.0000	.0000	.0000	.0000	.0001	.0002	.0006	.0015
36	.0000	.0000	.0000	.0000	.0000	.0000	.0000	.0001	.0003	.0008
37	.0000	.0000	.0000	.0000	.0000	.0000	.0000	.0001	.0002	.0004
38	.0000	.0000	.0000	.0000	.0000	.0000	.0000	.0000	.0001	.0002
39	.0000	.0000	.0000	.0000	.0000	.0000	.0000	.0000	.0000	.0001

Table G

r	25.0	30.0	40.0	50.0	λ 75.0	100.0
1	1.0000	1.0000	1.0000	1.0000	1.0000	1.0000
2	1.0000	1.0000	1.0000	1.0000	1.0000	1.0000
3	1.0000	1.0000	1.0000	1.0000	1.0000	1.0000
4	1.0000	1.0000	1.0000	1.0000	1.0000	1.0000
5	1.0000	1.0000	1.0000	1.0000	1.0000	1.0000
6	1.0000	1.0000	1.0000	1.0000	1.0000	1.0000
7	1.0000	1.0000	1.0000	1.0000	1.0000	1.0000
8	1.0000	1.0000	1.0000	1.0000	1.0000	1.0000
9	.9999	1.0000	1.0000	1.0000	1.0000	1.0000
10	.9998	1.0000	1.0000	1.0000	1.0000	1.0000
11	.9994	1.0000	1.0000	1.0000	1.0000	1.0000
12	.9986	.9999	1.0000	1.0000	1.0000	1.0000
13	.9969	.9998	1.0000	1.0000	1.0000	1.0000
14	.9935	.9996	1.0000	1.0000	1.0000	1.0000
15	.9876	.9991	1.0000	1.0000	1.0000	1.0000
16	.9777	.9981	1.0000	1.0000	1.0000	1.0000
17	.9623	.9961	1.0000	1.0000	1.0000	1.0000
18	.9395	.9927	1.0000	1.0000	1.0000	1.0000
19	.9080	.9871	.9999	1.0000	1.0000	1.0000
20	.8664	.9781	.9998	1.0000	1.0000	1.0000
21	.8145	.9647	.9996	1.0000	1.0000	1.0000
22	.7527	.9456	.9993	1.0000	1.0000	1.0000
23	.6825	.9194	.9986	1.0000	1.0000	1.0000
24	.6061	.8854	.9974	1.0000	1.0000	1.0000
25	.5266	.8428	.9955	1.0000	1.0000	1.0000
26	.4471	.7916	.9924	.9999	1.0000	1.0000
27	.3706	.7327	.9877	.9999	1.0000	1.0000
28	.2998	.6671	.9807	.9997	1.0000	1.0000
29	.2366	.5969	.9706	.9995	1.0000	1.0000
30	.1821	.5243	.9568	.9991	1.0000	1.0000
31	.1367	.4516	.9383	.9984	1.0000	1.0000
32	.1001	.3814	.9145	.9973	1.0000	1.0000
33	.0715	.3155	.8847	.9956	1.0000	1.0000
34	.0498	.2555	.8486	.9930	1.0000	1.0000
35	.0338	.2027	.8061	.9892	1.0000	1.0000
36	.0225	.1574	.7576	.9838	1.0000	1.0000
37	.0145	.1196	.7037	.9762	1.0000	1.0000
38	.0092	.0890	.6453	.9660	1.0000	1.0000
39	.0057	.0648	.5840	.9526	1.0000	1.0000
40	.0034	.0462	.5210	.9354	1.0000	1.0000
41	.0020	.0323	.4581	.9139	1.0000	1.0000
42	.0012	.0221	.3967	.8877	1.0000	1.0000
43	.0007	.0148	.3382	.8565	1.0000	1.0000
44	.0004	.0097	.2838	.8202	1.0000	1.0000
45	.0002	.0063	.2343	.7790	.9999	1.0000
46	.0001	.0040	.1903	.7331	.9999	1.0000
47	.0001	.0024	.1521	.6833	.9998	1.0000
48	.0000	.0015	.1196	.6303	.9996	1.0000
49	.0000	.0009	.0925	.5751	.9994	1.0000
50	.0000	.0005	.0703	.5188	.9991	1.0000
51	.0000	.0003	.0526	.4625	.9986	1.0000
52	.0000	.0002	.0387	.4073	.9979	1.0000
53	.0000	.0001	.0280	.3542	.9968	1.0000
54	.0000	.0000	.0200	.3041	.9953	1.0000
55	.0000	.0000	.0140	.2577	.9932	1.0000
56	.0000	.0000	.0097	.2155	.9904	1.0000
57	.0000	.0000	.0066	.1779	.9866	1.0000
58	.0000	.0000	.0044	.1449	.9816	1.0000
59	.0000	.0000	.0029	.1164	.9751	1.0000
60	.0000	.0000	.0019	.0923	.9669	1.0000
61	.0000	.0000	.0012	.0722	.9567	1.0000
62	.0000	.0000	.0007	.0557	.9440	1.0000
63	.0000	.0000	.0005	.0424	.9288	1.0000
64	.0000	.0000	.0003	.0318	.9106	1.0000
65	.0000	.0000	.0002	.0236	.8893	.9999
66	.0000	.0000	.0001	.0173	.8647	.9999
67	.0000	.0000	.0001	.0125	.8368	.9998
68	.0000	.0000	.0000	.0089	.8055	.9997
69	.0000	.0000	.0000	.0062	.7710	.9996
70	.0000	.0000	.0000	.0043	.7335	.9993

Table G

r	36.0	30.0	40.0	50.0	λ 75.0	100.0
71	.0000	.0000	.0000	.0030	.6934	.9990
72	.0000	.0000	.0000	.0020	.6510	.9986
73	.0000	.0000	.0000	.0013	.6068	.9980
74	.0000	.0000	.0000	.0009	.5614	.9972
75	.0000	.0000	.0000	.0006	.5153	.9960
76	.0000	.0000	.0000	.0004	.4693	.9945
77	.0000	.0000	.0000	.0002	.4239	.9926
78	.0000	.0000	.0000	.0001	.3797	.9900
79	.0000	.0000	.0000	.0001	.3372	.9867
80	.0000	.0000	.0000	.0000	.2968	.9825
81	.0000	.0000	.0000	.0000	.2589	.9774
82	.0000	.0000	.0000	.0000	.2239	.9709
83	.0000	.0000	.0000	.0000	.1918	.9631
84	.0000	.0000	.0000	.0000	.1629	.9537
85	.0000	.0000	.0000	.0000	.1370	.9425
86	.0000	.0000	.0000	.0000	.1142	.9292
87	.0000	.0000	.0000	.0000	.0943	.9139
88	.0000	.0000	.0000	.0000	.0771	.8962
89	.0000	.0000	.0000	.0000	.0625	.8762
90	.0000	.0000	.0000	.0000	.0502	.8537
91	.0000	.0000	.0000	.0000	.0399	.8286
92	.0000	.0000	.0000	.0000	.0314	.8011
93	.0000	.0000	.0000	.0000	.0245	.7712
94	.0000	.0000	.0000	.0000	.0190	.7390
95	.0000	.0000	.0000	.0000	.0145	.7048
96	.0000	.0000	.0000	.0000	.0110	.6688
97	.0000	.0000	.0000	.0000	.0083	.6313
98	.0000	.0000	.0000	.0000	.0062	.5926
99	.0000	.0000	.0000	.0000	.0046	.5532
100	.0000	.0000	.0000	.0000	.0033	.5133
101	.0000	.0000	.0000	.0000	.0024	.4734
102	.0000	.0000	.0000	.0000	.0017	.4340
103	.0000	.0000	.0000	.0000	.0012	.3953
104	.0000	.0000	.0000	.0000	.0009	.3577
105	.0000	.0000	.0000	.0000	.0006	.3216
106	.0000	.0000	.0000	.0000	.0004	.2872
107	.0000	.0000	.0000	.0000	.0003	.2547
108	.0000	.0000	.0000	.0000	.0002	.2244
109	.0000	.0000	.0000	.0000	.0001	.1963
110	.0000	.0000	.0000	.0000	.0001	.1705
111	.0000	.0000	.0000	.0000	.0000	.1471
112	.0000	.0000	.0000	.0000	.0000	.1260
113	.0000	.0000	.0000	.0000	.0000	.1072
114	.0000	.0000	.0000	.0000	.0000	.0905
115	.0000	.0000	.0000	.0000	.0000	.0759
116	.0000	.0000	.0000	.0000	.0000	.0632
117	.0000	.0000	.0000	.0000	.0000	.0522
118	.0000	.0000	.0000	.0000	.0000	.0428
119	.0000	.0000	.0000	.0000	.0000	.0349
120	.0000	.0000	.0000	.0000	.0000	.0282
121	.0000	.0000	.0000	.0000	.0000	.0227
122	.0000	.0000	.0000	.0000	.0000	.0181
123	.0000	.0000	.0000	.0000	.0000	.0143
124	.0000	.0000	.0000	.0000	.0000	.0112
125	.0000	.0000	.0000	.0000	.0000	.0088
126	.0000	.0000	.0000	.0000	.0000	.0068
127	.0000	.0000	.0000	.0000	.0000	.0052
128	.0000	.0000	.0000	.0000	.0000	.0040
129	.0000	.0000	.0000	.0000	.0000	.0030
130	.0000	.0000	.0000	.0000	.0000	.0023
131	.0000	.0000	.0000	.0000	.0000	.0017
132	.0000	.0000	.0000	.0000	.0000	.0012
133	.0000	.0000	.0000	.0000	.0000	.0009
134	.0000	.0000	.0000	.0000	.0000	.0007
135	.0000	.0000	.0000	.0000	.0000	.0005
136	.0000	.0000	.0000	.0000	.0000	.0003
137	.0000	.0000	.0000	.0000	.0000	.0002
138	.0000	.0000	.0000	.0000	.0000	.0002
139	.0000	.0000	.0000	.0000	.0000	.0001
140	.0000	.0000	.0000	.0000	.0000	.0001

Table G

AREAS AND ORDINATES OF THE NORMAL CURVE

Table of Areas
Column (2) Shows

Table of Ordinates
Column (3) Shows

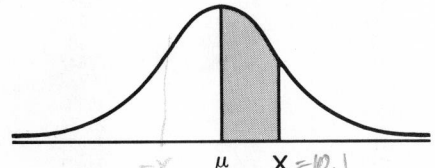

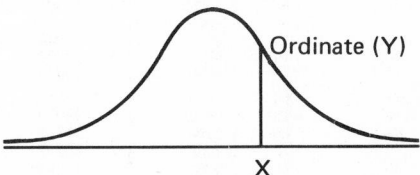

Ordinate (Y)

$-X$ μ $X = 10.1$

X

$\dfrac{X - \mu}{\sigma}$	Area under the curve between μ and X	Ordinate (Y) of the curve at X	$\dfrac{X - \mu}{\sigma}$	Area under the curve between μ and X	Ordinate (Y) of the curve at X
(1)	(2)	(3)	(1)	(2)	(3)
.00	.00000	.39894	.20	.07926	.39104
.01	.00399	.39892	.21	.08317	.39024
.02	.00798	.39886	.22	.08706	.38940
.03	.01197	.39876	.23	.09095	.38853
.04	.01595	.39862	.24	.09483	.38762
.05	.01994	.39844	.25	.09871	.38667
.06	.02392	.39822	.26	.10257	.38568
.07	.02790	.39797	.27	.10642	.38466
.08	.03188	.39767	.28	.11026	.38361
.09	.03586	.39733	.29	.11409	.38251
.10	.03983	.39695	.30	.11791	.38139
.11	.04380	.39654	.31	.12172	.38023
.12	.04776	.39608	.32	.12552	.37903
.13	.05172	.39559	.33	.12930	.37780
.14	.05567	.39505	.34	.13307	.37654
.15	.05962	.39448	.35	.13683	.37524
.16	.06356	.39387	.36	.14058	.37391
.17	.06749	.39322	.37	.14431	.37255
.18	.07142	.39253	.38	.14803	.37115
.19	.07535	.39181	.39	.15173	.36973

By permission from J. F. Kenney and E. S. Keeping, *Mathematics of Statistics*, (*Part I*), Copyright 1954, D. Van Nostrand Company, Inc., Princeton, N. J.

$\dfrac{X-\mu}{\sigma}$	Area under the curve between μ and X	Ordinate (Y) of the curve at X	$\dfrac{X-\mu}{\sigma}$	Area under the curve between μ and X	Ordinate (Y) of the curve at X
(1)	(2)	(3)	(1)	(2)	(3)
.40	.15542	.36827	.90	.31594	.26609
.41	.15910	.36678	.91	.31859	.26369
.42	.16276	.36526	.92	.32121	.26129
.43	.16640	.36371	.93	.32381	.25888
.44	.17003	.36213	.94	.32639	.25647
.45	.17364	.36053	.95	.32894	.25406
.46	.17724	.35889	.96	.33147	.25164
.47	.18082	.35723	.97	.33398	.24923
.48	.18439	.35553	.98	.33646	.24681
.49	.18793	.35381	.99	.33891	.24439
.50	.19146	.35207	1.00	.34134	.24197
.51	.19497	.35029	1.01	.34375	.23955
.52	.19847	.34849	1.02	.34614	.23713
.53	.20194	.34667	1.03	.34850	.23471
.54	.20540	.34482	1.04	.35083	.23230
.55	.20884	.34294	1.05	.35314	.22988
.56	.21226	.34105	1.06	.35543	.22747
.57	.21566	.33912	1.07	.35769	.22506
.58	.21904	.33718	1.08	.35993	.22265
.59	.22240	.33521	1.09	.36214	.22025
.60	.22575	.33322	1.10	.36433	.21785
.61	.22907	.33121	1.11	.36650	.21546
.62	.23237	.32918	1.12	.36864	.21307
.63	.23565	.32713	1.13	.37076	.21069
.64	.23891	.32506	1.14	.37286	.20831
.65	.24215	.32297	1.15	.37493	.20594
.66	.24537	.32086	1.16	.37698	.20357
.67	.24857	.31874	1.17	.37900	.20121
.68	.25175	.31659	1.18	.38100	.19886
.69	.25490	.31443	1.19	.38298	.19652
.70	.25804	.31225	1.20	.38493	.19419
.71	.26115	.31006	1.21	.38686	.19186
.72	.26424	.30785	1.22	.38877	.18954
.73	.26730	.30563	1.23	.39065	.18724
.74	.27035	.30339	1.24	.39251	.18494
.75	.27337	.30114	1.25	.39435	.18265
.76	.27637	.29887	1.26	.39617	.18037
.77	.27935	.29659	1.27	.39796	.17810
.78	.28230	.29431	1.28	.39973	.17585
.79	.28524	.29200	1.29	.40147	.17360
.80	.28814	.28969	1.30	.40320	.17137
.81	.29103	.28737	1.31	.40490	.16915
.82	.29389	.28504	1.32	.40658	.16694
.83	.29673	.28269	1.33	.40824	.16474
.84	.29955	.28034	1.34	.40988	.16256
.85	.30234	.27798	1.35	.41149	.16038
.86	.30511	.27562	1.36	.41309	.15822
.87	.30785	.27324	1.37	.41466	.15608
.88	.31057	.27086	1.38	.41621	.15395
.89	.31327	.26848	1.39	.41774	.15183

Table H

AREAS AND ORDINATES OF THE NORMAL CURVE

$\frac{X - \mu}{\sigma}$	Area under the curve between μ and X	Ordinate (Y) of the curve at X	$\frac{X - \mu}{\sigma}$	Area under the curve between μ and X	Ordinate (Y) of the curve at X
(1)	(2)	(3)	(1)	(2)	(3)
1.40	.41924	.14973	1.90	.47128	.06562
1.41	.42073	.14764	1.91	.47193	.06438
1.42	.42220	.14556	1.92	.47257	.06316
1.43	.42364	.14350	1.93	.47320	.06195
1.44	.42507	.14146	1.94	.47381	.06077
1.45	.42647	.13943	1.95	.47441	.05959
1.46	.42786	.13742	1.96	.47500	.05844
1.47	.42922	.13542	1.97	.47558	.05730
1.48	.43056	.13344	1.98	.47615	.05618
1.49	.43189	.13147	1.99	.47670	.05508
1.50	.43319	.12952	2.00	.47725	.05399
1.51	.43448	.12758	2.01	.47778	.05292
1.52	.43574	.12566	2.02	.47831	.05186
1.53	.43699	.12376	2.03	.47882	.05082
1.54	.43822	.12188	2.04	.47932	.04980
1.55	.43943	.12001	2.05	.47982	.04879
1.56	.44062	.11816	2.06	.48030	.04780
1.57	.44179	.11632	2.07	.48077	.04682
1.58	.44295	.11450	2.08	.48124	.04586
1.59	.44408	.11270	2.09	.48169	.04491
1.60	.44520	.11092	2.10	.48214	.04398
1.61	.44630	.10915	2.11	.48257	.04307
1.62	.44738	.10741	2.12	.48300	.04217
1.63	.44845	.10567	2.13	.48341	.04128
1.64	.44950	.10396	2.14	.48382	.04041
1.65	.45053	.10226	2.15	.48422	.03955
1.66	.45154	.10059	2.16	.48461	.03871
1.67	.45254	.09893	2.17	.48500	.03788
1.68	.45352	.09728	2.18	.48537	.03706
1.69	.45449	.09566	2.19	.48574	.03626
1.70	.45543	.09405	2.20	.48610	.03547
1.71	.45637	.09246	2.21	.48645	.03470
1.72	.45728	.09089	2.22	.48679	.03394
1.73	.45818	.08933	2.23	.48713	.03319
1.74	.45907	.08780	2.24	.48745	.03246
1.75	.45994	.08628	2.25	.48778	.03174
1.76	.46080	.08478	2.26	.48809	.03103
1.77	.46164	.08329	2.27	.48840	.03034
1.78	.46246	.08183	2.28	.48870	.02965
1.79	.46327	.08038	2.29	.48899	.02898
1.80	.46407	.07895	2.30	.48928	.02833
1.81	.46485	.07754	2.31	.48956	.02768
1.82	.46562	.07614	2.32	.48983	.02705
1.83	.46638	.07477	2.33	.49010	.02643
1.84	.46712	.07341	2.34	.49036	.02582
1.85	.46784	.07206	2.35	.49064	.02522
1.86	.46856	.07074	2.36	.49086	.02463
1.87	.46926	.06943	2.37	.49111	.02406
1.88	.46995	.06814	2.38	.49134	.02349
1.89	.47062	.06687	2.39	.49158	.02294

AREAS AND ORDINATES OF THE NORMAL CURVE

$\frac{X - \mu}{\sigma}$	Area under the curve between μ and X	Ordinate (Y) of the curve at X	$\frac{X - \mu}{\sigma}$	Area under the curve between μ and X	Ordinate (Y) of the curve at X
(1)	(2)	(3)	(1)	(2)	(3)
2.40	.49180	.02239	2.90	.49813	.00595
2.41	.49202	.02186	2.91	.49819	.00578
2.42	.49224	.02134	2.92	.49825	.00562
2.43	.49245	.02083	2.93	.49831	.00545
2.44	.49266	.02033	2.94	.49836	.00530
2.45	.49286	.01984	2.95	.49841	.00514
2.46	.49305	.01936	2.96	.49846	.00499
2.47	.49324	.01889	2.97	.49851	.00485
2.48	.49343	.01842	2.98	.49856	.00471
2.49	.49361	.01797	2.99	.49861	.00457
2.50	.49379	.01753	3.00	.49865	.00443
2.51	.49396	.01709	3.01	.49869	.00430
2.52	.49413	.01667	3.02	.49874	.00417
2.53	.49430	.01625	3.03	.49878	.00405
2.54	.49446	.01585	3.04	.49882	.00393
2.55	.49461	.01545	3.05	.49886	.00381
2.56	.49477	.01506	3.06	.49889	.00370
2.57	.49492	.01468	3.07	.49893	.00358
2.58	.49506	.01431	3.08	.49897	.00348
2.59	.49520	.01394	3.09	.49900	.00337
2.60	.49534	.01358	3.10	.49903	.00327
2.61	.49547	.01323	3.11	.49906	.00317
2.62	.49560	.01289	3.12	.49910	.00307
2.63	.49573	.01256	3.13	.49913	.00298
2.64	.49585	.01223	3.14	.49916	.00288
2.65	.49598	.01191	3.15	.49918	.00279
2.66	.49609	.01160	3.16	.49921	.00271
2.67	.49621	.01130	3.17	.49924	.00262
2.68	.49632	.01100	3.18	.49926	.00254
2.69	.49643	.01071	3.19	.49929	.00246
2.70	.49653	.01042	3.20	.49931	.00238
2.71	.49664	.01014	3.21	.49934	.00231
2.72	.49674	.00987	3.22	.49936	.00224
2.73	.49683	.00961	3.23	.49938	.00216
2.74	.49693	.00935	3.24	.49940	.00210
2.75	.49702	.00909	3.25	.49942	.00203
2.76	.49711	.00885	3.26	.49944	.00196
2.77	.49720	.00861	3.27	.49946	.00190
2.78	.49728	.00837	3.28	.49948	.00184
2.79	.49736	.00814	3.29	.49950	.00178
2.80	.49744	.00792	3.30	.49952	.00172
2.81	.49752	.00770	3.31	.49953	.00167
2.82	.49760	.00748	3.32	.49955	.00161
2.83	.49767	.00727	3.33	.49957	.00156
2.84	.49774	.00707	3.34	.49958	.00151
2.85	.49781	.00687	3.35	.49960	.00146
2.86	.49788	.00668	3.36	.49961	.00141
2.87	.49795	.00649	3.37	.49962	.00136
2.88	.49801	.00631	3.38	.49964	.00132
2.89	.49807	.00613	3.39	.49965	.00127

Table H

AREAS AND ORDINATES OF THE NORMAL CURVE

$\frac{X - \mu}{\sigma}$	Area under the curve between μ and X	Ordinate (Y) of the curve at X	$\frac{X - \mu}{\sigma}$	Area under the curve between μ and X	Ordinate (Y) of the curve at X
(1)	(2)	(3)	(1)	(2)	(3)
3.40	.49966	.00123	3.70	.49989	.00042
3.41	.49968	.00119	3.71	.49990	.00041
3.42	.49969	.00115	3.72	.49990	.00039
3.43	.49970	.00111	3.73	.49990	.00038
3.44	.49971	.00107	3.74	.49991	.00037
3.45	.49972	.00104	3.75	.49991	.00035
3.46	.49973	.00100	3.76	.49992	.00034
3.47	.49974	.00097	3.77	.49992	.00033
3.48	.49975	.00094	3.78	.49992	.00031
3.49	.49976	.00090	3.79	.49992	.00030
3.50	.49977	.00087	3.80	.49993	.00029
3.51	.49978	.00084	3.81	.49993	.00028
3.52	.49978	.00081	3.82	.49993	.00027
3.53	.49979	.00079	3.83	.49994	.00026
3.54	.49980	.00076	3.84	.49994	.00025
3.55	.49981	.00073	3.85	.49994	.00024
3.56	.49981	.00071	3.86	.49994	.00023
3.57	.49982	.00068	3.87	.49995	.00022
3.58	.49983	.00066	3.88	.49995	.00021
3.59	.49983	.00063	3.89	.49995	.00021
3.60	.49984	.00061	3.90	.49995	.00020
3.61	.49985	.00059	3.91	.49995	.00019
3.62	.49985	.00057	3.92	.49996	.00018
3.63	.49986	.00055	3.93	.49996	.00018
3.64	.49986	.00053	3.94	.49996	.00017
3.65	.49987	.00051	3.95	.49996	.00016
3.66	.49987	.00049	3.96	.49996	.00016
3.67	.49988	.00047	3.97	.49996	.00015
3.68	.49988	.00046	3.98	.49997	.00014
3.69	.49989	.00044	3.99	.49997	.00014

Table H

Areas in One Tail of the Normal Curve at Selected Values of z

This table shows the black area:

z	.00	.01	.02	.03	.04	.05	.06	.07	.08	.09
0.0	.5000	.4960	.4920	.4880	.4840	.4801	.4761	.4721	.4681	.4641
0.1	.4602	.4562	.4522	.4483	.4443	.4404	.4364	.4325	.4286	.4247
0.2	.4207	.4168	.4129	.4090	.4052	.4013	.3974	.3936	.3897	.3859
0.3	.3821	.3783	.3745	.3707	.3669	.3632	.3594	.3557	.3520	.3483
0.4	.3446	.3409	.3372	.3336	.3300	.3264	.3228	.3192	.3156	.3121
0.5	.3085	.3050	.3015	.2981	.2946	.2912	.2877	.2843	.2810	.2776
0.6	.2743	.2709	.2676	.2643	.2611	.2578	.2546	.2514	.2483	.2451
0.7	.2420	.2389	.2358	.2327	.2296	.2266	.2236	.2206	.2177	.2148
0.8	.2119	.2090	.2061	.2033	.2005	.1977	.1949	.1922	.1894	.1867
0.9	.1841	.1814	.1788	.1762	.1736	.1711	.1685	.1660	.1635	.1611
1.0	.1587	.1562	.1539	.1515	.1492	.1469	.1446	.1423	.1401	.1379
1.1	.1357	.1335	.1314	.1292	.1271	.1251	.1230	.1210	.1190	.1170
1.2	.1151	.1131	.1112	.1093	.1075	.1056	.1038	.1020	.1003	.0985
1.3	.0968	.0951	.0934	.0918	.0901	.0885	.0869	.0853	.0838	.0823
1.4	.0808	.0793	.0778	.0764	.0749	.0735	.0721	.0708	.0694	.0681
1.5	.0668	.0655	.0643	.0630	.0618	.0606	.0594	.0582	.0571	.0559
1.6	.0548	.0537	.0526	.0516	.0505	.0495	.0485	.0475	.0465	.0455
1.7	.0446	.0436	.0427	.0418	.0409	.0401	.0392	.0384	.0375	.0367
1.8	.0359	.0351	.0344	.0336	.0329	.0322	.0314	.0307	.0301	.0294
1.9	.0287	.0281	.0274	.0268	.0262	.0256	.0250	.0244	.0239	.0233
2.0	.0228	.0222	.0217	.0212	.0207	.0202	.0197	.0192	.0188	.0183
2.1	.0179	.0174	.0170	.0166	.0162	.0158	.0154	.0150	.0146	.0143
2.2	.0139	.0136	.0132	.0129	.0125	.0122	.0119	.0116	.0113	.0110
2.3	.0107	.0104	.0102	.00990	.00964	.00939	.00914	.00889	.00866	.00842
2.4	.00820	.00798	.00776	.00755	.00734	.00714	.00695	.00676	.00657	.00639
2.5	.00621	.00604	.00587	.00570	.00554	.00539	.00523	.00508	.00494	00480
2.6	.00466	.00453	.00440	.00427	.00415	.00402	.00391	.00379	.00368	.00357
2.7	.00347	.00336	.00326	.00317	.00307	.00298	.00289	.00280	.00272	.00264
2.8	.00256	.00248	.00240	.00233	.00226	.00219	.00212	.00205	.00199	.00193
2.9	.00187	.00181	.00175	.00169	.00164	.00159	.00154	.00149	.00144	.00139

z	.0	.1	.2	.3	.4	.5	.6	.7	.8	.9
3	.00135	$.0^3968$	$.0^3687$	$.0^4483$	$.0^3337$	$.0^3233$	$.0^3159$	$.0^3108$	$.0^4723$	$.0^4481$
4	$.0^4317$	$.0^4207$	$.0^4133$	$.0^5854$	$.0^5541$	$.0^5340$	$.0^5211$	$.0^5130$	$.0^5793$	$.0^5479$
5	$.0^6287$	$.0^6170$	$.0^7996$	$.0^7579$	$.0^7333$	$.0^7190$	$.0^7107$	$.0^8599$	$.0^8332$	$.0^8182$
6	$.0^9987$	$.0^9530$	$.0^9282$	$.0^9149$	$.0^{10}777$	$.0^{10}402$	$.0^{10}206$	$.0^{10}104$	$.0^{11}523$	$.0^{11}260$

From *Tables of Areas in Two Tails and in One Tail of the Normal Curve*, by Frederick E. Croxton. Copyright, 1949, by Prentice-Hall, Inc.

Table I

STUDENT'S t DISTRIBUTION

This table shows the
values of black area:

d.f.	Level of Significance												
	0.9	0.8	0.7	0.6	0.5	0.4	0.3	0.2	0.1	0.05	0.02	0.01	0.001
1	.158	.325	.510	.727	1.000	1.376	1.963	3.078	6.314	12.706	31.821	63.657	636.619
2	.142	.289	.445	.617	.816	1.061	1.386	1.886	2.910	4.303	6.965	9.925	31.598
3	.137	.277	.424	.584	.765	.978	1.250	1.638	2.353	3.182	4.541	5.841	12.941
4	.134	.271	.414	.569	.741	.941	1.190	1.533	2.132	2.776	3.747	4.604	8.610
5	.132	.267	.408	.559	.727	.920	1.156	1.476	2.015	2.571	3.365	4.032	6.859
6	.131	.265	.404	.553	.718	.906	1.134	1.440	1.943	2.447	3.143	3.707	5.959
7	.130	.263	.402	.549	.711	.896	1.119	1.415	1.895	2.365	2.998	3.499	5.405
8	.130	.262	.399	.546	.706	.889	1.108	1.397	1.860	2.306	2.896	3.355	5.041
9	.129	.261	.398	.543	.703	.883	1.100	1.383	1.833	2.262	2.821	3.250	4.781
10	.129	.260	.397	.542	.700	.879	1.093	1.372	1.812	2.228	2.764	3.169	4.587
11	.129	.260	.396	.540	.697	.876	1.088	1.363	1.796	2.201	2.718	3.106	4.437
12	.128	.259	.395	.539	.695	.873	1.083	1.356	1.782	2.179	2.681	3.055	4.318
13	.128	.259	.394	.538	.694	.870	1.079	1.350	1.771	2.160	2.650	3.012	4.221
14	.128	.258	.393	.537	.692	.868	1.076	1.345	1.761	2.145	2.624	2.977	4.140
15	.128	.258	.393	.536	.691	.866	1.074	1.341	1.753	2.131	2.602	2.947	4.073
16	.128	.258	.392	.535	.690	.865	1.071	1.337	1.746	2.120	2.583	2.921	4.015
17	.128	.257	.392	.534	.689	.863	1.069	1.333	1.740	2.110	2.567	2.898	3.965
18	.127	.257	.392	.534	.688	.862	1.067	1.330	1.734	2.101	2.552	2.878	3.922
19	.127	.257	.391	.533	.688	.861	1.066	1.328	1.729	2.093	2.539	2.861	3.883
20	.127	.257	.391	.533	.687	.860	1.064	1.325	1.725	2.086	2.528	2.845	3.850
21	.127	.257	.391	.532	.686	.859	1.063	1.323	1.721	2.080	2.518	2.831	3.819
22	.127	.256	.390	.532	.686	.858	1.061	1.321	1.717	2.074	2.508	2.819	3.792
23	.127	.256	.390	.532	.685	.858	1.060	1.319	1.714	2.069	2.500	2.807	3.767
24	.127	.256	.390	.531	.685	.857	1.059	1.318	1.711	2.064	2.492	2.797	3.745
25	.127	.256	.390	.531	.684	.856	1.058	1.316	1.708	2.060	2.485	2.787	3.725
26	.127	.256	.390	.531	.684	.856	1.058	1.315	1.706	2.056	2.479	2.779	3.707
27	.127	.256	.389	.531	.684	.855	1.057	1.314	1.703	2.052	2.473	2.771	3.690
28	.127	.256	.389	.530	.683	.855	1.056	1.313	1.701	2.048	2.467	2.763	3.674
29	.127	.256	.389	.530	.683	.854	1.055	1.311	1.699	2.045	2.462	2.756	3.659
30	.127	.256	.389	.530	.683	.854	1.055	1.310	1.697	2.042	2.457	2.750	3.646
40	.126	.255	.388	.529	.681	.851	1.050	1.303	1.684	2.021	2.423	2.704	3.551
60	.126	.254	.387	.527	.679	.848	1.046	1.296	1.671	2.000	2.390	2.660	3.460
120	.126	.254	.386	.526	.677	.845	1.041	1.289	1.658	1.980	2.358	2.617	3.373
∞	.126	.253	.385	.524	.674	.842	1.036	1.282	1.645	1.960	2.326	2.576	3.291

This table is reprinted from *Table III* of Fisher and Yates: *Statistical Tables for Biological, Agricultural, and Medical Research*, published by Oliver and Boyd Ltd., Edinburgh, by permission of the authors and publishers.

CHI SQUARE PROBABILITY DISTRIBUTION

This table shows
the black area:

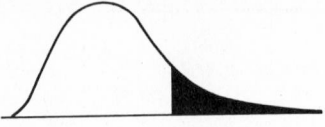

VALUES OF CHI SQUARE (χ^2)

d.f.	0.99	0.98	0.95	0.90	0.80	0.70
1	0.000157	0.000628	0.00393	0.0158	0.0642	0.148
2	0.0201	0.0404	0.103	0.211	0.446	0.713
3	0.115	0.185	0.352	0.584	1.005	1.424
4	0.297	0.429	0.711	1.064	1.649	2.195
5	0.554	0.752	1.145	1.610	2.343	3.000
6	0.872	1.134	1.635	2.204	3.070	3.828
7	1.239	1.564	2.167	2.833	3.822	4.671
8	1.646	2.032	2.733	3.490	4.594	5.527
9	2.088	2.532	3.325	4.168	5.380	6.393
10	2.558	3.059	3.940	4.865	6.179	7.267
11	3.053	3.609	4.575	5.578	6.989	8.148
12	3.571	4.178	5.226	6.304	7.807	9.034
13	4.107	4.765	5.892	7.042	8.634	9.926
14	4.660	5.368	6.571	7.790	9.467	10.821
15	5.229	5.985	7.261	8.547	10.307	11.721
16	5.812	6.614	7.962	9.312	11.152	12.624
17	6.408	7.255	8.672	10.085	12.002	13.531
18	7.015	7.906	9.390	10.865	12.857	14.440
19	7.633	8.567	10.117	11.651	13.716	15.352
20	8.260	9.237	10.851	12.443	14.578	16.266
21	8.897	9.915	11.591	13.240	15.445	17.182
22	9.542	10.600	12.338	14.041	16.314	18.101
23	10.196	11.293	13.091	14.848	17.187	19.021
24	10.856	11.992	13.848	15.659	18.062	19.943
25	11.524	12.697	14.611	16.473	18.940	20.867
26	12.198	13.409	15.379	17.292	19.820	21.792
27	12.879	14.125	16.151	18.114	20.703	22.719
28	13.565	14.847	16.928	18.939	21.588	23.647
29	14.256	15.574	17.708	19.768	22.475	24.577
30	14.953	16.306	18.493	20.599	23.364	25.508

From *Table III* of R. A. Fisher: *Statistical Methods for Research Workers*, Oliver & Boyd, Ltd., Edinburgh and London, 1936, by permission of the author and publishers.

† For larger values of n, the expression $\sqrt{2\chi^2} - \sqrt{(2df) - 1}$ may be used as a normal deviate with unit variance.

VALUES OF CHI SQUARE (χ^2)

d.f.	0.50	0.30	0.20	0.10	0.05	0.02	0.01
1	0.455	1.074	1.642	2.706	3.841	5.412	6.635
2	1.386	2.408	3.219	4.605	5.991	7.824	9.210
3	2.366	3.665	4.642	6.251	7.815	9.837	11.345
4	3.357	4.878	5.989	7.779	9.488	11.668	13.277
5	4.351	6.064	7.289	9.236	11.070	13.388	15.086
6	5.348	7.231	8.558	10.645	12.592	15.033	16.812
7	6.346	8.383	9.803	12.017	14.067	16.622	18.475
8	7.344	9.524	11.030	13.362	15.507	18.168	20.090
9	8.343	10.656	12.242	14.684	16.919	19.679	21.666
10	9.342	11.781	13.442	15.987	18.307	21.161	23.209
11	10.341	12.899	14.631	17.275	19.675	22.618	24.725
12	11.340	14.011	15.812	18.549	21.026	24.054	26.217
13	12.340	15.119	16.985	19.812	22.362	25.472	27.688
14	13.339	16.222	18.151	21.064	23.685	26.873	29.141
15	14.339	17.322	19.311	22.307	24.996	28.259	30.578
16	15.338	18.418	20.465	23.542	26.296	29.633	32.000
17	16.338	19.511	21.615	24.769	27.587	30.995	33.409
18	17.338	20.601	22.760	25.989	28.869	32.346	34.805
19	18.338	21.689	23.900	27.204	30.144	33.687	36.191
20	19.337	22.775	25.038	28.412	31.410	35.020	37.566
21	20.337	23.858	26.171	29.615	32.671	36.343	38.932
22	21.337	24.939	27.301	30.813	33.924	37.659	40.289
23	22.337	26.018	28.429	32.007	35.172	38.968	41.638
24	23.337	27.096	29.553	33.196	36.415	40.270	42.980
25	24.337	28.172	30.675	34.382	37.652	41.566	44.314
26	25.336	29.246	31.795	35.563	38.885	42.856	45.642
27	26.336	30.319	32.912	36.741	40.113	44.140	46.963
28	27.336	31.391	34.027	37.916	41.337	45.419	48.278
29	28.336	32.461	35.139	39.087	42.557	46.693	49.588
30	29.336	33.530	36.250	40.256	43.773	47.962	50.892

Table K

DISTRIBUTION OF F

$\alpha = .05$

$\alpha = .01$

5% (ROMAN TYPE) AND 1% (BOLD FACE TYPE) POINTS FOR THE DISTRIBUTION OF F

Handwritten annotations: first = 0.05, 2nd = 0.01

Each cell is given as: 5% point (roman) / **1% point (bold)**.

d.f.[1] = Degrees of Freedom (for greater mean square)

d.f.[2]	1	2	3	4	5	6	7	8	9	10	11	12	14	16	20	24	30	40	50	75	100	200	500	∞
1	161 / **4,052**	200 / **4,999**	216 / **5,403**	225 / **5,625**	230 / **5,764**	234 / **5,859**	237 / **5,928**	239 / **5,981**	241 / **6,022**	242 / **6,056**	243 / **6,082**	244 / **6,106**	245 / **6,142**	246 / **6,169**	248 / **6,208**	249 / **6,234**	250 / **6,261**	251 / **6,286**	252 / **6,302**	253 / **6,323**	253 / **6,334**	254 / **6,352**	254 / **6,361**	254 / **6,366**
2	18.51 / **98.49**	19.00 / **99.00**	19.16 / **99.17**	19.25 / **99.25**	19.30 / **99.30**	19.33 / **99.33**	19.36 / **99.36**	19.37 / **99.37**	19.38 / **99.39**	19.39 / **99.40**	19.40 / **99.41**	19.41 / **99.42**	19.42 / **99.43**	19.43 / **99.44**	19.44 / **99.45**	19.45 / **99.46**	19.46 / **99.47**	19.47 / **99.48**	19.47 / **99.48**	19.48 / **99.49**	19.49 / **99.49**	19.49 / **99.49**	19.50 / **99.50**	19.50 / **99.50**
3	10.13 / **34.12**	9.55 / **30.82**	9.28 / **29.46**	9.12 / **28.71**	9.01 / **28.24**	8.94 / **27.91**	8.88 / **27.67**	8.84 / **27.49**	8.81 / **27.34**	8.78 / **27.23**	8.76 / **27.13**	8.74 / **27.05**	8.71 / **26.92**	8.69 / **26.83**	8.66 / **26.69**	8.64 / **26.60**	8.62 / **26.50**	8.60 / **26.41**	8.58 / **26.35**	8.57 / **26.27**	8.56 / **26.23**	8.54 / **26.18**	8.54 / **26.14**	8.53 / **26.12**
4	7.71 / **21.20**	6.94 / **18.00**	6.59 / **16.69**	6.39 / **15.98**	6.26 / **15.52**	6.16 / **15.21**	6.09 / **14.98**	6.04 / **14.80**	6.00 / **14.66**	5.96 / **14.54**	5.93 / **14.45**	5.91 / **14.37**	5.87 / **14.24**	5.84 / **14.15**	5.80 / **14.02**	5.77 / **13.93**	5.74 / **13.83**	5.71 / **13.74**	5.70 / **13.69**	5.68 / **13.61**	5.66 / **13.57**	5.65 / **13.52**	5.64 / **13.48**	5.63 / **13.46**
5	6.61 / **16.26**	5.79 / **13.27**	5.41 / **12.06**	5.19 / **11.39**	5.05 / **10.97**	4.95 / **10.67**	4.88 / **10.45**	4.82 / **10.29**	4.78 / **10.15**	4.74 / **10.05**	4.70 / **9.96**	4.68 / **9.89**	4.64 / **9.77**	4.60 / **9.68**	4.56 / **9.55**	4.53 / **9.47**	4.50 / **9.38**	4.46 / **9.29**	4.44 / **9.24**	4.42 / **9.17**	4.40 / **9.13**	4.38 / **9.07**	4.37 / **9.04**	4.36 / **9.02**
6	5.99 / **13.74**	5.14 / **10.92**	4.76 / **9.78**	4.53 / **9.15**	4.39 / **8.75**	4.28 / **8.47**	4.21 / **8.26**	4.15 / **8.10**	4.10 / **7.98**	4.06 / **7.87**	4.03 / **7.79**	4.00 / **7.72**	3.96 / **7.60**	3.92 / **7.52**	3.87 / **7.39**	3.84 / **7.31**	3.81 / **7.23**	3.77 / **7.14**	3.75 / **7.09**	3.72 / **7.02**	3.71 / **6.99**	3.69 / **6.94**	3.68 / **6.90**	3.67 / **6.88**
7	5.59 / **12.25**	4.74 / **9.55**	4.34 / **8.45**	4.12 / **7.85**	3.97 / **7.46**	3.87 / **7.19**	3.79 / **7.00**	3.73 / **6.84**	3.68 / **6.71**	3.63 / **6.62**	3.60 / **6.54**	3.57 / **6.47**	3.52 / **6.35**	3.49 / **6.27**	3.44 / **6.15**	3.41 / **6.07**	3.38 / **5.98**	3.34 / **5.90**	3.32 / **5.85**	3.29 / **5.78**	3.28 / **5.75**	3.25 / **5.70**	3.24 / **5.67**	3.23 / **5.65**
8	5.32 / **11.26**	4.46 / **8.65**	4.07 / **7.59**	3.84 / **7.01**	3.69 / **6.63**	3.58 / **6.37**	3.50 / **6.19**	3.44 / **6.03**	3.39 / **5.91**	3.34 / **5.82**	3.31 / **5.74**	3.28 / **5.67**	3.23 / **5.56**	3.20 / **5.48**	3.15 / **5.36**	3.12 / **5.28**	3.08 / **5.20**	3.05 / **5.11**	3.03 / **5.06**	3.00 / **5.00**	2.98 / **4.96**	2.96 / **4.91**	2.94 / **4.88**	2.93 / **4.86**
9	5.12 / **10.56**	4.26 / **8.02**	3.86 / **6.99**	3.63 / **6.42**	3.48 / **6.06**	3.37 / **5.80**	3.29 / **5.62**	3.23 / **5.47**	3.18 / **5.35**	3.13 / **5.26**	3.10 / **5.18**	3.07 / **5.11**	3.02 / **5.00**	2.98 / **4.92**	2.93 / **4.80**	2.90 / **4.73**	2.86 / **4.64**	2.82 / **4.56**	2.80 / **4.51**	2.77 / **4.45**	2.76 / **4.41**	2.73 / **4.36**	2.72 / **4.33**	2.71 / **4.31**
10	4.96 / **10.04**	4.10 / **7.56**	3.71 / **6.55**	3.48 / **5.99**	3.33 / **5.64**	3.22 / **5.39**	3.14 / **5.21**	3.07 / **5.06**	3.02 / **4.95**	2.97 / **4.85**	2.94 / **4.78**	2.91 / **4.71**	2.86 / **4.60**	2.82 / **4.52**	2.77 / **4.41**	2.74 / **4.33**	2.70 / **4.25**	2.67 / **4.17**	2.64 / **4.12**	2.61 / **4.05**	2.59 / **4.01**	2.56 / **3.96**	2.55 / **3.93**	2.54 / **3.91**
11	4.84 / **9.65**	3.98 / **7.20**	3.59 / **6.22**	3.36 / **5.67**	3.20 / **5.32**	3.09 / **5.07**	3.01 / **4.88**	2.95 / **4.74**	2.90 / **4.63**	2.86 / **4.54**	2.82 / **4.46**	2.79 / **4.40**	2.74 / **4.29**	2.70 / **4.21**	2.65 / **4.10**	2.61 / **4.02**	2.57 / **3.94**	2.53 / **3.86**	2.50 / **3.80**	2.47 / **3.74**	2.45 / **3.70**	2.42 / **3.66**	2.41 / **3.62**	2.40 / **3.60**
12	4.75 / **9.33**	3.88 / **6.93**	3.49 / **5.95**	3.26 / **5.41**	3.11 / **5.06**	3.00 / **4.82**	2.92 / **4.65**	2.85 / **4.50**	2.80 / **4.39**	2.76 / **4.30**	2.72 / **4.22**	2.69 / **4.16**	2.64 / **4.05**	2.60 / **3.98**	2.54 / **3.86**	2.50 / **3.78**	2.46 / **3.70**	2.42 / **3.61**	2.40 / **3.56**	2.36 / **3.49**	2.35 / **3.46**	2.32 / **3.41**	2.31 / **3.38**	2.30 / **3.36**
13	4.67 / **9.07**	3.80 / **6.70**	3.41 / **5.74**	3.18 / **5.20**	3.02 / **4.86**	2.92 / **4.62**	2.84 / **4.44**	2.77 / **4.30**	2.72 / **4.19**	2.67 / **4.10**	2.63 / **4.02**	2.60 / **3.96**	2.55 / **3.85**	2.51 / **3.78**	2.46 / **3.67**	2.42 / **3.59**	2.38 / **3.51**	2.34 / **3.42**	2.32 / **3.37**	2.28 / **3.30**	2.26 / **3.27**	2.24 / **3.21**	2.22 / **3.18**	2.21 / **3.16**

Reprinted by permission from *Statistical Methods*, 6th edition, by George W. Snedecor and William C. Cochran, © 1967, by the Iowa State University Press, Ames, Iowa.

Table L

DISTRIBUTION OF F

$d.f.^1$ Degrees of Freedom (for greater mean square)

$d.f.^2$	1	2	3	4	5	6	7	8	9	10	11	12	14	16	20	24	30	40	50	75	100	200	500	∞	$d.f.^2$
14	4.60 / 8.86	3.74 / 6.51	3.34 / 5.56	3.11 / 5.03	2.96 / 4.69	2.85 / 4.46	2.77 / 4.28	2.70 / 4.14	2.65 / 4.03	2.60 / 3.94	2.56 / 3.86	2.53 / 3.80	2.48 / 3.70	2.44 / 3.62	2.39 / 3.51	2.35 / 3.43	2.31 / 3.34	2.27 / 3.26	2.24 / 3.21	2.21 / 3.14	2.19 / 3.11	2.16 / 3.06	2.14 / 3.02	2.13 / 3.00	14
15	4.54 / 8.68	3.68 / 6.36	3.29 / 5.42	3.06 / 4.89	2.90 / 4.56	2.79 / 4.32	2.70 / 4.14	2.64 / 4.00	2.59 / 3.89	2.55 / 3.80	2.51 / 3.73	2.48 / 3.67	2.43 / 3.56	2.39 / 3.48	2.33 / 3.36	2.29 / 3.29	2.25 / 3.20	2.21 / 3.12	2.18 / 3.07	2.15 / 3.00	2.12 / 2.97	2.10 / 2.92	2.08 / 2.89	2.07 / 2.87	15
16	4.49 / 8.53	3.63 / 6.23	3.24 / 5.29	3.01 / 4.77	2.85 / 4.44	2.74 / 4.20	2.66 / 4.03	2.59 / 3.89	2.54 / 3.78	2.49 / 3.69	2.45 / 3.61	2.42 / 3.55	2.37 / 3.45	2.33 / 3.37	2.28 / 3.25	2.24 / 3.18	2.20 / 3.10	2.16 / 3.01	2.13 / 2.96	2.09 / 2.89	2.07 / 2.86	2.04 / 2.80	2.02 / 2.77	2.01 / 2.75	16
17	4.45 / 8.40	3.59 / 6.11	3.20 / 5.18	2.96 / 4.67	2.81 / 4.34	2.70 / 4.10	2.62 / 3.93	2.55 / 3.79	2.50 / 3.68	2.45 / 3.59	2.41 / 3.52	2.38 / 3.45	2.33 / 3.35	2.29 / 3.27	2.23 / 3.16	2.19 / 3.08	2.15 / 3.00	2.11 / 2.92	2.08 / 2.86	2.04 / 2.79	2.02 / 2.76	1.99 / 2.70	1.97 / 2.67	1.96 / 2.65	17
18	4.41 / 8.28	3.55 / 6.01	3.16 / 5.09	2.93 / 4.58	2.77 / 4.25	2.66 / 4.01	2.58 / 3.85	2.51 / 3.71	2.46 / 3.60	2.41 / 3.51	2.37 / 3.44	2.34 / 3.37	2.29 / 3.27	2.25 / 3.19	2.19 / 3.07	2.15 / 3.00	2.11 / 2.91	2.07 / 2.83	2.04 / 2.78	2.00 / 2.71	1.98 / 2.68	1.95 / 2.62	1.93 / 2.59	1.92 / 2.57	18
19	4.38 / 8.18	3.52 / 5.93	3.13 / 5.01	2.90 / 4.50	2.74 / 4.17	2.63 / 3.94	2.55 / 3.77	2.48 / 3.63	2.43 / 3.52	2.38 / 3.43	2.34 / 3.36	2.31 / 3.30	2.26 / 3.19	2.21 / 3.12	2.15 / 3.00	2.11 / 2.92	2.07 / 2.84	2.02 / 2.76	2.00 / 2.70	1.96 / 2.63	1.94 / 2.60	1.91 / 2.54	1.90 / 2.51	1.88 / 2.49	19
20	4.35 / 8.10	3.49 / 5.85	3.10 / 4.94	2.87 / 4.43	2.71 / 4.10	2.60 / 3.87	2.52 / 3.71	2.45 / 3.56	2.40 / 3.45	2.35 / 3.37	2.31 / 3.30	2.28 / 3.23	2.23 / 3.13	2.18 / 3.05	2.12 / 2.94	2.08 / 2.86	2.04 / 2.77	1.99 / 2.69	1.96 / 2.63	1.92 / 2.56	1.90 / 2.53	1.87 / 2.47	1.85 / 2.44	1.84 / 2.42	20
21	4.32 / 8.02	3.47 / 5.78	3.07 / 4.87	2.84 / 4.37	2.68 / 4.04	2.57 / 3.81	2.49 / 3.65	2.42 / 3.51	2.37 / 3.40	2.32 / 3.31	2.28 / 3.24	2.25 / 3.17	2.20 / 3.07	2.15 / 2.99	2.09 / 2.88	2.05 / 2.80	2.00 / 2.72	1.96 / 2.63	1.93 / 2.58	1.89 / 2.51	1.87 / 2.47	1.84 / 2.42	1.82 / 2.38	1.81 / 2.36	21
22	4.30 / 7.94	3.44 / 5.72	3.05 / 4.82	2.82 / 4.31	2.66 / 3.99	2.55 / 3.76	2.47 / 3.59	2.40 / 3.45	2.35 / 3.35	2.30 / 3.26	2.26 / 3.18	2.23 / 3.12	2.18 / 3.02	2.13 / 2.94	2.07 / 2.83	2.03 / 2.75	1.98 / 2.67	1.93 / 2.58	1.91 / 2.53	1.87 / 2.46	1.84 / 2.42	1.81 / 2.37	1.80 / 2.33	1.78 / 2.31	22
23	4.28 / 7.88	3.42 / 5.66	3.03 / 4.76	2.80 / 4.26	2.64 / 3.94	2.53 / 3.71	2.45 / 3.54	2.38 / 3.41	2.32 / 3.30	2.28 / 3.21	2.24 / 3.14	2.20 / 3.07	2.14 / 2.97	2.10 / 2.89	2.04 / 2.78	2.00 / 2.70	1.96 / 2.62	1.91 / 2.53	1.88 / 2.48	1.84 / 2.41	1.82 / 2.37	1.79 / 2.32	1.77 / 2.28	1.76 / 2.26	23
24	4.26 / 7.82	3.40 / 5.61	3.01 / 4.72	2.78 / 4.22	2.62 / 3.90	2.51 / 3.67	2.43 / 3.50	2.36 / 3.36	2.30 / 3.25	2.26 / 3.17	2.22 / 3.09	2.18 / 3.03	2.13 / 2.93	2.09 / 2.85	2.02 / 2.74	1.98 / 2.66	1.94 / 2.58	1.89 / 2.49	1.86 / 2.44	1.82 / 2.36	1.80 / 2.33	1.76 / 2.27	1.74 / 2.23	1.73 / 2.21	24
25	4.24 / 7.77	3.38 / 5.57	2.99 / 4.68	2.76 / 4.18	2.60 / 3.86	2.49 / 3.63	2.41 / 3.46	2.34 / 3.32	2.28 / 3.21	2.24 / 3.13	2.20 / 3.05	2.16 / 2.99	2.11 / 2.89	2.06 / 2.81	2.00 / 2.70	1.96 / 2.62	1.92 / 2.54	1.87 / 2.45	1.84 / 2.40	1.80 / 2.32	1.77 / 2.29	1.74 / 2.23	1.72 / 2.19	1.71 / 2.17	25
26	4.22 / 7.72	3.37 / 5.53	2.98 / 4.64	2.74 / 4.14	2.59 / 3.82	2.47 / 3.59	2.39 / 3.42	2.32 / 3.29	2.27 / 3.17	2.22 / 3.09	2.18 / 3.02	2.15 / 2.96	2.10 / 2.86	2.05 / 2.77	1.99 / 2.66	1.95 / 2.58	1.90 / 2.50	1.85 / 2.41	1.82 / 2.36	1.78 / 2.28	1.76 / 2.25	1.72 / 2.19	1.70 / 2.15	1.69 / 2.13	26

The function, $F = e$ with exponent $2z$, is computed in part from Fisher's table VI (7). Additional entries are by interpolation, mostly graphical.

Table L   633

DISTRIBUTION OF F

$d.f.^1$ Degrees of Freedom (for greater mean square)

Each cell gives the 5% point (roman) over the 1% point (bold).

$d.f.^2$	1	2	3	4	5	6	7	8	9	10	11	12	14	16	20	24	30	40	50	75	100	200	500	∞	$d.f.^2$
27	4.21/**7.68**	3.35/**5.49**	2.96/**4.60**	2.73/**4.11**	2.57/**3.79**	2.46/**3.56**	2.37/**3.39**	2.30/**3.26**	2.25/**3.14**	2.20/**3.06**	2.16/**2.98**	2.13/**2.93**	2.08/**2.83**	2.03/**2.74**	1.97/**2.63**	1.93/**2.55**	1.88/**2.47**	1.84/**2.38**	1.80/**2.33**	1.76/**2.25**	1.74/**2.21**	1.71/**2.16**	1.68/**2.12**	1.67/**2.10**	27
28	4.20/**7.64**	3.34/**5.45**	2.95/**4.57**	2.71/**4.07**	2.56/**3.76**	2.44/**3.53**	2.36/**3.36**	2.29/**3.23**	2.24/**3.11**	2.19/**3.03**	2.15/**2.95**	2.12/**2.90**	2.06/**2.80**	2.02/**2.71**	1.96/**2.60**	1.91/**2.52**	1.87/**2.44**	1.81/**2.35**	1.78/**2.30**	1.75/**2.22**	1.72/**2.18**	1.69/**2.13**	1.67/**2.09**	1.65/**2.06**	28
29	4.18/**7.60**	3.33/**5.42**	2.93/**4.54**	2.70/**4.04**	2.54/**3.73**	2.43/**3.50**	2.35/**3.33**	2.28/**3.20**	2.22/**3.08**	2.18/**3.00**	2.14/**2.92**	2.10/**2.87**	2.05/**2.77**	2.00/**2.68**	1.94/**2.57**	1.90/**2.49**	1.85/**2.41**	1.80/**2.32**	1.77/**2.27**	1.73/**2.19**	1.71/**2.15**	1.68/**2.10**	1.65/**2.06**	1.64/**2.03**	29
30	4.17/**7.56**	3.32/**5.39**	2.92/**4.51**	2.69/**4.02**	2.53/**3.70**	2.42/**3.47**	2.34/**3.30**	2.27/**3.17**	2.21/**3.06**	2.16/**2.98**	2.12/**2.90**	2.09/**2.84**	2.04/**2.74**	1.99/**2.66**	1.93/**2.55**	1.89/**2.47**	1.84/**2.38**	1.79/**2.29**	1.76/**2.24**	1.72/**2.16**	1.69/**2.13**	1.66/**2.07**	1.64/**2.03**	1.62/**2.01**	30
32	4.15/**7.50**	3.30/**5.34**	2.90/**4.46**	2.67/**3.97**	2.51/**3.66**	2.40/**3.42**	2.32/**3.25**	2.25/**3.12**	2.19/**3.01**	2.14/**2.94**	2.10/**2.86**	2.07/**2.80**	2.02/**2.70**	1.97/**2.62**	1.91/**2.51**	1.86/**2.42**	1.82/**2.34**	1.76/**2.25**	1.74/**2.20**	1.69/**2.12**	1.67/**2.08**	1.64/**2.02**	1.61/**1.98**	1.59/**1.96**	32
34	4.13/**7.44**	3.28/**5.29**	2.88/**4.42**	2.65/**3.93**	2.49/**3.61**	2.38/**3.38**	2.30/**3.21**	2.23/**3.08**	2.17/**2.97**	2.12/**2.89**	2.08/**2.82**	2.05/**2.76**	2.00/**2.66**	1.95/**2.58**	1.89/**2.47**	1.84/**2.38**	1.80/**2.30**	1.74/**2.21**	1.71/**2.15**	1.67/**2.08**	1.64/**2.04**	1.61/**1.98**	1.59/**1.94**	1.57/**1.91**	34
36	4.11/**7.39**	3.26/**5.25**	2.86/**4.38**	2.63/**3.89**	2.48/**3.58**	2.36/**3.35**	2.28/**3.18**	2.21/**3.04**	2.15/**2.94**	2.10/**2.86**	2.06/**2.78**	2.03/**2.72**	1.98/**2.62**	1.93/**2.54**	1.87/**2.43**	1.82/**2.35**	1.78/**2.26**	1.72/**2.17**	1.69/**2.12**	1.65/**2.04**	1.62/**2.00**	1.59/**1.94**	1.56/**1.90**	1.55/**1.87**	36
38	4.10/**7.35**	3.25/**5.21**	2.85/**4.34**	2.62/**3.86**	2.46/**3.54**	2.35/**3.32**	2.26/**3.15**	2.19/**3.02**	2.14/**2.91**	2.09/**2.82**	2.05/**2.75**	2.02/**2.69**	1.96/**2.59**	1.92/**2.51**	1.85/**2.40**	1.80/**2.32**	1.76/**2.22**	1.71/**2.14**	1.67/**2.08**	1.63/**2.00**	1.60/**1.97**	1.57/**1.90**	1.54/**1.86**	1.53/**1.84**	38
40	4.08/**7.31**	3.23/**5.18**	2.84/**4.31**	2.61/**3.83**	2.45/**3.51**	2.34/**3.29**	2.25/**3.12**	2.18/**2.99**	2.12/**2.88**	2.07/**2.80**	2.04/**2.73**	2.00/**2.66**	1.95/**2.56**	1.90/**2.49**	1.84/**2.37**	1.79/**2.29**	1.74/**2.20**	1.69/**2.11**	1.66/**2.05**	1.61/**1.97**	1.59/**1.94**	1.55/**1.88**	1.53/**1.84**	1.51/**1.81**	40
42	4.07/**7.27**	3.22/**5.15**	2.83/**4.29**	2.59/**3.80**	2.44/**3.49**	2.32/**3.26**	2.24/**3.10**	2.17/**2.96**	2.11/**2.86**	2.06/**2.77**	2.02/**2.70**	1.99/**2.64**	1.94/**2.54**	1.89/**2.46**	1.82/**2.35**	1.78/**2.26**	1.73/**2.17**	1.68/**2.08**	1.64/**2.02**	1.60/**1.94**	1.57/**1.91**	1.54/**1.85**	1.51/**1.80**	1.49/**1.78**	42
44	4.06/**7.24**	3.21/**5.12**	2.82/**4.26**	2.58/**3.78**	2.43/**3.46**	2.31/**3.24**	2.23/**3.07**	2.16/**2.94**	2.10/**2.84**	2.05/**2.75**	2.01/**2.68**	1.98/**2.62**	1.92/**2.52**	1.88/**2.44**	1.81/**2.32**	1.76/**2.24**	1.72/**2.15**	1.66/**2.06**	1.63/**2.00**	1.58/**1.92**	1.56/**1.88**	1.52/**1.82**	1.50/**1.78**	1.48/**1.75**	44
46	4.05/**7.21**	3.20/**5.10**	2.81/**4.24**	2.57/**3.76**	2.42/**3.44**	2.30/**3.22**	2.22/**3.05**	2.14/**2.92**	2.09/**2.82**	2.04/**2.73**	2.00/**2.66**	1.97/**2.60**	1.91/**2.50**	1.87/**2.42**	1.80/**2.30**	1.75/**2.22**	1.71/**2.13**	1.65/**2.04**	1.62/**1.98**	1.57/**1.90**	1.54/**1.86**	1.51/**1.80**	1.48/**1.76**	1.46/**1.72**	46
48	4.04/**7.19**	3.19/**5.08**	2.80/**4.22**	2.56/**3.74**	2.41/**3.42**	2.30/**3.20**	2.21/**3.04**	2.14/**2.90**	2.08/**2.80**	2.03/**2.71**	1.99/**2.64**	1.96/**2.58**	1.90/**2.48**	1.86/**2.40**	1.79/**2.28**	1.74/**2.20**	1.70/**2.11**	1.64/**2.02**	1.61/**1.96**	1.56/**1.88**	1.53/**1.84**	1.50/**1.78**	1.47/**1.73**	1.45/**1.70**	48

Table L

DISTRIBUTION OF F

Table L

d.f.¹ Degrees of Freedom (for greater mean square)

Each cell shows the .05 point (top) and .01 point (bottom).

d.f.²	1	2	3	4	5	6	7	8	9	10	11	12	14	16	20	24	30	40	50	75	199	200	500	∞
50	4.03/7.17	3.18/5.06	2.79/4.20	2.56/3.72	2.40/3.41	2.29/3.18	2.20/3.02	2.13/2.88	2.07/2.78	2.02/2.70	1.98/2.62	1.95/2.56	1.90/2.46	1.85/2.39	1.78/2.26	1.74/2.18	1.69/2.10	1.63/2.00	1.60/1.94	1.55/1.86	1.52/1.82	1.48/1.76	1.46/1.71	1.44/1.68
55	4.02/7.12	3.17/5.01	2.78/4.16	2.54/3.68	2.38/3.37	2.27/3.15	2.18/2.98	2.11/2.85	2.05/2.75	2.00/2.66	1.97/2.59	1.93/2.53	1.88/2.43	1.83/2.35	1.76/2.23	1.72/2.15	1.67/2.06	1.61/1.96	1.58/1.90	1.52/1.82	1.50/1.78	1.46/1.71	1.43/1.66	1.41/1.64
60	4.00/7.08	3.15/4.98	2.76/4.13	2.52/3.65	2.37/3.34	2.25/3.12	2.17/2.95	2.10/2.82	2.04/2.72	1.99/2.63	1.95/2.56	1.92/2.50	1.86/2.40	1.81/2.32	1.75/2.20	1.70/2.12	1.65/2.03	1.59/1.93	1.56/1.87	1.50/1.79	1.48/1.74	1.44/1.68	1.41/1.63	1.39/1.60
65	3.99/7.04	3.14/4.95	2.75/4.10	2.51/3.62	2.36/3.31	2.24/3.09	2.15/2.93	2.08/2.79	2.02/2.70	1.98/2.61	1.94/2.54	1.90/2.47	1.85/2.37	1.80/2.30	1.73/2.18	1.68/2.09	1.63/2.00	1.57/1.90	1.54/1.84	1.49/1.76	1.46/1.71	1.42/1.64	1.39/1.60	1.37/1.56
70	3.98/7.01	3.13/4.92	2.74/4.08	2.50/3.60	2.35/3.29	2.23/3.07	2.14/2.91	2.07/2.77	2.01/2.67	1.97/2.59	1.93/2.51	1.89/2.45	1.84/2.35	1.79/2.28	1.72/2.15	1.67/2.07	1.62/1.98	1.56/1.88	1.53/1.82	1.47/1.74	1.45/1.69	1.40/1.62	1.37/1.56	1.35/1.53
80	3.96/6.96	3.11/4.88	2.72/4.04	2.48/3.56	2.33/3.25	2.21/3.04	2.12/2.87	2.05/2.74	1.99/2.64	1.95/2.55	1.91/2.48	1.88/2.41	1.82/2.32	1.77/2.24	1.70/2.11	1.65/2.03	1.60/1.94	1.54/1.84	1.51/1.78	1.45/1.70	1.42/1.65	1.38/1.57	1.35/1.52	1.32/1.49
100	3.94/6.90	3.09/4.82	2.70/3.98	2.46/3.51	2.30/3.20	2.19/2.99	2.10/2.82	2.03/2.69	1.97/2.59	1.92/2.51	1.88/2.43	1.85/2.36	1.79/2.26	1.75/2.19	1.68/2.06	1.63/1.98	1.57/1.89	1.51/1.79	1.48/1.73	1.42/1.64	1.39/1.59	1.34/1.51	1.30/1.46	1.28/1.43
125	3.92/6.84	3.07/4.78	2.68/3.94	2.44/3.47	2.29/3.17	2.17/2.95	2.08/2.79	2.01/2.65	1.95/2.56	1.90/2.47	1.86/2.40	1.83/2.33	1.77/2.23	1.72/2.15	1.65/2.03	1.60/1.94	1.55/1.85	1.49/1.75	1.45/1.68	1.39/1.59	1.36/1.54	1.31/1.46	1.27/1.40	1.25/1.37
150	3.91/6.81	3.06/4.75	2.67/3.91	2.43/3.44	2.27/3.14	2.16/2.92	2.07/2.76	2.00/2.62	1.94/2.53	1.89/2.44	1.85/2.37	1.82/2.30	1.76/2.20	1.71/2.12	1.64/2.00	1.59/1.91	1.54/1.83	1.47/1.72	1.44/1.66	1.37/1.56	1.34/1.51	1.29/1.43	1.25/1.37	1.22/1.33
200	3.89/6.76	3.04/4.71	2.65/3.88	2.41/3.41	2.26/3.11	2.14/2.90	2.05/2.73	1.98/2.60	1.92/2.50	1.87/2.41	1.83/2.34	1.80/2.28	1.74/2.17	1.69/2.09	1.62/1.97	1.57/1.88	1.52/1.79	1.45/1.69	1.42/1.62	1.35/1.53	1.32/1.48	1.26/1.39	1.22/1.33	1.19/1.28
400	3.86/6.70	3.02/4.66	2.62/3.83	2.39/3.36	2.23/3.06	2.12/2.85	2.03/2.69	1.96/2.55	1.90/2.46	1.85/2.37	1.81/2.29	1.78/2.23	1.72/2.12	1.67/2.04	1.60/1.92	1.54/1.84	1.49/1.74	1.42/1.64	1.38/1.57	1.32/1.47	1.28/1.42	1.22/1.32	1.16/1.24	1.13/1.19
1000	3.85/6.66	3.00/4.62	2.61/3.80	2.38/3.34	2.22/3.04	2.10/2.82	2.02/2.66	1.95/2.53	1.89/2.43	1.84/2.34	1.80/2.26	1.76/2.20	1.70/2.09	1.65/2.01	1.58/1.89	1.53/1.81	1.47/1.71	1.41/1.61	1.36/1.54	1.30/1.44	1.26/1.38	1.19/1.28	1.13/1.19	1.08/1.11
∞	3.84/6.64	2.99/4.60	2.60/3.78	2.37/3.32	2.21/3.02	2.09/2.80	2.01/2.64	1.94/2.51	1.88/2.41	1.83/2.32	1.79/2.24	1.75/2.18	1.69/2.07	1.64/1.99	1.57/1.87	1.52/1.79	1.46/1.69	1.40/1.59	1.35/1.52	1.28/1.41	1.24/1.36	1.17/1.25	1.11/1.15	1.00/1.00

VALUES OF THE CORRELATION COEFFICIENT
FOR DIFFERENT LEVELS OF SIGNIFICANCE*

$n - 2 =$ variable ↑

d.f.	.05	.02	.01
1	.996917	.9995066	.9998766
2	.95000	.98000	.990000
3	.8783	.93433	.95873
4	.8114	.8822	.91720
5	.7545	.8329	.8745
6	.7067	.7887	.8343
7	.6664	.7498	.7977
8	.6319	.7155	.7646
9	.6021	.6851	.7348
10	.5760	.6581	.7079
11	.5529	.6339	.6835
12	.5324	.6120	.6614
13	.5139	.5923	.6411
14	.4973	.5742	.6226
15	.4821	.5577	.6055
16	.4683	.5425	.5897
17	.4555	.5285	.5751
18	.4438	.5155	.5614
19	.4329	.5034	.5487
20	.4227	.4921	.5368
25	.3809	.4451	.4869
30	.3494	.4093	.4487
35	.3246	.3810	.4182
40	.3044	.3578	.3932
45	.2875	.3384	.3721
50	.2732	.3218	.3541
60	.2500	.2948	.3248
70	.2319	.2737	.3017
80	.2172	.2565	.2830
90	.2050	.2422	.2673
100	.1946	.2301	.2540

*This table is reprinted from Table V-A of Fisher: <u>Statistical Methods for Research Workers</u>, published by Oliver and Boyd Ltd., Edinburgh, by permission of the author and publishers.

For simple correlation, **d.f.** is 2 less than the number of pairs in the sample; for partial correlation, the number of secondary subscripts also should be subtracted.

Table M

RANDOM SAMPLING NUMBERS

FIRST 1,512 RANDOM DIGITS

	A	B	C	D	E	F	G
1	345769	953810	627280	423578	353511	899906	827008
	549075	004410	059309	271243	403382	248735	972383
	423480	950812	197145	556566	655917	046169	363201
	554518	514280	950974	482196	058868	474936	724289
	797165	670995	791954	188521	950156	086813	033365
	062730	163375	602168	908350	360861	152201	966097
2	356756	519371	679389	371912	502903	936741	636775
	700770	781547	916968	136999	801855	605975	295802
	279584	733750	487151	116069	274869	416181	610911
	862434	481154	391464	021094	761599	474456	582253
	199585	167701	170778	934765	761328	275799	323046
	048736	514507	977406	158840	846761	198016	933522
3	815218	609732	629295	517386	824505	676788	304971
	643021	527212	492869	261844	914505	354436	355772
	164332	245407	517804	422658	751712	583087	286872
	174303	085157	308590	535846	503131	266915	465641
	136325	414066	452293	649359	844625	674828	953396
	117780	407444	426115	108970	621527	601599	652376
4	435697	245510	946158	934221	824917	509832	362638
	912252	579474	848845	824321	049853	151126	052643
	754438	658573	717914	040054	630638	264060	594641
	322053	924909	048177	957012	801464	833319	978384
	897199	125506	708669	408374	737887	906201	599469
	046637	642050	435779	502427	027842	515775	811203
5	721653	260190	842505	797017	157497	179041	979346
	202312	011976	373248	374293	802292	646914	171322
	354014	356787	511271	904434	068589	329862	829316
	682909	809290	793392	098004	120575	469925	112743
	897690	572456	871574	465543	486529	507767	608677
	139029	160636	417690	191242	625269	104858	020808
6	341447	723998	905614	519309	926345	240082	395043
	415603	129727	894956	780924	227496	134056	023014
	014881	496311	750082	707823	738906	157591	072396
	827235	783798	324650	485324	568156	098331	768720
	261607	730824	341940	259028	253973	145183	658110
	527920	834376	972906	627959	654790	342497	593779

Appendix N is abridged with the permission of the author and publisher from "New Random Sampling Numbers," *Baylor Business Studies* No. 1, by H. N. Broom, published by The School of Business, Baylor University, Waco, Texas.

SECOND 1,512 RANDOM DIGITS

	A	B	C	D	E	F	G
1	835431	206253	467521	029822	700399	554652	450184
	512651	743206	118787	587401	921517	015407	206860
	376187	189133	154812	828785	667020	998697	579598
	092530	869028	483691	165063	847894	041617	762973
	238036	016856	290105	538530	079931	412195	838814
	308168	717698	919814	092230	215657	469994	805803
2	773429	915639	900911	276895	149505	540379	224349
	171626	601259	009905	572567	441960	299704	313987
	180570	665625	424048	713009	830314	664642	521021
	558715	965963	494210	875287	488595	898691	713010
	345067	361180	989224	138905	355519	045847	746266
	583819	310956	174728	099164	118461	758000	496302
3	615026	599459	722322	555090	572720	826686	456517
	812358	389535	166779	441968	105639	632418	340890
	784592	003651	279275	055646	341897	510689	026160
	094619	636747	934082	787345	772825	603866	565688
	450908	919891	157771	114333	710179	062848	615156
	593546	728768	984323	290410	970562	906724	315005
4	873778	491131	209695	604075	783895	862911	772026
	965705	317845	169619	921361	315606	990029	745251
	311163	943589	540958	556212	760508	129963	236556
	454554	284761	269019	924179	670780	389869	519229
	124330	819763	596075	064570	495169	030185	866211
	920765	122124	423205	596357	469969	072245	359269
5	183002	540547	312909	389818	464023	768381	377241
	600135	865974	929756	162716	415598	878513	994633
	235787	023117	895285	027055	943962	381112	530492
	953379	655834	283102	836259	437761	391976	940853
	009658	521970	537626	806052	715247	808585	252503
	176570	849057	387097	311529	893745	450267	182626
6	747456	304530	931013	678688	270736	355032	400713
	486876	631985	368395	154273	959983	672523	210456
	987193	268135	867829	025419	301168	409545	131960
	358155	950977	170562	246987	884126	785621	467942
	021394	182615	049084	942153	278313	872709	693590
	735047	428941	630704	893281	716045	267529	427605

Table N

THIRD 1,512 RANDOM DIGITS

	A	B	C	D	E	F	G
1	133877	894168	670664	007673	436272	479568	247014
	909935	172305	428979	775425	004071	896108	519806
	204092	380210	589306	421798	273014	842846	750253
	906975	390605	040857	206293	173991	258115	043825
	387430	513087	738318	344565	465609	416995	943451
	045890	563165	460571	633567	481740	951614	668403
2	837159	143979	698357	219259	924875	691935	843585
	796578	982105	540570	724307	369621	562203	757320
	509998	316652	678549	468115	387469	316301	013153
	067045	238296	042458	275413	499300	680274	026351
	207634	540337	350587	013692	412939	274513	984596
	980620	875228	496017	581165	251684	275169	588760
3	347609	157545	919210	690074	532650	922600	693037
	475802	466358	379889	594832	514118	205292	371756
	818821	932102	628457	533138	655279	704197	584316
	362078	838671	765113	410097	138149	701956	928874
	072228	759522	791735	398202	162345	294805	828520
	147935	014193	536872	552021	693458	018447	788748
4	419843	160700	338910	184107	235002	024298	449135
	825546	648481	916364	607857	436970	438087	798960
	082314	418158	781469	991818	721194	358904	450970
	915221	233704	129127	767232	098851	584646	353870
	765613	354681	367568	496453	308935	131432	204643
	036236	196087	690273	453073	595160	410830	466051
5	607104	305543	705229	623194	613727	696054	758402
	308792	376543	027151	165422	560769	814957	589180
	857280	462801	434761	324058	482908	294374	976175
	959721	758687	456782	568719	404563	154205	663418
	207153	231920	518416	804920	932735	082468	322964
	403778	187984	157069	719462	053157	953043	416342
6	286108	108539	428918	149527	723573	636055	737916
	411295	291930	481424	871000	172070	273030	456317
	679313	787369	159935	164716	835268	174221	959886
	405323	376852	057589	437497	357398	838285	098772
	917458	429205	795610	905859	676942	294087	791952
	659514	078457	711589	690730	104700	912369	848269

Table N

FOURTH 1,512 RANDOM DIGITS

	A	B	C	D	E	F	G
1	142582	838531	948535	204547	621651	329695	014694
	097086	190024	666521	170674	144070	124008	702818
	358324	034739	403012	692427	208539	381841	432976
	257091	654023	191287	731088	259167	352640	004388
	928731	264667	956546	240744	769932	574832	914694
	729816	278812	119374	895490	818386	267958	560523
2	781062	721128	169905	290611	024176	160727	856247
	093549	401262	079175	117813	842686	246713	649987
	829708	656390	804223	434596	134518	401187	589048
	550416	658096	352864	576572	178144	051421	836509
	072934	572971	564253	950363	656948	923152	790087
	646941	109528	073147	354187	771592	647850	086352
3	905725	867727	033964	579862	045061	896494	589268
	727696	156430	671765	127312	335860	407661	709388
	742859	985436	487786	403118	684839	561387	985352
	095217	375204	659737	001286	046025	616072	224715
	791020	730765	212021	763149	590401	433554	462302
	824304	754426	728896	070857	137631	634735	426189
4	194358	810596	051443	917458	855114	808348	568628
	364029	285129	651482	180425	166024	465370	467021
	675894	027149	802421	058779	786349	597533	917864
	009913	955754	981235	888191	437609	131287	967580
	605600	593586	200254	365462	154578	179723	358203
	792003	304109	298794	661389	720132	741928	088924
5	357790	028381	163072	758986	302348	248362	909435
	482034	980395	236510	516007	654864	890157	740017
	319302	713745	057612	027685	180265	981029	237304
	622343	241778	137067	061429	489784	439401	438854
	870846	008446	490322	136989	703895	591878	506804
	603242	818115	746069	437465	507246	713641	936584
6	143632	031587	688275	170345	823659	049277	970129
	954182	040683	787002	775349	571341	854167	020533
	283056	857426	252542	404561	546734	822595	481604
	891730	027420	126799	821731	195465	709433	240637
	497562	204798	343671	124740	855713	016508	282359
	862867	628369	179980	851292	200332	260919	634484

Table N

FIFTH 1,512 RANDOM DIGITS

	A	B	C	D	E	F	G
1	234903	977328	426289	059916	370504	472536	882774
	827916	836545	259741	351195	318902	035302	168872
	072531	890103	176448	541124	205121	123085	068264
	632794	206625	925039	624334	820835	334348	388207
	382872	097936	071964	621400	646309	247900	281703
	808573	394741	959638	247381	610565	709873	334815
2	354309	158909	153881	424752	783022	533624	175172
	906243	726658	251267	365360	579630	586949	158133
	525936	310872	970208	973742	569370	017236	474078
	728432	994758	280372	252475	231276	574619	494115
	133451	621863	348390	098228	347511	147196	784562
	689269	313634	060291	180301	975085	894513	576965
3	724364	808577	482097	323717	715709	476280	826741
	765851	353829	719547	543741	908672	823137	326739
	947243	118331	223157	039177	794272	801545	460983
	465051	280456	629658	126148	156208	857169	911700
	257697	776781	820503	296026	088363	662042	354276
	160987	935231	747978	651684	343587	645322	393694
4	821728	950392	695858	129173	969025	203142	691811
	133820	518328	195320	802857	715239	430737	837670
	676119	543864	713556	608730	542030	267639	272313
	358288	970868	823717	086731	757257	482576	776482
	845316	824309	503518	427637	685270	957076	892133
	942548	198829	493211	149531	094630	027693	329382
5	143233	887181	055337	249805	513691	817352	538149
	458184	837904	923458	391183	608420	216957	172575
	851984	813538	640801	612417	716166	250195	429326
	229237	475843	059797	909582	874102	515272	856061
	174277	763056	492535	469927	796518	647131	871689
	295226	004417	146345	143745	642136	818246	547348
6	517593	113209	334612	395850	971896	012245	572923
	354462	698717	874151	603057	392502	494365	797795
	468647	924887	108659	220318	201989	613680	679493
	684049	465801	098284	331425	284530	486915	763950
	030205	684076	497019	283971	842047	824963	909776
	561626	489302	597504	153984	534636	703728	628141

SIXTH 1,512 RANDOM DIGITS

	A	B	C	D	E	F	G
1	131002	982802	349586	732144	263958	525852	079077
	311036	948264	757246	999074	473250	301361	287480
	117900	967359	951340	206249	750614	757637	039561
	420108	719403	373353	805621	324985	382658	144203
	817917	014186	490768	918089	827877	872212	083869
	616038	432163	024784	280541	925802	715031	276156
2	028826	878944	125967	203556	380380	530327	766136
	306466	023143	957987	389181	042380	427260	725014
	212582	401308	784251	118122	369778	672765	370624
	904481	259462	613526	296340	417190	492514	683658
	039150	872354	091965	042174	578011	508348	598921
	124093	002854	421698	620839	128047	574933	431906
3	834925	709114	753692	497162	994578	072578	603677
	420841	566312	353244	740576	491964	624527	967488
	254108	159489	952679	167533	521907	193160	031448
	664232	516971	792650	400468	647852	170913	160213
	801813	559026	527213	527566	325794	825990	363411
	395837	431769	701261	078829	386268	265427	791021
4	854672	844120	509813	735713	856045	423249	847869
	713626	401301	541542	792042	627765	708281	990385
	152815	799642	172512	408639	477833	489620	492357
	043842	288755	982207	793857	146365	511024	040649
	621103	658201	406878	049460	736146	544352	951680
	907380	479835	173615	613129	135183	290643	711999
5	183424	225589	588245	751920	670401	465815	707089
	298105	197406	800758	377629	387216	804517	358658
	461943	527038	040083	821392	886273	541711	128572
	972720	500061	802028	649938	152578	108946	530986
	386414	603406	598381	649820	614989	999197	343017
	494412	721901	997552	293068	929691	279002	315891
6	454723	636448	877080	705018	817266	157453	836959
	623403	702369	575734	705190	611039	247033	465424
	375076	190955	175613	953498	527196	205576	322834
	432061	773509	782619	795283	630640	591027	437851
	685739	934795	409662	288493	105881	770890	454989
	474534	628374	913113	927692	876136	484264	370120

SEVENTH 1,512 RANDOM DIGITS

	A	B	C	D	E	F	G
1	709185	340438	460965	942000	429134	371533	349945
	803284	731331	947821	256570	084028	969352	614616
	613774	169070	625816	991975	931215	403052	246287
	840558	798060	559201	234095	772891	331445	380446
	013254	808899	049165	733968	452613	895842	679503
	183393	890935	491001	295887	522848	409359	015274
2	566494	363359	560313	713965	287916	894109	241842
	292683	864228	833304	918761	233059	183442	875803
	946842	039669	518435	878301	615978	651693	711543
	575525	980274	825670	462213	902406	126143	846392
	240843	754519	584210	651407	182782	817765	960782
	061360	041163	550463	510178	587647	072249	144505
3	851654	517546	483230	028541	136386	893299	538661
	612690	041734	207715	711009	782971	000545	435275
	631361	686831	035875	817705	491952	281547	411735
	124565	390685	177734	180255	932667	048215	962608
	734976	936074	295263	694131	048298	627197	793249
	769343	796105	839915	395087	007383	320656	373892
4	473105	964875	036127	406564	157278	560401	316867
	710915	231828	274369	485163	561230	207294	575026
	684251	094146	619711	251828	512906	312645	878060
	845885	102203	988634	298754	063181	813840	639183
	142951	585206	545267	473025	306256	308372	951465
	769678	251601	274652	427707	075091	948539	086764
5	461383	401090	268780	785630	978687	375917	384056
	730981	428921	742860	534632	393924	005326	864520
	924260	284374	892698	701835	915905	152546	503404
	832534	694104	015167	316561	124648	319627	136572
	080431	863062	566150	287352	095985	339957	697877
	518363	342832	630574	179853	396155	152035	875703
6	812252	414982	006162	592861	532436	487925	892949
	502404	563221	894242	402606	765101	528596	728298
	731967	783719	925607	347223	146852	957104	238921
	417986	204070	595380	562870	621398	174973	497973
	210968	130088	408564	905832	645304	500685	143622
	825692	263029	728499	199860	635831	054995	708355

Table N

EIGHTH 1,512 RANDOM DIGITS

	A	B	C	D	E	F	G
1	231708	504611	968036	591223	211096	777439	724687
	238155	252763	490318	537699	018264	611205	073090
	931326	566249	372390	235417	704547	162374	780520
	096931	857162	342793	866552	120717	346535	914120
	852194	201759	860169	753632	802716	534359	489785
	607691	970406	826115	282337	450421	678673	125376
2	512691	009320	072128	762442	318685	123608	673704
	353452	717059	585926	870062	914621	739670	408454
	420746	200515	694228	153715	636001	137873	425685
	519963	174622	015409	760736	287516	840116	023615
	540173	291088	064135	529330	163618	648945	204881
	421579	960813	843108	619981	051172	203138	880776
3	364778	497155	604345	743963	465583	293902	704439
	871259	627949	619511	713169	643386	815933	006967
	181627	620419	433130	481489	711163	000670	051126
	353905	752314	400977	062539	491624	629837	814535
	657714	902036	245805	732944	809022	127178	800521
	174209	839951	538710	577605	718761	892356	084388
4	725469	413439	902346	165419	490822	390429	499075
	671938	454482	417903	621828	864990	763056	423658
	885010	491779	058320	721145	083903	642452	930942
	226151	515549	670028	511374	761253	268230	009611
	745760	151626	366821	250137	238004	973980	121307
	717283	968736	706421	790072	049558	182425	836501
5	595867	272784	268703	536973	836325	100691	681035
	875626	533691	412573	958910	639313	480796	948218
	625030	856928	206125	378086	936909	163194	066165
	835819	791654	670319	395431	734718	968282	648931
	381220	405003	710916	721794	385418	144613	960278
	628938	749139	238325	787263	175396	941612	116823
6	579020	178087	342515	975848	963673	016366	577259
	485604	168520	649429	618405	738261	716550	051737
	906267	794639	751681	098745	935692	164279	691086
	290971	390334	714535	236290	638512	817957	294169
	005257	486575	021560	713492	147317	892418	382709
	609514	345261	433729	259272	964743	089464	219955

UNIT NORMAL LOSS FUNCTION

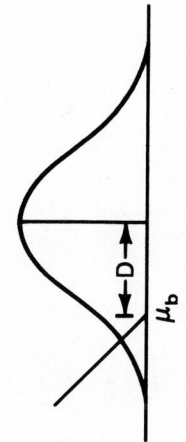

D	.00	.01	.02	.03	.04	.05	.06	.07	.08	.09
.0	.3989	.3940	.3890	.3841	.3793	.3744	.3697	.3649	.3602	.3556
.1	.3509	.3464	.3418	.3373	.3328	.3284	.3240	.3197	.3154	.3111
.2	.3069	.3027	.2986	.2944	.2904	.2863	.2824	.2784	.2745	.2706
.3	.2668	.2630	.2592	.2555	.2518	.2481	.2445	.2409	.2374	.2339
.4	.2304	.2270	.2236	.2203	.2169	.2137	.2104	.2072	.2040	.2009
.5	.1978	.1947	.1917	.1887	.1857	.1828	.1799	.1771	.1742	.1714
.6	.1687	.1659	.1633	.1606	.1580	.1554	.1528	.1503	.1478	.1453
.7	.1429	.1405	.1381	.1358	.1334	.1312	.1289	.1267	.1245	.1223
.8	.1202	.1181	.1160	.1140	.1120	.1100	.1080	.1061	.1042	.1023
.9	.1004	.09860	.09680	.09503	.09328	.09156	.08986	.08819	.08654	.08491
1.0	.08332	.08174	.08019	.07866	.07716	.07568	.07422	.07279	.07138	.06999
1.1	.06862	.06727	.06595	.06465	.06336	.06210	.06086	.05964	.05844	.05726
1.2	.05610	.05496	.05384	.05274	.05165	.05059	.04954	.04851	.04750	.04650
1.3	.04553	.04457	.04363	.04270	.04179	.04090	.04002	.03916	.03831	.03748
1.4	.03667	.03587	.03508	.03431	.03356	.03281	.03208	.03137	.03067	.02998
1.5	.02931	.02865	.02800	.02736	.02674	.02612	.02552	.02494	.02436	.02380
1.6	.02324	.02270	.02217	.02165	.02114	.02064	.02015	.01967	.01920	.01874
1.7	.01829	.01785	.01742	.01699	.01658	.01617	.01578	.01539	.01501	.01464
1.8	.01428	.01392	.01357	.01323	.01290	.01257	.01226	.01195	.01164	.01134
1.9	.01105	.01077	.01049	.01022	$.0^{2}9957$	$.0^{2}9698$	$.0^{2}9445$	$.0^{2}9198$	$.0^{2}8957$	$.0^{2}8721$

D	.00	.01	.02	.03	.04	.05	.06	.07	.08	.09
2.0	$.0^{2}8491$	$.0^{2}8266$	$.0^{2}8046$	$.0^{2}7832$	$.0^{2}7623$	$.0^{2}7418$	$.0^{2}7219$	$.0^{2}7024$	$.0^{2}6835$	$.0^{2}6649$
2.1	$.0^{2}6468$	$.0^{2}6292$	$.0^{2}6120$	$.0^{2}5952$	$.0^{2}5788$	$.0^{2}5628$	$.0^{2}5472$	$.0^{2}5320$	$.0^{2}5172$	$.0^{2}5028$
2.2	$.0^{2}4887$	$.0^{2}4750$	$.0^{2}4616$	$.0^{2}4486$	$.0^{2}4358$	$.0^{2}4235$	$.0^{2}4114$	$.0^{2}3996$	$.0^{2}3882$	$.0^{2}3770$
2.3	$.0^{2}3662$	$.0^{2}3556$	$.0^{2}3453$	$.0^{2}3352$	$.0^{2}3255$	$.0^{2}3159$	$.0^{2}3067$	$.0^{2}2977$	$.0^{2}2889$	$.0^{2}2804$
2.4	$.0^{2}2720$	$.0^{2}2640$	$.0^{2}2561$	$.0^{2}2484$	$.0^{2}2410$	$.0^{2}2337$	$.0^{2}2267$	$.0^{2}2199$	$.0^{2}2132$	$.0^{2}2067$
2.5	$.0^{2}2004$	$.0^{2}1943$	$.0^{2}1883$	$.0^{2}1826$	$.0^{2}1769$	$.0^{2}1715$	$.0^{2}1662$	$.0^{2}1610$	$.0^{2}1560$	$.0^{2}1511$
2.6	$.0^{2}1464$	$.0^{2}1418$	$.0^{2}1373$	$.0^{2}1330$	$.0^{2}1288$	$.0^{2}1247$	$.0^{2}1207$	$.0^{2}1169$	$.0^{2}1132$	$.0^{2}1095$
2.7	$.0^{2}1060$	$.0^{2}1026$	$.0^{3}9928$	$.0^{3}9607$	$.0^{3}9295$	$.0^{3}8992$	$.0^{3}8699$	$.0^{3}8414$	$.0^{3}8138$	$.0^{3}7870$
2.8	$.0^{3}7611$	$.0^{3}7359$	$.0^{3}7115$	$.0^{3}6879$	$.0^{3}6650$	$.0^{3}6428$	$.0^{3}6213$	$.0^{3}6004$	$.0^{3}5802$	$.0^{3}5606$
2.9	$.0^{3}5417$	$.0^{3}5233$	$.0^{3}5055$	$.0^{3}4883$	$.0^{3}4716$	$.0^{3}4555$	$.0^{3}4398$	$.0^{3}4247$	$.0^{3}4101$	$.0^{3}3959$
3.0	$.0^{3}3822$	$.0^{3}3689$	$.0^{3}3560$	$.0^{3}3436$	$.0^{3}3316$	$.0^{3}3199$	$.0^{3}3087$	$.0^{3}2978$	$.0^{3}2873$	$.0^{3}2771$
3.1	$.0^{3}2673$	$.0^{3}2577$	$.0^{3}2485$	$.0^{3}2396$	$.0^{3}2311$	$.0^{3}2227$	$.0^{3}2147$	$.0^{3}2070$	$.0^{3}1995$	$.0^{3}1922$
3.2	$.0^{3}1852$	$.0^{3}1785$	$.0^{3}1720$	$.0^{3}1657$	$.0^{3}1596$	$.0^{3}1537$	$.0^{3}1480$	$.0^{3}1426$	$.0^{3}1373$	$.0^{3}1322$
3.3	$.0^{3}1273$	$.0^{3}1225$	$.0^{3}1179$	$.0^{3}1135$	$.0^{3}1093$	$.0^{3}1051$	$.0^{3}1012$	$.0^{4}9734$	$.0^{4}9365$	$.0^{4}9009$
3.4	$.0^{4}8666$	$.0^{4}8335$	$.0^{4}8016$	$.0^{4}7709$	$.0^{4}7413$	$.0^{4}7127$	$.0^{4}6852$	$.0^{4}6587$	$.0^{4}6331$	$.0^{4}6085$
3.5	$.0^{4}5848$	$.0^{4}5620$	$.0^{4}5400$	$.0^{4}5188$	$.0^{4}4984$	$.0^{4}4788$	$.0^{4}4599$	$.0^{4}4417$	$.0^{4}4242$	$.0^{4}4073$
3.6	$.0^{4}3911$	$.0^{4}3755$	$.0^{4}3605$	$.0^{4}3460$	$.0^{4}3321$	$.0^{4}3188$	$.0^{4}3059$	$.0^{4}2935$	$.0^{4}2816$	$.0^{4}2702$
3.7	$.0^{4}2592$	$.0^{4}2486$	$.0^{4}2385$	$.0^{4}2287$	$.0^{4}2193$	$.0^{4}2103$	$.0^{4}2016$	$.0^{4}1933$	$.0^{4}1853$	$.0^{4}1776$
3.8	$.0^{4}1702$	$.0^{4}1632$	$.0^{4}1563$	$.0^{4}1498$	$.0^{4}1435$	$.0^{4}1375$	$.0^{4}1317$	$.0^{4}1262$	$.0^{4}1208$	$.0^{4}1157$
3.9	$.0^{4}1108$	$.0^{4}1061$	$.0^{4}1016$	$.0^{5}9723$	$.0^{5}9307$	$.0^{5}8908$	$.0^{5}8525$	$.0^{5}8158$	$.0^{5}7806$	$.0^{5}7469$
4.0	$.0^{5}7145$	$.0^{5}6835$	$.0^{5}6538$	$.0^{5}6253$	$.0^{5}5980$	$.0^{5}5718$	$.0^{5}5468$	$.0^{5}5227$	$.0^{5}4997$	$.0^{5}4777$
4.1	$.0^{5}4566$	$.0^{5}4364$	$.0^{5}4170$	$.0^{5}3985$	$.0^{5}3807$	$.0^{5}3637$	$.0^{5}3475$	$.0^{5}3319$	$.0^{5}3170$	$.0^{5}3027$
4.2	$.0^{5}2891$	$.0^{5}2760$	$.0^{5}2635$	$.0^{5}2516$	$.0^{5}2402$	$.0^{5}2292$	$.0^{5}2188$	$.0^{5}2088$	$.0^{5}1992$	$.0^{5}1901$
4.3	$.0^{5}1814$	$.0^{5}1730$	$.0^{5}1650$	$.0^{5}1574$	$.0^{5}1501$	$.0^{5}1431$	$.0^{5}1365$	$.0^{5}1301$	$.0^{5}1241$	$.0^{5}1183$
4.4	$.0^{5}1127$	$.0^{5}1074$	$.0^{5}1024$	$.0^{6}9756$	$.0^{6}9296$	$.0^{6}8857$	$.0^{6}8437$	$.0^{6}8037$	$.0^{6}7655$	$.0^{6}7290$
4.5	$.0^{6}6942$	$.0^{6}6610$	$.0^{6}6294$	$.0^{6}5992$	$.0^{6}5704$	$.0^{6}5429$	$.0^{6}5167$	$.0^{6}4917$	$.0^{6}4679$	$.0^{6}4452$
4.6	$.0^{6}4236$	$.0^{6}4029$	$.0^{6}3833$	$.0^{6}3645$	$.0^{6}3467$	$.0^{6}3297$	$.0^{6}3135$	$.0^{6}2981$	$.0^{6}2834$	$.0^{6}2694$
4.7	$.0^{6}2560$	$.0^{6}2433$	$.0^{6}2313$	$.0^{6}2197$	$.0^{6}2088$	$.0^{6}1984$	$.0^{6}1884$	$.0^{6}1790$	$.0^{6}1700$	$.0^{6}1615$
4.8	$.0^{6}1533$	$.0^{6}1456$	$.0^{6}1382$	$.0^{6}1312$	$.0^{6}1246$	$.0^{6}1182$	$.0^{6}1122$	$.0^{6}1065$	$.0^{6}1011$	$.0^{7}9588$
4.9	$.0^{7}9096$	$.0^{7}8629$	$.0^{7}8185$	$.0^{7}7763$	$.0^{7}7362$	$.0^{7}6982$	$.0^{7}6620$	$.0^{7}6276$	$.0^{7}5950$	$.0^{7}5640$

These tables of Unit Normal Loss Function appear in *Probability and Statistics for Business Decisions* by Robert Schlaifer, published by the McGraw-Hill Book Company in 1959. They are reproduced here by specific permission of the copyright holder, the President and Fellows of Harvard College.

ANSWERS TO ODD-NUMBERED PROBLEMS

Chapter 1

    1-1. a. 4–5   f. 2
          b. 3   g. 2–6
          c. 2   h. 2
          d. 8   i. 3
          e. 3
    1-3. a. 1.65   d. 600
          b. 2,400   e. 18,000
          c. 2,142.0   f. 891.4

Chapter 2

    2-1. a. 67.6 cents   c. 66
          b. 66
    2-3. a. 0.8125   c. Use μ for (a) and H for (b)
          b. 0.8054
    2-5. a. 111.96   b. 111.36
    2-7. a. 49 to 61 or 12   c. 4.03
          b. 4   d. 7.29%
    2-9. a. 11.82   c. 2.44%
          b. 0.288
   2-11. a. Frequencies are: 3, 9, 6, and 2   e. 27.78
          d. 28.5   f. 6.46
   2-13. a. Values are $25, 24, $20, $30, and $10   c. 105
          b. 15

Chapter 3

3–1. $5/9 = 0.56$

3–3. 3 to 1

3–5. The results will vary with conditions, but the tack should land with its point downward more often than with it upward.

3–7. $(0.4)(0.5)(0.6) = 0.12$

3–9. Five or more

3–11. a. $\{(HHH), (HHT), (HTH), (HTT), (THH), (THT), (TTH), (TTT)\}$

     b. *HHT, HTH,* and *THH*

     c. $3/8$

3–13. a. 0.9596   d. 0.0505

     b. 0.0400   e. 0.4800

     c. 0.4950   f. 0.4750

3–15. a. $P(0.1) = 0.295$ b. $P(C|dry) = 0.248$

3–17. $P(\text{CONSOLE}|\text{COLOR}) = 0.411$

3–19. $E(X) = \$5,100$

3–21. a. $P(0) = 0.2401, P(1) = 0.4116, P(2) = 0.2646, P(3) = 0.0756,$
$P(4) = 0.0081$

     b. $E(D) = 1.2$

3–23. $E(X) = 9.860$

Chapter 4

4–1. 0.2966

4–3. 0.3125

4–5. a. 0.0988   b. 0.0188

4–7. $\mu = np = 0.6, \sigma = \sqrt{npq} = 0.751$

4–9. a. 0.9885   c. 0.8784

     b. 1.000   d. 0.1821

4–11. a. 0.6676   b. 0.2461

4–13. $\mu = \lambda = 1.90$

r	Observed	Expected
0	14	14.96
1	28	28.42
2	27	27.00
3	19	17.10
4	9	8.12
5 or more	3	4.41

4–15. a. 0.6065   c. 0.9098

     b. 0.3935   d. 0.6065

4–17. a. 0.2592   b. 0.5533

4–19. a. 0.2143   b. 0.2143

4–21. 0.1786

4–23. a. 0.05906   c. 0.05002

     b. 0.03080

Chapter 5

5-1. 0.4

5-3. a. 0.34134   c. 0.24173
     b. 0.38292   d. 0.15982

5-5. a. 89   b. 43

5-7. 89.04%

5-9. a. $\sigma = 0.6$ c. $\sigma = 1.19$
     b. $\sigma = 0.75$

5-11. a. 0.1450   b. 0.12038

5-13. a. 0.67032   b. 0.45119

5-15. a. 0.30119   b. 0.45119

5-17. a. $\mu = 1.67$ b. 0.30119

Chapter 6

6-1. The results will differ with the random numbers used. One typical result is shown as follows:

Number of ships	Frequency	Cumulative frequency	Corresponding numbers	Empirical frequency
0	0.30	0.300	00–29	= 9
1	0.40	0.700	30–69	= 8
2	0.18	0.880	70–87	= 6
3	0.09	0.970	88–96	= 2
4	0.03	1.000	97–99	
				25

$$\mu = \frac{9(0) + 8(1) + 6(2) + 2(3)}{25} = 1.04 \text{ ships per day}$$

6-3. $\mu = \dfrac{\Sigma \overline{X}}{10} = 4$

6-5. 0.44

6-7. a. 0.98758   b. 0.95450

6-9. $\hat{\sigma} = 2.16$, $\hat{\sigma}_{\bar{x}} = 0.82$

6-11. 25,508, 26,492

6-13. 33.31, 46.69

6-15. a. $\overline{X} = 1.030$ c. 1.037
     b. 1.02, 1.04

6-17. a. 0.24   b. 0.069, 0.4109

6-19. 48.86 or 49

6-21. $\sigma = 1{,}493$, $n = 53.52$ or 54

6-23. 226.8 or 227

6-25. 21.7, 58.3

6-27. The means of subgroups 1, 3, 5, 8, 9, 11, 12, 15, 16, 19, and 20 lie beyond the control limits, indicating instability statistically.

Chapter 7

7-1. a. 6 and 12.18   b. 1.414
7-3. a. 6   c. 0.52
b. 279
7-5. $9.35 - 13.05$
7-7. 72, 55, 53, 14, and 6
7-9. 161, 103, and 36
. **7-11.** a. $M = 50$, $m = 6$, $\bar{n} = 4$, $n = 24$, $N = 500$, and $\bar{N} = 10$
b. Values of $\bar{x}_i$ are: 4.5, 3.0, 4.5, 5.0, 4.0, and 3.5. $\bar{\bar{x}} = 4.08$
c. $\hat{\sigma}_w^2 = 1.39$ and $\hat{\sigma}_b^2 = 0.5417$
d. $3.37 - 4.79$
7-13. a. $N = 250,000$, $\bar{N} = 20$, $M = 12,500$, $m = 10$, $\bar{n} = 5$, $n = 50$
b. 30
c. 53.11 and 5
d. 58.11
e. 2.32
f. $25.31 - 34.69$
7-15. 0.6842
7-17. $\delta = 0.26$, opt $\bar{n} = 6.75$ or 7, $m = 17.39$ or 17, $n = 17 \times 7 = 119$

Chapter 8

8-1. a. $x_{c_1} = 347.05$ b. $x_{c_2} = 352.95$
8-3. a. $x_{c_1} = 49.53$ b. $x_{c_2} = 50.47$
8-5. a. $H_0: \mu = 27$ b. 64
8-7. Values of z are: 3, -1.49, -2.67, -2.5, 1.4
8-9. $t = -1.40$, cannot reject H_0.
8-11. $t = -2.16$, reject H_0 and accept H_a.
8-13. $t = 1.42$, cannot reject H_0.
8-15. $t = 2.33$, cannot reject H_0.
8-17. Stop the machine if a sample of 100 guns has 16 or more defective.
8-19. a. $p_{c_1} = 0.317$ and $p_{c_2} = 0.443$
b. $p_{c_1} = 0.348$ and $p_{c_2} = 0.412$
8-21. $z = 2.10$
a. Cannot reject H_0
b. Can reject H_0
8-23. $z = 0.1935$, cannot reject H_0.
8-25. $z = 1.07$, cannot reject H_0.

Chapter 9

9-1. The value of chi-square $= 7.9$, eject H_0 and accept H_a.
9-3. The value of $\lambda = 1.4$, the value of chi-square $= 9.4$, cannot reject H_0.
9-5. The value of $D = 0.0416$, cannot reject H_0.

Answers to Odd-Numbered Problems

9–7. a. The value of chi-square $= 1.0504$, cannot reject H_0.

  b. The value of $D = 0.028$, cannot reject H_0.

9–9. The value of chi-square $= 19.21$, reject H_0 and accept H_a.

9–11. The value of chi-square $= 18.91$, reject H_0 and accept H_a. *19.736*

9–13. The value of chi-square is 8.56, reject H_0 and accept H_a.

9–15. The value of $D = 0.0725$, cannot reject H_0.

9–17. The value of $z = 1.61$, cannot reject H_0.

9–19. The value of $z = -2.31$, reject H_0 and accept H_a.

9–21. The value of $H = 10.582$, reject H_0 and accept H_a.

9–23. The value of $z = -.38$, cannot reject H_0.

9–25. The value of $z = 2.59$, reject H_0 and accept H_a.

Chapter 10

10–1. 30

10–3. -1.4

10–5. The utility function is concave from above, indicating a tendency to assume risk.

10–7. a_2, since largest of row minima $= 3$

  a_1, since largest of row maxima $= 7$

10–9. a_2, since smallest of row minima $= 3$

10–11. a_2, since maximum of row sums $= 4.8$

10–13. a_2, since maximum of row sums $= 4.25$

10–15. a_2, since maximum of row sums $= 4.3$

10–17. No, there is no dominated action.

10–19. a. a_3 is optimal

  b. $\$-1.85$

  c. $pc = \dfrac{\$5}{\$5 + \$2} = 0.71$

  d. $EVPI = \$24.90 - \$22.25 = \$2.65$

10–21. $pc = \dfrac{\$5}{\$5 + \$2} = 0.71$, and action a_3 is optimal.

10–23. a. $E(q) = 0.2(1,500) + 0.5(3,500) + 0.3(4,000) = 3,250$. Since $E(q) > q_b = 3,000$ and $B_1 > B_2$, action a_1 is optimal.

  b. $E(P_1) = \$1,500 > E(P_2) = 0$, action a_1 is optimal.

10–25. Expected loss for $a_1 = \$1,800 <$ expected loss for $a_2 = \$3,300$, and action a_1 is optimal.

10–27. a. $E(\mu) = 3,111 > \mu_b = 3,000, B_1 > B_2$, and action a_1 is optimal.

  b. $EVPI = \$6(740)(0.3284) = \$1,458.10$

10–29. $pc = \dfrac{25}{25 + 8} = 0.76, E(\mu) = 90 - 7.063 = 83$ units.

10–31. a. $E(p) = 0.285 > p_b = 0.263, B_1 > B_2$, and action a_1 is optimal.

  b. $\$117.56$

  c. Expected loss for $(10,2) = \$123.08$ and $\$117.31$ for $(20,5)$. Sample of 20 is best.

  d. $0.1252, 0.5836, 0.2913$

10–33. a. Sample of 6 is optimal, for *ENGS* is a maximum at $1,205.24.

b. $E_1(\mu) = 3,188.3$, $\sigma_1 = 264.72$, action a_1 is optimal, and $EVPI = \$206.32$.

c. *ENGS* for a sample of one is $-\$16.94$, and additional sampling is not warranted.

Chapter 11

11–1. The value of chi-square $= 64$, reject H_0 and accept H_a.

11–3. $0.00003723 - 0.00014738$

11–5. The value of $F = 1.50$, cannot reject H_0.

11–7. The value of $F = 3.04$, reject H_0 and accept H_a.

11–9. The value of $F = 2.67$, cannot reject H_0.

11–11. The value of $F = 3.096$, cannot reject H_0.

11–13. $F_C = 38.598$, $F_R = 3.718$, and $F_I = 2.828$, reject H_0 only for column means.

11–15. $F_C = 1.03$, $F_R = 0.41$, and $F_{TR} = 14.63$, reject H_0 only for treatments.

Chapter 12

12–1. b. $b = 0.8633$, $a = 4.9691$

c. $y_c = 4.9691 + 0.8633\ (7) = 11.0122$

d. $E(y|x = 6) \pm 2.306\ (0.7158) = 8.4983, 11.7995$

e. $\hat{\sigma}_b = 0.1784$, $t = 4.84$, b is significant at the 0.01 level.

12–3. $r = 0.8634$, $t = 4.8404$ and r is significantly different from zero.

12–5. b. $b = -2.2698$, $a = 31.9681$

c. $\hat{\sigma}_{yx} = 3.6893$, $\hat{\sigma}_b = 0.5556$, $t = -4.085$, and b is significant at the 0.01 level.

d. $E(y|x = 9) \pm 2,306\ (4.5474) = 1.0536, 22.0262$

12–7. $29.6983 \pm 2.306\ (2.5266) = 23.8720, 35.5246$

12–9. b. $b = 13.6371$, $a = 29.1067$

c. 83.6551

d. $E(y|x = 6) \pm 2.179\ (29.1073) = 47.51, 174.35$

e. $t = 2.179$ and b is not significant from zero.

12–11. $r = -0.8222$, $t = -4.0855$ and r is significant.

12–13. $r_s = 0.75$ and is significant.

12–15. $r_s = 0.7519$ and is significant.

12–17. a. $r_s = 0.9414$

b. $\sigma_{r_s} = 0.2294$, $z = 4.1037$, and r_s is significant.

Chapter 13

13–1. $\Sigma x = 15.82$ $\Sigma x^4 = 114.97448$

   $\Sigma y = 1,812.0$ $\Sigma xy = 3,304.03$

$$\Sigma x^2 = \quad 29.2082 \qquad \Sigma x^2 y = \quad 6{,}311.4773$$
$$\Sigma x^3 = \quad 56.634958 \qquad \Sigma y^2 = 377{,}550.0$$
b. $y_c = -320.72448 + 449.40095x - 109.62684x^2$
c. 244.5631
d. $\hat{\sigma}_{y.xx^2} = 9.7840$

13-3. $\Sigma x \ = \quad 1{,}164 \qquad \Sigma x^4 \ = 21{,}260{,}383{,}160$
$\phantom{\textbf{13-3.}} \Sigma y \ = \quad\quad 383 \qquad \Sigma xy \ = \quad\quad 19{,}931$
$\phantom{\textbf{13-3.}} \Sigma x^2 = \quad 260{,}890 \qquad \Sigma x^2 y = \quad 3{,}109{,}335$
$\phantom{\textbf{13-3.}} \Sigma x^3 = 71{,}319{,}018 \qquad \Sigma y^2 \ = \quad\quad 21{,}243$
b. $y_c = 74.27783 - 0.55528x + 0.00110x^2$
c. 36.89543
d. $\hat{\sigma}_{y.xx^2} = 7.9427$

13-5. a. $I^2_{y.xx^2} = 0.9549$
b. $r^2_{yx^2.x} = 0.7817$, $t = 4.635$ for 6 *d.f.*, and the coefficient is significant at the 0.01 level.

13-7. a. $I^2_{y.xx^2} = 0.9321$
b. $r^2_{yx^2.x} = 0.7417$, $t = 4.483$, and the coefficient is significant at the 0.01 level.

13-9. $\Sigma x \quad = \quad 9.70 \qquad \Sigma x \log y = 16.724898$
$\phantom{\textbf{13-9.}} \Sigma x^2 \quad = \quad 7.4182 \qquad \Sigma (\log y)^2 = 49.365451$
$\phantom{\textbf{13-9.}} \Sigma \log y = 27.046869$
c. $\log y_c = 2.23521 - 0.66817x$
$ \hat{\sigma}_{\log y.x} = 0.08092$
d. $\log y_c = 1.701$, $y_c = $ antilog $1.701 = 50.2$

13-11. $\Sigma y \quad = \quad 73.80 \qquad \Sigma x_1 y = 108.21$
$\phantom{\textbf{13-11.}} \Sigma x_1 \quad = \quad 12.20 \qquad \Sigma x_2 y = 777.59$
$\phantom{\textbf{13-11.}} \Sigma x_2 \quad = \quad 78.50 \qquad \Sigma x_1 x_2 = 118.47$
$\phantom{\textbf{13-11.}} \Sigma y^2 \ = 767.02 \qquad \bar{y} = \quad 9.225$
$\phantom{\textbf{13-11.}} \Sigma x_1^2 \ = \quad 18.96 \qquad \bar{x}_1 = \quad 1.525$
$\phantom{\textbf{13-11.}} \Sigma x_2^2 \ = 893.83 \qquad \bar{x}_2 = \quad 9.8125$
$\phantom{\textbf{13-11.}} \Sigma d_y^2 \ = \quad 86.2149 \qquad n = \quad 8$
a. $y_c = 22.98508 - 11.08801x_2 + 0.32093x_3$
b. $y_c \pm t_{0.05} \, \hat{\sigma}_{y.12} = 6.94201 \pm 2.571\,(2.049) = 1.674,\ 12.210$
c. $t = -3.166 < t_{0.05} = -2.571$ and b_1 is significant.
$ t = 1.710 < t_{0.10} = 2.015$ and b_2 is not significant.

13-13. $\Sigma y \quad = \quad 65 \qquad \Sigma x_1 y \ = \quad 514$
$\phantom{\textbf{13-13.}} \Sigma x_1 = \quad 68 \qquad \Sigma x_2 y = 1{,}397$
$\phantom{\textbf{13-13.}} \Sigma x_2 = \quad 220 \qquad \Sigma x_1 x_2 = 1{,}471$
$\phantom{\textbf{13-13.}} \Sigma y^2 \ = \quad 505 \qquad \bar{y} = \quad 6.5$
$\phantom{\textbf{13-13.}} \Sigma x_1^2 \ = \quad 532 \qquad \bar{x}_1 = \quad 6.8$
$\phantom{\textbf{13-13.}} \Sigma x_2^2 = 4{,}886 \qquad \bar{x}_2 = \quad 22.0$
$\phantom{\textbf{13-13.}} \Sigma d_y^2 = \quad 82.5 \qquad n = \quad 10$
a. $y_c = 4.17833579 + 0.96522549x_1 - 0.19281223x_2$
b. $y_c \pm t_{0.05} \, \hat{\sigma}_{y.12} = 7.07867 \pm 2.365\,(0.97402) = 4.7751,\ 9.33822$

13-15. $R^2_{y.12} = 0.75641$, $F = 7.763 > F_{0.05} = 5.79$ for $d.f._1 = 2$, $d.f._2 = 5$, and the coefficient is significant.

13-17. a. $R^2_{y.12} = 0.91950$, $F = 39.978 > F_{0.01} = 9.55$ for $d.f._1 = 2$,
$d.f._2 = 7$, and the coefficient is significant.

13-19.

$\Sigma y =$	8.7	$\Sigma x_1 y =$	8.74
$\Sigma x_1 =$	7.8	$\Sigma x_2 y =$	68.33
$\Sigma x_2 =$	67.2	$\Sigma x_3 y =$	312.80
$\Sigma x_3 =$	340.0	$\Sigma x_1 x_2 =$	62.02
$\Sigma y^2 =$	9.83	$\Sigma x_1 x_3 =$	297.0
$\Sigma x_1^2 =$	8.26	$\Sigma x_2 x_3 =$	2,542.0
$\Sigma x_2^2 =$	515.74	$\bar{y} =$	0.96667
$\Sigma x_3^2 =$	13,794.0	$\bar{x}_1 =$	0.86667
$\Sigma d_y^2 =$	1.4200	$\bar{x}_2 =$	7.46667
$n =$	9	$\bar{x}_3 =$	37.77778

a. $y_c = 0.58368 + 0.65368 x_1 + 0.06955 x_2 - 0.01860 x_3$

b. $y_c \pm t_{0.05}\, \hat{\sigma}_{y.123} = 2.0867 \pm 2.571\,(0.14560) = 1.7124,\ 2.4610$

c. $t = 3.098 > t_{0.05} = 2.571$ for 5 $d.f.$ and b_1 is significant.
   $t = 1.0075 < t_{0.30} = 1.119$ for 5 $d.f.$ and b_2 is not significant.
   $t = -3.925 < t_{0.02} = -3.365$ for 5 $d.f.$ and b_3 is significant.

d. $R^2_{y.123} = 0.92535$, $F = 20.660 > F_{0.01} = 12.06$ for $d.f._1 = 3$,
   $d.f._2 = 5$.

e. $r^2_{y1.23} = 0.65752$
   $r^2_{y2.13} = 0.16889$
   $r^2_{y3.12} = 0.75526$

Chapter 14

14-1. Graphs not shown.

14-3. a. $y_c = 20,140 + 629.697x$; origin is January 1, 1970; x unit = $\frac{1}{2}$ year; y unit = average dollar amount.

b. $\log y_c = 4.29692 + 0.0137441x$; origin is January 1, 1970; x unit = $\frac{1}{2}$ year; y unit is average dollar amount.

c. $y_c = 19,933.70 + 629.697x + 6.25x^2$; origin is January 1, 1970; x unit = $\frac{1}{2}$ year; y unit is average dollar amount.

d. Exponential trend is the best fit.

14-5. b. The trend equation for Japan: $\log y_c = 2.99635 + 0.0346429x$

c. The trend equation for Latin America: $\log y_c = 4.10189 + 0.0133826x$

d. Rate of increase for Japan is 8.3% per year.
   Rate of increase for Latin America is 3.1% per year.

14-7. The third-order polynomial gives the best fit.

14-9. a. Sales adjusted for seasonal variation for January through December: 6.02, 5.84, 5.51, 8.30, 7.41, 9.67, 7.53, 6.88, 8.27, 7.67, 8.38, and 8.99

b. Expected sales for March and August are 11.24 and 9.59 million dollars, respectively.

c. 110.11

14–11. a. trend, seasonal, cycle, and erratic

b. The trend equation is : $y_c = 168.56 + 24.96x$; origin July 1, 1973.

c. The index of seasonal variation for January through December is: 115.60, 75.11, 89.91, 83.83, 95.85, 76.77, 76.52, 84.90, 127.96, 125.99, 129.19, and 118.37.

d. Data after adjustment for trend, seasonal variation, and the moving average is shown for all of the months of 1972: 67.43, 71.39, 58.26, 66.71, 75.60, 81.40, 82.57, 70.89, 72.95, 69.72, 81.19, and 78.59.

14–13. a. 455.920

b. 454.00

Chapter 15

15–1. a. Values of the index are: 100.0, 116.11, 145.02, 177.25, 99.53, and 115.17.

b. Cannot be determined from the information given.

15–3. a. 190.89

b. 190.78

15–5. a. 155.47

b. 151.94

15–7. Values of the old index with 1970 = 100.0 are: 101.4, 100.0, 96.6, 91.1, 90.1, 80.0, 75.9, and 67.2.

15–9. The information given by the Consumer Price Index tells only how much the cost of living has increased in each city since the base period. It tells nothing about the relative cost of living in the two cities.

15–11. a. Index with 1969 = 100.0: 93.6, 100.0, 104.4, 107.3, 115.7, 120.8, 127.3, 143.1, and 152.4.

b. Index with 1973 = 100.0: 77.4, 82.8, 86.4, 88.8, 95.7, 100.0, 105.3, 118.5, and 126.1.

15–13. a. 133.32

b. 133.32

INDEX

A

absolute dispersion, 28–31; interquartile range, 29; quartile deviation, 29; range, 28; variance and standard deviation, 29–31

acceptance: number, 203; sampling, 203; and sequential sampling, 203

accuracy, of sample result, 180

action, 284; dominating, 285; optimal, 285

alienation, coefficient of, 390

allocation: Neyman, 192; optimum, 192

allowable error, 160

alpha error (α), 215

alternate hypothesis, 214

analysis: by association, 365, 425; incremental, 296; linear bivariate, 366; multivariate, notation for, 424; one-way, of variance, sample size equal, 328; problems of, time-series, 450; of variance table, 332, 336

ANOVA, 328

approximate number, 10

a priori probability distribution, 87

arbitrary sampling, 202

arbitrary selection, 203

area sample, 195

arithmetic mean: defined, 22; grouped data, 44; of base period index, 507; of price relatives, 496; weighted, 24

arithmetic progression, 456

assignable variations, 165

association: analysis by, 425; multivariate analysis by, 424; relationship with causation, 371

association analysis, 365; by classification, 368

attribute, 146, 169; control chart for, 169

autocorrelation, 475

average relationship, line of, 370

B

base period, 506

Bayesian criterion, 294

Bayes' Theorem, 77

Bernoulli process, success, 89

beta error (B), 215

bias, in estimate of universe dispersion, correction for, 144

binomial approximation, of hypergeometric probability, 104

binomial distribution: negative, 105; Poisson probability distribution as limiting form of, 99

binomial probability, 122; cumulative, 95; density function, 91; descriptive measures, 97; distribution, 89-99; negative, 105-107; table, 93

binomial sampling, and decision rules, 307

bivariate analysis, linear, 366

bivariate correlation, curvilinear, 420

bivariate distribution, 374

bivariate regression: curvilinear, 409; surface, 374; transformations in, 416

Box-Jenkins forecasting method, 475

C

causal law, 7

causation, relationship with association, 371

c chart, 170

central limit theorem, 140

central tendency, 40–45; arithmetic mean, 22; geometric mean, 26; measures of, 19; median, 21

certainty, 284

chain index, 499; number, 499

chance process, 66

chance variable, 66

chi-square: distribution, 246; relationship of with F, 355; tests, 248–258

chunk sampling, 195

class, open-end, 37

class interval, 35

class midpoints, 35

class limits: lower, 35; real, 35; upper, 35

classical statistical inference, 290; and statistical decision theory, 290

cluster sample: defined, 195; formulas, 197;

loss function, 300
loss matrix, 286
lower control limit, 166
LSD, 357

M

Mann-Whitney U test, 266–269
mathematical expectation, 80
matrix: defined, 47; loss, 286; payoff, 284
maximin, and maximax, 292
maximin criterion, 292
mean: arithmetic, grouped data, 44; for cluster sample, standard error of, 197; estimated standard error of, 157; of finite universe, interval estimate of, 163; interval estimate for, 152; sample, 138; of single sample, testing of, 223; small samples, interval estimates for, 158; of stratified sample, 190; for a stratum, 189; unbiased estimate of standard error of, 145
mean, standard error of, 140; for stratified sample, 190
mean square column, 331
mean square error, 332
median: defined, 21; grouped data, 43; sample, distribution of, 142
mesokurtic distribution, 33
method of least squares, 370, 400, 453; normal equations, 401; and polynomial regression, 412
minimax criterion, 292
minimax regret, 293
modal class, 20
mode: crude, 40; defined, 20; grouped data, 40
model: characteristics of, 3; in decision making, 3; with discrete prior probabilities, 295; forecasting, comparison of, 458; involving normal prior distribution, 301; of Latin square, 349; of one-way analysis of variance, 329; testing of, 4; time series, 452; of two-way analysis of variance, 339, 343; use in finding a solution, 4
modified exponential trend, 463
Monte Carlo method, 137
MSC, 331
MSE, 332
multicollinearity, 432
multiple correlation analysis, 433
multiple correlation, of more than three variables, 440
multiple determination, coefficient of, 433; significance test for, 434
multiple discriminate analysis, 2
multiplier, finite, 162
multivariate, 409
multivariate analysis: by association, 424; notation for, 424
mutually exclusive events, 57

N

negative binomial distribution, 105
negative binomial probability, 105–107
Neyman allocation, 192
nominal data, 14
nondetermination, universe coefficient of, 390
nonlinear trend, 456
nonparametric methods, 245; advantages of, 245
nonparametric test, 245
normal approximation of discrete probability distribution, 122
normal curve of error, 116
normal distribution, 116–125, 251; as limit of binomial distribution, 116; significance of, 124
normal distributions, and optimal sampling, 313
normal equations, for higher order polynomials, 415; method of least squares, 401
normal probability, 117–121, 122
normal probability density function, 116
normal probability distribution, 116
null hypothesis, 214
number: acceptance, 203; approximate, 10; criterion, 307; exact, 10; index, 493; random, 135, 136; rejection, 203; rounded, 12
numbers, large, law of, 140

O

objective probability, 58
observation, 57
observations, dependent, pairing of, 229
one-sample runs test, 271
one-sample test, Kolmogorov-Smirnov, 258
one-tail test, 221
one-way analysis of variance: sample size equal, 328; sample sizes unequal, 335
open-end class, 37
optimal action, 285; criteria for, 302
optimal sample size, 310
optimal sampling, with normal distributions, 313
optimum allocation, 192; cluster sample, 199; with fixed costs, 192; with varying costs, 193
ordinal data, 14

P

Paasche's price index, 498
pairing of dependent observations, 229
parameter, 89; defined, 8; infinite universe, estimation of, 148
parameter estimates, from sample data, 378
parametric methods, 245